Y0-CAH-897

Fedora™ 7 & Red Hat® Enterprise Linux: The Complete Reference

Richard Petersen

New York Chicago San Francisco
Lisbon London Madrid Mexico City
Milan New Delhi San Juan
Seoul Singapore Sydney Toronto

The McGraw-Hill Companies

Cataloging-in-Publication Data is on file with the Library of Congress

McGraw-Hill books are available at special quantity discounts to use as premiums and sales promotions, or for use in corporate training programs. For more information, please write to the Director of Special Sales, Professional Publishing, McGraw-Hill, Two Penn Plaza, New York, NY 10121-2298. Or contact your local bookstore.

Fedora™ 7 & Red Hat® Enterprise Linux: The Complete Reference

1234567890 DOC DOC 01987

ISBN-13: 978-0-07-148642-2
ISBN-10:   0-07-148642-9

Sponsoring Editor	**Technical Editor**	**Production Supervisor**
Jane Brownlow	Dr. Ibrahim Haddad	Jean Bodeaux
Editorial Supervisor	**Copy Editor**	**Composition**
Patty Mon	Robert Campbell	International Typesetting and Composition
Project Management	**Proofreading**	
International Typesetting and Composition	International Typesetting and Composition	**Illustration**
		International Typesetting and Composition
Acquisitions Coordinator	**Indexer**	
Jennifer Housh	Valerie Perry	**Art Director, Cover**
		Jeff Weeks

To my nephews,
Dylan, Christopher, and Justin

About the Author

Richard Petersen, MLIS, teaches UNIX and C/C++ courses at the University of California at Berkeley. He is the author of *Linux: The Complete Reference* (all six editions), *Red Hat Enterprise and Fedora Linux: The Complete Reference*, *Red Hat Linux, Linux Programming, Red Hat Linux Administrator's Reference, Linux Programmer's Reference, Introductory C with C++, Introductory Command Line Unix for Users*, and many other books. He is a contributor to the linux.syscon.com (*LinuxWorld Magazine*) with articles on IPv6, Fedora operating system, Yum, Fedora repositories, the Global File System (GFS), udev device management, and the Hardware Abstraction Layer (HAL).

About the Technical Editor

Dr. Ibrahim Haddad is currently Director of Embedded & Open Source Technology at Motorola. In this role he is responsible for defining and developing the requirements for Motorola Software Group's open source initiatives. Prior to Motorola, Dr. Haddad managed the Carrier Grade Linux and Mobile Linux Initiatives at the Open Source Development Lab (OSDL) which included promoting the development and adoption of Linux and Open Source software in the communications industry. He is the co-author of two books on Red Hat Linux and Fedora, a contributing editor of the *Linux Journal, Linux Planet*, and *Enterprise Open Source Magazine*, and a featured speaker and panelist at industry conferences such as Linux World, GlobalComm, Ottawa Linux Symposium, and at academic conferences hosted by IEEE, ACM, and USENIX. He received his B.Sc. and M.Sc. in Computer Science from the Lebanese American University, and his Ph.D. in Computer Science from Concordia University in Montreal, Canada.

Contents

Acknowledgments xxix
Introduction xxxi

Part I Getting Started

1 Introduction to Red Hat and Fedora Linux 3
Red Hat and Fedora Linux 5
    The Fedora Project 6
    Red Hat Enterprise Linux 6
    CENTOS: Community Enterprise Operating System 7
    Red Hat and Fedora Documentation 7
Fedora 7 9
Fedora Live CD 11
Operating Systems and Linux 12
History of Linux and Unix 13
    Unix 13
    Linux 14
Linux Overview 15
Open Source Software 16
Linux Software 17
    Fedora Software Repositories 17
    Third-Party Linux Software Repositories 18
    Linux Office and Database Software 19
    Internet Servers 19
    Development Resources 21
Online Linux Information Sources 21
Linux Documentation 21

2 Installing Fedora 25
Key Feature of Fedora Installation 25
Minimal Install Strategy with Desktop Spins:
    Making Use of Repositories 26
Minimal Install Strategy with Fedora Live CD: First Time Installs 26
Obtaining the CDs and DVDs 27
Installation Overview 28
    Install Sources 29
    Install Configurations 29
Install Procedures 29
    Installing Dual-Boot Systems 30
Simple Graphical Direct Install with DVD/CD-ROMs 30
Hardware, Software, and Information Requirements 32
    Hardware Requirements 32
    Hard Drive Configuration 33
    Information Requirements 33

CD-ROM, Hard Disk, and Mouse Information 33
Network Configuration Information 34
Boot Source Options 34
Install Methods 35
Virtual Network Computing 36
Automating Installation with Kickstart 36
Installing Linux 37
Starting the Installation Program 38
Install Hardware Detection 39
Initial Setup: Upgrade or Install 39
Partitions, RAID, and Logical Volumes 39
Partition 40
Custom and Review Partitioning 40
Boot Loaders 43
Network Configuration 43
System Configuration 44
Software Installation 44
Finishing Installation 46
GRUB on Restart 46
Setup 47
Firewall and SELinux 47
Date and Time 47
Hardware Profile Reporting 48
Create User 48
Sound Configuration 48
Login and Logout 48
Boot Disks 49
Rescue 49
Re-installing the Boot Loader 50
Creating Your Own Fedora Install Spins with Pungi 50

3   Interface Basics: Login, Desktop, Help, Repositories,
Multimedia, and Spins 55
User Accounts 55
Accessing Your Linux System 56
The Display Manager: GDM 56
The User Switcher 57
Accessing Linux from the Command Line Interface 58
Shutting Down Linux from the Command Line 59
The GNOME and KDE Desktops 59
Fedora Desktop 60
GNOME 60
GNOME Preferences 63
GNOME Applets 65
KDE 65
Starting a GUI from the Command Line 66
Desktop Operations 66
Desktop Font Sizes 66
Configuring Your Personal Information 66
Sessions 67
Beagle: Searching files 67

        Accessing File Systems, Devices, and Remote Hosts   69
        Using Removable Devices and Media   70
    Burning DVD/CDs with GNOME   71
        Installing Multimedia Support: MP3, DVD, and DivX   71
    Command Line Interface   72
    Help Resources   73
        Context-Sensitive Help   73
        Application Documentation   73
        The Man Pages   74
        The Info Pages   75
        Web Resources   75
    Using Fedora Software Repositories   75
        Using Repositories to Complete Your Installation   76
        Repository Incompatibilities   77
        Pirut   77
        Yum Extender: yumex   77
        Fedora Repository   79
        Livna   79
        Freshrpms   80
        Installing Some Popular Packages   81
        Java Applications: jpackage.org   83
    Windows Access and Applications   84
        Setting Up Windows Network Access: Samba   84
        Running Windows Software on Linux: Wine   85

 4 System Configuration   89
    Fedora Administrative Tools   90
    Editing Configuration Files Directly   90
    Simple Administrative Tasks   92
    Login Screen   93
    Configuring Users   93
    Printer Configuration   94
        New Printers   95
        Editing Printers   96
        Remote Printers   98
    X Window System Configuration: system-config-display and
        Vendor Drivers   99
        system-config-display   99
        Video Graphics Card Driver Support: ATI, NVIDIA, and Livna . . .   100
    Updating Fedora and Enterprise Linux: PUP and RHN   102
    Installing Software Packages   103
        Installing with Yum   104
        Pirut Package Manager: A Repository Model of
            Software Management   105
        Third-Party Kernel Module Updates   106
        Installing Packages Manually with the rpm Command   107
        Package Security Check   109
        Installing Source Code Applications   110
    Security Configuration   111
        Security Services   112
        Authentication Configuration   113

Unsupported Drivers 114
Installing Access for Local Windows NTFS File Systems 115
    NTFS Read/Write Access: ntfs-3g 115
    NTFS Project Read-Only: Livna 116
    DKMS 117
Bluetooth 117
    Bluetooth Configuration 117
    Personal Area Networks: PAN 118

5   Network Configuration **119**
Network Information: Dynamic and Static 119
Network Manager 121
Network Configuration with Fedora Network Tools 122
    system-config-network 123
    Configuring New Network Devices Manually 126
    Virtual Private Networks 128
    Interface Configuration Scripts:
        /etc/sysconfig/network-scripts 128
Command Line PPP Access: wvdial 129
Manual Wireless Configurations 131
    iwconfig 131
    iwpriv 132
    iwspy 133
    iwlist 133
    linux-wlan 133
Setting Up Your Firewall: system-config-securitylevel 133
InfiniBand Support 134
Configuring a Local Area Network 135

Part II   Environments

6   GNOME **139**
Fedora Desktop Look and Feel 140
GNOME 2.x Features 141
    GNOME 2.x Desktop Features 141
    GNOME 2.x File Manager Features 143
GTK+ 143
The GNOME Interface 144
    GNOME Components 145
    Quitting GNOME 146
    GNOME Help 146
The GNOME Desktop 146
    Drag and Drop Files to the Desktop 146
    Applications on the Desktop 147
    GNOME Desktop Menu 148
    Window Manager 148
The GNOME Volume Manager 149
The GNOME File Manager: Nautilus 150
    Nautilus Window 151
    Nautilus Sidebar: Tree, History, and Notes 152

Displaying Files and Folders 153
Nautilus Menu 153
Navigating Directories 153
Managing Files 154
Application Launcher 157
File and Directory Properties 157
Nautilus Preferences 158
Nautilus as a FTP Browser 159
The GNOME Panel 159
Panel Properties 160
Panel Objects 162
Special Panel Objects 164
GNOME Applets 164
Workspace Switcher 165
GNOME Window List 165
GNOME Configuration 165
GNOME Directories and Files 166
GNOME User Directories 166
The GConf Configuration Editor 166

7   **The K Desktop Environment: KDE** **171**
The Qt Library 173
Configuration and Administration Access with KDE 173
The KDE Desktop 174
KDE Menus 175
Quitting KDE 175
KDE Desktop Operations 176
Accessing System Resources from the File Manager 176
Configuring Your Desktop 177
Desktop Link Files and URL Locations 178
KDE Windows 178
Virtual Desktops: The KDE Desktop Pager 179
KDE Panel: Kicker 180
The KDE Help Center 181
Applications 181
Application Standard Links 182
Application Desktop Links 182
Mounting Devices from the Desktop 183
KDE File Manager and Internet Client: Konqueror 183
Konqueror Window 184
Navigation Panel 185
Search 185
Navigating Directories 186
Copy, Move, Delete, Rename, and Link Operations 187
Web and FTP Access 187
Configuring Konqueror 188
KDE Configuration: KDE Control Center 189
.kde and Desktop User Directories 191
MIME Types and Associated Applications 191
KDE Directories and Files 191

8   The Shell **193**
    The Command Line 193
        Command Line Editing 195
        Command and Filename Completion 196
    History 197
        History Events 198
        History Event Editing 200
        Configuring History: HISTFILE and HISTSAVE 201
    Filename Expansion: *, ?, [ ] 201
        Matching Multiple Characters 203
        Matching Single Characters 203
        Matching a Range of Characters 204
        Matching Shell Symbols 204
        Generating Patterns 205
    Standard Input/Output and Redirection 205
        Redirecting the Standard Output: > and >> 206
        The Standard Input 208
    Pipes: | 209
    Redirecting and Piping the Standard Error: >&, 2> 210
    Jobs: Background, Kills, and Interruptions 211
        Running Jobs in the Background 212
        Referencing Jobs 212
        Job Notification 212
        Bringing Jobs to the Foreground 213
        Canceling Jobs 213
        Suspending and Stopping Jobs 213
    Ending Processes: ps and kill 214
    Shell Variables 214
        Definition and Evaluation of Variables: =, $, set, unset ... 215
        Values from Linux Commands: Back Quotes 216
    Shell Scripts: User-Defined Commands 217
        Executing Scripts 217
        Script Arguments 218
    Control Structures 219
        Test Operations 219
        Conditional Control Structures 221
        Loop Control Structures 223
    Filters and Regular Expressions 224
        Searching Files: grep 225
        Regular Expressions 225

9   Shell Configuration **227**
    Aliases 228
        Aliasing Commands and Options 228
        Aliasing Commands and Arguments 229
        Aliasing Commands 229
    Controlling Shell Operations 230
    Environment Variables and Subshells: export 230
    Configuring Your Shell with Shell Parameters 231
        Shell Parameter Variables 233
        Configuring Your Login Shell: .bash_profile 238

Configuring the BASH Shell: .bashrc 242
The BASH Shell Logout File: .bash_logout 243
Initialization and Configuration Files 244
Configuration Directories and Files 245

**10 Managing Linux Files and Directories: Directories, Archives,
and Compression** 247
Linux Files 248
The File Structure 250
Home Directories 250
Pathnames 251
System Directories 252
Listing, Displaying, and Printing Files: ls, cat, more, less, and lpr 252
Displaying Files: cat, less, and more 254
Printing Files: lpr, lpq, and lprm 254
Managing Directories: mkdir, rmdir, ls, cd, and pwd 255
Creating and Deleting Directories 256
Displaying Directory Contents 256
Moving Through Directories 256
Referencing the Parent Directory 257
File and Directory Operations: find, cp, mv, rm, and ln 257
Searching Directories: find 258
Copying Files 259
Moving Files 262
Copying and Moving Directories 263
Erasing Files and Directories: the rm Command 263
Links: the ln Command 263
The mtools Utilities: msdos 265
Archiving and Compressing Files 266
Archiving and Compressing Files with File Roller 266
Archive Files and Devices: tar 267
File Compression: gzip, bzip2, and zip 272

Part III Applications

11 Office and Database Applications 277
Running Microsoft Office on Linux: CrossOver 278
OpenOffice 279
KOffice 280
KOffice Applications 281
KParts 282
GNOME Office 282
Document Viewers (PostScript, PDF, and DVI) 284
PDA Access 284
Database Management Systems 285
SQL Databases (RDMS) 286
Xbase Databases 287
Editors 288
GNOME Editor: Gedit 289
K Desktop Editors: Kate, KEdit, and KJots 289

	The Emacs Editor	289
	The Vi Editor: Vim and Gvim	290
12	**Graphics Tools and Multimedia**	**295**
	Graphics Tools	295
	Photo Management Tools: F-Spot and digiKam	295
	KDE Graphics Tools	297
	GNOME Graphics Tools	297
	X Window System Graphic Programs	297
	Multimedia	298
	GStreamer	299
	Sound Applications	301
	CD Burners and Rippers	302
	Video Applications	302
13	**Mail and News Clients**	**307**
	Mail Clients	307
	MIME	308
	Evolution	309
	Thunderbird	310
	GNOME Mail Clients: Evolution, Balsa, and Others	311
	The K Desktop Mail Client: KMail	312
	SquirrelMail Web Mail Client	313
	Emacs	313
	Command Line Mail Clients	313
	Notifications of Received Mail	316
	Accessing Mail on Remote POP Mail Servers	316
	Mailing Lists	317
	Usenet News	318
	Newsreaders	319
	News Transport Agents	320
14	**Web, FTP, and Java Clients**	**323**
	Web Clients	323
	URL Addresses	324
	Web Browsers	325
	Creating Your Own Web Site	329
	Java for Linux	329
	jpackage, Sun, and Java-like (java-gcj-compat)	330
	Installing the Java Runtime Environment: JRE	331
	Enabling the Java Runtime Environment for Mozilla/Firefox	331
	The Java Applications	332
	The Java 2 Software Development Kit	332
	FTP Clients	332
	Network File Transfer: FTP	333
	Web Browser–Based FTP: Firefox	334
	The K Desktop File Manager: Konqueror	334
	GNOME Desktop FTP: Nautilus	334
	gFTP	335
	wget	335
	curl	335
	ftp	336

Automatic Login and Macros: .netrc 339
lftp 341
NcFTP 342

15   Network Tools **343**
Network Information: ping, finger, traceroute, and host 343
   GNOME Network Tools: gnome-nettool 343
   ping 344
   finger and who 345
   host 345
   traceroute 345
Network Talk and Messenger Clients: VoIP, ICQ, IRC, AIM, and Talk 346
   Ekiga 346
   ICQ 347
   Instant Messenger 347
Telnet 348
RSH, Kerberos, and SSH Remote Access Commands 349
   Remote Access Information 350
   Remote Access Permission: .k5login 350
   rlogin, slogin, rcp, scp, rsh, and ssh 351

Part IV   Security

16   Encryption, Integrity Checks, and Signatures: GNU Privacy Guard **355**
Public Key Encryption, Integrity Checks, and Digital Signatures 355
   Public-Key Encryption 356
   Digital Signatures 356
   Integrity Checks 356
   Combining Encryption and Signatures 357
GNU Privacy Guard 358
   GnuPG Setup: gpg 358
   Using GnuPG 363
Checking Software Package Digital Signatures 365
   Importing Public Keys 365
   Validating Public Keys 366
   Checking RPM Packages 366
Intrusion Detection: Tripwire and AIDE 367
Encrypted File Systems: luks 367

17   Security-Enhanced Linux: SELinux **369**
Flask Architecture 370
SELinux Policy Packages 371
System Administration Access 372
Terminology 372
   Identity 373
   Domains 373
   Types 374
   Roles 374
   Security Context 374
   Transition: Labeling 374
   Policies 375

Multilayer Security (MLS) and Multicategory Security (MCS) 375
Management Operations for SELinux 375
   Turning Off SELinux 375
   Checking Status and Statistics 376
   Checking Security Context 376
SELinux Management Tools 376
   Configuration with system-config-selinux 377
   SELinux Troubleshooting and audit2allow 380
   semanage 381
   The Security Policy Analysis Tool: apol 382
   Checking SELinux Messages: seaudit 382
The SELinux Reference Policy 382
   Multilayer Security (MLS) 382
   Multicategory Security (MCS) 383
Policy Methods 383
   Type Enforcement 383
   Role-Based Access Control 383
   SELinux Users 383
   Policy Files 383
   SELinux Configuration 384
SELinux Policy Rules 384
   File Contexts 386
   User Roles 386
   Access Vector Rules: allow 386
   Role Allow Rules 387
   Transition and Vector Rule Macros 387
   Constraint Rules 387
SELinux Policy Configuration Files 387
   Compiling SELinux Modules 388
   Using SELinux Source Configuration 388
   InterfaceFiles 390
   Types Files 390
   Module Files 390
   Security Context Files 390
   User Configuration: Roles 390
   Policy Module Tools 391
   Application Configuration: appconfig 391
Creating an SELinux Policy: make and checkpolicy 391
SELinux: Administrative Operations 392
   Using Security Contexts: fixfiles, setfiles, restorecon, and chcon . . . 392
   Adding New Users 392
   Runtime Security Contexts and Types: Contexts 393

18 Internet Protocol Security: IPsec **395**
IPsec Protocols 396
IPsec Modes 396
IPsec Security Databases 397
   IPsec Tools 397
Configuring IPsec with system-config-network 397
Configuring Connections with setkey 399
   Security Associations: SA 399

Security Policy: SP 399
Receiving Hosts 400
Two-Way Transmissions 400
Configuring IPsec with racoon: IKE 401
Certificates 402
Connection Configuration with racoon 403
IPsec and IP Tables: Net Traversal 403
IPsec Tunnel Mode: Virtual Private Networks 403

19 **Secure Shell and Kerberos** **405**
The Secure Shell: OpenSSH 405
SSH Encryption and Authentication 406
SSH Tools 407
SSH Setup 408
SSH Clients 411
Port Forwarding (Tunneling) 413
SSH Configuration 414
Kerberos 414
Kerberos Servers 415
Authentication Process 416
Kerberized Services 417
Configuring Kerberos Servers 417

20 **Network Firewalls: Netfilter** **419**
Firewalls: IPtables, NAT, and ip6tables 419
IPtables 420
ip6tables 421
Modules 421
Packet Filtering 421
Chains 422
Targets 422
Firewall and NAT Chains 423
Adding and Changing Rules 423
IPtables Options 424
Accepting and Denying Packets: DROP and ACCEPT 424
User-Defined Chains 427
ICMP Packets 427
Controlling Port Access 428
Packet States: Connection Tracking 429
Specialized Connection Tracking: ftp, irc, Amanda, tftp 430
Network Address Translation (NAT) 431
Adding NAT Rules 431
Nat Targets and Chains 431
Nat Redirection: Transparent Proxies 433
Packet Mangling: the Mangle Table 433
IPtables Scripts 433
Red Hat and Fedora IPtables Support 434
Red Hat and Fedora ip6tables Support 437
An IPtables Script Example: IPv4 437
IP Masquerading 445
Masquerading Local Networks 446

Masquerading NAT Rules 446
IP Forwarding 447
Masquerading Selected Hosts 447

Part V   Red Hat and Fedora Servers

21   Managing Services **451**
System Startup Files: /etc/rc.d and /etc/sysconfig 451
rc.sysinit and rc.local 451
/etc/rc.d/init.d 452
SysV Init: init.d Scripts 453
Starting Services: Stand-Alone and xinetd 455
Starting Services Directly 455
Starting and Stopping Services with Service Scripts 456
Starting Services Automatically 456
Service Management Tools: chkconfig and system-config-services 457
system-config-services 457
chkconfig 458
Service Scripts: /etc/init.d 461
Service Script Functions 461
Service Script Tags 462
Service Script Example 463
Installing Service Scripts 465
Extended Internet Services Daemon (xinetd) 465
Starting and Stopping xinetd Services: system-config-services
On Demand 465
xinetd Configuration: xinetd.conf 466
xinetd Service Configuration Files: /etc/xinetd.d Directory 469
Configuring Services: xinetd Attributes 469
Disabling and Enabling xinetd Services 470
TCP Wrappers 471

22   FTP Servers **473**
FTP Servers 473
Available Servers 474
Fedora and Red Hat FTP Server Directories 474
FTP Users 475
Anonymous FTP: vsftpd 475
The FTP User Account: anonymous 476
FTP Group 476
Creating New FTP Users 476
Anonymous FTP Server Directories 477
Anonymous FTP Files 477
Using FTP with rsync 478
Accessing FTP Sites with rsync 478
Configuring an rsync Server 478
rsync Mirroring 479
The Very Secure FTP Server 480
Running vsftpd 480
Configuring vsftpd 480

vsftpd Access Controls 484
vsftpd Virtual Hosts 485
vsftpd Virtual Users 486

23   Web Servers: Apache **487**
Tux 487
Alternate Web Servers 488
Apache Web Server 489
Java: Apache Jakarta Project 489
Linux Apache Installations 490
Apache Multiprocessing Modules: MPM 490
Starting and Stopping the Web Server 490
Apache Configuration Files 492
Apache Configuration and Directives 493
Global Configuration 494
Server Configuration 496
Directory-Level Configuration: .htaccess and <Directory> . 497
Access Control 498
URL Pathnames 498
MIME Types 499
CGI Files 499
Automatic Directory Indexing 500
Authentication 500
Log Files 501
Virtual Hosting on Apache 503
IP-Based Virtual Hosting 503
Name-Based Virtual Hosting 503
Dynamic Virtual Hosting 504
Server-Side Includes 506
PHP 507
Apache Configuration Tool 508
Web Server Security: SSL 508

24   Proxy Servers: Squid **513**
Configuring Client Browsers 514
The squid.conf File 516
Security 516
Caches 519
Connecting to Caches 519
Memory and Disk Configuration 520
Administrative Settings 520
Logs 520
Web Server Acceleration: Reverse Proxy Cache 520

25   Mail Servers: SMTP, POP, and IMAP **523**
Mail Transport Agents 523
Received Mail: MX Records 524
Postfix 525
Postfix Commands 526
Postfix Configuration: main.cf 526
Postfix Greylisting Policy Server 528
Controlling User and Host Access 528

Sendmail 530
    Aliases and LDAP 532
    Sendmail Configuration 533
    Sendmail Masquerading 537
    Configuring Mail Servers and Mail Clients 539
    Configuring Sendmail for a Simple Network Configuration 540
    Configuring Sendmail for a Centralized Mail Server 540
    Configuring a Workstation with Direct ISP Connection 541
    The Mailer Table 541
    Virtual Domains: virtusertable 542
    Security 542
POP and IMAP Server: Dovecot 544
    Dovecot 545
    Other POP and IMAP Servers 546
Spam: SpamAssassin 546

26   Print, News, and Database Servers: CUPS, INN, and MySQL 549
Printer Devices and Configuration 550
    Printer Device Files 550
    Spool Directories 551
    Starting the CUPS Server 551
Installing Printers with CUPS 551
    Configuring Remote Printers on CUPS 552
    Configuring a Shared CUPS Printer 553
    CUPS Printer Classes 553
CUPS Configuration 553
    cupsd.conf 554
    CUPS Directives 554
CUPS Command Line Print Clients 554
    lpr 555
    lpc 555
    lpq and lpstat 556
    lprm 556
CUPS Command Line Administrative Tools 556
    lpadmin 557
    lpoptions 558
    enable and disable 558
    accept and reject 558
    lpinfo 558
News and Search Servers 558
    News Servers: INN 559
    Newsreader Access 560
    Overviews 560
    INN Implementation 561
Database Servers: MySQL and PostgreSQL 561
    Relational Database Structure 562
    SQL 562
    MySQL 563
    PostgreSQL 566

Part VI   System Administration

27   Basic System Administration **569**
   Superuser Control: the Root User 569
      Root User Password 570
      Root User Access: su 570
      Controlled Administrative Access: sudo 572
   System Time and Date 573
      Using the system-config-date Utility 573
      Using the date Command 574
   Scheduling Tasks: cron 574
      The crond Service 574
      crontab Entries 575
      Environment Variables for cron 575
      The cron.d Directory 576
      The crontab Command 576
      Editing in cron 576
      Organizing Scheduled Tasks 576
      Running cron Directory Scripts 577
      Cron Directory Names 578
      Anacron 578
   System Runlevels: telinit, initab, and shutdown 578
      Runlevels 578
      Runlevels in initab 580
      Changing Runlevels with telinit 580
      The runlevel Command 581
      Shutdown 581
   Managing Services 582
      chkconfig 582
      The service Command 583
      system-config-services 583
   Fedora Administration Tools 583
   System Directories 584
      Program Directories 584
   Configuration Directories and Files 585
      Configuration Files: /etc 585
      /etc/sysconfig 587
   System Logs: /var/log and syslogd 588
      syslogd and syslog.conf 589
      Entries in syslogd.conf 589
      Priorities 589
      Actions and Users 591
      An Example for /etc/syslog.conf 591
   The Linux Auditing System: auditd 592
   Performance Analysis Tools and Processes 593
      GNOME System Monitor 594
      The ps Command 594
      vmstat, free, top, iostat, Xload, and sar 595
      System Tap 595
      Frysk 595

GNOME Power Manager 595
GKrellM 596
KDE Task Manager and Performance Monitor (KSysguard) 597
Grand Unified Bootloader (GRUB) 597

28   Managing Users **601**
User Configuration Files 601
The Password Files 601
/etc/passwd 602
/etc/shadow and /etc/gshadow 603
Password Tools 603
Managing User Environments 604
Profile Scripts 604
/etc/skel 604
/etc/login.defs 604
/etc/login.access 605
Controlling User Passwords 605
Adding and Removing Users with useradd, usermod, and userdel . . . 606
useradd 607
usermod 608
userdel 609
Managing Groups 609
/etc/group and /etc/gshadow 609
User Private Groups 609
Group Directories 610
Managing Groups with the system-config-users 610
Managing Groups Using groupadd, groupmod, and groupdel 610
Controlling Access to Directories and Files: chmod 611
Permissions 611
chmod 612
Ownership 614
Changing a File's Owner or Group: chown and chgrp 614
Setting Permissions: Permission Symbols 615
Absolute Permissions: Binary Masks 616
Directory Permissions 617
Ownership Permissions 618
Sticky Bit Permissions 619
Permission Defaults: umask 619
Disk Quotas 620
Quota Tools 620
edquota 621
quotacheck, quotaon, and quotaoff 621
repquota and quota 622
Lightweight Directory Access Protocol 622
LDAP Clients and Servers 622
LDAP Configuration Files 623
Configuring the LDAP server: /etc/slapd.conf 623
LDAP Directory Database: ldif 624
LDAP Tools 629
LDAP and PAM 629

LDAP and the Name Service Switch Service 629
Pluggable Authentication Modules 630
    PAM Configuration Files 630
    PAM Modules 630

29   **Software Management** **633**
Software Repositories 634
    Software Package Types 635
Downloading ISO and DVD Distribution Images with BitTorrent 635
Updating Using yum and PUP 636
    PUP 637
    Update with the yum Command 637
    Automatic Yum Update 637
Installing Fedora Packages with YUM 638
Yum Configuration 638
    /etc/yum.conf 639
    Repository Files:/etc/yum.repos.d 639
    Fedora 640
    Livna 640
    Freshrpms 641
    jpackage 641
    Creating Local Yum Repositories 642
    Managing YUM Caches 642
APT 642
Red Hat Package Manager (RPM) 643
    RPM Tools 643
    RPM Packages 644
    Installing from the Desktop: rpm 644
Command Line Installation: rpm 644
    The rpm Command 644
    Querying Information from RPM Packages
      and Installed Software 647
    Installing and Updating Packages with rpm 648
    Installation Example 649
    Removing RPM Software Packages 650
    RPM: Verifying an RPM Installation 650
    Rebuilding the RPM Database 651
Installing Software from RPM Source Code Files: SRPMs 651
    Source Code RPM Directories 651
    Building the Source Code 651
Installing Software from Compressed Archives: .tar.gz 652
    Decompressing and Extracting Software in One Step 652
    Decompressing Software 652
    Selecting an Install Directory 653
    Extracting Software 653
    Compiling Software 654
    Configure Command Options 655
    Development Libraries 655
    Shared and Static Libraries 656
    Makefile File 656

Command and Program Directories: PATH 657
/etc/profile 657
.bash_profile 658
Subversion and CVS 658
Packaging Your Software with RPM 659

30 File System Management **661**
File Systems 662
Filesystem Hierarchy Standard 662
Root Directory: / 662
System Directories 664
The /usr Directory 665
The /media Directory 665
The /mnt Directory 666
The /home Directory 666
The /var Directory 666
The /proc File System 666
The sysfs File System: /sys 666
Device Files: /dev, udev, and HAL 668
Mounting File Systems 671
File System Information 671
Journaling 673
ext3 Journaling 673
ReiserFS 674
Mounting File Systems Automatically: /etc/fstab 674
Hal and fstab 674
fstab Fields 675
Auto Mounts 676
mount Options 676
Boot and Disk Check 677
fstab Sample 677
Partition Labels: e2label 678
Windows Partitions 679
Linux Kernel Interfaces 679
noauto 680
Mounting File Systems Manually: mount and umount 680
The mount Command 680
The umount Command 682
Mounting Floppy Disks 682
Mounting DVD/CD-ROMs 683
Mounting Hard Drive Partitions: Linux and Windows 684
Creating File Systems: mkfs, mke2fs, mkswap, parted, and fdisk 684
fdisk 686
parted 687
mkfs 687
mkswap 689
CD-ROM and DVD ROM Manual Recording 689
mkisofs 689
dvdrecord 691
dvd+rw Tools 691

31 RAID and LVM **693**
    Logical Volume Manager 694
        LVM Structure 694
        Creating LVMs During Installation 695
        system-config-lvm 695
        LVM Tools: Using the LVM Commands 697
        LVM Example for Multiple Hard Drives 700
        Using LVM to Replace Drives 703
        LVM Example for Partitions on Different Hard Drives 703
    Configuring RAID Devices 705
        Hardware RAID Support: dmraid 705
        Linux Software RAID Levels 706
        RAID Devices and Partitions: md and fd 708
        Booting from a RAID Device 708
        RAID Administration: mdadm 708
        Creating and Installing RAID Devices 709
        Corresponding Hard Disk Partitions 715
        RAID Example 716

32 Devices and Modules: udev, HAL, and MAKEDEV **719**
    Hardware Device Installation: Kudzu 720
    Device Information: /sys, /proc, and /etc/sysconfig/hwconf 720
        The sysfs File System: /sys 721
        The proc File System: /proc 721
    udev: Device Files 722
        udev Configuration 723
        Device Names and udev Rules: /etc/udev/rules.d 724
        Symbolic Links 726
        Program Fields and /lib/udev 728
        Creating udev Rules 728
        SYMLINK Rules 729
        Persistent Names: udevinfo 730
        Permission Fields: MODE, GROUP, OWNER 731
    Hardware Abstraction Layer: HAL 732
        The HAL Daemon and hal-device-manager (hal-gnome) 733
        HAL Configuration: /etc/hal/fdi, and /usr/share/hal/fdi 733
        Device Information Files: fdi 733
        Properties 734
        Device Information File Directives 735
    Manual Devices 737
        Device Types 738
        MAKEDEV 738
        mknod 739
    Mono and .NET Support 740
    Installing and Managing Terminals and Modems 740
        Serial Ports 741
        mingetty, mgetty, and agetty 741
        termcap and inittab Files 741
        tset 742
    Input Devices 742
    Installing Sound, Network, and Other Cards 742

Sound Devices 743
Video and TV Devices 743
PCMCIA Devices 744
Modules 744
Kernel Module Tools 745
Module Files and Directories: /lib/modules 745
Managing Modules with /etc/moprobe.conf 746
The depmod Command 746
The modprobe Command 746
The insmod Command 747
The rmmod Command 748
The /etc/modprobe.conf File 748
Installing New Modules from Vendors: Driver Packages 749
Kernel Header Files: /lib/modules/version/source 750
Installing New Modules from the Kernel 751

33   Kernel Administration: Virtualization **753**
Kernel Versions 753
References 754
Kernel Tuning: Kernel Runtime Parameters 755
Installing a New Kernel Version 755
CPU Kernel Packages 756
Installing Kernel Packages: /boot 756
Precautionary Steps for Modifying a Kernel of the Same Version 757
Boot Loader 758
Boot Disk 758
Compiling the Kernel from Source Code 759
Installing Kernel Sources with Fedora Core SRPM 759
Installing Kernel Sources: Kernel Archives and Patches 760
Configuring the Kernel 760
Kernel Configuration Tools 761
Important Kernel Configuration Features 762
Compiling and Installing the Kernel 764
Installing the Kernel Image Manually 766
Kernel Boot Disks 767
Boot Loader Configurations: GRUB 767
Module RAM Disks 768
Virtualization 769
Virtual Machine Manager: virt-manager 770
Kernel-based Virtualization Machine (KVM):
Hardware Virtualization 771
Xen Virtualization Kernel 773

34   Backup Management: rsync, Amanda, and dump/restore **779**
Individual Backups: archive and rsync 779
Amanda 781
Amanda Commands 781
Amanda Configuration 782
Enabling Amanda on the Network 783
Using Amanda 783
Backups with dump and restore 784

The dump Levels 784
Recording Backups 786
Operations with dump 786
Recovering Backups 787

Part VII   Network Administration

35   Administering TCP/IP Networks 793
TCP/IP Protocol Suite 793
IPv4 and IPv6 796
TCP/IP Network Addresses 797
IPv4 Network Addresses 797
Class-Based IP Addressing 797
Netmask 798
Classless Interdomain Routing (CIDR) 799
Obtaining an IP Address 802
Broadcast Addresses 804
Gateway Addresses 804
Name Server Addresses 805
IPv6 Addressing 805
IPv6 Address Format 805
IPv6 Interface Identifiers 806
IPv6 Address Types 806
IPv6 and IPv4 Coexistence Methods 808
TCP/IP Configuration Files 808
Identifying Hostnames: /etc/hosts 809
/etc/resolv.conf 810
/etc/sysconfig/network-scripts 810
/etc/sysconfig/networking 810
/etc/services 811
/etc/protocols 811
/etc/sysconfig/network 811
Domain Name Service (DNS) 811
host.conf 812
/etc/nsswitch.conf: Name Service Switch 813
Network Interfaces and Routes: ifconfig and route 815
Network Startup Script: /etc/rc.d/init.d/network 815
Interface Configuration Scripts:
/etc/sysconfig/network-scripts 816
ifconfig 817
Routing 818
Monitoring Your Network: ping, netstat, tcpdump, EtherApe, Ettercap,
and Wireshark 820
ping 820
Ettercap 821
Wireshark 821
tcpdump 823
netstat 823
IP Aliasing 824

36 Domain Name System **825**
    DNS Address Translations 825
        Fully Qualified Domain Names 825
        IPv4 Addresses 826
        IPv6 Addressing 826
        Manual Translations: /etc/hosts 826
        DNS Servers 826
        DNS Operation 827
        DNS Clients: Resolvers 827
    Local Area Network Addressing 828
        IPv4 Private Networks 828
        IPv6 Private Networks 828
        Local Network Address Example Using IPv4 829
    BIND 830
        Alternative DNS Servers 830
        BIND Servers and Tools 831
        Starting and Stopping the BIND Server 832
    Domain Name Service Configuration 832
        DNS Zones 832
        DNS Servers Types 833
        Location of Bind Server Files: /etc/named/chroot 834
    named.conf 834
        The zone Statement 835
        Configuration Statements 836
    The options Statement 837
        The directory Option 837
        The forwarders Option 838
        The notify Option 838
        An IPv4 named.conf Example 838
        An IPv6 named.conf Example 839
        Caching-Only Server 840
    Resource Records for Zone Files 840
        Resource Record Types 841
        Time To Live Directive and Field: $TTL 841
        Start of Authority: SOA 842
        Name Server: NS 843
        Address Record: A and A6 843
        Mail Exchanger: MX 844
        Aliases: CNAME 845
        Pointer Record: PTR 845
        Host Information: HINFO, RP, MINFO, and TXT 846
    Zone Files 846
        Zone Files for Internet Zones 846
        IPv6 Zone File Example 850
        Reverse Mapping File 850
        Localhost Reverse Mapping 853
    Subdomains and Slaves 854
        Subdomain Zones 854
        Subdomain Records 854
        Slave Servers 854
    IP Virtual Domains 856

Cache File 857
Dynamic Update: DHCP and Journal Files 857
    TSIG Signatures and Updates 858
    Manual Updates: nsupdate 858
DNS Security: Access Control Lists, TSIG, and DNSSEC 859
    Access Control Lists 859
    Secret Keys 860
    DNSSEC 860
    TSIG Keys 862
Split DNS: Views 863
    Internal and External Views 864
    Configuring Views 864
    Split View Example 865

37 Network Autoconfiguration: IPv6, DHCPv6, and DHCP **867**
IPv6 Stateless Autoconfiguration 867
    Generating the Local Address 868
    Generating the Full Address: Router Advertisements 868
    Router Renumbering 868
IPv6 Stateful Autoconfiguration: DHCPv6 870
    Linux as an IPv6 Router: radvd 871
DHCP for IPv4 872
    Configuring DHCP IPv4 Client Hosts 872
    Configuring the DHCP IPv4 Server 873
    Dynamic IPv4 Addresses for DHCP 876
    DHCP Dynamic DNS Updates 878
    DHCP Subnetworks 880
    DHCP Fixed Addresses 881

38 NFS, NIS, and GFS **885**
Network File Systems: NFS and /etc/exports 885
    NFSv4 885
    NFS Daemons 886
    Starting and Stopping NFS 886
    Configuring NFS with the NFS Configuration Tool 886
    NFS Configuration: /etc/exports 887
    NFS File and Directory Security with nfs4 Access Lists 891
    Controlling Accessing to NFS Serves 891
    Mounting NFS File Systems: NFS Clients 893
Network Information Service: NIS 896
    NIS Servers 896
    Netgroups 899
    NIS Clients 900
Distributed Network File Systems 901
    Parallel Virtual File System (PVFS) 902
    Coda 903
Red Hat Global File System (GFS and GFS 2) 903
    system-config-cluster 904
    GFS 2 Packages (Fedora Core 6 and on) 905
    GFS 2 Service Scripts 905

Implementing a GFS 2 File System 905
GFS Tools 906
GFS File System Operations 906
GFS 1 Packages (Red Hat Enterprise Linux 4, Fedora Core 4/5) ... 908

39   Samba 909
Samba Documentation 909
Samba Applications 910
Starting Up Samba 911
Firewalls 912
Testing Samba from Linux 912
Configuring Samba Access from Windows 912
Samba Configuration File and Tools 913
User Level Security 913
Samba Passwords: smbpasswd 915
Configuring Samba with system-config-samba 916
Server Configuration with system-config-samba 917
Adding Samba Users with system-config-samba 917
Specifying Samba Shares with system-config-samba 917
The Samba smb.conf Configuration File 917
SWAT and smb.conf 919
Activating SWAT 919
Accessing SWAT 920
SWAT Configuration Pages 921
Creating a New Share with SWAT 922
A SWAT-Generated smb.conf Example 922
Global Section 923
Passwords 925
Homes Section 925
Printer Section 925
Shares 926
Printers 927
Variable Substitutions 928
Testing the Samba Configuration 929
Domain Logons 929
Accessing Samba Services with Clients 930
Accessing Windows Samba Shares from GNOME 930
smbclient 930
mount.cifs: mount -t cifs 932
Sharing Windows Directories and Printers with Samba Clients 933
Windows Clients 934

Index 935

Acknowledgments

I would like to thank everyone at McGraw-Hill who made this book a reality, particularly Jane Brownlow, sponsoring editor, for her continued encouragement and analysis as well as management of such a complex project; Dr. Ibrahim Haddad, the technical editor, whose analysis and suggestions proved very insightful and helpful; Jennifer Housh, acquisitions coordinator, who provided needed resources and helpful advice; Robert Campbell, copy editor, for his excellent job of editing the book, as well as his insightful comments; project editor Patty Mon who, with project managers Sam RC and Vasundhara Sawhney, incorporated the large number of features found in this book as well as coordinating the intricate task of generating the final version. Thanks also to Scott Rogers who initiated the project.

Special thanks to Linus Torvalds, the creator of Linux, and to those who continue to develop Linux as an open, professional, and effective operating system accessible to anyone. Thanks also to the academic community whose special dedication has developed Unix as a flexible and versatile operating system. I would also like to thank professors and students at the University of California, Berkeley, for the experience and support in developing new and different ways of understanding operating system technologies.

I would also like to thank my parents, George and Cecelia, and my brothers, George, Robert, and Mark, for their support and encouragement with such a difficult project. Also Valerie and Marylou and my nieces and nephews, Aleina, Larisa, Justin, Christopher, and Dylan, for their support and deadline reminders.

Introduction

The Red Hat Linux and Fedora distributions have become one of the major Linux distributions, bringing to the PC all the power and flexibility of a Unix workstation as well as a complete set of Internet applications and a fully functional desktop interface. This book is designed not only to be a complete reference on Linux, but also to provide clear and detailed explanations of Linux features. No prior knowledge of Unix is assumed; Linux is an operating system anyone can use.

Fedora and Red Hat Enterprise

Red Hat has split its Linux development into two lines: Red Hat Enterprise Linux and the Fedora Project. The Red Hat Enterprise Linux product line consists of Red Hat Enterprise Linux WS (workstation), Red Hat Enterprise Linux ES (entry/mid server), and the Red Hat Enterprise Linux AS (advanced server). As a result, the enterprise family products are controlled releases from Red Hat for commercial deployments with new releases issued every two years or so. The second development line falls within the Fedora Project, an Open Source initiative supported by Red Hat. The Fedora releases will be issued every six months on average, incorporating the most recent development in the Linux kernel, as well as supported applications.

The Fedora release consists entirely of Open Source software. Developers from around the globe can contribute to the project following Open Source processes giving them freedom in promoting enhancements, new features, and new applications, while maintaining fast pace releases with the course of rapid online development. Unlike Red Hat Enterprise Linux, the Fedora version of Linux is entirely free and it is not a supported Red Hat product. You can download the most current version, including test betas, from **fedoraproject.org**. The Fedora Project release will replace the original standard Red Hat Linux distribution.

The Red Hat Enterprise line of products is designed for corporate, research, and business applications. These products focus on reliability, stability, and performance, in addition to supporting multiple processor architectures. They are released on a much more controlled schedule than the Fedora Project versions.

This book covers the current Fedora release, while maintaining compatibility with Red Hat Enterprise Linux. This book identifies seven major Linux topics: Basic setup, environments, applications, security, servers, administration, and network administration. Whereas the book details the latest Red Hat tools, desktops, and kernel features in the Fedora project, it also covers in depth the network servers, administrative tasks, and applications featured in Red Hat Enterprise Linux.

Important Features with Fedora 7

With Fedora, several key features are incorporated as standardized and stable components of the Linux operations system. These include changes to distribution methods, device detection, security support, and desktop use. Some of these are listed here, with a complete listing in Chapter 1.

- Fedora features automatic detection and configuration of removable devices like USB printers, digital cameras, and card readers, treating CD/DVD disks as removable devices, as well as fully detecting IDE CD/DVD devices.

- Fedora software is easily downloaded and updated from the Fedora software repository (formerly Core and Extras).

- Fedora is distributed using different spins (install disks) to perform an initial installation. You can then use the Fedora repository to install additional software. You can even create your own install spin.

- Fedora Red Hat provides full IPv6 network protocol support, including automatic addressing and renumbering.

- SE Linux is now a integral component of Fedora and Red Hat, providing system-wide security. You can set different levels of control and create your own policies.

- Extensive and simple virtualization support (full and para), using Xen, KVM, and the Virtual Machine Manager.

- The PUP software updater automatically updates your Fedora system and all its installed applications from the Yum Fedora online repositories.

- GFS version 2 support for a network distributed file system.

Linux Features

Fedora 4 includes features that have become a standard part of any Linux distribution, like the desktops, Unix compatibility, network servers, and numerous software applications like Office, multimedia, and Internet applications. GNOME and the K Desktop Environment (KDE) have become standard desktop Graphical User Interfaces (GUI) for Linux, noted for their power, flexibility, and ease-of-use. These are complete desktop environments that are more flexible than either Windows or the Mac/OS. KDE and GNOME have become the standard GUI interface for Linux systems. You can install both, run applications from either, and easily switch from one to the other. Both have become integrated components of Linux, with applications and tools for every kind of task and operation. Instead of treating GNOME and KDE as separate entities, GNOME and KDE tools and applications are presented throughout the book.

Linux is also a fully functional Unix operating system. It has all the standard features of a powerful Unix system, including a complete set of Unix shells such as BASH, TCSH, and the Z-shell. Those familiar with the Unix interface can use any of these shells, with the same Unix commands, filters, and configuration features.

For the Internet, Linux has become a platform for very powerful network applications. With Linux, you can become a part of the Internet by creating your own Web and FTP sites. Other users can access your Linux systems, several at the same time, using different services. You can also use very powerful GNOME, KDE, and Unix clients for mail and news.

Linux systems are not limited to the Internet. You can use them on any local intranet, setting up an ftp or Web site for your network. Red Hat Linux comes equipped with a variety of fully functional servers already installed and ready to use.

A wide array of applications operate on Red Hat and Fedora Linux. Numerous desktop applications are continually released on the Fedora repository, as well as on third-party Fedora-compliant repositories. The GNU general public licensed software provides professional-level applications such as programming development tools, editors and word processors, as well as numerous specialized applications such as those for graphics and sound.

How to Use This Book

The first two sections of the book are designed to cover tasks you would need to perform to get your system up and running. After an introduction to the working environment, including both GNOME and KDE desktops, you learn how to quickly update your system, manage users, groups, and set up your printer using the Red Hat and Fedora administrative tools. The software management is nearly automatic, letting you install software on your system with just a couple of mouse clicks. Internet access can be set up for modems, DSL, wireless, and Ethernet networks with easy-to-use administrative tools that guide you every step of the way. All these topics are covered in greater detail later in the book.

Since this book is really several books in one—a user interface book, a security book, a server book, and an administration book—how you choose to use it depends upon how you want to use your Fedora Linux system. Almost all Linux operations can be carried out using either the GNOME or KDE interface. You can focus on the GNOME and KDE sections and their corresponding tools and applications in the different chapters throughout the book. On the other hand, if you want to delve deeper into the Unix aspects of Linux, you can check out the shell chapters and the corresponding shell-based applications in other chapters. If you only want to use Linux for its Internet services, then concentrate on the Internet clients and servers. If you want to use Linux as a multiuser system servicing many users or integrate it into a local network, you can use the detailed system, file, and network administration information provided in the administration chapters. None of these tasks are in any way exclusive. If you are working in a business environment, you will probably make use of all three aspects. Single users may concentrate more on the desktops and the Internet features, whereas administrators may make more use of the security and networking features.

Section Topics

The first part of this book is designed to help you start using Fedora Linux quickly. It provides an introduction to Red Hat and Fedora Linux, their current features, providing a list of resources, including software repositories, documentation sites, newsgroups, and Linux news and development sites. The next chapter covers the streamlined installation procedure for most distributions, which takes about 30 minutes or less. The installation program provides excellent commentary, describing each step in detail. In this section you also learn the essentials of using desktop, along with the basic of working on the shell command line. System configuration tasks like adding printers and creating new user accounts are presented with the easiest methods, without much of the complex detail described in the administration chapters that is unnecessary for basic operation. Basic network configuration tasks are discussed such as setting up a LAN connection. You learn how to update and install new software easily using Fedora Yum repositories. With the Pirut software installer you can install the latest versions directly from a repository with a few clicks. The software updater (PUP) automatically detects updates and lets you perform all updates with a single click.

Part II of this book deals with Fedora Linux environments. Here you are introduced to the different kinds of user environments available for Linux, starting with KDE and GNOME. Different features such as applets, the Panel, and configuration tools are described in detail. With either of these interfaces, you can run all your applications using icons, menus, and windows. At any time, you can open up a terminal window through which you can enter standard Linux commands on a command line. You can also choose to use just the standard Unix command line interface to run any of the standard Unix commands. Next the BASH shell and its various file, directory, and filter commands are examined.

Part III of this book discusses in detail the many office, multimedia, and Internet applications you can use on your Linux system, beginning with Office suites like OpenOffice and KOffice. The different database management systems available are also discussed, along with the Web site locations where you can download them. A variety of different text editors are also available, including several GNOME and KDE editors, as well as the Vim (enhanced VI). Linux automatically installs mail, news, FTP, and Web browser applications, as well as FTP and Web servers. Both KDE and GNOME come with a full set of mail, news, FTP clients, and Web browsers. There are also many independent mail clients, newsreaders, and Internet tools that you can easily install from the Fedora repository.

Part IV demonstrates how to implement security precautions using encryption, authentication, and firewalls. Coverage of the General Public License Privacy Guard (GPG) shows you how to implement public and private key-based encryption. With Luks (Linux Unified Key Setup) you can easily encrypt file systems. SELinux provides comprehensive and refined control of all your network and system resources. IPsec tools let you use the IPSEC protocol to encrypt and authenticate network transmissions. Network security topics cover firewalls and encryption using netfilter (iptables) to protect your system, the Secure Shell (SSH) to provide secure remote transmissions, and Kerberos to provide secure authentication.

Part V discusses Internet servers you can run on Red Hat Linux, including FTP, Web, and Mail servers. The Apache Web server chapter covers standard configuration directives like those for automatic indexing, as well as the newer virtual host directives. Sendmail, Postfix, IMAP, and POP mail servers are covered. The INN news server, CUPS print server, MySQL database server, and the Squid proxy server are also examined.

Part VI discusses system administration topics, including user, software, file system, system, device, and kernel administration. There are detailed descriptions of the configuration files used in administration tasks and how to make entries in them. First, basic system administration tasks are covered, such as selecting runlevels, monitoring your system, and scheduling shutdowns. Then aspects of setting up and controlling users and groups are discussed. Presentations include both the GUI tools you can use for these tasks and the underlying configurations files and commands. Software installation has been simplified with package management systems, like the Red Hat Package Manager (RPM) and Pirut and Pup software manager and updater, as well as Yum supported repositories like the Fedora repository. Using, updating, and configuring the Linux kernel with its modules is covered in detail along with procedures for installing new kernels. Different methods of virtualization are covered, like full (KVM) and para-virtualizaton (Xen). With the Virtual Machine Manager, both can be used to easily install and run guest operation systems. Different file system tasks are covered, such as mounting file systems, managing file systems with HAL and udev, and configuring RAID devices and LVM volumes. Devices are automatically detected with udev and the Hardware Abstraction Layer (HAL). Fedora uses a hotplug model for managing all its devices. The udev utility automatically generates device interfaces, managing both fixed and removable devices using its own rules. HAL provides hotplug information about devices to applications, affording them direct access.

Part VII covers network administration, dealing with topics such as configuring remote file system access and setting up firewalls. Configuration files and features for the Domain Name System (DNS) and its BIND server are examined in detail, along with features like virtual domains and IP aliases. IPv6 support for Internet addressing and DNS configuration is discussed in detail, showing the new IPv6 formats replacing the older IPv4 versions. You also learn how to implement your own IPv4 Dynamic Host Configuration Protocol (DHCP) server to dynamically assign hosts IP addresses or how IPv6 automatic addressing and renumbering operate. The various network file system interfaces and services like GFS version 2, NFS for Unix, and NIS networks are presented. The chapter on Samba shows how to access Windows file systems and printers.

Getting Started

CHAPTER 1
Introduction to Red Hat
and Fedora Linux

CHAPTER 2
Installing Fedora

CHAPTER 3
Interface Basics: Login,
Desktop, Help, Repositories,
Multimedia, and Spins

CHAPTER 4
System Configuration

CHAPTER 5
Network Configuration

Introduction to Red Hat and Fedora Linux

*L*inux is a fast, stable, and open source operating system for PC computers and workstations that features professional-level Internet services, extensive development tools, fully functional graphical user interfaces (GUIs), and a massive number of applications ranging from office suites to multimedia applications. Linux was developed in the early 1990s by Linus Torvalds, along with other programmers around the world. As an operating system, Linux performs many of the same functions as Unix, Macintosh, Windows, and Windows NT. However, Linux is distinguished by its power and flexibility, along with being freely available. Most PC operating systems, such as Windows, began their development within the confines of small, restricted personal computers, which have only recently become more versatile machines. Such operating systems are constantly being upgraded to keep up with the ever-changing capabilities of PC hardware. Linux, on the other hand, was developed in a different context. Linux is a PC version of the Unix operating system that has been used for decades on mainframes and minicomputers and is currently the system of choice for network servers and workstations. Linux brings the speed, efficiency, scalability, and flexibility of Unix to your PC, taking advantage of all the capabilities that personal computers can now provide.

Technically, Linux consists of the operating system program, referred to as the *kernel*, which is the part originally developed by Linus Torvalds. But it has always been distributed with a massive number of software applications, ranging from network servers and security programs to office applications and development tools. Linux has evolved as part of the open source software movement, in which independent programmers joined together to provide free quality software to any user. Linux has become the premier platform for open source software, much of it developed by the Free Software Foundation's GNU project. Many of these applications are bundled as part of standard Linux distributions. Currently, thousands of open source applications are available for Linux from sites like the Open Source Development Network's (OSDN) **sourceforge.net**, the software depositories **rpmfind.net**, **rpm.livna.org**, **freshrpms.net**, KDE's **www.kde-apps.org**, and GNOME's **www.gnome.org**. Most of these applications are also incorporated into the Fedora repository, using packages that are Fedora compliant. You should always check the Fedora repository (Applications | Add/Remove Software) first for the software you want. Third party Fedora compliant software is also available from Livna and Freshrpms repositories (**rpm.livna.org** and **fresrpms.net**).

Along with Linux's operating system capabilities come powerful networking features, including support for Internet, intranets, and Windows networking. As a norm, Linux distributions include fast, efficient, and stable Internet servers, such as the Web, FTP, and DNS servers, along with proxy, news, and mail servers. In other words, Linux has everything you need to set up, support, and maintain a fully functional network.

With the both GNOME and K Desktop, Linux also provides GUI interfaces with that same level of flexibility and power. Unlike Windows and the Mac, Linux enables you to choose the interface you want and then customize it further, adding panels, applets, virtual desktops, and menus, all with full drag-and-drop capabilities and Internet-aware tools.

Linux does all this at the right price. Linux is free, including the network servers and GUI desktops. Unlike the official Unix operating system, Linux is distributed freely under a GNU General Public License as specified by the Free Software Foundation, making it available to anyone who wants to use it. GNU (the acronym stands for "GNU's Not Unix") is a project initiated and managed by the Free Software Foundation to provide free software to users, programmers, and developers. Linux is copyrighted, not public domain. However, a GNU public license has much the same effect as the software's being in the public domain. The GNU general public license is designed to ensure Linux remains free and, at the same time, standardized. Linux is technically the operating system kernel—the core operations— and only one official Linux kernel exists. People sometimes have the mistaken impression that Linux is somehow less than a professional operating system because it is free. Linux is, in fact, a PC, workstation, and server version of Unix. Many consider it far more stable and much more powerful than Windows. This power and stability have made Linux an operating system of choice as a network server.

To appreciate Linux completely, you need to understand the special context in which the Unix operating system was developed. Unix, unlike most other operating systems, was developed in a research and academic environment. In universities, research laboratories, data centers, and enterprises, Unix is the system most often used. Its development has paralleled the entire computer and communications revolution over the past several decades. Computer professionals often developed new computer technologies on Unix, such as those developed for the Internet. Although a sophisticated system, Unix was designed from the beginning to be flexible. The Unix system itself can be easily modified to create different versions. In fact, many different vendors maintain different official versions of Unix. IBM, Sun, and Hewlett-Packard all sell and maintain their own versions of Unix. The unique demands of research programs often require that Unix be tailored to their own special needs. This inherent flexibility in the Unix design in no way detracts from its quality. In fact, this flexibility attests to the ruggedness of Unix, allowing it to adapt to practically any environment. This is the context in which Linux was developed. Linux is, in this sense, one other version of Unix—a version for the PC. The development of Linux by computer professionals working in a research-like environment reflects the way Unix versions have usually been developed. Linux is publicly licensed and free—and reflects the deep roots Unix has in academic institutions, with their sense of public service and support. Linux is a top-rate operating system accessible to everyone, free of charge.

Red Hat and Fedora Linux

Red Hat Linux is currently the most popular Linux distribution. As a company, Red Hat provides software and services to implement and support professional and commercial Linux systems. Red Hat has split its Linux development into two lines, Red Hat Enterprise Linux and the Fedora Project. Red Hat Enterprise Linux features commercial enterprise products for servers and workstations, with controlled releases issued every two years or so. The Fedora Project is an Open Source initiative whose Fedora release will be issued every six months on average, incorporating the most recent development in Linux operating system features as well as supported applications. Red Hat freely distributes its Fedora version of Linux under the GNU General Public License; the company generates income by providing professional-level support, consulting services, and training services. The Red Hat Certified Engineers (RHCE) training and certification program is designed to provided reliable and highly capable administrators and developers to maintain and customize professional-level Red Hat systems. Red Hat has forged software alliances with major companies like Oracle, IBM, Dell, and Sun.

Currently, Red Hat provides several commercial products, known as Red Hat Enterprise Linux. These include the Red Hat Enterprise Advanced Server for intensive enterprise-level tasks; Red Hat Enterprise ES, which is a version of Linux designed for small businesses and networks; and Red Hat Enterprise Workstation. Red Hat also maintains for its customers the Red Hat Network, which provides automatic updating of the operating system and software packages on your system. Specialized products include the Stronghold secure Web server, versions of Linux tailored for IBM- and Itanium-based servers, and GNUPro development tools (**www.redhat.com/software/gnupro**).

Red Hat also maintains a strong commitment to open source Linux applications. Red Hat originated the RPM package system used on several distributions, which automatically installs and removes software packages. Red Hat is also providing much of the software development for the GNOME desktop, and it is a strong supporter of KDE.

Red Hat provides an extensive set of configuration tools designed to manage tasks such as adding users, starting servers, accessing remote directories, and configuring devices such as your monitor or printer. These tools are accessible on the System Settings and Server Settings menus and windows, as well as by their names, all beginning with the term "system-config" (see Chapters 4 and 5).

The new release of Fedora features key updates to critical applications as well as new tools replacing former ones. Fedora includes the GNOME desktop, the Apache Web server, the GNU Compiler Collection (GCC), and the GNU Java Compiler (GJC). Configuration tools, including Program Manager and the PUP updater for managing software and system-config-cluster for configuring your distribution, are included and others have been updated. The extensive collection of Fedora-compliant software that was held in the Fedora Extras repository has been merged into one large Fedora repository. The former Fedora Core and Fedora Extras repositories have been merged into a single Fedora repository.

Installing Fedora has been significantly simplified. A core set of applications are installed, and you add to them as you wish. Following installation, added software is taken from online repositories, not the disk. Install screens have been reduced to just a few screens, moving quickly through default partitioning, network detection, and time settings, to the package selection. Firewall and SELinux configuration are part of the post-install configuration procedure.

The Fedora distribution of Linux is available online at numerous FTP sites. Fedora maintains its own FTP site at **download.fedora.redhat.com** along with mirrors at **fedoraproject.org/Download/mirrors.html**, where you can download the entire current release of Fedora Linux, as well as updates and additional software. Red Hat was designed from its inception to work on numerous hardware platforms. Currently, Red Hat Enterprise supports the Sparc, Intel, and Alpha platforms. See **www.redhat.com** for more information, including extensive documentation such as Red Hat manuals, FAQs, and links to other Linux sites.

If you purchase Red Hat Enterprise Linux from Red Hat, you are entitled to online support services. Although Linux is free, Red Hat as a company specializes in support services, providing customers with its expertise in developing solutions to problems that may arise or using Linux to perform any of several possible tasks, such as e-commerce or database operations.

The Fedora Project

The Fedora release is maintained and developed by an Open Source project called the Fedora Project. The release consists entirely of open source software. Development is carried out using contributions from Linux developers, allowing them free rein to promote enhancements and new features. The project is designed to work much like other open source projects, with releases keeping pace with the course of rapid online development. The Fedora project features detailed documentation of certain topics like Installation and desktop user guides at **doc.fedoraproject.org**.

The Fedora versions of Linux are entirely free. You can download the most current version, including betas, from **www.fedoraproject.org** or **fedoraproject.org/Download/mirrors.html**. You can update Fedora using the Package Updater (PUP) to access the Fedora Yum repository. Updating can be supported by any one of several Yum Fedora repositories. Access is automatically configured during installation. The Fedora Project release replaces the original standard Red Hat Linux version that consisted of the entry-level Red Hat release. In addition to the Fedora software, the Fedora Project will also provide popular compatible packages (see Table 1-2 later in this chapter).

Red Hat Enterprise Linux

The Red Hat Enterprise line of products are designed for corporate, research, and business applications (**www.redhat.com**). These products focus on reliability and stability. They are released on a much more controlled schedule than the Fedora Project versions. What was once the low-cost consumer version of Red Hat Linux is replaced by a scaled-down commercial desktoop versions for consumers and small business.

Red Hat provides both desktop and server versions of Red Hat Enterprise Linux. The desktop versions are offered as a simple desktop, a full workstation, or either a simple desktop or workstation with virtualization support (multi-OS). Keep in mind that the lowest level product, the simple desktop, does not include certain networking features like Samba and NFS servers, limiting the ability to share data. The workstation desktop versions have no system memory limit, provides software development support, and include Samba and NFS servers. The workstation virtualization version features unlimited guest OS support.

Red Hat offers two Enterprise server versions, Red Hat Enterprise Linux and the Advanced Platform version. The Red Hat Enterprise version provides less server capability limiting both servers and virtual guests. The Advanced Platform includes storage cluster support (GFS) as well as unlimited servers and virtual guests. Both Red Hat Linux Enterprise server versions have standard and premium editions which vary in their level of customer support. A basic edition is also provided for the standard server version which provides minimal support.

All versions, both desktop and server, feature automatic software updating with the Red Hat Network (RHN).

Red Hat Enterprise Linux is valued for its stability, often providing more stable implementations than Fedora. It is licensed as an open source GPL product, so is technically available to anyone. The versions that Red Hat sells include commercial products and support that are not open source. Red Hat does, however, freely provide its open source enterprise versions for download from its FTP site, **ftp.redhat.com/pub/redhat/linux/enterprise**. Earlier Enterprise versions are available in binary and ISO formats, though without any commercial features. The current Enterprise version is available as source files only.

CENTOS: Community Enterprise Operating System

Should you want to take advantage of the stability and reliability of Red Hat Enterprise Linux and not purchase the product, you can, instead, use CENTOS, the Community Enterprise Operating System (**www.centos.org**). CENTOS make no claim to have any official association with Red Hat. Instead, under the GPL license and Red Hat's open source distribution policies, it makes use of Red Hat Enterprise Linux source files to provide its own Linux distribution. In effect, with CENTOS, you can enjoy the stability, reliability, and enterprise capability of Red Hat Enterprise Linux, without the commercial support. Keep in mind though that CENTOS is an independent operation that builds its own distribution. It has none of the support or guarantees that Red Hat provides for its products.

Red Hat and Fedora Documentation

Red Hat maintains an extensive library of documentation for Red Hat Enterprise Linux (see Table 1-1). From the Red Hat home page, you can click to its support page, and then on its Documentation page. The documentation page provides a pop-up menu from which to select products. Red Hat Enterprise Linux is selected by default. Click Go to open the Red Hat Enterprise Linux documentation page, which lists the complete set of Red Hat manuals. The documentation is arranged by version. Documentation covers topics like virtualization, the Global File System (GFS), Logical Volume Mangement (LVM), and the Installation Guide. Tip, HOW-TO, and FAQ documents are also provided. All the Red Hat documentation is freely available under the GNU General Public License. Before installing Red Hat Enterprise Linux on your system, you may want to check the online Installation guide. The Red Hat Magazine provides information on the latest features.

Documentation for Fedora can be found at **docs.fedoraproject.org**, with specialize topics provided at **fedoraproject.org/wiki/Docs**. The Fedora installation guide provides a detailed description of all your install procedures. The Fedora desktop users guide covers basic desktop operations like logging in, using office applications, and accessing the Web. Several dedicated Fedora support sites are available that provide helpful information, including **fedoraforums.org**, **www.fedoraproject.org**, and **fedoranews.org**. The **fedoraforums.org** is a

References	Description
www.redhat.com	The Red Hat Web site
www.redhat.com/magazine	Red Hat Magazine with specialized articles on latest developments
www.centos.org	Community Enterprise Operating System, CENTOS. (Linux distribution derived from Red Hat Enterprise open source packages)
fedoraproject.org	The Fedora Project (earlier page at **fedora.redhat.com**)
docs.fedoraproject.org **fedoraproject.org/wiki/Docs**	Documentation and support tutorials for Fedora releases. Includes release notes and specialized information like installation, desktop use, and SELinux
fedoraforums.org	End-user discussion support forum, endorsed by the Fedora Project; includes FAQs and news links
www.fedorafaq.org	Unofficial FAQ with quick help topics, such as enabling MP3 and 3-D graphic card support
fedoranews.org	Collects the latest news and developments on Fedora, as well as articles and blogs about recent changes
www.linux-foundation.org	The Linux Foundation, official Linux development
www.kernel.org	Latest Linux kernels

TABLE 1-1   Red Hat Linux and Fedora Resources

Fedora Project–sponsored forum for end-user support. Here you can post questions and check responses for common problems. One of the more useful sites is the unofficial Fedora FAQ at **www.fedorafaq.org**. Here you will find solutions to the more common problems like graphic card issues and enabling MP3 support.

TIP *Your Firefox Browser will already be configured with panels for accessing poplular documentation and support sites. These include the Fedora Project home page, the Fedora Weekly News, community support from Fedora forums, as well as communication page, the Fedora Package List, the Red Hat Magazine.*

Fedora maintains detailed specialized documentation, like information on understanding how udev is implemented or how SELinux is configured. For much of the documentation you will have to rely on installed documentation in **/usr/share/doc** or the Man and info pages, as well as the context help button for different applications running on your desktop. Web sites for software like those for GNOME, KDE, and OpenOffice.org will provide extensive applicable documentation. For installation, you can use the Fedora Installation Guide at **docs.fedoraproject.org/install-guide**.

Fedora 7

Fedora 7 features a much more streamlined look and feel, with new Echo icons and a more responsive desktop, as well as new administration tools for easier installation, software update, and management.

- Fedora Core and Fedora Extras repositories have been merged into one Fedora software repository.

- Fedora disks are released as a set of spins that collect software for different purposes. Currently there are three spins available: GNOME, KDE, and Fedora. The Fedora spin includes a collection of workstation and server software. Spins are created with Pungi, which you can use to develop your own customized spins.

- Fedora features a Live CD with which you can run Fedora from a CD-ROM drive.

- With the alternative compiz window manager, desktop AIGLX effects can be enabled. From the Administration | Preferences | Look And Feel | Desktop Effect entry, choose Enable Effects. You will see wobbling windows when moved, and rotating workspaces with the workspace switcher.

- Encrypted file system support is offered for swap and non-root partitions. Use **gnome-luks-format** or **crypsetup** to create the encrypted partition.

- Kernel-based Virtualization Machine (KVM) support is included with the kernel. KVM uses hardware virtualization enabled processors like Intel VT (Virtualization Technology) and AMD SVM (Secure Virtual Machine) processors to support hardware-level guest operating systems. Most standard Intel and AMD processors already provide this support.

- Use Virtual Machine Manger to manage and install both KVM and Xen virtual machines.

- To better manage SELinux configurations, you can use setroubleshooter, which will notify you of any problems.

- The java-gcj-compat collection provides Java runtime environment compatibility. It consists of GNU Java runtime (libgcj), the Eclipse Java compiler (ecj), and a set of wrappers and links (java-gcj-compat).

- Localized Common User Directories (**xdg-user-dirs**). Automatically sets up Documents, Video, and Music directories in user home directories.

- User-controlled screen resolution is available through System | Preferences | Screen Resolution.

- The Pirut Program Manager manages software directly from Yum online repositories.

- .NET is supported using Mono (Novell). .NET-supported packages such as F-Spot and Beagle desktop search are included.

- Features automatic detection of removable devices like USB printers, digital cameras, and card readers. CD/DVD disks are treated as removable devices, automatically displayed and accessed when inserted.

- The IDE hard disk drivers are now supported by the Serial ATA drivers. All IDE devices are named with an **sd** prefix, not the **hd** prefix.

- Fedora also provides full IPv6 network protocol support, including automatic addressing and renumbering.

- SELinux is an integral component of Fedora, providing system-wide security. You can set different levels of control and create your own policies. SELinux uses modules for configuration.

- A wide range of multimedia applications are included, such as a video player and a TV viewer, along with compatible support from various multimedia applications and libraries available from **freshrpms.net**, such as DVD and DivX support.

- With the Network Monitor, you can automatically select wireless connections.

- Information about hotplugged devices is provided to applications with the Hardware Abstraction Layer (HAL) from **freedesktop.org**. This allows applications like GNOME to easily display and manage removable devices.

- All devices are treated logically as removable, and automatically configured by udev. Fixed devices are simply ones that cannot be removed. This feature is meant to let Linux accommodate a wide variety of devices, such as digital cameras, PDAs, and cell phones. PCMCIA devices are managed by udev and HAL directly.

- Hard disk storage can be implemented with the Logical Volume Manager (LVM), letting you manage your storage more easily (default at installations).

- The PUP Package updater can be used to automatically update your Fedora system and all its installed applications, from the Yum Fedora online repositories.

- You can download free and licensed MP3 support from www.flluendo.com. The site also provides inexpensive multimedia codec licensing for gstreamer plugins.

- The current version of Office.org provides very effective and MS Office–competitive office applications, featuring support for document storage standards.

- CodeWeavers' CrossOver Office and Wine run Windows applications, including Office, directly in Linux windows.

- Kernel headers, used for module source and application compilation and development, are now included with the kernel binaries and installed at **/usr/src/kernels**. The full kernel source no longer needs to be installed.

- The Fedora kernel source SRPM packages are extracted to the Red Hat Build directories in **/usr/src/redhat**. The **/usr/src/linux** directory is no longer used for the kernel source. Original kernel sources in normal archives (tar) should be extracted in a user directory.

- The Xen Virtualization kernel is also provided, which allows the use of virtual machines on which you can run different operating systems adapted for use on Xen. You can also use the virtual machines to run different instances of the kernel, allowing developers and users to run and test new software without endangering the primary system. The single Xen kernel version incorporates both user and host support. Use virt-install for installing guest (user) access.

- Updated versions of all network servers are provided, including the Apache Web server, the vsftp FTP server, the BIND DNS server, and the Samba server.

- Fedora has a complete range of system and network administration tools featuring easy-to-use GUI interfaces (see Chapter 4, Table 4-1).

- InfiniBand high-speed connections are now supported by the kernel. Currently used for local clusters and supercomputers, they provide transmissions at 10 gigabits per second and can go much higher.

- For software development, Fedora includes the Eclipse IDE software tool.

- The Global File System (GFS2) cluster file system is included, supported directly by the kernel. GFS version 1 has been replaced by GFS version 2, with many changes to its package and support tools configurations (see Chapter 38).

- The kernel source is no longer included with the distribution binaries. You have to download it separately. It no longer uses **/usr/src/linux**, but the RPM **BUILD** and **SPEC** directories in **/usr/src/redhat**. You need to specify which version of the kernel to extract (see Chapter 33).

- You can compile modules using kernel headers in the **/lib/modules/***version***/source** directory (now a link to kernel headers in the **/usr/src/kernels** directory through the **build** link).

- Fedora uses the X.org X Windows server instead of XFree86. Configuration and server names are different from XFree86, for instance, the **xorg.conf** configuration file and xorg server. Configuration files are still located in **/etc/X11**.

Fedora Live CD

With the Fedora Live CD you can run Fedora from any CD-ROM drive. In effect, you can carry your operating system with you on just a CD-ROM. New users could also use the Live-CD to check out Fedora to see if they like it. Files and data can be written to removable devices like USB drives. You could also mount partitions from hard drives on the system you are running the Live CD on. You can find out more about the Fedora Live CD at **fedoraproject.org/wiki/FedoraLiveCD**.

The Live CD provide by Fedora includes a very limited set of software packages. OpenOffice applications are not provided, just Abiword for word processing and Gnumeric for spread sheets. Servers are not included. For desktop support you use GNOME. Other than these limitations, you have a fully operational Fedora desktop. You have the full set of administrative tools, with which you can add users and change configuration settings while the Live CD is running. When you shut down, the configuration information is lost.

You can, however, create your own Live CD which can include your favorite software. From an installed Fedora system, you can use the **livecd-creator** to create your own Live CD (**livecd-tools** package). The **livecd-creator** tool uses a configuration file set up in kickstart syntax to create a Live CD ISO image. Live CD kickstart configuration files for a minimal, desktop (GNOME), and KDE package selection is located at **/usr/share/livecdtools**.

The livecd-creator help option provides a complete listing of options with examples, `--help`. You use the `--config` option to specify a kickstart configuration file, the `--label` option to name your disk, and the `--repo` option to specify any special repositories. Check the

README file in **/usr/shard/doc/livecd-tools** *version* for detailed information. The livecd-creator tool will first create a disk image, then download specified packages and install them on the image, install the boot loader, and then create the ISO image. The image and packages are held in the **/var/tmp** directory. The following creates a simple GNOME dekstop Live CD (entered as one line).

```
livecd-creator --config=/usr/share/livecd-tools/livecd-fedora-desktop.ks \
   --fslabel=MyFedora-Live
```

In the configuration file you set start up options like language, firewall, xconfig for graphical start up, and specific services like NetworkManger and DHCP for network connections. The repositories used are specified in the repo entries. You can use the desktop, minimal, and KDE configuration files as a base to work from. Packages are listed after the **%packages** entry. For individual packages you simply specify the package's unique name. Kickstart syntax for groups of packages conforms to the same categories and subheadings use in Add/Remove Software Browse panel (Pirut). These are useful when you have to select an extensive set of packages like those used for the GNOME or KDE desktops. Be sure to prefix a group name with the @ symbol, like @**Base** for the base packages.

TIP *Keep in mind that running Fedora Live using the hard disk is not the same as installing Fedora on the hard disk. Running Fedora using the hard disk is the standard Fedora Live operation that uses some hard disk space for running the Live CD disk image. Install to Hard Drive (icon on the desktop) actually runs a standard Fedora install process, putting Fedora on your system, just as you would with a normal installation (see Chapter 2).*

You can also install your Fedora Live ISO image on a USB drive, instead of burning a CD-ROM disk. Use the **livecd-iso-to-stick** command, as in **/usr/bin/livecd-iso-to-stick F-7-Live-i386.iso /dev/***usb-device*. When you first boot, you have the options of running Fedora Live entirely from system memory (RAM), or the normal option of using some disk space as a disk image. These will be listed as options on the Grub boot screen. After your system starts up, you will be presented with the standard Login screen. Enter the user **fedora** or **root** for access.

The Live CD can also be used as an installation disk, providing its limited collection of software on a system, but installing a full fledged Fedora operating system that can be expanded and updated from Fedora online repositories (see Chapter 2). Double-click on the "Install to Hard Drive" icon.

Operating Systems and Linux

An *operating system* is a program that manages computer hardware and software for the user. Operating systems were originally designed to perform repetitive hardware tasks, which centered around managing files, running programs, and receiving commands from the user. You interact with an operating system through a *user interface*, which allows the operating system to receive and interpret instructions sent by the user. You only need to send an instruction to the operating system to perform a task, such as reading a file or printing a document. An operating system's user interface can be as simple as entering commands on a line or as complex as selecting menus and icons on a desktop.

An operating system also manages software applications. To perform different tasks, such as editing documents or performing calculations, you need specific software applications. An *editor* is an example of a software application that enables you to edit a document, making changes and adding new text. The editor itself is a program consisting of instructions to be executed by the computer. For the program to be used, it must first be loaded into computer memory, and then its instructions are executed. The operating system controls the loading and execution of all programs, including any software applications. When you want to use an editor, simply instruct the operating system to load the editor application and execute it.

File management, program management, and user interaction are traditional features common to all operating systems. Linux, like all versions of Unix, adds two more features. Linux is a multiuser and multitasking system. As it is a *multitasking* system, you can ask the system to perform several tasks at the same time. While one task is being done, you can work on another. For example, you can edit a file while another file is being printed. You do not have to wait for the other file to finish printing before you edit. As it is a *multiuser* system, several users can log in to the system at the same time, each interacting with the system through his or her own terminal.

As a version of Unix, Linux shares that system's flexibility, a flexibility stemming from Unix's research origins. Developed by Ken Thompson at AT&T Bell Laboratories in the late 1960s and early 1970s, the Unix system incorporated many new developments in operating system design. Originally, Unix was designed as an operating system for researchers. One major goal was to create a system that could support the researchers' changing demands. To do this, Thompson had to design a system that could deal with many different kinds of tasks. Flexibility became more important than hardware efficiency. Like Unix, Linux has the advantage of being able to deal with the variety of tasks any user may face. The user is not confined to limited and rigid interactions with the operating system. Instead, the operating system is thought of as making a set of highly effective tools available to the user. This user-oriented philosophy means you can configure and program the system to meet your specific needs. With Linux, the operating system becomes an operating environment.

History of Linux and Unix

As a version of Unix, the history of Linux naturally begins with Unix. The story begins in the late 1960s, when a concerted effort to develop new operating system techniques occurred. In 1968, a consortium of researchers from General Electric, AT&T Bell Laboratories, and the Massachusetts Institute of Technology carried out a special operating system research project called MULTICS (the Multiplexed Information and Computing Service). MULTICS incorporated many new concepts in multitasking, file management, and user interaction.

Unix

In 1969, Ken Thompson, Dennis Ritchie, and the researchers at AT&T Bell Laboratories developed the Unix operating system, incorporating many of the features of the MULTICS research project. They tailored the system for the needs of a research environment, designing it to run on minicomputers. From its inception, Unix was an affordable and efficient multiuser and multitasking operating system.

The Unix system became popular at Bell Labs as more and more researchers started using the system. In 1973, Dennis Ritchie collaborated with Ken Thompson to rewrite the programming code for the Unix system in the C programming language. Unix gradually grew from one person's tailored design to a standard software product distributed by many different vendors, such as Novell and IBM. Initially, Unix was treated as a research product. The first versions of Unix were distributed free to the computer science departments of many noted universities. Throughout the 1970s, Bell Labs began issuing official versions of Unix and licensing the systems to different users. One of these users was the Computer Science department of the University of California, Berkeley. Berkeley added many new features to the system that later became standard. In 1975, Berkeley released its own version of Unix, known by its distribution arm, Berkeley Software Distribution (BSD). This BSD version of Unix became a major contender to the AT&T Bell Labs version. AT&T developed several research versions of Unix, and in 1983, it released the first commercial version, called System 3. This was later followed by System V, which became a supported commercial software product.

At the same time, the BSD version of Unix was developing through several releases. In the late 1970s, BSD Unix became the basis of a research project by the Department of Defense's Advanced Research Projects Agency (DARPA). As a result, in 1983, Berkeley released a powerful version of Unix called BSD release 4.2. This release included sophisticated file management as well as networking features based on Internet network protocols—the same protocols now used for the Internet. BSD release 4.2 was widely distributed and adopted by many vendors, such as Sun Microsystems.

In the mid-1980s, two competing standards emerged, one based on the AT&T version of Unix and the other based on the BSD version. AT&T's Unix System Laboratories developed System V release 4. Several other companies, such as IBM and Hewlett-Packard, established the Open Software Foundation (OSF) to create their own standard version of Unix. Two commercial standard versions of Unix existed then—the OSF version and System V release 4.

Linux

Originally designed specifically for Intel-based personal computers, Linux started out as a personal project of a computer science student named Linus Torvalds at the University of Helsinki. At that time, students were making use of a program called *Minix,* which highlighted different Unix features. Minix was created by Professor Andrew Tanenbaum and widely distributed over the Internet to students around the world. Linus' intention was to create an effective PC version of Unix for Minix users. It was named Linux, and in 1991, Linus released version 0.11. Linux was widely distributed over the Internet, and in the following years, other programmers refined and added to it, incorporating most of the applications and features now found in standard Unix systems. All the major window managers have been ported to Linux. Linux has all the networking tools, such as FTP file transfer support, Web browsers, and the whole range of network services such as e-mail, the domain name service, and dynamic host configuration, along with FTP, Web, and print servers. It also has a full set of program development utilities, such as C++ compilers and debuggers. Given all its features, the Linux operating system remains small, stable, and fast. In its simplest format, Linux can run effectively on only 2 MB of memory.

Although Linux has developed in the free and open environment of the Internet, it adheres to official Unix standards. Because of the proliferation of Unix versions in the previous decades, the Institute of Electrical and Electronics Engineers (IEEE) developed an independent Unix standard for the American National Standards Institute (ANSI). This new ANSI-standard Unix is called the Portable Operating System Interface for Computer

Environments (POSIX). The standard defines how a Unix-like system needs to operate, specifying details such as system calls and interfaces. POSIX defines a universal standard to which all Unix versions must adhere. Most popular versions of Unix are now POSIX-compliant. Linux was developed from the beginning according to the POSIX standard. Linux also adheres to the Linux file system hierarchy standard (FHS), which specifies the location of files and directories in the Linux file structure. See **www.pathname.com/fhs** for more details.

Linux development is now overseen by The Linux Foundation (**www.linux-foundation.org**), which is a merger of The Free Standards Group and Open Source Development Labs(OSDL). This is the group that Linux Torvalds works with to develop new Linux versions. Actual Linux kernels are released at **www.kernel.org**.

Linux Overview

Like Unix, Linux can be generally divided into three major components: the kernel, the environment, and the file structure. The *kernel* is the core program that runs programs and manages hardware devices, such as disks and printers. The *environment* provides an interface for the user. It receives commands from the user and sends those commands to the kernel for execution. The *file structure* organizes the way files are stored on a storage device, such as a disk. Files are organized into directories. Each directory may contain any number of subdirectories, each holding files. Together, the kernel, the environment, and the file structure form the basic operating system structure. With these three, you can run programs, manage files, and interact with the system.

An environment provides an interface between the kernel and the user. It can be described as an interpreter. Such an interface interprets commands entered by the user and sends them to the kernel. Linux provides several kinds of environments: desktops, window managers, and command line shells. Each user on a Linux system has his or her own user interface. Users can tailor their environments to their own special needs, whether they be shells, window managers, or desktops. In this sense, for the user, the operating system functions more as an operating environment, which the user can control.

In Linux, files are organized into directories, much as they are in Windows. The entire Linux file system is one large interconnected set of directories, each containing files. Some directories are standard directories reserved for system use. You can create your own directories for your own files, as well as easily move files from one directory to another. You can even move entire directories, and share directories and files with other users on your system. With Linux, you can also set permissions on directories and files, allowing others to access them or restricting access to yourself alone. The directories of each user are, in fact, ultimately connected to the directories of other users. Directories are organized into a hierarchical tree structure, beginning with an initial root directory. All other directories are ultimately derived from this first root directory.

With the K Desktop Environment (KDE) and the GNU Network Object Model Environment (GNOME), Linux now has a completely integrated GUI interface. You can perform all your Linux operations entirely from either interface. KDE and GNOME are fully operational desktops supporting drag-and-drop operations, enabling you to drag icons to your desktop and to set up your own menus on an Applications panel. Both rely on an underlying X Window System, which means as long as they are both installed on your system, applications from one can run on the other desktop. The GNOME and KDE sites are particularly helpful for documentation, news, and software you can download for those desktops. Both desktops can run any X Window System program, as well as any cursor-based program such as Emacs and Vi, which were designed to work in a shell environment. At the same time, a great many applications are written just for those desktops and included with your distributions. The K Desktop has a complete set of Internet tools, along with editors and graphic, multimedia, and system applications. GNOME has slightly fewer applications, but a great many are currently in the works. Check their Web sites at **www.gnome.org** and **www.kde.org** for latest developments. As new versions are released, they include new software.

Open Source Software

Linux was developed as a cooperative Open Source effort over the Internet, so no company or institution controls Linux. Software developed for Linux reflects this background. Development often takes place when Linux users decide to work on a project together. The software is posted at an Internet site, and any Linux user can then access the site and download the software. Linux software development has always operated in an Internet environment and is global in scope, enlisting programmers from around the world. The only thing you need to start a Linux-based software project is a Web site.

Most Linux software is developed as Open Source software. This means that the source code for an application is freely distributed along with the application. Programmers over the Internet can make their own contributions to a software package's development, modifying and correcting the source code. Linux is an open source operating system. Its source code is included in all its distributions and is freely available on the Internet. Many major software development efforts are also open source projects, as are the KDE and GNOME desktops along with most of their applications. The Netscape Communicator Web browser package has also become open source, with its source code freely available. The OpenOffice office suite supported by Sun is an open source project based on the StarOffice office suite (StarOffice is essentially Sun's commercial version of OpenOffice). Many of the open source applications that run on Linux have located their Web sites at SourceForge (**sourceforge.net**), which is a hosting site designed specifically to support open source projects. You can find more information about the Open Source movement at **www.opensource.org**.

Open source software is protected by public licenses. These prevent commercial companies from taking control of open source software by adding a few modifications of their own, copyrighting those changes, and selling the software as their own product. The most popular public license is the GNU General Public License provided by the Free Software Foundation. This is the license that Linux is distributed under. The GNU General Public License retains the copyright, freely licensing the software with the requirement that the software and any modifications made to it always be freely available. Other public licenses have also been created to support the demands of different kinds of open source projects. The GNU Lesser General Public License (LGPL) lets commercial applications use GNU licensed software libraries. The Qt Public License (QPL) lets open source developers use the Qt libraries essential to the KDE desktop. You can find a complete listing at **www.opensource.org**.

Linux is currently copyrighted under a GNU public license provided by the Free Software Foundation, and it is often referred to as GNU software (see **www.gnu.org**). GNU software is distributed free, provided it is freely distributed to others. GNU software has proved both reliable and effective. Many of the popular Linux utilities, such as C compilers, shells, and editors, are GNU software applications. Installed with your Linux distribution are the GNU C++ and Lisp compilers, Vi and Emacs editors, BASH and TCSH shells, as well as TeX and Ghostscript document formatters. In addition, there are many open source software projects that are licensed under the GNU General Public License (GPL). Many of these software applications are available at different Internet sites, and these are listed in Table 1-4. Chapter 4 and Chapter 29 describe in detail the process of downloading software applications from Internet sites and installing them on your system.

Under the terms of the GNU General Public License, the original author retains the copyright, although anyone can modify the software and redistribute it, provided the source code is included, made public, and provided free. Also, no restriction exists on selling the software or giving it away free. One distributor could charge for the software, while another one could provide it free of charge. Major software companies are also providing Linux versions of their most popular applications. Oracle provides a Linux version of its Oracle database. (At present, no plans seem in the works for Microsoft applications.)

Linux Software

All Linux software is currently available from online repositories. You can download applications for desktops, Internet servers, office suites, and programming packages, among others. Software packages are primarily distributed in through Yum-enabled repositories, the largest of which is the official Fedora repository. Downloads and updates are handled automatically by your desktop software manager and updater.

In addition, you could download from third-party sources software that is in the form of compressed archives or in RPM packages. RPM packages are those archived using the Red Hat Package Manager. Compressed archives have an extension such as .tar.gz or .tar.Z, whereas RPM packages have an .rpm extension. Any RPM package that you download directly, from whatever site, can be installed easily with the click of a button using the Pirut Package Manager on either the GNOME or KDE desktop. You could also download the source version and compile it directly on your system. This has become a simple process, almost as simple as installing the compiled RPM versions.

Red Hat and Fedora also have a large number of mirror sites from which you can download their software packages for current releases (**fedoraproject.org/Download/ mirrors.html**). If you have trouble connecting to a main FTP site, try one of its mirrors.

Fedora Software Repositories

For Fedora, you can update to the latest software from the Fedora Yum repository using the software updater (see Chapter 4). For Red Hat Enterprise Linux, you can automatically download upgrades for your system using the Red Hat Network. Updates for Red Hat Enterprise are handled directly by Red Hat, whereas updates for Fedora use Fedora Yum software repositories. Your software updater is already configured to access the standard repositories.

The Fedora distribution provides a comprehensive selection of software ranging from office and multimedia applications to Internet servers and administration services (see Table 1-2). Many popular applications are not included, though Fedora-compliant versions are provided on associated software sites. During installation, Yum is configured to access Fedora repositories.

The Fedora repository does contain support for the NTFS file system, the file system used for Windows XP, NT, and 2000 systems. The NTFS support is implemented by the **ntfs-3g** package. You can install this directly with the program manager. You can choose to

URL	Internet Site
fedoraproject.org/wiki/Distribution/Download	Download page for the latest Fedora releases
fedoraproject.org/Download/mirrors.html	Page listing Fedora mirrors
download.fedora.redhat.com/pub/fedora/linux/	Fedora Yum repository for Fedora software
download.fedora.redhat.com/pub/fedora/linux/updates	Fedora Yum repository for Fedora updates
linux.duke.edu/projects/yum	Yellow Dog Updater, Modified (Yum) update tool, with listings of Yum repositories for updating Fedora Linux
moin.conectiva.com.br/AptRpm	APT-RPM Red Hat repository for APT-enabled RPM packages (see Chapter 4)
rpm.livna.org/fedora	Fedora applications not included with the distribution due to licensing and other restrictions. This is an official extension of the Fedora Project.
www.freshrpms.net	Linux multimedia applications and support libraries; specifically lists Fedora-version RPM packages
sources.redhat.com	Open source software hosted by Red Hat
torrent.fedoraproject.org	Fedora BitTorrent site for BitTorrent downloads of Fedora distribution ISO images

TABLE 1-2   Fedora Software Repositories

enable or disable write support. Be careful of this option. It should work but is not guaranteed. There are also third-party NTFS support packages from Livna and freshrpms. They are not compatible. Use one or the other.

Due to licensing restrictions, multimedia support for popular operations like MP3, DVD, and DivX is not included with Fedora distributions. A Fedora Project–associated site, **rpm.livna.org/fedora**, does provided support for these functions. You can download free licensed MP3 gstreamer plugin from **www.fluendo.com**. Any software you do not find at those sites can usually be found at **freshrpms.net**, Fedora does not provide support for the official Nvidia- or ATI-released Linux graphics drivers. Support for these can be found at **rpm.livna .org/fedora** (see Chapter 4). Fedora does include the generic X.org Nvidia and ATI drivers, which will enable your graphics cards to work.

TIP   *The software management tools, Program Manager and PUP, will list software from all configured Yum repositories. Initially these include Fedora, update, and development. If you add configurations for **rpm.livna.org** or **freshrpms.net**, their software will also be listed and managed by Program Manager and PUP.*

Third-Party Linux Software Repositories

Though almost all application should be included in the Fedora software repository, you could download and install software from third-party repositories. Always check first to see if the software you want is already in the Fedora repository. Open Add/Remove Software from the Applications menu and click on the Search menu, and then search for the software using a pattern. If it is not available, then you would download from a third-party repository. Some repositories will be Yum-enabled, like Livna, freshrpms, and jpackage. Their sites will have Fedora-compliant Yum configuration files that you can download and install as an RPM package. You can then use the software manager or the **yum** command to select, download, and install software from the third-party repository directly.

Several third-party repositories make it easy to locate an application and find information about it. Of particular note are **sourceforge.net**, **www.gnu.org**, **rpmfind.net**, **freshrpms.net**, **www.gnomefiles.org**, and **www.kde-apps.org**. The following tables list different sites for Linux software. Repositories and archives for Linux software are listed in Table 1-3, along with several specialized sites, such as those for commercial and game software. When downloading software packages, always check to see if versions are packaged for your particular distribution. For example, **rpmfind.net**, **freshmeat.net**, and **sourceforge.net** are also good places for locating RPM packages.

Linux Office and Database Software

Many professional-level databases and office suites are now available for Linux. These include Oracle and IBM databases, as well as the OpenOffice and KOffice suites. Table 1-4 lists sites for office suites and databases. Most of the Office suites as well as Mysql and Postgrresql are already included on the Fedora repository and may be part of your Fedora spin. Many of the other sites provide free personal versions of their software for Linux, and others are entirely free. You can download them directly and install the software on your Linux system.

Internet Servers

One of the most important features of Linux, as of all Unix systems, is its set of Internet clients and servers. The Internet was designed and developed on Unix systems, and

URL	Internet Site
sourceforge.net	SourceForge, open source software development sites for Linux applications and software repository
rpm.livna.org	Fedora Yum–compliant repository specializing in drivers
www.freshrpms.net	Fedora Yum–compliant repository specializing in Linux multimedia applications and support libraries
jpackage.org	Fedora Yum–compliant repository for Java applications and tools.
www.gnomefiles.org	GNOME applications
www.kde-apps.org	KDE software repository
freshmeat.net	New Linux software
rpmfind.net	RPM package repository
www.gnu.org	GNU archive
www.happypenguin.org	Linux Game Tome
www.linuxgames.com	Linux games

TABLE **1-3**   Third-Party Linux Software Archives, Repositories, and Links

URL	Software
Database Software	
www.oracle.com	Oracle database
www.sybase.com	Sybase database
www.software.ibm.com/data/db2/linux	IBM DB2 database
www.mysql.com	MySQL database (Fedora)
www.gnu.org/software/gnowsys	GNOWSYS
www.postgresql.org	PostgreSQL database (Fedora)
Office Software	
www.openoffice.org	OpenOffice (Fedora)
koffice.kde.org	KOffice (Fedora)
www.sun.com/star/staroffice	StarOffice
www.gnomefiles.org	GNOME Office and Productivity applications (Fedora)

TABLE 1-4   Database and Office Software

Internet clients and servers, such as those for FTP and the Web, were first implemented on BSD versions of Unix. DARPANET, the precursor to the Internet, was set up to link Unix systems at different universities across the nation. Linux contains a full set of Internet clients and servers, including mail, news, FTP, and Web, as well as proxy clients and servers. Sites for Internet server software available for Linux are listed in Table 1-5. All of these are already included on the Fedora repository and may be part of your Fedora spin; however, you can obtain news and documentation directly from the server's Web sites.

URL	Servers
www.apache.org	Apache Web server
vsftpd.beasts.org	Very secure FTP server
www.proftpd.org	ProFTPD FTP server
www.isc.org	Internet Software Consortium: BIND, INN, and DHCPD
www.sendmail.org	Sendmail mail server
www.postfix.org	Postfix mail server
www.squid-cache.org	Squid proxy server
www.samba.org	Samba SMB (Windows network) server
www.netfilter.org	IP Tables firewall
web.mit.edu/kerberos/www	Kerberos network authentication protocol
www.openssh.com	Open Secure Shell (free version of SSH)

TABLE 1-5   Network Servers and Security Available on Fedora

URL	Internet Sites
www.gnu.org	Linux compilers and tools (gcc)
java.sun.com	Sun Java Web site
www.perl.com	Perl Web site with Perl software
developer.gnome.org	GNOME developer's Web site
developer.kde.org	Developer's library for KDE

TABLE 1-6   Linux Programming

Development Resources

Linux has always provided strong support for programming languages and tools. All distributions include the GNU C and C++ compiler (gcc) with supporting tools such as make. Fedora comes with full development support for the KDE and GNOME desktops, letting you create your own GNOME and KDE applications. You can also download the Linux version of the Java Software Development Kit for creating Java programs. A version of Perl for Linux is also included with most distributions. You can download current versions from their Web sites. Table 1-6 lists different sites of interest for Linux programming.

Online Linux Information Sources

Extensive online resources are available on almost any Linux topic. The tables in this chapter list sites where you can obtain software, display documentation, and read articles on the latest developments. Many Linux Web sites provide news, articles, and information about Linux. Several, such as **www.linuxjournal.com** and **www.linuxworldmagazine.com,** are based on popular Linux magazines. Check the Fedora Portal page on **fedoranews.org** for links to Fedora sites. Some specialize in particular area, such as **www.linuxgames.com** for the latest games ported for Linux. Currently, many Linux Web sites provide news, information, and articles on Linux developments, as well as documentation, software links, and other resources. These are listed in Table 1-7.

Linux Documentation

Linux documentation has also been developed over the Internet. Much of the documentation currently available for Linux can be downloaded from Internet FTP sites. A special Linux project called the Linux Documentation Project (LDP), headed by Matt Welsh, has developed a complete set of Linux manuals. The documentation is available at the LDP home site at **www.tldp.org**. Linux documents provided by the LDP are listed in Table 1-8, along with their Internet sites. The Linux documentation for your installed software will be available at your **/usr/share/doc** directory. As previously noted, some Fedora-specific documentation is available at **doc.fedoraproject.org**.

An extensive number of mirrors are maintained for the Linux Documentation Project. You can link to any of them through a variety of sources, such as the LDP home site, **www.tldp.org**, and **www.linuxjournal.org**. The documentation includes a user's guide, an introduction, and

URL	Internet Site
www.tldp.org	Web site for the Linux Documentation Project
www.lwn.net	Linux Weekly News
www.linux.com	Linux.com
www.linuxtoday.com	Linux Today
www.linuxplanet.com	Linux Planet
www.linuxfocus.org	Linux Focus
www.linuxworldmagazine.com	Linux World Magazine
www.linuxjournal.com	Linux Journal
www.linuxgazette.com	Linux Gazette
www.linux.org	Linux Online
slashdot.org	Linux forum
www.opensource.org	Open source information
fedoraforum.org	Fedora support forums
fedoranews.org	Latest developments for Fedora Project
fedoraproject.org	The Fedora Project
fcp.homelinux.org	Fedora Community Portal
www.redhat.com/magazine	Red Hat Magazine

TABLE 1-7   Linux Information and News Sites

Sites	Web Sites
www.tldp.org	LDP Web site
Guides	**Document Format**
Linux Installation and Getting Started Guide	DVI, PostScript, LaTeX, PDF, and HTML
Linux User's Guide	DVI, PostScript, HTML, LaTeX, and PDF
Linux System Administrator's Guide	PostScript, PDF, LaTeX, and HTML
Linux Network Administrator's Guide	DVI, PostScript, PDF, and HTML
Linux Programmer's Guide	DVI, PostScript, PDF, LaTeX, and HTML
The Linux Kernel	HTML, LaTeX, DVI, and PostScript
Linux Kernel Hacker's Guide	DVI, PostScript, and HTML
Linux HOW TOs	HTML, PostScript, SGML, and DVI
Linux FAQs	HTML, PostScript, and DVI
Linux Man Pages	Man page format

TABLE 1-8   Linux Documentation Project

Newsgroup	Title
comp.os.linux.announce	Announcements of Linux developments
comp.os.linux.development.apps	For programmers developing Linux applications
comp.os.linux.development.system	For programmers working on the Linux operating system
comp.os.linux.hardware	Linux hardware specifications
comp.os.linux.admin	System administration questions
comp.os.linux.misc	Special questions and issues
comp.os.linux.setup	Installation problems
comp.os.linux.answers	Answers to command problems
comp.os.linux.help	Questions and answers for particular problems
comp.os.linux.networking	Linux network questions and issues
linux.dev._group_	Numerous development newsgroups beginning with **linux.dev**, such as **linux.dev.admin** and **linux.dev.doc**

TABLE 1-9   Linux Usenet Newsgroups

administrative guides. These are available in text, PostScript, or Web page format. Table 1-8 lists these guides. You can also find briefer explanations, in what are referred to as HOW-TO documents.

Distribution Web sites, such as **www.redhat.com** and **fedora.redhat.com**, provide extensive Linux documentation and software. The **www.gnome.org** site holds documentation for the GNOME desktop, while **www.kde.org** holds documentation for the KDE desktop. The tables in this chapter list many of the available sites. You can find other sites through resource pages that hold links to other Web sites—for example, the Linux Web site on the World Wide Web at **www.tldp.org/links.html**.

In addition to Web sites, Linux Usenet newsgroups are also available. Through your Internet connection, you can access Linux newsgroups to read the comments of other Linux users and to post messages of your own. Several Linux newsgroups exist, each beginning with **comp.os.linux**. One of particular interest to the beginner is **comp.os.linux.help**, where you can post questions. Table 1-9 lists some of the Usenet Linux newsgroups you can check out, particularly for posting questions.

Installing Fedora

This chapter describes the installation procedure for Fedora Linux. The installation includes the Linux operating system, a great many Linux applications, and a complete set of network servers. Red Hat Enterprise Linux and Fedora use the same Anaconda installation program; it is designed to be easy to use and helpful, while at the same time efficient and brief, installing as many services and applications as possible. Detailed help panels explain each procedure, every step of the way. A Fedora Installation Guide is also available online. First check the new Fedora Installation guide at

`http://docs.fedoraproject.org/fedora-install-guide-en`

For the Red Hat Linux Enterprise installation, check the appropriate install guide at

`http://www.redhat.com/docs/manuals/enterprise/`

As a Red Hat Enterprise owner, you would also be eligible for customer support with your installation.

Key Feature of Fedora Installation

There are several key features in the installation procedure:

- The software install tool, Pirut Package Manager, is designed to work with Yum repositories.
- Firewall and SELinux configuration is part of the post-install process.
- Default software configurations include: Office and Productivity, Software development, and Web server.
- Fedora Spins: Fedora is now offered in various DVD versions, each with a different bias (see Chapter 3). Currently Fedora offers three official spins: Gnome, KDE, and Fedora. The Gnome spin just provides the Gnome desktop with various supporting workstation software. The KDE does the same but with the KDE dekstop instead. Fedora is a collection of both workstation and server software, and includes both Gnome and KDE. It is offered only as a DVD.

- Custom Spins: You can create your own customize Fedora installation disk with Pungi. Pungi is desribed at the end of this chapter. You run Pungi from an installed Fedora Linux system to create a custon install spin you can use install on other systems.

Minimal Install Strategy with Desktop Spins: Making Use of Repositories

Perhaps a more sensible install strategy is to install a minimal desktop, using just a Fedora desktop spin (Gnome or KDE). You would only need to download a desktop spin, use it to install or upgrade, and then rely on the Fedora repository to update and install any other software.

The reasoning behind this approach takes into consideration the dramatic impact of software repositories used for Fedora software installations, along with the very painless and simple process for automatically updating software. Keep in mind that software is continually being updated. This includes all software applications, including office, Internet, and graphics applications. Software is, in a sense, dynamic and fluid, in a state of constant change. On Fedora with its Yum repositories, updates are performed for you automatically. This means that the software on the CD/DVD distribution disks becomes obsolete rapidly. In as little as one month after the release, much of the software has to be updated. In effect, the initial install of applications from the disk becomes redundant. You will have to download the current versions of your software from the software repository anyway.

So a more effective strategy is to skip the software install from the disk and go directly to the repositories. You can do this during installation, but it is better to install first and then take your time with the software installs, once your system is up and running.

Alternatively, if you have no high-speed network connection to support extensive downloads, and you are content to use the disk versions of the software, the opposite strategy should be used. In this case you would need to download the Fedora spin. The Fedora spin is an extensive collection of the more popular applications (servers, development, and desktop). It is available in DVD and CD ISO image format.

Keep in mind, though, that a download to update a single package on a standard high-speed connection can take as little as a few seconds.

Minimal Install Strategy with Fedora Live CD: First Time Installs

If you are installing Fedora for the first time, and want to download the software quickly, you can just install from the Fedora Live-CD. The Live-CD also allows you to first see what Fedora is like, without having to install it. Should you then want to install Fedora on your system, you can do so using just the Live-CD. You would not have to separately download an installation spin like the KDE desktop or Fedora spin. You can then download and install software you want from the Fedora repository.

Once you download and burn the Fedora Live-CD, boot your system from it to display the login screen. Enter fedora as your login (no password will be required) to start up Fedora from the CD.

On the screen there will be a icon of the Fedora F symbol with the lable "Install to Hard Drive." If you want to install Fedora directly on your system, just as you would from an install spin, click this button. Clicking this button will start the standard install procedure (anaconda) as described in this chapter. You will be installing Fedora just as you would from a standard install CD/DVD disk like the Fedora spin. The only difference is that only the small subset of applications already on the Fedora Live-CD will be installed. You will not have the option to choose applications during the install process. Given that most applications have to update from the Fedora repository anyway, this is not much of an issue. Just use Add/Remove Sofware (Pirut) to install the software you want, after you have finished installation. However, if do not have any online access and need certain applications, you would have to use a standard installation CD/DVD spin like Fedora.

When you start the Install to Hard Drive process, a window will open, showing the initial install screen, letting you choose to install Fedora. The install process shows fewer screens than the standard process, but performs all necessary tasks. The screens shown are as follows:

- **Partitions**   Here you set up your partitions. You have the option to use a default set up, or mange your own. See the section on Partition, Raid, and Logical volumes for more information.

- **Network**   Specify your network configuration, usually DHCP.

- **Time**   Set the time.

- **Password**   Enter a password for the root user. This is your administrative password.

- **Format, software install, and post-installation**   Your partitions are formatted and all the software from the Live-CD is installed. Then post install procedures are performed like setting up the Grub boot loader.

When you reboot, you will start up the Fedora installation on your hard disk. Initially you will only have the same software available as was on the Live-CD, but you can use Applications | Add/Remove Software to install other applications, like OpenOffice. You may also have to update many of the applications installed from the Live-CD. Click the update notification, which will automatically appear, to start the update process. Applications and updates will be downloaded from the Fedora repository and automatically installed.

Obtaining the CDs and DVDs

The preferred method for obtaining Fedora is to download it from a Fedora mirror site. Red Hat Enterprise Linux, however, is a commercial product whose disks Red Hat will send you. Red Hat Enterprise Linux updates can then be downloaded from the Red Hat Network, now a commercial service.

A detailed description for all the Fedora download options, including all the ISO disks you will need and links to mirror sites, is available at

```
http://fedoraproject.org/wiki/Distribution/Download
```

Check this site for the latest download procedures.

You can download directly from the Fedora download site at the following link, where you will find directories for the Fedora distributions.

```
http://download.fedora.redhat.com/pub/fedora/linux/
```

The connection can be very fast with broadband, DSL or cable, using an FTP client like **gFTP** or **wget**. **wget** operates from the command line. Web-client downloads with browsers like Firefox tend to be slower.

To download Fedora for installation from a DVD/CD-ROM drive, you download the CD or DVD ISO images. These are very large files that reside in the **iso** directory on the download site and have the extension **.iso**. Once they are downloaded, you burn them to a disk using your CD or DVD writer and burner software, like the GNOME Nautilus file manager or K3b.

There are ISO images for 64-bit system support and for the standard x86 (32-bit) support. Download the appropriate one. You cannot run a 64-bit version on a x86 (32-bit) system.

Several ISO images, called spins, are provided, each with a different software configuration. Fedora currently provides three spins, Gnome, KDE, and Fedora. Choose the one you want. You only need one. Gnome and KDE are desktop workstation collections, whereas the Fedora spin adds server software. The Fedora spin is meant to be the most comprehensive collection available on disk, though it still holds only part of the packages available on the Fedora repository.

You do not have to download the images to a Linux system. You can just as easily download them on a Windows system and use Windows CD/DVD burner software to make the disks.

Though you can use any FTP or Web client, such as gFTP or Firefox, to download the image files, these are very large files that can take a long time to download, especially if the FTP site is very busy or if you have a slow Internet connection. The preferred alternative for such very large files is to use BitTorrent. BitTorrent is a safe distributed download operation that is ideal for large files, letting many participants download and upload the same file, building a torrent that can run very fast for all participants (three hours for a DVD binary at broadband speed). The Fedora BitTorrent files are located at

```
torrent.fedoraproject.org
```

You will first need to install the BitTorrent client. For Fedora, there are several BitTorrent clients available, including **azureus**, **rtorrent**, and the original **bittorrent**. A search on "bittorrent" in Pirut will display them If you are installing several months after the Fedora release, you will have very large number of updates to download, possibly several hundred packages. To avoid such a lengthy update, you could, instead, install from the Fedora Unity project's Fedora re-spin. The Fedora Unix project collects all updates and incorporates them into a distribution re-spin every few months, letting you install directly with the latest updates (**fedoraunity.org/respins**).

Installation Overview

Installing Linux involves several steps. First, you need to determine whether your computer meets the basic hardware requirements. These days, most Intel-based PC computers do. The Fedora Installation Guide is now available at **fedora.redhat.com/docs/fedora-install-guide-en**. Check this guide before installing Fedora. It provides detailed screen examples and is geared to the x86 version.

Install Sources

Fedora supports several methods for installing Linux. You can install from a local source such as a CD-ROM or a hard disk, or from a network or Internet source. For a network or Internet source, Fedora supports NFS, FTP, and HTTP installations. With FTP, you can install from an FTP site. With HTTP, you can install from a Web site. NFS enables you to install over a local network. For a local source, you can install from a CD-ROM or a hard disk. You can start the installation process by booting from your DVD-ROM, or from boot disks that can then use the DVD-ROM or hard disk repository. Fedora documentation covers each of these methods in detail.

To select an install source, you will need to first boot the install kernel, either from a Fedora CD or DVD disk or from a Fedora CD or USB boot image disk or drive. You can also use VFAT USB disks and PXE servers. At the boot prompt you enter the option **linux askmethod**, as shown here:

```
boot: linux askmethod
```

For a USB boot drive, check the section "Preparing USB Boot Media" in the Fedora Installation Guide.

Install Configurations

Fedora currently supports three pre-selection install configurations: Office and Productivity, Software development, and Web server. They differ in the partition they will set up by default and the group of packages they will install. Office and Productivity are selected by default. If you know what packages you want, you can select the Customize Now option. This will invoke the Pirut Package Manager to let you choose the packages by group or individually that you want on your system. This will be the only time you can easily install software from your CD/DVD disk. All future software installations will download and install software from Fedora Yum–enabled online repositories.

- **Office and Productivity**   Home or desktop systems
- **Software Development**   Includes software development
- **Web Server**   Includes the Apache Web server
- **Customize Now**   Select from all software packages

Install Procedures

Once the installation program begins, you simply follow the instructions, screen by screen. Most of the time, you only need to make simple selections or provide yes and no answers. The installation program progresses through several phases. First, you create Linux partitions on your hard drive, configure your network connection, and then install the software packages. After that, you can configure your X Window System for graphical user interface support. Both the X Window System and network configurations can be performed independently at a later time.

Once your system is installed, you are ready to start it and log in. Normally, you will log in using a graphical login, selecting the desktop you want and entering your username and password. Alternatively, you can log in to a simple command line interface. From the command line, you can then invoke a desktop such as GNOME or KDE that provides you with a full graphical user interface.

Installing Dual-Boot Systems

If you want to have another operating system on the same computer as your Linux system, you will have to configure your system to be dual-booted. The boot loader, GRUB, already supports dual-booting. Should you have both Linux and Windows systems installed on your hard disks, GRUB will let you choose to boot either the Linux system or a Windows system. Configuring dual boots can be complicated. If you want a Windows system on your computer, you should install it first if it is not already installed. Windows would overwrite the boot loader that a previous Linux system installed, cutting off access to the Linux system. Check the link for "Configuring a Dual-Boot System" on

```
http://fedoraproject.org/wiki/Distribution/Download
```

Simple Graphical Direct Install with DVD/CD-ROMs

If you are installing from DVD/CD-ROMs, installation is a straightforward process. A graphical installation is very easy to use, providing full mouse support and explaining each step with detailed instructions on a help pane.

- Most systems today already meet hardware requirements and have automatic connections to the Internet (DHCP).
- They also support booting a DVD-ROM or CD-ROM disk, though this support may have to be explicitly configured in the system BIOS.
- Also, if you know how you want Linux installed on your hard disk partitions, or if you are performing a simple update that uses the same partitions, installing Fedora is a fairly simple process. Fedora features an automatic partitioning function that will perform the partitioning for you.
- If you choose one of the three preconfigured packaging installations, you will not even have to select packages.

For a quick installation you can simply start up the installation process, placing your DVD or CD disk in your optical drive and starting up your system. Graphical installation is a simple matter of following the instructions in each window as you progress. Many of them are self-explanatory (for LCD displays you may have to use the **nofb** option at the boot prompt). The steps involved are as follows:

- **Boot Menu or Prompt** At the initial menu select Install or Upgrade and press ENTER. For text installs, press ENTER at the boot prompt.
- **Media Check** DVDs and CDs are often burned disks from downloaded ISO images. The media check can make sure your DVD/CD-ROMs are being read correctly.
- **Language Selection** A default is chosen for you, like English, so you can usually just press Next.

- **Keyboard Configuration**   A default is chosen for you; you can usually press Next.
- **Upgrade/Install Option**   Choose whether to install or to upgrade. If you already have a Fedora system installed, Upgrade will already be chosen.
- **Install Configurations**   Here you choose one or more of the following: Office and Productivity, Software Development, Web Server. You can also choose to Customize Now, enabling yourself to select particular packages.
- **Disk Partitions**   For automatic partitioning you have the option of replacing any partitions already present: either all partitions or just Linux partitions (preserving any Windows partitions). You can also choose no partitions and use available free space. This is used to either preserve your old partitions or for new drives. Check the Review option to have the Disk Druid partitioning tool show your partitioning selections and let you make changes.
- **Boot Loader**   You can then configure your boot loader (GRUB). Primarily this is used to choose a different operating system such as Windows to boot by default; otherwise, you can accept the current configuration and press Next.
- **Network Configuration**   Most ISPs and routers now use DHCP, and this will be selected for you by default. Just press Next. You do have the option of entering in your own network information, including IP addresses and DNS servers.
- **Time Zone**   Use the map to choose your time zone or select it from the pop-up menu.
- **Root Password**   Select a password to use for the root users. This enables administrative access. Be sure to remember the password.
- **About to Install**   At this point nothing has been done to your system. You can opt out of the installation at this point. If you click Next, then the install process will take place, making actual changes. The system will first be formatted, then packages installed, with installation progress shown, and then a post-install will perform default configurations for your packages.
- **Exit**   After the install, you will be asked to remove your DVD/CD-ROM and click the Exit button. This will reboot your system (do not reboot yourself).
- **First Boot**   On reboot, you will enter a Fedora Setup Agent procedure where you will be able to set the date and time, set up your firewall, and check your sound card. You will also be asked to create a standard user, which you can use to log in for normal use (not as root). More users can be created later.
- **Firewall and SELinux**   This is the iptables firewall configuration. It will be enabled by default. Here you select the level of support you want for SELinux. Enforcing is selected by default, but it is recommended that you change this to the Permissive level until you can configure SELinux yourself. For the firewall, you can check services to allow through. Trusted interfaces allow any host connected to that interface to access all services provided by your system. They are usually used if your system operates as a server for your local network. You may want to select **smb** to allow Samba browsing from your desktop.
- **Login**   After Setup your login screen will display and installation will be complete.

Hardware, Software, and Information Requirements

Before installing Linux, you must ensure that your computer meets certain minimum hardware requirements. Most hardware today meets these requirements. Linux can be installed on a wide variety of systems, ranging from the very weak to the very powerful. All the requirements are presented in detail in the following sections. Be sure to read them carefully before you begin installation. During the installation program, you need to provide responses that reflect the configuration of your computer. For older or unusual hardware configurations you might need to have certain specific information ready concerning your mouse and CD-ROM drive.

Hardware Requirements

Listed here are the minimum hardware requirements for installing a standard installation of the Linux system on an Intel-based PC:

- A 32-bit or 64-bit Intel- or AMD-based personal computer. At least an Intel or compatible (AMD) Pentium-class microprocessor is required. A 400 MHz Pentium II or more is recommended for a graphical interface and 200 MHz for text. Fedora is currently optimized for a Pentium 4.

- For 64-bit systems, be sure to use the 64-bit version of Fedora, which includes a supporting kernel.

- A CD-ROM or DVD-ROM drive. Should you need to create a bootable DVD/CD-ROM, you will need a DVD/CD-RW drive.

- Normally you will need at least 64MB RAM for text, and 192 MB for a graphical interface, with 256 MB recommended. For 64-bit systems, you will need 128 MB for text and 256 MB for graphical, with 512 MB recommended. (Linux can run on as little as 12 MB RAM.) 3 GB or more is recommended for desktop installation and 700 MB for a command line interface–only installation. You will also need 64 MB to 2 GB for swap space, depending on the amount of RAM memory you have.

- Hard disk requirements depend on the kind of installation you want. The three choices, Office and Productivity, Software Development, and Web Server, each add a basic configuration package for those tasks. You can then add as many more as you wish in different categories. Fedora now uses a new software manager to install software. The software manager is able to download packages from Fedora repositories during installation, which will provide you with a massive selection of software to choose from during installation. You can also use the software manager after installation to install packages from any Fedora–supported repository. This kind of capability means that install sizes for different systems can vary greatly, depending on each system's particular needs. Approximate install sizes for command line and desktop systems are shown here:
  - Command line (minimum): 700 MB

  - Desktop: 3 GB

  - Keep in mind that the disk space requirements represent the amount of space used after installation. The install process will also require an additional amount of space for the install image (**/Fedora/base/stage2.img**) and selected RPM packages. Figure on 100 MB for a minimum install and 200 MB for a full installation.

Hard Drive Configuration

These days, Linux is usually run on its own hard drive, though it can also be run on a hard drive that contains a separate partition for a different operating system such as Windows.

If you want to install Linux and Windows on the same hard drive, you can use a partition management software package, such as **fdisk**, **fips**, **Parted**, or **PartitionMagic**, to set up your Windows and Linux partitions. If you have already installed Windows on your hard drive and configured it to take up the entire hard drive, you would resize its partition to free up unused space. The freed space could then be used for a Linux partition.

TIP   You can also use the Fedora Live CD or another Linux Live CD like Ubuntu to start up Linux and perform the needed hard disk partitioning.

Information Requirements

Part of adapting a powerful operating system like Linux to the PC entails making the most efficient use of the computer hardware at hand. In almost all configurations, your Linux installation process will automatically detect and configure your hardware components. Sometimes, however, particularly with older or very recent hardware, your installer may not be able to correctly identify a component.

You will also need to determine how you want to use hardware resources; for example, how much of your hard disk you want to devote to Linux.

CD-ROM, Hard Disk, and Mouse Information

In rare instances, for some older SCSI CD-ROM drives, you need the manufacturer's name and model.

Decide how much of your hard drive (in megabytes) you want to dedicate to your Linux system. If you are sharing with Windows, decide how much you want for Windows and how much for Linux.

Decide how much space you want for your swap partition. Your swap partition should be about the same size as your RAM memory, but it can work with as little as 64 MB. For systems with smaller RAM configurations, the swap disk should be twice the size of the RAM. Your swap partition is used by Linux as an extension of your computer's RAM.

Know where you live so that you can select the appropriate time zone.

Mice are now automatically detected. Fedora no longer supports serial mice. The system-config-mouse utility has been dropped. If you should need to later configure your mouse, you can use the GNOME or KDE mouse configuration tool.

---

*NOTE   Monitors and video cards are automatically configured during installation. If you have problems, you will have to configure your system after installation using tools like system-config-display (see Chapter 4). You still need to provide the manufacturer's make and model, in case the detection is wrong. Find out the manufacturer for your monitor and its model, such as Dell 2405. You can find a complete list of supported cards at **www.x.org**. For older CRT monitors, the vertical and horizontal refresh rates are particularly important.*

Network Configuration Information

If your ISP service or network uses DHCP, you will most likely not have to provide any configuration information. Most local networks, cable connections, and DSL connections now use DHCP to automatically configure hosts. Network information is provided automatically by a DHCP server. During the installation process, you will be given the option of either automatically configuring your network connection (DHCP) or entering the network information manually.

If you need to configure your network connection, you can also put configuration off until a later time and use network configuration utilities provided by your distribution to perform network configuration. All you need to do during installation is provide a hostname.

If you decide to manually configure your network connection, you will need the following information, usually obtainable from your network administrator:

- The name for your computer (this is called a hostname). Your computer will be identified by this name on the Internet. Do not use "localhost," which is reserved for special use by your system.

- The Internet Protocol (IP) address assigned to your machine. Every host on the Internet is assigned an IP address.

- Your network IP address. This address is usually similar to the IP address, but with one or more zeros at the end.

- The netmask address. This is usually 255.255.255.0 for class C IP addresses. If, however, you are part of a large network, check with your network administrator.

- The broadcast address for your network, if available. Usually, your broadcast address is the same as your IP address with the number 255 used for the last number.

- The gateway IP address for your network. The gateway connects your network to a larger one like the Internet.

- The IP address of any name servers your network uses.

- The NIS domain and IP address if your network uses an NIS server.

- The Samba server if your network is connected to a Windows network.

Boot Source Options

Fedora supports several booting options should your DVD-ROM not be bootable for some reason. Take note that floppy disk boots are no longer supported. The 2.6 kernel is too large to fit on a floppy.

Normally you would boot from a DVD-ROM. Most systems currently support booting from a DVD-ROM drive. However, if you have an older system or DVD-ROM that will not support booting, and you can boot from a CD-ROM disk, you can create a CD-ROM boot disk, using **images/boot.iso** to burn the disk. Alternatively, you could use a USB drive or PXE network boot if these are supported for your system. Once installation begins, your DVD-ROM will be used to continue installation.

- If you are installing with DVD/CD-ROMs, most systems and DVD/CD-ROM drives are now bootable. You can use the DVD/CDs directly. If for some reason your system does not support bootable DVD/CD-ROMs, you will have to set up an alternative boot method such as a USB disk with **diskboot.img** or a PXE server.

- You can create a bootable DVD/CD-ROM disk with which to start the installation. The DVD/CD-ROM boot disk image is located in the **images** directory and is called **boot.iso**. You can also use this disk to install from alternate sources such as a hard drive or a network location such as an NFS, FTP, or Web site.

- With the **diskboot.img** file (also in the **images** directory) you can boot from small USB drives or any bootable device large enough to hold the 2.6 kernel (the size of the **diskboot.img** file, about 6 MB). This is a VFAT file system. Check first if your system can boot from the USB drive.

- You can also boot from the PXE (Pre-Execution Environment) server using the **initrd.img** file in the **images/pxeboot** directory. A PXE server operates through DHCP and TFTP servers off a Linux system. Check the PXE documentation file, **pxelinux.doc**, in the **/usr/share/syslinux-2.11** directory (version number may differ).

If you are installing from a Fedora DVD-ROM, you will need a DVD-ROM drive on your computer to read the DVD-ROM disk. If your system supports bootable DVD/CD-ROMs, then it will boot from this DVD-ROM, letting you install your Fedora system from the DVD-ROM directly.

Install Methods

Fedora supports various methods for installation. Other than the graphical install, you can user a text install or a low-resolution (lowres) graphical install, which is helpful if your graphics card was not correctly detected. If you have difficulty with detecting your hardware, you can use the noprobe option, which will let you provide your own drivers, or the expert option, which will let you choose all your hardware. You may also need to use **nofb** for some LCD monitors, or set **acpi=off** to disable ACPI if it stops your installation.

For text installs, you would add these options at the boot prompt. If you are using the graphical menu, as would normally be the case, press the TAB key to display the command line listing your current options. Add in the one you want. Use backspace to delete current options. Press the ESC key to return to the menu.

- **linux text**   Use a text-based install interface employing a text cursor to make selections with the arrow, TAB, and ENTER keys.
- **linux lowres**   Use a low-resolution graphical interface that is video card independent.
- **linux nofb**   Disable the frame buffer (needed for some LCD monitors like Dell).
- **linux noprobe**   Do not probe hardware.
- **linux acpi=off**   Turn off ACPI, which can interfere with the install procedure.
- **linux expert**   Select all hardware.
- **linux askmethod**   Select a method of installation, as from a hard disk or a network site.
- **linux vnc**   Start a VNC install from a VNC site.
- **linux ks**=*filelocation*   Start an automated install using a kickstart configuration file.

Virtual Network Computing

A VNC (Virtual Network Computing) installation lets you boot the installation normally on the install system, and then lets the installation be managed from another Linux host, stepping through the install system's installation screen. It is a kind of remotely controlled installation, over a network connection. A VNC install requires that the host computer be running a VNC server. This is managed by the vncserver script, which can be controlled with system-config-services (System | Administration | Server Settings | Services on the main menu). You can also use the **service** tool.

```
service vncserver start
```

Once vncserver is started, the host then becomes a VNC server that can access and control installations being performed on other systems. As the VNC server, the host uses the vncviewer client to interact with the installation process on the install system. The client is invoked with the **-listen** option that checks for reverse connections from a VNC server.

```
vncviewer -listen
```

The install system has to then start the installation procedure by specifying a VNC install at the boot prompt or the graphical menu options, and providing the host computer IP address along with a password.

```
boot: linux vnc vncconnect=192.168.0.2 vncpassword=geo4455
```

On the install system you will have to first configure your language, keyboard, and network connection. Once you have configured the network connection for your install system, then a connection can be made to the VNC server. You can then move to the VNC host system and continue installation from there.

Automating Installation with Kickstart

Kickstart is a method for providing a predetermined installation configuration for installing Fedora. Instead of having a user enter responses on the install screens, the responses can be listed in a kickstart file the install process can read from. You will need to create a kickstart configuration file on a working Fedora system. (Kickstart configuration files have the extension **.cfg**.) A kickstart file is created for every Fedora system that holds the install responses used for that installation. It is located in the root directory at

```
/root/anaconda-ks.cfg
```

If you plan to perform the same kind of install on computers that would be configured in the same way, say on a local network with hosts that have the same hardware, you could use this kickstart file as a model for performing installations. It is a text file that you can edit, with entries for each install response, like the following for keyboard and time zone:

```
keyboard us
timezone America/LosAngeles
```

More complex responses may take options such as `network`, which uses `--device` for the device interface and **bootproto** for the boot client.

```
network --device eth0 --bootproto dhcp
```

Display configuration is more complex, specifying a video card and monitor type, which could vary. You can have the system skip this with **xskip**.

The first entry is the install source. This will be **cdrom** for a CD/DVD-ROM install. If you want to use an NFS or Web install instead, you could place that here, specifying the server name or Web site Kickstart also support installing packages from other repositories (**repo** option). You can also specify services to start up (**services** option), as well as create new users (**user** option). Packages will be listed after the %**packages** entry. Prefix package groups with @.

You can also use the **system-config-kickstart** file to create your kickstart file. This provides a graphical interface for each install screen. To start it, enter **system-config-kickstart** in a terminal window. The help manual provides a detailed description on how to use this tool.

The name of the configuration file should be **ks.cfg**.

Once you have created your kickstart file, you can copy it to CD/DVD or to a floppy disk. You could also place the file on a local hard disk partition (such as a Windows or Linux partition), if you already have one. For a network, you could place the file on an NFS server, provided your network is running a DHCP server to enable automatic network configuration on the install computer.

When you start the installation, at the boot prompt you specify the kickstart file and its location.

You can use **hd:***device* to specify a particular device such as a hard drive or second CD-ROM drive. For an NFS site, you would use **nfs:**.

Installing Linux

Installing Linux involves several processes, beginning with creating Linux partitions, and then loading the Linux software, configuring your X Window System interface, installing the Linux boot loader (GRUB or LILO) that will boot your system, and creating new user accounts. The installation program used on Fedora is a screen-based program that takes you through all these processes, step-by-step, as one continuous procedure. You can use either your mouse or the keyboard to make selections. When you finish with a screen, click the Next button at the bottom to move to the next screen. If you need to move back to the previous screen, click Back. You can also use TAB, the arrow keys, SPACEBAR, and ENTER to make selections. The installation screens will display a help panel explaining each step in detail. You have little to do other than make selections and choose options. Some screens provide a list of options from which you make a selection. In a few cases, you are asked for information you should already have if you followed the steps earlier in this chapter. Hardware components will be automatically detected and displayed as you progress. During installation, you will be able to perform administrative tasks such as configuring your network connections, creating users, and setting the time. Keep in mind that such administrative tasks can also be performed after installation. You are now ready to begin installation. The steps for each part of the procedure are delineated in the following sections. This should not take more than an hour.

The installation process will first install your Linux, including all selected packages, on your system. It will then reboot and start a Setup process to let you fine-tune certain settings, including your display settings, sound check, and time and date.

Starting the Installation Program

If your computer can boot from the DVD/CD-ROM, you can start the installation directly from the CD-ROMs or the DVD-ROM. Just place the CD-ROM in the CD-ROM drive, or the DVD-ROM in the DVD drive, before you start your computer. After you turn on your computer, the installation program will start up.

To boot from a CD-ROM or DVD-ROM, you may first have to change the boot sequence setting in your computer's BIOS so that the computer will try to boot first from the CD-ROM. This requires some technical ability and knowledge of how to set your motherboard's BIOS configuration.

The installation program will start, presenting you with a menu listing the following options:

- Install or Upgrade an existing system
- Install or Upgrade an existing system (text mode)
- Rescue installed system
- Boot from local drive

Use the arrow keys to move from one menu entry to the next, and then press ENTER to select the entry. Should you need to add options, say to the Install or Upgrade entry, press the TAB key. A command line is displayed where you can enter the options. Current options will already be listed. Use the backspace key to delete and arrow keys to move through the line. Press the ESC key to return to the menu.

Your system then detects your hardware, providing any configuration specifications that may be needed. For example, if you have an IDE CD-RW or DVD-RW drive, it will be configured automatically. If for some reason it cannot do so, your system will ask you to select your CD-ROM from a list. If you still have difficulty, you may have to specify the CD-ROM at the boot prompt or in the option command line.

```
hdx=cdrom
```

Replace the *x* with one of the following letters, depending on the interface the unit is connected to, and whether it is configured as master or a slave: a (first IDE controller master), b (first IDE controller slave), c (second IDE controller master), d (second IDE controller slave).

If you cannot start the install process and you are using an LCD display, you should press TAB on the Install entry and enter **nofb** (no frame buffer) in the options command line.

```
nofb
```

As each screen appears in the installation, default entries will be already selected, usually by the autoprobing capability of the installation program. Selected entries will appear highlighted. If these entries are correct, you can simply click Next to accept them and go on to the next screen.

Install Hardware Detection

When the install first starts, a series of text screens appear that select your language and keyboard automatically. You have the option to change the selections. Press the ENTER key to continue on, and use the arrow keys to change selections. Use the TAB or arrow keys to move between buttons.

You will then be asked to select your language, and then a keyboard configuration. A default language will already be selected, usually English.

You will then be asked to select a keyboard—the default is already selected, such as U.S. English.

You are then asked to choose an installation method, such as Local CDROM, hard drive, NFS directory, FTP, or HTTP. For your DVD/CD disk choose Local CDROM. This is selected by default. Just press ENTER.

If your DVD/CD drive was not detected correctly, you will be asked to select a driver. There will be options for Select a driver, Use a driver disk, or Back. Select a driver is the default and will list most drivers. Press ENTER on the select driver button. Then use the arrow key to select a driver entry from the list. Check your motherboard or computer documentation for the appropriate driver to use.

You are then asked to check the DVD/CD disk for errors. This check can take several minutes. You can skip the procedure by pressing the TAB or arrow keys to move to the Skip button, then press ENTER.

Your graphical install screens will then start up.

Initial Setup: Upgrade or Install

If your basic device and hardware configuration was appropriately detected, a Welcome screen will be displayed, with a Next button on the lower-right corner. Once finished with a step, you click Next to move on. In some cases you will be able to click a Back button to return to a previous step.

The first screen will welcome you to the Fedora installation, with a button for displaying the release notes. Press Next to start the install process.

You are then given the option to either Upgrade an older installed version or Install an entirely new system. For upgrading, the root partition of the installed system will be shown.

Partitions, RAID, and Logical Volumes

Then you will be asked to designate the Linux partitions and hard disk configurations you want to use on your hard drives. Fedora provides automatic partitioning options if you just want to use available drives and free space for your Linux system. To manually configure your hard disks, Fedora uses a very detailed and graphic-oriented partitioning tool called Partd. With Partd, you can create specific partitions, or configure RAID devices, or set up logical volumes.

No partitions will be changed or formatted until you select your packages later in the install process. You can opt out of the installation at any time until that point, and your original partitions will remain untouched. A default layout used in the first three partition sets up a swap partition, a boot partition of type ext3 (Linux native) for the kernel, and an LVM partition that will hold all your apps and files.

Partition

The partition screen will display a pop-up menu with the automatic partition selections, which provides four options: Remove All Partitions on selected drive and create default layout, Remove Linux partitions on selected drive and create default layout, Use Free Space on selected drive and create default layout, and Create custom layout. For the first three, default partitions will be created. The Remove All Linux Partitions option (2) is selected by default.

- **Remove Linux partitions on selected drives**   This removes just Linux partitions that are already on your disks. Any Windows or other OS partitions will remain untouched.

- **Remove all partitions on selected drives**   This removes all the partitions on the disk, effectively erasing it. You will lose any existing partitions, including Windows partitions.

- **Use existing free space on selected drives**   This is for disks that might be partially used, such as a partition for Windows that uses only part of the hard disk. This assumes that there is a significant amount of free space already on the disk.

- **Create custom layout**   This options open Partd directly and lets you create your own partitions or manually select current ones. This option provides the most control, but you need to know how partitions work and how they are implemented on a hard drive.

In a pane below the options is a list of all the hard drives on your system. You can select the one you want Linux installed on. If you have only one, it will be selected for you.

An option at the bottom of the screen lets you review all your partitions in Partd, letting you modify them if you need to. This will not be checked by default. Check this to see exactly how Partd will partition your system. You can also make changes if needed.

- **Review and modify partitioning layout**   This allows you to make changes manually to the partitions as well as see exactly what partitions will be created on your drives. Like the Create custom layout option you are place in the Partd partition manager where you can modify your partitions as you wish.

If you want to organize your data using several partitions, such as **/home**, **/**, and **/var**, as well as boot, you will have to manually configure them. Automatic partitioning will set up a boot partition and an LVM Linux partition only.

The Advanced Storage Configuration button lets you either select an iSCSI device or disable your motherboard RAID device controller (dmraid).

Custom and Review Partitioning

If you choose the Create custom layout option or checked the Review option, the partitioning screen is displayed, placing you into the Partd partition configurator. Here, you can manually create Linux partitions or select the one where you want to install Fedora. The top pane lists the hard drives with their partitions on your computer (many computers will have only one hard drive), and the lower pane lists the partitions. Selecting a hard drive will list its partitions. The buttons above the partitions pane enable you to create, edit, and delete partitions. The Partitions screen is actually an interactive interface where you configure partitions as well as create new ones.

If you are reviewing after default partitioning, then the hard disk partitions set up for you will be displayed. The panel will show the specific partitions that will be created for your system.

If you are formatting any old Linux partitions that still have data on them, a dialog box will appear listing them and asking you to confirm that you want to format them (new Linux partitions that you created will automatically be formatted). If you already have a Linux system, you will most likely have several Linux partitions already. Some of these may be used for just the system software, such as the boot and root partitions. These should be formatted. Others may have extensive user files, such as a **/home** partition that normally holds user home directories and all the files they have created. You should *not* format such partitions.

Recommended Partitions

If you are manually creating your partitions, you are required to set up at least two Linux partitions: a swap partition and a root partition. The *root partition* is where the Linux system and application files are installed. In addition, it is recommended that you also set up a boot partition that would contain just your Linux kernel, and a **/home** partition that would hold all user files. Separating system files on the root and boot partitions from the user files on the home partition allows you to replace the system files should they ever become corrupt, without touching the user files. Similarly, if just your kernel becomes corrupt, you would have to replace only the kernel files on your boot partition, leaving the system files on the root partition untouched. This strategy of separating system directories into different partitions can be carried further to ensure a more robust system. For example, the **/var** directory, which now holds Web and FTP server files, can be assigned its own partition, physically separating the servers from the rest of your system. The **/usr** directory, which holds most user applications, can be placed in its own partition and then be shared and mounted by other systems. One drawback to this strategy is that you would need to know ahead of time the maximum space you would want to use for each partition. For system and kernel files, this can be easily determined, but for directories whose disk usage can change dramatically, like **/home**, **/var**, and even **/usr**, this can be difficult to determine. As an alternative to creating separate physical partitions for each directory, you could use logical volumes (described later). A basic partition configuration is shown here:

- **Swap partition** No mount point
- **/** Root partition for system files (and all other files if no other partition is defined)
- **/boot** Boot partition holding the Linux kernel (approximately 200 MB)
- **/home** User home directories and files

Except for the swap partition, when setting up a Linux partition, you must specify a mountpoint. A *mountpoint* is a directory where the files on that partition are connected to the overall Linux file structure for your system. The mountpoint for your root partition is the root directory, represented by a single slash (/). The mountpoint for your boot partition is the path **/boot**. For a user's partition, it would be **/home**.

The size of the swap partition should be the same size as your RAM memory, with a recommended minimum size of 64 MB. With 512 MB of RAM, you could use a 512 MB swap partition. If your disk space is limited, you should make your swap size at least 64 MB.

Creating Partitions

To create the new partition, click the New button to display a dialog box where you can enter the mountpoint, the size (in megabytes), the partition type, and the hard disk on which you want to create the partition. By default you can select a fixed size, specifying the megabytes to use. You can also select a "Fill to maximum allowable size" option to have the partition automatically expand to the size of the remaining free space on the disk. You can have this option selected for more than one partition. In that case, the partition size will be taken as a required minimum and the remaining free space will be shared equally among the partitions. For partition type, select ext3 for standard Linux partitions and select the Linux swap type for your swap partition. You can even use Partd to create Windows vfat partitions (16 bit). There are five kinds of partitions supported during installation, ext2, ext3, swap, physical volume, software RAID, and vfat. The ext2 partition is an older form of the Linux standard partition type, ext3. You would use software RAID if you are setting up RAID arrays using the Linux RAID software instead of your motherboard RAID device support. Physical volumes is used to set up Logical volumes. If you choose to set up default partitions, you will see that a physical volume has already been created (LVM pv), with a corresponding Logical group and its volumes on which your swap and root partitions reside.

To make any changes later, you can edit a partition by selecting it and clicking the Edit button.

Logical Volumes

Fedora also supports Logical Volume Management (LVM), letting you create *logical volumes,* which you can use instead of using hard disk partitions directly. Logical volumes are implemented by Logical Volume Management (LVM). They provide a more flexible and powerful way of dealing with disk storage, organizing physical partitions into logical volumes in which memory can be managed easily. Disk storage for a logical volume is treated as one pool of memory, though the volume may in fact contain several hard disk partitions spread across different hard disks. There is one restriction. The boot partition cannot be a logical volume. You still have to create a separate hard disk partition as your boot partition with the **/boot** mountpoint in which your kernel will be installed. If you selected default partitioning, the **/boot** partition will have already been set up for you, along with an LVM volume partition for the rest of the system.

If you choose to let the install program set up a default partition layout for you, a logical group will be set up with volumes for both the swap and root partitions. The logical group will be labeled Logical0 by default. You can elect to change this name later by editing its properties with logical volume manager, system-config-lvm.

Creating logical volumes involves several steps. First you create physical LVM partitions, then the volume groups you place these partitions in, and then from the volume groups you create the logical volumes, for which you then specify mountpoints and file system types. To create your physical LVM partitions, click New and select Physical Volume (LVM) for the File System Type. Create an LVM physical partition for each partition you want on your hard disks. Once you have created LVM physical partitions, you click the LVM button to create your logical volumes. You first need to assign the LVM physical partitions to volume groups. Volume groups are essentially logical hard drives. You could assign LVM physical partitions from different hard disks to the same volume group, letting the volume group span different hard drives. Once the volume groups are created, you are ready to create your logical volumes. You can create several logical volumes within each group. The logical volumes function like partitions. You will have to specify a file system type and a mountpoint for each logical volume you create. In a default configuration, two logical volumes have already been set up for the root and swap partitions.

RAID Disks

You also have the option of creating Linux software RAID disks. Such disk are for use with the Linux software RAID service, and are not used for your motherboard or computer's RAID devices. If you have already decided to use the motherboard RAID support, you do not need Linux software RAID. Linux supports both motherboard/computer RAID devices (dmraid) as well as its own Linux software RAID.

To create Linux software RAID device, first create partitions and select as their type Software RAID. Once you have created your partitions, you can create a RAID disk. Click the RAID button and then select the partitions you previously created that you want to make up the RAID disk, choosing also the type of RAID disk. RAID disks are used primarily for servers or for systems with several hard disks that can make use of RAID's recovery capabilities.

Boot Loaders

Once your partitions are prepared, you install a boot loader. Fedora uses the Grand Unified Bootloader (GRUB). You use a boot loader to start Linux from your hard drive. The screen will display the partition to boot by default, listing all partitions with different operating systems installed on them, for instance, with a check box to select the default. Your Windows system will simply be labeled as Other. The New button to the side will let you add a new entry, specifying its label, the partition it uses, and whether it should be the default. By selecting a current entry and clicking the Edit button, you can change any of these features, such as changing the Other entry name to Windows.

Clicking the Advanced options lets you refine your boot procedure, enabling you to choose where to install the boot loader or determine the drive boot order. You have two choices as to where to install the boot loader: the Master Boot Record (MBR) or the root partition. The recommended place is the MBR.

You can also set a boot loader password. When any user boots with GRUB, they can change the boot loader options (the Force LBA option is used for old hard drives and motherboards). A password will prevent other users on your system from changing the boot loader options.

Network Configuration

The Network Configuration screen displays entries in the top part for the different network devices on your computer. The screen displays segments for your network devices, hostname, and miscellaneous settings. If you use DHCP to automatically configure your network connection, as most networks do, you will most likely not need to do anything on this screen.

The Network devices segment at the top will list your network connection devices, such as your Ethernet device. For computers already connected to a network with an Ethernet card, the first entry is usually labeled eth0. If you need to manually configure your device, entering an IP address for it, you can click Edit to display the device's configuration panel.

This panel has two segments, one for IPv4 options and the other for IPv6 options. There are check boxes for each allowing you to enable for disable IPv4 or IPv6 support. For IPv4 support you can choose to either manually configure the device or use DHCP to automatically configure it. For manual configuration, you can enter the device's IP address (usually your computer's IP address) and your network's prefix. For IPv6 support you can choose Automatic Neighborhood discovery (similar effect as DHCP, but different process), Dynamic IP Conficuration which requires the use of a DHCPv6 server on your network (similar to DHCP), and manual configuration where you can enter in the IPv6 address directly. Keep in mind that a manual IPv6 can be very lengthy and complicated. See Chapter 37 for more information on IPv6.

In the Hostname segment, you can choose either to manually provide your network information or to use DHCP to automatically obtain it.

If you choose to manually provide your network information, you can enter a hostname along with your network's gateway and DNS servers' IP addresses. To choose a manual configuration, you first have to edit the network device in the top panel and choose to manual configuration, entering in your IP address. Only the will you be allowed to make gateway and DNS entries in the Miscellaneous section. Otherwise these enteries will be grayed out.

System Configuration

On the Time Zone Configuration screen, you have the option of setting the time by using a map to specify your location or by using Universal Coordinated Time (UTC) entries. The Time Zone tool uses a new map feature that expands first to your region to let you easily select your Zone. You can also select your time zone from the pop up menu directly.

On the next screen, you can set the root password for the root account on your system. This is the account used for system administration operations, such as installing software and managing users. After installation, a similar screen will let you also add an ordinary user account.

Software Installation

The next screen displays three install options. You will also have the option to Customize Now and select the particular packages you want.

- **Office and Productivity**   Home or desktop systems
- **Software Development**   Includes software development
- **Web Server**   Includes the Apache Web server, FTP servers, Samba and NFS file servers, and the DNS server

The options provide a quick install process, using a standard selection of software packages. The Customize Now button will let you select the packages you want, including all packages, as well as give you more control over configuring your partitions.

In addition you can choose to install software for additional software repositories. These can include software for critical software like proprietary graphics drivers from Nvidia or AMD, as well as multimedia support like MP3 or DVD which is not included with software repositories. Your company or institution may also run its own repository that holds a collection of customized software. For graphical proprietary devices, the recomended repository is rpm.livna.org. For example, to install a proprietary graphics driver during instlalation, you would add rpm.livna.org as an additional repository, and then check Customize Now. Then choose the graphics drivers you need.

Keep in mind that adding software repositories will complicate and lengthen your installation. A safer approach would be to add software from repositories later, after your system is up and running.

Depending on the kind of install you choose, Fedora will select a set of predetermined software collections tailored to Customize Later (the default) or to Customize Now. If you customize now, you can add packages to be installed from the CD/DVD-ROM. If you customize later, packages will be downloaded and installed from online repositories.

TIP   *If you are installing well after the distribution release date, you may want to install as little software as possible. Much of the software may need updating, requiring a download from the online Fedora repository anyway. You may as well download the updated version directly, after you set up your system.*

If you choose the Customize Now option, you will be placed in the Fedora Software Manager. A base selection is automatically made. You can then choose to add optional software packages or remove those selected. The Package Manager first displays two panes, one for a small set of major software categories like Desktops and Applications, and the other for subcategories depending on the major category selected. The subcategories will have check boxes for software selected. Within each subcategory an optional panel will list specific packages you can add or remove. The major categories are Desktop Environments, Applications, Development, Base System, Servers, and Languages. Desktop Environments will have only the subcategories GNOME and KDE, of which only GNOME will be selected by default. Servers will list all the servers, most of which will not be selected. The Base System will hold your Administration and System Tools entries as well as Java. Applications have several subcategories including Graphical Internet, Office/Productivity, and Sound and Video. To see what packages are actually selected for installation, as well as to add or remove others, select a subcategory and then click the Optional Packages button. This opens a new window listing all the packages that can be installed for this subcategory, each with a check box next to its entry. Check boxes with checkmarks in them will be installed; those that are empty will not. Click the check box to toggle between the two.

Only the Fedora spin will have a Server category listing all the Linux servers. The GNOME spin will have neither KDE or servers, and the KDE spin will not have GNOME or servers.

Take the time to check out what packages are not being installed and select the ones you want. Chances are a package you are expecting to be installed won't be. For example, in the Internet collection (Applications | Graphical Internet) you will find that such useful tools as the gFTP application are not selected by default. You will need to manually select it by clicking the Optional Packages button to display the list of packages, and then click the check box for gFTP. In multimedia (Applications I Sound and Video) the popular K3b CD/DVD burning application also is not selected. This is just one of the popular applications you will have to select in the Multimedia optional panel. Other packages you may want to include are Thunderbird (Applications I Graphical Internet) and Samba configuration (Servers I Windows File Server).

You can no longer just install everything or even everything in a category. Users are becoming more and more specialized in their tasks, and there is no sense in installing software they will never need. The initial install becomes more like a base collection that users can then add to as they want. This reflects the massive expansion of Linux software packages now available. The Fedora Extras repository along with additional repositories like **freshrpms.net** now provide far more software than could possibly be included in a few disks.

Many software packages require that other software packages also be installed. This is called a dependency. If you don't have these already selected for installation, they will be selected for you.

After selecting your software, the next screen lets you start the installation. This is your last chance to back out of the installation. You can press the Back button to reselect packages, or simply press your system's reset button to end the install process, leaving your original system untouched. Once you click the Next button, if you chose to format partitions, they will be formatted.

The packages are then installed, showing each package as it is installed and the progress of the installation. (For the Fedora DVD-ROM, the install program detects all packages as residing on the single DVD-ROM. If you are using CD-ROMs instead, you will be prompted when to install the next CD-ROM. The current one will automatically be ejected for you.) When the installation finishes, a postinstall process will complete. You are then usually given the option to create a boot disk. You can use this disk to access your Linux system should your hard disk boot somehow fail.

Finishing Installation

Once your installation is finished, you can click the Reboot button to reboot. Be sure to remove the install or boot DVD/CD-ROM. If you booted from a CD, your CD will be ejected before rebooting. If you booted directly from the CD-ROM, you may want to change your boot sequence in your BIOS back to your original settings.

GRUB on Restart

When you reboot, a GRUB boot loader menu will be displayed listing Linux and other operating systems you specified, such as Windows. Use the arrow keys to move to the Linux entry, if it is not already highlighted, and press ENTER. The screen will appear for a few seconds and then run the default operating system. If you want to remain at the menu display until you specifically choose a system, you can press any key when GRUB starts up.

For graphical installations, some displays may have difficulty running the graphical start up display known as the red hat graphical boot tool, **rhgb**. If you have this problem, you can edit your Linux GRUB entry and remove the **rhgb quiet** terms at the end of the Grub start up line. Press the **e** key to edit a Grub entry. You system will start up initially using text display for all the start up tasks, then shift to the graphical login. The Linux GRUB line will look something like this.

```
kernel /vmlinuz-2.6.20-1.3094.fc7 ro root=/dev/fedora7/fedora70 rhgb quiet
```

Setup

The first time you start up Fedora, the Setup Agent is run. This agent will help you perform basic configuration of your system, letting you set the date and time, configure your display (graphics card and monitor), and configure your sound card, as well as set up user accounts. The different steps will be listed on a side pane, with an arrow progressing through each one as you complete a task. For Fedora, you will be initially asked to approve the GNU General Public License for this distribution. The steps are listed here:

- License Agreement
- Firewall
- SELinux
- Date and Time
- Hardware Profile
- Create User
- Sound Card
- Finish Setup

Firewall and SELinux

The Firewall Configuration screen then lets you create basic default levels of network security. A pop-up menu lets you enable or disable the firewall (it is enabled by default). You can also specify services you may be running that permit others to access to your system, such as Web or FTP services. One service you may want to include is Samba to allow browsing of your Samba shares. The Other Ports entry expands to a panel where you can add ports that should be allowed access, like ports you want to use for bittorrent.

The next screen lets you configure Security-Enhanced Linux (SELinux). SELinux provides a very high level of security administration. You have three settings: enforcing, permissive, and disable. Enforcing is the default, but Permissive may be the better choice until you are sure how you want SELinux configured in detail. The Enforcing setting will deny access by unauthorized users to files and applications. If your security policy is not accurately configured, access could be denied to valid users. At the Permissive level you can see how SELinux performs and adjust its configuration appropriately. SELinux may not be fully compatible with older software.

Date and Time

The Date And Time Configuration panel will automatically probe for the date and time, displaying the date on a calendar and the time in hours, minutes, and seconds. You can easily change any entry with the click of a button. You can also choose to use the Network Time Protocol, which will obtain the time automatically from a time server on the Internet, making sure your time is always correct. You can choose from server pools listed, for instance, **0.fedora.pool.ntp.org**. The advanced options let you synchornize before using a service or use a local time source.

TIP *The display is automatically detected during installation. You can later configure it after the install process is completed. Should you have an ATI or Nvidia graphics card on your system, you can later download and install its Linux driver from rpm.livna.org (see Chapter 4).*

Hardware Profile Reporting

The Smolt hardware profile screen lets you allow your hardware configuration to be registered with the Fedora project, so statistics on hardware compatibility can be compiled directly from users. See **fedoraproject.org/wiki/Releases/Smolt** for more information.

Create User

The Create User panel then lets you create a normal user account. You should have at least one, other than root. A dialog box is displayed with entries for the username, the user's full name, the password, and the password confirmation. Once you have entered the information and clicked Next, the new user will be created.

You can also select LDAP, Windbind, Hesiod, or NIS to configure a user's network login process. Click the Use Network Login button. Here you can configure the servers. This starts up system-config-authentication. Use this also if your network supports the authentication server. Three panels are displayed: User Information, Authentication, and Options. On the User Information panel, you can configure LDAP, Kerberos, Windbind, and SMB (Samba) authentication. On the Autnehntication panel, you can enable and configure support for each, specifying NIS, LDAB, Kerberos, or SMB servers that your network may use. The options panel lists support for password authentication.

Sound Configuration

On the Sound panel, your sound card will be automatically detected and configured. You can click a button to test the sound. You also have mixer options for dynamic keys and to disable software mixing. If you have more than one device, they will all be displayed with their own panels.

Click the Finish button to finish your setup.

Login and Logout

The Setup Agent then concludes and the login prompt or the login screen will appear. A graphical install will use the login screen. You can then log in to your Linux system using a login name and a password for any of the users you have set up. An entry box will be displayed in the middle of the screen and labeled User. Just type in your user name and press ENTER. The label of the box will then change to password and the box will clear. Then enter your password and press ENTER.

If you log in as the root user, you can perform administrative operations, such as installing new software or creating more users. To log in as the root user, enter **root** at the entry box and the root user password in the entry box when the password label appears.

On the login screen, two pop-up menus and one button are displayed in the middle of the screen: Language, Options, and Shutdown. The Options menu lets you choose what desktop graphical interface to use, such as KDE or GNOME, as well as to shut down or restart the system. You use the Shutdown button to shut down. To reboot, select Restart from the Options menu. The Language menu lets you select a language to use.

When you finish, you can shut down your system. If you are using a command line interface, use the command **halt**. From GNOME, you can elect to shut down the entire system. If you log out from either GNOME or KDE and return to the login screen, you can click the Shutdown button.

If the system should freeze on you for any reason, you can hold down the CTRL and ALT keys and press DEL (CTRL-ALT-DEL) to safely restart it. Never just turn it off. You can also use CTRL-ALT-F3 to shift to a command line prompt and log in to check out your system, shutting down with the **halt** command.

Boot Disks

You can use **mkbootdisk** to create a boot CD-ROM. Use the **--iso** option and the **--device** option with the name of an ISO image file to create. You then use CD-ROM-burning software to create the CD-ROM from the image file. The following example creates an CD-ROM image file called **mybootcd.iso** that can be used as a boot CD-ROM.

```
mkbootdisk --iso --device mybootcd.iso 2.6.15-1.2504_FC5
```

Rescue

If for some reason you are not able to boot or access your system, it may be due to conflicting configurations, libraries, or applications. In this case, you can boot your Linux system in a rescue mode and then edit configuration files with a text editor such as Vi, remove the suspect libraries, or reinstall damaged software with RPM. To enter the rescue mode, CD-ROM or the DVD-ROM boot disk, select Rescue Installed System on the initial menu.

You will boot into the command line mode with your system's files mounted at **/mnt/ sysimage**. You will be notified that you can use the **chroot** command to set your system to the / directory as the root directory. Issue the following command at the command line prompt:

```
chroot /mnt/sysimage
```

Use the **cd** command to move between directories. Check **/etc** and **/etc/sysconfig** for your configuration files. You can use Vi to edit your files and the **less** command to view them. To reinstall files, use the **rpm** command. When you are finished, enter the **exit** command.

If you have a command line system, at the boot prompt, enter

```
linux rescue
```

You can also download and create the Linux rescue CD. Just download the Linux rescue CD iso from the Fedora repository and boot with this disk.

Re-installing the Boot Loader

If you have a dual-boot system, where you are running both Windows and Linux on the same machine, you may run into a situation where you have to re-install your GRUB boot loader. This problem occurs if your Windows system completely crashes beyond repair and you have to install a new version of Windows, or you are adding Windows to your machine after having installed Linux. Windows will automatically overwrite your boot loader (alternatively, you could install your boot loader on your Linux partition instead of the MBR). You will no longer be able to access your Linux system.

All you need to do is to reinstall your boot loader. First boot from your Linux DVD/ CD-ROM installation disk, and at the menu select Rescue Installed System.

As noted in the preceding section, this boots your system in rescue mode. Then use **grub-install** and the device name of your first partition to install the boot loader. Windows normally wants to be on the first partition with the MBR, the master boot record. You would specify this partition. At the prompt enter

```
grub-install /dev/hda1
```

TIP *If even your Linux rescue disks are unable to access your system, you could use a Fedora Live CD to start up Fedora, and then manually mount your Fedora partitions. You will need to know your partition device names (use GParted). Once mounted, you can access the system files on the mounted partition and make any needed changes.*

Creating Your Own Fedora Install Spins with Pungi

You can create your own distribution discs with Pungi. The Pungi tool uses configuration files in the /**etc/pungi** directory. It will generate a basic collection of packages, downloading them from the Fedora repository. Default settings are listed in the **pungi.conf** file. The packages to add to the spin are listed by category in the **minimal-manifest** file. It uses the same syntax as kickstart. The **comps.xml** file in the /**etc/pungi** directory defines the package grouping for your release. The /**etc/pungi/comps-fc7.xml** file will hold the package grouping for Fedora 7. These are the same grouping that you see in the Add/Remove Software Browse panel. In your manifest file you can use the grouping names to add whole groups of packages to your installation disc, such as Desktop for all desktops or Servers for all your servers. For just subgroupings, just indicate their name, like GNOME for just the GNOME desktop and its software, or Editors for just the editors. For particular packages, select their unique prefix, like **kmod-fgrlx** for the ATI drivers.

The default directories used are /**srv/pungi/cache** and /**srv/pungi/Fedora**. Other defaults are designed for your current installation. You can change the destination directory either by changing the product_name entry in the /**etc/pungi/pungi.conf** file or by specifying a directory with the **--destir=** option when you invoke Pungi. Pungi also needs to know whether to use 32- or 64-bit versions of the software. This is specified with the **arch** option. Also Pungi has to inform Yum what repository directories to use and whether to use the 64- or 32-bit packages. The **yumconf** option is set to a Yum configuration file that holds all the repositories you want to check. By default these will include only the Fedora repository, but you can add others if you wish. This file holds much the same information as appears in your /**etc/yum/yum.conf** file and your various repository files in /**etc/yum.conf.d** directory.

There are separate Yum configuration files for 64 bits and 32 bits. These files are in the **/etc/pungi** directory.

In the **/etc/pungi** directory you will find several possible Pungi configuration and Yum configuration files, along with a default version. The Pungi configuration files will have the prefix **pungi**, and the Yum configuration files will have the prefix **yum.conf**. The configuration files will then be further distinguished by architecture: i386, x86_64, source, and ppc. There will already be a default **pungi.conf** file that is set up for 64-bit architecture. To create a distribution disc, you will first have to decide which architecture to use and the Yum repositories to download from. When setting up your **pungi.conf** file, first make a copy or pungi-fc7 configuration file for the architecture you want, and then be sure to specify the appropriate Yum configuration file in the **pungi.conf** file.

For example, to create a distribution for a 64-bit machine, you would specify x86_64 options in the **pungi.conf** file. Be sure that the **yumconf** option in the **pungi.conf** file is set to the **yum.conf.x86_64** file. In effect, the architecture and the Yum configuration have to correspond. A 64-bit architecture uses a 64-bit Yum repository, whereas a ppc architecture will use a ppc repository. In your **pungi.conf** file make sure that the **arch** option is set to the same architecture that your **yumconf** option is using. The **arch** option for a 64-bit architecture would be set to **x86_64**, and its **yumconf** option would use the Yum 64-bit repositories, **yum.conf.x86_64**. For a source code disc you would use a **source** architecture and the corresponding Yum configuration file for source code of the architecture you want.

The default Pungi configuration file is **/etc/pungi/pungi.conf**. Here you will find options for creating a distribution spin. Should you want to make changes, you can either back up the file first or use it to create a copy, which you can then edit. With the **--conf=** option you can then direct Pungi to use your new configuration file. In any case, make sure to keep a copy of the original **pungi.conf** file for reference. The Pungi options are listed in Table 2-1.

The default **pungi.conf** file is shown here:

pungi.conf

```
product_name = myFedora ; The name used during install
product_path = Fedora ; The directory where RPMS go
iso_basename = F ; The first part of the ISO image file name
bugurl = http://bugzilla.redhat.com ; Used for betanag
comps = /etc/pungi/comps-fc7.xml ; Package groupings and default installs
manifest = /etc/pungi/minimal-manifest ; Determine what to bring in. Kickstart syntax
yumconf = /etc/pungi/yum.conf.x86_64 ; Where to gather packages from
destdir = /srv/pungi/Fedora ; Top level composition directory, must be clean
cachedir = /srv/pungi/cache ; Cache used for repeat runs
arch = x86_64 ; What architecture to compose (must be same arch as system)
version = 7 ; Used both in install and part of the destination tree
flavor = Custom ; Further define a given cut of the package set
discs = 1 ; Number of discs needed to fit data.
#cdsize = 4608.0 ; Not used if disc count is 1
getsource = YES ; Used to determine if we want source packages or not
```

The files to gather into the distribution are listed in a manifest file specified by the **manifest** option in the **pungi.conf** file. By default this is set to **/etc/pungi/minimal-manifest**, which holds the minimal set of packages you need for any distribution. You can then add to this or change some settings. One strategy is to copy the **minimal-manifest** file and make changes to the copy. Then make the changed copy the manifest file for Pungi to use, changing

Option	Description
product_name	The name used during install; default is Fedora.
product_path	The directory where RPMS goes; default is Fedora.
iso_basename	The first part of the ISO filename; default is F.
bugurl	Used for bug reports; default is **http://bugzilla.redhat.com**.
comps	Used to define package groupings and default installs; default is **/etc/pungi/comps-fc7.xml** for Fedora 7.
manifest	Used to determine what to bring in. Supports kickstart syntax; default is **/etc/pungi/minimal-manifest**, also in **/etc/pungi**.
yumconf	Specify Yum configuration file with Yum repositories to gather packages from. Be sure to distinguish according to architecture: i386, x86_64, ppc. Default configuration files have the prefix **yum.conf** with the distribution name, and end with the architecture, like **yum.conf.fc7.i386** for 32-bit systems.
destdir	Top-level composition directory, must be clean; default is **/srv/pungi/Fedora**, use **--destdir** for Pungi command option.
cachedir	Cache used for repeat runs; default is **/srv/pungi/cache**.
arch	What architecture to compose (must be same architecture as system), use same as current system, **x86_64** for 64 bit and **i386** for 32 bit.
version	Used both in install and part of the destination tree. Default for Fedora 7 is 7.
flavor	Further define a given selection of the package set; default is Custom.
discs	Number of discs needed to fit data; default is 1.
cdsize	Not used if disc count is 1, commented out by default; default value is 4608.0.
getsource	Used to determine if we want source packages or not; default is YES.

TABLE 2-1 Pungi Options

the manifest option to that file. Gathered packages will be listed in your destination directory. You can examine them to see exactly what your distribution will include.

A copy of the **minimal-manifest** file is shown here. Packages include the kernel, Xorg X Server drivers and fonts, SELinux targeted policy, the GRUB boot loader, the Man pages, and the joe text editor.

/etc/pungi/minimal-manifest
```
kernel
xorg-x11-fonts-ISO8859-1-75dpi
busybox-anaconda
dejavu-lgc-fonts
xorg-x11-fonts-base
memtest86+
xorg-x11-drivers
selinux-policy-targeted
```

```
anaconda-runtime
man
joe
grub
```

The manifest file uses the same syntax as kickstart. The package groups you can use have the same names as listed in the Add/Remove Software (Pirut) Browse panel. To specify a group, prefix the group name with the @ symbol (no space). In the following example, the **my-manifest** file will use all the packages in the GNOME Desktop Environment, Editors, and Windows File Server (Samba) groups. Editors is a subgroup of Applications. All dependent software, such as X Windows System software needed for the desktops, will be automatically included, though for desktops it would be helpful to include the X Windows System group. Be sure to use the name exactly as it is shown in Add/Remove Software, such as @GNOME Desktop Environment, not just GNOME. Should you just want the KDE desktop instead of the GNOME desktop, you could enter @KDE (K Desktop Environment). Be sure to check that the packages for a group are all included on the disc. If not, specify them singly. Groups are specified in the Pungi comps file, for instance, **/etc/pungi/comps-fc7.xml**. This is an XML file that you could modify to add your own groups. A sample manifest file is shown here using groups to specify packages.

/etc/pungi/my-manifest
```
kernel
busybox-anaconda
dejavu-lgc-fonts
memtest86+
selinux-policy-targeted
anaconda-runtime
man
@X Window System
@GNOME Desktop Environment
@Editors
@Windows File Server
grub
```

TIP *Downloaded packages are kept by Pungi in the */srv/pungi/cache* file. If you are generating a new disc version by just adding new packages, Pungi will make use of packages already in the cache directory, so you will not have to download them again.*

If you want to include third-party software such as the vendor drivers supplied by Livna or multimedia software like MPlayer with its DVD support, you will have to modify the Pungi Yum configuration file you want to use to include the third-party repository Yum configuration. This is a simple matter of editing the Yum configuration file and performing a copy and paste from the third-party repo file in **/etc/yum.repos.d** directory. For example, to add the support for the Livna repository, you would edit the **/etc/yum.repos.d/livna.repo** file, copy its contents, and paste them to the bottom of your **/etc/pungi** Yum configuration file. You could then specify Livna packages in your Pungi manifest file, such as kmod-nvidia for the NVIDIA vendor graphics driver, or mplayer for MPlayer. You could do the same with your **freshrpms.repo** file to let you access packages on the Freshrpms repository.

Pungi moves through different stages to create your spin. You can have Pungi perform these all at once with the **--all-stages** option, or you can proceed stage by stage. There are options for each stage:

- **Gather , -G**   First Pungi will gather the packages to install on your spin. These will be downloaded from the Fedora repository.
- **BuildInstall, -B**   In the buildinstall stage the gathered packages are synchronized with Anaconda for installation.
- **Package Order, -P**   The install packages are organized into a sequence that Anaconda can install, making sure dependent packages are installed first as needed.
- **SplitTree, -S**   If the collection of packages are too large to fit on a single disc, the Split Tree stage will split the collection accordingly.
- **CreateISO, -I**   The CreateISO stage then creates the ISO image for the distribution. If you need more than one disc, several ISO image files will be generated. You can then burn the images, and you should be able to install from those discs.

All these stages can be performed at once with the **--all-stages** option.

The ISO image or images will be placed in the *destination/version/flavor/architecture/iso* subdirectory. The default directory is **Fedora/7/custom/i386/iso**. The name is made up of the iso_basename, the version, the architecture, and the media type. The default would be **F-7-i386-DVD.iso**. Pungi should also create a rescue image.

Pungi will generate a log of all its actions when creating a distribution disc. This log is kept in the destination folder under the **logs** directory with the name of the distribution flavor name. The default directory will be **/srv/pungi/Fedora/logs**. For an i386 version the log would be named **Custom.i386.log**. If you have problems, consult this log for a detailed listing of all Pungi actions.

Pungi will generate all needed Fedora repository keys as well as use the standard Fedora release notes.

You can then burn your image. You can just right-click the ISO image file and select Open With CD/DVD Creator. Insert a DVD or CD, and burn the image.

When you boot from your distribution disc, the standard Fedora installation screen will be displayed with options to install, update, rescue, or edit parameters. The title for the distribution will be the same as the product name you specified. Installation will proceed just as it would for a normal installation, as described in this chapter, but using only those packages you specified for your disk.

Interface Basics: Login, Desktop, Help, Repositories, Multimedia, and Spins

This chapter reviews quickly the basics of using a Fedora desktop, along with changes in the GDM login interface, changes to the Removable Devices and Multimedia configuration, and the new Fedora desktop.

Using Linux has become an almost intuitive process, with easy-to-use interfaces, including graphical logins and graphical user interfaces (GUIs) like GNOME and KDE. Even the standard Linux command line interface has become more user-friendly with editable commands, history lists, and cursor-based tools. To start using Linux, you have to know how to access your Linux system and, once you are on the system, how to execute commands and run applications. Access is supported through either the default graphical login or a command line login. For the graphical login, a simple window appears with menus for selecting login options and text boxes for entering your username and password. Once you access your system, you can then interact with it using either a command line interface or a graphical user interface (GUI). With GUI interfaces like GNOME and KDE, you can use windows, menus, and icons to interact with your system.

Linux is noted for providing easy access to extensive help documentation. It's easy to obtain information quickly about any Linux command and utility while logged in to the system. You can access an online manual that describes each command or obtain help that provides more detailed explanations of different Linux features. A complete set of manuals provided by the Linux Documentation Project is on your system and available for you to browse through or print. Both the GNOME and KDE desktops provide help systems that give you easy access to desktop, system, and application help files.

User Accounts

You never directly access a Linux system. Instead, Linux sets up an interface called a *shell* through which you can interact with it. Linux is a multiuser system that can support several user shells at once, accommodating several users simultaneously, each connected through his or her own terminal or from a remote system.

User access to the system is provided through *accounts.* Unix, which Linux is based on, was first used on large minicomputers and mainframes that could accommodate hundreds of users at the same time. Using one of many terminals connected to the computer, users could log in to the Unix system using their usernames and passwords. To gain access to the system, you need to have a user account set up for you. A system administrator creates the account, assigning a username and password for it. You then use your account to log in and use the system.

You can, in fact, create other new user accounts using special system administration tools like system-config-users. These tools become available to you when you log in as the root user. The *root user* is a special user account reserved for system administration tasks, such as creating users and installing new software.

Accessing Your Linux System

To access and use your Linux system, you must carefully follow required startup and shutdown procedures. You do not simply turn off your computer. Fedora does, however, implement journaling, which allows you to automatically recover your system from situations where the computer suddenly loses power and is shut off.

If you have installed the boot loader GRUB, when you turn on or reset your computer, the boot loader first decides what operating system to load and run. GRUB will display a menu of operating systems to choose.

If, instead, you wait a moment or press the ENTER key, the boot loader loads the default operating system. If a Windows system is listed, you can choose to start that instead.

You can think of your Linux operating system as operating on two different levels, one running on top of the other. The first level is when you start your Linux system, and where the system loads and runs. It has control of your computer and all its peripherals. You still are not able to interact with it, however. After Linux starts, it displays a login screen, waiting for a user to log in to the system and start using it. You cannot gain access to Linux, unless you log in first.

You can think of logging in and using Linux as the next level. Now you can issue commands instructing Linux to perform tasks. You can use utilities and programs such as editors or compilers, or even games. Depending on a choice you made during installation, however, you may be interacting with the system either using a simple command line interface or using the desktop directly. There are both command line login prompts and graphical login windows. Fedora will use a graphical interface by default, presenting you with a graphical login window at which you enter your username and password. If you choose not to use the graphical interface, you are presented with a simple command line prompt to enter your username.

The Display Manager: GDM

With the graphical login, your GUI interface starts up immediately and displays a login window with boxes for a username and password. When you enter your username and password, and then press ENTER, your default GUI starts up. On Fedora, this is GNOME by default.

For Fedora, graphical logins are handled by the GNOME Display Manager (GDM). The GDM manages the login interface along with authenticating a user password and username, and then starting up a selected desktop. If problems ever occur using the GUI interface, you can force an exit of the GUI with the CTRL-ALT-BACKSPACE keys, returning to the Login screen (or the command line if you started your GUI from there). Also, from the GDM, you can shift to the command line interface with the CTRL-ALT-F1 keys, and then shift back to the GUI with the CTRL-ALT-F7 keys.

When the GDM starts up, it shows a login window with a box for login. Various GDM themes are available, which you can select using the GDM configuration tool. The default theme currently used is the Fedora Flying High theme. Three pop-up menus are located at the center of the screen, labeled Language, Options, and Shutdown. To log in, enter your username in the entry box labeled Username and press ENTER. You are prompted to enter your password. Do so, and press ENTER. By default, the GNOME desktop is then started up.

TIP *You can configure your GDM login window with different features like background images and user icons. The GDM even has its own selection of themes to choose from. Select Login Screen entry on the Administration menu to configure your login window.*

When you log out from the desktop, you return to the GDM login window. To shut down your Linux system, click the Shutdown button. To restart, select Restart from the Options menu. Alternatively, you can also shut down from GNOME. From the System menu, select the Shutdown entry. GNOME will display a dialog screen with the buttons Suspend, Shutdown, or Reboot. Shutdown is the default and will occur automatically after a few seconds. Selecting Reboot will shut down and restart your system. (You can also open a terminal window and enter the **shutdown**, **halt**, or **reboot** command as described in the next section; **halt** will log out and shut down your system.)

From the Options menu, you can select the desktop or window manager you want to start up. Here you can select KDE to start up the K Desktop, for example, instead of GNOME. On Fedora, both KDE and GNOME will use similar themes, appearing much the same. The Language menu lists a variety of different languages that Linux supports. Choose one to change the language interface.

You can configure the GDM with the GDM configuration tool, which is accessible from either the login screen or the desktop. From the login screen, select Configure Login screen from the Options menu. You will be first prompted to enter the root password. Then the GDM configuration panel will be displayed (see Chapter 4 for more details). Use the Local panel to choose the theme you want. The Users panel lets you choose what User icons you want displayed on the login screen. To access the GDM configuration tool from the desktop, you select the System | Administration | Login Screen entry.

The User Switcher

Once you have logged in to GNOME, you can add the User Switcher to your desktop. This lets you switch to another user, without having to log out or end your current user session. Once the User Switcher is installed (right-click the panel and select Add To Panel), the switcher will appear on the panel as the name of the currently logged in user. If you left-click the name, a list of all other users will be displayed. Check boxes next to each show which users are logged in and running. To switch a user, select the user from this menu. If the user is not already logged in, the login manager (GDM) will appear and you can enter that user's password. If the user is already logged in, then the login window for the lock screen will appear (you can disable the lock screen). Just enter the user's password. The user's original session will continue with the same open windows and applications running when the user switched off. You can easily switch back and forth between logged-in users, with all users retaining their session from where they left off. When you switch off from a user, that user's running programs will continue in the background.

Right-clicking the switcher will list several user management items, like configuring the Login screen, managing users, or changing the user's password and personal information. The Preferences item lets you configure how the User Switcher is displayed on your panel. Instead of the user's name, you could use the term Users or a user icon. You can also choose whether to use a lock screen when the user switches. Disabling the lock screen option will let you switch seamlessly between logged-in users.

Accessing Linux from the Command Line Interface

For the command line interface, you are initially given a login prompt. The system is now running and waiting for a user to log in and use it. You can enter your username and password to use the system. The login prompt is preceded by the hostname you gave your system. In this example, the hostname is **turtle**. When you finish using Linux, you first log out. Linux then displays exactly the same login prompt, waiting for you or another user to log in again. This is the equivalent of the login window provided by the GDM. You can then log in to another account.

```
Fedora release 7.0
Kernel 2.6 on an i686

turtle login:
```

Logging In and Out with the Command Line

Once you log in to an account, you can enter and execute commands. Logging in to your Linux account involves two steps: entering your username and then entering your password. Type in the username for your user account. If you make a mistake, you can erase characters with the BACKSPACE key. In the next example, the user enters the username **richlp** and is then prompted to enter the password:

```
Fedora release 7.0
Kernel 2.6 on an i686

turtle login: richlp
Password:
```

When you type in your password, it does not appear on the screen. This is to protect your password from being seen by others. If you enter either the username or the password incorrectly, the system will respond with the error message "Login incorrect" and will ask for your username again, starting the login process over. You can then reenter your username and password.

Once you enter your username and password correctly, you are logged in to the system. Your command line prompt is displayed, waiting for you to enter a command. Notice the command line prompt is a dollar sign ($), not a number sign (#). The $ is the prompt for regular users, whereas the # is the prompt solely for the root user. In this version of Fedora, your prompt is preceded by the hostname and the directory you are in. Both are bounded by a set of brackets.

```
[turtle /home/richlp]$
```

To end your session, issue the **logout** or **exit** command. This returns you to the login prompt, and Linux waits for another user to log in.

```
[turtle /home/richlp]$ logout
```

Shutting Down Linux from the Command Line

If you want to turn off your computer, you must first shut down Linux. If you don't shut down Linux, you could require Linux to perform a lengthy systems check when it starts up again. You shut down your system in either of two ways. First log in to an account and then enter the **halt** command. This command will log you out and shut down the system.

```
$ halt
```

Alternatively, you can use the **shutdown** command with the **-h** option. With the **-r** option, it shuts down the system and then reboots it. In the next example, the system is shut down after five minutes. To shut down the system immediately, you can use **+0** or the word **now**.

```
# shutdown -h now
```

TIP *Shutting down involves a series of important actions, such as unmounting file systems and shutting down any servers. You should never simply turn off the computer, though it can normally recover.*

You can also force your system to reboot at the login prompt, by holding down the CTRL and ALT keys and then pressing the DEL key (CTRL-ALT-DEL). Your system will go through the standard shutdown procedure and then reboot your computer.

The functionality of the GNOME desktop is similar to previous versions, with Application, Places, and System menus.

The GNOME and KDE Desktops

Two alternative desktop GUI interfaces can be installed on Fedora Linux: GNOME and KDE. Each has its own style and appearance. GNOME uses the Clearlooks theme for its interface with the Fedora screen background and menu icon as its default.

It is important to keep in mind that though the GNOME and KDE interfaces appear similar, they are really two very different desktop interfaces with separate tools for selecting preferences. The Preferences menus on GNOME and KDE display a very different selection of desktop configuration tools. These are discussed in Chapters 6 and 7.

Though GNOME and KDE are wholly integrated desktops, they in fact interact with the operating system through a window manager, Metacity in the case of GNOME and the KDE window manager for KDE. You can use a different GNOME- or KDE-compliant window manager if you wish, or simply use a window manager in place of either KDE or GNOME.

You can find out detailed information about different window managers available for Linux from the X11 Web site at **www.xwinman.org**.

GNOME also includes a window manager called compiz that provides 3-D effects. To use compiz, select System | Preferences | Look And Feel | Desktop Effects, and then click Enable Desktop Effects. You can select Windows wobble and Workspace cubes. When you log in to GNOME again, compiz will be used with your desktop effects enabled.

Fedora Desktop

Fedora features a Fedora desktop look and feel with a Fedora logo, as well as default Fedora screen background. The logo depicts an F encased in a blue circle. On the main panel you will now see the blue Fedora logo as the icon for the Applications menu, instead of Red Hat's hat. There are several Fedora backgrounds, including the Fedora Bubbles, Fedora DNA, and Fedora Flying High. The logos even have their own package, Fedora-logos.

The default theme is Clearlooks with the Echo icons (the Fedora theme). Numerous other themes are available from the theme manager (System | Preferences | Look and Feel | Theme). The terminal window is located in Applications | System Tools.

GNOME

The Clearlooks/Fedora GNOME desktop display, shown in Figure 3-1, initially displays two panels at the top and bottom of the screen, as well as any file manager folder icons for

FIGURE 3-1   The Fedora GNOME desktop

your home directory and for the system. The top panel is used for menus, application icons, and notification tasks like your clock. There are three menus:

- **Applications**   With category entries like Office and Internet, these submenus will list the applications installed on your system. Use this menu to start your applications.

- **Places**   This menu lets you easily access commonly used locations like your home directory, the desktop folder for any files on your desktop, and the Computer window, through which you can access devices, shared file systems, and all the directories on your local system. It also has entries for searching for files (Search For Files), accessing recently used documents, and logging in to remote servers, such as NFS and FTP servers. The Places menu has a CD/DVD creator entry for using Nautilus to burn data CD/DVD-ROMs. A Recent Documents menu lists all your recently accessed files.

- **System**   This includes Preferences and Administration menus. The Preferences menu is used for configuring your GNOME settings, such as the theme you want to user and the behavior of your mouse. The Administration menu holds all the Fedora system configuration tools used to perform administrative tasks like adding users, setting up printers, configuring network connections, and managing network services like a Web server or Samba Windows access. This menu also holds entries for locking the screen (Lock) and logging out of the system (Logout).

Next to the menus are application icons for commonly used applications. These include Firefox (the Fox and World logo), the Evolution mail utility, and several OpenOffice applications. Click one to start that application. You can also start applications using the Applications menu.

On the right you will see icons for the date/time and the sound volume control.

The bottom panel is used for interactive tasks like selecting workspaces and docking applications. The workspace switcher for virtual desktops appears as four squares in the lower-left corner. Clicking a square moves you to that area. To the right of the workspace switcher is the trash space that shows what items you have in your trash.

When you click the folder for your home directory on your desktop, a file manager window opens showing your home directory. The file manager uses a spatial design by default, opening a new window for each subdirectory you open. A directory window will show only the menus for managing files and the icons. The menu entries provide the full range of tasks involved in managing your files. On the lower-left bar of the window is a pop-up menu to access parent directories. The name of the currently displayed directory is shown.

TIP   *If your desktop becomes too cluttered with open windows and you want to clear it by just minimizing all the windows, you can click on the Show Desktop Button at the left side of the lower panel.*

Your home directory will already have default directories created for commonly used files. These include Pictures, Documents, Music, and Videos. Your office applications will automatically save files to the Documents directory by default. A Download directory functions as your automatic download directory. The Desktop folder will hold all files and directories saved to your desktop.

The file manager also supports a browser view that has more displayed components, including a browser toolbar, a location box, and a sidebar commonly found on most traditional file managers. To use this format, right-click the folder's icon to display a pop-up menu, and then select Browser Folder. This will open that folder with the enhanced format. Also, from within a special window, you can select a folder and then select Browser view from the File menu to open it. When you open a new directory from a Browser Folder window, the same window is used to display it, and you can use the forward and back arrows to move through previously opened directories. In the location window, you can enter the pathname for a directory to move directly to it. Figure 3-2 shows both the spatial and browser views for the file manager windows.

NOTE *For both GNOME and KDE, the file manager is Internet-aware. You can use it to access remote FTP directories and to display or download their files, though in KDE the file manager is also a fully functional Web browser.*

To move a window, left-click and drag its title bar. Each window supports Maximize, Minimize, and Close buttons. Double-clicking the title bar will maximize the window. Each window will have a corresponding button on the bottom panel. You can use this button to minimize and restore the window. The desktop supports full drag-and-drop capabilities. You can drag folders, icons, and applications to the desktop or other file manager windows open to other folders. The move operation is the default drag operation (you can also press the SHIFT key while dragging). To copy files, press the CTRL key and then click and drag before releasing the mouse button. To create a link, hold both the CTRL and SHIFT keys while dragging the icon to where you want the link, such as the desktop.

To quit the GNOME desktop, select the Log Out entry from the System menu. If you entered from a login window, you are then logged out of your account and returned to the login window. If you started GNOME from the command line, you are returned to the command line prompt, still logged in to your account.

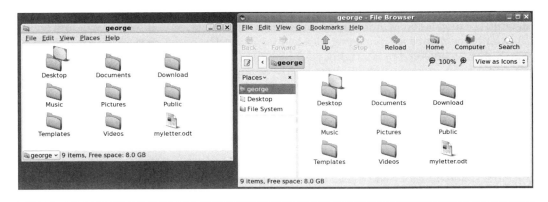

FIGURE 3-2   File manager spatial and browser views

GNOME Preferences

Fedora provides several tools for configuring your GNOME desktop. These are listed in the System | Preferences menu. Configuration preference tools are organized into several submenus: Personal, Look and Feel, Internet and Network, Hardware, and System. Those that do not fall into any category are listed directly. The GNOME preferences are listed in Table 3-1. Several are discussed in different sections in this and other chapters. The Help button on each preference window will display detailed descriptions and examples. Some of the more important tools are discussed here.

Personal	
About Me	Personal information like image, addresses, and password (see About Me later in this chapter).
Assistive Technology Preferences	Enables features like screen reader, keboard display, and magnifier.
File Managment	Default methods for file and director displays.
Input Method	Specify custom input methods.
Keyboard Accessibility	Set features like repeating, slow, and sticking, and mouse keys.
Keyboard Shortcuts	Configure keys for special tasks, like multimedia operations.
Preferred Applications	Set default Web browser, Mail application, and Terminal window.
Sessions	Manage your session with start up programs and save options (see Sessions later in this chapter).
Volume Control	Sound Mixer for setting volume control.
Look and Feel	
Desktop Background	Choose a desktop background; you can choose your own image.
Desktop Effects	Choose to use a 3d window manager like
Font	Change fonts and font sizes for different components on your desktop (see Desktop Font Sizes later in this chapter).
Main Menu	Add or remove categories and menu items for the Applications and System menus.
Menus and Toolbar	Simple menu and toolbar preferences; display icons in menus and enable detachable toolbars.
Theme	Select a theme to use for your desktop.
Screensaver	Select and manage your screen saver.
Windows	Enable certain window capabilities like roll up on title bar, movement key, window selection.
Internet and Network	
Bluetooth Preferences	Bluetooth notification icon display options.

TABLE 3-1   GNOME Desktop Preferences *(continued)*

Internet and Network	
Internet Proxy	Specify proxy configuration if needed: manual or automatic.
Personal File Sharing	Permit sharing public files on network; may require password.
Remote Desktop	Allow remote users to view or control your desktop; can control access with password.
Hardware	
Default Printer	Choose a default printer if more than one.
Keyboard	Configure your keyboard: selecting options, models, and typing breaks.
Mouse	Mouse configuration: select hand orientation, mouse image, and motion.
Removable Drives and Media	Set removable drives and media preferences (see Using Removable Devices and Media later in this chapter).
Screen Resolution	Change your screen resolution, refresh rate, and screen orientation.
Sound	Select the sound driver for events, video and music, and conferencing; also select sounds to use for desktop events.
System	
Power Managment	Power managment options for battery use and sleep options.
Search and Indexing	Set search and indexing preferences for Desktop searches.

Table 3-1   GNOME Desktop Preferences

The keyboard shortcuts configuration (Personal | Keyboard Shortcuts) lets you map keys to certain tasks, like mapping multimedia keys on a keyboard to media tasks like play and pause. Just select the task and then press the key. There are tasks for the desktop, multimedia, and window management. With window management you can also map keys to perform workspace switching. Keys that are already assigned will be shown.

The File Management configuration (Personal | File Managment) lets you determine the way files and directories are displayed along with added information to show in icon captions or list views. You can also specify double click behavior and files that can be previewed.

The Windows configuration (Look and Feel | Windows) is where you can enable features like window roll up, window movement key, and mouse window selection.

The Mouse and Keyboard preferences are the primary tools for configuring your mouse and keyboard (Hardware | Keyboard and Hardware | Mouse). The Mouse preferences let you choose a mouse image, configure its motion, and hand orientation. The Keyboard preferences window shows several panels for selecting your keyboard mdoel (layout), configuring keys (Layout Options), repeat delay (Keyboard), and even enforcing breaks from power typing as a health precaution.

There are three sound configuration tools to keep track up, each with very different tasks. To set the actual volume control and mixing for different sound sources like CD, speakers, microphone, and video, you use the GNOME Volume Control tool (Personal | Volume Control). You can also invoke it with the Volume Control applet on your panel.

To select a sound driver to use for different tasks, as well as specify the sounds to use for desktop events, you use the Hardware Sound configuration tool (Hardware | Sound). On the Devices panel you can select the sound driver to use, if more than one, for the Sound Events, Music and Videos, and conferencing. Defaults will already be choosen. On the Sounds panel you can enable software sound mixing letting you choose the sound you want for different desktop events. The System Beep panel lets you turn off the system beep sound and use visual beep instead like flashing window title bar.

The Sound entry in the Administration menu just detects sound devices and makes sure they are working (System | Administration | Sound Card Detection). Use this to detect new sound cards, or select a sound device should you have more than one.

GNOME Applets

GNOME applets are small programs that operate off your panel. It is very easy to add applets. Right-click the panel and select the Add entry. This lists all available applets. Some helpful applets are dictionary lookup, the current weather, the system monitor, which shows your CPU usage, the CPU Frequency Scaling Monitor for Cool and Quiet processors, and Search, which searches your system for files, as well as Lock, Shutdown, and Logout buttons. Some of these, including find, lock, and logout, are already on the Places menu. You could drag these directly from the menu to the panel to add the applet. Figure 3-3 shows some of the more common applets. Following the Web browser and e-mail icons, you have, from left to right: Search for files, dictionary lookup, Tomboy note taker, Network connection monitor, CPU scaling monitor, System monitor, Weather report, Eyes that follow your mouse around, User switcher, logout, shutdown, and lock screen buttons.

KDE

The K Desktop Environment (KDE) displays a panel at the bottom of the screen that looks very similar to one displayed on the top of the GNOME desktop. The file manager appears slightly different but operates much the same way as the GNOME file manager. There is a Control Center entry in the main menu that opens the KDE control center, from which you can configure every aspect of the KDE environment, such as themes, panels, peripherals like printers and keyboards (already handled by Fedora system tools), even the KDE file manager's Web browsing capabilities.

NOTE *The XFce4 desktop is a new lightweight desktop designed to run fast without the kind of overhead seen in full-featured desktops like KDE and GNOME. It includes its own file manager and panel, but the emphasis is on modularity and simplicity. The desktop consists of a collection of modules, including the xffm file manager, the xfce4-panel panel, and the xfwm4 window manager. In keeping with its focus on simplicity, its small scale makes it appropriate for laptops or dedicated systems that have no need for the complex overhead found in other desktops.*

FIGURE 3-3   GNOME applets

Starting a GUI from the Command Line

Once logged in to the system from the command line, you still have the option of starting an X Window System GUI, such as GNOME or KDE. In Linux, the command **startx** starts a desktop. The **startx** command starts the GNOME desktop by default. Once you shut down the desktop, you will return to your command line interface, still logged in.

```
$ startx
```

On Fedora, you can use the Desktop Switcher while in your desktop to switch between GNOME or KDE. The Desktop Switcher is accessible from the System | Preferences menu as the Desktop Switching Tool, or with the **switchdesk** command. You will have to install the switchdesk software packages first (use Add/Remove software and search on **switchdesk**).

Desktop Operations

There are several desktop operations that you may want to take advantage of when first setting up your desktop. These include setting your font sizes larger for high resolution monitors, burning CD/DVD disks, searching your desktop for files, and using removable media like USB drives, along with access to remote host.

Desktop Font Sizes

With very large monitors and their high resolutions becoming more common, one feature users find helpful is the ability to increase the desktop font sizes. On a large widescreen monitor, resolutions less than the native one tend not to scale well. A monitor always looks best in its native resolution. However, with a large native resolution like 1900 × 1200, text sizes become so small they are hard to read. You can overcome this issue by increasing the font size. The default size is 10; increasing it to 12 makes text in all desktop features like windows and menus much more readable.

To increase the font size, open the Font Preferences dialog by clicking System | Preferences | Look And Feel | Fonts. The Font Preferences dialog is shown in Figure 3-4. You can even change the font itself as well as choose bold or italic. You can further refine your fonts display by clicking the Details button to open a window where you can set features like the dots-per-inch, hinting, and smoothing. To examine a font in more detail, click the Go To Fonts Folder button and click the font.

Configuring Your Personal Information

The About Me peferences dialog (see Figure 3-5) lets you set up personal information to be used with your desktop applications, as well as change your password. Clicking on the image icon in the top left corner opens a browser where you can select the image to use. The Faces directory is selected by default with images you can use. The selected image is displayed to the left on the browser. For a personal photograph you can select the Picture folder. This the Picture folder on your home directory. Should you place a photograph or image there, you could then select it for your personal image. The image will be use in the login screen when showing your user entry. Should you want to change your password, you can click on the Change password button at the top right.

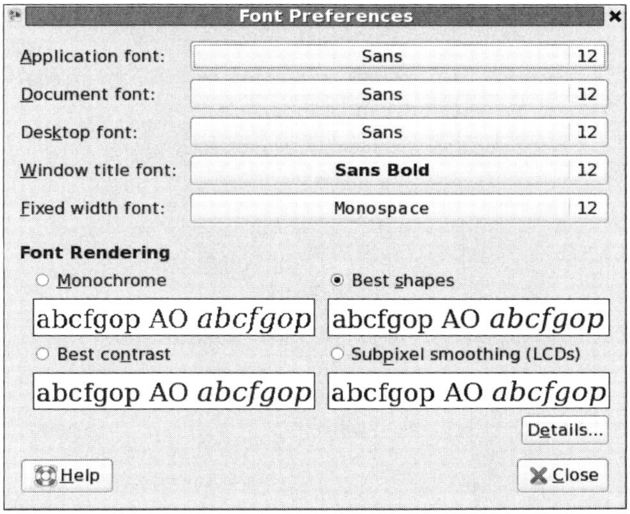

FIGURE **3-4**
Setting Font Sizes

There are three panels: Contact, Addresss, and Personal Info. The Contact panel you enter email (home and work), telephone, and instant messaging addresses. On the Address panel you enter your home and work addresses, and on the Person Info panel you list your Web addresses and work information.

Sessions

You can configure your desktop to restore your previously opened windows and applications, as well as specify startup programs. When you log out, you may want the windows you have open and the applications you have running to be automatically started when you log back in. In effect, you are saving you current session, and having it restored it when you log back in. For example, if you are in the middle of working on a spread sheet, you can save your work, but not close the file. Then logout. When you log back in, your spreadsheet will be opened automatically to where you left off.

Saving sessions is not turned on by default. You use the the Sessions preferences dialog's Sesssion Options panel (System | Preferences | Personal | Sessions) to save sessions. You can save your current session manually, opt to have all your sessions saved automatically when you logout, restoring them whenever you login.

You can also use the Sessions preferences dialog to select programs that you may want started up automatically. Some are already selected like the Software updater and the SELinux troubleshooter. On the Start Up Programs panel you can select programs you want started, as well as un-select the ones you don't want.

Beagle: Searching files

Beagle is a desktop search tool (**beaglewiki.org**). To start Beagle, select Search from the Places menu. Beagle will search all the files on your system, including images, e-mails, media files, and program source code.

FIGURE 3-5
About Me
information:
System |
Preferences |
Personal |
About Me

FIGURE 3-5
About Me
information:
System |
Preferences |
Personal |
About Me

About Richard Petersen   ✕

User name: richard

Richard Petersen   Change Password...

Contact Address Personal Info

Email

Work: [   ]

Home: [   ]

Telephone

Work: [   ]   Work fax: [   ]

Home: [   ]   Mobile: [   ]

Instant Messaging

Jabber: [   ]   Yahoo: [   ]

MSN: [   ]   AIM/iChat: [   ]

ICQ: [   ]   Groupwise: [   ]

✕ Close

On Fedora, to index files so that they can be searched, Beagle uses extended attributes
for file systems, an option specified automatically for **ext3** file systems by HAL (the user_
xatter option). Beagle runs as the daemon **beagled**, which you can start or stop using
system-config-services or the `beagled` services script. Keep in mind that Beagle does not
run on the root user account, only on ordinary user accounts.

By default Beagle performs indexing automatically in the background. Your home
directory is indexed by default. Use the Indexing panel in the Search Preferences window
to add other directories, as well as specify which directories to exclude (see Figure 3-6).

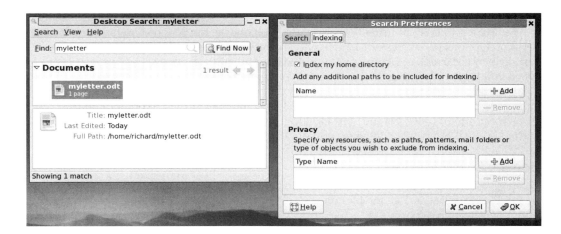

FIGURE 3-6   Beagle search

The **beagle-info** tool with the **--status** and **--index-info** options provides information about Beagle's current indexing state. Beagle also allows you to do static indexing of directories that do not change often, instead of constantly performing live background indexing.

For specific kinds of application data like MS Word files, Evolution address books, or Adobe PDF files, you can install supporting tools to let Beagle extract indexing information from them. See **beagle-project.org/Optional_prerequisites** for a detailed listing. The evolution-sharp tool will let Beagle index e-mail addresses, wv1 allows Word files to be indexed, and pdfinfo indexes PDF files, both metadata and text. A Firefox extension will index viewed Web sites. To index metadata from video files, you will have to have MPlayer installed.

Accessing File Systems, Devices, and Remote Hosts

Removable media such as CD and DVD discs, USB storage disks, digital cameras, and floppy disks will be displayed as icons on your desktop. These icons will not appear until you place the disks into their devices. To open a disk, double-click it to display a file manager window and the files on it.

The desktop will also display a Computer folder. Opening this folder will also list your removable devices, along with icons for your file system and network connections (see Figure 3-7). The file system icon can be used to access the entire file system on your computer, starting from the root directory. Regular users will have only read access to many of these directories, whereas the root user will have full read and write access.

Opening Network will list any hosts on your system with shared directories, like Windows systems accessible with Samba (see Chapter 39). GNOME uses DNS-based service discovery to automatically detect these hosts. Opening a host's icons will list the shared directories available on that system. When opening a shared directory, you will be asked for a user and password, like the user and password for a directory owned by a Windows user. The first time you access a shared directory, you will also be asked to save this user and

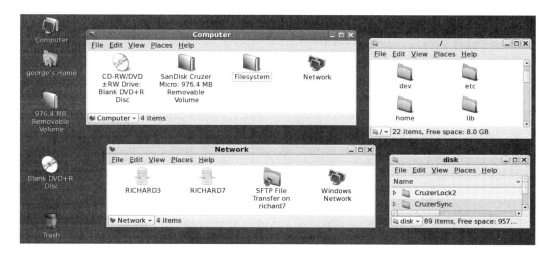

FIGURE 3-7   Removable devices, Computer folder, and shared network folders (Echo icons)

password in a keyring, which itself can be password protected. This allows repeated access without have to always enter the password.

Using Removable Devices and Media

Fedora now supports removable devices and media like digital cameras, PDAs, card readers, and even USB printers. These devices are handled automatically with an appropriate device interface set up on the fly when needed. Such hotplugged devices are identified, and where appropriate, their icons will appear in the file manager window. For example, when you connect a USB drive to your system, it will be detected and displayed as storage device with its own file system. If you copied any files to the disk, be sure to unmount it first before removing it (right-click and select Unmount Volume).

Digital cameras are also automatically detected. Photo applications like gThumb will be able to access the photos on your digital camera.

TIP *Fedora cannot play MP3, DVD, or DivX files as installed. You need to download and install supporting tools and libraries from either **rpm.livna.org/fedora** or **freshrmps.net**.*

DVD and CD discs are also treated like removable devices, with an icon for a disc automatically displayed when your put one in your CD/DVD drive. You can then double-click the CD/DVD disc icon to open a file manager window for it, displaying its contents. For media discs, such as music CDs, your system is configured to play the appropriate application. Music CDs will start up the CD player, which will let you play the music. For DVDs, however, you will need to download and install supporting video codecs, libraries, and applications from **freshrpms.net** or **rpm.livna.org**, both of which are Fedora Yum–supported repositories. Once you have configured Yum to use them, you can use Pirut to download to install them. DivX support must also be downloaded and installed separately (**labs.divx.com/DivXLinuxCodec**).

To set the preferences for how removable media are treated, you use the Removable Drives and Media Preferences tool, accessible with the Removable Drives and Media entry in the System | Preferences | Hardware menu. This displays the Removable Drives and Media Preferences window with six panels: for storage devices, multimedia devices, cameras, PDAs, Printers and Scanners, and Input devices. Certain settings are already set. Removable and hotplugged media will be automatically mounted. This includes floppy disks and data CD/DVDs. Blank CDs can be configured to be opened for burning by Nautilus.

On the multimedia panel, there are settings for audio CDs, video DVDs, and portable music players (see Figure 3-8). Audio CDs and video CDs will be played by the Totem player. There is currently no default for music players. Digital cameras will use gThumb to import photos. You can change any of the default applications used for these actions, as well as turn off default operations, such as automatically mounting or playing Audio CDs. Keep in mind that Totem will not play commercial DVDs. You would have to install a DVD-enabled player for commercial discs such as PowerDVD or the MPlayer, Xine, or Totem-zine players available on **freshrpms.net**. Once you have installed your DVD player, you can then use the Drives and Removable Media tool to have the DVD movie automatically start up in your selected player.

TIP *Fedora now treats all devices as if they were hotplugged, automatically generating device interfaces even for fixed devices like hard disks.*

PART I

Figure 3-8
Multimedia
preferences

Burning DVD/CDs with GNOME

With GNOME, burning data to a DVD or CD is a simple matter of dragging files to an open blank CD or DVD and clicking the Write To Disk button. When you insert a blank DVD/ CD, a window will open labeled CD/DVD Creator. To burn files, just drag them to that window. All Read/Write disks, even if they are not blank, are also recognized as writable disks and opened up in a DVD/CD Creator window. Click Write To Disk when ready to burn a DVD/CD. A dialog will open as shown in Figure 3-9. You can specify write speed, the DVD/CD writer to use (if you have more than one), and the disk label.

When you click Write, a dialog opens showing the write progress. Once finished, you can then eject the disk, and then make another copy if you wish.

GNOME also support burning ISO images. Just double-click the ISO image file or right-click the file and select Open With CD/DVD Creator. This opens the CD/DVD Creator dialog, which prompts you to burn the image. Be sure to first insert a blank CD or DVD into your CD/DVD burner.

Installing Multimedia Support: MP3, DVD, and DivX

Due to licensing and other restrictions, the Fedora distribution does not include MP3, DVD, or DivX media support. You cannot play MP3 files, DVD disks, or DivX files after installing Fedora. You will not find these on the Fedora repository. However, an independent operation at **freshrpms.net** does provide the needed libraries and support files for these media formats. All packages are RPM packages that you can install with Yum, after first downloading and installing their Yum repository configuration files. DivX support can be obtained from **labs.divx.com/DivXLinuxCodec**. Check **fedoraproject.org/wiki/Multimedia** for more information.

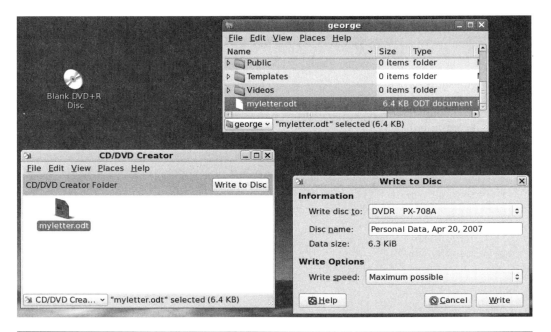

FIGURE 3-9   Writing to a DVD/CD

NOTE   *There are many forbidden items that cannot be included with Fedora due to licensing restrictions, including MP3 support, Adobe reader, and Nvidia vendor provided drivers. Check* **fedoraproject.org/wiki/ForbiddenItems** *for details.*

Command Line Interface

When using the command line interface, you are given a simple prompt at which you type in your command. Even with a GUI, you sometimes need to execute commands on a command line. The terminal window is no longer available on the GNOME desktop menu. You now have to access it from the Applications | System Tools menu. If you use terminal windows frequently, you may want to just drag the menu entry to the desktop to create a desktop icon for the terminal window. Just click to open.

Linux commands make extensive use of options and arguments. Be careful to place your arguments and options in their correct order on the command line. The format for a Linux command is the command name followed by options, and then by arguments, as shown here:

```
$ command-name options arguments
```

An *option* is a one-letter code preceded by one or two hyphens, which modifies the type of action the command takes. Options and arguments may or may not be optional, depending on the command. For example, the **ls** command can take an option, **-s**. The **ls** command displays a listing of files in your directory, and the **-s** option adds the size of each file in blocks. You enter the command and its option on the command line as follows:

```
$ ls -s
```

An *argument* is data the command may need to execute its task. In many cases, this is a filename. An argument is entered as a word on the command line after any options. For example, to display the contents of a file, you can use the **more** command with the file's name as its argument. The **less** or **more** command used with the filename **mydata** would be entered on the command line as follows:

```
$ less mydata
```

The command line is actually a buffer of text you can edit. Before you press ENTER, you can perform editing commands on the existing text. The editing capabilities provide a way to correct mistakes you may make when typing in a command and its options. The BACKSPACE and DEL keys let you erase the character you just typed in. With this character-erasing capability, you can BACKSPACE over the entire line if you want, erasing what you entered. CTRL-U erases the whole line and enables you to start over again at the prompt.

TIP *You can use the up arrow key to redisplay your last-executed command. You can then reexecute that command, or you can edit it and execute the modified command. This is helpful when you have to repeat certain operations over and over, such as editing the same file. This is also helpful when you've already executed a command you entered incorrectly.*

Help Resources

A great deal of support documentation is already installed on your system, as well as accessible from online sources. Table 3-2 lists Help tools and resources accessible on your Fedora Linux system. Both the GNOME and KDE desktops feature Help systems that use a browser-like interface to display help files. To start the GNOME or KDE Help browser, select the Help entry in the main menu. You can then choose from the respective desktop user guides, including the KDE manual, Linux Man pages, and GNU info pages. The GNOME Help Browser also accesses documents for GNOME applications such as the File Roller archive tool and Evolution mail client. The GNOME Help browser and the KDE Help Center also incorporate browser capabilities, including bookmarks and history lists for documents you view.

Context-Sensitive Help

Both GNOME and KDE, along with applications, provide context-sensitive help. Each KDE and GNOME application features detailed manuals that are displayed using their respective Help browsers. Also, system administrative tools feature detailed explanations for each task.

Application Documentation

On your system, the **/usr/share/doc** directory contains documentation files installed by each application. Within each directory, you can usually find HOW-TO, README, and INSTALL documents for that application.

Resource	Description
KDE Help Center	KDE Help tool; GUI interface for documentation on KDE desktop and applications, Man pages, and info documents.
GNOME Help Browser	GNOME Help tool; GUI interface for accessing documentation for the GNOME desktop and applications, Man pages, and info documents.
/usr/share/doc	Location of application documentation.
man *command*	Linux Man pages; detailed information on Linux commands, including syntax and options.
info *application*	GNU info pages, documentation on GNU applications.
www.redhat.com	Red Hat Enterprise documentation, guides, HOWTOs, and FAQs; located under "Support and Documentation;" much of the Red Hat Linux documentation may be helpful.
doc.fedoraproject.org	Online Fedora documentation, install and desktop guides.
fedoraforum.org	End-user discussion support forum, endorsed by the Fedora Project; includes FAQs and news links.
www.fedorafaq.org	Unofficial FAQ with quick help topics.
fedorasolved.org	Solutions to common problems.
fedoranews.org	Collects the latest news and developments on Fedora, as well as articles and blogs about recent changes.
fedoraproject.org	Fedora Project site, with numerous Documentation, FAQ, and Help resources along with links to forums, newsgroups, and community Web sites.
fcp.homelinux.org	Fedora community portal; Fedora forums, FAQs, questions, and news.

Table **3-2**   Help Tools

The Man Pages

You can also access the Man pages, which are manuals for Linux commands available from the command line interface, using the **man** command. Enter **man** with the command on which you want information. The following example asks for information on the **ls** command:

```
$ man ls
```

Pressing the SPACEBAR key advances you to the next page. Pressing the B key moves you back a page. When you finish, press the Q key to quit the Man utility and return to the command line. You activate a search by pressing either the slash (/) or question mark (?). The / searches forward; the ? searches backward. When you press the /, a line opens at the bottom of your screen, and you then enter a word to search for. Press ENTER to activate the search. You can repeat the same search by pressing the N key. You needn't reenter the pattern.

TIP You can also use either the GNOME or KDE Help system to display Man and info pages.

The Info Pages

Online documentation for GNU applications, such as the gcc compiler and the Emacs editor, also exist as *info* pages accessible from the GNOME and KDE Help Centers. You can also access this documentation by entering the command **info.** This brings up a special screen listing different GNU applications. The info interface has its own set of commands. You can learn more about it by entering **info info**. Typing **m** opens a line at the bottom of the screen where you can enter the first few letters of the application. Pressing ENTER brings up the info file on that application.

Web Resources

You can obtain documentation for Fedora at the Fedora and Red Hat Web sites. Some of the Red Hat documentation is still applicable to Fedora. Most Linux applications are covered by the Linux Documentation Project. The GNOME and KDE Web sites also contain extensive documentation showing you how to use the desktop and taking you through a detailed explanation of Linux applications. Several dedicated Fedora support sites are also available.

- **fedoraforum.org**   Provides specific end-user support you can check the support forums on.
- **www.fedorafaq.org**   Lists quick answers to some common issues such as enabling MP3 support.
- **fedoranews.org**   Provides the latest news and collection of recent articles as well as blog resources you can check.
- **fcp.homelinux.org**   This is the Fedora Community Portal, a Fedora online support community.
- **fedorasolved.org**   Provides solutions to common problems.

Using Fedora Software Repositories

Fedora software has grown so large and undergoes such frequent updates that it no longer makes sense to use disks as the primary means of distribution. Instead distribution is effected using an online Fedora software repository. This repository contains an extensive collection of Fedora-compliant software, merging the Fedora Core and Fedora Extras used in previous releases into one large repository.

For Fedora, you can add software to your system by accessing any software repositories supporting Yum (Yellowdog Updater, Modified). Many software applications, particularly multimedia ones, have potential licensing conflicts. Such software can be found in third-party repositories, allowing Fedora to avoid possible legal issues. Many of the popular multimedia applications, such as video and digital music support, can be obtained from third-party repositories using the same simple Yum commands you would use for Fedora-sponsored software. One of the more frustrating features of a Fedora installation is its lack of popular multimedia and driver support. With a few simple steps you can easily add such software to your system, using Yum.

This entire approach heralds a move from thinking of most Linux software as something included on a few disks, to viewing the disk as just a core from which you can expand your installed software as you like from online repositories. Most software is now located on the

Internet-connected repositories. With the integration of Yum into your Fedora system, you can now think of that software as an easily installed extension of your current collection. Relying on disk media for your software becomes, in a sense, obsolete. You can find out more about how Yum is used on Fedora by reading Managing Software with Yum, located on the Fedora documentation page: **doc.fedoraproject.org/yum/en/.**

Using Repositories to Complete Your Installation

A few repositories provide much of the software you will normally need. The main Fedora software repository will most likely contain the software you want. Always check this repository first, before trying a third-party repository. Some specialized applications like vendor-supplied graphics drivers can be located at **rpm.livna.org/fedora.** A more complete collection of multimedia support packages can be located at **freshprms.net.** Java applications are located at **jpackage.org**, though some are already in the Fedora repository. Together these repositories make up a set of software sites you can use to provide most of the functionality users expect from a desktop system. All are Yum compliant, with Yum configuration files for Fedora. You can use Yum to install and update software from these repositories. Each will have its own Yum configuration file. The sites and their repository files are shown here.

download.fedora.redhat .com/pub/fedora/linux/	The Fedora repository: Fedora-compliant software. **fedora.repo**
freshrpms.net	Freshrpms: customized RPM packages featuring multimedia apps. **fresrpms.repo**
rpm.livna.org/fedora	Livna: repository for driver, multimedia, and other RPM packages, **lvn. livna.repo**
jpackage.org	Java applications. **jpackage.repo**

To see what packages are available, you can use your Web browser to access the sites. Fedora provides **repodata** directories for detailed listings. Livna provides simple directory file listings, whereas Freshrpms uses a detailed Web interface. Livna packages are further identified with the term **lvn** in their name.

All these sites support Yum, allowing you to use a simple **yum** command to both download and install a package, as well as any supporting libraries. This makes installation a very simple procedure.

To use Yum on a software repository, Yum has to be configured to access them. This is a simple matter of listing the site's URL, both its Web address and directory location. Configurations for repositories are placed in **repo** files located in the **/etc/yum.repos.d** directory on your Linux system. You will have to add configurations for Livna and Freshrpms before you can access them with Yum. However, both Livna and Freshrpms provide RPM packages on their Web sites, that, when installed, automatically set up the needed Yum configuration files. For Livna this is the **livna-release** package, and for Freshrpms it is **freshrpms-release**.

To install packages, use Pirut, yumex, or the **yum** command. All will automatically use the repo files to check your enabled repositories.

Alternatively, you can download a package directly using your browser. Your Fedora Web browsers will let you perform both a download and install in one simple operation.

On a GNOME desktop already-downloaded packages can be installed with a simple right-click and install selection, invoking Pirut to perform the installation.

Repository Incompatibilities

When an application requires several packages, it is important to be sure that the supporting packages are compatible. In the past there have been—and there may still be—incompatibilities between the Livna repository and the Freshrpms repository. Given the comprehensive multimedia support provided by Freshrpms, it may be best to use that repository on a regular basis, instead of Livna. On the other hand, the Livna repository contains key drivers missing in Freshrpms, such as the vendor-supplied ATI and NVIDIA graphics drivers.

If you are planning to use the vendor-supplied ATI or NVIDIA drivers, then the simplest approach would be to enable Livna and disable Freshrpms. New kernel drivers are provided by Livna each time you update to a new kernel version. These will be automatically downloaded and installed for you, with Livna enabled. The same would also be true should you decide to use the NTFS project's NTFS modules, which are supplied by Livna, instead of the ntfs-3g support included with Fedora.

An alternative approach would be to install both repository configurations and then enable Freshrpms, but disable Livna. This would allow you to install and update the numerous multimedia applications available on **freshrpms.net**. You could then temporarily enable Livna when installing a particular driver from their site. The **yum** option **--enablerepo** option on a command line operation will temporarily enable a repository. You have to perform this task each time you update your kernel.

```
yum install --enablerepo=livna kmod-nvidia
```

To disable a repository, you edit its repo file in **/etc/yum.repos.d**, setting the **enabled** option to 0.

```
enabled = 0
```

Pirut

All software listed in all your Yum repositories can be accessed and installed using Pirut (see Chapter 4). Pirut will use all the repo files in **/etc/yum.repos.d** to list available software. So, though you can still use a command line Yum operation to install and update software, you could just as easily use Pirut. To see the packages from all the repositories, you will need to use the List view or Search option on Pirut. The Browse view will list only Fedora packages.

In many cases, only latest versions will be available; the originals will no longer be considered viable. At the same time, several updates for the same packages may be available. And the some package releases may be designed to work together. This is often the case with multipackage services like GFS, where an update will include several packages.

Yum Extender: yumex

The Yum Extender is an alternative GUI interface for managing software packages on your Yum repositories (see Figure 3-10); yumex is included with Fedora. Open Add/Remove Software and on the Browse panel select Base System, then Administration Tools, and then

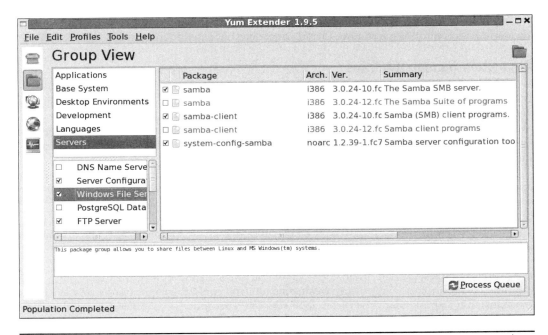

FIGURE 3-10 Yum Extender group view

click the Optional Packages to see yumex listed. Check to install. You can also just search for **yumex** on the Search panel or use the following command in a terminal window:

```
yum install yumex
```

You can then access yumex with the Yum Extender entry in the Applications | System Tools menu. The Yum Extender screen has five panels, each accessed by view icons on the left column, as shown in Figure 3-10. You can select a package using either the Package or the Groups button. The Package button will list all possible packages, whereas the Groups panel shows the categories. Uninstalled packages are shown in red.

The Package panel features ways to narrow your displayed packages. You can choose to display updates, installed packages, or uninstalled packages only. You can further specify categories, like repositories, displaying only packages from a certain repository. Clicking a package will display detailed information about it on the panel below, where you can select the description, files included with the package, and the change log if available.

To select a package, just check the one you want to install. Once selected, the package is added to the Process Queue panel.

Once you have added packages to the Queue, click the Queue icon to see the list of packages you want to install. From this panel you can choose to delete items or just save the list for later installation. To perform the installation, click the Process Queue button. All dependent packages will also be displayed. The install process will be shown on the Output panel.

One of the more convenient features of yumex is the Repos panel, which lists all your repository configuration files. From this panel you can enable or disable any repositories you want. For example, if you need to temporarily enable the Livna repository, you can select it on this panel, and then install software from that repository. Once finished, you could then disable the repository using the Repos panel.

NOTE   *The Fedora Extras repository was designed for those packages that either duplicated or were not considered essential to the Fedora Core collection. With Fedora 7, both Fedora Core and Fedora Extras have been merged into one Fedora repository.*

Fedora Repository

The Fedora repository is already configured for use by Yum. To download any Fedora package, simply use the Pirut program manager (Applications | Add/Remove Software), or enter the **yum** command with the install option on a command line. The package will be detected, along with any dependent software, and you will be asked to confirm installation. The download and installation will be automatic. Check the **repodata** files on a Fedora repository to list the available Fedora files. There will be one in the **os** directory for respective version, **i386, x86_64** for 64-bit, and **ppc** for PowerPC versions. You can then click a particular package to display its RPM package data, showing version information and links to download the package, as well as to the package development Web site. Though you could download the package, it is preferable to use Yum or a Yum interface like Pirut.

The **repodata** directory page features several ways to access the very extensive collection of Fedora packages. The page first lists recent additions and updates, and then provides groups for different packages. The groups are also listed at links in the left-hand pane. Should you know the beginning letter of a package, you can use the Jump to Letter index at the top right, displaying pages with packages beginning with just that letter.

To download a Fedora package, you should use either Pirut (Applications | Add/ Remove Software) or yumex (Applications | System Tools | Yum Extender) or the **yum** command. On Pirut, the List or Search views will let you access all the packages, not just those organized into a browsing category. Alternatively, you can use a **yum** command in a terminal window with the **install** option as shown here. The following command installs Gnumeric:

```
yum install gnumeric
```

The following command installs KOffice from the Fedora repository:

```
yum install koffice
```

The first time you install a package from the Fedora repository, you will be prompted to install the Fedora GPG key, used to authenticate the packages. Just click Yes to install the key.

Livna

The **rpm.livna.org** site provides popular software for many software applications, including multimedia applications like MPlayer, as well as those not included with Fedora due to licensing issues. Several of the more popular packages include the vendor ATI and NVIDIA graphics drivers. Livna specializes in configuring sometimes difficult drivers for compatibility with Fedora. For example, you can download the NVIDIA Linux driver directly from the NVIDIA Web site and try to install it on your Fedora system. But there can be complications and the driver could require additional configuration. As an alternative, Livna provides a version of the driver that has already been configured for Fedora. A safer and more reliable approach is to simply install the Livna package for the NVIDIA driver. Livna also provides ATI driver packages.

To configure Yum on your system to access **rpm.livna.org**, just install the **livna-release** package for Fedora. This will install the **livna.repo** configuration file in the **/etc/yum.repos.d** directory, as well as download the Livna GPG key. You can install the GPG manually or just wait until you first install a package from Livna, in which case Yum will install it for you, after prompting for your approval. Check the Livna configuration page at **rpm.livna.org** for details. The name of the package will be something like

```
livna-release-7.noarch.rpm
```

You can download and install the package directly with **rpm** command from within a terminal window.

```
rpm -ivh http://rpm.livna.org/livna-release-7.rpm
```

Alternatively, you can install directly from your browser by selecting Open With "Software Installer", or download it, right-click it, and select Open With "Software Installer". The package will be listed in the Livna category for the Livna Web display of the Fedora release.

You could also install it later with the **rpm** command as shown here:

```
rpm -ivh rpm.livna.org/livna-release-7.norarch.rpm
```

To manually install the GPG key, you would use the following:

```
rpm --import http://rpm.livna.org/RPM-LIVNA-GPG-KEY
```

Once the repository is installed, all packages will be accessible with Yum. You will find them listed as with the term **lvn** in the name on Pirut and yumex package listings.

To see what packages are available on Livna, use your Web browser to go to **www.livna .org/fedora**. Here you will find a listing of directories for each supported release. Selecting your release directory, you then choose your architecture, such as i386 (32 bit) or x86_64 (64 bit). Here you will see a simple file listing of all available packages.

Freshrpms

Freshrpms.net provides an extensive listing of multimedia packages, including packages for DVD video like MPlayer along with needed supporting libraries. Here you will also find MP3 support. Several of these packages are also available on Livna, but the collection on Freshrpms is a bit more extensive.

For Freshrpms just download and install the **freshrpms-release** package. There is a direct link on the **freshrpms.net** Web site. A link to this package can also be found on

ayo.freshrpms.net. Click on the Fedora link to list the **freshrpms-release** packages for Fedora. The package you want is something like

```
freshrpms-release-1.1-1.fc.noarch.rpm
```

With your Web browser you can choose to download and install at once. The install procedure will warn that there is no key for the packages, but install anyway. The key is included with the **freshrpms-release** package and will be automatically installed. Alternatively, you could download the package first, and then install it either from GNOME or using the **rpm** command. With GNOME, just right-click and select Open With "Software Installer." With the **rpm** command, download the package first, and then just use the following:

```
rpm -ivh freshrpms-release-1.1-1.fc.noarch.rpm
```

This will install the **freshrpms.repo** configuration file in the **/etc/yum.repos.d** directory, as well as download the Freshrpms GPG key. You can then install the GPG manually or just wait until you first install a package from Freshrpms, in which case Yum will install it for you, after prompting for your approval. The following will import the Freshrpms key manually:

```
rpm --import http://freshrpms.net/RPM-GPG-KEY-freshrpms
```

Installing Some Popular Packages

Once configured, installation is a simple matter of opening a terminal window and entering the command **yum** along with the **install** option followed by the name of the software package you want to install.

If you are installing a package from Fedora repository, you are set to go. You can use Pirut or the **yum** command. Be sure to use the Search or List views of Pirut to access all packages. For example, to install Abiword from a command line, you just enter

```
yum install abiword
```

Yum does the rest, first locating the package, then downloading it, and then performing the installation. It will also be careful to select the package for your architecture, like x86_64 for 64 bit or i686 for 32 bit. Yum will first ask for confirmation before installing, listing any dependent packages that will also have to be installed. You can also use Yum to remove and update packages. Check the **yum** Man page for options. Some detailed examples are shown here for some of the more popular packages such as MPlayer and Xine, as well as GStreamer and MP3 support.

Before installing multimedia packages, you will first need to install the Yum configuration file for a repository that carries them. You could use **freshrpms.net**, which carries a collection of multimedia packages, including GStreamer and MPlayer. If you have installed the Yum configuration file for Livna, be sure to disable the repository if you have not already done so.

GStreamer Support: Multimedia Plug-ins

Many GNOME multimedia applications such as Totem use GStreamer to provide multimedia support. To use such features as DVD video and MP3, you have to install additional GStreamer plug-ins. You can find out more information about GStreamer and its supporting packages at **gstreamer.freedesktop.org**.

You can obtain additional GStreamer plug-in and supporting packages from either Livna or Freshrpms.

The current version of GStreamer is 1.0. The supporting packages can be confusing. For version 1.0, GStreamer establishes four different support packages called the base, the good, the bad, and the ugly. The base package is a set of useful plug-ins that are reliable. The good package is a set of supported and tested plug-ins that meet all licensing requirements. Both the base and good packages are part of the Fedora repository and are installed by default.

The bad is a set of unsupported plug-ins whose performance is not guaranteed and may crash, but still meets licensing requirements. The ugly package contains plug-ins that work fine but may not meet licensing requirements, such as for DVD support. These you will find on Freshrpms or GStreamer repositories.

- **The base**   Reliable, commonly used plug-ins (Fedora repository)
- **The good**   Additional reliable and useful plug-ins (Fedora repository)
- **The ugly**   Reliable but not fully licensed plug-ins (DVD/MP3 support)
- **The bad**   Possibly unreliable but useful plug-ins (possible crashes)

To download and install the GStreamer plug-in packages, just search for **gstreamer** on Add/Remove Software (Pirut). If you have enabled either Livna or Freshrpms repositories, you will also see entries for the ugly and bad packages. Alternatively, you could use the following Yum command to install all plug-ins at once. Be sure to include the asterisk to match on all the plug-in packages. Your architecture (i586, i686, or x86_64) will automatically be detected.

```
yum install gstreamer-plugins*
```

Other plug-ins for GStreamer 1.0 that you may want to include are **ffmpeg** and **pitfdll**, **gstreamer-ffmpeg**, and **gstreamer-pitfdll**. **ffmpeg** provides several popular codecs, including Ogg and .264. The **pitdfdll** package provides support for media files in proprietary formats like Microsoft's WM9.

MPlayer

MPlayer is a very popular multimedia player. You can find out more about MPlayer at **www.mplayerhq.hu**. If this is your first multimedia package, numerous supporting packages will be selected. Assuming the configuration for a repository that carries MPlayer has been installed, you can then use Pirut or the **yum** command to select, download, and install MPlayer. For more details, check the MPlayer documentation.

If all goes well, MPlayer will be installed with an entry in your Applications | Sound And Video menu.

To install MPlayer from the command line, just enter

```
yum install mplayer
```

Yum will then retrieve the needed packages, including a long list of dependent packages.

Once the packages are selected, you are prompted to install. Enter **y**. The packages are then downloaded and installed on your system. If this is the first time you have downloaded from Freshrpms or from Fedora, you will also be prompted to install their GPG keys (separate prompt for each key). Enter **y** to install the keys.

Xine

Perhaps the easiest player to use for music, video, and DVD playback, Xine has a very easy-to-use interface. Both Xine and MPlayer use many of the same supporting packages, so you may see a much shorter list of dependencies for the one installed later. There is also a Totem version with a Xine plug-in that will allow Totem to support DVD video. You would first have to uninstall the original version of Totem already installed.

```
yum install xine
```

DVD Support

DVD support requires an additional set of packages. Again make sure you have installed the Yum configuration for a repository that carries it, like **freshrpms.net**. From Pirut use the Search view and enter **dvd**. To access Video-DVDs, multimedia players will need support libraries like **libdvdnav** and **libdvdplay.**

Additional Support: FFmpeg and DivX

For additional multimedia codecs you may want to download FFmpeg. It can be installed easily with Yum using a Pirut Search or the following command line entry, provided access to the **livna** or **freshrpms** repository has been configured:

```
yum install ffmpeg
```

DivX 6 is not available on any of the repositories, though XviD (xvidcore) is. For DivX 6, you will have to go to **labs.divx.com/DivXLinuxCodec** and download and install the Linux version manually. It does not require any supporting packages.

VideoLAN is another popular player requiring a list of supporting packages. You can install the VideoLAN client with Yum from Freshrpms. You can search for it on Pirut or use the following command line entry:

```
yum install videolan-client
```

MP3 with Lame

LAME originally stood for Lame Ain't an Mp3 Encoder, but the product has long since become a full-featured MP3 encoder whose software is available under the LPGL license. It is included with VideoLAN and FFmpeg, and Yum will download in support of MPlayer or Xine. You can download it separately with:

```
yum install lame
```

Java Applications: jpackage.org

To download Java applications, it is easiest to just download and install Fedora-compliant versions from **jpackage.org**. Simply use their Yum repository for Java packages. Keep in mind that **jpackage.org** does not provide the JRE. This you will have to download and install from Sun. Also, development packages on **jpackage.org** are commercial.

First download and install the **jpackage.repo**. Place **jpackage.repo** in the **/etc/yum.repos.d** directory. Check first to see if the repository has been set up for your particular version of Fedora. If not, you will have to use the generic version. Use the **enabled** option to activate or deactivate a version. Generic will be set by default.

The packages will show up in Pirut (List or Search views). They will have the identifier jpp.

Windows Access and Applications

In many cases, certain accommodations need to be made for Windows systems. Most Linux systems are part of networks that also run Windows systems. Using Linux Samba servers, your Linux and Windows systems can share directories and printers. In addition you may also need to run a Windows applications directly on your Linux system. Though there is an enormous amount of Linux software available, in some cases you many need or prefer to run a Windows application. The Wine compatibility layer allows you to do just that, for many Windows applications (not all).

Setting Up Windows Network Access: Samba

Most local and home networks may include some systems working on Microsoft Windows and others on Linux. You may need to let a Windows computer access a Linux system or vice versa. Windows, due to its massive market presence, tends to benefit from both drivers and applications support not found for Linux. Though there are equivalent applications on Linux, many of which are as good or better, some applications run best on Windows, if for no other reason than that the vendor only develops drivers for Windows.

One solution is to use the superior server and storage capabilities of Linux to manage and hold data, while using Windows systems with their unique applications and drivers to run applications. For example, you could use a Linux system to hold pictures and videos, while using Windows systems to show or run them. Video or pictures could be streamed through your router to the system that wants to run them. In fact many commercial DVR systems use a version of Linux to manage video recording and storage. Another use would be to enable Windows systems to use devices like printers that may be connected to a Linux system, or vice versa.

To allow Windows to access a Linux system, as well as Linux to access a Windows system, you use the Samba server (see Chapter 39 for more details). First be sure that Samba is installed along with the Services tool. Open the Add/Remove Software tool in the Applications menu. Click the Browse panel, and scroll down and select the Servers entry in the left box. Then check the Windows File Server entry in the right box. It will be the last entry. If the item is not checked, check it. Also make sure Server Configuration Tools is also checked. If they were not installed, click Apply to install them.

Samba has two methods of authentication, shares and users. User authentication requires that there be corresponding accounts in the the Windows and Linux systems. They can have the same name, though a Windows user can be mapped to a Linux account. A share can be made open to any user and function as an extension of the user's storage space (see Chapter 39 for more details).

To have Samba start up automatically, select the system-config-services configuration tool by choosing System | Administration | Server Settings | Services. Then on the Background Services panel click the check boxed for both the **smb** and **nmb** entries. Click Save to save the startup specification and click Restart to start the Samba server.

To set up simple file sharing on a Linux system, you first need to configure your Samba server. You can do this by directly editing the **/etc/samba/samba.conf** file or by using the system-config-samba configuration tool (System | Administration | Server Settings | Samba). If you just edit the **/etc/samba/samba.conf** file, you first need to specify the name of your Windows network (see Chapter 39).

Open the system-config-samba tool by selecting System | Administration | Server Settings | Samba. Then under the Preferences menu, select Server Settings. On the Basic panel you enter the name of your Windows network workgroup. The default names given by Windows are MSHOME or WORKGROUP. Use the name already given to your Windows network. For home networks, you can decide on your own. Just make sure all your computers use the same network name. Check your Windows Control Panel's System applet to make sure.

To set up a simple share, click Add Share, which opens a Create A Share window. On the Basic panel you select the Linux directory to share (click Browse to find it), and then specify whether it will be writable and visible. On the Access panel you can choose to open it to everyone, or just to specific users.

On the Security panel you can select the kind of authentication you want to use. By default, User security is used. You could also use share or server security; these are more open, but both have been deprecated and may be dropped in later versions. For user authentication you will have to associate a Windows user with a particular Linux account. Select Samba Users in the Preferences window. Then select a Linux user to use, then enter the corresponding Windows user, and then a password that user can use to access Linux. This is the Samba password for that user. Samba maintains its own set of passwords that a user will need to access a Samba share. When a Windows user wants to access a Samba share, they will need their Samba password.

To restart Samba with your new configuration use the Services tool, restarting both **nmb** and **smb** (System | Administration | Server Settings | Services). Be sure that the firewall on your Windows system is not blocking Samba.

When a Windows user wants to access the share on the Linux system, they open their My Network Places and then "Add a network place" to add a network place entry for the share, or View workgroup computers to see computers on your Windows network. Selecting the Linux Samba server will display your Samba shares. To access the share, the user will be required to enter in the user name and the Samba password. You have the option of having the username and password remembered for automatic access.

NOTE *The fuse-smb tool lets you browse your entire Windows network at once.*

Running Windows Software on Linux: Wine

Wine is a Windows compatibility layer that will allow you to run many Windows applications natively on Linux. Though you could run the Windows OS on it, the actual Windows operating system is not required. Windows applications will run as if they were Linux applications, able to access the entire Linux file system and use Linux-connected devices. Applications that are heavily driver dependent, like graphic intensive games, most likely will not run. Others, like new readers, that do not rely on any specialized drivers, may run very well. For some applications, you may also need to copy over specific Windows DLLs from a working Windows system to your Wine Windows system32 or system directory.

Wine is helpful for running certain useful applications that have been written only for Windows. Installation may require you to install certain DLL files from a working Windows operating system to your Wine emulator system32 directory.

To install Wine on your system, search for **wine** on Add/Remove Applications (Pirut). You will see several packages listed. You will need to select only the Wine package. Others will be selected by Yum as dependent packages, including wine-twain and wine-tools. Some are already included with the Wine package but are presented as separate packages, such as wine-arts, in case you do not want to install everything.

TIP   *To play Windows games on Linux, you can try using cedega. These are inexpensive commercial drivers that are configured to support many popular games, **www.cedega.com**, enabling full graphics accelleration.*

Once installed, a Wine menu will appear in the Applications menu. The Wine menu holds entries for Wine configuration, the Wine software uninstaller, and Wine file browser, as well as a regedit registry editor, a notepad, and a Wine help tool.

To set up Wine, a user starts the Wine Configuration tool. This opens a window with panels for Applications, Libraries (DLL selection), Audio (sound drivers), Drives, Desktop Integration, and Graphics. On the Applications window you can select which version of Windows an application is designed for. The Drives panel will list your detected partitions, as well as your Windows-emulated drives, such as drive C. The C: drive is really just a directory, **.wine/drive_c**, not a partition of a fixed size. Your actual Linux file system will be listed as the Z drive.

Once configured, Wine will set up a **.wine** directory on the user's home directory (the directory is hidden, so enable Show Hidden Files in the file browser View menu to display it). Within that directory will be the **drive_c** directory, which functions as the C: drive holding your Windows system files and program files in the Windows and Program File subdirectories. The System and System32 directories are located in the Windows directory. Here is where you would place any needed DLL files. The Program Files directory will hold your installed Windows programs, just as they would be installed on a Windows Program Files directory.

To install a Windows application with Wine, you can either use the Wine configuration tool or just open a terminal window and run the **wine** command with the Windows application as an argument. The following example installs the popular newsbin program:

```
$ wine newsbin.exe
```

To install with the Windows Configuration tool, select the Applications panel and then click Add.

Some applications like newsbin will also require that you use certain DLL files from a working Windows operating system. The DLL files are normally copied to the user's **.wine/drive_c/Windows/system32** directory.

Icons for installed Windows software will appear on your desktop. Just double-click an icon to start up the application. It will run normally within a Linux window as would any Linux application.

Installing Windows fonts on Wine is a simple matter of copying fonts from a Windows font directory to your Wine **.wine/drive_c/Windows/fonts** directory. You can just copy any Windows **.ttf** file to this directory to install a font.

Wine will use a stripped down window style for features like buttons and titlebar. If you want to use the XP style, download and install the Royal theme from Microsoft. Keep in mind though that supporting this theme is very resource intensive and will likely slow down your system.

TIP *Alternatively, you can use the commercial Windows compatibility layer called CrossoverOffice. This is a commercial product tested to run certain applications like Microsoft Office. Check* **www.codeweavers.com** *for more details. CrossoverOffice is based on Wine, which CodeWeavers supports directly.*

System Configuration

This chapter reviews the key system configuration task and tools you may normally use. Most are familiar from earlier releases. A complete overview helps to establish a better context for those tools that are new or have been changed.

To make effective use of your Linux system, you must know how to configure certain features and services. Administrative operations such as adding users and installing software can now be performed with user-friendly system tools. This chapter discusses basic system administration operations that you need to get your system up and running, as well as to perform basic maintenance such as adding new users or printers.

TIP *If you have difficulties with your system configuration, check the **fedorasolved.org** site for possible solutions. The site offers helpful solutions ranging from video and network problems to games, browsers, and multimedia solutions.*

There are four basic system configuration tasks that you most likely will have to deal with: user management, printer setup, display configuration, and software management. You can manage users, adding new ones, removing others, and updating user properties. Different kinds of printers, remote and local, can be set up for your system. For your video card and monitor, you can select the resolutions and color depths you want. You can also install new software packages and update or remove current ones. You were asked to perform all of these tasks during installation. In addition, there are other tools you can use to configure devices such as your keyboard, sound card, and mouse, as well as perform tasks such as setting the system date and time or selecting a language to use. You can make changes or additions easily using the administrative tools described in this chapter.

Configuration operations can be performed from a GUI interface such as GNOME or KDE, or they can be performed using a simple shell command line at which you type configuration commands. You can manually access system configuration files, editing them and making entries yourself. For example, the domain name server entries are kept in the **/etc/resolv.conf** file. You can edit this file and type in the addresses for the servers.

NOTE *Configuration tools are accessible only to the root user. You will first need to log in using **root** as your username and providing the root password you specified during installation.*

Fedora Administrative Tools

On Fedora, administration is handled by a set of separate specialized administrative tools developed and supported by Fedora, such as those for user management and display configuration (see Table 4-1). To access the GUI-based Fedora tools, you log in as the root user to the GNOME desktop and select the main menu. System administrative tools are listed on the System Administration menu included in the main menu. Here you will find tools to set the time and date, manage users, configure printers, and update software. Users & Groups lets you create and modify users and groups. Printing lets you install and reconfigure printers. All tools provide very intuitive GUI interfaces that are easy to use. In the System Administration menu, tools are identified by simple descriptive terms, whereas their actual names normally begin with the term system-config. For example, the printer configuration tool is listed as Printing, but its actual name is system-config-printer. You can separately invoke any tool by entering its name in a terminal window.

NOTE *Many configuration tasks can also be handled on a command line, invoking programs directly. To use the command line, open a terminal window by selecting the Terminal entry in the Applications | System Tools menu. This opens a terminal window with a command line prompt. Commands like **rpm** and **make** discussed later will require a terminal window.*

Editing Configuration Files Directly

Though the administrative tools will handle all configuration settings for you, there may be times when you will need to make changes by directly editing configuration files. These are usually text files in the **/etc** directory or dot files in a user home directory, like **.bash_profile**. To change any of these files, you will need administrative access, requiring you to first log in as the **root** user.

You can use any standard editor such as Vi or Emacs to edit these files, though one of the easiest ways to edit them is to use the Gedit editor on the GNOME desktop. Select Text Editor from the Accessories menu. This opens a Gedit window. Click Open to open a file browser where you can move through the file system to locate the file you want to edit.

CAUTION *Be careful when editing your configuration files. Editing mistakes can corrupt your configurations. It is advisable to make a backup of any configuration files you are working on first, before making major changes to the original.*

Gedit will let you edit several files at once, opening a tabbed pane for each. You can use Gedit to edit any text file, including ones you create yourself. In Figure 4-1 three configuration files are opened: **.bash_profile**, **/boot/grub/grub.conf**, and **/etc/fstab**. The **.bash_profile** file configures your login shell, **/etc/fstab** lists all your file systems and how they are mounted, and **/boot/grub/grub.conf** is the configuration file for your Grub boot loader.

Dot files like **.bash_profile** have to be chosen from the file manager window. First configure the file manager to display dot files by opening the Preferences dialog (select Preferences in the Edit menu of any file manager window) and then check the Show Hidden Files entry and close the dialog. Then choose Restore Default Settings in the View menu. This displays the dot files in your file manager window. Double-click to open one in Gedit.

Fedora Administration Tools	Description
Pirut Package Manager	Yum Software management using online repositories
Package Update Program (PUP)	Update tool using Yum repositories (replaces RHN)
System I Administration	Fedora menu for accessing administrative tools
System I Preferences	Fedora menu for GNOME desktop configuration
Applications I System Tools	Fedora menu for accessing specialized administrative applications
system-config-authentication	Sets authentication settings
system-config-boot	Sets operating system to boot default
system-config-date	Changes system time and date
system-config-display	Fedora display configuration tool (video card and monitor)
system-config-httpd	Configures Apache Web server
system-config-keyboard	Changes the keyboard configuration
system-config-kickstart	Configures Automatic install scripts
system-config-language	Selects a language to use
system-config-lvm	Configures LVM file system volumes
system-config-nfs	Configures your network interfaces
system-config-network	Configures your network interfaces
system-config-network-tui	Configures your network interfaces using the command line; it is cursor based, with no GUI
system-config-language	Selects a language to use
system-config-cluster	Global File System (GFS) management
system-config-printer	Printer configuration tool
system-config-rootpassword	Changes the root user password
system-config-samba	Configures your Samba server
system-config-securitylevel	Configures your network firewall
system-config-securitylevel-tui	Configures your network firewall on a command line interface
system-config-selinux	Manages and configures SELinux policy
system-config-services	Manages system and network services, such as starting and stopping servers
system-config-soundcard	Configures your sound card (see "Simple Administrative Tasks" later in this chapter)
system-config-switch-mail	Selects mail transport agent (server)
system-config-users	User and Group configuration tool

TABLE 4-1   Fedora Administrative Tools

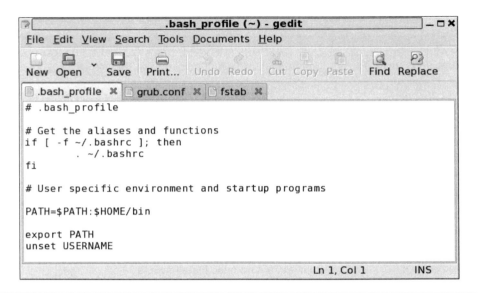

FIGURE 4-1 Gedit text editor and configuration files

Simple Administrative Tasks

Certain simple administrative tasks can be performed using some of the system-config tools. Most of these have obvious entries in the Administration menu. Others like Login Screen use their own configuration tools.

- **system-config-rootpassword (Root Password)** Use this tool to change your root password, something you may want to do regularly.

- **system-config-date (Date & Time)** Use this to set the date and time, as well as select a time server for automatic time settings.

- **system-config-boot (Bootloader)** Use this tool if you have set up a dual-boot system, with several operating systems on the same hard disks. This will list your operating systems and let you choose the default. This is useful for selecting either Window or Linux on the same computer, or, say, a stable or test kernel. If you install a new kernel, it will become the default. Use system-config-boot to set the default back to the one you want.

- **system-config-soundcard (Soundcard Detection)** This will detect and test a sound card.

Mouse configuration and display of logs are now handled by GNOME tools. Check GNOME preferences for mouse configuration, and System Logviewer (**gnome-system-log**) to display logs.

Login Screen

If you want to change the login screen, you can use the Login Screen Setup window accessible from Login Screen entry in the Administration menu. This configures the GNOME Display Manager, which runs your login process. Here you can set the background image, icons to be displayed, the theme to use, users to list, and even the welcome message. Login screens can be configured for local or remote users. You can choose between a plain screen, a plain screen with face browser, or a themed screen. The local panel lets you selects what screen to use for local logins, as well as browse among available themes. From the remote panel you can select plain, select plain with browser, or use the same configuration as your local logins.

On the users panel, you can select which users you want displayed when using a face browser. On the local panel you can choose from a number of themes. The latest Fedora theme is selected by default, like the Fedora Flying High theme with face browser, which is the default for Fedora 7. You can also opt to have the theme randomly selected.

On the security panel, you can set up an automatic login, skipping the login screen on startup. You can even set a timed login, automatically logging in a specific user after displaying the login screen for a given amount of time. In the Security segment of the panel you can set security options such as whether to allow root logins or allow TCP (Internet) access, as well as setting the number of allowable logins. Click the Configure X Server button on this panel to open a window for configuring X server access. Check the GNOME Display Manager Reference Manual, accessible with the Help button, for details.

Configuring Users

Currently, the easiest and most effective way to add new users on Fedora is to use system-config-users, also known as the Fedora User Manager. You can access it from the GNOME Desktop menu, System | Administration menu | Users And Groups entry. The system-config-users window will display panels for listing both users and groups (see Figure 4-2).

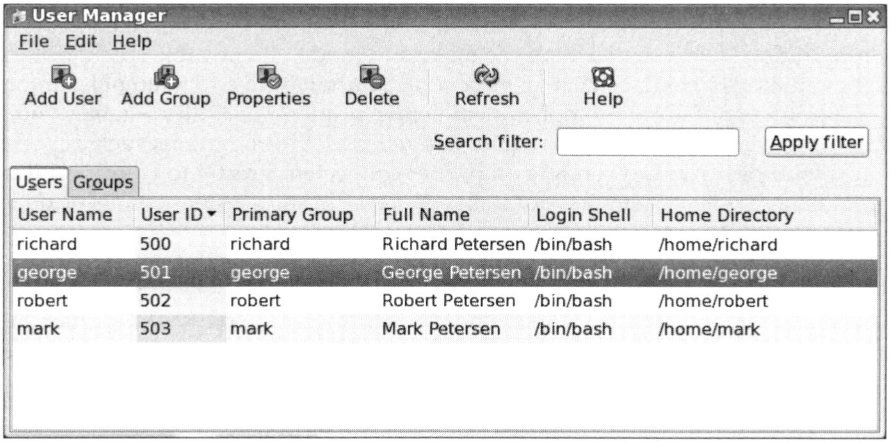

FIGURE 4-2   The Fedora User Manager, system-config-users

A button bar will list various tasks you can perform, including creating new users or groups, editing current ones (Edit), or deleting a selected user or group.

To create a new user, click Add User. This opens a window with entries for the username, password, and login shell, along with options to create a home directory and a new group for that user. Once you have created a user, you can edit its properties to add or change features. Select the user's entry and click Edit and select Properties. This displays a window with tabbed panels for User Data, Account Info, Password Info, and Groups. On the Groups panel, you can select the groups that the user belongs to, adding or removing group memberships.

Alternatively, you can use the useradd command in a terminal window or command line to add user accounts and the userdel command to remove them. The following example adds the user **dylan** to the system:

```
$ useradd dylan
```

One common operation performed from the command line is to change a password. Any user can change her own password with the passwd command. The command prompts you for your current password. After entering your current password and pressing ENTER, you are then prompted for your new password. After entering the new password, you are asked to reenter it. This is to make sure you actually entered the password you intended to enter.

```
$ passwd
Old password:
New password:
Retype new password:
$
```

TIP *You can use the system-config-rootpassword tool (Root Password on System | Administration) to change the password for the root user.*

Printer Configuration

Whenever you first attach a local printer, like a USB printer, you will be asked to perform basic configuration such as confirming the make and model. Removable local printers are managed by udev and HAL. To change your configuration or to add a remote printer, you can use the printer configuration tool, system-config-printer. This utility enables you to select the appropriate driver for your printer, as well as set print options such as paper size and print resolutions. You can configure a printer connected directly to your local computer or a printer on a remote system on your network. You can start system-config-printer by selecting the Printing entry in the System | Administration menu.

When you start up system-config-printer, you are presented with a window that displays two panes, one that lists your servers and the other for configuration panels for those printers (see Figure 4-3). To display the configuration for a particular printer, just click its entry in the Server Settings pane, where printers will be listed in an expandable tree under the servers that the printers are connected to. Printers connected directly to your computer will be listed under Local Printers. Clicking the Server Settings entry will display a pane for setting global printing options such as allowing users to cancel their own print jobs or sharing your printers on your network.

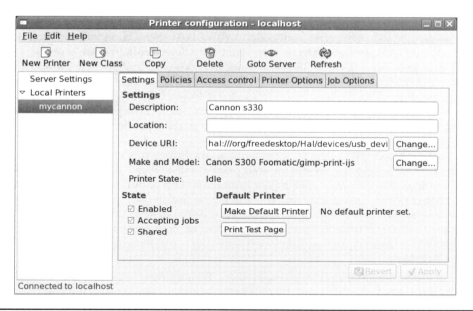

FIGURE 4-3   The system-config-printer tool

To add a new printer, click New Printer. To edit an installed printer, click its entry in the Server Settings pane to display its configuration panels. There are panels for Settings, Policies, Access Control, Printer Options, and Job Control. Once you have made your changes, you can click Apply to save your changes and restart the printer daemon. If you have more than one printer on your system, you can make one the default by clicking Make Default Printer button in its Settings panel. The Delete button will remove a printer configuration. You can test your printer with a PostScript, A4, or ASCII test sheet selected from the Test menu.

New Printers

When you click New Printer, a series of dialog boxes are displayed where you can enter the printer name, its type, and its model. In the Printer Name dialog box, give the printer a name along with any particular description.

On the following Select Connection screen, you select the appropriate printer connection information. Connected local printer brands will be listed by name, such as Canon, whereas for remote printers you specify the type of network connection, like Windows printers via Samba for printers connected to a Windows system, or Internet Printing Protocol (ipp) for printers connected to other Linux systems, or AppSocket/HP Direct for HP printers connected directly to your network.

For most connected printers, your connection is usually determined by the device hotplug services udev and HAL, which now manage all devices. This will be the first entry in the list, and the description will show that it was detected by HAL (see Figure 4-4). It is always preferable to use the HAL connection. With a HAL connection you can plug the printer into any USB port and HAL will automatically detect it. If, instead, you always want the USB printer to use a specific USB port, you can choose the USB-specific connection, such as Canon S330 USB #1. If for some reason your device is not detected, you can use the Other entry to enter the device name.

For an older local printer, you will need to specify the port the printer is connected to, such as LPT1 for the first parallel port used for older parallel printers, or Serial Port #1 for a printer connected to the first serial port.

On the next screen you select your printer manufacturer's model along with its driver (see Figure 4-5). The selected drivers for your printer will be listed. You can find out more about the printer and driver by clicking the Printer and Driver buttons at the bottom of the screen. Then click the Forward button. You will be notified that the printer configuration is about to be created. Click Finish. You then see your printer listed in the system-config-printer window, with its configuration panel displayed. You are now ready to print.

Editing Printers

You can also edit a printer to change any settings. For editing, a set of five tabbed panes are displayed for the Settings, Policies, Access Control, Printer Options, and Job Options (see Figure 4-6). On the Settings panel you can change configuration settings like the driver and the printer name, enable or disable the printer, or specify whether to share it or not. You can also make it the default printer. The Policies panel lets you specify a start and end banner, as

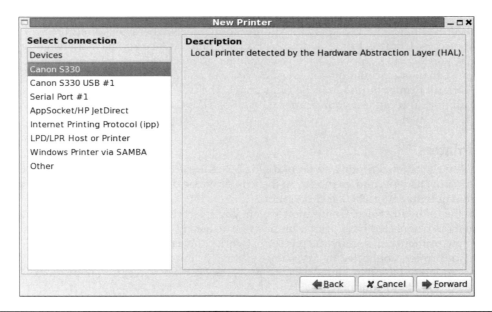

FIGURE 4-4 New Printer Select Connection dialog

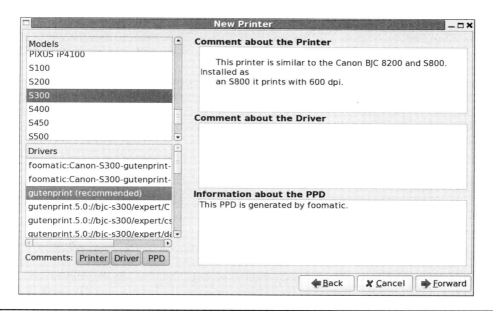

FIGURE 4-5 Printer model for new printers

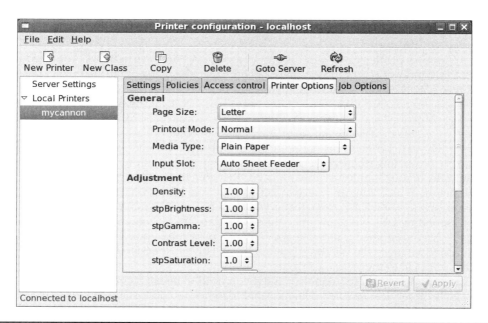

FIGURE 4-6 Printer Options panel

well as an error policy which specifies whether to retry or abort the print job, or stop the printer should an error occur. The Access Control panel allows you to deny access to certain users. The Printer Options panel is where you set particular printing features like paper size and type, print quality, and the input tray to use.

On the Job Options panel you can select default printing features. A pop-up menu provides a list of printing feature categories to choose from. You then click the Add button to add the category, selecting a particular feature from a pop-up menu. You can set such features as the number of copies (copies); letter, glossy, or A4-sized paper (media); the kind of document, for instance, text, PDF, PostScript, or image (document format); and single- or double-sided printing (sides).

Remote Printers

You can also use system-config-printer to set up a remote printer on Linux, Unix, or Windows networks. When you add a new printer or edit one, the New Printer/Select Connection dialog will list possible remote connection types. When you select a remote connection entry, a panel will be displayed where you can enter configuration information. For a remote Linux or UNIX printer, select either Internet Printing Protocol (ipp), which is used for newer systems, or LPD/LPR Host or Printer, which is used for older systems. Both panels display entries for the Host name and the Printer name. For the Host name, enter the hostname for the system that controls the printer. For the Printer name, enter the device name on that host for the printer. The LPD/LPR dialog also has a probe button for detecting the printer.

A Networked Novell (NCP) screen will add entries for the user and the password. A Networked Windows (SMB) screen will have entries for different connected printers. To add one, click Specify to open a window where you can enter the share name, host IP address, workgroup, user, and password. Networked CUPS (IPP) will have entries for the CUPS server and its directory.

A "Windows printer via Samba" is one located on a Windows network. You need to specify the Windows server (host name or IP address), the name of the share, the name of the printer's workgroup, and the username and password. The share is the hostname and printer name in the **smb** URL format *hostname**printername*. The server is the computer where the printer is located. The username and password can be for the printer resource itself, or for access by a particular user. The panel will display a box at the top where you can enter the share host and printer name as an **smb** URL. Instead of typing in the URL, you can use the box below to select the printer from a listing of Windows hosts on your network. For example, if your Windows network is WORKGROUP, then the entry WORKGROUP will be shown, which you can then expand to list all the Windows hosts on that network (if your network is MSHOME, then that is what will be listed). When you make your selection, the corresponding URL will show up in the smb:// box. At the bottom of the panel, enter in any needed Samba authentication like user name or password. You can then use a print client like **lpr** to print a file to the Windows printer; **lpr** will invoke the Samba client **smbclient** to send the print job to the Windows printer.

To access an SMB shared remote printer, you need to install Samba and have the Server Message Block services enabled using the **smb** daemon. To do this, be sure to start Samba with the **smb** entry in system-config-services (System | Administration | Servers Settings | Services menu) and check its box to have it start each time you boot. Printer sharing must, in turn, be enabled on the Windows network.

X Window System Configuration: system-config-display and Vendor Drivers

The GUI interface for your desktop display is implemented by the X Window System. The version used on Fedora is X.org (**x.org**). X.org provides its own drivers for various graphics cards and monitors. You can configure your display settings using the system-config-display tool to change screen resolution settings, as well as select monitor or video card drivers.

As an alternative, you could download and install the drivers and video configuration tools supplied by graphics card vendors like ATI or Nvidia. These are provided by third-party repositories, in particular Livna. Due to licensing issues they are not part of the Fedora repository. Once installed you can use their own configurations tools to configure your display (Applications | System Tools menu). The vendor drivers often provide many more options, such as 3d acceleration, than the X.org drivers, though the X.org drivers tend to be more stable.

system-config-display

If you want to change your display settings, or if you are having trouble with your X Window System configuration, you can use system-config-display to change your configuration. You can run system-config-display by selecting Display on the System | Administration menu. The system-config-display tool opens a Display Settings window with three panels: Settings, Hardware, and Dual Head (shown in Figure 4-7).

FIGURE 4-7
The system-config-display Display Settings window

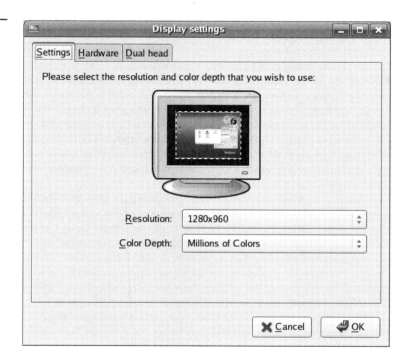

The Settings panel shows pop-up menus for selecting your resolution and color depth. Your current resolution and color depth will already be selected.

To change your monitor or video card settings, click the Hardware tab. This displays a panel with entries for Monitor and Video Card. Each will have a Configure button. Clicking the Video Card Configure button displays a list of supported video cards. Initially only Generic CRT and LCD entries will show. Click the Show All Available Monitors check box to display a complete listing with expandable vendor entries. A Reset default button will return to your default entries. The Video card configuration should not normally be used, though it can be useful for switching between different drivers for the same card, for instance, the X.org nv NVIDIA driver and the NVIDIA-supplied nvidia driver.

For video cards that support dual-head connections, you can use the Dual Head panel to configure your second monitor. First you enable dual head, and then you can configure the monitor connected to the second connection. For the Desktop Layout, you can have individual desktops or a spanning desktop over both monitors.

The system-config-display tool then generates an X Window System configuration file called **/etc/X11/xorg.conf**. This is the file the X Window System uses to start up. Fedora uses the X.org drivers for the X Window System. You can find out more about X.org at **www.x.org**. Whenever you change your settings, your current configuration is saved to **/etc/X11/xorg.backup.conf**. Should you need to restore your old settings manually, you can just replace your current **xorg.conf** with the backup file.

Video Graphics Card Driver Support: ATI, NVIDIA, and Livna

Though a generic Xorg NVIDIA and ATI driver is included with Fedora, to make full use of your graphics driver, you will have to use the vendor-supplied NVIDIA or ATI drivers. Both NVIDIA and ATI provide Linux-compatible versions of their drivers, released almost monthly. The drivers contain updated bug fixes and enhancements.

You can download and install these drivers either directly from the vendor Web site or with Yum using the Livna-prepared versions. It is always preferable to use the Livna versions of the vendor graphics drivers. The Livna versions have been tested and configured specifically for use on Fedora, whereas the direct vendor packages are generic, designed for all Linux systems. Most likely you will have difficulties trying to use the vendor graphics packages directly, whereas the Livna versions usually have no problems. Livna remains perhaps the best repository for specialized kernel drivers and modules, even though some of its other multimedia packages may conflict with those from other repositories. Even if you leave Livna disabled, you will still want to use it for your graphics and NTFS drivers, along with other specialized drivers.

The Livna-supplied graphic drivers use two packages, one for the supporting software and another for the kernel. At the **rpm.livna.org** site, you will find listed ATI and NVIDIA modules for each kernel version. Yum will automatically detect your kernel version and select the correct module package. In addition, there are kernel modules for different kinds of kernels, like Xen or PAE. Again, Yum will detect the correct module package to use. If you want to manually install the module package, you will have to know your kernel version and type to select the correct package. To find out your kernel version, you can use the command **uname -r**.

NVIDIA organizes its drivers into three driver packages: the package for current cards, a 96xx package for 9600 series cards, and a legacy package for obsolete cards. In addition,

Livna provides a development package for supporting software, as well as source code packages for the drivers in its SRPMS directory. The following are the NVIDIA drivers packages for current video cards:

```
xorg-x11-drv-nvidia-driver-version.i386.rpm
kmod-nvidia-kernel-verson_FC7.i586.rpm
```

The ATI packages use the term **fglrx**, not ATI. ATI uses only a single driver collection, with a package for the supporting software and one for the kernel module. Livna provides module packages for each kernel version and kernel type, which Yum will automatically detect. Like NVIDIA, ATI also provides a development package for supporting software. The Livna site also provides source code packages for the drivers in its SRPMS directory.

```
xorg-x11-drv-fglrx-driver-version.i386.rpm
kmod-fglrx-kernel-verson_FC7.i686.rpm
```

It is always best to use Yum to install the drivers. Yum will automatically detect the correct kernel version. You only need to use the initial unique term for the kernel module, like **kmod-fgrlx** for ATI. The ATI driver software will also be selected as a dependency, in this case **xorg-x11-drv-fgrlx**. Yum will detect the rest of the package name, selecting the package appropriate for your kernel. For NVIDIA, you would use **kmod-nvidia** in a **yum** command, which will also detect and select **xorg-x11-drv-nvidia**, the NVIDIA driver software.

To install your graphics driver using Yum, be sure that Linva Yum repository support is already installed. Download and install the **livna-release** package for your Fedora release from the **rpm.livna.org** site. Once it is installed, you can then access all Livna software with Yum. You can use either Pirut (Applications | Add/Remove Software) or the **yum** command in a terminal window. With Pirut, select the Search panel and enter in the string **kmod-nvidia** for NVIDIA or **kmod-fgrlx** for ATI. Then select the kernel module package you want installed.

For example, to install the ATI driver and supporting software, you would enter the appropriate Yum command on a command line (terminal window). If Livna is not disabled, you can simply use the following:

```
yum install kmod-fgrlx
```

If you have Livna disabled in its repo configuration file, you could use the **-enablerepo** option to temporarily enable it, allowing Yum to access the Livna repository:

```
yum install --enablerepo=livna  kmod-fgrlx
```

If this happens to be first time you have downloaded anything from this repository and you have not already imported its GPG key, you will also be prompted to approve the import of the Livna GPG key.

Using the vendor drivers directly can be risky. The package is designed for use on all Linux systems and has not been tested for Fedora systems specifically. Be sure to read the install instructions on the vendor Web site first. You may want to back up your **/etc/ xorg.conf** file first, should you need to restore it. The vendor drivers uses just one package, which will have to be run with the X Window System shut down. You would first download the package, and then open a terminal window and run the `telinit` command with the argument **3**, `telinit 3`. This will place you in the command line interface with a login prompt (you may have to press ENTER to display the prompt). If you put the graphics package in a subdirectory, then use the `cd` command to change to that directory. Then issue the `sh` command with the package name. Once installation is complete, return to X with the `telinit 5` command. If X does not start, you can use CTRL-SHIFT-F1 to return the command line interface and then restore your original **/etc/xorg.conf** file (copy the current one over with the backup using the `cp` command).

As an alternative to both the Livna and vendor-direct packages, you could also use the DKMS versions provided by **freshrpms.net**. These versions will dynamically generate a new graphics kernel module each time you update your kernel. There is no need to download anything further. Keep in mind, though, that the Livna modules are designed for specific Fedora kernels, whereas the DKMS versions are generated by your compiler.

Updating Fedora and Enterprise Linux: PUP and RHN

New versions of Fedora are released every few months. In the meantime, new updates are continually being prepared for particular software packages. These are posted as updates you can download from software repositories and install on your system. These include new versions of applications, servers, and even the kernel. Such updates may range from single software packages to whole components—for instance, all the core, application, and development packages issued when a new release of GNOME, KDE, or X11 is made available.

TIP *If you are installing or updating several months after the official Fedora release, it may be easier to use a Fedora Re-Spin disk. This is disk with the latest updates. This way you avoid having to download numerous updates to the original packages from online repositories. Fedora Re-Spins are issued every three months by the Fedora Unity project. Fedora Re-Spins disks can be downloaded using BitTorrent from **torrents.fedoraunity.org**.*

Updating your Linux system has become a very simple procedure, using the automatic update tools. For Fedora, you can update your system by accessing software repositories supporting the Yum (Yellowdog Updater, Modified) update methods. Yum uses RPM headers to determine which packages need to be updated. You can find out more about Yum, including a listing of Yum repositories, at **linux.duke.edu/projects/yum**.

To update your packages, you now use the Package Updater Program (PUP). PUP is a graphical update interface for Yum, which now performs all updates. With PUP you no longer have to update using a **yum** update command entered in a terminal window.

PUP makes use of the PUP applet on your GNOME panel, which will automatically check for updates whenever you log in. If updates are detected, PUP will flash its icon on the panel and display a message telling you that updates are available and how many there are. Click the PUP button to start PUP. You can also select PUP manually from its Software Updater entry in the Applications | System Tools menu.

All needed updates will be selected automatically when PUP starts up. The check boxes for each entry let you deselect any particular packages you may not want to update. Click the Apply button to start updating. Dependencies will be checked first. Then the packages will be downloaded from their appropriate repository. Once downloaded, the packages are updated.

All the Yum-compatible repositories that are configured on your system will be checked. Again, software is now seen as a set of collections on different online repositories, rather than particular disks.

Be sure to check down the list for critical installs, like a new kernel. You may or may not want such an install. Should a new kernel be installed, you will be prompted to reboot your system. You will, however, be booted into your current working kernel. To choose the new kernel, you will need to select it from the GRUB boot screen. To make it the default, you can either select it with the Bootloader configuration screen (System | Administration | Bootloader) or set the default option in the **/etc/grub/grub.conf** file to 0.

As a standard practice, you may want to perform an update before installing new packages, as they will always be the most recent version downloaded from the repository and may require updated dependencies.

TIP   *To update to a new Fedora release, you can download Fedora CD/DVD-ROM ISO images from **download.fedora.redhat.com/download** or from one of the Fedora download mirrors, **fedoraproject.org/Download/mirrors.html**. You can then burn the ISO image and update from that install CD/DVD. Fedora ISO images can also be downloaded using the BitTorrent service, **torrent.fedoraproject.org**. BitTorrent provides a very fast method for downloading ISO images.*

Installing Software Packages

Now that you know how to start Linux and access the root user account, you can install any other software packages you may want. Installing software is an administrative function performed by the root user. Unless you chose to install all your packages during your installation, only some of the many applications and utilities available for users on Linux were installed on your system. On Fedora, you can easily install or remove software from your system with either the Pirut tool (Update/Remove Software) or the **rpm** command. Alternatively, you can install software by downloading and compiling its source code. The procedure for installing software using its source code has been simplified to just a few commands, though you have a great deal of flexibility in tailoring an application to your specific system.

An RPM software package operates like its own installation program for a software application. A Linux software application often consists of several files that must be installed in different directories. The program itself is most likely placed in a directory called **/usr/bin**, online manual files go in another directory, and library files go in yet another directory. In addition, the installation may require modification of certain configuration files on your system. The RPM software packages perform all these tasks for you. Also, if you later decide you don't want a specific application, you can uninstall packages to remove all the files and configuration information from your system.

The software packages on your DVD/CD-ROMs, as extensive as they are, represent only some of the software packages available for Fedora Linux. Many multimedia applications and support libraries can be found at **rpm.livna.org/fedora** and **freshrpms.net**. Table 4-2 lists several Fedora and Linux software sites. Fedora, Livna, and Freshrpms are all Yum supported, meaning that a simple Yum configuration enables you to directly download and install software from those sites using the **yum** command or the Pirut software manager. Fedora is already installed, and both Livna and Freshrpms provide their own Yum configuration files.

Internet Sites	Description
ftp.redhat.com	Red Hat distribution RPM packages
download.fedora.redhat.com/ pub/fedora/linux	Fedora-compliant software, Yum (see **repodata** files for listings)
freshrpms.net	Fedora-compliant RPM package repository, includes multimedia packages, Yum
rpm.livna.org/fedora	Repository for devices and multimedia and other RPM packages, Yum (Fedora Project extension)
rpmfind.net	RPM package repository
sourceforge.net	SourceForge open source software repository and development site
freshmeat.net	New Linux software
kde-apps.org	KDE software applications
www.gnomefiles.org	GNOME software applications
fedoraproject.org/wiki/ ForbiddenItems	Packages not included in the main Fedora software repository.
fedoraproject.org/wiki/ Multimedia.	Information on multimedia packages available for Fedora

TABLE 4-2   Fedora and Linux Software Sites

TIP   For information on multimedia applications available for Fedora see **fedoraproject.org/wiki/** **Multimedia***.*

Fedora provides only open source applications in its own repository. For proprietary applications like NVIDIA's own graphics drivers or multimedia application that may have patent issues, you need to use third-party repositories like **freshrpms.net** or **rpm.livna.org**. The list of forbidden items for the official Fedora repository can be found at **fedoraproject .org/wiki/ForbiddenItems**. These include items like the NVIDIA and ATI graphics drivers (those you can obtain from rpm.livna.org).

You can download additional software from online software sites such as GNOME's **gnomefiles.org**, KDE's **kde-apps.net**, and **sourceforge.net**. The **sourceforge.net** site not only distributes software but also serves as the primary development site for a massive number of open source software projects. You can also locate many of the newest Linux applications from **freshmeat.net** or **rpmfind.net**.

Installing with Yum

Downloading Fedora software or software from any configured Fedora Yum repository is a simple matter of entering the **yum** utility with the install option and the name of the package in a terminal window. Yum will detect the software and any dependencies, and it will prompt you to download and install it. For example, the following command will install Abiword:

```
yum install abiword
```

Alternatively, you can use Pirut, which provides a GUI interface for Yum, letting you download software from any Yum-configured software repository.

Pirut Package Manager: A Repository Model of Software Management

The Pirut Package Manager is a new package management tool that now replaces the older system-config-packages, which was used primarily for the disk-based packages. The Package Manager is Internet-based, installing from online repositories only, using Yum to download and install.

Pirut is the same tool used during the installation procedure to select packages, only now you can uninstall packages. Check **fedoraproject.org/wiki/Tools/yum** for tips on using Yum, including a script to let you perform partial installs. Yum by default stops the entire process if there is any configuration or dependency problem with any one repository or package.

As described in Chapter 3, to use Pirut you select the Add/Remove Software entry from the Applications menu. Pirut will start up by gathering information on all your packages. You then have three different ways to use Pirut: Search, Categories, and List. The Categories method accesses Fedora packages only, whereas the List and Search methods access all the software on all your enabled repositories (you can turn a repository off by setting its **enabled** bit to 0 in its repo configuration file, see Chapter 29). Due to the very large number of packages available, you may find yourself using the Search method frequently. Figure 4-8 shows Pirut used to list gconf (GNOME configuration tool) packages.

With Package Manager, Yum is now integrated as the primary install packages tool. When you install a package with Package Manager, Yum will be invoked and it will automatically select and download the package from the appropriate online repository. This is a major

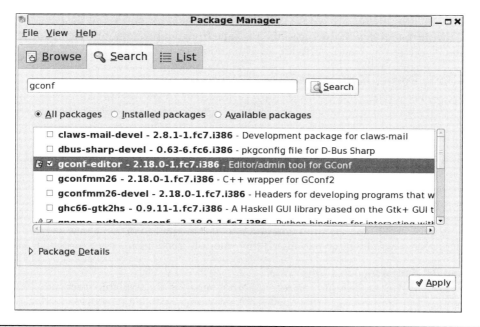

FIGURE 4-8   Pirut Package Manager

change that users may not be aware of at first glance. After having installed your system, when you then want to install additional packages, the install packages tool will now use Yum to install from an online repository, rather than retrieving the packages from your CD- or DVD-ROM. This will include all Yum online repositories you may have enabled such as sites like **freshrpms.net**, not just the Fedora distribution and update repositories configured for you during installation.

Keep in mind that when you use Pirut to list your available software, it is listing software on all the enabled repositories taken together. The software on your disk is not being referenced. Pirut, using Yum, will see all the packages on your enabled repositories and can access and update any of them, including their dependencies. When you click List on the package manager and you see the list of software, you are seeing the collections of all repositories together. Pirut is literally a front end for Yum.

This means that the repositories with their updated versions become the primary software source, not the disks. On the other hand, if you want to install a package from the disk, you have to do it manually. You will need to use a command line operation entered in a terminal window. You have the choice of using either RPM or Yum with the **localinstall** option. You would have to open a terminal window, change to the disk's RPMS software directory, and then enter either the **yum** command with the **localinstall** option or the **rpm** command with the **-i** option. Be careful, though. If you used PUP to update, you may already have updated dependent packages to versions beyond which the older packages on the disk can handle. In this respect, the repository model is far more effective in giving you the most up-to-date software. A side effect is that your disk software may very quickly become out of date and useless. In fact after your first update as much as a third of the disk software may already be obsolete.

You might think that trying to install a disk package by right-clicking it from GNOME and selecting install-software would install that disk package. This is not the case. Pirut will still be invoked, and it will download the package from a repository. In effect, your disks are completely ignored by install-software after the initial install.

Third-Party Kernel Module Updates

Third-party kernel drivers are provided for certain devices and system support, such as the ATI or NVIDIA Linux graphics drivers for their video cards. You could download and try to install these drivers directly, but it is recommended that you use a third-party package designed for use with Fedora. There are two approaches to providing additional kernel modules: a precompiled module for each kernel version, or a dynamically compiled version using Dynamic Kernel Module Support (DKMS).

The issue here is that each new kernel version requires its own set of kernel drivers. For example, whenever you update to a new kernel, you then have to install new kernel modules for that kernel for the ATI and NVIDIA graphics drivers. You will not have access to the NVIDIA or ATI drivers until you do. Also, if you want to install a new version of the graphics drivers, you then have to install their module versions for your particular kernel.

Precompiled Kernel Modules from Livna

Precompiled kernel modules for all recent kernel versions are available from the Livna repository. Each time you update your kernel, or want to install a new drivers release for a kernel, you download and install the appropriate kernel package from the Livna repository. Yum can do this for you automatically. This, however, requires that the module package be available and that you have the Internet connection to download it.

Using the Livna kernel modules is preferable. The Livna modules are specially configured to work with Fedora. They have proven to be very stable, much more so than even the original versions release from vendors. This is particularly true for graphics drivers like ATI and NVIDIA. It is always best to use the Livna versions of the NVIDIA or ATI graphics drivers and modules.

Updating Kernel Modules Using Dynamic Kernel Module Support: Freshrpms

The Dynamic Kernel Module Support (DKMS) is designed to make the installation of driver releases independent from kernel versions. Though not as reliable as the Livna kernel modules, it has the advantage that you never have to worry about installing the appropriate kernel module for a kernel version. You just have to download and install new driver software, like graphic drivers, as they are released. DKMS takes care of the needed kernel modules. DKMS was originally developed by Dell Corporation to provide easy driver updates for users, **linux.dell.com/dkms**.

To use DKMS for a particular driver, you need to download and install its DKMS driver package. DKMS driver versions for certain drivers can be obtained from the **freshrpms.net** repository. Some will have the prefix dkms. The NVIDIA and ATI drives will not have this prefix. DKMS is designed to automatically generate kernel modules whenever you update your kernel. There is no need to download a precompiled package. To use DKMS drivers, you will first have to install the DKMS software package.

A DKMS package will install the driver source code in the **/usr/src** directory. With the driver source code will be a **dkms.conf** configuration file for creating the module.

Installing Packages Manually with the rpm Command

If you are installing a package that is not part of a Yum repository, and you do not have access to the desktop or you prefer to work from the command line interface, you can use the **rpm** command to manage and install software packages (you can also open a terminal window by selecting the Terminal entry in the Applications | System Tools menu). In most cases you will not need to use the **rpm** command. Most software now resides on Yum-supported, Fedora-compliant repositories. You would just use the **yum** command to install your package. Yum has the advantage of automatically installing any dependent packages, whereas the **rpm** command, though it will detect needed packages, will not install them. You will have to separately install any dependent packages in the correct order.

For packages that are not part of any Yum-supported repository, such as custom-made packages, and that have few or no dependent packages, you can use the **rpm** command directly. You could also use the **rpm** command to bypass Yum, forcing installation of a particular package instead of from Yum repositories (Yum's `localinstall` option will achieve the same purpose).

The **rpm** command performs installation, removal, and verification of software packages. Each software package is actually an RPM package, consisting of an archive of software files and information about how to install those files. Each archive resides as a single file with a name that ends with **.rpm**, indicating it is a software package that can be installed by the Red Hat Package Manager.

You can use the **rpm** command to either install or uninstall a package. The **rpm** command uses a set of options to determine what action to take. The `-i` option installs the specified software package, and the `-U` option updates a package. With an `-e` option, **rpm** uninstalls the package. A **q** placed before an **i** (**-qi**) queries the system to see if a software package is already installed and displays information about the software (**-qpi** queries an uninstalled package file). The **rpm** command with no options provides a complete list of rpm options. A set of commonly used options is shown here:

Option	Action
-U	Updates package
-i	Installs package
-e	Uninstalls package
-qi	Displays information for an installed package
-ql	Displays file list for installed package
-qpi	Displays information from an RPM package file (used for uninstalled packages)
-qpl	Displays file list from an RPM package file (used for uninstalled packages)
-K	Authenticates and performs integrity check on a package

The software package name is usually quite lengthy, including information about the version and release date in its name. All end with **.rpm**. In the next example, the user installs the freeciv package using the **rpm** command. Notice that the full filename is entered. To list the full name, you can use the **ls** command with the first few characters and an asterisk. The following examples use the DivX xvidcore RPM packages downloaded from **rpm.livna.org** (you can also download more recent versions of xvidcore from **freshrpms.net**).

```
ls xvid*
```

You can also use the * to match the remainder of the name, as in the following:

```
ls xvidccore-1*.rpm
```

In most cases, you are installing packages with the **-U** option, for update. Even if the package is not already installed, **-U** still installs it.

```
$ rpm -Uvh xvidcore-1.2.0-4.lvn.i386.rpm
```

When RPM performs an installation, it first checks for any dependent packages. These are other software packages with programs the application you are installing needs to use. If other dependent packages must be installed first, RPM cancels the installation and lists those packages. You can install those packages and then repeat the installation of the application. To determine if a package is already installed, use the **-qi** option with **rpm**. The **-q** stands for query. To obtain a list of all the files the package has installed, as well as the directories it installed to, use the **-ql** option. To query package files, add the **p** option. The **-qpi** option displays information about a package, and **-qpl** lists the files in it. The following example lists all the files in the freeciv package:

```
$ rpm -qpl xvidcore-1.2.0-4.lvn.i386.rpm
```

To remove a software package from your system, first use **rpm -qi** to make sure it is actually installed, and then use the **-e** option to uninstall it. As with the **-qi** option, you needn't use the full name of the installed file. You only need the name of the application. In the next example, the user removes the DivX xvidcore from the system:

```
$ rpm -e xvidcore
```

Package Security Check

If you download a software package, you may want to check its integrity and authentication, making sure the package was not tampered with and that it was obtained from a valid source. Yum is configured to automatically perform this check on all software downloaded from your Fedora-compliant repositories. Each repository configuration file in the **/etd/ yum.repos.d** directory will have its **gpgcheck** option set to 1. Should you want to turn off this check for a particular repository, you can set its **gpgcheck** option to 0.

To authenticate a package, its digital signature is checked. Packages are signed with encrypted digital keys that can be decrypted using the public key provided by the author of the package. This public key has to first be downloaded and installed on the encryption tool used on your system. Fedora, along with most Linux systems, uses the GNU Privacy Guard (GPG) encryption tool. To use a public key to authenticate an RPM package, you first have to install it in the RPM key database. For all RPM packages that are part of the Fedora distribution, you can use the Fedora public key, placed during installation in the **/usr/share/ doc/fedora-release-7/RPM-GPG-KEY** file.

You need to import the key to the RPM database before you can check Fedora packages. The first time you use Pirut to install a package, you will be prompted to import the GPG key. Once it is imported, you need not import it again. Alternatively, you can manually import the key as shown here:

```
rpm --import /usr/share/doc/fedora-release-7/RPM-GPG-KEY
```

If you have downloaded an RPM package from another site, you can also download and install its public key, with which you can authenticate that package. For example, there are public keys for both the Livna and Freshrpms Fedora Yum repositories. These are included in the Yum configuration files, which you can download and install, for instance, **livna-release-7.rpm** for Livna. The keys will be automatically installed along with the configuration.

Once the public key is installed, you can check the package's authentication using the **rpm** command with the **-K** option.

```
$ rpm -K xvidcore-1.2.0-4.lvn7.i386.rpm
```

To see a list of all the keys you have imported, you can use the **-qa** option and match on the gpg-pubkey* pattern. Using **rpm** with the **-qi** option and the public key, you can display detailed information about the key. The following example shows the Fedora public key:

```
$ rpm -qa gpg-pubkey*
gpg-pubkey-4f2a6fd2-3f9d9d3b
gpg-pubkey-db42a60e-37ea5438
```

You can manually check just a package's integrity with the **rpm** command with the **-K** and the **--nosignature** options. A value called the MD5 digest measures the contents of a package. If the value is incorrect, the package has been tampered with. Some packages provide just digest values, allowing only integrity checks. In the next example, the user checks whether the freeciv package has been tampered with. The **--nosignature** option says not to perform authentication, doing the integrity check only.

```
$ rpm -K --nosignature xvidcore-1.2.0-4.lvn.i386.rpm
```

Installing Source Code Applications

Many programs are available for Linux in source code format. These programs are stored in a compressed archive that you need to decompress and then extract. The resulting source code can then be configured, compiled, and installed on your system. The process has been simplified to the extent that it involves not much more than installing an RPM package. The following example shows the common method to extract, compile, and install software, in this case the kat program, a desktop search and indexing tool. Always check the included README and INSTALL files that come with the source code to check the appropriate method for creating and installing that software.

TIP *Be sure that you have installed all development packages onto your system. Development packages contain the key components such as the compiler, GNOME and KDE headers and libraries, and preprocessors. You cannot compile source code software without them.*

First you locate the software and then you download it to your system. It is downloaded in a file named **freeciv-2.0.8-7.tar.bz2**. Then decompress and extract the file either with the Archive Manager on the desktop, or with the **tar** command in a terminal window.

Extracting the Archive

The easiest way to extract compressed archives is to use the Archive Manager (Applications | System Tools | Archive Manager) on GNOME. Either double-click the compressed archive file or right-click and select Open With "Archive Manager". This displays the top-level contents of the archive, which you can browse if you wish, even reading text files like README and INSTALL files. You can also see what files will actually be installed. Use the Back, Forward, and Up buttons to navigate, and double-click a directory to open it. Nothing is extracted at this point. To extract the archive, click Extract.

To use the **tar** command, first open a terminal window (select Terminal in the Applications | System Tools menu). At the prompt, enter the **tar** command with the **xvjf** options (**j** for **bz2** and **z** for **gz**), as shown here:

```
tar xvjf freeciv-2.0.8-7.tar.bz2
```

Configure, Compile, and Install

Extracting the archive will create a directory with the name of the software, in this case **freeciv-2.0.1**. Once it is extracted, you have to configure, compile, and install the software. This usually needs to be done from a terminal window.

Change to the software directory with the cd command:

```
cd freeciv-2.0.8-7
```

First read the INSTALL or README files included with the software and follow the instructions. Most software just uses the three following commands, but there are variations. Issue the command `./configure`. This generates a compiler configuration for your particular system.

```
./configure
```

Compile the software with the **make** command:

```
make
```

Then install the program with the **make install** command:

```
make install
```

Most KDE- and GNOME-compliant software will also place an entry for the program in the appropriate menus—for example, a freeciv entry will be placed in the KDE Applications menu. You can then run freeciv from the menu entry. You could also open a terminal window and enter the program's name.

Security Configuration

Once you have installed your Linux system, you should carry out some basic security measures to protect your system from outside attacks. Systems connected to the Internet are open to attempts by outside users to gain unauthorized access. This usually takes the following forms:

- Trying to break into the system
- Having broken in, changing or replacing system files with hacked or corrupt versions
- Attempting to intercept communications from remote users
- Changing or replacing messages sent to or from users
- Pretending to be a valid user

Firewalls, intrusion protection, encryption, data integrity, and authentication are ways of protecting against such attacks.

- A firewall prevents any direct unauthorized attempts at access.
- Intrusion detection checks the state of your system files to see if they have been tampered with by someone who has broken in.
- Encryption protects transmissions by authorized remote users, providing privacy.
- Integrity checks such as modification digests guarantee that messages and data have not been intercepted and changed or substituted en route.
- Authentication methods such as digital signatures can verify that the user claiming to send a message or access your system is actually that person.

Security Services

Fedora includes several security services for protecting your system and your network transmissions (see Table 4-3). Using GNU Privacy Guard (GPG), you can encrypt your e-mail messages or files you want to send, as well as sign them with an encrypted digital signature authenticating that the message was sent by you. The digital signature also includes encrypted modification digest information that provides an integrity check, allowing the recipient to verify that the message received is the original and not one that has been changed or substituted.

With Security-Enhanced Linux a refined administrative approach is provided for greater security controls. User access to different parts of the operating system can be limited using roles and security contexts. Only qualified users can have access to certain objects like files and applications. Security-Enhanced Linux policy can be either strict or targeted. A targeted policy applies restrictions to daemons like Internet servers, restricting access for users that access those servers. You can choose which servers you want controlled. Use the system-config-securitylevel tool's SE Linux panel to select the servers you want managed by SE Linux.

A good foundation for your network security is to set up a Linux system to operate as a firewall for your network, protecting it from unauthorized access. You can use a firewall to implement either packet filtering or proxies. *Packet filtering* is simply the process of deciding whether a packet received by the firewall host should be passed on into the local

Applications	Description
GNU Privacy Guard (GPG)	Encryption and digital signatures **www.gnupg.org**
Netfilter (iptables)	Firewall packet filtering **www.netfilter.org**
Security-Enhanced Linux (SELinux)	Security-Enhanced Linux **www.nsa.gov/selinux**
system-config-selinux	Fedora tool to configure and manage your SELinux policy
ClamAV	Virus protection with automatic update. **www.clamav.net**
OpenSSH	Secure Shell encryption and authentication for remote access **www.openssh.org**
Kerberos	User authentication for access to services **web.mit.edu/kerberos/www**
Pluggable Authorization Modules (PAM)	Authentication management and configuration
Shadow passwords	Password encryption
Lightweight Directory Access Protocol (LDAP)	User management and authorization **www.openldap.org**
system-config-authentication	Fedora tool to enable and configure authentication tools: Kerberos, LDAP, and shadow passwords
Internet Protocol Security (IPsec)	Protocol to implement Virtual Private Networks

TABLE 4-3   Security Applications

system or network. The firewall package currently in use is Netfilter (iptables). To implement a firewall, you simply provide a series of rules to govern what kind of access you want to allow on your system. If that system is also a gateway for a private network, the system's firewall capability can effectively protect the network from outside attacks. You can provide a simple configuration for your own system using system-config-securitylevel, as well as a more complete configuration and management with system-config-selinux. Be sure to check the Fedora SE Linux FAQ at **fedora.redhat.com/docs/selinux-faq** for implementation details and problems on using SE Linux on Fedora.

For virus protection, you can use the ClamAV virus tools (Fedora repository). **kclamav** and **clamtk** provide desktop interfaces. Though designed for mail servers, on access and user initiated scanning is supported (**clamscan** and **clamd**). See **www.clamav.net** for more details.

To further control access to your system, you can provide secure user authentication with encrypted passwords, a Lightweight Directory Access Protocol (LDAP) service, and Pluggable Authentication Modules (PAM). User authentication can further be controlled for certain services by Kerberos servers. Kerberos authentication provides another level of security whereby individual services can be protected, allowing use of a service only to users who are cleared for access. LDAP and Kerberos are all enabled and configured with system-config-authentication (Authentication in the System Administration menu).

To protect remote connections from hosts outside your network, transmissions can be encrypted. For Linux systems, you can use the Secure Shell (SSH) suite of programs to encrypt any transmissions, preventing them from being read by anyone else. The SSH programs are meant to replace the remote tools such as **rsh** and **rcp**, which perform no encryption.

The IPsec protocol also provides encryption of network transmissions, but integrated into the IP packet structure. With IPsec you can both encrypt and authenticate transmissions, ensuring that they were not intercepted and tampered with, and you can implement virtual private networks (VPNs), using encrypted transmissions to connect one local network to another using a larger network like the Internet.

You can find the latest news on security issues at the Red Hat Web site (**www.redhat .com**) along with other Linux sites such as Linux Security (**www.linuxsecurity.com**), Linux Weekly News (**lwn.net**), and Linux Today (**linuxtoday.com**).

NOTE *Numerous older security applications are also available for Linux such as COPS (Computer Oracle and Password System) to check password security; Tiger, which scans your system for unusual or unprotected files; and SATAN (Security Administration Tool for Analyzing Networks), which checks your system for security holes. Crack is a newer password auditing tool that you can use to check how well your password security performs under dictionary attacks.*

Authentication Configuration

To confirm that user identities are valid, your network may provide several authentication services. These can be enabled on your system using system-config-authentication (system-config-authentication). You can invoke system-config-authentication by selecting Authentication from the System Administration menu. The system-config-authentication tool consists of three panels, User Information, Authentication, and Options. Configuration consists primarily of specifying the address of the service's server on your network. The User Information panel is used for services like NIS and LDAP, which maintain configuration information about systems and users on your network. The Authentication panel lists services for authenticating users. If your network also maintains LDAP, Kerberos, and SMB authentication servers, you can enable support for them here, specifying their servers and domains. The Options panel provides authentication options like Shadow and MD5 Password support, which are selected by default and provide password protection.

Unsupported Drivers

Drivers for most network devices are already included in your Fedora distribution and managed automatically by udev and HAL. However, if you have a new or specialized device that is currently not supported, you should check with the provider's Web site for the appropriate Linux driver. Also, many popular third-party drivers can be obtained from **livna.org**.

A driver takes the form of a module that is loaded dynamically by the Linux kernel when your system starts up (see Chapters 32 and 33). Normally, compiled versions of a module are provided that you can download and then install on your system. To install a module, you use the **modprobe** command. Once installed, the module will be loaded automatically by the kernel each time you start your system. Should something go wrong with the install, you can always uninstall the module using the **modprobe** command with the **-r** option.

Many unsupported modules are provided as source code only. In this case, you will have to unpack and compile the module first, using the **tar** command as noted in the preceding section. Check the README or INSTALL files normally included with the source code for detailed instructions. If none are included, try the **./configure** and **make** commands. Usually a **make** command with the **install** option will install the module in your system's module library directory. The **install** option may also run the **depmod** command to update the module dependencies, allowing **modprobe** to load it.

```
./configure
make
make install
```

If you are using a precompiled version, you need to follow any instruction for installing the module in the module library. This is located in **/lib/modules/***version* directory, which has several subdirectories for different kinds of modules. Here *version* is the kernel version number, like **2.6.20-1.3038_FC7** on Fedora 7. Modules for network cards are kept in the **kernel/drivers/net** directory, as in **/lib/modules/ 2.6.20-1.3038_FC7 /kernel/drivers/net**. You can copy a precompiled module for a network card to that directory.

Once you have created the module and installed it in the module library directory, the module needs to be checked for any dependent modules that may also need to be loaded with it to make it work. This is done by the **depmod** tool. If you installed from a source code version, **depmod** may have already been run. In this case, you can directly load the module with **modprobe**. If, however, you copied the precompiled version directly to the module library, or if your source code version did not run **depmod**, you should then restart your system. On restart, the **depmod** tool will run automatically and check for any module dependencies. You can then manually load the using the **modprobe** command and the module name. The **lsmod** command will list your currently loaded modules.

You can add any parameters the module may require. To discover what parameters a module takes, you can use the **modinfo** command with the **-p** option. The **-v** option (verbose) lists all actions taken as they occur. In the next example, **modprobe** loads the **bcm4400.o** module for a Broadcom network device (do not use the **.o** suffix in the name):

```
# modprobe -v bcm4400
```

Options for the **modprobe** command are placed in the **/etc/modprobe.conf** file. Here, you can enter configuration options, such as default directories and aliases. An alias provides a simple name for a module. For example, the following entry enables you to reference the bcm4400.o Ethernet card module as **eth0** (Kmod, the Kernel module loader, automatically detects the Broadcom card and loads the bcm4400 module):

```
alias eth0 bcm4400
```

Once it is loaded, you need to restart your system. On restart, the new hardware will be detected and you will be asked to configure it. You can configure it at this time, specifying any network information, or wait and use system-config-network after your system starts up. With system-config-network, you can create a new device for the hardware connection and provide configuration information such as whether to use DHCP for automatic configuration or manually supply network IP and DNS addresses.

Installing Access for Local Windows NTFS File Systems

If you have installed Fedora on a dual-boot system with Windows XP, NT, or 2000, or otherwise need access to NTFS partitions, you will not be able to access them until you install the Linux NTFS file system support. There are three methods for providing this support: the ntfs-3g read/write drivers, which are available on the Fedora repository, the original read-only NTFS Project drivers available from Livna, and the DKMS version provided by Freshrpms. The ntfs-3g driver is the preferred method, though write support is not yet fully guaranteed.

The NTFS Project provides a set of tools for access to NTFS partitions that are used by both the ntfs-3g and the original NTFS Project drivers. These tools include **mktfs** to format NTFS partitions, **ntfsresize** to resize a partition, and **ntfsls** to list files in a partition. These tools are included on the Fedora repository as the **ntfsprogs** package. Just search for and install this package with Add/Remove software. To support GNOME browsing, you would install NTFS project's **ntfs-gnomevfs** package, also on the Fedora repository.

NTFS Read/Write Access: ntfs-3g

The simplest and easiest approach is to use the ntfs-3g NTFS driver. The ntfs-3g drivers developed from the NTFS Project. Check the ntfs-3g Web site for more details, **www.ntfs-3g.org**. As noted, ntfs-3g uses the same support tools, **ntfsprogs**. Unlike the original NTFS Project driver, ntfs-3g provides write support. You can write to and delete from NTFS partitions. Though writing should work, for safety's sake, you have the option to turn off write capability. Once ntfs-3g is installed, there is no need to install further kernel support.

You can install ntfs-3g from Pirut by performing a search for **ntfs-3g**. You should also install the **ntfs-config** package. This provides a GUI interface for configuring ng3 NTFS access. Once it is installed, select Applications | System Tools | NTFS Configuration Tool. The first time you use this, you will be prompted to enter in a name to use for your Windows partition.

The directory name will be created in the **/media** directory. You can then choose to enable or disable write support. Though **ntfs-3g** does support write access, it is not guaranteed. A safer approach is to turn off write access.

Once configured, entries for your partitions will be placed in the **/etc/fstab** file. Note that the file system type used is **ntfs-3g**, not **ntfs**. The file systems will be automatically mounted when you start up your system.

NTFS Project Read-Only: Livna

The Linux NTFS Project has developed read-only NTFS support that is available from Livna as a kernel module. You can find detailed information and help at its Web site, **www.linux-ntfs.org**. In the future it is expected to incorporate ntfs-3g for write support. If you have not already done so, configure your system to use the **rpm.livna.org** repository by downloading and installing the livna-release package from the configuration page for your particular Fedora version. You can then use Pirut or Yum directly to download and install the NTFS module. Search on **ntfs** and select the Livna NTFS package. It will have the prefix **kmod-ntfs**. Selecting it will also install the NTFS common package, **ntfs-kmod-common**.

Whenever you update your kernel, an NTFS module for that kernel will have to be downloaded and installed from Livna.

If you have disabled Livna and want to enable it just to install the NTFS module, you can run Yum with the **--enablerepo** option. Yum will detect the correct kernel module for NTFS to use.

```
yum install --enablerepo=livna kmod-ntfs
```

As noted previously, the Linux NTFS Project provides an extensive set of tools for managing NTFS partitions from Linux included on the Fedora repository as the **ntfsprogs** package.

Once the module is installed, you can then mount your NTFS file systems. First set up a directory where you want the Windows files system mounted. Usually this is in the **/mnt** directory under a subdirectory that could be named **windows**.

```
mkdir /mnt/windows
```

You will need to know your hard drive names for any NTFS partitions. You can find this out by entering the **fdisk -l** command. In the following example, the NTFS file system is located at **/dev/sda1**:

To mount, use the **mount** command and specify the type with the **-t ntfs** option. List the directory first and then the file system name. Though the NTFS module supports limited write capability, it does not support full write operations. To be safe, you may want to limit it to just read capability. Do this with the **-o ro** option.

```
mount /dev/sda1  /mnt/windows  -t ntfs  -o ro
```

If you want the partition mounted automatically when you log in, you have to make an entry for it in the **/etc/fstab** file. You can use the text editor (Gedit) to edit the file. Be very careful editing this file. You may want to make a backup of it first. Using the previous example, the corresponding fstab entry would be:

```
/dev/sda1    /mnt/windows    ntfs    ro    0 0
```

DKMS

Alternatively you could try to use the DKMS method for generating NTFS modules, which is available from the **freshrpms.net** repository. As with ntfs-3g, you install the package only once. Whenever your kernel is updated, an appropriate kernel module is generated and installed automatically. For access you would use the same **ntfsprogs** tools, as well as ntfspros-gnomevfs for browsing. You will also have to mount your partitions as you would for the Livna NTFS module.

Bluetooth

Fedora Linux now provides Bluetooth support for both serial connections and BlueZ protocol–supported devices. Bluetooth is a wireless connection method for locally connected devices such as keyboards, mice, printers, and even PDAs and Bluetooth-capable cell phones. You can think of it as a small local network dedicated to your peripheral devices, eliminating the needs for wires. Bluetooth devices can be directly connected through your serial ports or through specialized Bluetooth cards connected to USB ports or inserted in a PCI slot. BlueZ is the official Linux Bluetooth protocol and has been integrated into the Linux kernel since version 2.4.6. The BlueZ protocol was developed originally by Qualcomm and is now an open source project, located at **bluez.sourceforge.net**. It is included with Fedora in the bluez-utils and bluez-libs packages, among others. Check the BlueZ site for a complete list of supported hardware, including adapters, PCMCIA cards, and serial connectors.

Both GNOME and KDE provide Bluetooth configuration and management tools. GNOME provides the GNOME Bluetooth subsystem, which features a device manager, a plug-in for Nautilus to let the GNOME file browser access Bluetooth devices, and a file server. GNOME Bluetooth subsystem provides a GNOME interface for administering and accessing your Bluetooth devices (gnome-bluetooth-admin). Check the gnome-bluetooth RPM package. Fedora also includes the Bluetooth File Sharing applet for receiving Bluetooth files (Applications | System Tools | Bluetooth File Sharing).

For KDE, the KDE Bluetooth Utilities provides similar tools for accessing Bluetooth devices. To connect mobile phones to a system using Bluetooth, you can use the GNOME Phone Manager or KDE's K68 tool.

NOTE *The Affix Frontend Environment (AFE) is an alternative to Bluez that provides an easy-to-use method for accessing Bluetooth devices (**affix.sourceforge.net**).*

Bluetooth Configuration

Configuration information is located in the **/etc/bluetooth** directory, along with the **/etc/pcmcia** directory for notebooks. Use the **hciconfig** command to configure Bluetooth devices, **hcitool** to configure Bluetooth connections. Use **hciattach** to attach serial devices to a serial port such as **/dev/ttyS1**, and **rfcomm** to configure and attach RFCOMM devices. The HCI information is saved in **/etc/bluetooth/hcid.conf**, and RFCOMM configuration information is in **/etc/bluetooth/rfcomm.conf**. With **l2ping**, you can detect a Bluetooth device.

You can start and stop the Bluetooth service using the **service** command and the Bluetooth service script, **/etc/rc.d/init.d/bluetooth**.

```
service bluetooth start
```

This script will start up the Bluetooth daemon for HCI devices, **hcid**, and run any detection and configuration tools, including **sdpd** for the Service Discovery Protocol, and **rfcomm**. It will also activate any serial Bluetooth devices, using `hciattach` to detect them.

BlueZ includes several modules and drivers, including the core Bluetooth protocols for HCI (Host Controller Interface) devices, HCI USB, UART, PCMCIA, and virtual HCI drivers, along with modules to support protocols for L2CAP (Logical Link Control and Adaptation Protocol), serial port emulation (RFCOMM), Ethernet emulation (BNEP), SCO (Synchronous Connection-Oriented links for real-time voice), and the Service Discovery Protocol (SDP), which automatically detects services available for an application. In addition, extended services are supported such as PAN (personal area networking), and LAP (LAN access over PPP).

Personal Area Networks: PAN

PAN allows you to use Bluetooth to implement a personal area network supporting IP protocols, much like a wireless LAN for a small number of computers and devices. Bluetooth supports a much smaller bandwidth (1 to 2 megabits) than that used for a standard LAN, but it is sufficient for connecting and transferring data from handheld devices such as Palm Pilots. Several devices and computers can be configured as PAN users, connecting through a central Group Network (GN) computer. Alternatively, the PAN users could connect to a gateway system operating as a network access point connecting the Bluetooth personal network to a large LAN network. The PAN nodes run their own service daemon, **pand**. PAN user clients will also load the **bnep.o** module implementing a Bluetooth network device. The PAN server then needs to instruct its **pand** daemon to list the address for that device (alternatively, you could use SDP). On both the server and user systems, a virtual network device is created called **bnep0**, which can be configured using local IP protocol addresses. On Fedora, you can create a **ifcfg-bnep0** file and have it configured to use either static or dynamic (DHCP) addressing (**/etc/sysconfig/network-scripts/**). Check the HOWTO-PAN file on the BlueZ site for more details (currently, there is no Fedora Bluetooth networking tool).

Network Configuration

There are few changes in network configuration. With Fedora, network configuration is now managed primarily by the Network Manager, though the standard tools from previous releases are still used.

Network configuration differs depending on whether you are connected to a local area network (LAN) with an Ethernet card or are using a DSL or ISDN modem, a wireless connection, or a dial-up modem connection. You had the opportunity to enter your LAN network settings during the installation process. For modifying your LAN settings and for configuring other kinds of interfaces such as DSL, wireless, or ISDN connections, you can configure your network connection using system-config-network. Table 5-1 lists several different network configuration tools.

Network Information: Dynamic and Static

If you are on a network, you may need to obtain certain information to configure your interface. Most networks now support dynamic configuration using either the older Dynamic Host Configuration Protocol (DHCP) or the new IPv6 Protocol and its automatic address configuration. In this case, you need only check the DHCP entry in most network configuration tools. For IPv6, you would check the Enable IPv6 configuration entry in the system-config-network device configuration window (see Figure 5-3 later in this chapter). However, if your network does not support DHCP or IPv6 automatic addressing, you will have to provide detailed information about your connection. Such connections are known as static connections, whereas DCHP and IPv6 connections are dynamic. In a static connection, you need to manually enter your connection information such as your IP address and DNS servers, whereas in a dynamic connection this information is automatically provided to your system by a DHCP server or generated by IPv6 when you connect to the network. For DHCP, a DHCP client on each host will obtain the information from a DHCP server serving that network. IPv6 generates its addresses directly from the device and router information such as the device hardware MAC address.

In addition, if you are using a DSL dynamic, ISDN, or modem connection, you will also have to supply provider, login, and password information, whether your system is dynamic or static. You may also need to supply specialized information such as DSL or modem compression methods, dial-up number, or wireless channels to select.

Network Configuration Tool	Description
system-config-network	Fedora network configuration tool for all types of connections.
Network Manager	Automates wireless and standard network connection selection and notification.
KNetworkManager	KDE tool to automate wireless and standard network connection selection and notification.
system-config-services	Starts and stops servers, including network servers (smb for Samba, httpd for Web, bind for DNS, and nfs for NFS).
system-config-securitylevel	Sets up a network firewall.
system-config-bind	Configures a domain name server.
wvdial	PPP modem connection, enter on a command line.
pand	Implements the Bluetooth Personal Network.
system-config-samba	Configures Samba shares.
system-config-nfs	Configures NFS shares.
system-config-httpd	Configures an Apache Web server.
system-config-netboot	Configures diskless workstations and network installation.

TABLE 5-1 Fedora Network Configuration Tools

You can obtain most of your static network information from your network administrator or from your ISP (Internet service provider). You would need the following information:

- **The device name for your network interface**   For LAN and wireless connections, this is usually an Ethernet card with the name **eth0** or **eth1**. For a modem, DSL, or ISDN connection, this is a PPP device named **ppp0** (**ippp0** for ISDN). Virtual private network (VPN) connections are also supported with Crypto IP Encapsulation devices named **cipcb**.

- **Hostname**   Your computer will be identified by this name on the Internet. Do not use localhost; that name is reserved for special use by your system. The name of the host should be a simple word, which can include numbers, but not punctuation such as periods and backslashes. The hostname includes both the name of the host and its domain. For example, a hostname for a machine could be **turtle**, whose domain is **mytrek.com**, giving it a hostname of **turtle.mytrek.com**.

- **Domain name**   This is the name of your network.

- **The Internet Protocol (IP) address assigned to your machine**   This is needed only for static Internet connections. Dynamic connections use the DHCP protocol to automatically assign an IP address for you. Every host on the Internet is assigned an IP address. Traditionally, this address used an IPv4 format consisting of a set of four numbers, separated by periods, which uniquely identifies a single location on the

Internet, allowing information from other locations to reach that computer. Networks are now converting to the new IP protocol version 6, IPv6, which uses a new format with a much more complex numbering sequence.

- **Your network IP address**   Static connections only. This address is usually similar to the IP address, but with one or more zeros at the end.

- **The netmask**   Static connections only. This is usually 255.255.255.0 for most networks. If, however, you are part of a large network, check with your network administrator or ISP.

- **The broadcast address for your network, if available (optional)**   Static connections only. Usually, your broadcast address is the same as your IP address with the number 255 added at the end.

- **The IP address of your network's gateway computer**   Static connections only. This is the computer that connects your local network to a larger one like the Internet.

- **Name servers**   Static connections only. The IP address of the name servers your network uses. These enable the use of URLs.

- **NIS domain and IP address for an NIS server**   Necessary if your network uses an NIS server (optional).

- **Login and password information**   Needed for dynamic DSL, ISDN, and modem connections.

Network Manager

Fedora uses Network Manager to detect your network connections, both wired and wireless. Network Manager makes use of the automatic device detection capabilities of udev and HAL to configure your connections. Network Manager is not turned on by default. Use the Services tool under the System | Administration | Servers menu to start both the Network Manager daemon and the Network Manager dispatcher. Once started, Network Manager will display a Network icon to the right on the top panel. Left-click to see a list of all possible network connections, including all wireless connections available. Right-click to have the option of shutting off your connection (work offline), or to see information about the connection.

NOTE *The KDE version of Network Manager, knetworkmanager, also detects network connections. In addition it allows you to configure PPP dial up connections as well as manage wireless connections. To start kdenetworkmanager, select its entry in Applications | Network Tools.*

With multiple wireless access points for Internet connections, a system could have several different network connections to choose from, instead of a single-line connection like DSL or cable. This is particularly true for notebook computers that could access different wireless connections at different locations. Instead of manually configuring a new connection each time one is encountered, the Network Manager tool can automatically configure and select a connection to use.

By default, an Ethernet connection will be preferred if available. Direct lines that support Ethernet connections are normally considered faster than wireless ones. For wireless connections, you will need to choose the one you want.

Network Manager is designed to work in the background, providing status information for your connection and switching from one configured connection to another as needed. For initial configuration, it detects as much information as possible about the new connection. It operates as a GNOME Panel applet, monitoring your connection, and can work on any Linux distribution.

Network Manager operates as a daemon with the name NetworkManager. It is managed with the NetworkManager service script, which you can start and stop using the Services tool in System | Administration | Servers, or by using the service command in a terminal window.

```
service NetworkManager start
```

To have it start up automatically, you can use the Services tool in System | Administration | Servers, or use **chkconfig**.

```
chkconfig NetworkManager on
```

If no Ethernet connection is available, Network Manager will scan for wireless connection, check for Extended Service Set Identifiers (ESSIDs). If an ESSID identifies a previously used connection, then it is automatically selected. If several are found, then the most recently used one is chosen. If only a new connection is available, then Network Manager waits for the user to choose one. A connection is selected only if the user is logged in. If an Ethernet connection is later made, then Network Manager will switch to it from wireless.

Network Manager is user specific. When a user logs in, it selects the one preferred by that user. The first time a user runs NetworkManager, the notification applet will display a list of current possible connections. The user can then choose one.

Clicking the Network Manager icon in the panel will list available network connections. Password-protected access points will display a lock next to them. You will have to configure hidden access points yourself. Select Other Wireless Networks from the applets listing to open a dialog where you can enter the ESSID of the network, the key type, and the password.

Network Interface Connection (NIC cards) hardware is detected using HAL. Information provided by Network Manager is made available to other applications over D-Bus. Features currently under development include VPN and application notification. Network Manager uses the DHCPCD client to gather network information. For user interaction and notification, it uses NetworkManagerInfo.

Network Configuration with Fedora Network Tools

Fedora provides an easy-to-use network configuration and activation tool, which you can use to configure and control any kind of network connection, including Ethernet cards, modems, DSL and ISDN modems, and wireless connections (at this time, Bluetooth Personal Networks are not configured). All are supported with standard configuration panels like those for IP address settings, along with specialized panels used only for a particular kind of connection, such as Compression for modem connections or Wireless Settings for a wireless card. New connections are initially configured using system-config-network, which will detect and prompt for basic configuration information and then place you in the system-config-network tool to let you refine your configuration, making or changing entries as you require. For more illustrations on how to configure network connections using the Fedora's network tools, check the Official Red Hat Linux Customization Guide for Red Hat Linux.

system-config-network

You can access the system-config-network tool directly from the System Administration menu (Network entry). This tool opens a Network Configuration window that has five tabbed panels: Devices, Hardware, IPsec, Hosts, and DNS (see Figure 5-1). These panels are used for configuring the network settings for your entire system. The Devices panel lists all your network connections, and Hardware lists all the network components on your system, such as Ethernet cards and modems. The DNS panel is where you enter your own system's hostname and your network's name and server addresses. The Hosts panel lists static host IP addresses and their domain names, including those for your own system. The IPsec panel is used to create secure encrypted and authenticated network connections, using the Internet Protocol. It is commonly used to create virtual private networks (VPNs), creating secure connections between hosts and local networks across a larger network such as the Internet.

DNS Settings

The DNS panel has a box at the top, labeled Hostname (see Figure 5-2). Here, you enter your system's fully qualified domain name. There are boxes for entering the IP addresses for your system's primary, secondary, and tertiary DNS servers, needed for static configurations. You can then list your search domain. Both the search domain and the name server addresses are saved in the **/etc/resolv.conf** file.

Hosts

You use the Hosts panel to associate static IP addresses with certain hosts. The panel has a single pane with New, Edit, Copy, and Delete buttons. This panel lists entries that associate hostnames with static IP addresses. You can also add aliases (nicknames). The Hosts panel actually displays the contents of the **/etc/hosts** file and saves any entries you make to that

FIGURE 5-1
The system-config-network Network Configuration window.

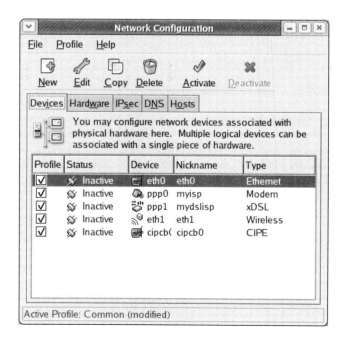

FIGURE 5-2
The system-config-
network DNS panel.

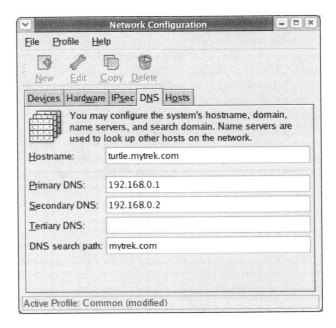

file. To add an entry, click New. A window opens with boxes for the hostname, IP address, and nicknames. When you finish, the entry is added to the Hosts list. To edit an entry, click Edit and a similar window opens, enabling you to change any of the fields. To delete an entry, select it and click Delete.

***

NOTE *If you are having trouble connecting with an Ethernet device using a static network connection, make sure that the Hosts panel lists your hostname and IP address, not just localhost. If your hostname is not there, add it.*

Device Configuration: Automatic or Static

The Devices panel will list the configured network devices on your system. An entry shows the device name and its type. Use the New, Edit, Copy, and Delete buttons to manage the device entries. To edit a device, you can just double-click its entry. For example, when you edit an Ethernet device, you open a tabbed panel for configuring it, enabling you to specify whether it is dynamic or static (see Figure 5-3). There is an entry for automatically activating it when the system starts. You can choose to use IPv6 for automatic addressing. For DHCP you can automatically obtain DNS information. For a static connection you will be able to enter an IP address, netmask, and gateway. A Hardware panel will let you choose the actual hardware device to use. The configuration panels will differ, depending on the device you edit. For example, a modem device will add panels for provider, compression, and modem options, whereas a DSL connection will have panels for provider, route (gateway), and hardware device. An Ethernet connection will have only general, route, and hardware device panels. Making entries here performs the same function as `ifconfig`.

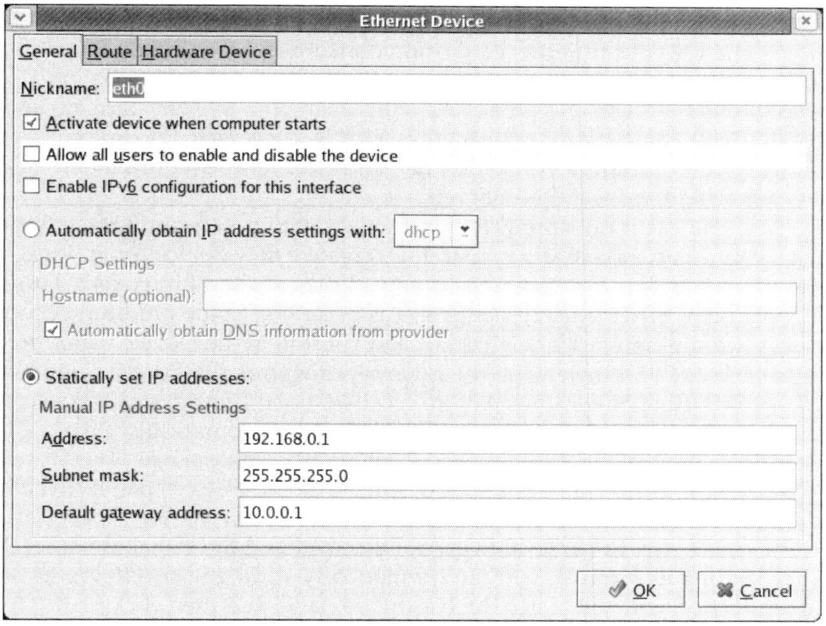

FIGURE 5-3
Device
configuration
in system-
config-network.

When you finish and are ready to save your configuration, select the Save entry from the File menu. If you want to abandon the changes you made, you can close without saving. You can run system-config-network at any time to make changes in your network configuration.

Profiles

The system-config-network tool also supports profiles. *Profiles* are commonly used for portable computers that may be moved from one environment to another. For example, at your office you could have an Office profile that uses an Ethernet card to connect to the office LAN. At home, you could use a Home profile that uses a modem to connect to the Internet. Profiles are integrated into the configuration process, with a Common profile functioning as the default configuration. The Common profile will be inherited by all other profiles, so make your basic configuration with that profile.

Profiles are accessed from the Profile menu. Select the profile you want, or select New to create a new profile. The name of the currently selected profile will be displayed at the bottom of the Network Configuration screen. The Delete entry in the Profile menu will delete the current profile. By default, the Common profile will be selected. To create a profile, click the New entry and enter the name of the profile. It will be added to the Profile menu. You can also remove or rename a profile. The new profile will inherit the setting of the common profile. Once you have selected a profile, you can then select devices or change DNS or host information. On the Devices panel of system-config-network, each device entry will have a check box. Selecting this check box selects the device for the current profiles. To select a device for a given profile, first be sure to select the profile you are configuring, and then click the device's check box. For other profiles, the device will be unchecked. Select the Save entry from the File menu when you are finished. The changes you make will be part of that profile, and not of any other.

Configuring Replaced or Unsupported Ethernet Cards

If you change your Ethernet card or if your card is not supported and you need to manually load a driver for it, you will have to manually configure the card. For supported cards, Kudzu will automatically detect the card when your system starts up and prompt you to configure it. For dynamic connections, simply select DHCP to automatically determine your network configuration. For static connections, enter the required network information, such as your IP address and DNS servers.

If the device is not supported or if you elected not to configure it with Kudzu, you can use system-network-config to manually create a new device for the card. For unsupported devices, make sure you have first obtained the required Linux kernel module for it and have installed that module using **modprobe** as described in the preceding chapter. Then, start up system-config-network and click the New button in the Device panel. Select Ethernet as the type of device and then select the Ethernet card from the list provided. On the Configure Network Setting panel, click Automatically Obtain IP Address, and select the method from the drop-down menu, usually DHCP. Also click Automatically Obtain DNS Information. For static connections, enter the required information, such as your IP and DNS server addresses. Your new device will now appear in the Devices panel. To activate it, select it and then click Activate.

If your network hardware was not detected and did not show up in the Hardware panel after loading its module, you can try manually adding it, specifying its parameters and identification yourself. Click the Hardware panel and then click New. This opens a Choose Hardware Type dialog with a pop-up menu for different types of network cards. Choosing one opens a Network Adapter Configuration screen, where you select the kind of adapter, its device name, and resources used, such as IRQ.

Configuring New Network Devices Manually

If the device was detected but not configured, you will need to configure it manually. In this case the Hardware device will appear in the Hardware panel, but not in the Devices panel. To configure a new network connection manually, first open system-config-network to the Devices panel and click New. The Add New Device Type window opens and displays a list of all possible network connections (see Figure 5-4). When you select an entry, panels will

FIGURE 5-4
Add New Device
Type window in
system-config-
network.

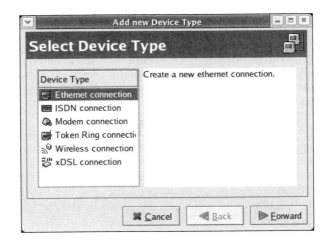

prompt you to enter basic information about a connection; this will include phone number, username, and password for modem, DSL, and ISDN connections, whereas Ethernet connections will prompt only for IP addresses. The types of connections and devices currently supported are Ethernet (**eth**), ISDN (**ippp**), Modem (**ppp**), xDSL (**ppp**), Token Ring (**tr**), and wireless connections (**eth**). After you complete your entries, your connection setting is configured and the new connection will be ready for use.

Modem Configuration

You can also use a modem with telephone lines to connect to a network. For a modem connection, your modem will be probed and detected. A window will then display entries for the serial device, baud rate, hardware control, and modem volume, which you can modify. You are then prompted to enter the phone number, provider, username, and password for your ISP account. The system-config-network tool is then started up, listing your modem device as a **ppp** connection (**ppp** stands for the *Point-to-Point Protocol [PPP]* protocol that transmits IP communications across telephone lines). You can then edit the **ppp** device to modify your settings and enter any other settings; for instance, you can enter IP addresses for static connections, specify compression methods, or list your DNS servers.

DSL and ISDN Configuration

To configure DSL, you will need to provide login and password information for DSL (Digital Subscriber Line) and ISDN. In other respects, DSL and ISDN connections operate much like a local area network (LAN), treating a host as an integrated part of a network. On Fedora, you can set up a DSL or ISDN connection. For DSL, a dialog box displays for entering your login name, your password, and the Ethernet interface your DSL modem is attached to. You will also need to enter the IP addresses for the DNS servers provided by your ISP. You can elect to have the connection automatically made up when your system starts up (depending upon your selected network profile).

Wireless Configuration

Wireless connections are now detected and configured by Network Manager. Should you need to, you can also configure a wireless connection manually as shown here. A wireless connection operates much like a standard Ethernet connection, requiring only an IP address and DNS server information to connect to the Internet. In addition, you will have to specify wireless connection information such as the network name and channel used. To add a new wireless connection, you start system-config-network, click New, and then select the wireless connection. If system-config-network is open, you can click Add on the Devices panel to start the configuration. You are prompted to select your wireless card.

On the Configure Wireless Connection panel, you then configure your wireless connection, selecting the mode, network name, channel, transmit, and key information.

- **Mode** Normally, you can leave this on Auto. For a simple network, one that does not require roaming, the mode is usually Ad Hoc. Managed networks allow roaming among different access points.

- **Network Name (SSID)** Can be left on Auto for a simple network. The Network Name is used to identify a cell as part of a virtual network.

- **Channel** Starting from 1, choose one with least interference.

- **Transmit Rate**   Usually set to Auto to adjust automatically to degraded transmissions. But you can set a specific rate such as 11M or 1M from the pop-up menu.
- **Key**   This is the encryption key for your wireless network. It must be the same for each cell on your network.

On the Configure Network Settings panel, you specify your IP address, whether it is obtained automatically with DHCP or one you enter yourself. For most company wireless networks, the IP address will be obtained automatically. Normally, the DNS servers are also provided. You can, if you wish, also specify a host name.

If you are setting up a local or home network, you will most likely use static IP addresses you select yourself from the private IP pool, beginning with 192.168, such as 192.168.0.1. The static subnet mask for a small local network is usually 255.255.255.0. The Gateway is the IP address for the computer on your network that connects to the Internet, or to a larger network.

You can later edit a wireless connection, making changes. Wireless configuration has the same General and Hardware Device panels as an Ethernet or DSL connection, but instead of a Route panel, it has a Wireless Settings panel, where you can set your mode and network name along with channel, transmit, and key information.

Your configuration setting will be saved in an Ethernet configuration file in the **/etc/sysconfig/network-scripts** directory. For example, if your wireless card is designated **eth1**, then its configuration information is saved in the **ifcfg-eth1** file. Here you will find the standard Ethernet connection parameters such as the IP address and gateway, as well as wireless parameters such as the channel used, the mode specified, and the encryption key. The standard setting can be modified using system-config-network on that device. You could also modify this file directly to enter additional parameters, like the frequency (FREQ) or sensitivity level (SENS). You can also specify any of the `iwconfig` parameters using the IWCONFIG option. Enter **IWCONFIG** followed by an assignment of an option with a value. For example, the following option sets the fragment threshold for packets:

```
IWCONFIG="frag 512"
```

Virtual Private Networks

A virtual private network lets you create your own private logical network on top of physical network connections, such as the Internet. Using encryption, your private network transmissions are kept secure from the physical network. Though a virtual private network (VPN) has no physical connections of its own and is not a actual network, the secure transmissions it sends have the effect of operating as if the network did exist as separate entity. VPNs make use of tunneling, in which secure transmissions are sent directly through interconnecting systems on a large network like the Internet without being intercepted or, at any point, translated. To implement a VPN, each node has to use the same encryption support software. On Fedora you can choose to use either the newer IPsec tools or the older third-party Crypto IP Encapsulation (CIPE) tool. To use IPsec to set up a VPN, you click the IPsec panel in system-config-network and create a new connection.

Interface Configuration Scripts: /etc/sysconfig/network-scripts

A network configuration implemented by system-config-network is saved in interface configuration scripts located in the **/etc/sysconfig/network-scripts** directory. You can edit these scripts directly, changing specific parameters, as discussed previously for wireless connection. Interface configuration files bear the names of the network interfaces currently configured, such as **ifcfg-eth0** for the first Ethernet device, or **ifcfg-ppp0** for the first PPP modem device. These files define shell variables that hold information on the interface, such as whether to start them at boot time. For example, the **ifcfg-eth0** file holds definitions for NETWORK, BROADCAST, and IPADDR, which are assigned the network, broadcast, and IP addresses that the device uses. You can also manually edit these interface configuration files, making changes as noted previously for the wireless connection. A sample **ifcfg-eth0** file is shown here using a DHCP address.

/etc/sysconfig/network-scripts/ifcfg-eth0

```
DEVICE=eth0
BOOTPROTO=DHCP
HWDADDR=00:00:00:EF:AF:00
ONBOOT=yes
TYPE=Ethernet
```

Command Line PPP Access: wvdial

If, for some reason, you have been unable to set up a modem connection on your X Window System, you may have to set it up from the command line interface instead of a desktop. For a dial-up PPP connection, you can use the wvdial dialer, which is an intelligent dialer that not only dials up an ISP service but also performs login operations, supplying your username and password. The wvdial program first loads its configuration from the **/etc/wvdial.conf** file. In here, you can place modem and account information, including the modem speed and serial device, as well as the ISP phone number, username, and password. The **wvdial.conf** file is organized into sections, beginning with a section label enclosed in brackets. A section holds variables for different parameters that are assigned values, such as **username = chris**. The default section holds default values inherited by other sections, so you needn't repeat them. Table 5-2 lists the wvdial variables.

You can use the wvdialconf utility to create a default **wvdial.conf** file for you automatically; wvdialconf will detect your modem and set default values for basic features. You can then edit the **wvdial.conf** file and modify the Phone, Username, and Password entries with your ISP dial-up information. Remove the preceding semicolon (;) to unquote the entry. Any line beginning with a semicolon is ignored as a comment.

```
$ wvdialconf
```

You can also create a named dialer, such as *myisp* in the following example. This is helpful if you have different ISPs you log in to. The following example shows the **/etc/wvdial.conf** file:

/etc/wvdial.conf [Modem0]
```
Modem = /dev/ttyS0
Baud = 57600
Init1 = ATZ
SetVolume = 0
Dial Command = ATDT
```

```
[Dialer Defaults]
Modem = /dev/ttyS0
Baud = 57600
Init1 = ATZ
SetVolume = 0
Dial Command = ATDT

[Dialer myisp]
Username = chris
Password = mypassword
Modem = /dev/ttyS0
Phone = 555-5555
Area Code = 555
Baud = 57600
Stupid mode = 0
```

Variable	Description
Inherits	Explicitly inherits from the specified section. By default, sections inherit from the [Dialer Defaults] section.
Modem	The device wvdial should use as your modem. The default is **/dev/modem**.
Baud	The speed at which wvdial communicates with your modem. The default is 57,600 baud.
Init1...Init9	Specifies the initialization strings to be used by your modem; wvdial can use up to 9. The default is "ATZ" for Init1.
Phone	The phone number you want wvdial to dial.
Area Code	Specifies the area code, if any.
Dial Prefix	Specifies any needed dialing prefix—for example, 70 to disable call waiting or 9 for an outside line.
Dial Command	Specifies the dial operation. The default is "ATDT."
Login	Specifies the username you use at your ISP.
Login Prompt	If your ISP has an unusual login prompt, you can specify it here.
Password	Specifies the password you use at your ISP.
Password Prompt	If your ISP has an unusual password prompt, you can specify it here.
Force Address	Specifies a static IP address to use (for ISPs that provide static IP addresses to users).
Stupid Mode	In Stupid Mode, wvdial does not attempt to interpret any prompts from the terminal server and starts pppd after the modem connects.
Auto Reconnect	If enabled, wvdial attempts to reestablish a connection automatically if you are randomly disconnected by the other side. This option is on by default.

TABLE 5-2 Variables for wvdial

To start wvdial, enter the command **wvdial**, which then reads the connection configuration information from the **/etc/wvdial.conf** file; wvdial dials the ISP and initiates the PPP connection, providing your username and password when requested.

```
$ wvdial
```

You can set up connection configurations for any number of connections in the **/etc/wvdial.conf** file. To select one, enter its label as an argument to the **wvdial** command, as shown here:

```
$ wvdial myisp
```

Manual Wireless Configurations

NetworkManager will automatically detect and configure your wireless connections, as will KNetworkmanager. However, you can manually configure your connections with wireless tools like ifwconfig. Wireless configuration makes use of the same set of Wireless Extensions. The Wireless Tools package is a set of network configuration and reporting tools for wireless devices installed on a Linux system. They are currently supported and developed as part of the Linux Wireless Extension and Wireless Tools Project, an open source project maintained by Hewlett-Packard.

Wireless Tools consists of the configuration and report tools listed here:

Tool	Description
iwconfig	Sets the wireless configuration options basic to most wireless devices.
iwlist	Displays current status information of a device.
iwspy	Sets the list of IP addresses in a wireless network and checks the quality of their connections.
iwpriv	Accesses configuration options specific to a particular device.

The wireless LAN device will have an Ethernet name just like an Ethernet card. The appropriate modules will automatically be loaded, listing their aliases in the **/etc/modprobe.conf** file.

iwconfig

The **iwconfig** command works much like **ifconfig**, configuring a network connection. It is the tool used by system-config-network to configure a wireless card. Alternatively, you can run **iwconfig** directly on a command line, specifying certain parameters. Added parameters let you set wireless-specific features such as the network name (nwid), the frequency or channel the card uses (freq or channel), and the bit rate for transmissions (rate). See the **iwconfig** Man page for a complete listing of accepted parameters. Some of the commonly used parameters are listed in Table 5-3.

For example, to set the channel used for the wireless device installed as the first Ethernet device, you would use the following, setting the channel to 2:

```
iwconfig eth0 channel 2
```

Parameter	Description
essid	A network name
freq	The frequency of the connection
channel	The channel used
nwid or domain	The network ID or domain
mode	The operating mode used for the device, such as Ad Hoc, Managed, or Auto. Ad Hoc = one cell with no access point; Managed = network with several access points and supports roaming; Master = the node is an access point; Repeater = node forwards packets to other nodes; Secondary = backup master or repeater; Monitor = only receives packets
sens	The sensitivity, the lowest signal level at which data can be received
key or enc	The encryption key used
frag	Cut packets into smaller fragments to increase better transmission
bit or rate	Speed at which bits are transmitted. The auto option automatically falls back to lower rates for noisy channels.
ap	Specify a specific access point
power	Power management for wakeup and sleep operations

TABLE 5-3   Commonly Used Parameters

You can also use **iwconfig** to display statistics for your wireless devices, just as **ifconfig** does. Enter the **iwconfig** command with no arguments or with the name of the device. Information such as the name, frequency, sensitivity, and bit rate is listed. Check also **/proc/net/wireless** for statistics.

Instead of using **iwconfig** directly to set parameters, you can specify them in the wireless device's configuration file. The wireless device configuration file will be located in the **/etc/sysconfig/network-scripts** directory and given a name like **ifcfg-eth1**, depending on the name of the device. This file will already contain many **iwconfig** settings. Any further setting can be set by assigning **iwconfig** values to the IWCONFIG parameter as shown here:

```
IWCONFIG="rate 11M"
```

iwpriv

The **iwpriv** command works in conjunction with **iwconfig**, allowing you set options specific to a particular kind of wireless device. With **iwpriv**, you can also turn on roaming or select the port to use. You use the *private-command* parameter to enter the device-specific options. The following example sets roaming on:

```
iwpriv eth0 roam on
```

iwspy

Your wireless device can check its connection to another wireless device it is receiving data from, reporting the quality, signal strength, and noise level of the transmissions. Your device can maintain a list of addresses for different devices it may receive data from. You use the `iwspy` tool to set or add the addresses that you want checked. You can list either IP addresses or the hardware versions. A + sign will add the address, instead of replacing the entire list:

```
iwspy eth0 +192.168.2.5
```

To display the quality, signal, and noise levels for your connections, you use the `iwspy` command with just the device name:

```
iwspy eth0
```

iwlist

To obtain more detailed information about your wireless device, such as all the frequencies or channels available, you use the `iwlist` tool. Using the device name with a particular parameter, you can obtain specific information about a device, including the frequency, access points, rate, power features, retry limits, and encryption keys used. You can use `iwlist` to obtain information about faulty connections. The following example will list the frequencies used on the **eth0** wireless device:

```
iwlist eth0 freq
```

linux-wlan

The linux-wlan project (**www.linux-wlan.org**) has developed a separate set of wireless drivers designed for Prism-based wireless cards supporting the new 802.11 wireless standard. The linux-wlan drivers are not currently included with Fedora; you will have to download the drivers. The original source code package is available from the linux-wlan site at **www.linux-wlan.org**. The current package is linux-wlan-ng. You will have to unpack and compile the drivers as noted for source code software packages in the preceding chapter.

The drivers will install WLAN devices, with device configurations placed in the **/etc/sysconfig/network-scripts** directory. For example, the configuration for the first WLAN device will be in the **ifcfg-wlan0** script. General wireless options are placed in the **/etc/wlan.conf** configuration file.

Setting Up Your Firewall: system-config-securitylevel

To set up your firewall , run system-config-securitylevel on your system (Security Level in the System Administration window and menu). In version 1.8, you can enable or disable your firewall with the Enable and Disable buttons (see Figure 5-5). You can run your firewall on a stand-alone system directly connected to the Internet, or on a gateway system that connects a local network to the Internet. Most small networks now use dedicated routers for Internet access which have their own firewalls. Version 1.7 of system-config-securitylevel also includes a panel for enabling and disabling SELinux (which can also be done with system-config-selinux.There is no separate panel for other firewall ports.

FIGURE **5-5**
The system-config-
securitylevel tool,
version 1.8.

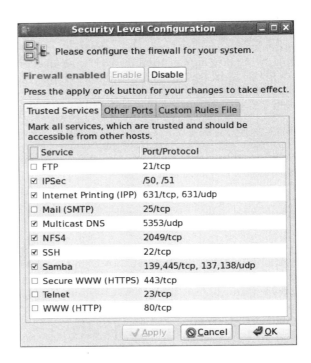

The Custom Rules panel lets you load a IP-tables file that can hold customized firewall rules. Instead of having to choose whether to use system-config-securitylevel or to create a entire set of rules in an IP-tables file, you can use system-config-securitylevel to automatically configure the standard firewall rules and then set up an IP-tables file that holds only customized rules for your system. These will be added to the standard set implemented by system-config-securitylevel. See Chapter 20 for a detailed discussion of IP-tables firewall rules.

Often a Linux system will be used as a router if it is also used to run servers for wider network. If you are creating a strong firewall but still want to run a service such as a Web server, allow users to perform FTP file transfers on the Internet, permit Samba desktop browsing, or allow remote encrypted connections such as SSH, you will have to specify them in the Trusted Services panel. Samba desktop browsing lets you access your Samba shares, like remote Windows file systems, from your GNOME or KDE desktops.

The Custom Ports panel lets you specify ports that you may want opened for certain services, like BitTorrent. Click the Add button to open a dialog where you can enter the port number along with the protocol to control (tcp or udp).

InfiniBand Support

Fedora, since the 2.6.10 kernel, includes InfiniBand support. This is a new I/O architecture that is used to replace the older bus architectures used in current systems. Often InfiniBand is used as a replacement for local network connections. It is currently implemented in supercomputer and network server clusters. You can find more about InfiniBand at the

Linux InfiniBand Project at **infiniband.sourceforge.net**. Support for InfiniBand is being carried out as an open source project by OpenIB Alliance, **www.openib.org**.

Systems today use the PCI bus or its enhanced versions, PCI X or PCI Express. This PCI I/O architecture uses a shared bus that can only reach about a half gigabit of throughput. Clustered servers are already reaching the limits of this I/O method. One alternative technology is the InfiniBand I/O architecture. InfiniBand uses serial channels instead of a shared bus. Speeds start at 2.6 gigabits per second and go as high as 30 gigabits per second. Instead of having a bus processing transactions controlled by a single host, InfiniBand uses peer-to-peer channel architecture where multiple connections can be managed using different channels. This fabric switch architecture enables InfiniBand to switch among different nodes. PCI Express is limited to use as a local bus, connecting a CPU with peripherals. InfiniBand, by contrast, supports networking connections, letting you implement essentially a local high-speed intranet as well as shared high-speed connections to stand-alone storage devices like hard drives. Using an InfiniBand cable instead of an Ethernet cable, you can connect your hosts and shared devices (within up to 50 feet). The IPoIB (IP over InfiniBand) protocol lets you implement IP networking over InfiniBand connections, and the RDMA protocol can be used for remote storage devices. The higher speed of an InfiniBand connection is particularly important for servers needing high-bandwidth capability. In addition, the Sockets Direct Protocol can set up high-speed InfiniBand connections for streams, and the SCSI RDMA Protocol (SRP) manages connections to hard drives.

Machines with PCI Express can handle the greater bandwidth provided by a InfiniBand connection. A Host Channel Adapter (HCA) card placed in a PCI slot has InfiniBand connectors and will interface InfiniBand transmissions with the PCI Express bus. Drivers for several HCAs are already incorporated in the kernel, as are protocol drivers.

TIP *Network configuration and Internet access is usually handled by a dedicated network router. You could, though, set up your Linux system to operate as a router, with its own firewall protecting an entire network (see Chapter 20). You could also set up a very simple configuration with a proxy server to provide Web access only.*

Configuring a Local Area Network

For most networks, dedicated routers are used to set up networks, providing domain name services (DNS), firewalls, and network addressing. You can set up a Linux system to provide these operations, but normally that would only be needed if you require a uniquely customized network configuration or want direct control over the firewall, DNS, and network addressing software, instead of relying on the router software. For some networks, it may be appropriate to use Linux just to provide certain network services like a DNS server that you control or a complex firewall, letting the router handle just network addressing. In such a case, a Linux system would run a DNS server and an IP tables firewall configured to manage a network. If your network is tied into subnetworks, you may need to configure proxy services.

NOTE *You can use system-config-bind to configure a domain name server (System | Administration | Server Settings | Domain Name System).*

A Linux system could also run mail and print servers for a local network, as well as Web and FTP services. Such services are designed to work with any DNS or firewall service, not just the Linux versions. You could set up Web and printer servers with Linux, leaving your dedicated router to handle firewall and DNS services.

The following table lists the network services commonly used in a local network:

Service Name	Service Program
Domain Name Service (DNS) (Chapter 36)	named
Network Connections (Chapter 37)	network
Firewall (Chapter 20)	iptables
Squid Proxy service (Chapter 24)	squid
Samba Windows network client (Chapter 39)	smb
Apache Web server (Chapter 23)	httpd
FTP server (Chapter 22)	vsftpd
Sendmail mail service (Chapter 25)	sendmail
Postfix mail service (Chapter 25)	postfix

These can all be started or stopped using system-config-services (System | Administration | Server Settings | Services), or the **service** command with the **start**, **stop**, and **restart** arguments. To restart the DNS service, you could use the following:

```
service named restart
```

PART

II

Environments

CHAPTER 6
GNOME

CHAPTER 7
The K Desktop Environment:
KDE

CHAPTER 8
The Shell

CHAPTER 9
Shell Configuration

CHAPTER 10
Managing Linux Files and
Directories: Directories,
Archives, and Compression

GNOME

The GNU Network Object Model Environment, also known as *GNOME*, is a powerful and easy-to-use environment consisting primarily of a panel, a desktop, and a set of GUI tools with which program interfaces can be constructed. GNOME is designed to provide a flexible platform for the development of powerful applications. Currently, GNOME is supported by several distributions and is the primary interface for Fedora. GNOME is free and released under the GNU Public License. You can download the source code, as well as documentation and other GNOME software, directly from the GNOME Web site at **www .gnome.org**. Several companies have joined together to form the GNOME Foundation, an organization dedicated to coordinating the development of GNOME and GNOME software applications. These include such companies as Sun, IBM, and Hewlett-Packard as well as Linux distributors such as Mandrake, Fedora, and TurboLinux. Modeled on the Apache Software Foundation, which developed the Apache Web server, the GNOME Foundation will provide direction to GNOME development, as well as organization, financial, and legal support.

The core components of the GNOME desktop consist of a panel for starting programs and desktop functionality. Other components normally found in a desktop, such as a file manager, a Web browser, and a window manager, are provided by GNOME-compliant applications. GNOME provides libraries of GNOME GUI tools that developers can use to create GNOME applications. Programs that use buttons, menus, and windows that adhere to a GNOME standard can be said to be GNOME-compliant. The official file manager for the GNOME desktop is Nautilus. The GNOME desktop does not have its own window manager as KDE does. Instead, it uses any GNOME-compliant window manager. The Metacity window manager is the one bundled with the GNOME distribution.

Support for component model interfaces is integrated into GNOME, allowing software components to interconnect regardless of the computer language in which they are implemented or the kind of machine on which they are running. The standard used in GNOME for such interfaces is the Common Object Request Broker Architecture (CORBA), developed by the Object Model Group for use on Unix systems. GNOME uses the ORBit implementation of CORBA. With such a framework, GNOME applications and clients can directly communicate with each other, enabling you to use components of one application in another. With GNOME 2.0, GNOME officially adopted GConf and its libraries as the underlying method for configuring GNOME and its applications. GConf can configure independently coordinating programs such as those that make up the Nautilus file manager.

Web Sites	Descriptions
www.gnome.org	Official GNOME Web site
developer.gnome.org	GNOME developer Web site
art.gnome.org	Desktop themes and background art
http://www.gnomefiles.org	GNOME software applications, applets, and tools
www.gnome.org/gnome-office	GNOME office applications

TABLE 6-1   GNOME Resources

You can find out more about GNOME at its Web site, **www.gnome.org**. The Web site provides online documentation, such as the GNOME User's Guide and FAQs, and also maintains extensive mailing lists for GNOME projects to which you can subscribe. The **www.gnomefiles.org** site provides a detailed software listing of current GNOME applications and projects. If you want to develop GNOME programs, check the GNOME developer's Web site at **developer.gnome.org.** The site provides tutorials, programming guides, and development tools. Here you can find the complete API reference manual online, as well as extensive support tools such as tutorials and integrated development environments (IDEs). The site also includes detailed online documentation for the GTK+ library, GNOME widgets, and the GNOME desktop. Table 6-1 offers a listing of useful GNOME sites.

Fedora Desktop Look and Feel

Fedora features a desktop look and feel with the Fedora logo, as well as default Fedora logo screen background. The logo depicts an F encased in a blue circle. On the main panel you will see the blue Fedora logo as the icon for the Applications menu, instead of Red Hat's hat. The logos even have their own package, fedora-logos. There are several Fedora background images to choose from, including the Fedora blue F logo encased in a bubble and surrounded by other rising bubbles, the Fedora double helix, and the Fedora hot air balloon image.

The default theme is clearlooks, but the latest clearlooks has a very comforting feel to it. The desktop images are based on Cairo with more intuitive and user-friendly icons. Buttons and windows are easier to use and appear more pleasing to the eye. The Cairo images theme is compliant with the TANGO style guidelines. TANGO is an open source standard for desktop images, providing the same image style across all open source desktops. See **tango.freedesktop.org** for more information. In addition, GNOME also adheres to the freedesktop.org standard naming specifications. KDE, GNOME, and XFce all adhere to the same naming specifications, using the same standard names for icons on their desktops.

The GNOME Control Center provides an intuitive organization and access for your desktop configuration. This is integrated into Fedora as submenus in the System | Preferences menu. Preferences are organized into Personal, Look and Feel, Internet and Network, Hardware, and System categories. The GNOME Control Center is also implemented as a GUI interface that will display a dialog with icons on the left for the different categories like Personal and Hardware, and a continuous display of preferences on the right. Selecting a category moves to and highlights the appropriate preferences. You can invoke the control center GUI by entering **gnome-control-center** in a terminal window.

TIP *There are three menus with the name System in it: the main System menu with its own button listed next to Applications and Places, the System Tools submenu in the Applications main menu (used for specialized system tools like the Disk Usage Analyser, the Terminal window, and the PUP Package Updater), and finally the System submenu in the Preferences main menu used for GNOME configuration tools, like the GNOME Power Management tool.*

GNOME 2.x Features

Check **www.gnome.org** for a detailed description of GNOME features and enhancements, with screen shots and references. GNOME releases new revisions on a frequent schedule. Several versions since the 2.0 release have added many new capabilities. Many applications and applets like Deskbar and Gconf are not installed by default.

GNOME features include interface changes to Evolution, Gnome meeting, and Eye of GNOME as well as efficiencies in load time and memory use, making for a faster response time. GEdit has been reworked to adhere to the Multiple Documentation Interface specs. New tools like F-Spot image and camera managers and the Beagle search tool are emphasized (both are .NET Mono–supported packages). The new menu editor, Alacarte, lets you customize your menus easily. The disk usage analyzer, Baobab, lets you quickly see how much disk space is used. The GNOME video player, Totem, supports Web access, featuring Windows media player support.

For GPG encryption, signing, and decryption of files and text, GNOME provides the Seahorse Encryption Key Manager, accessible from the System menu as the Encryption Preferences entry. With Seahorse you can manage your encryption keys stored in the GNOME Keyring, as well as OpenPGP SSH keys and passphrases. You can import existing keys, search for remote keys, and create your own keys. Default key servers are listed on the Key Servers panel, to which you can add new ones. Plug-ins are provided for Gedit editor to encrypt text files, the Epiphany Web browser for text phrases, and Nautilus to perform encryption from the context menu. A panel applet lets you encrypt, sign, and decrypt clipboard content.

GNOME 2.x Desktop Features

Some of GNOME desktop features added since version 2.0 are described here:

- Seahorse integrates GPG encryption, decryption, and signing of files and text (System | Encryption Preferences).
- GNOME uses a TANGO-compliant icon images theme, CAIRO.
- The GNOME Control Center for basic preferences is integrated into Fedora as submenus in the System | Preferences menu.
- An easy-to-use file permissions dialog allows changing permissions for all files in a folder, as well as setting SELinux attributes.
- Mouse and logging configuration are now handled by GNOME administrative tools instead of by the Fedora system tools.
- Support is included for 3-D effects for windows (wobble, shrink, and explode).

- The Places menu has a CD/DVD creator entry for using Nautilus to burn data CD/DVD-ROMs.
- On Fedora home directories now have data specific folders set up including Pictures, Documents, Videos, and Music (Common Use Directory Structure).
- You will find the terminal window tool in Applications | System Tools.
- RPIntegrated power management is controlled with Power Management Preferences (System | Preferences | System).
- Menu editing is simplified with Alacarte, via the Menus And Toolbars entry in the System | Preferences | Look and Feel menu.
- The Disk Usage Analyzer (Applications | System Tools | Disk Usage Analyzer) details disk and partition usage, as well as usage by directory, with totals for your entire file systems with space availability.
- Tomboy offers integrated note taking using links. Create your own links to different notes.
- Baobab, the disk usage analyzer, lets you see instantly how much disk space is used and by what.
- Assistive technology provider interface support includes the Orca screen reader, integrating speech synthesis, magnification, and Braille support.
- Desktop search is supported using Deskbar.
- Font support tools let you more easily configure your fonts, enabling you to select and display fonts as they will appear for different components such as applications or windows.
- For archive management, File Roller provides integrated archive content display, archive creation, and extraction. It is the simplest way to view either tar or RPM package contents, letting you extract individual files and view text files directly.
- The Epiphany Web browser, the Evolution mail client, and the Totem video player are integrated parts of the GNOME desktop.
- Ekiga provides voice/video over IP.
- The GNOME panel has a single panel type with different possible features, instead of separate panel types. Panel applets now include a network monitor and keyboard indicator. Panel applet selection has been simplified. The clock applet now connects to the Evolution calendar, the network monitor supports wireless connections, and the battery monitor for laptops has been improved. Addition panel applets include a trash can, mounting for removable media like CD/DVD discs and card readers, a sound mixer, and a CPU frequency monitor for notebooks.
- To support those with disabilities, GNOME provides the Gnopernicus magnifier and reader, and the GOK dynamic onscreen keyboard.
- With the GNOME Volume Manager, a computer window is now included listing your file system devices, including CD-ROMs as well as network file system devices. The network device icon opens to a network window, where you can access your remote systems, such as Samba Windows shares.

- A lockdown feature lets administrators restrict remote systems, preventing actions like changing applets, entering certain kinds of URLs, editing bookmarks or toolbars, and accessing the command line.

- GNOME also supports automatic mounting of removable devices. Connecting a removable DVD or CD device, as well as a Memory Stick, will automatically display the device icon in a file manager window. This feature relies on the hardware abstraction layer (HAL) developed by **freedesktop.org**.

- Like KDE, GNOME now includes a range of system administration tools for basic administrative tasks such as setting the time, managing users, and configuring network connections. (See Chapters 4 and 5 for descriptions of these tools.) In addition, GNOME also provides a network monitor tool, integrating tasks like ping, netstat, and traceroute. GNOME also includes a virtual networking computing client (VNC) to allow administrators to remotely control a user's desktop.

GNOME 2.x File Manager Features

Originally developed by Eazel, Nautilus is now the official file manager for the GNOME desktop. You can find out more about Nautilus from the Nautilus user's manual that is part of the GNOME User's Guide at **www.gnome.org**. The Nautilus file manager, as part of GNOME, also has several new features added.

- It is now more integrated into other applications such as File Roller for archives, the image viewer for pictures, and the GNOME media player for audio and video. You can now preview sound and video files within a Nautilus window.

- Nautilus can also now burn files and ISO images to DVD/CD writers.

- Context-sensitive menus let you perform appropriate actions, such as extracting archive files. An Open With option lets you choose from a selection of appropriate applications. Multiple applications can now be registered for use with a file.

- With a spatial interface, only one window is used for each folder, remembering how that folder was displayed. A folder is always opened in a new window, instead of using the same file manager window for different folders. Using the SHIFT key when opening a folder lets you use the same window. The lower corner of a folder window will display a pop-up menu displaying all the parent directories for that folder, allowing you to move to any of them quickly.

- The file manager can display network shares on local networks, using DNS-based service discovery (Rendezvous in Apple). The file manager also supports access to password-protected FTP sites.

GTK+

GTK+ is the widget set used for GNOME applications. Its look and feel was originally derived from Motif. The widget set is designed from the ground up for power and flexibility. For example, buttons can have labels, images, or any combination thereof. Objects can be dynamically queried and modified at runtime. It also includes a theme engine that enables users to change the look and feel of applications using these widgets. At the same time, the GTK+ widget set remains small and efficient.

The GTK+ widget set is entirely free under the Lesser General Public License (LGPL). The LGPL enables developers to use the widget set with proprietary software, as well as free software (the GPL would restrict it to just free software). The widget set also features an extensive set of programming language bindings, including C++, Perl, Python, Pascal, Objective C, Guile, and Ada. Internalization is fully supported, permitting GTK+-based applications to be used with other character sets, such as those in Asian languages. The drag-and-drop functionality supports drag-and-drop operations with other widget sets that support these protocols, such as Qt.

The GNOME Interface

The GNOME interface consists of the panel and a desktop, as shown in Figure 6-1. The panel appears as a long bar across the bottom of the screen. It holds menus, programs, and applets. (An *applet* is a small program designed to be run within the panel.) On the top panel is a menu labeled Applications. The menu operates like the Start menu, listing entries for applications you can run on your desktop. You can display panels horizontally or vertically, and have them automatically hide to show you a full screen. The Applications menu is reserved for applications. Other tasks like opening a home directory window or logging out are located in the Places menu. The System menu holds the Preferences menu for configuring your GNOME interface, as well as the Administration menu for accessing the Fedora administrative tools.

FIGURE 6-1 GNOME with Preferences menu

NOTE *The current Fedora GNOME interface uses two panels, one on top for menus and notification tasks like your clock, and one on the bottom for interactive features for workspaces and docking applications. Three main menus are now used instead of one: an Applications menu, a Places menu, and the System. The System menu is used to log out of your session.*

The remainder of the screen is the desktop. Here, you can place directories, files, or programs. You can create them on the desktop directly or drag them from a file manager window. A click-and-drag operation will move a file from one window to another or to the desktop. A click and drag with the CTRL key held down will copy a file. A click-and-drag operation with the middle mouse button (two buttons at once on a two-button mouse) enables you to create links on the desktop to installed programs. Initially, the desktop holds only an icon for your home directory. Clicking it opens a file manager window to that directory. A right-click anywhere on the desktop displays a desktop menu with which you can open new windows and create new folders.

TIP *You can display your GNOME desktop using different themes that change the appearance of desktop objects such as windows, buttons, and scroll bars. GNOME functionality is not affected in any way. You can choose from a variety of themes. Many are posted on the Internet at **art .gnome.org**. Technically referred to as GTK themes, these allow the GTK widget set to change its look and feel. To select a theme, select Theme in the Preferences | Look and Feel menu. The default GNOME theme is Clearlooks.*

GNOME Components

From a user's point of view, you can think of the GNOME interface as having four components: the desktop, the panel, the main menus, and the file manager.

In its standard default configuration, the GNOME desktop displays a Folder icon for your home directory in the upper-left corner, along with a trash can to delete items. In addition, the desktop also displays a Computer window for accessing the entire file system, CD/DVD drives, and network shares. Double-clicking the home directory icon will open the file manager, displaying files in your home directory. On Red Hat and Fedora Linux, you have two panels displayed, one used for menus, application icons, and running applets at the top of the screen, and one at the bottom of the screen used primarily for managing your windows and desktop spaces.

The top bar has several menus and application icons: the Applications menu, the Places menu, the System menu, the Mozilla Firefox Web browser (globe with fox), and the Evolution mail tool (envelope). To the right are the time and date icons. An update button will appear if updates are available. You can use the update icon to automatically update your system. The bottom bar holds icons for minimized windows as well as running applets. These include a Workspace Switcher (squares) placed to the right. An icon to the left lets you minimize all your open windows. When you open a window, a corresponding button for it will be displayed in the lower panel, which you can use to minimize and restore the window.

To start a program, you can select its entry in the Applications menu. You can also click its application icon in the panel (if there is one) or drag a data file to its icon.

Quitting GNOME

To quit GNOME, you select the Logout or Shutdown entries in the System menu. The Logout entry quits GNOME, returning you to the login window (or command line shell, still logged in to your Linux account, if you started GNOME with `startx`). The Shut Down entry displays a dialog which allows you to hibernate, shutdown, cancel, or restart your system. A Restart entry shuts down and reboots your system. You must separately quit a window manager that is not GNOME-compliant after logging out of GNOME.

GNOME Help

The GNOME Help browser (Yelp) provides a browser-like interface for displaying the GNOME user's manual, Man pages, and info documents. You can select it from the System menu. It features a toolbar that enables you to move through the list of previously viewed documents. You can even bookmark specific items. A browser interface enables you to use links to connect to different documents. On the main page, expandable links for several GNOME desktop topics are displayed on the left side, with entries for the GNOME User Manual, Administration Guide, and Fedora release notes on the right side. At the bottom of the left side listing are links for the Man and Info pages. You can use these links to display Man and Info pages easily. Use the Search box to quickly locate help documents. YSpecial URL-like protocols are supported for the different types of documents: **ghelp**, for GNOME help; **man**, for Man pages; and **info**, for the info documents, like **man:fstab** to display the Man page for the **fstab** file.

The GNOME Help Browser provides a detailed manual on every aspect of your GNOME interface. The left hand links display GNOME categories for different application categories like the System tools, Gnome Applets. The GNOME Applets entry will provide detailed descriptions of all available GNOME applets. Applications categories like Internet, Programming, System Tools, and Sound and Video will provide help documents for applications developed as part of the GNOME project, like the Evolution mail client, the Totem movie player, the Disk Usage Analyzer, and the GNOME System Monitor. Click on the Desktop entry at the top of the left hand list, to display links for GNOME User and Administration manuals.

The GNOME Desktop

The GNOME desktop provides you with all the capabilities of GUI-based operating systems (see Figure 6-1). You can drag files, applications, and directories to the desktop, and then back to GNOME-compliant applications. If the desktop stops functioning, you can restart it by starting the GNOME file manager (Nautilus). The desktop is actually a back-end process in the GNOME file manager. But you needn't have the file manager open to use the desktop.

NOTE   *As an alternative to using the desktop, you can drag any program, file, or directory to the panel and use the panel instead.*

Drag and Drop Files to the Desktop

Any icon for an item that you drag from a file manager window to the desktop also appears on the desktop. However, the default drag-and-drop operation is a **move** operation. If you select a file in your file manager window and drag it to the desktop, you are actually moving the file from its current directory to the GNOME desktop directory, which is located in your home directory and holds all items on the desktop. For GNOME, the desktop directory is **DESKTOP**. In the case of dragging directory folders to the desktop, the entire directory and its subdirectories will be moved to the GNOME desktop directory. To remove an icon from the desktop, you move it to the trash.

You can also copy a file to your desktop by pressing the CTRL key and then clicking and dragging it from a file manager window to your desktop. You will see the small arrow in the upper-right corner of the copied icon change to a + symbol, indicating that you are creating a copy, instead of moving the original.

CAUTION   *Be careful when removing icons from the desktop. If you have moved the file to the desktop, then its original is residing in the DESKTOP folder, and when you remove it you are erasing the original. If you have copied or linked the original, then you are simply deleting the link or the copy. When you drag applications from the menu or panel to the desktop, you are just creating a copy of the application launcher button in the DESKTOP directory. These you can safely remove.*

You can also create a link on the desktop to any file. This is useful if you want to keep a single version in a specified directory and just be able to access it from the desktop. You could also use links for customized programs that you may not want on the menu or panel. There are two ways to create a link. While holding down the CTRL and SHIFT keys, CTRL-SHIFT, drag the file to where you want the link created. A copy of the icon then appears with a small arrow in the right corner indicating it is a link. You can click this link to start the program, open the file, or open the directory, depending on what kind of file you linked to. Alternatively, first click and drag the file out of the window, and after moving the file but before lifting up the mouse button, press the ALT key. This will display a pop-up menu with selections for Cut, Copy, and Link. Select the Link option to create a link.

GNOME's drag-and-drop file operation works on virtual desktops provided by the GNOME Workspace Switcher. The GNOME Workspace Switcher on the bottom panel creates icons for each virtual desktop in the panel, along with task buttons for any applications open on them.

NOTE   *Although the GNOME desktop supports drag-and-drop operations, these normally work only for applications that are GNOME-compliant. You can drag any items from a GNOME-compliant application to your desktop, and vice versa.*

Applications on the Desktop

In most cases, you only want to create on the desktop another way to access a file without moving it from its original directory. You can do this either by using a GNOME application launcher button or by creating a link to the original program. Application launcher buttons are the GNOME components used in menus and panels to display and access applications. The Open Office buttons on the top panel are application launcher buttons. To place an icon for the application on your desktop, you can simply drag the application button from the panel or from a menu. For example, to place an icon for the Firefox Web browser on your desktop, just drag the Web browser icon on the top panel to anywhere on your desktop space.

For applications that are not on the panel or in the menu, you can either create an application launcher button for it or create a direct link, as described in the preceding section.

To create an application launcher, first right-click the desktop background to display the desktop menu. Then select the Create Launcher entry.

GNOME Desktop Menu

You can also right-click anywhere on the empty desktop to display the GNOME desktop menu. This will list entries for common tasks, such as creating an application launcher, creating a new folder, or organizing the icon display. Keep in mind that the New Folder entry creates a new directory on your desktop, specifically in your GNOME desktop directory (**DESKTOP**), not your home directory. The entries for this menu are listed in Table 6-2.

Window Manager

GNOME works with any window manager. However, desktop functionality, such as drag-and-drop capabilities and the GNOME workspace switcher (discussed later), works only with window managers that are GNOME-compliant. The current release of GNOME uses the Metacity window manager. It is completely GNOME-compliant and is designed to integrate with the GNOME desktop without any duplication of functionality. Other window managers such as Enlightenment, IceWM, and Window Maker can also be used. Check a window manager's documentation to see if it is GNOME-compliant.

For 3D support you can use compositing window managers like Compiz or Beryl. Windows are displayed using window decorators, allowing windows to wobble, bend, and move in unusual ways. They employ features similar to current Mac and Vista desktops. A compositing window manager relies on a graphics card OpenGL 3D acceleration support. Be sure your graphics card is supported. C Compiz is installed as the default 3D support, and can be activated by enabling desktop effects (System | Preferences | Look and Feel | Desktop Effects). See **compiz.org** for more information. Beryl was developed from Compiz and features its own window decorators. It is also available on the Fedora repository. You can find more about Beryl at **beryl-project.org**. Both projects plan to merge providing a single compositing window manager for Linux.

Menu Item	Description
Create Launcher	Creates a new desktop icon for an application.
Create Folder	Creates a new directory on your desktop, within your DESKTOP directory.
Create Document	Creates files using installed templates
Clean Up by Name	Arranges your desktop icons.
Keep Aligned	Aligns your desktop icons.
Cut, Copy, Paste	Cuts, copies, or pastes files, letting you move or copy files between folders.
Change Desktop Background	Opens a Background Preferences dialog to let you select a new background for your desktop.

TABLE 6-2   The GNOME Desktop Menu

Metacity employs much the same window operations as used on other window managers. You can resize a window by clicking any of its sides or corners and dragging. You can move the window with a click-and-drag operation on its title bar. You can also right-click and drag any border to move the window, as well as ALT-click anywhere on the window. The upper-right corner shows the Maximize, Minimize, and Close buttons. Minimize creates a button for the window in the panel that you can click to restore it. You can right-click the title bar of a window to display a window menu with entries for window operations. These include workspace entries to move the window to another workspace (virtual desktop) or to all workspaces, which displays the window no matter to what workspace you move.

The GNOME Volume Manager

Managing DVD/CD-ROMs, card readers, floppy disks, digital cameras, and other removable media is the task of the GNOME Volume Manager. This is a lower-level utility that remains transparent to the user, though how you treat removable media can be configured with the Drives and Removable Media preferences tool. The GNOME Volume Manager allows you not only to access removable media, but to access all your mounted file systems, remote and local, including any Windows shared directories accessible from Samba. You can browse all your file systems directly from GNOME, which implements this capability with the gnome virtual file system (gnome-vfs) mapping to your drives, storage devices, and removable media. The GNOME Volume Manager uses HAL and udev to access removable media directly, and Samba to provide Windows networking support. Media are mounted by **gnome-mount**, a wrapper for accessing Hal and udev, which perform the mount (/etc/fstab is no longer used).

You can access your file systems and removable media using the Computer icon on the desktop. This opens a top-level window showing icons for all removable media (mounted CD-ROMs, floppies, etc.), your local file system, and your network shared resources (see Figure 6-2). Double-click any icon to open a file manager window displaying its contents. The file system icon will open a window showing the root-level directory, the top directory for your file system. Access will be restricted for system directories, unless you log in as the root user. The network icon will open a window listing your connected network hosts. Opening these will display the shares, such as shared directories, that you can have access to. Drag-and-drop operations are supported for all shared directories, letting you copy files and folders between a shared directory on another host with a directory on your system. To browse Windows systems on GNOME using Samba, you first have to configure your

FIGURE 6-2
GNOME Computer window (GNOME Volume Manager)

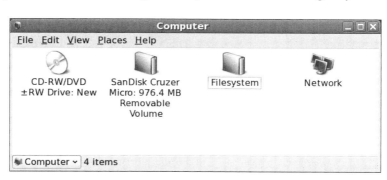

firewall to accept Samba connections. Using system-config-sercuritylevel (Firewall and SELinux on the System | Administration menu) check the Samba entry, if you have not already done so. You also should set access through SELinux. On the SELinux panel, open Modify SELinux Policy, expand the Samba entry and click the two Allow entries.

Removable media will also appear automatically as icons directly on your desktop. A DVD/CD-ROM is automatically mounted when you insert it into your DVD/CD-ROM drive, displaying an icon for it with its label. The same kind of access is also provided for card readers, digital cameras, and USB drives. Be sure to unmount the USB drives before removing them so that data will be written.

You can then access the disk in the DVD/CD-ROM drive either by double-clicking it or by right-clicking and selecting the Open entry. A file manager window opens to display the contents of the CD-ROM disk. To eject a CD-ROM, you can right-click its icon and select Eject from the pop-up menu. The same procedure works for floppy disks, using the Floppy Disk icon. Be sure you don't remove a mounted floppy disk until you have first unmounted it, selecting the Eject entry in the pop-up menu.

Burning a data DVD/CD is a simple matter of placing a blank DVD in your drive. Nautilus automatically recognizes it as a blank disk and allows you to write to it. All Read/Write disks, even if they are not blank, are also recognized as writable disks and opened up in a DVD/CD writer window. To burn a disk, just drag the files you want to copy to the blank disk window and then click Write To Disk. A dialog will open up with buttons to set options like the write speed and disk label. After writing, a dialog will then list buttons to eject, burn again, or close. Keep in mind that the newly written disk is not mounted. You can eject it at any time.

Nautilus can also burn ISO DVD and CD images. Just insert a blank DVD or CD disk and then drag to ISO disk image file to a blank CD/DVD icon on your desktop. A dialog will open up asking you if you want to burn the DVD/CD image. Nautilus works with ISO images, files ending with a **.iso** suffix. For other image files like **.img** you can just change the suffix to **.iso** and Nautilus will recognize and burn the image file normally.

GNOME will display icons for any removable media and perform certain default actions on them. For example, Audio CDs will be automatically played in the CD player. DVD movies can be started up in a DVD player. To set the preferences for how removable media are treated, you use the Drives and Removable Media preferences tool, accessible with the Removable Media entry in the System | Preferences | Hardware menu. Certain settings are already set.

NOTE *GNOME now manages all removable media directly with HAL, instead of using fstab entries.*

The GNOME File Manager: Nautilus

Nautilus is the GNOME file manager, supporting the standard features for copying, removing, and deleting items as well as setting permissions and displaying items. It also provides enhancements such as zooming capabilities, user levels, and theme support. You can enlarge or reduce the size of your file icons, select from novice, intermediate, or expert levels of use, and customize the look and feel of Nautilus with different themes. Nautilus also lets you set up customized views of file listings, enabling you to display images for directory icons and run component applications within the file manager window. Nautilus implements a spatial approach to file browsing. A new window is opened for each new folder.

Nautilus Window

Nautilus was designed as a desktop shell in which different components can be employed to add functionality. For example, within Nautilus, a Web browser can be executed to provide Web browser capabilities in a Nautilus file manager window. An image viewer can display images. The GNOME media player can run sound and video files. The GNOME File Roller tool can archive files, as well as extract them from archives. With the implementation of GStreamer, multimedia tools such as the GNOME audio recorder are now more easily integrated into Nautilus.

By default, the Nautilus windows are displayed with the spatial view. This provides a streamlined display with no toolbars or sidebar (see Figure 6-3). Much of its functionality has been moved to menus and pop-up windows, leaving more space to display files and folders. You can, however, open a Nautilus window in the browser view, which will display the traditional menu bar and location toolbars. You can open a window in the browser view by right-clicking the folder icon and selecting Browse Folder from the pop-up menu.

The Spatial view of a Nautilus window displays a menu bar at the top with menus for managing your files. An information bar at the bottom displays information about the directory or selected files. To the lower left is a pop-up window displaying the parent directories for your current working directory. You can select any entry to open a window for that directory.

With the Browser view, a Nautilus window displays toolbars, including a menu bar of file manager commands and a Location toolbar at the top which can toggle between a location box or button views (see Figure 6-4), along with a sidebar for file and directory information. The rest of the window is divided into two panes. The left pane is a side pane used to display information about the current working directory. The right pane is the main panel that displays the list of files and subdirectories in the current working directory. A status bar at the bottom of the window displays information about a selected file or directory. You can turn any of these elements on or off by selecting their entries in the View menu.

Figure 6-3
Spatial view—
Nautilus window

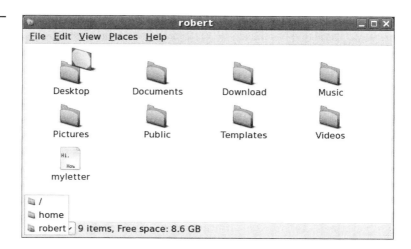

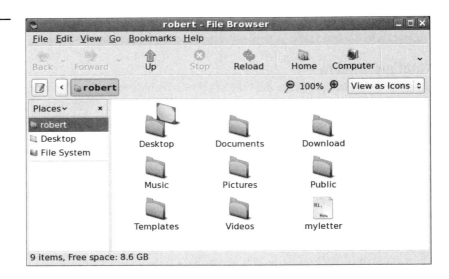

Figure 6-4
Browser view—
Nautilus file
manager window

Next to the Location bar (box or button) is an element for zooming in and out of the view of the files. Click the + button to zoom in and the – button to zoom out. Next to the zoom element is a drop-down menu for selecting the different views for your files, such as icons, small icons, or details.

Nautilus Sidebar: Tree, History, and Notes

The sidebar has several different views, selectable from a pop-up menu, for displaying additional information about files and directories: Places, Information, Tree, History, and Notes. Places show your file system locations that you would normally access, starting with your home directory. File System places you at the top of the file system, letting you move to any accessible part of it. Information displays detailed information about the current directory or selected file. For example, if you double-click an image file, the Information pane will display detailed data on the image, while the window pane displays the full image. The Tree view will display a tree-based hierarchical view of the directories and files on your system, highlighting the one you have currently selected. You can use this tree to move to other directories and files. The tree maps all the directories on your system, starting from the root directory. You can expand or shrink any directory by clicking the + or – symbol before its name. Select a directory by clicking the directory name. The contents of that directory are then displayed in the main panel. The History view shows previous files or directories you have accessed, handy for moving back and forth between directories or files.

The Notes view will display notes you have entered about an item or directory. The Notes view opens an editable text window within the side pane. Just select the Notes view and type in your notes. To add a note for a particular item, such as an image or sound file, just double-click the item to display or run it, and then select the Note view to type in your note. You can also right-click the item, to display the item's pop-up menu and select preferences, from which you can click a Notes panel. After you have added a note, you will see a note image added to the item's icon in the Nautilus window.

Displaying Files and Folders

You can view a directory's contents as icons or as a detailed list. In the spatial view, you select the different options from the View menu. In the Browser view, you use the pop-up menu located on the right side of the Location bar. The List view provides the name, permissions, size, date, owner, and group. In the "View as List" view, buttons are displayed for each field across the top of the main panel. You can use these buttons to sort the lists according to that field. For example, to sort the files by date, click the Date button; to sort by size, click Size.

In the Icon view, you can sort icons and preview their contents without opening them. To sort items in the Icon view, select the Arrange Items entry in the View menu (spatial or browser views) and then select a layout option. Certain types of file icons will display previews of their contents—for example, the icons for image files will display a small version of the image. A text file will display in its icon the first few words of its text. The Zoom In entry enlarges your view of the window, making icons bigger, and Zoom Out reduces your view, making them smaller. Normal Size restores them to the standard size. You can also use the + and – buttons on the Location bar to change sizes.

In both the spatial and browser views, you can also change the size of individual icons. Select the icon and then choose the Stretch entry from the Edit menu. Handles will appear on the icon image. Click and drag the handles to change its size. To restore the icon, select Restore Icon's Original Size in the Edit menu.

To add an emblem to any file or directory icon, just select the Background & Emblems entry from the Edit menu to open the Background And Emblems window. Here you will see three icons to display panels for color and pattern backgrounds, as well as file and directory emblems. Click emblems to display the selection of emblems. To add a emblem to a file or directory icon, click and drag the emblem from the Emblem panel to the file or directory icon. The emblem will appear on that icon. If you want to add your own emblem, click the Add Emblem button search for an emblem image file by name, or browse your file system for the image you want to use (click the image icon).

Nautilus Menu

You can click anywhere on the main panel to display a pop-up menu with entries for managing and arranging your file manager icons (see Table 6-3). The menu is the same for both spatial and browser views. To create a new folder, select Create Folder. The Arrange Items entry displays a submenu with entries for sorting your icons by name, size, type, date, or even emblem. The Manually entry lets you move icons wherever you want on the main panel. You can also cut, copy, and paste files to more easily move or copy them between folders.

***

TIP *To change the background used on the File Manager window, you now select Background & Emblems from the Edit menu, dragging the background you want to the file manager window. Choose from either colors or patterns.*

Navigating Directories

The spatial and browser views use different tools for navigating directories. The spatial view relies more on direct window operations, whereas the browse view works more like a browser. Recall that to open a directory with the browser view, you need to right-click the directory icon and select Browse Folder.

Menu Item	Description
Create Folder	Creates a new subdirectory in the directory.
Create Document	Creates a new document using installed templates.
Arrange Items	Displays a submenu to arrange files by name, size, type, date, or emblem.
Cut, Copy, Paste	Cuts, copies, or pastes files, letting you move or copy files between folders.
Zoom In	Provides a close-up view of icons, making them appear larger.
Zoom Out	Provides a distant view of icons, making them appear smaller.
Normal Size	Restores view of icons to standard size.
Properties	Opens the Properties panels for the directory opened in the window.
Clean Up by Name	Arranges icons by name.

TABLE 6-3   Nautilus File Manager Menu

Navigating in the Spatial View

In the spatial view, Nautilus will open a new window for each directory selected. To open a directory, either double-click it or right-click and select the Open entry. The parent directory pop-up menu at the bottom left lets you open a window for any parent directories, in effect, moving to a previous directory. To jump to a specific directory, select the Open Location entry from the File menu. This will, of course, open a new window for that directory. The Open Parent entry on the File menu lets you quickly open a new window for your parent. You will quickly find that moving to different directories entails opening many new windows.

Navigating in the Browser View

The browser view of the Nautilus file manager operates similarly to a Web browser, using the same window to display opened directories. It maintains a list of previously viewed directories, and you can move back and forth through that list using the toolbar buttons. The left arrow button moves you to the previously displayed directory, and the right arrow button moves you to the next displayed directory. The up arrow button moves you to the parent directory, and the Home button moves you to your home directory. To use a pathname to go directly to a given directory, you can type the pathname in the Location box and press ENTER. Use the toggle icon at the left of the location bar to toggle between box and button location views.

To open a subdirectory, you can double-click its icon or single-click the icon and select Open from the File menu. If you want to open a separate Nautilus browser view window for that directory, right-click the directory's icon and select Open In A New Window.

Managing Files

As a GNOME-compliant file manager, Nautilus supports GUI drag-and-drop operations for copying and moving files. To move a file or directory, click and drag from one directory to another as you would on Windows or Mac interfaces. The move operation is the default drag-and-drop operation in GNOME. To copy a file, click and drag normally while pressing the CTRL key.

NOTE *If you move a file to a directory on another partition (file system), it will be copied instead of moved.*

NOTE *Nautilus features built-in DVD/CD-burning support with the Nautilus-cd-burner package. Just copy a file to a blank DVD/CD disk.*

The File Menu
You can also perform remove, rename, and link creation operations on a file by right-clicking its icon and selecting the action you want from the pop-up menu that appears (see Table 6-4). For example, to remove an item, right-click it and select the Move To Trash entry from the pop-up menu. This places it in the Trash directory, where you can later delete it by selecting Empty Trash from the Nautilus File menu. To create a link, right-click the file and select Make Link from the pop-up menu. This creates a new link file that begins with the term "link."

Renaming Files
To rename a file, you can either right-click the file's icon and select the Rename entry from the pop-up menu or click the name of the file shown below its icon. The name of the icon will be highlighted in a black background, encased in a small text box. You can then click the name and delete the old name, typing a new one. You can also rename a file by entering

Menu Item	Description
Open	Opens the file with its associated application. Directories are opened in the file manager. Associated applications will be listed.
Open In A New Window	Opens a file or directory in a separate window. Browser view only.
Open With Other Application	Selects an application with which to open this file. A submenu of possible applications is displayed.
Cut, Copy, Paste files	Entries to cut, copy, paste files.
Make Link	Creates a link to that file in the same directory.
Rename	Renames the file.
Move To Trash	Moves a file to the Trash directory, where you can later delete it.
Create Archive	Archives file using File Roller.
Send To	E-mails the file.
Properties	Displays the Properties dialog box for this file. There are three panels: Statistics, Options, and Permissions.

TABLE 6-4   The Nautilus File Pop-Up Menu

a new name in its Properties dialog box. Use a right-click and select Properties from the pop-up menu to display the Properties dialog box. On the Basic tab, you can change the name of the file.

File Grouping

File operations can be performed on a selected group of files and directories. You can select a group of items in several ways. You can click the first item and then hold down the SHIFT key while clicking the last item. You can also click and drag the mouse across items you want to select. To select separated items, hold the CTRL key down as you click the individual icons. If you want to select all the items in the directory, choose the Select All entry in the Edit menu. You can then click and drag a set of items at once. This enables you to copy, move, or even delete several files at once.

Applications and Files: Open With

You can start any application in the file manager by double-clicking either the application itself or a data file used for that application. If you want to open the file with a specific application, you can right-click the file and select the Open With entry. A submenu displays a list of possible applications. If your application is not listed, you can select Other Application to open a Select An Application dialog box where you can choose the application with which you want to open this file. You can also use a text viewer to display the bare contents of a file within the file manager window. Drag-and-drop operations are also supported for applications. You can drag a data file to its associated application icon (say, one on the desktop); the application then starts up using that data file.

To change or set the default application to use for a certain type of file, you open a file's Properties and select the Open With panel. Here you can choose the default application to use for that kind of file. For example changing the default for an image file from Image Viewer to KView will make KView the default viewer for all image files. If the application you want is not listed, click the Add button in the Open With panel to display a listing of applications. Choose the one you want. This displays an Add Application box and a Browse button. Commonly used applications are already listed. If you already know the full pathname of the application, you can enter it directly. If the application is not listed, you can click Browse to display a Select An Application box that will list applications you can choose. Initially, applications in the **/usr/bin** directory are listed, though you can browse to other directories. Once you select your application, it will appear in the Open With list for this file.

Also, on the Open With panel, if there is an application you do not want listed in the Open With options, select it and click the Remove button.

For example, to associate BitTorrent files, with the original BitTorrent application, you would right-click any BitTorrent file (one with a **.torrent** extension), select the Properties entry, and then select the Open With panel. A list of installed applications will be displayed, such as Ktorrent, Azureus, and BitTorrent. Click BitTorrent to use the original BitTorrent application, then close. BitTorrent is now the default for .torrent files.

TIP *The Preferred Applications tool will let you set default applications for Internet and System applications, namely the Web browser, mail client, and terminal window console. Available applications are listed in pop-up menus. You can even select from a list of installed applications or select a custom program. You access the Preferred Applications tool from the Personal submenu located in the System | Preferences menu.*

Application Launcher

Certain files, such as shell scripts, are meant to be executed as applications. To run the file using an icon as you would other installed applications, you can create an application launcher for it. You can create application launchers using the Create Launcher tool. This tool is accessible either from the desktop menu as the Create Launcher entry, or from the panel menu's Add To box as the Custom Application Launcher entry. When accessed from the desktop, the new launcher is placed on the desktop, and from the panel, it will be placed directly on the panel.

The Create Launcher tool will prompt you for the application name, the command that invokes it, and its type. For the type, you have the choice for application, file, or file within a terminal. For shell scripts, you would use an Application In Terminal option, running the script within a shell.

Use the file type for a data file for which an associated application will be automatically started, opening the file, for example, a Web page, which will then start a Web browser. Instead of a command, you will be prompted to enter the location of the file.

For Applications and Applications In Terminal, you will be prompted to select the command to use. To select the command to use (the actual application or script file), you can either enter its pathname, if you know it, or use the Browse button to open a file browser window to select it.

To select an icon for your launcher, click the Icon button, initially labeled No Icon. This opens the Icon Browser window, listing icons from which you can choose. You have the option of selecting your own images.

File and Directory Properties

With the Properties dialog box, you can view detailed information on a file and set options and permissions (see Figure 6-5). A Properties box has five panels: Basic, Emblems, Permissions, Open With, and Notes. The *Basic* panel shows detailed information such as type, size, location, and date modified. The type is a MIME type, indicating the type of application associated with it. The file's icon is displayed at the top with a text box showing the file's name. You can edit the filename in this text box, changing that name. If you want to change the icon image used for the file or folder, just click the icon image on the Basic panel (next to the name). A Select Custom Icon dialog will open showing available icons you can use. You can select the one you want from that window. The **pixmaps** directory holds the set of current default images, though you can select your own images also. Click the image entry to see its icon displayed in the right panel. Double-clicking effects the icon image change.

The *Emblems* panel enables you to set the emblem you want displayed for this file, displaying all the emblems available. An emblem will appear in the upper-right corner of the icon, giving an indication of the file's contents or importance.

The *Permissions* panel for files shows the read, write, and execute permissions for owner, group, and other, as set for this file. You can change any of the permissions here, provided the file belongs to you. You configure access for owner, group, and others, using pop-up menus. You can set owner permissions as Read Only or Read And Write. For group and others, you can also set the None option, denying access. The group name expands to a pop-up menu listing different groups, allowing you to select one to change the file's group. If you want to execute this as an application (say a shell script) you check the Allow Executing File As Program entry. This has the effect of setting the execute permission.

The *Permissions* panel for directories operates much the same way, but it includes two access entries, Folder Access and File Access. The Folder Access entry controls access to the folder with options for List Files Only, Access Files, and Create And Delete Files. These correspond to read, read and execute, and read/write/execute permissions given to directories. The File Access entry lets you set permissions for all those files in the directory. They are the same as for files: for the owner, Read or Read and Write; for the group and others, the entry adds a None option to deny access. To set the permissions for all the files in the directory accordingly (not just the folder), you click the Apply Permissions To Enclosed Files button.

The Open With panel lists all the applications associated with this kind of file. You can select which one you want as the default. This can be particularly useful for media files, where you may prefer a specific player for a certain file, or a particular image viewer for pictures. The *Notes* panel will list any notes you want to make for the file or directory. It is an editable text window, so you can change or add to your notes, directly.

Certain kinds of files will have added panels, providing information about the item. For example, an audio file will have an *Audio* panel listing the type of audio file and any other information, such as the song title or compressions method used. An image file will have an *Image* panel listing the resolution and type of image. A video file will contain a *Video* panel showing the type of video file along with compression and resolution information.

Nautilus Preferences

You can set preferences for your Nautilus file manager in the Preferences dialog box. Access this dialog box by selecting the Preferences item in the Edit menu. The Preferences dialog box shows a main panel with a sidebar with several configuration entries, including Views, Behavior, Display, List Columns, and Preview. You use these dialog boxes to set the default display properties for your Nautilus file manager.

- The Views panel allows you to select how files are displayed by default, such as the list or icon view.

- Behavior lets you choose how to select files, manage the trash, and handle scripts, as well as whether to use the Browser view as the default.
- Display lets you choose what added information you want displayed in a icon caption, like the size or date.
- List Columns view lets you choose both the features to display in the detailed list and the order to display them in. In addition to the already-selected Name, Size, Date, and Type, you can add permissions, group, MIME type, and owner.
- The Preview panel lets you choose whether you want small preview content displayed in the icons, like beginning text for text files.

Nautilus as a FTP Browser

Nautilus works as an operational FTP browser. You can use the Location box (toggle to box view) or the Open Location entry on the File menu to access any FTP site. Just enter the URL for the FTP site in the Location box and press ENTER (you do not need to specify **ftp://**). Folders on the FTP site will be displayed, and you can drag files to a local directory to download them. The first time you connect to a site, an Authentication dialog will open letting you select either Anonymous access or access as a User. If you select User, you can then enter your username and password for that site. You can then choose to remember the password for just this session or permanently by storing it in a keyring.

Once you have accessed the site, you can navigate through the folders as you would with any Nautilus folder, opening directories or returning to parent directories. To download a file, just drag it from the ftp window to a local directory window. A small dialog will appear showing download progress. To upload a file, just drag it from your local folder to the window for the open ftp directory. Your file will be uploaded to that ftp site (should you have permission to do so). You can also delete files on the site's directories.

NOTE *Unlike KDE's Konqueror file manager, Nautilus is not a functional Web browser. It is preferable that you use the Web browsers for accessing the Web.*

The GNOME Panel

The *panel* is the center of the GNOME interface (see Figures 6-6 through 6-8). Through it you can start your applications, run applets, and access desktop areas. You can think of the GNOME panel as a type of tool you can use on your desktop. You can have several GNOME panels displayed on your desktop, each with applets and menus you have placed in them. In this respect, GNOME is flexible, enabling you to configure your panels any way you want. In fact, the default GNOME desktop that Red Hat and Fedora use features two panels, a menu panel at the top for your applications and actions, and a panel at the bottom used for minimized windows and the workspace switcher. You can customize a panel to fit your own needs, holding applets and menus of your own selection. You may add new panels, add applications to the panel, and add various applets.

Applications Places System   2:01 PM

FIGURE 6-6 The GNOME panel, at the top of Fedora desktop

FIGURE 6-7
Add To Panel box
listing panel
objects

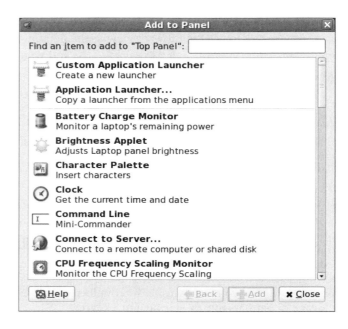

Panel configuration tasks such as adding applications, selecting applets, setting up menus, and creating new panels are handled from the Panel pop-up menu. Just right-click anywhere on your panel to display a menu with entries for Properties, New Panel, Add To Panel, and Delete This Panel, along with Help and About entries. New Panel lets you create other panels; Add To Panel lets you add items to the panel such as application launchers, applets for simple tasks like the Workspace Switcher, and menus like the main applications menu. The Properties entry will display a dialog for configuring the features for that panel, like the position of the panel and its hiding capabilities.

To add a new panel, select the New Panel entry in the Panel pop-up menu. A new expanded panel is automatically created and displayed on the side of your screen. You can then use the panel's properties box to set different display and background features, as described in the following sections.

Panel Properties

To configure individual panels, you use the Panel Properties dialog box. To display this dialog box, you right-click the particular panel and select the Properties entry in the pop-up menu. For individual panels, you can set general configuration features and the background. The Panel Properties dialog box includes a tabbed pane, General and Background. With version 2.4, GNOME abandoned the different panel types in favor of just one kind of panel with different possible features that give it the same capabilities as the old panel types.

FIGURE 6-8   Panel with Workspace Switcher and Window List, at the bottom of the Fedora desktop

Displaying Panels

On the General pane of a panel's properties box, you determine how you want the panel displayed. Here you have options for orientation, size, and whether to expand, auto-hide, or display hide buttons. The Orientation entry lets you select which side of the screen you want the panel placed on. You can then choose whether you want a panel expanded or not. An expanded panel will fill the edges of the screen, whereas a non-expanded panel is sized to the number of items in the panel and shows handles at each end. Expanded panels will remain fixed to the edge of screen, whereas unexpanded panels can be moved, provided the Show Hide Buttons feature is not selected.

Moving and Hiding Expanded Panels

Expanded panels can be positioned at any edge of your screen. You can move expanded panels from one edge of a screen to another by simply dragging the panel to another edge. If a panel is already there, the new one will stack on top of the current one. You cannot move unexpanded panels in this way. Bear in mind that if you place an expanded panel on the side edge, any menus will be displayed across at the top corner to allow proper pop-up display. The panel on the side edge will expand in size to accommodate its menus. If you have several menus or a menu with a lengthy names, you could end up with a very large panel.

You can hide expanded panels either automatically or manually. These are features specified in the panel properties General box as Auto Hide and Show Hide Buttons. To automatically hide panels, select the Auto Hide feature. To redisplay the panel, move your mouse to the edge where the panel is located. You can enable or disable the Hide buttons in the panel's properties window.

If you want to be able to hide a panel manually, select the Show Hide Buttons. Two handles will be displayed at either end of the panel. You can further choose whether to have these handles display arrows or not. You can then hide the panel at any time by clicking either of the Hide buttons located on each end of the panel. The Hide buttons are thin buttons showing a small arrow. This is the direction in which the panel will hide.

Unexpanded Panels: Movable and Fixed

Whereas an expanded panel is always located at the edge of the screen, an unexpanded panel is movable. It can be located at the edge of a screen, working like a shrunken version of an Expanded panel, or you can move it to any place on your desktop, just as you would an icon.

An unexpanded panel will shrink to the number of its components, showing handles at either end. You can then move the panel by dragging its handles. To access the panel menu with its properties entry, right-click either of its handles.

To fix an unexpanded panel at its current position, select the Show Hide Buttons feature on its properties box. This will replace the handles with Hide buttons and make the panel fixed. Clicking a Hide button will hide the panel to the edge of the screen, just as with Expanded panels. If an expanded panel is already located on that edge, the button for a hidden unexpanded panel will be on top of it, just as with a hidden expanded panel. The Auto Hide feature will work for unexpanded panels placed at the edge of a screen.

If you want to fix an unexpanded panel to the edge of a screen, make sure it is placed at the edge you want, and then set its Show Hide Buttons feature.

Panel Background

With a panel's Background pane on its properties box, you can change the panel's background color or image. For a color background you click a color button to display a color selection window where you can choose a color from a color circle and its intensity from an inner color triangle. You can enter its number if you know it. Once your color is selected, you can use the Style slide bar to make it more transparent or opaque. To use an image instead of a color, select the image entry and use the Browse button to locate the image file you want. For an image, you can also drag and drop an image file from the file manager to the panel; that image then becomes the background image for the panel.

Panel Objects

A panel can contain several different types of objects. These include menus, launchers, applets, drawers, and special objects.

- **Menus**   The Applications menu is an example of a panel menu. Launchers are buttons used to start an application or execute a command.

- **Launchers**   The Web browser icon is an example of a launcher button. You can select any application entry in the Applications menu and create a launcher for it on the panel.

- **Applets**   An applet is a small application designed to run within the panel. The Workspace Switcher showing the different desktops is an example of a GNOME applet.

- **Drawers**   A drawer is an extension of the panel that can be open or closed. You can think of a drawer as a shrinkable part of the panel. You can add anything to it that you can to a regular panel, including applets, menus, and even other drawers.

- **Special objects**   These are used for special tasks not supported by other panel objects. For example, the Logout and Lock buttons are special objects.

Moving, Removing, and Locking Objects

To move any object within the panel, right-click it and choose Move Entry. You can move it either to a different place on the same panel or to a different panel. For launchers, you can just drag the object directly where you want it to be. To remove an object from the panel, right-click it to display a pop-up menu for it, and then choose the Remove From Panel entry. To prevent an object from being moved or removed, you set its lock feature (right-click the object and select the Lock entry). To later allow it to be moved, you first have to unlock the object (right-click it and select Unlock).

TIP   *On the panel Add To list, common objects like the clock and the CD player are intermixed with object types like menus and applications. When adding a kind of object, like an application, you will have to search through the list to find the entry for that type; in the case of applications, it is the application launcher entry.*

Adding Objects

To add an object to a panel, select the object from the panel's Add To box (see Figure 6-7). To display the Add To box, right-click the panel and select the Add To Panel entry. This Add To box displays a lengthy list of common objects as well as object types. For example, it will display the Main menu as well as an entry for creating custom menus. You can choose to add an application that is already in the GNOME Application menu or create an application launcher for one that is not. Launchers can be added to a panel by just dragging them directly. Launchers include applications, windows, and files.

Application Launchers

If an application already has an application launcher, to add it to a panel is easy. You just have to drag the application launcher to the panel. This will automatically create a copy of the launcher for use on that panel. Launchers can be menu items or desktop icons. All the entries in your Application menu are application launchers. To add an application from the menu, just select it and drag it to the panel. You can also drag any desktop application icon to a panel to add a copy of it to that panel.

For any menu item, you can also go to its entry and right-click it. Then select the Add This Launcher To Panel entry. An application launcher for that application is then automatically added to the panel. Suppose you use Gedit frequently and want to add its icon to the panel, instead of having to go through the Application menu all the time. Right-click the Text Editor menu entry in the Accessories menu, and select the Add This Launcher To Panel option. The Gedit icon now appears in your panel.

You can also select the Add To Panel entry from the panel menu and then choose the Application Launcher entry. This will display a box with a listing of all the Application menu entries along with Preferences and Administration menus, expandable to their items. Just find the application you want added and select it. This may be an easier approach if you are working with many different panels.

Keep in mind that for any launcher that you previously created on the desktop, you can just drag it to the panel to have a copy of the launcher placed on the panel.

Folder and File Launchers

To add a folder to a panel, just drag it directly from the file manager window or from the desktop. To add a file, also drag it directly to the panel, but you will then have to create a launcher for it. The Create Launcher window will be displayed, and you can give the file launcher a name and select an icon for it.

Adding Drawers

You can also group applications under a Drawer icon. Clicking the Drawer icon displays a list of the different application icons you can then select. To add a drawer to your panel, right-click the panel and select the Add To Panel entry to display the Add To list. From that list select the Drawer entry. This will create a drawer on your panel. You can then drag any items from desktop, menus, or windows to the drawer icon on the panel to have them listed in the drawer.

If you want to add, as a drawer, a whole menu of applications on the main menu to your panel, right-click any item in that menu, and then select Entire Menu from the pop-up menu, and then select the Add This As Drawer To Panel entry. The entire menu appears as a drawer on your panel, holding icons instead of menu entries. For example, suppose you want to place the Internet Applications menu on your panel. Right-click any entry item, selecting Entire Menu, and select Add This As Drawer To Panel. A drawer appears on your panel labeled Internet, and clicking it displays a pop-up list of icons for all the Internet applications.

Adding Menus

A menu differs from a drawer in that a *drawer* holds application icons instead of menu entries. You can add menus to your panel, much as you add drawers. To add a submenu from the Applications menu to your panel, right-click any item and select Entire Menu, and then select the Add This As Menu To Panel entry. The menu title appears in the panel; you can click it to display the menu entries.

You can also add a menu from the panel's Add To list, by selecting Custom menu.

Adding Folders

You can also add directory folders to a panel. Click and drag the Folder icon from the file manager window to your panel. Whenever you click this Folder button, a file manager window opens, displaying that directory. You already have a Folder button for your home directory. You can add directory folders to any drawer on your panel.

Special Panel Objects

Special panel objects perform operations not supported by other panel objects. Currently, these include the Lock, Logout, and Launcher buttons, as well as the status dock. The Lock button, which displays a padlock, will lock your desktop, running the screensaver in its place. To access your desktop, click it and then enter your user password at the password prompt. The Logout button shows an open door. Clicking it will display the Logout dialog box, and you can then log out. It is the same as selecting Logout from the desktop menu. The Launcher button shows a launcher icon. It opens the Create Launcher dialog box, which allows you to enter or select an application to run.

The status dock is designed to hold status docklets. A status docklet provides current status information on an application. KDE applications that support status docklets can use the GNOME status dock, when run under GNOME.

GNOME Applets

Applets are small programs that perform tasks within the panel. To add an applet, right-click the panel and select Add To Panel from the pop-up menu. This displays the Add To box, listing common applets along with other types of objects, such as launchers. Select the one you want. For example, to add the clock to your panel, select Clock from the panel's Add To box. Once added, the applet will show up in the panel. If you want to remove an applet, right-click it and select the Remove From Panel entry.

GNOME features a number of helpful applets. Some applets monitor your system, such as the Battery Charge Monitor, which checks the battery in laptops, and System Monitor, which shows a graph indicating your current CPU and memory use. The Volume Control applet displays a small scroll bar for adjusting sound levels. The Deskbar tool searches for files on your desktop. Network Monitor lets you monitor a network connection.

Several helpful utility applets provide added functionality to your desktop. The Clock applet can display time in a 12- or 24-hour format. Right-click the Clock applet and select the Preferences entry to change its setup. The CPU Frequency Scaling Monitor displays CPU usage for CPUs like AMD and the new Intel processors that run at lower speeds when idle.

Workspace Switcher

The *Workspace Switcher* appears in the panel and shows a view of your virtual desktops (see Figure 6-8). Virtual desktops are defined in the window manager. Located on the right side of the lower panel, the Workspace Switcher lets you easily move from one desktop to another with the click of a mouse. It is a panel applet that works only in the panel. You can add the Workspace Switcher to any panel by selecting it from that panel's Add To box.

The Workspace Switcher shows your entire virtual desktop as separate rectangles listed next to each other. Open windows show up as small colored rectangles in these squares. You can move any window from one virtual desktop to another by clicking and dragging its image in the Workspace Switcher. To configure the Workspace Switcher, right-click it and select Preferences to display the Preferences dialog box. Here, you can select the number of workspaces. The default is four.

GNOME Window List

The *Window List* shows currently opened windows (see Figure 6-8). The Window List arranges opened windows in a series of buttons, one for each window. A window can include applications such as a Web browser or be a file manager window displaying a directory. You can move from one window to another by clicking its button. When you minimize a window, you can later restore it by clicking its entry in the Window List.

Right-clicking a window's Window List button opens a menu that lets you Minimize or Unminimize, Roll Up, Move, Resize, Maximize or Unmaximize, or Close the window. The Minimize operation will reduce the window to its Window List entry. Right-clicking the entry will display the menu with an Unminimize option instead of a Minimize one, which you can then use to redisplay the window. The Roll Up entry will reduce the window to its title bar. The Close entry will close the window, ending its application.

If there is not enough space on the Window List applet to display a separate button for each window, then common windows will be grouped under a button that will expand like a menu, listing each window in that group. For example, all open terminal windows would be grouped under a single button, which when clicked would pop up a list of their buttons.

The Window List applet is represented by a small serrated bar at the beginning of the window button list. To configure the Window List, right-click this bar and select the Properties entry. Here, you can set features such as the size in pixels, whether to group windows, whether to show all open windows or those from just the current workspace, or which workspace to restore windows to.

GNOME Configuration

You can configure different parts of your GNOME interface using tools listed in the Preferences menu in the System menu. This menu will display entries for the primary GNOME preferences organized into submenu categories like Hardware and Personal, along with preferences listing task-specific tools, like that for the Palm Pilot or Desktop Switcher. Selecting one will open a window labeled with the tool name, like mouse preferences.

Your GNOME system provides several desktop tools you can use to configure your desktop, such as Desktop Background, Screensaver, and Themes. You use the Desktop Background applet to select a background color or image, the Screensaver to select the screen saver images and wait time, and the Theme tool to choose a theme (see Figure 6-9).

FIGURE 6-9
Selecting GNOME themes

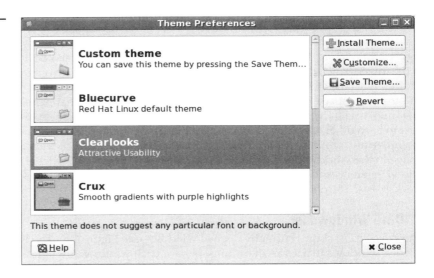

The Removable Drives and Media preferences tools lets you set what actions to perform on removable drives, CD and DVD discs, and digital cameras.

For the sound configuration, the Sound tool lets you select sound files to play for events in different GNOME applications. For your keyboard, you can set the repeat sensitivity and click sound with the Keyboard tool. You can configure mouse buttons for your right or left hand, and adjust the mouse motion.

GNOME Directories and Files

Fedora installs GNOME binaries in the **/usr/bin** directory on your system. GNOME libraries are located in the **/usr/lib** directory. GNOME also has its own **include** directories with header files for use in compiling and developing GNOME applications, **/usr/include/libgnome-2.0/libgnome** and **/usr/include/libgnomeui** (see Table 6-5). These are installed from the GNOME development packages. The directories located in **/usr/share/gnome** contain files used to configure your GNOME environment.

GNOME User Directories

GNOME sets up several configuration files and directories in your home directory. The **.gnome, .gnome2**, and **.gconf** directories hold configuration files for different desktop components, such as **nautilus** for the file manager and **panel** for the panels. The **DESKTOP** directory holds all the items you placed on your desktop. The **.gtckrc** file is the user configuration file for the GTK+ libraries, which contains current desktop configuration directives for resources such as key bindings, colors, and window styles.

The GConf Configuration Editor

GConf provides underlying configuration support (not installed by default). GConf corresponds to the Registry used on a Windows system. It consists of a series of libraries used to implement a configuration database for a GNOME desktop. This standardized

System GNOME Directories	Contents
/usr/bin	GNOME programs
/usr/lib	GNOME libraries
/usr/include/libgnome-2.0/libgnome	Header files for use in compiling and developing GNOME applications
/usr/include/libgnomeui	Header files for use in compiling and developing GNOME user interface components
/usr/share/gnome	Files used by GNOME applications
/usr/share/doc/gnome*	Documentation for various GNOME packages, including libraries
/etc/gconf	GConf configuration files
User GNOME Directories	**Contents**
.gnome, .gnome2	Holds configuration files for the user's GNOME desktop and GNOME applications; includes configuration files for the panel, background, MIME types, and sessions
DESKTOP	Directory where files, directories, and links you place on the desktop will reside
.gnome2_private	The user's private GNOME directory
.gtkrc	GTK+ configuration file
.gconf	GConf configuration database
.gconfd	GConf **gconfd** daemon management files
.gstreamer	GNOME GStreamer multimedia configuration files
.nautilus	Configuration files for the Nautilus file manager

TABLE 6-5   GNOME Configuration Directories

configuration database allows for consistent interactions between GNOME applications. GNOME applications that are built from a variety of other programs, as Nautilus is, can use GConf to configure all those programs according to a single standard, maintaining configurations in a single database. Currently the GConf database is implemented as XML files in the user's **.gconf** directory. Database interaction and access is carried out by the GConf daemon, **gconfd**.

You can use the GConf editor to configure different GNOME applications and desktop functions. To start the GConf editor, enter `gconf-editor` in a terminal window, or select Configuration Editor from the Applications | System Tools menu (Applications menu). Be sure to install the gconf-editor package first (you can use Pirut - Add/Remove Software).

Configuration elements are specified keys that are organized by application and program. You can edit the keys, changing their values. Figure 6-10 shows the GConf editor settings for the dialog display features used for the GNOME interface.

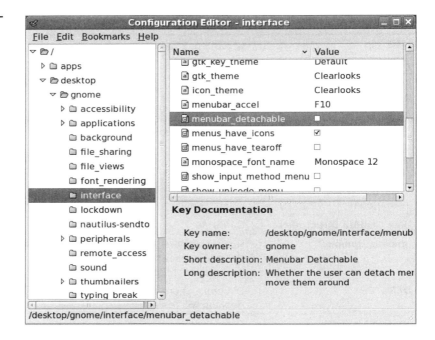

FIGURE 6-10
GConf editor

The GConf editor has four panes (see Figure 6-10):

- **Tree**   A tree pane for navigating keys, with expandable trees for each application, is located on the left. Application entries expand to subentries, grouping keys into different parts or functions for the application.

- **Modification**   A modification pane to the top right will display the keys for a selected entry. The name field will include an icon indicating its type, and the Value field is an editable field showing the current value. You can directly change this value.

- **Documentation**   The documentation field at the bottom right displays information about the selected key, showing the key name, the application that owns it, and a short and detailed description.

- **Results**   The results pane, displayed at the bottom, only appears when you do a search for a key.

A key has a specific type such as numeric or string, and you will only be able to make changes using the appropriate type. Each key entry has an icon specifying its type, such as a check mark for the Boolean values, a number *1* for numeric values, and a letter *a* for string values. Some keys have pop-up menus with limited selections to choose from, represented by an icon with a row of lines. To change the value of a key, click its value field. You can then edit the value. For pop-up menus, you right-click the value field to display the menu.

There are many keys distributed over several applications and groups. To locate one, you can use the search function. Select Find from the Edit menu and enter a pattern. The results are displayed in a Results pane, which you can use to scroll through matching keys, selecting the one you want.

Changes can be made either by users or by administrators. Administrators can set default or mandatory values for keys. Mandatory values will prevent users from making changes. For user changes, you can open a Settings window by selecting Settings from the File menu. This opens an identical GConf Editor window. For administrative changes, you first log in as the root user. For default changes, you select the Default entry from the File menu, and for mandatory changes, select the Mandatory entry.

PART II

The K Desktop Environment: KDE

The *K Desktop Environment (KDE)* is a network-transparent desktop that includes the standard desktop features, such as a window manager and a file manager, as well as an extensive set of applications that cover most Linux tasks. KDE is an Internet-aware system that includes a full set of integrated network/Internet applications, including a mailer, a newsreader, and a Web browser. The file manager doubles as a Web and FTP client, enabling you to access Internet sites directly from your desktop. KDE aims to provide a level of desktop functionality and ease of use found in Macintosh and Windows systems, combined with the power and flexibility of the Unix operating system.

The KDE desktop is developed and distributed by the KDE Project, which is a large open group of hundreds of programmers around the world. KDE is entirely free and open software provided under a GNU Public License and is available free of charge along with its source code. KDE development is managed by a core group: the KDE Core Team. Anyone can apply, though membership is based on merit.

NOTE *KDE applications are developed using several supporting KDE technologies. These include KIO, which offers seamless and modular access to files and directories across a network. For interprocess communication, KDE uses the Desktop Communications Protocol (DCOP). KParts is the KDE component object model used to embed one application within another, such as a spreadsheet within a word processor. The XML GUI uses XML to generate and place GUI objects such as menus and toolbars. KHTML is an HTML rendering and drawing engine.*

Numerous applications written specifically for KDE are easily accessible from the desktop. These include editors, photo and paint image applications, spreadsheets, and office applications. Such applications usually have the letter *K* as part of their name—for example, KWord or KMail. A variety of tools are provided with the KDE desktop. These include calculators, console windows, notepads, and even software package managers. On a system administration level, KDE provides several tools for configuring your system. With KUser, you can manage user accounts, adding new ones or removing old ones. Practically all your Linux tasks can be performed from the KDE desktop. KDE applications also feature a built-in Help application. Choosing the Contents entry in the Help menu starts the KDE Help viewer, which provides a Web page—like interface with links for navigating through the Help documents. KDE version 3.0 includes support for the office application suite KOffice, based on KDE's KParts technology. KOffice includes a presentation application, a spreadsheet, an illustrator, and a word processor, among other components (see Chapter 11 for more details). In addition, an integrated development environment (IDE), called KDevelop, is available to help programmers create KDE-based software.

NOTE *On KDE, menus will show more KDE applications than are shown on GNOME, including access to the KDE Control Center on the main menu.*

KDE, initiated by Matthias Ettrich in October 1996, has an extensive list of sponsors, including SUSE, Red Hat, Fedora, Mandrake, O'Reilly, and others. KDE is designed to run on any Unix implementation, including Linux, Solaris, HP-UX, and FreeBSD. The official KDE Web site is **www.kde.org**, which provides news updates, download links, and documentation. KDE software packages can be downloaded from the KDE FTP site at **ftp.kde.org** and its mirror sites. Several KDE mailing lists are available for users and developers, including announcements, administration, and other topics (see the KDE Web site to subscribe). A great many software applications are currently available for KDE at **www.kde-apps.org**. Development support and documentation can be obtained at **developer.kde.org**. Various KDE Web sites are listed in Table 7-1.

NOTE *Currently, new versions of KDE are being released frequently, sometimes every few months. KDE releases are designed to enable users to upgrade their older versions easily. The Package Updater (PUP) on your Fedora system will automatically update KDE from Fedora Yum repositories, as updates become available. Alternatively, you can download new KDE packages from your distribution's FTP site and install them manually. Packages tailored for various distributions can be also downloaded through the KDE Web site at **www.kde.org** or directly from the KDE FTP site at **ftp.kde.org** and its mirror sites in the **stable** directory.*

Web Site	Description
www.kde.org	KDE Web site
ftp.kde.org	KDE FTP site
www.kde-apps.org	KDE software repository
developer.kde.org	KDE developer site
www.trolltech.com	Site for Qt libraries
www.koffice.org	KOffice office suite
www.kde-look.org	KDE desktop themes; select KDE entry
lists.kde.org	KDE mailing lists

TABLE 7-1 KDE Web Sites

The Qt Library

KDE uses as its library of GUI tools the Qt library, developed and supported by Trolltech (**www.trolltech.com**). Qt is considered one of the best GUI libraries available for Unix/ Linux systems. Using Qt has the advantage of relying on a commercially developed and supported GUI library. Also, using the Qt libraries drastically reduces the development time for KDE. Trolltech provides the Qt libraries as Open Source software that is freely distributable. Certain restrictions exist, however: Qt-based (KDE) applications must be free and open-sourced, with no modifications made to the Qt libraries. If you develop an application with the Qt libraries and want to sell it, then you have to buy a license from Trolltech. In other words, the Qt library is free for free and Open Source applications, but not for commercial ones.

Configuration and Administration Access with KDE

KDE uses a different set of menus and access points than GNOME for accessing system administration tools. There are also different ways to access KDE configuration tasks, as well as KDE system administration tools not available through GNOME.

Access Fedora system administration tools from the Main Menu | Administration entry. Here you will find system-config Fedora administration tools like Users and Groups, Printing, Display, and Network. One significant addition is Kyum, which you can use to access your software repositories, instead of Pirut, installing and updating your software.

- **Control Center**   Accessible from Main Menu | Control Center, or from any file manager window's Go | Settings entry, this is the comprehensive KDE configuration tool, which lists all the KDE configuration panels for your managing your desktop, file manager, and system, as well as KDE's own administration tools that could be used instead of the Fedora ones.

- **System**   Accessible from Main Menu | System, this is a collection of system tools corresponding to those found in your GNOME System Tools menu, with the addition of certain other Fedora administration tools, like Add/Remove Software (Pirut) and the Software Updater (PUP). Many Fedora tools, including Display, Samba, and Services, are repeated here. Here you will also find KDE equivalents of many Fedora administration tools, such as KUser for managing users.

- **Settings**   Accessible from Main Menu | Settings, this is a smaller collection of desktop configuration features for tasks such as setting your login photo, configuring the panel, and configuring printers.

- **Utilities**   Accessible from Main Menu | Utilities, this is where you will find tools for specific tasks, such as Kpilot for Palm handhelds (under Peripherals) and Beagle for searches.

One point of confusion is that Settings is used differently in the main menu and in the file manager Go menu. In the main menu it refers to an ad hoc collection of desktop configuration tools like mail notification, whereas in the file manager window Go menu, it will display the Control Center, but in window icon format.

The term System is also used differently. In the file manager it displays desktop resources like your Home directory or Network shares, whereas in the main menu it lists the System tools like the Software updater. Also, on the Panel you can add a System applet, which also lists the file manager System resources.

To initially configure your desktop, you may want to run the Desktop Configuration Wizard, accessible from the Main Menu | Settings. Here you can set your country and language, your desktop appearance, the eye-candy feature level, and the desktop theme you want.

Keep in mind that Control Center will let you accesses all KDE configurations, whereas Main Menu | Administration lets you access all Fedora administration tools. To run software updates, you will have to access the Software Updater entry in the Main Menu | System Tools menu, which will start PUP.

Finally, to just configure your desktop, you can right-click anywhere on it to display a pop-up menu that will have a Desktop Configuration entry. Selecting this opens the desktop configuration panels. These are the same ones used on the Control Center's Desktop selection.

The KDE Desktop

One of KDE's aims is to provide users with a consistent integrated desktop, where all applications use GUI interfaces (see Figure 7-1). To this end, KDE provides its own window manager (KWM), file manager (Konqueror), program manager, and desktop panel (Kicker). You can run any other X Window System—compliant application, such as Firefox, in KDE, as well as any GNOME application. In turn, you can also run any KDE application, including the Konqueror file manager in GNOME.

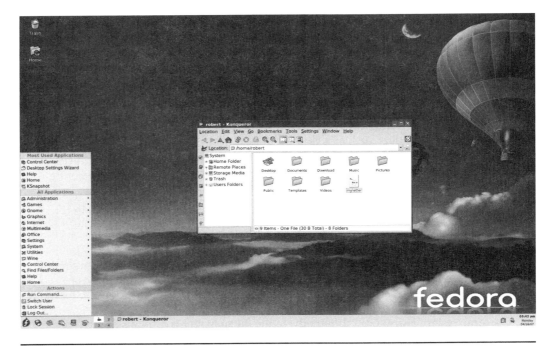

FIGURE 7-1   The KDE desktop.

NOTE *When you start KDE for the first time, you will be prompted to configure the Knemo network device monitor. Here you can specify your network devices, for instance, eth0 for the first Ethernet device, ppp0 for a dial-up connection, or wlan0 for a wireless connection. You can also specify tooltips to use, the icon for monitoring, even the color.*

KDE Menus

When you start KDE, the KDE panel is displayed at the bottom of the screen. Located on the panel are icons for menus and programs, as well as buttons for different desktop screens. The button for the main menu shows an *f*, the Fedora icon. This is the button for the KDE main menu. Click this button to display the menu of applications you run (you can also open the main menu by pressing ALT-F1). From the KDE menu, you can access numerous submenus for different kinds of applications. The menu also includes certain key items such as Logout, to log out of KDE; Lock Screen, to lock your desktop; Control Center, to configure your KDE desktop; Run Command, to run programs from a command line; your Home directory, to quickly browse your home directory; and Help, which starts the KDE help tool.

TIP *You can run the Desktop Settings Wizard on the Settings menu, to easily change your desktop settings.*

The standard KDE applications installed with the KDE can be accessed through this menu. The main menu has most of the same entries as those found on GNOME. The entries have been standardized for both interfaces. You can find entries for categories such as Internet, System Settings, Graphics, and Office. These menus list both GNOME and KDE applications you can use. However, some of the KDE menus contain entries for a few more alternate KDE applications, like KMail on the Internet menu. Some entries will invoke the KDE version of a tool, like the Terminal entry in the System Tools menu, which will invoke the KDE terminal window, KConsole. There is no Preferences menu. To configure KDE, you use the KDE Control Center referenced by the Control Center item in the main menu. The System menu will list KDE system tools like KCron, though it also includes the Pup and Pirut Software manager and updater, whereas the System | More Applications will list many of the configuration tools found on the Gnome Applications | System Tools menu. The Administration menu will list the same Fedora Administration tools found on Gnome's System | Administration menu.

TIP *If your CD or DVD-ROM device icons are not displayed when you insert a CD/DVD disk, you will need to enable a device icon display on your desktop. Right-click on the desktop and choose Config-Desktop from the pop-up menu. This shows the desktop entries only of the Control Center. Select Behavior, and then on the Device Icons pane, select the Show Device Icons check box. A long list of connectable devices is displayed, with default devices already selected. You select and de-select the ones you want shown or hidden. For most devices, you have both mounted and unmounted options. For example, an unmounted entry for the DVD-ROM will display a DVD-ROM icon even if the DVD-ROM device is empty.*

Quitting KDE

To quit KDE, you can select the Logout entry in the main menu, or you can right-click anywhere on the desktop and select the Logout entry from the pop-up menu. If you leave any KDE or X11 applications or windows open when you quit, they are automatically restored when you start up again. If you just want to lock your desktop, you can select the Lock Screen entry on the main menu and your screen saver will appear. To access a locked desktop, click on the screen and a box appears prompting you for your login password. When you enter the password, your desktop reappears.

Note *You can use the Create New menus to create new folders or files on the desktop, as well as links for applications and devices.*

KDE Desktop Operations

Initially the Trash icon is shown on the left side. The Trash icon operates like the Recycle Bin in Windows or the trash can on the Mac. Drag items to it to hold them for deletion. You can use the floppy and DVD/CD-ROM icons to mount, unmount, and display the contents of CD-ROMs and floppy disks. The DVD/CD-ROM icons will appear as disks are inserted and mounted, disappearing when ejected. Your home directory is accessed initially from the Home directory in the main menu. To place this folder on the desktop, right-click on the menu entry and select Add to Desktop from the pop-up menu. You also have the option to display the Home directory on your panel by selecting Add to Panel. A home directory icon then appears permanently on your desktop.

The KDE panel displayed across the bottom of the screen initially shows small buttons for the KDE main menu, the Web browser, office tools, and a clock, as well as buttons for virtual desktops, among others. The desktop supports drag-and-drop operations. For example, to print a document, drag it to the Printer icon. You can place any directories on the desktop by simply dragging them from a file manager window to the desktop. A small menu will appear with options to copy or link the folder. To just create an icon on the desktop for the same folder, select the link entry.

The desktop also supports copy-and-paste operations, holding text you copied from one application in a desktop clipboard that you can then use to paste to another application. You can even copy and paste from a Konsole window. For example, you can copy a Web address from a Web page and then paste it into an e-mail message or a word processing document. This feature is supported by the Klipper utility located on the panel.

You can create new directories on the desktop by right-clicking anywhere on the desktop and selecting Create New and then Directory from the pop-up menu. All items that appear on the desktop are located in the **Desktop** directory in your home directory. There you can find the **Trash** directory, along with any others you place on the desktop. You can also create simple text files and HTML files using the same menu.

Accessing System Resources from the File Manager

You can access system resources, including network shares, user directories, or storage media like CD-ROMs, from any file manager window (see Figure 7-2). Some of these resources can be opened directly, like the Trash and CD-ROM icons on your desktop, or the Home directory entry in the main menu. To open an initial file manager window, select the Home Directory entry in the main menu. Then click the system icon on the lower-left side of the file manager window. Icons are displayed that you can use to access various system resources such as storage media, remote hosts, Samba network shares, and your trash folder. You will see icons labeled Home Folder, Remote Places, Storage Media, and Trash. You can also access

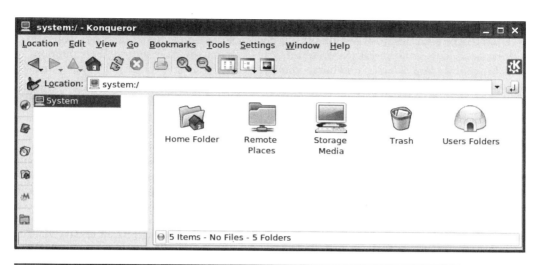

FIGURE 7-2   System resources access from the file manager.

any of these directly from the file manager Go menu. The Storage Media entry will expand to list all your DVD/CD media, removable media, and other partitions. Under Remote Places you will find icons for your local network, network services, and Samba shares, as well as a tool to add network folders. Through the Samba Shares icon you can access your shared Windows folders and printers. The Storage Media icon lists your storage media such as your CD-ROMs. You can open these to access their contents. Certain resources have their own URLs that you can enter into a file manager location box to directly access them. Remote Places has the URL **remote:/,** Samba uses **smb:/,** and Storage Media uses **media:/.**

Configuring Your Desktop

To configure your desktop, right-click the desktop and select the Configure Desktop entry. This displays a window with entries for Behavior, Multiple Desktops, Display, Background, and Screensaver. All these features can be configured also using the KDE Control Center's Appearance & Themes panels.

- Display lets you set the display resolution and orientation.

- Behavior lets you enable the display of certain features, such as displaying a desktop menu across the top of the screen, or showing icons on the desktop. You can also select the operations for a mouse click on the desktop (by default, a right-click displays the desktop menu) or specify which devices to display on the desktop.

- The Multiple Desktop panel lets you select the number of virtual desktops to display.

- Background lets you choose a background color or image for each virtual desktop.

- Screensaver lets you select a screen saver along with its timing. Numerous screen savers are already configured.

For your desktop, you can also select a variety of different themes. A *theme* changes the look and feel of your desktop, affecting the appearance of GUI elements, such as scroll bars, buttons, and icons. For example, you use the Mac OS theme to make your K Desktop look like a Macintosh. You can use the Theme Manager in the KDE Control Center (Appearance & Themes) to select a theme and install new ones. Several may be installed for you, including Bluecurve (the current theme) or the Default (the KDE theme). Additional themes for the K Desktop can be downloaded from the **www.kde-look.org** Web site.

Desktop Link Files and URL Locations

On the KDE desktop, special files called *link* files are used to access a variety of elements, including Web sites, application programs, and even devices. You create a link file by right-clicking the desktop and then selecting Create New. From this menu, you choose the type of link file you want to create.

The Link To Application entry is for launching applications. The Link To Location (URL) entry holds a URL address that you can use to access a Web or FTP site. The Link To Device submenu lets you create links to different kinds of devices, including CD-ROMs, hard disks, and cameras. Bear in mind that these are links only. You would rarely need to use them. Device icons that display on your desktop are now automatically generate directly by udev and HAL as needed (see Chapter 32).

To create a URL desktop file, right-click the desktop and select the Create New menu, and then the File submenu. Then select the Link To Location (URL) entry. A window appears that displays a box that prompts you to enter a name for the file and the URL address. Be sure to precede the URL with the appropriate protocol, like **http://** for Web pages. Alternatively, you can simply drag and drop a URL directly from the Location box on a Web browser such as Firefox. You can later edit the desktop file by right-clicking it and selecting Properties. A desktop dialog box for URL access is then displayed. This dialog box has three tabbed panels: General, Permissions, and URL. On the General panel is the name of your desktop file. It will have as its name the name that you entered. An Icon button on this panel shows the icon that will be displayed for this desktop file on your desktop. You can select an icon by clicking the Icon button to open a window that lists icons you can choose from. Click OK when you are finished. The desktop file then appears on your desktop with that icon. On the URL panel, you will see a box labeled URL with a URL you entered already in it. You can change it if you want. For example, for online themes, the URL would be **http://www.kde-look.org**. Be sure to include the protocol, such as **http://** or **ftp://**.

On your desktop, you can click the URL icon anytime to access that Web site. An alternative and easier way to create a URL desktop file is simply to drag a URL for a Web page displayed on the file manager to your desktop. A pop-up window will let you select Copy or Link. Choose Link to create a URL desktop file (Copy will create local copy of that page). A desktop file is automatically generated with that URL. To change the default icon used, you can right-click the file and choose Properties to display the desktop dialog box.

KDE Windows

A KDE window has the same functionality you find in other window managers and desktops. You can resize the window by clicking and dragging any of its corners or sides. A click-and-drag operation on a side extends the window in that dimension, whereas a corner extends both height and width at the same time. Notice that the corners are slightly enhanced. The top of the window has a title bar showing the name of the window, the program name in the case of applications, and the current directory name for the file manager windows. The active window has the title bar highlighted. To move the window, click this title bar and drag it where you want. Right-clicking the window title bar displays a drop-down menu with entries for window operations, such as closing or resizing the window. Within the window, menus, icons, and toolbars for the particular application are displayed.

You can configure the appearance and operation of a window by selecting the Configure Window Behavior entry from the Window menu (right-click the title bar). Here you can set appearance (Window Decorations), button and key operations (Actions), the focus policy such as a mouse click on the window or just passing the mouse over it (Focus), how the window is displayed when moving it (Moving), and advanced features like moving a window directly to another virtual desktop, Active Desktop Borders. All these features can be configured also using the KDE Control Center's Appearance & Themes panels.

Opened windows are also shown as buttons on the KDE taskbar located on the panel. The taskbar shows the different programs you are running or windows you have open. This is essentially a docking mechanism that lets you change to a window or application just by clicking its button. When you minimize (iconify) a window, it is reduced to its taskbar button. You can then restore the window by clicking its taskbar button.

To the right of the title bar are three small buttons for minimizing, maximizing, or closing the window. You can switch to a window at any time by clicking its taskbar button. From the keyboard, you can use the ALT-TAB key combination to display a list of current applications. Holding down the ALT key and sequentially pressing TAB moves you through the list.

Application windows may display a Help Notes button, shown next to the iconify button and displaying a question mark. Clicking this button changes your cursor to a question mark. You can then move the cursor to an item such as an icon on a toolbar, and then click it to display a small help note explaining what the item does. For example, moving the mouse to the Forward button in the file manager taskbar will show a note explaining that this button performs a browser forward operation.

TIP *The taskbar and pager have three styles: elegant, classic, and transparent.*

Virtual Desktops: The KDE Desktop Pager

KDE, like most Linux window managers, supports virtual desktops. In effect, this extends the desktop area on which you can work. You could have Mozilla running on one desktop and be using a text editor in another. KDE can support up to 16 virtual desktops, though the default is 4. Your virtual desktops can be displayed and accessed using the KDE Desktop Pager located on the panel. The KDE Desktop Pager represents your virtual desktops as miniature screens showing small squares for each desktop. It is made to look similar to the GNOME Workspace Switcher. By default, there are 4 squares, numbered 1, 2, 3, and 4. You can have up to 16. To move from one desktop to another, click the square for the destination desktop. Clicking 3 displays the third desktop, and clicking 1 moves you back to the first desktop. If you want to move a window to a different desktop, first open the window's menu by right-clicking the window's title bar. Then select the To Desktop entry, which lists the available desktops. Choose the one you want.

You can also configure KDE so that if you move the mouse over the edge of a desktop screen, it automatically moves to the adjoining desktop. You need to imagine the desktops arranged in a four-square configuration, with two top desktops next to each other and two desktops below them. You enable this feature by enabling the Active Desktop Borders feature in the Desktop | Window Behavior | Advanced panel in the KDE Control Center.

To change the number of virtual desktops, you use the KDE Control Center's Desktop entry. Either select the Configure Desktop entry in the Desktop pop-up menu (right-click anywhere on the desktop background) and choose Multiple Desktops, or select Control Center from the main menu and open the Desktop heading to select the Multiple Desktops entry. The visible bar controls the number of desktops. Slide this to the right to add more and to the left to reduce the number. You can change any of the desktop names by clicking a name and entering a new one. In the Appearance & Theme's Background entry, you can change the appearance for particular desktops such as color background and wallpaper (deselect Common background first).

KDE Panel: Kicker

The KDE panel (Kicker), located at the bottom of the screen, provides access to most KDE functions (see Figure 7-3). The panel includes icons for menus, directory windows, specific programs, and virtual desktops. At the left end of the panel is an button for the main menu (also know as the K menu), a fedora *f* icon on Fedora.

To add an application to the panel, right-click anywhere on the panel and select Add from the pop-up menu. The Add menu displays the kind of objects you can add, including applets, applications, panels extensions, and special buttons. For KDE applications, select the applications entry. This lists all installed KDE applications on your main menu. Click the application entry to add an application button to the panel. You can also drag applications from a file manager window or from the main menu to the panel directly and have them automatically placed in the panel. The panel displays only desktop files. When you drag and drop a file to the panel, a desktop file for it is automatically generated.

Kicker also support numerous applets and several panel extensions, as well as special buttons.

- Applets are designed to run as icons in the panel. These include a clock, a pager, and a system monitor.

- Panel extensions add components to your desktop (select Panel from the Add menu). For example, the Kasbar extension sets up its own panel and list icons for each window you open. You can easily move from one window to another by clicking their corresponding icon in the Kasbar extension panel.

- Special buttons included buttons for KDE-specific operations like the KDE Window list, a Kterm terminal window, the KDE print manager, and KDE preferences.

To configure the panel position and behavior, right-click the panel and select the Configure Panel entry. This displays a customized control module window that collects the Panel configuration entries from the KDE Control Center. There are five configuration windows.

Figure 7-3   KDE panel.

The first four let you determine how the panel is displayed, and the last, Taskbar, configures how windows are shown on the taskbar. These conform to the KDE Control center's Desktop | Panels | Taskbar entries.

The first four panes are Arrangement, Hiding, Menus, and Appearance. The Arrangement pane enables you to specify the edges of the screen where you want your panel and taskbar displayed. You can also enlarge or reduce it in size. The Hiding pane lets you set the hiding mode, whether to enable auto-hiding or to manually hide and display the taskbar. The Menus pane lets you control the size of your menus as well as whether to display recently opened documents as menu items. You can also select certain default entries like Preferences and Bookmarks, as well as edit the K menu directly, adding or removing items. The Appearance pane lets you set button colors for buttons and background image for the taskbar. With the Taskbar pane, you can control windows and tasks displayed on the taskbar, as well as set the button actions.

The KDE Help Center

The KDE Help Center provides a browser-like interface for accessing and displaying both KDE Help files and Linux Man and info files. You can start the Help Center by selecting its entry in the main menu (the life preserver), or by right-clicking the desktop and selecting the Help entry. The Help window is divided into two frames. The left frame of the Help screen holds two tabbed panels, one listing contents and the other providing a glossary. The right frame displays currently selected documents. A help tree on the contents panel lets you choose the kind of Help documents you want to access. Here you can choose manuals, Man pages, or info documents, even application manuals. The Help Center includes a detailed user manual, a FAQ, and KDE Web site access.

A navigation toolbar enables you to move through previously viewed documents. KDE Help documents use an HTML format with links you can click to access other documents. The Back and Forward commands move you through the list of previously viewed documents. The KDE Help system provides an effective search tool for searching for patterns in Help documents, including Man and info pages. Select the Find entry from the Edit menu to display a page where you can enter your pattern.

Applications

You can start an application in KDE in several ways. If an entry for it is in the main menu, you can select that entry to start the application. Some applications also have buttons on the KDE panel you can click to start them. On Fedora, the panel already holds the same applications as shown on the GNOME panel, including the Evolution mail client, the Firefox Web browser, and several Office.org applications. You can also use the file manager to locate a file using that application or the application program itself. Clicking its icon starts the application. Or you can open a shell window and enter the name of the application at the shell prompt and press ENTER to start an application. You can also select Run Command from the main menu (or press ALT-F2) to open a small window consisting of a box to enter a single command. Previous commands can be accessed from a pop-up menu. An Options button will list options for running the program, such as priority or within a terminal window.

NOTE *You can create a desktop file on your desktop for any application already on your KDE menu by simply clicking and dragging its menu entry to the desktop. Select Copy and a desktop file for that application is created for you on your desktop, showing its icon.*

Application Standard Links

You can also access applications directly from your desktop. To access an application from the desktop, create either a desktop file or a standard link file that can link to the original application program. With a desktop file, you can choose your own icon and specify a tooltip comment. You can also use a desktop file to start a shell-based application running in its own terminal window. A standard link, on the other hand, is a simple reference to the original program file. Using a link starts the program up directly with no arguments. To create a standard link file, either select and drag the application in the main menu to the desktop or locate the application on your file system, usually in the **/bin**, **/usr/bin**, or **/usr/sbin** directory, and then click and drag the application icon to your desktop. In the pop-up menu, select Link. The link has the same icon as the original application. Whenever you then double-click that icon, the application will start. You can also use this method to run a application program you have created yourself, locating it in your own directory and creating a link for it on your desktop.

Application Desktop Links

To create a new desktop file for an application, right-click anywhere on the empty desktop, select Create New from the pop-up menu, and then within the File submenu, choose Link To Application. Enter the name for the program and a desktop file for it appears on the desktop with that name. A Properties dialog box then opens with four panels: General, Permissions, and Application. The General panel displays the name of the link. To select an icon image for the desktop file, click the icon. The Select Icon window is displayed, listing icons from which you can choose.

On the Permissions panel, be sure to set execute permissions so that the program can be run. You can set permissions for yourself, for your group, or for any user on the system. The Meta Info panel will list the type of file system used.

To specify the application the desktop file runs, go to the Application panel and either enter the application's program name in the Command box or click Browse to select it. On this panel, you also specify the description and comment. For the description, enter the application name. This is the name used for the link, if you use the file manager to display it. The comment is the Help note that appears when you pass your mouse over the icon.

In the Application panel, you can also specify the type of documents to be associated with this application. The bottom of the panel shows Add and Remove buttons. To specify a MIME type, click Add. This displays a list of file types and their descriptions. Select the one you want associated with this program. Desktop files needn't reside on the desktop. You can place them in any directory and access them through the file manager. You can later make changes to a desktop file by right-clicking its icon and selecting Properties from the pop-up menu. This again displays the dialog box for this file. You can change its icon and even the application it runs.

The Advanced Options button contains execute options for the application, such as running it in a shell window, or as a certain user. To run a shell-based program such as Vi, select the Run In Terminal check box and specify any terminal options. Startup options let you list the program in the system tray.

> ***Tip*** *You can have KDE automatically display selected directories or start certain applications whenever it starts up. To do so, place links for these windows and applications in the **AutoStart** directory located in your **.kde** directory.*

Mounting Devices from the Desktop

To access a CD-ROM disk, place the CD-ROM disk in your CD-ROM drive and double-click the CD-ROM icon. The file manager window then opens, displaying the contents of the CD-ROM's top-level directory. To eject the CD, right-click the CD-ROM's icon and select Eject from the pop-up menu (you can also elect to just unmount the CD-ROM). To access a floppy disk, you can perform a similar operation using the Floppy Disk icon. Place the floppy disk in the disk drive and double-click the Floppy Disk icon. This displays a file manager window with the contents of the floppy disk. Be careful not to remove the disk unless you first unmount it. To unmount the disk, right-click its icon and select Unmount from the icon's pop-up menu. You can perform one added operation with floppy disks. If you put in a blank disk, you can format it. You can choose from several file system formats, including MS-DOS. To format a standard Linux file system, select the ext3 entry.

KDE File Manager and Internet Client: Konqueror

The KDE file manager, known as Konqueror, is a multifunctional utility with which you can manage files, start programs, browse the Web, and download files from remote sites (see Figure 7-4). Traditionally, the term "file manager" was used to refer to managing files on a local hard disk. The KDE file manager extends its functionality well beyond this traditional function because it is Internet capable, seamlessly displaying remote file systems as if they were your own, as well as viewing Web pages with browser capabilities. It is capable of displaying a multitude of different kinds of files, including image, PostScript, and text files. KOffice applications can be run within the Konqueror window. You can even open a separate pane within a file manager window to run a terminal window where you can enter shell commands (Window menu).

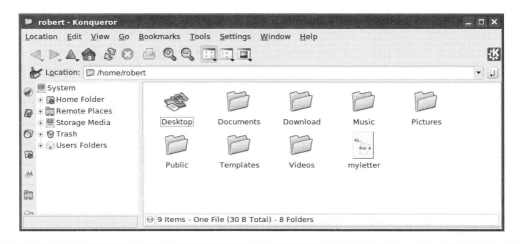

FIGURE 7-4   The KDE file manager.

Konqueror Window

A KDE file manager window consists of a menu bar, a navigation toolbar, a location field, a status bar, and a sidebar that provides different views of user resources such as a tree view of file and directory icons for your home directory. When you first display the file manager window, it displays the file and subdirectory icons for your home directory. Files and directories are automatically refreshed. Thus if you add or remove directories, you do not have to manually refresh the file manager window. It automatically updates for your listing, showing added files or eliminating deleted ones. The files listed in a directory can be viewed in several different ways such as icons, multicolumn (small icons), expandable trees, file information, or in a detailed listing. The different views are listed in the View Mode submenu within the View menu, and the commonly used ones are listed as icons at the end of the icon bar. The Tree mode lists your subdirectories as expandable trees whose contents you can display by clicking their plus signs. The Info mode lists file information such as the number of lines and characters in the file. The detailed listing provides permissions, owner, group, and size information. Permissions are the permissions controlling access to this file (see Chapter 28). The Text view does the same but does not display an icon next to the filename.

Konqueror also supports tabbed displays. Instead of opening a folder in a the same file manager window or a new one, you can open a new tab for it using the same file manager window. One tab can display the initial folder opened, and other tabs can be used for folders opened later. You can then move from viewing one folder to another by simply clicking the latter folder's tab. This way you can view multiple folders with just one file manager window. To open a folder as a tab, right-click its icon and select Open In New Tab. To later close the folder, right-click its tab label and select Close Tab. You can also detach a tab, opening it up in its own file manager window.

Tip *Configuration files, known as hidden files, are not usually displayed. To have the file manager display these files, select Show Hidden Files from the View menu. Konqueror also supports split views, letting you view different directories in the same window (Windows menu). You can split it vertically or horizontally.*

You can open a file either by clicking it or by selecting it and then choosing the Open entry in the File menu. If you want to select the file or directory, you need to hold down the CTRL key while you click it, or single-click. A double-click opens the file. If the file is a program, that program starts up. If it is a data file, such as a text file, the associated application is run using that data file. For example, if you double-click a text file, the Kate application starts displaying that file. If Konqueror cannot determine the application to use, it opens a dialog box prompting you to enter the application name. You can click the Browse button on this box to use a directory tree to locate the application program you want.

The file manager can also extract tar archives and install RPM packages. An *archive* is a file ending in **.tar.gz**, **.tar**, or **.tgz**. Clicking the archive lists the files in it. You can extract a particular file simply by dragging it out of the window. Clicking a text file in the archive displays it with Kate, while clicking an image file displays it with KView. Selecting an RPM package opens it with the system-config-packages utility, which you can then use to install the package.

If the folder is a CVS folder, used for managing different versions of a project, you can use the Cervisia tool listed in the View Mode submenu to display and examine CVS archives.

Navigation Panel

The navigation panel is a sidebar that lists different resources that a user can access with Konqueror. You can turn the navigation panel on or off by selecting its entry in the Windows menu. The sidebar is configured with the Navigation Panel Configuration tool, accessible as the first button on the Navigation panel's button bar.

TIP *Konqueror also provides a sidebar media player for running selected media files within your file manager window.*

The navigation panel features a vertical button bar for displaying items such as your bookmarks, devices, home directory, services, and network resources. Dragging the mouse over the resource icon displays its full name. When you click an item, its icon will expand to the name of that resource. Resources such as bookmarks, devices, and your home directory are listed in an expandable tree. Click an entry to expand it. Double-click it to access it with Konqueror. For example, to move to a subdirectory, expand your home directory entry and then double-click the subdirectory you want. Konqueror will now display that subdirectory. To go to a previously bookmarked directory or Web page, find its entry in the Bookmarks listing and select it. The network button lists network resources you have access to, such as FTP and Web sites. The root folder button displays your system's root directory and its subdirectories.

To configure the Navigation panel, click its configure button in the sidebar button bar. Select the Multiple Views entry to allow the display of several resource listings at once, each in its separate subsidebar. You can also add a new resource listing, choosing from a bookmark, history, or directory type. A button will appear for the new listing. You can right-click the button to select a new icon for it or select a URL, either a directory pathname or a network address. To remove a button and its listing, right-click it and select the Remove entry.

TIP *If the multiple views feature is enabled in the Navigation Panel Configuration, you can display several of these resources at once, just by clicking the ones you want. If this feature is not enabled, the previous listing is replaced by the selected one. Turn off a display by clicking its button again.*

Search

To search for files, select the Find entry in the Tools menu. This opens a pane within the file manager window in which you can search for filenames using wildcard matching symbols, such as *. Click Find to run the search and Stop to stop it. The search results are displayed in a pane in the lower half of the file manager window. You can click a file and have it open with its appropriate application. Text files are displayed by the Kate text editor. Images are displayed by KView, and PostScript files by KGhostView. Applications are run. The search program also enables you to save your search results for later reference. You can even select files from the search and add them to an archive.

Navigating Directories

Within a file manager window, a double-click on a directory icon moves to that directory and displays its file and subdirectory icons. To move back up to the parent directory, you click the up arrow button located on the left end of the navigation toolbar. A double-click on a directory icon moves you down the directory tree, one directory at a time. By clicking the up arrow button, you move up the tree. To move directly to a specific directory, you can enter its pathname in the Location box located just above the pane that displays the file and directory icons. Like a Web browser, the file manager remembers the previous directories it has displayed. You can use the back and forward arrow buttons to move through this list of prior directories. You can also use several keyboard shortcuts to perform such operations, as listed in Table 7-2.

If you know you want to access particular directories again, you can bookmark them, much as you do a Web page. Just open the directory and select the Add Bookmarks entry in the Bookmarks menu. An entry for that directory is then placed in the file manager's Bookmark menu. To move to the directory again, select its entry in the Bookmark menu. To navigate from one directory to another, you can use the Location field or the directory tree. In the Location field, you can enter the pathname of a directory, if you know it, and press ENTER. The directory tree provides a tree listing all directories on your system and in your home directory. To display the directory tree, select the Tree View from the View menu's View Mode submenu, or click the Tree View icon in the icon bar. To see the Tree View for your home or root directory directly, you can use the Navigation Panel's Home or Root Folder resources.

Keys	Description
ALT-LEFT ARROW, ALT-RIGHT ARROW	Backward and forward in history
ALT-UP ARROW	One directory up
ENTER	Open a file/directory
ESC	Open a pop-up menu for the current file
LEFT/RIGHT/UP/DOWN ARROWS	Move among the icons
SPACEBAR	Select/unselect file
PAGE UP, PAGE DOWN	Scroll up fast
CTRL-C	Copy selected file to clipboard
CTRL-V	Paste files from clipboard to current directory
CTRL-S	Select files by pattern
CTRL-L	Open new location
CTRL-F	Find files
CTRL-W	Close window

TABLE 7-2   KDE File Manager Keyboard Shortcuts

Copy, Move, Delete, Rename, and Link Operations

To perform an operation on a file or directory, you first have to select it. To select a file or directory, you click the file's icon or listing. To select more than one file, continue to hold the CTRL key down while you click the files you want. You can also use the keyboard arrow keys to move from one file icon to another and then use the ENTER key to select the file you want.

To copy and move files, you can use the standard drag-and-drop method with your mouse. To copy a file, you locate it by using the file manager. Open another file manager window to the directory to which you want the file copied. Then click and drag the File icon to that window. A pop-up menu appears with selections for Move, Copy, or Link. Choose Copy. To move a file to another directory, follow the same procedure, but select Move from the pop-up menu. To copy or move a directory, use the same procedure as for files. All the directory's files and subdirectories are also copied or moved.

To rename a file, click its icon and press F2, or right-click the icon and select Rename from the pop-up menu. The name below the icon will become boxed, editable text that you can then change.

You delete a file either by removing it immediately or placing it in a Trash folder to delete later. To delete a file, select it and then choose the Delete entry in the Edit menu. You can also right-click the icon and select Delete. To place a file in the Trash folder, click and drag it to the Trash icon on your desktop or select Move To Trash from the Edit menu. You can later open the Trash folder and delete the files. To delete all the files in the Trash folder, right-click the Trash icon and select Empty Trash Bin from the pop-up menu. To restore any files in the Trash bin, open the Trash bin and drag them out of the Trash folder.

Each file or directory has properties associated with it that include permissions, the filename, and its directory. To display the Properties window for a given file, right-click the file's icon and select the Properties entry. On the General panel, you see the name of the file displayed. To change the file's name, replace the name there with a new one. Permissions are set on the Permissions panel. Here, you can set read, write, and execute permissions for user, group, or other access to the file (see Chapter 28 for a discussion of permissions). The Group entry enables you to change the group for a file. The Meta Info panel lists information specific to that kind of file, for example, the number of lines and characters in a text file. An image file will list features like resolution, bit depth, and color.

TIP *KDE automatically searches for and reads an existing **.directory** file located in a directory. A **.directory** file holds KDE configuration information used to determine how the directory is displayed. You can create such a file in a directory and place a setting in it to set display features, such as the icon to use to display the directory folder.*

Web and FTP Access

The KDE file manager also doubles as a full-featured Web browser and an FTP client. It includes a box for entering either a pathname for a local file or a URL for a Web page on the Internet or your intranet. A navigation toolbar can be used to display previous Web pages or previous directories. The Home button will always return you to your home directory. When accessing a Web page, the page is displayed as on any Web browser. With the navigation toolbar, you can move back and forth through the list of previously displayed pages in that session.

The KDE file manager also operates as an FTP client. When you access an FTP site, you navigate the remote directories as you would your own. The operations to download a file are the same as copying a file on your local system. Just select the file's icon or entry in the file manager window and drag it to a window showing the local directory to which you want it downloaded. Then, select the Copy entry from the pop-up menu that appears. Konqueror also includes KSSL, which provides full SSL support for secure connections, featuring a secure connection status display.

TIP *KDE features the KGet tool for Konqueror, which manages FTP downloads, letting you select, queue, suspend, and schedule downloads, while displaying status information on current downloads.*

Configuring Konqueror

As a file browser, Web and FTP browser, and integral part of the KDE desktop, Konqueror has numerous configuration options. To configure Konqueror, open the Configure Konqueror window by selecting Configure Konqueror from a Konqueror window Settings menu (see Figure 7-5). This window displays a category listing on a sidebar. The initial categories deal with basic file management options like appearance, behavior, previews, and file associations. In Behavior, you specify such actions as displaying tooltips and opening folders in new windows.

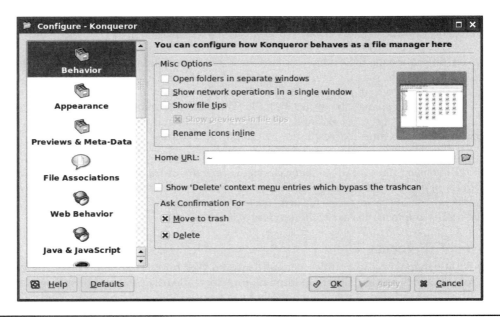

FIGURE 7-5 Konqueror Configure window.

Appearance lets you select the font and size. With Previews you can set the size of previewed icons, as well as specify the kind of files to retrieve metadata on. File Associations lets you set default applications for different kinds of files (same as File Association in KDE Components in Control Center).

The remaining categories deal with Web browser configurations, including configuring proxies, and Web page displays, as well as such basic behavior as highlighting URLs, fonts to use, managing cookies, and selecting encryption methods. The History category lets you specify the number of history items and their expiration date. With the Plugins category you can see a listing of current browser plug-ins as well as scan for new ones.

KDE Configuration: KDE Control Center

With the KDE Control Center, you can configure your desktop and system, changing the way it is displayed and the features it supports (see Figure 7-6). The Control Center can be directly started by selecting Control Center from the main menu.

The Control Center window is divided into two panes. The left pane shows a tree view of all the components you can configure, and the right pane displays the dialog windows for a

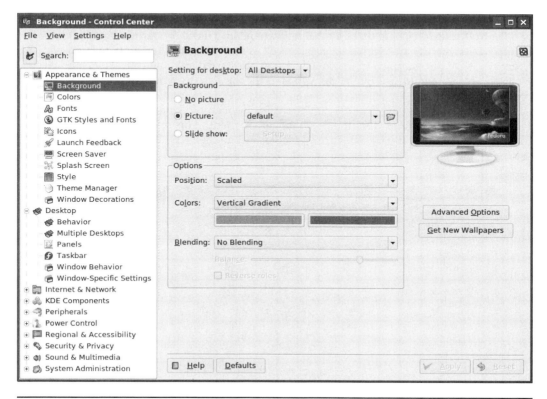

FIGURE 7-6   KDE Control Center.

selected component. See the Help viewer for a current listing of K Desktop configuration modules.

On the left pane, components are arranged into categories whose titles you can expand or shrink. The Internet and Network heading holds entries for configuring the KDE file manager's network tools, including Web browser features as well as Samba (Windows) access and wireless connectivity. Under Appearances & Themes, you can set different features for displaying and controlling your desktop. For example, the Background entry enables you to select a different background color or image for each one of your virtual desktops. Other entries enable you to configure components such as the screen saver, the language used, and the window style. The Peripheral heading holds entries that let you to configure your mouse, keyboard, and printer. The Sound and Multimedia heading contains panels for configuring sound components. From the Control Center, you can also access a set of specialized KDE system configuration tools. Currently these include a login manager and a font manager.

The KDE components category configure the behavior of your KDE interface. The Component Chooser lets you choose default components for applications, including the mail client to use, the default terminal tool, and the Web browser. File Associations associates file MIME types with default applications. The File Manager entry lets you set file manager features such as the font used and the files to preview. With the Session Manager, you can configure session startup and shutdown actions, for instance, restoring previous sessions on startup or automatically shutting down the system when you exit KDE. The Service Manager will list KDE daemons, both those loaded on demand and those on startup. You can elect whether to have a daemon run at startup, as well as manually start and stop daemons. Currently, KDE file sharing and Internet daemons are started automatically. You could elect instead to have them turned off, letting you start them manually when you want that kind of connectivity.

You can also access the Control Center entries from any file manager window (see Figure 7-7). Select Settings from the file manager Go menu. This opens a folder listing icons for all the KDE configuration categories as icons and folders. KDE configuration uses **settings:/** URL.

FIGURE 7-7   System settings access (Control Center) from the file manager.

.kde and Desktop User Directories

Your **.kde** directory holds files and directories used to maintain your KDE desktop. As with GNOME, the **Desktop** directory holds KDE desktop files whose icons are displayed on the desktop. Configuration files are located in the **.kde/share/config** directory. Here you can find the general configuration files for different KDE components: **kwinrc** holds configuration commands for the window manager, **kmailrc** for mail, and **kickerrc** for your panel, while **kdeglobals** holds keyboard shortcuts along with other global definitions. You can place configuration directives directly in any of these files; **.kde/share/mimelnk** holds the desktop files for the menu entries added by the user. The **.kde/share/apps** directory contains files and directories for configuring KDE applications, including **koffice**, **kmail**, and even **konqueror**.

MIME Types and Associated Applications

As you install new kinds of programs, they may use files of a certain type. In that case, you will need to register the type with KDE so that it can be associated with a given application or group of applications. For example, the MIME type for GIF images is **image/gif**, which is associated with image-viewing programs. You use the KDE Control Center to set up a new MIME type or to change MIME type associations with applications. Select the File Association entry under KDE Components. This will list known MIME types and their associated filename extensions. Select an entry to edit it, where you can change the applications associated with it. KDE saves its MIME type information in a separate file called **mimelnk** in the KDE configuration directory.

KDE Directories and Files

When KDE is installed on your system, its system-wide application, configuration, and support files may be installed in the same system directories as other GUIs and user applications. On Red Hat Enterprise Linux and Fedora, KDE is installed in the standard system directories with some variations, such as **/usr/bin** for KDE program files, **/usr/lib/kde3**, which holds KDE libraries, and **/usr/include/kde**, which contains KDE header files used in application development.

The directories located in **share** directory contain files used to configure system defaults for your KDE environment (the system **share** directory is located at **/usr/share**). The **share/mimelnk** directory maps its files to KDE icons and specifies MIME type definitions. Their contents consist of desktop files having the extension **.desktop**, one for each menu entry. The **share/apps** directory contains files and directories set up by KDE applications; **share/config** contains the configuration files for particular KDE applications. These are the system-wide defaults that can be overridden by users' own configurations in their own **.kde/share/config** directories. The **share/icons** directory holds the default icons used on your KDE desktop and by KDE applications as well as for the Bluecurve interface. As noted previously, in the user's home directory, the **.kde** directory holds a user's own KDE configuration for the desktop and its applications.

As noted previously, each user has a **Desktop** directory that holds KDE link files for all icons and folders on the user's desktop (see Table 7-3). These include the Trash folders and the CD-ROM and home directory links.

System KDE Directories	Description
/usr/bin	KDE programs
/usr/lib/kde3	KDE libraries
/usr/include/kde	Header files for use in compiling and developing KDE applications
/usr/share/config	KDE desktop and application configuration files
/usr/share/mimelnk	Desktop files used to build the main menu
/usr/share/apps	Files used by KDE applications
/usr/share/icons	Icons used in KDE desktop and applications
/usr/share/doc	KDE Help system
User KDE Directories	**Description**
.kde/AutoStart	Applications automatically started up with KDE
.kde/share/config	User KDE desktop and application configuration files for user-specified features
.kde/share/mimelnk	Desktop files used to build the user's menu entries on the KDE main menu
.kde/share/apps	Directories and files used by KDE applications
Desktop	Desktop files for icons and folders displayed on the user's KDE desktop
Desktop/Trash	Trash folder for files marked for deletion

TABLE 7-3   KDE Installation Directories

The Shell

The *shell* is a command interpreter that provides a line-oriented interactive and noninteractive interface between the user and the operating system. You enter commands on a command line; they are interpreted by the shell and then sent as instructions to the operating system (the command line interface is accessible from Gnome and KDE through a Terminal windows—Applications/Accessories menu). You can also place commands in a script file to be consecutively executed much like a program. This interpretive capability of the shell provides for many sophisticated features. For example, the shell has a set of file expansion characters that can generate filenames. The shell can redirect input and output, as well as run operations in the background, freeing you to perform other tasks.

Several different types of shells have been developed for Linux: the Bourne Again shell (BASH), the Korn shell, the TCSH shell, and the Z shell. All shells are available for your use, although the BASH shell is the default. You only need one type of shell to do your work. Fedora Linux includes all the major shells, although it installs and uses the BASH shell as the default. If you use the command line shell, you will be using the BASH shell unless you specify another. This chapter discusses the BASH shell, which shares many of the same features as other shells.

You can find out more about shells at their respective Web sites as listed in Table 8-1. Also, a detailed online manual is available for each installed shell. Use the **man** command and the shell's keyword to access them, **bash** for the BASH shell, **ksh** for the Korn shell, **zsh** for the Z shell, and **tsch** for the TSCH shell. For example, the command **man bash** will access the BASH shell online manual.

NOTE *You can find out more about the BASH shell at **www.gnu.org/software/bash**. A detailed online manual is available on your Linux system using the **man** command with the **bash** keyword.*

The Command Line

The Linux command line interface consists of a single line into which you enter commands with any of their options and arguments. From GNOME or KDE, you can access the command line interface by opening a terminal window. Should you start Linux with the command line interface, you will be presented with a BASH shell command line when you log in.

Shell	Web Site
www.gnu.org/software/bash	BASH Web site with online manual, FAQ, and current releases
www.gnu.org/software/ bash/manual/bash.html	BASH online manual
www.zsh.org	Z shell Web site with referrals to FAQs and current downloads.
www.tcsh.org	TCSH Web site with detailed support including manual, tips, FAQ, and recent releases
www.kornshell.com	Korn shell site with manual, FAQ, and references

TABLE 8-1   Linux Shells

By default, the BASH shell has a dollar sign (**$**) prompt, but Linux has several other types of shells, each with its own prompt (like % for the C shell). The root user will have a different prompt, the **#**. A shell *prompt,* such as the one shown here, marks the beginning of the command line:

```
$
```

You can enter a command along with options and arguments at the prompt. For example, with an **-l** option, the **ls** command will display a line of information about each file, listing such data as its size and the date and time it was last modified. In the next example, the user enters the **ls** command followed by a **-l** option. The dash before the **-l** option is required. Linux uses it to distinguish an option from an argument.

```
$ ls -l
```

If you wanted only the information displayed for a particular file, you could add that file's name as the argument, following the **-l** option:

```
$ ls -l mydata
-rw-r--r-- 1 chris weather 207 Feb 20 11:55 mydata
```

TIP   *Some commands can be complex and take some time to execute. When you mistakenly execute the wrong command, you can interrupt and stop such commands with the interrupt key—*CTRL-C.

You can enter a command on several lines by typing a backslash just before you press ENTER. The backslash "escapes" the ENTER key, effectively continuing the same command line to the next line. In the next example, the **cp** command is entered on three lines. The first two lines end in a backslash, effectively making all three lines one command line.

```
$ cp -i \
mydata \
/home/george/myproject/newdata
```

You can also enter several commands on the same line by separating them with a semicolon (;). In effect the semicolon operates as an execute operation. Commands will be executed in the sequence they are entered. The following command executes an **ls** command followed by a **date** command.

```
$ ls ; date
```

You can also conditionally run several commands on the same line with the **&&** operator (see Chapter 9). A command is executed only if the previous one is true. This feature is useful for running several dependent scripts on the same line. In the next example, the **ls** command is run only if the **date** command is successfully executed.

```
$ date && ls
```

TIP *Command can also be run as arguments on a command line, using their results for other commands. To run a command within a command line, you encase the command in back quotes, see Values from Linux Commands later in this chapter.*

Command Line Editing

The BASH shell, which is your default shell, has special command line editing capabilities that you may find helpful as you learn Linux (see Table 8-2). You can easily modify commands you have entered before executing them, moving anywhere on the command line and inserting or deleting characters. This is particularly helpful for complex commands. You can use the CTRL-F or RIGHT ARROW key to move forward a character, or the CTRL-B or LEFT ARROW key to move back a character. CTRL-D or DEL deletes the character the cursor is on, and CTRL-H or BACKSPACE deletes the character before the cursor. To add text, you use the arrow keys to move the cursor to where you want to insert text and type the new characters. You can even cut words with the CTRL-W or ALT-D key and then use the CTRL-Y key to paste them back in at a different position, effectively moving the words. As a rule, the CTRL version of the command operates on characters, and the ALT version works on words, such as CTRL-T to transpose characters and ALT-T to transpose words. At any time, you can press ENTER to execute the command. For example, if you make a spelling mistake when entering a command, rather than reentering the entire command, you can use the editing operations to correct the mistake. The actual associations of keys and their tasks, along with global settings, are specified in the **/etc/inputrc** file.

TIP *The editing capabilities of the BASH shell command line are provided by Readline. Readline supports numerous editing operations. You can even bind a key to a selected editing operation. Readline uses the /etc/inputrc file to configure key bindings. This file is read automatically by your /etc/profile shell configuration file when you log in (see Chapter 9). Users can customize their editing commands by creating an .inputrc file in their home directory (this is a dot file). It may be best to first copy the /etc/inputrc file as your .inputrc file and then edit it. /etc/profile will first check for a **local** .inputrc file before accessing the /etc/inputrc file. You can find out more about Readline in the BASH shell reference manual at **www.gnu.org/manual/bash**.*

Movement Commands	Operation
CTRL-F, RIGHT-ARROW	Move forward a character
CTRL-B, LEFT-ARROW	Move backward a character
CTRL-A or HOME	Move to beginning of line
CTRL-E or END	Move to end of line
ALT-F	Move forward a word
ALT-B	Move backward a word
CTRL-L	Clear screen and place line at top
Editing Commands	**Operation**
CTRL-D or DEL	Delete character cursor is on
CTRL-H or BACKSPACE	Delete character before the cursor
CTRL-K	Cut remainder of line from cursor position
CTRL-U	Cut from cursor position to beginning of line
CTRL-W	Cut previous word
CTRL-C	Cut entire line
ALT-D	Cut the remainder of a word
ALT-DEL	Cut from the cursor to the beginning of a word
CTRL-Y	Paste previous cut text
ALT-Y	Paste from set of previously cut text
CTRL-Y	Paste previous cut text
CTRL-V	Insert quoted text, used for inserting control or meta (ALT) keys as text, such as CTRL-B for backspace or CTRL-T for tabs
ALT-T	Transpose current and previous word
ALT-L	Lowercase current word
ALT-U	Uppercase current word
ALT-C	Capitalize current word
CTRL-SHIFT-_	Undo previous change

TABLE 8-2 Command Line Editing Operations

Command and Filename Completion

The BASH command line has a built-in feature that performs command line and file name completion. Automatic completions can be effected using the TAB key. If you enter an incomplete pattern as a command or filename argument, you can then press the TAB key to activate the command and filename completion feature, which completes the pattern. Directories will have a / attached to their name. If more than one command or file has the same prefix, the shell simply beeps and waits for you to enter the TAB key again. It then displays a list of possible command completions and waits for you to add enough characters to select a unique command or filename. For situations where you know there are likely multiple possibilities, you can just press the ESC key instead of two TABS. In the next example, the user issues a **cat** command with an incomplete filename. When the user presses the TAB key, the system searches for a match and, when it finds one, fills in the filename. The user can then press ENTER to execute the command.

```
$ cat pre tab
$ cat preface
```

The automatic completions also works with the names of variables, users, and hosts. In this case, the partial text needs to be preceded by a special character, indicating the type of name. Variables begin with a $ sign, so any text beginning with a dollar sign is treated as a variable to be completed. Variables are selected from previously defined variables, like system shell variables (see Chapter 9). User names begin with a tilde (~). Host names begin with a @ sign, with possible names taken from the **/etc/hosts** file. A listing of possible automatic completions follows:

- Filenames begin with any text or /.
- Shell variable text begins with a $ sign.
- User name text begins with a ~ sign.
- Host name text begins with a @.
- Commands, aliases, and text in files begin with normal text.

For example, to complete the variable HOME given just $HOM, simple enter a tab character.

```
$ echo $HOM <tab>
$ echo $HOME
```

If you entered just an H, then you could enter two tabs to see all possible variables beginning with H. The command line is redisplayed, letting you complete the name.

```
$ echo $H <tab> <tab>
$HISTCMD $HISTFILE $HOME $HOSTTYPE HISTFILE  $HISTSIZE $HISTNAME
$ echo $H
```

You can also specifically select the kind of text to complete, using corresponding command keys. In this case, it does not matter what kind of sign a name begins with. For example, the ALT-~ will treat the current text as a user name. ALT-@ will treat it as a host name, and ALT-$, as a variable. ALT-! will treat it as a command. To display a list of possible completions, use the CTRL-X key with the appropriate completion key, as in CTRL-X-$ to list possible variable completions. See Table 8-3 for a complete listing.

History

The BASH shell keeps a list, called a *history list,* of your previously entered commands. You can display each command, in turn, on your command line by pressing the UP ARROW key. The DOWN ARROW key moves you down the list. You can modify and execute any of these previous commands when you display them on your command line.

Command (CTRL-R for listing possible completions)	Description
TAB	Automatic completion
TAB TAB or ESC	List possible completions
ALT-/, CTRL-R-/	Filename completion, normal text for automatic
ALT-$, CTRL-R-$	Shell variable completion, $ for automatic
ALT-~, CTRL-R-~	User name completion, ~ for automatic
ALT-@, CTRL-R-@	Host name completion, @ for automatic
ALT-!, CTRL-R-!	Command name completion, normal text for automatic

TABLE 8-3   Command Line Editing Operations

TIP   *The capability to redisplay a previous command is helpful when you've already executed a command you had entered incorrectly. In this case, you would be presented with an error message and a new, empty command line. By pressing the UP ARROW key, you can redisplay your previous command, make corrections to it, and then execute it again. This way, you would not have to enter the whole command again.*

History Events

In the BASH shell, the *history utility* keeps a record of the most recent commands you have executed. The commands are numbered starting at 1, and a limit exists to the number of commands remembered—the default is 500. The history utility is a kind of short-term memory, keeping track of the most recent commands you have executed. To see the set of your most recent commands, type **history** on the command line and press ENTER. A list of your most recent commands is then displayed, preceded by a number.

```
$ history
1 cp mydata today
2 vi mydata
3 mv mydata reports
4 cd reports
5 ls
```

Each of these commands is technically referred to as an event. An *event* describes an action that has been taken—a command that has been executed. The events are numbered according to their sequence of execution. The most recent event has the highest number. Each of these events can be identified by its number or beginning characters in the command.

The history utility enables you to reference a former event, placing it on your command line and enabling you to execute it. The easiest way to do this is to use the UP ARROW and DOWN ARROW keys to place history events on your command line, one at a time. You needn't display the list first with **history**. Pressing the UP ARROW key once places the last history event on your command line. Pressing it again places the next history event on your command. Pressing the DOWN ARROW key places the previous event on the command line.

You can use certain control and meta keys to perform other history operations like searching the history list. A meta key is the ALT key, and the ESC key on keyboards that have no ALT key. The ALT key is used here. ALT-< will move you to the beginning of the history list; ALT-N will search it. CTRL-S and CTRL-R will perform incremental searches, display matching commands as you type in a search string. Table 8-4 lists the different commands for referencing the history list.

TIP *If more than one history event matches what you have entered, you will hear a beep, and you can then enter more characters to help uniquely identify the event.*

You can also reference and execute history events using the **!** history command. The **!** is followed by a reference that identifies the command. The reference can be either the number

History Commands	Description
CTRL-N or DOWN ARROW	Moves down to the next event in the history list
CTRL-P or UP ARROW	Moves up to the previous event in the history list
ALT-<	Moves to the beginning of the history event list
ALT->	Moves to the end of the history event list
ALT-N	Forward Search, next matching item
ALT-P	Backward Search, previous matching item
CTRL-S	Forward Search History, forward incremental search
CTRL-R	Reverse Search History, reverse incremental search
fc *event-reference*	Edits an event with the standard editor and then executes it **Options** **-l** List recent history events; same as **history** command **-e** *editor event-reference* Invokes a specified editor to edit a specific event
History Event References	**Description**
! *event num*	References an event with an event number
! !	References the previous command
! *characters*	References an event with beginning characters
! ? *pattern* **?**	References an event with a pattern in the event
! *-event num*	References an event with an offset from the first event
! *num* *-num*	References a range of events

TABLE 8-4 History Commands and History Event References

of the event or a beginning set of characters in the event. In the next example, the third command in the history list is referenced first by number and then by the beginning characters:

```
$ !3
mv mydata reports
$ !mv my
mv mydata reports
```

You can also reference an event using an offset from the end of the list. A negative number will offset from the end of the list to that event, thereby referencing it. In the next example, the fourth command, **cd mydata**, is referenced using a negative offset, and then executed. Remember that you are offsetting from the end of the list—in this case, event 5—up toward the beginning of the list, event 1. An offset of 4 beginning from event 5 places you at event 2.

```
$ !-4
vi mydata
```

To reference the last event, you use a following !, as in **! !**. In the next example, the command **! !** executes the last command the user executed—in this case, **ls**:

```
$ !!
ls
mydata today reports
```

History Event Editing

You can also edit any event in the history list before you execute it. In the BASH shell, you can do this two ways. You can use the command line editor capability to reference and edit any event in the history list. You can also use a history **fc** command option to reference an event and edit it with the full Vi editor. Each approach involves two different editing capabilities. The first is limited to the commands in the command line editor, which edits only a single line with a subset of Emacs commands. At the same time, however, it enables you to reference events easily in the history list. The second approach invokes the standard Vi editor with all its features, but only for a specified history event.

With the command line editor, not only can you edit the current command, you can also move to a previous event in the history list to edit and execute it. The CTRL-P command then moves you up to the prior event in the list. The CTRL-N command moves you down the list. The ALT-< command moves you to the top of the list, and the ALT-> command moves you to the bottom. You can even use a pattern to search for a given event. The slash followed by a pattern searches backward in the list, and the question mark followed by a pattern searches forward in the list. The **n** command repeats the search.

Once you locate the event you want to edit, you use the Emacs command line editing commands to edit the line. CTRL-D deletes a character. CTRL-F or the RIGHT ARROW moves you forward a character, and CTRL-B or the LEFT ARROW moves you back a character. To add text, you position your cursor and type in the characters you want.

If you want to edit an event using a standard editor instead, you need to reference the event using the **fc** command and a specific event reference, such as an event number.

The editor used is the one specified by the shell in the **EDITOR** variable. This serves as the default editor for the **fc** command. You can assign to the **EDITOR** variable a different editor if you wish, such as Emacs instead of Vi. The next example will edit the fourth event, **cd reports**, with the standard editor and then execute the edited event:

```
$ fc 4
```

You can select more than one command at a time to be edited and executed by referencing a range of commands. You select a range of commands by indicating an identifier for the first command followed by an identifier for the last command in the range. An identifier can be the command number or the beginning characters in the command. In the next example, the range of commands 2–4 is edited and executed, first using event numbers and then using beginning characters in those events:

```
$ fc 2 4
$ fc vi c
```

The **fc** command uses the default editor specified in the **FCEDIT** special variable. Usually, this is the Vi editor. If you want to use the Emacs editor instead, you use the **-e** option and the term **emacs** when you invoke **fc**. The next example will edit the fourth event, **cd reports**, with the Emacs editor and then execute the edited event:

```
$ fc -e emacs 4
```

Configuring History: HISTFILE and HISTSAVE

The number of events saved by your system is kept in a special system variable called **HISTSIZE**. By default, this is usually set to 500. You can change this to another number by simply assigning a new value to **HISTSIZE**. In the next example, the user changes the number of history events saved to 10 by resetting the **HISTSIZE** variable:

```
$ HISTSIZE=10
```

The actual history events are saved in a file whose name is held in a special variable called **HISTFILE**. By default, this file is the **.bash_history** file. You can change the file in which history events are saved, however, by assigning its name to the **HISTFILE** variable. In the next example, the value of **HISTFILE** is displayed. Then a new filename is assigned to it, **newhist**. History events are then saved in the **newhist** file.

```
$ echo $HISTFILE
.bash_history
$ HISTFILE="newhist"
$ echo $HISTFILE
newhist
```

Filename Expansion: *, ?, [ ]

Filenames are the most common arguments used in a command. Often you may know only part of the filename, or you may want to reference several filenames that have the same extension or begin with the same characters. The shell provides a set of special characters that search out, match, and generate a list of filenames. These are the asterisk, the question mark, and brackets (*****, **?**, **[]**). Given a partial filename, the shell uses these matching operators to search for files and expand to a list of filenames found. The shell replaces the partial filename argument with the expanded list of matched filenames. This list of filenames can then become the arguments for commands such as **ls**, which can operate on many files. Table 8-5 lists the shell's file expansion characters.

Common Shell Symbols	Execution
ENTER	Execute a command line.
;	Separate commands on the same command line.
`command`	Execute a command.
$ (command)	Execute a command.
[]	Match on a class of possible characters in filenames.
\	Quote the following character. Used to quote special characters.
|	Pipe the standard output of one command as input for another command.
&	Execute a command in the background.
!	History command.
File Expansion Symbols	**Execution**
*	Match on any set of characters in filenames.
?	Match on any single character in filenames.
[]	Match on a class of characters in filenames.
Redirection Symbols	**Execution**
>	Redirect the standard output to a file or device, creating the file if it does not exist and overwriting the file if it does exist.
>!	The exclamation point forces the overwriting of a file if it already exists. This overrides the **noclobber** option.
<	Redirect the standard input from a file or device to a program.
>>	Redirect the standard output to a file or device, appending the output to the end of the file.
Standard Error Redirection Symbols	**Execution**
2>	Redirect the standard error to a file or device.
2>>	Redirect and append the standard error to a file or device.
2>&1	Redirect the standard error to the standard output.
>&	Redirect the standard error to a file or device.
|&	Pipe the standard error as input to another command.

TABLE 8-5   Shell Symbols

Matching Multiple Characters

The asterisk (*) references files beginning or ending with a specific set of characters. You place the asterisk before or after a set of characters that form a pattern to be searched for in filenames. If the asterisk is placed before the pattern, filenames that end in that pattern are searched for. If the asterisk is placed after the pattern, filenames that begin with that pattern are searched for. Any matching filename is copied into a list of filenames generated by this operation. In the next example, all filenames beginning with the pattern "doc" are searched for and a list generated. Then all filenames ending with the pattern "day" are searched for and a list is generated. The last example shows how the * can be used in any combination of characters.

```
$ ls
doc1 doc2 document docs mydoc monday tuesday
$ ls doc*
doc1 doc2 document docs
$ ls *day
monday tuesday
$ ls m*d*
monday
$
```

Filenames often include an extension specified with a period and followed by a string denoting the file type, such as **.c** for C files, **.cpp** for C++ files, or even **.jpg** for JPEG image files. The extension has no special status and is only part of the characters making up the filename. Using the asterisk makes it easy to select files with a given extension. In the next example, the asterisk is used to list only those files with a .c extension. The asterisk placed before the **.c** constitutes the argument for **ls**.

```
$ ls *.c
calc.c main.c
```

You can use * with the **rm** command to erase several files at once. The asterisk first selects a list of files with a given extension, or beginning or ending with a given set of characters, and then it presents this list of files to the **rm** command to be erased. In the next example, the **rm** command erases all files beginning with the pattern "doc":

```
$ rm doc*
```

TIP *Use the * file expansion character carefully and sparingly with the **rm** command. The combination can be dangerous. A misplaced * in an **rm** command without the **-i** option could easily erase all the files in your current directory. The **-i** option will first prompt the user to confirm whether the file should be deleted.*

Matching Single Characters

The question mark (?) matches only a single incomplete character in filenames. Suppose you want to match the files **doc1** and **docA**, but not the file **document**. Whereas the asterisk will match filenames of any length, the question mark limits the match to just one extra character. The next example matches files that begin with the word "doc" followed by a single differing letter:

```
$ ls
doc1 docA document
$ ls doc?
doc1 docA
```

Matching a Range of Characters

Whereas the * and ? file expansion characters specify incomplete portions of a filename, the brackets ([]) enable you to specify a set of valid characters to search for. Any character placed within the brackets will be matched in the filename. Suppose you want to list files beginning with "doc", but only ending in *1* or *A.* You are not interested in filenames ending in *2* or *B,* or any other character. Here is how it's done:

```
$ ls
doc1 doc2 doc3 docA docB docD document
$ ls doc[1A]
doc1 docA
```

You can also specify a set of characters as a range, rather than listing them one by one. A dash placed between the upper and lower bounds of a set of characters selects all characters within that range. The range is usually determined by the character set in use. In an ASCII character set, the range "a-g" will select all lowercase alphabetic characters from *a* through *g,* inclusive. In the next example, files beginning with the pattern "doc" and ending in characters *1* through *3* are selected. Then, those ending in characters *B* through *E* are matched.

```
$ ls doc[1-3]
doc1 doc2 doc3
$ ls doc[B-E]
docB docD
```

You can combine the brackets with other file expansion characters to form flexible matching operators. Suppose you want to list only filenames ending in either a **.c** or **.o** extension, but no other extension. You can use a combination of the asterisk and brackets: * [co]. The asterisk matches all filenames, and the brackets match only filenames with extension **.c** or **.o**.

```
$ ls *.[co]
main.c  main.o  calc.c
```

Matching Shell Symbols

At times, a file expansion character is actually part of a filename. In these cases, you need to quote the character by preceding it with a backslash to reference the file. In the next example, the user needs to reference a file that ends with the **?** character, **answers?**. The **?** is, however, a file expansion character and would match any filename beginning with "answers" that has one or more characters. In this case, the user quotes the **?** with a preceding backslash to reference the filename.

```
$ ls answers\?
answers?
```

Placing the filename in double quotes will also quote the character.

```
$ ls "answers?"
answers?
```

This is also true for filenames or directories that have white space characters like the space character. In this case you could either use the backslash to quote the space character in the file or directory name, or place the entire name in double quotes.

```
$ ls My\ Documents
My Documents
$ ls "My Documents"
My Documents
```

Generating Patterns

Though not a file expansion operation, **{ }** is often useful for generating names that you can use to create or modify files and directories. The braces operation only generates a list of names. It does not match on existing filenames. Patterns are placed within the braces and separated with commas. Any pattern placed within the braces will be used to generate a version of the pattern, using either the preceding or following pattern, or both. Suppose you want to generate a list of names beginning with "doc", but only ending in the patterns "ument", "final", and "draft". Here is how it's done:

```
$ echo doc{ument,final,draft}
document docfinal docdraft
```

Since the names generated do not have to exist, you could use the **{ }** operation in a command to create directories, as shown here:

```
$ mkdir {fall,winter,spring}report
$ ls
fallreport springreport winterreport
```

Standard Input/Output and Redirection

The data in input and output operations is organized like a file. Data input at the keyboard is placed in a data stream arranged as a continuous set of bytes. Data output from a command or program is also placed in a data stream and arranged as a continuous set of bytes. This input data stream is referred to in Linux as the *standard input,* while the output data stream is called the *standard output.* There is also a separate output data stream reserved solely for error messages, called the *standard error* (see the section "Redirecting and Piping the Standard Error: >&, 2>" later in this chapter).

Because the standard input and standard output have the same organization as that of a file, they can easily interact with files. Linux has a redirection capability that lets you easily move data in and out of files. You can redirect the standard output so that, instead of displaying the output on a screen, you can save it in a file. You can also redirect the standard input away from the keyboard to a file, so that input is read from a file instead of from your keyboard.

When a Linux command is executed that produces output, this output is placed in the standard output data stream. The default destination for the standard output data stream is a device—in this case, the screen. *Devices,* such as the keyboard and screen, are treated as files. They receive and send out streams of bytes with the same organization as that of a byte-stream file. The screen is a device that displays a continuous stream of bytes. By default, the standard output will send its data to the screen device, which will then display the data.

For example, the `ls` command generates a list of all filenames and outputs this list to the standard output. Next, this stream of bytes in the standard output is directed to the screen device. The list of filenames is then printed on the screen. The `cat` command also sends output to the standard output. The contents of a file are copied to the standard output, whose default destination is the screen. The contents of the file are then displayed on the screen.

Redirecting the Standard Output: > and >>

Suppose that instead of displaying a list of files on the screen, you would like to save this list in a file. In other words, you would like to direct the standard output to a file rather than the screen. To do this, you place the output redirection operator, the greater-than sign (`>`), followed by the name of a file on the command line after the Linux command. Table 8-6 lists the different ways you can use the redirection operators. In the next example, the output of the `ls` command is redirected from the screen device to a file:

```
$ ls -l *.c > programlist
```

The redirection operation creates the new destination file. If the file already exists, it will be overwritten with the data in the standard output. You can set the **noclobber** feature to prevent overwriting an existing file with the redirection operation. In this case, the redirection operation on an existing file will fail. You can overcome the **noclobber** feature by placing an exclamation point after the redirection operator. You can place the **noclobber** command in a shell configuration file to make it an automatic default operation (see Chapter 9). The next example sets the **noclobber** feature for the BASH shell and then forces the overwriting of the **oldletter** file if it already exists:

```
$ set -o noclobber
$ cat myletter >! oldletter
```

Although the redirection operator and the filename are placed after the command, the redirection operation is not executed after the command. In fact, it is executed before the command. The redirection operation creates the file and sets up the redirection before it receives any data from the standard output. If the file already exists, it will be destroyed and replaced by a file of the same name. In effect, the command generating the output is executed only after the redirected file has been created.

Command	Execution
ENTER	Execute a command line.
;	Separate commands on the same command line.
command\ *opts args*	Enter backslash before carriage return to continue entering a command on the next line.
'*command*'	Execute a command.
$(*command*)	Execute a command.
Special Characters for Filename Expansion	**Execution**
*	Match on any set of characters.
?	Match on any single characters.
[]	Match on a class of possible characters.
\	Quote the following character. Used to quote special characters.
Redirection	**Execution**
command > *filename*	Redirect the standard output to a file or device, creating the file if it does not exist and overwriting the file if it does exist.
command < *filename*	Redirect the standard input from a file or device to a program.
command >> *filename*	Redirect the standard output to a file or device, appending the output to the end of the file.
command >! *filename*	In the C shell and the Korn shell, the exclamation point forces the overwriting of a file if it already exists. This overrides the **noclobber** option.
command 2> *filename*	Redirect the standard error to a file or device in the Bourne shell.
command 2>> *filename*	Redirect and append the standard error to a file or device in the Bourne shell.
command 2>&1	Redirect the standard error to the standard output in the Bourne shell.
command >& *filename*	Redirect the standard error to a file or device in the C shell.
Pipes	**Execution**
command | *command*	Pipe the standard output of one command as input for another command.
command |& *command*	Pipe the standard error as input to another command in the C shell.

TABLE 8-6   The Shell Operations

In the next example, the output of the **ls** command is redirected from the screen device to a file. First the **ls** command lists files, and in the next command, **ls** redirects its file list to the **listf** file. Then the **cat** command displays the list of files saved in **listf**. Notice the list of files in **listf** includes the **listf** filename. The list of filenames generated by the **ls** command includes the name of the file created by the redirection operation—in this case, **listf**. The **listf** file is first created by the redirection operation, and then the **ls** command lists it along with other files. This file list output by **ls** is then redirected to the **listf** file, instead of being printed on the screen.

```
$ ls
mydata intro preface
$ ls > listf
$ cat listf
mydata intro listf preface
```

TIP *Errors occur when you try to use the same filename for both an input file for the command and the redirected destination file. In this case, because the redirection operation is executed first, the input file, because it exists, is destroyed and replaced by a file of the same name. When the command is executed, it finds an input file that is empty.*

You can also append the standard output to an existing file using the **>>** redirection operator. Instead of overwriting the file, the data in the standard output is added at the end of the file. In the next example, the **myletter** and **oldletter** files are appended to the **alletters** file. The **alletters** file will then contain the contents of both **myletter** and **oldletter**.

```
$ cat myletter >> alletters
$ cat oldletter >> alletters
```

The Standard Input

Many Linux commands can receive data from the standard input. The standard input itself receives data from a device or a file. The default device for the standard input is the keyboard. Characters typed on the keyboard are placed in the standard input, which is then directed to the Linux command. Just as with the standard output, you can also redirect the standard input, receiving input from a file rather than the keyboard. The operator for redirecting the standard input is the less-than sign (<). In the next example, the standard input is redirected to receive input from the **myletter** file, rather than the keyboard device (use CTRL-D to end the typed input). The contents of **myletter** are read into the standard input by the redirection operation. Then the **cat** command reads the standard input and displays the contents of **myletter**.

```
$ cat < myletter
hello Christopher
How are you today
$
```

You can combine the redirection operations for both standard input and standard output. In the next example, the **cat** command has no filename arguments. Without filename arguments, the **cat** command receives input from the standard input and sends output to the standard output. However, the standard input has been redirected to receive its data from a file, while the standard output has been redirected to place its data in a file.

```
$ cat < myletter > newletter
```

Pipes: |

You may find yourself in situations in which you need to send data from one command to another. In other words, you may want to send the standard output of a command to another command, not to a destination file. Suppose you want to send a list of your filenames to the printer to be printed. You need two commands to do this: the **ls** command to generate a list of filenames and the **lpr** command to send the list to the printer. In effect, you need to take the output of the **ls** command and use it as input for the **lpr** command. You can think of the data as flowing from one command to another. To form such a connection in Linux, you use what is called a *pipe*. The *pipe operator* (|, the vertical bar character) placed between two commands forms a connection between them. The standard output of one command becomes the standard input for the other. The pipe operation receives output from the command placed before the pipe and sends this data as input to the command placed after the pipe. As shown in the next example, you can connect the **ls** command and the **lpr** command with a pipe. The list of filenames output by the **ls** command is piped into the **lpr** command.

```
$ ls | lpr
```

You can combine the **pipe** operation with other shell features, such as file expansion characters, to perform specialized operations. The next example prints only files with a **.c** extension. The **ls** command is used with the asterisk and ".c" to generate a list of filenames with the **.c** extension. Then this list is piped to the **lpr** command.

```
$ ls *.c | lpr
```

In the preceding example, a list of filenames was used as input, but what is important to note is that pipes operate on the standard output of a command, whatever that might be. The contents of whole files or even several files can be piped from one command to another. In the next example, the **cat** command reads and outputs the contents of the **mydata** file, which are then piped to the **lpr** command:

```
$ cat mydata | lpr
```

Linux has many commands that generate modified output. For example, the **sort** command takes the contents of a file and generates a version with each line sorted in alphabetic order. The **sort** command works best with files that are lists of items. Commands such as **sort** that output a modified version of its input are referred to as *filters*. Filters are often used with pipes. In the next example, a sorted version of **mylist** is generated and piped into the **more** command for display on the screen. Note that the original file, **mylist**, has not been changed and is not itself sorted. Only the output of **sort** in the standard output is sorted.

```
$ sort mylist | more
```

The standard input piped into a command can be more carefully controlled with the standard input argument (**-**). When you use the dash as an argument for a command, it represents the standard input.

Redirecting and Piping the Standard Error: >&, 2>

When you execute commands, an error could possibly occur. You may give the wrong number of arguments, or some kind of system error could take place. When an error occurs, the system issues an error message. Usually such error messages are displayed on the screen, along with the standard output. Linux distinguishes between standard output and error messages, however. Error messages are placed in yet another standard byte stream, called the *standard error*. In the next example, the **cat** command is given as its argument the name of a file that does not exist, **myintro**. In this case, the **cat** command simply issues an error:

```
$ cat myintro
cat : myintro not found
$
```

Because error messages are in a separate data stream from the standard output, error messages still appear on the screen for you to see even if you have redirected the standard output to a file. In the next example, the standard output of the **cat** command is redirected to the file **mydata**. However, the standard error, containing the error messages, is still directed to the screen.

```
$ cat myintro > mydata
cat : myintro not found
$
```

You can redirect the standard error, as you can the standard output. This means you can save your error messages in a file for future reference. This is helpful if you need a record of the error messages. Like the standard output, the standard error has the screen device for its default destination. However, you can redirect the standard error to any file or device you choose using special redirection operators. In this case, the error messages will not be displayed on the screen.

Redirection of the standard error relies on a special feature of shell redirection. You can reference all the standard byte streams in redirection operations with numbers. The numbers 0, 1, and 2 reference the standard input, standard output, and standard error, respectively. By default, an output redirection, **>**, operates on the standard output, 1. You can modify the output redirection to operate on the standard error, however, by preceding the output redirection operator with the number 2. In the next example, the **cat** command again will generate an error. The error message is redirected to the standard byte stream represented by the number 2, the standard error.

```
$ cat nodata 2> myerrors
$ cat myerrors
cat : nodata not found
$
```

You can also append the standard error to a file by using the number 2 and the redirection append operator (**>>**). In the next example, the user appends the standard error to the **myerrors** file, which then functions as a log of errors:

```
$ cat nodata 2>> myerrors
```

Jobs: Background, Kills, and Interruptions

In Linux, you not only have control over a command's input and output, but also over its execution. You can run a job in the background while you execute other commands. You can also cancel commands before they have finished executing. You can even interrupt a command, starting it again later from where you left off. Background operations are particularly useful for long jobs. Instead of waiting at the terminal until a command has finished execution, you can place it in the background. You can then continue executing other Linux commands. You can, for example, edit a file while other files are printing. The background commands, as well as commands to cancel and interrupt jobs, are listed in Table 8-7.

Background Jobs	Execution
%*jobnum*	References job by job number, use the **jobs** command to display job numbers.
%	References recent job.
%*string*	References job by an exact matching string.
%?*string*?	References job that contains unique string.
%--	References job before recent job.
&	Execute a command in the background.
fg %*jobnum*	Bring a command in the background to the foreground or resume an interrupted program.
bg	Place a command in the foreground into the background.
CTRL-Z	Interrupt and stop the currently running program. The program remains stopped and waiting in the background for you to resume it.
notify %*jobnum*	Notify you when a job ends.
kill %*jobnum* **kill** *processnum*	Cancel and end a job running in the background.
jobs	List all background jobs. The **jobs** command is not available in the Bourne shell, unless it is using the jsh shell.
ps -a	List all currently running processes, including background jobs.
at *time date*	Execute commands at a specified time and date. The time can be entered with hours and minutes and qualified as am or pm.

TABLE 8-7 Job Management Operations

Running Jobs in the Background

You execute a command in the background by placing an ampersand (**&**) on the command line at the end of the command. When you place a job in the background, a user job number and a system process number are displayed. The user job number, placed in brackets, is the number by which the user references the job. The system process number is the number by which the system identifies the job. In the next example, the command to print the file **mydata** is placed in the background:

```
$ lpr mydata &
[1]   534
$
```

You can place more than one command in the background. Each is classified as a job and given a name and a job number. The command **jobs** lists the jobs being run in the background. Each entry in the list consists of the job number in brackets, whether it is stopped or running, and the name of the job. The **+** sign indicates the job currently being processed, and the **-** sign indicates the next job to be executed. In the next example, two commands have been placed in the background. The **jobs** command then lists those jobs, showing which one is currently being executed.

```
$ lpr intro &
[1]   547
$ cat *.c > myprogs &
[2]   548
$ jobs
[1]   +   Running   lpr intro
[2]   -   Running   cat *.c > myprogs
$
```

Referencing Jobs

Normally jobs are referenced using the job number, preceded by a **%** symbol. You can obtain this number with the **jobs** command, which will list all background jobs, as shown in the preceding example. In addition you can also reference a job using an identifying string (see Table 8-7). The string must be either an exact match or a partial unique match. If there is no exact or unique match, you will receive an error message. Also, the **%** symbol itself without any job number references the recent background job. Followed by a **- -** it references the second previous background job. The following example brings job 1 in the previous example to the foreground.

```
fg %lpr
```

Job Notification

After you execute any command in Linux, the system tells you what background jobs, if you have any running, have been completed so far. The system does not interrupt any operation, such as editing, to notify you about a completed job. If you want to be notified immediately when a certain job ends, no matter what you are doing on the system, you can use the **notify** command to instruct the system to tell you. The **notify** command takes a job number as its argument. When that job is finished, the system interrupts what you are doing to notify you the job has ended. The next example tells the system to notify the user when job 2 has finished:

```
$ notify %2
```

Bringing Jobs to the Foreground

You can bring a job out of the background with the foreground command, **fg**. If only one job is in the background, the **fg** command alone will bring it to the foreground. If more than one job is in the background, you must use the job's number with the command. You place the job number after the **fg** command, preceded with a percent sign. A **bg** command also places a job in the background. This command is usually used for interrupted jobs. In the next example, the second job is brought back into the foreground. You may not immediately receive a prompt again because the second command is now in the foreground and executing. When the command is finished executing, the prompt appears and you can execute another command.

```
$ fg %2
cat *.c > myprogs
$
```

Canceling Jobs

If you want to cancel a job running in the background, you can force it to end with the **kill** command. The **kill** command takes as its argument either the user job number or the system process number. The user job number must be preceded by a percent sign (%). You can find out the job number from the **jobs** command. In the next example, the **jobs** command lists the background jobs; then job 2 is canceled:

```
$ jobs
[1]  +  Running  lpr intro
[2]  -  Running  cat *.c > myprogs
$ kill %2
```

Suspending and Stopping Jobs

You can suspend a job and stop it with the CTRL-Z key. This places the job to the side until it is restarted. The job is not ended; it merely remains suspended until you want to continue. When you're ready, you can continue with the job in either the foreground or the background using the **fg** or **bg** command. The **fg** command restarts a suspended job in the foreground. The **bg** command places the suspended job in the background.

At times, you may need to place a currently running job in the foreground into the background. However, you cannot move a currently running job directly into the background. You first need to suspend it with CTRL-Z and then place it in the background with the **bg** command. In the next example, the current command to list and redirect **.c** files is first suspended with CTRL-Z. Then that job is placed in the background.

```
$ cat *.c > myprogs
^Z
$ bg
```

> **Note** *You can also use* CTRL-Z *to stop currently running jobs like Vi, suspending them in the background until you are ready to resume them. The Vi session remains a stopped job in the background until resumed with the* **bg** *command.*

Ending Processes: ps and kill

You can also cancel a job using the system process number, which you can obtain with the **ps** command. The **ps** command will display your proceses and you can use a process number to end any running process. The **ps** command displays a great deal more information than the **jobs** command does. The next example lists the processes a user is running. The PID is the system process number, also known as the process ID. TTY is the terminal identifier. The time is how long the process has taken so far. COMMAND is the name of the process.

```
$ ps
PID     TTY      TIME     COMMAND
523     tty24    0:05     sh
567     tty24    0:01     lpr
570     tty24    0:00     ps
```

You can then reference the system process number in a `kill` command. Use the process number without any preceding percent sign. The next example kills process 567:

```
$ kill 567
```

Check the **ps** man page for more detailed information about detecting and displaying process information. To just display a process id number use the output options **-o pid=**. Combined with the **-C** command option you can display just the process id for a particular command. If there is more than one process for that command, like multiple bash shells, then all the pids will be displayed.

```
$ ps -C lpr -o pid=
567
```

For unique commands, those you know have only one process running, you can safely combine the previous command with the **kill** command to end the process on one line. This avoids interactively having to display and enter the pid to kill the process. The technique can be useful for non-interactive operations like **cron** (see Chapter 27), and helpful for ending open-ended operations like video recording. In the following example, a command using just one process, **getatsc**, is ended in a single kill operation. The **getatsc** is a third party hdtv recording command. Backquotes are used to first executp the **ps** command to obtain the pid (see Values from Linux Commands section later in this chapter).

```
kill `ps -C getatsc -o pid=`
```

Shell Variables

The Bash, Korn, and Z shells described previously are actually types of shells. A *shell*, by definition, is an interpretive environment within which you execute commands. You could have many environments running at the same time, either of the same type or of different types of shells. So you could have several shells running at the same time that are of the Bash shell type.

Within each shell, you could enter and execute commands. You can further enhance the capabilities of a shell using shell variables. With a shell variable, you can hold data that you could reference over and over again as you execute different commands within a given shell. For example, you could define a shell variable to hold the name of complex filename. Instead of retyping the filename in different commands, you could reference it with the shell variable.

You define variables within a shell, and such variables are known as *shell variables*. Many different shells exist. Some utilities, such as the Mail utility, have their own shells with their own shell variables. You can also create your own shell using what are called *shell scripts*. You have a user shell that becomes active as soon as you log in. This is often referred to as the *login shell*. Special system-level parameter variables are defined within this login shell. Shell variables can also be used to define a shell's environment, as described in Chapter 9.

NOTE *Shell variables exist as long as your shell is active—that is, until you exit the shell. For example, logging out will exit the login shell. When you log in again, any variables you may need in your login shell must be defined again.*

Definition and Evaluation of Variables: =, $, set, unset

You define a variable in a shell when you first use the variable's name. A variable's name may be any set of alphabetic characters, including the underscore. The name may also include a number, but the number cannot be the first character in the name. A name may not have any other type of character, such as an exclamation point, an ampersand, or even a space. Such symbols are reserved by the shell for its own use. Also, a variable name may not include more than one word. The shell uses spaces on the command line to distinguish different components of a command such as options, arguments, and the name of the command.

You assign a value to a variable with the assignment operator (=). You type the variable name, the assignment operator, and then the value assigned. Do not place any spaces around the assignment operator. The assignment operation **poet = Virgil**, for example, will fail. (The C shell has a slightly different type of assignment operation.) You can assign any set of characters to a variable. In the next example, the variable **poet** is assigned the string **Virgil**:

```
$ poet=Virgil
```

Once you have assigned a value to a variable, you can then use the variable name to reference the value. Often you use the values of variables as arguments for a command. You can reference the value of a variable using the variable name preceded by the $ operator. The dollar sign is a special operator that uses the variable name to reference a variable's value, in effect evaluating the variable. Evaluation retrieves a variable's value, usually a set of characters. This set of characters then replaces the variable name on the command line. Wherever a $ is placed before the variable name, the variable name is replaced with the value of the variable. In the next example, the shell variable **poet** is evaluated and its contents, **Virgil**, are then used as the argument for an **echo** command. The **echo** command simply echoes or prints a set of characters to the screen.

```
$ echo $poet
Virgil
```

You must be careful to distinguish between the evaluation of a variable and its name alone. If you leave out the **$** operator before the variable name, all you have is the variable name itself. In the next example, the **$** operator is absent from the variable name. In this case, the **echo** command has as its argument the word "poet", and so prints out "poet":

```
$ echo poet
poet
```

The contents of a variable are often used as command arguments. A common command argument is a directory pathname. It can be tedious to retype a directory path that is being used over and over again. If you assign the directory pathname to a variable, you can simply use the evaluated variable in its place. The directory path you assign to the variable is retrieved when the variable is evaluated with the **$** operator. The next example assigns a directory pathname to a variable and then uses the evaluated variable in a copy command. The evaluation of **ldir** (which is **$ldir**) results in the pathname **/home/chris/letters**. The copy command evaluates to **cp myletter /home/chris/letters**.

```
$ ldir=/home/chris/letters
$ cp myletter $ldir
```

You can obtain a list of all the defined variables with the **set** command. If you decide you do not want a certain variable, you can remove it with the **unset** command. The **unset** command undefines a variable.

Values from Linux Commands: Back Quotes

Although you can create variable values by typing in characters or character strings, you can also obtain values from other Linux commands. To assign the result of Linux command to a variable, you first need to execute the command. If you place a Linux command within back quotes on the command line, that command is first executed and its result becomes an argument on the command line. In the case of assignments, the result of a command can be assigned to a variable by placing the command within back quotes to first execute it. The back quotes can be thought of as a kind of expression consisting of a command to be executed whose result is then assigned to the variable. The characters making up the command itself are not assigned. In the next example, the command ls *.c is executed and its result is then assigned to the variable listc. ls *.c generates a list of all files with an .c extension. This list of files will then be assigned to the listc variable.

```
$ listc=`ls *.c`
$ echo $listc
main.c prog.c lib.c
```

You need to keep in mind the difference between single quotes and back quotes. Single quotes treat a Linux command as a set of characters. Back quotes force execution of the Linux command. There may be times when you accidentally enter in single quotes, when you mean to use back quotes. In the following first example, the assignment for the lscc variable, has single quotes, not back quotes, placed around the ls *.c command. In this case, ls *.c are just characters to be assigned to the variable lscc. In the second example, backquotes are placed around the ls *.c command, forcing evaluation of the command. A list of file names ending in .c is generated and assigned as the value of lscc.

```
$ lscc='ls *.c'
$ echo $lscc
ls *.c

$ lscc='ls *.c'
$ echo $lscc
main.c  prog.c
```

Shell Scripts: User-Defined Commands

You can place shell commands within a file and then have the shell read and execute the commands in the file. In this sense, the file functions as a shell program, executing shell commands as if they were statements in a program. A file that contains shell commands is called a *shell script.*

You enter shell commands into a script file using a standard text editor such as the Vi editor. The **sh** or **.** command used with the script's filename will read the script file and execute the commands. In the next example, the text file called **lsc** contains an **ls** command that displays only files with the extension **.c**:

lsc
ls *.c

A run of the **lsc** script is shown here:

```
$ sh lsc
main.c calc.c
$ . lsc
main.c calc.c
```

Executing Scripts

You can dispense with the **sh** and **.** commands by setting the executable permission of a script file. When the script file is first created by your text editor, it is given only read and write permission. The **chmod** command with the **+x** option will give the script file executable permission. (Permissions are discussed in Chapter 30.) Once it is executable, entering the name of the script file at the shell prompt and pressing ENTER will execute the script file and the shell commands in it. In effect, the script's filename becomes a new shell command. In this way, you can use shell scripts to design and create your own Linux commands. You need to set the permission only once. In the next example, the **lsc** file's executable permission for the owner is set to on. Then the **lsc** shell script is directly executed like any Linux command.

```
$ chmod u+x lsc
$ lsc
main.c calc.c
```

You may have to specify that the script you are using is in your current working directory. You do this by prefixing the script name with a period and slash combination, `./`, as in `./lsc`. The period is a special character representing the name of your current working directory. The slash is a directory pathname separator, as explained more fully in Chapter 32 (you could also add the current directory to your PATH variable as discussed in Chapter 9). The following example would show how you would execute the `lsc` script:

```
$ ./lsc
main.c calc.c
```

Script Arguments

Just as any Linux command can take arguments, so also can a shell script. Arguments on the command line are referenced sequentially starting with 1. An argument is referenced using the `$` operator and the number of its position. The first argument is referenced with `$1`, the second, with `$2`, and so on. In the next example, the `lsext` script prints out files with a specified extension. The first argument is the extension. The script is then executed with the argument `c` (of course, the executable permission must have been set).

lsext
```
ls *.$1
```

A run of the `lsext` script with an argument is shown here:

```
$ lsext c
main.c calc.c
```

In the next example, the commands to print out a file with line numbers have been placed in an executable file called `lpnum`, which takes a filename as its argument. The `cat` command with the `-n` option first outputs the contents of the file with line numbers. Then this output is piped into the `lpr` command, which prints it. The command to print out the line numbers is executed in the background.

lpnum
```
cat -n $1 | lpr &
```

A run of the `lpnum` script with an argument is shown here:

```
$ lpnum mydata
```

You may need to reference more than one argument at a time. The number of arguments used may vary. In `lpnum`, you may want to print out three files at one time and five files at some other time. The `$` operator with the asterisk, `$*`, references all the arguments on the command line. Using `$*` enables you to create scripts that take a varying number of arguments. In the next example, `lpnum` is rewritten using `$*` so that it can take a different number of arguments each time you use it:

lpnum
```
cat -n $* | lpr &
```

A run of the **lpnum** script with multiple arguments is shown here:

```
$ lpnum mydata preface
```

Control Structures

You can control the execution of Linux commands in a shell script with control structures. Control structures allow you to repeat commands and to select certain commands over others. A control structure consists of two major components: a test and commands. If the test is successful, then the commands are executed. In this way, you can use control structures to make decisions as to whether commands should be executed.

There are two different kinds of control structures: *loops* and *conditions*. A loop repeats commands, whereas a condition executes a command when certain conditions are met. The BASH shell has three loop control structures: **while**, **for**, and **for-in**. There are two condition structures: **if** and **case**. The control structures have as their test the execution of a Linux command. All Linux commands return an exit status after they have finished executing. If a command is successful, its exit status will be 0. If the command fails for any reason, its exit status will be a positive value referencing the type of failure that occurred. The control structures check to see if the exit status of a Linux command is 0 or some other value. In the case of the **if** and **while** structures, if the exit status is a zero value, then the command was successful and the structure continues.

Test Operations

With the **test** command, you can compare integers, compare strings, and even perform logical operations. The command consists of the keyword **test** followed by the values being compared, separated by an option that specifies what kind of comparison is taking place. The option can be thought of as the operator, but it is written, like other options, with a minus sign and letter codes. For example, **-eq** is the option that represents the equality comparison. However, there are two string operations that actually use an operator instead of an option. When you compare two strings for equality, you use the equal sign (=). For inequality you use ! =. Table 8-8 lists some of the commonly used options and operators used by **test**. The syntax for the **test** command is shown here:

```
test value -option value
test string = string
```

In the next example, the user compares two integer values to see if they are equal. In this case, you need to use the equality option, **-eq**. The exit status of the **test** command is examined to find out the result of the test operation. The shell special variable **$?** holds the exit status of the most recently executed Linux command.

```
$ num=5
$ test $num -eq 10
$ echo $?
1
```

Integer Comparisons	Function
`-gt`	Greater-than
`-lt`	Less-than
`-ge`	Greater-than-or-equal-to
`-le`	Less-than-or-equal-to
`-eq`	Equal
`-ne`	Not-equal
String Comparisons	**Function**
`-z`	Tests for empty string
`=`	Equal strings
`!=`	Not-equal strings
Logical Operations	**Function**
`-a`	Logical AND
`-o`	Logical OR
`!`	Logical NOT
File Tests	**Function**
`-f`	File exists and is a regular file
`-s`	File is not empty
`-r`	File is readable
`-w`	File can be written to, modified
`-x`	File is executable
`-d`	Filename is a directory name

TABLE 8-8   BASH Shell Test Operators

Instead of using the keyword **test** for the **test** command, you can use enclosing brackets. The command **test $greeting = "hi"** can be written as

```
$ [ $greeting = "hi" ]
```

Similarly, the test command **test $num -eq 10** can be written as

```
$ [ $num -eq 10 ]
```

The brackets themselves must be surrounded by white space: a space, TAB, or ENTER. Without the spaces, it would be invalid.

Conditional Control Structures

The BASH shell has a set of conditional control structures that allow you to choose what Linux commands to execute. Many of these are similar to conditional control structures found in programming languages, but there are some differences. The **if** condition tests the success of a Linux command, not an expression. Furthermore, the end of an **if-then** command must be indicated with the keyword **fi**, and the end of a **case** command is indicated with the keyword **esac**. The condition control structures are listed in Table 8-9.

Condition Control Structures: if, else, elif, case	Function
if *command* **then** *command* fi	**if** executes an action if its test command is true.

if *command* **then**
   command
else
   command
fi
	if-else executes an action if the exit status of its test command is true; if false, then the **else** action is executed.

if *command* **then**
   command
elif *command* **then**
   command
else
   command
fi
	elif allows you to nest **if** structures, enabling selection among several alternatives; at the first true **if** structure, its commands are executed and control leaves the entire **elif** structure.

case *string* in pattern) *command*; ; esac	**case** matches the string value to any of several patterns; if a pattern is matched, its associated commands are executed.
command && *command*	The logical AND condition returns a true 0 value if both commands return a true 0 value; if one returns a nonzero value, then the AND condition is false and also returns a nonzero value.
command || *command*	The logical OR condition returns a true 0 value if one or the other command returns a true 0 value; if both commands return a nonzero value, then the OR condition is false and also returns a nonzero value.
! *command*	The logical NOT condition inverts the return value of the command.

TABLE 8-9   BASH Shell Control Structures *(continued)*

Loop Control Structures: while, until, for, for-in, select	Function

`while` *command*
`do`
command
`done`
	`while` executes an action as long as its test command is true.

`until` *command*
`do`
command
`done`
	`until` executes an action as long as its test command is false.

`for` *variable* `in` *list-values*
`do`
command
`done`
	`for-in` is designed for use with lists of values; the variable operand is consecutively assigned the values in the list.

`for` *variable*
`do`
command
`done`
	`for` is designed for reference script arguments; the variable operand is consecutively assigned each argument value.

`select` *string* `in` *item-list*
`do`
command
`done`
	`select` creates a menu based on the items in the *item-list*; then it executes the command; the command is usually a `case`.

TABLE 8-9   BASH Shell Control Structures *(continued)*

elsels
```
echo Enter s to list file sizes,
echo         otherwise all file information is listed.
echo -n "Please enter option: "
read choice
if [  "$choice" = s  ]
    then
        ls -s
    else
            ls -l
fi
echo Good-bye
```

A run of the program follows:

```
$ elsels
Enter s to list file sizes,
otherwise all file information is listed.
Please enter option: s
total 2
    1 monday     2 today
$
```

The **if** structure places a condition on commands. That condition is the exit status of a specific Linux command. If a command is successful, returning an exit status of 0, then the commands within the **if** structure are executed. If the exit status is anything other than 0, then the command has failed and the commands within the **if** structure are not executed. The **if** command begins with the keyword **if** and is followed by a Linux command whose exit condition will be evaluated. The keyword **fi** ends the command. The **elsels** script in the next example executes the **ls** command to list files with two different possible options, either by size or with all file information. If the user enters an **s**, files are listed by size; otherwise, all file information is listed.

Loop Control Structures

The **while** loop repeats commands. A **while** loop begins with the keyword **while** and is followed by a Linux command. The keyword **do** follows on the next line. The end of the loop is specified by the keyword **done**. The Linux command used in **while** structures is often a test command indicated by enclosing brackets.

The **for-in** structure is designed to reference a list of values sequentially. It takes two operands—a variable and a list of values. The values in the list are assigned one by one to the variable in the **for-in** structure. Like the **while** command, the **for-in** structure is a loop. Each time through the loop, the next value in the list is assigned to the variable. When the end of the list is reached, the loop stops. Like the **while** loop, the body of a **for-in** loop begins with the keyword **do** and ends with the keyword **done**. The **cbackup** script makes a backup of each file and places it in a directory called **sourcebak**. Notice the use of the * special character to generate a list of all filenames with a **.c** extension.

cbackup
```
for backfile in *.c
do
    cp $backfile sourcebak/$backfile
 echo $backfile
done
```

A run of the program follows:

```
$ cbackup
io.c
lib.c
main.c
$
```

The **for** structure without a specified list of values takes as its list of values the command line arguments. The arguments specified on the command line when the shell file is invoked become a list of values referenced by the **for** command. The variable used in the **for** command is set automatically to each argument value in sequence. The first time through the loop, the variable is set to the value of the first argument. The second time, it is set to the value of the second argument.

Filters and Regular Expressions

Filters are commands that read data, perform operations on that data, and then send the results to the standard output. Filters generate different kinds of output, depending on their task. Some filters generate information only about the input, other filters output selected parts of the input, and still other filters output an entire version of the input, but in a modified way. Some filters are limited to one of these, while others have options that specify one or the other. You can think of a filter as operating on a stream of data—receiving data and generating modified output. As data is passed through the filter, it is analyzed, screened, or modified.

The data stream input to a filter consists of a sequence of bytes that can be received from files, devices, or the output of other commands or filters. The filter operates on the data stream, but it does not modify the source of the data. If a filter receives input from a file, the file itself is not modified. Only its data is read and fed into the filter.

The output of a filter is usually sent to the standard output. It can then be redirected to another file or device, or piped as input to another utility or filter. All the features of redirection and pipes apply to filters. Often data is read by one filter and its modified output piped into another filter.

NOTE *Data could easily undergo several modifications as it is passed from one filter to another. However, it is always important to realize the original source of the data is never changed.*

Many utilities and filters use patterns to locate and select specific text in your file. Sometimes, you may need to use patterns in a more flexible and powerful way, searching for several different variations on a given pattern. You can include a set of special characters in your pattern to enable a flexible search. A pattern that contains such special characters is called a *regular expression*. Regular expressions can be used in most filters and utilities that employ pattern searches such as **sed**, **awk**, **grep**, and **egrep**.

TIP *Although many of the special characters used for regular expressions are similar to the shell file expansion characters, they are used in a different way. Shell file expansion characters operate on filenames. Regular expressions search text.*

You can save the output of a filter in a file or send it to a printer. To do so, you need to use redirection or pipes. To save the output of a filter to a file, you redirect it to a file using the redirection operation (>). To send output to the printer, you pipe the output to the **lpr** utility, which then prints it. In the next command, the **cat** command pipes its output to the **lpr** command, which then prints it.

```
$ cat complist | lpr
```

All filters accept input from the standard input. In fact, the output of one filter can be piped as the input for another filter. Many filters also accept input directly from files, however. Such filters can take filenames as their arguments and read data directly from those files.

Searching Files: grep

The **grep** and **fgrep** filters search the contents of files for a pattern. They then inform you of what file the pattern was found in and print the lines in which it occurred in each file. Preceding each line is the name of the file in which the line is located. The **grep** command can search for only one pattern, whereas **fgrep** can search for more than one pattern at a time.

The **grep** filter takes two types of arguments. The first argument is the pattern to be searched for; the second argument is a list of filenames, which are the files to be searched. You enter the filenames on the command line after the pattern. You can also use special characters, such as the asterisk, to generate a file list.

```
$ grep pattern filenames-list
```

If you want to include more than one word in the pattern search, you enclose the words within single quotation marks. This is to quote the spaces between the words in the pattern. Otherwise, the shell would interpret the space as a delimiter or argument on the command line, and **grep** would try to interpret words in the pattern as part of the file list. In the next example, **grep** searches for the pattern "text file":

```
$ grep 'text file' preface
A text file in Linux
text files, changing or
```

If you use more than one file in the file list, **grep** will output the name of the file before the matching line. In the next example, two files, **preface** and **intro**, are searched for the pattern "data". Before each occurrence, the filename is output.

```
$ grep data preface intro
 preface: data in the file.
 intro: new data
```

As mentioned earlier, you can also use shell file expansion characters to generate a list of files to be searched. In the next example, the asterisk file expansion character is used to generate a list of all files in your directory. This is a simple way of searching all of a directory's files for a pattern.

```
$ grep data *
```

The special characters are often useful for searching a selected set of files. For example, if you want to search all your C program source code files for a particular pattern, you can specify the set of source code files with ***.c**. Suppose you have an unintended infinite loop in your program and you need to locate all instances of iterations. The next example searches only those files with a **.c** extension for the pattern "while" and displays the lines of code that perform iterations:

```
$ grep while *.c
```

Regular Expressions

Regular expressions enable you to match possible variations on a pattern, as well as patterns located at different points in the text. You can search for patterns in your text that have different ending or beginning letters, or you can match text at the beginning or end of a line.

Character	Match	Operation
^	Start of a line	References the beginning of a line.
$	End of a line	References the end of a line.
.	Any character	Matches on any one possible character in a pattern.
*	Repeated characters	Matches on repeated characters in a pattern.
[]	Classes	Matches on classes of characters (a set of characters) in the pattern.

TABLE **8-10**   Regular Expression Special Characters

The regular expression special characters are the circumflex, dollar sign, asterisk, period, and brackets: ^, $, *, ., []. The circumflex and dollar sign match on the beginning and end of a line. The asterisk matches repeated characters, the period matches single characters, and the brackets match on classes of characters. See Table 8-10 for a listing of the regular expression special characters.

NOTE *Regular expressions are used extensively in many Linux filters and applications to perform searches and matching operations. The Vi and Emacs editors and the **sed, diff, grep**, and **gawk** filters all use regular expressions.*

Suppose you want to use the long-form output of **ls** to display just your directories. One way to do this is to generate a list of all directories in the long form and pipe this list to **grep**, which can then pick out the directory entries. You can do this by using the ^ special character to specify the beginning of a line. Remember, in the long-form output of **ls**, the first character indicates the file type. A **d** represents a directory, an **l** represents a symbolic link, and an **a** represents a regular file. Using the pattern '^d', **grep** will match only on those lines beginning with a *d*.

```
$ ls -l | grep '^d'
drwxr-x---  2  chris 512 Feb 10 04:30   reports
drwxr-x---  2  chris 512 Jan 6  01:20   letters
```

Shell Configuration

Four different major shells are commonly used on Linux systems: the Bourne Again shell (BASH), the AT&T Korn shell, the TCSH shell, and the Z shell. The BASH shell is an advanced version of the Bourne shell, which includes most of the advanced features developed for the Korn shell and the C shell. TCSH is an enhanced version of the C shell, originally developed for BSD versions of Unix. The AT&T Unix Korn shell, included with Fedora, is open source. The Z shell is an enhanced version of the Korn shell. The PDKSH shell (Public Domain Korn Shell), a subset of the Unix Korn shell, is no longer provided for Fedora Linux. Although their Unix counterparts differ greatly, the Linux shells share many of the same features. In Unix, the Bourne shell lacks many capabilities found in the other Unix shells. In Linux, however, the BASH shell incorporates all the advanced features of the Korn shell and C shell, as well as the TCSH shell. All four shells are available for your use, though the BASH shell is the default.

So far, all examples in this book have used the BASH shell, which is the default shell for Red Hat and Fedora. If you are logging in to a command line interface, you will be placed in the default shell automatically and given a shell prompt at which to enter your commands. The shell prompt for the BASH shell is a dollar sign (**$**). In the GUI interface, like GNOME or KDE, you can open a terminal window that will display a command line interface with the prompt for the default shell (BASH). Though you log in to your default shell or display it automatically in a terminal window, you can change to another shell by entering its name. **tcsh** invokes the TCSH shell, **bash** the BASH shell, **ksh** the Korn shell, and **zsh** the Z shell. You can leave a shell with the CTRL-D or **exit** command. You only need one type of shell to do your work. Table 9-1 shows the different commands you can use to invoke different shells. Some shells have added links you can use the invoke the same shell, like **sh** and **bsh**, which link to and invoke the **bash** command for the BASH shell.

This chapter describes common features of the BASH shell, such as aliases, as well as how to configure the shell to your own needs using shell variables and initialization files. The other shells share many of the same features and use similar variables and initialization files.

Though the basic shell features and configurations are shown here, you should consult the respective online manuals and FAQs for each shell for more detailed examples and explanations (see Table 8-1 in Chapter 8).

Features	Description
`bash`	BASH shell, **/bin/bash**
`bsh`	BASH shell, **/bin/bsh** (link to **/bin/bash**)
`sh`	BASH shell, **/bin/sh** (link to **/bin/bash**)
`tcsh`	TCSH shell, **/usr/tcsh**
`csh`	TCSH shell, **/bin/csh** (link to **/bin/tcsh**)
`ksh`	Korn shell, **/bin/ksh** (also added link **/usr/bin/ksh**)
`zsh`	Z shell, **/bin/zsh**

TABLE 9-1 Shell Invocation Command Names

Aliases

You use the **alias** command to create another name for a command. The **alias** command operates like a macro that expands to the command it represents. The alias does not literally replace the name of the command; it simply gives another name to that command. An **alias** command begins with the keyword **alias** and the new name for the command, followed by an equal sign and the command the alias will reference.

NOTE *No spaces can be around the equal sign used in the* **alias** *command.*

In the next example, **list** becomes another name for the **ls** command:

```
$ alias list=ls
$ ls
mydata today
$ list
mydata today
$
```

Aliasing Commands and Options

You can also use an alias to substitute for a command and its option, but you need to enclose both the command and the option within single quotes. Any command you alias that contains spaces must be enclosed in single quotes. In the next example, the alias **lss** references the **ls** command with its **-s** option, and the alias **lsa** references the **ls** command with the **-F** option. The **ls** command with the **-s** option lists files and their sizes in blocks, and **ls** with the **-F** option places a slash after directory names. Notice how single quotes enclose the command and its option.

```
$ alias lss='ls -s'
$ lss
mydata 14    today  6    reports  1
$ alias lsa='ls -F'
$ lsa
mydata today reports/
$
```

Aliases are helpful for simplifying complex operations. In the next example, `listlong` becomes another name for the **ls** command with the **-l** option (the long format that lists all file information), as well as the **-h** option for using a human-readable format for file sizes. Be sure to encase the command and its arguments within single quotes so that they are taken as one argument and not parsed by the shell.

```
$ alias listlong='ls -lh'
$ listlong
-rw-r--r--    1 root    root    51K Sep  18  2003 mydata
-rw-r--r--    1 root    root    16K Sep  27  2003 today
```

Aliasing Commands and Arguments

You may often use an alias to include a command name with an argument. If you execute a command that has an argument with a complex combination of special characters on a regular basis, you may want to alias it. For example, suppose you often list just your source code and object code files—those files ending in either a **.c** or **.o**. You would need to use as an argument for **ls** a combination of special characters such as `*.[co]`. Instead, you could alias **ls** with the `.[co]` argument, giving it a simple name. In the next example, the user creates an alias called **lsc** for the command `ls.[co]`:

```
$ alias lsc='ls *.[co]'
$ lsc
main.c main.o lib.c lib.o
```

Aliasing Commands

You can also use the name of a command as an alias. This can be helpful in cases where you should use a command only with a specific option. In the case of the **rm**, **cp**, and **mv** commands, the **-i** option should always be used to ensure an existing file is not overwritten. Instead of constantly being careful to use the **-i** option each time you use one of these commands, you can alias the command name to include the option. In the next example, the **rm**, **cp**, and **mv** commands have been aliased to include the **-i** option:

```
$ alias rm='rm -i'
$ alias mv='mv -i'
$ alias cp='cp -i'
```

The **alias** command by itself provides a list of all aliases that have been defined, showing the commands they represent. You can remove an alias by using the **unalias** command. In the next example, the user lists the current aliases and then removes the **lsa** alias:

```
$ alias
lsa=ls -F
list=ls
rm=rm -i
$ unalias lsa
```

Controlling Shell Operations

The BASH shell has several features that enable you to control the way different shell operations work. For example, setting the **noclobber** feature prevents redirection from overwriting files. You can turn these features on and off like a toggle, using the **set** command. The **set** command takes two arguments: an option specifying on or off and the name of the feature. To set a feature on, you use the **-o** option, and to set it off, you use the **+o** option. Here is the basic form:

```
$ set -o feature          turn the feature on
$ set +o feature          turn the feature off
```

Three of the most common features are **ignoreeof**, **noclobber**, and **noglob**. Table 9-2 lists these different features, as well as the **set** command. Setting **ignoreeof** enables a feature that prevents you from logging out of the user shell with CTRL-D. CTRL-D is not only used to log out of the user shell, but also to end user input entered directly into the standard input. CTRL-D is used often for the Mail program or for utilities such as **cat**. You could easily enter an extra CTRL-D in such circumstances and accidentally log yourself out. The **ignoreeof** feature prevents such accidental logouts. In the next example, the **ignoreeof** feature is turned on using the **set** command with the **-o** option. The user can now log out only by entering the **logout** command.

```
$ set -o ignoreeof
$ CTRL-D
Use exit to logout
$
```

Environment Variables and Subshells: export

When you log in to your account, Linux generates your user shell. Within this shell, you can issue commands and declare variables. You can also create and execute shell scripts. When you execute a shell script, however, the system generates a subshell. You then have two shells, the one you logged in to and the one generated for the script. Within the script shell, you could execute another shell script, which would have its own shell. When a script has

Features	Description
`$ set -+o` _feature_	BASH shell features are turned on and off with the **set** command; **-o** sets a feature on and **+o** turns it off: `$ set -o noclobber` set _noclobber on_ `$ set +o noclobber` set _noclobber off_
`ignoreeof`	Disables CTRL-D logout
`noclobber`	Does not overwrite files through redirection
`noglob`	Disables special characters used for filename expansion: *****, **?**, **~**, and **[]**

TABLE 9-2 BASH Shell Special Features

finished execution, its shell terminates and you return to the shell from which it was executed. In this sense, you can have many shells, each nested within the other. Variables you define within a shell are local to it. If you define a variable in a shell script, then, when the script is run, the variable is defined with that script's shell and is local to it. No other shell can reference that variable. In a sense, the variable is hidden within its shell.

You can define environment variables in all types of shells, including the BASH shell, the Z shell, and the TCSH shell. The strategy used to implement environment variables in the BASH shell, however, is different from that of the TCSH shell. In the BASH shell, environment variables are exported. That is to say, a copy of an environment variable is made in each subshell. For example, if the **EDITOR** variable is exported, a copy is automatically defined in each subshell for you. In the TCSH shell, on the other hand, an environment variable is defined only once and can be directly referenced by any subshell.

In the BASH shell, an environment variable can be thought of as a regular variable with added capabilities. To make an environment variable, you apply the **export** command to a variable you have already defined. The **export** command instructs the system to define a copy of that variable for each new shell generated. Each new shell will have its own copy of the environment variable. This process is called *exporting variables.* To think of exported environment variables as global variables is a mistake. A new shell can never reference a variable outside of itself. Instead, a copy of the variable with its value is generated for the new shell.

NOTE   *You can think of exported variables as exporting their values to a shell, not to themselves. If you are familiar with programming structures, think of exported variables as a form of "call by value."*

Configuring Your Shell with Shell Parameters

When you log in to your account, the system generates a shell for you. This shell is referred to as either your login shell or your user shell. When you execute scripts, you are generating subshells of your user shell. You can define variables within your user shell, and you can also define environment variables that can be referenced by any subshells you generate.

When you log in, Linux will set certain parameters for your login shell. These parameters can take the form of variables or features. See the previous section "Controlling Shell Operations" for a description of how to set features. Linux reserves a predefined set of variables for shell and system use. These are assigned system values, in effect, setting parameters. Linux sets up parameter shell variables you can use to configure your user shell. Many of these parameter shell variables are defined by the system when you log in. Some parameter shell variables are set by the shell automatically, and others are set by initialization scripts, described later. Certain shell variables are set directly by the shell, and others are simply used by it. Many of these other variables are application specific, used for such tasks as mail, history, or editing. Functionally, it may be better to think of these as system-level variables, as they are used to configure your entire system, setting values such as the location of executable commands on your system, or the number of history commands allowable. See Table 9-3 for a list of those shell variables set by the shell for shell-specific tasks; Table 9-4 lists those used by the shell for supporting other applications.

Shell Variables	Description
BASH	Holds full pathname of BASH command
BASH_VERSION	Displays the current BASH version number
GROUPS	Groups that the user belongs to
HISTCMD	Number of the current command in the history list
HOME	Pathname for user's home directory
HOSTNAME	The host name
HOSTTYPE	Displays the type of machine the host runs on
OLDPWD	Previous working directory
OSTYPE	Operating system in use
PATH	List of pathnames for directories searched for executable commands
PPID	Process ID for shell's parent shell
PWD	User's working directory
RANDOM	Generates random number when referenced
SHLVL	Current shell level, number of shells invoked
UID	User ID of the current user

TABLE 9-3   Shell Variables, Set by the Shell

Shell Variables	Description
BASH_VERSION	Displays the current BASH version number
CDPATH	Search path for the **cd** command
EXINIT	Initialization commands for Ex/Vi editor
FCEDIT	Editor used by the history **fc** command.
GROUPS	Groups that the user belongs to
HISTFILE	The pathname of the history file
HISTSIZE	Number of commands allowed for history
HISTFILESIZE	Size of the history file in lines
HISTCMD	Number of the current command in the history list
HOME	Pathname for user's home directory
HOSTFILE	Sets the name of the hosts file, if other than **/etc/hosts**
IFS	Interfield delimiter symbol
IGNOREEOF	If not set, EOF character will close the shell. Can be set to the number of EOF characters to ignore before accepting one to close the shell (default is 10)

TABLE 9-4   System Environment Variables Used by the Shell *(continued)*

Shell Variables	Description
INPUTRC	Set the **inputrc** configuration file for Readline (command line). Default is current directory, **.inputrc**. Red Hat and Fedora set this to **/etc/inputrc**
KDEDIR	The pathname location for the KDE desktop
LOGNAME	Login name
MAIL	Name of specific mail file checked by Mail utility for received messages, if MAILPATH is not set
MAILCHECK	Interval for checking for received mail
MAILPATH	List of mail files to be checked by Mail for received messages
HOSTTYPE	Linux platforms, like i686, x86_64, or ppc
PROMPT_COMMAND	Command to be executed before each prompt, integrating the result as part of the prompt
HISTFILE	The pathname of the history file
PS1	Primary shell prompt
PS2	Secondary shell prompt
QTDIR	Location of the Qt library (used for KDE)
SHELL	Pathname of program for type of shell you are using
TERM	Terminal type
TMOUT	Time that the shell remains active awaiting input
USER	User name
UID	Real user ID (numeric)
EUID	Effective user ID (numeric). This is usually the same as the UID but can be different when the user changes IDs, as with the **su** command, which allows a user to become an effective root user.

TABLE 9-4   System Environment Variables Used by the Shell

A reserved set of keywords is used for the names of these system variables. You should not use these keywords as the names of any of your own variable names. The system shell variables are all specified in uppercase letters, making them easy to identify. Shell feature variables are in lowercase letters. For example, the keyword **HOME** is used by the system to define the **HOME** variable. **HOME** is a special environment variable that holds the pathname of the user's home directory. On the other hand, the keyword **noclobber** is used to set the **noclobber** feature on or off.

Shell Parameter Variables

Many of the shell parameter variables automatically defined and assigned initial values by the system when you log in can be changed, if you wish. Some parameter variables exist whose values should not be changed, however. For example, the **HOME** variable holds the pathname for your home directory. Commands such as **cd** reference the pathname in the **HOME** shell variable to locate your home directory. Some of the more common of these parameter variables are described in this section. Other parameter variables are defined by the system and given an initial value that you are free to change. To do this, you redefine them and assign a new value. For example, the **PATH** variable is defined by the system and given an initial value; it contains the pathnames of directories where commands are located. Whenever you execute a command, the shell searches for it in these directories. You can add a new directory to be searched by redefining the **PATH** variable yourself, so that it will include the new directory's pathname. Still other parameter variables exist that the system does not define. These are usually optional features, such as the **EXINIT** variable that enables you to set options for the Vi editor. Each time you log in, you must define and assign a value to such variables. Some of the more common parameter variables are **SHELL**, **PATH**, **PS1**, **PS2**, and **MAIL**. The **SHELL** variable holds the pathname of the program for the type of shell you log in to. The **PATH** variable lists the different directories to be searched for a Linux command. The **PS1** and **PS2** variables hold the prompt symbols. The **MAIL** variable holds the pathname of your mailbox file. You can modify the values for any of them to customize your shell.

NOTE   *You can obtain a listing of the currently defined shell variables using the* **env** *command. The* **env** *command operates like the* **set** *command, but it lists only parameter variables.*

Using Initialization Files

You can automatically define parameter variables using special shell scripts called initialization files. An *initialization file* is a specially named shell script executed whenever you enter a certain shell. You can edit the initialization file and place in it definitions and assignments for parameter variables. When you enter the shell, the initialization file will execute these definitions and assignments, effectively initializing parameter variables with your own values. For example, the BASH shell's **.bash_profile** file is an initialization file executed every time you log in. It contains definitions and assignments of parameter variables. However, the **.bash_profile** file is basically only a shell script, which you can edit with any text editor such as the Vi editor; changing, if you wish, the values assigned to parameter variables.

In the BASH shell, all the parameter variables are designed to be environment variables. When you define or redefine a parameter variable, you also need to export it to make it an environment variable. This means any change you make to a parameter variable must be accompanied by an **export** command. You will see that at the end of the login initialization file, **.bash_profile**, there is usually an **export** command for all the parameter variables defined in it.

Your Home Directory: HOME

The **HOME** variable contains the pathname of your home directory. Your home directory is determined by the parameter administrator when your account is created. The pathname for your home directory is automatically read into your **HOME** variable when you log in. In the next example, the **echo** command displays the contents of the **HOME** variable:

```
$ echo $HOME
/home/chris
```

The **HOME** variable is often used when you need to specify the absolute pathname of your home directory. In the next example, the absolute pathname of **reports** is specified using **HOME** for the home directory's path:

```
$ ls $HOME/reports
```

Command Locations: PATH

The **PATH** variable contains a series of directory paths separated by colons. Each time a command is executed, the paths listed in the **PATH** variable are searched one by one for that command. For example, the **cp** command resides on the system in the directory **/usr/bin**. This directory path is one of the directories listed in the **PATH** variable. Each time you execute the **cp** command, this path is searched and the **cp** command located. The system defines and assigns **PATH** an initial set of pathnames. In Linux, the initial pathnames are **/usr/bin** and **usr/sbin**.

The shell can execute any executable file, including programs and scripts you have created. For this reason, the **PATH** variable can also reference your working directory; so if you want to execute one of your own scripts or programs in your working directory, the shell can locate it. No spaces are allowed between the pathnames in the string. A colon with no pathname specified references your working directory. Usually, a single colon is placed at the end of the pathnames as an empty entry specifying your working directory. For example, the pathname **/usr/bin:/usr/sbin:** references three directories: **/usr/bin**, **/usr/sbin**, and your current working directory.

```
$ echo $PATH
/usr/bin:/usr/sbin:
```

You can add any new directory path you want to the **PATH** variable. This can be useful if you have created several of your own Linux commands using shell scripts. You could place these new shell script commands in a directory you created and then add that directory to the **PATH** list. Then, no matter what directory you are in, you can execute one of your shell scripts. The **PATH** variable will contain the directory for that script, so that directory will be searched each time you issue a command.

You add a directory to the **PATH** variable with a variable assignment. You can execute this assignment directly in your shell. In the next example, the user **chris** adds a new directory, called **mybin,** to the **PATH**. Although you could carefully type in the complete pathnames listed in **PATH** for the assignment, you can also use an evaluation of **PATH**—**$PATH**—in their place. In this example, an evaluation of **HOME** is also used to designate the user's **home** directory in the new directory's pathname. Notice the empty entry between two colons, which specifies the working directory:

```
$ PATH=$PATH:$HOME/mybin:
$ export PATH
$ echo $PATH
/usr/bin:/usr/sbin::/home/chris/mybin
```

If you add a directory to **PATH** yourself while you are logged in, the directory will be added only for the duration of your login session. When you log back in, the login initialization file, **.bash_profile**, will again initialize your **PATH** with its original set of directories. The **.bash_profile** file is described in detail a bit later in this chapter. To add a new directory to your **PATH** permanently, you need to edit your **.bash_profile** file and find the assignment for the **PATH** variable. Then, you simply insert the directory, preceded by a colon, into the set of pathnames assigned to **PATH**.

Specifying the BASH Environment: BASH_ENV

The **BASH_ENV** variable holds the name of the BASH shell initialization file to be executed whenever a BASH shell is generated. For example, when a BASH shell script is executed, the **BASH_ENV** variable is checked and the name of the script that it holds is executed before the shell script. The **BASH_ENV** variable usually holds **$HOME/.bashrc**. This is the **.bashrc** file in the user's home directory. (The **.bashrc** file is discussed later in this chapter.) You could specify a different file if you wish, using that instead of the **.bashrc** file for BASH shell scripts.

Configuring the Shell Prompt

The **PS1** and **PS2** variables contain the primary and secondary prompt symbols, respectively. The primary prompt symbol for the BASH shell is a dollar sign (**$**). You can change the prompt symbol by assigning a new set of characters to the **PS1** variable. In the next example, the shell prompt is changed to the **->** symbol:

```
$ PS1= '->'
-> export PS1
->
```

You can change the prompt to be any set of characters, including a string, as shown in the next example:

```
$ PS1="Please enter a command: "
Please enter a command: export PS1
Please enter a command: ls
mydata /reports
Please enter a command:
```

The **PS2** variable holds the secondary prompt symbol, which is used for commands that take several lines to complete. The default secondary prompt is **>**. The added command lines begin with the secondary prompt instead of the primary prompt. You can change the secondary prompt just as easily as the primary prompt, as shown here:

```
$ PS2="@"
```

Like the TCSH shell, the BASH shell provides you with a predefined set of codes you can use to configure your prompt. With them you can make the time, your username, or your directory pathname a part of your prompt. You can even have your prompt display the history event number of the current command you are about to enter. Each code is preceded by a \ symbol: **\w** represents the current working directory, **\t** the time, and **\u** your username; **\!** will display the next history event number. In the next example, the user adds the current working directory to the prompt:

```
$ PS1="\w $"
/home/dylan $
```

The codes must be included within a quoted string. If no quotes exist, the code characters are not evaluated and are themselves used as the prompt. **PS1=\w** sets the prompt to the characters \w, not the working directory. The next example incorporates both the time and the history event number with a new prompt:

```
$ PS1="\t \! ->"
```

The following table lists the codes for configuring your prompt:

Prompt Codes	Description
\!	Current history number
\$	Use $ as prompt for all users except the root user, which has the # as its prompt
\d	Current date
\#	History command number for just the current shell
\h	Host name
\s	Shell type currently active
\t	Time of day in hours, minutes, and seconds.
\u	Username
\v	Shell version
\w	Full pathname of the current working directory
\W	Name of the current working directory
\\	Displays a backslash character.
\n	Inserts a newline
\[\]	Allows entry of terminal specific display characters for features like color or bold font.
\nnn	Character specified in octal format

The default BASH prompt is \s-\v\$ to display the type of shell, the shell version, and the $ symbol as the prompt. Fedora and Red Hat have changed this to a more complex command consisting of the user, the hostname, and the name of the current working directory. The actual operation is carried out in the **/etc/bashrc** file discussed in the later section "The System **/etc/ bashrc** BASH Script and the /etc/profile.d Directory." A sample configuration is shown here. The **/etc/ bashrc** file uses USER, HOSTNAME, and PWD environment variables to set these values. A simple equivalent is show here with @ sign in the hostname, and a $ for the final prompt symbol. The home directory is represented with a tilde (~).

```
$ PS1="\u@\h:\w$"
richard@turtle.com:~$
```

Specifying Your News Server

Several shell parameter variables are used to set values used by network applications, such as Web browsers or newsreaders. **NNTPSERVER** is used to set the value of a remote news server accessible on your network. If you are using an ISP, the ISP usually provides a news server you can access with your newsreader applications. However, you first have to provide your newsreaders with the Internet address of the news server. This is the role of the **NNTPSERVER** variable. News servers on the Internet usually use the NNTP protocol. **NNTPSERVER** should hold the address of such a news server. For many ISPs, the news server address is a domain name that begins with **nntp**. The following example assigns the news server address **nntp.myservice.com** to the **NNTPSERVER** shell variable. Newsreader applications automatically obtain the news server address from **NNTPSERVER**. Usually, this assignment is placed in the shell initialization file, **.bash_profile**, so that it is automatically set each time a user logs in.

```
NNTPSERVER=news.myservice.com
export NNTPSERVER
```

Configuring Your Login Shell: .bash_profile

The **.bash_profile** file is the BASH shell's login initialization file, which can also be named **.profile** (as in SUSE Linux). It is a script file that is automatically executed whenever a user logs in. The file contains shell commands that define system environment variables used to manage your shell. They may be either redefinitions of system-defined variables or definitions of user-defined variables. For example, when you log in, your user shell needs to know what directories hold Linux commands. It will reference the **PATH** variable to find the pathnames for these directories. However, first, the **PATH** variable must be assigned those pathnames. In the **.bash_profile** file, an assignment operation does just this. Because it is in the **.bash_profile** file, the assignment is executed automatically when the user logs in.

Exporting Variables

Parameter variables also need to be exported, using the **export** command, to make them accessible to any subshells you may enter. You can export several variables in one **export** command by listing them as arguments. Usually, the **.bash_profile** file ends with an **export** command with a list of all the variables defined in the file. If a variable is missing from this list, you may be unable to access it. Notice the **export** command at the end of the **.profile** file in the example described next. You can also combine the assignment and **export** command into one operation as shown here for **NNTPSERVER**:

```
export NNTPSERVER=news.myservice.com
```

Variable Assignments

A copy of the standard **.bash_profile** file provided for you when your account is created is listed in the next example. Notice how **PATH** is assigned, as is the value of **$HOME**. Both **PATH** and **HOME** are parameter variables the system has already defined. **PATH** holds the pathnames of directories searched for any command you enter, and **HOME** holds the pathname of your home directory. The assignment **PATH=$PATH:$HOME/bin** has the effect of redefining **PATH** to include your **bin** directory within your home directory so that your **bin** directory will also be searched for any commands, including ones you create yourself, such as scripts or programs. Notice **PATH** is then exported, so that it can be accessed by any subshells.

.bash_profile
```
# .bash_profile

# Get the aliases and functions
```

```
if [ -f ~/.bashrc ]; then
        . ~/.bashrc
fi

# User specific environment and startup programs
PATH=$PATH:$HOME/bin
export  PATH
```

The root user version of **.bash_profile** adds an entry to unset the **USERNAME** variable, which contains the user's text name.

```
unset USERNAME
```

Should you want to have your home directory searched also, you can use any text editor to modify this line in your **.bash_profile** file to **PATH=$PATH:$HOME/bin:$HOME**, adding **:$HOME** at the end. In fact, you can change this entry to add as many directories as you want searched. If you add a colon at the end, then your current working directory will also be searched for commands. Making commands automatically executable in your current working directory could be a security risk, allowing files in any directory to be executed, instead of in certain specified directories. An example of how to modify your **.bash_profile** file is shown in the following section.

```
PATH=$PATH:$HOME/bin:$HOME:
```

Editing Your BASH Profile Script

Your **.bash_profile** initialization file is a text file that can be edited by a text editor, like any other text file. You can easily add new directories to your **PATH** by editing **.bash_profile** and using editing commands to insert a new directory pathname in the list of directory pathnames assigned to the **PATH** variable. You can even add new variable definitions. If you do so, however, be sure to include the new variable's name in the **export** command's argument list. For example, if your **.bash_profile** file does not have any definition of the **EXINIT** variable, you can edit the file and add a new line that assigns a value to **EXINIT**. The definition **EXINIT='set nu ai'** will configure the Vi editor with line numbering and indentation. You then need to add **EXINIT** to the **export** command's argument list. When the **.bash_profile** file executes again, the **EXINIT** variable will be set to the command **set nu ai**. When the Vi editor is invoked, the command in the **EXINIT** variable will be executed, setting the line number and auto-indent options automatically.

In the following example, the user's **.bash_profile** has been modified to include definitions of **EXINIT** and redefinitions of **PATH**, **PS1**, and **HISTSIZE**. The **PATH** variable has **$HOME:** added to its value. **$HOME** is a variable that evaluates to the user's home directory, and the ending colon specifies the current working directory, enabling you to execute commands that may be located in either the home directory or the working directory. The redefinition of **HISTSIZE** reduces the number of history events saved, from 1,000 defined in the system's **.profile** file, to 30. The redefinition of the **PS1** parameter variable changes the prompt to include the pathname of the current working directory. Any changes you make to parameter variables within your **.bash_profile** file override those made earlier by the system's **.profile** file. All these parameter variables are then exported with the **export** command.

.bash_profile
```
# .bash_profile
# Get the aliases and functions
if [ -f ~/.bashrc ];
 then
    . ~/.bashrc
fi
# User-specific environment and startup programs
PATH=$PATH:$HOME/bin:$HOME:
 unset USERNAME
HISTSIZE=30
NNTPSERVER=news.myserver.com
EXINIT='set nu ai'
PS1="\w \$"
export PATH HISTSIZE EXINIT PS1 NNTPSERVER
```

Manually Reexecuting the .bash_profile Script

Although **.bash_profile** is executed each time you log in, it is not automatically reexecuted after you make changes to it. The **.bash_profile** file is an initialization file that is executed *only* whenever you log in. If you want to take advantage of any changes you make to it without having to log out and log in again, you can reexecute **.bash_profile** with the dot (**.**) command. The **.bash_profile** file is a shell script and, like any shell script, can be executed with the **.** command.

```
$ . .bash_profile
```

Alternatively, you can use the **source** command to execute the **.bash_profile** initialization file, or any initialization file such as **.login** used in the TCSH shell, or **.bashrc**.

```
$ source .bash_profile
```

System Shell Profile Script

Your Linux system also has its own profile file that it executes whenever any user logs in. This system initialization file is simply called **profile** and is found in the **/etc** directory, **/etc/profile**. This file contains parameter variable definitions the system needs to provide for each user. A copy of the system's **.profile** file follows. Fedora and Red Hat use a **pathmunge** function to generate a directory list for the **PATH** variable. Normal user paths will lack the system directories (those with **sbin** in the path) but include the name of their home directory, along with **/usr/kerberos/bin** for Kerberos tools. The path generated for the root user (Effective User ID of 0, EUID = 0) will include both system and user application directories, adding **/usr/kerberos/sbin**, **/sbin**, **/usr/sbin**, and **/usr/local/sbin**, as well as the root user local application directory, **/root/bin**.

```
# echo $PATH
/usr/kerberos/bin/usr/local/bin:usr/sbin:/bin:/usr/X11R6/bin:/home/richard/bin
```

A special work-around is included for the Korn Shell to set the User and Effective User IDs (**EUID** and **UID**).

The **USER**, **MAIL**, and **LOGNAME** variables are then set, provided that **/usr/bin/id**, which provides the User ID, is executable. The **id** command with the **-un** option provides the user ID's text name only, like **chris** or **richard**.

HISTSIZE is also redefined to include a larger number of history events. An entry has been added here for the **NNTPSERVER** variable. Normally, a news server address is a value that needs to be set for all users. Such assignments should be made in the system's **/etc/profile** file by the system administrator, rather than in each individual user's own **.bash_profile** file.

NOTE   *The /etc/profile file also executes any scripts in the directory /etc/profile.d. This design allows for a more modular structure. Rather than make entries by editing the /etc/profile file, you can just add a script to **profile.d** directory.*

The **/etc/profile** file also runs the **/etc/inputrc** file, which configures your command line editor. Here you will find key assignments for different tasks, such as moving to the end of a line or deleting characters. Global options are set as well. Keys are represented in hexadecimal format.

The number of aliases and variable settings needed for different applications would make the **/etc/profile** file much to large to manage. Instead, application- and task-specific aliases and variables are placed in separate configuration files located in the **/etc/profile.d** directory. There are corresponding scripts for both the BASH and C shells. The BASH shell scripts are run by **/etc/profile**. The scripts are named for the kinds of tasks and applications they configure. For example, **colorls.sh** sets the file type color coding when the **ls** command displays files and directories. The **vim.sh** file sets the an alias for the **vi** command, executing **vim** whenever the user enters just **vi**. The **kde.sh** file sets the global environment variable **KDEDIR**, specifying the KDE Desktop applications directory, in this case **/usr**. The **krb5.sh** file adds the pathnames for Kerberos, **/usr/kerberos**, to the **PATH** variable. Files run by the BASH shell end in the extension **.sh**, and those run by the C shell have the extension **.csh**.

/etc/profile

```
# /etc/profile

# System-wide environment and startup programs, for login setup
# Functions and aliases go in /etc/bashrc

pathmunge () {
        if ! echo $PATH | /bin/egrep -q "(^|:)$1($|:)" ; then
            if [ "$2" = "after" ] ; then
                    PATH=$PATH:$1
            else
                    PATH=$1:$PATH
            fi
        fi
}

# ksh workaround
```

```
if [ -z "$EUID" -a -x /usr/bin/id ]; then
        EUID='id -u'
        UID='id -ru'
fi

# Path manipulation
if [ "$EUID" = "0" ]; then
        pathmunge /sbin
        pathmunge /usr/sbin
        pathmunge /usr/local/sbin
fi

# No core files by default
ulimit -S -c 0 > /dev/null 2>&1

if [ -x /usr/bin/id ]; then
        USER="'id -un'"
        LOGNAME=$USER
        MAIL="/var/spool/mail/$USER"
fi

HOSTNAME='/bin/hostname'
HISTSIZE=1000

if [ -z "$INPUTRC" -a ! -f "$HOME/.inputrc" ]; then
    INPUTRC=/etc/inputrc
fi

export PATH USER LOGNAME MAIL HOSTNAME HISTSIZE INPUTRC

for i in /etc/profile.d/*.sh ; do
    if [ -r "$i" ]; then
            . $i
    fi
done

unset i
unset pathmunge
```

Configuring the BASH Shell: .bashrc

The **.bashrc** file is a configuration file executed each time you enter the BASH shell or
generate any subshells. If the BASH shell is your login shell, **.bashrc** is executed along with
your **.bash_login** file when you log in. If you enter the BASH shell from another shell, the
.bashrc file is automatically executed, and the variable and alias definitions it contains will
be defined. If you enter a different type of shell, the configuration file for that shell will be
executed instead. For example, if you were to enter the TCSH shell with the **tcsh** command,
the **.tcshrc** configuration file would be executed instead of **.bashrc**.

The User .bashrc BASH Script

The **.bashrc** shell configuration file is actually executed each time you generate a BASH
shell, such as when you run a shell script. In other words, each time a subshell is created,

the **.bashrc** file is executed. This has the effect of exporting any local variables or aliases you have defined in the **.bashrc** shell initialization file. The **.bashrc** file usually contains the definition of aliases and any feature variables used to turn on shell features. Aliases and feature variables are locally defined within the shell. But the **.bashrc** file defines them in every shell. For this reason, the **.bashrc** file usually holds aliases and options you would want defined for each shell. In this example, the standard **.bashrc** installed by Fedora for users would included only the execution of the system **/etc/bashrc** file. As an example of how you can add your own aliases and options, aliases for the **rm**, **cp**, and **mv** commands and the shell **noclobber** and **ignoreeof** options have been added. For the root user **.bashrc**, the **rm**, **cp**, and **mv** aliases have already been included in the root's **.bashrc** file.

.bashrc
```
# Source global definitions
if [ -f /etc/bashrc ];
 then
     . /etc/bashrc
fi
set  -o ignoreeof
set  -o noclobber
alias rm='rm -i'
alias mv='mv -i'
alias cp='cp -i'
```

You can add any commands or definitions of your own to your **.bashrc** file. If you have made changes to **.bashrc** and you want them to take effect during your current login session, you need to reexecute the file with either the **.** or the **source** command.

```
$ . .bashrc
```

The System /etc/bashrc BASH Script and the /etc/profile.d Directory

Linux systems usually contain a system **bashrc** file executed for all users. The file contains certain global aliases and features needed by all users whenever they enter a BASH shell. This is located in the **/etc** directory, **/etc/bashrc**. A user's own **.bashrc** file, located in the home directory, contains commands to execute this system **.bashrc** file. The **. /etc/bashrc** command in the previous example of **.bashrc** does just that. Currently the **/etc/bashrc** file sets the default shell prompt, one for a terminal window and another for a screen interface. Several other specialized aliases and variables are then set using configuration files located in the **/etc/profile.d** directory. These scripts are executed by **/etc/bashrc** if the shell is not the user login shell.

The BASH Shell Logout File: .bash_logout

The **.bash_logout** file is also a configuration file, but it is executed when the user logs out. It is designed to perform any operations you want done whenever you log out. Instead of variable definitions, the **.bash_logout** file usually contains shell commands that form a kind of shutdown procedure—actions you always want taken before you log out. One common logout command is to clear the screen and then issue a farewell message.

As with **.bash_profile**, you can add your own shell commands to **.bash_logout**. In fact, the **.bash_logout** file is not automatically set up for you when your account is first created. You need to create it yourself, using the Vi or Emacs editor. You could then add a farewell message or other operations. In the next example, the user has a `clear` command and an `echo` command in the **.bash_logout** file. When the user logs out, the `clear` command clears the screen, and then the `echo` command displays the message "Good-bye for now."

.bash_logout
```
# ~/.bash_logout
/usr/bin/clear
echo "Good-bye for now"
```

Initialization and Configuration Files

Each type of shell has its own set of initialization and configuration files. The BASH shell configuration files were discussed previously. The TCSH shell uses **.login**, **.tcshrc**, and **.logout** files in place of **.bash_profile**, **.bashrc**, and **.bash_logout**. The Z shell has several initialization files: **.zshenv**, **.zlogin**, **.zprofile**, **.zschrc**, and **.zlogout**. See Table 9-5 for a listing. Check the Man pages for each shell to see how they are usually configured. When you install a shell, default versions of these files are automatically placed in the users' home directories.

BASH Shell	Function
.bash_profile	Login initialization file
.bashrc	BASH shell configuration file
.bash_logout	Logout name
.bash_history	History file
/etc/profile	System login initialization file
/etc/bashrc	System BASH shell configuration file
/etc/profile.d	Directory for specialized BASH shell configuration files
TCSH Shell	**Function**
.login	Login initialization file
.tcshrc	TCSH shell configuration file
.logout	Logout file
Z Shell	**Function**
.zshenv	Shell login file (first read)
.zprofile	Login initialization file
.zlogin	Shell login file
.zshrc	Z shell configuration file
.zlogout	Logout file
Korn Shell	**Function**
.profile	Login initialization file
.kshrc	KORN shell configuration file

TABLE 9-5 Shell Configuration Files

Except for the TCSH shell, all shells use much the same syntax for variable definitions and assigning values (TCSH uses a slightly different syntax, described in its Man pages).

Configuration Directories and Files

Applications often install configuration files in a user's home directory that contain specific configuration information, which tailors the application to the needs of that particular user. This may take the form of a single configuration file that begins with a period, or a directory that contains several configuration files. The directory name will also begin with a period. For example, Mozilla installs a directory called **.mozilla** in the user's home directory that contains configuration files. On the other hand, many mail application uses a single file called **.mailrc** to hold alias and feature settings set up by the user, though others like Evolution also have their own, **.evolution**. Most single configuration files end in the letters **rc**. **FTP** uses a file called **.netrc**. Most newsreaders use a file called **.newsrc**. Entries in configuration files are usually set by the application, though you can usually make entries directly by editing the file. Applications have their own set of special variables to which you can define and assign values. You can list the configuration files in your home directory with the **ls -a** command.

Managing Linux Files and Directories: Directories, Archives, and Compression

I n Linux, all files are organized into directories that, in turn, are hierarchically connected to each other in one overall file structure. A file is referenced not just according to its name, but also according to its place in this file structure. You can create as many new directories as you want, adding more directories to the file structure. The Linux file commands can perform sophisticated operations, such as moving or copying whole directories along with their subdirectories. You can use file operations such as **find**, **cp**, **mv**, and **ln** to locate files and copy, move, or link them from one directory to another. Desktop file managers, such as Konqueror and Nautilus used on the KDE and GNOME desktops, provide a graphical user interface to perform the same operations using icons, windows, and menus (see Chapters 6 and 7). This chapter will focus on the commands you use in the shell command line to manage files, such as **cp** and **mv**. However, whether you use the command line or a GUI file manager, the underlying file structure is the same.

The organization of the Linux file structure into its various system and network administration directories is discussed in detail in Chapter 30. Though not part of the Linux file structure, there are also special tools you can use to access Windows partitions and floppy disks. These follow much the same format as Linux file commands.

Archives are used to back up files or to combine them into a package, which can then be transferred as one file over the Internet or posted on an FTP site for easy downloading. The standard archive utility used on Linux and Unix systems is tar, for which several GUI front ends exist. You have several compression programs to choose from, including GNU zip (gzip), Zip, bzip, and compress.

NOTE *Linux also allows you to mount and access file systems used by other operating systems such as Unix or Windows. Linux itself supports a variety of different file systems such as ext2, ext3, and ReiserFS. File systems are discussed in Chapter 30. Access to remote file systems is discussed in Chapter 39.*

Linux Files

You can name a file using any letters, underscores, and numbers. You can also include periods and commas. Except in certain special cases, you should never begin a filename with a period. Other characters, such as slashes, question marks, or asterisks, are reserved for use as special characters by the system and should not be part of a filename. Filenames can be as long as 256 characters. Filenames can also include spaces, though to reference such filenames from the command line, be sure to encase them in quotes. On a desktop like GNOME or KDE you do not need quotes.

You can include an extension as part of a filename. A period is used to distinguish the filename proper from the extension. Extensions can be useful for categorizing your files. You are probably familiar with certain standard extensions that have been adopted by convention. For example, C source code files always have an extension of **.c**. Files that contain compiled object code have a **.o** extension. You can, of course, make up your own file extensions. The following examples are all valid Linux filenames. Keep in mind that to reference the last of these names on the command line, you would have to encase it in quotes as "New book review":

```
preface
chapter2
9700info
New_Revisions
calc.c
intro.bk1
New book review
```

Special initialization files are also used to hold shell configuration commands. These are the hidden, or dot, files, which begin with a period. Dot files used by commands and applications have predetermined names, such as the **.mozilla** directory used to hold your Mozilla data and configuration files. Recall that when you use **ls** to display your filenames, the dot files will not be displayed. To include the dot files, you need to use **ls** with the **-a** option. Dot files are discussed in more detail in the chapter on shell configuration, Chapter 9.

As shown in Figure 10-1, the **ls -l** command displays detailed information about a file. First the permissions are displayed, followed by the number of links, the owner of the file, the name of the group the user belongs to, the file size in bytes, the date and time the file was last modified, and the name of the file. Permissions indicate who can access the file: the user, members of a group, or all other users. Permissions are discussed in detail later in this chapter. The group name indicates the group permitted to access the file object. In Figure 10-1, the file type for **mydata** is that of an ordinary file. Only one link exists, indicating the file has no other names and no other links. The owner's name is **chris**, the same as the login name, and the group name is **weather**. Other users probably also belong to the **weather** group. The size of the file is 207 bytes, and it was last modified on February 20, at 11:55 A.M. The name of the file is **mydata**.

If you want to display this detailed information for all the files in a directory, simply use the **ls -l** command without an argument.

```
$ ls -l
-rw-r--r-- 1 chris weather 207 Feb 20 11:55 mydata
-rw-rw-r-- 1 chris weather 568 Feb 14 10:30 today
-rw-rw-r-- 1 chris weather 308 Feb 17 12:40 monday
```

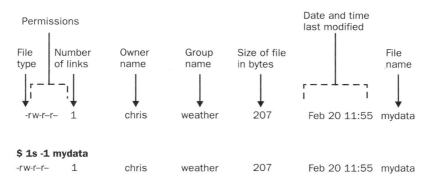

FIGURE 10-1   File information displayed using the `-l` option for the `ls` command

All files in Linux have one physical format—a byte stream. A *byte stream* is just a sequence of bytes. This allows Linux to apply the file concept to every data component in the system. Directories are classified as files, as are devices. Treating everything as a file allows Linux to organize and exchange data more easily. The data in a file can be sent directly to a device such as a screen because a device interfaces with the system using the same byte-stream file format as regular files.

This same file format is used to implement other operating system components. The interface to a device, such as the screen or keyboard, is designated as a file. Other components, such as directories, are themselves byte-stream files, but they have a special internal organization. A directory file contains information about a directory, organized in a special directory format. Because these different components are treated as files, they can be said to constitute different *file types.* A character device is one file type. A directory is another file type. The number of these file types may vary according to your specific implementation of Linux. Five common types of files exist, however: ordinary files, directory files, first-in first-out pipes, character device files, and block device files. Although you may rarely reference a file's type, it can be useful when searching for directories or devices. Later in the chapter, you see how to use the file type in a search criterion with the **find** command to search specifically for directory or device names.

Although all ordinary files have a byte-stream format, they may be used in different ways. The most significant difference is between binary and text files. Compiled programs are examples of binary files. However, even text files can be classified according to their different uses. You can have files that contain C programming source code or shell commands, or even a file that is empty. The file could be an executable program or a directory file. The Linux **file** command helps you determine what a file is used for. It examines the first few lines of a file and tries to determine a classification for it. The **file** command looks for special keywords or special numbers in those first few lines, but it is not always accurate. In the next example, the **file** command examines the contents of two files and determines a classification for them:

```
$ file monday reports
monday: text
reports: directory
```

If you need to examine the entire file byte by byte, you can do so with the **od** (octal dump) command. The **od** command performs a dump of a file. By default, it prints every byte in its octal representation. However, you can also specify a character, decimal, or hexadecimal representation. The **od** command is helpful when you need to detect any special character in your file or if you want to display a binary file.

The File Structure

Linux organizes files into a hierarchically connected set of directories. Each directory may contain either files or other directories. In this respect, directories perform two important functions. A *directory* holds files, much like files held in a file drawer, and a directory connects to other directories, much as a branch in a tree is connected to other branches. Because of the similarities to a tree, such a structure is often referred to as a *tree structure.*

The Linux file structure branches into several directories beginning with a root directory, */.* Within the root directory several system directories contain files and programs that are features of the Linux system. The root directory also contains a directory called **/home** that contains the home directories of all the users in the system. Each user's home directory, in turn, contains the directories the user has made for his or her own use. Each of these could also contain directories. Such nested directories would branch out from the user's home directory, as shown in Figure 10-2.

NOTE *The user's home directory can be any directory, though it is usually the directory that bears the user's login name. This directory is located in the directory named **/home** on your Linux system. For example, a user named **dylan** will have a home directory called **dylan** located in the system's **/home** directory. The user's home directory is a subdirectory of the directory called* **/home** *on your system.*

Home Directories

When you log in to the system, you are placed within your home directory. The name given to this directory by the system is the same as your login name. Any files you create when you first log in are organized within your home directory. Within your home directory, however, you can create more directories. You can then change to these directories and store

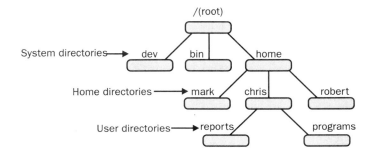

FIGURE 10-2 The Linux file structure beginning at the root directory

files in them. The same is true for other users on the system. Each user has his own home directory, identified by the appropriate login name. Users, in turn, can create their own directories.

You can access a directory either through its name or by making it the default directory. Each directory is given a name when it is created. You can use this name in file operations to access files in that directory. You can also make the directory your default directory. If you do not use any directory names in a file operation, the default directory will be accessed. The default directory is referred to as the *working directory.* In this sense, the working directory is the one from which you are currently working. When you log in, the working directory is your home directory, usually having the same name as your login name. You can change the working directory by using the **cd** command to designate another directory as the working directory.

Pathnames

The name you give to a directory or file when you create it is not its full name. The full name of a directory is its *pathname.* The hierarchically nested relationship among directories forms paths, and these paths can be used to identify and reference any directory or file unambiguously. Each directory in the file structure can be said to have its own unique path. The actual name by which the system identifies a directory always begins with the root directory and consists of all directories nested below that directory.

In Linux, you write a pathname by listing each directory in the path separated from the last by a forward slash. A slash preceding the first directory in the path represents the root. The pathname for the **robert** directory is **/home/robert**. The pathname for the **reports** directory is **/home/chris/reports**. Pathnames also apply to files. When you create a file within a directory, you give the file a name. The actual name by which the system identifies the file, however, is the filename combined with the path of directories from the root to the file's directory. In Figure 10-3, the path for the **weather** file consists of the root, **home**, and **chris** directories and the filename **weather**. The pathname for **weather** is **/home/chris/weather** (the root directory is represented by the first slash).

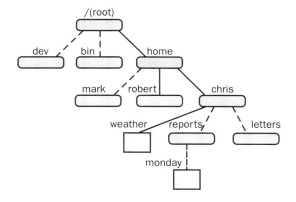

FIGURE 10-3   Linux pathnames

Pathnames may be absolute or relative. An *absolute pathname* is the complete pathname of a file or directory beginning with the root directory. A *relative pathname* begins from your working directory; it is the path of a file relative to your working directory. The working directory is the one you are currently operating in. Using the directory structure described in Figure 10-3, if **chris** is your working directory, the relative pathname for the file **monday** is **reports/monday**. The absolute pathname for **monday** is **/home/chris/reports/monday**.

The absolute pathname from the root to your home directory could be especially complex and, at times, even subject to change by the system administrator. To make it easier to reference, you can use a special character, the tilde (**~**), which represents the absolute pathname of your home directory. In the next example, from the **thankyou** directory, the user references the **weather** file in the home directory by placing a tilde and slash before **weather**:

```
$ pwd
/home/chris/letters/thankyou
$ cat ~/weather
raining and warm
$
```

You must specify the rest of the path from your home directory. In the next example, the user references the **monday** file in the **reports** directory. The tilde represents the path to the user's home directory, **/home/chris**, and then the rest of the path to the **monday** file is specified.

```
$ cat ~/reports/monday
```

System Directories

The root directory that begins the Linux file structure contains several system directories. The system directories contain files and programs used to run and maintain the system. Many contain other subdirectories with programs for executing specific features of Linux. For example, the directory **/usr/bin** contains the various Linux commands that users execute, such as **cp** and **mv**. The directory **/bin** holds interfaces with different system devices, such as the printer or the terminal. Table 10-1 lists the basic system directories.

NOTE *The overall organization of the Linux file structure for system directories and other useful directories, such as those used for the kernel, are discussed in detail in Chapter 30.*

Listing, Displaying, and Printing Files: ls, cat, more, less, and lpr

One of the primary functions of an operating system is the management of files. You may need to perform certain basic output operations on your files, such as displaying them on your screen or printing them. The Linux system provides a set of commands that perform basic file-management operations, such as listing, displaying, and printing files, as well as copying, renaming, and erasing files. These commands are usually made up of abbreviated versions of words. For example, the **ls** command is a shortened form of "list" and lists the files in your directory. The **lpr** command is an abbreviated form of "line print" and will print a file. The **cat**, **less**, and **more** commands display the contents of a file on the screen. Table 10-2 lists these commands with their different options. When you log in to your Linux

Directory	Function
/	Begins the file system structure, called the *root*.
/home	Contains users' home directories.
/bin	Holds all the standard commands and utility programs.
/usr	Holds those files and commands used by the system; this directory breaks down into several subdirectories.
/usr/bin	Holds user-oriented commands and utility programs.
/usr/sbin	Holds system administration commands.
/usr/lib	Holds libraries for programming languages.
/usr/share/doc	Holds Linux documentation.
/usr/share/man	Holds the online manual man files.
/var/spool	Holds spooled files, such as those generated for printing jobs and network transfers.
/sbin	Holds system administration commands for booting the system.
/var	Holds files that vary, such as mailbox files.
/dev	Holds file interfaces for devices such as the terminals and printers (dynamically generated by udev, do not edit, see Chapter 32).
/etc	Holds system configuration files and any other system files.

TABLE 10-1   Standard System Directories in Linux

Command	Execution
ls	This command lists file and directory names.
cat *filenames*	This command can be used to display a file. It can take filenames for its arguments. It outputs the contents of those files directly to the standard output, which, by default, is directed to the screen.
more *filenames*	This utility displays a file screen by screen. Press the SPACEBAR to continue to the next screen and **q** to quit.
less *filenames*	This utility also displays a file screen by screen. Press the SPACEBAR to continue to the next screen and **q** to quit.
lpr *filenames*	Sends a file to the line printer to be printed; a list of files may be used as arguments. Use the **-P** option to specify a printer.
lpq	Lists the print queue for printing jobs.
lprm	Removes a printing job from the print queue.

TABLE 10-2   Listing, Displaying, and Printing Files

system, you may want a list of the files in your home directory. The **ls** command, which outputs a list of your file and directory names, is useful for this. The **ls** command has many possible options for displaying filenames according to specific features.

Displaying Files: cat, less, and more

You may also need to look at the contents of a file. The **cat** and **more** commands display the contents of a file on the screen. The name **cat** stands for *concatenate*.

```
$ cat mydata
computers
```

The **cat** command outputs the entire text of a file to the screen at once. This presents a problem when the file is large because its text quickly speeds past on the screen. The **more** and **less** commands are designed to overcome this limitation by displaying one screen of text at a time. You can then move forward or backward in the text at your leisure. You invoke the **more** or **less** command by entering the command name followed by the name of the file you want to view (**less** is a more powerful and configurable display utility).

```
$ less mydata
```

When **more** or **less** invoke a file, the first screen of text is displayed. To continue to the next screen, you press the F key or the SPACEBAR. To move back in the text, you press the B key. You can quit at any time by pressing the Q key.

Printing Files: lpr, lpq, and lprm

With the printer commands such as **lpr** and **lprm**, you can perform printing operations such as printing files or canceling print jobs (see Table 10-2). When you need to print files, use the **lpr** command to send files to the printer connected to your system. See Chapter 26 to learn more about printing. In the next example, the user prints the **mydata** file:

```
$ lpr mydata
```

If you want to print several files at once, you can specify more than one file on the command line after the **lpr** command. In the next example, the user prints out both the **mydata** and **preface** files:

```
$ lpr mydata preface
```

Printing jobs are placed in a queue and printed one at a time in the background. You can continue with other work as your files print. You can see the position of a particular printing job at any given time with the **lpq** command, which gives the owner of the printing job (the login name of the user who sent the job), the print job ID, the size in bytes, and the temporary file in which it is currently held.

If you need to cancel an unwanted printing job, you can do so with the **lprm** command, which takes as its argument either the ID number of the printing job or the owner's name. It then removes the print job from the print queue. For this task, **lpq** is helpful, as it provides you with the ID number and owner of the printing job you need to use with **lprm**.

Managing Directories: mkdir, rmdir, ls, cd, and pwd

You can create and remove your own directories, as well as change your working directory, with the **mkdir**, **rmdir**, and **cd** commands. Each of these commands can take as its argument the pathname for a directory. The **pwd** command displays the absolute pathname of your working directory. In addition to these commands, the special characters represented by a single dot, a double dot, and a tilde can be used to reference the working directory, the parent of the working directory, and the home directory, respectively. Taken together, these commands enable you to manage your directories. You can create nested directories, move from one directory to another, and use pathnames to reference any of your directories. Those commands commonly used to manage directories are listed in Table 10-3.

Command	Execution
mkdir *directory*	Creates a directory.
rmdir *directory*	Erases a directory.
ls -F	Lists directory names with a preceding slash.
ls -R	Lists working directory as well as all subdirectories.
cd *directory name*	Changes to the specified directory, making it the working directory. **cd** without a directory name changes back to the home directory.
pwd	Displays the pathname of the working directory.
Pathname References	**Remarks**
directory name / filename	A slash is used in pathnames to separate each directory name. In the case of pathnames for files, a slash separates the preceding directory names from the filename.

..	References the parent directory. You can use it as an argument or as part of a pathname:
	$ cd ..
	$ mv ../larisa oldletters

.	References the working directory. You can use it as an argument or as part of a pathname: $ ls .
~/*pathname*	The tilde is a special character that represents the pathname for the home directory. It is useful when you need to use an absolute pathname for a file or directory: $ cp monday ~/today

TABLE 10-3 Directory Commands

Creating and Deleting Directories

You create and remove directories with the **mkdir** and **rmdir** commands. In either case, you can also use pathnames for the directories. In the next example, the user creates the directory **reports** in the current working directory. Then the user creates the directory **letters** using a pathname:

```
$ mkdir reports
$ mkdir /home/chris/letters
```

You can remove a directory with the **rmdir** command followed by the directory name. In the next example, the user removes the directory **reports** with the **rmdir** command:

```
$ rmdir reports
```

To remove a directory and all its subdirectories, you use the **rm** command with the **-r** option. This is a very powerful command and could easily be used to erase all your files. By default, **rm** is aliased with the **-i** option so that you will be prompted to verify removal of each file. To simply remove all files and subdirectories without prompts, add the **-f** option. The following example deletes the **reports** directory and all its subdirectories:

```
$ rm -rf reports
```

Displaying Directory Contents

You have seen how to use the **ls** command to list the files and directories within your working directory. To distinguish between file and directory names, however, you need to use the **ls** command with the **-F** option. A slash is then placed after each directory name in the list.

```
$ ls
weather reports letters
$ ls -F
weather reports/ letters/
```

The **ls** command also takes as an argument any directory name or directory pathname. This enables you to list the files in any directory without first having to change to that directory. In the next example, the **ls** command takes as its argument the name of a directory, **reports**. Then the **ls** command is executed again, only this time the absolute pathname of **reports** is used.

```
$ ls reports
monday tuesday
$ ls /home/chris/reports
monday tuesday
$
```

Moving Through Directories

The **cd** command takes as its argument the name of the directory to which you want to change. The name of the directory can be the name of a subdirectory in your working directory or the full pathname of any directory on the system. If you want to change back to your home directory, you only need to enter the **cd** command by itself, without a filename argument.

```
$ cd props
$ pwd
/home/dylan/props
```

Referencing the Parent Directory

A directory always has a parent (except, of course, for the root). For example, in the preceding listing, the parent for reports is Dylan's home directory (**/home/dylan**). When a directory is created, two entries are made: one represented with a dot (**.**), and the other with double dots (**..**). The dot represents the pathname of the directory, and the double dots represent the pathname of its parent directory. Double dots, used as an argument in a command, reference a parent directory. The single dot references the directory itself.

You can use the single dot to reference your working directory, instead of using its pathname. For example, to copy a file to the working directory retaining the same name, the dot can be used in place of the working directory's pathname. In this sense, the dot is another name for the working directory. In the next example, the user copies the **weather** file from the **chris** directory to the **reports** directory. The **reports** directory is the working directory and can be represented with the single dot.

```
$ cd reports
$ cp /home/chris/weather .
```

The **..** symbol is often used to reference files in the parent directory. In the next example, the **cat** command displays the **weather** file in the parent directory. The pathname for the file is the **..** symbol followed by a slash and the filename.

```
$ cat ../weather
raining and warm
```

TIP   *You can use the* **cd** *command with the* **..** *symbol to step back through successive parent directories of the directory tree from a lower directory.*

File and Directory Operations: find, cp, mv, rm, and ln

As you create more and more files, you may want to back them up, change their names, erase some of them, or even give them added names. Linux provides you with several file commands that enable you to search for files, copy files, rename files, or remove files (see Tables 10-5). If you have a large number of files, you can also search them to locate a specific one. The commands are shortened forms of full words, consisting of only two characters. The **cp** command stands for "copy" and copies a file, **mv** stands for "move" and renames or moves a file, **rm** stands for "remove" and erases a file, and **ln** stands for "link" and adds another name for a file, often used as a shortcut to the original. One exception to the two-character rule is the **find** command, which performs searches of your filenames to find a file. All these operations can be handled by the GUI desktops, like GNOME and KDE (see Chapters 6 and 7).

Searching Directories: find

Once you have a large number of files in many different directories, you may need to search them to locate a specific file, or files, of a certain type. The **find** command enables you to perform such a search from the command line. The **find** command takes as its arguments directory names followed by several possible options that specify the type of search and the criteria for the search; it then searches within the directories listed and their subdirectories for files that meet these criteria. The **find** command can search for a file by name, type, owner, and even the time of the last update.

```
$ find directory-list -option criteria
```

TIP From the GNOME desktop you can use the "Search" tool in the Places menu to search for files. From the KDE Desktop you can use the find tool in the file manager. Select find from the file manager (Konqueror) tools menu.

The **-name** option has as its criteria a pattern and instructs **find** to search for the filename that matches that pattern. To search for a file by name, you use the **find** command with the directory name followed by the **-name** option and the name of the file.

```
$ find directory-list -name filename
```

The **find** command also has options that merely perform actions, such as outputting the results of a search. If you want **find** to display the filenames it has found, you simply include the **-print** option on the command line along with any other options. The **-print** option is an action that instructs **find** to write to the standard output the names of all the files it locates (you can also use the **-ls** option instead to list files in the long format). In the next example, the user searches for all the files in the **reports** directory with the name **monday**. Once located, the file, with its relative pathname, is printed.

```
$ find reports -name monday -print
reports/monday
```

The **find** command prints out the filenames using the directory name specified in the directory list. If you specify an absolute pathname, the absolute path of the found directories will be output. If you specify a relative pathname, only the relative pathname is output. In the preceding example, the user specified a relative pathname, **reports**, in the directory list. Located filenames were output beginning with this relative pathname. In the next example, the user specifies an absolute pathname in the directory list. Located filenames are then output using this absolute pathname.

```
$ find /home/chris -name monday -print
/home/chris/reports/monday
```

---

*TIP Should you need to find the location of a specific program or configuration file, you could use **find** to search for the file from the root directory. Log in as the root user and use / as the directory. This command searched for the location of the **more** command and files on the entire file system: **find / -name more -print**.*

Searching the Working Directory

If you want to search your working directory, you can use the dot as the directory pathname to represent your working directory. The double dots would represent the parent directory. The next example searches all files and subdirectories in the working directory, using the dot to represent the working directory. If you are located in your home directory, this is a convenient way to search through all your own directories. Notice the located filenames are output beginning with a dot.

```
$ find . -name weather -print
./weather
```

You can use shell wildcard characters as part of the pattern criteria for searching files. The special character must be quoted, however, to avoid evaluation by the shell. In the next example, all files with the **.c** extension in the **programs** directory are searched for and then displayed in the long format using the **-ls** action:

```
$ find programs -name '*.c' -ls
```

Locating Directories

You can also use the **find** command to locate directories. In Linux, a directory is officially classified as a special type of file. Although all files have a byte-stream format, some files, such as directories, are used in special ways. In this sense, a file can be said to have a file type. The **find** command has an option called **-type** that searches for a file of a given type. The **-type** option takes a one-character modifier that represents the file type. The modifier that represents a directory is a **d**. In the next example, both the directory name and the directory file type are used to search for the directory called **thankyou**:

```
$ find /home/chris -name thankyou -type d -print
/home/chris/letters/thankyou
$
```

File types are not so much different types of files as they are the file format applied to other components of the operating system, such as devices. In this sense, a device is treated as a type of file, and you can use **find** to search for devices and directories, as well as ordinary files. Table 10-4 lists the different types available for the **find** command's **-type** option.

You can also use the find operation to search for files by ownership or security criteria, like those belonging to a specific user or those with a certain security context. The user option allows you to locate all files belonging to a certain user. The following example lists all files that the user **chris** has created or owns on the entire system. To list those just in the users' home directories, you would use **/home** for the starting search directory. This would find all those in a user's home directory as well as any owned by that user in other user directories.

```
$ find / -user chris -print
```

Copying Files

To make a copy of a file, you simply give **cp** two filenames as its arguments (see Table 10-5). The first filename is the name of the file to be copied—the one that already exists. This is often referred to as the *source file*. The second filename is the name you want for the copy.

Command	Execution
`find`	Searches directories for files according to search criteria. This command has several options that specify the type of criteria and actions to be taken.

Option	Execution
`-name` *pattern*	Searches for files with the *pattern* in the name.
`-lname` *pattern*	Searches for symbolic link files.
`-group` *name*	Searches for files belonging to the group *name*.
`-gid` *num*	Searches for files belonging to a group according to group ID.
`-user` *name*	Searches for files belonging to a user.
`-uid` *num*	Searches for files belonging to a user according to user ID.
`-size` *numc*	Searches for files with the size *num* in blocks. If **c** is added after *num*, the size in bytes (characters) is searched for.
`-mtime` *num*	Searches for files last modified *num* days ago.
`-newer` *pattern*	Searches for files modified after the one matched by *pattern*.
`-context` *scontext*	Searches for files according to security context (SE Linux).
`-print`	Outputs the result of the search to the standard output. The result is usually a list of filenames, including their full pathnames.
`-type` *filetype*	Searches for files with the specified file type. File type can be **b** for block device, **c** for character device, **d** for directory, **f** for file, or **l** for symbolic link.
`-perm` *permission*	Searches for files with certain permissions set. Use octal or symbolic format for permissions (see Chapter 29).
`-ls`	Provides a detailed listing of each file, with owner, permission, size, and date information.
`-exec` *command*	Executes command when files found.

TABLE 10-4   The `find` Command

This will be a new file containing a copy of all the data in the source file. This second argument is often referred to as the *destination file*. The syntax for the **cp** command follows:

```
$ cp source-file destination-file
```

In the next example, the user copies a file called **proposal** to a new file called **oldprop**:

```
$ cp proposal oldprop
```

You could unintentionally destroy another file with the **cp** command. The **cp** command generates a copy by first creating a file and then copying data into it. If another file has the same name as the destination file, that file is destroyed and a new file with that name is created. By default Red Hat configures your system to check for an existing copy by the

Command	Execution
cp *filename filename*	Copies a file. **cp** takes two arguments: the original file and the name of the new copy. You can use pathnames for the files to copy across directories: `$ cp today reports/Monday`
cp -r *dirname dirname*	Copies a subdirectory from one directory to another. The copied directory includes all its own subdirectories: `$ cp -r letters/thankyou oldletters`
mv *filename filename*	Moves (renames) a file. The **mv** command takes two arguments: the first is the file to be moved. The second argument can be the new filename or the pathname of a directory. If it is the name of a directory, then the file is literally moved to that directory, changing the file's pathname: `$ mv today /home/chris/reports`
mv *dirname dirname*	Moves directories. In this case, the first and last arguments are directories: `$ mv letters/thankyou oldletters`
ln *filename filename*	Creates added names for files referred to as links. A link can be created in one directory that references a file in another directory: `$ ln today reports/Monday`
rm *filenames*	Removes (erases) a file. Can take any number of filenames as its arguments. Literally removes links to a file. If a file has more than one link, you need to remove all of them to erase a file: `$rm today weather weekend`

TABLE 10-5 File Operations

same name (**cp** is aliased with the **-i** option, see Chapter 9). To copy a file from your working directory to another directory, you only need to use that directory name as the second argument in the **cp** command. In the next example, the **proposal** file is overwritten by the **newprop** file. The **proposal** file already exists.

```
$ cp newprop proposal
```

You can use any of the wildcard characters to generate a list of filenames to use with **cp** or **mv**. For example, suppose you need to copy all your C source code files to a given directory. Instead of listing each one individually on the command line, you could use an ***** character with the **.c** extension to match on and generate a list of C source code files (all files with a **.c** extension). In the next example, the user copies all source code files in the current directory to the **sourcebks** directory:

```
$ cp *.c sourcebks
```

If you want to copy all the files in a given directory to another directory, you could use **∗** to match on and generate a list of all those files in a **cp** command. In the next example, the user copies all the files in the **props** directory to the **oldprop** directory. Notice the use of a **props** pathname preceding the **∗** special character. In this context, **props** is a pathname that will be appended before each file in the list that **∗** generates.

```
$ cp props/* oldprop
```

You can, of course, use any of the other special characters, such as **.** , **?**, or **[]**. In the next example, the user copies both source code and object code files (**.c** and **.o**) to the **projbk** directory:

```
$ cp *.[oc] projbk
```

When you copy a file, you may want to give the copy a different name than the original. To do so, place the new filename after the directory name, separated by a slash.

```
$ cp filename directory-name/new-filename
```

Moving Files

You can use the **mv** command either to rename a file or to move a file from one directory to another. When using **mv** to rename a file, you simply use the new filename as the second argument. The first argument is the current name of the file you are renaming. If you want to rename a file when you move it, you can specify the new name of the file after the directory name. In the next example, the **proposal** file is renamed with the name **version1**:

```
$ mv proposal version1
```

As with **cp**, it is easy for **mv** to erase a file accidentally. When renaming a file, you might accidentally choose a filename already used by another file. In this case, that other file will be erased. The **mv** command also has an **-i** option that checks first to see if a file by that name already exists.

You can also use any of the special characters described in Chapter 8 to generate a list of filenames to use with **mv**. In the next example, the user moves all source code files in the current directory to the **newproj** directory:

```
$ mv *.c newproj
```

If you want to move all the files in a given directory to another directory, you can use **∗** to match on and generate a list of all those files. In the next example, the user moves all the files in the **reports** directory to the **repbks** directory:

```
$ mv reports/* repbks
```

NOTE *The easiest way to copy files to a CD-R/RW or DVD-R/RW disc is to use the built-in Nautilus burning capability. Just insert a blank disk, open it as a folder, and drag and drop files on to it. You will be prompted automatically to burn the files. You can also use any number of CD/DVD burning tools, such as K3B (see Chapter 3).*

Copying and Moving Directories

You can also copy or move whole directories at once. Both **cp** and **mv** can take as their first argument a directory name, enabling you to copy or move subdirectories from one directory into another (see Table 10-5). The first argument is the name of the directory to be moved or copied, while the second argument is the name of the directory within which it is to be placed. The same pathname structure used for files applies to moving or copying directories.

You can just as easily copy subdirectories from one directory to another. To copy a directory, the **cp** command requires you to use the **-r** option. The **-r** option stands for "recursive." It directs the **cp** command to copy a directory, as well as any subdirectories it may contain. In other words, the entire directory subtree, from that directory on, will be copied. In the next example, the **thankyou** directory is copied to the **oldletters** directory. Now two **thankyou** subdirectories exist, one in **letters** and one in **oldletters**.

```
$ cp -r letters/thankyou oldletters
$ ls -F letters
/thankyou
$ ls -F oldletters
/thankyou
```

Erasing Files and Directories: the rm Command

As you use Linux, you will find the number of files you use increases rapidly. Generating files in Linux is easy. Applications such as editors, and commands such as **cp**, easily create files. Eventually, many of these files may become outdated and useless. You can then remove them with the **rm** command. The **rm** command can take any number of arguments, enabling you to list several filenames and erase them all at the same time. In the next example, the user erases the file **oldprop**:

```
$ rm oldprop
```

Be careful when using the **rm** command, because it is irrevocable. Once a file is removed, it cannot be restored (there is no undo). With the **-i** option, you are prompted separately for each file and asked whether to remove it. If you enter **y**, the file will be removed. If you enter anything else, the file is not removed. In the next example, the **rm** command is instructed to erase the files **proposal** and **oldprop**. The **rm** command then asks for confirmation for each file. The user decides to remove **oldprop**, but not **proposal**.

```
$ rm -i proposal oldprop
Remove proposal? n
Remove oldprop? y
$
```

Links: the ln Command

You can give a file more than one name using the **ln** command. You might want to reference a file using different filenames to access it from different directories. The added names are often referred to as *links*. Linux supports two different types of links, hard and symbolic. *Hard* links are literally another name for the same file, whereas *symbolic* links function like shortcuts referencing another file. Symbolic links are much more flexible and can work over many different file systems, whereas hard links are limited to your local file system. Furthermore, hard links introduce security concerns, as they allow direct access from a link that may have public access to an original file that you may want protected. Links are usually implemented as symbolic links.

Symbolic Links

To set up a symbolic link, you use the **ln** command with the **-s** option and two arguments: the name of the original file and the new, added filename. The **ls** operation lists both filenames, but only one physical file will exist.

```
$ ln -s original-file-name added-file-name
```

In the next example, the **today** file is given the additional name **weather**. It is just another name for the **today** file.

```
$ ls
today
$ ln -s today weather
$ ls
today weather
```

You can give the same file several names by using the **ln** command on the same file many times. In the next example, the file **today** is given both the names **weather** and **weekend**:

```
$ ln -s today weather
$ ln -s today weekend
$ ls
today weather weekend
```

If you list the full information about a symbolic link and its file, you will find the information displayed is different. In the next example, the user lists the full information for both **lunch** and **/home/george/veglist** using the **ls** command with the **-l** option. The first character in the line specifies the file type. Symbolic links have their own file type, represented by an l. The file type for **lunch** is l, indicating it is a symbolic link, not an ordinary file. The number after the term "group" is the size of the file. Notice the sizes differ. The size of the **lunch** file is only four bytes. This is because **lunch** is only a symbolic link—a file that holds the pathname of another file—and a pathname takes up only a few bytes. It is not a direct hard link to the **veglist** file.

```
$ ls -l lunch /home/george/veglist
lrw-rw-r-- 1 chris group 4 Feb 14 10:30 lunch
-rw-rw-r-- 1 george group 793 Feb 14 10:30 veglist
```

To erase a file, you need to remove only its original name (and any hard links to it). If any symbolic links are left over, they will be unable to access the file. In this case, a symbolic link would hold the pathname of a file that no longer exists.

Hard Links

You can give the same file several names by using the **ln** command on the same file many times. To set up a hard link, you use the **ln** command with no **-s** option and two arguments: the name of the original file and the new, added filename. The **ls** operation lists both file-names, but only one physical file will exist.

```
$ ln original-file-name added-file-name
```

In the next example, the **monday** file is given the additional name **storm**. It is just another name for the **monday** file.

```
$ ls
today
$ ln monday storm
$ ls
monday storm
```

To erase a file that has hard links, you need to remove all its hard links. The name of a file is actually considered a link to that file—hence the command **rm** that removes the link to the file. If you have several links to the file and remove only one of them, the others stay in place and you can reference the file through them. The same is true even if you remove the original link—the original name of the file. Any added links will work just as well. In the next example, the **today** file is removed with the **rm** command. However, a link to that same file exists, called **weather**. The file can then be referenced under the name **weather**.

```
$ ln today weather
$ rm today
$ cat weather
The storm broke today
and the sun came out.
$
```

NOTE *Each file and directory in Linux contains a set of permissions that determine who can access them and how. You set these permissions to limit access in one of three ways: You can restrict access to yourself alone, you can allow users in a group to have access, or you can permit anyone on your system to have access. You can also control how a given file or directory is accessed. A file and directory may have read, write, and execute permissions. When a file is created, it is automatically given read and write permissions for the owner, enabling you to display and modify the file. You may change these permissions to any combination you want (see Chapter 28 for more details).*

The mtools Utilities: msdos

Your Linux system provides a set of utilities, known as *mtools,* that enable you to access floppy and hard disks formatted for MS-DOS easily. They work only with the old MS-DOS or FAT32 file systems, and not with Windows XP, NT, or 2000, which use the NTFS file system. The **mcopy** command enables you to copy files to and from an MS-DOS floppy disk in your floppy drive or a Windows FAT32 partition on your hard drive. No special operations, such as mounting, are required. With mtools, you needn't mount an MS-DOS partition to access it. For an MS-DOS floppy disk, place the disk in your floppy drive, and you can then use mtool commands to access those files. For example, to copy a file from an MS-DOS floppy disk to your Linux system, use the **mcopy** command. You specify the MS-DOS disk with **a:** for the A drive. Unlike normal DOS pathnames, pathnames used with mtool commands use forward slashes instead of backslashes. The directory **docs** on the A drive would be referenced by the pathname **a:/docs**, not **a:\docs**. Unlike MS-DOS, which defaults the second argument to the current directory, you always need to supply the second argument for **mcopy**. The next example copies the file **mydata** to the MS-DOS disk and then copies the **preface** file from the disk to the current Linux directory.

```
$ mcopy mydata a:
$ mcopy a:/preface   .
```

TIP *You can use mtools to copy data to Windows-formatted floppy disks or to a Windows FAT32 partition, which can also be read or written to by Windows XP, but you cannot access Windows XP, NT, or 2000 hard disk file systems (NTFS) with mtools. The NTFS partitions require a different tool, the NTFS kernel module (see Chapter 4).*

You can use the **mdir** command to list files on your MS-DOS disk, and you can use the **mcd** command to change directories on it. The next example lists the files on the MS-DOS disk in your floppy drive and then changes to the **docs** directory on that drive:

```
$ mdir a:
$ mcd a:/docs
```

Access to MS-DOS or Windows 95, 98, or ME partitions by mtools is configured by the **/etc/mtools.conf** file. This file lists several different default MS-DOS or Windows partitions and disk drives. Each drive or partition is identified with a particular device name.

Archiving and Compressing Files

Archives are used to back up files or to combine them into a package, which can then be transferred as one file over the Internet or posted on an FTP site for easy downloading. The standard archive utility used on Linux and Unix systems is tar, for which several GUI front ends exist. You have several compression programs to choose from, including GNU zip (gzip), Zip, bzip, and compress.

Archiving and Compressing Files with File Roller

Red Hat and Fedora provide the File Roller tool (accessible from the Accessories menu, labeled Archive Manager) that operates as a GUI front end to archive and compress files, letting you perform Zip, gzip, tar, and bzip2 operation using a GUI interface (see Figure 10-4). You can examine the contents of archives, extract the files you want, and create new compressed archives. When you create an archive, you determine its compression method by specifying its filename extension, such as **.gz** for gzip or **.bz2** for bzip2. You can select the different extensions from the File Type menu or enter the extension yourself. To both archive and

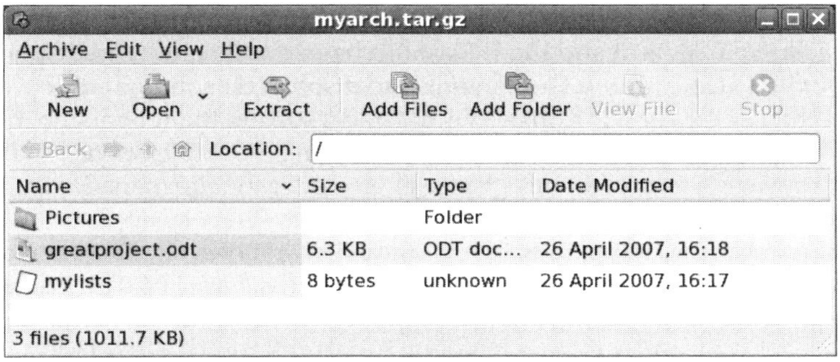

FIGURE 10-4 File Roller archiving and compression tool

compress files, you can choose a combined extension like **.tar.bz2**, which both archives with tar and compresses with bzip2. Click Add to add files to your archive. To extract files from an archive, open the archive to display the list of archive files. You can then click Extract to extract particular files or the entire archive.

TIP *For the popular rar archives, you can use the unrar tool to read and extract rar archives, but not to create them. unrar is available from rpm.livna.org and can be downloaded and installed with yum. Graphical front ends like Xarchiver and Linrar are available from freshmeat.net. To create rar archives, you have to purchase the archiver from Rarlab at www.rarlab.com.*

File Roller can also be use to examine the contents of an archive file easily. From the file manager, right-click the archive and select Open With "Archive Manager." The list of files and directories in that archive will be displayed. For subdirectories, double-click their entries. This method also works for RPM software files, letting you browse all the files that make up a software package.

Archive Files and Devices: tar

The tar utility creates archives for files and directories. With tar, you can archive specific files, update them in the archive, and add new files as you want to that archive. You can even archive entire directories with all their files and subdirectories, all of which can be restored from the archive. The tar utility was originally designed to create archives on tapes. (the term "tar" stands for tape archive), but you can create archives on any device, such as a floppy disk, or you can create an archive file to hold the archive. The tar utility is ideal for making backups of your files or combining several files into a single file for transmission across a network (File Roller is a GUI interface for tar).

NOTE *As an alternative to tar, you can use pax, which is designed to work with different kinds of Unix archive formats such as cpio, bcpio, and tar. You can extract, list, and create archives. The pax utility is helpful if you are handling archives created on Unix systems that are using different archive formats.*

Displaying Archive Contents

Both file managers in GNOME and the K Desktop have the capability to display the contents of a tar archive file automatically. The contents are displayed as though they were files in a directory. You can list the files as icons or with details, sorting them by name, type, or other fields. You can even display the contents of files. Clicking a text file opens it with a text editor, and an image is displayed with an image viewer. If the file manager cannot determine what program to use to display the file, it prompts you to select an application. Both file managers can perform the same kinds of operations on archives residing on remote file systems, such as tar archives on FTP sites. You can obtain a listing of their contents and even read their readme files. The Nautilus file manager (GNOME) can also extract an archive. Right-click the Archive icon and select Extract.

Creating Archives

On Linux, tar is often used to create archives on devices or in files. You can direct tar to archive files to a specific device or a file by using the **f** option with the name of the device or file. The syntax for the **tar** command using the **f** option is shown in the next example. The device or filename is often referred to as the archive name. When creating a file for a tar archive, the filename is usually given the extension **.tar**. This is a convention only and is not required. You can list as many filenames as you want. If a directory name is specified, all its subdirectories are included in the archive.

```
$ tar optionsf archive-name.tar directory-and-file-names
```

To create an archive, use the **c** option. Combined with the **f** option, **c** creates an archive on a file or device. You enter this option before the **f** option. You can also add the **v** option before the **f** option to allow you to see the results of the **tar** command (**v** stands for verbose). Notice no dash precedes a tar option. Table 10-6 lists the different options you can use with tar. In the next example, the directory **mydir** and all its subdirectories are saved in the file **myarch.tar**. In this example, the **mydir** directory holds two files, **mymeeting** and **party**, as well as a directory called **reports** that has three files: **weather**, **monday**, and **friday**.

```
$ tar cvf myarch.tar mydir
mydir/
mydir/reports/
mydir/reports/weather
mydir/reports/monday
mydir/reports/friday
mydir/mymeeting
mydir/party
```

Extracting Archives

The user can later extract the directories from the tape using the **x** option. The **xf** option extracts files from an archive file or device. The tar extraction operation generates all subdirectories. In the next example, the **xvf** option directs **tar** to extract all the files and subdirectories from the tar file **myarch.tar** and display the names of the extracted files on the screen:

```
$ tar xvf myarch.tar
mydir/
mydir/reports/
mydir/reports/weather
mydir/reports/monday
```

```
mydir/reports/friday
mydir/mymeeting
mydir/party
```

You use the **r** option to add files to an already-created archive. The **r** option appends the files to the archive. In the next example, the user appends the files in the **letters** directory to the **myarch.tar** archive. Here, the directory **mydocs** and its files are added to the **myarch.tar** archive:

```
$ tar rvf myarch.tar mydocs
mydocs/
mydocs/doc1
```

Commands	Execution
tar *options files*	Backs up files to default tape, device, or archive file.
tar *options*f *archive_ name filelist*	Backs up files to a specific file or device specified as *archive_ name*. *filelist*; can be filenames or directories.
Options	**Execution**
c	Creates a new archive.
t	Lists the names of files in an archive.
r	Appends files to an archive.
U	Updates an archive with new and changed files; adds only those files modified since they were archived or files not already present in the archive.
--delete	Removes a file from the archive.
w	Waits for a confirmation from the user before archiving each file; enables you to update an archive selectively.
x	Extracts files from an archive.
m	When extracting a file from an archive, no new timestamp is assigned.
M	Creates a multiple-volume archive that may be stored on several floppy disks.
f *archive-name*	Saves the tape archive to the file archive name, instead of to the default tape device. When given an archive name, the **f** option saves the tar archive in a file of that name.
f *device-name*	Saves a tar archive to a device such as a floppy disk or tape. **/dev/fd0** is the device name for your floppy disk; the default device is held in **/etc/default/tar-file**.
v	Displays each filename as it is archived.
z	Compresses or decompresses archived files using gzip.
j	Compresses or decompresses archived files using bzip2.

TABLE 10-6 File Archives: `tar`

Updating Archives

If you change any of the files in directories you previously archived, you can use the **u** option to instruct tar to update the archive with any modified files. The **tar** command compares the time of the last update for each archived file with those in the user's directory and copies into the archive any files that have been changed since they were last archived. Any newly created files in these directories are also added to the archive. In the next example, the user updates the **myarch.tar** file with any recently modified or newly created files in the **mydir** directory. In this case, the **gifts** file was added to the **mydir** directory.

```
tar uvf myarch.tar mydir
mydir/
mydir/gifts
```

If you need to see what files are stored in an archive, you can use the **tar** command with the **t** option. The next example lists all the files stored in the **myarch.tar** archive:

```
tar tvf myarch.tar
drwxr-xr-x root/root 0 2006-10-24 21:38:18 mydir/
drwxr-xr-x root/root 0 2006-10-24 21:38:51 mydir/reports/
-rw-r--r-- root/root 22 2006-10-24 21:38:40 mydir/reports/weather
-rw-r--r-- root/root 22 2006-10-24 21:38:45 mydir/reports/monday
-rw-r--r-- root/root 22 2006-10-24 21:38:51 mydir/reports/friday
-rw-r--r-- root/root 22 2006-10-24 21:38:18 mydir/mymeeting
-rw-r--r-- root/root 22 2006-10-24 21:36:42 mydir/party
drwxr-xr-x root/root 0 2006-10-24 21:48:45 mydocs/
-rw-r--r-- root/root 22 2006-10-24 21:48:45 mydocs/doc1
drwxr-xr-x root/root 0 2006-10-24 21:54:03 mydir/
-rw-r--r-- root/root 22 2006-10-24 21:54:03 mydir/gifts
```

Archiving to Floppies

To back up the files to a specific device, specify the device as the archive. For a floppy disk, you can specify the floppy drive. Be sure to use a blank floppy disk. Any data previously placed on it will be erased by this operation. In the next example, the user creates an archive on the floppy disk in the **/dev/fd0** device and copies into it all the files in the **mydir** directory:

```
$ tar cf /dev/fd0 mydir
```

To extract the backed-up files on the disk in the device, use the **xf** option:

```
$ tar xf /dev/fd0
```

Compressing Archives

The **tar** operation does not perform compression on archived files. If you want to compress the archived files, you can instruct tar to invoke the gzip utility to compress them. With the lowercase **z** option, tar first uses gzip to compress files before archiving them. The same **z** option invokes gzip to decompress them when extracting files.

```
$ tar czf myarch.tar.gz mydir
```

To use bzip instead of gzip to compress files before archiving them, you use the **j** option. The same **j** option invokes bzip to decompress them when extracting files.

```
$ tar cjf myarch.tar.bz2 mydir
```

Remember, a difference exists between compressing individual files in an archive and compressing the entire archive as a whole. Often, an archive is created for transferring several files at once as one tar file. To shorten transmission time, the archive should be as small as possible. You can use the compression utility gzip on the archive tar file to compress it, reducing its size, and then send the compressed version. The person receiving it can decompress it, restoring the tar file. Using gzip on a tar file often results in a file with the extension **.tar.gz**. The extension **.gz** is added to a compressed gzip file. The next example creates a compressed version of **myarch.tar** using the same name with the extension **.gz**:

```
$ gzip myarch.tar
$ ls
$ myarch.tar.gz
```

Instead of retyping the tar command for different files, you could place the command in a script and pass the files to it. Be sure to make the script executable. In the following example, a simple **myarchprog** script is created that will archive filenames listed as its arguments.

myarchprog
```
tar   cvf    myarch.tar    $*
```

A run of the **myarchprog** script with multiple arguments is shown here:

```
$ myarchprog mydata preface
mydata
preface
```

Archiving to Tape

If you have a default device specified, such as a tape, and you want to create an archive on it, you can simply use **tar** without the **f** option and a device or filename. This can be helpful for making backups of your files. The name of the default device is held in a file called **/etc/default/tar**. The syntax for the **tar** command using the default tape device is shown in the following example. If a directory name is specified, all its subdirectories are included in the archive.

```
$ tar option directory-and-file-names
```

In the next example, the directory **mydir** and all its subdirectories are saved on a tape in the default tape device:

```
$ tar c mydir
```

In this example, the **mydir** directory and all its files and subdirectories are extracted from the default tape device and placed in the user's working directory:

```
$ tar x mydir
```

> **NOTE** *There are other archive programs you can use such as cpio, pax, and shar. However, tar is the one most commonly used for archiving application software.*

File Compression: gzip, bzip2, and zip

Several reasons exist for reducing the size of a file. The two most common are to save space or, if you are transferring the file across a network, to save transmission time. You can effectively reduce a file size by creating a compressed copy of it. Anytime you need the file again, you decompress it. Compression is used in combination with archiving to enable you to compress whole directories and their files at once. Decompression generates a copy of the archive file, which can then be extracted, generating a copy of those files and directories. File Roller provides a GUI interface for these tasks.

Compression with gzip

Several compression utilities are available for use on Linux and Unix systems. Most software for Linux systems uses the GNU gzip and gunzip utilities. The gzip utility compresses files, and gunzip decompresses them. To compress a file, enter the command **gzip** and the filename. This replaces the file with a compressed version of it, with the extension **.gz**.

```
$ gzip mydata
$ ls
mydata.gz
```

To decompress a gzip file, use either **gzip** with the **-d** option or the command **gunzip**. These commands decompress a compressed file with the **.gz** extension and replace it with a decompressed version with the same root name, but without the **.gz** extension. When you use gunzip, you needn't even type in the **.gz** extension; **gunzip** and **gzip -d** assume it. Table 10-7 lists the different gzip options.

```
$ gunzip mydata.gz
$ ls
mydata
```

> **TIP** *On your desktop, you can extract the contents of an archive by locating it with the file manager and double-clicking it. You can also right-click and choose "Open with Archive Manager." This will start the File Roller application, which will open the archive, listing its contents. You can then choose to extract the archive. File Roller will use the appropriate tools to decompress the archive (bzip2, zip, or gzip) if compressed, and then extract the archive (tar) (see Chapter 4).*

You can also compress archived tar files. This results in files with the extensions **.tar.gz**. Compressed archived files are often used for transmitting extremely large files across networks.

```
$ gzip myarch.tar
$ ls
myarch.tar.gz
```

You can compress tar file members individually using the **tar z** option that invokes gzip. With the **z** option, tar invokes gzip to compress a file before placing it in an archive.

Option	Execution
`-c`	Sends compressed version of file to standard output; each file listed is separately compressed: `gzip -c mydata preface > myfiles.gz`

`-d`	Decompresses a compressed file; or you can use gunzip:
	`gzip -d myfiles.gz`
	`gunzip myfiles.gz`

`-h`	Displays help listing.
`-l` *file-list*	Displays compressed and uncompressed size of each file listed: `gzip -l myfiles.gz.`
`-r` *directory-name*	Recursively searches for specified directories and compresses all the files in them; the search begins from the current working directory. When used with `gunzip`, compressed files of a specified directory are uncompressed.
`-v` *file-list*	For each compressed or decompressed file, displays its name and the percentage of its reduction in size.
-num	Determines the speed and size of the compression; the range is from –1 to –9. A lower number gives greater speed but less compression, resulting in a larger file that compresses and decompresses quickly. Thus –1 gives the quickest compression, but with the largest size; –9 results in a very small file that takes longer to compress and decompress. The default is –6.

TABLE 10-7   The `gzip` Options

Archives with members compressed with the **z** option, however, cannot be updated, nor is it possible to add to them. All members must be compressed, and all must be added at the same time.

The compress and uncompress Commands

You can also use the **compress** and **uncompress** commands to create compressed files. They generate a file that has a **.Z** extension and use a different compression format than gzip. The **compress** and **uncompress** commands are not that widely used, but you may run across **.Z** files occasionally. You can use the **uncompress** command to decompress a .Z file. The gzip utility is the standard GNU compression utility and should be used instead of **compress**.

Compressing with bzip2

Another popular compression utility is **bzip2**. It compresses files using the Burrows-Wheeler block-sorting text compression algorithm and Huffman coding. The command line options are similar to gzip by design, but they are not exactly the same. (See the bzip2 Man page for a complete listing.) You compress files using the **bzip2** command and decompress with **bunzip2**. The **bzip2** command creates files with the extension **.bz2**. You can use **bzcat** to output compressed data to the standard output. The **bzip2** command compresses files in blocks and enables you to specify their size (larger blocks give you greater compression). As when using gzip, you can use bzip2 to compress tar archive files. The following example compresses the **mydata** file into a bzip compressed file with the extension **.bz2**:

```
$ bzip2 mydata
$ ls
mydata.bz2
```

To decompress, use the **bunzip2** command on a bzip file.

```
$ bunzip2 mydata.bz2
```

Using Zip

Zip is a compression and archive utility modeled on PKZIP, which was used originally on DOS systems. Zip is a cross-platform utility used on Windows, Mac, MS-DOS, OS/2, Unix, and Linux systems. Zip commands can work with archives created by PKZIP and can use Zip archives. You compress a file using the **zip** command. This creates a Zip file with the **.zip** extension. If no files are listed, **zip** outputs the compressed data to the standard output. You can also use the—argument to have **zip** read from the standard input. To compress a directory, you include the **-r** option. The first example archives and compresses a file:

```
$ zip mydata
$ ls
mydata.zip
```

The next example archives and compresses the **reports** directory:

```
$ zip -r reports
```

A full set of archive operations is supported. With the **-f** option, you can update a particular file in the Zip archive with a newer version. The **-u** option replaces or adds files, and the **-d** option deletes files from the Zip archive. Options also exist for encrypting files, making DOS-to-Unix end-of-line translations, and including hidden files.

To decompress and extract the Zip file, you use the **unzip** command.

```
$ unzip mydata.zip
```

Applications

PART III

CHAPTER 11
Office and Database
Applications

CHAPTER 12
Graphics Tools and
Multimedia

CHAPTER 13
Mail and News Clients

CHAPTER 14
Web, FTP, and Java Clients

CHAPTER 15
Network Tools

Office and Database Applications

A variety of office suites are now available for Linux (see Table 11-1). These include professional-level word processors, presentation managers, drawing tools, and spreadsheets. The freely available versions are described in this chapter. Sun has initiated development of an Open Source office suite using StarOffice code. The applications, known as OpenOffice, provide Office applications integrated with GNOME. OpenOffice is currently the primary office application supported by Fedora and Red Hat. KOffice is an entirely free office suite designed for use with KDE. The GNOME Office suite integrates GNOME applications into a productivity suite that is freely available. CodeWeavers CrossOver Office provides reliable support for running MS Office Windows applications directly on Linux, integrating with them with KDE and GNOME. You can also purchase commercial office suites such as StarOffice from Sun. For desktop publishing, especially PDF generation, you can use Scribus, a cross-platform tool available from the Fedora repository.

A variety of database management systems are also available for Linux. These include high-powered, commercial-level database management systems, such as Oracle, IBM's DB2, and Sybase. Most of the database management systems available for Linux are designed to support large relational databases. Fedora and Red Hat include both MySQL and PostgreSQL databases in its distribution. For small personal databases, you can use the desktop database management systems being developed for KDE and GNOME. In addition, some software is available for databases accessed with the Xbase database programming language. These are smaller databases using formats originally developed for dBase on the PC. Various database management systems available to run under Linux are listed in Table 11-6 later in this chapter.

Fedora and Red Hat Linux also provides several text editors that range from simple text editors for simple notes to editors with more complex features such as spell-checkers, buffers, or pattern matching. All generate character text files and can be used to edit any Linux text files. Text editors are often used in system administration tasks to change or add entries in Linux configuration files found in the /etc directory or a user's initialization or application dot files located in a user's home directory. You can use any text editor to work on source code files for any of the programming languages or shell program scripts.

Web Site	Description
www.openoffice.org	OpenOffice open source office suite based on StarOffice
www.koffice.org	KOffice Suite, for KDE
www.gnome.org/gnome-office	GNOME Office, for GNOME
www.sun.com/staroffice	StarOffice Suite
www.codeweavers.com	CrossOver Office (MS Office support)
www.scribus.net	Scribus desktop publishing tool

TABLE 11-1 Linux Office Suites

Running Microsoft Office on Linux: CrossOver

One of the primary concerns for new Linux users is what kind of access they will have to their Microsoft Office files, particularly Word files. The Linux operating system and many applications for it are designed to provide seamless access to MS Office files. The major Linux Office suites, including KOffice, OpenOffice, and StarOffice, all read and manage any Microsoft Office files. In addition, these office suites are fast approaching the same level of features and support for office tasks as found in Microsoft Office.

If you want to use any Windows application on Linux, three important alternatives are the Wine virtual windows API support, VMware virtual platform technology, and the CrossOver Office by CodeWeavers. VMware and CrossOver are commercial packages. Wine allows you to run many Windows applications directly, using a supporting virtual windows API. See the Wine Web site for a list of supported applications, **www.winehq.com**.

CrossOver Office also lets you install and run most Microsoft Office applications. CrossOver Office was developed by CodeWeavers, which also supports Windows Web browser plug-ins as well as several popular Windows applications like Adobe Photoshop. CrossOver features both standard and professional versions, providing reliable application support. You can find out more about CrossOver Office at **www.codeweavers.com**.

CrossOver can be installed either for private multiuser mode or managed multiuser mode. In private multiuser mode, each user installs his or her own Windows software, such as full versions of Office. In managed multiuser mode, the Windows software is installed once and all users share it. When you install new software, you first open the CrossOver startup tool, and then on the Add/Remove panel you will see a list of supported software. This will include Office applications as well as some Adobe applications, including earlier versions of Photoshop. An Install Software panel will then let you select whether to install from a CD-ROM or an .exe file. For Office on a CD-ROM, select CD-ROM, place the Windows CD-ROM in your CD-ROM drive, and then click Next. The Windows Office installer will start up in a Linux window and will proceed as if you were on a Windows system. When the install requires a restart of the system, CrossOver will simulate it for you. Once the software is installed, you will see a Windows Applications menu on the main menu, from which you can start your installed Windows software. The applications will run within a Linux window, just as if they were running in Windows.

You can also try CrossOver for unsupported applications. They may or may not run.

With VMware, you can run Windows under Linux, allowing you to run Windows applications, including Microsoft Office, on your Linux system. For more information, check the VMware Web site at **www.vmware.com**.

NOTE *Though Linux allows users to directly mount and access any of the old DOS or FAT32 partitions used for Windows 95, 98, and ME, it can mount NTFS partitions (Windows XP, 2000, and NT) reliably as read only, with possible write support. There are two drivers for mounting NTFS, **ntfs-3g** and the original NTFS project support. The **ntfs-3g** driver supports writing NTFS partitions and is included on the Fedora repository. The orginal NTFS project driver is read only and can be downloaded from the Livna repository. (see Chapter 4).*

OpenOffice

OpenOffice (OO) is a fully integrated suite of office applications developed as an open source project and freely distributed to all. It is included as the primary office suite for Fedora and Red Hat Linux, accessible from the Office menu. It includes word processing, spreadsheet, presentation, and drawing applications (see Table 11-2). Versions of OpenOffice exist for Linux, Windows, and Mac OS. You can obtain information such as online manuals and FAQs as well as current versions from the OpenOffice.org Web site at **www.openoffice.org**.

NOTE *Development for OpenOffice is being carried out as an open source project called openoffice .org. The core code is based on the original StarOffice. The code developed in the openoffice.org project will then be incorporated into future releases of StarOffice.*

OpenOffice is an integrated suite of applications. You can open the writer, spreadsheet, or presentation application directly. Also, in most OpenOffice applications, you can select New from the File menu and select a different application if you wish. The Writer word processor supports standard word processing features, such as cut and paste, spell-checker, and text formatting, as well as paragraph styles (see Figure 11-1). You can embed objects within documents, such as using Draw to create figures that you can then drag and drop to the Writer document. You can find out more about each component at their respective product pages listed at, **www.openoffice.org/product**.

Application	Description
Calc	OpenOffice spreadsheet
Draw	OpenOffice drawing application
Writer	OpenOffice word processor
Math	OpenOffice mathematical formula composer
Impress	OpenOffice presentation manager
Base	Database front end for accessing and managing a variety of different databases

TABLE 11-2   OpenOffice.org Applications

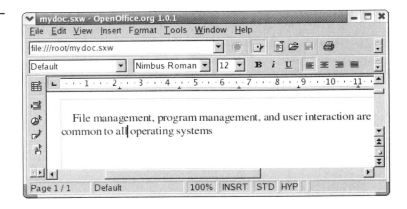

FIGURE 11-1
OpenOffice.org's
Writer word
processor.

Calc is a professional-level spreadsheet. With Math, you can create formulas that you can then embed in a text document. With the presentation manager (Impress), you can create images for presentations, such as circles, rectangles, and connecting elements like arrows, as well as vector-based illustrations. Impress supports advanced features such as morphing objects, grouping objects, and defining gradients. Draw is a sophisticated drawing tool that includes 3-D modeling tools. You can create simple or complex images, including animation text aligned on curves. OpenOffice also includes a printer setup tool with which you can select printers, fonts, paper sizes, and page formats.

NOTE *StarOffice is a fully integrated and Microsoft Office–compatible suite of office applications developed and supported by Sun Microsystems, **www.sun.com/staroffice**. Sun provides StarOffice as a commercial product, though educational use is free.*

OpenOffice also provides access to many database files. File types supported include ODBC 3.0 (Open Database Connectivity), JDBC (Java), ADO, MySQL, dBase, CSV, PostgresSQL, and MDB (Microsoft Access) database files. Check the OpenOffice.orgBase page and Project page (**dba.openoffice.org**) for detailed information on drivers and supported databases.

OpenOffice features an underlying component model that can be programmed to develop customized applications. Check the OpenOffice API project for more details (**api.openoffice .org**). The OpenOffice Software Development Kit (SDK) provides support for using OpenOffice components in applications written in C++ or Java. The Unified Network Objects (UNO) model is the component model for OpenOffice, providing interaction between programming languages, other object models, and network connections.

KOffice

KOffice is an integrated office suite for the KDE (K Desktop Environment) consisting of several office applications, including a word processor, a spreadsheet, and graphic applications. KOffice is part of the Fedora. You can download it using Pirut/Yum (Add/Remove Sofware). All applications are written for the KOM component model, which allows components from any one application to be used in another. This means you can embed a spreadsheet from

KSpread or diagrams from Karbon14 in a KWord document. You can obtain more information about KOffice from the KOffice Web site at **www.koffice.org**.

Tip *KOffice applications have import and export filters that allow them to import or export files from popular applications like Abiword, OpenOffice.org applications, MS Word, and even Palm documents. The reliability of these filters varies, and you should check the KOffice Filters Web page for a listing of the different filters and their stability.*

KOffice Applications

Currently, KOffice includes KSpread, KPresenter, KWord, Karbon14, KFormula, KChart, Kugar, Krita, and Kivio (see Table 11-3). The contact application, Kontact, has been spun off as a separate project. Kontact is an integrated contact application including Kmail, Korganizer, Kaddressbook, and Knotes. KSpread is a spreadsheet, KPresenter is a presentation application, Karbon14 is a vector graphics program, KWord is a Publisher-like word processor, KFormula is a formula editor, and KChart generates charts and diagrams. Kugar is a report generator, Krita is a bitmap image editor, and Kivio creates flow charts. Kexi provides database integration with KOffice applications, currently supporting PostgreSQL and MySQL.

KSpread is the spreadsheet application, which incorporates the basic operations found in most spreadsheets, with formulas similar to those used in Excel. You can also embed charts, pictures, or formulas using KChart, Krita, Karbon14, or KFormula.

With KChart, you can create different kinds of charts, such as bar graphs, pie charts, and line graphs, as well as create diagrams. To generate a chart, you can use data in KSpread to enter your data. With KPresenter, you can create presentations consisting of text and

Application	Description
KSpread	Spreadsheet
KPresenter	Presentation program
Kontour	Vector drawing program
Karbon14	Vector graphics program
KWord	Word processor (desktop publisher)
KFormula	Mathematical formula editor
KChart	Tool for drawing charts and diagrams
Kugar	Report generator
Krita	Paint and image manipulation program
Kivio	Flow chart generator and editor (similar to Vivio)
Kexi	Database integration
KPlato	Project management and planning
Kontact (separate project)	Contact application including mail, address book, and organizer

Table 11-3 KOffice Applications

graphics modeled using different fonts, orientations, and attributes such as colors. You can add such elements as speech bubbles, arrows, and clip art, as well as embed any KOffice component. Karbon14 is a vector-based graphics program, much like Adobe Illustrator and OpenOffice Draw. It supports the standard graphic operations such as rotating, scaling, and aligning objects.

KWord can best be described as a desktop publisher, with many of the features found in publishing applications like Microsoft Publisher and FrameMaker. Although it is also a fully functional word processor, KWord is not page-based like Word or WordPerfect. Instead, text is set up in frames that are placed on the page like objects. Frames, like objects in a drawing program, can be moved, resized, and even reoriented. You can organize frames into a frame set, having text flow from one to the other.

KParts

Embedded components support real-time updates. For example, if you use KChart to generate a chart in a KWord document using data in a KSpread spreadsheet and then change the selected data in the spreadsheet, KChart automatically updates the chart in the KWord document. In effect, you are creating a compound document—one made up of several applications. This capability is implemented by the KDE component model known as KParts. KParts provides communication between distributed objects. In this respect, you can think of an application working also as a server, providing other applications with the services it specializes in. A word processor, specializing in services such as paragraph formatting or spell-checking, could provide these services to all KOffice applications. In that way, other applications do not need to have their own text formatting functions written into them.

KParts is implemented with DCOP, the Desktop Communications Protocol. This is a very simple, small, and fast IPC/RPC mechanism for interprocess communication (IPC) that is based on the X Window System's ICE (Inter-Client Exchange) protocol. KDE applications now use DCOP libraries to manage their communications with each other. DCOP makes development of KOffice applications much easier and more stable.

GNOME Office

The GNOME Office project supports three office applications: AbiWord, Gnumeric, and GNOME-DB. Former members of GNOME Office still provide certain Office tasks, like Novell's Evolution e-mail and contact client. Many former members are still GNOME projects, with information listed for them at **www.gnome.org/projects**. The GNOME Office applications, as well as other GNOME-based Office applications, are part of Fedora and can be downloaded with Add/Remove Software (Yum). You can find out more from the GNOME Office site at **www.gnome.org/gnome-office**. A current listing for common GNOME Office applications, including those not part of the GNOME Office suite, is shown in Table 11-4. All implement the CORBA model for embedding components, ensuring drag-and-drop capability throughout the GNOME interface.

AbiWord is a word processor, Gnumeric is a spreadsheet, GNOME-DB provides database connectivity. Gnumeric is a GNOME spreadsheet, a professional-level program meant to replace commercial spreadsheets. Like GNOME, Gnumeric is freely available under the GNU Public License. Gnumeric is included with the GNOME release, and you will find it

Application	
GNOME **Office**	**Description**
AbiWord	Cross-platform word processor
Gnumeric	Spreadsheet
GNOME-DB	Database connectivity
Other GNOME Office Apps	
GNOME **Office**	**Description**
Evolution	Integrated e-mail, calendar, and personal organizer (Novell)
Dia	Diagram and flow chart editor (GNOME project)
GnuCash	Personal finance manager (GNOME project)
Balsa	E-mail client (GNOME project)
GnuCash	Personal finance manager (GNOME project)
Planner	Project manager (GNOME project)
OpenOffice	OpenOffice office suite

TABLE 11-4   GNOME Office and Other Office Applications for GNOME

installed with GNOME on any distribution that supports GNOME. You can download current versions from **www.gnome.org/projects/gnumeric**. Gnumeric supports standard GUI spreadsheet features, including autofilling and cell formatting, and it provides an extensive number of formats. It supports drag-and-drop operations, enabling you to select and then move or copy cells to another location. Gnumeric also supports plug-ins, making it possible to extend and customize its capabilities easily.

AbiWord is an open source word processor that aims to be a complete cross-platform solution, running on Mac, Unix, and Windows, as well as Linux. It is part of a set of desktop productivity applications being developed by the AbiSource project (**www.abisource.com**).

The GNOME-DB project provides a GNOME Data Access (GDA) library supporting several kinds of databases, such as PostgreSQL, MySQL, Microsoft Access, and unixODBC. It provides an API to which databases can plug in. These back-end connections are based on CORBA. Through this API, GNOME applications can then access a database. You can find out more about GNOME-DB at **www.gnome-db.org**.

Dia is a drawing program designed to create diagrams (GNOME project). You can select different kinds of diagrams to create, such as database, circuit object, flow chart, and network diagrams. You can easily create elements along with lines and arcs with different types of endpoints such as arrows or diamonds. Data can be saved in XML format, making it easily transportable to other applications.

GnuCash (**www.gnucash.org**) is a personal finance application for managing accounts, stocks, and expenses (GNOME project). It includes support for home banking with the OpenHBCI interface. OpenHBCI is the open source home banking computer interface (**openhbci.sourceforge.net**).

Viewer	Description
Evince	Document viewer for PostScript and PDF files
KPDF	KDE tool for displaying PDF files
KGhostView	KDE interface for displaying PostScript and PDF files
xpdf	X Window System tool for displaying PDF files only
KDVI	KDE tool for displaying TeX DVI files (plug-in to KViewShell)
Acrobat Reader for Linux	Adobe PDF and PostScript display application
Scribus	Desktop publisher for generating PDF documents
gv	X Window System viewer for ghostscript files
pdfedit	Edit PDF documents

TABLE 11-5 PostScript, PDF, and DVI viewers

Document Viewers (PostScript, PDF, and DVI)

Though located under Graphic headings in the main menu, PostScript, PDF, and DVI viewers are more commonly used with Office applications (see Table 11-5). Evince and Ghostview can display both PostScript (.ps) and PDF (.pdf) files. Its X Window System front end is gv. KPDF and Xpdf are PDF viewers. KPDF includes many of the standard Adobe reader features such as zoom, two-page display, and full-screen mode. Alternatively, you can download Acrobat reader for Linux from Adobe to display PDF files. All these viewers also have the ability to print documents. To generate PDF documents you can use Scribus desktop publisher (**www.scribus.net**), and to edit PDF documents you can use pdfedit.

Linux also features a professional-level typesetting tool, called TeX, commonly used to compose complex mathematical formulas. TeX generates a DVI document that can then be displayed by DVI viewers, of which there are several for Linux. DVI files generated by the TeX document application can be viewed by KDVI, which is a plug-in to the KViewShell tool. KViewShell can display and print any kind of document for which it has a plug-in. You can access KDVI as the DVI Viewer in the Graphics menu.

PDA Access

For many PDAs you can use the pilot tools to access your handheld, transferring information between it and your system. The **pilot-link** package holds the tools you use to access your PDA. Check **www.pilot-link.org** for detailed documentation and useful links. The tool name usually begin with "pilot"; for instance, **pilot-addresses** reads addresses from an address book. Other tools whose names begin with "read" allow you to convert Palm data for access by other applications; **read-expenses**, for instance, outputs expense data as standard text. One of the more useful tools is **pilot-xfer**, used to back up your Palm.

Instead of using command line commands directly, you can use the J-Pilot, KPilot, and GnomePilot applications to access your Palm PDA. To use your PDA on GNOME, you can use the gnome-pilot applet from your GNOME panel to configure your connection. In the gnome-pilot applet's Preferences windows (right-click Applet), the Conduits panel lets you enable several hotsync operations to perform automatically, including e-mail, memos, and installing files. Click the Help button for a detailed manual.

J-Pilot provides a GUI interface that lets you perform basic tasks such as synchronizing address book and writing memos. J-Pilot is accessible from the Office menu and is part of Fedora. KPilot is included with the **kpim** package installed as part of the KDE Desktop. On Fedora you need to open a terminal window and enter the **kpilot** command to run it. It will first let you automatically sync with your PDA. You then have the option to use either Evolution or KContact with your PDA, or just perform backups. You can then perform operations like hotsyncs, viewing addresses, and installing files. For text and Palm format conversions, you can use KPalmDoc. This tool will convert text files to Palm files, and Palm files to text files.

TIP *The device name used for your PDA is* **/dev/pilot***, which is managed by* **udev***. Should you need to manually specify a port for your handheld, you would have to modify udev rules, not change the* **/dev/pilot** *file directly (see Chapter 32).*

Database Management Systems

Database software can be generally organized into three categories: SQL, Xbase, and desktop databases. *SQL-based databases* are professional-level relational databases whose files are managed by a central database server program. Applications that use the database do not access the files directly. Instead, they send requests to the database server, which then performs the actual access. *SQL* is the query language used on these industrial-strength databases. Fedora and Red Hat Linux include both MySQL and PostgreSQL databases. Both are open source projects freely available for your use. Table 11-6 lists DBMSs currently available for Linux.

The *Xbase language* is an enhanced version of the dBase programming language used to access database files whose formats were originally developed for dBase on the PC. With

System	Site
PostgreSQL	The PostgreSQL database: **www.postgresql.org**
MySQL	MySQL database: **www.mysql.com**
Oracle	Oracle database: **www.oracle.com**
Sybase	Sybase database: **www.sybase.com**
DB2	IBM database: **www.software.ibm.com/data/db2/linux**
Informix	Informix database: **www.informix.com/linux**
MaxDB	SAP database now supported by MySQL: **www.mysql.com**
GNU SQL	The GNU SQL database: **www.ispras.ru/~kml/gss**
Flagship	Interface for Xbase database files: **www.fship.com/free.html**
XBase	Xbase tools and libraries: **linux.techass.com/projects/xdb**

TABLE 11-6   Database Management Systems for Linux

Xbase, database management systems can directly access the database files. Xbase is used mainly for smaller personal databases, with database files often located on a user's own system.

SQL Databases (RDMS)

SQL databases are relational database management systems (RDMSs) designed for extensive database management tasks. Many of the major SQL databases now have Linux versions, including Oracle, Informix, Sybase, and IBM (but not, of course, Microsoft). These are commercial and professional database management systems of the highest order. Linux has proved itself capable of supporting complex and demanding database management tasks. In addition, many free SQL databases are available for Linux that offer much the same functionality. Most commercial databases also provide free personal versions, as do Oracle, Adabas D, and MySQL.

PostgreSQL

PostgreSQL is based on the POSTGRES database management system, though it uses SQL as its query language. POSTGRES is a next-generation research prototype developed at the University of California, Berkeley. Linux versions of PostgreSQL are included in most distributions, including the Red Hat, Fedora, Debian, and Mandrake distributions. You can find more information on it from the PostgreSQL Web site at **www.postgresql.org**. PostgreSQL is an open source project, developed under the GPL license. See Chapter 26 for a detailed discussion.

MySQL

MySQL, included with Fedora and Red Hat, is a true multiuser, multithreaded SQL database server, supported by MySQL AB. MySQL is an open source product available free under the GPL license. You can obtain current information on it from its Web site, **www.mysql.com**. The site includes detailed documentation, including manuals and FAQs. See Chapter 26 for a detailed discussion.

Oracle

Oracle offers a fully functional version of its Oracle9*i* database management system for Linux, as well as the Oracle Application Server. You can download trial versions from the Oracle Web site at **www.oracle.com**. Oracle is a professional DBMS for large databases specifically designed for Internet e-business tasks. The Oracle Application Server provides support for real-time and commercial applications on the Web. As Linux is a fully functional version of Unix, Oracle is particularly effective on it. Oracle was originally designed to operate on Unix, and Linux is a far better platform for it than other PC operating systems.

Oracle offers extensive documentation for its Linux version that you can download from its Documentation page, to which you can link from the Support pages on its Web site. The documentation available includes an installation guide, an administrator's reference, and release notes, as well as the generic documentation. You can find specific information on installing and configuring Oracle for Linux in the Oracle Database HOW-TO.

Informix

Informix (now controlled by IBM) offers an integrated platform of Internet-based applications called Informix Internet Foundation.2000 on Linux. These include the Informix Dynamic Server, their database server. Informix Dynamic Server features Dynamic Scalable Architecture, making it capable of effectively using any hardware setup. Informix provides only commercial products. No free versions exist, though the company currently provides special promotions for Linux products. You can find out more about Informix at **www-4.ibm.com/software/data/ informix**. Informix strongly supports Linux development of its Informix line. You can find out more about Informix for Linux at **www-306.ibm.com/software/data/informix/linux**.

Sybase

For Linux, Sybase offers the Sybase Adaptive Server Enterprise server (see **www.sybase.com**). You can currently download the Adaptive Server Enterprise server from the Web site. The Sybase Enterprise database features data integration that coordinates all information resources on a network. SQL Anywhere is a database system designed for smaller databases, though with the same level of complexity found in larger databases.

DB2

IBM provides a Linux version of its DB2 Universal Database software. You can download it free from the IBM DB2 Web page for Linux, **www.software.ibm.com/data/db2/linux**. DB2 Universal Database for Linux includes Internet functionality along with support for Java and Perl. With the Web Control Center, administrators can maintain databases from a Web browser. DB2 features scalability to expand the database easily, support for Binary Large Objects, and cost-based optimization for fast access. DB2 is still very much a mainframe database, though IBM is currently working on refining its Unix/Linux version.

MaxDB

MaxDB is a SAP-certified database, originally developed by SAP. It provides capabilities comparable to many of the professional-level databases. MaxDB is now developed by the MySQL AB project, **www.mysql.com**. Recently, the MySQL AB project also added MAX DB, formerly SAP DB.

GNU SQL

GNU SQL is the GNU relational database developed by a group at the Institute for System Programming of the Russian Academy of Sciences and supported by the GNU organization. It is a portable multiuser database management system with a client/server structure that supports SQL. The server process requests and performs basic administrative operations, such as unloading parts of the database used infrequently. The clients can reside on any computer of a local network. GNU SQL uses a dialect of SQL based on the SQL-89 standard and is designed for use on a Unix-like environment. You can download the database software from the GNU FTP site at **ftp.gnu.org**. For more information, contact the GNU SQL Web site at **www.ispras.ru/~kml/gss**.

Xbase Databases

Databases accessed with Xbase are smaller in scale, designed for small networks or for personal use. Many are originally PC database programs, such as dBase III, Clipper, FoxPro, and Quicksilver. Currently, only Flagship provides an interface for accessing Xbase database files.

Flagship is a compiler with which you can create interfaces for querying Xbase database files. The interfaces support menus and dialog boxes, and they have function calls that execute certain database queries. Flagship can compile dBase III+ code and up. It is compatible with dBase and Clipper and can access most Xbase file formats, such as **.dbf**, **.dbt**, **.fmt**, and **.frm**.

One of Flagship's key features is that its interfaces can be attached to a Web page, enabling users to update databases. Flagship is commercial software, though you can download a free personal version from its Web site at **www.fship.com/free.html**.

Editors

Traditionally, most Linux distributions, including Fedora and Red Hat, install the cursor-based editors Vim and Emacs. *Vim* is an enhanced version of the Vi text editor used on the Unix system. These editors use simple, cursor-based operations to give you a full-screen format. You can start these editors from the shell command line without any kind of X Window System support. In this mode, their cursor-based operations do not have the ease of use normally found in window-based editors. There are no menus, scroll bars, or mouse-click features. However, the K Desktop and GNOME do support powerful GUI text editors with all these features. These editors operate much more like those found on Macintosh and Windows systems. They have full mouse support, scroll bars, and menus. You may find them much easier to use than the Vi and Emacs editors. These editors operate from their respective desktops, requiring you first have either KDE or GNOME installed, though the editors can run on either desktop. Vi and Emacs have powerful editing features that have been refined over the years. Emacs, in particular, is extensible to a full-development environment for programming new applications. Newer versions of Emacs, such as GNU Emacs and XEmacs, provide X Window System support with mouse, menu, and window operations. They can run on any window manager or desktop. In addition, the gvim version of the Vim editor also provides basic window operations. You can access it on both GNOME and KDE desktops. Table 11-7 lists several GUI-based editors for Linux.

The K Desktop	Description
KEdit	Text editor
Kate	Text and program editor
KJots	Notebook editor
KWord	Desktop publisher, part of KOffice
GNOME	**Description**
Gedit	Text editor
AbiWord	Word processor
X Window System	**Description**
GNU Emacs	Emacs editor with X Window System support
XEmacs	X Window System version of Emacs editor
gvim	Vim version with X Window System support (vim-x11)
OpenWriter	OpenOffice word processor that can edit text files

TABLE **11-7**   Desktop Editors

NOTE *Fedora Linux includes a fully functional word processor, Writer (OpenOffice). AbiWord is now part of Fedora, along with Kword, which is part of KOffice. You can find out more at www.abiword.com.*

GNOME Editor: Gedit

The Gedit editor is a basic text editor for the GNOME desktop (see Chapter 4). It provides full mouse support, implementing standard GUI operations, such as cut and paste to move text, and click and drag to select text. It supports standard text editing operations such as Find and Replace. You can use Gedit to create and modify your text files, including configuration files. Gedit also provides more advanced features such as print preview and configurable levels of undo/redo operations, and it can read data from pipes. It features a plug-in menu that provides added functionality, and it includes plug-ins for spell-checking, encryption, e-mail, and text-based Web page display.

K Desktop Editors: Kate, KEdit, and KJots

All the K Desktop editors provide full mouse support, implementing standard GUI operations, such as cut and paste to move text, and click and drag to select text. The K Desktop editors are accessible from the Utilities | Editors menu on the K Desktop (you have to log in using the K-Desktop, check KDE entry in login screen's Options | Select Session menu), though you can start any of them up from GNOME using the terminal window and the command name. Kate is an advanced editor, with such features as spell-checking, font selection, and highlighting. Most commands can be selected using menus. A toolbar of icons for common operations is displayed across the top of the Kate window. A sidebar displays panels for a file selector and a file list. With the file selector, you can navigate through the file system selecting files to work on. Kate also supports multiple views of a document, letting you display segments in their own windows, vertically or horizontally. You can also open several documents at the same time, moving between them with the file list. Kate is designed to be a program editor for editing software programming/development-related source code files. Although Kate does not have all the features of Emacs or Vi, it can handle most major tasks. Kate can format the syntax for different programming languages, such as C, Perl, Java, and XML. In addition, Kate has the capability to access and edit files on an FTP or Web site.

    KEdit is an older simple text editor meant for editing simple text files such as configuration files. A toolbar of buttons at the top of the KEdit window enables you to execute common editing commands easily using just a mouse click. With KEdit, you can also mail files you are editing over a network. The entry for KEdit in the K menu is listed simply as Text Editor.

    The editor KJots is designed to enable you to jot down notes in a notebook. It organizes notes you write into notebooks, called simply *books*. You can select the one you want to view or add to from the Books menu. To start KJots, select its entry in the Utilities | Pim menu or enter the `kjots` command in a terminal window.

The Emacs Editor

Emacs can best be described as a working environment featuring an editor, a mailer, a newsreader, and a Lisp interpreter. The editor is tailored for program development, enabling you to format source code according to the programming language you use. Many versions of Emacs are currently available for use on Unix and Linux systems. The versions usually included with Linux distributions are either GNU Emacs or XEmacs. The current version for GNU Emacs is 20.*x*; it is X Window System–capable, enabling GUI features such as menus, scroll bars, and mouse-based editing operations. (See Chapter 13 for a discussion of the GNU Emacs mailer and its newsreader.) Check the update FTP sites for your distribution for new versions as they come out, and also check the GNU Web site at **www.gnu.org** and the Emacs Web site at **www.emacs.org**. You can find out more information about XEmacs at its Web site, **www.xemacs.org**.

Emacs derives much of its power and flexibility from its capability to manipulate buffers. Emacs can be described as a buffer-oriented editor. Whenever you edit a file in any editor, the file is copied into a work buffer, and editing operations are made on the work buffer. Emacs can manage many work buffers at once, enabling you to edit several files at the same time. You can edit buffers that hold deleted or copied text. You can even create buffers of your own, fill them with text, and later save them to a file. Emacs extends the concept of buffers to cover any task. When you compose mail, you open a mail buffer; when you read news, you open a news buffer. Switching from one task to another is simply a matter of switching to another buffer.

The Emacs editor operates much like a standard word processor. The keys on your keyboard represent input characters. Commands are implemented with special keys, such as control (CTRL) keys and alternate (ALT) keys. There is no special input mode, as in Vi or Ed. You type in your text, and if you need to execute an editing command, such as moving the cursor or saving text, you use a CTRL key. Such an organization makes the Emacs editor easy to use. However, Emacs is anything but simple—it is a sophisticated and flexible editor with several hundred commands. Emacs also has special features, such as multiple windows. You can display two windows for text at the same time. You can also open and work on more than one file at a time, displaying each on the screen in its own window. You invoke the Emacs editor with the command **emacs**. You can enter the name of the file you want to edit, and if the file does not exist, it is created. In the next example, the user prepares to edit the file **mydata** with Emacs:

```
$ emacs mydata
```

The GNU Emacs editor now supports an X Window System graphical user interface. To enable X support, start Emacs within an X Window System environment, such as a KDE, GNOME, or XFce desktop. The basic GUI editing operations are supported: selection of text with click-and-drag mouse operations; cut, copy, and paste; and a scroll bar for moving through text. The Mode line and Echo areas are displayed at the bottom of the window, where you can enter keyboard commands. The scroll bar is located on the left side. To move the scroll bar down, click it with the left mouse button. To move the scroll bar up, click it with the right mouse button.

NOTE *XEmacs is the complete Emacs editor with a graphical user interface and Internet applications, including a Web browser, a mail utility, and a newsreader. XEmacs is available on the Fedora repository.*

The Vi Editor: Vim and Gvim

The Vim editor included with most Linux distributions is an enhanced version of the Vi editor. It includes all the commands and features of the Vi editor. Vi, which stands for *visual*, remains one of the most widely used editors in Linux. Keyboard-based editors like Vim and Emacs use a keyboard for two different operations: to specify editing commands and to receive character input. Used for editing commands, certain keys perform deletions, some execute changes, and others perform cursor movement. Used for character input, keys represent characters that can be entered into the file being edited. Usually, these two different functions are divided among different keys on the keyboard. Alphabetic keys are reserved for character input, while function keys and control keys specify editing commands, such as deleting text or moving the cursor. Such editors can rely on the existence of an extended keyboard that includes function and control keys. Editors in Unix, however, were designed to assume a minimal keyboard with alphanumeric characters and some control characters, as well as the ESC and ENTER keys. Instead of dividing the command and input functions among different keys, the Vi editor has three separate modes of operation for the keyboard: command and input modes, and a line editing mode. In *command* mode, all the keys on the keyboard become editing commands; in the *input* mode, the keys on the keyboard become input characters. Some of the editing commands, such as **a** or **i**, enter the input mode. On typing **i**, you leave the command mode and enter the input mode. Each key now represents a character to be input to the text. Pressing ESC automatically returns you to the command mode, and the keys once again become editor commands. As you edit text, you are constantly moving from the command mode to the input mode and back again. With Vim, you can use the CTRL-O command to jump quickly to the command mode and enter a command, and then automatically return to the input mode. Table 11-8 lists a very basic set of Vi commands to get you started.

Although the Vi command mode handles most editing operations, it cannot perform some, such as file saving and global substitutions. For such operations, you need to execute line editing commands. You enter the line editing mode using the Vi colon command. The colon is a special command that enables you to perform a one-line editing operation. When you type the colon, a line opens up at the bottom of the screen with the cursor placed at the beginning of the line. You are now in the line editing mode. In this mode, you enter an editing command on a line, press ENTER, and the command is executed. Entry into this mode is usually only temporary. Upon pressing ENTER, you are automatically returned to the Vi command mode, and the cursor returns to its previous position on the screen.

Although you can create, save, close, and quit files with the Vi editor, the commands for each are not all that similar. Saving and quitting a file involves the use of special line editing commands, whereas closing a file is a Vi editing command. Creation of a file is usually specified on the same shell command line that invokes the Vi editor. To edit a file, type **vi** or **vim** and the name of a file on the shell command line. If a file by that name does not exist, the system creates it. In effect, giving the name of a file that does not yet exist instructs the Vi editor to create that file. The following command invokes the Vi editor, working on the file **booklist**. If **booklist** does not yet exist, the Vi editor creates it.

```
$ vim booklist
```

After executing the **vim** command, you enter Vi's command mode. Each key becomes a Vi editing command, and the screen becomes a window onto the text file. Text is displayed screen by screen. The first screen of text is displayed, and the cursor is positioned in the upper-left corner. With a newly created file, there is no text to display. This fact is indicated by a column of tildes at the left side of the screen. The tildes represent the part of a screen that is not part of the file.

Command	Cursor Movement
h	Moves the cursor left one character.
l	Moves the cursor right one character.
k	Moves the cursor up one line.
j	Moves the cursor down one line.
CTRL-F	Moves forward by a screen of text; the next screen of text is displayed.
CTRL-B	Moves backward by a screen of text; the previous screen of text is displayed.
Input	(*All input commands place the user in input; the user leaves input with* ESC.)
a	Enters input after the cursor.
i	Enters input before the cursor.
o	Enters input below the line the cursor is on; inserts a new empty line below the one the cursor is currently on.
Text Selection (Vim)	**Cursor Movement**
v	Visual mode; move the cursor to expand selected text by character. Once selected, press key to execute action: **c** change, **d** delete, **y** copy, **:** line editing command, **J** join lines, **U** uppercase, **u** lowercase.
V	Visual mode; move cursor to expand selected text by line.
Delete	**Effect**
x	Deletes the character the cursor is on.
dd	Deletes the line the cursor is on.
Change	(*Except for the replace command,* **r**, *all change commands place the user into input after deleting text.*)
cw	Deletes the word the cursor is on and places the user into the input mode.
r	Replaces the character the cursor is on. After pressing **r**, the user enters the replacement character. The change is made without entering input; the user remains in the Vi command mode.
R	First places into input mode, and then overwrites character by character. Appears as an overwrite mode on the screen but actually is in input mode.
Move	Moves text by first deleting it, moving the cursor to desired place of insertion, and then pressing the **p** command. (When text is deleted, it is automatically held in a special buffer.)
p	Inserts deleted or copied text after the character or line the cursor is on.

TABLE 11-8   Vi Editor Commands (*continued*)

Commands	Effect
P	Inserts deleted or copied text before the character or line the cursor is on.
dw p	Deletes a word, and then moves it to the place you indicate with the cursor (press **p** to insert the word *after* the word the cursor is on).
yy *or* Y p	Copies the line the cursor is on.
Search	The two search commands open up a line at the bottom of the screen and enable the user to enter a pattern to be searched for; press ENTER after typing in the pattern.
/*pattern*	Searches forward in the text for a pattern.
?*pattern*	Searches backward in the text for a pattern.
n	Repeats the previous search, whether it was forward or backward.
Line Editing Commands	**Effect**
w	Saves file.
q	Quits editor; **q!** quits without saving.

TABLE **11-8**   Vi Editor Commands

Remember, when you first enter the Vi editor, you are in the command mode. To enter text, you need to enter the input mode. In the command mode, **a** is the editor command for appending text. Pressing this key places you in the input mode. Now the keyboard operates like a typewriter and you can input text to the file. If you press ENTER, you merely start a new line of text. With Vim, you can use the arrow keys to move from one part of the entered text to another and work on different parts of the text. After entering text, you can leave the input mode and return to the command mode by pressing ESC. Once finished with the editing session, you exit Vi by typing two capital Zs, **zz**. Hold down the SHIFT key and press **z** twice. This sequence first saves the file and then exits the Vi editor, returning you to the Linux shell. To save a file while editing, you use the line editing command **w**, which writes a file to the disk; **w** is equivalent to the Save command found in other word processors. You first type a colon to access the line editing mode, and then type **w** and press ENTER.

You can use the **:q** command to quit an editing session. Unlike the **zz** command, the **:q** command does not perform any save operation before it quits. In this respect, it has one major constraint. If any modifications have been made to your file since the last save operation, the **:q** command will fail and you will not leave the editor. However, you can override this restriction by placing a ! qualifier after the **:q** command. The command **:q!** will quit the Vi editor without saving any modifications made to the file in that session since the last save (the combination **:wq** is the same as **zz**).

To obtain online help, enter the **:help** command. This is a line editing command. Type a colon, enter the word **help** on the line that opens at the bottom of the screen, and then press ENTER. You can add the name of a specific command after the word **help**. The F1 key also brings up online help.

   As an alternative to using Vim in a command line interface, you can use gvim, which provides X Window System–based menus for basic file, editing, and window operations. Gvim is installed as the **vim-x11** package, which includes several links to Gvim such as **evim**, **gview**, and **gex** (open Ex editor line). To use Gvim, you can select it from the Programming menu as VIM Improved, or enter the `gvim` command at an X Window System terminal prompt. You can also right-click a text file and select VIM Improved from the list under Open With Other Application. After selecting it once, it will always appear as a possible option when you right-click a text file.

   The standard Vi interface is displayed, but with several menu buttons displayed across the top along with a toolbar with button for common commands like searches and file saves. All the standard Vi commands work just as described previously. However, you can use your mouse to select items on these menus. You can open and close a file, or open several files using split windows or different windows. The editing menu enables you to cut, copy, and paste text as well as undo or redo operations. In the editing mode, you can select text with your mouse with a click-and-drag operation, or use the Editing menu to cut or copy and then paste the selected text. Text entry, however, is still performed using the **a**, **i**, or **o** command to enter the input mode. Searches and replacements are supported through a dialog window. There are also buttons on the toolbar for finding next and previous instances. Gview also features programming support, with color coding for programming syntax, for both shell scripts and C++ programs. There is even a Make button for running Make files.

Graphics Tools and Multimedia

Fedora includes a wide range of both graphic and multimedia applications and tools. such as simple image viewers like KView, sophisticated image manipulation programs like GIMP, music and CD players like Rhythmbox, and TV viewers like Totem. Graphics tools available for use under Linux are listed later in Table 12-2. Additionally, there is strong support for multimedia tasks from video and DVD to sound and music editing (see Table 12-3). Thousands of multimedia and graphic projects, as well as standard projects, are under development or currently available from **www.sourceforge.net**, **rpm.livna.org**, and **freshrpms .net**. Be sure to check the SourceForge site for any kind of application you may need.

Support for many popular multimedia operations, specifically MP3, DVD, and DivX, are not included with the Fedora distribution because of licensing and other restrictions. To play MP3, DVD, or DivX files, you will have to download and install support packages manually. Precompiled RPM binary packages for many popular media applications and libraries, such as MPlayer and XviD, are available at **rpm.livna.org** and **freshrpms.net**. These include many that are not part of the Fedora distribution. The **rpm.livna.org** site is an official Fedora repository that provides RPM Fedora-compatible packages for many multimedia and other applications that cannot be included with the Fedora distribution. These include MP3 support, DVD and DivX codecs, and even NTFS file system support. The **freshrpms.net** site contains more packages, though the **rpm.livna.org** site packages may be more compatible. If you cannot find a package at **rpm.livna.org**, you should check **freshrpms.net**. Current multimedia sites are listed in Table 12-1.

Graphics Tools

GNOME, KDE, and the X Window System support an impressive number of graphics tools, including image viewers, window grabbers, image editors, and paint tools. On the KDE and GNOME desktops, these tools can be found under either a Graphics submenu or the Utilities menu.

Photo Management Tools: F-Spot and digiKam

The F-Spot Photo Manager provides a simple and powerful way to manage, display, and import your photos and images (**www.f-spot.org**). Photos can be organized by different categories such as events, people, and places. You can perform standard display operations

Projects and Sites	Description
SourceForge	This site holds a massive amount of multimedia software for Linux, much under development: **sourceforge.net**
KDE multimedia applications	KDE supports an extensive set of multimedia software applications: **www.kde-apps.org**
GNOME multimedia applications	Many multimedia applications have been developed for GNOME: **www.gnomefiles.org**
Sound & MIDI Software for Linux	Lists a wide range of multimedia and sound software. **linux-sound.org**
Advanced Linux Sound Architecture (ALSA)	The Advanced Linux Sound Architecture (ALSA) project is under development on Linux under the GPL: **www.alsa-project.org**
Fedora Gaming	Games you can play on Fedora: **fedoraproject.org/wiki/games**
rpm.livna.org	Repository for RPM binary packages for popular applications and libraries, including ones for media that are not included with Fedora. This is an official extension of the Fedora project and contains RPM file specifically designed for Fedora.
freshrpms.net	Repository for RPM binary packages for popular media applications and libraries, many of which are not included with Red Hat Fedora. Holds a wide variety of current applications and libraries, Fedora compatible.

TABLE 12-1   Linux Multimedia Sites

like rotation or full-screen viewing, along with slide shows. Image editing support is provided. Selected photos can be directly burned to a CD (uses Nautilus burning capabilities).

Features include a simple and easy-to-use interface. A timeline feature lets you see photos as they were taken. You can also display photos in full-screen mode or as slide shows. F-Spot includes a photo editor that provides basic adjustments and changes like rotation, red eye correction, and standard color settings including temperature and saturation. You can tag photos placing them in groups, making them easier to access. With a tag you can label a collection of photos. Then use the tag to instantly access them. The tag itself can be a user-selected icon, including one that the user can create with the included Tag icon editor. F-Spot provides several ways to upload photos to a Web site using a Flickr account (**www.flickr.com**)

digiKam is a KDE photo manager with many of the same features (**www.digiKam.org**). A side panel allows easy access by album, date, tags, or previous searches. digiKam also provides image editing capabilities, with numerous effects. digiKam configuration (Settings menu) provides extensive options including image editing, digitial camera support, and interface configuration.

KDE Graphics Tools

KView is a simple image viewer for GIF and JPEG image files. The KSnapshot program is a simple screen grabber for KDE, which currently supports only a few image formats. KFourier is an image-processing tool that uses the Fourier transform to apply several filters to an image at once. KuickShow is an easy-to-use, comfortable image browser and viewer supporting slide shows and numerous image formats, based on imlib. KolourPaint is a simple paint program with brushes, shapes, and color effects; it supports numerous image formats. Krita is the KOffice professional image paint and editing application, with a wide range of features, such as creating Web images and modifying photographs (formerly known as Krayon and KImageShop).

GNOME Graphics Tools

GNOME features several powerful and easy-to-use graphic tools. Some are installed with Red Hat Fedora, whereas you can download others, such as GView and gtKam, from **www .gnomefiles.org**. Also, many of the KDE tools work just as effectively in GNOME and are accessible from the GNOME desktop.

The gThumb application is a thumbnail image viewer that lets you browse images using thumbnails, display them, and organize them into catalogs or easy reference. See **sourceforge.net** for more information.

GIMP is the GNU Image Manipulation Program, a sophisticated image application much like Adobe Photoshop. You can use GIMP for such tasks as photo retouching, image composition, and image authoring. It supports features such as layers, channels, blends, and gradients. GIMP makes particular use of the GTK+ widget set. You can find out more about GIMP and download the newest versions from its Web site at **www.gimp.org**. GIMP is freely distributed under the GNU Public License.

Inkscape is a Gnome based vector graphics application for SVG (scalable vector graphics) images with features and capabilities similar to professional level vector graphics applications like Adobe Illustrator. The SVG format allows easy generation of images for Web use, as well as complex art. Though its native format is SVG, it can also export to PNG format. It features layers and easy object creation, including stars and spirals. A color bar lets you quickly change color fills.

The gPhoto project provides software for accessing digital cameras (**www.gphoto.org**). Several front-end interfaces are provided for a core library, called libgphoto2, consisting of drivers and tools that can access numerous digital cameras.

X Window System Graphic Programs

X Window System–based applications run directly on the underlying X Window System, which supports the more complex desktops like GNOME and KDE. These applications tend to be simpler, lacking the desktop functionality found in GNOME or KDE applications. Xpaint is a paint program, much like MacPaint. You can load graphics or photographs, and then create shapes, add text, and add colors. You can use brush tools with various sizes and colors. Xfig is a drawing program, and Xmorph enables you to morph images, changing their shapes. ImageMagick lets you convert images from one format to another; you can, for instance, change a TIFF image to a JPEG image. Table 12-2 lists some popular graphics tools for Linux.

Tools	Description
F-Spot	GNOME digital camera application and image library manager (**f-spot.org**)
digiKam	KDE digital camera application and image library manager (**www.digikam.org**)
KDE	**Description**
KView	Simple image viewer for GIF and JPEG image files
ShowFoto	Simple image viewer, works with digiKam (**www.digikam.org**)
KSnapshot	Screen grabber
KFourier	Image processing tool that uses the Fourier transform
KuickShow	Image browser and viewer
KolourPaint	Paint program
Krita	Image editor (**www.koffice.org/krita**)
GNOME	**Description**
gThumb	Image browser, viewer, and cataloger (**gthumb.sourceforge.net**)
GIMP	GNU Image Manipulation Program (**www.gimp.org**)
Inkscape	GNOME Vector graphics application (**www.inkscape.org**)
X Window System	**Description**
Xpaint	Paint program
Xfig	Drawing program
Xmorph	Tool that morphs images
Xfractals	Fractal image generator
ImageMagick	Image format conversion and editing tool

TABLE 12-2   Graphics Tools for Linux

Multimedia

Many applications are available for both video and sound, including sound editors, MP3 players, and video players (see Table 12-3). Linux sound applications include mixers, digital audio tools, CD audio writers, MP3 players, and network audio support. Multimedia applications use various codecs to run different kinds of media, like MP3 for music files. The Codec Buddy tool will detect the codec you need and download it if not installed. For Fedora, you can purchase third party commercial codec like Window media or Dolby codecs from Fluendo (www.fluendo.com). Many applications designed specifically for the GNOME or KDE user interface can be found at their respective software sites (**www.gnomefiles.org** and **www.kde-apps.org**). Precompiled binary RPM packages for most applications are at the Fedora repository.

Application	Description
Xine	Multimedia player for video, DVD, and audio
Rhythmbox	Music management (GStreamer)
Sound Juicer	GNOME CD audio ripper (GStreamer)
Grip	CD audio ripper
aKtion	KDE video player
Kscd	Music CD player
Krec	KDE sound recorder
Kaboodle	A media player
GNOME CD Player	CD player
GNOME Sound Recorder	Sound recorder
Pulse	Pulse sound server
XMMS	CD player
Xplaycd	Music CD player
Noatun	KDE multimedia player
codec buddy	Codec detection tool
Fluendo	Commercial codecs for Fedora (**www.fluendo.com**)
HelixPlayer	Open source version of Real Player (**www.real.com**)
K3b	KDE CD writing interface for cdrecord, mkisofs, and cdda2wav
KAudioCreator	KDE CD burner and ripper
dvdauthor	Tools for creating DVDs (**dvdauthor.sourceforge.net**). Download RPM from **rpm.livna.org**
Qauthor	KDE front end for dvdauthor (**www.kde-apps.org**)
DVDStyler	DVD authoring application for GNOME (**dvdstyler.sourceforge.net**)

TABLE 12-3   Multimedia and Sound Applications

GStreamer

Many of the GNOME-based applications make use of GStreamer. GStreamer is a streaming media framework based on graphs and filters. Using a plug-in structure, GStreamer applications can accommodate a wide variety of media types. You can download modules and plug-ins from **gstreamer.freedesktop.org**. Fedora includes several GStreamer applications:

- The Totem video player uses GStreamer to play DVDs, VCDs, and MPEG media.

- Rhythmbox provides integrated music management; it is similar to the Apple iTunes music player.

- Sound Juicer is an audio CD ripper.
- A CD player, a sound recorder, and a volume control are all provided as part of the GStreamer GNOME Media package.

Multimedia System Selector

GStreamer can be configured to use different input and output sound and video drivers and servers. You can make these selections using the GStreamer properties tool. To open this tool from the Desktop menu, first select Preferences, then More Preferences, and then the Multimedia Systems Selector entry. You can also enter `gstreamer-properties` in a terminal window. The properties window displays two tabbed panels, one for sound and the other for video. The output drivers and servers are labeled Default Sink, and the input divers are labeled Default Source. There are pop-up menus for each listing the available sound or video drivers or servers. For example the sound server used is ALSA, but you can change that to OSS.

Gstreamer Plug-ins: the Good, the Bad, and the Ugly

Many GNOME multimedia applications like Totem use Gstreamer to provide multimedia support. To use such features as DVD Video and MP3, you have to install Gstreamer extra plug-ins. You can find out more information about Gstreamer and its supporting packages at **gstreamer.freedesktop.org**. For valid third p

The supporting packages can be confusing. For version 1.0 and above, Gstreamer establishes four different support packages called the base, the good, the bad, and the ugly. The base package is a set of useful plug-ins that are reliable. These are in Fedora repository. The good package is a set of supported and tested plug-ins that meet all licensing requirements. This is also part of the Fedora repository. The bad is a set of unsupported plug-ins whose performance is not guaranteed and may crash, but still meet licensing requirements. The ugly package contains plug-ins that work fine, but may not meet licensing requirements, like DVD support. These you will find on Freshrpms or or Livna repositories.

- **The base**   Reliable commonly used plug-ins
- **The good**   Reliable additional and useful plug-ins
- **The ugly**   Reliable but not fully licensed plug-ins (DVD/MP3 support)
- **The bad**   Possibly unreliable but useful plug-ins (possible crashes)

You can download and install the Gstreamer plug-in packages using the yum command or Pirut (Add/Remove Software). Codec Buddy will automatically detect the codec you will need to use for your Gstreamer application. For commercial codecs, like DVD, MP3, or Dolby, Fedora recommends that you purchase and download the codec plugins from Fluendo (www.fluendo.com). The fluendo codec plugins are inexpensive as well as reliable and supported.

Other plug-ins for Gstreamer that you may want include are **ffmpeg** and **pitfdll**, **gstreamer-ffmpeg** and **gstreamer-pitfdll** (Freshrpms and Livna repositories). ffmpeg provides several popular codecs, including ogg and .264. The **pitdfdll** package provides support for media files in proprietary formats like Microsoft's WM9. For Pulse (sound server) and Farsight (video conferencing) support, use their respective gtreamer plugins on the Fedora repository.

GStreamer MP3 Compatibility: iPod

For your iPod and other MP3 devices to work with GNOME applications like Rhythmbox, you will need to install MP3 support for GStreamer. MP3 support is not included with Red Hat distributions because of licensing issues. You can, however, download and install the GStreamer **gstreamer-plugins-ugly** support package as noted previously, which maintains most multimedia support packages for Fedora that are not included with the distribution. You can download the package from **freshrpms.net**.

To sync and import from your iPod, you can use iPod management software such as GUI for iPod (gtkpod). Several scripts and tools are currently available for iPod operations; they include SyncPOD, myPod, gtkpod (a GUI for iPod), and iPod for Linux. Check **sourceforge.net** and search for iPod.

Sound Applications

Sound devices on Linux are supported by drivers forming a sound system. With the current Fedora kernel, sound support is implemented by the Advanced Linux Sound Architecture (ALSA) system. ALSA replaces the free version of the Open Sound System used in previous releases, as well as the original built-in sound drivers (see Chapter 32). You can find more about ALSA at **www.alsa-project.org**.

MP3 with Lame

LAME originally stood for **L**ame **A**in't an **M**p3 Encoder, but it has long since evolved into a full MP3 encoder whose software is available under the LPGL license. It is included with VideoLAN and FFmpeg, and Yum will download from **Freshrpms.net** in support of MPlayer or Xine. You can download it separately with

```
yum install lame
```

Due to licensing and patent issues, Red Hat Linux has removed support for MP3 files. MP3 playback capability has been removed from multimedia players like XMMS and Noatun. As an alternative to MP3, you can use Ogg Vorbis compression for music files (**www.vorbis.com**).

NOTE *Linux has become a platform of choice for many professional-level multimedia tasks such as generating computer-generated images (CGI) and animation for movie special effects, using such demanding software as Maya and Softimage. Linux graphic libraries include those for OpenGL, MESA, and SGI.*

Music Applications

Many music applications are currently available for GNOME, including sound editors, MP3 players, and audio players. You can use the GNOME CD Player to play music CDs and the GNOME Sound Recorder to record sound sources. Check the software map at **www.gnomefiles.org** for current releases. A variety of applications are also available for KDE, including two media players (Kaiman and Kaboodle), a mixer (KMix), and a CD player (Kscd). Check **www.kde-apps.org** for recent additions. Several X Window System-based multimedia applications are installed with most distributions. These include XMMS and Xplaycd, CD music players, and Xanim, an animation and video player.

Red Hat and Fedora feature the XMMS multimedia player, the GNOME CD Player, the GNOME Sound Recorder, and the GNOME Volume Control in the Sound And Video menu. The Extra Sound And Video menus list several KDE applications, including KMidi, Kaboodle, and Noatun. Fedora also includes HelixPlayer, the open source project used for RealPlayer. HelixPlayer runs only open source media like Ogg Vorbis files (though you can obtain RealPlayer audio and video codecs for the player). See **helixcommunity.org** for more information. You can also download a copy of RealPlayer, the Internet streaming media player, from **www.real.com**. Be sure to choose RealPlayer for Unix, and as your OS. The Pulse sound server lets you direct and manage sound streams from a device, letting you direct and modify sound to different clients. The Sound & Midi Software for Linux site currently at **linux-sound.org** hold links to Web and FTP sites for many of sound applications.

CD Burners and Rippers

Several CD writer programs that can be used for CD music and MP3 writing (burners and rippers) are available from **www.kde-apps.org**. These include K3b, CD-Rchive, and KAudioCreator (CD ripper). For GNOME, you can use CD-REC and the Nautilus CD burner, which is integrated into the Nautilus file manager, the default file manager for the GNOME desktop. All use mkisofs, cdrecord, and cdda2wav CD writing programs, which are installed as part of the Red Hat distribution. GNOME also features two CD audio rippers installed with Red Hat Fedora, Grip, and Sound Juicer.

TIP   *If your CD or DVD application has difficulty finding your CD/DVD player or burner, you may need to check whether HAL is creating an appropriate link to your CD/DVD device using /dev/cdrom or /dev/dvdrom. These links should be generated automatically (see Chapter 32).*

Video Applications

Several projects are under way to provide TV, video, DivX, DVD, and DTV support for Linux (see Table 12-4). Many of these applications are not on the Red Hat or Fedora repositories. In most cases, the most recent versions will be in source code format on the original site. For these you will have to download the source code, which you will then need to compile and install. Many applications, though, are already available in binary RPM packages at **rpm .livna.org** and **freshrpms.net**. The **freshrpms.net site** will have a larger and more recent collection of packages, though **rpm.livna.org** might be more reliable with Fedora. It is recommended that you install the Freshrpms or Livna Yum configuration file first, and then use Pirut (Add/Remove Software), Yumex (Applications | System Tools), or the **yum** command on a command line (Terminal window). Yumex has the added capability of letting you disable or enable a repository. This can be a concern when mixing Livna and Freshrpms repositories. You could disable Livna and use Freshrpms for all your multimedia applications, while enabling Livna when you want to update drivers like vendor graphics drivers.

You can also opt to download and install a packages manually, though you would have to also manually install any dependencies. For packages like mplayer which has numerous dependencies, this is not practical. For smaller packages with no dependencies, this will work fine. For RPM packages, Firefox will give you the option to automatically install the RPM with system-config-packages. For compressed archives such as **.tar.bz** files, FireFox

Projects and Players	Sites
LinuxTV.org	Links to video, TV, and DVD sites, **linuxtv.org**
DVD players list	**dvd.sourceforge.net**
xine	Xine video player, **xinehq.de**
Totem	Totem video and DVD player for GNOME based on Xine and using GStreamer, **xinehq.de**
VideoLAN	Network multimedia streaming, includes x264 high definition support, **www.videolan.org**
MPlayer	MPlayer DVD/multimedia player, **www.mplayerhq.hu**
PowerDVD	Cyberlink PowerDVD for Linux, **gocyberlink.com**
DVD::rip	DVD transcoding and DivX software, **www.exit1.org/dvdrip**
kdetv	KDE TV viewer, **www.kdetv.org**
tvtime	TV viewer, **tvtime.sourceforge.net**
DivX for Linux	**labs.divx.com/DivXLinuxCodec**
XviD	Open Source DivX, **www.xvid.org**

TABLE 12-4   Video and DVD Projects and Applications

will automatically invoke File Roller, letting you immediately decompress and extract source code files to a selected directory.

TIP   For HDTV reception you can use the PCHDTV video card (www.pdhdtv.org). For the latest PCHDTV card, you can use the c88-dvb drivers included with Fedora. For earlier versions you would have to download, compile, and install a separate driver. The DVB kernel driver is not installed by default. You would use modprobe to manually install. Use the dvd tools available to manage access. You can use MythTV and vdr to view and record.

Video and DVD Players

Access to current DVD and media players is provided at **dvd.sourceforge.net**. Here you will find links for players like VideoLAN, MPlayer, and Xine.

- The VideoLAN project (**www.videolan.org**) offers network streaming support for most media formats, including MPEG-4, x264, and MPEG-2. It includes a multimedia player, VLC, that can work on any kind of system.

- MPlayer is one of the most popular and capable multimedia/DVD players in use. It is a cross-platform open source alternative to RealPlayer and Windows Media Player. MPlayer includes support for DivX. You can download MPlayer from **www .mplayerhq.hu**. MPlayer uses an extensive set of supporting libraries and supporting applications like **lirc**, **lame**, **lzo**, and **aalib**. If you have trouble displaying video, be sure to check the preferences for different Video devices, selecting one that works best.

- Xine is a multipurpose video player for Linux/Unix systems that can play video, DVD, and audio discs. See **xinehq.de** for more information. Xine is available in source code form, which you will have to compile and install, though you can download an RPM binary from **freshrpm.net**.

- Totem, installed with Fedora, is a GNOME movie player based on Xine that uses GStreamer. To expand Totem capabilities, you need to install added GStreamer plug-ins.

- PowerDVD provides a commercial version of its DVD player for Linux (**www.cyberlink.com**).

- For DVD transcoding and DivX support, check the DVD::rip project. **www.exit1.org/dvdrip**.

- kdtv KDE television viewer

- tvtime TV viewer

- Additional codec support is supplied by ffmeg and x264. The x264 codec is an open source version, developed by Videolan, of the high definition H.264 codec.

None of the open source software hosted at SourceForge performs CSS decryption of commercial DVDs. You could, however, download and install the **libdvdcss** library, which works around CSS decryption by treating the DVD as a block device, allowing you to use any of the DVD players to run commercial DVDs. It is also provides region-free access. Bear in mind that this may not be legal in certain countries that require CSS licenses for DVD players.

NOTE *To play DivX media on Red Hat and Fedora, you use the Divx for Linux codec at* **labs.divx.com/DivXLinuxCodec***.*

Originally, many of these players did not support DVD menus. With the **libdvdnav** and **libdvdplay** libraries, these player now feature full DVD menu support. The **libdvdread** library provides basic DVD interface support such as reading IFO files. You can download RPM binaries for these packages from **freshrpms.net**.

TV Players

The site **linuxtv.org** provides detailed links to DVD, digital video broadcasting (DVB), and multicasting. The site also provides downloads of many Linux video applications.

The primary TV player on Fedora is tvtime, which works with many common video capture cards, relying on drivers developed for TV tuner chips on those cards like the Conexant chips. It can only display a TV image. It has no recording or file playback capabilities. Check **tvtime.sourceforge.net** for more information.

For KDE, several video applications are available or currently under development, including kdetv. Check **www.kde-apps.org** for downloads. For Gnome based players, check **www.gnomefiles.org**.

DivX and Xvid on Linux

DivX is a commercial video compression technology (free for personal use) for providing DVD-quality video with relatively small file sizes. You can compress 60 minutes of DVD video into about 400 MB, while maintaining very good quality. DivX is based on the MPEG-4 compression format, whereas DVD is MPEG-2. You can download the Linux version of DivX for free from **labs.divx.com/DivXLinuxCodec**. You have to manually install the package. If you download with Firefox, you can choose to extract the archive directly.

Instead of trying to get DivX to work, you can just use the open source version of DivX known as Xvid. Most DivX files can be run using XviD. XviD is an entirely independent open source project, but compatible with DivX files. Binary RPM versions can be obtained for Fedora from **rpm.livna.org** and **freshrpms.net**. If you have configured these repositories for use by Yum on your system, you can just use Pirut or the yum command to install the xvid package.

```
yum install xvid
```

You could also download the XviD source code from **www.xvid.org**. If you use Firefox to download, you will automatically have the option to download the original compressed **.tar.bz** file or open File Roller and immediately extract the compressed archive. Once it is extracted, you can compile the source code and install the codec. The Linux version is built in the **build/generic** subdirectory, using the `./configure`, `make`, and `make install` commands (see Chapter 4). Open a terminal window and use the `cd` command to change to that directory, then run the commands.

Mail and News Clients

Your Linux system supports a wide range of both electronic mail and news clients. Mail clients enable you to send and receive messages with other users on your system or accessible from your network. News clients let you read articles and messages posted in newsgroups, which are open to access by all users. This chapter reviews mail and news clients installed with Fedora Linux.

Mail Clients

You can send and receive e-mail messages in a variety of ways, depending on the type of mail client you use. Although all electronic mail utilities perform the same basic tasks of receiving and sending messages, they tend to have different interfaces. Some mail clients operate on a desktop, such as KDE or GNOME. Others run on any X Window System manager. Several popular mail clients were designed to use a screen-based interface and can be started only from the command line. Other traditional mail clients were developed for just the command line interface, which requires you to type your commands on a single command line. Most mail clients described here are included in standard Linux distributions and come in a standard RPM package for easy installation. For Web-based Internet mail services, such as Hotmail, Google, and Yahoo, you use a Web browser instead of a mail client to access mail accounts provided by those services. Table 13-1 lists several popular Linux mail clients. Mail is transported to and from destinations using mail transport agents. Sendmail, Exim, and Smail send and receive mail from destinations on the Internet or other sites on a network (see Chapter 25). To send mail over the Internet, they use the Simple Mail Transport Protocol (SMTP). Most Linux distributions, including Fedora, automatically install and locally configure Sendmail for you. On starting up your system, having configured your network connections, you can send and receive messages over the Internet.

You can sign your e-mail message with the same standard signature information, such as your name, Internet address or addresses, or farewell phrase. Having your signature information automatically added to your messages is helpful. To do so, you need to create a signature file in your home directory and enter your signature information in it. A *signature file* is a standard text file you can edit using any text editor. Mail clients such as KMail enable you to specify a file to function as your signature file. Others, such as Mail, expect the signature file to be named **.signature**.

Mail Client	Description
Kontact (KMail, KAddressbook, KOrganizer)	Includes the K Desktop mail client, KMail; integrated mail, address book, and scheduler
Evolution	E-mail client
Balsa	GNOME mail client
Thunderbird	Mozilla group stand-alone mail client and newsreader
Netscape	Web browser–based mail client
GNUEmacs and XEmacs	Emacs mail clients
Mutt	Screen-based mail client
Sylpheed	Gtk mail and news client
Mail	Original Unix-based command line mail client
SquirrelMail	Web-based mail client

TABLE 13-1   Linux Mail Clients

MIME

MIME (the term stands for *Multipurpose Internet Mail Extensions*) is used to enable mail clients to send and receive multimedia files and files using different character sets such as those for different languages. Multimedia files can be images, sound clips, or even video. Mail clients that support MIME can send binary files automatically as attachments to messages. MIME-capable mail clients maintain a file called **mailcap** that maps different types of MIME messages to applications on your system that can view or display them. For example, an image file will be mapped to an application that can display images. Your mail clients can then run that program to display the image message. A sound file will be mapped to an application that can play sound files on your speakers. Most mail clients have MIME capabilities built in and use their own version of the **mailcap** file. Others use a program called metamail that adds MIME support. MIME is not only used in mail clients. As noted in Chapters 6 and 7, both the KDE and GNOME file managers use MIME to map a file to a particular application so that you can launch the application directly from the file.

The mime.types File

Applications are associated with binary files by means of the **mailcap** and **mime.types** files. The **mime.types** file defines different MIME types, associating a MIME type with a certain application. The **mailcap** file then associates each MIME type with a specified application. Your system maintains its own MIME types file, usually **/etc/mime.types**.

    Entries in the MIME types file associate a MIME type and possible subtype of an application with a set of possible file extensions used for files that run on a given kind of application. The MIME type is usually further qualified by a subtype, separated from the major type by a slash. For example, a MIME type image can have several subtypes such as jpeg, gif, or tiff. A sample MIME type entry defining a MIME type for JPEG files is shown here. The MIME type is image/jpeg, and the list of possible file extensions is "jpeg jpg jpe":

```
image/jpeg jpeg jpg jpe
```

The applications specified will depend on those available on your particular system. The MIME type is separated from the application with a semicolon. In many cases, X Window System–based programs are specified. Comments are indicated with a **#**. A ***** used in a MIME subtype references all subtypes. The entry **image/*** would be used for an application that can run all types of image files. A formatting code, **%s**, is used to reference the attachment file that will be run on this application. Sample **mailcap** entries are shown here. The first entry associates all **image** files with the xv image viewer. The next two associate video and video MPEG files with the XAnim application.

```
image/*; xv %s
video/*; xanim %s
video/mpeg; xanim %s
```

MIME Associations on GNOME and KDE

You can also create and edit MIME types on the GNOME and KDE desktops. For GNOME, use the GNOME Control Center's MIME types capplet. This capplet will list the MIME types defined for your system along with their associated filename extensions. Edit an entry to change the application and icon associated with that MIME type, i.e. that type of file. On KDE, use the KDE Control Center's File Association entry under KDE Components. This will list MIME types and their associated filename extensions. Select an entry to edit it and change the applications associated with it. KDE saves its MIME type information in a separate file called **mimelnk** in the KDE configuration directory.

MIME Standard Associations

Though you can create your own MIME types, a standard set is already in use. The types text, image, audio, video, application, multipart, and message, along with their subtypes, have already been defined for your system. You will find that commonly used file extensions such as **.tif** and **.jpg** for TIFF and JPEG image files are already associated with a MIME type and an application. Though you can easily change the associated application, it is best to keep the MIME types already installed. The current official MIME types are listed at the IANA Web site (**www.iana.org**) under the name Media Types, provided as part of their Assignment Services. You can access the media types file directly on their site.

OpenPGP/MIME and S/MIME Authentication and Encryption Protocols

S/MIME and OpenPGP/MIME are authentication protocols for signing and encrypting mail messages. S/MIME was originally developed by the RSA Data Security. OpenPGP is an open standard based on the PGP/MIME protocol developed by the PGP (Pretty Good Privacy) group. Clients like KMail and Evolution can use OpenPGP/MIME to authenticate messages. Check the Internet Mail Consortium for more information, **www.imc.org**.

Evolution

Evolution is the primary mail client for the GNOME desktop. It is installed by default along with OpenOffice. Though designed for GNOME, it will work equally well on KDE. Evolution is an integrated mail client, calendar, and address book, currently being developed by Novell and now known as Novell Evolution. The Evolution mailer is a powerful tool with support for numerous protocols (SMTP, POP, and IMAP), multiple mail accounts, and encryption. With Evolution, you can create multiple mail accounts on different servers, including those that use different protocols such as POP or IMAP. You can also decrypt PGP- or GPG-encrypted messages.

The Evolution mailer provides a simple GUI interface, with a toolbar for commonly used commands and a sidebar for shortcuts. A menu of Evolution commands allows access to other operations. The main panel is divided into two panes, one for listing the mail headers and the other for displaying the currently selected message. You can click any header title to sort your headers by that category. Evolution also supports the use of virtual folders. These are folders created by the user to hold mail that meets specified criteria. Incoming mail can be automatically distributed to specified virtual folders. For automatic mail notification, you use the mail-notification plug-in for Evolution, now a separate package in Fedora Extras.

Thunderbird

Thunderbird is a full-featured stand-alone e-mail client provided by the Mozilla project (**www.mozilla.org**). It is designed to be easy to use, highly customized, and heavily secure. It features advanced intelligent spam filtering, as well as security features like encryption, digital signatures, and S/MIME. To protect against viruses, e-mail attachments can be examined without being run. Thunderbird supports both IMAP and POP, as well as functioning as a newsreader. It also features a built-in RSS reader. Thunderbird also supports the use of LDAP address books. Thunderbird is an extensible application, allowing customized modules to be added to enhance its capabilities. You can download extensions such as a dictionary search and contact sidebars from its Web site. GPG encryption can be supported with the enigmail extension (see Chapter 16).

The interface uses a standard three-pane format, with a side pane for listing mail accounts and their boxes. The top pane lists main entries, and the bottom pane shows text. Commands can be run using the toolbar, menus, or keyboard shortcuts. You can even change the appearance using different themes. Thunderbird also support HTML mail, displaying Web components like URLs in mail messages.

The message list pane will show several fields by which you can sort your messages. Some use just symbols like the Threads, Attachments, and Read icons. Clicking Threads will gather the messages into respective threads with replies grouped together. The last icon in the message list fields is a pop-up menu letting you choose which fields to display. Thunderbird provides a variety of customizable display filters, such as People I Know, which displays only messages from those in your address book, and Attachments, which displays messages with attached files. You can even create your own display filters. Search and sorting capabilities also include filters that can match selected patterns in any field, including subject, date, or the message body.

When you first start up Thunderbird, you will be prompted to create an e-mail account. You can add more e-mail accounts or modify your current ones by selecting Account Settings from the Edit menu. Then click Add Account to open a dialog with four options, one of which is an e-mail account. Upon selecting the Email option, you are prompted to enter your e-mail address and name. In the next panel you specify either the POP or IMAP protocol and enter the name of the incoming e-mail server, such as **smtp.myemailserver.com**. You then specify an incoming user name, the user name given you by your e-mail service. Then you enter an account name label to identify the account on Thunderbird. A final verification screen lets you confirm your entries. In the Account Settings window you will see an entry for your news server, with panels for Server Settings, Copies & Folders, Composition & Addressing, Offline & Disk Space, Return Receipt, and Security. The Server Settings panel has entries for your server name, port, user name, and connection and task configurations, such as automatically downloading new messages. The Security panel opens the Certificate Manager, where you can select security certificates to use to digitally sign or encrypt messages.

Thunderbird provides an address book where you can enter complete contact information, including e-mail addresses, street addresses, phone numbers, and notes. Select Address Book from the Tools menu to open the Address Book window. There are three panes, one for the address books available, one listing the address entries with field entries like name, e-mail, and organization, and one for displaying address information. You can sort the entries by these fields. Clicking an entry will display the address information, including e-mail address, street addresses, and phone. Only fields with values are displayed. To create a new entry in an address book, click New Card to open a window with panels for Contact and Address information. To create mailing lists from the address book entries, you click the New List button, specify the name of the list, and enter the e-mail addresses.

Once you have your address book set up, you can easily use its addresses when creating mail messages. On the Compose window, click the Contacts button to open a Contacts pane. Your address book entries will be listed using the contact's name. Just click the name to add it to the address box of your e-mail message. Alternatively, you can open the address book and drag and drop addresses to the address box on your message window.

A user's e-mail messages, addresses, and configuration information are kept in files located in the **.thunderbird** directory within the user's home directory. Backing up this information is as simple as making a copy of that directory. Messages for the different mail boxes are kept in a **Mail** subdirectory. If you are migrating to a new system, you can just copy the directory from the older system. To back up the mail for any given mail account, just copy the **Mail** subdirectory for that account. Though the default address books, **abook.mab** and **history.mab**, can be interchangeably copied, non-default address books need to be exported to an LDIF format and then imported to the new Thunderbird application. It is advisable to regularly export your address books to LDIF files as backups.

NOTE *Netscape Communicator includes a mail client called Messenger. Account information, such as your mail server, username, and password, must be entered in the Mail panel in the Preferences window, accessible from the Edit menu. Fedora no longer includes Netscape in its distribution, though you can download and install it if you wish.*

GNOME Mail Clients: Evolution, Balsa, and Others

Several GNOME-based mail clients are now available on Fedora Extras (see Table 13-2). These include Evolution, Balsa, and Sylpheed (Evolution is included with Fedora). Check **www.gnomefiles.org** for more mail clients as they come out. Many are based on the GNOME mail client libraries (camel), which provides support for standard mail operations. Balsa is a GNOME mail client with extensive features, though it can operate under any window manager, including KDE, as long as GNOME is installed on your system. As noted previously, Evolution is an integrated mail client, calendar, and contact manager from Novell. Sylpheed is a mail and news client with an interface similar to Windows mail clients.

Balsa provides a full-featured GUI interface for composing, sending, and receiving mail messages. The Balsa window displays three panes for folders, headers, and messages. The left pane displays your mail folders. You initially have three folders: an inbox folder for received mail, an outbox folder for mail you have composed but have not sent yet, and a

Application	Description
Balsa	E-mail client for GNOME that supports POP3, IMAP, local folders, and multithreading
Evolution	Integrated mail client, calendar, and contact manager
Sylpheed	Mail and news client similar to Windows clients
gnubiff	E-mail checker and notification tool
Mail Notification	E-mail checker and notification that works with numerous mail clients, including MH, Sylpheed, Gmail, Evolution, and Mail

TABLE 13-2   GNOME Mail Clients

trash folder for messages you have deleted. You can also create your own mail folders in which you can store particular messages. To place a message in a folder you have created, click and drag the message header for that message to the folder.

The K Desktop Mail Client: KMail

The K Desktop mail client, KMail, provides a full-featured GUI interface for composing, sending, and receiving mail messages. KMail is now part of the KDE Personal Information Management suite, KDE-PIM, which also includes an address book (KAddressBook), an organizer and scheduler (KOrganizer), and a note writer (KNotes). All these components are also directly integrated on the desktop into Kontact. To start up KMail, you start the Kontact application. The KMail window displays three panes for folders, headers, and messages. The upper-left pane displays your mail folders. You have an inbox folder for received mail, an outbox folder for mail you have composed but have not sent yet, and a sent-mail folder for messages you have previously sent. You can create your own mail folders and save selected messages in them, if you wish. The top-right pane displays mail headers for the currently selected mail folder. To display a message, click its header. The message is then displayed in the large pane below the header list. You can also send and receive attachments, including binary files. Pictures and movies that are received are displayed using the appropriate K Desktop utility. If you right-click the message, a pop-up menu displays options for actions you may want to perform on it. You can move or copy it to another folder, or simply delete it. You can also compose a reply or forward the message. KMail, along with Kontact, KOrganizer, and KaddressBook, is accessible from the KDE Desktop, Office, and Internet menus.

To set up KMail for use with your mail accounts, you must enter account information. Select the Configure entry in the Settings menu. Several panels are available on the Settings window, which you can display by clicking their icons in the left column. For accounts, you select the Network panel. You may have more than one mail account on mail servers maintained by your ISP or LAN. A Configure window is displayed where you can enter login, password, and host information. For secure access, KMail now supports SSL, provided OpenSSL is installed. Messages can now be encrypted and decoded by users. It also supports IMAP in addition to POP and SMTP protocols.

SquirrelMail Web Mail Client

You can use the SquirrelMail Web mail tool to access mail on a Linux system using your Web browser. It will display a login screen for mail users. It features an inbox list and message reader, support for editing and sending new messages, and a plug-in structure for adding new features. You can find out more about SquirrelMail at **www.squirrelmail.org**. The Apache configuration file is **/etc/httpd/conf.d/squirrelmail.conf**, and SquirrelMail is installed in **/usr/share/squirrelmail**. Be sure that the IMAP mail server is also installed.

To configure SquirrelMail, you use the **config.pl** script in the **/usr/share/squirrelmail/config** directory. This displays a simple text-based menu where you can configure settings like the server to use, folder defaults, general options, and organizational preferences.

```
./config.pl
```

To access SquirrelMail, use the Web server address with the **/squirrelmail** extension, as in **localhost/squirrelmail** for users on the local system, or **www.mytrek.com/squirrelmail** for remote users.

Emacs

The Emacs mail clients are integrated into the Emacs environment, of which the Emacs editor is the primary application. They are, however, fully functional mail clients. The GNU version of Emacs includes a mail client along with other components, such as a newsreader and editor. GNU Emacs is included on Fedora distributions. Check the Emacs Web site at **www.gnu.org/software/emacs** for more information. When you start up GNU Emacs, menu buttons are displayed across the top of the screen. If you are running Emacs in an X Window System environment, you have full GUI capabilities and can select menus using your mouse. To access the Emacs mail client, select from the mail entries in the Tools menu. To compose and send messages, just select the Send Mail item in the Tools menu. This opens a screen with prompts for To and Subject header entries. You then type the message below them, using any of the Emacs editing capabilities. GNU Emacs is a working environment within which you can perform a variety of tasks, with each task having its own buffer. When you read mail, a buffer is opened to hold the header list, and when you read a message, another buffer will hold the contents. When you compose a message, yet another buffer holds the text you wrote. The buffers you have opened for mail, news, or editing notes or files are listed in the Buffers menu. You can use this menu to switch among them.

XEmacs is another version of Emacs, designed to operate solely with a GUI interface. The Internet applications, which you can easily access from the main XEmacs button bar, include a Web browser, a mail utility, and a newsreader. When composing a message, you have full use of the Emacs editor with all its features, including the spell-checker and search/replace functions.

Command Line Mail Clients

Several mail clients use a simple command line interface. They can be run without any other kind of support, such as the X Window System, desktops, or cursor support. They are simple and easy to use but include an extensive set of features and options. Two of the more widely used mail clients of this type are Mail and Mutt. Mail is the mailx mail client that was developed for the Unix system. It is considered a kind of default mail client that can be found on all Unix and Linux systems. Mutt is a cursor-based client that can be run from the command line.

NOTE *You can also use the Emacs mail client from the command line, as described in the previous section.*

Mutt

Mutt has an easy-to-use screen-based interface. Mutt has an extensive set of features, such as MIME support. You can find more information about Mutt from the Mutt Web site, **www.mutt.org**. Here you can download recent versions of Mutt and access online manuals and help resources. On most distributions, the Mutt manual is located in the **/usr/doc** directory under Mutt. The Mutt newsgroup is **comp.mail.mutt**, where you can post queries and discuss recent Mutt developments.

Mail

What is known now as the Mail utility was originally created for BSD Unix and called, simply, mail. Later versions of Unix System V adopted the BSD mail utility and renamed it mailx. Now, it is simply referred to as Mail. Mail functions as a de facto default mail client on Unix and Linux systems. All systems have the mail client called Mail, whereas they may not have other mail clients.

To send a message with Mail, type **mail** along with the address of the person to whom you are sending the message. Press ENTER and you are prompted for a subject. Enter the subject of the message and press ENTER again. At this point, you are placed in input mode. Anything typed in is taken as the contents of the message. Pressing ENTER adds a new line to the text. When you finish typing your message, press CTRL-D on a line of its own to end the message. You will then be prompted to enter a user to whom to send a carbon copy of the message (Cc). If you do not want to sent a carbon copy, just press ENTER. You will then see *EOT (end-of-transmission)* displayed after you press CTRL-D.

You can send a message to several users at the same time by listing those users' addresses as arguments on the command line following the **mail** command. In the next example, the user sends the same message to both **chris** and **aleina**.

```
$ mail chris aleina
```

To receive mail, you enter only the **mail** command and press ENTER. This invokes a Mail shell with its own prompt and mail commands. A list of message headers is displayed. Header information is arranged into fields beginning with the status of the message and the message number. The status of a message is indicated by a single uppercase letter, usually **N** for *new* or **U** for *unread*. A message number, used for easy reference to your messages, follows the status field. The next field is the address of the sender, followed by the date and time the message was received, and then the number of lines and characters in the message. The last field contains the subject the sender gave for the message. After the headers, the Mail shell displays its prompt, an ampersand (**&**). At the Mail prompt, you enter commands that operate on the messages. An example of a Mail header and prompt follows:

```
$ mail
Mail version 8.1 6/6/93. Type ? for help.
"/var/spool/mail/larisa": 3 messages 2 unread
```

```
 1 chris@turtle.mytrek. Thu Jun 7 14:17 22/554 "trip"
>U 2 aleina@turtle.mytrek Thu Jun 7 14:18 22/525 "party"
 U 3 dylan@turtle.mytrek. Thu Jun 7 14:18 22/528 "newsletter"
& q
```

Mail references messages either through a message list or through the current message marker (**>**). The greater-than sign (**>**) is placed before a message considered the current message. The current message is referenced by default when no message number is included with a Mail command. You can also reference messages using a message list consisting of several message numbers. Given the messages in the preceding example, you can reference all three messages with **1-3**.

You use the **R** and **r** commands to reply to a message you have received. The **R** command entered with a message number generates a header for sending a message and then places you into the input mode to type in the message. The **q** command quits Mail. When you quit, messages you have already read are placed in a file called **mbox** in your home directory. Instead of saving messages in the **mbox** file, you can use the **s** command to save a message explicitly to a file of your choice. Mail has its own initialization file, called **.mailrc**, that is executed each time Mail is invoked for either sending or receiving messages. Within it, you can define Mail options and create Mail aliases. You can set options that add different features to mail, such as changing the prompt or saving copies of messages you send. To define an alias, you enter the keyword **alias**, followed by the alias you have chosen and then the list of addresses it represents. In the next example, the alias **myclass** is defined in the **.mailrc** file.

.mailrc

```
alias myclass chris dylan aleina justin larisa
```

In the next example, the contents of the file **homework** are sent to all the users whose addresses are aliased by **myclass**.

```
$ mail myclass < homework
```

Notifications of Received Mail

As your mail messages are received, they are automatically placed in your mailbox file, but you are not automatically notified when you receive a message. You can use a mail client to retrieve any new messages, or you can use a mail monitor tool to tell you if you have any mail waiting. Several mail notification tools are also available, such as gnubiff and Mail Notification. Mail Notification will support Gmail, as well as Evolution (for Evolution, install the separate plug-in package). When you first log in after Mail Notification has been installed, the Mail Notification configuration window is displayed. Here you can add new mail accounts to check, such as Gmail accounts, as well as set other features like summary pop-ups. When you receive mail, a mail icon will appear in the notification applet of your panel. Move your cursor over it to check for any new mail. Clicking it will display the Mail Notification configuration window, though you can configure this to go directly to your e-mail application. gnubiff will notify you of any POP3 or IMAP mail arrivals.

The KDE Desktop has a mail monitor utility called Korn that works in much the same way. Korn shows an empty inbox tray when there is no mail and a tray with slanted letters in it when mail arrives. If old mail is still in your mailbox, letters are displayed in a neat square. You can set these icons as any image you want. You can also specify the mail client to use and the polling interval for checking for new mail. If you have several mail accounts, you can set up a Korn profile for each one. Different icons can appear for each account, telling you when mail arrives in one of them.

For command line interfaces, you can use the biff utility. The biff utility notifies you immediately when a message is received. This is helpful when you are expecting a message and want to know as soon as it arrives. Then biff automatically displays the header and beginning lines of messages as they are received. To turn on biff, you enter **biff y** on the command line. To turn it off, you enter **biff n**. To find out if biff is turned on, enter **biff** alone.

You can temporarily block biff by using the **mesg n** command to prevent any message displays on your screen. The **mesg n** command not only stops any Write and Talk messages, it also stops biff and Notify messages. Later, you can unblock biff with a **mesg y** command. A **mesg n** command comes in handy if you don't want to be disturbed while working on some project.

Accessing Mail on Remote POP Mail Servers

Most newer mail clients are equipped to access mail accounts on remote servers. For such mail clients, you can specify a separate mail account with its own mailbox. For example, if you are using an ISP, most likely you will use that ISP's mail server to receive mail. You will have set up a mail account with a username and password for accessing your mail. Your e-mail address is usually your username and the ISP's domain name. For example, a username of **justin** for an ISP domain named **mynet.com** would have the address **justin@mynet.com**. The address of the actual mail server could be something like **mail.mynet.com**. The user **justin** would log in to the **mail.mynet.com** server using his username and password to access mail sent to the address **justin@mynet.com**. Mail clients, such as Evolution, KMail, Balsa, and Thunderbird, enable you to set up a mailbox for such an account and access your ISP's mail server to check for and download received mail. You must specify what protocol a mail server uses. This is usually either the Post Office Protocol (POP) or the IMAP protocol (IMAP). This procedure is used for any remote mail server. Using a mail server address, you can access your account with your username and password.

Should you have several remote e-mail accounts, instead of creating separate mailboxes for each in a mail client, you can arrange to have mail from those accounts sent directly to the inbox maintained by your Linux system for your Linux account. All your mail, whether from other users on your Linux system or from remote mail accounts, will appear in your local inbox. Such a feature is helpful if you are using a mail client, such as Mail, that does not have the capability to access mail on your ISP's mail server. You can implement this feature with Fetchmail. Fetchmail checks for mail on remote mail servers and downloads it to your local inbox, where it appears as newly received mail (you will have to be connected to the Internet or the remote mail server's network).

To use Fetchmail, you have to know a remote mail server's Internet address and mail protocol. Most remote mail servers use the POP3 protocol, but others may use the IMAP or POP2 protocols. Enter **fetchmail** on the command line with the mail server address and any needed options. The mail protocol is indicated with the **-p** option and the mail server type, usually POP3. If your e-mail username is different from your Linux login name, you use the **-u** option and the e-mail name. Once you execute the **fetchmail** command, you are prompted for a password. The syntax for the **fetchmail** command for a POP3 mail server follows:

```
fetchmail -p POP3 -u username mail-server
```

To use Fetchmail, connect to your ISP and then enter the **fetchmail** command with the options and the POP server name on the command line. You will see messages telling you if mail is there and, if so, how many messages are being downloaded. You can then use a mail client to read the messages from your inbox. You can run Fetchmail in daemon mode to have it automatically check for mail. You have to include an option specifying the interval in seconds for checking mail.

```
fetchmail -d 1200
```

You can specify options such as the server type, username, and password in a **.fetchmailrc** file in your home directory. You can also have entries for other mail servers and accounts you may have. Once it is configured, you can enter **fetchmail** with no arguments and it will read the entries from your **.fetchmailrc** file. You can also make entries directly in the **.fetchmailrc** file. An entry in the **.fetchmailrc** file for a particular mail account consists of several fields and their values: poll, protocol, username, and password. *Poll* is used to specify the mail server name, and *protocol,* the type of protocol used. Notice you can also specify your password, instead of having to enter it each time Fetchmail accesses the mail server.

Mailing Lists

As an alternative to newsgroups, you can subscribe to mailing lists. Users on mailing lists automatically receive messages and articles sent to the lists. Mailing lists work much like a mail alias, broadcasting messages to all users on the list. Mailing lists were designed to serve small, specialized groups of people. Instead of posting articles for anyone to see, only those who subscribe receive them. Numerous mailing lists are available for Linux as well as other subjects. For example, at the **www.gnome.org** site, you can subscribe to any of several mailing lists on GNOME topics, such as **gnome-themes-list@gnome.org**, which deals with GNOME desktop themes. You can do the same at **lists.kde.org** for KDE topics. At **www .liszt.com**, you can search for mailing lists on various topics. By convention, to subscribe to a list, you send a request to the mailing list address with a **–request** term added to its username. For example, to subscribe to **gnome-themes-list@gnome.org**, you send a request to **gnome-themes-list-request@gnome.org**. At **www.linux.org**, you can link to sites that support Linux-oriented mailing lists, such as the Red Hat mailing lists page and the Linux Mailing Lists Web site. Lists exist for such topics as the Linux kernel, administration, security, and different distributions. For example, **linux-admin** covers administration topics, and **linux-apps** discusses software applications; **vger.kernel.org** provides mailing list services for Linux kernel developers.

NOTE   *You can use the Mailman and Majordomo programs to automatically manage your mailing lists. Mailman is the GNU mailing list manager included with Fedora (**www.list.org**). You can find out more about Majordomo at **www.greatcircle.com/majordomo**, and about Mailman at **sourceforge.net**.*

Usenet News

Usenet is an open mail system on which users post messages that include news, discussions, and opinions. It operates like a mailbox that any user on your Linux system can read or send messages to. Users' messages are incorporated into Usenet files, which are distributed to any system signed up to receive them. Each system that receives Usenet files is referred to as a *site*. Certain sites perform organizational and distribution operations for Usenet, receiving messages from other sites and organizing them into Usenet files, which are then broadcast to many other sites. Such sites are called *backbone sites*, and they operate like publishers, receiving articles and organizing them into different groups.

To access Usenet news, you need access to a news server. A news server receives the daily Usenet newsfeeds and makes them accessible to other systems. Your network may have a system that operates as a news server. If you are using an Internet service provider (ISP), a news server is probably maintained by your ISP for your use. To read Usenet articles, you use a *newsreader*—a client program that connects to a news server and accesses the articles. On the Internet and in TCP/IP networks, news servers communicate with newsreaders using the Network News Transfer Protocol (NNTP) and are often referred to as NNTP news servers. Or you could also create your own news server on your Linux system to run a local Usenet news service or to download and maintain the full set of Usenet articles. Several Linux programs, called *news transport agents*, can be used to create such a server. This chapter focuses on the variety of newsreaders available for the Linux platform. The configuration administration and architecture of the NNTP server are covered in Chapter 26.

Usenet files were originally designed to function like journals. Messages contained in the files are referred to as *articles*. A user could write an article, post it in Usenet, and have it immediately distributed to other systems around the world. Someone could then read the article on Usenet, instead of waiting for a journal publication. Usenet files themselves were organized as journal publications. Because journals are designed to address specific groups, Usenet files were organized according to groups called *newsgroups*. When a user posts an article, it is assigned to a specific newsgroup. If another user wants to read that article, he or she looks at the articles in that newsgroup. You can think of each newsgroup as a constantly updated magazine. For example, to read articles on the Linux operating system, you would access the Usenet newsgroup on Linux. Usenet files are also used as bulletin boards on which people carry on debates. Again, such files are classified into newsgroups, though their articles read more like conversations than journal articles. You can also create articles of your own, which you can then add to a newsgroup for others to read. Adding an article to a newsgroup is called *posting* the article.

NOTE *The Google Web site maintains online access to Usenet newsgroups. It has the added capability of letting you search extensive newsgroup archives. You can easily locate articles on similar topics that may reside in different newsgroups. Other sites such as Yahoo maintain their own groups that operate much like Usenet newsgroups, but with more supervision.*

Linux has newsgroups on various topics. Some are for discussion, and others are sources of information about recent developments. On some, you can ask for help for specific problems. A selection of some of the popular Linux newsgroups is provided here:

Newsgroup	Topic
comp.os.linux.announce	Announcements of Linux developments
comp.os.linux.admin	System administration questions
comp.os.linux.misc	Special questions and issues
comp.os.linux.setup	Installation problems
comp.os.linux.help	Questions and answers for particular problems
linux.help	Obtain help for Linux problems

Newsreaders

You read Usenet articles with a newsreader, such as KNode, Pan, Mozilla, trn, or tin, which enables you to first select a specific newsgroup and then read the articles in it. A newsreader operates like a user interface, enabling you to browse through and select available articles for reading, saving, or printing. Most newsreaders employ a sophisticated retrieval feature called *threads* that pulls together articles on the same discussion or topic. Newsreaders are designed to operate using certain kinds of interfaces. For example, KNode is a KDE newsreader that has a KDE interface and is designed for the KDE desktop. Pan has a GNOME interface and is designed to operate on the GNOME desktop. Pine is a cursor-based newsreader, meaning that it provides a full-screen interface that you can work with using a simple screen-based cursor that you can move with arrow keys. It does not support a mouse or any other GUI feature. The tin program uses a simple command line interface with limited cursor support. Most commands you type in and press ENTER to execute. Several popular newsreaders are listed in Table 13-3.

NOTE *Numerous newsreaders currently are under development for both GNOME and KDE. You can check for KDE newsreaders on the software list on the K Desktop Web site at **www.kde-apps.org**. For GNOME newsreaders, check Internet tools on the software map on the GNOME Web site at **www.gnome-files.org**.*

Newsreader	Description
Pan	GNOME Desktop newsreader
KNode	KDE Desktop newsreader
Thunderbird	Mail client with newsreader capabilities (X-based)
Sylpheed	GNOME Windows-like newsreader
Slrn	Newsreader (cursor-based)
Emacs	Emacs editor, mail client, and newsreader (cursor-based)
trn	Newsreader (command line interface)
NewsBin	Newsreader (Windows version works under Wine)

TABLE 13-3   Linux Newsreaders

Most newsreaders can read Usenet news provided on remote news servers that use the NNTP. Many such remote news servers are available through the Internet. Desktop newsreaders, such as KNode and Pan, have you specify the Internet address for the remote news server in their own configuration settings. Several shell-based newsreaders, however, such as trn and tin, obtain the news server's Internet address from the **NNTPSERVER** shell variable. Before you can connect to a remote news server with such newsreaders, you first have to assign the Internet address of the news server to the **NNTPSERVER** shell variable, and then export that variable. You can place the assignment and export of **NNTPSERVER** in a login initialization file, such as **.bash_profile**, so that it is performed automatically whenever you log in. Administrators could place this entry in the **/etc/profile** file for a news server available to all users on the system.

```
$ NNTPSERVER=news.domain.com
$ export NNTPSERVER
```

The slrn newsreader is screen-based. Commands are displayed across the top of the screen and can be executed using the listed keys. Different types of screens exist for the newsgroup list, article list, and article content, each with its own set of commands. An initial screen lists your subscribed newsgroups with commands for posting, listing, and subscribing to your newsgroups. When you start slrn for the first time, you will have to create a **.jnewsrc** file in your home directory. Use the following command: `slrn -f .jnewsrc -create`. Also, you will have to set the **NNTPSERVER** variable and make sure it is exported.

The slrn newsreader features a new utility called slrnpull that you can use to automatically download articles in specified newsgroups. This allows you to view your selected newsgroups offline. The slrnpull utility was designed as a simple single-user version of Leafnode; it will access a news server and download its designated newsgroups, making them available through slrn whenever the user chooses to examine them. Newsgroup articles are downloaded to the **SLRNPULL_ROOT** directory. On Fedora, this is **/var/spool/srlnpull**. The selected newsgroups to be downloaded are entered in the **slrnpull.conf** configuration file placed in the **SLRNPULL_ROOT** directory. In this file, you can specify how many articles to download for each group and when they should expire. To use **slrn** with slrnpull, you will have to further configure the **.slrnrc** file to reference the slrnpull directories where newsgroup files are kept.

NOTE *Several Windows-based newsreaders, like the popular Newsbin, will run under Linux, using the Wine Windows emulation on Fedora. You can download and install Wine using Pirut (Add/Remove Applications). To get the newsreader working you will have to follow configuration directions, often requiring specific Windows DLLs. For Newsbin, check the Newsbin forum for Linux. Be sure to add DLLs to your* **.wine/drive_c/Windows/System32** *directory. Also, for 64 bit Fedora Linux systems you will need to use the DLLs from a "Windows XP x64" system.*

News Transport Agents

Usenet news is provided over the Internet as a daily newsfeed of articles and postings for thousands of newsgroups. This newsfeed is sent to sites that can then provide access to the news for other systems through newsreaders. These sites operate as news servers; the newsreaders used to access them are their clients. The news server software, called *news transport agents,* is what provides newsreaders with news, enabling you to read newsgroups and post articles. For Linux, three of the popular news transport agents are INN, Leafnode, and Cnews. Both Cnews and Leafnode are small, simple, and useful for small networks. INN is more powerful and complex, designed with large systems in mind (see **www.isc.org** for more details).

Daily newsfeeds on Usenet are often large and consume much of a news server's resources in both time and memory. For this reason, you may not want to set up your own Linux system to receive such newsfeeds. If you are operating in a network of Linux systems, you can designate one of them as the news server and install the news transport agent on it to receive and manage the Usenet newsfeeds. Users on other systems on your network can then access that news server with their own newsreaders.

If your network already has a news server, you needn't install a news transport agent at all. You only have to use your newsreaders to remotely access that server (see **NNTPSERVER** in the preceding section). In the case of an ISP, such providers often operate their own news servers, which you can also remotely access using your own newsreaders, such as KNode and Pan. Remember, though, that newsreaders must take the time to download the articles for selected newsgroups, as well as updated information on all the newsgroups.

You can also use news transport agents to run local versions of news for only the users on your system or your local network. To do this, install INN, Leafnode, slrnpull, or Cnews and configure them just to manage local newsgroups. Users on your system could then post articles and read local news.

Web, FTP, and Java Clients

Most Linux distributions will provide powerful Web and FTP clients for accessing the Internet. Many are installed automatically and are ready to use when you first start up your Linux system. Linux also includes full Java development support, letting you run and construct Java applets. This chapter will cover some of the more popular Web, Java, and FTP clients available on Linux. Web and FTP clients connect to sites that run servers, using Web pages and FTP files to provide services to users.

Web Clients

The World Wide Web (WWW, or the Web) is a hypertext database of different types of information, distributed across many different sites on the Internet. A *hypertext database* consists of items linked to other items, which, in turn, may be linked to yet other items, and so on. Upon retrieving an item, you can use that item to retrieve any related items. For example, you could retrieve an article on the Amazon rain forest and then use it to retrieve a map or a picture of the rain forest. In this respect, a hypertext database is like a web of interconnected data you can trace from one data item to another. Information is displayed in pages known as *Web pages.* On a Web page, certain keywords or graphics are highlighted that form links to other Web pages or to items, such as pictures, articles, or files.

On your Linux system, you can choose from several Web browsers, including Firefox, Konqueror, Epiphany, and Lynx. Firefox, Konqueror, and Epiphany are X Window System–based browsers that provide full picture, sound, and video display capabilities. Most distributions also include the Lynx browser, a line-mode browser that displays only lines of text. The K Desktop incorporates Web browser capabilities into its file manager, letting a directory window operate as a Web browser. GNOME-based browsers, such as Express and Mnemonic, are also designed to be easily enhanced.

Web browsers and FTP clients are commonly used to conduct secure transactions such as logging in to remote sites, ordering items, or transferring files. Such operations are currently secured by encryption methods provided by the Secure Sockets Layer (SSL). See Chapters 19 and 23 for more information about SSL and its counterpart, SSH, the Secure Shell. If you use a browser for secure transactions, it should be SSL enabled. Most browsers such as Mozilla and ELinks include SSL support. For FTP operations, you can use the SSH version of ftp, sftp, or the Kerberos 5 version (see Chapter 19). Linux distributions include SSL as part of a standard installation.

URL Addresses

An Internet resource is accessed using a Universal Resource Locator (URL). A URL is composed of three elements: the transfer protocol, the hostname, and the pathname. The transfer protocol and the hostname are separated by a colon and two slashes, **://**. The *pathname* always begins with a single slash:

```
transfer-protocol://host-name/path-name
```

The *transfer protocol* is usually HTTP (Hypertext Transfer Protocol), indicating a Web page. Other possible values for transfer protocols are **ftp**, and **file**. As their names suggest, **ftp** initiates FTP sessions, whereas **file** displays a local file on your own system, such as a text or HTML file. Table 14-1 lists the various transfer protocols.

The *hostname* is the computer on which a particular Web site is located. You can think of this as the address of the Web site. By convention, most hostnames begin with www. In the next example, the URL locates a Web page called **guides.html** on the **tldp.org** Web site:

```
http://tldp.org/guides.html
```

If you do not want to access a particular Web page, you can leave the file reference out, and then you automatically access the Web site's home page. To access a Web site directly, use its hostname. If no home page is specified for a Web site, the file **index.html** in the top directory is often used as the home page. In the next example, the user brings up the Red Hat home page:

```
http://www.redhat.com/
```

The pathname specifies the directory where the resource can be found on the host system, as well as the name of the resource's file. For example, **/pub/Linux/newdat.html** references an HTML document called **newdat** located in the **/pub/Linux** directory.

The resource file's extension indicates the type of action to be taken on it. A picture has a **.gif** or **.jpeg** extension and is converted for display. A sound file has an **.au** or **.wav** extension and is played. The following URL references a **.gif** file. Instead of displaying a Web page, your browser invokes a graphics viewer to display the picture. Table 14-2 provides a list of the more common file extensions.

```
http://www.train.com/engine/engine1.gif
```

Protocol	Description
http	Uses Hypertext Transfer Protocol for Web site access.
ftp	Uses File Transfer Protocol for anonymous FTP connections.
telnet	Makes a Telnet connection.
news	Reads Usenet news; uses Network News Transfer Protocol (NNTP).

TABLE 14-1 Web Protocols

File Type	Description
.html	Web page document formatted using HTML, the Hypertext Markup Language
Graphics Files	**Description**
.gif	Graphics, using GIF compression
.jpeg	Graphics, using JPEG compression
.png	Graphics, using PNG compression (Portable Network Graphics)
Sound Files	**Description**
.au	Sun (Unix) sound file
.wav	Microsoft Windows sound file
.aiff	Macintosh sound file
Video Files	**Description**
.QT	QuickTime video file, multiplatform
.mpeg	Video file
.avi	Microsoft Windows video file

TABLE 14-2   Web File Types

Web Browsers

Most Web browsers are designed to access several different kinds of information. Web browsers can access a Web page on a remote Web site or a file on your own system. Some browsers can also access a remote news server or an FTP site. The type of information for a site is specified by the keyword **http** for Web sites, **nntp** for news servers, **ftp** for FTP sites, or **file** for files on your own system. As noted previously, several popular browsers are available for Linux. Three distinctive ones are described here: Mozilla, Konqueror, and Lynx. Mozilla is an X Window System–based Web browser capable of displaying graphics, video, and sound, as well as operating as a newsreader and mailer. Konqueror is the K Desktop file manager. KDE has integrated full Web-browsing capability into the Konqueror file manager, letting you seamlessly access the Web and your file system with the same application. Lynx and ELinks are command line–based browsers with no graphics capabilities, but in every other respect they are fully functional Web browsers.

To search for files on FTP sites, you can use search engines provided by Web sites, such as Yahoo!, Google, or Lycos. These usually search for both Web pages and FTP files. To find a particular Web page you want on the Internet, you can use any of these search engines or perform searches from any number of Web portals. Web searches have become a standard service of most Web sites. Searches carried out on documents within a Web site may use local search indexes set up and maintained by indexing programs like ht:/Dig. Sites using ht:/Dig use a standard Web page search interface. Hypertext databases are designed to access any kind of data, whether it is text, graphics, sound, or even video. Whether you can actually access such data depends to a large extent on the type of browser you use.

The Mozilla Framework

The Mozilla project is an open source project based on the original Netscape browser code that provides a development framework for Web-based applications, primarily the Web browser and e-mail client. Originally, the aim of the Mozilla project was to provide an end-user Web browser called Mozilla. Its purpose has since changed to providing a development framework that anyone can use to create Web applications, though the project also provides its own browser. Table 14-3 lists some Mozilla resources.

Currently the development framework is used for Mozilla products like the Firefox Web browser and the Thunderbird mail client, as well for non-Mozilla products like the Netscape, Epiphany, and Galeon Web browsers. In addition, the framework is easily extensible, supporting numerous add-ons in the form of plug-ins and extensions. The Mozilla project site is **www.mozilla.org**, and the site commonly used for plug-in and extension development is **www.mozdev.org**.

The first-generation product of the Mozilla project was the Mozilla Web browser, which is still available. Like the original Netscape, it included a mail client and newsreader, all in one integrated interface. The second generation products have split this integrated package into separate stand-alone applications, the Firefox Web browser and the Thunderbird e-mail/newsreader client. Also under development is the Camino Web browser for Mac OS X and the Sunbird calendar application.

In 1998, Netscape made its source code freely available under the Netscape Public License (NPL). Mozilla is developed on an open source model much like Linux, KDE, and GNOME. Developers can submit modifications and additions over the Internet to the Mozilla Web site. Mozilla releases are referred to as Milestones. Mozilla products are currently released under both the NPL license for modifications of mozilla code and the MPL license (Mozilla Public License) for new additions.

The Firefox Web Browser

Firefox is the next generation of browsers based on the Netscape core source code known as mozilla. In current releases, Red Hat and Fedora use Firefox as its primary browser, in place of Netscape. Firefox is a streamlined browser featuring fast Web access and secure protection from invasive spyware.

Firefox is an X Window System application you can operate from any desktop, including GNOME, KDE, and XFce. On Red Hat Fedora, Firefox is installed by default with both a menu entry in the Main menu's Internet menu and an icon on the different desktop panels.

Web Site	Description
www.mozilla.org	The Mozilla project
www.mozdev.org	Mozilla plug-ins and extensions
www.oreillynet.com/mozilla	Mozilla documentation and news
www.mozillazine.org	Mozilla news and articles
www.mozillanews.org	Mozilla news and articles
www.bugzilla.org	Mozilla bug reporting and tracking system

TABLE 14-3 Mozilla Resources

When opened, Firefox displays an area at the top of the screen for entering a URL address and a series of buttons for various Web page operations like page navigation. Drop-down menus on the top menu bar provide access to such Firefox features as Tools, View, and Bookmarks.

To the right of the URL box is a search box where you can use different search engines for searching the Web, selected sites, or particular items. A pop-up menu lets you select a search engine. Currently included are Google, Yahoo, Amazon, and eBay, along with Dictionary.com for looking up word definitions. Firefox also features button links and tabbed pages. You can drag the URL from the URL box to the button link bar to create a button with which to quickly access the site. Use this for frequently accessed sites.

For easy browsing, Firefox features tabbed panels for displaying Web pages. To open an empty tabbed panel, press CTRL-T or select New Tab from the File menu. To display a page in that panel, drag its URL from the URL box or from the bookmark list to the panel. You can have several panels open at once, moving from one page to the next by clicking their tabs. You can elect to open all your link buttons as tabbed panels by right-clicking the link bar and selecting Open In Tabs.

Firefox refers to the URLs of Web pages you want to keep as *bookmarks,* marking pages you want to access directly. The Bookmarks menu enables you to add your favorite Web pages. You can then view your bookmarks and select one to view. You can also edit your list of bookmarks, adding new ones or removing old ones. History is a list of previous URLs you have accessed. The URL box also features a pop-up menu listing your previous history sites. Bookmarks and History can be viewed as sidebars, selectable from the View menu.

When you download a file using Firefox, the download is managed by the Download Manager. You can download several files at once. Progress can be displayed in the Download Manager window, accessible from the Tools menu. You can cancel a download at any time, or just pause a download, resuming it later. Right-clicking a download entry will display the site it was downloaded from, as well as the directory you saved it in. To remove an entry, click Remove. To clear out the entire list, click Clean Up.

The Preferences menu (Edit | Preferences) in Firefox enables you to set several different options. Firefox also supports such advanced features as cookie, form, image, and password management. You can elect to suppress cookies from sites, automatically fill in forms, not display site images, and set up login information such as usernames and passwords for selected sites. You can set preferences for general features, privacy, Web, and download management, as well as advanced features. In General preferences, you can determine your home page, page fonts, and colors, as well as connection settings such as proxy information. For Privacy you can control information saved (such as the number of history sites to remember and the download history), set policy for saving cookies, and set the size of your cache. All of these you can manually clear. Under Web Features you can control pop-ups, allow software installs, and enable JavaScript. The Download Manager panel lets you configure your downloading operations, letting you specify a default download directory, whether to automatically prompt for one, and what plug-ins you may want run automatically on certain kinds of files, such as Adobe Acrobat for Adobe PDF files. The Advanced panel lets you control more complex features of browsing such as scrolling, security levels, and certificate management.

If you are on a network that connects to the Internet through a firewall, you must use the Proxies screen to enter the address of your network's firewall gateway computer. A *firewall* is a computer that operates as a controlled gateway to the Internet for your network. Several types of firewalls exist. One of the most restrictive uses programs called *proxies,* which receive Internet requests from users and then make those requests on their behalf. There is no direct connection to the Internet.

NOTE *The Privoxy Web proxy filters Web content to protect user privacy, intercepting unwanted advertising or blocking invasive cookies. Privoxy will execute rules listed in its action files, such as action.default, located in the /etc/privoxy directory. You can start Privoxy with the Services tool or the **service** command. To have your browser use Privoxy, configure it to use the host running Privoxy as a proxy.*

The K Desktop File Manager: Konqueror

If you are using the K Desktop, you can use a file manager window as a Web browser. The K Desktop's file manager is automatically configured to act as a Web browser. It can display Web pages, including graphics and links. The K Desktop's file manager supports standard Web page operation, such as moving forward and backward through accessed pages. Clicking a link accesses and displays the Web page referenced. In this respect, the Web becomes seamlessly integrated into the K Desktop.

GNOME Web Browsers: Galeon and Epiphany

Several other GNOME-based Web browsers are also available. Epiphany, Galeon, and Kazehakase support standard Web operations. Epiphany is a GNOME Web browser designed to be fast with a simple interface. You can find out more about Epiphany at **epiphany.mozdev.org**. Epiphany is included with Red Hat and Fedora. Epiphany works well as a simple browser with a clean interface. It is also integrated with the desktop, featuring a download applet that will continue even after closing Epiphany. Epiphany also support tabbed panels for multiple Web site access. Galeon is a fast, light browser also based on the Mozilla browser engine (Gecko). Kazehakase emphasizes a customizable interface with download boxes and RSS bookmarks.

For GNOME, you can also download numerous support tools, such as the RSSOwl to display news feeds and the GNOME Download Manager (Gwget) for controlling Web-based downloads. The Downloader for X client is useful for both FTP and Web file downloads. It has numerous features, letting you control download speeds, as well as downloading subdirectories. Though it is not part of the Red Hat Fedora distribution, you can download it from **rpmfind.net**.

NOTE *Epiphany and Galeon can both be downloaded with Add/Remove Software's Graphical Internet Browse panel.*

Lynx and ELinks: Line-Mode Browsers

Lynx is a line-mode browser you can use without the X Window System. A Web page is displayed as text only. A text page can contain links to other Internet resources but does not display any graphics, video, or sound. Except for the display limitations, Lynx is a fully functional Web browser. You can use Lynx to download files or to make Telnet connections. All information on the Web is still accessible to you. Because it does not require much of the overhead that graphics-based browsers need, Lynx can operate much faster, quickly displaying Web page text. To start the Lynx browser, you enter **lynx** on the command line and press ENTER.

Another useful text-based browser shipped with most distributions is ELinks. ELinks is a powerful screen-based browser that includes features such as frame, form, and table support. It also supports SSL secure encryption. To start ELinks, enter the **elinks** command in a terminal window.

Creating Your Own Web Site

To create your own Web site, you need access to a Web server. Red Hat automatically installs the Apache Web server on its Linux systems. You can also rent Web page space on a remote server—a service many ISPs provide, some for free. On Red Hat systems, the directory set up by your Apache Web server for your Web site pages is **/var/httpd/html**. Other servers provide you with a directory for your home page. Place the Web pages you create in that directory. You place your home page here. You can make other subdirectories with their own Web pages to which these can link. Web pages are not difficult to create. Links from one page to another move users through your Web site. You can even create links to Web pages or resources on other sites. Many excellent texts are available on Web page creation and management.

Web pages are created using either HTML, the Hypertext Markup Language, or the newer extended version, XML, the Extended Markup Language. They are a subset of Standard Generalized Markup Language (SGML). Creating an HTML or XML document is a matter of inserting HTML or XML tags in a text file. In this respect, creating a Web page is as simple as using a tag-based word processor. You use the HTML tags to format text for display as a Web page. XML tags can include more detailed information about a particular connection such as object data or transaction characteristics. The Web page itself is a text file you can create using any text editor, such as Vi. If you are familiar with tag-based word processing on Unix systems, you will find it conceptually similar to nroff. Some HTML tags indicate headings, lists, and paragraphs, as well as links to reference Web resources.

Instead of manually entering HTML or XML code, you can use Web page composers. A Web page composer provides a graphical interface for constructing Web pages. Special Web page creation programs can easily help you create complex Web pages without ever having to type any HTML tags explicitly. Remember, though, no matter what tool you use to create your Web page, the Web page itself will be an HTML document. As part of the KDE project, KDE Web Dev (**www.kdewebdev.org**) provides several Web development applications, like the Quanta Plus Web editor and the Kommander dialog builder.

NOTE *Many of the standard editors for the K Desktop and GNOME include Web page construction features. Many enable you to insert links or format headings. For example, the KEdit program supports basic text-based Web page components. You can add headings, links, or lines, but not graphics.*

Java for Linux

To develop Java applications, use Java tools, and run many Java products, you must install the Java 2 Software Development Kit (SDK) and the Java 2 Runtime Environment (JRE) on your system. Together, they make up the Java 2 Platform, Standard Edition (J2SE). Sun currently supports and distributes Linux versions of these products. You can download them from Sun at **java.sun.com/j2se** and install them on your system. Java packages and applications are listed in Table 14-4.

jpackage, Sun, and Java-like (java-gcj-compat)

Fedora includes numerous free Java applications and support, like Jakarta. Check the fedoraproject.org/wiki/JavaFAQ for information on how Java is implemented on Fedora. You should use the Fedora versions of Java packages, as they have been specially modified for use on Fedora. However, the main Java Runtime Environment and SDK are not included. Instead you either use an included compatible set of GNU packages (Java-like) that allow you to run Java applets, install the JRE and SDK from JPackage, or download and install the original JRE and SDK from Sun. None of these options are exclusive.

Fedora now includes a Java-like collection of support packages that enable the use of Java Runtime operations. There is no official name for this collection, though it is referred to as java-gci-compat, as well as Java-like. This collection provides a free and open source environment included with Fedora, consisting of three packages: GNU Java runtime (libgcj), the Eclipse Java compiler (ecj), and a set of wrappers and links (java-gcj-compat).

Application	Description
Java 2 Software Development Kit (SDK)	A Java development environment with a compiler, interpreters, debugger, and more, **java.sun.com/j2se**. SDK is part of the Java 2 platform. Download the Linux port from JPackage or directly from Sun.
Java 2 Runtime Environment 1.4 (J2RE)	A Java Runtime Environment used to run Java applets. Download the Linux port from **.java.com** or **jpackage.org**.
Java 3D for Linux	Sun's 3-D Application Program Interface for 3-D Java programs.
Java-like environment	The Java-like Free and Open Environment, consisting of the GNU Java runtime (libgcj), the Eclipse Java compiler (ecj), and supporting wrappers and links (java-gcj-compat). Included with Fedora (**fedoraproject.org/wiki/JavaFAQ**).
Java Advanced Imaging (JAI) for Linux	Java Advanced Imaging API.
Java 1.1 Development Kit (JDK) and Java 1.1 Runtime Environment (JRE) for Linux	The older Java 1.1 development environment with a compiler, interpreters, debugger, and more. Download the Linux port for your distribution's update through **jpackage.org**.
Java System Web Server	A Web server implemented with Java. Available at Java Web site at **java.sun.com** (commercial).
GNU Java Compiler	GNU Public Licensed Java Compiler (GJC) to compile Java programs, **gcc.gnu.org/java**. Included with Fedora (libgjc).
Jakarta Project	Apache Software Foundation project for open source Java applications, **jakarta.apache.org**.

TABLE 14-4 Java Packages and Java Web Applications

Fedora recommends that you download additional Java and Java applications from JPackage, which designs its Java packages so that they do not conflict and are compatible with the specified Linux release. With JPackage versions of Java you can safely install and uninstall the numerous Java applications and support tools. The best way to use JPackage is to download its Yum repository configuration file. Be sure to select the one for the appropriate Fedora distribution (when available). Unfortunately, due to licensing restrictions, JPackage has to charge for the main JRE as well as the SDK Java application. These are included in their Java package. Alternatively, you can download and install the JRE or JDK directly from Sun for free. Should you install alternative Java environments from JPackage, you can switch between them with the **alternatives** command.

NOTE   *Check fedoraproject.org/wiki/JavaFAQ possible compatibility issues.*

Installing the Java Runtime Environment: JRE

Many Web sites will run applications that require the Java Runtime Environment (JRE). Fedora does not come with the Java Runtime Environment already installed. But Java-like already supports compatible applications like Office.org and Eclipse. For Sun's Java, you will have to download and install the JRE on your Linux system. You can obtain a copy from either the Sun Java site (**www.java.com**) or JPackage. The SDK and JRE are available in the form of self-extracting compressed archives, with a **.bin** extension. These files are actually shell scripts with an embedded compressed archive. (Separate install instructions are available.) Because of filename conflicts, you should not use the Sun RPM package (.bin.rpm). Instead you should download the **.bin** package and extract it in the **/opt** directory. Alternatively, you can use the RPM package from JPackage. You will have to make the self-extracting bin file executable with the **chmod** command. The following command will change the JRE file, **jre-1_5_0_02-linux-i586-rpm.bin**, to an executable. You will be prompted first to accept the license agreement.

```
chmod a+x jre-1_5_0_02-linux-i586-rpm.bin
./ jre-1_5_0_02-linux-i586-rpm.bin
```

The JRE would be installed in the **/opt** directory, in this case under **/opt/jre1.5.0_02**.

Enabling the Java Runtime Environment for Mozilla/Firefox

To allow either the Mozilla or the Firefox Web browser to use the JRE, you need to create a link from the Mozilla plug-in directory to the Java plug-in libraries. Be sure you have first installed the JRE. Within the **/usr/lib/mozilla/plugins** directory, you will have to create a link to the **libjavaplugin_oji.so** library in the JRE's **/plugin/i386/ns7** subdirectory, where "ns7" indicates Netscape 7.

```
# cd /usr/lib/mozilla/plugins
# ln -s /opt/jre1.5.0_06/plugin/i386/ns7/libjavaplugin_oji.so libjavaplugin_oji.so
```

NOTE   *On Firefox and Mozilla, be sure Java support is enabled.*

The Java Applications

Numerous additional Java-based products and tools are currently adaptable for Linux. Tools include Java 3D, Java Media Framework (JMF), and Java Advanced Imaging (JAI). Many of the products, such as the Java Web server, run directly as provided by Sun. You can download several applications directly from the Sun Java Web site at **java.sun.com**. The Jakarta project (**jakarta.apache.org**), part of the Apache Software Foundation, provides open source Java tools and applications, including libraries, server applications, and engines. Jakarta along with other packages are included with Fedora. These are derived from the JPackage Project at **jpackage.org**, which also includes some packages that are not in Fedora, which you can download and install. JPackage is a Fedora Yum–supported repository.

The Java 2 Software Development Kit

The Java Software Development Kit (SDK) provides tools for creating and debugging your own Java applets and provides support for Java applications. The kit includes demonstration applets with source code. You can obtain detailed documentation about the SDK from the Sun Web site at **java.sun.com**. Four major releases of the SDK are currently available—1.2, 1.3, 1.4.*x*, and 1.5 (also known as 5.0)—with corresponding versions for the Java 2 Runtime Environment (J2RE) for 1.2, 1.3, 1.4, and 1.5 (5.0). The Java SDK adds capabilities for security, GUI support with JFC (also know as Swing), and running Java enhancements, such as Java 3D and Java Sound.

The SDK includes standard features found in the JDK features for internationalization, signed applets, the JAR file format, AWT (window toolkit) enhancements, the JavaBeans component model, networking enhancements, a math package for large numbers, database connectivity (JDBC), object serialization, and inner classes. Java applications include a Java compiler (javac), a Java debugger (jdb), and an applet viewer (appletviewer). Detailed descriptions of these features can be found in the SDK documentation, **java.sun.com/docs**.

You create a Java applet much as you would create a program using a standard programming language. You first use a text editor to create the source code, which is saved in a file with a **.java** extension. Then you can use the **javac** compiler to compile the source code file, generating a Java applet. Numerous integrated development environment (IDE) applications are available for composing Java applets and applications. Although most are commercial, some provide free shareware versions. An IDE provides a GUI interface for constructing Java applets. Eclipse, included with Fedora, can operate as a development platform for Java applets.

FTP Clients

With FTP clients, you can connect to a corresponding FTP site and download files from it. FTP clients are commonly used to download software from public FTP sites that operate as software repositories. Most Linux software applications can be downloaded to your Linux system from such sites. These sites feature anonymous logins that let any user access their files. A distribution site like **ftp.redhat.com** is an example of one such FTP site, holding an extensive set of packaged Linux applications you can download using an FTP client and then easily install on your system. Basic FTP client capabilities are incorporated into the Konqueror (KDE) and Nautilus (GNOME) file managers. You can use a file manager window to access an FTP site and drag files to local directories to download them. Effective FTP clients are also now incorporated into most Web browsers, making Web browsers a primary downloading tool. Firefox in particular has strong FTP download capabilities.

Though file managers and Web browsers provide effective access to public (anonymous login) sites, to access private sites, you may need a stand-alone FTP client like curl, wget, gFTP or ftp. These clients let you enter user names and passwords with which you can access a private FTP site. The stand-alone clients are also useful for large downloads from public FTP sites, especially those with little or no Web display support. Popular Linux FTP clients are listed in Table 14-5.

Network File Transfer: FTP

With File Transfer Protocol (FTP) clients you can transfer extremely large files directly from one site to another. FTP can handle both text and binary files. This is one of the TCP/IP protocols, and it operates on systems connected to networks that use the TCP/IP protocols, such as the Internet. FTP performs a remote login to another account on another system connected to you on a network. Once logged in to that other system, you can transfer files to and from it. To log in, you need to know the login name and password for the account on the remote system. For example, if you have accounts at two different sites on the Internet, you can use FTP to transfer files from one to the other. Many sites on the Internet allow public access using FTP, however. Such sites serve as depositories for large files anyone can access and download. These sites are often referred to as *FTP sites,* and in many cases, their Internet addresses begin with the word *ftp,* such as **ftp.gnome.org** or **ftp.redhat.com**. Others begin with other names, such as **metalab.unc.edu**. These public sites allow anonymous FTP login from any user. For the login name, you use the word "anonymous," and for the password, you use your email address. You can then transfer files from that site to your own system.

You can perform FTP operations using any one of a number of FTP client programs. For Linux systems, you can choose from several FTP clients. Many now operate using GUI interfaces such as GNOME. Some, such as Firefox, have limited capabilities, whereas others, such as NcFTP, include an extensive set of enhancements. The original FTP client is just as effective, though not as easy to use. It operates using a simple command line interface and requires no GUI or cursor support, as do other clients.

FTP Clients	Description
Firefox	Mozilla Web and FTP browser
Konqueror	K Desktop file manager
Nautilus	GNOME file manager
gFTP	GNOME FTP client
ftp	Command line FTP client
lftp	Command line FTP client capable of multiple connections
NcFTP	Screen-based FTP client
curl	Internet transfer client (FTP and HTTP)

TABLE 14-5   Linux FTP Clients

The Internet has a great many sites open to public access. They contain files anyone can obtain using file transfer programs. Unless you already know where a file is located, however, finding it can be difficult. To search for files on FTP sites, you can use search engines provided by Web sites, such as Yahoo!, Google, or Lycos. For Linux software, you can check sites such as **freshmeat.net, sourceforge.net**, **rpmfind.net**, **freshrpms.net**, **apps.kde.com**, and **www.gnome.org**. These sites usually search for both Web pages and FTP files.

Web Browser–Based FTP: Firefox

You access an FTP site and download files from it with any Web browser. A Web browser is effective for checking out an FTP sit
e to see what files are listed there. When you access an FTP site with a Web browser, the entire list of files in a directory is listed as a Web page. You can move to a subdirectory by clicking its entry. With Firefox, you can easily browse through an FTP site to download files. To download a file with Firefox, click the download link. This will start the transfer operation, opening a box for selecting your local directory and the name for the file. The default name is the same as on the remote system. You can manage your downloads with the download manager, which will let you cancel a download operation in progress or remove other downloads requested. The manager will show the time remaining, the speed, and the amount transferred for the current download. Browsers are useful for locating individual files, though not for downloading a large set of files, as is usually required for a system update.

The K Desktop File Manager: Konqueror

On the K Desktop, the desktop file manager (Konqueror) has a built-in FTP capability. The FTP operation has been seamlessly integrated into standard desktop file operations. Downloading files from an FTP site is as simple as copying files by dragging them from one directory window to another, but one of the directories happens to be located on a remote FTP site. On the K Desktop, you can use a file manager window to access a remote FTP site. Files in the remote directory are listed just as your local files are. To download files from an FTP site, you open a window to access that site, entering the URL for the FTP site in the window's location box. Open the directory you want, and then open another window for the local directory to which you want the remote files copied. In the window showing the FTP files, select the ones you want to download. Then simply click and drag those files to the window for the local directory. A pop-up menu appears with choices for Copy, Link, or Move. Select Copy. The selected files are then downloaded. Another window then opens, showing the download progress and displaying the name of each file in turn, along with a bar indicating the percentage downloaded so far.

GNOME Desktop FTP: Nautilus

The easiest way to download files is to use the built-in FTP capabilities of the GNOME file manager, Nautilus. On GNOME, the desktop file manager—Nautilus—has a built-in FTP capability much like the KDE file manager. The FTP operation has been seamlessly integrated into standard desktop file operations. Downloading files from an FTP site is as simple as dragging files from one directory window to another, where one of the directories happens to be located on a remote FTP site. Just as local files are listed in the GNOME file manager, you can access a remote FTP site, and list files in the remote directory. Just enter the FTP URL following the prefix **ftp://** and press ENTER. The top directory of the remote FTP site will be displayed. Simply use the file manager to progress through the remote FTP site's directory tree until you find the file you want. Then open another window for the local directory to which you want the remote files copied. In the window showing the FTP files, select those you want to download. Then CTRL-click and drag those files to the window for the local directory. CTRL-clicking performs a copy operation, not a move. As files are downloaded, a dialog window appears showing the progress.

gFTP

The gFTP program is a simpler GNOME FTP client designed to let you make standard FTP file transfers. The gFTP window consists of several panes. The top-left pane lists files in your local directory, and the top-right pane lists your remote directory. Subdirectories have folder icons preceding their names. The parent directory can be referenced by the double period entry (..) with an up arrow at the top of each list. Double-click a directory entry to access it. The pathnames for all directories are displayed in boxes above each pane. You can enter a new pathname for a different directory to change to it, if you want.

Two buttons between the panes are used for transferring files. The left arrow button, <-, downloads selected files in the remote directory, and the right arrow button, ->, uploads files from the local directory. To download a file, click it in the right-side pane and then click the left arrow button, <-. When the file is downloaded, its name appears in the left pane, your local directory. Menus across the top of the window can be used to manage your transfers. A connection manager enables you to enter login information about a specific site. You can specify whether to perform an anonymous login or to provide a username and password. Click Connect to connect to that site. A drop-down menu for sites enables you to choose the site you want. Interrupted downloads can be restarted easily.

wget

The wget tool lets you easily access Web and FTP sites for particular directories and files. Directories can be recursively downloaded, letting you copy an entire Web site. **wget** takes as its option the URL for the file or directory you want. Helpful options include **-q** for quiet, **-r** for recursive (directories), **-b** to download in the background, and **-c** to continue downloading an interrupted file. One of the drawbacks is that your URL reference can be very complex. You have to know the URL already. You cannot interactively locate an item as you would with an FTP client. The following would download the Fedora DVD in the background.

```
wget -b  ftp://download.fedora.redhat.com/pub/fedora/linux/core/7/i386/iso/
FC-7-i386-DVD.iso
```

TIP *With the Gnome Wget tool you can run wget downloads using a GUI interface. Select Applications | Internet | Download Manager to display Gnome Wget.*

curl

The curl Internet client operates much like wget, but with much more flexibility. With curl you can specify multiple URLs on its command line. You can also use braces to specify multiple matching URLs, like different Web sites with the same domain name. You can list the different Web site host names within braces, followed by their domain name (or visa versa). You can also use brackets to specify a range of multiple items. This can be very useful for downloading archived files that have the same root name with varying extensions, like different issues of the same magazine. curl can download using any protocol, and will try to intelligently guess the protocol to use if none is given. Check the curl man page for more information.

ftp

The name ftp designates the original FTP client used on Unix and Linux systems. The ftp client uses a command line interface, and it has an extensive set of commands and options you can use to manage your FTP transfers. You start the ftp client by entering the command **ftp** at a shell prompt. If you have a specific site you want to connect to, you can include the name of that site on the command line after the ftp keyword. Otherwise, you need to connect to the remote system with the ftp command **open**. You are then prompted for the name of the remote system with the prompt "(to)". When you enter the remote system name, ftp connects you to the system and then prompts you for a login name. The prompt for the login name consists of the word "Name" and, in parentheses, the system name and your local login name. Sometimes the login name on the remote system is the same as the login name on your own system. If the names are the same, press ENTER at the prompt. If they are different, enter the remote system's login name. After entering the login name, you are prompted for the password. In the next example, the user connects to the remote system **garnet** and logs in to the **robert** account:

```
$ ftp
ftp> open
(to) garnet
Connected to garnet.berkeley.edu.
220 garnet.berkeley.edu FTP server ready.
Name (garnet.berkeley.edu:root): robert
password required
Password:
user robert logged in
ftp>
```

Once logged in, you can execute Linux commands on either the remote system or your local system. You execute a command on your local system in ftp by preceding the command with an exclamation point. Any Linux commands without an exclamation point are executed on the remote system. One exception exists to this rule. Whereas you can change directories on the remote system with the **cd** command, to change directories on your local system, you need to use a special ftp command called **lcd** (local **cd**). In the next example, the first command lists files in the remote system, while the second command lists files in the local system:

```
ftp> ls
ftp> !ls
```

The ftp program provides a basic set of commands for managing files and directories on your remote site, provided you have the permission to do so (see Table 14-6). You can use **mkdir** to create a remote directory, and **rmdir** to remove one. Use the **delete** command to erase a remote file. With the **rename** command, you can change the names of files. You close

Command	Effect
`ftp`	Invokes the ftp program.
open *site-address*	Opens a connection to another system.
`close`	Closes connection to a system.
`quit` or **bye**	Ends ftp session.
`ls`	Lists the contents of a directory.
`dir`	Lists the contents of a directory in long form.
get *filename*	Sends file from remote system to local system.
put *filename*	Sends file from local system to remote system.
mget *regular-expression*	Enables you to download several files at once from a remote system. You can use special characters to specify the files; you are prompted to transfer each file in turn.
mput *regular-expression*	Enables you to send several files at once to a remote system. You can use special characters to specify the files; you are prompted for each file to be transferred.
`runique`	Toggles storing of files with unique filenames. If a file already exists with the same filename on the local system, a new filename is generated.
reget *filename*	Resumes transfer of an interrupted file from where you left off.
`binary`	Transfers files in binary mode.
`ascii`	Transfers files in ASCII mode.
cd *directory*	Changes directories on the remote system.
lcd *directory*	Changes directories on the local system.
help or **?**	Lists ftp commands.
mkdir *directory*	Creates a directory on the remote system.
`rmdir`	Deletes a remote directory.
delete *filename*	Deletes a file on the remote system.
mdelete *file-list*	Deletes several remote files at once.
`rename`	Renames a file on a remote system.
`hash`	Displays progressive hash signs during download.
`status`	Displays current status of ftp.

TABLE **14-6**   The ftp Client Commands

your connection to a system with the **close** command. You can then open another connection if you want. To end the ftp session, use the **quit** or **bye** command.

```
ftp> close
ftp> bye
Good-bye
$
```

To transfer files to and from the remote system, use the **get** and **put** commands. The **get** command receives files from the remote system to your local system, and the **put** command sends files from your local system to the remote system. In a sense, your local system gets files *from* the remote and puts files *to* the remote. In the next example, the file **weather** is sent from the local system to the remote system using the **put** command:

```
ftp> put weather
PORT command successful.
ASCII data connection
ASCII Transfer complete.
ftp>
```

If a download is ever interrupted, you can resume the download with **reget**. This is helpful for an extremely large file. The download resumes from where it left off, so the whole file needn't be downloaded again. Also, be sure to download binary files in binary mode. For most FTP sites, the binary mode is the default, but some sites might have ASCII (text) as the default. The command **ascii** sets the character mode, and the command **binary** sets the binary mode. Most software packages available at Internet sites are archived and compressed files, which are binary files. In the next example, the transfer mode is set to binary, and the archived software package **mydata.tar.gz** is sent from the remote system to your local system using the **get** command:

```
ftp> binary
ftp> get mydata.tar.gz
PORT command successful.
Binary data connection
Binary Transfer complete.
ftp>
```

You may often want to send several files, specifying their names with wildcard characters. The **put** and **get** commands, however, operate only on a single file and do not work with special characters. To transfer several files at a time, you have to use two other commands, **mput** and **mget**. When you use **mput** or **mget**, you are prompted for a file list. You can then either enter the list of files or a file-list specification using special characters. For example, ***.c** specifies all the files with a .c extension, and ***** specifies all files in the current directory. In the case of **mget**, files are sent one by one from the remote system to your local system. Each time, you are prompted with the name of the file being sent. You can type **y** to send the file or **n** to cancel the transmission. You are then prompted for the next file. The **mput** command works in the same way, but it sends files from your local system to the remote system. In the next example, all files with a **.c** extension are sent to your local system using **mget**:

```
ftp> mget
(remote-files) *.c
mget calc.c? y
PORT command successful
ASCII data connection
ASCII transfer complete
mget main.c? y
PORT command successful
ASCII data connection
ASCII transfer complete
ftp>
```

Answering the prompt for each file can be a tedious prospect if you plan to download a large number of files, such as those for a system update. In this case, you can turn off the prompt with the **prompt** command, which toggles the interactive mode on and off. The **mget** operation then downloads all files it matches, one after the other.

```
ftp> prompt
Interactive mode off.
ftp> mget
(remote-files) *.c
 PORT command successful
ASCII data connection
ASCII transfer complete
PORT command successful
ASCII data connection
ASCII transfer complete
ftp>
```

NOTE   *To access a public FTP site, you have to perform an anonymous login. Instead of a login name, you enter the keyword **anonymous** (or **ftp**). Then, for the password, you enter your email address. Once the ftp prompt is displayed, you are ready to transfer files. You may need to change to the appropriate directory first or set the transfer mode to binary.*

Automatic Login and Macros: .netrc

The ftp client has an automatic login capability and support for macros. Both are entered in a user's ftp configuration file called **.netrc**. Each time you connect to a site, the **.netrc** file is checked for connection information, such as a login name and password. In this way, you needn't enter a login name and password each time you connect to a site. This feature is particularly useful for anonymous logins. Instead of your having to enter the username "anonymous" and your e-mail address as your password, they can be automatically read from the **.netrc** file. You can even make anonymous login information your default so that, unless otherwise specified, an anonymous login is attempted for any FTP site to which you try to connect. If you have sites you must log in to, you can specify them in the **.netrc** file and, when you connect, either automatically log in with your username and password for that site or be prompted for them.

Entries in the **.netrc** file have the following syntax. An entry for a site begins with the term "machine," followed by the network or Internet address, and then the login and password information.

```
machine system-address login remote-login-name password password
```

The following example shows an entry for logging in to the **dylan** account on the **turtle.trek.com** system:

```
machine golf.mygames.com login dylan password legogolf
```

For a site you would anonymously log in to, you enter the word "anonymous" for the login name and your e-mail address for the password.

```
machine ftp.redhat.com login anonymous password dylan@turtle.trek.com
```

In most cases, you are using ftp to access anonymous FTP sites. Instead of trying to make an entry for each one, you can make a default entry for anonymous FTP login. When you connect to a site, ftp looks for a machine entry for it in the **.netrc** file. If none exists, ftp looks for a default entry and uses that. A default entry begins with the word "default" with no network address. To make anonymous logins your default, enter **anonymous** and your e-mail address as your login and password.

```
default login anonymous password dylan@turtle.trek.com
```

A sample **.netrc** file with a machine definition and a default entry is shown here:

.netrc
```
machine golf.mygames.com login dylan password legogolf
default login anonymous password dylan@turtle.trek.com
```

You can also define macros in your **.netrc** file. With a macro, you can execute several ftp operations at once using only the macro name. Macros remain in effect during a connection. When you close a connection, the macros are undefined. Although a macro can be defined on your ftp command line, defining them in **.netrc** entries makes more sense. This way, you needn't redefine them again. They are read automatically from the **.netrc** file and defined for you. You can place macro definitions within a particular machine entry in the **.netrc** file or in the default entry. Macros defined in machine entries are defined only when you connect to that site. Macros in the default entry are defined whenever you make a connection to any site.

The syntax for a macro definition follows. It begins with the keyword **macdef**, followed by the macro name you want to give it, and ends with an empty line. An ftp macro can take arguments, referenced within the macro with **$n**, where **$1** references the first argument, and **$2** the second, and so on. If you need to use a **$** character in a macro, you have to quote it using the backslash, **\$**.

```
macdef macro-name
ftp commands
empty-line
```

The **redupd** macro, defined next, changes to a directory where it then downloads Red Hat updates for the current release. It also changes to a local directory where the update files are to be placed. The **prompt** command turns off the download prompts for each file.

The **mget** command then downloads the files. The macro assumes you are connected to the Red Hat FTP site.

```
macdef redupd
cd pub/redhat/current
lcd /root/redupdate
prompt
mget *
```

A sample **.netrc** file follows with macros defined for both specific and default entries. An empty line is placed after each macro definition. You can define several macros for a machine or the default entry. The macro definitions following a machine entry up to the next machine entry are automatically defined for that machine connection.

```
machine updates.redhat.com login anonymous password dylan@turtle.trek.com
# define a macro for downloading updated from the Red Hat site
macdef redupd
 cd pub/redhat/current
 lcd /root/redupdate
 prompt
 mget *

default login anonymous password dylan@turtle.trek.com
macdef lls
!ls
```

lftp

The **lftp** program is an enhanced FTP client with advanced features such as the capabilities to download mirror sites and to run several FTP operations in the background at the same time. It uses a command set similar to that for the ftp client. You use **get** and **mget** commands to download files, using the **-o** option to specify local locations for them. Use **lcd** and **cd** to change local and remote directories.

To manage background commands, you use many of the same commands as for the shell (see Chapter 8). The **&** placed at the end of a command puts it into the background. Use CTRL-Z to pause a job that is already running, and then **bg** to put it into the background. Commands can be grouped with parentheses and placed together into the background. Use the **jobs** command to list your background jobs, and the **wait** or **fg** command to move jobs from the background to the foreground. When you exit lftp, the program will continue to run any background jobs. In effect, lftp becomes a background job itself.

When you connect to a site, you can queue commands with the **queue** command, setting up a list of FTP operations to perform. With this feature, you could queue several download operations to a site. The queue can be reordered and entries deleted if you wish. You can also connect to several sites and set up a queue for each one. The **mirror** command lets you maintain a local version of a mirror site. You can download an entire site or just update newer files, as well as remove files no longer present on the mirror.

You can tailor lftp with options set in the **.lftprc** file. System-wide settings are placed in the **/etc/lftp.conf** file. Here, you can set features like the prompt to use and your anonymous password. The **.lftp** directory holds support files for command history, logs, bookmarks, and startup commands. The lftp program also supports the **.netrc** file, checking it for login information.

NcFTP

The NcFTP program has a screen-based interface that can be run from any shell command line. It does not use a desktop interface. To start up NcFTP, you enter the `ncftp` command on the command line. If you are working in a window manager, such as KDE, GNOME, or XFce, open a shell terminal window and enter the command at its prompt. The main NcFTP screen consists of an input line at the bottom of the screen with a status line above it. The remainder of the screen is used to display commands and responses from remote systems. For example, when you download files, a message specifying the files to be downloaded is displayed in the status line. NcFTP lets you set preferences for different features, such as anonymous login, progress meters, or a download directory. Enter the `pref` command to open the preferences screen. From there, you can select and modify the listed preferences.

To connect to an FTP site, you enter the `open` command on the input line, followed by the site's address. The address can be either an IP address or a domain name, such as **ftp.gnome.org**. If you don't supply an address, a list of your bookmarked sites is displayed, and you can choose one from there. By default, NcFTP attempts an anonymous login, using the term "anonymous" as your username and your e-mail address as the password. When you successfully connect, the status bar displays the remote site's name on the left and the remote directory name.

If you want to log in to a specific account on a remote site, have yourself prompted for the username and password by using the `-u` option with the `open` command. The `open` command remembers the last kind of login you performed for a specific site and repeats it. If you want to change back to an anonymous login from a user login, you use the `-a` option with the `open` command.

Once connected, you enter commands on the input line to perform FTP operations such as displaying file lists, changing directories, or downloading files. With the `ls` command, you can list the contents of the current remote directory. Use the `cd` command to change to another remote directory. The `dir` command displays a detailed listing of files. With the `page` command, you view the contents of a remote file, a screen at a time. To download files, you use the `get` command, and to upload files, you use the `put` command. During a download, a progress meter above the status bar displays how much of the file has been downloaded so far. The `get` command has several features described in more detail in the following section. When you finish, you can disconnect from the site with the `close` command. You can then use `open` to connect to another site, or quit the NcFTP program with the `quit` command. The `help` command lists all NcFTP commands. You can use the `help` command followed by the name of a command to display specific information on it.

The NcFTP `get` command differs significantly from the original FTP client's `get` command. Whereas the original FTP client uses two commands, `get` and `mget`, to perform download operations, NcFTP uses only the `get` command. However, the NcFTP `get` command combines the capabilities of both `mget` and `get` into the `get` command, as well as adding several new features. By default, the NcFTP `get` command performs wildcard matching for filenames. If you enter only part of a filename, the `get` command tries to download all files beginning with that name. You can turn off wildcard matching with the `-G` option, in which case you must enter the full names of the files you want.

CHAPTER

Network Tools

You can use a variety of network tools to perform tasks such as obtaining information about other systems on your network, accessing other systems, and communicating directly with other users. Network information can be obtained using utilities such as **ping**, **finger**, **traceroute**, and **host**. Talk, ICQ, and IRC clients enable you to communicate directly with other users on your network. Telnet performs a remote login to an account you may have on another system connected on your network. Some tools have a corresponding K Desktop or GNOME version. In addition, your network may make use of network remote access commands. These are useful for smaller networks and enable you to access remote systems directly to copy files or execute commands.

Network Information: ping, finger, traceroute, and host

You can use the **ping**, **finger**, **traceroute**, and **host** commands to find out status information about systems and users on your network. The **ping** command is used to check if a remote system is up and running. You use **finger** to find out information about other users on your network, seeing if they are logged in or if they have received mail; **host** displays address information about a system on your network, giving you a system's IP and domain name addresses; and **traceroute** can be used to track the sequence of computer networks and systems your message passed through on its way to you. Table 15-1 lists various network information tools.

GNOME Network Tools: gnome-nettool

For the GNOME desktop, the **gnome-nettool** utility provides a GNOME interface for entering the **ping** and **traceroute** commands, as well as Finger, Whois, and Lookup for querying users and hosts on the network Applications | System Tools | Network Tools. Whois will provide domain name information about a particular domain, and Lookup will provide both domain name and IP addresses. You can access **gnome-nettool** with the Network Tools entry in the System Tools menu. It also includes network status tools such as **netstat** and **portscan**, which are described in more detail in Chapter 35. The first panel, Devices, describes your connected network devices, including configuration and transmission information about each device, such as the hardware address and bytes transmitted. Both IPv4 and IPv6 host IP addresses will be listed (see Chapter 35 for more information on addresses).

Network Information Tools	Description
ping	Detects whether a system is connected to the network.
finger	Obtains information about users on the network.
who	Checks what users are currently online.
whois	Obtains domain information.
host	Obtains network address information about a remote host.
traceroute	Tracks the sequence of computer networks and hosts your message passes through.
ethereal	Protocol analyzer to examine network traffic.
gnome-nettool	GNOME interface for various network tools including ping, finger, and traceroute.
mtr and xmtr	My traceroute combines both ping and traceroute operations (Traceroute on System Tools menu).

TABLE 15-1   Network Tools

ping

The **ping** command detects whether a system is up and running. **ping** takes as its argument the name of the system you want to check. If the system you want to check is down, **ping** issues a timeout message indicating a connection could not be made. The next example checks to see if **www.redhat.com** is up and connected to the network:

```
# ping www.redhat.com
PING www.redhat.com (209.132.177.50) 56(84) bytes of data.
64 bytes from www.redhat.com (209.132.177.50): icmp_seq=1 ttl=118 time=36.7 ms
64 bytes from www.redhat.com (209.132.177.50): icmp_seq=2 ttl=118 time=36.9 ms
64 bytes from www.redhat.com (209.132.177.50): icmp_seq=3 ttl=118 time=37.4 ms

--- www.redhat.com ping statistics ---
4 packets transmitted, 3 received, 25% packet loss, time 3000ms
rtt min/avg/max/mdev = 36.752/37.046/37.476/0.348 ms
```

You can also use **ping** with an IP address instead of a domain name. With an IP address, **ping** can try to detect the remote system directly without having to go through a domain name server to translate the domain name to an IP address. This can be helpful for situations where your network's domain name server may be temporarily down and you want to check if a particular remote host on your network is connected. In the next example, the user checks the Red Hat site using its IP address:

```
# ping 209.132.177.50
PING 209.132.177.50 (209.132.177.50) 56(84) bytes of data.
64 bytes from 209.132.177.50: icmp_seq=1 ttl=118 time=37.4 ms
64 bytes from 209.132.177.50: icmp_seq=2 ttl=118 time=37.0 ms
64 bytes from 209.132.177.50: icmp_seq=3 ttl=118 time=36.3 ms
```

```
--- 209.132.177.50 ping statistics ---
3 packets transmitted, 3 received, 0% packet loss, time 2001ms
rtt min/avg/max/mdev = 36.385/36.969/37.436/0.436 ms
```

NOTE *A* **ping** *operation could also fail if* **ping** *access is denied by a network's firewall. See Chapter 20 for more details.*

finger and who

You can use the **finger** command to obtain information about other users on your network and the **who** command to see what users are currently online on your system. The **who** and **w** commands lists all users currently connected, along with when, how long, and where they logged in. The **w** command provides more detailed information. It has several options for specifying the level of detail. The **who** command is meant to operate on a local system or network; **finger** can operate on large networks, including the Internet, though most systems block it for security reasons.

NOTE *Ethereal is a protocol analyzer that can capture network packets and display detailed information about them. You can detect what kind of information is being transmitted on your network as well as its source and destination. Ethereal is used primarily for network and server administration. Ethereal is discussed in detail in Chapter 35.*

host

With the **host** command, you can find network address information about a remote system connected to your network. This information usually consists of a system's IP address, domain name address, domain name nicknames, and mail server. This information is obtained from your network's domain name server. For the Internet, this includes all systems you can connect to over the Internet.

The **host** command is an effective way to determine a remote site's IP address or URL. If you have only the IP address of a site, you can use **host** to find out its domain name. For network administration, an IP address can be helpful for making your own domain name entries in your **/etc/host** file. That way, you needn't rely on a remote domain name server (DNS) for locating a site.

```
# host gnomefiles.org
gnomefiles.org has address 67.18.254.188
gnomefiles.org mail is handled by 10 mx.zayda.net.

# host 67.18.254.188
188.254.18.67.in-addr.arpa domain name pointer gnomefiles.org.
```

traceroute

Internet connections are made through various routes, traveling through a series of interconnected gateway hosts. The path from one system to another could take different routes, some of which may be faster than others. For a slow connection, you can use **traceroute** to check the route through which you are connected to a host, monitoring the speed and the number of intervening gateway connections a route takes. The **traceroute** command takes as its argument the hostname or IP addresses for the system whose route you want to check. Options are available for specifying parameters like the type of service (**-t**) or the source host (**-s**). The **traceroute** command will return a list of hosts the route traverses, along with the times for three probes sent to each gateway. Times greater than five seconds are displayed with a asterisk, *.

```
traceroute rabbit.mytrek.com
```

You can also use the mtr or xmtr tools to perform both ping and traces (Traceroute on the System Tools menu).

Network Talk and Messenger Clients: VoIP, ICQ, IRC, AIM, and Talk

You may, at times, want to communicate directly with other users on your network. You can do so with VoIP, Talk, ICQ, instant messenger, and IRC utilities, provided the other user is also logged in to a connected system at the same time (see Table 15-2). With Voice over the Internet Protocol applications, you can speak over Internet connections, talking as if on a telephone. The Talk utility operates like a two-way text messaging tool, enabling you to have a direct two-way conversation with another user. Talk is designed for users on the same system or connected on a local network. ICQ (I Seek You) is an Internet tool that notifies you when other users are online and enables you to communicate with them. ICQ works much like an instant messenger. With an Internet Relay Chat utility (IRC), you can connect to a remote server where other users are also connected and talk with them. Instant messenger (IM) clients operate much the same way, allowing users on the same IM system to communicate anywhere across the Internet. Currently the major IM systems are AOL (AIM), Microsoft Network (MSN), Yahoo, ICQ, and Jabber. Unlike the others, Jabber is an open source instant messenger service (**www.jabber.org**).

Ekiga

Ekiga is GNOME's new VoIP application providing Internet IP Telephone and video conferencing support. It was formerly called GnomeMeeting, and its web site is still at

Clients	Description
Ekiga	VoIP application
GnomeICU	GNOME ICQ client
X-Chat	Internet Relay Chat (IRC) client
Konversation	KDE IRC client
Gabber	Jabber client
Gaim	GNOME AIM client
psi	Jabber client using QT (KDE)
nalm	Command line cursor-based IRC, ICQ, and AIM client

TABLE 15-2   Talk and Messenger Clients

www.gnomemeeting.org. Ekiga supports both the H.323 and SIP (Session Initiation Protocol) protocols. It is compatible with Microsoft's NetMeeting. H.323 is a comprehensive protocol that includes the digital broadcasting protocols like DVB and H.261 for video streaming, as well as the supporting protocols like the H.450 series for managing calls.

To use Ekiga you will need a SIP address. You can obtain a free one from **ekiga.net**. You will first have to subscribe to the service. When you first start Ekiga, you will be prompted to configure your connection. Here you can provide information like contact information, your connection method, sound driver, and video device. Use the address book to connect to another Ekiga user. A white pages directory lets you search for people who are also using Ekiga.

ICQ

The ICQ protocol enables you to communicate directly with other users online, like an instant messenger utility. Using an ICQ client, you can send users messages, chat with them, or send files. You can set up a contact list of users you may want to contact when they are online. You are then notified in real time when they connect, and you can communicate with them if you wish. Several modes of communication are supported. These include chat, message, e-mail, file transfer, and games. To use ICQ, you register with an ICQ server that provides you with an ICQ number, also known as a Universal Internet Number (UIN). You can find out more about the ICQ protocol at **www.icq.com**.

Internet Relay Chat (IRC) operates like a chat room, where you can enter channels and talk to other users already there. First, you select an IRC server to connect to. Various servers are available for different locales and topics. Once connected to a server, you can choose from a list of channels to enter. The interface works much like a chat room. When you connect to the server, you can choose a nickname by which you will be known. Several Internet Relay Chat clients are available for use on Linux systems. Most operate on either the X Window System, KDE, or GNOME platforms.

Several GNOME- and KDE-based ICQ and IRC clients are available for your use. Check the GNOME software listings at **www.gnomefiles.org** for new versions and recent updates. For KDE-based ICQ clients, check **www.kde-apps.org** (Network | Chat).

Instant Messenger

AOL Instant Messenger (AIM) is a free service provided by AOL for anyone who registers for it, as well as those who are already members of AOL. With AIM, you can send messages to members instantly, play games with them, and receive stock alerts. You can even share images, sounds, and photographs. AOL already provides clients for Windows and Macintosh. A new version called AIM Express is designed to run on any Web browser and will run on systems with JDK 1.1 or greater. You can find out more about AIM at **www.aim.com**.

Several GNOME instant messaging clients are designed to work with all instant messaging systems, including AIM, Yahoo, MSN, and ICQ. Gaim has plug-ins that let you connect to ICQ, Yahoo, MSN, IRC, Jabber, and Zephyr. Gabber, a Jabber client, is an open source instant messaging system that allows communication with all other systems, including AIM, Yahoo, MSN, and ICQ.

NOTE *Talk is the original Unix talk utility designed to set up an interactive two-way communication between you and another user using a command line interface. It works much like an instant messenger. Due to security concerns, you should use talk only on a locally secure system. A K Desktop version of Talk called KTalk displays user screens as panes in a K Desktop window. GNU Talk is a GNOME version of Talk that supports multiple clients, file transfers, encryption, shared applications, auto-answer, and call forwarding.*

Telnet

You use the **telnet** command to log in remotely to another system on your network. The system can be on your local area network or available through an Internet connection. Telnet operates as if you were logging in to another system from a remote terminal. You will be asked for a login name and, in some cases, a password. In effect, you are logging in to another account on another system. In fact, if you have an account on another system, you could use Telnet to log in to it.

CAUTION *The original version of Telnet is noted for being very insecure. For secure connections over a network or the Internet, you should use the SSH or Kerberos versions of Telnet (see Chapter 19). They operate in the same way as the original but use authentication and encryption to secure the Telnet connection. Even so, it is advisable never to use Telnet to log in to your root account.*

You invoke the Telnet utility with the keyword **telnet**. If you know the name of the site you want to connect with, you can enter **telnet** and the name of the site on the Linux command line. As an alternative, you can use the K Desktop KTelnet utility. This provides a GUI interface for connecting and logging in to remote systems.

```
$ telnet garnet.berkeley.edu
Connected to garnet
login:
```

The Telnet program also has a command mode with a series of commands you can use to configure your connection. You can enter the **telnet** command mode either by invoking Telnet with the keyword **telnet** or by pressing CTRL-] during a session. The Telnet **help** command lists all the Telnet commands you can use. A comprehensive list is available on the Man pages (**man telnet**). In the next example, the user first invokes the Telnet utility. A prompt is displayed next, indicating the command mode, **telnet>**. The Telnet command **open** then connects to another system.

```
$ telnet
telnet> open garnet.berkeley.edu
Connected to garnet.berkeley.edu
login:
```

Once connected, you follow the login procedure for that system. If you are logging in to a regular system, you must provide a login name and password. Once logged in, you are provided with the operating system prompt; in the case of Linux or Unix, this will be either $ or %. You are then directly connected to an account on that system and can issue any commands you want. When you finish your work, you log out. This breaks the connection and returns you to the Telnet prompt on your own system. You can then quit Telnet with the `quit` command.

```
telnet> quit
```

When using Telnet to connect to a site that provides public access, you needn't provide a login name or password. Access is usually controlled by a series of menus that restrict what you can do on that system. If you are logging in to a specific account on another system, you can use the `-1` option to specify the login name of that account.

RSH, Kerberos, and SSH Remote Access Commands

The remote access commands were designed for smaller networks, such as intranets. They enable you to log in remotely to another account on another system and to copy files from one system to another. You can also obtain information about another system, such as who is currently logged on (see Table 15-3). Many of the remote commands have comparable network communication utilities used for the Internet. For example, **rlogin**, which remotely logs in to a system, is similar to **telnet**. The **rcp** command, which remotely copies files, performs much the same function as **ftp**.

Remote Command	Effect
`rwho`	Displays all users logged in to systems in your network.
`ruptime`	Displays information about each system on your network.
`rlogin` *system-name*	Allows you to log in remotely to an account on another system. Kerberos version used by default. The `-1` option allows you to specify the login name of the account.
`slogin` *system-name*	Secure login to an account on another system.
`rcp` *sys-name:file1* *sys-name:file2*	Allows you to copy a file from an account on one system to an account on another system. The `-p` option, preserves the modification times and modes of source files. Kerberos version used by default.
`scp` *sys-name:file1* *sys-name:file2*	Secure copy of a file from an account on one system to an account on another system.
`rsh` *sys-name Linux-command*	Allows you to remotely execute a command on another system. The `-1` option allows you to specify the login name; `-n` redirects input from the null special device, **/dev/null**. Kerberos version used by default.
`ssh` *sys-name Linux-command*	Secure remote execution of a command on another system.

TABLE 15-3   Remote Access Commands

Due to security risks with the original versions of the remote operations **rcp**, **rlogin**, and **rsh** (RSH package), secure implementations are now installed with Fedora. Secure versions of these commands are provided by Kerberos and the Secure Shell (SSH). The Kerberos versions are configured as the default (**/etc/profile.d/krb5-workstation.sh**). Whenever you enter a **rcp** or **rsh** command, you are actually invoking the Kerberos version of the command. Kerberos provides versions for **telnet**, **rlogin**, **rcp**, **rsh**, and **ftp**, which provide authentication and encryption. These versions operate using the same commands and options as the originals, making their use transparent to the user. When Kerberos is installed on your system, Fedora configures the user's PATH variable to access the Kerberos versions of the remote commands, located at **/usr/kerberos/bin** instead of **/usr/bin**.

The Secure Shell (SSH) versions use slightly different names, using an initial *s* in the commands, such as **ssh**, **slogin**, or **scp** (see Chapter 19). SSH commands are encrypted, providing a very high level of security.

Even the original remote commands now include Kerberos support, enabling them to use more secure access configurations like those provided by **.k5login** (discussed below). Still, these commands could allow easy unencrypted remote access to a Linux system. They should be used only within a local secure network.

Remote Access Information

You can use several commands to obtain information about different systems on your network. You can find out who is logged in, get information about a user on another system, or find out if a system is up and running. For example, the **rwho** command functions in the same way as the **who** command. It displays all the users currently logged in to each system in your network.

```
$ rwho
violet robert:tty1 Sept 10 10:34
garnet chris:tty2 Sept 10 09:22
```

The **ruptime** command displays information about each system on your network. The information shows how each system has been performing: **ruptime** shows whether a system is up or down, how long it has been up or down, the number of users on the system, and the average load on the system for the last five, ten, and fifteen minutes.

```
$ ruptime
violet up 11+04:10, 8 users, load 1.20 1.10 1.00
garnet up 11+04:10, 20 users, load 1.50 1.40 1.30
```

Remote Access Permission: .k5login

The remote commands on Fedora are Kerberos enabled, allowing you to use Kerberos authentication to control access. For ease of use you can use the **.k5login** file to control access to your account by users using remote commands (**.rhosts** is not used). Users create this file on their own accounts using a standard editor. The file must be located in the user's home directory.

The **.k5login** file is a simple way to allow other people access to your account without giving out your password. To deny access to a user, simply delete the system's name and the user's login name from your **.k5login** file. If a user's login name and system are in an **.k5login** file, that user can directly access your account without knowing the password (in place of using **.k5login**, you could use a password). The **.k5login** file will contain Kerberos names for users, including user names and realms. Such a user will undergo Kerberos authentication to gain access. A **.k5login** file is required for other remote commands, such as remotely copying files or remotely executing Linux commands.

The type of access **.k5login** provides enables you to use remote commands to directly access accounts that you might have on other systems. You do not have to log in to them first. In effect, you can treat your accounts on other systems as extensions of the one you are currently logged in to. Using the **rcp** command, you can copy any files from one directory to another no matter which of your accounts they are on. With the **rsh** command, you can execute any Linux command you want on any of your other accounts.

rlogin, slogin, rcp, scp, rsh, and ssh

You may have accounts on different systems in your network, or you may be permitted to access someone else's account on another system. You could access an account on another system by first logging in to your own account, and then remotely logging in across your network to the account on the other system. You can perform such a remote login using the **rlogin** command, which takes as its argument a system name. The command connects you to the other system and begins login procedures. Bear in mind that if you are using an SSH-enabled network connection, you could use **slogin** instead of **rlogin**. Either **slogin** or Kerberos **rlogin** will provide secure encrypted login access.

You can use the **rcp** command to copy files to and from remote and local systems. For SSH-enabled network connections, you would use **scp** instead of **rcp**. The **rcp** and **scp** commands are file transfer tools that operate like the **cp** command, but across a network connection to a remote system. The **rcp** command begins with the keyword **rcp** and has as its arguments the names of the source file and the copy file. To specify the file on the remote system, you need to place the remote system name before the filename, separated from it by a colon. When you are copying a file on the remote system to your own, the source file is a remote file and requires the remote system's name. The copy file is a file on your own system and does not require a system name:

```
$ rcp remote-system-name:source-file copy-file
```

In the next example, the user copies the file **wednesday** from the remote system **violet** to her own system and renames the file **today**:

```
$ rcp violet:wednesday today
```

You can also use **scp** or **rcp** to copy whole directories to or from a remote system. The **scp** command with the **-r** option copies a directory and all its subdirectories from one system to another. Like the **cp** command, these commands require source and destination directories. The directory on the remote system requires that the system name and colon be placed before the directory name. When you copy a directory from your own system to a remote system, the copy directory is on the remote system and requires the remote system's name. In the next example, the user uses the **scp** command to copy the directory **letters** to the directory **oldnotes** on the remote system **violet**:

```
$ scp -r letters violet:oldnotes
```

NOTE *For backups or copying a large number of files you would use* **rsync**, *described in Chapter 34.*

At times, you may need to execute a single command on a remote system. The **rsh** command executes a Linux command on another system and displays the results on your own. Your system name and login name must, of course, be in the remote system's **.k5login** file. For SSH-enabled network connections, you could use **ssh** instead of **rsh**. The **ssh** and **rsh** commands take two general arguments: a system name and a Linux command. The syntax is as follows:

```
$ rsh remote-system-name Linux-command
```

In the next example, the **rsh** command executes an **ls** command on the remote system **violet** to list the files in the **/home/robert** directory:

```
$ rsh violet ls /home/robert
```

Special characters are evaluated by the local system unless quoted. If you quote a special character, it becomes part of the Linux command evaluated on the remote system. Quoting redirection operators enables you to perform redirection operations on the remote system. In the next example, the redirection operator is quoted. It becomes part of the Linux command, including its argument, the filename **myfiles**. The **ls** command then generates a list of filenames that is redirected on the remote system to a file called **myfiles**, also located on the remote system.

```
$ ssh violet ls /home/robert '>' myfiles
```

The same is true for pipes. The first command (shown next) prints the list of files on the local system's printer. The standard output is piped to your own line printer. In the second command, the list of files is printed on the remote system's printer. The pipe is quoted and evaluated by the remote system, piping the standard output to the printer on the remote system.

```
$ ssh violet ls /home/robert | lpr
$ ssh violet ls /home/robert '|' lpr
```

NOTE *The Kerberos versions of the remote commands also let you specify Kerberos realms and credentials.*

Security

CHAPTER 16
Encryption, Integrity Checks, and Signatures: GNU Privacy Guard

CHAPTER 17
Security Enhanced Linux: SELinux

CHAPTER 18
Internet Protocol Security: IPsec

CHAPTER 19
Secure Shell and Kerberos

CHAPTER 20
Network Firewalls: Netfilter

Encryption, Integrity Checks, and Signatures: GNU Privacy Guard

You can use encryption, integrity checks, and digital signatures to protect data transmitted over a network. For example, the GNU Privacy Guard encryption package lets you encrypt your e-mail messages or files you want to send, as well as letting you sign them with an encrypted digital signature authenticating that the message was sent by you. The digital signature also includes encrypted modification digest information that provides an integrity check, allowing the recipient to verify that the message received is the original and not one that has been changed or substituted.

Encryption was originally implemented with Pretty Good Privacy (PGP). Originally a privately controlled methodology, it was handed over to the Internet Engineering Task Force (IETF) to support an open standard for PGP called OpenPGP (see Table 16-1). Any project can use OpenPGP to create encryption applications, such as GnuPGP. Commercial products for PGP are still developed by the PGP Corporation, which also uses the OpenPGP standard.

> **NOTE** *An intrusion detection system is not included with Fedora Red Hat, but you can use the Linux Intrusion Detection System (LIDS) at **www.lids.org** to implement one. Be sure to use the RPM for the kernel version you are using.*

Public Key Encryption, Integrity Checks, and Digital Signatures

Encrypting data is the only sure way to secure data transmitted over a network. Encrypt data with a key, and the receiver or receivers can later decrypt it. To fully protect data transmitted over a network, you should not only encrypt it but also check that it has not been modified, as well as confirm that it was actually created by the claimed author. An encrypted message could still be intercepted and modified, and then reencrypted. Integrity checks such as modification digests make sure that the data was not altered. Though encryption and integrity checks protect the data, they do not authenticate it. You also need

Web Site	Description
www.gnupg.org	GnuPGP, Gnu Privacy Guard
www.openpgp.org	IETF open standard for Pretty Good Privacy (PGP)
www.pgp.com	PGP Corporation, Pretty Good Privacy commercial products

TABLE 16-1   PGP Sites

to know that the person from whom the message claims to be, is the one who actually, sent it, rather than an imposter. To authenticate a message, the author can sign it using a digital signature. This signature can also be encrypted, allowing the receiver to validate it. Digital signatures ensure that the message you receive is authentic.

Public-Key Encryption

Encryption uses a key to encrypt data in such a way that a corresponding key can decrypt it. In the past, older forms of encryption used the same key to both encrypt and decrypt a message. This, however, involved providing the receiver with the key, opening up the possibility that anyone who obtained the key could decrypt the data. Public-key encryption uses two keys to encrypt and decrypt a message, a private key and a public key. The *private* key you always keep and use to decrypt messages you have received. The *public* key you make available to those you send messages to. They then use your public key to encrypt any message they want to send to you. The private key decrypts messages, and the public key encrypts them. Each user has a set of private and public keys. Reciprocally, if you want to send messages to another user, you would first obtain the user's public key and use it to encrypt the message you want to send to the user. The user then decrypts the messages with his or her own private key. In other words, your public key is used by others to encrypt the messages you receive, and you use other users' public keys to encrypt messages you send to them. All the users on your Linux system can have their own public and private keys. They will use the **gpg** program to generate them and keep their private key in their own directory.

Digital Signatures

A *digital signature* is used to both authenticate a message and provide an integrity check. Authentication guarantees that the message has not been modified—that it is the original message sent by you—and the integrity check verifies that it has not been changed. Though usually combined with encrypted messages to provide a greater level of security, digital signatures can also be used for messages that can be sent in the clear. For example, you would want to know if a public notice of upgrades of a Red Hat release was actually sent by Red Hat, and not by someone trying to spread confusion. Such a message still needs to be authenticated, checked to see if it was actually sent by the sender or, if sent by the original sender, was not somehow changed en route. Verification like this protects against modification or substitution of the message by someone pretending to be the sender.

Integrity Checks

Digitally signing a message involves generating a checksum value from the contents of the message using an encryption hash algorithm such as the SHA2 modification digest algorithm. This is a unique value that accurately represents the size and contents of your message. Any changes to the message of any kind would generate a different value. Such a value provides a way to check the integrity of the data. The value is commonly known as the MD5 value, reflective of the MD5 hash algorithm that was used to encrypt the value. The MD5 algorithm has since been replaced by the more secure SHA2 algorithms.

The MD5 value is then itself encrypted with your private key. When the user receives your message, they decrypt your digital signature with your public key. The user then generates an MD5 value of the message received and compares it with the MD5 value you sent. If they are the same, the message is authenticated—it is the original message sent by you, not a false one sent by a user pretending to be you. The user can use GnuPG (described in the next section) to decrypt and check digital signatures.

Combining Encryption and Signatures

Normally, digital signatures are combined with encryption to provide a more secure level of transmission. The message would be encrypted with the recipient's public key, and the digital signature encrypted with your private key. The user would decrypt both the message (with that user's own private key) and then the signature (with your public key). The user would then compare the signature with one that the user generates from the message to authenticate it. When GnuPG decodes a message, it will also decode and check a digital signature automatically. Figure 16-1 shows the process for encrypting and digitally signing a message.

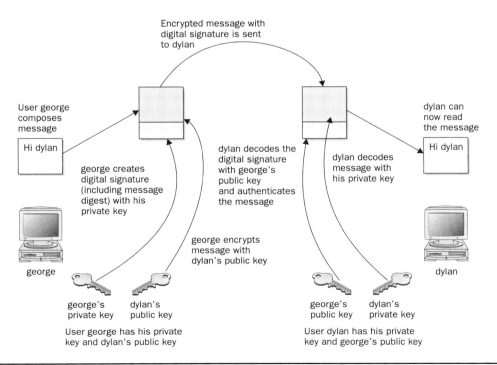

FIGURE 16-1 Public-key encryption and digital signatures

GNU Privacy Guard

To protect messages that you send by e-mail, most Linux distributions provide GNU Privacy Guard (GnuPG) encryption and authentication (**www.gnupg.org**). GnuPG is GNU open source software that works much like Pretty Good Privacy (PGP) encryption. It is the OpenPGP encryption and signing tool, and OpenPGP is the open source version of PGP. With GnuPG, you can both encrypt your messages and digitally sign them—protecting the message and authenticating that it is from you. Currently, Evolution and KMail both support GnuPG encryption and authentication, as does Thunderbird with the added use of GPG extensions. On Evolution, you can select PGP encryption and signatures from the Security menu to use GnuPG (the PGP options use GnuPG on Fedora and Red Hat Linux). On KMail, you can select the encryption to use on the Security panel in the Options window. For Thunderbird you can use the **enigmail** extension to support OpenGPG and PGP encryption (**enigmail.mozdev.org**).

GNU Privacy Guard (GnuPG) operations are carried out with the **gpg** command, which uses both commands and options to perform tasks. Commonly used commands and options are listed in Table 16-2. Some commands and options have a short form that uses only one hyphen. Normally, two hyphens are used. If you just want to verify the validity of a digital signature, you can use **gpgv** instead. This is a stripped-down version of **gpg** used just for signature verification.

The first time you use **gpg**, a **.gnugpg** directory is created in your home directory with a file named **options**. The **.gnugpg/gpg.conf** file contains commented default options for GPG operations. You can edit this file and uncomment or change any default options you want implemented for GPG. You can use a different options file by specifying it with the **--options** parameter when invoking **gpg**. Helpful options include keyserver entries. The **.gnugpg** directory will also hold encryption files such as **secring.gpg** for your secret keys (secret keyring), **pubring.gpg** for your public keys (public keyring), and **trustdb.gpg**, which is a database for trusted keys.

TIP *You can use GNOME Keyring Manager (**gnome-keyring**) to manage your PGP secret keys.*

GnuPG Setup: gpg

Before you can use GnuPG, you will have to generate your private and public keys. On the command line (terminal window), enter the **gpg** command with the **--gen-key** command. The **gpg** program will then prompt with different options for creating your private and public keys. You can check the **gpg** Man page for information on using the **gpg** program.

```
gpg --gen-key
```

Creating Your Key

You are first asked to select the kind of key you want. Normally, you would just select the default entry, which you can do by pressing the ENTER key. Then you choose the key size, usually the default 1024. You then specify how long the key is to be valid—usually, there is no expiration. You will be asked to enter a user ID, a comment, and an e-mail address. Press ENTER to be prompted for each in turn. These elements, any of which can be used as the key's name, identify the key. You use the key name when performing certain GPG tasks such as signing a key or creating a revocation certificate. For example, the following

GPG Commands	Description
`-s, --sign`	Signs a document, creating a signature. May be combined with `--encrypt`.
`--clearsign`	Creates a clear-text signature.
`-b, --detach-sign`	Creates a detached signature.
`-e, --encrypt`	Encrypts data. May be combined with `--sign`.
`--decrypt` [*file*]	Decrypts file (or stdin if no file is specified) and writes it to stdout (or the file specified with `--output`). If the decrypted file is signed, the signature is verified.
`--verify` [[*sigfile*] [*signed-files*]]	Verifies a signed file. The signature can either be contained with the file or be a separate detached signature file.
`--list-keys` [*names*]	Lists all keys from the keyrings or those specified.
`--list-public-keys` [*names*]	Lists all keys from the public keyrings or those specified.
`--list-secret-keys` [*names*]	Lists your private (secret) keys.
`--list-sigs` [*names*]	Lists your keys along with any signatures they have.
`--check-sigs` [*names*]	Lists keys and their signatures and verify the signatures.
`--fingerprint` [*names*]	Lists fingerprints for specified keys.
`--gen-key`	Generates a new set of private and public keys.
`--edit-key` *name*	Edits your keys. Use commands to perform most key operations such as **sign** to sign a key or **passwd** to change your passphrase.
`--sign-key` *name*	Signs a public key with your private key. Same as **sign** in `--edit-key`.
`--delete-key` *name*	Removes a public key from the public keyring.
`--delete-secret-key` *name*	Removes private and public keys from both the secret and public keyrings.
`--gen-revoke`	Generates a revocation certificate for your own key.
`--export` [*names*]	Exports a specified key from your keyring. With no arguments, exports all keys.
`--send-keys` [*names*]	Exports and sends specified keys to a keyserver. The option –keyserver must be used to give the name of this **keyserver**.
`--import` [*files*]	Imports keys contained in files into your public keyring.
GPG Options	**Description**
`-a, --armor`	Creates ASCII armored output, ASCII version of encrypted data.
`-o, --output` *file*	Writes output to a specified file.

TABLE 16-2   GPG Commands and Options *(continued)*

GPG Options	Description
`--default-key` name	Specifies the default private key to use for signatures.
`--keyserver` site	The keyserver to look up public keys not on your keyring. Can also specify the site to send your public key to. `host -l pgp.net	grep www.keys` will list the keyservers.
`-r, --recipient` names	Encrypts data for the specified user, using that user's public key.
`--default-recipient` names	Specifies the default recipient to use for encrypting data.

TABLE 16-2 GPG Commands and Options

elements create a key for the user richlp with the comment "author" and the e-mail address richlp@turtle.mytrek.com:

```
Richard Petersen (author) <richlp@turtle.mytrek.com>
```

You can use any unique part of a key's identity to reference that key. For example, the string "Richard" would reference the preceding key, provided there are no other keys that have the string "Richard" in them. The string "richlp" would also reference the key, as would "author". Where a string matches more than one key, all the matched ones would be referenced.

Protecting Your Key

The **gpg** program will then ask you to enter a passphrase, which is used to protect your private key. Be sure to use a real phrase, including spaces, not just a password. **gpg** then generates your public and private keys and places them in the **.gnupg** directory. The private keys are kept in a file called **secring.gpg** in your **.gnupg** directory. The public key is placed in the **pubring.gpg** file, to which you can add the public keys of other users. You can list these keys with the `--list-keys` command.

In case you later need to change your keys, you can create a revocation certificate to notify others that the public key is no longer valid. For example, if you forget your password or someone else discovers it, you can use the revocation certificate to tell others that your public key should no longer be used. In the next example, the user creates a revocation certificate for the key richlp and places it in the file **myrevoke.asc**:

```
$ gpg --output myrevoke.asc --gen-revoke richlp
```

Making Your Public Key Available

For other users to decrypt your messages, you have to make your public key available to them. They, in turn, have to send you their public keys so that you can decrypt any messages you receive from them. In effect, enabling encrypted communications between users involves all of them exchanging their public keys. The public keys then have to be verified and signed by each user that receives them. The public keys can then be trusted to safely decrypt messages.

If you are sending messages to just a few users, you can manually e-mail them your public key. For general public use, you can post your public key on a keyserver, which anyone can then download and use to decrypt any message they receive from you. A keyserver can be accessed using e-mail, LDAP, or the HTTP Horwitz Keyserver Protocol (HKP). The OpenPGP Public Keyserver project is located at **pks.sourceforge.net**. Several public keyservers are available. **hkp://subkeys.pgp.net** is listed in your **.gnupg/gpg.conf** file, though commented out. You can send directly to the keyserver with the **-keyserver** option and **--send-key** command. The **--send-key** command takes as its argument your e-mail address. You need to send to only one keyserver, as it will share your key with other keyservers automatically.

```
gpg --keyserver search.keyserver.net --send-key chris@turtle.mytrek.com
```

If you want to send your key directly to another user, you should generate an armored text version of the key that you can then e-mail. You do this with the **--armor** and **--export** options, using the **--output** option to specify a file to place the key in. The **--armor** option will generate an ASCII text version of the encrypted file so that it can be e-mailed directly, instead of as an attached binary. Files that hold an ASCII-encoded version of the encryption normally have the extension **.asc**, by convention. Binary encrypted files normally use the extension **.gpg**. You can then e-mail the file to users to whom you want to send encrypted messages.

```
# gpg --armor --export richlp@turtle.mytrek.com --output richlp.asc
# mail -s 'mypubkey' george@rabbit.mytrek.com < richlp.asc
```

Many companies and institutions post their public key files on their Web sites, where they can be downloaded and used to verify encrypted software downloads or official announcements.

NOTE *Some commands and options for GPG have both long and short forms. For example, the* **--armor** *command can be written as* **-a,** **--output** *as* **-o,** **--sign** *as* **-s,** *and* **--encrypt** *as* **-e.** *Most others, like* **--export,** *have no short form.*

Obtaining Public Keys

To decode messages from other users, you will need to have their public keys. Either they can send them to you or you can download them from a keyserver. Save the message or Web page containing the public key to a file. You will then need to import, verify, and sign the key. Use the file you received to import the public key to your **pubring** file. In the following example, the user imports George's public key, which he has received as the file **georgekey.asc**.

```
gpg --import georgekey.asc
```

All Linux distribution sites have their own public keys available for download. You should, for example, download the Red Hat public key, which can be accessed from the Red Hat site on its security resources page (**www.redhat.com**). Click the Public Encryption Key link. From there, you can access a page that displays just the public key. You can save this page as a file and use that file to import the Red Hat public key to your keyring. (Your Red Hat distribution also places the Red Hat public key in the **/usr/share/doc/rpm4-1** directory with versions for both GPG and PGP encryption, **RPM-GPG-KEY** and **RPM-PGP-KEY** files.) In the following example, the user saved the page showing just the Red Hat public key as **myredhat.asc**, and then imported that file:

```
gpg --import myredhat.asc
```

NOTE *You can remove any key, including your own private key, with the* **--delete-key** *and* **--delete-secret-key** *commands.*

Validating Keys

To manually check that a public key file was not modified in transit, you can check its fingerprint. This is a hash value generated from the contents of the key, much like a modification digest. Using the **--fingerprint** option, you can generate a hash value from the key you installed, and then contact the sender and ask them what the hash value should really be. If they are not the same, you know the key was tampered with in transit.

```
gpg --fingerprint george@rabbit
```

You do not have to check the fingerprint to have **gpg** operate. This is just an advisable precaution you can perform on your own. The point is that you need to be confident that the key you received is valid. Normally you can accept most keys from public servers or known sites as valid, though it is easy to check their posted fingerprints. Once assured of the key's validity, you can then sign it with your private key. Signing a key notifies **gpg** that you officially accept the key.

To sign a key, you use the **gpg** command with the **--sign-key** command and the key's name.

```
gpg --sign-key george@rabbit
```

Alternatively, you can edit the key with the **--edit-key** command to start an interactive session in which you can enter the command **sign** to sign the key and **save** to save the change. Signing a key involves accessing your private key, so you will be prompted for your passphrase. When you are finished, leave the interactive session with the **quit** command.

Normally, you would want to post a version of your public key that has been signed by one or more users. You can do the same for other users. Signing a public key provides a way to vouch for the validity of a key. It indicates that someone has already checked it out. Many different users could sign the same public key. For a key that you have received from another user, and that you have verified, you can sign the key, generate a file containing the signed public version, and return the signed version to that user. This process builds a Web of Trust, where many users vouch for the validity of public keys.

```
gpg -a --export george@rabbit --output  georgesig.asc
```

The user would then import the signed key and export it to a keyserver.

TIP *If you want to start over from scratch, you can just erase your* **.gnupg** *directory, though this is a drastic measure, as you will lose any keys you have collected.*

Using GnuPG

GnuPG encryption is currently supported by most mail clients, including Kmail, Thunderbird, and Evolution. You can also use the GNU Privacy Assistant (GPA), a GUI front end, to manage GPG tasks, or you can use the **gpg** command to manually encode and decode messages, including digital signatures, if you wish. As you perform GPG tasks, you will need to reference the keys you have using their key names. Bear in mind that you only need a unique identifying substring to select the key you want. GPG performs a pattern search on the string you specify as the key name in any given command. If the string matches more than one key, all those matching values will be selected. In the following example, the "Sendmail" string selects matches on the identities of two keys.

```
# gpg --list-keys "Sendmail"
pub   1024R/CC374F2D 2000-12-14
            Sendmail Signing Key/2001 <sendmail@Sendmail.ORG>
pub   1024R/E35C5635 1999-12-13
            Sendmail Signing Key/2000 <sendmail@Sendmail.ORG>
```

Encrypting Messages

The **gpg** command provides several options for managing secure messages. The **e** option encrypts messages, the **a** option generates an armored text version, and the **s** option adds a digital signature. You will need to specify the recipient's public key, which you should already have imported into your **pubring** file. It is this key that is used to encrypt the message. The recipient will then be able to decode the message with their private key. Use the **--recipient** or **-r** option to specify the name of the recipient key. You can use any unique substring in the user's public key name. The e-mail address usually suffices. You use the **d** option to decode received messages. In the following example, the user encrypts (**e**) and signs (**s**) a file generated in armored text format (**a**). The **-r** option indicates the recipient for the message (whose public key is used to encrypt the message).

```
gpg e -s -a -o myfile.asc -r george@rabbit.mytrek.com myfile
# mail george@rabbit.mytrek.com < myrile.asc
```

You can leave out the ASCII armor option if you want to send or transfer the file as a binary attachment. Without the **--armor** or **-a** option, **gpg** generates an encoded binary file, not an encoded text file. A binary file can be transmitted through e-mail only as an attachment. As noted previously, ASCII armored versions usually have an extension of **.asc**, whereas binary versions use **.gpg**.

NOTE *You can use **gpgsplit** to split a GPG message into its components in order to examine them separately.*

Decrypting Messages

When the other user receives the file, they can save it to a file named something like **myfile.asc** and then decode the file with the **-d** option. The **-o** option will specify a file to save the decoded version in. GPG will automatically determine if it is a binary file or an ASCII armored version.

```
gpg -d -o myfile.txt myfile.asc
```

To check the digital signature of the file, you use the **gpg** command with the **--verify** option. This assumes that the sender has signed the file.

```
$ gpg --verify myfile.asc
```

Decrypting a Digital Signature
You will need to have the signer's public key to decode and check the digital signature. If you do not, you will receive a message saying that the public key was not found. In this case, you will first have to obtain the signer's public key. You could access a keyserver that you think may have the public key, or request the public key directly from a Web site or from the signer. Then import the key as described previously.

Signing Messages
You do not have to encrypt a file to sign it. A digital signature is a separate component. You can either combine the signature with a given file or generate one separately. To combine a signature with a file, you generate a new version that incorporates both. Use the **--sign** or **-s** option to generate a version of the document that includes the digital signature. In the following example, the **mydoc** file is digitally signed with the **mydoc.gpg** file containing both the original file and the signature.

```
$ gpg  -o mydoc.gpg  --sign mydoc
```

If, instead, you want to just generate a separate signature file, you use the **--detach-sig** command. This has the advantage of not having to generate a complete copy of the original file. That file remains untouched. The signature file usually has an extension like **.sig**. In the following example, the user creates a signature file called **mydoc2.sig** for the **mydoc2** file.

```
$ gpg -o mydoc2.sig --detach-sig mydoc2
```

To verify the file using a detached signature, the recipient user specifies both the signature file and the original file.

```
$ gpg --verify mydoc2.sig  mydoc2
```

To verify a trusted signature you can use **gpgv**.

You could also generate a clear sign signature to be used in text files. A *clear sign* signature is a text version of the signature that can be attached to a text file. The text file can be further edited by any text editor. Use the **--clearsign** option to create a clear sign signature. The following example creates a clear signed version of a text file called **mynotice.txt**.

```
$ gpg -o mysignotice.txt --clearsign mynotice.txt
```

NOTE *Numerous GUI front ends and filters are available for GnuPG at **www.gnupg.org**. GPA (GNU Privacy Assistant) provides a GNOME-based front end to easily encrypt and decrypt files. You can select files to encode, choose the recipients (public keys to use), and add a digital signature if you wish. You can also use GPA to decode encoded files you receive. You can also manage your collection of public keys—the keys in your keyring file.*

TIP *Steganography is a form of encryption that hides data in other kinds of objects, such as images. You can use JPEG Hide and Seek software (JPHS) to encode and retrieve data in a JPEG image (* **jphide** *and* **jpseek**). *See* **linux01.gwdg.de/~alatham/stego.html** *for more details.*

Checking Software Package Digital Signatures

One very effective use for digital signatures is to verify that a software package has not been tampered with. It is possible that a software package could be intercepted in transmission and some of its system-level files changed or substituted. Software packages from your distribution, as well as those by reputable GNU and Linux projects, are digitally signed. The signature provides modification digest information with which to check the integrity of the package. The digital signature may be included with the package file or posted as a separate file. You use the **gpg** command with the **--verify** option to check the digital signature for a file.

TIP *Fedora and Red Hat will install the Red Hat public key in the RPM documentation directory in a file called* **RPM-GPG-KEY, /usr/share/doc/rpm-4.4.2.** *Fedora and Red Hat use this key to check RPM packages during installation. The version number will change with future RPM releases.*

Importing Public Keys

First, however, you will need to make sure that you have the signer's public key. The digital signature was encrypted with the software distributor's private key. That distributor is the signer. Once you have that signer's public key, you can check any data you receive from them. In the case of software repositories like Fedora, **rpm.livna.org**, or **freshrpms.net**, you will be asked to install their public key the first time you try to install any software from their site. Once the key is installed, you do not have to install it again. With Yum, this is usually just a prompt to install the key, requesting a y or n confirmation, or a dialog requesting an OK click. Repositories like Livna and **Fresprms.net** will include their keys with their Yum configuration packages. You can also, if you wish, download and install them manually from their Web sites.

In the case of a software distributor, you can download their public key from their Web site or from their keyserver. Once you have their public key, you can check any software they distribute.

As noted previously, you can download the Red Hat public key from the Red Hat Web site security resources page or use the version installed in the RPM documentation directory. Once you have obtained the public key, you can add to your keyring with the **-import** option, specifying the name you gave to the downloaded key file (in this case, **myredhat.asc**):

```
# gpg --import redhat.asc
gpg: key CBA29BF9: public key imported
gpg: Total number processed: 1
gpg:               imported: 1 (RSA: 1)
```

To download from a keyserver instead, you use the **--keyserver** option and the keyserver name.

To import the Red Hat public key from the RPM directory, you would specify the **RPM-GPG-KEY** file. This is the key provided by the Red Hat distribution on your DVD-ROM or CD-ROMs. Though used during installation, the key has to be imported to verify packages again after they have been installed.

```
# rpm --import /usr/share/doc/rpm-4.2.2/RPM-GPG-KEY
```

Validating Public Keys

You can use the `--fingerprint` option to check a key's validity if you wish. If you are confident that the key is valid, you can then sign it with the `--sign-key` command. In the following example, the user signs the Red Hat key, using the string "Red Hat" in the key's name to reference it. The user is also asked to enter his passphrase to allow use of his private key to sign the Red Hat public key.

```
# gpg --sign-key "Red Hat"
pub  1024R/CBA29BF9  created: 1996-02-20 expires: never  trust: -/q
(1). Red Hat Software, Inc. <redhat@redhat.com>
pub  1024R/CBA29BF9  created: 1996-02-20 expires: never  trust: -/q
 Fingerprint: 6D 9C BA DF D9 60 52 06  23 46 75 4E 73 4C FB 50
 Red Hat Software, Inc. <redhat@redhat.com>

Are you really sure that you want to sign this key
with your key: "Richard Petersen (author) <richlp@turtle.mytrek.com>"
Really sign? yes
You need a passphrase to unlock the secret key for
user: "Richard Petersen (author) <richlp@turtle.mytrek.com>"
1024-bit DSA key, ID 73F0A73C, created 2001-09-26
Enter passphrase:
#
```

Checking RPM Packages

RPM packages from any Yum repository like Fedora will check the public key automatically. Should you download an RPM package separately, you can check the package manually. Once you have the software provider's public key, you can check any RPM software packages for Fedora or Red Hat with the **rpm** command and **-K** option. The following example checks the validity of the xcdroast software packages:

```
# rpm -K xcdroast-0.98alpha9-1.i386.rpm
xcdroast-0.98alpha9-1.i386.rpm: md5 OK
```

Many software packages in the form of compressed archives, **.tar.gz** or **tar.bz2**, will provide signatures in separate files that end with the **.sig** extension. To check these, you use the **gpg** command with the **--verify** option. For example, the most recent Sendmail package is distributed in the form of a compressed archive, **.tar.gz**. Its digital signature is provided in a separate **.sig** file. First you would download and install the public key for Sendmail software obtained from the Sendmail Web site (the key may have the year as part of its name).

```
# gpg --import sendmail2006.asc
```

You should then sign the Sendmail public key that you just imported. In this example, the e-mail address was used for the key name.

```
# gpg --sign-key sendmail@Sendmail.ORG
```

You could also check the fingerprint of the key for added verification.

You would then download both the compressed archive and the digital signature files. For the compressed archive (**.tar.gz**) you can use the **.sig** file ending in **.gz.sig**, and for the uncompressed archive use **.tar.sig**. Then, with the **gpg** command and the **--verify** option, use the digital signature in the **.sig** file to check the authenticity and integrity of the software compressed archive.

```
# gpg --verify sendmail.8.13.8.tar.gz.sig sendmail.8.13.8.tar.gz
gpg: Signature made Tue 08 Aug 2006 10:24:45 PM PDT using RSA key ID AF959625
gpg: Good signature from "Sendmail Signing Key/2006 <sendmail@Sendmail.ORG>"
```

You could also just specify the signature file and **gpg** will automatically search for and select a file of the same name, but without the **.sig** or **.asc** extension.

```
# gpg --verify sendmail.8.12.0.tar.sig
```

In the future, when you download any software from the Sendmail site that uses this key, you just have to perform the **--verify** operation. Bear in mind, though, that different software packages from the same site may use different keys. You would have to make sure that you have imported and signed the appropriate key for the software you are checking.

Intrusion Detection: Tripwire and AIDE

When someone breaks into a system, they will usually try to gain control by making their own changes to system administration files, such as password files. They could create their own user and password information, allowing them access at any time, or simply change the root user password. They could also replace entire programs, such as the login program, with their own version. One method of detecting such actions is to use an integrity checking tool such as Tripwire or AIDE to detect any changes to system administration files. AIDE (Advanced Intrusion Detection Environment) is an alternative to Tripwire. It provides easy configuration and detailed reporting. Both are available on the Fedora repository.

An integrity checking tool works by first creating a database of unique identifiers for each file or program to be checked. These can include features such as permissions and file size, but also, more importantly, checksum numbers generated by encryption algorithms from the file's contents. For example, in Tripwire, the default identifiers are checksum numbers created by algorithms like the SHA2 modification digest algorithm and Snefru (Xerox secure hash algorithm). An encrypted value that provides such a unique identification of a file is known as a signature. In effect, a signature provides an accurate snapshot of the contents of a file. Files and programs are then periodically checked by generating their identifiers again and matching them with those in the database. Tripwire will generate signatures of the current files and programs and match them against the values previously generated for its database. Any differences are noted as changes to the file, and Tripwire then notifies you of the changes.

Encrypted File Systems: luks

You are now able to encrypt non-root and swap file systems using luks. These are partitions or disks that do not include your root directory.

PART IV

NOTE *You can also employ sniffers to check our network traffic. This kind of intrusion detection is provided by Kismet and Snort, also available on the Fedora repository.*

Encrypted File Systems

Fedora lets you encrypt non-root and swap file systems, allowing access only to those users with the appropriate encrypted password. You can apply encryption to both fixed and removable file systems like USB devices. It is recommended that you use the Luks (Linux Unified Key Setup) encryption tools to encrypt file systems. The easiest way to set up an encrypted file system is to use gnome-luks-format tool. This tool lets you specify the file system, the encryption cypher and passphrase, and the file system type and name. Be sure the file system is not mounted. Instead of gnome-luks-format, you can use luks-format command.

Once formatted, restart your system. You can then access the encrypted partition or removable drive. For a USB drive or disk, from file system window double click on the USB drive icon. This opens a window in which you are prompted for a password with the option to forget, remember for the session, or always remember. A message tells you the device is encrypted. Once you enter your password, you can then mount and access the device (double click it again). The volume name will appear with an icon on your desktop. HAL will handle all mounting and access for removable media. Use the same procedure for fixed partitions. Instead of restarting your system after the initialization and format, you can use luks-setup or crypsetup with the luksOpen option to open the encrypted file system. If you want to manage fixed drives manually, you can place entries in the **/etc/crypttab** and **/etc/fstab** files for them.

Instead of using gnome-luks-format, you can use the cryptsetup command directly to manually setup your encrypted file system. You first use the cryptsetup command with the luksFormat option to initialize and create an encrypted volume. You will be prompted to specify a key (or add the key file as an argument). Add an entry for the volume in the **/etc/crypttab** file. Then either reboot or use the cryptsetup command with the luksOpen option to access the volume. You will be prompted for the key (or use **--keyfile** to specify the key). You can then format the file system, specifying its name and type. Place an entry for the new file system in the **/etc/fstab** file.

If you did not use Luks, you will have to specify a encryption method with the cypher option. Use the **--cypher** option with cryptsetup the cypher option in the **/etc/crypttab** entry. For an ESSIV cypher you would use aes-cbc-essiv:sha256. For a plain cypher you would use aes-cbc-plain.

Security-Enhanced Linux: SELinux

Though numerous security tools exist for protecting specific services, as well as user information and data, no tool has been available for protecting the entire system at the administrative level. Security-Enhanced Linux provides built-in administrative protection for aspects of your Linux system. Instead of relying on users to protect their files or on a specific network program to control access, security measures are built into the basic file management system and the network access methods. All controls can be managed directly by an administrator as part of Linux system administration.

Security-Enhanced Linux (SELinux) is a project developed and maintained by the National Security Agency (NSA), which chose Linux as its platform for implementing a secure operating system. Fedora Linux has embraced SELinux and has incorporated it as a standard feature of its distribution. Detailed documentation is available from the resources listed in Table 17-1, including sites provided by the NSA, SourceForge, and Fedora. A very detailed manual for SELinux on Red Hat is provided by the Red Hat Enterprise Linux SELinux Guide, located on the Documentation Web page for Red Hat Enterprise Linux Documentation at the Red Hat site, **www.redhat.com**. It is advised that you read this guide. Its content is also applicable to Fedora. Also check out the Fedora FAQs on SELinux for new features like MLS and documentation links. The site located at

```
fedoraproject.org/wiki/SELinux
```

Linux and Unix systems normally use a discretionary access control (DAC) method for restricting access. In this approach users and the objects they own, such as files, determine permissions. The user has complete discretion over the objects it owns. The weak point in many Linux/Unix systems has been the user administrative accounts. If an attacker managed to gain access to an administrative account, that person would have complete control over the service the account managed. Access to the root user would give control over the entire system, all its users, and any network services it was running. To counter this weakness, the NSA set up a mandatory access control (MAC) structure. Instead of an all-or-nothing set of privileges based on accounts, services and administrative tasks are compartmentalized and separately controlled, with policies detailing what can and cannot be done. Access is granted not just because one is an authenticated user, but when specific

Resource	Location
Red Hat Enterprise SE Linux Guide	**www.redhat.com/docs/manuals/enterprise/ RHEL-4-Manual/selinux-guide/**
Fedora SELinux FAQs	**fedoraproject.org/wiki/SELinux**
NSA SELinux	**www.nsa.gov/selinux**
NSA SELinux FAQs	**www.nsa.gov/selinux/info/faq.cfm**
SELinux at sourceforge.net	**selinux.sourceforge.net**
Writing SELinux Policy HOWTO	Accessible from the "SELinux resources at sourceforge" link at **selinux.sourceforge.net**
NSA SELinux Documentation	**www.nsa.gov/selinux/info/docs.cfm**
Configuring SELinux Policy	Accessible from NSA SELinux Documentation
SELinux on Fedora, tutorials, references, and links	**fedoraproject.org/wiki/SELinux**
SELinux Reference Policy Project	**oss.tresys.com/projects/refpolicy**

TABLE 17-1 SELinux Resources

security criteria are met. Users, applications, processes, files, and devices can be given just the access they need to do their job, and nothing more.

TIP *Fedora features two tools for more easily managing your SELinux policy: System-Config-SELinux for directly managing your policy, and SELinux Troubleshooter for fixing SELinux access permissions for certain applications or operations.*

Flask Architecture

The Flask architecture organizes operating system components and data into subjects and objects. Subjects are processes: applications, drivers, and system tasks that are currently running. Objects are fixed components such as files, directories, sockets, network interfaces, and devices. For each subject and object, a security context is defined. A *security context* is a set of security attributes that determine how a subject or object can be used. This approach provides a very fine-grained control over every element in the operating system as well as all data on your computer.

The attributes designated for the security contexts and the degree to which they are enforced are determined by an overall security policy. The policies are enforced by a security server. Fedora provides three policies, each in its own package—strict, targeted, and MLS—which are all variations of a single reference policy.

SELinux uses a combination of the type enforcement (TE), role-based access control (RBAC), and multilevel security (MLS) security models. Type enforcement focuses on objects and processes like directories and applications, whereas role-based access enforcement controls user access. For the type enforcement model, the security attributes assigned to an object are known as either domains or types. Types are used for fixed objects such as files, and domains are used for processes such as running applications. For user access to processes and objects, SELinux makes use of the role-based access control model. When new processes or objects are created, transition rules specify the type or domain they belong to in their security contexts.

With the RBAC model, users are assigned roles for which permissions are defined. The roles restrict what objects and processes a user can access. The security context for processes will include a role attribute, controlling what objects it can assess. The new multilevel security (MLS) model adds security levels, containing both a sensitivity and capability value.

Users are given separate SELinux user identities. Normally these correspond to the user IDs set up under the standard Linux user creation operations. Though they may have the same name, they are not the same identifiers. Standard Linux identities can be easily changed with commands like **setuid** and **su**. Changes to the Linux user ID will not affect the SELinux ID. This means that even if a user changes its ID, SELinux will still be able to track it, maintaining control over that user.

SELinux Policy Packages

Fedora Linux provides several SELinux policy packages. The targeted one is installed by default. You can use Pirut to download the others. The source code, along with the source code documentation, is now kept in separate RPMS packages, which you download and manually install.

selinux-policy	SELinux documentation
selinux-policy-targeted	SELinux targeted policy configuration
selinux-policy-strict	SELinux strict policy configuration
selinux-policy-mls	SELinux MLS policy configuration
selinux-policy-*version*-src.rpms	SELinux Reference Policy source files
selinux-doc	Binary documentation
selinux-doc-*version*-src.rpms	SELinux Reference Policy documentation
selinux-development	SELinux development modules, **/usr/share/ selinux/devl**

NOTE *You can also use* **setroubleshoot** *to check and locate problems you may be having with SELinux.*

Each policy installs its configuration files in **/etc/selinux**. If you want to add your own module, you need to use the policy headers and module **.pp** files, which are located in **/usr/ share/selinux**. The **selinux-development** package installs the main development module headers in **/usr/share/selinux/devel**. Other packages, such as targeted-policy, then install their own module **.pp** files, with links to the **devel** directory.

Check the **/usr/share/doc/selinux*** directory for examples on how to create a module of your own.

Keep in mind that these are not the source files. There are no **.te** files. The source files have to be installed separately from the **selnux-policy-*version*-src.rpms** file located in the **source/ SRPMS** directory of the Fedora distribution. You will have to manually access the site and download them directly using a Web browser like Firefox or an FTP client. The source packages will not show up in Pirut or Yum.

So there are two selinux-policy creation packages, which are very different from each other, one RPM and one source: **selnux-development** and **selnux-policy-*version*-src.rpms**. The RPM one, which you can install with Pirut or Yum, contains just the headers and **.pp** files needed so that you can compile your own additional modules. The selinux-policy source SRPMS file is the entire SELinux reference policy with all the source code files, including the **.te** files for each module.

You see the same kind of structure for kernel modules. The selinux-development RPM contains only the **header/pp** files needed to create modules, much as you need only the kernel headers to create kernel modules, not the entire kernel source.

System Administration Access

It is critically important that you make sure you have system administrative access under SELinux before you enforce its policies. This is especially true if you are using a strict or MLS policy, which imposes restrictions on administrative access. You should always use SELinux in permissive mode first and check for any messages denying access. With SELinux enforced, it may no longer matter whether you can access the root user or not. What matters is whether your user, even the root user, has sysadm_r role and sysadm_t object access and an administrative security level. You may not be able to just use the **su** command to access the root user and expect to have root user administrative access. Recall that SELinux keeps its own security identities that are not the same as Linux user IDs. Though you might change your user ID with **su**, you still have not changed your security ID.

The targeted policy will set up rules that allow standard system administrator access using normal Linux procedures. The root user will be able to access the root user account normally. In the strict policy, however, the root user needs to access its account using the appropriate security ID. Both are now part of a single reference policy. If you want administrative access through the **su** command (from another user), you would first use the **su** command to log in as the root user. You then have to change your role to that of the sysadm_r role, as well as already be configured by SELinux policy rules to be allowed to take on the sysadm_r role. A user can have several allowed possible roles it could assume.

To change the role, you use the **newrole** command with the **-r** option:

```
newrole -r sysadm_r
```

Terminology

SELinux uses several terms that have different meanings in other contexts. The terminology can be confusing because some of the terms, such as domain, have different meanings in other, related, areas. For example, a domain in SELinux is a process as opposed to an object, whereas in networking the term refers to network DNS addresses.

Identity

SELinux creates identities with which to control access. Identities are not the same as traditional user IDs. At the same time, each user normally has an SELinux identity, though the two are not linked. Affecting a user does not affect the corresponding SELinux identity. SELinux can set up a separate corresponding identity for each user, though on the less secure policies, such as targeted policies, general identities are used. A general user identity is used for all normal users, restricting users to user-level access, whereas administrators are given administrative identities. You can further define security identities for particular users.

The identity makes up part of a security context that determines what a user can or cannot do. Should a user change user IDs, that user's security identity will not change. A user will always have the same security identity. In traditional Linux systems, a user could use commands like **su** to change their user ID and becoming a different user. On SELinux, even though a user could still change his or her Linux user ID, the user still retains the same original security ID. You always know what a particular person is doing on your system, no matter what user ID that person may assume.

The security identity can have limited access. So even though a user may use the Linux **su** command to become the root user, the user's security identity could prevent him or her from performing any root user administrative commands. As noted previously, to gain an administrative access, the role for their security identity would have to change as well.

Use **id -Z** to see what the security context for your security identity is, what roles you have, and what kind of object you can access. This will list the user security context that starts with the security ID, followed by a colon, and then the roles a user has and the objects the user can control. Security identities can have roles that control what they can do. A user role is user_r, and a system administration role is system_r. The general security identity is user_u, whereas a particular security identity will normally use the user name. The following example shows a standard user with the general security identity:

```
$ id -Z
 user_u:user_r:user_t
```

In this example the user has a security identity called george:

```
$ id -Z
 george:user_r:user_t
```

You can use the **newrole** command to change the role a user is allowed. Changing to a system administrative role, the user can then have equivalent root access:

```
$ id -Z
 george:sysadm_r:sysadm_t
```

Domains

Domains are used to identify and control processes. Each process is assigned a domain within which it can run. A domain sets restrictions on what a process can do. Traditionally, a process was given a user ID to determine what it could do, and many had to have the root user ID to gain access to the full file system. This also could be used to gain full administrative access over the entire system. A domain, on the other hand, can be tailored to access some areas but not others. Attempts to break into another domain, say the administrative domain, would be blocked. For example, the administrative domain is sysadm_t, whereas the DNS server uses only named_t and users have a user_t domain.

Types

Whereas domains control processes, *types* control objects like files and directories. Files and directories are grouped into types that can be used to control who can have access to them. The type names have the same format as the domain names, ending with a _t suffix. Unlike domains, types reference objects, including files, devices, and network interfaces.

Roles

Types and domains are assigned to roles. Users (security identities) with a given role can access types and domains assigned to that role. For example, most users can access user_t type objects, but not sysadm_t objects. The types and domains a user can access are set by the role entry in configuration files. The following example allows the user to access objects with the user password type:

```
role user_r types user_passwd_t
```

Security Context

Each object has a security context that sets its security attributes. These include identity, role, domain, or type. A file will have a security context listing the kind of identity that can assess it, the role under which it can be accessed, and the security type it belongs to. Each component adds its own refined level of security. Passive objects are usually assigned a generic role, **object_r**, which has no effect, as such objects cannot initiate actions.

For a normal file created by users in their own directories, you would have the following identity, role, and type. The identity is a user, and the role is that of an object. The type is the user's home directory. This type is used for all subdirectories and their files created within a user's home directory.

```
user_u:object_r:user_home_t
```

A file or directory created by that same user in a different part of the file system will have a different type. For example, the type for files created in the **/tmp** directory will be tmp_t.

```
user_u:object_r:tmp_t
```

Transition: Labeling

A *transition,* also known as labeling, assigns a security context to a process or file. For a file, the security context is assigned when it is created, whereas for a process the security context is determined when the process is run.

Making sure every file has an appropriate security context is called *labeling.* Adding another file system would require that you label (add security contexts) to the directories and files on it. Labeling varies, depending on the policy you use. Each policy may have different security contexts for objects and processes. Relabeling is carried out using the **fixfiles** command in the policy source directory.

```
fixfiles relabel
```

Policies

A *policy* is a set of rules to determine the relationships between users, roles, and types or domains. These rules state what types a role can access and what roles a user can have.

Multilayer Security (MLS) and Multicategory Security (MCS)

Multilayer security (MLS) adds a more refined security access method, designed for servers. MLS adds a security level value to resources. Only users with access to certain levels can access the corresponding files and applications. Within each level access can be further controlled with the use of categories. Categories work much like groups, allowing access only to users cleared for that category. Access becomes more refined, instead of an all-or-nothing situation.

Multicategory security (MCS) extends SELinux to use not only by administrators, but also by users. Users can set categories to restrict and control access to their files and applications. Though based on MLS, MCS uses only categories, not security levels. Users can select a category for a file, but only the administrator can create a category and determine what users can access it. Though similar in concept to an ACL (access control list), MCS differs in that it makes use of the SELinux security structure, providing user-level controls enforced by SELinux.

Management Operations for SELinux

Certain basic operations such as checking the SELinux status, checking a user's or file's security context, or disabling SELinux at boot can be very useful.

Turning Off SELinux

Check the Fedora SELinux FAQs for details on how to turn off SELinux. Should you want to turn off SELinux before you even start up your system, you can turn it off at the boot prompt. Just add the following parameter to the end of your GRUB boot line:

```
selinux=0
```

To turn off SELinux permanently, you can use the system-config-selinux Status tab to set the System Default Enforcing Mode to Disabled, or set the **SELINUX** variable in the **/etc/selinux/config** file to **disabled**:

```
SELINUX=disabled
```

To turn off (permissive mode) SELinux temporarily without rebooting, use the **setenforce** command with the 0 option; use 1 to turn it back on (enforcing mode). You can also use the terms **permissive** or **enforcing** in the arguments instead of 0 or 1. You must first have the sysadm_r role, which you can obtain by logging in as the root user.

```
setenforce 1
```

Checking Status and Statistics

To check the current status of your SELinux system, you can use **sestatus** . Add the **-v** option to also display process and file contexts, as listed in **/etc/sestatus.conf**. The contexts will specify the roles and types assigned to a particular process, file, or directory.

```
sestatus -v
```

Use the **seinfo** command to display your current SELinux statistics.

```
# seinfo
Statistics for policy file: /etc/selinux/targeted/policy/policy.21
Policy Version & Type: v.21 (binary, MLS)

    Classes:              55    Permissions:         206
    Types:              1043    Attributes:           85
    Users:                 3    Roles:                 6
    Booleans:            135    Cond. Expr.:         138
    Sensitivities:         1    Categories:          256
    Allow:             46050    Neverallow:            0
    Auditallow:           97    Dontaudit:          3465
    Role allow:            5    Role trans:            0
    Type_trans:          987    Type_change:          14
    Type_member:           0    Range_trans:          10
    Constraints:           0    Validatetrans:         0
    Fs_use:               12    Genfscon:             52
    Portcon:             190    Netifcon:              0
    Nodecon:               8    Initial SIDs:          0
```

Checking Security Context

The **-Z** option used with the **ls**, **id**, and **ps** commands can be used to check the security context for files, users, and processes, respectively. The security context tells you the roles that users must have to access given processes or objects:

```
ls -lZ
id -Z
ps -eZ
```

SELinux Management Tools

SELinux provides a number of tools to let you manage your SELinux configuration and policy implementation, including semanage to configure your policy. The Fedora system configuration tool for SELinux is system-config-selinux. The setools packages provides SELinux configuration and analysis tools including apol, the Security Policy Analysis tool for domain transition analysis, sediffx for policy differences, and seaudit to examine the auditd logs (see Table 17-2). The setools collection also has corresponding GUI interfaces, in the setool-gui package. These will be listed in the System | Administration menu as SELinux Audit Log Analysis, SELinux Policy Analysis, and SELinux Policy Differences. The command line user management tools, useradd, usermod, and userdel, all have SELinux options that can be applied when SELinux is installed. In addition, the **audit2allow** tool will

Command	Description
`seinfo`	Display policy statistics
`sestatus`	Check status of SELinux on your system, including the contexts of processes and files
`sesearch`	Search for type enforcement rules in policies
`seaudit`	Examine SELinux log files
`sediffx`	Examine SELinux policy differences
`autid2allow`	Generate policy allow rules for modules using audit AVC denial messages.
`apol`	SELinux Policy Analysis
`system-config-selinux`	Fedora SELinux GUI configuration tool
`setroubleshoot`	SELinux GUI troubleshooting tool
`checkpolicy`	The SELinux policy compiler
`fixfiles`	Check file systems and set security contexts
`restorecon`	Set security features for particular files
`newrole`	New role
`setfiles`	Set security context for files
`chcon`	Change context
`chsid`	Change security ID

Table 17-2   SELinux Tools

convert SELinux denial messages into policy modules that will allow access. See a complete listing of SELinux commands at **fedoraproject.org/wiki/SELinux/Commands**.

With the modular version of SELinux, policy management is no longer handled by editing configuration files directly. Instead you use the SELinux management tools such as the command line tool semanage and system-config-selinux (System | Administration | SELinux Managment). These tools make use of interface files to generate changed policies.

Configuration with system-config-selinux

With system-config-selinux you can manage and configure your SELinux policies, though you cannot create new policies (see Figure 17-1). You can access system-config-selinux from the System | Administration menu by selecting the SELinux Management entry.

The system-config-selinux window will list several panes with a sidebar menu for Status, Boolean, File Labeling, User Mapping, SELinux User, Translation, Network Port, and Policy Module. system-config-selinux will invoke the SELinux management tools like sestatus and semanage with appropriate options to make configuration changes.

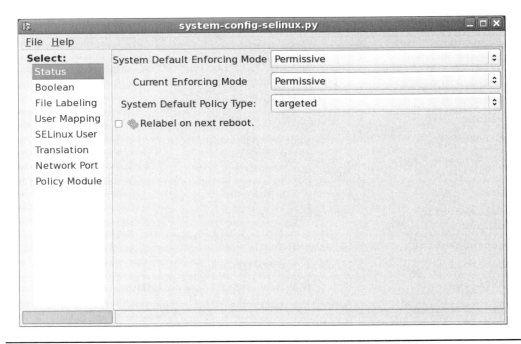

Figure 17-1 The system-config-selinux

The Status pane lists pop-up menus for selecting policy and enforcement defaults, as well as the current enforcing mode. A check box to relabel on reboot lets you force relabeling of your file security contexts when you reboot (see Figure 17-1).

The Boolean pane lists various options for targeted services like Web and FTP servers, NFS, and Samba. With these you can further modify how each service is controlled. There are expandable menus for different services like FTP, Apache Web server, and Samba. For example, the FTP entry lets you choose whether to allow access to home directories or to NFS transfers..

The File Labeling pane will list your system directories and files, showing their security contexts and types. You can edit a file's properties by selecting the entry and then clicking Properties. This displays a dialog with the File Name, Type, SELinux Type, and MLS Level. You can change the SELinux type or the MLS level. For a permissive policy, the MLS level will be s0, allowing access to anyone. You can also add or delete entries.

User Mapping shows the mapping of user login names to SELinux users. Initially there will be two mappings: the root user and the default user.

The SELinux Users pane shows the different kinds of SELinux users. Initially there will be three user types: root, system_u, and user_u (see Figure 17-2). The root user is the root user, which has full and total administrative access to the entire system. The system_u user allows users to take on administrative access where needed. The user_u user is used for normal users. Each entry lists its SELinux User, SELinux prefix, MLS level, MLS range, and SELinux roles. MLS level is the access level (s0 on a permissive policy), and MLS range is the range of access from SystemLow to SystemHigh. A given user has certain roles available. The root user has the system_r, sysadm_r, and user_r roles, allowing it system access, administration

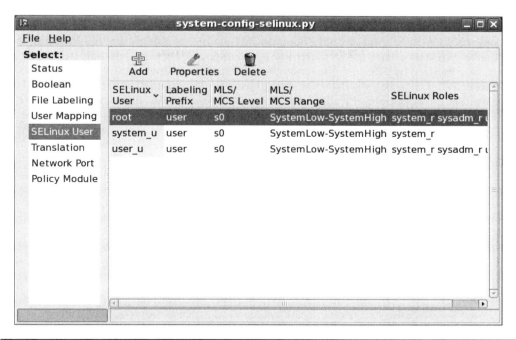

FIGURE 17-2   system-config-selinux SELinux User pane

capability, and standard user access. The same roles are applied to user_u, allowing the user to perform system administration if that user has the root user password. The system_u role has only system access and cannot perform system administration.

The Translation pane lets you set MLS symbols. Initially you will have symbols for SystemHigh and the SystemLow–SystemHigh range. You change the MLS levels for a mapping, changing the security level access across the system.

The Network Port pane lists the network protocol, the SELinux type, and the MLS security level for ports on your system. Select an entry and click Properties to change the SELinux type or the MLS level for the port. The Group View button will display the SELinux type along with a list of the ports they apply to. This view does not display the MLS level, as these apply to ports individually.

The Policy modules pane lists the different SELinux policy modules. Here you will see modules for different applications like Thunderbird and Evolution, as well as device services like USB and HAL. Listed also are desktops like GNOME. The pane allows you to add or remove a module. You can also enable or add additional audit rules for a module for logging.

NOTE   *You can use system-config-securitylevel to configure basic settings for SELinux (see Chapter 4 for more details). Here you can choose whether to enable SELinux, and if so, whether to enforce it or use the permissive option. The permissive option will issue warnings only.*

SELinux Troubleshooting and audit2allow

Fedora includes the SELinux troubleshooter, which notifies problems that SELinux detects. Whenever SELinux denies access to a file or application, the kernel issues an AVC notice. These are analyzed by SELinux troubleshooter to detect problems that users may have to deal with. When a problem is detected, the SELinux troubleshooter notification will be displayed in the desktop notification area along with the a troubleshooter icon. Clicking on the icon or notice will open the SELinux troubleshooter window. You can also access it at any time from System | Administration | SELinux troubleshooter. You can find out more information about SELinux troubleshooter at **hosted.fedoraproject.org/projects/setroubleshoot**.

The SELinux troubleshooter window will display a list of notices, along with their date, the number of times it has occurred, its category, and a brief explanation. The Filter entry lets you turn off future notification of this event. Selecting an entry will display detailed information about the notice in four sections: Summary, Detailed Description, Allowing Access, and Additional Information (see Figure 17-3).

In many cases the problem may be simple to fix, as shown in the Allowing Access section in Figure 17-3. Often, the security context of a file has to be renamed to allow access. You use the **chcon** command to change a file's security context. In this rename access needs

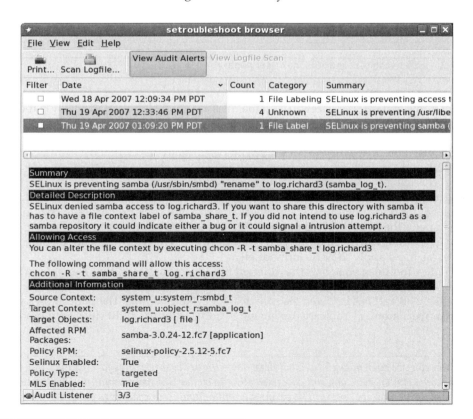

FIGURE 17-3 SELinux troubleshooter

to be granted to the Samba server for a **log.richard3** file in the **/var/lib/samba** directory. The SELinux troubleshooter will take no action of its own. Instead it recommends possible actions. In this example, the user just issues the following **chcon** command:

```
chcon -R -t samba_share_t log.richard3
```

More complicated problems, especially ones that are unknown, may require you to create a new policy module using the AVC messages in the audit log. To do this, you can use the **audit2allow** command. This command will take an audit AVC message and generate commands to allow SELinux access. The audit log used in Fedora is **/var/log/autid/audit.log**. This log is outputed to **audit2allow,** which then can use its **-M** option to create a policy module.

```
cat /var/log/audit/audit.log | audit2allow -M local
```

You then use the semodule command to load the module.

```
semodule -i local.pp
```

If you want to first edit the allowable entries, you can use the following to create a **.te** file of the local module, **local.te**, which you can then edit:

```
audit2allow -m local -i  /var/log/audit/audit.log   >  local.te
```

Once you have edited the **.te** file, you can then use **checkmodule** to compile the module, and then **semodule_package** to create the policy module, **local.pp**. Then you can install it with **semodule**. You first create a **.mod** file with **checkmodule**, and then a **.pp** file with **semodule_package**.

```
checkmodule -M -m -o local.mod local.te
semodule_package -o local.pp  -m local.mod
semodule -i local.pp
```

In this example the policy module is just called **local**. If you later want to create a new module with **audit2allow**, you should either use a different name or just append the output to the **.te** file using the **-o** option.

semanage

Using **semanage**, you can change your SELinux configuration without having to edit SELinux source files directly. It covers several major categories, including users, ports, file contexts, and logins. Check the main page for **semanage** for detailed descriptions. Options let you modify specific security features such as **-s** for the user name, **-R** for the role, **-t** for the type, and **-r** for an MLS security range. The following example adds a user with role user_r:

```
semanage user -a -R user_r  justin
```

semanage is configured with the **/etc/selinux/semanage.conf** file, where you can set **semanage** to write directly on modules (the default) or work on the source.

The Security Policy Analysis Tool: apol

The SELinux Policy Analysis tool, **apol**, provides a complex and detailed analysis of a selected policy (System | Administration | SELinux Policy Analysis). Check the Red Hat Enterprise Linux SELinux Guide for a detailed description. Select the **apol** entry in the Administration menu to start it.

Checking SELinux Messages: seaudit

SELinux AVC messages are now saved in the **/var/log/audit/audit.log** file. These are particularly important if you are using the permissive mode to test a policy you want to later enforce. You need to find out if you are being denied access where appropriate and afforded control when needed. To see just the SELinux messages, you can use the **seaudit** tool (System | Administration | SELinux Audit Log Analysis). Check the Red Hat Enterprise Linux SELinux Guide for a detailed description on using **seaudit**. Startup messages for the SELinux service are still logged in **/var/log/messages**.

The SELinux Reference Policy

A system is secured using a policy. SELinux now uses a single policy, the reference policy, instead of the two separate targeted and strict policies used in previous editions (see **serefpolicy.sourceforge.net**). Instead of giving users just two alternatives, strict and targeted, the SELinux reference policy project aims to provide a basic policy that can be easily adapted and expanded as needed. The SELinux reference policy configures SELinux into modules that can be handled separately. You still have strict and targeted policies, but these are variations on a basic reference policy. In addition, you can have an MLS policy for multilayer security. The targeted policy is installed by default, and you can install the strict or MLS policies yourself.

So for Fedora, there are currently three effective policies provided: **targeted**, **strict**, and **mls**. The targeted policy is used to control specific services, like network and Internet servers such as Web, DNS, and FTP servers. It also can control local services with network connections. The policy will not affect just the daemon itself, but all the resources it uses on your system. Fedora 5 has a large number of daemons that are now controlled by the targeted policy. See the Fedora SELinux FAQ at **http://fedoraproject.org/wiki/SELinux/Domains** for a complete listing.

The strict policy provides complete control over your system. It is under this kind of policy that your users and even administrators can be inadvertently locked out of the system. A strict policy needs to be carefully tested to make sure access is denied and granted where appropriate.

There will be **targeted**, **strict**, and **mls** subdirectories in your **/etc/selinux** directory, but they now each contain a modules directory. It is here that you will find your SELinux configurations.

Multilayer Security (MLS)

Multilayer security (MLS) adds a more refined security access method. MLS adds a security level value to resources. Only users with access to certain levels can access the corresponding files and applications. Within each level access can be further controlled with the use of categories. Categories work much like groups, allowing access only to users cleared for each category. Access becomes more refined, instead of an all-or-nothing situation.

Multicategory Security (MCS)

Multicategory security (MCS) extends SELinux not only to use by administrators, but also by users. Users can set categories that restrict and control access to their files and applications. Though based on MLS, MCS uses only categories, not security levels. Users can select a category for a file, but only the administrator can create a category and determine what users can access it. Though similar in concept to an ACL (access control list), it differs in that it makes use of the SELinux security structure, providing user-level controls enforced by SELinux.

Policy Methods

Operating system services and components are categorized in SELinux by their type and their role. Rules controlling these objects can be type-based or role-based. Policies are implemented using two different kinds of rules, type enforcement (TE) and role-based access control (RBAC). Multilayer security (MLS) is an additional method further restricting access by security level. Security contexts now feature both the role of an object, such as a user, and that object's security level.

Type Enforcement

With a type structure, the operating system resources are partitioned off into types, with each object assigned a type. Processes are assigned to domains. Users are restricted to certain domains, allowed to use only objects accessible in those domains.

Role-Based Access Control

A role-based approach focuses on controlling users. Users are assigned roles, which define what resources they can use. In a standard system, file permissions, such as those for groups, can control user access to files and directories. With roles, permissions become more flexible and refined. Certain users can have more access to services than others.

SELinux Users

Users will retain the permissions available on a standard system. In addition, SELinux can set up its own controls for a given user, defining a role for that user. General security identities created by SELinux include

- **system_u**   The user for system processes
- **user_u**   Allows normal users to use a service
- **root**   For the root user

Policy Files

Policies are implemented in policy files. These are binary files compiled from source files. On Fedora you have just a targeted policy file. The policy binary files are in policy subdirectories in the **/etc/selinux** configuration directory, **/etc/selinux/targeted**. For example, the policy file for the targeted policy is

```
/etc/selinux/targeted/policy/policy.20
```

The targeted development file that holds the interface files is installed at **/usr/share/selinux**:

```
/usr/share/selinux/targeted
```

You can use the development files to create your own policy modules that you can then load.

SELinux Configuration

Configuration for general SELinux server settings is carried out in the **/etc/selinux/config** directory. Currently there are only two settings to make: the state and the policy. You set the SELINUX variable to the state, such as enforcing or permissive, and the SELINUXTYPE variable to the kind of policy you want. These correspond to the Securitylevel-config SELinux settings for disabled and enforcing, as well as the policy to use, such as targeted. A sample config file is shown here:

```
# This file controls the state of SELinux on the system.
# SELINUX= can take one of these three values:
#     enforcing - SELinux security policy is enforced.
#     permissive - SELinux prints warnings instead of enforcing.
#     disabled - SELinux is fully disabled.
SELINUX=permissive
# SELINUXTYPE= type of policy in use. Possible values are:
#     targeted - Only targeted network daemons are protected.
#     strict - Full SELinux protection.
SELINUXTYPE=targeted
```

SELinux Policy Rules

Policy rules can be made up of either type (type enforcement) or RBAC (role-based access control) statements, along with security levels (multilevel security). A type statement can be a type or attribute declaration, or a transition, change, or assertion rule. The RBAC statements can be role declarations or dominance or allow roles. A security level specifies a number corresponding to the level of access permitted. Policy configuration can be difficult, using extensive and complicated rules. For this reason, many rules are implemented using M4 macros in **fi** files that will in turn generate the appropriate rules (Sendmail uses M4 macros in a similar way). You will find these rules in files in the SELinux reference policy source code package, which you need to download and install. The reference policy package is **selinux-policy**, located in the **RPMS** source code repository of Fedora. See the following section on SELinux configuration files.

Type and Role Declarations

A type declaration starts with the keyword **type**, followed by the type name (identifier) and any optional attributes or aliases. The type name will have a _t suffix. Standard type definitions are included for objects such as files. The following is a default type for any file, with attributes file_type and sysadmfile:

```
type file_t, file_type, sysadmfile;
```

The root will have its own type declaration.

```
type root_t, file_type, sysadmfile;
```

Specialized directories such as the boot directory will also have their own type.

```
type boot_t, file_type, sysadmfile;
```

More specialized rules are set up for specific targets like the Amanda server. The following example is the general type definition for amanda_t objects, those objects used by the Amanda backup server, as listed in the targeted policy's **src/program/amanda.te** file:

```
type amanda_t, domain, privlog, auth, nscd_client_domain ;
```

A role declaration determines the roles that can access objects of a certain type. These rules begin with the keyword **role** followed by the role and the objects associated with that role. In this example, the amanda objects (amanda_t) can be accessed by a user or process with the system role (system_r).

```
role system_r types amanda_t;
```

A more specific type declaration is provided for executables, such as the following for the Amanda server (amanda_exec_t). This defines the Amanda executable as a system administration–controlled executable file.

```
type amanda_exec_t, file_type, sysadmfile, exec_type;
```

Associated configuration files often have their own rules.

```
type amanda_config_t, file_type, sysadmfile;
```

In the targeted policy a general, unconfined type is created that user and system roles can access, giving complete, unrestricted access to the system. More specific rules will restrict access to certain targets like the Web server.

```
type unconfined_t, domain, privuser, privhome, privrole, privowner, admin,
auth_write, fs_domain, privmem;
role system_r types unconfined_t;
role user_r types unconfined_t;
role sysadm_r types unconfined_t;
```

Types are also set up for the files created in the user home directory.

```
type user_home_t, file_type, sysadmfile, home_type;
type user_home_dir_t, file_type, sysadmfile, home_dir_type;
```

File Contexts

File contexts associate specific files with security contexts. The file or files are listed first, with multiple files represented with regular expressions. Then the role, type, and security level are specified. The following creates a security context for all files in the **/etc** directory (configuration files). These are accessible from the system user (system_u) and are objects of the etc_t type with a security level of 0, s0.

```
/etc(/.*)?                system_u:object_r:etc_t:s0
```

Certain files can belong to other types; for instance, the **resolve.conf** configuration file belongs to the net_conf type.

```
/etc/resolv\.conf.*    --    system_u:object_r:net_conf_t:s0
```

Certain services will have their own security contexts for their configuration files.

```
/etc/amanda(/.*)?           system_u:object_r:amanda_config_t:s0
```

File contexts are located in the **file_contexts** file in the policy's contexts directory, such as **/etc/selinux/targeted/contexts/files/file_contexts**. The version used to create or modify the policy is located in the policy modules active directory, as in **targeted/modules/active/ file_contexts**.

User Roles

User roles define what roles a user can take on. Such a role begins with the keyword **user** followed by the user name, then the keyword **roles**, and finally the roles it can use. You will find these rules in the selinux reference policy source code files. The following example is a definition of the system_u user:

```
user system_u roles system_r;
```

If a user can have several roles, then they are listed in brackets. The following is the definition of the standard user role in the targeted policy, which allows users to take on system administrative roles:

```
user user_u roles { user_r sysadm_r system_r };
```

The strict policy lists only the user_r role.

```
user user_u roles { user_r };
```

Access Vector Rules: allow

Access vector rules are used to define permissions for objects and processes. The **allow** keyword is followed by the object or process type, and then the types it can access or be accessed by and the permissions used. The following allows processes in the amanda_t domain to search the Amanda configuration directories (any directories of type amanda_config_t):

```
allow amanda_t amanda_config_t:dir search;
```

The following example allows Amanda to read the files in a user home directory:

```
allow amanda_t user_home_type:file { getattr read };
```

The next example allows Amanda to read, search, and write files in the Amanda data directories:

```
allow amanda_t amanda_data_t:dir { read search write };
```

Role Allow Rules

Roles can also allow rules. Though they can be used for domains and objects, they are usually used to control role transitions, specifying whether a role can transition to another role. These rules are listed in the rbac configuration file. The following entry allows the user to transition to a system administrator role:

```
allow user_r sysadm_r;
```

Transition and Vector Rule Macros

The type transition rules set the type used for rules to create objects. Transition rules also require corresponding access vector rules to enable permissions for the objects or processes. Instead of creating separate rules, macros are used that will generate the needed rules. The following example sets the transition and access rules for user files in the home directory using the file_type_auto_trans macro:

```
file_type_auto_trans(privhome, user_home_dir_t, user_home_t)
```

The next example sets the Amanda process transition and access rules for creating processes:

```
domain_auto_trans(inetd_t, amanda_inetd_exec_t, amanda_t)
```

Constraint Rules

Restrictions can be further placed on processes such as transitions to ensure greater security. These are implemented with constraint definitions in the constraints file. Constraint rules are often applied to transition operations, such as requiring that, in a process transition, user identities remain the same, or that process 1 be in a domain that has the privuser attribute and process 2 be in a domain with the userdomain attribute. The characters **u**, **t**, and **r** refer to user, type, and role.

```
constrain process transition
     ( u1 == u2 or ( t1 == privuser and t2 == userdomain )
```

SELinux Policy Configuration Files

Configuration files are normally changed using **.te** and **.fc** files. These are missing from the module headers in **/usr/share/selinux**. If you are adding a module, you will need to create the **.te** and **.fc** files for it. Then you can create a module and add it as described in the next section.

If you want to create or modify your own policy, you will need to download and install the source code files for the SELinux reference policy as described in the section after that. The reference policy code holds the complete set of .te and .fc configuration files.

Compiling SELinux Modules

Instead of compiling the entire source each time you want to make a change, you can just compile a module for the area you changed. The modules directory holds the different modules. Each module is built from a corresponding .te file. The **checkmodule** command is used to create a .mod module file from the .te file, and then the **semanage_module** command is used to create the loadable .pp module file as well as an .fc file context file. As noted in the SELinux documentation, if you need to just change the configuration for **syslogd**, you would first use the following to create a **syslogd.mod** file using **syslogd.te**. The **-M** option specifies support for MLS security levels.

```
checkmodule -M -m syslogd.te  -o syslogd.mod
```

Then use the **semanage_module** command to create a **syslogd.pp** file from the **syslogd.mod** file. The **-f** opton specifies the file context file.

```
semanage_module -m syslogd.mod  -o syslogd.pp -f syslogd.fc
```

To add the module, you use **semodule** and the **-i** option. You can check if a module is loaded with the **-l** option.

```
semodule -i syslogd.pp
```

Changes to the base policy are made to the **policy.conf** file, which is compiled into the **base.pp** module.

Using SELinux Source Configuration

To perform your own configuration, you will have to download and install the source code file **selinux-policy** from the **SRPMS** directory (**source**). The .te files used for configuring SELinux are no longer part of the SELinux binary packages.

Once the SRPMS file is downloaded, you would then have to use an **rpm** command with the **-i** option in a terminal window to install the source code.

```
rpm -i selinux-policy-2.3.18-10.noarch.srpms
```

The compressed archive of the source, a **tgz** file, along with various policy configuration files, will be installed to **/usr/src/redhat/SOURCES**. (Be sure you have already installed **rpm-build**; it is not installed by default.) Documentation for using the source files appears in another source SRPMS file, called **selinux-doc**.

You use an **rpmbuild** operation to extract the file to the **serefpolicy** directory in **/usr/src/redhat/BUILD**. Within this directory you will find a **policy/modules** subdirectory. There, organized into several directories, **admin**, **apps**, and others, you will find the .tc, .fc, and .if configuration files.

```
rpmbuild -bp  security-policy.spec
```

Then you change to the **/usr/src/redhat/BUILD/seref-policy** directory and run the following command to install selinux source to **/etc/selinux/serefpolicy/src**:

```
make install-src
```

The rules are held in configuration files located in various subdirectories in a policy's **src** directory. Within this directory you will find a **policy/modules** subdirectory. There, organized into several directories, **admin**, **apps**, and others, you will find the **.tc**, **.fc**, and **.if** configuration files.

You will have configuration files for both type enforcement and security contexts. Type enforcement files have the extension **.te**, whereas security contexts have an **.sc** extension.

Reflecting the fine-grained control that SELinux provides, you have numerous module configuration files for the many kinds of objects and processes on your system. The primary configuration files and directories are listed in Table 17-3, but several expand to detailed listings of subdirectories and files.

Directories and Files	Description
assert.te	Access vector assertions
config/appconfig-*	Application runtime configuration files
policy/booleans.conf	Tunable features
file_contexts	Security contexts for files and directories
policy/flask	Flask configuration
policy/mcs	Multicategory security (MCS) configuration
doc	Policy documentation support
policy/modules	Security policy modules
policy/modules.conf	Module list and use
policy/modules/admin	Administration modules
policy/modules/apps	Application modules
policy/modules/kernel	Kernel modules
policy/modules/services	Services and server modules
policy/modules/system	System modules
policy/rolemap	User domain types and roles
policy/users	General users definition
config/local.users	Define your own SELinux users
policy/constraints	Additional constraints for role transition and object access
policygentool	Script to generate policies
policy/global_tunables	Defines policy tunables for customization
policy/mls	Multilevel security (MLS) configuration

TABLE 17-3 SELinux Policy Configuration Files

InterfaceFiles

File interface files allow management tools to generate policy modules. They define interface macros for your current policy. The **refpolicy** SELinux source file will hold **.if** files for each module, along with **.te** and **.fc** files. Also, **.if** files in the **/usr/share/selinux/devel** directory can be used to generate modules.

Types Files

In the targeted policy, the modules directory that defines types holds a range of files, including **nfs.te** and **network.te** configuration files. Here you will find type declarations for the different kinds of objects on your system. The **.te** files are no longer included with your standard SELinux installation. Instead, you have to download and install the **serefpolicy** source package. This is the original source and allows you to completely reconfigure your SELinux policy, instead of managing modules with management tools like **semanage**. The modules directory will hold **.te** files for each module listing their TE rules.

Module Files

Modules are located among several subdirectories in the **policy/modules** directory. Here you will find three corresponding files for each application or service. There will be a **.te** file that contains the actual type enforcement rules, an **.fi**, or interface, file that allows other applications to interact with the module, and the **.fc** files that define the file contexts.

Security Context Files

Security contexts for different files are detailed in security context files. The **file_contexts** file holds security context configurations for different groups, directories, and files. Each configuration file has an **.fc** extension. The **types.fc** file holds security contexts for various system files and directories, particularly access to configuration files in the **/etc** directory. In the SELinux **refpolicy** source, each module will have its own **.fc** file, along with corresponding **.te** and **.if** files. The **distros.fc** file defines distribution-dependent configurations, including security contexts for all the Fedora system configuration tools. The **homedir_template** file defines security contexts for dot files that may be set up in a user's home directory, such as **.mozilla**, **.gconf**, and **.java**.

A modules directory has context files for particular applications and services. For example, **apache.fc** has the security contexts for all the files and directories used by the Apache Web server, such as **/var/www** and **/etc/httpd**.

User Configuration: Roles

Global user configuration is defined in the policy directory's **users** file. Here you find the user definitions and the roles they have for standard users (user_u) and administrators (admin_u). To add your own users, you use the **local.users** file. Here you will find examples for entering your own SELinux users. Both the strict and targeted policies use the general **user_u** SELinux identity for users. To set up a separate SELinux identity for a user, you would define that user in the **local.users** file.

The **rbac** file defines the allowed roles one role can transition to. For example, can the user role transition to a system administration role? The targeted policy has several entries allowing a user to freely transition to an administrator, and vice versa. The strict policy has no such definitions.

Role transitions are further restricted by rules in the **constraints** file. Here the change to other users is controlled, and changing object security contexts (labeling) is restricted.

Policy Module Tools

To create a policy module and load it, you use several policy module tools. First the `checkmodule` command is used to create a .mod file from a .te file. Then the **semodule_ package** tool takes the **.mod** file and any supporting **.fc** file and generates a module policy package file, **.pp**. Finally the **semodule** tool can take the policy package file and install it as part of your SELinux policy.

Application Configuration: appconfig

Certain services and applications are security aware and will request default security contexts and types from SELinux (see also the upcoming section "Runtime Security Contexts and Types: contexts"). The configuration is kept in files located in the **policy/config/appconfig-*** directory. The **default_types** file holds type defaults; **default_contexts** holds default security contexts. The **initrc_context** file has the default security context for running **/etc/rc.d** scripts. A special **root_default_contexts** file details how the root user can be accessed. The **removable_ context** file holds the security context for removable devices, and **media** lists media devices, such as cdrom for CD-ROMs. Runtime values can also be entered in corresponding files in the policy contexts directory, such as **/etc/selinux/targeted/contexts**.

Creating a SELinux Policy: make and checkpolicy

If you want to create an entirely new policy, you use the SELinux reference policy source, **/etc/selinux/serefpolicy**. Once you have configured your policy, you can create it with the `make policy` and `checkpolicy` commands. The `make policy` command generates a **policy.conf** file for your configuration files, which `checkpolicy` can then use to generate a policy binary file. A policy binary file will be created in the **policy** subdirectory with a numeric extension for the policy version, such as **policy.20**.

You will have to generate a new policy **policy.conf** file. To do this, you enter the following command in the policy src directory, which will be **/etc/selinux/serefpolicy/src/policy**:

```
make policy
```

Then you can use **checkpolicy** to create the new policy.

Instead of compiling the entire source each time you want to make a change, you can just compile a module for the area you changed. In the previous SELinux version, you always had to recompile the entire policy every time you made a change. The modules directory holds the different modules. Each module is built from a corresponding .te file. The `checkmodule` command is used to create a **.mod** module file from the **.te** file, and then the `semanage_module` command is used to create the loadable policy package **.pp** module file. As noted in the SELinux documentation, if you need to just change the configuration for **syslogd**, you would first use the following to create a **syslogd.mod** file using **syslogd.te**. The **-M** option specifies support for MLS security levels.

```
checkmodule -M  -m syslogd.te  -o syslogd.mod
```

Then use the **semanage_module** command to create a **syslogd.pp** file from the syslogd.mod file. The **-f** option specifies the file context file.

```
semanage_module -m syslogd.mod  -o syslogd.pp -f syslogd.fc
```

To add the module you use **semodule** and the **-i** option. You can check if a module is loaded with the **-l** option.

```
semodule -i syslogd.pp
```

Changes to the base policy are made to the **policy.conf** file, which is compiled into the **base.pp** module.

To perform your own configuration, you will now have to download the source code file selinux-policy from the SRPMS directory. The **.te** files used for configuring SELinux are no longer part of the SELinux binary packages. The source files will be installed to **/usr/src/ redhat/SOURCES**. (Be sure you have already installed rpm-build; it is not installed by default.) Once installed, the source will be in the **sefepolicy** directory in **/etc/selinux.** Documentation for using the source files is included in another source SRPMS file, called selinux-doc.

For **fixfiles**, you use:

```
fixfiles relabel
```

SELinux: Administrative Operations

There are several tasks you can perform on your SELinux system without having to recompile your entire configuration. Security contexts for certain files and directories can be changed as needed. For example, when you add a new file system, you will need to label it with the appropriate security contexts. Also, when you add users, you may need to have a user given special attention by the system. For detecting and fixing problems, you can use **setroubleshoot**.

Using Security Contexts: fixfiles, setfiles, restorecon, and chcon

Several tools are available for changing your objects' security contexts. The **fixfiles** command can set the security context for file systems. You use the **relabel** option to set security contexts, and the **check** option to see what should be changed. The **fixfiles** tool is a script that uses **setfiles** and **restorecon** to make actual changes.

The **restorecon** command will let you restore the security context for files and directories, but **setfiles** is the basic tool for setting security contexts. It can be applied to individual files or directories. It is used to label the file when a policy is first installed.

With **chcon,** you can change the permissions of individual files and directories, much as **chmod** does for general permissions.

Adding New Users

If a new user needs no special access, you can generally just use the generic SELinux user_u identity. If, however, you need to allow the user to take on roles that would otherwise be restricted, such as a system administrator role in the strict policy, you need to configure the user accordingly. To do this, you add the user to the **local.users** file in the policy users directory, as in **/etc/selinux/targeted/policy/users/local.users**. Note that this is different from the **local.users** file in the src directory, which is compiled directly into the policy. The user rules have the syntax

```
user username roles { rolelist };
```

The following example adds the sysadm role to the **george** user:

```
user george roles { user_r sysadm_r };
```

Once the role is added, you have to reload the policy.

```
make reload
```

You can also manage users with the **seuser** command. To see what users are currently active, you can list them with the **seuser** command and the **show users** option.

```
# seuser show users
system_u: system_r
user_u: user_r sysadm_r system_r
root: user_r sysadm_r system_r
```

The **seuser** command has **add**, **delete**, **change**, and **rename** options for managing users. The **add** and **change** options let you specify roles to add to a user, whereas the **delete** option will remove the user.

Runtime Security Contexts and Types: Contexts

Several applications and services are security aware and will need default security configuration information such as security contexts. Runtime configurations for default security contexts and types are kept in files located in the policy context directory, such as **/etc/selinux/targeted/contexts**. Types files will have the suffix **_types**, and security context files will use **_context**. For example, the default security context for removable files is located in the **removable_context** file. The contents of that file are shown here:

```
system_u:object_r:removable_t
```

The **default_context** file is used to assign a default security context for applications. In the strict policy it is used to control system admin access, providing it where needed, for instance, during the login process.

The following example sets the default roles for users in the login process:

```
system_r:local_login_t user_r:user_t
```

This would allows users to log in either as administrators or as regular users.

```
system_r:local_login_t sysadm_r:sysadm_t user_r:user_t
```

This next example is for remote user logins, where system administration is not included:

```
system_r:remote_login_t user_r:user_t staff_r:staff_t
```

The **default_types** file defines default types for roles. This files has role/type entries, and when a transition takes place to a new role, the default type specified here is used. For example, the default type for the sysadm_r role is sysadm_t.

```
sysadm_r:sysadm_t
user_r:user_t
```

Of particular interest is the **initrc_context** file, which sets the context for running the system scripts in the **/etc/rc.d** directory. In the targeted policy these are open to all users.

```
user_u:system_r:unconfined_t
```

In the strict policy these are limited to the system user.

```
system_u:system_r:initrc_t
```

users

Default security contexts may also need to be set up for particular users such as the root user. In the **sesuers** file you will find a root file that lists roles, types, and security levels the root user can take on, such as the following example for the su operation:

```
sysadm_r:sysadm_su_t sysadm_r:sysadm_t staff_r:staff_t user_r:user_t
```

context/files

Default security contexts for your files and directories are located in the **contexts/files** directory. The **file_contexts** directory lists the default security contexts for all your files and directories as set up by your policy. The **file_context.homedirs** directory sets the file contexts for user home directory files as well as the root directory, including dot configuration files like **.mozilla** and **.gconf**. The media file sets the default context for media devices such as CD-ROMs and disks.

```
cdrom system_u:object_r:removable_device_t
floppy system_u:object_r:removable_device_t
disk system_u:object_r:fixed_disk_device_t
```

Internet Protocol Security: IPsec

The Internet Security Protocol, IPsec, incorporates security for network transmission into the Internet Protocol (IP) directly. IPsec is integrated into the new IPv6 protocol (Internet Protocol version 6). It can also be used with the older IPv4 protocol (see Chapter 37). IPsec provides methods for both encrypting data and authenticating the host or network it is sent to. The process can be handled manually or be automated using the IPsec **racoon** key exchange tool. With IPsec, the kernel can automatically detect and decrypt incoming transmissions, as well as encrypt outgoing ones. You can also use IPsec to implement virtual private networks, encrypting data sent over the Internet from one local network to another. Although IPsec is a relatively new security method, its integration into the Internet Protocol will eventually provide it wide acceptance. Check the IPsec Howto for a detailed explanation of IPsec implementation on Linux, **www.ipsec-howto.org**. The Red Hat Linux Enterprise Security Guide provides a helpful description on using IPsec on a Red Hat system in its Virtual Private Network section. The Guide can be found at the Red Hat Linux Enterprise Documentation page on the Red Hat site, **www.redhat.com**.

Several projects currently provide development and implementation of IPsec tools (see Table 18-1). The original IPsec tools are provided by the KAME project, **www.kame.net**. Current versions can be obtained from **ipsec-tools.sourceforge.net**. RPM packages are included with Red Hat Fedora and can also be obtained from **rpmfind.net**. Other IPsec tool projects include the Open Secure/Wide Area Network project (Openswan) at **www.openswan.org**, which provides a Linux implementation of IPsec tools, and the VPN Consortium (VPNC) at **www.vpnc.org**, which supports Windows and Macintosh versions. Openswan is now included with Fedora. Documentation will be located at **/usr/doc/openswan-***version*. Detailed documentation is held in the **openswan-doc** package, which will be installed at **/usr/doc/openswan-doc-***version.*

NOTE *Fedora also provides the **vpnc** client for use with Cisco Easy VPM implementations, and **l2tpd**, which implements the Layer 2 Tunneling Protocol. L2TP supports tunneling operations over dial-up PPP connections.*

Web Site	Project
www.kame.net	KAME project for IPsec tools
www.openswan.org	Open Secure/Wide Area Network project (Fedora)
www.vpnc.org	VPN Consortium
www.ipsec-howto.org	IPsec Howto documentation
ipsec-tools.sourceforge.net	IPsec tools and resources

TABLE 18-1   IPsec Resources

NOTE *Red Hat and Fedora include support for IPsec tools. The system-config-network tool includes panels for IPsec support.*

IPsec Protocols

IPsec is made up of several protocols that provide authentication, encryption, and the secure exchange of encryption keys. The Authentication Header protocol (AH) confirms that the packet was sent by the sender, and not by someone else. IPsec also includes an integrity check to detect any tampering in transit. Packets are encrypted using the Encapsulating Security Payload (ESP). Encryption and decryption are performed using secret keys shared by the sender and the receiver. These keys are themselves transmitted using the Internet Key Exchange (IKE) protocol, which provides a secure exchange. ESP encryption can degrade certain compression transmission methods, such as PPP for dial-up Internet connections. To accommodate these compression methods, IPsec provides the IP Payload Compression Protocol (IPComp), with which packets can be compressed before being sent.

Encrypted authentication and integrity checks are included using Hash Methods Authentication Codes (HMAC) generated from hash security methods like SHA2 using a secret key. The HMAC is included in the IPsec header, which the receiver can then check with the secret key. Encryption of transmitted data is performed by symmetric encryption methods like 3DES, Blowfish, and DES.

The AH, ESP, and IPComp protocols are incorporated into the Linux kernel. The IKE protocol is implemented as a separate daemon. It simply provides a way to share secret keys, and can be replaced by other sharing methods.

IPsec Modes

You can use IPsec capabilities for either normal transport or packet tunneling. With normal transport, packets are encrypted and sent to the next destination. The normal transport mode is used to implement direct host-to-host encryption, where each host handles the IPsec encryption process. Packet tunneling is used to encrypt transmissions between gateways, letting the gateways handle the IPsec encryption process for traffic directed to or from an entire network, rather than having to configure IPsec encryption for each host. With packet tunneling, the packets are encapsulated with new headers for a specific destination, enabling you to implement virtual private networks (VPNs). Packets are directed to VPN gateways, which encrypt and send on local network packets.

NOTE *You can choose to encrypt packets for certain hosts or for those passing through specific ports.*

IPsec Security Databases

The packets you choose to encrypt are designated by the IPsec Security Policy Database (SPD). The method you use to encrypt them is determined by the IPsec Security Association Database (SAD). The SAD associates an encryption method and key with a particular connection or kind of connection. The connections to be encrypted are designated in the Security Policy Database.

IPsec Tools

Several IPsec tools are provided with which you can manage your IPsec connections (see Table 18-2). All are included in the Red Hat Fedora ipsec-tools RPM package. With **setkey**, you can manage both the policy and association databases. The **racoon** tool configures the key exchange process to implement secure decryption key exchanges across connections. To administer your IPsec connections you can use **racoonctl**. For example, the **show-sa** option will display your security associations and the **vpn-connect** will establish a VPN connection.

NOTE *To enable IPsec in the kernel, be sure to enable the PF_KEY, AH, and ESP options in Cryptographic Options.*

Configuring IPsec with system-config-network

The system-config-network tool now provides support for implementing IPsec connections. On the system-config-network tool, select the IPsec panel (see Figure 18-1) and click New to start the IPsec settings wizard for creating an IPsec connection. You are first asked to enter a nickname for the connection and to specify if you want it started automatically. You then choose the connection type. This can be either a direct host-to-host connection or a connection between two networks. A network connection implements a virtual private network (VPN) and runs IPsec in tunnel mode. (Both the host and VPN connections are described in detail in the following sections.) You then select the kind of encryption you want to use. This can either be manual or use IKE, letting **racoon** automatically manage the encryption and authentication process.

You then will configure both your local and remote connections, starting with the local settings. For a host-to-host connection, you need only enter the IP address for the remote host. For a VPN, you will have to enter corresponding addresses for the local and remote networks. For the local network, you will need to enter the IP addresses for the local network, the local network's gateway computer, and the local network's netmask. For the

Tools	Description
plainrsa-gen	Generate a Plain RSA key.
setkey	Manage policy (SPD) and association (SAD) databases
racoon	Configure and implement secure key exchanges using IPsec Key Exchange (IKE)
racoonctl	Administer IPsec connections

TABLE 18-2   IPsec Tools

FIGURE 18-1 IPsec on system-config-network

remote VPN connection, you will need the remote IP address, the remote network's address, its netmask, and its gateway address. Finally, you enter the authentication key. Click the Generate button to create this key.

A final screen will display your entries. Click Apply to save them. Your connection will appear in the IPsec panel, showing its type, destination, and nickname. To establish a connection, select the IPsec connection and click Activate. This will run the **ifup-ipsec** script in the **/etc/sysconfig/network-scripts** directory, which will execute IPsec tools such as **setkey** and **racoon** to establish your connection. Configuration data will be kept in the **/etc/sysconfig/networking/devices** directory, using the name of the IPsec connections. For example, configuration information on the **myipsec** IPsec connection is kept in the **ifcfg-myipsec** file. Corresponding keys for each connection are kept in the keys files, including **keys-myipsec**. A sample **ifcfg** configuration file for a VPN is shown here. The IKE method is a private shared key (PSK). The destination (remote) gateway is 10.0.0.1, and the source (local) gateway is 192.168.0.1. The destination (remote) network address is 10.0.0.0/24, and the source (local) address is 192.168.0.0/24. The destination host is 10.0.0.2.

```
ONBOOT=no
IKE_METHOD=PSK
DSTGW=10.0.0.1
SRCGW=192.168.0.1
DSTNET=10.0.0.0/24
SRCNET=192.168.0.0/24
DST=10.0.0.2
TYPE=IPSEC
```

The corresponding keys file would specify the key used.

```
IKE_PSK=myvpnkey
```

Configuring Connections with setkey

To configure your IPsec connections, you can use the **setkey** tool. This tool contains several instructions for managing rules in the IPsec policy and security databases. You use the **add** instruction to add a security association to the security database (SAD), and the **spdadd** instruction to add a policy to the policy database (SPD). The **ah** term designates that the instruction is being applied to the authentication header (AH), and **esp** indicates the encryption is to be implemented by the encryption security payload (ESP). To implement **setkey** operations, it is best to use a script invoking **setkey** with the **-f** option and listing the **setkey** instructions. The following example creates a simple script to add authentication and encryption instructions for a particular connection, as well as create a security policy for it:

```
#!/sbin/setkey -f
add 192.168.0.2 192.168.0.5 ah 15700 -A hmac-md5 "secret key";
add 192.168.0.2 192.168.0.5  esp 15701 -E 3des-cbc "secret key ";
spdadd 192.168.0.2 192.168.0.5  any -P out ipsec
   esp/transport//require
   ah/transport//require;
```

Security Associations: SA

You use security associations to indicate that you want the authentication header (AH) and encryption payload (ESP) encrypted. A particular connection, such as that between two hosts, can have those hosts' authentication headers encrypted using specified encryption methods and designated secret keys. The same can be done for the encryption payload, the main content of transmissions. A secret key can be determined manually or automatically using key exchanges. The following example specifies that for the connection between 192.168.0.2 and 192.168.0.5, the **hmac-md5** authentication method and a secret key (here designated by the placeholder **secret key**) will be used for the authentication header, **ah**.

```
add 192.168.0.2 192.168.0.5 ah 15700 -A hmac-md5 "secret key";
```

The security association for the encryption payload uses the 3des-cbc encryption method and a different secret key.

```
add 192.168.0.2 192.168.0.5 esp 15701 -E 3des-cbc "secret key";
```

Each instruction is identified with a security parameter index (SPI), in this case, 15700 and 15701. In fact, identical instructions with different SPIs are considered different instructions.

Bear in mind that the security associations only specify possible encryption procedures. They do not implement them. For that, you need to set security policies.

Security Policy: SP

A security policy will implement an IPsec security procedure for a connection. You can designate a host or port connection. Once a policy is set for a connection, the kernel will determine what security associations to apply, using the SAD database. A security policy is added with the **spdadd** instruction. Either encryption, authentication, or both can be required.

The following example will encrypt and authenticate transmissions between hosts 192.168.0.2 and 192.168.0.5. Any outgoing transmissions between these hosts will be both encrypted and authenticated:

```
spdadd 192.168.0.2 192.168.0.5 any -P out ipsec esp/transport//require
ah/transport/require;
```

In the **spdadd** instruction, you will need to specify the connection, such as one between two hosts or two networks. For two hosts, you would use their IP addresses, in this example, 192.168.0.2 and 192.168.0.5. You then specify the kind of packet and its direction, in this case any outgoing packet, **any -P out**. Then you can specify the **ipsec** directives for either the ESP or AH protocol, or both. For each entry, you specify the mode (transport or tunnel), the hosts involved (this can be different in tunnel mode), and the policy for the encryption, usually **require**. This example shows that the ESP protocol will use the transport mode for connections between 192.168.02 and 192.168.0.5, and it will be required:

```
esp/transport/192.168.02-192.168.0.5/require
```

You can leave out the host information if it is the same, as in the prior example.

```
esp/transport//require
```

Receiving Hosts

For a host to receive an encrypted IPsec transmission, it must have corresponding security association instructions in its own SAD database that tell it how to authenticate and decrypt the received instructions. The security association instructions would mirror those of the sender's instructions, using the same encryption method, secret keys, and security indexes. A corresponding policy, though, is not required.

```
#!/sbin/setkey -f
add 192.168.0.2 192.168.0.5 ah 15700 -A hmac-md5 "secret key";
add 192.168.0.2 192.168.0.5 esp 15701 -E 3des-cbc "secret key";
```

Receiving hosts may want to set up policies to screen incoming packets on secure connections, discarding those that are not encrypted. The following policy will accept only incoming IPsec encrypted and authenticated transmissions from 192.168.0.2.

```
spdadd 192.168.0.2 192.168.0.5 any -P in ipsec esp/transport//require
ah/transport//require;
```

Two-Way Transmissions

The preceding example set up a secure connection between two hosts going only one way, from 192.168.0.2 to 192.168.0.5, not the other way, from 192.168.0.5 to 192.168.0.2. To implement two-way secure transmissions between two hosts, both need to be configured as the sender and the receiver, with corresponding security associations to match. The following scripts are based on common examples of a simple two-way IPsec connection between two hosts. They set up a secure two-way IPsec connection between hosts 192.168.0.2 and 192.168.0.5. Corresponding incoming policies are also included, but not required.

First is the configuration for host 192.168.0.2:

```
#!/sbin/setkey -f
add 192.168.0.2 192.168.0.5 ah 15700 -A hmac-md5 "secret key";
add 192.168.0.5 192.168.0.2 ah 24500 -A hmac-md5 "secret key";

add 192.168.0.2 192.168.0.5 esp 15701 -E 3des-cbc "secret key";
add 192.168.0.5 192.168.0.2 esp 24501 -E 3des-cbc "secret key";

spdadd 192.168.0.2 192.168.0.5 any -P out ipsec esp/transport//require
ah/transport//require;
spdadd 192.168.0.5 192.168.0.2 any -P in ipsec esp/transport//require
ah/transport//require;
```

The corresponding host, 192.168.0.5, would uses the same instructions, but with the IP connections reversed. Notice that the security indexes for instructions for the sender and receiver at each end correspond:

```
#!/sbin/setkey -f
add 192.168.0.5 192.168.0.2 ah 15700 -A hmac-md5 "secret key";
add 192.168.0.2 192.168.0.5 ah 24500 -A hmac-md5 "secret key";

add 192.168.0.5 192.168.0.2 esp 15701 -E 3des-cbc "secret key";
add 192.168.0.2 192.168.0.5 esp 24501 -E 3des-cbc "secret key";

spdadd 192.168.0.5 192.168.0.2 any -P out ipsec esp/transport//require ah/
transport//require;
spdadd 192.168.0.2 192.168.0.5 any -P in ipsec esp/transport//require
ah/transport//require;
```

Configuring IPsec with racoon: IKE

IPsec keys can be implemented as manual keys, as shared keys, or with certificates. Manual keys are explicitly exchanged and are prone to security problems. Both shared keys and certificates are managed using the IPsec Key Exchange protocol, which will automatically exchange keys, changing them randomly to avoid detection.

One of the advantages of using IKE is that it will automatically generate any needed security associations, if none are provided. This means that to configure secure connections, with IKE you would need to specify only a security policy, not the security associations.

The **racoon** tool is the key exchange daemon for the IPsec IKE protocol. In the case of shared keys, hosts are authenticated dynamically by **racoon** using preshared secret keys. With the certificate method, hosts are authenticated using certificate files. The **racoon** configuration file is located at **/etc/racoon/racoon.conf**. Here you can set general parameters. You can use the default **racoon.conf** file for most connections.

The **racoon** configuration consists of stanzas containing parameters for possible connections. A very simple configuration is shown in the following example, which uses a simple shared secret key. The location is specified by the **path pre_shared_key** option, in this case **/etc/racoon/psk.txt**. Certificate keys, a more secure method using public and private keys, are discussed later.

```
path pre_shared_key "/etc/racoon/psk.txt";

remote anonymous
{
        exchange_mode aggressive,main;
        doi ipsec_doi;
        situation identity_only;

        my_identifier address;

        lifetime time 2 min;    # sec,min,hour
        initial_contact on;
        proposal_check obey;      # obey, strict or claim

        proposal {
                encryption_algorithm 3des;
                hash_algorithm sha1;
                authentication_method pre_shared_key;
                dh_group 2 ;
        }
}
sainfo anonymous
{
        pfs_group 1;
        lifetime time 2 min;
        encryption_algorithm 3des, blowfish, des, cast128, rijndael ;
        authentication_algorithm hmac_sha1, hmac_md5;
                compression_algorithm deflate ;
}
```

This configuration defines stanzas for default (anonymous) connections. The **remote anonymous** stanza defines parameters for connecting to remote systems, and the **sainfo anonymous** section provides information for security association instructions, such as the encryption and authentication methods to use.

Certificates

To use certificates instead of shared keys, you first have to create certificates using OpenSSL. Then instruct **racoon** to use them. Specify the path for the certificates.

```
path certificate "/usr/local/etc/racoon/certs";
```

You can now configure **racoon** to use the public and private keys generated by the certificates. In the appropriate stanza in the **/etc/racoon/racoon.conf** file, the **certificate_type** directive specifies the public and private keys for this system. The **peers_certfile** directive specifies the location of the remote system's public key. The **authentication_method** directive is now set to **rsasig**, the RSA public/private keys. Make sure each system has its corresponding public and private keys.

```
certificate_type x509 "192.168.0.2.public" "192.168.0.2.private";
peers_certfile "192.168.0.5.public";
authentication_method rsasig;
```

Connection Configuration with racoon

With **racoon**, you will only need to specify the security policy for the connection configuration, as shown here for the sender. The receiver will have corresponding policies:

```
spdadd 192.168.0.5 192.168.0.2 any -P out ipsec
         esp/transport//require
         ah/transport//require;
spdadd 192.168.0.2 192.168.0.5 any -P in ipsec
         esp/transport//require
         ah/transport//require;
```

IPsec and IP Tables: Net Traversal

IPtables netfiltering will stop many IPsec packets. To enable IPtables to pass IPsec packets, use the following IPtables commands. The number for the AH protocol is 51, and for the ESP protocol, it is 50. To allow IPsec packets, you should set policy rules such as the following:

```
iptables -A INPUT -p 50 -j ACCEPT
iptables -A OUTPUT -p 51 -j ACCEPT
```

For netfiltering that implements IP masquerading, you will need to add a **net_traversal** option to your raccoon IPsec configuration. With Net Traversal, the IPsec connection will bypass the IP address substitution performed by IP Tables when masquerading IP addresses. In addition, the **nat_keepalive** option will maintain the connection, and with the **iskamp_natt** option you specify the IP address and port to connect to.

IPsec Tunnel Mode: Virtual Private Networks

Instead of encrypting two hosts directly, you could use IPsec to just encrypt the gateways between the networks those hosts belong to, assuming that communication within those networks can be trusted. This would significantly reduce the encryption configuration setup, letting hosts from an entire network reach those of another network, using an intermediate secure IPsec connection between their gateways. For connections between gateways, transmissions sent through intervening routers can be tunneled. This is known as the tunnel mode for IPsec, which is used to implement virtual private networks (VPNs). Encrypting transmissions between gateways effectively implements a VPN, securing transmissions across a larger network from one local net to another.

To tunnel transmissions from a host through a gateway to a network, you would use the **-m tunnel** option. The IPsec connection would be between the two gateways. The following example is the security association on gateway 10.0.0.1 that encrypts transmissions from gateway 10.0.0.1 to gateway 10.0.23.5. The examples used here are for a gateway-to-gateway connection, set up as a direct connection between two hosts using manual keys.

```
add 10.0.0.1 10.0.23.5 esp 34501 -m tunnel -E 3des-cbc "secretkey";
```

The security policy on 10.0.0.1 then implements encryption for communication from one network to another using their respective gateways. The two networks are 192.168.0.0 and 192.168.1.0. Transmissions from hosts on the 192.168.0.0 network are encrypted by their gateway, 10.0.0.1, and are then sent to the gateway for the 192.168.1.0 network, 10.0.23.5, which then decrypts them.

```
spdadd 192.168.0.0/24 192.168.1.0/24 any -P out ipsec esp/tunnel/10.0.0.1-
10.0.23.5/require;
```

Notice that the gateway IP addresses are specified in the **spdadd** instruction's **ipsec** directive. The mode specified is the tunnel mode, rather than the transport mode.

```
ipsec esp/tunnel/10.0.0.1-10.0.23.5/require
```

The receiving gateway, 10.0.23.5, will have a corresponding security association and policy, as shown here. The policy is set for incoming transmissions. In both gateway configurations, other than specifying the tunnel option and using network addresses in the security policy, the security associations and policies are the same as those used for host-to-host connections.

```
add 10.0.0.1 10.0.23.5 esp 34501 -m tunnel -E 3des-cbc "secretkey";

spdadd 192.168.0.0/24 192.168.1.0/16 any -P in ipsec esp/tunnel/10.0.0.1-
10.0.23.5/require;
```

To set up full two-way communication, the two gateways would have corresponding security associations and policies to handle traffic in both directions. The following example is for the configuration on gateway 10.0.0.1 and handles two-way traffic to and from gateway 10.0.23.5. Gateway 10.0.23.5 would have a similar configuration:

```
add 10.0.0.1 10.0.23.5 esp 34501 -m tunnel -E 3des-cbc "secretkey";
add 10.0.23.5 10.0.03.1 esp 34501 -m tunnel -E 3des-cbc "secretkey";

spdadd 192.168.0.0/24 192.168.1.0/24 any -P out ipsec esp/tunnel/10.0.0.1-
10.0.23.5/require;


spdadd 192.168.1.0/16 192.168.0.0/24 any -P in ipsec esp/tunnel/10.0.23.5-
10.0.0.1/require;
```

If you use **racoon** to configure gateway connections, you only have to set the security policies on each gateway, letting the **racoon** server generate the needed security associations.

19

Secure Shell and Kerberos

To protect remote connections from hosts outside your network, transmissions can be encrypted (see Table 19-1). For Linux systems, you can use the Secure Shell (SSH) suite of programs to encrypt and authenticate transmissions, preventing them from being read or modified by anyone else, as well confirming the identity of the sender. The SSH programs are meant to replace the remote tools such as **rsh** and **rcp** (see Chapter 15), which perform no encryption and include security risks such as transmitting passwords in clear text. User authentication can be controlled for certain services by Kerberos servers. Kerberos authentication provides another level of security whereby individual services can be protected, allowing use of a service only to users who are cleared for access.

The Secure Shell: OpenSSH

Although a firewall can protect a network from attempts to break into it from the outside, the problem of securing legitimate communications to the network from outside sources still exists. A particular problem is the one of users who want to connect to your network remotely. Such connections could be monitored, and information such as passwords and user IDs used when the user logs in to your network could be copied and used later to break in. One solution is to use SSH for remote logins and other kinds of remote connections such as FTP transfers. SSH encrypts any communications between the remote user and a system on your network.

Two different implementations of SSH currently use what are, in effect, two different and incompatible protocols. The first version of SSH, known as SSH1, uses the original SSH protocol. Version 2.0, known as SSH2, uses a completely rewritten version of the SSH protocol. Encryption is performed in different ways, encrypting different parts of a packet. SSH1 uses server and host keys to authenticate systems, whereas SSH2 uses only host keys. Furthermore, certain functions, such as sftp, are supported only by SSH2.

NOTE *A commercial version of SSH is available from SSH Communications Security, whose Web site is **www.ssh.com**. SSH Communications Security provides an entirely commercial version called SSH Tectia, designed for enterprise and government use. The older noncommercial SSH package is still freely available, which you can download and use.*

Web Site	Description
www.openssh.org	OpenSSH open source version of SSH
www.ssh.com	SSH Communications Security, commercial SSH version
web.mit.edu/kerberos	Kerberos authentication

TABLE 19-1 SSH and Kerberos Resources

The SSH protocol has become an official Internet Engineering Task Force (IETF) standard. A free and open source version is developed and maintained by the OpenSSH project, currently supported by the OpenBSD project. OpenSSH is the version supplied with most Linux distributions, including Fedora, Red Hat, Mandrake, Novell, and Debian. You can find out more about OpenSSH at **www.openssh.org**, where you can download the most recent version, though your distribution will provide current RPM versions.

SSH Encryption and Authentication

SSH secures connections by both authenticating users and encrypting their transmissions. The authentication process is handled with public key encryption (see Chapter 16). Once authenticated, transmissions are encrypted by a cipher agreed upon by the SSH server and client for use in a particular session. SSH supports multiple ciphers. Authentication is applied to both hosts and users. SSH first authenticates a particular host, verifying that it is a valid SSH host that can be securely communicated with. Then the user is authenticated, verifying that the user is who they say they are.

SSH uses strong encryption methods, and their export from the United States may be restricted. Currently, SSH can deal with the following kinds of attacks:

- IP spoofing, where a remote host sends out packets that pretend to come from another, trusted host

- IP source routing, where a host can pretend an IP packet comes from another, trusted host

- DNS spoofing, where an attacker forges name server records

- Interception of clear-text passwords and other data by intermediate hosts

- Manipulation of data by people in control of intermediate hosts

- Attacks based on listening to X authentication data and spoofed connections to the X11 server

Encryption

The public key encryption used in SSH authentication makes use of two keys: a public key and a private key. The *public key* is used to encrypt data, while the *private key* decrypts it. Each host or user has its own public and private keys. The public key is distributed to other hosts, who can then use it to encrypt authentication data that only the host's private key can decrypt. For example, when a host sends data to a user on another system, the host encrypts the authentication data with a public key, which it previously received from that user. The data can be decrypted only by the user's corresponding private key. The public key can safely be sent in the open from one host to another, allowing it to be installed safely on different hosts. You can think of the process as taking place between a client and a server. When the client sends data to the server, it first encrypts the data using the server's public key. The server can then decrypt the data using its own private key.

It is recommended that SSH transmissions be authenticated with public-private keys controlled by passphrases. Unlike PGP, SSH uses public-key encryption for the authentication process only. Once authenticated, participants agree on a common cipher to use to encrypt transmission. Authentication will verify the identity of the participants. Each user who intends to use SSH to access a remote account first needs to create the public and private keys, along with a passphrase to use for the authentication process. A user then sends their public key to the remote account they want to access and installs the public key on that account. When the user attempts to access the remote account, that account can then use the user's public key to authenticate that the user is who they claim to be. The process assumes that the remote account has set up its own SSH private and public key. For the user to access the remote account, they will have know the remote account's SSH passphrase. SSH is often used in situations where a user has two or more accounts located on different systems and wants to be able to securely access them from each other. In that case, the user already has access to each account and can install SSH on each, giving each its own private and public keys along with their passphrases.

Authentication

The mechanics of authentication in SSH version 1 and version 2 differ slightly. However, the procedure on the part of users is the same. Essentially, a user creates both public and private keys. For this you use the **ssh-keygen** command. The user's public key then has to be distributed to those users that the original user wants access to. Often this is an account a user has on another host. A passphrase further protects access. The original user will need to know the other user's passphrase to access it.

SSH version 1 uses RSA authentication. When a remote user tries to log in to an account, that account is checked to see if it has the remote user's public key. That public key is then used to encrypt a challenge (usually a random number) that can be decrypted only by the remote user's private key. When the remote user receives the encrypted challenge, that user decrypts the challenge with its private key. SSH version 2 can use either RSA or DSA authentication. The remote user will first encrypt a session identifier using its private key, before signing it. The encrypted session identifier is then decrypted by the account using the remote user's public key. The session identifier has been previously set up by SSH for that session.

SSH authentication is first carried out with the host, and then with users. Each host has its own host keys, public and private keys used for authentication. Once the host is authenticated, the user is queried. Each user has their own public and private keys. Users on an SSH server who want to receive connections from remote users will have to keep a list of those remote user's public keys. Similarly, an SSH host will maintain a list of public keys for other SSH hosts.

SSH Tools

SSH is implemented on Linux systems with OpenSSH. The full set of OpenSSH packages includes the general OpenSSH package (openssh), the OpenSSH server (openssh-server), and the OpenSSH clients (openssh-clients). These packages also require OpenSSL (openssl), which installs the cryptographic libraries that SSH uses.

The SSH tools are listed in Table 19-2. They include several client programs like **scp** and ssh, as well as the ssh server. The ssh server (sshd) provides secure connections to anyone from the outside using the ssh client to connect. Several configuration utilities are also included, such as ssh-add, which adds valid hosts to the authentication agent, and ssh-keygen, which generates the keys used for encryption.

On Red Hat Fedora, you can start, restart, and stop the sshd server with the **service** command or redhat-config-services (Services on the Server Settings window and menu):

```
# service sshd restart
```

For version 2, names of the actual tools have a 2 suffix. Version 1 tools have a 1 as their suffix. During installation, however, links are set for each tool to use only the name with the suffix. For example, if you have installed version 2, there is a link called scp to the scp2 application. You can then use the link to invoke the tool. Using scp starts scp2. Table 19-2 specifies only the link names, as these are the same for each version. Remember, though, some applications, such as sftp, are available only with version 2.

SSH Setup

Using SSH involves creating your own public and private keys and then distributing your public key to other users you want to access. These can be different users or simply user accounts of your own that you have on remote systems. Often people remotely log in from

Application	Description
ssh	SSH client
sshd	SSH server (daemon)
sftp	SSH FTP client, Secure File Transfer Program. Version 2 only. Use **?** to list sftp commands (SFTP protocol).
sftp-server	SSH FTP server. Version 2 only (SFTP protocol).
scp	SSH copy command client
ssh-keygen	Utility for generating keys. Use **-h** for help.
ssh-keyscan	Tool to automatically gather public host keys to generate **ssh_known_hosts** files
ssh-add	Adds RSD and DSA identities to the authentication agent
ssh-agent	SSH authentication agent that holds private keys for public key authentication (RSA, DSA)
ssh-askpass	X Window System utility for querying passwords, invoked by **ssh-add** (openssh-askpass)
ssh-askpass-gnome	GNOME utility for querying passwords, invoked by **ssh-add**
ssh-signer	Signs host-based authentication packets. Version 2 only. Must be suid root (performed by installation).
slogin	Remote login (version 1)

TABLE 19-2 SSH Tools

a local client to an account on a remote server, perhaps from a home computer to a company computer. Your home computer would be your client account, and the account on your company computer would be your server account. On your client account, you would need to generate your public and private keys. Then you would have to place a copy of your public key in the server account. You can do this by simply e-mailing the key file or copying the file from a floppy disk. Once the account on your server has a copy of your client user's public key, you can access the server account from your client account. You will be also prompted for the server account's passphrase. You will have to know this to access that account. Figure 19-1 illustrates the SSH setup that allows a user **george** to access the account **cecelia**.

The following steps are needed to allow you to use SSH to access other accounts:

- Create public and private keys on your account along with a passphrase. You will need to use this passphrase to access your account from another account.
- Distribute your public key to other accounts you want to access, placing them in the **.ssh/authorized_keys** file.
- Other accounts also have to set up public and private keys along with a passphrase.
- You will need to also know the other account's passphrase to access it.

Creating SSH Keys with ssh-keygen

You create your public and private keys using the **ssh-keygen** command. You need to specify the kind of encryption you want to use. You can use either DSA or RSA encryption. Specify the type using the **-t** option and the encryption name in lowercase (**dsa** or **rsa**). In the following example, the user creates a key with the RSA encryption:

```
$ ssh-keygen -t rsa
```

The **ssh-keygen** command prompts you for a passphrase, which it will use as a kind of password to protect your private key. The passphrase should be several words long. You are also prompted to enter a filename for the keys. If you do not enter one, SSH will use its defaults. The public key will be given the extension **.pub**. The **ssh-keygen** command generates the public key and places it in your **.ssh/id_dsa.pub** or **.ssh/id_drsa.pub** file,

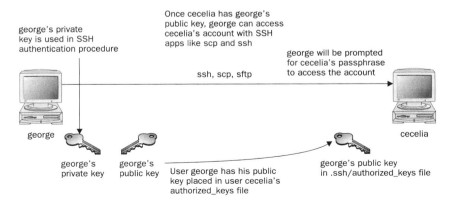

FIGURE 19-1   SSH setup and access

depending on the type of key you specified; it places the private key in the corresponding
.ssh/id_dsa or **.ssh/id_rsa.pub** file.

> **NOTE** *The .ssh/identity filename is used in SSH version 1; it may be installed by default on older distribution versions. SSH version 2 uses a different filename, .ssh/id_dsa or .ssh/id_rsa, depending on whether RSA or DSA authentication is used.*

If you need to change your passphrase, you can do so with the **ssh-keygen** command
and the **-p** option. Each user will have their own SSH configuration directory, called **.ssh**,
located in their own home directory. The public and private keys, as well as SSH configuration
files, are placed here. If you build from the source code, the **make install** operation will
automatically run **ssh-keygen**. Table 19-3 lists the SSH configuration files.

File	Description
$HOME/.ssh/known_hosts	Records host keys for all hosts the user has logged in to (that are not in **/etc/ssh/ssh_known_hosts**)
$HOME/.ssh/random_seed	Used for seeding the random number generator
$HOME/.ssh/id_rsa	Contains the RSA authentication identity of the user
$HOME/.ssh/ id_dsa	Contains the DSA authentication identity of the user
$HOME/.ssh/id_rsa.pub	Contains the RSA public key for authentication—the contents of this file should be added to **$HOME/.ssh/ authorized_keys** on all machines where you want to log in using RSA authentication.
$HOME/.ssh/id_dsa.pub	Contains the DSA public key for authentication. The contents of this file should be added to **$HOME/.ssh/ authorized_keys** on all machines where you want to log in using DSA authentication.
$HOME/.ssh/config	The per-user configuration file
$HOME/.ssh/authorized_ keys	Lists the RSA or DSA keys that can be used for logging in as this user
/etc/ssh/ssh_known_hosts	System-wide list of known host keys
/etc/ssh/ssh_config	System-wide configuration file—this file provides defaults for those values not specified in the user's configuration file.
/etc/ssh/sshd_config	SSH server configuration file
/etc/ssh/sshrc	System default—commands in this file are executed by ssh when the user logs in just before the user's shell (or command) is started.
$HOME/.ssh/rc	Commands in this file are executed by ssh when the user logs in just before the user's shell (or command) is started.

TABLE 19-3   SSH Configuration Files

Authorized Keys

A public key is used to authenticate a user and its host. You use the public key on a remote system to allow that user access. The public key is placed in the remote user account's **.ssh/authorized_keys** file. Recall that the public key is held in the **.ssh/id_dsa.pub** file. If a user wants to log in remotely from a local account to an account on a remote system, they would first place their public key in the **.ssh/authorized_keys** file in the account on the remote system they want to access. If the user **larisa** on **turtle.mytrek.com** wants to access the **aleina** account on **rabbit.mytrek.com**, **larisa**'s public key from **/home/larisa/.ssh/id_dsa.pub** first must be placed in **aleina**'s **authorized_keys** file, **/home/aleina/.ssh/authorized_keys**. User **larisa** could send the key or have it copied over. A simple cat operation can append a key to the authorized key file. In the next example, the user adds the public key for **aleina** in the **larisa.pub** file to the authorized key file. The **larisa.pub** file is a copy of the **/home/larisa/.ssh/id_dsa.pub** file that the user received earlier.

```
$ cat larisa.pub >> .ssh/authorized_keys
```

Loading Keys

If you regularly make connections to a variety of remote hosts, you can use the **ssh-agent** command to place private keys in memory where they can be accessed quickly to decrypt received transmissions. The **ssh-agent** command is intended for use at the beginning of a login session. For GNOME, you can use the openssh-askpass-gnome utility, invoked by **ssh-add**, which allows you to enter a password when you log in to GNOME. GNOME will automatically supply that password whenever you use an SSH client.

Although the **ssh-agent** command enables you to use private keys in memory, you also must specifically load your private keys into memory using the **ssh-add** command. **ssh-add** with no arguments loads your private key from your **.ssh/id_dsa** or **.ssh/id_rsa .pub** file. You are prompted for your passphrase for this private key. To remove the key from memory, use **ssh-add** with the **-d** option. If you have several private keys, you can load them all into memory. **ssh-add** with the **-l** option lists those currently loaded.

SSH Clients

SSH was originally designed to replace remote access operations, such as **rlogin**, **rcp**, and Telnet (see Chapter 15), which perform no encryption and introduce security risks such as transmitting passwords in clear text. You can also use SSH to encode X server sessions as well as FTP transmissions (**sftp**). The ssh-clients package contains corresponding SSH clients to replace these applications. With **slogin** or **ssh**, you can log in from a remote host to execute commands and run applications, much as you can with **rlogin** and **rsh**. With **scp**, you can copy files between the remote host and a network host, just as with **rcp**. With **sftp**, you can transfer FTP files secured by encryption.

ssh

With **ssh**, you can remotely log in from a local client to a remote system on your network operating as the SSH server. The term *local client* here refers to one outside the network, such as your home computer, and the term *remote* refers to a host system on the network to which you are connecting. In effect, you connect from your local system to the remote network host. It is designed to replace **rlogin**, which performs remote logins, and **rsh**, which executes remote commands. With **ssh**, you can log in from a local site to a remote host on your network and then send commands to be executed on that host. The ssh command is also capable of supporting X Window System connections. This feature is automatically enabled if you make an ssh connection from an X Window System environment, such as GNOME or KDE. A connection is set up for you between the local X server and the remote X server. The remote host sets up a dummy X server and sends any X Window System data through it to your local system to be processed by your own local X server.

The ssh login operation function is much like the **rlogin** command. You enter the **ssh** command with the address of the remote host, followed by a **-l** option and the login name (username) of the remote account you are logging in to. The following example logs in to the **aleina** user account on the **rabbit.mytrek.com** host:

```
$ ssh rabbit.mytrek.com -l aleina
```

You can also use the username in an address format with **ssh**, as in

```
$ ssh aleian@rabbit.mytrek.com
```

The following listing shows how the user **george** accesses the **cecelia** account on **turtle.mytrek.com**:

```
[george@turtle george]$ ssh turtle.mytrek.com -l cecelia
cecelia@turtle.mytrek.com's password:
[cecelia@turtle cecelia]$
```

A variety of options are available to enable you to configure your connection. Most have corresponding configuration options that can be set in the configuration file. For example, with the **-c** option, you can designate which encryption method you want to use, for instance, **idea**, **des**, **blowfish**, or **arcfour**. With the **-i** option, you can select a particular private key to use. The **-C** option enables you to have transmissions compressed at specified levels (see the **ssh** Man page for a complete list of options).

scp

You use **scp** to copy files from one host to another on a network. Designed to replace **rcp**, **scp** actually uses ssh to transfer data and employs the same authentication and encryption methods. If authentication requires it, **scp** requests a password or passphrase. The **scp** program operates much like rcp. Directories and files on remote hosts are specified using the username and the host address before the filename or directory. The username specifies the remote user account that **scp** is accessing, and the host is the remote system where that account is located. You separate the user from the host address with an @, and you separate the host address from the file or directory name with a colon. The following example copies the file **party** from a user's current directory to the user **aleina's birthday** directory, located on the **rabbit.mytrek.com** host:

```
$ scp party aleina@rabbit.mytrek.com:/birthday/party
```

Of particular interest is the **-r** (recursive) option, which enables you to copy whole directories. See the **scp** Man page for a complete list of options. In the next example, the user copies the entire **reports** directory to the user **justin's projects** directory:

```
$ scp -r reports justin@rabbit.mytrek.com:/projects
```

In the next example, the user **george** copies the **mydoc1** file from the user **cecelia**'s home directory:

```
[george@turtle george]$ scp cecelia@turtle.mytrek.com:mydoc1  .
cecelia@turtle.mytrek.com's password:
mydoc1     0% |                                    |    0 --:--
ETA
mydoc1   100% |****************************|   17 00:00
[george@turtle george]$
```

From a Windows system, you can also use **scp** clients such as **winscp**, which will interact with Linux scp-enabled systems.

sftp and sftp-server

With **sftp**, you can transfer FTP files secured by encryption. The **sftp** client, which works only with ssh version 2, operates much like **ftp**, with many of the same commands (see Chapter 14). Use **sftp** instead of **ftp** to invoke the sftp client.

```
$ sftp ftp.redhat.com
```

To use the **sftp** client to connect to an FTP server, that server needs to be operating the sftp-server application. The ssh server invokes sftp-server to provide encrypted FTP transmissions to those using the **sftp** client. The **sftp** server and client use the SSH File Transfer Protocol (SFTP) to perform FTP operations securely.

Port Forwarding (Tunneling)

If, for some reason, you can connect to a secure host only by going through an insecure host, ssh provides a feature called port forwarding. With *port forwarding*, you can secure the insecure segment of your connection. This involves simply specifying the port at which the insecure host is to connect to the secure one. This sets up a direct connection between the local host and the remote host, through the intermediary insecure host. Encrypted data is passed through directly. This process is referred to as tunneling, creating a secure tunnel of encrypted data through connected servers.

You can set up port forwarding to a port on the remote system or to one on your local system. To forward a port on the remote system to a port on your local system, use **ssh** with the **-R** option, followed by an argument holding the local port, the remote host address, and the remote port to be forwarded, each separated from the next by a colon. This works by allocating a socket to listen to the port on the remote side. Whenever a connection is made to this port, the connection is forwarded over the secure channel, and a connection is made to a remote port from the local machine. In the following example, port 22 on the local system is connected to port 23 on the **rabbit.mytrek.com** remote system:

```
$ ssh -R 22:rabbit.mytrek.com:23
```

To forward a port on your local system to a port on a remote system, use **ssh** with the **-L** option, followed by an argument holding the local port, the remote host address, and the remote port to be forwarded, with each of the arguments separated by a colon. A socket is allocated to listen to the port on the local side. Whenever a connection is made to this port, the connection is forwarded over the secure channel and a connection is made to the remote port on the remote machine. In the following example, port 22 on the local system is connected to port 23 on the **rabbit.mytrek.com** remote system:

```
$ ssh -L 22:rabbit.mytrek.com:23
```

You can use the LocalForward and RemoteForward options in your **.ssh/config** file to set up port forwarding for particular hosts or to specify a default for all hosts you connect to.

SSH Configuration

The SSH configuration file for each user is in their **.ssh/config** file. The **/etc/ssh/ssh_config** file is used to set site-wide defaults. In the configuration file, you can set various options, as listed in the **ssh_config** Man document. The configuration file is designed to specify options for different remote hosts to which you might connect. It is organized into segments, where each segment begins with the keyword **HOST**, followed by the IP address or name of the host. The following lines hold the options you have set for that host. A segment ends at the next **HOST** entry. Of particular interest are the **User** and **Cipher** options. Use the **User** option to specify the names of users on the remote system who are allowed access. With the **Cipher** option, you can select which encryption method to use for a particular host. Encryption methods include IDEA, DES (standard), triple-DES (3DES), Blowfish (128 bit), Arcfour (RSA's RC4), and Twofish. The following example allows access from **larisa** at **turtle .mytrek.com** and uses Blowfish encryption for transmissions:

```
Host turtle.mytrek.com
     User larisa
     Compression no
     Cipher blowfish
```

To specify global options that apply to any host you connect to, create a **HOST** entry with the asterisk as its host, **HOST *.** This entry must be placed at the end of the configuration file because an option is changed only the first time it is set. Any subsequent entries for an option are ignored. Because a host matches on both its own entry and the global one, its specific entry should come before the global entry. The asterisk (*****) and the question mark (**?**) are both wildcard matching operators that enable you to specify a group of hosts with the same suffix or prefix.

```
Host *
  FallBackToRsh yes
  KeepAlive no
  Cipher idea
```

Kerberos

User authentication can further be controlled for certain services by Kerberos servers, discussed in this chapter. Kerberos authentication provides another level of security whereby individual services can be protected, allowing use of a service only to users who are cleared for access. Kerberos servers are all enabled and configured with **authconfig-gtk** (Authentication in the System Settings menu).

Kerberos is a network authentication protocol that provides encrypted authentication to connections between a client and a server. As an authentication protocol, Kerberos requires a client to prove its identity using encryption methods before it can access a server. Once authenticated, the client and server can conduct all communications using encryption. Whereas firewalls protect only from outside attacks, Kerberos is designed to also protect from attacks from those inside the network. Users already within a network could try to break into local servers. Kerberos places protection around the servers themselves, rather than an entire network or computer. A free version is available from the Massachusetts Institute of Technology at **web.mit.edu/kerberos** under the MIT Public License, which is similar to the GNU Public License. The name *Kerberos* comes from Greek mythology and is the name of the three-headed watchdog for Hades. Be sure to check the **web.mit.edu/ kerberos** site for recent upgrades and detailed documentation, including FAQs, manuals, and tutorials.

TIP *The Kerberos V5 package includes its own versions of network tools such as Telnet, RCP, FTP, and RSH. These provide secure authenticated access by remote users. The tools operate in the same way as their original counterparts described in Chapter 15. The package also contains a Kerberos version of the* **su** *administrative login command,* **ksu***. Priority is given to Kerberos tools by the* **/etc/profile.d/krb5-workstation.sh** *script which places the Kerberos directory before all others in the user's PATH variable.*

Kerberos Servers

The key to Kerberos is a Kerberos server through which all requests for any server services are channeled. The Kerberos server then authenticates a client, identifying the client and validating the client's right to use a particular server. The server maintains a database of authorized users. Kerberos then issues the client an encrypted ticket that the client can use to gain access to the server. For example, if a user needs to check their mail, a request for use of the mail server is sent to the Kerberos server, which then authenticates the user and issues a ticket that is then used to access the mail server. Without a Kerberos-issued ticket, no one can access any of the servers. Originally, this process required that users undergo a separate authentication procedure for each server they wanted to access. However, users now only need to perform an initial authentication that is valid for all servers.

This process actually involves the use of two servers, an authentication server (AS) and a ticket-granting server (TGS). Together they make up what is known as the key distribution center (KDC). In effect, they distribute keys used to unlock access to services. The authentication server first validates a user's identity. The AS issues a ticket called the ticket-granting ticket (TGT) that allows the user to access the ticket-granting server. The TGS then issues the user another ticket to actually access a service. This way, the user never has any direct access of any kind to a server during the authentication process. The process is somewhat more complex than described. An authenticator using information such as the current time, a checksum, and an optional encryption key is sent along with the ticket and is decrypted with the session key. This authenticator is used by a service to verify your identity.

NOTE *You can view your list of current tickets with the* **klist** *command.*

Authentication Process

The authentication server validates a user using information in its user database. Each user needs to be registered in the authentication server's database. The database will include a user password and other user information. To access the authentication server, the user provides the username and the password. The password is used to generate a user key with which communication between the AS and the user is encrypted. The user will have their own copy of the user key with which to decrypt communications. The authentication process is illustrated in Figure 19-2.

Accessing a service with Kerberos involves the following steps:

1. The user has to be validated by the authentication server and granted access to the ticket-granting server with a ticket access key. You do this by issuing the **kinit** command, which will ask you enter your Kerberos username and then send it on to the authentication server (the Kerberos username is usually the same as your username).

   ```
   $ kinit
   ```

2. The AS generates a ticket-granting ticket with which to access the ticket-granting server. This ticket will include a session key that will be used to let you access the TGS. The TGT is sent back to you encrypted with your user key (password).

3. The **kinit** program then prompts you to enter your Kerberos password, which it then uses to decrypt the TGT. You can manage your Kerberos password with the **kpasswd** command.

4. Now you can use a client program such as a mail client program to access the mail server, for instance. When you do so, the TGT is used to access the TGS, which then will generate a ticket for accessing the mail server. The TGS will generate a new session key for use with just the mail server. This will be provided in the ticket sent to you for accessing the mail server. In effect, there is a TGT session key used for

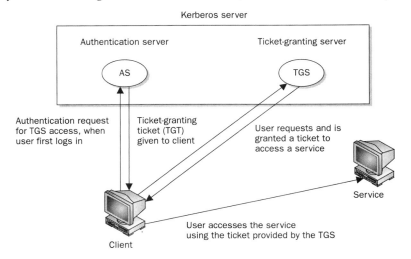

FIGURE 19-2 Kerberos authentication

accessing the TGS, and a mail session key used for accessing the mail server. The ticket for the mail server is sent to you encrypted with the TGS session key.

5. The client then uses the mail ticket received from the TGS to access the mail server.

6. If you want to use another service such as FTP, when your FTP client sends a request to the TGS for a ticket, the TGS will automatically obtain authorization from the authentication server and issue an FTP ticket with an FTP session key. This kind of support remains in effect for a limited period of time, usually several hours, after which you again have to use **kinit** to undergo the authentication process and access the TGS. You can manually destroy any tickets you have with the **kdestroy** command.

NOTE *With Kerberos V5 (version 5), a Kerberos login utility is provided whereby users are automatically granted ticket-granting tickets when they log in normally. This avoids the need to use* **kinit** *to manually obtain a TGT.*

Kerberized Services

Setting up a particular service to use Kerberos (known as Kerberizing) can be a complicated process. A Kerberized service needs to check the user's identity and credentials, check for a ticket for the service, and if one is not present, obtain one. Once they are set up, use of Kerberized services is nearly transparent to the user. Tickets are automatically issued and authentication carried out without any extra effort by the user. The **/etc/services** file should contain a listing of specific Kerberized services. These are services such as **kpasswd**, **ksu**, and **klogin** that provide Kerberos password, superuser access, and login services, respectively.

Kerberos also provides its own kerberized network tools for **ftp**, **rsh**, **rcp**, and **rlogin** (see Chapter 15). These are located at **/usr/kerberos/bin**, and most have the same name as the original network tools. In the Red Hat Fedora installation, the PATH variable, which contains the directories for all your commands, will list **/usr/kerberos/bin** before **/usr/bin**. This means that when you invoke **ftp**, you are actually using the Kerberos version of **ftp** **/usr/kerberos/bin**, instead of the original **ftp**, which is still located in **/usr/bin**. The same is true for **rlogin** and **rcp**. The original name for the kerberized network tools had a **k** prefix, and there are still links with some of these original names, such as **krlogin**, which links to the kerberos **rlogin**.

Configuring Kerberos Servers

Installing and configuring a Kerberos server is also a complex process. Carefully check the documentation for installing the current versions. Some of the key areas are listed here. In the Kerberos configuration file, **krb5.conf**, you can set such features as the encryption method used and the database name. When installing Kerberos, be sure to carefully follow the instructions for providing administrative access. To run Kerberos, you start the Kerberos server with the **service** command and the **krb5kdc**, **kadmin**, and **krb524** scripts.

TIP *Check the Red Hat Linux Reference Manual for more detailed instructions on setting up Kerberos servers and clients on your system.*

Consult the Red Hat Linux Reference Guide for detailed instructions on how to install and configure Kerberos on Red Hat. You will need to configure the server for your network, along with clients for each host (**krb5-server** package for servers and **krb5-workstation** for clients). To configure your server, you first specify your Kerberos realm and domain by manually replacing the lowercase **example.com** and the uppercase **EXAMPLE.COM** entries in the **/etc/krb5.conf** and **/var/kerberos/krb5kdc/kdc.conf** files with your own domain name. Maintain the same case for each entry. Realms are specified in uppercase, and simple host and domain names are in lowercase. You then create a database with the **kdb5_util** command and the **create** option. You will be prompted to enter a master key.

```
# kdb5_util create -s
```

Full administrative access to the server is controlled by user entries in the **var/kerberos/krb5kdc/kadm5.acl** file. Replace the **EXAMPLE.COM** text with your Kerberos realm (usually your domain name in uppercase). You then need to add a local principal, a local user with full administrative access from the host the server runs on. Start the **kadmin.local** tool and use the **addprinc** command to add the local principal. You can then start your **krb5kdc**, **kadmin**, and **krb524** servers.

On each client host, use the **kadmin** tool with the **addprincipal** command to add a principal for the host. Also add a host principal for each host on your network with **host/** qualifier, as in **host/rabbit.mytrek.com**. You can use the **-randkey** option to specify a random key. Then save local copies of the host keys, using the **ktadd** command to save them in its **/etc/krb5.keytab** file. Each host needs to also have the same **/etc/krb5.conf** configuration file on its system, specifying the Kerberos server and the kdc host.

NOTE *When you configure Kerberos with the Authentication tool, you will be able to enter the realm, kdc server, and Kerberos server. Default entries will be displayed using the domain "example.com." Be sure to specify the realm in uppercase. A new entry for your realm will be made in the realms segment of the /etc/krb5.conf, listing the kdc and server entries you made.*

Network Firewalls: Netfilter

Most systems currently connected to the Internet are open to attempts by outside users to gain unauthorized access. Outside users can try to gain access directly by setting up an illegal connection, by intercepting valid communications from users remotely connected to the system, or by pretending to be a valid user. Firewalls, encryption, and authentication procedures are ways of protecting against such attacks. A *firewall* prevents any direct unauthorized attempts at access, *encryption* protects transmissions from authorized remote users, and *authentication* verifies that a user requesting access has the right to do so. The current Linux kernel incorporates support for firewalls using the Netfilter (IPtables) packet filtering package (the previous version, IP Chains, is used on older kernel versions). To implement a firewall, you simply provide a series of rules to govern what kind of access you want to allow on your system. If that system is also a gateway for a private network, the system's firewall capability can effectively help protect the network from outside attacks.

NOTE *You can set up basic Netfilter firewall protection with the system-config-securitylevel tool (Firewall on the System | Administration menu). This tool will generate a basic set of IPtables rules to protect your system and network (see Chapter 5).*

To provide protection for remote communications, transmission can be simply encrypted. For Linux systems, you can use the Secure Shell (SSH) suite of programs to encrypt any transmissions, to prevent them from being read by anyone else (see Chapter 19). Kerberos authentication provides another level of security whereby individual services can be protected, allowing use of a service only to users who are cleared for access (see Chapter 19). Outside users may also try to gain unauthorized access through any Internet services you may be hosting, such as a Web site. In such a case, you can set up a proxy to protect your site from attack. For Linux systems, use Squid proxy software to set up a proxy to protect your Web server (see Chapter 24). Table 20-1 lists several network security applications commonly used on Linux.

Firewalls: IPtables, NAT, and ip6tables

A good foundation for your network's security is to set up a Linux system to operate as a firewall for your network, protecting it from unauthorized access. You can use a firewall to implement either packet filtering or proxies. *Packet filtering* is simply the process of deciding

Web Site	Security Application
www.netfilter.org	Netfilter project, Iptables, and NAT
www.netfilter.org/ipchains	IP Chains firewall
www.openssh.org	Secure Shell encryption
www.squid-cache.org	Squid Web Proxy server
web.mit.edu/Kerberos	Kerberos network authentication

TABLE 20-1   Network Security Applications

whether a packet received by the firewall host should be passed on into the local network. The packet-filtering software checks the source and destination addresses of the packet and sends the packet on, if it's allowed. Even if your system is not part of a network but connects directly to the Internet, you can still use the firewall feature to control access to your system. Of course, this also provides you with much more security.

With proxies, you can control access to specific services, such as Web or FTP servers. You need a proxy for each service you want to control. The Web server has its own Web proxy, while an FTP server has an FTP proxy. Proxies can also be used to cache commonly used data, such as Web pages, so that users needn't constantly access the originating site. The proxy software commonly used on Linux systems is Squid, discussed in Chapter 24.

An additional task performed by firewalls is network address translation (NAT). Network address translation redirects packets to appropriate destinations. It performs tasks such as redirecting packets to certain hosts, forwarding packets to other networks, and changing the host source of packets to implement IP masquerading.

NOTE   *The IP Chains package is the precursor to IPtables that was used on Linux systems running the 2.2 kernel. It is still in use on many Linux systems. The Linux Web site for IP Chains, which is the successor to ipfwadm used on older versions of Linux, is currently* **www.netfilter.org/ipchains**. *IP Chains is no longer included with Fedora Linux.*

The Netfilter software package implements both packet-filtering and NAT tasks for the Linux 2.4 kernel and above. The Netfilter software is developed by the Netfilter Project, which you can find out more about at **www.netfilter.org**. The Red Hat Enterprise Linux Security Guide provides a helpful description on using Netfilter on Red Hat systems (**www.redhat.com**, Red Hat Enterprise Linux Documentation page).

IPtables

The command used to execute packet filtering and NAT tasks is **iptables**, and the software is commonly referred to as simply IPtables. However, Netfilter implements packet-filtering and NAT tasks separately using different tables and commands. A table will hold the set of commands for its application. This approach streamlines the packet-filtering task, letting IPtables perform packet-filtering checks without the overhead of also having to do address translations. NAT operations are also freed from being mixed in with packet-filtering checks. You use the **iptables** command for both packet-filtering and NAT tasks, but for NAT you add the **-nat** option. The IPtables software can be built directly into the kernel or loaded as a kernel module, **iptable_filter.o**.

ip6tables

The ip6tables package provides support for IPv6 addressing. It is identical to IPtables except that it allows the use of IPv6 addresses instead of IPv4 addresses (see Chapter 37). Both filter and mangle tables are supported in ip6tables, but not NAT tables. The filter tables support the same options and commands as in IPtables. The mangle tables will allow specialized packet changes like those for IPtables, using PREROUTING, INPUT, OUTPUT, FORWARD, and POSTROUTING rules. Some extensions have ipv6 labels for their names, such as ipv6-icmp, which corresponds to the IPtables icmp extension. The ipv6headers extension is used to select IPv6 headers.

Modules

Unlike its predecessor, IP Chains, Netfilter is designed to be modularized and extensible. Capabilities can be added in the form of modules such as the state module, which adds connection tracking. Most modules are loaded as part of the IPtables service. Others are optional; you can elect to load them before installing rules. The IPtables modules on your Red Hat Fedora system are located at /usr/lib/*kernel-version*/kernel/net/ipv4/netfilter, where *kernel-version* is your kernel number. For IPv6 modules, check the **ipv6/netfilter** directory. Modules that load automatically will have an **ipt_** prefix, and optional ones have just an **ip_** prefix.

Optional modules can be specified as a list assigned to the IPTABLES_MODULES parameters located in the **/etc/sysconfig/iptables-config** file, which is used by the iptables service script. Whenever you start IPtables with the iptables service script, they will be automatically loaded. For IPv6 configuration, you use the **ip6tables-config** file.

```
# service iptables start
```

If you are writing you own iptables script, instead of using the Red Hat or Fedora service iptables script, you would have to add **modpobe** commands to load optional modules directly.

NOTE *The IPtables package includes backward-compatible modules for both ipfwadm and IP Chains. In fact, IPtables is very similar to IP Chains. You can still use IP Chains and the earlier ipfwadm commands by loading the **ipchains.o** or **ipfwadm.o** module provided with the Netfilter software. These provide full backward compatibility.*

Packet Filtering

Netfilter is essentially a framework for packet management that can check packets for particular network protocols and notify parts of the kernel listening for them. Built on the Netfilter framework is the packet selection system implemented by IPtables. With IPtables, different tables of rules can be set up to select packets according to differing criteria. Netfilter currently supports three tables: filter, nat, and mangle. Packet filtering is implemented using a filter table that holds rules for dropping or accepting packets. Network address translation operations such as IP masquerading are implemented using the NAT table that holds IP masquerading rules. The mangle table is used for specialized packet changes. Changes can be made to packets before they are sent out, when they are received, or as they are being forwarded. This structure is extensible in that new modules can define their own tables with their own rules. It also greatly improves efficiency. Instead of all packets checking one large table, they access only the table of rules they need to.

IP table rules are managed using the `iptables` command. For this command, you will need to specify the table you want to manage. The default is the filter table, which need not be specified. You can list the rules you have added at any time with the `-L` and `-n` options, as shown below. The `-n` option says to use only numeric output for both IP addresses and ports, avoiding a DNS lookup for hostnames. You could, however, just use the `-L` option to see the port labels and hostnames:

```
iptables -L -n
```

NOTE *In IPtables commands, chain names have to be entered in uppercase, as with the chain names INPUT, OUTPUT, and FORWARD.*

Chains

Rules are combined into different chains. The kernel uses chains to manage packets it receives and sends out. A *chain* is simply a checklist of rules. These rules specify what action to take for packets containing certain headers. The rules operate with an if-then-else structure. If a packet does not match the first rule, the next rule is then checked, and so on. If the packet does not match any rules, the kernel consults chain policy. Usually, at this point the packet is rejected. If the packet does match a rule, it is passed to its target, which determines what to do with the packet. The standard targets are listed in Table 20-2. If a packet does not match any of the rules, it is passed to the chain's default target.

Targets

A *target* could, in turn, be another chain of rules, even a chain of user-defined rules. A packet could be passed through several chains before finally reaching a target. In the case of user-defined chains, the default target is always the next rule in the chains from which it was called. This sets up a procedure- or function call–like flow of control found in programming languages. When a rule has a user-defined chain as its target, when activated, that user-defined chain is executed. If no rules are matched, execution returns to the next rule in the originating chain.

Target	Function
ACCEPT	Allow packet to pass through the firewall.
DROP	Deny access by the packet.
REJECT	Deny access and notify the sender.
QUEUE	Send packets to user space.
RETURN	Jump to the end of the chain and let the default target process it.

TABLE 20-2 IPtables Targets

TIP *Specialized targets and options can be added by means of kernel patches provided by the*
Netfilter site. For example, the SAME patch returns the same address for all connections.
A patch-o-matic option for the Netfilter file will patch your kernel source code, adding support
for the new target and options. You can then rebuild and install your kernel.

Firewall and NAT Chains

The kernel uses three firewall chains: INPUT, OUTPUT, and FORWARD. When a packet is
received through an interface, the INPUT chain is used to determine what to do with it. The
kernel then uses its routing information to decide where to send it. If the kernel sends the
packet to another host, the FORWARD chain is checked. Before the packet is actually sent,
the OUTPUT chain is also checked. In addition, two NAT table chains, POSTROUTING and
PREROUTING, are implemented to handle masquerading and packet address
modifications. The built-in Netfilter chains are listed in Table 20-3.

Adding and Changing Rules

You add and modify chain rules using the **iptables** commands. An **iptables** command
consists of the keyword **iptables**, followed by an argument denoting the command to
execute. For example, **iptables -A** is the command to add a new rule, whereas **iptables**
-D is the command to delete a rule. The **iptables** commands are listed in Table 20-4. The
following command simply lists the chains along with their rules currently defined for your
system. The output shows the default values created by **iptables** commands.

```
iptables -L -n
Chain input (policy ACCEPT):
Chain forward (policy ACCEPT):
Chain output (policy ACCEPT):
```

To add a new rule to a chain, you use **-A**. Use **-D** to remove it, and **-R** to replace it.
Following the command, list the chain to which the rule applies, such as the INPUT,
OUTPUT, or FORWARD chain, or a user-defined chain. Next, you list different options that
specify the actions you want taken (most are the same as those used for IP Chains, with
a few exceptions). The **-s** option specifies the source address attached to the packet, **-d**
specifies the destination address, and the **-j** option specifies the target of the rule. The
ACCEPT target will allow a packet to pass. The **-i** option now indicates the input device
and can be used only with the INPUT and FORWARD chains. The **-o** option indicates the

Chain	Description
INPUT	Rules for incoming packets
OUTPUT	Rules for outgoing packets
FORWARD	Rules for forwarded packets
PREROUTING	Rules for redirecting or modifying incoming packets, NAT table only
POSTROUTING	Rules for redirecting or modifying outgoing packets, NAT table only

TABLE 20-3 Netfilter Built-in Chains

Option	Function
-A *chain*	Appends a rule to a chain.
-D *chain* [*rulenum*]	Deletes matching rules from a chain. Deletes rule *rulenum* (1 = first) from *chain*.
-I *chain* [*rulenum*]	Inserts in *chain* as *rulenum* (default 1 = first).
-R *chain rulenum*	Replaces rule *rulenum* (1 = first) in *chain*.
-L [*chain*]	Lists the rules in *chain* or all chains.
-E [*chain*]	Renames a chain.
-F [*chain*]	Deletes (flushes) all rules in *chain* or all chains.
-R *chain*	Replaces a rule; rules are numbered from 1.
-Z [*chain*]	Zero counters in *chain* or all chains.
-N *chain*	Creates a new user-defined chain.
-X *chain*	Deletes a user-defined chain.
-P *chain target*	Changes policy on *chain* to *target*.

TABLE 20-4   IPtables Commands

output device and can be used only for OUTPUT and FORWARD chains. Table 20-5 lists several basic options.

IPtables Options

The IPtables package is designed to be extensible, and there are number of options with selection criteria that can be included with IPtables. For example, the TCP extension includes the **--syn** option that checks for SYN packets. The ICMP extension provides the **--icmp-type** option for specifying ICMP packets as those used in ping operations. The limit extension includes the **--limit** option, with which you can limit the maximum number of matching packets in a specified time period, such as a second.

In the following example, the user adds a rule to the INPUT chain to accept all packets originating from the address 192.168.0.55. Any packets that are received (**INPUT**) whose source address (**-s**) matches 192.168.0.55 are accepted and passed through (**-j ACCEPT**):

```
iptables -A INPUT -s 192.168.0.55 -j ACCEPT
```

Accepting and Denying Packets: DROP and ACCEPT

There are two built-in targets, DROP and ACCEPT. Other targets can be either user-defined chains or extensions added on, such as REJECT. Two special targets are used to manage chains, RETURN and QUEUE. RETURN indicates the end of a chain and returns to the chain it started from. QUEUE is used to send packets to user space.

```
iptables -A INPUT -s www.myjunk.com -j DROP
```

Option	Function
-p [!] *proto*	Specifies a protocol, such as TCP, UDP, ICMP, or ALL.
-s [!] *address* [/*mask*] [!] [*port* [:*port*]]	Source address to match. With the *port* argument, you can specify the port.
--sport [!] [*port* [:*port*]]	Source port specification. You can specify a range of ports using the colon, *port:port.*
-d [!] *address* [/*mask*] [!] [*port* [:*port*]]	Destination address to match. With the *port* argument, you can specify the port.
--dport [!] [*port* [:*port*]]	Destination port specification.
--icmp-type [!] *typename*	Specifies ICMP type.
-i [!] *name* [+]	Specifies an input network interface using its name (for example, **eth0**). The + symbol functions as a wildcard. The + attached to the end of the name matches all interfaces with that prefix (**eth+** matches all Ethernet interfaces). Can be used only with the INPUT chain.
-j *target* [**port**]	Specifies the target for a rule (specify [**port**] for REDIRECT target).
--to-source < *ipaddr*> [-< *ipaddr*>] [: *port- port*]	Used with the SNAT target, rewrites packets with new source IP address.
--to-destination <*ipaddr*> [-< *ipaddr*>] [: *port- port*]	Used with the DNAT target, rewrites packets with new destination IP address.
-n	Numeric output of addresses and ports, used with **-L**.
-o [!] *name* [+]	Specifies an output network interface using its name (for example, **eth0**). Can be used only with FORWARD and OUTPUT chains.
-t *table*	Specifies a table to use, as in **-t nat** for the NAT table.
-v	Verbose mode, shows rule details, used with **-L**.
-x	Expands numbers (displays exact values), used with **-L**.
[!] **-f**	Matches second through last fragments of a fragmented packet.
[!] **-V**	Prints package version.
!	Negates an option or address.
-m	Specifies a module to use, such as state.
--state	Specifies options for the state module such as NEW, INVALID, RELATED, and ESTABLISHED. Used to detect packet's state. NEW references SYN packets (new connections).
--syn	SYN packets, new connections.

TABLE 20-5   IPtables Options *(continued)*

Option	Function
`--tcp-flags`	TCP flags: SYN, ACK, FIN, RST, URG, PS, and ALL for all flags.
`--limit`	Option for the limit module (`-m limit`). Used to control the rate of matches, matching a given number of times per second.
`--limit-burst`	Option for the limit module (`-m limit`). Specifies maximum burst before the limit kicks in. Used to control denial-of-service attacks.

TABLE 20-5   IPtables Options

You can turn a rule into its inverse with an **!** symbol. For example, to accept all incoming packets except those from a specific address, place an **!** symbol before the **-s** option and that address. The following example will accept all packets except those from the IP address 192.168.0.45:

```
iptables -A INPUT -j ACCEPT ! -s 192.168.0.45
```

You can specify an individual address using its domain name or its IP number. For a range of addresses, you can use the IP number of their network and the network IP mask. The IP mask can be an IP number or simply the number of bits making up the mask. For example, all of the addresses in network 192.168.0 can be represented by 192.168.0.0/ 225.255.255.0 or by 192.168.0.0/24. To specify any address, you can use 0.0.0.0/0.0.0.0 or simply 0/0. By default, rules reference any address if no **-s** or **-d** specification exists. The following example accepts messages coming in that are from (source) any host in the 192.168.0.0 network and that are going (destination) anywhere at all (the **-d** option is left out or could be written as **-d 0/0**):

```
iptables -A INPUT -s 192.168.0.0/24  -j ACCEPT
```

The IPtables rules are usually applied to a specific network interface such as the Ethernet interface used to connect to the Internet. For a single system connected to the Internet, you will have two interfaces, one that is your Internet connection and a localhost interface (**lo**) for internal connections between users on your system. The network interface for the Internet is referenced using the device name for the interface. For example, an Ethernet card with the device name **/dev/eth0** would be referenced by the name **eth0**. A modem using PPP protocols with the device name **/dev/ppp0** would have the name **ppp0**. In IPtables rules, you use the **-i** option to indicate the input device; it can be used only with the INPUT and FORWARD chains. The **-o** option indicates the output device and can be used only for OUTPUT and FORWARD chains. Rules can then be applied to packets arriving and leaving on particular network devices. In the following examples, the first rule references the Ethernet device **eth0**, and the second, the localhost:

```
iptables -A INPUT -j DROP -i eth0 -s 192.168.0.45
iptables -A INPUT -j ACCEPT  -i lo
```

User-Defined Chains

With IPtables, the FORWARD and INPUT chains are evaluated separately. One does not feed into the other. This means that if you want to completely block certain addresses from passing through your system, you will need to add both a FORWARD rule and an INPUT rule for them.

```
iptables -A INPUT -j DROP -i eth0 -s 192.168.0.45
iptables -A FORWARD -j DROP -i eth0 -s 192.168.0.45
```

A common method for reducing repeated INPUT and FORWARD rules is to create a user chain that both the INPUT and FORWARD chains feed into. You define a user chain with the **-N** option. The next example shows the basic format for this arrangement. A new chain is created called incoming (it can be any name you choose). The rules you would define for your FORWARD and INPUT chains are now defined for the incoming chain. The INPUT and FORWARD chains then use the incoming chain as a target, jumping directly to it and using its rules to process any packets they receive.

```
iptables -N incoming

iptables -A incoming -j DROP -i eth0 -s 192.168.0.45
iptables -A incoming -j ACCEPT  -i lo

iptables -A FORWARD -j incoming
iptables -A INPUT -j incoming
```

ICMP Packets

Firewalls often block certain Internet Control Message Protocol (ICMP) messages. ICMP redirect messages, in particular, can take control of your routing tasks. You need to enable some ICMP messages, however, such as those needed for ping, traceroute, and particularly destination-unreachable operations. In most cases, you always need to make sure destination-unreachable packets are allowed; otherwise, domain name queries could hang. Some of the more common ICMP packet types are listed in Table 20-6. You can enable an ICMP type of packet with the **--icmp-type** option, which takes as its argument a number or a name representing the message. The following examples enable the use of echo-reply, echo-request, and destination-unreachable messages, which have the numbers 0, 8, and 3:

```
iptables -A INPUT -j ACCEPT  -p icmp -i eth0 --icmp -type  echo-reply -d 10.0.0.1
iptables -A INPUT -j ACCEPT  -p icmp -i eth0 --icmp-type  echo-request -d 10.0.0.1
iptables -A INPUT -j ACCEPT -p icmp -i eth0 --icmp-type  destination-unreachable -d
10.0.0.1
```

Their rule listing will look like this:

```
ACCEPT     icmp --  0.0.0.0/0              10.0.0.1            icmp type 0
ACCEPT     icmp --  0.0.0.0/0              10.0.0.1            icmp type 8
ACCEPT     icmp --  0.0.0.0/0              10.0.0.1            icmp type 3
```

Ping operations need to be further controlled to avoid the ping-of-death security threat. You can do this several ways. One way is to deny any ping fragments. Ping packets are

Number	Name	Required By
0	echo-reply	ping
3	destination-unreachable	Any TCP/UDP traffic
5	redirect	Routing if not running routing daemon
8	echo-request	ping
11	time-exceeded	traceroute

TABLE 20-6   Common ICMP Packets

normally very small. You can block ping-of-death attacks by denying any ICMP packet that is a fragment. Use the **-f** option to indicate fragments.

```
iptables -A INPUT -p icmp -j DROP -f
```

Another way is to limit the number of matches received for ping packets. You use the limit module to control the number of matches on the ICMP ping operation. Use **-m limit** to use the limit module and **--limit** to specify the number of allowed matches. **1/s** will allow one match per second.

```
iptables -A FORWARD -p icmp --icmp-type echo-request -m limit --limit 1/s -j ACCEPT
```

Controlling Port Access

If your system is hosting an Internet service, such as a Web or FTP server, you can use IPtables to control access to it. You can specify a particular service by using the source port (**--sport**) or destination port (**--dport**) options with the port that the service uses. IPtables lets you use names for ports such as **www** for the Web server port. The names of services and the ports they use are listed in the **/etc/services** file, which maps ports to particular services. For a domain name server, the port would be **domain**. You can also use the port number if you want, preceding the number with a colon. The following example accepts all messages to the Web server located at 192.168.0.43:

```
iptables -A INPUT -d 192.168.0.43 --dport www -j ACCEPT
```

You can also use port references to protect certain services and deny others. This approach is often used if you are designing a firewall that is much more open to the Internet, letting users make freer use of Internet connections. Certain services you know can be harmful, such as Telnet and NTP, can be denied selectively. For example, to deny any kind of Telnet operation on your firewall, you can drop all packets coming in on the Telnet port, 23. To protect NFS operations, you can deny access to the port used for the portmapper, 111. You can use either the port number or the port name.

```
# deny outside access to portmapper port on firewall.
iptables -A arriving  -j DROP -p tcp -i eth0  --dport 111
# deny outside access to telnet port on firewall.
iptables -A arriving  -j DROP -p tcp -i eth0  --dport telnet
```

The rule listing will look like this:

```
DROP     tcp  --  0.0.0.0/0    0.0.0.0/0       tcp dpt:111
DROP     tcp  --  0.0.0.0/0    0.0.0.0/0       tcp dpt:23
```

One port-related security problem is access to your X server on the XFree86 ports that range from 6000 to 6009. On a relatively open firewall, these ports could be used to illegally access your system through your X server. A range of ports can be specified with a colon, as in 6000:6009. You can also use x11 for the first port, x11:6009. Sessions on the X server can be secured by using SSH, which normally accesses the X server on port 6010.

```
iptables -A arriving  -j DROP -p tcp -i eth0  --dport 6000:6009
```

Common ports checked and their labels are shown here:

Service	Port Number	Port Label
Auth	113	auth
Finger	79	finger
FTP	21	ftp
NTP	123	ntp
Portmapper	111	sunrpc
Telnet	23	telnet
Web server	80	www
XFree86	6000:6009	x11:6009

Packet States: Connection Tracking

One of the more useful extensions is the state extension, which can easily detect tracking information for a packet. Connection tracking maintains information about a connection such as its source, destination, and port. It provides an effective means for determining which packets belong to an established or related connection. To use connection tracking, you specify the state module first with **-m state**. Then you can use the **--state** option. Here you can specify any of the following states:

State	Description
NEW	A packet that creates a new connection
ESTABLISHED	A packet that belongs to an existing connection
RELATED	A packet that is related to, but not part of, an existing connection, such as an ICMP error or a packet establishing an FTP data connection
INVALID	A packet that could not be identified for some reason
RELATED+REPLY	A packet that is related to an established connection, but not part of one directly

PART IV

If you are designing a firewall that is meant to protect your local network from any attempts to penetrate it from an outside network, you may want to restrict packets coming in. Simply denying access by all packets is unfeasible because users connected to outside servers—say, on the Internet—must receive information from them. You can, instead, deny access by a particular kind of packet used to initiate a connection. The idea is that an attacker must initiate a connection from the outside. The headers of these kinds of packets have their SYN bit set on and their FIN and ACK bits empty. The state module's NEW state matches on any such SYN packet. By specifying a DROP target for such packets, you deny access by any packet that is part of an attempt to make a connection with your system. Anyone trying to connect to your system from the outside is unable to do so. Users on your local system who have initiated connections with outside hosts can still communicate with them. The following example will drop any packets trying to create a new connection on the **eth0** interface, though they will be accepted on any other interface:

```
iptables -A INPUT -m state --state NEW -i eth0 -j DROP
```

You can use the **!** operator on the **eth0** device combined with an ACCEPT target to compose a rule that will accept any new packets except those on the **eth0** device. If the **eth0** device is the only one that connects to the Internet, this still effectively blocks outside access. At the same time, input operation for other devices such as your localhost are free to make new connections. This kind of conditional INPUT rule is used to allow access overall with exceptions. It usually assumes that a later rule such as a chain policy will drop remaining packets.

```
iptables -A INPUT -m state --state NEW ! -i eth0 -j ACCEPT
```

The next example will accept any packets that are part of an established connection or related to such a connection on the **eth0** interface:

```
iptables -A INPUT -m state --state ESTABLISHED,RELATED -j ACCEPT
```

TIP *You can use the iptstate tool to display the current state table.*

Specialized Connection Tracking: ftp, irc, Amanda, tftp

To track certain kinds of packets, IPtables uses specialized connection tracking modules. These are optional modules that you have to have loaded manually. To track passive FTP connections, you would have to load the ip_conntrack_ftp module. To add NAT table support, you would also load the ip_nat_ftp module. For IRC connections, you use ip_conntrack_irc and ip_nat_irc. There are corresponding modules for Amanda (the backup server) and TFTP (Trivial FTP).

To have these modules loaded automatically by the Red Hat Fedora iptables service script, you have to list them in the IPTABLES_MODULE parameter in the **/etc/sysconfig/iptables-config** file. For example, the following assignment adds support for both FTP and Amanda:

```
IPTABLES_MODULES="ip_conntrack, ip_conntrack_ftp, ip_nat_ftp, ip_conntrack_
amanda, ip_nat_amanda"
```

If you were writing your own iptables script, instead of using the service iptables script, you would have to add **modprobe** commands to load the modules.

```
modprobe ip_conntrack ip_conntrack_ftp ip_nat_ftp
modprobe ip_conntrack_amanda ip_nat_amanda
```

Network Address Translation (NAT)

Network address translation (NAT) is the process whereby a system will change the destination or source of packets as they pass through the system. A packet will traverse several linked systems on a network before it reaches its final destination. Normally, they will simply pass the packet on. However, if one of these systems performs a NAT on a packet, it can change the source or destination. A packet sent to a particular destination could have its destination address changed. To make this work, the system also needs to remember such changes so that the source and destination for any reply packets are altered back to the original addresses of the packet being replied to.

NAT is often used to provide access to systems that may be connected to the Internet through only one IP address. Such is the case with networking features such as IP masquerading, support for multiple servers, and transparent proxying. With IP masquerading, NAT operations will change the destination and source of a packet moving through a firewall/gateway linking the Internet to computers on a local network. The gateway has a single IP address that the other local computers can use through NAT operations. If you have multiple servers but only one IP address, you can use NAT operations to send packets to the alternate servers. You can also use NAT operations to have your IP address reference a particular server application such as a Web server (transparent proxy). NAT tables are not implemented for ip6tables.

Adding NAT Rules

Packet selection rules for NAT operations are added to the NAT table managed by the **iptables** command. To add rules to the NAT table, you have to specify the NAT table with the **-t** option. Thus, to add a rule to the NAT table, you would have to specify the NAT table with the **-t nat** option as shown here:

```
iptables -t nat
```

With the **-L** option, you can list the rules you have added to the NAT table:

```
iptables -t nat -L -n
```

Adding the **-n** option will list IP addresses and ports in numeric form. This will speed up the listing, as iptables will not attempt to do a DNS lookup to determine the hostname for the IP address.

Nat Targets and Chains

In addition, there are two types of NAT operations: source NAT, specified as SNAT target, and destination NAT, specified as DNAT target. SNAT target is used for rules that alter source addresses, and DNAT target, for those that alter destination addresses.

Three chains in the NAT table are used by the kernel for NAT operations. These are PREROUTING, POSTROUTING, and OUTPUT. PREROUTING is used for destination NAT (DNAT) rules. These are packets that are arriving. POSTROUTING is used for source NAT (SNAT) rules. These are for packets leaving. OUTPUT is used for destination NAT rules for locally generated packets.

As with packet filtering, you can specify source (**-s**) and destination (**-d**) addresses, as well as the input (**-i**) and output (**-o**) devices. The **-j** option will specify a target such as MASQUERADE. You would implement IP masquerading by adding a MASQUERADE rule to the POSTROUTING chain:

```
# iptables -t nat -A POSTROUTING -o eth0 -j MASQUERADE
```

To change the source address of a packet leaving your system, you would use the POSTROUTING rule with the SNAT target. For the SNAT target, you use the **--to-source** option to specify the source address:

```
# iptables -t nat -A POSTROUTING -o eth0 -j SNAT --to-source 192.168.0.4
```

To change the destination address of packets arriving on your system, you would use the PREROUTING rule with the DNAT target and the **--to-destination** option:

```
# iptables -t nat -A PREROUTING -i eth0 \
          -j DNAT --to-destination 192.168.0.3
```

Specifying a port lets you change destinations for packets arriving on a particular port. In effect, this lets you implement port forwarding. In the next example, every packet arriving on port 80 (the Web service port) is redirected to 10.0.0.3, which in this case would be a system running a Web server.

```
# iptables -t nat -A PREROUTING -i eth0 -dport 80 \
          -j DNAT --to-destination 10.0.0.3
```

With the TOS and MARK targets, you can mangle the packet to control its routing or priority. A TOS target sets the type of service for a packet, which can set the priority using criteria such as normal-service, minimize-cost, or maximize-throughput, among others.

The targets valid only for the NAT table are shown here:

SNAT	Modify source address, use **--to-source** option to specify new source address.
DNAT	Modify destination address, use **--to-destination** option to specify new destination address.
REDIRECT	Redirect a packet.
MASQUERADE	IP masquerading.
MIRROR	Reverse source and destination and send back to sender.
MARK	Modify the Mark field to control message routing.

Nat Redirection: Transparent Proxies

NAT tables can be used to implement any kind of packet redirection, a process transparent to the user. Redirection is communing used to implement a transparent proxy. Redirection of packets is carried out with the REDIRECT target. With transparent proxies, packets received can be automatically redirected to a proxy server. For example, packets arriving on the Web service port, 80, can be redirected to the Squid Proxy service port, usually 3128. This involves a command to redirect a packet, using the REDIRECT target on the PREROUTING chain:

```
# iptables -t nat -A PREROUTING -i eth1 --dport 80 -j REDIRECT --to-port 3128
```

Packet Mangling: the Mangle Table

The *packet mangling* table is used to actually modify packet information. Rules applied specifically to this table are often designed to control the mundane behavior of packets, like routing, connection size, and priority. Rules that actually modify a packet, rather than simply redirect or stop it, can be used only in the mangle table. For example, the TOS target can be used directly in the mangle table to change the Type of Service field to modifying a packet's priority. A TCPMSS target could be set to control the size of a connection. The ECN target lets you work around ECN black holes, and the DSCP target will let you change DSCP bits. Several extensions such as the ROUTE extension will change a packet, in this case, rewriting its destination, rather than just redirecting it.

The mangle table is indicated with the **-t mangle** option. Use the following command to see what chains are listed in your mangle table:

```
iptables -t mangle  -L
```

Several mangle table targets are shown here:

TOS	Modify the Type of Service field to manage the priority of the packet.
TCPMSS	Modify the allowed size of packets for a connection, enabling larger transmissions.
ECN	Remove ECN black hole information.
DSCP	Change DSCP bits.
ROUTE	Extension TARGET to modify destination information in the packet.

NOTE *The IPtables package is designed to be extensible, allowing customized targets to be added easily. This involves applying patches to the kernel and rebuilding it. See **www.netfilter.org** for more details, along with a listing of extended targets.*

IPtables Scripts

Though you can enter IPtables rules from the shell command line, when you shut down your system, these commands will be lost. On Fedora and Red Hat, you can make use of the built-in support for saving and reading IPtables rules using the iptables service script.

Alternatively, you can manage the process yourself, saving to files of your own choosing. In either event, you will most likely need to place your IPtables rules in a script that can then be executed directly. This way you can edit and manage a complex set of rules, adding comments and maintaining their ordering.

NOTE *On Red Hat binaries, IPtables support in the kernel is enabled by default. If you recompile the kernel be sure support for packet filtering is turned on, check Networking Options in the 2.4 kernel, and Networking Support/Networking Options under Device Drivers in the 2.6 kernel.*

Red Hat and Fedora IPtables Support

Red Hat provides support for IPtables as part of their system configuration using various scripts and configuration files (see Table 20-7). When you install the RPM package for IPtables, an iptables service script is installed that will read and save IPtables commands using the **/etc/sysconfig/iptables** file. If you have set IPtables to be started up automatically when you boot your system, this file will be checked to see if it exists and is not empty. If so, IPtables will automatically read the IPtables commands that it holds. This helps to integrate IPtables more smoothly into the system setup process.

IPtables Rules: /etc/sysconfig/iptables and system-config-security-level

The `/etc/sysconfig/iptables` script is automatically generated by **system-config-securitylevel**, which is run during the installation process. When you first start up your system, the **/etc/sysconfig/iptables** file will contain the IPtables rules for the configuration you selected when you ran **system-config-securitylevel**. If you run **system-config-securitylevel** again, changing your configuration, the **/etc/sysconfig/iptables** file will be overwritten with the new IPtables rules. You can access **system-config-securitylevel** as the Firewall entry on the System | Administration menu.

You can sidestep this automatic IPtables setup by simply deleting the **/etc/sysconfig/iptables** file. (Running **system-config-securitylevel** and clicking the Disable button will do the same.) Be sure you back it up first in case it has important commands. It is possible to

Script and Tool	Description
`/etc/sysconfig/iptables`	Red Hat IPtables script to create IPtables rules.
`/etc/sysconfig/iptables.save`	Red Hat IPtables backup script to create IPtables rules. This is a copy made of original IPtables, when a new IPtables file is generated with the save option.
/etc/sysconfig/iptables-config	Configuration file for **/etc/rc.d/init.d/iptables** service script, containing shell variable definitions.
`/etc/rc.d/init.d/iptables`	Red Hat iptables service script to manage IPtables rules in **/etc/sysconfig/iptables.**
`system-config-securitylevel`	Red Hat and Fedora tool for creating basic IPtables firewall rules for **/etc/syscofig/iptables**.

TABLE 20-7   Red Hat Fedora IPtables Scripts and Tools

edit the **/etc/sysconfig/iptables** file directly and enter IPtables commands, but it is not recommended. Instead, you should think of this file as holding a final installation of your IPtables commands.

The iptables Service Script: /etc/rc.d/init.d/iptables and /etc/sysconfig/iptables-config

You should think of the iptables service script that Red Hat Fedora provides as a versatile management tool, not as a service startup script. The use of the `service` command for this script can be confusing. The iptables script only manages IPtables rules, flushing, adding, or reporting them. It does not start and stop the IPtables service. If Netfilter is not running, you will need to specify that it be started up when your system boots. For this, you can use **system-config-service** (Services in the Server Settings window) and then select IPtables from the list of services.

The iptables service script makes use of several predefined shell parameters for specifying modules along with start and stop options. Default definitions are placed within the iptables service script, whereas corresponding custom definitions are located in a special file called **/etc/sysconfig/iptables-config**. Here the system administrator can set options like what modules to load or whether to save rules whenever IPtables is stopped, without having to edit the IPtables service script directly. For IPv6, you would use **ip6tables-config**. Table 20-8 lists the current IPtables parameters. Each time the iptables service script is used to start IPtables, it will load the modules specified in IPTABLES_MODULES as listed in **iptables-config**.

The service script `/etc/rc.d/init.d/iptables` supports several options with which to manage your rules. The `status` option displays a listing of all your current rules. The `stop` option will flush your current rules. Unlike `stop` and `status`, the `start` and `save` options are tied directly to the **/etc/sysconfig/iptables** file. The `start` option will flush your current IPtables rules and add those in the **/etc/sysconfig/iptables** file. The `save` option will save your current rules to the **/etc/sysconfig/iptables** file. Keep in mind that the `stop` and `status` operations work on the current IPtables rules, no matter if they were

Parameter	Description
IPTABLES_MODULES	List of IPtables modules to load. Empty by default.
IPTABLES_MODULES_UNLOAD	Default is yes; set to yes to unload modules at service script start and stop operations.
IPTABLES_SAVE_ON_STOP	Default is no; if set to yes, will save all rules when service script stops firewall.
IPTABLES_ SAVE_ON_RESTART	Default is no; if set to yes, will save all rules when service script restarts firewall.
IPTABLES_SAVE_COUNTERS	Default is no; if set to yes, will save counters if saved for stopping or restarting is enabled.
IPTABLES_STATUS_NUMERIC	Default is yes; if set to yes, will display addresses and ports numerically.

TABLE 20-8   Configuration Parameters for iptables-config

added manually on the command line, added by your own script, or added by the **start** option from **/etc/sysconfig/iptables**. The following command will list your current rules:

```
service iptables status
```

Perhaps the most effective way to think of the iptables service script is as an IPtables development tool. When creating complex firewall rules (beyond the simple set generated by **system-config-securitylevel**), you should first create a script and place your rules in it, as described later in the IPtables script example. Make the script executable. Any changes you need to make as you debug your firewall, you make to this script. Before you run it, run the iptables service script with the **stop** option to clear out any previous rules:

```
service iptables stop
```

Then run your script, as shown here for the **myfilters** script:

```
./myfilters
```

To see how the commands have been interpreted by IPtables, use the service script with the **status** option:

```
service iptables status
```

For any changes, edit your iptables script. Then run the service script again to clear out the old rules. Run the iptables script again, and use the **status** option with the service script to see how they were implemented:

```
service iptables stop
./myfilters
service iptables status
```

Saving IPtables Rules

Once you are satisfied that your IPtables rules are working correctly, you can save your rules to the **/etc/sysconfig/iptables** file (for IPv6 you use **/etc/sysconfig/ip6tables**). Use the iptables service script with the **save** option. Now your rules will be read automatically when your system starts up. You can think of the save operation as installing your IPtables rules on your system, making them part of your system setup whenever you start your system.

```
service iptables save
```

To make changes, modify your iptables script, run the service script with **stop** to clear out the old rules, run the iptables script, and then use the service script with the **save** option to generate a new **/etc/sysconfig/iptables** file. A backup of the original is saved in **/etc/sysconfig/iptables.save**, in case you to need to restore the older rules.

Instead of using the service script, you can save your rules using the **iptables-save** script. The recommended file to use is **/etc/iptables.rules**. The service script actually uses **iptables-save** with the **-c** option to save rules to the **/etc/sysconfig/iptables** file. The **-c** option for **iptables-save** includes counters in the output (the iptables service script is designed to parse counter information along with the commands). The **iptables-save** command outputs rules to the standard output. To save them in a file, you must redirect the output to a file with the redirection operator, **>**, as shown here:

```
iptables-save -c > /etc/sysconfig/iptables
```

You can also save your rules to a file of your choosing, such as **/etc/iptables.rules**. The **/etc/rc.d/init.d/iptables** service script defines the IPTABLES_CONFIG variable, which holds the name of the IPtables configuration file, **/etc/sysconfig/iptables**.

```
iptables-save > /etc/iptables.rules
```

Then, to restore the rules, use the **iptables-restore** script to read the IPtables commands from that saved file:

```
iptables-restore < /etc/iptables.rules
```

Red Hat and Fedora ip6tables Support

For ip6tables, Red Hat and Fedora use a different, corresponding set of supporting scripts and configuration files. ip6tables has its own service script, **ip6tables**, as well as its own restore and save scripts, **ip6tables-save** and **ip6tables-restore**. In their names, they have the number 6, as in **/etc/sysconfig/ip6tables**. The ip6tables configuration scripts and files are shown in Table 20-9.

An IPtables Script Example: IPv4

You now have enough information to create a simple IPtables script that will provide basic protection for a single system connected to the Internet. The following script, **myfilter**, provides an IPtables filtering process to protect a local network and a Web site from outside attacks. This example uses IPtables and IPv4 addressing (see Chapter 37). For IPv6 addressing you would use ip6tables, which has corresponding commands, except for the NAT rules, which would be implemented as mangle rules.

Script and Tool	Description
`/etc/sysconfig/ip6tables`	Fedora Red Hat ip6tables script to create IPv6 IPtables rules.
`/etc/sysconfig/ip6tables-config`	Configuration file for `/etc/rc.d/init.d/ip6tables` service script, containing shell variable definitions.
`/etc/rc.d/init.d/ip6tables`	Fedora Red Hat ip6tables service script to manage ip6tables rules in `/etc/sysconfig/ip6tables`.
`ip6tables-save`	Ip6tables save script, operates like **ip6tables-save** (see previous section).
`ip6tables-restore`	Ip6tables restore script, operates like **ip6tables-restore** (see previous section).

TABLE **20-9**   Configuration File and Support Scripts for ip6tables

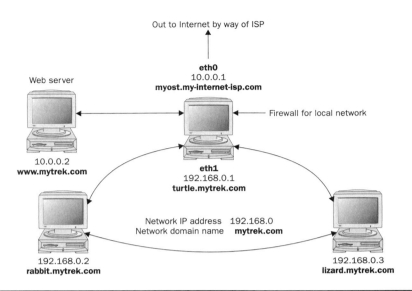

FIGURE 20-1   A network with a firewall

The script configures a simple firewall for a private network (check the IPtables HOWTO for a more complex example). If you have a local network, you could adapt this script to it. In this configuration, all remote access initiated from the outside is blocked, but two-way communication is allowed for connections that users in the network make with outside systems. In this example, the firewall system functions as a gateway for a private network whose network address is 192.168.0.0 (see Figure 20-1). The Internet address is, for the sake of this example, 10.0.0.1. The system has two Ethernet devices: one for the private network (**eth1**) and one for the Internet (**eth0**). The gateway firewall system also supports a Web server at address 10.0.0.2. Entries in this example that are too large to fit on one line are continued on a second line, with the newline quoted with a backslash.

The basic rules as they apply to different parts of the network are illustrated in Figure 20-2.

myfilter

```
Firewall Gateway system IP address is 10.0.0.1 using Ethernet device eth0
# Private network address is 192.168.0.0 using Ethernet device eth1
# Web site address is 10.0.0.2
# turn off IP forwarding
echo 0 > /proc/sys/net/ipv4/ip_forward
# Flush chain rules
iptables -F INPUT
iptables -F OUTPUT
iptables -F FORWARD
# set default (policy) rules
iptables -P INPUT DROP
iptables -P OUTPUT ACCEPT
iptables -P FORWARD ACCEPT

# IP spoofing, deny any packets on the internal network that have an
external source address.
```

```
iptables -A INPUT -j LOG  -i eth1 \! -s 192.168.0.0/24
iptables -A INPUT -j DROP  -i eth1 \! -s 192.168.0.0/24
iptables -A FORWARD -j DROP  -i eth1 \! -s 192.168.0.0/24
# IP spoofing, deny any outside packets (any not on eth1) that have the
source address of the internal network
iptables -A INPUT -j DROP \! -i eth1 -s 192.168.0.0/24
iptables -A FORWARD -j DROP \! -i eth1 -s 192.168.0.0/24
# IP spoofing, deny any outside packets with localhost address
# (packets not on the lo interface (any on eth0 or eth1) that have the
source address of localhost)
iptables -A INPUT -j DROP  -i \! lo  -s  127.0.0.0/255.0.0.0
iptables -A FORWARD -j DROP  -i \! lo  -s  127.0.0.0/255.0.0.0

# allow all incoming messages for users on your firewall system
iptables -A INPUT -j ACCEPT  -i lo

# allow  communication to the Web server (address 10.0.0.2), port www
iptables -A INPUT  -j ACCEPT -p tcp -i eth0  --dport www -s 10.0.0.2
# Allow  established connections from Web servers to internal network
iptables -A INPUT -m state --state ESTABLISHED,RELATED -i eth0 -p tcp
--sport www -s 10.0.0.2 -d 192.168.0.0/24  -j ACCEPT
# Prevent new  connections from Web servers to internal network
iptables -A OUTPUT -m state --state  NEW -o eth0 -p tcp  --sport www -d
192.168.0.0/24  -j DROP

# allow established and related outside communication to your system
# allow outside communication to the firewall, except for ICMP packets
iptables -A INPUT -m state --state ESTABLISHED,RELATED -i eth0 -p \! icmp
-j ACCEPT
# prevent outside initiated connections
iptables -A INPUT -m state --state NEW -i eth0 -j DROP
iptables -A FORWARD -m state --state NEW -i eth0 -j DROP
```

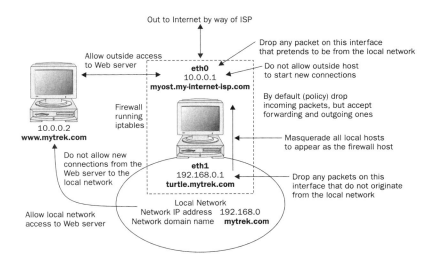

FIGURE 20-2   Firewall rules applied to a local network example

```
# allow all local communication to and from the firewall on eth1  from
the local network
iptables -A INPUT -j ACCEPT -p all -i eth1 -s 192.168.0.0/24
# Set up masquerading to allow internal machines access to outside
network
iptables -t nat -A POSTROUTING -o eth0 -j MASQUERADE
# Accept ICMP Ping and Destination unreachable messages
# Others will be rejected by INPUT and OUTPUT DROP policy
iptables -A INPUT -j ACCEPT  -p icmp -i eth0 --icmp-type  echo-reply -d
10.0.0.1
iptables -A INPUT -j ACCEPT  -p icmp -i eth0 --icmp-type  echo-request -d
10.0.0.1
iptables -A INPUT -j ACCEPT -p icmp -i eth0 --icmp-type  destination-
unreachable -d 10.0.0.1
# Turn on IP Forwarding
echo 1 > /proc/sys/net/ipv4/ip_forward
```

Initially, in the script you would clear your current IPtables with the flush option (-F) and then set the policies (default targets) for the non-user-defined rules. IP forwarding should also be turned off while the chain rules are being set:

```
echo 0 > /proc/sys/net/ipv4/ip_forward
```

Drop Policy

First, a DROP policy is set up for INPUT and FORWARD built-in IP chains. This means that if a packet does not meet a criterion in any of the rules to let it pass, it will be dropped. Then both IP spoofing attacks and any attempts from the outside to initiate connections (SYN packets) are rejected. Outside connection attempts are also logged. This is a very basic configuration that can easily be refined to your own needs by adding IPtables rules.

```
iptables -P INPUT DROP
iptables -P OUTPUT ACCEPT
iptables -P FORWARD ACCEPT
```

IP Spoofing

One way to protect a private network from the IP spoofing of any packets is to check for any outside addresses on the Ethernet device dedicated to the private network. In this example, any packet on device **eth1** (dedicated to the private network) whose source address is not that of the private network (! -s 192.168.0.0) is denied. Also, check to see if any packets coming from the outside are designating the private network as their source. In this example, any packets with the source address of the private network on any Ethernet device other than for the private network (**eth1**) are denied. The same strategy can be applied to the local host.

```
# IP spoofing, deny any packets on the internal network
# that has an external source address.
iptables -A INPUT -j LOG  -i eth1 \! -s 192.168.0.0/24
iptables -A INPUT -j DROP  -i eth1 \! -s 192.168.0.0/24
iptables -A FORWARD -j DROP  -i eth1 \! -s 192.168.0.0/24
# IP spoofing, deny any outside packets (any not on eth1)
# that have the source address of the internal network
```

```
iptables -A INPUT -j DROP \! -i eth1 -s 192.168.0.0/24
iptables -A FORWARD -j DROP \! -i eth1 -s 192.168.0.0/24
# IP spoofing, deny any outside packets with localhost address
# (packets not on the lo interface (any on eth0 or eth1)
# that have the source address of localhost)
iptables -A INPUT -j DROP  -i \! lo  -s  127.0.0.0/255.0.0.0
iptables -A FORWARD -j DROP  -i \! lo  -s  127.0.0.0/255.0.0.0
```

Then, you would set up rules to allow all packets sent and received within your system (localhost) to pass.

```
iptables -A INPUT -j ACCEPT  -i lo
```

Server Access

For the Web server, you want to allow access by outside users but block access by anyone attempting to initiate a connection from the Web server into the private network. In the next example, all messages are accepted to the Web server, but the Web server cannot initiate contact with the private network. This prevents anyone from breaking into the local network through the Web server, which is open to outside access. Established connections are allowed, permitting the private network to use the Web server.

```
# allow  communication to the Web server (address 10.0.0.2), port www
iptables -A INPUT  -j ACCEPT -p tcp -i eth0  --dport www -s 10.0.0.2
# Allow  established connections from Web servers to internal network
iptables -A INPUT -m state --state ESTABLISHED,RELATED -i eth0 \
   -p tcp  --sport www -s 10.0.0.2 -d 192.168.0.0/24  -j ACCEPT
# Prevent new  connections from Web servers to internal network
iptables -A OUTPUT -m state --state  NEW -o eth0 -p tcp \
  --sport www -d 192.168.0.1.0/24  -j DROP
```

Firewall Outside Access

To allow access by the firewall to outside networks, you allow input by all packets except for ICMP packets. These are handled later. The firewall is specified by the firewall device, **eth0**. First your firewall should allow established and related connections to proceed, as shown here. Then you would block outside access as described later.

```
# allow outside communication to the firewall,
# except for ICMP packets
iptables -A INPUT -m state --state ESTABLISHED,RELATED \
         -i eth0 -p \! icmp -j ACCEPT
```

Blocking Outside Initiated Access

To prevent outsiders from initiating any access to your system, create a rule to block access by SYN packets from the outside using the **state** option with NEW. Drop any new connections on the **eth0** connection (assumes only **eth0** is connected to the Internet or outside network).

```
# prevent outside initiated connections
iptables -A INPUT -m state --state NEW -i eth0 -j DROP
iptables -A FORWARD -m state --state NEW -i eth0 -j DROP
```

Local Network Access

To allow interaction by the internal network with the firewall, you allow input by all packets on the internal Ethernet connection, **eth1**. The valid internal network addresses are designated as the input source.

```
iptables -A INPUT -j ACCEPT -p all -i eth1 -s 192.168.0.0/24
```

Masquerading Local Networks

To implement masquerading, where systems on the private network can use the gateway's Internet address to connect to Internet hosts, you create a NAT table (**-t nat**) POSTROUTING rule with a MASQUERADE target.

```
iptables -t nat -A POSTROUTING -o eth0 -j MASQUERADE
```

Controlling ICMP Packets

In addition, to allow ping and destination-reachable ICMP packets, you enter INPUT rules with the firewall as the destination. To enable ping operations, you use both echo-reply and echo-request ICMP types, and for destination unreachable, you use the destination-unreachable type.

```
iptables -A INPUT -j ACCEPT  -p icmp -i eth0 --icmp-type \
   echo-reply -d 10.0.0.1
iptables -A INPUT -j ACCEPT  -p icmp -i eth0 --icmp-type \
   echo-request -d 10.0.0.1
iptables -A INPUT -j ACCEPT -p icmp -i eth0 --icmp-type \
   destination-unreachable -d 10.0.0.1
```

At the end, IP forwarding is turned on again.

```
echo 1 > /proc/sys/net/ipv4/ip_forward
```

Listing Rules

A listing of these **iptables** options shows the different rules for each option, as shown here:

```
# iptables -L
Chain INPUT (policy DROP)
target   prot opt source            destination
LOG      all  --  !192.168.0.0/24   anywhere            LOG level warning
DROP     all  --  !192.168.0.0/24   anywhere
DROP     all  --  192.168.0.0/24    anywhere
DROP     all  --  127.0.0.0/8       anywhere
ACCEPT   all  --  anywhere          anywhere
ACCEPT   tcp  --  10.0.0.2          anywhere            tcp dpt:http
ACCEPT   tcp  --  10.0.0.2          192.168.0.0/24      state RELATED,ESTABLISHED
                                                                    tcp spt:http
ACCEPT   !icmp --  anywhere         anywhere            state RELATED,ESTABLISHED
DROP     all  --  anywhere          anywhere            state NEW
ACCEPT   all  --  192.168.0.0/24    anywhere
ACCEPT   icmp --  anywhere          10.0.0.1            icmp echo-reply
ACCEPT   icmp --  anywhere          10.0.0.1            icmp echo-request
```

```
ACCEPT   icmp -- anywhere          10.0.0.1              icmp destination-unreachable
Chain FORWARD (policy ACCEPT)
target   prot opt source           destination
DROP     all  -- !192.168.0.0/24   anywhere
DROP     all  -- 192.168.0.0/24    anywhere
DROP     all  -- 127.0.0.0/8       anywhere
DROP     all  -- anywhere          anywhere          state NEW

Chain OUTPUT (policy ACCEPT)
target   prot opt source        destination
DROP       tcp  -- anywhere      192.168.0.0/24   state NEW tcp spt:http

# iptables -t nat -L
Chain PREROUTING (policy ACCEPT)
target      prot opt source         destination
Chain POSTROUTING (policy ACCEPT)
target      prot opt source         destination
MASQUERADE  all  -- anywhere          anywhere
Chain OUTPUT (policy ACCEPT)
target      prot opt source         destination
```

User-Defined Rules

For more complex rules, you may want to create your own chain to reduce repetition. A common method is to define a user chain for both INPUT and FORWARD chains, so that you do not have to repeat DROP operations for each. Instead, you would have only one user chain that both FORWARD and INPUT chains would feed into for DROP operations. Keep in mind that both FORWARD and INPUT operations may have separate rules in addition to the ones they share. In the next example, a user-defined chain called arriving is created. The chain is defined with the **-N** option at the top of the script:

```
iptables -N arriving
```

A user chain has to be defined before it can be used as a target in other rules. So you have to first define and add all the rules for that chain, and then use it as a target. The arriving chain is first defined and its rules added. Then, at the end of the file, it is used as a target for both the INPUT and FORWARD chains. The INPUT chain lists rules for accepting packets, whereas the FORWARD chain has an ACCEPT policy that will accept them by default.

```
iptables -N arriving
iptables -F arriving
# IP spoofing, deny any packets on the internal network
# that has an external source address.
iptables -A arriving -j LOG  -i eth1 \! -s 192.168.0.0/24
iptables -A arriving -j DROP  -i eth1 \! -s 192.168.0.0/24
iptables -A arriving -j DROP \! -i eth1 -s 192.168.0.0/24
..............................
# entries at end of script
iptables -A INPUT -j arriving
iptables -A FORWARD -j arriving
```

A listing of the corresponding rules is shown here:

```
Chain INPUT (policy DROP)
target     prot opt source          destination
arriving   all  --  0.0.0.0/0        0.0.0.0/0
Chain FORWARD (policy ACCEPT)
target     prot opt source          destination
arriving   all  --  0.0.0.0/0        0.0.0.0/0
Chain arriving (2 references)
target     prot opt source          destination
LOG        all  --  !192.168.0.0/24  0.0.0.0/0       LOG flags 0 level 4
DROP       all  --  !192.168.0.0/24  0.0.0.0/0
DROP       all  --  192.168.0.0/24   0.0.0.0/0
```

For rules where chains may differ, you will still need to enter separate rules. In the **myfilter** script, the FORWARD chain has an ACCEPT policy, allowing all forwarded packets to the local network to pass through the firewall. If the FORWARD chain had a DROP policy, like the INPUT chain, then you may need to define separate rules under which the FORWARD chain could accept packets. In this example, the FORWARD and INPUT chains have different rules for accepting packets on the **eth1** device. The INPUT rule is more restrictive. To enable the local network to receive forwarded packets through the firewall, you could enable forwarding on its device using a separate FORWARD rule, as shown here:

```
iptables -A FORWARD -j ACCEPT -p all -i eth1
```

The INPUT chain would accept packets only from the local network.

```
iptables -A INPUT -j ACCEPT -p all -i eth1 -s 192.168.0.0/24
```

Simple LAN Configuration

To create a script to support a simple LAN without any Internet services like Web servers, you would just not include rules for supporting those services. You would still need FORWARD and POSTROUTING rules for connecting your local hosts to the Internet, as well as rules governing interaction between the hosts and the firewall. To modify the example script to support a simple LAN without the Web server, just remove the three rules governing the Web server. Leave everything else the same.

LAN Configuration with Internet Services on the Firewall System

Often, the same system that functions as a firewall is also used to run Internet servers, like Web and FTP servers. In this case the firewall rules are applied to the ports used for those services. The example script dealt with a Web server running on a separate host system. If the Web server were instead running on the firewall system, you would apply the Web server firewall rules to the port that the Web server uses. Normally the port used for a Web server is 80. In the following example, the IPtables rules for the Web server have been applied to port www, port 80, on the firewall system. The modification simply requires removing the old Web server host address references, 10.0.0.2.

```
# allow  communication to the Web server, port www (port 80)
iptables -A INPUT  -j ACCEPT -p tcp -i eth0  --dport www
# Allow  established connections from Web servers to internal network
```

```
iptables -A INPUT -m state --state ESTABLISHED,RELATED -i eth0 \
   -p tcp  --sport www -d 192.168.0.0/24  -j ACCEPT
# Prevent new  connections from Web servers to internal network
iptables -A OUTPUT -m state --state  NEW -o eth0 -p tcp \
  --sport www -d 192.168.0.1.0/24 -j DROP
```

Similar entries could be set up for an FTP server. Should you run several Internet services, you could use a user-defined rule to run the same rules on each service, rather than repeating three separate rules per service. Working from the example script, you would use two defined rules, one for INPUT and one for OUTPUT, controlling incoming and outgoing packets for the services.

```
iptables -N inputservice
iptables -N outputservice
iptables -F inputservice
iptables -F outputservice
# allow  communication to the service
iptables -A inputservice  -j ACCEPT -p tcp -i eth0
# Allow  established connections from the service to internal network
iptables -A inputservice -m state --state ESTABLISHED,RELATED -i eth0 \
    -p tcp  -d 192.168.0.0/24  -j ACCEPT
# Prevent new  connections from service to internal network
iptables -A outputservice -m state --state  NEW -o eth0 -p tcp \
  -d 192.168.0.1.0/24 -j DROP
.............................
# Run rules for the Web server, port www (port 80)
iptables -A INPUT  --dport www -j inputservice
iptables -A INPUT  --dport www -j outputservice
# Run rules for the FTP server, port ftp (port 21)
iptables -A OUTPUT  --dport ftp -j inputservice
iptables -A OUTPUT  --dport ftp -j outputservice
```

IP Masquerading

On Linux systems, you can set up a network in which you can have one connection to the Internet, which several systems on your network can use. This way, using only one IP address, several different systems can connect to the Internet. This method is called *IP masquerading,* where a system masquerades as another system, using that system's IP address. In such a network, one system is connected to the Internet with its own IP address, while the other systems are connected on a local area network (LAN) to this system. When a local system wants to access the network, it masquerades as the Internet-connected system, borrowing its IP address.

IP masquerading is implemented on Linux using the IPtables firewalling tool. In effect, you set up a firewall, which you then configure to do IP masquerading. Currently, IP masquerading supports all the common network services—as does IPtables firewalling—such as Web browsing, Telnet, and ping. Other services, such as IRC, FTP, and RealAudio, require the use of certain modules. Any services you want local systems to access must also be on the firewall system because requests and responses actually are handled by services on that system.

You can find out more information on IP masquerading at the IP Masquerade Resource Web site at **ipmasq.webhop.net**. In particular, the Linux IP Masquerade mini-HOWTO provides a detailed, step-by-step guide to setting up IP masquerading on your system. IP masquerading must be supported by the kernel before you can use it. If your kernel does not support it, you may have to rebuild the kernel, including IP masquerade support, or use loadable modules to add it. See the IP Masquerade mini-HOWTO for more information.

With IP masquerading, as implemented on Linux systems, the machine with the Internet address is also the firewall and gateway for the LAN of machines that use the firewall's Internet address to connect to the Internet. Firewalls that also implement IP masquerading are sometimes referred to as *MASQ gates.* With IP masquerading, the Internet-connected system (the firewall) listens for Internet requests from hosts on its LAN. When it receives one, it replaces the requesting local host's IP address with the Internet IP address of the firewall and then passes the request out to the Internet, as if the request were its own. Replies from the Internet are then sent to the firewall system. The replies the firewall receives are addressed to the firewall using its Internet address. The firewall then determines the local system to whose request the reply is responding. It then strips off its IP address and sends the response on to the local host across the LAN. The connection is transparent from the perspective of the local machines. They appear to be connected directly to the Internet.

Masquerading Local Networks

IP masquerading is often used to allow machines on a private network to access the Internet. These could be machines in a home network or a small LAN, such as for a small business. Such a network might have only one machine with Internet access and, as such, only the one Internet address. The local private network would have IP addresses chosen from the private network allocations (10., 172.16., or 192.168.). Ideally, the firewall has two Ethernet cards: one for an interface to the LAN (for example, **eth1**) and one for an interface to the Internet, such as **eth0** (for dial-up ISPs, this would be **ppp0** for the modem). The card for the Internet connection (**eth0**) would be assigned the Internet IP address. The Ethernet interface for the local network (**eth1**, in this example) is the firewall Ethernet interface. Your private LAN would have a network address like 192.168.0. Its Ethernet firewall interface (**eth1**) would be assigned the IP address 192.168.0.1. In effect, the firewall interface lets the firewall operate as the local network's gateway. The firewall is then configured to masquerade any packets coming from the private network. Your LAN needs to have its own domain name server, identifying the machines on your network, including your firewall. Each local machine needs to have the firewall specified as its gateway. Try not to use IP aliasing to assign both the firewall and Internet IP addresses to the same physical interface. Use separate interfaces for them, such as two Ethernet cards, or an Ethernet card and a modem (**ppp0**).

Masquerading NAT Rules

In Netfilter, IP masquerading is a NAT operation and is not integrated with packet filtering as in IP Chains. IP masquerading commands are placed on the NAT table and treated separately from the packet-filtering commands. Use IPtables to place a masquerade rule on the NAT table. First reference the NAT table with the **-t nat** option. Then add a rule to the POSTROUTING chain with the **-o** option specifying the output device and the **-j** option with the MASQUERADE command.

```
iptables -t nat -A POSTROUTING -o eth0 -j MASQUERADE
```

IP Forwarding

The next step is to turn on IP forwarding, either manually or by setting the **net.ipv4.ip_forward** variable in the **/etc/sysctl.conf** file and running **sysctl** with the -p option. IP forwarding will be turned off by default. For IPv6, use **net.ipv6.conf.all.forwarding**. The **/etc/sysctl.conf** entries are shown here:

```
net.ipv4.ip_forward = 1
net.ipv6.conf.all.forwarding = 1
```

You then run **sysctl** with the **-p** option.

```
sysctl -p
```

You can directly change the respective forwarding files with an **echo** command as shown here:

```
echo 1 > /proc/sys/net/ipv4/ip_forward
```

For IPv6, you would to use the forwarding file in the corresponding **/proc/sys/net/ipv6** directory, **conf/all/forwarding**.

```
echo 1 > /proc/sys/net/ipv6/conf/all/forwarding
```

Masquerading Selected Hosts

Instead of masquerading all local hosts as the single IP address of the firewall/gateway host, you could use the NAT table to rewrite addresses for a few selected hosts. Such an approach is often applied to setups where you want several local hosts to appear as Internet servers. Using the DNAT and SNAT targets, you can direct packets to specific local hosts. You would use rules on the PREROUTING and POSTROUTING chains to direct input and output packets.

For example, the Web server described in the previous example could have been configured as a local host to which a DNAT target could redirect any packets originally received for 10.0.0.2. Say the Web server was set up on 192.168.0.5. It could appear as having the address 10.0.0.2 on the Internet. Packets sent to 10.0.0.2 would be rewritten and directed to 192.168.0.5 by the NAT table. You would use the PREROUTING chain with the **-d** option to handle incoming packets and POSTROUTING with the **-s** option for outgoing packets.

```
iptables -t nat -A PREROUTING -d 10.0.0.2  \
          --to-destination 192.168.0.5 -j DNAT
iptables -t nat -A POSTROUTING -s 192.168.0.5 \
          --to-source 10.0.0.2 -j SNAT
```

TIP *Bear in mind that with IPtables, masquerading is not combined with the FORWARD chain, as it is with IP Chains. So, if you specify a DROP policy for the FORWARD chain, you will also have to specifically enable FORWARD operation for the network that is being masqueraded. You will need both a POSTROUTING rule and a FORWARD rule.*

PART

V

Red Hat and
Fedora Servers

Chapter 21
Managing Services

Chapter 22
FTP Servers

Chapter 23
Web Servers: Apache

Chapter 24
Proxy Servers: Squid

Chapter 25
Mail Servers: SMTP, POP, and IMAP

Chapter 26
Print, News, and Database Servers: CUPS, INN, and MySQL

Managing Services

A single Linux system can provide several different kinds of services, ranging from security to administration, and including more obvious Internet services like Web and FTP sites, e-mail, and printing. Security tools such as SSH and Kerberos run as services, along with administrative network tools such as DHCP and LDAP. The network connection interface is itself a service that you can restart at will. Each service operates as a continually running daemon looking for requests for its particular services. In the case of a Web service, the requests will come from remote users. You can turn services on or off by starting or shutting down their daemons.

The process of starting up or shutting down a service is handled by service scripts, described in detail in this chapter. It applies to all services, including those discussed in the Security, System Administration, and Network Administration sections, as well as the Red Hat and Fedora Servers section. It is covered at this point since you will most likely use them to start and stop Internet services like Web and mail servers.

System Startup Files: /etc/rc.d and /etc/sysconfig

Each time you start your system, it reads a series of startup commands from system initialization files located in your **/etc/rc.d** directory. These initialization files are organized according to different tasks. Some are located in the **/etc/rc.d** directory itself, while others are located in a subdirectory called **init.d**. You should not have to change any of these files. The organization of system initialization files varies among Linux distributions. The Red Hat and Fedora organizations are described here. Some of the files you find in **/etc/rc.d** are listed in Table 21-1.

rc.sysinit and rc.local

The **/etc/rc.d/rc.sysinit** file holds the commands for initializing your system, including the mounting and unmounting of your file systems. The **/etc/rc.d/rc.local** file is the last initialization file executed. You can place commands of your own here. When you shut down your system, the system calls the **halt** file, which contains shutdown commands. The files in **init.d** are then called to shut down daemons, and the file systems are unmounted. **halt** is located in the **init.d** directory.

File	Description
/etc/sysconfig	Directory that holds system configuration files and directories.
/etc/rc.d	Directory that holds system startup and shutdown files.
/etc/rc.d/ rc.sysinit	Initialization file for your system.
/etc/rc.d/rc.local	Initialization file for your own commands; you can freely edit this file to add your own startup commands; this is the last startup file executed.
/etc/rc.d/init.d	Directory that holds network scripts to start up network connections.
/etc/rc.d/rcnum**.d**	Directories for different runlevels, where *num* is the runlevel. The directories hold links to scripts in the **/etc/rc.d/init.d** directory.
/etc/rc.d/init.d	Directory that holds system service scripts. See Table 21-2.
/etc/rc.d/ init.d/halt	Operations performed each time you shut down the system, such as unmounting file systems; called rc.halt in other distributions.

TABLE 21-1 System Startup Files and Directories

/etc/rc.d/init.d

The **/etc/rc.d/init.d** directory is designed primarily to hold scripts that start up and shut down different specialized daemons, such as network and printer daemons and those for font and Web servers. These files perform double duty, starting a daemon when the system starts up and shutting down the daemon when the system shuts down. The files in **init.d** are designed in a way to make it easy to write scripts for starting up and shutting down specialized applications. They use functions defined in the **functions** file. Many of these files are set up for you automatically. You shouldn't need to change them. If you do change them, be sure you know how these files work first.

When your system starts up, several programs are automatically started and run continuously to provide services, such as a Web site or print servers. Depending on what kinds of services you want your system to provide, you can add or remove items in a list of services to be started automatically. For example, the Web server is run automatically when your system starts up. If you are not hosting a Web site, you would have no need for the Web server. You could prevent the service from starting, removing an extra task the system does not need to perform, freeing up resources, and possibly reducing potential security holes. Several of the servers and daemons perform necessary tasks. The **sendmail** server enables you to send messages across networks, and the **cupsd** server performs printing operations.

To configure a service to start up automatically at boot, you can use the system-config-services tool available on the desktop or the **chkconfig** tool, which is run at a command line. The system-config-services tool displays a list of available services, letting you choose the ones you want to start or prevent from starting. The **chkconfig** command uses the **on** and **off** options to select and deselect services for startup at boot (see the section "chkconfig" later in this chapter).

```
chkconfig httpd on
```

To start and stop services manually at any time, you can use either system-config-services or the **service** command. With the **service** command, you list the service with the **stop** argument to stop it, the **start** argument to start it, and the **restart** argument to restart it.

```
service httpd start
```

TIP *When your system starts up, it uses links in special runlevel directories in the /etc/rc.d/ directory to run the service scripts in the /etc/rc.d/init.d directory. A runlevel directory bears the number of its runlevel, as in /etc/rc.d/rc3.d for runlevel 3 and /etc/rc.d/rc5.d for runlevel 5. To prevent a service from starting up, remove its link from that runlevel directory, or change the first letter in the name of the link from S to K.*

SysV Init: init.d Scripts

You can manage the startup and shutdown of server daemons with special service scripts located in the **/etc/rc.d/init.d** directory. These scripts often have the same name as the service's program. For example, for the **/usr/sbin/httpd** Web server program, the corresponding script is called **/etc/rc.d/init.d/httpd**. This script starts and stops the Web server. This method of using **init.d** service scripts to start servers is called *SysV Init*, after the method used in Unix System V. Some of the more commonly used service scripts are listed in Table 21-2.

TIP *If you change the configuration of a server, you may need to start and stop it several times as you refine the configuration. Several servers provide special management tools that enable you to perform this task easily. The **apachectl** utility enables you to start and stop the Apache Web server easily. It is functionally equivalent to using the /etc/rc.d/init.d/httpd script to start and stop the server. For the domain name server, the **ndc** utility enables you to start and stop the **named** server, the DNS server discussed in Chapter 36. However, it is not advisable to mix the use of **init.d** scripts and the management tools.*

The service scripts in the **/etc/rc.d/init.d** directory can be executed automatically whenever you boot your system. Be careful when accessing these scripts, however. These start essential programs, such as your network interface and your printer daemon. These init scripts are accessed from links in subdirectories set up for each possible runlevel. The **/etc/rc.d** directory holds a set of subdirectories whose names have the format **rc**n**.d**, where *n* is a number referring to a runlevel (there are also links in the **/etc** directory directly to the **/etc/rc.d** runlevel subdirectories). The **rc** script detects the runlevel in which the system was started, and then executes only the service scripts specified in the subdirectory for that runlevel. When you start your system, the **rc** script executes the service scripts specified in the **rc3.d** directory, if you are performing a command line login, or the **rc5.d** directory, if you are using a graphical login. The **rc3.d** and **rc5.d** directories hold symbolic links to certain service scripts in the **/etc/rc.d/init.d** directory. Thus, the **httpd** script in the **/etc/rc.d/init.d** directory is actually called through a symbolic link in the **rc3.d** or the **rc5.d** directory. The symbolic link for the **/etc/rc.d/httpd** script in the **rc3.d** directory is **S85httpd**. The *S* prefixing the link stands for "startup"; thus, the link calls the corresponding **init.d** script

Service Script	Description
network	Operations to start up or shut down your network connections
xinetd	Operations to start up or shut down the **xinetd** daemon
autofs	Automatic file system mounting (see Chapter 30)
cups	The CUPS printer daemon (see Chapter 26)
cpuspeed	Service to manage CPU speed (Athlon Cool and Quiet)
dhcpd	Dynamic Host Configuration Protocol daemon (see Chapter 37)
httpd	Apache Web server (see Chapter 23)
innd	Internet News service (see Chapter 26)
ipsec	IPsec secure VPN service (see Chapter 18)
iptables	Controls the IPtables daemon
ip6tables	IPtables for IP protocol version 6 (see Chapter 20)
krb5kdc	Kerberos kdc server (see Chapter 19)
kudzu	Detects new hardware
ldap	LDAP service (see Chapter 28)
nfs	Network Filesystem (see Chapter 38)
postfix	Postfix mail server (see Chapter 25)
sendmail	The Sendmail MTA daemon (see Chapter 25)
smb	Samba for Windows hosts (see Chapter 39)
squid	Squid proxy-cache server (see Chapter 24)
sshd	Secure Shell daemon (see Chapter 19)
syslog	System logging daemon (see Chapter 27)
vsftpd	Very Secure FTP server (see Chapter 22)
xfs	X Window System font server
ypbind	Network Information Service (NIS) (see Chapter 38)
yumupdatesd	Yum Updates service

TABLE 21-2   Selection of Service Scripts in /etc/rc.d/init.d

with the **start** option. The number indicates the order in which service scripts are run; lower numbers run first. **S85httpd** invokes **/etc/rc.d/init.d/httpd** with the option **start**. If you change the name of the link to start with a *K*, the script is invoked with the **stop** option, stopping it. Such links are used in the runlevels 0 and 6 directories, **rc6.d** and **rc0.d**. Runlevel 0 halts the system, and runlevel 6 reboots it. You can use the **runlevel** command to find out what runlevel you are currently operating at (see Chapter 27 for more details on runlevels). A listing of runlevels is shown in Table 21-3.

Runlevel	rc.d Directory	Description
0	**rc0.d**	Halt (shut down) the system
1	**rc1.d**	Single-user mode (no networking, limited capabilities)
2	**rc2.d**	Multiuser mode with no NFS support (limited capabilities)
3	**rc3.d**	Multiuser mode (full operational mode)
4	**rc4.d**	User-defined, implemented by default on Red Hat and Fedora as the same as runlevel 3, multiuser mode
5	**rc5.d**	Multiuser mode with graphical login (full operation mode with graphical login added)
6	**rc6.d**	Reboot system

TABLE 21-3   System Runlevels

Starting Services: Stand-Alone and xinetd

A *service* is a daemon that runs concurrently with your other programs, continually looking for a request for its services, either from other users on your system or from remote users connecting to your system through a network. When a server receives a request from a user, it starts up a *session* to provide its services. For example, if users want to download a file from your system, they can use their own FTP client to connect to your FTP server and start up a session. In the session, they can access and download files from your system. Your server needs to be running for a user to access its services. For example, if you set up a Web site on your system with HTML files, you must have the **httpd** Web server program running before users can access your Web site and display those files.

Starting Services Directly

You can start a server in several ways. One way is to do it manually from the command line by entering the name of the server program and its arguments. When you press ENTER, the server starts, although your command line prompt reappears. The server runs concurrently as you perform other tasks. To see if your server is running, you can use the **service** command with the **status** option.

```
# service httpd status
```

Alternatively, you can use the **ps** command with the **-aux** option to list all currently running processes. You should see a process for the server program you started. To refine the list, you can add a **grep** operation with a pattern for the server name you want. The second command lists the process for the Web server.

```
# ps -aux
# ps -aux | grep 'httpd'
```

You could just as easily check for the **httpd** process on the Gnome System Monitor (System | Administration | System Monitor).

Starting and Stopping Services with Service Scripts

On Red Hat Linux and Fedora systems, you use service scripts to start and stop your server manually. These scripts are located in the **/etc/rc.d/init.d** directory and have the same names as the server programs. For example, the **/etc/rc.d/init.d/httpd** script with the **start** option starts the Web server. Using this script with the **stop** option stops it. Instead of using the complete pathname for the script, you can use the **service** command and the script name. The following commands are equivalent:

```
/etc/rc.d/init.d/httpd stop
service httpd stop
```

Starting Services Automatically

Instead of manually executing all the server programs each time you boot your system, you can have your system automatically start the servers for you. You can do this in two ways, depending on how you want to use a server. You can have a server running continuously from the time you start your system until you shut it down, or you can have the server start only when it receives a request from a user for its services. If a server is being used frequently, you may want to have it running all the time. If it is used rarely, you may want the server to start only when it receives a request. For example, if you are hosting a Web site, your Web server is receiving requests all the time from remote users on the Internet. For an FTP site, however, you may receive requests infrequently, in which case you may want to have the FTP server start only when it receives a request. Of course, certain FTP sites receive frequent requests, which would warrant a continuously running FTP server.

Stand-Alone Servers

A server that starts automatically and runs continuously is referred to as a *stand-alone* server. Red Hat and Fedora use the SysV Init procedure to start servers automatically whenever your system boots. This procedure uses service scripts for the servers located in the **/etc/rc.d/init.d** directory. Most Linux systems configure the Web server to start automatically and to run continuously by default. A script for it called **httpd** is in the **/etc/rc.d/init.d** directory.

xinetd Servers

To start the server only when a request for its services is received, you configure it using the **xinetd** daemon. If you add, change, or delete server entries in the **/etc/xinetd** files, you will have to restart the **xinetd** daemon for these changes to take effect. On Red Hat and Fedora, you can restart the **xinetd** daemon using the **/etc/rc.d/init.d/xinetd** script with the **restart** argument, as shown here:

```
# service xinetd restart
```

You can also use the **xinetd** script to start and stop the **xinetd** daemon. Stopping effectively shuts down all the servers that the **xinetd** daemon manages (those listed in the **/etc/xinetd.conf** file or the **xinetd.d** directory).

```
# service xinetd stop
# service xinetd start
```

You can also directly restart **xinetd** by stopping its process directly. To do this, you use the `killall` command with the `-HUP` signal and the name `xinetd`.

```
# killall -HUP xinetd
```

TIP *Versions prior to Red Hat 7.0 used the **inetd** daemon (the term stands for the Internet Services Daemon) instead of **xinetd**, which is meant to be the enhanced replacement for **inetd**. If you are upgrading from **inetd**, you can use the `inetdconvert` command to convert **inetd** entries into **xinetd** configurations.*

Service Management Tools: chkconfig and system-config-services

On Red Hat and Fedora, system-config-services and the `chkconfig` command provide simple interfaces you can use to choose what servers you want started up and how you want them to run. You use these tools to control any daemon you want started up, including system services such as **cron**, the print server, remote file servers for Samba and NFS, authentication servers for Kerberos, and, of course, Internet servers for FTP or HTTP. Such daemons are referred to as *services,* and you should think of these tools as managing these services. Any of these services can be set up to start or stop at different runlevels.

These tools manage services that are started up by scripts in the **/etc/rc.d/init.d** directory. If you add a new service, either `chkconfig` or system-config-services can manage it. As described in the following section, services are started up at specific runlevels using service links in various runlevel directories. These links are connected to the service scripts in the **init.d** directory. Runlevel directories are numbered from 0 to 6 in the **/etc/rc.d** directory, such as **/etc/rc.d/rc3.d** for runlevel 3 and **/etc/rc.d/rc5.d** for runlevel 5. Removing a service from a runlevel only changes its link in the corresponding runlevel **rc.d** directory. It does not touch the service script in the **init.d** directory.

system-config-services

With the Red Hat and Fedora system-config-services utility, you can simply select from a list of commonly used services those that you want to run when your system boots up. You can access system-config-services from the Services icon in the Server Settings window or menu, located under System Settings. The system-config-services tool lets you start, stop, and restart a server, much like the `service` command (see Figure 21-1), providing a GNOME GUI interface for easy use. It displays a list of your installed stand-alone servers on the Background Services panel, with checked check boxes for those currently chosen to start up. You can start, stop, or restart any particular service by selecting it and choosing either Start Service, Stop Service, or Restart Service from the Action menu.

You can also set startup runlevels for services, just as you can with `chkconfig`, though you are limited to levels 3, 4, and 5. The list of checked entries differs depending on the runlevel you choose from the Edit Runlevel menu. In effect, you are choosing which services to start at a given runlevel. The default is runlevel 5, the GUI startup level. You may want a different set of services started or stopped for runlevel 3, the command line startup level. In that case, you would select Runlevel 3 from the Edit Runlevel menu to display the services with selected check boxes for runlevel 3.

FIGURE 21-1
The system-config-services tool background panel for stand-alone servers

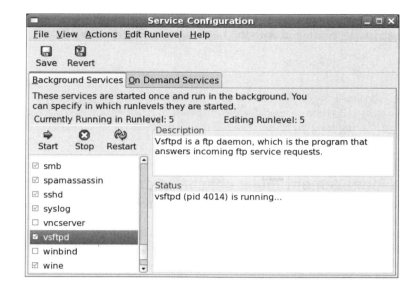

FIGURE 21-1
The system-config-services tool background panel for stand-alone servers

The system-config-services tool also lets you manage **xinetd** "On Demand" services. (The **xinetd** service is described later in this chapter.) First you have to have **xinetd** installed and running. Then, clicking on the On Demand panel lets you manage your **xinetd**-supported services.

chkconfig

You can specify the service you want to start and the level you want to start it at with the **chkconfig** command. Unlike other service management tools, **chkconfig** works equally well on stand-alone and **xinetd** services. Though stand-alone services can be run at any runlevel, you can also turn **xinetd** services on or off for the runlevels that **xinetd** runs in. Table 21-4 lists the different **chkconfig** options.

Listing Services with chkconfig

To see a list of services, use the **--list** option. A sampling of services managed by **chkconfig** are shown here. The on or off status of the service is shown at each runlevel, as are **xinetd** services and their statuses:

```
chkconfig -list
dhcpd   0:off 1:off 2:off 3:off 4:off 5:off 6:off
httpd   0:off 1:off 2:off 3:off 4:off 5:off 6:off
named   0:off 1:off 2:off 3:off 4:off 5:off 6:off
lpd     0:off 1:off 2:on  3:on  4:on  5:on  6:off
nfs     0:off 1:off 2:off 3:off 4:off 5:off 6:off
crond   0:off 1:off 2:on  3:on  4:on  5:on  6:off
xinetd  0:off 1:off 2:off 3:on  4:on  5:on  6:off
xinetd based services:
     time:        off
     finger:      off
     pop3s:       off
     swat:        on
```

Option	Description
`--level` *runlevel*	Specifies a runlevel to turn on, turn off, or reset a service.
`--list` *service*	Lists startup information for services at different runlevels. **xinetd** services are just **on** or **off**. With no argument, all services are listed, including **xinetd** services.
`--add` *service*	Adds a service, creating links in the default-specified runlevels (or all runlevels, if none are specified).
`--del` *service*	Deletes all links for the service (startup and shutdown) in all runlevel directories.
service **on**	Turns a service on, creating a service link in the specified or default runlevel directories.
service **off**	Turns a service off, creating shutdown links in specified or default directories.
service **reset**	Resets service startup information, creating default links as specified in the **chkconfig** entry in the service's **init.d** service script.

TABLE 21-4   Options for chkconfig

Starting and Stopping Services with chkconfig

You use the **on** option to have a service started at specified runlevels, and the **off** option to disable it. You can specify the runlevel to affect with the `--level` option. If no level is specified, **chkconfig** will use any **chkconfig** default information in a service's **init.d** service script. Red Hat and Fedora install their services with **chkconfig** default information already entered (if this is missing, **chkconfig** will use runlevels 3, 4, and 5). The following example has the Web server (**httpd**) started at runlevel 5:

```
chkconfig --level 5 httpd on
```

The **off** option configures a service to shut down if the system enters a specified runlevel. The next example shuts down the Web server if runlevel 3 is entered. If the service is not running, it remains shut down:

```
chkconfig --level 3 httpd off
```

The **reset** option restores a service to its **chkconfig** default options as specified in the service's **init.d** service script:

```
chkconfig httpd reset
```

To see just the startup information for a service, you use just the service name with the `--list` option:

```
chkconfig --list httpd
httpd   0:off  1:off 2:off 3:on 4:off 5:on 6:off
```

Enabling and Disabling xinetd Services with chkconfig

Unlike system-config-services, **chkconfig** can also enable or disable **xinetd** services. Simply enter the **xinetd** service with either an **on** or **off** option. The service will be started up or shut down, and the disable line in its **xinetd** configuration script in the **/etc/xinetd.d** directory will be edited accordingly. For example, to start swat, the Samba configuration server, which runs on **xinetd**, you simply enter

```
chkconfig swat on
chkconfig --list swat
    swat            on
```

The **swat** configuration file for **xinetd**, **/etc/xinetd.d/swat**, will have its disable line edited to no, as shown here:

```
disable=no
```

If you want to shut down the swat server, you can use the **off** option. This will change the disable line in **/etc/xinetd.d/swat** to read "disable=yes".

```
chkconfig swat off
```

The same procedure works for other **xinetd** services such as the POP3 server and **finger**.

Removing and Adding Services with chkconfig

If you want a service removed entirely from the entire startup and shutdown process in all runlevels, you can use the **--del** option. This removes all startup and shutdown links in all the runlevel directories.

```
chkconfig --del httpd
```

You can also add services to **chkconfig** management with the **--add** option; **chkconfig** will create startup links for the new service in the appropriate startup directories, **/etc/rc.d/rc***n*.**d**. If you have previously removed all links for a service, you can restore them with the **add** option.

```
chkconfig --add httpd
```

Configuring xinetd Services for Use by chkconfig

Default runlevel information should be placed in the service scripts that are to be managed by **chkconfig**. Red Hat and Fedora have already placed this information in the service scripts for the services that are installed with its distribution. You can edit these scripts to change the default information if you wish. This information is entered as a line beginning with a # sign and followed by the **chkconfig** keyword and a colon. Then you list the default runlevels that the service should start up on, along with the start and stop priorities. The following entry lists runlevels 3 and 5 with a start priority of 85 and a stop of 15. See the section "Service Script Tags" for more information:

```
# chkconfig: 35 85 15
```

Thus, when a user turns on the **httpd** service with no level option specified, `chkconfig` will start up **httpd** at runlevels 3 and 5.

```
chkconfig httpd on
```

How chkconfig Works

The `chkconfig` tool works by creating startup and shutdown links in the appropriate runlevel directories in the **/etc/rc.d** directory. For example, when `chkconfig` adds the **httpd** service at runlevel 5, it creates a link in the **/etc/rc.d/rc5.d** directory to the service script **httpd** in the **/etc/rc.d/init.d** directory. When it turns off the Web service from runlevel 3, it creates a shutdown link in the **/etc/rc.d/rc3.d** directory to use the script **httpd** in the **/etc/rc.d/initd** directory to make sure the Web service is not started. In the following example, the user turns on the Web service (**httpd**) on runlevel 3, creating the startup link in **rc5.d**, **S85httpd**, and then turns off the Web service on runlevel 3, creating a shutdown link in **rc3.d**, **K15httpd**.

```
chkconfig --level 5 httpd on
ls /etc/rc.d/rc5.d/*httpd
   /etc/rc.d/rc5.d/S85httpd
chkconfig -level 3 httpd off
ls /etc/rc.d/rc3.d/*httpd
  /etc/rc.d/rc3.d/K15httpd
```

Service Scripts: /etc/init.d

Most software using RPM packages will automatically install any appropriate service scripts and create the needed links in the appropriate **rc**_n_**.d** directories, where _n_ is the runlevel number. Service scripts, though, can be used for any program you may want run when your system starts up. To have such a program start automatically, you first create a service script for it in the **/etc/rc.d/init.d** directory and then create symbolic links to that script in the **/etc/rc.d/rc3.d** and **/etc/rc.d/rc5.d** directories. A shutdown link (_K_) should also be placed in the **rc6.d** directory used for runlevel 6 (reboot).

Service Script Functions

A simplified version of the service script **httpd** uses on Red Hat and Fedora systems is shown in a later section. You can see the different options, listed in the `/etc/rc.d/init.d/httpd` example, under the **case** statement: **start**, **stop**, **status**, **restart**, and **reload**. If no option is provided (*****), the script usage syntax is displayed. The **httpd** script first executes a script to define functions used in these service scripts. The **daemon** function with **httpd** actually executes the **/usr/sbin/httpd** server program.

```
echo -n "Starting httpd: "
 daemon httpd
 echo
 touch /var/lock/subsys/httpd
```

The `killproc` function shuts down the daemon. The lock file and the process ID file (**httpd.pid**) are then deleted:

```
killproc httpd
echo
rm -f /var/lock/subsys/httpd
rm -f /var/run/httpd.pid
```

The **daemon**, **killproc**, and **status** functions are shell scripts defined in the **functions** script, also located in the **inet.d** directory. The **functions** script is executed at the beginning of each service script to activate these functions. A list of these functions is provided in Table 21-5.

```
. /etc/rc.d/init.d/functions
```

Service Script Tags

The beginning of the service script holds tags used to configure the server. These tags, which begin with an initial **#** symbol, are used to provide runtime information about the service to your system. The tags are listed in Table 21-6, along with the service functions. You enter a tag with a preceding **#** symbol, the tag name with a colon, and then the tag arguments. For example, the **processname** tag specifies the name of the program being executed, in this example **httpd**:

```
# processname: httpd
```

If your script starts more than one daemon, you should have a **processname** entry for each. For example, the Samba service starts up both the **smdb** and **nmdb** daemons.

```
# processname: smdb
# processname: nmdb
```

The end of the tag section is indicated by an empty line. After this line, any lines beginning with a **#** are treated as comments. The **chkconfig** line lists the default runlevels

Init Script Function	Description
`daemon` [+/-*nicelevel*] *program* [*arguments*] [&]	Starts a daemon, if it is not already running.
`killproc` *program* [*signal*]	Sends a signal to the program; by default it sends a **SIGTERM**, and if the process doesn't stop, it sends a **SIGKILL**. It will also remove any PID files, if it can.
`pidofproc` *program*	Used by another function, it determines the PID of a program.
`status` *program*	Displays status information.

TABLE 21-5 Init Script Functions

Init Script Tags	Description
# chkconfig: *startlevellist startpriority endpriority*	Required. Specifies the default start levels for this service as well as start and end priorities.
# description [*ln*]: *description of service*	Required. The description of the service, continued with \ characters. Use an initial # for any added lines. With the *ln* option, you can specify the language the description is written in.
# autoreload: true	Optional. If this line exists, the daemon checks its configuration files and reloads them automatically when they change.
# processname: *program*	Optional, multiple entries allowed. The name of the program or daemon started in the script.
# config: *configuration-file*	Optional, multiple entries allowed. Specifies a configuration file used by the server.
# pidfile: *pid-file*	Optional, multiple entries allowed. Specifies the PID file.
# probe: true	Optional, used *in place* of **autoreload**, **processname**, **config**, and **pidfile** entries to automatically probe and start the service.

TABLE 21-6   System V init Script Tags

that the service should start up on, along with the start and stop priorities. The following entry lists runlevels 3, 4, and 5 with a start priority of 85 and a stop of 15:

```
# chkconfig: 345 85 15
```

For the description, you enter a short explanation of the service, using the \ symbol before a new line to use more than one line.

```
# description: Apache Web server
```

With **config** tags, you specify the configuration files the server may use. In the case of the Apache Web server, there may be three configuration files:

```
# config: /etc/httpd/conf/access.conf
# config: /etc/httpd/conf/httpd.conf
# config: /etc/httpd/conf/srm.conf
```

The **pidfile** entry indicates the file where the server's process ID is held.

Service Script Example

As an example, a simplified version of the Web server service script, **/etc.rc.d/init.d/ httpd**, is shown here. Most scripts are much more complicated, particularly when

determining any arguments or variables a server may need to specify when it starts up. This
script has the same name as the Web server daemon, **httpd**:

```
#!/bin/sh
#
# Service script for the Apache Web Server
#
# chkconfig: 35 85 15
# description: Apache is a World Wide Web server. \
# It is used to serve HTML files and CGI.
# processname: httpd
# pidfile: /var/run/httpd.pid
# config: /etc/httpd/conf/access.conf
# config: /etc/httpd/conf/httpd.conf
# config: /etc/httpd/conf/srm.conf
# Source function library.
. /etc/rc.d/init.d/functions

# See how we were called.
case "$1" in
 start)
   echo -n "Starting httpd: "
    daemon httpd
    echo
    touch /var/lock/subsys/httpd
    ;;
   stop)
    killproc httpd
    echo
    rm -f /var/lock/subsys/httpd
    rm -f /var/run/httpd.pid
    ;;
 status)
    status httpd
    ;;
 restart)
    $0 stop
    $0 start
    ;;
 reload)
    echo -n "Reloading httpd: "
    killproc httpd -HUP
    echo
    ;;
 *)
    echo "Usage: $0 {start|stop|restart}"
    exit 1
 esac
exit 0
```

Installing Service Scripts

The RPM-packaged version for a service includes a service script. For example, an Internet server package includes the service script for that server. Installing the RPM package installs the script in the **/etc/rc.d/init.d** directory and creates its appropriate links in the runlevel directories, such as **/etc/rc.h/rc3.d**. If you decide, instead, to create the server using its source code files, you can then manually install the service script. If no service script exists, you first make a copy of the `httpd` script—renaming it—and then edit the copy to replace all references to `httpd` with the name of the server daemon program. Then place the copy of the script in the **/etc/rc.d/init.d** directory and make a symbolic link to it in the **/etc/rc.d/rc3.d** directory. Or you could use system-config-services to create the link in the **/etc/rc.d/rc3.d** directory. Select File | Refresh Services. When you start your system now, the new server is automatically started up, running concurrently and waiting for requests.

Extended Internet Services Daemon (xinetd)

If your system averages only a few requests for a specific service, you don't need the server for that service running all the time. You need it only when a remote user is accessing its service. The Extended Internet Services Daemon (**xinetd**) manages Internet servers, invoking them only when your system receives a request for their services. **xinetd** checks continuously for any requests by remote users for a particular Internet service; when it receives a request, it then starts the appropriate server daemon.

The **xinetd** program is designed to be a replacement for **inetd**, providing security enhancements, logging support, and even user notifications. For example, with **xinetd** you can send banner notices to users when they are not able to access a service, telling them why. **xinetd** security capabilities can be used to prevent denial-of-service attacks, limiting remote hosts' simultaneous connections or restricting the rate of incoming connections. **xinetd** also incorporates TCP, providing TCP security without the need to invoke the **tcpd** daemon. Furthermore, you do not have to have a service listed in the **/etc/services** file. **xinetd** can be set up to start any kind of special-purpose server. The Red Hat Linux versions 7.0 and up, as well as all Fedora versions, use **xinetd**.

Starting and Stopping xinetd Services: system-config-services On Demand

You can start, stop, and restart **xinetd** using its service script in the **/etc/rc.d/init.d** directory, as shown here:

```
# service xinetd stop
# service xinetd start
# service xinetd restart
```

On Red Hat and Fedora, you can also turn on and off particular **xinetd** services with `chkconfig`, as described earlier. Use the **on** and **off** options to enable or disable a service; `chkconfig` will edit the disable option for the service, changing its value to "yes" for off and "no" for on. For example, to enable the swat server, you could enter

```
chkconfig swat on
```

You can also use system-config-services to start and stop particular **xinetd** services. Once **xinetd** is started, the On Demand panel will list the available **xinetd**-supported services.

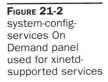

FIGURE 21-2
system-config-
services On
Demand panel
used for xinetd-
supported services

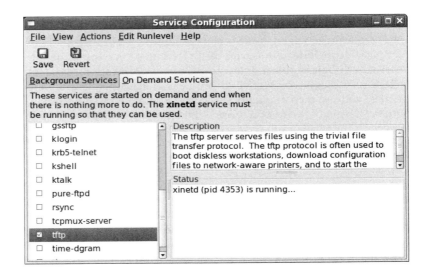

You can select, start, and stop a service just as you would regular services. Figure 21-2 shows the tftpd service selected.

xinetd Configuration: xinetd.conf

The xinetd.conf file contains settings for your xinetd server, like logging and security attributes (see Table 21-7). This file can also contain server configuration entries, but on Red Hat and Fedora, these are placed into separate configuration files located in the **/etc/xinetd.d** directory. The **includedir** attribute specifies this directory:

```
includedir /etc/xinetd.d
```

Logging xinetd Services

You can further add a variety of other attributes such as logging information about connections and server priority (**nice**). In the following example, the **log_on_success** attribute logs the duration (**DURATION**) and the user ID (**USERID**) for connections to a service, **log_on_failure** logs the users that failed to connect, and **nice** sets the priority of the service to 10.

```
log_on_success += DURATION USERID
log_on_failure += USERID
nice = 10
```

The default attributes defined in the defaults block often set global attributes such as default logging activity and security restrictions: **log_type** specifies where logging information is to be sent, such as to a specific file (**FILE**) or to the system logger (**SYSLOG**), **log_on_success** specifies information to be logged when connections are made, and **log_on_failure** specifies information to be logged when they fail.

```
log_type = SYSLOG daemon info
log_on_failure = HOST
log_on_success = PID HOST EXIT
```

Attribute	Description
`ids`	Identifies a service. By default, the service ID is the same as the service name.
`type`	Type of service: `RPC`, `INTERNAL` (provided by **xinetd**), or `UNLISTED` (not listed in a standard system file).
`flags`	Possible flags include `REUSE`, `INTERCEPT`, `NORETRY`, `IDONLY`, `NAMEINARGS` (allows use of `tcpd`), `NODELAY`, and `DISABLE` (disable the service). See the **xinetd.conf** Main page for more details.
`disable`	Specify **yes** to disable the service.
`socket_type`	Specify **stream** for a stream-based service, **dgram** for a datagram-based service, **raw** for a service that requires direct access to IP, and **seqpacket** for reliable sequential datagram transmission.
`protocol`	Specifies a protocol for the service. The protocol must exist in **/etc/protocols**. If this attribute is not defined, the default protocol employed by the service will be used.
`wait`	Specifies whether the service is single-threaded or multithreaded (**yes** or **no**). If **yes**, the service is single-threaded, which means that **xinetd** will start the server and then stop handling requests for the service until the server stops. If **no**, the service is multithreaded and **xinetd** will continue to handle new requests for it.
`user`	Specifies the user ID (UID) for the server process. The user name must exist in **/etc/passwd**.
`group`	Specifies the GID for the server process. The group name must exist in **/etc/group**.
`instances`	Specifies the number of server processes that can be simultaneously active for a service.
`nice`	Specifies the server priority.
`server`	Specifies the program to execute for this service.
`server_args`	Lists the arguments passed to the server. This does not include the server name.
`only_from`	Controls the remote hosts to which the particular service is available. Its value is a list of IP addresses. With no value, service is denied to all remote hosts.
`no_access`	Controls the remote hosts to which the particular service is unavailable.
`access_times`	Specifies the time intervals when the service is available. An interval has the form hour:min-hour:min.
`log_type`	Specifies where the output of the service log is sent, either the syslog facility (**SYSLOG**) or a file (**FILE**).

TABLE 21-7 Attributes for xinetd *(continued)*

Attribute	Description
`log_on_success`	Specifies the information that is logged when a server starts and stops. Information you can specify includes **PID** (server process ID), **HOST** (the remote host address), **USERID** (the remote user), **EXIT** (exit status and termination signal), and **DURATION** (duration of a service session).
`log_on_failure`	Specifies the information that is logged when a server cannot be started. Information you can specify includes **HOST** (the remote host address), **USERID** (user ID of the remote user), **ATTEMPT** (logs a failed attempt), and **RECORD** (records information from the remote host to allow monitoring of attempts to access the server).
`rpc_version`	Specifies the RPC version for a RPC service.
`rpc_number`	Specifies the number for an UNLISTED RPC service.
`env`	Defines environment variables for a service.
`passenv`	The list of environment variables from **xinetd**'s environment that will be passed to the server.
`port`	Specifies the service port.
`redirect`	Allows a TCP service to be redirected to another host.
`bind`	Allows a service to be bound to a specific interface on the machine.
`interface`	Synonym for **bind.**
`banner`	The name of a file to be displayed for a remote host when a connection to that service is established.
`banner_success`	The name of a file to be displayed at the remote host when a connection to that service is granted.
`banner_fail`	The name of a file to be displayed at the remote host when a connection to that service is denied.
`groups`	Allows access to groups the service has access to (**yes** or **no**).
`enabled`	Specifies the list of service names to enable.
`include`	Inserts the contents of a specified file as part of the configuration file.
`includedir`	Takes a directory name in the form of **includedir /etc/xinetd.d**. Every file inside that directory will be read sequentially as an **xinetd** configuration file, combining to form the **xinetd** configuration.

TABLE 21-7   Attributes for xinetd

xinetd Network Security

For security restrictions, you can use **only_from** to restrict access by certain remote hosts. The **no_access** attribute denies access from the listed hosts, but no others. These controls take IP addresses as their values. You can list individual IP addresses, a range of IP addresses, or a network, using the network address. The **instances** attribute limits the number of server processes that can be active at the same time for a particular service. The following examples restrict access to a local network 192.168.1.0 and the localhost, deny access from 192.168.1.15, and use the **instances** attribute to limit the number of server processes at one time to 60:

```
only_from = 192.168.1.0
only_from = localhost
no_access = 192.168.1.15
instances = 60
```

The **xinetd** program also provides several internal services, including **time**, **services**, **servers**, and **xadmin**: **services** provides a list of currently active services, and **servers** provides information about servers; **xadmin** provides **xinetd** administrative support.

xinetd Service Configuration Files: /etc/xinetd.d Directory

Instead of having one large **xinetd.conf** file for all services, the service configurations are split it into several configuration files, one for each service. The directory is specified in **xinetd.conf** file with an **includedir** option. In the following example, the **xinetd.d** directory holds **xinetd** configuration files for services like swat. This approach has the advantage of letting you add services by just creating a new configuration file for them. Modifying a service involves editing only its configuration file, not an entire **xinetd.conf** file.

As an example, the **swat** file in the **xinetd.d** directory is shown here. Notice that it is disabled by default.

```
# default: off
# description: SWAT is the Samba Web Admin Tool.\
# Use swat to configure your Samba server. \
# To use SWAT, connect to port 901 with your \
# favorite web browser.
service swat
{
    port            = 901
    socket_type     = stream
    wait            = no
    only_from       = 127.0.0.1
    user            = root
    server          = /usr/sbin/swat
    log_on_failure  += USERID
    disable         yes
}
```

Configuring Services: xinetd Attributes

Entries in an **xinetd** service file define the server to be activated when requested along with any options and security precautions. An entry consists of a block of attributes defined for different features, such as the name of the server program, the protocol used, and security restrictions. Each block for an Internet service such as a server is preceded by the keyword **service** and the name by which you want to identify the service. A pair of braces encloses the block of attributes. Each attribute entry begins with the attribute name, followed by an assignment operator, such as **=**, and then the value or values assigned. A special block specified by the keyword **default** contains default attributes for services. The syntax is shown here:

```
service <service_name>
{
<attribute> <assign_op> <value> <value> ...
 ...
}
```

Most attributes take a single value for which you use the standard assignment operator, **=**. Some attributes can take a list of values. You can assign values with the **=** operator, but you can also add or remove items from these lists with the **=+** and **=-** operators. Use **=+** to add values and **=-** to remove values. You often use the **=+** and **=-** operators to add values to attributes that may have an initial value assigned in the default block.

Attributes are listed in Table 21-7. Certain attributes are required for a service. These include **socket_type** and **wait**. For a standard Internet service, you also need to provide the **user** (user ID for the service), the **server** (name of the server program), and the **protocol** (protocol used by the server). With **server_args**, you can also list any arguments you want passed to the server program (this does not include the server name). If **protocol** is not defined, the default protocol for the service is used.

Disabling and Enabling xinetd Services

You can turn services on or off manually, or use the system-config-services On Demand panel. Services are turned on and off with the **disable** attribute in their configuration file. To enable a service, you set the disable attribute to **no**, as shown here:

```
disable = no
```

You then have to restart **xinetd** to start the service.

```
# /etc/rc.d/init.d/xinetd restart
```

TIP *Red Hat or Fedora currently disables all the services it initially sets up when it installs **xinetd**. To enable a particular service, you will have to set its disable attribute to **no**.*

To enable management by **chkconfig**, a commented default and description entry need to be placed before each service segment. Where separate files are used, the entry is placed at the head of each file. Red Hat and Fedora already provide these for the services they install with their distributions, such as **tftp** and SWAT. A default entry can be either on or off. For example, the **chkconfig** default and description entries for the FTP service are shown here:

```
# default: off
# description: The tftp server serves files using the trivial file transfer \
#       protocol.  The tftp protocol is often used to boot diskless \
#       workstations, download configuration files to network-aware printers, \
#       and to start the installation process for some operating systems.
```

If you want to turn on a service that is off by default, you can set its **disable** attribute to **no** and restart **xinetd** (alternatively, use system-config-services On Demand panel). The entry for the TFtp FTP server, **tftpd**, is shown here. An initial comment tells you that it is off by default, but then the **disable** attribute turns it on:

```
service tftp
{
    socket_type        = dgram
    protocol           = udp
    wait               = yes
    user               = root
    server             = /usr/sbin/in.tftpd
    server_args        = -s /tftpboot
    disable            = yes
    per_source         = 11
    cps                = 100 2
    flags              = IPv4
}
```

TCP Wrappers

TCP wrappers add another level of security to **xinetd**-managed servers. In effect, the server is wrapped with an intervening level of security, monitoring connections and controlling access. A server connection made through **xinetd** is monitored, verifying remote user identities and checking to make sure they are making valid requests. Connections are logged with the **syslogd** daemon (see Chapter 27) and may be found in **syslogd** files such as **/var/log/secure**. With TCP wrappers, you can also restrict access to your system by remote hosts. Lists of hosts are kept in the **hosts.allow** and **hosts.deny** files. Entries in these files have the format **service:hostname:domain**. The domain is optional. For the service, you can specify a particular service, such as FTP, or you can enter **ALL** for all services. For the hostname, you can specify a particular host or use a wildcard to match several hosts. For example, **ALL** will match on all hosts. Table 21-8 lists the available wildcards. In the following example, the first entry allows access by all hosts to the Web service, **http**. The second entry

Wildcard	Description
ALL	Matches all hosts or services.
LOCAL	Matches any host specified with just a hostname without a domain name. Used to match on hosts in the local domain.
UNKNOWN	Matches any user or host whose name or address is unknown.
KNOWN	Matches any user or host whose name or address is known.
PARANOID	Matches any host whose hostname does not match its IP address.
EXCEPT	An operator that lets you provide exceptions to matches. It takes the form of *list1* **EXCEPT** *list2* where those hosts matched in *list1* that are also matched in *list2* are excluded.

TABLE 21-8 TCP Wrapper Wildcards

allows access to all services by the **pango1.train.com** host. The third and fourth entries allow FTP access to **rabbit.trek.com** and **sparrow.com**.

```
http:ALL
ALL:pango1.train.com
ftp:rabbit.trek.com
ftp:sparrow.com
```

The **hosts.allow** file holds hosts to which you allow access. If you want to allow access to all but a few specific hosts, you can specify **ALL** for a service in the **hosts.allow** file but list the ones you are denying access to in the **hosts.deny** file. Using IP addresses instead of hostnames is more secure because hostnames can be compromised through the DNS records by spoofing attacks where an attacker pretends to be another host.

When **xinetd** receives a request for an FTP service, a TCP wrapper monitors the connection and starts up the **in.ftpd** server program. By default, all requests are allowed. To allow all requests specifically for the FTP service, you would enter the following in your **/etc/hosts.allow** file. The entry **ALL:ALL** opens your system to all hosts for all services.

```
ftp:ALL
```

TIP   *Originally, TCP wrappers were managed by the **tcpd** daemon. However, **xinetd** has since integrated support for TCP wrappers into its own program. You can explicitly invoke the **tcpd** daemon to handle services if you wish. The **tcpd** Man pages (**man tcpd**) provide more detailed information about **tcpd**.*

FTP Servers

The File Transfer Protocol (FTP) is designed to transfer large files across a network from one system to another. Like most Internet operations, FTP works on a client/server model. FTP client programs can enable users to transfer files to and from a remote system running an FTP server program. Chapter 14 discusses FTP clients. Any Linux system can operate as an FTP server. It only has to run the server software—an FTP daemon with the appropriate configuration. Transfers are made between user accounts on client and server systems. A user on the remote system has to log in to an account on a server and can then transfer files to and from that account's directories only. A special kind of user account, named *ftp*, allows any user to log in to it with the username "anonymous." This account has its own set of directories and files that are considered public, available to anyone on the network who wants to download them. The numerous FTP sites on the Internet are FTP servers supporting FTP user accounts with the anonymous login. Any Linux system can be configured to support anonymous FTP access, turning them into network FTP sites. Such sites can work on an intranet or on the Internet.

FTP Servers

FTP server software consists of an FTP daemon and configuration files. The *daemon* is a program that continuously checks for FTP requests from remote users. When a request is received, it manages a login, sets up the connection to the requested user account, and executes any FTP commands the remote user sends. For anonymous FTP access, the FTP daemon allows the remote user to log in to the FTP account using anonymous or ftp as the username. The user then has access to the directories and files set up for the FTP account. As a further security measure, however, the daemon changes the root directory for that session to be the FTP home directory. This hides the rest of the system from the remote user. Normally, any user on a system can move around to any directories open to him or her. A user logging in with anonymous FTP can see only the FTP home directory and its subdirectories. The remainder of the system is hidden from that user. This effect is achieved by the **chroot** operation (discussed later) that literally changes the system root directory for that user to that of the FTP directory. By default, the FTP server also requires a user be using a valid shell. It checks for a list of valid shells in the **/etc/shells** file. Most daemons have options for turning off this feature.

Available Servers

Several FTP servers are available for use on Fedora and Red Hat systems (see Table 22-1). Three Fedora-compliant servers included with Fedora are **vsftpd**, **pureftpd**, and **proftpd**. The Very Secure FTP Server, **vsftpd,** provides a simple and very secure FTP server. The Pure FTPD, **pureftpd,** server is a lightweight, fast, and secure FTP server, based upon Troll-FTPd. Documentation and the latest sources are available from **www.pureftpd.org**.

ProFTPD, **proftpd,** is a popular FTP daemon based on an Apache Web server design. It features simplified configuration and support for virtual FTP hosts. The compressed archive of the most up-to-date version, along with documentation, is available at the ProFTPD Web site at **www.proftpd.org**. Another FTP daemon, NcFTPd, is a commercial product produced by the same programmers who did the NcFTP FTP client. NcFTPd is free for academic use and features a reduced fee for small networks. Check **www.ncftpd.org** for more information.

Several security-based FTP servers are also available, including SSLFTP and SSH **sftpd**, along with **gssftpd**. SSLFTP uses SSL (Secure Sockets Layer) to encrypt and authenticate transmissions, as well as MD5 digests to check the integrity of transmitted files. SSH **sftpd** is an FTP server that is now part of the Open SSH package, using SSH encryption and authentication to establish secure FTP connections. The **gssftpd** server is part of the Kerberos 5 package and provides Kerberos-level security for FTP operations.

Fedora and Red Hat FTP Server Directories

The **vsftpd** server package is part of Fedora. If you choose to install an FTP server, the **vsftpd** server package is installed along with anonymous FTP support. An **ftp** directory is created along with several subdirectories where you can place files for FTP access. The directories are configured to control access by remote users, restricting use to only the **ftp** directories and any subdirectories. The **ftp** directory is placed in the **/var** directory, **/var/ftp**. Place the files you want to allow access to in the **/var/ftp/pub** directory.

You can also create subdirectories and place files there. Once you are connected to a network, a remote user can connect to your system and download files you placed in **/var/ftp/pub** or any of its subdirectories. The **vsftpd** FTP package implements a default configuration for those directories and their files. You can change these if you want. If you

FTP Servers	Site
Very Secure FTP Server (vsftpd)	**vsftpd.beasts.org (Fedora)**
ProFTPD	**www.proftpd.org**
PureFTP	**www.pureftpd.org**
NcFTPd	**www.ncftpd.org**
SSH sftp-server	**www.openssh.org**
Washington University Web server (WU-FTPD)	**www.wu-ftpd.org**
Tux	Web server with FTP capabilities
gssftpd	Kerberos FTP server

TABLE 22-1   FTP Servers

are installing an FTP server yourself, you need to know the procedures detailed in the following sections to install an FTP server and create its data directories.

The **vsftpd** FTP package does not create a directory where users can upload files to the FTP site. Such a directory is usually named the incoming directory, located at **ftp/pub/incoming**. If you want such a directory, you will have to create it, make it part of the **ftp** group, and then set its permissions to allow users write access.

```
# chgrp ftp ./var/ftp/pub/incoming
# chmod g+w /var/ftp/pub/incoming
```

FTP Users

Normal users with accounts on an FTP server can gain full FTP access simply by logging into their accounts. Such users can access and transfer files directly from their own accounts or any directories they may have access to. You can also create users, known as guest users, that have restricted access to the FTP publicly accessible directories. This involves setting standard user restrictions, with the FTP public directory as their home directory. Users can also log in as anonymous users, allowing anyone on the network or Internet to access files on an FTP server.

Anonymous FTP: vsftpd

An anonymous FTP site is essentially a special kind of user on your system with publicly accessible directories and files in its home directory. Anyone can log in to this account and access its files. Because anyone can log in to an anonymous FTP account, you must be careful to restrict a remote FTP user to only the files on that anonymous FTP directory. Normally, a user's files are interconnected to the entire file structure of your system. Normal users have write access that lets them create or delete files and directories. The anonymous FTP files and directories can be configured in such a way that the rest of the file system is hidden from them and remote users are given only read access. In ProFTPD, this is achieved through configuration directives placed in its configuration file. An older approach implemented by the vsftpd package involves having copies of certain system configuration, command, and library files placed within subdirectories of the FTP home directory. Restrictions placed on those subdirectories then control access by other users. Within the FTP home directory, you then have a publicly accessible directory that holds the files you want to make available to remote users. This directory usually has the name **pub**, for public.

An FTP site is made up of an FTP user account, an FTP home directory, and certain copies of system directories containing selected configuration and support files. Newer FTP daemons, such as ProFTPD, do not need the system directories and support files. Most distributions, including Fedora and Red Hat, have already set up an FTP user account when you installed your system.

NOTE *The **vsftpd** RPM package will set up the home directory and the copies of the system directories when it is installed. If, for some reason, you do not want to use the **vsftpd** RPM package (if, for instance, you are recompiling the source code), you may have to create these system directories yourself.*

The FTP User Account: anonymous

To allow anonymous FTP access by other users to your system, you must have a user account named *FTP*. Most distributions already create this account for you. If your system does not have such an account, you will have to create one. You can then place restrictions on the FTP account to keep any remote FTP users from accessing any other part of your system. You must also modify the entry for this account in your **/etc/passwd** file to prevent normal user access to it. The following is the entry you find in your **/etc/passwd** file that sets up an FTP login as an anonymous user:

```
ftp:x:14:50:FTP User:/var/ftp:
```

The **x** in the password field blocks the account, which prevents any other users from gaining access to it, thereby gaining control over its files or access to other parts of your system. The user ID, 14, is a unique ID. The comment field is FTP User. The login directory is **/var/ftp**. When FTP users log in to your system, they are placed in this directory. If a home directory has not been set up, create one and then change its ownership to the FTP user with the **chown** command.

FTP Group

The group ID is the ID of the **ftp** group, which is set up only for anonymous FTP users. You can set up restrictions on the **ftp** group, thereby restricting any anonymous FTP users. Here is the entry for the **ftp** group you find in the **/etc/group** file. If your system does not have one, you should add it:

```
ftp::50:
```

Creating New FTP Users

If you are creating virtual FTP hosts, you will need to create an FTP user for each one, along with its directories. For example, to create an FTP server for a host1-ftp host, you would create a **host1-ftp** user with its own directory.

```
# useradd -d /var/host1-ftp host1-ftp
```

This would create a user such as that described here:

```
host1-ftp:x:14:50:FTP User:/var/host1-ftp:
```

You would also need to create the corresponding home directory, **/var/host1-ftp** in this example, and set its permissions to give users restricted access.

```
# mkdir /var/host1-ftp
# chmod 755 /var/host1-ftp
```

You also need to make sure that the root user owns the directory, not the new FTP users. This gives control of the directory only to the root user, not to any user that logs in.

```
# chown root.root /var/host1-ftp
```

Anonymous FTP Server Directories

As previously noted, the FTP home directory is named **ftp** and is placed in the **/var** directory. When users log in anonymously, they are placed in this directory. An important part of protecting your system is preventing remote users from using any commands or programs not in the restricted directories. For example, you would not let a user use your **ls** command to list filenames, because **ls** is located in your **/bin** directory. At the same time, you want to let the FTP user list filenames using an **ls** command. Newer FTP daemons like vsftpd and ProFTPD solve this problem by creating secure access to needed system commands and files, while restricting remote users to only the FTP site's directories. In any event, make sure that the FTP home directory is owned by the root user, not by the FTP user. Use the **ls -d** command to check on the ownership of the FTP directory.

```
# ls -d /var/ftp
```

To change a directory's ownership, you use the **chown** command, as shown in this example:

```
# chown  root.root /var/ftp
```

Another, more traditional, solution is to create copies of certain system directories and files needed by remote users and to place them in the **ftp** directory where users can access them. A **bin** directory is placed in the **ftp** directory and remote users are restricted to it, instead of the system's **bin** directory. Whenever they use the **ls** command, remote users are using the one in **ftp/bin**, not the one you use in **/bin**. If, for some reason, you set up the anonymous FTP directories yourself, you must use the **chmod** command to change the access permissions for the directories so that remote users cannot access the rest of your system. Create an **ftp** directory and use the **chmod** command with the permission 555 to turn off write access: **chmod 555 ftp**. Next, make a new **bin** directory in the **ftp** directory, and then make a copy of the **ls** command and place it in **ftp/bin**. Do this for any commands you want to make available to FTP users. Then create an **ftp/etc** directory to hold a copy of your **passwd** and **group** files. Again, the idea is to prevent any access to the original files in the **/etc** directory by FTP users. The **ftp/etc/passwd** file should be edited to remove any entries for regular users on your system. All other entries should have their passwords set to **x** to block access. For the **group** file, remove all user groups and set all passwords to **x**. Create an **ftp/lib** directory, and then make copies of the libraries you need to run the commands you placed in the **bin** directory.

Anonymous FTP Files

A directory named **pub**, located in the FTP home directory, usually holds the files you are making available for downloading by remote FTP users. When FTP users log in, they are placed in the FTP home directory (**/var/ftp**), and they can then change to the **pub** directory to start accessing those files (**/var/ftp/pub**). Within the **pub** directory, you can add as many files and directories as you want. You can even designate some directories as upload directories, enabling FTP users to transfer files to your system.

In each subdirectory set up under the **pub** directory to hold FTP files, you should create a **README** file and an **INDEX** file as a courtesy to FTP users. The **README** file contains a brief description of the kind of files held in this directory. The **INDEX** file contains a listing of the files and a description of what each one holds.

Using FTP with rsync

Many FTP servers also support rsync operations using **rsync** as a daemon. This allows intelligent incremental updates of files from an FTP server. You can update multiple files in a directory or a single file such as a large ISO image.

Accessing FTP Sites with rsync

To access the FTP server running an rsync server, you enter the **rsync** command, and following the host name, you enter a double colon and then either the path of the directory you want to access or one of the FTP server's modules. In the following example, the user updates a local **myproject** directory from the one on the **mytrek.com** FTP site:

```
$ rsync ftp.mytrek.com::/var/ftp/pub/myproject  /home/myproject
```

To find out what directories are supported by rsync, you check for rsync modules on that site. These are defined by the site's **/etc/rsyncd.conf** configuration file. A *module* is just a directory with all its subdirectories. To find available modules, you enter the FTP site with a double colon only.

```
$ rsync ftp.mytrek.com::
ftp
```

This tells you that the **ftp.mytrek.com** site has an FTP module. To list the files and directories on the module, you can use the **rsync** command with the **-r** option.

```
$ rsync -r ftp.mytrek.com::ftp
```

Many sites that run the rsync server will have an rsync protocol that will already be set to access the available rsync module (directory). For example, the following URL can be used with rsync to access the ibiblio location for the Fedora distribution. The module is named fedora-linux-core, which follows the host name.

```
$ rsync://distro.ibiblio.org/fedora-linux-core/
```

You can even use rsync to update just a single file, such as an ISO image that may have been changed. The following example updates the Fedora 7 ISO disk 1 image. The **--progress** option will show the download progress.

```
$ rsync -a --progress rsync://distro.ibiblio.org/fedora-linux-core/7/i386/
iso/FC7-i386-disc1.iso
```

Configuring an rsync Server

To configure your FTP server to let clients use rsync on your site, you need to first run rsync on the server. Use system-config-services or **chkconfig** to turn on the rsync daemon, commonly known as **rsyncd**. This will run the rsync daemon through **xinetd**, using an **rsync** script in **/etc/xinetd.d** to turn it on and set parameters.

```
# chkconfig rsync on
```

When run as a daemon, rsync will read the **/etc/rsyncd.conf** file for its configuration options. Here you can specify FTP options such as the location for the FTP site files.

The configuration file is segmented into modules, each with its own options. A module is a symbolic representation of a exported tree (a directory and its subdirectories). The module name is enclosed in brackets, for instance, **[ftp]** for an FTP module. You can then enter options for that module, e.g., by using the path option to specify the location of your FTP site directories and files. The user and group IDs can be specified with the **uid** and **gid** options. The default is nobody. A sample FTP module for anonymous access is shown here:

```
[ftp]
        path = /var/ftp/pub
        comment = ftp site
```

For more restricted access, you could add an **auth users** option to specify authorized users; rsync will allow anonymous access to all users by default. Use hosts allow or deny to control access from specific hosts. Access to areas on the FTP site by rsync can be further controlled using a secrets file, like **/etc/rsyncd.secrets**. This is a colon-separated list of user names and passwords.

```
aleina:mypass3
larisa:yourp5
```

A corresponding module to the controlled area would look like this:

```
[specialftp]
        path = /var/projects/special
        command = restricted access
        auth users = aleina,larisa
        secrets file = /etc/rsyncd.secrets
```

If you are on your FTP server and want to see what modules will be made available, you can run **rsync** with the **localhost** option and nothing following the double colon.

```
$ rsync localhost::
ftp
specialftp
```

Remote users can find out what modules you have by entering your host name and double colon only.

```
$ rsync ftp.mytrek.com::
```

rsync Mirroring

Some sites will allow you to use rsync to perform mirroring operations. With rsync you would not have to copy the entire site, just those files that have been changed. The following example will mirror the **mytrek** FTP site to the **/var/ftp/mirror/mytrek** directory on a local system:

```
$ rsync -a --delete ftp.mytrek.com::ftp /var/ftp/mirror/mytrek
```

The options uses are as follows: the **-a** option is archive mode, which includes several other options, such as **-r** (recursive) to include all subdirectories, **-t** to preserves file times and dates, **-l** to recreate symbolic links, and **-p** to preserve all permissions. In addition, the **--delete** option is added to delete files that don't exist on the sending side, removing obsolete files.

PART V

The Very Secure FTP Server

The Very Secure FTP Server (vsftpd) is small, fast, easy, and secure. It is designed to avoid the overhead of large FTP server applications like ProFTPD, while maintaining a very high level of security. It can also handle a very large workload, managing high traffic levels on an FTP site. It is perhaps best for sites where many anonymous and guest users will be downloading the same files. Beginning with Red Hat 9, it replaced the Washington University FTP server, WU-FTPD.

The Very Secure FTP Server is inherently designed to provide as much security as possible, taking full advantage of Unix and Linux operating system features. The server is separated into privileged and unprivileged processes. The unprivileged process receives all FTP requests, interpreting them and then sending them over a socket to the privileged process, which then securely filters all requests. Even the privileged process does not run with full root capabilities, using only those that are necessary to perform its tasks. In addition, the Very Secure FTP Server uses its own version of directory commands like **ls**, instead of the system's versions.

Running vsftpd

The Very Secure FTP Server's daemon is named **vsftpd**. It is designed to be run as a stand-alone server, which can be started and stopped using the **/etc/rc.d/init.d/vsftpd** server script. To start, stop, and restart **vsftpd**, you can use the **service** command.

```
$ service vsftpd start
```

To have the server start automatically, you can turn it on with the **chkconfig** command and the **on** argument, as shown here. Use the **off** argument to disable the server. If you previously enabled another FTP server such as ProFTPD, be sure to disable it first.

```
$ chkconfig vsftpd on
```

You can also use system-config-services to start and stop **vsftpd**, or to have it started automatically.

Alternatively, you can implement **vsftpd** to be run by **xinetd**, running the server only when a request is made by a user. The use of **xinetd** for the servers is described in detail in Chapter 21. The **xinetd** daemon will run an **xinetd** script file called **vsftpd** located in the **/etc/xinetd.d** directory.

Initially, the server will be turned off. You can turn it on in **xinetd** with the **chkconfig** command and the **on** argument, as shown here. Use the **off** argument to disable the server.

```
$ chkconfig vsftpd on
```

Should you make configuration changes, restart **xinetd** with the **service** command (or system-config-services) to restart the **vsftpd** server.

```
# service xinetd restart
```

Configuring vsftpd

You configure **vsftpd** using one configuration file, **/etc/vsftpd/vsftpd.conf**. Configuration options are simple and kept to a minimum, making it less flexible than ProFTPD, but much faster (see Table 22-2). The **vsftpd.conf** file contains a set of directives where an option is assigned a value. Options can be on and off flags assigned a YES or NO value, features that

Option	Description
`listen`	Set stand-alone mode.
`listen_port`	Specify port for stand-alone mode.
`anonymous_enable`	Enable anonymous user access.
`local_enable`	Enable access by local users.
`no_anon_password`	Specify whether anonymous users must submit a password.
`anon_upload_enable`	Enable uploading by anonymous users.
`anon_mkdir_write_enable`	Allow anonymous users to create directories.
`aonon_world_readable_only`	Make uploaded files read only to all users.
`idle_session_timeout`	Time limit in seconds for idle sessions.
`data_connection_timeouts`	Time limit in seconds for failed connections.
`dirmessage_enable`	Display directory messages.
`ftpd_banner`	Display FTP login message.
`xferlog_enable`	Enable logging of transmission transactions.
`xferlog_file`	Specify log file.
`deny_email_enable`	Enable denying anonymous users whose e-mail addresses are specified in **vsftpd.banned**.
`userlist_enable`	Deny access to users specified in the **vsftp.user_list** file.
`userlist_file`	Deny or allow users access depending on setting of `userlist_deny`.
`userlist_deny`	When set to YES, **userlist_file** list users are denied access. When set to NO, **userlist_file** list users, and only those users, are allowed access.
`chroot_list_enable`	Restrict users to their home directories.
`chroot_list_file`	Allow users access to home directories. Unless `chroot_local_user` is set to YES, this file contains a list of users not allowed access to their home directories.
`chroot_local_user`	Allow access by all users to their home directories.
`pam_service_name`	Specify PAM script.
`ls_recurse_enable`	Enable recursive listing.

TABLE **22-2**   Configuration Options for **vsftpd.conf**

take a numeric value, or ones that are assigned a string. A default **vsftpd.conf** file is installed in the **/etc/vsftpd** directory. This file lists some of the commonly used options available with detailed explanations for each. Those not used are commented out with a preceding # character. Option names are very understandable. For example, `anon_upload_enable` allows anonymous users to upload files, whereas `anon_mkdir_write_enable` lets anonymous users create directories. The Man page for **vsftpd.conf** lists all options, providing a detailed explanation for each.

NOTE *When setting options in the **vsftpd.conf** file, there are no spaces around the = sign.*

Enabling Stand-Alone Access
To run **vsftpd** as a stand-alone server, you set the listen option to YES. This instructs **vsftpd** to continually listen on its assigned port for requests. You can specify the port it listens on with the `listen_port` option.

```
listen=YES
```

Enabling Login Access
In the following example, taken from the **vsftpd.conf** file, anonymous FTP is enabled by assigning the YES value to the **anonymous_enable** option. The `local_enable` option allows local users on your system to use the FTP server.

```
# Allow anonymous FTP?
anonymous_enable=YES
#
# Uncomment this to allow local users to log in.
local_enable=YES
```

Should you want to let anonymous users log in without providing a password, you can set **no_anon_password** to YES.

Local User Permissions
A variety of user permissions control how local users can access files on the server. If you want to allow local users to create, rename, and delete files and directories on their account, you have to enable write access with the **write_enable** option. This way, any files they upload, they can also delete. Literally, the **write_enable** option activates a range of commands for changing the file system, including creating, renaming, and deleting both files and directories.

```
write_enable=YES
```

You can further specify the permissions for uploaded files using the `local_umask` option (022 is the default set in **vsftpd.conf**, indicating read and write for the owner and read only for all other users, 644).

```
local_umask=022
```

Though ASCII uploads are disabled by default, you can also enable this feature. ASCII uploads entail certain security risks and are turned off by default. But if you are uploading large text files, you may want to enable them in special cases. Use `ascii_upload_enable` to allow ASCII uploads.

Anonymous User Permissions
You can also allow anonymous users to upload and delete files, as well as create or remove directories. Uploading by anonymous users is enabled with the **anon_upload_enable** option. To let anonymous users also rename or delete their files, you set the **anon_other_write_enable** option. To also let them create directories, you set the **anon_mkdir_write_enable** option.

```
anon_upload_enable=YES
anon_other_write_enable=YES
anon_mkdir_write_enable=YES
```

The **anon_world_readable_only** option will make uploaded files read only (downloadable), restricting write access to the user that created them. Only the user that uploaded a file could delete it.

All uploaded files are owned by the anonymous FTP user. You can have the files owned by another user, adding greater possible security. In effect, the actual user owning the uploaded files becomes hidden from anonymous users. To enable this option, you use **chown_uploads** and specify the new user with **chown_username**. Never make the user an administrative user like root.

```
chown_uploads=YES
chown_username=myftpfiles
```

The upload directory itself should be given write permission by other users.

```
# chmod 777 /var/ftp/upload
```

You can control the kind of access that users have to files with the **anon_mask** option, setting default read/write permissions for uploaded files. The default is 077, which gives read/write permission to the owner only (600). To allow all users read access, you would set the umask to 022, where the 2 turns off write permission but sets read permission (644). The value 000 would allow both read and write for all users.

Connection Time Limits

To more efficiently control the workload on a server, you can set time limits on idle users and failed transmissions. The **idle_session_timeout** option will cut off idle users after a specified time, and **data_connection_timeouts** will cut off failed data connections. The defaults are shown here:

```
idle_session_timeout=600
data_connection_timeout=120
```

Messages

The **dirmessage_enable** option will allow a message held in a directory's **.message** file to be displayed whenever a user accesses that directory. The **ftpd_banner** option lets you set up your own FTP login message. The default is shown here:

```
ftpd_banner=Welcome to blah FTP service.
```

Logging

A set of **xferlog** options control logging. You can enable logging, as well as specify the format and the location of the file.

```
xferlog_enable=YES
```

Use **xferlog_file** option to specify the log file you want to use. The default is shown here:

```
xferlog_file=/var/log/vsftpd.log
```

vsftpd Access Controls

Certain options control access to the FTP site. As previously noted, the **anonymous_enable** option allows anonymous users access, and **local_enable** permits local users to log in to their accounts.

Denying Access

The **deny_email_enable** option lets you deny access by anonymous users, and the **banned_email** file option designates the file (usually **vstfpd.banned**) that holds the e-mail addresses of those users. The **vsftpd.ftpusers** file lists those users that can never be accessed. These are usually system users like root, mail, and nobody. See Table 22-3 for a list of vsftpd files.

User Access

The **userlist_enable** option controls access by users, denying access to those listed in the file designated by the **userlist_file** option (usually **vsftpd.user_list**). If, instead, you want to restrict access to just certain select users, you can change the meaning and usage of the **vsftpd.user_list** file to indicate only those users allowed access, instead of those denied access. To do this, you set the **userlist_deny** option to NO (its default is YES). Only users listed in the **vsftpd.user_list** file will be granted access to the FTP site.

User Restrictions

The **chroot_list_enable** option controls access by local users, letting them access only their home directories, while restricting system access. The **chroot_list_file** option designates the file (usually **vstfpd.chroot**) that lists those users allowed access. You can allow access by all local users with the **chroot_local_user** option. If this option is set, then the file designated by **chroot_list_file** will have an inverse meaning, listing those users not allowed access. In the following example, access by local users is limited to those listed in **vsftpd.chroot_list**:

```
chroot_list_enable=YES
chroot_list_file=/etc/vsftpd.chroot_list
```

File	Description
vsftpd.ftpusers	Users always denied access
vsftpd.user_list	Specified users denied access (allowed access if **userlist_deny** is NO)
vsftpd.chroot_list	Local users allowed access (denied access if **chroot_local_user** is on)
/etc/vsftpd/vsftpd.conf	vsftpd configuration file
/etc/pam.d/vsftpd	PAM vsftpd script
/etc/rc.d/init.d/vsftpd	Service vsftpd server script, stand-alone
/etc/xinetd.d/vsftpd	Xinetd vsftpd server script

TABLE 22-3   Files for **vsftpd**

User Authentication

The **vsftpd** server makes use of the PAM service to authenticate local users that are remotely accessing their accounts through FTP. In the **vsftpd.conf** file, the PAM script used for the server is specified with the **pam_service_name** option.

```
pam_service_name=vsftpd
```

In the **etc/pam.d** directory, you will find a PAM file named **vsftpd** with entries for controlling access to the **vsftpd** server. PAM is currently set up to authenticate users with valid accounts, as well as deny access to users in the **/etc/vsftpd.ftpusers** file. The default **/etc/pam.d/vsftpd** file is shown here:

```
#%PAM-1.0
auth required pam_listfile.so item=user sense=deny
                file=/etc/vsftpd.ftpusers onerr=succeed
auth     required   pam_stack.so service=system-auth
auth     required   pam_shells.so
account required   pam_stack.so service=system-auth
session required   pam_stack.so service=system-auth
```

Command Access

Command usage is highly restricted by **vsftpd**. Most options for the `ls` command that lists files are not allowed. Only the asterisk file-matching operation is supported (see Chapter 8). To enable recursive listing of files in subdirectories, you have to enable the use of the `-R` option by setting the `ls_recurse_enable` option to YES. Some clients, such as **ncftp** (see Chapter 14), will assume that the recursive option is enabled.

vsftpd Virtual Hosts

Though the capability is not inherently built in to **vsftpd**, you can configure and set up the **vsftpd** server to support virtual hosts. *Virtual hosting* is where a single FTP server operates as if it has two or more IP addresses. Several IP addresses can then be used to access the same server. The server will then use a separate FTP user directory and files for each host. With **vsftpd**, this involves manually creating separate FTP users and directories for each virtual host, along with separate **vsftpd** configuration files for each virtual host in the **/etc/vsftpd** directory. **vsftpd** is configured to run as a stand-alone service. Its `/etc/rc.d/init.d/vsftpd` start-up script will automatically search for and read any configuration files listed in the **/etc/vsftpd** directory.

If, on the other hand, you wish to run **vsftpd** as a, **xinetd** service, you would have to create a separate **xinetd** service script for each host in the **/etc/xinetd.d** directory. In effect, you have several **vsftpd** services running in parallel for each separate virtual host. The following example uses two IP addresses for an FTP server:

- First, create an FTP user for each host. Create directories for each host (you could use the one already set up for one of the users). For example, for the first virtual host you could use **FTP-host1**. Be sure to set root ownership and the appropriate permissions.

  ```
  useradd -d /var/ftp-host1 FTP-host1
  chown root.root /var/ftp-host1
  chmod a+rx /var/ftp-host1
  umask 022
  mkdir /var/ftp-host1/pub
  ```

- Set up two corresponding vsftpd service scripts in the **/etc/xinetd.d** directory. The **vsftpd** directory in **/usr/share/doc** has an **xinetd** example script, **vsftpd.xinetd**. Within each, enter a **bind** command to specify the IP address the server will respond to.

```
bind  192.168.0.34
```

- Within the same scripts, enter a **server_args** entry specifying the name of the configuration file to use.

```
server_args = vsftpd-host1.conf
```

- Within the **/etc/vsftpd** directory, create separate configuration files for each virtual host. Within each, specify the FTP user you created for each, using the **ftp_username** entry.

```
ftp_username = FTP-host1
```

vsftpd Virtual Users

Virtual users can be implemented by making use of PAM to authenticate authorized users. In effect, you are allowing access to certain users, while not having to actually set up accounts for them on the FTP server system. First create a PAM login database file to use along with a PAM file in the **/etc/pam.d** directory that will access the database. Then create a virtual FTP user along with corresponding directories that the virtual users will access (see the **vsftpd** documentation at **vsftpd.beasts.org** for more detailed information). Then in the **vsftpd.conf** file, you can disable anonymous FTP:

```
anonymous_enable=NO
local_enable=YES
```

and then enable guest access:

```
guest_enable=YES
guest_username=virtual
```

Web Servers: Apache

L inux distributions provide several Web servers for use on your system. The primary
Web server is Apache, which has almost become the standard Web server for Red Hat
Linux and Fedora distributions. It is a very powerful, stable, and fairly easy-to-
configure system. Other Web servers are also available, such as Tux. Tux is smaller, but very
fast, and is very efficient at handling Web data that does not change. Red Hat and Fedora
Linux provide default configurations for the Web servers, making them usable as soon as
they are installed.

Apache freely supports full secure shell encryption using OpenSSL. There are also
private cryptographic products available only with licensing fees. Instead of obtaining the
licensing directly, you can simply buy a commercial version of Apache that includes such
licensing such as Stronghold and Raven (**www.covalent.net**). Formerly, this kind of restriction
applied to the use of RSA technology only in the United States, where it was once patented.
The RSA patent has since expired, and RSA is now available for use in freely distributed
products like OpenSSL.

Tux

Tux, the Red Hat Content Accelerator, is a static-content Web server designed to be run
very fast from within the Linux kernel. In effect, it runs in kernel space, making response
times much faster than standard user-space Web servers like Apache. As a kernel-space
server, Tux can handle static content such as images very efficiently. At the same time, it can
coordinate with a user-space Web server, like Apache, to provide the dynamic content, like
CGI programs. Tux can even make use of a cache to hold previously generated dynamic
content, using it as if it were static. The ability to coordinate with a user-space Web server
lets you use Tux as your primary Web server. Anything that Tux cannot handle, it will pass
off to the user-space Web server.

NOTE *Tux is freely distributed under the GNU Public License and is included with many distributions.*

The Tux configuration file is located in **/proc/sys/net/tux**. Here you enter parameters
such as `serverport`, `max_doc_size`, and `logfile` (check the Tux reference manual at
www.redhat.com/docs/manuals/tux for a detailed listing). Defaults are already entered;
`serverport`, `clientport`, and `documentroot` are required parameters that must be set.

serverport is the port Tux will use—80 if it is the primary Web server. **clientport** is the port used by the user-space Web server Tux coordinates with, like Apache. **documentroot** specifies the root directory for your Web documents (**/var/www/html** on Red Hat and Fedora).

Ideally, Tux is run as the primary Web server and Apache as the secondary Web server. To configure Apache to run with Tux, the port entry in the Apache **httpd.conf** file needs to be changed from 80 to 8080.

```
Port 8080
```

You can start, stop, and restart the server with the **service** command and the **/etc/rd.d/ init.d/tux** script. Several parameters like **DOCROOT** can be specified as arguments to this Tux command. You can enter them in the **/etc/sysconfig/tux** file.

NOTE *You can also run Tux as an FTP server. In the **/proc/sys/net/tux** directory, you change the contents of the file **serverport** to 21, **application_protocol** to 1, and **nonagle** to 0, and then restart Tux. Use the **generatetuxlist** command in the document root directory to generate FTP directory listings.*

Alternate Web Servers

Other Web servers available for Linux include the Stronghold Enterprise Server and the Apache-SSL server. A listing is provided here.

- Apache-SSL (**www.apache-ssl.org**) is an encrypting Web server based on Apache and OpenSSL (**www.openssl.org**).

- lighthttpd (**www.lighttpd.net/**) is a small, very fast, Web server, included with Fedora.

- Sun Java System Web server (**www.sun.com**) features Java development support and security.

- Zope application server (**www.zope.org**) is an open source Web server with integrated security, Web-based administration and development, and database interface features. It was developed by the Zope Corporation, which also developed the Python programming language.

- Stronghold Enterprise Server (**www.redhat.com/software/stronghold**) is a commercial version of the Apache Web server featuring improved security and administration tools.

- Netscape Enterprise Server (**enterprise.netscape.com**), part of Netscape security solutions, features open standards with high performance.

- You can also use the original NCSA Web server, though it is no longer under development and is not supported (**hoohoo.ncsa.uiuc.edu**).

Apache Web Server

The Apache Web server is a full-featured free HTTP (Web) server developed and maintained by the Apache Server Project. The aim of the project is to provide a reliable, efficient, and easily extensible Web server, with free open source code made available under its own Apache Software License. The server software includes the server daemon, configuration files, management tools, and documentation. The Apache Server Project is maintained by a core group of volunteer programmers and supported by a great many contributors worldwide. The Apache Server Project is one of several projects currently supported by the Apache Software Foundation (formerly known as the Apache Group). This nonprofit organization provides financial, legal, and organizational support for various Apache Open Source software projects, including the Apache HTTPD Server, Java Apache, Jakarta, and XML-Apache. The Web site for the Apache Software Foundation is **www.apache.org**. Table 23-1 lists various Apache-related Web sites.

Apache was originally based on the NCSA Web server developed at the National Center for Supercomputing Applications, University of Illinois, Urbana-Champaign. Apache has since emerged as a server in its own right and has become one of the most popular Web servers in use. Although originally developed for Linux and Unix systems, Apache has become a cross-platform application with Windows and OS/2 versions. Apache provides online support and documentation for its Web server at **httpd.apache.org**. An HTML-based manual is also provided with the server installation. You can use the Apache Configuration Tool to help configure your Apache server easily. It operates on any X Window System window manager, including GNOME and KDE. In addition, you can use the Comanche configuration tool. Webmin conf also provides Apache configuration support.

Java: Apache Jakarta Project

The Apache Jakarta Project supports the development of Open Source Java software; its Web site is located at **jakarta.apache.org**. Currently, the Jakarta Project supports numerous

Web Site	Description
www.apache.org	Apache Software Foundation
httpd.apache.org	Apache HTTP Server Project
jakarta.apache.org	Jakarta Apache Project
www.apache-gui.com	Apache GUI Project
www.comanche.org	Comanche (Configuration Manager for Apache)
www.apache-ssl.org	Apache-SSL server
www.openssl.org	OpenSSL project (Secure Socket Layer)
www.modssl.org	The SSL module (mod_ssl) project to add SSL encryption to an Apache Web server
www.php.net	PHP Hypertext Preprocessor, embedded Web page programming language

TABLE 23-1   Apache-Related Web Sites

projects, including libraries, tools, frameworks, engines, and server applications. Tomcat is an open source implementation of the Java Servlet and JavaServer Pages specifications. Tomcat is designed for use in Apache servers. JMeter is a Java desktop tool to test performance of server resources, such as servlets and CGI scripts. Velocity is a template engine that provides easy access to Java objects. Watchdog is a tool that checks the compatibility of servlet containers. Struts, Cactus, and Tapestry are Java frameworks, established methods for developing Java Web applications.

Linux Apache Installations

Your Linux distribution will normally provide you with the option of installing the Apache Web server during the initial installation of your Linux system. All the necessary directories and configuration files are automatically generated for you. Then, whenever you run Linux, your system is already a fully-functional Web site. Every time you start your system, the Web server will also start up, running continuously. On most distributions, the directory reserved for your Web site data files is **/var/www/html**. Place your Web pages in this directory or in any subdirectories. Your system is already configured to operate as a Web server. All you need to do is perform any needed network server configurations, and then designate the files and directories open to remote users. You needn't do anything else. Once your Web site is connected to a network, remote users can access it.

The Web server normally sets up your Web site in the **/var/www** directory. It also sets up several directories for managing the site. The **/var/www/cgi-bin** directory holds the CGI scripts, and **/var/www/html/manual** holds the Apache manual in HTML format. You can use your browser to examine it. Your Web pages are to be placed in the **/var/www/html** directory. Place your Web site home page there. Your configuration files are located in a different directory, **/etc/httpd/conf**. Table 23-2 lists the various Apache Web server directories and configuration files.

Apache Multiprocessing Modules: MPM

Apache now uses a new architecture that uses multiprocessing modules (MPMs), which are designed to customize Apache to different operating systems, as well as handle certain multiprocessing operations. For the main MPM, a Linux system would use either the prefork or worker MPM, whereas Windows would use the mpm_winnt MPM. The prefork is a standard MPM module designed to be compatible with older Unix and Linux systems, particularly those that do not support threading. It is the module loaded by default by Fedora. The worker MPM implements threading for Apache server processes, a feature supported by the Native POSIX Thread Libraries (NPTL) that are part of Red Hat and Fedora. You can configure the workload parameters for both in the Apache configuration file, **/etc/httpd/conf/httpd.conf**.

Many directives that once resided in the Apache core are now placed in respective modules and MPMs. With this modular design, several directives have been dropped, such as ServerType. Configuration files for these module are located in the **/etc/httpd/conf.d** directory.

Starting and Stopping the Web Server

On most systems, Apache is installed as a stand-alone server, continually running. As noted in Chapter 21, in the discussion of init scripts, your system automatically starts up the Web server daemon, invoking it whenever you start your system. A service script for the Web

Web Site Directories	Description
/var/www/html	Web site Web files
/var/www/cgi-bin	CGI program files
/var/www/html/manual	Apache Web server manual
Configuration Files	**Description**
.htaccess	Directory-based configuration files; an **.htaccess** file holds directives to control access to files within the directory in which it is located
/etc/httpd/conf	Directory for Apache Web server configuration files
/etc/httpd/conf/httpd.conf	Apache Web server configuration file
/etc/httpd/conf.d	Directory holding module configuration files like **ssl.conf** for SSL and **php.conf** for PHP
Service Scripts	**Description**
/etc/rc.d/init.d/httpd	Service script for Web server daemon
/etc/sysconfig/httpd	Red Hat and Fedora configuration options for Web server daemon, as used by the httpd service script
Application and Module Files	**Description**
/usr/sbin	Location of the Apache Web server program file and utilities
/usr/share/doc/	Apache Web server documentation
/var/log/http	Location of Apache log files
/etc/httpd/modules	Directory holding Apache modules
/etc/httpd/run	Directory holding Apache process IDs

TABLE 23-2   Apache Web Server Files and Directories (RPM Installation)

server called **httpd** is in the **/etc/rc.d/init.d** directory. Symbolic links through which this script is run are located in corresponding runlevel directories. You will usually find the **S85httpd** link to **/etc/rc.d/init.d/httpd** in the runlevel 3 and 5 directories, **/etc/rc.d/rc3.d** and **/etc/rc.d/rc5.d**. You can use the **chkconfig** command or the System V Init Editor to set the runlevels at which the httpd server will start, creating links in appropriate runlevel directories. The following command will set up the Web server (httpd) to start up at runlevels 3 and 5 (see Chapters 21 and 27 for more details on runlevels):

```
# chkconfig --level 35 httpd on
```

You can also use the **service** command to start and stop the httpd server manually. This may be helpful when you are testing or modifying your server. The **httpd** script with the **start** option starts the server, the **stop** option stops it, and **restart** will restart it. Simply killing the Web process directly is not advisable.

```
# service httpd restart
```

The **service** command uses the **/etc/sysconfig/httpd** configuration file to set options for the **httpd** service script. Here you can specify such options as whether to use the worker or prefork Apache MPM modules.

Apache also provides a control tool called **apachectl** (Apache control) for managing your Web server. With **apachectl**, you can start, stop, and restart the server from the command line. The **apachectl** command takes several arguments: **start** to start the server, **stop** to stop it, **restart** to shut down and restart the server, and **graceful** to shut down and restart gracefully. In addition, you can use **apachectl** to check the syntax of your configuration files with the **config** argument. You can also use **apachectl** as a system service file for your server in the **/etc/rc.d** directory.

Remember, **httpd** is a script that calls the actual **httpd** daemon. You could call the daemon directly using its full pathname. This daemon has several options. The **-d** option enables you to specify a directory for the **httpd** program if it is different from the default directory. With the **-f** option, you can specify a configuration file different from **httpd.conf**. The **-v** option displays the version.

```
# /usr/sbin/httpd -v
```

To check your Web server, start your Web browser and enter the Internet domain name address of your system. For the system **turtle.mytrek.com**, the user enters **http://turtle.mytrek.com**. This should display the home page you placed in your Web root directory. A simple way to do this is to use Lynx, the command line Web browser. Start Lynx, and type **g** to open a line where you can enter a URL for your own system. Lynx displays your Web site's home page. Be sure to place an **index.html** file in the **/var/www/html** directory first.

Once you have your server running, you can check its performance with the **ab** benchmarking tool, also provided by Apache: **ab** shows you how many requests at a time your server can handle. Options include **-v,** which enables you to control the level of detail displayed, **-n,** which specifies the number of requests to handle (default is 1), and **-t,** which specifies a time limit.

NOTE *Currently there is no support for running Apache under* **xinetd***. In Apache 2.0, such support is determined by choosing an MPM module designed to run on* **xinetd***.*

Apache Configuration Files

Configuration directives are placed in the **httpd.conf** configuration file. A documented version of the **httpd.conf** configuration file is installed automatically in **/etc/httpd/conf**. It is strongly recommended that you consult this file on your system. It contains detailed descriptions and default entries for Apache directives.

Any of the directives in the main configuration files can be overridden on a per-directory basis using a **.htaccess** file located within a directory. Although originally designed only for access directives, the **.htaccess** file can also hold any resource directives, enabling you to tailor how Web pages are displayed in a particular directory. You can configure access to **.htaccess** files in the **httpd.conf** file.

In addition, many of the modules provided for Apache have their own configuration files. These are places in the **/etc/httpd/conf.d** directory.

Apache Configuration and Directives

Apache configuration operations take the form of directives entered into the Apache configuration files. With these directives, you can enter basic configuration information, such as your server name, or perform more complex operations, such as implementing virtual hosts. The design is flexible enough to enable you to define configuration features for particular directories and different virtual hosts. Apache has a variety of different directives performing operations as diverse as controlling directory access, assigning file icon formats, and creating log files. Most directives set values such as **DirectoryRoot**, which holds the root directory for the server's Web pages, or **Port**, which holds the port on the system that the server listens on for requests. The syntax for a simple directive is shown here:

```
directive option option ...
```

Certain directives create blocks able to hold directives that apply to specific server components (also referred to as sectional directives). For example, the **Directory** directive is used to define a block within which you place directives that apply only to a particular directory. Block directives are entered in pairs: a beginning directive and a terminating directive. The terminating directive defines the end of the block and consists of the same name beginning with a slash. Block directives take an argument that specifies the particular object to which the directives apply. For the **Directory** block directive, you must specify a directory name to which it will apply. The **<Directory** *mydir***>** block directive creates a block whose directives within it apply to the *mydir* directory. The block is terminated by a **</Directory>** directive. The **<VirtualHost** *hostaddress***>** block directive is used to configure a specific virtual Web server and must include the IP or domain name address used for that server. **</VirtualHost>** is its terminating directive. Any directives you place within this block are applied to that virtual Web server. The **<Limit** *method***>** directive specifies the kind of access method you want to limit, such as GET or POST. The access control directives located within the block list the controls you are placing on those methods. The syntax for a block directive is as follows:

```
<block-directive option ... >
  directive option ...
  directive option ...
</block-directive>
```

Usually, directives are placed in one of the main configuration files. Directory directives in those files can be used to configure a particular directory. However, Apache also makes use of directory-based configuration files. Any directory may have its own **.htaccess** file that holds directives to configure only that directory. If your site has many directories, or if any directories have special configuration needs, you can place their configuration directives in their **.htaccess** files, instead of filling the main configuration file with specific **Directory** directives for each one. You can control what directives in a **.htaccess** file take precedence over those in the main configuration files. If your site allows user- or client-controlled directories, you may want to carefully monitor or disable the use of **.htaccess** files in them. (It is possible for directives in a **.htaccess** file to override those in the standard configuration files unless disabled with AllowOverride directives.)

Global Configuration

The standard Apache configuration has three sections: Global Settings, Server Settings, and Virtual Hosts. The Global settings control the basic operation and performance of the Web server. Here you set configuration locations, process ID files, timing, settings for the MPM module used, and what Apache modules to load.

The **ServerTokens** directive prevents disclosure of any optional modules your server is using. The **ServerRoot** directive specifies where your Web server configuration, error, and log files are kept. This is **/etc/httpd** on Fedora, which will also include your error and log files, as well as the server modules. This server root directory is then used as a prefix to other directory entries.

```
ServerRoot /etc/httpd
```

The server's process ID (PID) file is usually **/etc/httpd/run/httpd.pid**, as set by **PidFile**.

```
PidFile run/httpd.pid
```

Connection and request timing is handled by **Timeout**, **KeepAlive**, **MaxKeepAlive**, and **KeepAliveTimeout** directives. **Timeout** is the time in seconds that the Web server times out a send or receive request. **KeepAlive** allows persistent connections, several requests from a client on the same connection. This is turned off by default. **KeepAliveRequests** sets the maximum number of requests on a persistent connection. **KeepAliveTimeout** is the time that a given connection to a client is kept open to receive more requests from that client.

The **Listen** directive will bind the server to a specific port or IP address. By default this is port 80.

```
Listen 80
```

Modules

Much of the power and flexibility of the Apache Web server comes from its use of modules to extend its capabilities. Apache is implemented with a core set of directives. Modules can be created that hold definitions of other directives. They can be loaded into Apache, enabling you to use those directives for your server. A standard set of modules is included with the Apache distribution, though you can download others and even create your own. For example, the mod_autoindex module holds the directives for automatically indexing directories (as described in the following section). The mod_mime module holds the MIME type and handler directives. Modules are loaded with the **LoadModule** directive. You can find **LoadModule** directives in the **httpd.conf** configuration file for most of the standard modules.

```
LoadModule mime_module modules/mod_mime.so
```

LoadModule takes as its arguments the name of the module and its location. The modules are stored in the **/etc/httpd/modules** directory, referenced here by the **modules/** prefix.

Configuration files for different modules are located in **/etc/httpd/conf.d** directory. These are also loaded using the **Include** directive. The following inserts all configuration files (those with a .conf extension) in the **/etc/httpd/conf.d** directory.

```
Include conf.d/*.conf
```

The **apxs** application provided with the Apache package can be used to build Apache extension modules. With the **apxs** application, you can compile Apache module source code in C and create dynamically shared objects that can be loaded with the **LoadModule** directive. The **apxs** application requires that the mod_so module be part of your Apache application. It includes extensive options such as **-n** to specify the module name, **-a** to add an entry for it in the **httpd.conf** file, and **-i** to install the module on your Web server.

You can find a complete listing of Apache Web configuration directives at the Apache Web site, **httpd.apache.org**, and in the Apache manual located in your site's Web site root directory. On many systems, this is located in the manual subdirectory in the Web site default directory set up by the distribution (this is **/var/www/manual**).

MPM Configuration

Configuration settings for MPM prefork and worker modules let you tailor your Apache Web server to your workload demands. Default entries will already be set for a standard Web server operating under a light load. You can modify these settings for different demands.

Fedora conditionally configures two MPM modules commonly available to Unix and Linux systems, prefork and worker. The prefork module supports one thread per process, which maintains compatibility with older systems and modules. The worker module supports multiple threads for each process, placing a much lower load on system resources. They share several of the same directives, such as **StartServer** and **MaxRequestPerChild**. You can decide which module to load with the **httpd** service script by setting the HTTPD option in the **/etc/sysconfig/httpd** file. The prefork module is loaded by default.

Apache runs a single parent process with as many child process as are needed to handle requests. Configuration for MPM modules focuses on the number of processes that should be available. The prefork module will list server numbers, as a process is started for each server; worker will control threads, since it uses threads for each process. The **StartServer** directives lists the number of server processes to start for both modules. This will normally be larger for prefork than for worker.

In the prefork module you need to set minimum and maximum settings for spare servers. **MaxClients** sets the maximum number of servers that can be started, and **ServerLimit** sets the number of servers allowed. The **MaxRequestsPerChild** sets the maximum number of requests allowed for a server.

In the worker module, **MaxClients** also sets the maximum number of client threads, and **ThreadsPerChild** sets the number of threads for each server. **MaxRequestsPerChild** limits the maximum number of requests for a server. Spare thread limits are also configured.

The directives serve as a kind of throttle on the Web server access, controlling processes to keep available and limit the resources that can be used. In the prefork configuration, Fedora sets the **StartServer** number to 8, and the spare minimum to 5, with the maximum spare as 20. This means that initially 8 server processes with be started up, waiting for requests, along with 5 spare processes. When server processes are no longer being used, they will be terminated until the number of these spare processes is less than 20. The maximum number of server processes that can be started is 256. The maximum number of connections per server process is set at 4,000.

In the worker MPM, only 2 server processes are initially started. Spare threads are set at 25 and 75. The maximum number of threads is set at 150, with the threads per child at 25.

Server Configuration

Certain directives are used to configure your server's overall operations. These directives are placed midway in the **httpd.conf** configuration file, directly under the section labeled Server Settings. Some directives require pathnames, whereas others only need to be turned on or off with the keywords **on** and **off**. The default **httpd.conf** file already contains these directives. Some are commented out with a preceding **#** symbol. You can activate a directive by removing its **#** sign. Many of the entries are preceded by comments explaining their purpose.

The following is an example of the **ServerAdmin** directive used to set the address where users can send mail for administrative issues. You replace the **you@your.address** entry with the address you want to use to receive system administration mail. By default, this is set to **root@localhost**.

```
# ServerAdmin: Your address, where problems should be e-mailed.
ServerAdmin you@your.address
```

A Web server usually uses port 80, which is the Apache default. If you want to use a different port, specify it with the **Port** directive.

```
Port 80
```

The **ServerName** directive holds the hostname for your Web server. Specifying a hostname is important to avoid unnecessary DNS lookup failures that can hang your server. Notice the entry is commented with a preceding **#**. Simply remove the **#** and type your Web server's hostname in place of *new.host.name.* If you are using a different port than 80, be sure to specify it attached to the host name, as in **turtle.mytrek.com:80**. Here is the original default entry:

```
# ServerName allows you to set a hostname which is sent
# back to clients for your server if it's different than the
# one the program would get (i.e. use
# "www" instead of the host's real name).

#ServerName new.host.name:80
```

A modified **ServerName** entry would look like this:

```
ServerName turtle.mytrek.com
```

When receiving URL requests for the server system, like those for local files on the system, the **UseCanonicalName** directive will use the **ServerName** and **Port** directives to generate the host URL server name. When off, it will just use the name supplied by the client request. This can be confusing if the Web server is referenced by one name but uses another, like **www.mytrek.com** used to reference **turtle.mytrek.com**. **UseCanonicalName** set to on will overcomes this problem, generating the correct local URL.

On Fedora systems, entries have already been made for the standard Web server installation using **/var/www** as your Web site directory. You can tailor your Web site to your own needs by changing the appropriate directives. The **DocumentRoot** directive determines the home directory for your Web pages.

```
DocumentRoot /var/www/html
```

NOTE *You can also configure Apache to operate as just a proxy and/or cache server. Default proxy and cache server directives are already included in the **httpd.conf** file. The **ProxyRequests** directive turns proxy activity on. Caching can be configured with directives like **CacheRoot** to specify the cache directory, **CacheSize** for the cache size (500KB default), and **CacheMaxExpire** to set a time limit on unmodified documents.*

Directory-Level Configuration: .htaccess and <Directory>

One of the most flexible aspects of Apache is its ability to configure individual directories. With the **Directory** directive, you can define a block of directives that apply only to a particular directory. Such a directive can be placed in the **httpd.conf** or **access.conf** configuration files. You can also use a **.htaccess** file within a particular directory to hold configuration directives. Those directives are then applied only to that directory. The name ".htaccess" is actually set with the **AccessFileName** directive. You can change this if you want.

```
AccessFileName .htaccess
```

A Directory block begins with a `<Directory` *pathname>* directive, where *pathname* is the directory to be configured. The ending directive uses the same `<>` symbols, but with a slash preceding the word "Directory": `</Directory>`. Directives placed within this block apply only to the specified directory. The following example denies access to only the **mypics** directory by requests from **www.myvids.com**.

```
<Directory /var/www/html/mypics>
 Order Deny,Allow
 Deny from www.myvids.com
</Directory>
```

With the **Options** directive, you can enable certain features in a directory, such as the use of symbolic links, automatic indexing, execution of CGI scripts, and content negotiation. The default is the **All** option, which turns on all features except content negotiation (**Multiviews**). The following example enables automatic indexing (**Indexes**), symbolic links (**FollowSymLinks**), and content negotiation (**Multiviews**).

```
Options Indexes FollowSymLinks Multiviews
```

Configurations made by directives in main configuration files or in upper-level directories are inherited by lower-level directories. Directives for a particular directory held in **.htaccess** files and Directory blocks can be allowed to override those configurations. This capability can be controlled by the **AllowOverride** directive. With the **all** argument, **.htaccess** files can override any previous configurations. The **none** argument disallows overrides, effectively disabling the **.htaccess** file. You can further control the override of specific groups of directives. **AuthConfig** enables use of authorization directives, **FileInfo** is for type directives, **Indexes** is for indexing directives, **Limit** is for access control directives, and **Options** is for the options directive.

```
AllowOverride all
```

Access Control

With access control directives, such as **allow** and **deny**, you can control access to your Web site by remote users and hosts. The **allow** directive followed by a list of hostnames restricts access to only those hosts. The **deny** directive with a list of hostnames denies access by those systems. The argument `all` applies the directive to all hosts. The **order** directive specifies in what order the access control directives are to be applied. Other access control directives, such as **require**, can establish authentication controls, requiring users to log in. The access control directives can be used globally to control access to the entire site or placed within **Directory** directives to control access to individual directives. In the following example, all users are allowed access:

```
order allow,deny
allow from all
```

URL Pathnames

Certain directives can modify or complete pathname segments of a URL used to access your site. The pathname segment of the URL specifies a particular directory or Web page on your site. Directives enable you to alias or redirect pathnames, as well as to select a default Web page. With the **Alias** directive, you can let users access resources located in other parts of your system, on other file systems, or on other Web sites. An alias can use a URL for sites on the Internet, instead of a pathname for a directory on your system. With the **Redirect** directive, you can redirect a user to another site.

```
Alias /mytrain /home/dylan/trainproj
Redirect /mycars http://www.myautos.com/mycars
```

If Apache is given only a directory to access, rather than a specific Web page, it looks for an index Web page located in that directory and displays it. The possible names for a default Web page are listed by the **DirectoryIndex** directive. The name usually used is **index.html**, but you can add others. The standard names are shown here. When Apache is given only a Web directory to access, it looks for and displays the **index.html** Web page located in it.

```
DirectoryIndex index.html index.shtml index.cgi
```

Apache also lets a user maintain Web pages located in a special subdirectory in the user's home directory, rather than in the main Web site directory. Using a ~ followed by the username accesses this directory. The name of this directory is specified with the **UserDir** directive. The default name is **public_html**, as shown here. The site **turtle.mytrek.com/~dylan** accesses the directory **turtle.mytrek.com/home/dylan/public_html** on the host **turtle.mytrek.com**.

```
UserDir public_html
```

If you want, instead, to allow people to use a full pathname, then use a pathname reference. For example, for the user **dylan**, **/usr/www** would translate to a URL reference of **/usr/www/dylan**, where the HTML files would be located; **/home/*/www** would translate to **/home/dylan/www**, a www directory in the user **dylan**'s home directory.

```
UserDir /usr/www
UserDir /home/*/www
```

Userdir access is commented out by default in the standard configuration file. Usually there are users like **root** that you want access denied to. With the disable and enable options, you can open access to certain users, while disabling access to others, as shown here:

```
UserDir disable root
UserDir disabled
UserDir enabled dylan chris justin
```

MIME Types

When a browser accesses Web pages on a Web site, it is often accessing many different kinds of objects, including HTML files, picture or sound files, and script files. To display these objects correctly, the browser must have some indication of what kind of objects they are. A JPEG picture file is handled differently from a simple text file. The server provides this type information in the form of MIME types (see Chapter 13). MIME types are the same types used for sending attached files through Internet mailers, such as Pine. Each kind of object is associated with a given MIME type. Provided with the MIME type, the browser can correctly handle and display the object.

The MIME protocol associates a certain type with files of a given extension. For example, files with a **.jpg** extension would have the MIME type image/jpeg. The **TypesConfig** directive holds the location of the **mime.types** file, which lists all the MIME types and their associated file extensions. **DefaultType** is the default MIME type for any file whose type cannot be determined. **AddType** enables you to modify the **mime.type** types list without editing the MIME file.

```
TypesConfig /etc/mime.types
DefaultType text/plain
```

Other type directives are used to specify actions to be taken on certain documents. **AddEncoding** lets browsers decompress compressed files on the fly. **AddHandler** maps file extensions to actions, and **AddLanguage** enables you to specify the language for a document. The following example marks filenames with the **.gz** extension as gzip-encoded files and files with the **.fr** extension as French language files:

```
AddEncoding x-gzip gz
AddLanguage fr .fr
```

A Web server can display and execute many different types of files and programs. Not all Web browsers are able to display all those files, though. Older browsers are the most limited. Some browsers, such as Lynx, are not designed to display even simple graphics. To allow a Web browser to display a page, the server negotiates with it to determine the type of files it can handle. To enable such negotiation, you need to enable the **multiviews** option.

```
Option multiviews
```

CGI Files

Common Gateway Interface (CGI) files are programs that can be executed by Web browsers accessing your site. CGI files are usually initiated by Web pages that execute the program as part of the content they display. Traditionally, CGI programs were placed in a directory called **cgi-bin** and could be executed only if they resided in such a special directory.

Usually, only one **cgi-bin** directory exists per Web site. Distributions will normally set up a **cgi-bin** directory in the default Web server directory (**/var/www/cgi-bin** on Fedora). Here, you place any CGI programs that can be executed on your Web site. The **ScriptAlias** directive specifies an alias for your **cgi-bin** directory. Any Web pages or browsers can use the alias to reference this directory.

```
ScriptAlias /cgi-bin/ /var/www/cgi-bin/
```

Automatic Directory Indexing

When given a URL for a directory instead of an HTML file, and when no default Web page is in the directory, Apache creates a page on the fly and displays it. This is usually only a listing of the different files in the directory. In effect, Apache indexes the items in the directory for you. You can set several options for generating and displaying such an index. If **FancyIndexing** is turned on, Web page items are displayed with icons and column headers that can be used to sort the listing.

```
FancyIndexing on
```

Authentication

Your Web server can also control access on a per-user or per-group basis to particular directories on your Web site. You can require various levels for authentication. Access can be limited to particular users and require passwords, or expanded to allow members of a group access. You can dispense with passwords altogether or set up an anonymous type of access, as used with FTP.

To apply authentication directives to a certain directory, you place those directives within either a **Directory** block or the directory's **.htaccess** file. You use the **require** directive to determine what users can access the directory. You can list particular users or groups. The **AuthName** directive provides the authentication realm to the user, the name used to identify the particular set of resources accessed by this authentication process. The **AuthType** directive specifies the type of authentication, such as basic or digest. A **require** directive requires also **AuthType**, **AuthName**, and directives specifying the locations of group and user authentication files. In the following example, only the users **george**, **robert**, and **mark** are allowed access to the **newpics** directory:

```
<Directory /var/www/html/newpics
    AuthType Basic
    AuthName Newpics
    AuthUserFile /web/users
    AuthGroupFile /web/groups
    <Limit GET POST>
        require users george robert mark
    </Limit>
</Directory>
```

The next example allows group access by administrators to the CGI directory:

```
<Directory /var/www/html/cgi-bin
    AuthType Basic
```

```
    AuthName CGI
    AuthGroupFile /web/groups
    <Limit GET POST>
        require groups admin
    </Limit>
s</Directory>
```

To set up anonymous access for a directory, place the **Anonymous** directive with the user anonymous as its argument in the directory's Directory block or **.htaccess** file. You can also use the **Anonymous** directive to provide access to particular users without requiring passwords from them.

Apache maintains its own user and group authentication files specifying what users and groups are allowed access to which directories. These files are normally simple flat files, such as your system's password and group files. They can become large, however, possibly slowing down authentication lookups. As an alternative, many sites have used database management files in place of these flat files. Database methods are then used to access the files, providing a faster response time. Apache has directives for specifying the authentication files, depending on the type of file you are using. The **AuthUserfile** and **AuthGroupFile** directives are used to specify the location of authentication files that have a standard flat file format. The **AuthDBUserFile** and **AuthDBGroupFile** directives are used for DB database files, and the **AuthDBMGUserFIle** and **AuthDBMGGroupFile** are used for DBMG database files.

The programs **htdigest**, **htpasswd**, and **dbmmanage** are tools provided with the Apache software package for creating and maintaining *user authentication files*, which are user password files listing users who have access to specific directories or resources on your Web site. The **htdigest** and **htpasswd** programs manage a simple flat file of user authentication records, whereas **dbmmanage** uses a more complex database management format. If your user list is extensive, you may want to use a database file for fast lookups. **htdigest** takes as its arguments the authentication file, the realm, and the username, creating or updating the user entry. **htpasswd** can also employ encryption on the password. **dbmmanage** has an extensive set of options to add, delete, and update user entries. A variety of different database formats are used to set up such files. Three common ones are Berkeley DB2, NDBM, and GNU GBDM. **dbmmanage** looks for the system libraries for these formats in that order. Be careful to be consistent in using the same format for your authentication files.

Log Files

Apache maintains logs of all requests by users to your Web site. By default, these logs include records using the Common Log Format (CLF). The record for each request takes up a line composed of several fields: host, identity check, authenticated user (for logins), the date, the request line submitted by the client, the status sent to the client, and the size of the object sent in bytes.

Webalizer

Reports on Web logs can be generated using the Webalizer tool. Webalizer will display information on your Web site usage. When you run the `webalizer` command, usage reports will be placed in the **/var/www/html/usage** directory. Access the index page to display a page with links to monthly reports, **file:/var/www/html/usage/index.html**. Report configuration is specified in the **/etc/webalizer.conf** file. Previous summaries are kept in the **/etc/webalizer.history** file.

Customizing Logs

Using the **LogFormat** and **CustomLog** directives, you can customize your log record to add more fields with varying levels of detail. These directives use a format string consisting of field specifiers to determine the fields to record in a log record. You add whatever fields you want and in any order. A field specifier consists of a percent (%) symbol followed by an identifying character. For example, **%h** is the field specifier for a remote host, **%b** for the size in bytes, and **%s** for the status. See the documentation for the mod_log_config module for a complete listing. You should quote fields whose contents may take up more than one word. The quotes themselves must be quoted with a backslash to be included in the format string. The following example is the Common Log Format implemented as a **FormatLog** directive:

```
FormatLog "%h %l %u %t \"%r\" %s %b"
```

Certain field specifiers in the log format can be qualified to record specific information. The **%i** specifier records header lines in requests the server receives. The reference for the specific header line to record is placed within braces between the **%** and the field specifier. For example, **User-agent** is the header line that indicates the browser software used in the request. To record User-agent header information, use the conversion specifier **%{User-agent}i**.

To maintain compatibility with NCSA servers, Apache originally implemented **AgentLog** and **RefererLog** directives to record User-agent and Referer headers. These have since been replaced by qualified **%i** field specifiers used for the **LogFormat** and **CustomLog** directives. A Referer header records link information from clients, detecting who may have links to your site. The following is an NCSA-compliant log format:

```
"%h %l %u %t \"%r\" %s %b\"%{Referer}i\" \"%{User-agent}i\"".
```

Generating and Managing Log Files

Instead of maintaining one large log file, you can create several log files using the **CustomLog** or **TransferLog** directive. This is helpful for virtual hosts where you may want to maintain a separate log file for each host. You use the **FormatLog** directive to define a default format for log records. The **TransferLog** then uses this default as its format when creating a new log file. **CustomLog** combines both operations, enabling you to create a new file and to define a format for it.

```
FormatLog "%h %l %u %t \"%r\" %s %b"
# Create a new log file called myprojlog using the FormatLog format
TransferLog myprojlog
# Create a new log file called mypicslog using its own format
CustomLog mypicslog "%h %l %u %t \"%r\" %s %b"
```

Apache provides two utilities for processing and managing log files: **logresolve** resolves IP addresses in your log file to hostnames; **rotatelogs** rotates log files without having to kill the server. You can specify the rotation time.

NOTE *The Apache Web server can also provide detailed reports on server activity and configuration, letting you display this information to remote servers. The **Location** directive server-info will display the configuration details of your Web server, and the **server-status** directive will show Web processes. The pages server-info and server-status will display the reports, as in **http://localhost/server-info**. Use the **ExtendedStatus** directive to enable detailed reports.*

Virtual Hosting on Apache

Virtual hosting allows the Apache Web server to host multiple Web sites as part of its own. In effect, the server can act as several servers, each hosted Web site appearing separate to outside users. Apache supports both IP address–based and name-based virtual hosting. IP address–based virtual hosts use valid registered IP addresses, whereas name-based virtual hosts use fully qualified domain addresses. These domain addresses are provided by the host header from the requesting browser. The server can then determine the correct virtual host to use on the basis of the domain name alone. Note that SSL servers require IP virtual hosting. See **httpd.apache.org** for more information.

IP-Based Virtual Hosting

In the IP address–based virtual hosting method, your server must have a different IP address for each virtual host. The IP address you use is already set up to reference your system. Network system administration operations can set up your machine to support several IP addresses. Your machine could have separate physical network connections for each one, or a particular connection could be configured to listen for several IP addresses at once. In effect, any of the IP addresses can access your system.

You can configure Apache to run a separate daemon for each virtual host, separately listening for each IP address, or you can have a single daemon running that listens for requests for all the virtual hosts. To set up a single daemon to manage all virtual hosts, use **VirtualHost** directives. To set up a separate daemon for each host, also use the **Listen** directive.

Name-Based Virtual Hosting

With IP-based virtual hosting, you are limited to the number of IP addresses your system supports. With name-based virtual hosting, you can support any number of virtual hosts using no additional IP addresses. With only a single IP address for your machine, you can still support an unlimited number of virtual hosts. Such a capability is made possible by the HTTP/1.1 protocol, which lets a server identify the name by which it is being accessed. This method requires the client, the remote user, to use a browser that supports the HTTP/1.1 protocol, as current browsers do (though older ones may not). A browser using such a protocol can send a host header specifying the particular host to use on a machine.

If your system has only one IP address, implementing virtual hosts prevents access to your main server with that address. You could no longer use your main server as a Web server directly; you could use it only indirectly to manage your virtual hosts. You could configure a virtual host to manage your main server's Web pages. You would then use your main server to support a set of virtual hosts that would function as Web sites, rather than the main server operating as one site directly. If your machine has two or more IP addresses, you can use one for the main server and the other for your virtual hosts. You can even mix

IP-based virtual hosts and name-based virtual hosts on your server. You can also use separate IP addresses to support different sets of virtual hosts. You can further have several domain addresses access the same virtual host. To do so, place a **ServerAlias** directive listing the domain names within the selected **VirtualHost** block.

```
ServerAlias www.mypics.com www.greatpics.com
```

Requests sent to the IP address used for your virtual hosts have to match one of the configured virtual domain names. To catch requests that do not match one of these virtual hosts, you can set up a default virtual host using _default_:*. Unmatched requests are then handled by this virtual host.

```
<VirtualHost _default_:*>
```

Dynamic Virtual Hosting

If you have implemented many virtual hosts that have the same configuration on your server, you can use a technique called *dynamic virtual hosting* to have these virtual hosts generated dynamically. The code for implementing your virtual hosts becomes much smaller, and as a result, your server accesses them faster. Adding yet more virtual hosts becomes a simple matter of creating appropriate directories and adding entries for them in the DNS server.

To make dynamic virtual hosting work, the server uses commands in the mod_vhost_ alias module (supported in Apache versions 1.3.6 and up) to rewrite both the server name and the document root to those of the appropriate virtual server (for older Apache versions before 1.3.6, you use the mod_rewrite module). Dynamic virtual hosting can be either name-based or IP-based. In either case, you have to set the **UseCanonicalName** directive in such a way as to allow the server to use the virtual hostname instead of the server's own name. For name-based hosting, you simply turn off **UseCanonicalName**. This allows your server to obtain the hostname from the host header of the user request. For IP-based hosting, you set the **UseCanonicalName** directive to DNS. This allows the server to look up the host in the DNS server.

```
UseCanonicalName Off
UseCanonicalName DNS
```

You then have to enable the server to locate the different document root directories and CGI bin directories for your various virtual hosts. You use the **VirtualDocumentRoot** directive to specify the template for virtual hosts' directories. For example, if you place the different host directories in the **/var/www/hosts** directory, then you could set the **VirtualDocumentRoot** directive accordingly.

```
VirtualDocumentRoot /var/www/hosts/%0/html
```

The %0 will be replaced with the virtual host's name when that virtual host is accessed. It is important that you create the dynamic virtual host's directory using that host's name. For example, for a dynamic virtual host called **www.mygolf.org**, you would create a directory named **/var/www/hosts/www.mygolf.org**. Then create subdirectories for the document root and CGI programs, as in **/var/www/hosts/www.mygolf.org/html**. For the CGI directory, use the **VirtualScriptAlias** directive to specify the CGI subdirectory you use.

```
VirtualScriptAlias /var/www/hosts/%0/cgi-bin
```

A simple example of name-based dynamic virtual hosting directives follows:

```
UseCanonicalName Off
VirtualDocumentRoot /var/www/hosts/%0/html
VirtualScriptAlias /var/www/hosts/%0/cgi-bin
```

If a request was made for **www.mygolf.com/html/mypage**, that would evaluate to

```
/var/www/hosts/www.mygolf.com/html/mypage
```

A simple example of dynamic virtual hosting is shown here:

```
UseCanonicalName Off

NameVirtualHost 192.168.1.5

<VirtualHost 192.168.1.5>
 ServerName www.mygolf.com
 ServerAdmin webmaster@mail.mygolf.com
 VirtualDocumentRoot /var/www/hosts/%0/html
 VirtualScriptAlias /var/www/hosts/%0/cgi-bin
 ...
</VirtualHost>
```

To implement IP-based dynamic virtual hosting instead, set the **UseCanonicalName** to DNS instead of Off.

```
UseCanonicalName DNS
VirtualDocumentRoot /var/www/hosts/%0/html
VirtualScriptAlias /var/www/hosts/%0/cgi-bin
```

Interpolated Strings

The mod_vhost_alias module supports various interpolated strings, each beginning with a **%** symbol and followed by a number. As you have seen, **%0** references the entire Web address. **%1** references only the first segment, **%2** references the second, **%-1** references the last part, and **%2+** references from the second part on. For example, if you want to use only the second part of a Web address for the directory name, you would use the following directives:

```
VirtualDocumentRoot /var/www/hosts/%2/html
VirtualScriptAlias /var/www/hosts/%2/cgi-bin
```

In this case, a request made for **www.mygolf.com/html/mypage** would use only the second part of the Web address. This would be "mygolf" in **www.mygolf.com**, and would evaluate to

```
/var/www/hosts/mygolf/html/mypage
```

If you used **%2+** instead, as in **/var/www/hosts/%2+/html**, the request for **www.mygolf .com/html/mypage** would evaluate to

```
/var/www/hosts/mygolf.com/html/mypage
```

The same method works for IP addresses, where `%1` references the first IP address segment, `%2` references the second, and so on.

Logs for Virtual Hosts

One drawback of dynamic virtual hosting is that you can set up only one log for all your hosts. However, you can create your own shell program to simply cut out the entries for the different hosts in that log.

```
LogFormat "%V %h %l %u %t \"%r\" %s %b" vcommon
CustomLog logs/access_log vcommon
```

IP Addressing

Implementing dynamic virtual hosting in the standard way as shown previously will slow down the process, as your server will have to perform a DNS lookup to discover the name of your server using its IP address. You can avoid this step by simply using the IP address for your virtual host's directory. So, for IP virtual host 192.198.1.6, you would create a directory **/var/www/hosts/192.198.1.6**, with an **html** subdirectory for that host's document root. You would use the **VirtualDocumentRootIP** and **VirtualScriptAliasIP** directives to use IP addresses as directory names. Now the IP address can be mapped directly to the document root directory name, no longer requiring a DNS lookup. Also be sure to include the IP address in your log, **%A**.

```
UseCanonicalName DNS
LogFormat "%A %h %l %u %t \"%r\" %s %b" vcommon
CustomLog logs/access_log vcommon
VirtualDocumentRootIP /var/www/hosts/%0/html
VirtualScriptAliasIP /var/www/hosts/%0/cgi-bin
```

Server-Side Includes

Server-side includes (SSIs) are designed to provide a much more refined control of your Web site content, namely the Web pages themselves. Server-side includes are Apache directives placed within particular Web pages as part of the page's HTML code. You can configure your Apache Web server to look for SSI directives in particular Web pages and execute them. First, you have to use the **Options** directive with the **include** option to allow SSI directives,

```
Options Includes
```

You need to instruct the server to parse particular Web pages. The easiest way to enable parsing is to instruct Apache to parse HTML files with specified extensions. Usually, the extension **.shtml** is used for Web pages that have SSI directories. In fact, in the default Apache configuration files, you can find the following entry to enable parsing for SSI directives in HTML files. The **AddType** directive here adds the **.shtml** type as an HTML type of file, and the **AddHandler** directive specifies that **.shtml** files are to be parsed (server-parsed):

```
# To use server-parsed HTML files
AddType text/html .shtml
AddHandler server-parsed .shtml
```

Instead of creating a separate type of file, you can use the **XBitHack** directive to have Apache parse any executable file for SSI directives. In other words, any file with execute permission (see Chapter 30) will be parsed for SSI directives.

SSI directives operate much like statements in a programming language. You can define variables, create loops, and use tests to select alternate directives. An SSI directive consists of an element followed by attributes that can be assigned values. The syntax for a SSI directive is shown here:

```
<!--#element attribute=value ... -->
```

You can think of an element as operating much like a command in a programming language, and attributes as its arguments. For example, to assign a value to a variable, you use the **set** element with the variable assignment as its attribute. The **if** directive displays any following text on the given Web page. The **if** directive takes as its attribute **expr**, which is assigned the expression to test. The test is able to compare two strings using standard comparison operators such as <=, !=, or =. Variables used in the test are evaluated with the $ operator.

```
<!--#set myvar="Goodbye" -->
<!--#if expr="$myvar = Hello" -->
```

Other helpful SSI elements are **exec**, which executes CGI programs, or shell commands, which read the contents of a file into the Web page and also execute CGI files. The **echo** element displays values such as the date, the document's name, and the page's URL. With the **config** element, you can configure certain values, such as the date or file size.

PHP

PHP (PHP: Hypertext Preprocessor) is a scripting language designed for use in Web pages. PHP-enabled pages allow you to create dynamic Web pages that can perform tasks instead of just displaying data. PHP is an official project of the Apache Software Foundation. You can find out more about PHP at **www.php.net**.

Unlike CGI programs, which are executed separately from a Web page, PHP commands are embedded as tags within the page itself, much as SSI commands are. PHP support to interpret and execute these commands is provided directly by the Web server. This embedded support is enabled in Apache with the mod_php module (**/etc/httpd/conf.d/php.conf** configuration file). Instead of having to separately construct programs to be invoked and run outside the Web server, with PHP, such commands are embedded within a Web page and run by the Web server. The Web server maintains complete control at all times whenever tasks are being performed. It is possible, however, to implement PHP in a CGI mode, where PHP pages are constructed as separate programs, invoked by a Web page much as a Perl-based CGP program is.

PHP has flexible and powerful programming capabilities on the same level as C and Perl. As in those languages, you can create control structures such as if statements and loops. In addition, PHP has capabilities specifically suited to Web page tasks. PHP can interact directly with databases such as Oracle, MySQL, and IBM DB2. It can easily interact with all the standard protocols, such as IMAP, LDAP, HTTP, and POP3. It even has text processing abilities such as interpreting regular expressions and displaying XML documents. There are also extensions for searches, compression tools like **gzip**, and language translations. PHP supports a massive collection of possible operations. Check its Web site for a complete listing, as well as online manuals and tutorials.

Apache Configuration Tool

The Apache Configuration Tool (System | Administration | Server Settings | HTTP) opens with a window displaying panels for Main, Virtual Hosts, Server, and Performance Tuning. In each of these you will see buttons to open dialog boxes where you can enter default settings. You will also be able to enter settings for particular items such as virtual hosts and directories. For example, in the Virtual Hosts panel you can enter default settings for all virtual hosts, as well as add and edit particular virtual hosts. Click the Help button to display a Web page–based reference manual that details how to use each panel.

- On the Main panel, you enter your Web server address, the Web master's e-mail address, and the ports the Web server will be listening on.

- On the Virtual Hosts panel, be sure to select Default Virtual Host and click Edit to set the default settings for server options, pages searches, SSL support, log files, CGI environment support, and directories (Performance). To add a virtual host, click Add to open a window where you can enter host information such as the virtual hostname and IP address. You can select different configuration panels for the virtual host, such as log files and directory controls.

- On the server panel, you set administrative settings such as the Apache server's user ID and the process ID file, along with the user and group.

- The Performance Tuning panel lets you set different usage limits such as the maximum number of requests and the number of requests per connection.

When the Apache Configuration Tool saves its settings, it will overwrite the Apache configuration file, **/etc/httpd/conf/httpd.conf**. It is advisable that you first make a backup copy of your **httpd.conf** file in case you want to restore the original settings created by your distribution for Apache. If you have already manually edited this file, you will receive a warning, and the Apache Configuration Tool will make a backup copy in **/etc/httpd/conf/httpd.conf.bak.**

Web Server Security: SSL

Web server security deals with two different tasks: protecting your Web server from unauthorized access, and providing security for transactions carried out between a Web browser client and your Web server. To protect your server from unauthorized access, you use a proxy server such as Squid. Squid is a GNU proxy server often used with Apache on Linux systems. (See Chapter 24 for a detailed explanation of the Squid server.) Apache itself has several modules that provide security capabilities. These include mod_access for mandatory controls; mod_auth, mod_auth_db, mod_auth_digest, and mod_auth_dbm, which provide authentication support; and mod_auth_anon for anonymous FTP-like logging (see previous sections on access control and authentication).

To secure transmissions, you need to perform three tasks. You have to verify identities, check the integrity of the data, and ensure the privacy of the transmission. To verify the identities of the hosts participating in the transmission, you perform authentication procedures. To check the integrity of the data, you add digital signatures containing a digest value for the data. The digest value is a value that uniquely represents the data. Finally, to secure the privacy of the transmission, you encrypt it. Transactions between a browser and your server can then be encrypted, with the browser and your server alone able to decrypt the transmissions. The protocol most often used to implement secure transmissions with Linux Apache Web servers is the Secure Sockets Layer (SSL) protocol, which was originally developed by Netscape for secure transactions on the Web.

Like the Secure Shell (SSH) described in Chapter 19 and the GNU Privacy Guard discussed in Chapter 16, SSL uses a form of public- and private-key encryption for authentication. Data is encrypted with the public key but can be decrypted only with the private key. Once the data is authenticated, an agreed-upon cipher is used to encrypt it. Digital signatures encrypt an MD5 digest value for data to ensure integrity. Authentication is carried out with the use of certificates of authority. Certificates identify the different parties in a secure transmission, verifying that they are who they say they are. A Web server will have a certificate verifying its identity, verifying that it is the server it claims to be. The browser contacting the server will also have a certificate identifying who it is. These certificates are, in turn, both signed by a certificate authority, verifying that they are valid certificates. A certificate authority is an independent entity that both parties trust.

A certificate contains the public key of the particular server or browser it is given to, along with the digital signature of the certificate authority and identity information such as the name of the user or company running the server or browser. The effectiveness of a certificate depends directly on the reliability of the certificate authority issuing it. To run a secure Web server on the Internet, you should obtain a certificate from a noted certificate authority such as VeriSign. A commercial vendor such as Stronghold can do this for you. Many established companies already maintain their own certificate authority, securing transmissions within their company networks. An SSL session is set up using a handshake sequence in which the server and browser are authenticated by exchanging certificates, a cipher is agreed upon to encrypt the transmissions, and the kind of digest integrity check is chosen. There is also a choice in the kind of public key encryption used for authentication, either RSA or DSA. For each session, a unique session key is set up that the browser and server use.

A free open source version of SSL called OpenSSL is available for use with Apache (see **www.openssl.org**). It is based on SSLeay from Eric A. Young and Tim J. Hudson. However, U.S. government restrictions prevent the Apache Web server from being freely distributed with SSL capabilities built in. You have to separately obtain SSL and update your Apache server to incorporate this capability.

The U.S. government maintains export restrictions on encryption technology over 40 bits. SSL, however, supports a number of ciphers using 168-, 128-, and 40-bit keys (128 is considered secure, and so by comparison the exportable 40-bit versions are useless). This means that if Apache included SSL, it could not be distributed outside the United States. Outside the United States, however, there are projects that do distribute SSL for Apache using OpenSSL. These are free for noncommercial use in the United States, though export restrictions apply. The Apache-SSL project freely distributes Apache with SSL built in, apache+ssl. You can download this from their Web site at **www.apache-ssl.org** (though there are restrictions on exporting encryption technology, there are none on importing it). In addition, the mod_ssl project provides an SSL module with patches you can use to update your Apache Web server to incorporate SSL (**www.modsll.org**). mod_ssl is free for both commercial and noncommercial use under an Apache-style license. Red Hat and Fedora include the mod_ssl module with their distributions in the mod_ssl package (**/etc/httpd/conf.d/ssl.conf** configuration file).

The mod_ssl implementation of SSL provides an alternate access to your Web server using a different port (443) and a different protocol, https. In effect, you have both an SSL server and a nonsecure version. To access the secure SSL version, you use the protocol https instead of http for the Web server's URL address. For example, to access the SSL version for the Web server running at **www.mytrek.com**, you would use the protocol https in its URL, as shown here:

```
https://www.mytrek.com
```

You can configure mod_ssl using a number of configuration directives in the Apache configuration file, **smb.conf**. On Fedora, the default configuration file installed with Apache contains a section for the SSL directives along with detailed comments. Check the online documentation for mod_ssl at **www.modssl.org** for a detailed reference listing all the directives. There are global, server-based, and directory-based directives available.

In the Fedora **smb.conf** file, the inclusion of SSL directives are controlled by IfDefine blocks enabled by the HAVE_SSL flag. For example, the following code will load the SSL module:

```
<IfDefine HAVE_SSL>
LoadModule ssl_module        modules/libssl.so
</IfDefine>
```

The SSL version for your Apache Web server is set up in the **smb.conf** file as a virtual host. The SSL directives are enabled by an ifDefine block using the HAVE_SSL flag. Several default directives are implemented such as the location of SSL key directories and the port that the SSL version of the server will listen on (443). Others are commented out. You can enable them by removing the preceding # symbol, setting your own options. Several of the directives are shown here:

```
<IfDefine HAVE_SSL>
## SSL Virtual Host Context

#  Server Certificate:
SSLCertificateFile /etc/httpd/conf/ssl.crt/server.crt

#  Server Private Key:
SSLCertificateKeyFile /etc/httpd/conf/ssl.key/server.key

#  Certificate Authority (CA):
#SSLCACertificatePath /etc/httpd/conf/ssl.crt
#SSLCACertificateFile /etc/httpd/conf/ssl.crt/ca-bundle.crt
```

In the **/etc/httpd/conf** directory, mod_ssl will set up several SSL directories that will contain SSL authentication and encryption keys and data. The **ssl.crt** directory will hold certificates for the server. The **ssl.key** directory holds the public and private keys used in authentication encryption. Revocation lists for revoking expired certificates are kept in **ssl.crl**. The **ssl.csr** directory holds the certificate signing request used to request an official certificate from a certificate authority. **ssl.prm** holds parameter files used by the DSA key encryption method. Check the README files in each directory for details on the SSL files they contain.

The mod_ssl installation will provide you with a demonstration certificate called snakeoil that you can use to test your SSL configuration. When you have an official certificate, you can install it with the `make certificate` command within the **ssl.crt** directory. This will overwrite the **server.crt** server certificate file.

Proxy Servers: Squid

Proxy servers operate as an intermediary between a local network and services available on a larger one, such as the Internet. Requests from local clients for Web services can be handled by the proxy server, speeding transactions as well as controlling access. Proxy servers maintain current copies of commonly accessed Web pages, speeding Web access times by eliminating the need to access the original site constantly. They also perform security functions, protecting servers from unauthorized access. *Squid* is a free, open source, proxy-caching server for Web clients, designed to speed Internet access and provide security controls for Web servers. It implements a proxy-caching service for Web clients that caches Web pages as users make requests. Copies of Web pages accessed by users are kept in the Squid cache, and as requests are made, Squid checks to see if it has a current copy. If Squid does have a current copy, it returns the copy from its cache instead of querying the original site. If it does not have a current copy, it will retrieve one from the original site. Replacement algorithms periodically replace old objects in the cache. In this way, Web browsers can then use the local Squid cache as a proxy HTTP server. Squid currently handles Web pages supporting the HTTP, FTP, and SSL protocols (Squid cannot be used with FTP clients), each with an associated default port (see Table 24-1). It also supports ICP (Internet Cache Protocol), HTCP (Hypertext Caching Protocol) for Web caching, and SNMP (Simple Network Management Protocol) for providing status information.

You can find out more about Squid at **www.squid-cache.org**. For detailed information check the Squid FAQ and the user manual located at their Web site. The FAQ is also installed in your **/usr/share/doc** under the **squid** directory.

As a proxy, Squid does more that just cache Web objects. It operates as an intermediary between the Web browsers (clients) and the servers they access. Instead of connections being made directly to the server, a client connects to the proxy server. The proxy then relays requests to the Web server. This is useful for situations where a Web server is placed behind a firewall server, protecting it from outside access. The proxy is accessible on the firewall, which can then transfer requests and responses back and forth between the client and the Web server. The design is often used to allow Web servers to operate on protected local networks and still be accessible on the Internet. You can also use a Squid proxy to provide Web access to the Internet by local hosts. Instead of using a gateway providing complete access to the Internet, local hosts can use a proxy to allow them just Web access (see Chapter 5). You can also combine the two, allowing gateway access, but using the proxy server to provide more control for Web access. In addition, the caching capabilities of Squid can provide local hosts with faster Web access.

Protocol	Description and Port
HTTP	Web pages, port 3128
FTP	FTP transfers through Web sites, port 3128
ICP	Internet Caching Protocol, port 3130
HTCP	Hypertext Caching Protocol, port 4827
CARP	Cache Array Routing Protocol
SNMP	Simple Network Management Protocol, port 3401
SSL	Secure Socket Layer

TABLE 24-1 Protocols Supported by Squid

Technically, you could use a proxy server to simply manage traffic between a Web server and the clients that want to communicate with it, without doing caching at all. Squid combines both capabilities as a proxy-caching server.

Squid also provides security capabilities that let you exercise control over hosts accessing your Web server. You can deny access by certain hosts and allow access by others. Squid also supports the use of encrypted protocols such as SSL (see Chapter 23). Encrypted communications are tunneled (passed through without reading) through the Squid server directly to the Web server.

Squid is supported and distributed under a GNU Public License by the National Laboratory for Applied Network Research (NLANR) at the University of California, San Diego. The work is based on the Harvest Project to create a Web indexing system that included a high-performance cache daemon called **cached**. You can obtain current source code versions and online documentation from the Squid home page at **www.squid-cache.org**. The Squid software package consists of the Squid server, several support scripts for services like LDAP and HTTP, and a cache manager script called **cachemgr.cgi**. The **cachemgr.cgi** lets you view statistics for the Squid server as it runs.

You can start, stop, and restart the Squid server using the **squid** script, as shown here:

```
# service squid restart
```

You can also set the Squid server to start up automatically using the system-config-services tool (System | Administration | Server Settings | Services) or **chkconfig**.

Configuring Client Browsers

Squid supports both standard proxy caches and transparent caches. With a standard proxy cache, users will need to configure their browsers to specifically access the Squid server. A transparent cache, on the other hand, requires no browser configuration by users. The cache is transparent, allowing access as if it were a normal Web site. Transparent caches are implemented by IPtables using net filtering to intercept requests and direct them to the proxy cache (see Chapter 20).

With a standard proxy cache, users need to specify their proxy server in their Web browser configuration. For this they will need the IP address of the host running the Squid proxy server, as well as the port it is using. Proxies usually make use of port 3128. To configure use of a proxy server running on the local sample network described in Chapter 5, you would enter the following in the Proxy configuration settings of your browser. The proxy server is running on **turtle.mytrek.com** (192.168.0.1) and using port 3128.

```
192.168.0.1 3128
```

On Firefox, Mozilla, and Netscape, the user on the sample local network would first select the Proxy panel located in Preferences under the Edit menu. Then, in the Manual proxy configuration's View panel, enter the previous information. The user will see entries for FTP, Gopher, HTTP, and Security proxies. For standard Web access, enter the IP address in the FTP, Gopher, and Web boxes. For their port boxes, enter 3128.

For GNOME, select Network Proxy in the Preferences menu or window, and for Konqueror on the KDE Desktop, select the Proxies panel on the Preferences | Web Browsing menu window. Here, you can enter the proxy server address and port numbers. If your local host is using Internet Explorer (such as a Windows system does), you set the proxy entries in the Local Area Network settings accessible from the Internet Options window.

On Linux or Unix systems, local hosts can set the **http_proxy, gopher_proxy** and **ftp_proxy** shell variables to configure access by Linux-supported Web browsers such as Lynx. You can place these definitions in your **.bash_profile** or **/etc/profile** file to have them automatically defined whenever you log in.

```
http_proxy=192.168.0.1:3128
ftp proxy=192.168.0.1:3128
gopher_proxy=192.168.0.1:3128
export http_proxy ftp_proxy gopher_proxy
```

Alternatively, you can use the proxy's URL.

```
http_proxy=http://turtle.mytrek.com:3128
```

For the Elinks browser, you can specify a proxy in its configuration file, **/etc/elinks.conf**. Set both FTP and Web proxy host options, as in:

```
protocol.http.proxy.host   turtle.mytrek.com:3128
protocol.ftp.proxy.host    turtle.mytrek.com:3128
```

Before a client on a local host could use the proxy server, access permission would have to be given to it in the server's **squid.conf** file, described in the later section "Security." Access can easily be provided to an entire network. For the sample network used here, you would have to place the following entries in the **squid.conf** file. These are explained in detail in the following sections:

```
acl mylan src 192.168.0.0/255.255.255.0
http_access allow mylan
```

TIP *Web clients that need to access your Squid server as a standard proxy cache will need to know the server's address and the port for Squid's HTTP services, which by default is 3128.*

The squid.conf File

The Squid configuration file is **squid.conf**, located in the **/etc/squid** directory. In the **/etc/squid/squid.conf** file, you set general options such as ports used, security options controlling access to the server, and cache options for configuring caching operations. You can use a backup version called **/etc/squid/squid.conf.default** to restore your original defaults. The default version of **squid.conf** provided with the Squid software includes detailed explanations of all standard entries, along with commented default entries. Entries consist of tags that specify different attributes. For example, **maximum_object_size** and **maximum_object** set limits on objects transferred.

```
maximum_object_size 4096 KB
```

As a proxy, Squid will use certain ports for specific services, such as port 3128 for HTTP services like Web browsers. Default port numbers are already set for Squid. Should you need to use other ports, you can set them in the **/etc/squid/squid.conf** file. The following entry shows how you would set the Web browser port:

```
http_port 3128
```

NOTE *Squid uses the Simple Network Management Protocol (SNMP) to provide status information and statistics to SNMP agents managing your network. You can control SNMP with the **snmp access** and **port** configurations in the **squid.conf** file.*

Security

Squid can use its role as an intermediary between Web clients and a Web server to implement access controls, determining who can access the Web server and how. Squid does this by checking access control lists (ACLs) of hosts and domains that have had controls placed on them. When it finds a Web client from one of those hosts attempting to connect to the Web server, it executes the control. Squid supports a number of controls with which it can deny or allow access to the Web server by the remote host's Web client (see Table 24-2). In effect, Squid sets up a firewall just for the Web server.

The first step in configuring Squid security is to create ACLs. These are lists of hosts and domains for which you want to set up controls. You define ACLs using the **acl** command, in which you create a label for the systems on which you are setting controls. You then use commands such as **http_access** to define these controls. You can define a system, or a group of systems, by use of several **acl** options, such as the source IP address, the domain name, or even the time and date. For example, the **src** option is used to define a system or group of systems with a certain source address. To define an **acl** entry for a group of systems in a local network referred to as mylan with the addresses 192.168.0.0 through 192.168.0.255, use the following ACL definition:

```
acl mylan src 192.168.0.0/255.255.255.0
```

Once it is defined, you can use an ACL definition in a Squid option to specify a control you want to place on those systems. For example, to allow access by the mylan group of local systems to the Web through the proxy, use an **http_access** option with the **allow** action specifying **mylan** as the **acl** definition to use, as shown here:

```
http_access allow mylan
```

Options	Description
src *ip-address/netmask*	Client's IP address
src *addr1-addr2/netmask*	Range of addresses
dst *ip-address/netmask*	Destination IP address
myip *ip-address/netmask*	Local socket IP address
srcdomain *domain*	Reverse lookup, client IP
dstdomain *domain*	Destination server from URL; for **dstdomain** and **dstdom_regex**, a reverse lookup is tried if an IP-based URL is used
srcdom_regex **[-i]** *expression*	Regular expression matching client name
dstdom_regex **[-i]** *expression*	Regular expression matching destination
time *[day-abbrevs]* *[h1:m1-h2:m2]*	Time as specified by day, hour, and minutes. Day abbreviations: S = Sunday, M = Monday, T = Tuesday, W = Wednesday, H = Thursday, F = Friday, A = Saturday
url_regex **[-i]** *expression*	Regular expression matching on whole URL
urlpath_regex **[-i]** *expression*	Regular expression matching on URL path
port *ports*	Specify a port or range of ports
proto *protocol*	Specify a protocol, such as HTTP or FTP
method *method*	Specify methods, such as GET and POST
browser **[-i]** *regexp*	Pattern match on user-agent header
ident *username*	String match on **ident** output
src_as *number*	Used for routing of requests to specific caches
dst_as *number*	Used for routing of requests to specific caches
proxy_auth *username*	List of valid usernames
snmp_community *string*	A community string to limit access to your SNMP agent

TABLE **24-2**   Squid ACL Options

By defining ACLs and using them in Squid options, you can tailor your Web site with the kind of security you want. The following example allows access to the Web through the proxy by only the **mylan** group of local systems, denying access to all others. Two **acl** entries are set up: one for the local system and one for all others; **http_access** options first allow access to the local system and then deny access to all others.

```
acl mylan src 192.168.0.0/255.255.255.0
acl all src 0.0.0.0/0.0.0.0
http_access allow mylan
http_access deny all
```

The default entries that you will find in your **squid.conf** file, along with an entry for the mylan sample network, are shown here. You will find these entries in the ACCESS CONTROLS section of the **squid.conf** file.

```
acl all src 0.0.0.0/0.0.0.0
acl manager proto cache_object
acl localhost src 127.0.0.1/255.255.255.255
acl mylan src 192.168.0.0/255.255.255.0
acl SSL_ports port 443 563
```

The order of the **http_access** options is important. Squid starts from the first and works its way down, stopping at the first **http_access** option with an ACL entry that matches. In the preceding example, local systems that match the first **http_access** command are allowed, whereas others fall through to the second **http_access** command and are denied.

For systems using the proxy, you can also control what sites they can access. For a destination address, you create an **acl** entry with the **dst** qualifier. The **dst** qualifier takes as its argument the site address. Then you can create an **http_access** option to control access to that address. The following example denies access by anyone using the proxy to the destination site **rabbit.mytrek.com**. If you have a local network accessing the Web through the proxy, you can use such commands to restrict access to certain sites.

```
acl myrabbit dst rabbit.mytrek.com
http_access deny myrabbit
```

The **http_access** entries already defined in the **squid.conf** file, along with an entry for the **mylan** network, are shown here. Access to outside users is denied, whereas access by hosts on the local network and the local host (Squid server host) is allowed.

```
http_access allow localhost
http_access allow mylan
http_access deny all
```

You can also qualify addresses by domain. Often, Web sites can be referenced using only the domain. For example, a site called **www.mybeach.com** can be referenced using just the domain **mybeach.com**. To create an **acl** entry to reference a domain, use the **dstdomain** or **srcdomain** option for destination and source domains, respectively. Remember, such a reference refers to all hosts in that domain. An **acl** entry with the **dstdomain** option for **mybeach.com** restricts access to **www.mybeach.com**, **ftp.mybeach.com**, **surf.mybeach.com**, and so on. The following example restricts access to the **www.mybeach.com** site along with all other **.mybeach.com** sites and any hosts in the **mybeach.com** domain:

```
acl thebeach dstdomain .mybeach.com
http_access deny thebeach
```

You can list several domains or addresses in an **acl** entry to reference them as a group, but you cannot have one domain that is a subdomain of another. For example, if **mybeachblanket.com** is a subdomain of **mybeach.com**, you cannot list both in the same **acl** list. The following example restricts access to both **mybeach.com** and **mysurf.com**:

```
acl beaches dstdomain .mybeach.com .mysurf.com
http_access deny beaches
```

An **acl** entry can also use a pattern to specify certain addresses and domains. In the following example, access is denied to any URL with the pattern "chocolate" but allowed to all others:

```
acl Choc1 url_regex chocolate
http_access deny Choc1
http_access allow all
```

Squid also supports ident and proxy authentication methods to control user access. The following example allows only the users **dylan** and **chris** to use the Squid cache:

```
ident_lookup on
acl goodusers user chris dylan
http_access allow goodusers
http_access deny all
```

Caches

Squid primarily uses the Internet Cache Protocol (ICP) to communicate with other Web caches. It also provides support for the more experimental Hypertext Cache Protocol (HTCP) and the Cache Array Routing Protocol (CARP).

Using the ICP protocols, your Squid cache can connect to other Squid caches or other cache servers, such as Microsoft proxy server, Netscape proxy server, and Novell BorderManager. This way, if your network's Squid cache does not have a copy of a requested Web page, it can contact another cache to see if it is there instead of accessing the original site. You can configure Squid to connect to other Squid caches by connecting it to a cache hierarchy. Squid supports a hierarchy of caches denoted by the terms *child, sibling,* and *parent.* Sibling and child caches are accessible on the same level and are automatically queried whenever a request cannot be located in your own Squid's cache. If these queries fail, a parent cache is queried, which then searches its own child and sibling caches—or its own parent cache, if needed—and so on.

You can set up a cache hierarchy to connect to the main NLANR server by registering your cache using the following entries in your **squid.conf** file:

```
cache_announce 24
announce_to sd.cache.nlanr.net:3131
```

Connecting to Caches

Use **cache_peer** to set up parent, sibling, and child connections to other caches. This option has five fields. The first two consist of the hostname or IP address of the queried cache and the cache type (parent, child, or sibling). The third and fourth are the HTTP and the ICP ports of that cache, usually 3128 and 3130. The last is used for **cache_peer** options such as **proxy-only** to not save fetched objects locally, **no-query** for those caches that do not support ICP, and **weight**, which assigns priority to a parent cache. The following example sets up a connection to a parent cache:

```
cache_peer sd.cache.nlanr.net parent 3128 3130
```

Memory and Disk Configuration

Squid provides several options for configuring cache memory. The **cache_mem** option sets the memory allocated primarily for objects currently in use (objects in transit). If available, the space can also be use for frequently accessed objects (hot objects) and failed requests (negative-cache objects). The default is 8MB. The following example sets it to 256 MB:

```
cache_mem 256 MB
```

You can further specify the minimum and maximum sizes of objects saved either on disk or in memory. On disk, you use **maximum_object_size** and **minimum_object_size**. The default maximum is 4 KB. The default minimum is set to 0, indicating no minimum. For memory, you use **maximum_object_size_in_memory** and **minimum_object_size_in_memory**.

The **cache_swap_low** and **cache_swap_low** options let you set bars for replacing objects in your cache.

To designate where cache objects are to be located, you use the **cache_dir** option. Here you specify what directories to use for your cache.

Administrative Settings

The e-mail address for the administrator for your Squid cache is specified in the **cache_mgr** option.

If you run Squid as the root user, then Squid will change its user and group ID from **root** to **nobody**. The group ID will be changed to **nogroup**. This is to protect root user access. Should you run Squid as a user other than root, Squid will retain that original user as its user ID. If, when running Squid from the root user, you want to designate another user other than **nobody**, you can use **cache_effective_user** to change user IDs, and **cache_effective_group** to change the group.

You can also specify a special host name to be displayed in error messages. Use **visible_hostname** to set the name.

Logs

Squid keeps several logs detailing access, cache performance, and error messages.

- **access.log** holds requests sent to your proxy.
- **cache.log** holds Squid server messages such as errors and startup messages.
- **store.log** holds information about the Squid cache, such as objects added or removed.

You can use the cache manager (**cachemgr.cgi**) to manage the cache and view statistics on the cache manager as it runs. To run the cache manager, use your browser to execute the **cachemgr.cgi** script (this script should be placed in your Web server's **cgi-bin** directory).

Web Server Acceleration: Reverse Proxy Cache

Though Squid caches can enhance access by clients to a Web server, Squid can also reduce the load on a Web server. Web servers that become overwhelmed by requests can move their cachable pages to a Squid proxy server that can serve as a kind of alternate site, handling requests for those pages. In effect, the Web server becomes accelerated. Such a cache is known as a reverse proxy cache, focusing on the server instead of the client. A reverse proxy cache will intercept requests to a server, processing any for its cached pages. Only requests for noncached pages are forwarded to the original Web server.

To configure a reverse proxy cache, you use the http_port directive with the **accel** option (for Squid 2.4 and earlier you use **httpd_accel** directives). To specify a particular location for the accelerators, you use **defaultsite** (this replaces httpd_accel_host used in Squid 2.4 and earlier).

```
http_port 3128
http_port 192.168.0.25:80 accel defaultsite=rabbit.mytrek.com
```

If your Squid proxy server and the Web server are operating on the same host, you need to specify the port that the Web server is using. This cannot be the same port as Squid is using. You use the **cache_peer** directive with the **port** option to specify the server port. You then specify the address of the Web server with the **cache_peer** directive and the **originserver** option. In the following example, the Web server is using port 80, whereas Squid is using port 3128:

```
http_port 3128 # Port of Squid proxy
cache_peer port 80
cache_peer originserver localhost # IP address of web server
```

With Squid 2.6, transparent caches are supported directly as an **http_port** option, **transparent**.

```
http_port 3218 transparent
```

To specify the use of host directives (virtual hosts), you use the **vhost** option. This replaces the **httpd_accel_uses_host_header** directive used in earlier versions. For virtual IP hosts you use **vport**.

```
http_port vhost
```

In addition, DNS entries for the external network would use the IP address of the proxy server for the Web server host name, directing all the Web server requests to the proxy server. DNS entries for the internal network would use the Web server's IP address for the Web server host name, allowing the proxy to redirect noncached requests on to the Web server. If your network uses only one DNS server, you can set up a Split DNS server to specify internal and external addresses (see Chapter 36).

Mail Servers: SMTP, POP, and IMAP

Mail servers provide Internet users with electronic mail services. They have their own TCP/IP protocols such as the Simple Mail Transfer Protocol (SMTP), the Post Office Protocol (POP), and the Internet Mail Access Protocol (IMAP). Messages are sent across the Internet through mail servers that service local domains. A *domain* can be seen as a subnet of the larger Internet, with its own server to handle mail messages sent from or received for users on that subnet. When a user mails a message, it is first sent from their host system to the mail server. The mail server then sends the message to another mail server on the Internet, the one servicing the subnet on which the recipient user is located. The receiving mail server then sends the message to the recipient's host system.

At each stage, a different type of operation takes place using different agents (programs). A mail user agent (MUA) is a mail client program, such as mail or Elm. With an MUA, a user composes a mail message and sends it. Then a mail transfer agent (MTA) transports the messages over the Internet. MTAs are mail servers that use SMTP to send messages across the Internet from one mail server to another, transporting them among subnets. On Linux and Unix systems, the commonly used MTA is Sendmail, a mail server daemon that constantly checks for incoming messages from other mail servers and sends outgoing messages to appropriate servers. Other MTAs becoming more popular are Postfix, Exim, Courier, and Qmail (see Table 25-1). Incoming messages received by a mail server are distributed to a user with mail delivery agents (MDAs). Most Linux systems use procmail as their MDA, taking messages received by the mail server and delivering them to user accounts (see **www.procmail.org** for more information).

Mail Transport Agents

Red Hat Linux and Fedora automatically install and configure both Sendmail and Postfix for you. On starting your system, you can send and receive messages between local users using Sendmail or Postfix. Red Hat and Fedora include a special tool called the Mail Transport Agent Switcher, accessible from the System Settings menu or window, to let you switch between the two. You can also set up your Linux system to run a POP server.

Agent	Description
Sendmail	Sendmail mail transfer agent, supported by the Sendmail consortium **www.sendmail.org**
Postfix	Fast, easy-to-configure, and secure mail transfer agent compatible with Sendmail and designed to replace it **www.postfix.org**
Qmail	Fast, flexible, and secure MTA with its own implementation and competitive with Postfix **www.qmail.org**
Exim	MTA based on smail3 **www.exim.org**
Courier	Courier MTA **www.courier-mta.org**
Mail Transport Agent Switcher	Red Hat and Fedora tool to let you switch between using Sendmail and Postfix (System I Administration I Mail Transport Agent Switcher)

TABLE 25-1   Mail Transfer Agents

POP servers hold users' mail until they log in to access their messages, instead of having mail sent to their hosts directly. Both Postfix and Sendmail will be discussed in this chapter.

Courier is a fast, small, and secure MTA that maintains some compatibility with Sendmail. The Courier software package also includes POP, IMAP, and webmail servers along with mailing list services. It supports extensive authentication methods including shadow passwords, PAM, and LDAP.

Exim is a fast and flexible MTA similar to Smail. Developed at the University of Cambridge, it has a very different implementation than Sendmail.

Qmail is also a fast and secure MTA, but it has little compatibility with Sendmail. It has its own configuration and maintenance files. Like Postfix, it has a modular design, using a different program for each mail task. It also focuses on security, speed, and easy configuration.

NOTE *Messages sent within a single stand-alone system require a loopback interface. Most Linux distributions, including Fedora, do this automatically for you during the installation process. A loopback interface enables your system to address itself, allowing it to send and receive mail to and from itself. A loopback interface uses the hostname **localhost** and a special IP address reserved for use by local systems, 127.0.0.1. You can examine your **/etc/hosts** file to see if your loopback interface has been configured as the local host. You should see **127.0.0.1 localhost** listed as the first entry.*

Received Mail: MX Records

A mail address consists of a username and a host address. The host address takes the form of a fully qualified domain name, listing the hostname and the domain name, separated by periods. Most uses of a hostname, such as FTP connections, translate the hostname into an IP address and use the IP address to locate the host system. Mail messages operate nearly the same way. However, they make use of the Domain Name Service to determine which host to actually send a message to. The host specified in the mail address may not be the host to which delivery should actually be made. Different networks will often specify a mail server to which mail for the hosts in a network should be delivered. For example, mail addressed to the **rabbit.mytrek.com** host may actually be delivered to the **turtle.mytrek.com** host. **turtle.mytrek.com** may be running a POP mail server that users on **rabbit.mytrek.com** can access to read their mail.

Such mail servers are associated with different hosts by mail exchange records, known as MX records, in a network's DNS configuration (see Chapter 36). When mail is received in a network, the network's DNS configuration is first checked for MX records to determine if the mail is to be delivered to a host different from that in the mail message address. For example, the following MX record says that any mail for the **rabbit.mytrek.com** host is to be delivered to the **turtle.mytrek.com** host; **turtle.mytrek.com** is the mail exchanger for **rabbit .mytrek.com**:

```
rabbit.mytrek.com. IN   MX   0   turtle.mytrek.com.
```

A host could have several mail exchangers, each with a different priority. If one is down, the one with next highest priority will be accessed. Such a design provides for more robust mail delivery, letting a few well-maintained servers handle received mail, instead of each host on its own.

Mail exchange records are also used for mail addresses for which there are no hosts. For example, you could designate virtual hosts or use the domain name as an address. To use a domain name, you would have an MX record with the domain name mapped to a mail server on the network. Mail addressed to the domain name would be sent to the mail server. For example, with the following MX record, mail sent to **mytrek.com** would be delivered to **turtle.mytrek.com**, which would be running a mail server like Sendmail:

```
mytrek.com. IN   MX   0   turtle.mytrek.com.
```

Mail addressed to george@mytrek.com would be sent to george@turtle.mytrek.com.

MX records come into play with certain mail configurations such as masquerading or centralized mail services. MX records are not required. If you have a stand-alone system or a small network with only a few hosts, you may want mail received directly by different hosts.

***

NOTE *MX records are used not only for incoming mail, but also for outgoing mail. An MX record can specify a mail server to use for relaying mail from a given host out to a larger network.* .

Postfix

Postfix is a fast, secure, and flexible MTA designed to replace Sendmail while maintaining as much compatibility as possible. Written by Wietse Venema and originally released as the IBM Secure Mailer, it is now available under the GNU license (**www.postfix.org**). Postfix is included as part of the Fedora distribution. Postfix was created with security in mind, treating all incoming mail as potential security risks. Postfix uses many of the same Sendmail directories and files and makes use of Sendmail wrappers, letting Sendmail clients interact seamlessly with Postfix servers. Postfix is also easier to configure, using its own configuration file. Fedora now provides Postfix along with Sendmail.

Instead of one large program, Postfix is implemented as a collection of smaller programs, each designed to perform a specific mail-related task. A Postfix master daemon runs continuously and manages the use of the other Postfix daemons, running them only as needed. A **bounce** daemon handles undeliverable mail, a **trivial-rewrite** daemon redirects messages, and the **showq** daemon provides information on the print queues.

Postfix Commands

Several Postfix commands allow you to manage your server tasks. The **sendmail** command sends messages. You use **mailq** to display the status of your mail queues. The **newaliases** command takes mail aliases listed in the aliases files and stores them in a database file that can be used by Postfix. The **postmap** command is used to maintain various database files used by Postfix, such as the alias file for mail aliases and the access file that restricts messages received by the server. In addition, Postfix provides lower-level tools, all beginning with the term **post**, such as the **postalias** command, which maintains the alias database, and **postcat**, which displays print queue files.

Postfix Configuration: main.cf

Postfix configuration is handled by setting parameters in its configuration file, **main.cf**. Fedora installs a default **/etc/postfix/main.cf** file with Postfix, with most of the essential configuration values already set. Parameter names tend to be user friendly. For example, directory locations are specified by parameters ending in the term **directory**, such as **queue_directory** for the location of Postfix queues and **daemon_directory** for the location of the Postfix daemons. Defaults are already implemented for most parameters. For example, defaults are set for particular resource controls, such as message size, time limits, and the number of allowed messages per queue. You can edit the **main.cf** file to change the parameter values to meet your own needs. After making any changes, you only need to reload the configuration using the **postfix reload** command:

```
postfix reload
```

Network Parameters

You will most likely need to set several network parameters. To ease this process, Postfix defines parameters that hold key network information, such as **myhostname**, which holds the hostname of your system, and **mydomain**, which holds the domain name of your network. For example, **myhostname** would be set to the host **turtle.mytrek.com**, whereas **mydomain** would be just **mytrek.com**. Parameters like **myhostname** and **mydomain** are themselves used as values assigned to other parameters. In the next example, **myhostname** and **mydomain** are set to the host the mail server is running on and its network domain:

```
myhostname=turtle.mytrek.com
mydomain=mytrek.com
```

The **myorigin** parameter specifies the origin address for e-mail sent by the server. By default, this is set to the value of the parameter **myhostname**, as shown here. Note that a **$** precedes the **myhostname** variable to evaluate it.

```
myorigin=$myhostname
```

If you are using a single system directly attached to the Internet, you may want to keep this configuration, labeling mail as being sent by your host. However, if your system is operating as a gateway for a network, your mail server is sending out mail from different hosts on that network. You may wish to change the origin address to the domain name, so that mail is perceived as sent from the domain.

```
myorigin=$mydomain
```

Local Networks

The **mydestination** parameter holds the list of domains that your mail server will receive mail for. By default, these include **localhost** and your system's hostname.

```
mydestination = $myhostname localhost.$mydomain
```

If you want the mail server to receive mail for an entire local network, you need to also specify its domain name. That way, the server can receive mail addressed just to the domain, instead of your specific host.

```
mydestination = $myhostname localhost.$mydomain $mydomain
```

Also, if your host goes by other hostnames and there are DNS records identifying your host by those names, you need to specify those names as well. For example, your host could also be a Web server to which mail could be directed. A host **turtle.mytrek.com** may also be identified as the Web site **www.mytrek.com**. Both names would have to be listed in the **mydestination** parameter.

```
mydestination = $myhostname localhost.$mydomain $mydomain www.$mydomain
```

If your system is a gateway for one or more local networks, you can specify them with the **mynetworks** parameter. This allows your mail server to relay mail addressed to those networks. Networks are specified using their IP addresses. The **relay_domains** parameter lets you specify domain addresses of networks for which you can relay messages. By default, this is set to **mydestination**:

```
mynetworks=192.168.0.0
relay_domains=$mydestination
```

Hosts within the local network connected to the Internet by a gateway need to know the identity of the relay host, the mail server. You set this with the **relayhost** parameter. Also, **myorigin** should be set to just **mydomain**. If there is a DNS server identifying the gateway as the mail server, you can just set **relayhost** to the value of **mydomain**. If not, then **relayhost** should be set to the specific hostname of the gateway/mail server. If your local network is not running a DNS server, be sure to set **disable_dns_lookups** to **yes**.

```
relay_host=$mydomain
```

Direct Connections

If your system is directly connected to the Internet and you use an ISP for receiving mail, you can configure Postfix as a null client to just send mail. Set the **relay_host** parameter to just your own domain name. Also, in the **master.cf** file, comment out the SMTP server and local delivery agent entries.

```
relayhost = $mydomain
```

Masquerading

If your mail server is operating on a gateway for a local network and you want to hide the hosts in that network, you can opt to masquerade the local hosts, letting it appear that all mail is coming from the domain in general, instead of a particular host. To set this option, you use the **masquerade_domains** parameter. In the following example, all mail sent by a local host such as **rabbit.mytrek.com** will be addressed as just coming from **mytrek.com**. Thus a message sent by the user **chris@rabbit.mytrek.com** is sent out as coming from **chris@mytrek.com**:

```
masquerade_domains = $mydomain
```

Received mail is not masqueraded by default. This allows Postfix to still deliver received mail to particular hosts. If you want received mail to also be masqueraded, you have to add the **envelope_recipients** parameter to the list of values assigned to the **masquerade_class** parameter. In that case, Postfix will no longer be able to deliver received mail.

Virtual Domains

If your network has implemented virtual domains, you will need to set up a virtual domain table and then specify that table with the **virtual_maps** option. Setting up a table is a simple matter of listing virtual names and their real addresses in a text file such as **/etc/postfix/virtual**. Then use the **postmap** command to create a Postfix table:

```
postmap /etc/postfix/virtual
```

In the **main.cf** file, specify the table with the **virtual_maps** parameter. Postfix will then use this table to look up virtual domains.

```
virtual_maps = hash:/etc/postfix/virtual
```

NOTE *See the Postfix FAQ at **www.postfix.org** for detailed information on how to set up Postfix for a gateway, a local workstation, or a host directly connected to the Internet (null server).*

Postfix Greylisting Policy Server

Postfix also supports greylisting with the Postfix Greylisting Policy Server. Greylisting blocks spammers based on their mailing methods rather than content, relying on the fact that spammers will not attempt retries if rejected (**www.greylisting.org**). Messages from new previously unknown sources are rejected, whereupon a valid MTA will retry, whereas a spammer will not. To support the Greylisting Policy Server, Postfix is configured to delegate Policy access to a server. In the **/etc/postfix** directory you can use the postgrey_whitelist files to exclude email addresses from greylisting.

The Greylisting Policy Server is run as a stand-alone server, using its own startup script. It can be managed with system-config-services under the postgrey entry. The postgrey man page provides detailed information about the server's options.

Controlling User and Host Access

With an access file, you can control access by certain users, hosts, and domains. The access file works much like the one used for Sendmail. Entries are made in a text file beginning with the user, host, or domain name or address, followed by an action to take. A user, host, or domain can be accepted, rejected, or rejected with a message. Once entries are made, they can be installed in a Postfix database file with the **postmap** command:

```
postmap /etc/postfix/access
```

You can then use the access file in various Postfix operations to control clients, recipients, and senders.

Access can also be controlled by use of the Mail Abuse Prevention System (MAPS), which provides the RBL+ service, a collection of mail address DNS-based databases (**mailabuse.com**). These databases, like the Realtime Blackhole List (RBL), list mail addresses that are known to be used by mail abusers. A domain or host is matched against a list maintained by the service, which can be accessed on a local server or directly from an online site. Various Postfix operations let you use MAPS databases to control access by clients, recipients, or senders.

Header and Body Checks

With the **header_checks** parameter, you can specify a Postfix table where you can list criteria for rejecting messages. Check the **/etc/postfix/header_checks** file for details. The criteria are patterns that can match message headers. You can have matching messages rejected, rejected with a reply, simply deleted, or logged with a warning. You have the option of taking several actions, including REJECT, DISCARD, WARN, HOLD, and IGNORE.

```
header_checks = regexp:/etc/postfix/header_checks
```

The database, in this case **/etc/postfix/header_checks**, will have lines, each with a regular expression and a corresponding action. The regular expression can either be a standard regular expression as denoted by **regexp** in the header_checks parameter (see Chapter 8) or conform to a Perl Compatible Regular Expression, **prece**.

The **body_checks** parameter lets you check the body of a text message, line by line, using regular expressions and actions like those used for **header_checks** in an **/etc/postfix/ body_checks** file.

Controlling Client, Senders, and Recipients

With the **smtpd_client_restrictions** parameter, you can restrict access to the mail server by certain clients. Restrictions you can apply include **reject_unknown_client_ hostname**, which will reject any clients with unresolved addresses, **permit_mynetworks**, which allows access by any clients defined by **mynetworks**, and **check_client_access**, which will check an access database to see if a client should be accepted or rejected. The **reject_rbl_client** and **reject_rhsbl_client** parameters will reject clients from specified domains.

```
smtpd_client_restrictions = permit_mynetworks, \
              reject_unknown_client, check_client_access, reject_maps_rbl
```

The **reject_rbl_client** restriction rejects domain addresses according to a specified MAPS service. The site can be an online site or a local one set up to provide the service. The **reject_rhsbl_client** restriction rejects host addresses.

```
smtpd_client_restrictions = reject_rbl_client relays.mail-abuse.org
```

To implement restrictions from an access file, you can use the **hash** directive and the name of the file.

```
smtpd_client_restrictions = hash:/etc/postfix/access
```

The corresponding **smtpd_sender_restrictions** parameter works much the same way as its client counterpart but controls access from specific senders. It has many of the same restrictions but adds **reject_non_fqdn_sender**, which will reject any mail header without a fully qualified domain name, and **reject_sender_login_mismatch**, which will require sender verification. The **reject_rhsbl_sender** restriction rejects domain addresses according to a specified MAPS service.

The **smtpd_recipient_restrictions** parameter will restrict the recipients the server will accept mail for. Restrictions include **permit_auth_destination**, which allows authorized messages, and **reject_unauth_destination**, which rejects unauthorized messages. The **check_recipient_access** restriction will check local networks for a recipient address. The **reject_unknown_recipient_domain** restriction rejects recipient addresses with no DNS entry. The **reject_rhsbl_recipient** restriction rejects domain addresses according to a specified MAPS service.

You can further refine restrictions with parameters like **smtpd_helo_restrictions**, which requires a HELO command from a client. Restriction parameters include **reject_invalid_hostname**, which checks for faulty syntax, **reject_unknown_hostname** for hosts with no DNS entry, and **reject_non_fqdn_hostname** for hosts whose names are not fully qualified. The **strict_rfc821_envelopes** parameter will implement strict envelope protocol compliance.

Sendmail

Sendmail operates as a server to both receive and send mail messages. Sendmail listens for any mail messages received from other hosts and addressed to users on the network hosts it serves. At the same time, Sendmail handles messages users are sending out to remote users, determining what hosts to send them to. You can learn more about Sendmail at **www.sendmail.org**, including online documentation and current software packages. The Sendmail newsgroup is **comp.mail.sendmail**. You can also obtain a commercial version from **www.sendmail.com**.

The domain name server for your network designates the host that runs the Sendmail server. This is your mail host. Messages are sent to this host, whose Sendmail server then sends the message to the appropriate user and its host. In your domain name server configuration file, the mail host entry is specified with an MX entry. To print the mail queue of messages for future delivery, you can use **mailq** (or **sendmail -v -q**). This runs Sendmail with instructions to print the mail queue.

The Sendmail software package contains several utilities for managing your Sendmail server. These include mailq, which displays the queue of outgoing messages; mailstats, which shows statistics on mail server use; hoststat, which provides the stats of remote hosts that have connected with the mail server; and praliases, which prints out the mail aliases listed in the **/etc/aliases** file. Some, like mailq and hoststat, simply invoke Sendmail with certain options. Others, like mailstats and praliases, are separate programs.

Sendmail now maintains all configuration and database files in the **/etc/mail** directory. Here you will find the Sendmail macro configuration file, **sendmail.mc**, as well as several database files (see Table 25-2). Many have changed their names with the release of

File	Description
/etc/mail/sendmail.cf	Sendmail configuration file
/etc/mail/sendmail.mc	Sendmail M4 macro configuration file
/etc/mail/submit.cf	Sendmail configuration file for mail submission mode where Sendmail does not run as a server but merely submits mail
/etc/mail/submit.mc	Sendmail M4 macro configuration file for Sendmail mail submission mode
/etc/aliases	Sendmail aliases file for mailing lists
/etc/aliases.db	Sendmail aliases database file generated by the **newaliases** command using the aliases file
/etc/mail/access	Sendmail access text file. Access control for screening or relaying messages from different hosts, networks, or users. Used to generate the **access.db** file
/etc/mail/access.db	Sendmail access database file. Generated from the access text file
/etc/mail/local-host-names	Sendmail local hosts file for multiple hosts using the same mail server (formerly **sendmail.cw**)
/etc/mail/trusted-users	Sendmail trusted users file (formerly **sendmail.ct**)
/etc/mail/error-header	Sendmail error header file (formerly **sendmail.oE**)
/etc/mail/helpfile	Sendmail help file (formerly **sendmail.ht**)
/etc/mail/statistics	Sendmail statistics file (formerly **sendmail.st**)
/etc/mail/virtusertable	Sendmail virtual user table text file. Maps user virtual domain addresses, allowing virtual domains to be hosted on one system. Make entries in this file and then use it to generate the **virtusertable.db** file
/etc/mail/virtusertable.db	Sendmail virtual user table database generated from the **virtusertable** file
/etc/mail/mailertable	Sendmail mailer table text file, used to override routing for your domains
/etc/mail/mailertable.db	Sendmail mailer table database file, generated from the **mailertable** file
/etc/mail/userdb	Sendmail user database file
/etc/mail/domaintable	Sendmail **domaintable** file, maps a domain name to another domain name
/etc/mail/domaintable.db	Sendmail **domaintable** database file, generated from the **domaintable** file
/var/spool/mail	Incoming mail
/var/spool/mqueue	Outgoing mail
/var/spool/maillog	Mail log file

TABLE 25-2   Sendmail Files and Directories

Sendmail 8.10. For example, the help file is now **/etc/mail/helpfile** instead of **/etc/sendmail.ht**. Specialized files provide support for certain features such as **access**, which lets you control access by different hosts and networks to your mail server, and virtusertable, which lets you designate virtual hosts. These files have both text and database versions. The database version ends with the extension **.db** and is the file actually used by Sendmail. You would make your entries in the text version and then effect the changes by generating a corresponding database version. Database versions are generated using the **makemap** command with the **hash** option and a redirection operation for the text and database file. For example, to deny access to a particular host, you would place the appropriate entry for it in the **/etc/mail/access** file, editing the file using any text word processor. Then, to generate the **/etc/mail/access.db** version of the access file, you would change to the **/etc/mail** directory and use the following command:

```
cd /etc/mail
makemap hash access < access
```

To regenerate all the database files, just use the **make** command in the **/etc/mail** directory:

```
make
```

Certain files and directories are used to manage the mail received and sent. Incoming mail is usually kept in the **/var/spool/mail** directory, and outgoing messages are held in the **/var/spool/mqueue** directory, with subdirectories for different users. Monitoring and error messages are logged in the **/var/log/maillog** file.

NOTE *Red Hat and Fedora place the Sendmail configuration file, **sendmail.cf**, in the /etc/mail directory instead of the /etc directory as they did in previous versions (7.3 and earlier).*

NOTE *If your mail server services several hosts, you will need to enter them in the /etc/mail/local-host-names file.*

Aliases and LDAP

Sendmail can now support the Lightweight Directory Access Protocol (LDAP). LDAP enables the use of a separate server to manage Sendmail queries about user mail addresses. Instead of maintaining aliases and **virtusertable** files on different servers, Sendmail uses LDAP support to simply use one centralized LDAP server to locate recipients. Mail addresses are looked up in the LDAP server, instead of having to search several aliases and **virtusertable** files on different servers. LDAP also provides secure authentication of users, allowing controlled access to mail accounts. The following example enables LDAP support on Sendmail in the **sendmail.mc** file:

```
FEATURE('ldap_routing')dnl
LDAPROUTE_DOMAIN('mytrek.com')dnl
```

Alternatively, Sendmail still supports the use of aliases, for either sent or received mail. It checks an aliases database file called **aliases.db** that holds alias names and their associated e-mail addresses. This is often used for administrator mail, where mail may be sent to the system's root user and then redirected to the mail address of the actual system administrator.

You can also alias host addresses, enabling you to address hosts on your network using only their aliases. Alias entries are kept in the **/etc/aliases** file. This file consists of one-line alias records associating aliases with user addresses. You can edit this file to add new entries or to change old ones. They are then stored for lookup in the **aliases.db** file using the command `newaliases`, which runs Sendmail with instructions to update the **aliases.db** file.

Aliases allow you to give different names for an e-mail address or collection of e-mail addresses. One of its most useful features is to create a mailing list of users. Mail addresses to an alias will be sent to the user or list of users associated with the alias. An alias entry consists of an alias name terminated by a colon and followed by a username or a comma-separated list of users. For example, to alias **filmcritic** with the user **george@rabbit.mytrek.com**, you would use the following entry:

```
filmcritic:    george@rabbit.mytrek.com
```

To alias **singers** with the local users **aleina** and **larisa**, you would use

```
singers:     aleina, larisa
```

You can also use aliases as the target addresses, in which case they will expand to their respective user addresses. For example, the **performers** alias will expand through the **filmcritic** and **singers** aliases to the users **george@rabbit.mytrek.com**, **aleina**, and **larisa**:

```
performers:    filmcritic, singers
```

Once you have made your entries in the **/etc/mail/aliases** file, you need to generate a database version using the `newaliases` command:

```
newaliases
```

NOTE *Sendmail now supports a mail submission mode. In this mode, Sendmal does not run as a server along with the corresponding root privileges. Instead it merely submits mail. In this mode, Sendmail can be invoked directly by Email clients to send mail. The mail submission mode uses the /etc/mail/submit.cf configuration file, which can be configured using macros in the /etc/mail.submit.mc file.*

Sendmail Configuration

The main Sendmail configuration file is **sendmail.cf**, located in the **/etc** directory. This file consists of a sometimes lengthy list of mail definitions that set general options, designate MTAs, and define the address rewrite rules. A series of options set features, such as the maximum size of mail messages or the name of host files. The MTAs are those mailers through which Sendmail routes messages. The rewrite rules "rewrite" a mail address to route through the appropriate Internet connections to its destination (these rules can be complex). Check the Sendmail HOW-TO and the online documentation for a detailed explanation.

The **sendmail.cf** definitions can be complex and confusing. To simplify the configuration process, Sendmail supports the use of macros you can use to generate the **sendmail.cf** file using the M4 preprocessor (this requires installation of the sendmail-cf package). Macros are placed in the **/etc/mail/sendmail.mc** file. Here, you can use macros to designate the definitions and features you want for Sendmail, and then the macros are used to generate the appropriate definitions and rewrite rules in the **sendmail.cf** file. As part of the Sendmail package, several specialized versions of the **sendmail.mc** file are made available in the **/usr/share/sendmail-cf** directory. These begin with a system name and have the suffix **.mc**. On many distributions, a specialized version tailored to your distribution is already installed as your **/etc/mail/sendmail.mc** file.

Once you configure your **sendmail.mc** file, you use the following command to generate a **sendmail.cf** file (be sure first to back up your original **sendmail.cf** file). You can rename the **sendmail.mc** file to reflect the specific configuration. You can have as many different **.mc** files as you want and use them to implement different configurations. On Red Hat and Fedora you can use the following command in the **/etc/mail** directory:

```
make -C /etc/mail
```

Alternatively, you can use the original **m4** macro command:

```
m4 sendmail.mc > /etc/mail/sendmail.cf
```

You will then need to restart the Sendmail server to make the configuration effective:

```
service sendmail restart
```

In the **sendmail.mc** file, you configure different aspects of Sendmail using either a **define** command to set the value of Sendmail variables or a Sendmail macro that has already been defined to set a particular Sendmail feature. For example, to assign the **PROCMAIL_PATH** variable to the directory **/usr/bin/procmail**, you would use the following:

```
define('PROCMAIL_MAILER_PATH','/usr/bin/procmail')
```

Similarly, if there are variables that you do not want defined, you can remove them with the **undefine** command:

```
undefine('UUCP_RELAY')
```

To specify the type of operating system that your Sendmail server is running on, you would use the **OSTYPE** Sendmail macro. The following example specifies the Linux operating system:

```
OSTYPE('linux')
```

The **MAILER** macro specifies the mail delivery agents (MDAs) to be used. You may have more than one. Usually, you will need a mail delivery agent such as procmail for delivering mail to hosts on your network. In addition, Sendmail in effect operates as an MDA to receive messages from hosts in its local network, which it will then send out to the larger network.

```
MAILER(procmail)
MAILER(smtp)
```

Sendmail also supports an extensive number of features that you need to explicitly turn on. You can do this with the Sendmail **FEATURE** macro. See Table 25-3 for a list of commonly

Feature	Description
`use_cw_file`	Checks for hosts served by the mail server **/etc/mail/local-host-names** file.
`use_ct_file`	Reads a list of users from the **/etc/trusted-users** file. These are trusted users that can change the sender name for their messages.
`redirect`	Rejects all mail addressed to "address.REDIRECT", providing a forwarding address is placed in the **/etc/aliases** file.
`mailertable`	Uses a mailer table file, **/etc/mail/mailertable**, to override routing for particular domains.
`domaintable`	Uses a domain table file, **/etc/mail/domaintable**, to map one domain to another. Useful if you change your domain name.
`allmasquerade`	Causes recipient addresses to also masquerade as being from the masquerade host.
`masquerade_entire_domain`	Masquerades all hosts within the domain specified in **MASQUERADE_AS**.
`masquerade_envelope`	Masquerades envelope sender and recipient along with headers.
`virtusertable`	For virtual hosts, maps virtual addresses to real addresses.
`nullclient`	Turns a Sendmail server into a null client, which simply forwards mail messages to a central mail server for processing.
`local_procmail`	Uses procmail as the local mailer.
`smrsh`	Uses the Sendmail Restricted Shell (smrsh) for mailing.
`promiscuous_relay`	Allows you to relay mail, allowing mail to be received from outside your domain and sent on to hosts outside your domain.
`relay_entire_domain`	Allows any host in your domain to relay mail (default limits this to hosts in the access database).
`relay_hosts_only`	Checks for relay permission for particular hosts instead of domains.
`accept_unqualified_senders`	Allows sender e-mail addresses to be single usernames instead of just fully qualified names that include domain names.

TABLE 25-3   Sendmail Features *(continued)*

Feature	Description
`accept_unresolvable_domains`	Allows Sendmail to accept unresolvable domain names. Useful for those users in a local network blocked by a firewall from the full DNS namespace. By default, Sendmail requires domains in addresses to be resolvable with DNS.
`access_db`	Accepts or rejects mail from domains and hosts in the access database.
`blacklist_recipients`	Blocks mail to certain users, such as those that should never receive mail—like the users **nobody** and **host**.
`dnsbl`	Rejects hosts in the Realtime Blackhole List. Managed by MAPS (Mail Abuse Prevention System LLC) and designed to limit transport of unwanted mass e-mail (**mail-abuse.org**).
`ldap_routing`	Enables LDAP use.

TABLE 25-3   Sendmail Features

used Sendmail features. The following example turns on the **redirect** feature, which is used to inform a sender that a recipient is now at a different address:

```
FEATURE(redirect)
```

In addition, you can set certain configuration options. These are variables beginning with the prefix **conf** that you can set and assign values to using the **define** command. There are an extensive number of configuration options, most of which you will not need to change. The following example defines the **confAUTO_REBUILD** configuration option, which will automatically rebuild the aliases database if needed:

```
define('confAUTO_REBUILD')
```

Certain macros and types of macros need to be placed in the **sendmail.mc** file in a particular sequence as shown here. Notice that **MAILER** is toward the end and **OSTYPE** at the beginning. Local macro definitions (**define**) and **FEATURE** entries follow the **OSTYPE** and **DOMAIN** entries:

```
VERSIONID
OSTYPE
DOMAIN
define
FEATURE
local macro definitions
MAILER
LOCAL_RULE_*
LOCAL_RULESETS
```

The local macro and configuration option definitions that affect a particular feature need to be entered before the **FEATURE** entry. For example, the **redirect** feature uses the aliases file. Any local definition of the aliases file needs to be entered before the **redirect** feature.

```
define('ALIAS_FILE','/etc/aliases')
FEATURE(redirect)
```

You need to be careful how you enter comments into a **sendmail.mc** file. This file is read as a stream of macros, ignoring all white spaces, including newlines. No special comment characters are looked for. Instead, you have to simulate comment indicators using the **dnl** or **divert** commands. The **dnl** command instructs that all characters following that **dnl** command up to and including the next newline are to be ignored. If you place a **dnl** command at the beginning of a text line in the **sendmail.mc** file, it has the effect of turning that line into a comment, ignoring everything on that line—including its newline. Even empty lines will require a **dnl** entry to ignore the newline character:

```
dnl you will have to /etc/mail/sendmail.cf by running this the m4
dnl macro config through preprocessor:
dnl
```

Alternatively, you can use the **divert** command. The **divert** command will ignore all data until another **divert** command is reached:

```
divert(-1)
 This is the macro config file used to generate
 the /etc/mail/sendmail.cf file. If you modify the file regenerate
 you will have to regenerate /etc/mail/sendmail.cf by running the m4
 macro
divert(0)
```

For Sendmail to work at all, it requires only that the **OSTYPE** and **MAILERS** macros be defined, along with any needed features and options. A very simple Sendmail file is shown here:

mysendmail.mc
```
dnl My sendmail.mc file
OSTYPE('linux')
define('PROCMAIL_MAILER_PATH','/usr/bin/procmail')
FEATURE(redirect)
MAILER(procmail)
MAILER(smtp)
```

A **sendmail.mc** file usually contains many more entries, particularly for parameters and features. Check the **/etc/mail/sendmail.mc** file on your Red Hat or Fedora system to see the standard default entries for Sendmail.

Sendmail Masquerading

For a mail server that is relaying messages from local hosts to the Internet, you may want to masquerade the source of the messages. In large networks that have their own mail servers connected to the Internet, Sendmail masquerading can make messages sent by local hosts appear to be sent by the mail server. Their host address will be replaced by the mail server's address. Returned mail can then be sent to the mail server and held in POP or IMAP server mailboxes that can be accessed later by users on the local hosts. Also, entries in the server's virtual user table could forward mail to corresponding users in local hosts.

Masquerading is often used to mask local hosts with a domain name. Any subdomains can also be masqueraded. This method can be applied to situations where an ISP or your network administrator has assigned your network its own domain name. You can then mask all mail messages as coming from your domain name instead of from particular hosts or from any subdomains you may have. For example, if a network's official domain name is **mytrek .com**, all messages from the hosts in the **mytrek.com** network, such as **rabbit.mytrek.com** and **turtle.mytrek.com**, could be masqueraded to appear as just coming from **mytrek.com**. Should the **mytrek.com** network have a subnetwork whose domain is **mybeach.com**, any messages from **mybeach.com** could also be masqueraded as coming from **mytrek.com**.

Masquerading is turned on with the **MASQUERADE_AS** command. This takes as its argument the name you want to masquerade your mail as. Normally, the name used is just the domain name, without the mail host. In the following example, the mail is masqueraded as simply **mytrek.com**. Mail sent from a local host like **turtle.mytrek.com** will appear to be sent by just **mytrek.com**:

```
MASQUERADE_AS('mytrek.com')dnl
```

You will also have to specify the hosts and domains on your local network that your Sendmail server should masquerade. If you have decided to masquerade all the hosts in your local network, you just need to set the **masquerade_entire_domain** feature, as in

```
FEATURE('masquerade_entire_domain')dnl
```

If, instead, you want to masquerade particular hosts or your domain has several subdomains that you want masqueraded, you list them in the **MASQUERADE_DOMAIN** entry. You can list either particular hosts or entire domains. For example, given a local network with the local hosts **turtle.mytrek.com** and **rabbit.mytrek.com**, you can list them with the **MASQUERADE_DOMAIN** to have them masqueraded. The domain they are masqueraded as is specified in the **MASQUERADE_AS** entry.

```
MASQUERADE_DOMAIN('turtle.mytrek.com rabbit.mytrek.com')dnl
```

If you want to masquerade all the hosts in your local network, you can simply list your local network's domain name. If your local network also supports several subdomains, you can list those as well to masquerade them. For example, to masquerade all the hosts in the **mybeach.com** domain, you would use the following entry:

```
MASQUERADE_DOMAIN('mytrek.com mybeach.com')dnl
```

If you have a long list of domains or hosts, or if you want to be able to easily change those that should be masqueraded, you can place them in a file to be read by Sendmail. Specify the file with the **MASQUERADE_DOMAIN_FILE** command:

```
MASQUERADE_DOMAIN_FILE('mydomains')dnl
```

If you just want to masquerade all the hosts in your local domain, you use the **masquerade_entire_domain** feature:

```
FEATURE(masquerade_entire_domain)dnl
```

A common configuration for a local network would specify the domain name in the **MASQUERADE_AS** entry and in the **MASQUERADE_DOMAIN** entry. Using the example **myisp .com** for the domain, the entries would look like this:

```
MASQUERADE_AS('mytrek.com')dnl
FEATURE(masquerade_entire_domain)dnl
```

If you wanted to masquerade as an ISP's mail domain, you would use the ISP's domain in the **MASQUERADE_AS** entry as shown here:

```
MASQUERADE_AS('myisp.com')dnl
MASQUERADE_DOMAIN('mytrek.com')dnl
```

When mail is received from the outside bearing just the address **mytrek.com**, your network needs to know what host to send it to. This is the host designated as the mail server for the **mytrek.com** network. This information is provided by a mail exchange record (MX) in your DNS configuration that will specify that mail sent to **mytrek.com** will be handled by the mail server—in this case, **turtle.mytrek.com**:

```
mytrek.com.    IN    MX    0    turtle.mytrek.com.
```

You further have to be sure that MX relaying is enabled with the **relay_based_on_MX** feature:

```
FEATURE(relay_based_on_MX)dnl
```

All messages will appear to originate from the mail server's host. For example, if your Sendmail mail server is running on **turtle.mytrek.com**, mail sent from a local host called **rabbit.mytrek.com** will appear to have been sent from **turtle.mytrek.com**.

You can also masquerade recipient addresses, so that mail sent to users on your local host will be sent instead to the masqueraded address. Use the **allmasquerade** feature to enable recipient masquerading:

```
FEATURE(allmasquerade)dnl
```

Configuring Mail Servers and Mail Clients

Sendmail can be used either as a mail server, handling mail for various hosts on a network, or as a mail client, managing mail for local users on a particular host. In a simple network configuration, you would have each host running Sendmail in a client configuration, and one host operating as a mail server, relaying mail for the network hosts. For a local network connected to the Internet, your local hosts would run Sendmail in a client configuration, and your gateway would run Sendmail in a server configuration (though the mail server would not have to necessarily run on the gateway). The mail server would relay messages from the local network hosts out to the Internet. The mail server could also be used to block unwanted access from outside hosts, such as those sending spam mail. A basic client or server Sendmail configuration involves just a few features in the **/etc/mail/sendmail.mc** file. The default Fedora configuration installed on your system allows use on a single host, managing messages between users on that host. To enable client and server use, you will need to make changes to the **/etc/mail/sendmail.mc** file.

Configuring Sendmail for a Simple Network Configuration

Fedora initially configures Sendmail to work only on the system it is running on, **localhost**. To use Sendmail to send messages to other hosts on a local network, you need to change and add settings in the **sendmail.mc** and **/etc/mail/access** files. A simple network configuration would have Sendmail running on each host, handling both mail sent between users on that host and mail to and from users on other hosts. For each Sendmail server configuration, you would make the changes described in the following section on simple local network configuration.

For messages sent between hosts on your network, you only need to run the Sendmail server on each, making a few changes to their Sendmail configurations. The Sendmail server on one of your hosts can be configured to handle the task of relaying messages between hosts. Using the network example described earlier, the hosts **turtle**, **rabbit**, and **lizard** will be running their own Sendmail servers. The Sendmail server on the **turtle** host will be configured to relay messages between all the hosts, itself included.

On each host on your network, edit the **/etc/mail/sendmail.mc** file and make the following changes. Comment out the **DAEMON_OPTIONS** line in the default **sendmail.mc** file by placing a **dnl** word in front of it, as shown here. Removing this feature will allow you to receive messages over your local network. This entry is restricting Sendmail to the **localhost** (127.0.0.1):

```
dnl DAEMON_OPTIONS('Port=smtp,Addr=127.0.0.1, Name=MTA')dnl
```

In the **sendmail.mc** file located on the host that you want to have handle the relaying of messages, you need to also add the following line:

```
FEATURE(relay_entire_domain)dnl
```

Run the **m4** operation to install the changed configuration and then restart the server with the service operation, as described earlier.

You can now e-mail messages from one user to another across your network. For example, **george@turtle.mytrek.com** can now e-mail a message to **larisa@rabbit.mytrek.com**. The local Sendmail servers will take care of sending and delivering mail both to users within their hosts and those located on other network hosts.

Configuring Sendmail for a Centralized Mail Server

Alternatively, you could set up a central mail server to handle all the mail on your network. Mail clients on various hosts could send their messages to the central mail server, which would then relay them out to the larger network or Internet. Mail could then be received at the central mail server, where clients could later retrieve it. There are several ways to set up a central mail server. One of the simplest is to run a central mail server on your gateway host, and then have null client versions of the Sendmail server running on local hosts.

Any mail sent from local hosts would be automatically forwarded to the central mail server. Received mail could only be delivered to the central server, usually to a POP or IMAP server also running on the central server's host. Users could then access the POP server to retrieve their mail.

For a centralized configuration, it would make sense to treat users as having their network domain as their address, rather than separate hosts in their network. Thus the user **cece** on **rabbit.mytrek.com** would use the mail address **cece@mytrek.com**, not **cece@rabbit .mytrek.com**. Users could have the same name as those on their respective hosts, but corresponding users would be set up on the gateway host to handle received mail managed by the POP or IMAP servers.

An effective simple mail server would involve several components:

- A central mail server running on the gateway host
- Each client running Sendmail as a null client
- Masquerading all mail to use the domain address only, not host addresses
- A POP or IMAP server running on the gateway host to handle received mail

Configuring a Workstation with Direct ISP Connection

If you are running a Linux system that is not part of a network but does have a direct connection to the Internet through an ISP (Internet service provider), you could simply use the ISP mail servers for sending and receiving mail. Normally, you would have an SMTP mail server for outgoing mail and a POP server for incoming mail. However, you can also configure Sendmail to interface with your ISP.

Be sure to first comment out the **DAEMON_OPTIONS** option as shown in the previous sections.

Normally, your ISP will provide a mail server that will handle mail for its hosts. To make use of the ISP mail server, you can define it with the **SMART_HOST** option. Mail will be sent through the ISP mail server. **SMART_HOST** has the format *type:hostname,* where *type* is the kind of mail server used, usually SMTP. The default is relay. Define the **SMART_HOST** option to use your ISP to send and receive mail:

```
define ('SMART_HOST', 'smtp:mail.my-isp.com')dnl
```

The **SMART_HOST** option is used to indicate a specific remote mail server that you want to have handle the relaying of your network messages. It can be an ISP mail server, as well as any mail server in a larger network.

For a dial-up connection over a modem, you can use various configuration options to control your connection. The **confMESSAGE_TIMEOUT** option lets you control how long mail can remain on the output queue, letting you keep mail until you are ready to dial in and send it. Setting the **confDELIVERY_MODE** option to **queueonly** lets you send mail only when you are ready.

The Mailer Table

The mailer table lets you route messages addressed to a specified host or domain to particular mail server. You can use the mailer table to have mail addressed to a virtual domain routed to the mail server for your network. To reference an entire domain, prefix the domain name with a period. The host to which the mail is routed is prefixed by the mailer used, usually **smtp** for Sendmail. The following entry will route mail addressed to **.mybeach.com** to the mail server **turtle.mytrek.com**:

```
.mybeach.com          smtp:turtle.mytrek.com
```

Entries are placed in the **/etc/mail/mailertable** file. Once you have made your entries, generate the **mailertable.db** database file with the **make** command:

```
make mailertable
```

Virtual Domains: virtusertable

As you will see in Chapter 36, you can define virtual domains for your network. These virtual domains are mapped to one or more real domains by your DNS server. However, you can receive messages with mail addresses for users on your virtual domains. In this case, you need to map these addresses to users on your real domain so that the mail can be delivered to an existing location. This mapping is carried out by the virtual user table called **/etc/mail/virtusertable**. The virtual user table lets you map mail addresses for virtual domains to users on real domains. Once you have made your entries, generate the **virtusertable.db** database file with the **make** command:

```
make virtusertable
```

Security

For security, Sendmail lets you screen specific messages as well as provide authentication and encryption for Sendmail transmissions. With version 8.11, Sendmail incorporated support for the Secure Sockets Layer (SSL) and the Simple Authentication and Security Layer (SASL). Support for SSL goes by the Sendmail command **STARTTLS**, which stands for "start transport layer security." SSL provides authentication, encryption, and integrity checks for Sendmail operations (see Chapter 19). OpenSSL must first be installed to allow use of SSL encryption and authentication methods.

The SASL is implemented by the **AUTH** command and is referred to as SMTP AUTH. SASL provides authentication for mail users and servers. It can make use of already-installed Kerberos services to provide authentication.

Sendmail also provides you with the capability of screening out messages from specific domain, host, IP, and user addresses. Rules to perform such screening are kept in the **/etc/mail/access** file. You can edit this file and add your own rules. A rule consists of an address followed by an action to take. (The actions supported are listed in Table 25-4.) For example, to remove all messages from the **myannoyingad.com** domain, you would enter

```
myannoyingad.com DISCARD
```

The next example rejects any message from **larisa@turtle.mycar.com** and sends a notice of the rejection:

```
larisa@turtle.mycar.com REJECT
```

Action	Description
`OK`	Accepts message even if other rules would reject (exception to the rules).
`DISCARD`	Discards the message completely.
`REJECT`	Rejects the message, sending a rejection notice to the sender.
`RELAY`	Relays messages for specified domain.
SMTP-code message	Code and message to be sent to sender.

TABLE 25-4   Access Actions

You can also specify an error message to return, as shown here:

```
cecelia@rabbit.mytrek.com     ERROR:"Retired yesterday"
```

To send an error message to spammers, you could include a message as shown here. The first number is an error code:

```
cyberspammer.com     ERROR:"550 We don't accept mail from spammers"
```

An **/etc/mail/access** file with the previous entries would look like the following:

```
myannoyingad.com              DISCARD
larisa@turtle.mycar.com       REJECT
cecelia@rabbit.mytrek.com     ERROR:"Retired yesterday"
cyberspammer.com              ERROR:"550 We don't accept mail from spammers"
```

Sendmail actually reads the access rules from a database file called **access.db**, also located in the **/etc/mail** directory. To implement your rules, you have to regenerate the **access.db** file using the access file. You can do this with the **make** command using **access** as the argument, as shown here:

```
make access
```

Sendmail then has to be restarted to read the new **access.db** file.

The use of the access file is enabled in the **sendmail.mc** file with the **access_db** feature:

```
FEATURE('access_db')dnl
```

The access file will deny mail received from the listed addresses. However, you can also reject any mail sent to them. Additionally, you can also receive mail for certain hosts on your network. You do this by enabling the **blacklist_recipients** option in the **sendmail.mc** file. This option governs recipients, whereas **access** normally governs senders. Those addresses listed will not be able to receive any mail. This feature is also used for certain administrative users that should never receive mail, such as **nobody** (the guest user) or **ftp** (the FTP user):

```
FEATURE('blacklist_recipients')dnl
```

The following example will not allow mail to be sent to **cyberspammer.com** (a recipient), nor can mail be received for **justin@lizard.mytrek.com**, **secretproject@rabbit.mytrek.com**, or **mysurfboard.com**:

```
mysurfboard.com                     ERROR:"Domain does not exist"
justin@lizard.mytrek.com            "Moved to Hawaii"
secretproject@rabbit.mytrek.com     REJECT
cyberspammer.com                    REJECT
```

Your distribution version of **smb.conf** may configure Sendmail to use **access_db** (as is the case with Fedora). Access is granted only to users on the local host. If your system is being used as a mail server for a network and you have not enabled the **relay_entire_domain** feature, you will need to allow access by other hosts on your network. In the access file, you can place a **RELAY** rule for your network. The **RELAY** rule will let other hosts use your mail server to send messages out to other hosts. This is normally done for a gateway host that needs to relay messages from a local network out to the Internet. The following example allows access from the **mytrek.com** network:

```
mytrek.com      RELAY
```

For a specific host, place an entry for it in the access file as shown here:

```
rabbit.mytrek.com      RELAY
```

To further secure Sendmail, you should disable the use of **VRFY**. This option allows remote users to try to verify the existence of a user address. This can be used to guess valid users on your system. This option is disabled with the **noverify** feature:

```
FEATURE('noverify')dnl
```

Another potential security breach is the **EXPN** option, which expands mailing lists and aliases to their actual addresses. Use the **noexpn** feature to turn it off:

```
FEATURE('noexpn')dnl
```

By default, Sendmail will refuse mail from any domain that cannot be resolved. You can override this restriction with the **accept_unresolvable_domains** feature. Sendmail will also reject mail whose addresses do not have fully qualified domain names. You can override this feature with **accept_unqualified_senders**.

POP and IMAP Server: Dovecot

The protocols Internet Mail Access Protocol (IMAP) and Post Office Protocol (POP) allow a remote server to hold mail for users who can then fetch their mail from it when they are ready. Unlike procmail, which delivers mail messages directly to a user account on a Linux system, the IMAP and POP protocols hold mail until a user accesses an account on the IMAP or POP server. The servers then transfer any received messages to the user's local mailbox. Such servers are often used by ISPs to provide Internet mail services for users. Instead of being sent directly to a user's machine, the mail resides in the IMAP or POP server until it's retrieved. Red Hat Linux and Fedora install Dovecot as both its IMAP and POP servers, and it also includes the Cyrus IMAP server. Other popular IMAP and POP servers available are Qpopper, the Qmail POP server, the Washington University POP and IMAP servers, and the Courier POP and IMAP servers.

You can access the POP server from different hosts; however, when you do, all the messages are transferred to that host. They are not kept on the POP server (though you can set an option to keep them). The POP server simply forwards your messages on the requesting host. When you access your messages from a certain computer, they will be transferred to that computer and erased from the POP server. If you access your POP server again from a different computer, those previous messages will be gone.

The Internet Mail Access Protocol (IMAP) allows a remote server to hold mail for users who can then log in to access their mail. Unlike the POP servers, IMAP servers retain user mail messages. Users can even save their mail on the IMAP mail server. This has the advantage of keeping a user's mail in one centralized location accessible anywhere on the network. Users can log in to the mail server from any host on the network and read, send, and save their mail.

Unlike POP, IMAP allows users to set up multiple folders on their mail server in which they can organize their mail. IMAP also supports the use of shared folders to which several users can access mail on a given topic.

Dovecot

Dovecot is a combination IMAP and POP server. Using its own indexing methods, Dovecot is able to handle a great deal of e-mail traffic. It features support for SSL, along with numerous authentication methods. Password database support includes shadow passwords, LDAP, PAM, and MySQL. The **/etc/dovecot.conf** file is configured to use plain password authentication with PAM, using the **passwd** file.

Dovecot is a service that is managed with a service script: **/etc/rc.d/init.d/dovecot**. You can start, stop, or restart with either the `service` command or system-config-services.

```
service dovecot start
```

Configuration options are placed in **/etc/dovecot.conf**. This file contains commented default settings with detail explanations for each. Options specific to **imap** and **pop3** are placed in their own sections. These are some basic settings to configure:

- **protocols**   This can be set to imap and pop as well as imaps and pops for SSL-encrypted connections.
- **listen**   These can be set to IPv4 or IPv4 protocols; IPv6 is set by default. The listen option is set in the respective protocol sections, like **protocol imap** or **protocol pop3**.
- **auth default** section   This section holds your default authentication options.
- **mechanism** in **auth** section is plain by default. digest-MD5 and cran-MD5 are supported, but they are not needed if you are using SSL.
- **passwd** in **auth** section**mail_location**   The default mail storage method and location.

Dovecot supports either mailbox or maildir (IMAP) storage formats. The mailbox format uses single, large mailbox files to hold several mail messages. Updates can be time consuming. The Maildir format uses a separate file for each message, making updates much more efficient. Dovecot will automatically detect the kind of storage use, referencing the MAIL environment variable. This will be the user's mbox file at **/var/mail**. You can configure Dovecot to use a Maildir format by setting the **mail_location** option to use a maildir setting, specifying the directory to use. The **%u** symbol can be used to represent the user name, **%h** for the home directory. Messages will be stored in a user's Maildir directory instead of an mbox file. Be sure to create the Maildir directory and give it read, write, and execute access.

```
mail_location=maildir:/var/mail/%1u/%u/maildir
```

Other POP and IMAP Servers

Fedora also includes the Cyrus IMAP server, which you can install and use instead of Dovecot. In addition, several other IMAP and POP servers are available for use on Linux:

- The University of Washington POP and IMAP servers (**ftp.cac.washington.edu/imap**) are part of the University of Washington's **imap** RPM package. The POP server daemons are called **ipop2d** and **ipop3d**. Your Linux system then runs as a POP2 and POP3 server for your network. These servers are run through **xinetd**. The POP3 server uses the **ipop3** file in the **/etc/xinetd.d**, and the IMAP uses **imap**.

- The Cyrus IMAP server (**asg.web.cmu.edu/cyrus**) is included with Fedora. Cyrus IMAP servers feature security controls and authentication, using a private mailbox structure that is easily scalable. Designed to be run on dedicated mail servers, it is supported and maintained by Carnegie Mellon. The name of the Cyrus IMAP server daemon is **imapd**. On Fedora, there will be a file called **imap** in the **/etc/xinetd.d** directory. You turn it on or off with the **chkconfig** command.

- The Courier-IMAP server (**www.courier-mta.org**) is a small, fast IMAP server that provides extensive authentication support including LDAP and PAM.

- Qpopper is the Berkeley POP server (popper). Qpopper is unsupported software, currently available from Qualcomm, makers of Eudora e-mail software. The Qpopper Web page is located at the Eudora site archives (**www.eudora.com**).

NOTE *The IMAP and POP servers included with Fedora provide SSL encryption for secure e-mail transmissions. You can also run IMAP and POP servers using Stunnel to provide similar security. Stunnel is an SSL wrapper for daemons like **imapd**, **popd**, and even **pppd** (modem connections). In the service's **xinetd** script, you can invoke the server with the **stunnel** command instead of running the server directly.*

Spam: SpamAssassin

With SpamAssassin, you can filter sent and received e-mail for spam. The filter examines both headers and content, drawing on rules designed to detect common spam messages. When they are detected, it then tags the message as spam, so that a mail client can then discard it. SpamAssassin will also report spam messages to spam detection databases. The version of SpamAssassin distributed for Linux is the open source version developed by the

Apache project, located at **spamassassin.apache.org**. There you can find detailed documentation, FAQs, mailing lists, and even a listing of the tests that SpamAssassin performs.

SpamAssassin rule files are located at **/usr/share/spamassassin**. The files contain rules for running tests such as detecting the fake hello in the header. Configuration files for SpamAssassin are located at **/etc/mail/spamassassin**. The **local.cf** file lists system-wide SpamAssassin options such as how to rewrite headers. The **init.pre** file holds spam system configurations. The **spamassassin-spamc.rc** file will redirect all mail to the **spamc** client.

Users can set their own SpamAssassin option in their **.spamassassin/user_prefs** file. Common options include `required_score`, which sets a threshold for classifying a message as SPAM, numerous whitelist and blacklist options that accept and reject messages from certain users and domains, and tagging options that either rewrite or just add SPAM labels. Check the Mail::SpamAssassin::Conf Man page for details.

SpamAssassin is run as a service using the `/etc/init.d/spamassassin` service script. This runs the **spamd** server, which in turn is accessed by the **spamc** client. Using the server/client structure greatly enhances SpamAssassin's efficiency. Options for **spamd** can be set in the **/etc/sysconfig/spamassassin** file.

```
service spamassassin start
```

To configure procmail to use SpamAssassin, you need to have procmail run the **/etc/mail/spamassassin/spamassassin-spamc.rc** file. This will filter all mail through SpamAssassin. The **spamassassin-spamc.rc** file uses the **spamd** daemon, which means you have to have the SpamAssassin service running. The **spamassassin-default.rc** file runs a less efficient script to use SpamAssassin, instead of the daemon. If you want system-wide procmail filtering, you use the **/etc/procmailrc** file, whereas to implement filtering on a per-user basis, use a **.procmail** file in the user's home directory. Within the respective procmail files add the following at the top:

```
INCLUDERC=/etc/mail/spamassassin/spamassassin-spamc.rc
```

Configuring Postfix for use with SpamAssassin can be complicated. A helpful tool for this task is **amavisd-new**, an interface between a mail transport agent like Sendmail or Postfix, and content checkers like SpamAssassin and virus checkers. Check **www.ijs.si/ software/amavisd** for more details. This tool is currently part of Fedora.

PART V

Print, News, and Database Servers: CUPS, INN, and MySQL

Once treated as devices attached to a system directly, printers are now treated as network resources managed by print servers. In the case of a single printer attached directly to a system, the networking features become transparent and the printer appears as just one more device. On the other hand, you could easily make use of a print server's networking capability to let several systems use the same printer. Although printer installation is almost automatic on most Linux distributions, it helps to understand the underlying process. Printing sites and resources are listed in Table 26-1.

The Common Unix Printing System (CUPS) provides printing services. It is freely available under the GNU Public License. Though it is now included with most distributions, you can also download the most recent source-code version of CUPS from **www.cups.org**. The site also provides detailed documentation on installing and managing printers. CUPS is based on the Internet Printing Protocol (IPP), which is designed to establish a printing standard for the Internet (for more information, see **www.pwg.org/ipp**). Whereas the older LPD-based printing systems focused primarily on line printers, an IPP-based system provides networking, PostScript, and Web support. CUPS works like an Internet server and employs a configuration setup much like that of the Apache Web server. Its network support lets clients directly access printers on remote servers, without having to configure the printers themselves. Configuration needs to be maintained only on the print servers.

The Common Unix Printing System (CUPS) is the primary print server for Fedora and Red Hat Linux, and it has always been the primary server for Fedora. CUPS is the print server supported by system-config-printer. With libgnomecups, GNOME now provides integrated support for CUPS, allowing GNOME-based applications to directly access CUPS printers.

Once you have installed your printers and configured your print server, you can print and manage your print queue using print clients. There are a variety of printer clients available for the CUPS server, including system-config-printer, GNOME print manager, the CUPS configuration tool, and various line printing tools like **lpq** and **lpc**. These are

Resource	Description
www.cups.org	Common Unix Printing System
www.pwg.org/ipp	Internet Printing Protocol
sourceforge.net/projects/lprng	LPRng Print server

TABLE 26-1   Linux Printing Resources

described in further detail later in this chapter. The CUPS configuration tool is a Web-based configuration tool that can also manage printers and print jobs (open your browser and enter the URL **http://localhost:631**). A Web page is displayed with entries for managing jobs, managing printers, and administrative tasks. Select the Manage Jobs entry to remove or reorder jobs you have submitted.

NOTE *Line Printer, Next Generation (LPRng) was the traditional print server for Linux and Unix systems, but it has since been dropped from the Red Hat and Fedora distributions. You can find out more about LPRng at **sourceforge.net/projects/lprng**.*

Printer Devices and Configuration

Before you can use any printer, you first have to install it on a Linux system on your network. A local printer is installed directly on your own system. This involves creating an entry for the printer in a printer configuration file that defines the kind of printer it is, along with other features such as the device file and spool directory it uses. On CUPS, the printer configuration file is **/etc/cups/printers.conf**. Installing a printer is fairly simple: determine which device file to use for the printer and the configuration entries for it. On Red Hat and Fedora, you can use the system-config-printer configuration tool to set up and configure your printer easily. Depending on the interface you are using, system-config-printer will invoke either system-config-printer-gui, a GUI GNOME printer configuration tool, or system-config-printer-tui, the same tool with a screen-based cursor-driven interface.

TIP *If you cannot find the drivers for your printer, you may be able to download them from **www.openprinting.org**. The site maintains an extensive listing of drivers.*

Printer Device Files

Linux dynamically creates the device names for printers that are installed (see Chapter 32). For parallel printers, the device names will be **lp0**, **lp1**, and **lp2**, depending on how many parallel printers are connected. The number used in these names corresponds to a parallel port on your PC; **lp0** references the LPT1 parallel port and **lp1** references the LPT2 parallel port. Serial printers will use serial ports, referenced by the device names like **ttyS0**, **ttyS1**, **ttyS2**, and so on. USB-connected printers will have a Hardware Abstract Layer (HAL) device connection. HAL is designed for removable devices that can easily be attached to other connections and still be recognized.

Spool Directories

When your system prints a file, it makes use of special directories called *spool directories*. A *print job* is a file to be printed. When you send a file to a printer, a copy of it is made and placed in a spool directory set up for that printer. The location of the spool directory is obtained from the printer's entry in its configuration file. In Linux, the spool directory is located at **/var/spool/cups** under a directory with the name of the printer. For example, the spool directory for the **myepson** printer would be located at **/var/spool/cups/myepson**. The spool directory contains several files for managing print jobs. Some files use the name of the printer as their extension. For example, the **myepson** printer has the files **control .myepson**, which provides printer queue control, and **active.myepson** for the active print job, as well as **log.myepson,** which is the log file.

Starting the CUPS Server

With the RPM (Remote Print Manager) version used by Red Hat and Fedora, a **cups** startup script is installed in the **/etc/rc.d/init.d** directory. You can start, stop, and restart CUPS using the **service** command and the **cups** script or system-config-services (System I Administration I Server Settings I Services). When you make changes or install printers, be sure to restart CUPS to have your changes take effect. You can use the following command:

```
# service cups restart
```

Installing Printers with CUPS

The easiest way to configure and install printers with CUPS is to use system-config printer, as described in Chapter 4, or use the CUPS configuration tool, which is a Web browser–based configuration tool. To ensure browser access, be sure to first select CUPS with the Printer System Switcher, or if you are using **xinetd** for CUPS, turn on **cups** with the **chkconfig** command.

```
# chkconfig cups on
```

To start the Web interface, enter the following URL into your Web browser:

```
http://localhost:631
```

This opens an administration screen where you can manage and add printers. You will first be asked to enter the administrator's username (usually **root**) and password (usually the root user's password).

With the CUPS configuration tool, you install a printer on CUPS through a series of Web pages, each of which requests different information. To install a printer, click the Add Printer button to display a page where you enter the printer name and location. The location is the host to which the printer is connected.

Subsequent pages will prompt you to enter the model of the printer and driver, which you select from available listings. Once you have added the printer, you can configure it. Clicking the Manage Printers entry in the Administration page lists your installed printers. You can then click a printer to display a page that lets you control the printer. You can stop the printer, configure its printing, modify its installation, and even delete the printer.

Clicking the Configure Printer button displays a page where you can configure how your printer prints, by specifying the resolution or paper size.

Configured information for a printer will be stored in the **/etc/cups/printers.conf** file. You can examine this file directly, and edit it as desired. Here is an example of a printer configuration entry. Notice that it was created using system-config-printer. The **DeviceURI** entry specifies the device used, in this case a USB printer managed by HAL. It is currently idle, with no jobs:

```
# Printer configuration file for CUPS
# Written by cupsd
<Printer mycannon>
Info Cannon s330
Location
DeviceURI
hal:///org/freedesktop/Hal/devices/usb_device_4a9_1074_300HCR_if0_printer_noserial
State Idle
StateTime 1166554036
Accepting Yes
Shared Yes
JobSheets none none
QuotaPeriod 0
PageLimit 0
KLimit 0
OpPolicy default
ErrorPolicy stop-printer
</Printer>
```

NOTE *You can perform all administrative tasks from the command line using the* **lpadmin** *command. See the CUPS documentation for more details.*

Configuring Remote Printers on CUPS

To install a remote printer that is attached to a Windows system or another Linux system running CUPS, you specify its location using special URL protocols. For another CUPS printer on a remote host, the protocol used is **ipp**, (Internet Printing Protocol), whereas for a Windows printer, it would be **smb**. Older Unix or Linux systems using LPRng would use the **lpd** protocol.

As shown in Chapter 4, you can use system-config-printer to configure a remote printer with CUPS. Create a new printer and select a network type. The entries displayed are different for some network types. A CUPS or LPD remote server will just need the IP address and queue name, whereas the Windows server will need a Samba share name. You can also use the CUPS configuration tool to configure a remote Windows printer. Select the Windows Printer Via Samba entry and then enter the appropriate SMB URL.

In the **cupsd.conf** file, for a remote printer, the DeviceURI entry, instead of listing the device, will have an Internet address, along with its protocol. For example, a remote printer on a CUPS server (**ipp**) would be indicated as shown here (a Windows printer would use an **smb** protocol):

```
DeviceURI ipp://mytsuff.com/printers/queue1
```

For a Windows printer, you first need to install, configure, and run Samba. (CUPS uses Samba, which is covered in Chapter 39, to access Windows printers.) When you install the Windows printer on CUPS, you specify its location using the URL protocol **smb**. The user allowed to log in to the printer is entered before the hostname and separated from it by an **@** sign. On most configurations, this is the **guest** user. The location entry for a Windows printer called **myhp** attached to a Windows host named **lizard** is shown here. Its Samba share reference would be **//lizard/myhp**:

```
DeviceURI smb://guest@lizard/myhp
```

To enable CUPS on Samba, you also have to set the printing option in the **/etc/samba/smb.conf** file to **cups**, as shown here:

```
printing = cups
printcap name = cups
```

To enable CUPS to work with Samba, you have to link the **smbspool** to the CUPS **smb** spool directory:

```
ln -s /usr/bin/smbspool   /usr/cups/backend/smb
```

Configuring a Shared CUPS Printer

To allow a printer to be accessed by the hosts on your local network, you can simply enable printer sharing for that printer. On the host to which the printer is directly connected, use system-config-printer to select its printer entry. On the Settings panel for that printer, check the Shared box under the State heading. You can also limit access by users on the Access tab. The Server Settings tab list an option to share printers on your system.

NOTE   *To configure a shared Linux printer for access by Windows hosts, you need to configure it as a SMB shared printer. You do this with Samba (see Chapter 39).*

CUPS Printer Classes

CUPS features a way to let you select a group of printers to receive a print job, instead of selecting just one. That way, if one printer is busy or down, another printer can be automatically selected to perform the job. Such groupings of printers are called *classes*. Once you have installed your printers, you can then group them into different classes. For example, you may want to group all inkjet printers into one class and laser printers into another, or you may want to group printers connected to one specific printer server in their own class. To create a class, select Classes on the Administration page and enter the name of the class. You can then add printers to it.

CUPS Configuration

CUPS configuration files are placed in the **/etc/cups** directory. These files are listed in Table 26-2. The **classes.conf**, **printers.conf**, and **client.conf** files can be managed by the Web interface. The **printers.conf** file contains the configuration information for the different printers you have installed. Any of these files can be edited manually, if you wish.

Filename	Description
classes.conf	Configurations for different local printer classes
client.conf	Lists specific options for specified clients
cupsd.conf	Configures the CUPS server, **cupsd**
printers.conf	Printer configurations for available local printers

TABLE 26-2   CUPS Configuration Files

cupsd.conf

The CUPS server is configured with the **cupsd.conf** file located in **/etc/cups**. You must edit configuration options manually; the server is not configured with the Web interface. Your installation of CUPS installs a commented version of the **cupsd.conf** file with each option listed, though most options will be commented out. Commented lines are preceded with a **#** symbol. Each option is documented in detail. The server configuration uses an Apache Web server syntax consisting of a set of directives. As with Apache, several of these directives can group other directives into blocks.

CUPS Directives

Certain directives allow you to place access controls on specific locations. These can be printers or resources, such as the administrative tool or the spool directories. Location controls are implemented with the **Location** directive. **Allow From** and **Deny From** directives can permit or deny access from specific hosts. CUPS supports both Basic and Digest forms of authentication, specified in the **AuthType** directive. Basic authentication uses a user and password. For example, to use the Web interface, you are prompted to enter the root user and the root user password. Digest authentication makes use of user and password information kept in the CUPS **/etc/cups/passwd.md5** file, using MD5 versions of a user and password for authentication. The **AuthClass** directive specifies the class allowed access. The **System** class includes the **root**, **sys**, and **system** users. The following example shows the **Location** directive for the **/admin** resource, the administrative tool:

```
<Location /admin>

AuthType Basic
AuthClass System

## Restrict access to local domain
Order Deny,Allow
Deny From All
Allow From 127.0.0.1

</Location>
```

CUPS Command Line Print Clients

Once a print job is placed in a print queue, you can use any of several print clients to manage the printing jobs on your printer or printers, such as Klpq, the GNOME Print Manager, and the CUPS Printer Configuration tool for CUPS. You can also use several command line print

CUPS clients. These include the **lpr**, **lpc**, **lpq**, and **lprm** commands (see Chapter 10). The Printer System Switcher moves you from one set to the other. With these clients, you can print documents, list a print queue, reorder it, and remove print jobs, effectively canceling them. For network connections, CUPS features an encryption option for its commands, **-E**, to encrypt print jobs and print information sent over a network. Table 26-3 shows various printer commands.

NOTE *The command line clients have the same name, and much the same syntax, as the older LPR and LPRng command line clients used in Unix and older Linux systems.*

lpr

The **lpr** client submits a job, and **lpd** then takes it in turn and places it in the appropriate print queue; **lpr** takes as its argument the name of a file. If no printer is specified, then the default printer is used. The **-P** option enables you to specify a particular printer. In the next example, the user first prints the file **preface** and then prints the file **report** to the printer with the name **myepson**:

```
$ lpr preface
$ lpr -P myepson report
```

lpc

You can use **lpc** to enable or disable printers, reorder their print queues, and reexecute configuration files. To use **lpc**, enter the command **lpc** at the shell prompt. You are then given an **lpc>** prompt at which you can enter **lpc** commands to manage your printers and reorder their jobs. The **status** command with the name of the printer displays whether the

Printer Management	Description
GNOME Print Manager	GNOME print queue management tool (CUPS).
CUPS Configuration Tool	Print, manage, and configure CUPS.
lpr *options file-list*	Prints a file, copies the file to the printer's spool directory, and places it in the print queue to be printed in turn. **-P** *printer* prints the file on the specified printer.
lpq *options*	Displays the print jobs in the print queue. **-P** *printer* prints the queue for the specified printer. **-l** prints a detailed listing.
lpstat *options*	Displays printer status.
lprm *options printjob-id* **or** *printer*	Removes a print job from the print queue. You identify a particular print job by its number as listed by **lpq**. **-P** *printer* removes all print jobs for the specified printer.
lpc	Manages your printers. At the **lpc>** prompt, you can enter commands to check the status of your printers and take other actions.

TABLE 26-3 CUPS Printer Management

printer is ready, how many print jobs it has, and so on. The **stop** and **start** commands can stop a printer and start it back up. The printers shown depend on the printers configured for a particular print server. A printer configured on CUPS will only show if you have switched to CUPS.

```
# lpc
lpc> status myepson
myepson:
 printer is on device 'hal' speed -1
 queuing is enabled
 printing is enabled
 1 entry in spool area
```

lpq and lpstat

You can manage the print queue using the **lpq** and **lprm** commands. The **lpq** command lists the print jobs currently in the print queue. With the **-P** option and the printer name, you can list the jobs for a particular printer. If you specify a username, you can list the print jobs for that user. With the **-l** option, **lpq** displays detailed information about each job. If you want information on a specific job, simply use that job's ID number with **lpq**. To check the status of a printer, use **lpstat**.

```
# lpq
myepson is ready and printing
Rank    Owner  Jobs  File(s)        Total Size
active  chris   1    report         1024
```

lprm

The **lprm** command enables you to remove a print job from the queue, erasing the job before it can be printed. The **lprm** command takes many of the same options as **lpq**. To remove a specific job, use **lprm** with the job number. To remove all print jobs for a particular printer, use the **-P** option with the printer name. **lprm** with no options removes the job that is currently printing. The following command removes the first print job in the queue (use **lpq** to obtain the job number):

```
# lprm 1
```

CUPS Command Line Administrative Tools

CUPS provides command line administrative tools like **lpadmin**, **lpoptions**, **lpinfo**, **enable**, **disable**, **accept**, and **reject**. The **enable** and **disable** commands start and stop print queues directly, whereas the **accept** and **reject** commands start and stop particular jobs. The **lpinfo** command provides information about printers, and **lpoptions** lets you set printing options. The **lpadmin** command lets you perform administrative tasks like adding printers and changing configurations. CUPS administrative tools are listed in Table 26-4.

Administration Tool	Description
lpadmin	CUPS printer configuration
lpoptions	Set printing options
enable	Activate a printer
disable	Stop a printer
accept	Allow a printer to accept new jobs
reject	Prevent a printer from accepting new print jobs
lpinfo	List CUPS devices available

TABLE 26-4   CUPS Administrative Tools

lpadmin

You can use the **lpadmin** command to either set the default printer or configure various options for a printer. You can use the **-d** option to specify a particular printer as the default destination (you can also do this in system-config-printer). Here **myepson** is made the default printer:

```
lpadmin -d myepson
```

The **-p** option lets you designate a printer for which to set various options. The following example sets printer description information:

```
lpadmin -p myepson   -D  Epson550
```

Certain options let you control per-user quotas for print jobs. The **job-k-limit** option sets the size of a job allowed per user, **job-page-limit** sets the page limit for a job, and **job-quota-period** limits the number of jobs within a specified time frame. The following command set a page limit of 100 for each user:

```
lpadmin -p myepson   -o job-page-limit=100
```

User access control is determined with the **-u** option with an **allow** or **deny** list. Users allowed access are listed following the **allow:** entry, and those denied access are listed with a **deny:** entry. Here access is granted to **chris** but denied to **aleina** and **larisa**.

```
lpadmin -p myepson -u allow:chris   deny:aleina,larisa
```

Use **all** or **none** to permit or deny access to all or no users. You can create exceptions by using **all** or **none** in combination with user-specific access. The following example allows access to all users except **justin**:

```
lpadmin -p myepson   -u allow:all   deny:justin
```

lpoptions

The `lpoptions` command lets you set printing options and defaults that mostly govern how your print jobs will be printed. For example, you can set the color or page format to be used with a particular printer. Default settings for all users are maintained by the root user in the **/etc/cups/lpoptions** file, and each user can create their own configurations, which are saved in their **.lpoptions** files. The `-l` option lists current options for a printer, and the `-p` option designates a printer (you can also set the default printer to use with the `-d` option).

```
lpoptions -p myepson -l
```

Printer options are set using the `-o` option along with the option name and value, `-o` *option=value*. You can remove a printer option with the `-r` option. For example, to print on both sides of your sheets, you can set the **sides** option to **two-sided**:

```
lpoptions -p myepson -o sides=two-sided
```

To remove the option, use `-r`.

```
lpoptions -p myepson -r sides
```

To display a listing of available options, check the standard printing options in the CUPS Software Manual at **www.cups.org**.

enable and disable

The **enable** command starts a printer, and the **disable** command stops it. With the `-c` option, you can also cancel all jobs in the printer's queue, and with the `-r` option, you broadcast a message explaining the shutdown.

```
disable myepson
```

accept and reject

The **accept** and **reject** commands let you control access to the printer queues for specific printers. The **reject** command prevents a printer from accepting new jobs, whereas **accept** allows new print jobs.

```
reject myepson
```

lpinfo

The **lpinfo** command is a handy tool for letting you know what CUPS devices and drivers that are available on your system. Use the `-v` option for devices, and the `-m` option for drivers.

```
lpinfo -m
```

News and Search Servers

News servers provide Internet users with Usenet news services. They have their own TCP/IP protocol, the Network News Transfer Protocol (NNTP). On most Linux systems, including Red Hat, the InterNetNews (INN) news server provides news services (**www.isc.org**).

In addition, servers exist that provide better access to Internet resources. The search and indexing server ht://Dig enables document searches of Web and FTP sites (**www.htdig.org**). With it, you can index documents and carry out complex search requests.

News Servers: INN

The InterNetNews (INN) news server accesses Usenet newsfeeds, providing news clients on your network with the full range of newsgroups and their articles. Newsgroup articles are transferred using NNTP, and servers that support this protocol are known as *NNTP servers*. INN was written by Rich Salz and is currently maintained and supported by the Internet Software Consortium (ISC). You can download current versions from its Web site at **www.isc.org**. INN is also included with most Linux distributions. The documentation directory for INN in **/usr/share/doc** contains extensive samples. The primary program for INN is the **innd** daemon.

INN Configuration Files

Various INN configuration files can be found in **/etc/news**, including **inn.conf, storage.conf, readers.conf**, and **incoming.conf** (see Table 26-5); **inn.conf** sets options for INN, and **incoming.conf** holds the hosts from which you receive newsfeeds. Place entries for remote hosts in the **readers.conf** file to allow them access to your news server. Actual newsfeeds are managed in directories in the **/var/spool/news** directory. Here you will find directories such as **article**, which holds newsgroup articles, **outgoing** for articles being posted by your users

File	Description
inn.conf	General INN configuration file.
incoming.conf	Specifies hosts from which newsfeeds are received.
cycbuff.conf	Configures buffers used in cnfs storage format.
storage.conf	Defines storage classes. These consist of a storage method and the newsgroups that use it. Storage methods are the storage formats: tradspool, timehash, timecaf, and cnfs. An additional method, trash, throws out the articles.
expire.ctl	Sets the expiration policy for articles on the news server.
readers.conf	Designates hosts whose users can access the news server with newsreaders.
ovdb.conf	Configures ovdb storage method for overviews.
newsfeeds	Defines how your news server feeds articles to other news servers.
moderated	Moderated newsgroups.
active	Supported newsgroups.
history	Record of posted articles.
innfeed.conf	Configures newsfeed processes for innfeed.
innreport.conf	Configures innreport utility for generating log-based reports.
buffindexed.conf	Configures overview buffer for buffindexed method.

TABLE 26-5   INN Configuration Files

to newsgroups, and **overview,** which holds summary information about articles. Correct configuration of INN can be a complex and time-consuming process, so be sure to consult references and online resources, such as the documents. When you change configurations, be sure to restart the INN server. An **innd** script is in the **/etc/rc.d/init.d** directory, which has similar arguments to the Web **httpd** script. You can use **start**, **restart**, and **stop** arguments with the **innd** script to start, restart, and stop the INN server.

TIP *There is a Man page for each configuration file in INN, providing detailed information on how to configure their features.*

---

inn.conf

On many distributions, a basic **inn.conf** file is already set up for you with default settings. Several of the initial parameters you will have to set yourself, such as **domain**, which holds the domain name for your server; **pathhost**, in which you specify the name for your newsreader as you want it to appear in the path header field for news articles you post; and **server**, in which you specify your newsreader's IP or fully-qualified domain name address, as in **mynews.mytrek.com**. Different path options have already been set up for you defining the location of different INN directories, such as **patharticles**, set to **/var/spool/ news** articles that holds your newsgroup articles, and **pathetc**, set to **/etc/news** for your configuration files.

Storage Formats

Storage formats for the vast number of news articles that are often downloaded and accessed are a central concern for a full-scale news server like INN. INN lets you choose among four possible storage formats: tradspool, timehash, timecaf, and cnfs. The tradspool format is the traditional method whereby articles are arranged in a simple directory structure according to their newsgroups. This is known to be very time-consuming to access and store. timehash stores articles in directories organized by the time they were received, making it easier to remove outdated articles. timecaf is similar to timehash, but articles received at a given time are placed in the same file, making access much faster. cnfs stores articles into buffer files that have already been set up. When a buffer file becomes full, the older articles are overwritten by new ones as they come in. This is an extremely fast method, since no new files are created. There is no need to set maximum article limits, but there is also no control on how long an article is retained. In the **storage.conf** file, storage formats are assigned to different newsgroups as storage methods.

Newsreader Access

Users access your news server using newsreaders, as described in Chapter 13. You can place controls on users with options in the **readers.conf** file. Control is specified in two components: authentication and access definitions. The authentication definition creates a user category and the hosts and their authentication tools for users. The access definition applies restrictions to a user category, such as what newsgroups can be accessed and whether posting articles is allowed.

Overviews

INN also supports overviews. These are summaries of articles that readers can check, instead of having to download the entire article to see what it is. Overviews have their own storage methods: tradindexed, buffindexed, and ovdb. You specify the one you want to use in the ovmethod feature in **inn.conf**. tradindexed is fast for readers but difficult for the server to generate. buffindexed is fast for news servers but slow for readers. ovdb uses Berkeley DB database files and is very fast for both readers and servers but uses more disk space. If you choose ovdb, you can set configuration parameters for it in **ovdb.conf**.

INN Implementation

On many distributions, a **news** user is already created with a newsgroup for use by your INN daemon and sets up the news directories in **/var/spool/news**. INN software also installs **cron** scripts, which are used to update your news server, removing old articles and fetching new ones. These are usually placed in the **/etc/cron.daily** directory, though they may reside anywhere. `inn-cron-expire` removes old articles, and `inn-cron-rnews` retrieves new ones. `inn-cron-nntpsend` sends articles posted from your system to other news servers.

INN also includes several support programs to provide maintenance and crash recovery, and to perform statistical analysis on server performance and usage. cleanfeed implements spam protection, and innreport generates INN reports based on logs. INN also features a very strong filter system for screening unwanted articles.

NOTE *Leafnode is an NNTP news server designed for small networks that may have slow connections to the Internet. You can obtain the Leafnode software package along with documentation from its Web site at www.leafnode.org. Along with the Leafnode NNTP server, the software package includes several utilities such as Fetchnews, Texpire, and Newsq that send, delete, and display news articles. slrnpull is a simple single-user version of Leafnode that can be used only with the slrn newsreader.*

Database Servers: MySQL and PostgreSQL

As noted in Chapter 11, Red Hat Linux and Fedora include two fully functional database servers in their distribution, MySQL and PostgreSQL. MySQL is by far the more popular of the two, though PostgreSQL is noted for providing more features. Recently, the MySQL AB project added MaxDB, formerly SAP DB, which provides capabilities comparable to many professional-level database management systems. This chapter will cover how to set up and manage a MySQL database and will offer a brief introduction to PostgreSQL. You can learn more about these products through the sites listed in Table 26-6.

Database	Resource
MySQL	**www.mysql.com**
PostgreSQL	**www.postgresql.org**
MaxDB	**www.mysql.com**

TABLE 26-6   Database Resources

Relational Database Structure

Both MySQL and PostgreSQL use a relational database structure. Essentially, this means data is placed in tables, with identifier fields used to relate the data to entries in other tables. Each row in the table is a record, and each has a unique identifier, like a record number. The connections between records in different tables are implemented by special tables that associate the unique identifiers from records in one table with those of another. Relational database theory and implementation are subjects beyond the scope of this chapter.

A simple, single-table database would have no need for a unique identifier. A simple address book listing names and addresses is an example of a single-table database. However, most databases access complex information of different types, related in various ways. Instead of having large records with repeated information, you would divide the data in different tables, each holding the unique instance of the data. In this way, data is not repeated. You would have only one table that held a single record for person's name, rather than repeating that person's name each time the data references him or her. The relational organization then takes on the task of relating one piece of data to another. In this way, you can store a great deal of information using relatively small database files.

Though there are many ways to implement a relational database, a simple rule of thumb is to organize data into tables where you have a unique instance of each item of data. Each record is given a unique identifier, usually a number. To associate the records in one table with another, you create tables that associate their identifiers.

SQL

The SQL query language is the language used by most relational database management systems (RDBMSs), including both MySQL and PostgreSQL. Though many RDBMSs use administrative tools to manage databases, on Linux MySQL and PostgreSQL, you still have to use the SQL commands directly. Common SQL commands that you may use are listed in Table 26-7. The commands are often written in uppercase by convention, though they can be in lowercase.

Command	Description
CREATE DATABASE *name*	Create a database.
CREATE TABLE *name* (*fields*, ...)	Create a table within a database, specifying fields.
INSERT INTO *table-name* VALUES (*value list*)	Create and insert a record into a table.
INSERT INTO *table-name* VALUES (*value list*), (*value list*), ...	Insert multiple records at once.
SELECT *field* FROM *table-name* WHERE *value*	Search operation, selecting certain records in a table based on a value in a specified field.
USE *database*	Use a particular database; following commands will operate on it.

TABLE 26-7   SQL Commands

Using the previously described relational database, the following command will create the database:

```
CREATE DATABASE myphotos
```

Before performing any operations on a database, you first access it with the USE command.

```
USE myphotos
```

The tables are created using the CREATE TABLE command; the fields for each table are listed within parentheses following the table name. For each field, you need to specify a name, data type, and other options, such as whether it can have a null value or not.

```
CREATE TABLE names (
    personid INT(5) UNSIGNED NOT NULL,
    name VARCHAR(20) NOT NULL,
    street VARCHAR(30) NOT NULL,
    phone CHAR(8)
    );
```

To insert a record into a table, you can use the INSERT INTO command, though many databases support using data files that can be read all at once. To add records, you use the INSERT INTO command with the table name followed by the VALUES option, which is followed in turn by a comma-delimited list of values, one for each field. Character values are quoted with single quotes. The list is enclosed in parentheses. If you have not done so previously, you access the database with the USE command.

```
INSERT INTO names VALUES (1, 'justin','111 mordor','555-7543');
```

Once values are added to the tables, you can search for them with the SELECT command, specifying field, table name, and the value to be searched.

```
SELECT phone FROM names WHERE phone='555-7543';
```

MySQL

MySQL is structured on a client/server model with a server daemon (**mysqld**) filling requests from client programs. MySQL is designed for speed, reliability, and ease of use. It is meant to be a fast database management system for large databases and, at the same time, a reliable one, suitable for intensive use.

To create databases, you use the standard SQL language. User access can be controlled by assigning privileges.

MySQL Configuration

The MySQL supports three different configuration files, one for global settings, another for server-specific settings, and an optional one for user-customized settings.

- The **/etc/my.cnf** configuration file is used for global settings applied to both clients and servers. The **/etc/my.cnf** file provides information such as the data directory

(**/var/lib/mysql**) and log file (**/var/log/mysql.log**) locations, as well as the server base directory (**/var/lib**).

- The **/var/lib/mysql/my.cnf** file is used for server settings only.
- The **.my.cnf** file allows users to customize their access to MySQL. It is located in a user's home directory. Note that this is a dot file.

Sample configuration **my.cnf** files can be found in the **mysql-server** directory in **/usr/share/doc**. The **mysql-server** directory lists configurations for small, medium, large, and huge implementations. The administrative manual is located in the **mysql** directory in **/usr/share/doc**. It is in the info format. Use `info mysql` to start it, and the arrow and ENTER keys to move through the menus. Here you can find more information about different options.

Global Configuration:/etc/my.cnf
MySQL specifies options according to different groups, usually the names of server tools. The options are arranged in group segments. The group name is placed within brackets, and options applied to it follow. The default **/etc/my.cnf** file is shown here:

```
[mysqld]
datadir=/var/lib/mysql
socket=/var/lib/mysql/mysql.sock

[mysql.server]
user=mysql
basedir=/var/lib

[safe_mysqld]
err-log=/var/log/mysqld.log
pid-file=/var/run/mysqld/mysqld.pid
```

Mysql global options are listed in the **/etc/my.cnf** file. Options are set up according to groups that control different behaviors of the MySQL server: **mysqld** for the daemon, **mysql.server** for server options, and **safe_mysqld** for the MySQL startup script, **safe_mysqld**. The **datadir** directory, **/var/lib/mysql**, is where your database files will be placed. Server tools and daemons are located in the **basedir** directory, **/var/lib**, and the user that MySQL will run as has the name **mysql**, as specified in the **user** option.

A client group will set up options to be sent to clients, such as the port and socket to use to access the MySQL database.

```
[client]
port=3306
socket=/var/lib/mysql/mysql.sock
```

To see what options are currently set for both client and server, you run **mysqld** directly with the **--help** option.

```
/usr/libexec/mysqld --help
```

User Configuration: .my.cnf

Users who access the database server will have their own configuration file in their home directory: **.my.cnf**. Here the user can specify connection options such as the password used to access the database and the connection timeouts.

```
[client]
password=mypassword

[mysql]
no-auto-rehash
set-variable = connect_timeout=2

[mysql-hotcopy]
interactive-timeout
```

Starting and Stopping the MySQL Server

The MySQL server, **mysqld**, can be managed with the **service** command or the services tool.

```
service mysqld start
```

The **mysqld** script invokes **safe_mysqld**, which is designed to run MySQL on Unix systems, making sure that data directories are set and log files are running. The **safe_mysqld** script in turn will start up the **mysqld** daemon.

MySQL Tools

MySQL provides a variety of tools (as shown in Table 26-8), including server, client, and administrative tools. Backups can be handled with the **mysqldump** command. The **mysqlshow** command will display a database, just as issuing the SQL command SELECT *.* does, and **mysqlimport** can import text files, just like LOAD INFILE.

MySQL Management with mysql and mysqladmin

To manage your MySQL database, you use **mysql** as the **root** user. The **mysql** client starts up the MySQL monitor. As the **root** user, you can enter administrative commands to create databases and database tables, add or remove entries, as well as carry out standard client tasks such as displaying data.

Command	Description
mysqld	MySQL server
mysql	MySQL client
mysqladmin	Create and administer databases
mysqldump	Database backup
mysqlimport	Import text files
mysqlshow	Display databases

TABLE 26-8   MySQL Commands

Log in as the root user and open a terminal window. Then enter the **mysql** command. This will start a MySQL monitor shell with a **mysql>** prompt. Be sure to end your commands with a semicolon; otherwise, the monitor will provide an indented arrow prompt waiting for added arguments. In the monitor, the semicolon, not the ENTER key, ends commands.

```
# mysql -u root -p
mysql>
```

If you have set up a MySQL root user, you can use the **-u root** with the **-p** option. You will be prompted for a password.

```
# mysql -u root -p
```

Once the **mysql** client has started, you can use the **status** command to check the status of your server, and **show databases** to list current databases.

```
mysql> status;
mysql> show databases;
```

Initially two databases set up by MySQL for its own management are displayed: mysql and test. The mysql database holds MySQL user information, and the test database is used to test the server.

PostgreSQL

PostgreSQL is based on the POSTGRES database management system, though it uses SQL as its query language. POSTGRES is a next-generation research prototype developed at the University of California, Berkeley. You can find more information on it from the PostgreSQL Web site at **www.postgresql.org**. PostgreSQL is an open source project, developed under the GPL license.

PostgreSQL is often used to provide database support for Internet servers with heavy demands, such as Web servers. With a few simple commands, you can create relational database tables. Use the **createuser** command to create a PostgreSQL user that you can then log in to the server with. You can then create a database with the **createdb** command and construct relational tables using the **create table** directive. With an **insert** command, you can add records and then view them with the **select** command. Access to the server by remote users is controlled by entries in the **pg_hba.conf** file located in PostgreSQL directory, usually **/var/lib/pgsql**.

The Red Hat Linux edition of PostgreSQL also includes the Red Hat Database Graphical tools used to easily manage and access PostgreSQL databases. With the administrator tool, you can browse and manage databases, the Visual Explain tool analyzes query processes, and the Control Center lets you manage databases on servers.

VI

PART

System Administration

CHAPTER 27
Basic System Administration

CHAPTER 28
Managing Users

CHAPTER 29
Software Management

CHAPTER 30
File System Management

CHAPTER 31
RAID and LVM

CHAPTER 32
Devices and Modules: udev,
HAL, and MAKEDEV

CHAPTER 33
Kernel Administration:
Virtualization

CHAPTER 34
Backup Management: rsync,
Amanda, and dump/restore

Basic System Administration

L inux is designed to serve many users at the same time, providing an interface between the users and the system with its resources, services, and devices. Users have their own shells through which they interact with the operating system, but you may need to configure the operating system itself in different ways. You may need to add new users, devices like printers and scanners, and even file systems. Such operations come under the heading of system administration. The person who performs such actions is referred to as either a *system administrator* or a *superuser*. In this sense, there are two types of interaction with Linux: regular users' interactions, and those of the superuser, who performs system administration tasks. The chapters in this book cover operations such as changing system runlevels, managing users, configuring printers, adding file systems, and compiling the kernel. You perform most of these tasks only rarely, such as adding a new printer or mounting a file system. Other tasks, such as adding or removing users, you perform on a regular basis. Basic system administration covers topics such as system access by superusers, selecting the runlevel to start, system configuration files, and performance monitoring.

With Linux, you have the ability to load different versions of the Linux kernel as well as other operating systems that you have installed on your system. The task of selecting and starting up an operating system or kernel is managed by a boot management utility, the Grand Unified Bootloader (GRUB). This is a versatile tool, letting you load operating systems that share the same disk drive, as well as letting you choose from different Linux kernels that may be installed on the same Linux system.

Superuser Control: the Root User

To perform system administration operations, you must first have access rights such as the correct password that enables you to log in as the root user, making you the superuser. Because a superuser has the power to change almost anything on the system, such a password is usually a carefully guarded secret, changed very frequently, and given only to those whose job it is to manage the system. With the correct password, you can log in to the system as a system administrator and configure the system in different ways. You can start up and shut down the system, as well as change to a different operating mode, such as a single-user mode. You can also add or remove users, add or remove whole file systems, back up and restore files, and even designate the system's name and address.

NOTE *If SELinux is enabled, superuser access will be controlled by SELinux rules. See Chapter 17.*

To become a superuser, you log in to the *root user account.* This is a special account reserved for system management operations with unrestricted access to all components of your Linux operating system. You can log in as the root user from either the GUI (graphical user interface) login screen or the command line login prompt. You then have access to all administrative tools. Using a GUI interface like GNOME, the root user has access to a number of Red Hat and Fedora GUI administrative tool such as system-config-users for managing users. If you log in from the command line interface, you can run corresponding administrative commands like **rpm** to install packages or **useradd** to add a new user. From your GUI desktop, you can also run command line administrative tools using a terminal window. The command line interface for the root user uses a special prompt, the sharp sign, **#**. In the next example, the user logs in to the system as the root user and receives the **#** prompt.

```
login: root
password:
#
```

Root User Password

As the root user, you can use the **passwd** command to change the password for the root login, as well as for any other user on the system. The **passwd** command will check your password with Pluggable Authentication Modules (PAM), as discussed in Chapter 28, to see if you've selected one that can be easily cracked. To more easily change your root password from a GUI interface, you can use the system-config-rootpassword tool.

```
# passwd root
New password:
Re-enter new password:
#
```

You must take precautions to protect your root password. Anyone who gains access as the root user will have complete control over your system. The online manual for the **passwd** command provides detailed recommendations for handling and choosing your password. For example, never store your password in a file on your system, and never choose one based on any accessible information, such as your phone number or date of birth. A basic guideline is to make your password as complex as possible, using a phrase of several words with numbers and upper- and lowercase letters, yet something you can still remember easily so that you never have to write it down. You can access the **passwd** online manual page with the command

```
# man passwd
```

Root User Access: su

While you are logged in to a regular user account, it may be necessary for you to log in as the root and become a superuser. Ordinarily, you would have to log out of your user account first, and then log in to the root. Instead, you can use the **su** command (switch user) to log in directly to the root while remaining logged in to your user account. If you are using a GUI desktop like GNOME, you can enter the **su** command from a terminal window, or use

ALT-CTRL-F1 to switch to a command line interface (ALT-CTRL-F10 returns you to the GUI interface). A CTRL-D or **exit** command returns you to your own user login. When you are logged in as the root, you can use **su** to log in as any user, without providing the password. In the next example, the user is logged in already. The **su** command then logs in as the root user, making the user a superuser. Some basic superuser commands are shown in Table 27-1.

```
$ pwd
/home/chris
$su
 password:
# cd
# pwd
/root
# exit
$
```

CAUTION *For security reasons, Linux distributions do not allow the use of **su** in a telnet session to access the root user. For SSH- or Kerberos-enabled systems, Fedora provides secure login access using slogin (SSH) and rlogin (Kerberos version).*

Command	Description
`su root`	Logs a superuser into the root from a user login; the superuser returns to the original login with a CTRL-D.
`sudo` *command*	Restricted administrative access for specified users.
`passwd` *login-name*	Sets a new password for the login name.
`crontab` *options filename*	With *filename* as an argument, installs `crontab` entries in the file to a **crontab** file; these entries are operations executed at specified times (see later section): `-e` Edits the **crontab** file `-l` Lists the contents of the **crontab** file `-r` Deletes the **crontab** file
`telinit` *runlevel*	Changes the system runlevels.
`shutdown` *options time*	Shuts down the system.
`date`	Sets the date and time for the system.
system-config-date	GUI tool to set system time and date (System I Administration I Date & Time).
Kcron	KDE GUI interface **cron** management tool (Applications I System Tools I KCron).
gnome-schedule	GNOME GUI interface **cron** management tool (Applications I System Tools I Schedule).
system-config-rootpassword	GUI tool to change the root user (administrator) password. (System I Administration I Root Password).

TABLE 27-1 Basic System Administration Tools

Controlled Administrative Access: sudo

With the sudo tool you can allow ordinary users to have limited root user–level administrative access for certain tasks. This allows other users to perform specific superuser operations without having full root level control. You can find more about sudo at **www.sudo.ws**. To use sudo to run an administrative command, the user precedes the command with the **sudo** command. The user is issued a time-sensitive ticket to allow access.

```
sudo date
```

Access is controlled by the **/etc/sudoers** file. This file lists users and the commands they can run, along with the password for access. If the NOPASSWD option is set, then users will not need a password. ALL, depending on the context, can refer to all hosts on your network, all root-level commands, or all users.

To make changes or add entries, you have to edit the file with the special sudo editing command **visudo**. This invokes the Vi editor to edit the **/etc/sudoers** file. Unlike a standard editor, **visudo** will lock the **/etc/sodoers** file and check the syntax of your entries. You are not allowed to save changes unless the syntax is correct. If you want to use a different editor, you can assign it to the EDITOR shell variable.

A **sudoers** entry has the following syntax:

```
user    host=command
```

The host is a host on your network. You can specify all hosts with the ALL term. The command can be a list of commands, some or all qualified by options such as whether a password is required. To specify all commands, you can also use the ALL term. The following gives the user **george** full root-level access to all commands on all hosts:

```
george  ALL = ALL
```

In addition, you can let a user run as another user on a given host. Such alternate users are placed within parentheses before the commands. For example, if you want to give **george** access to the **beach** host as the user **mydns**, you use the following:

```
george beach = (mydns) ALL
```

By default sudo will deny access to all users, including the root. For this reason, the default **/etc/sudoers** file sets full access for the root user to all commands. The ALL=(ALL) ALL entry allows access by the root to all hosts as all users to all commands.

```
root    ALL=(ALL)    ALL
```

To specify a group name, you prefix the group with a % sign, as in **%mygroup**. This way, you can give the same access to a group of users. The **/etc/sudoers** file contains samples for a **%wheel** group.

To give **robert** access on all hosts to the **date** command, you would use

```
robert ALL=/usr/bin/system-config-date
```

If a user wants to see what commands he or she can run, that user would use the **sudo** command with the **-l** option.

```
sudo -l
```

System Time and Date

You can set the system time and date using the shell **date** command or the Fedora GUI tool system-config-date. You probably set the time and date when you first installed your system. You should not need to do so again. If you entered the time incorrectly or moved to a different time zone, though, you could use this utility to change your time.

Using the system-config-date Utility

The preferred way to set the system time and date is to use the Fedora Date and Time Properties utility (system-config-date). Select the System | Administration | Date & Time entry. There are three panels, one for the date and time, one for the Network Time Protocol, and one for the time zone (see Figure 27-1). Use the calendar to select the year, month, and date. Then use the Time box to set the hour, minute, and second. The Time Zone panel shows a map with locations. Select the one nearest you to set your time zone.

The Network Time Protocol (NTP) allows a remote server to set the date and time, instead of using local settings. NTP allows for the most accurate synchronization of your system's clock. It is often used to manage the time and date for networked systems, freeing the administrator from having to synchronize clocks manually. You can download current documentation and NTP software from the **www.ntp.org** site.

FIGURE 27-1
system-config-date

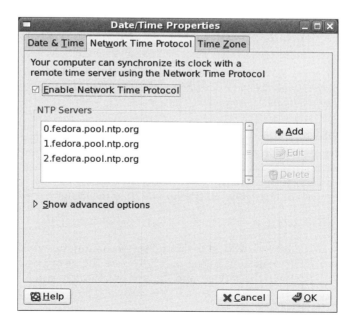

On the Network Time Protocol panel you can choose to enable NTP and select the server to use. NTP servers operate through pools that will randomly select an available server to increase efficiency. A set of pools designated for use by Fedora is already installed for you, beginning with **0.fedora.pool.ntp.org**. If access with one pool is slow, you change to another. The **pool.ntp.org** pool servers support worldwide access. Pools for specific geographical locations can be found at the NTP Public Services Project site (Time Servers link), **ntp.isc.org**. A closer server could be faster.

Using the date Command

You can also use the **date** command on your root user command line to set the date and time for the system. As an argument to **date**, you list (with no delimiters) the month, day, time, and year. In the next example, the date is set to 2:59 P.M., April 6, 2007 (04 for April, 06 for the day, 1459 for the time, and 03 for the year 2007):

```
# date 0406145903
Tue Mar 6 02:59:27 PST 2007
```

> **NOTE** *You can also set the time and date with the Date & Time tool in the KDE Control Center.*

Scheduling Tasks: cron

Scheduling regular maintenance tasks, such as backups, is managed by the **cron** service on Linux, implemented by a **cron** daemon. A daemon is a continually running server that constantly checks for certain actions to take. These tasks are listed in the **crontab** file. The **cron** daemon constantly checks the user's **crontab** file to see if it is time to take these actions. Any user can set up a **crontab** file of his or her own. The root user can set up a **crontab** file to take system administrative actions, such as backing up files at a certain time each week or month.

> **TIP** *You can use the KCron or Schedule to set up cron jobs (Applications | System Tools). The GUI interfaces let you set specific or recurring times. They execute a command line version of a command with listed arguments.*

The crond Service

The name of the **cron** daemon is **crond**. Normally it is started automatically when your system starts up. You can set this feature using system-config-services Background Services panel or **chkconfig**, as described in Chapter 21. The following example starts the **crond** service automatically whenever you boot the system:

```
chkconfig crond on
```

You can also start and stop the **crond** service manually, which you may want to do for emergency maintenance or during upgrades. Use the **service** command and the **stop** option to shut down the service, and the **start** option to run it again:

```
service crond stop
```

crontab Entries

A **crontab** entry has six fields: the first five are used to specify the time for an action, while the last field is the action itself. The first field specifies minutes (0–59), the second field specifies the hour (0–23), the third field specifies the day of the month (1–31), the fourth field specifies the month of the year (1–12, or month prefixes like *Jan* and *Sep*), and the fifth field specifies the day of the week (0–6, or day prefixes like *Wed* and *Fri*), starting with 0 as Sunday. In each of the time fields, you can specify a range, specify a set of values, or use the asterisk to indicate all values. For example, **1-5** for the day-of-week field specifies Monday through Friday. In the hour field, **8, 12, 17** would specify 8 A.M., 12 noon, and 5 P.M. An ***** in the month-of-year field indicates every month. The format of a **crontab** field follows:

```
minute  hour  day-month  month  day(s)-week  task
```

The following example backs up the **projects** directory at 2:00 A.M. every weekday:

```
0 2 * * 1-5   tar cf /home/backp /home/projects
```

The same entry is listed here again using prefixes for the month and weekday:

```
0 2 * * Mon-Fri tar cf /home/backp /home/projects
```

To specify particular months, days, weeks, or hours, you can list them individually, separated by commas. For example, to perform the previous task on Sunday, Wednesday, and Friday, you could use **0,3,5** in the day-of-week field, or their prefix equivalents, **Sun,Wed,Fri**.

```
0 2 * * 0,3,5   tar cf /home/backp /home/projects
```

cron also supports comments. A comment is any line beginning with a **#** sign.

```
# Weekly backup for Chris's projects
0 2 * * Mon-Fri  tar cf /home/backp /home/projects
```

Environment Variables for cron

The **cron** service also lets you define environment variables for use with tasks performed. Fedora defines variables for **SHELL**, **PATH**, **HOME**, and **MAILTO**. **SHELL** designates the shell to use for tasks, in this case the BASH shell. **PATH** lists the directories where programs and scripts can be found. This example lists the standard directories, **/usr/bin** and **/bin**, as well as the system directories reserved for system applications, **/usr/sbin** and **/sbin**. **MAILTO** designates to whom the results of a task are to be mailed. By default, these are mailed to the user who schedules it, but you can have the results sent to a specific user, such as the administrator's e-mail address or an account on another system in a network. **HOME** is the home directory for a task, in this case the top directory.

```
SHELL=/bin/bash
PATH=/sbin:/bin:/usr/sbin:/usr/bin
MAILTO=root
HOME=/
```

The cron.d Directory

On a heavily used system, the **/etc/crontab** file can become crowded easily. There may also be instances where certain entries require different variables. For example, you may need to run some task under a different shell. To help better organize your `crontab` tasks, you can place `crontab` entries in files within the **cron.d** directory. The files in the **cron.d** directory all contain `crontab` entries of the same format as **/etc/crontab**. They may be given any name. They are treated as added `crontab` files, with **cron** checking them for tasks to run. For example, Fedora installs a **smolt** file in the **cron.d** that contains `crontab` entries to run system statistics for the SMOLT hardware reporting service.

The crontab Command

You use the `crontab` command to install your entries into a **crontab** file. To do this, first create a text file and type your `crontab` entries. Save this file with any name you want, such as **mycronfile**. Then, to install these entries, enter **crontab** and the name of the text file. The `crontab` command takes the contents of the text file and creates a **crontab** file in the **/var/spool/cron** directory, adding the name of the user who issued the command. In the following example, the root user installs the contents of **mycronfile** as the root's **crontab** file. This creates a file called **/var/spool/cron/root**. If a user named **justin** installed a **crontab** file, it would create a file called **/var/spool/cron/justin**. You can control use of the `crontab` command by regular users with the **/etc/cron.allow** file. Only users with their names in this file can create **crontab** files of their own. Conversely, the **/etc/cron.deny** file lists those users denied use of the **cron** tool, preventing them for scheduling tasks. If neither file exists, access is denied to all users. If a user is not in an **/etc/cron.allow** file, access is denied. However, if the **/etc/cron.allow** file does not exist, and the **/etc/cron.deny** file does, then all users not listed in **/etc/cron.deny** are automatically allowed access.

```
# crontab mycronfile
```

Editing in cron

Never try to edit your **crontab** file directly. Instead, use the `crontab` command with the `-e` option. This opens your **crontab** file in the **/var/spool/cron** directory with the standard text editor, such as Vi—`crontab` uses the default editor as specified by the `EDITOR` shell environment variable. To use a different editor for `crontab`, change the default editor by assigning the editor's program name to the `EDITOR` variable and exporting that variable. Normally, the editor variable is set in the **/etc/profile** script. Running `crontab` with the `-l` option displays the contents of your **crontab** file, and the `-r` option deletes the entire file. Invoking `crontab` with another text file of `crontab` entries overwrites your current **crontab** file, replacing it with the contents of the text file.

Organizing Scheduled Tasks

You can organize administrative **cron** tasks into two general groups: common administrative tasks that can be run at regular intervals, and specialized tasks that need to be run at a unique time. Unique tasks can be run as entries in the **/etc/crontab** file, as described in the next section. Common administrative tasks, though they can be run from the **/etc/crontab** file, are better organized into specialized **cron** directories. Within such directories, each task is placed in its own shell script that will invoke the task when run. For example, there may be several administrative tasks that all need to be run each week on the same day, say if maintenance for a system is scheduled on a Sunday morning. For these kinds of tasks, **cron** provides several specialized directories for automatic daily, weekly, monthly, and yearly tasks. Each contains a **cron** prefix and a suffix for the time interval. The **/etc/cron.daily** directory is used for tasks that need to be performed every day, whereas weekly tasks can be placed in the **/etc/cron.weekly** directory. The **cron** directories are listed in Table 27-2.

Running cron Directory Scripts

Each directory contains scripts that are all run at the same time. The scheduling for each group is determined by an entry in the **/etc/crontab** file. The actual execution of the scripts is performed by the **/usr/bin/run-parts** script, which runs all the scripts and programs in a given directory. Scheduling for all the tasks in a given directory is handled by an entry in the **/etc/crontab** file. Fedora provides entries with designated times, which you may change for your own needs. The default Fedora **crontab** file is shown here, with times for running scripts in the different **cron** directories. Here you can see that most scripts are run at about 4 A.M. either daily (4:02), Sunday (4:22), or the first day of each month (4:42). Hourly ones are run one minute after the hour.

```
SHELL=/bin/bash
PATH=/sbin:/bin:/usr/sbin:/usr/bin
MAILTO=root
HOME=/
# run-parts
01 * * * * root run-parts /etc/cron.hourly
02 4 * * * root run-parts /etc/cron.daily
22 4 * * 0 root run-parts /etc/cron.weekly
42 4 1 * * root run-parts /etc/cron.monthly
```

cron Files and Directories	Description
/etc/crontab	System `crontab` file, accessible only by the root user
/etc/cron.d	Directory containing multiple `crontab` files, accessible only by the root user
/etc/cron.hourly	Directory for tasks performed hourly
/etc/cron.daily	Directory for tasks performed daily
/etc/cron.weekly	Directory for tasks performed weekly
/etc/cron.monthly	Directory for tasks performed monthly
/etc/cron.yearly	Directory for tasks performed yearly
/etc/cron.allow	Users allowed to submit `cron` tasks
/etc/cron.deny	Users denied access to `cron`

TABLE 27-2   Cron Files and Directories

TIP *Scripts within a **cron** directory are run alphabetically. If you need a certain script to run before any others, you may have to alter its name. One method is to prefix the name with a numeral. For example, in the **/cron.weekly** directory, the **anacron** script is named **0anacron** so that it will run before any others.*

Keep in mind though that these are simply directories that contain executable files. The actual scheduling is performed by the entries in the **/etc/crontab** file. For example, if the weekly field in the `cron.weekly crontab` entry is changed to * instead of **0**, and the monthly field to **1** (`22 4 1 * *` instead of `22 4 * * 0`), tasks in the **cron.weekly** file would end up running monthly instead of weekly.

Cron Directory Names

The names used for these directories are merely conventions. They have no special meaning to the **cron** daemon. You could, in fact, create your own directory, place scripts within it, and schedule run-parts to run those scripts at a given time. In the next example, scripts placed in the **/etc/cron.mydocs** directory will run at 12 noon every Wednesday.

```
* 12 * * 3 root run-parts /etc/cron.mydocs
```

Anacron

For a system that may normally be shut down during times that **cron** is likely to run, you may want to supplement **cron** with **anacron**. **anacron** activates only when scheduled tasks need to be executed. For example, if a system is shut down on a weekend when **cron** jobs are scheduled, then the jobs will not be performed; **anacron**, however, checks to see what jobs need to be performed when the system is turned on again, and then runs them. It is designed only for jobs that run daily or weekly.

For **anacron** jobs, you place `crontab` entries in the **/etc/anacrontab** file. For each scheduled task, you specify the number of intervening days when it is executed (7 is weekly, 30 is monthly), the time of day it is run (numbered in minutes), a description of the task, and the command to be executed. For backups, the command used would be **tar** operation. You can use system-config-services to turn on the **anacron** service or have it start up automatically at boot time.

System Runlevels: telinit, initab, and shutdown

A Linux system can run on different levels, depending on the capabilities you want to give it. For example, you can run your system at an administrative level, locking out user access. Normal full operations are activated by simply running your system at a certain level of operational capability such as supporting multiuser access or graphical interfaces. These levels (also known as states or modes) are referred to as *runlevels*, the level of support that you are running your system at.

Runlevels

A Linux system has several runlevels, numbered from 0 to 6. When you power up your system, you enter the default runlevel. Runlevels 0, 1, and 6 are special runlevels that perform specific functions. Runlevel 0 is the power-down state and is invoked by the **halt** command to shut down the system. Runlevel 6 is the reboot state—it shuts down the system and reboots. Runlevel 1 is the single-user state, which allows access only to the superuser and does not run any network services. This enables you, as the administrator, to perform administrative actions without interference from others.

Other runlevels reflect how you want the system to be used. Runlevel 2 is a partial multiuser state, allowing access by multiple users, but without network services like NFS or **xinetd** (eXtended InterNET services daemon). This level is useful for a system that is not part of a network. Both runlevel 3 and runlevel 5 run a fully operational Linux system, with multiuser support and remote file sharing access. They differ in terms of the interface they use. Runlevel 3 starts up your system with the command line interface (also known as the text mode interface). Runlevel 5 starts up your system with an X session, running the X Window System server and invoking a graphical login, using display managers, such as gdm or xdm. If you choose to use graphical logins during installation, runlevel 5 will be your default runlevel. Linux provides two keyboard sequences to let you switch between the two during a login session: CTRL-ALT-F1 changes from the graphical interface (runlevel 5) to the command line interface (runlevel 3), and CTRL-ALT-F7 changes from the command line interface to the graphical interface. The runlevels are listed in Table 27-3.

Changing runlevels can be helpful if you have problems at a particular runlevel. For example, if your video card is not installed properly, then any attempt to start up in runlevel 5 will likely fail, as this level immediately starts your graphical interface. Instead, you should use the command line interface, runlevel 3, to fix your video card installation.

Tip *You can use the single-user runlevel (1) as a recovery mode state, allowing you to start up your system without running startup scripts for services like DNS. This is helpful if your system hangs when you try to start such services. Networking is disabled, as well as any multiuser access. You can also use* **linux -s** *at the boot prompt to enter runlevel 1. If you want to enter the single-user state and also run the startup scripts, you can use the special* **s** *or* **S** *runlevel.*

State	Description
0	Halt (do *not* set the default to this level); shuts down the system completely.
1	Administrative single-user mode; denies other users access to the system, but allows root access to the entire multiuser file system. Startup scripts are not run. (Use **s** or **S** to enter single-user mode with startup scripts run.)
2	Multiuser, without network services like NFS, **xinetd**, and NIS (the same as 3, but you do not have networking).
3	Full multiuser mode with login to command line interface; allows remote file sharing with other systems on your network. Also referred to as the *text mode state*.
4	Unused.
5	Full multiuser mode that starts up in an X session, initiating a graphical login; allows remote file sharing with other systems on your network (same as 3, but with graphical login).
6	Reboots; shuts down and restarts the system (do *not* set the default to this).

TABLE **27-3**   System Runlevels (States)

Runlevels in initab

When your system starts up, it uses the default runlevel as specified in the default `init` entry in the **/etc/inittab** file. For example, if your default init runlevel is 5 (the graphical login), the default `init` entry in the **/etc/inittab** file would be

```
id:5:initdefault:
```

You can change the default runlevel by editing the **/etc/inittab** file and changing the `init` default entry. Editing the **/etc/inittab** file can be dangerous. You should do this with great care. As an example, if the default runlevel is 3 (command line), the entry for your default runlevel in the **/etc/inittab** file should look like the following:

```
id:3:initdefault:
```

You can change the 3 to a 5, to change your default runlevel from the command line interface (3) to the graphical login (5). Change only this number and nothing else.

```
id:5:initdefault:
```

TIP *If your /etc/inittab file becomes corrupted, you can reboot and enter* **linux single** *at the boot prompt to start up your system, bypassing the* **inittab** *file. You can then edit the file to fix it.*

Changing Runlevels with telinit

No matter what runlevel you start in, you can change from one runlevel to another with the `telinit` command. If your default runlevel is 3, you power up in runlevel 3, but you can change to, say, runlevel 5 with `telinit 5`. The command `telinit 0` shuts down your system. In the next example, the `telinit` command changes to runlevel 1, the administrative state:

```
# telinit 1
```

The `telinit` command is really a symbolic link (another name for a command) to the `init` command. The `init` command performs the actual startup operations and is automatically invoked when your system starts up. Though you could use `init` to change runlevels, it is best to use `telinit`. When invoked as `telinit`, `init` merely changes runlevels.

One use for telinit is to shutdown the X Windows server when installing the vendor graphics drivers. Open a terminal window and enter the following:

```
telinit 3
```

This starts the command line interface where you can login and run commands. Use the following to return to the X Windows desktop:

```
telinit 5
```

Should you want to use init, you would enter the **init** command and the runlevel number on a command line. If you were in runlevel 3 (command line), the following would place you in runlevel 5 (graphical interface):

```
init 5
```

The runlevel Command

Use the `runlevel` command to see what state you are currently running in. It lists the previous state followed by the current one. If you have not changed states, the previous state will be listed as N, indicating no previous state. This is the case for the state you boot up in. In the next example, the system is running in state 3, with no previous state change:

```
# runlevel
N 3
```

Shutdown

Although you can power down the system with the `telinit` command and the 0 state, you can also use the **shutdown** command. The **shutdown** command has a time argument that gives users on the system a warning before you power down. You can specify an exact time to shut down, or a period of minutes from the current time. The exact time is specified by *hh:mm* for the hour and minutes. The period of time is indicated by a **+** and the number of minutes. The **shutdown** command takes several options with which you can specify how you want your system shut down. The **-h** option, which stands for halt, simply shuts down the system, whereas the **-r** option shuts down the system and then reboots it. In the next example, the system is shut down after 10 minutes:

```
# shutdown -h +10
```

To shut down the system immediately, you can use **+0** or the word **now**. The following example shuts down the system immediately and then reboots:

```
# shutdown -r now
```

With the **shutdown** command, you can include a warning message to be sent to all users currently logged in, giving them time to finish what they are doing before you shut them down.

```
# shutdown -h +5 "System needs a rest"
```

If you do not specify either the **-h** or the **-r** option, the **shutdown** command shuts down the multiuser mode and shifts you to an administrative single-user mode. In effect, your system state changes from 3 (multiuser state) to 1 (administrative single-user state). Only the root user is active, allowing the root user to perform any necessary system administrative operations with which other users might interfere.

TIP *You can also shut down your system from the GNOME or KDE desktops, or from the login screen (see Chapter 3).*

The shutdown options are listed in Table 27-4.

PART VI

Command	Description
`shutdown [-rkhncft]` *time* [*warning-message*]	Shuts the system down after the specified time period, issuing warnings to users; you can specify a warning message of your own after the time argument; if neither `-h` nor `-r` is specified to shut down the system, the system sets to the administrative mode, runlevel state 1.
Argument	
Time	Has two possible formats: it can be an absolute time in the format *hh*:*mm*, with *hh* as the hour (one or two digits) and *mm* as the minute (in two digits); it can also be in the format +*m*, with *m* as the number of minutes to wait; the word **now** is an alias for `+0`.
Option	
`-t` *sec*	Tells **init** to wait *sec* seconds between sending processes the warning and the kill signals, before changing to another runlevel.
`-k`	Doesn't actually shut down; only sends the warning messages to everybody.
`-r`	Reboots after shutdown, runlevel state 6.
`-h`	Halts after shutdown, runlevel state 0.
`-n`	Doesn't call **init** to do the shutdown; you do it yourself.
`-f`	Skips file system checking (fsck) on reboot.
`-c`	Cancels an already running shutdown; no time argument.

TABLE 27-4   System Shutdown Options

Managing Services

As noted previously for the **crond** service, you can select certain services to run and the runlevel at which to run them. Most services are servers like a Web server or proxy server. Other services provide security, such as SSH or Kerberos. You can decide which services to use with the **chkconfig**, service, or system-config-services tools. These are described here briefly, and in more detail in Chapter 21.

chkconfig

To configure a service to start up automatically, you can use the system-config-services tool available on the desktop or the **chkconfig** tool, which is run on a command line. The system-config-services tool will display a list of available services, letting you choose the ones you want to start and deselect. The **chkconfig** command uses the **on** and **off** options to select and deselect services for startup (see Chapter 21 for more details).

```
chkconfig httpd on
```

The service Command

To start and stop services manually, you can user either system-config-services or the `service` command. With the `service` command, you list the service with the `stop` argument to stop it, the `start` argument to start it, and the `restart` argument to restart it.

```
service httpd start
```

system-config-services

The system-config-services tool provides an interface displaying a simple list of services from which you can select the ones you want to start up (System | Administration | Server Settings | Services). On the system-config-services tool, the main panel lists different daemons and servers that you can have start by just clicking a checkbox. The system-config-services tool displays two panels, one for Background Services and one for On Demand Services. Background Services will hold most of the daemons and servers you will need for administrative tasks. Several are already selected by default, like **network,** which runs your network connections, and an **haldaemon,** which detects your hardware. Others, such as Network Manager, which detects wireless networks, and **smb,** which runs Samba Windows network support, are optional. You can use system-config-services to run them. The On Demand Services are fewer and run only when invoked. These include special tools like Swat, the Samba Web administration tool. Initially this panel will be empty, with tools added as you install them. See Chapter 21 for more information on system-config-services.

Fedora Administration Tools

On Fedora, most administration tasks can be handled by a set of separate specialized administrative tools developed and supported by Red Hat Linux and Fedora, such as those for user management and display configuration. Many of these are GUI-based and will work on any X Window System environment, such as GNOME or KDE. To access the GUI-based Red Hat and Fedora tools, you log in as the root user to the GNOME desktop and select the System menu. System administrative tools are listed on the Administration menu. Here you will find tools to set the time and date, manage users, configure printers, and update software. Users & Groups lets you create and edit users. Printing lets you install and reconfigure printers. All tools provide very intuitive GUI interfaces that are easy to use. In the System | Administration menu, tools are identified by simple descriptive terms, whereas their actual names normally begin with the term system-config. For example, the printer configuration tool is listed as Printing, but its actual name is system-config-printer. You can separately invoke any tool by entering its name in a terminal window. Table 27-5 provides a listing of basic Red Hat and Fedora administration tools.

Certain hardware configuration tasks are now handled by your desktop. In GNOME, mouse and detailed keyboard configuration as well as screen resolution and sound configuration are handled by GNOME tools listed in the System | Preferences | Hardware menu.

Fedora Administration Tool	Description
System I Administration	Menu for accessing administrative tools
system-config-users	User and Group configuration tool (Users and Groups)
system-config-printer	Printer configuration tool (Printing)
system-config-display	Display configuration tool, video card and monitor (Display). Just to change resolutions use System I Preferences I Hardware I Screen resolution
system-config-packages	Software management (Applications I Add/Remove Software)
system-config-rootpassword	Changes the root user password (Root Password)
system-config-keyboard	Changes the keyboard detection (Keyboard)
system-config-date	Changes system time and date (Date & Time)
system-config-language	Selects a language to use (Language)
system-config-soundcard	Detects your sound card (Soundcard Detection)
system-config-boot	Grub boot loader configuration (Bootloader)
system-config-lvm	Configure hard disk storage with Logical Volumes, see Chapter 31 (Logical Volume Management)
Mouse, Keyboard, Sound	For detailed mouse, keyboard, and sound configuration you use the desktop tools like those for GNOME. See the menu System I Preferences I Hardware

TABLE 27-5   Fedora Basic Configuration Tools

System Directories

Your Linux file system is organized into directories whose files are used for different system functions (see Table 27-6). For basic system administration, you should be familiar with the system program directories where applications are kept, the system configuration directory (**/etc**) where most configuration files are placed, and the system log directory (**/var/log**) that holds the system logs, recording activity on your system. Other system directories are covered in their respective chapters, with many discussed in Chapter 30.

Program Directories

Directories with "bin" in the name are used to hold programs. The **/bin** directory holds basic user programs, such as login shells (BASH, TCSH, and ZSH) and file commands (**cp**, **mv**, **rm**, **ln**, and so on). The **/sbin** directory holds specialized system programs for such tasks as file system management (**fsck, fdisk, mkfs**) and system operations like shutdown and startup (**init**). The **/usr/bin** directory holds program files designed for user tasks. The **/usr/sbin** directory holds user-related system operations, such as **useradd** to add new users. The **/lib** directory holds all the libraries your system makes use of, including the main Linux library, **libc**, and subdirectories such as **modules**, which holds all the current kernel modules.

Directory	Description
/bin	System-related programs
/sbin	System programs for specialized tasks
/lib	System and application libraries
/etc	Configuration files for system and network services and applications
/home	The location of user home directories and server data directories, such as Web and FTP site files
/mnt	The location where CD-ROM and floppy disk file systems are mounted (Chapter 30)
/var	The location of system directories whose files continually change, such as logs, printer spool files, and lock files (Chapter 30)
/usr	User-related programs and files. Includes several key subdirectories, such as **/usr/bin**, **/usr/X11**, and **/usr/doc**
/usr/bin	Programs for users
/dev	Dynamically generated directory for device files (Chapter 32)
/etc/X11	X Window System configuration files
/usr/share	Shared files
/usr/share/doc	Documentation for applications
/tmp	Directory for system temporary files
/var/log	Logging directory
/var/log/	System logs generated by **syslogd**
/var/log/audit	Audit logs generated by **auditd**

TABLE 27-6 System Directories

Configuration Directories and Files

When you configure different elements of your system, like users, applications, servers, or network connections, you make use of configuration files kept in certain system directories. Configuration files are placed in the **/etc** directory, with more specific device and service configurations located in the **/etc/sysconfig** directory.

Configuration Files: /etc

The **/etc** directory holds your system, network, server, and application configuration files. Here you can find the **fstab** file listing your file systems, the **hosts** file with IP addresses for hosts on your system, and **grub.conf** (a link to **/boot/grub/grub.conf**) for the boot systems supported by the GRUB boot loader. This directory includes various subdirectories, such as **/etc/apache** for the Apache Web server configuration files, **/etc/X11** for the X Window System and window manager configuration files, and **/etc/udev** for rules to generate device files in **/dev**. You can configure many applications and services by directly editing their configuration files, though it is best to use a corresponding administration tool. Table 27-7 lists several commonly used configuration files found in the **/etc** directory.

File	Description
/etc/bashrc	Default shell configuration file Bash shell
/etc/group	Contains a list of groups with configurations for each
/etc/fstab	Automatically mounts file systems when you start your system
/boot/grub/grub.conf	The GRUB configuration file for the GRUB boot loader, linked to by /etc/grub.conf
/etc/inittab	Sets the default state, as well as terminal connections
/etc/profile	Default shell configuration file for users
/etc/modprobe.conf	Modules on your system to be automatically loaded
/etc/motd	System administrator's message of the day
/etc/mtab	Currently mounted file systems
/etc/passwd	Contains user password and login configurations
/etc/services	Services run on the system and the ports they use
/etc/shadow	Contains user-encrypted passwords
/etc/shells	Shells installed on the system that users can use
/etc/sudoers	Sudo configuration to control administrative access
/etc/termcap	Contains a list of terminal type specifications for terminals that could be connected to the system
/etc/xinetd.conf	Xinetd server configuration
Directory	**Description**
/etc/cron.d	Cron scripts
/etc/cups	CUPS printer configuration files
/etc/init.d	Service scripts
/etc/mail	Sendmail configuration files
/etc/openldap	Configuration for Open LDAP server
/etc/rc.d	Startup scripts for different runlevels
/etc/skel	Directory that holds the versions of initialization files, such as **.bash_profile**, which are copied to new users' home directories
/etc/sysconfig	Red Hat and Fedora device and service configuration environments and support
/etc/X11	X Window System configuration files
/etc/xinetd.d	Configuration scripts for services managed by Xinetd server
/etc/udev	Rules for generating devices (Chapter 32)
/etc/hal	Rules for generating removable devices (Chapter 32)

TABLE 27-7   Configuration Files and Directories

/etc/sysconfig

On Red Hat and Fedora systems, configuration and startup information is also kept in the **/etc/sysconfig** directory. Here you will find files containing definitions of system variables used to configure devices such as your keyboard and mouse, along with settings for network connections, as well as options for service scripts, covering services such as the Web server and the IPtables firewall. These entries were defined for you when you configured your devices during installation or installed your service software.

A sample of the keyboard file, **/etc/sysconfig/keyboard**, is shown here:

```
KEYBOARDTYPE="pc"
KEYTABLE="us"
```

Several of these files are generated by Fedora administration tools such as system-config-mouse, system-config-keyboard, or system-config-network. Table 27-8 lists several commonly used tools and the sysconfig files they control. For example, system-config-mouse generates configuration variables for the mouse device name, type, and certain features, placing them in the **/etc/sysconfig/mouse** file, shown here:

```
FULLNAME="Generic - 3 Button Mouse (PS/2)"
MOUSETYPE="PS/2"
XMOUSETYPE="PS/2"
XEMU3="no"
DEVICE=/dev/mouse
```

Other files, like **hwconf**, list all your hardware devices, defining configuration variables such as its class (video, CD-ROM, hard drive), the bus it uses (PCI, IDE), its device name (such as **hdd** or **st0**), the drivers it uses, and a description of the device. A CD-ROM entry is shown here:

```
class: CDROM
bus: IDE
detached: 0
device: hdd
driver: ignore
desc: "TOSHIBA DVD-ROM SD-M1402"
```

Some files provide global or system configuration support for service scripts, like **iptables**, **samba**, **httpd** (Apache), or **spamassassin**. Other files provide configuration settings for corresponding tools like system-config-users.

Several directories are included, such as **network-scripts**, which lists several startup scripts for network connections—an example is **ifup-ppp**, which starts up PPP connections.

Some administration tools use more than one **sysconfig** file; for example, system-config-network places its network configuration information such as the hostname and gateway in the **/etc/sysconfig/network** file. Specific Ethernet device configurations, which would include your IP address and netmask, are placed in the appropriate Ethernet device configuration file in the **/etc/sysconfig/network-scripts** directory. For example, the IP address and netmask used for the **eth0** Ethernet device can be found in **/etc/sysconfig/network-scripts/ifcfg-eth0**. Local host settings are in **/etc/sysconfig/network-scripts/ifcfg-lo**.

Tools	Configuration Files	Description
system-config-authentication	**/etc/sysconfig/authconfig** **/etc/sysconfig/network**	Authentication options, such as enabling NIS, shadow passwords, Kerberos, and LDAP.
system-config-securitylevel	**/etc/sysconfig/iptables**	Selects the level of firewall protection: High, Medium, and None.
system-config-keyboard	**/etc/sysconfig/keyboard**	Selects the keyboard type.
system-config-network	**/etc/sysconfig/network** **/etc/sysconfig/network-scripts/ifcfg-eth**N	Sets your network settings.
system-config-date	**/etc/sysconfig/clock**	Sets the time and date.
system-config-users	**/etc/sysconfig/system-config-users**	Settings for system-config-users.
system-config-samba	**/etc/sysconfig/samba**	Settings for Samba service.
system-config-httpd	**/etc/sysconfig/httpd**	Settings for Apache Web server.
system-config-securitylevel	**/etc/sysconfig/system-config-securitylevel**	Settings for system-config-securitylevel.

TABLE 27-8 Sysconfig Files with Corresponding Fedora System Administration Tools

TIP Some administration tools, like system-config-authentication, will further configure configuration files for the services selected. The system-config-authentication tool configures /etc/sysconfig/authconfig, as well as /etc/krb5.conf for Kerberos authentication, /etc/yp.conf for NIS support, and /etc/openldap/ldap.conf for LDAP authentication.

System Logs: /var/log and syslogd

Various system logs for tasks performed on your system are stored in the **/var/log** directory. Here you can find logs for mail, news, and all other system operations, such as Web server logs. The **/var/log/messages** file is a log of all system tasks not covered by other logs. This usually includes startup tasks, such as loading drivers and mounting file systems. If a driver for a card failed to load at startup, you find an error message for it here. Logins are also recorded in this file, showing you who attempted to log in to what account. The **/var/log/maillog** file logs mail message transmissions and news transfers.

NOTE To view logs, you can use the GNOME System Log Viewer (System | Administration | System Log).

syslogd and syslog.conf

The **syslogd** daemon manages all the logs on your system, as well as coordinating with any of the logging operations of other systems on your network. Configuration information for **syslogd** is held in the **/etc/syslog.conf** file, which contains the names and locations for your system log files. Here you find entries for **/var/log/messages** and **/var/log/maillog**, among others. Whenever you make changes to the **syslog.conf** file, you need to restart the **syslogd** daemon using the following command (or use system-config-services, System | Administration | Server Settings | Services):

```
service syslog restart
```

Entries in syslogd.conf

An entry in **syslog.conf** consists of two fields: a *selector* and an *action*. The selector is the kind of service to be logged, such as mail or news, and the action is the location where messages are to be placed. The action is usually a log file, but it can also be a remote host or a pipe to another program. The kind of service is referred to as a *facility*. The **syslogd** daemon has several terms it uses to specify certain kinds of service (see Table 27-9). A facility can be further qualified by a priority. A *priority* specifies the kind of message generated by the facility; **syslogd** uses several designated terms to indicate different priorities. A *sector* is constructed from both the facility and the priority, separated by a period. For example, to save error messages generated by mail systems, you use a sector consisting of the `mail` facility and the `err` priority, as shown here:

```
mail.err
```

To save these messages to the **/var/log/maillog** file, you specify that file as the action, giving you the following entry:

```
mail.err /var/log/maillog
```

The **syslogd** daemon also supports the use of * as a matching character to match either all the facilities or all the priorities in a sector: `cron.*` would match on all **cron** messages no matter what the priority, `*.err` would match on error messages from all the facilities, and `*.*` would match on all messages. The following example saves all mail messages to the **/var/log/maillog** file and all critical messages to the **/var/log/mycritical** file:

```
mail.* /var/log/maillog
*.crit /var/log/mycritical
```

Priorities

When you specify a priority for a facility, all messages with a higher priority are also included. Thus the `err` priority also includes the `crit`, `alert`, and `emerg` priorities. If you just want to select the message for a specific priority, you qualify the priority with the = operator. For example, `mail.=err` will select only error messages, not `crit`, `alert`, or `emerg` messages. You can also restrict priorities with the ! operator. This will eliminate messages with the specified priority and higher. For example, `mail.!crit` will exclude `crit` messages, as well as the higher `alert` and `emerg` messages. To specifically exclude

Facilities	Description
auth-priv	Security/authorization messages (private)
cron	Clock daemon (cron and at) messages
daemon	Other system daemon messages
kern	Kernel messages
lpr	Line printer subsystem messages
mail	Mail subsystem messages
mark	Internal use only
news	Usenet news subsystem messages
syslog	Syslog internal messages
user	Generic user-level messages
uucp	UUCP subsystem messages
local0 through local7	Reserved for local use
Priorities	**Description**
debug	7, Debugging messages, lowest priority
info	6, Informational messages
notice	5, Notifications, normal, but significant, condition
warning	4, Warnings
err	3, Error messages
crit	2, Critical conditions
alert	1, Alerts, action must be taken immediately
emerg	0, Emergency messages, system is unusable, highest priority
Operators	**Description**
*	Matches all facilities or priorities in a sector
=	Restrict to a specified priority
!	Exclude specified priority and higher ones
/	A file to save messages to
@	A host to send messages to
|	A FIFO pipe to send messages to

TABLE 27-9   Syslogd Facilities, Priorities, and Operators

all the messages for an entire facility, you use the **none** priority; for instance, **mail.none** excludes all mail messages. This is usually used when you're defining several sectors in the same entry.

You can list several priorities or facilities in a given sector by separating them with commas. You can also have several sectors in the same entry by separating them with semicolons.

The first example saves to the **/var/log/messages** file all messages with `info` priority, excluding all mail and authentication messages (`authpriv`). The second saves all `crit` messages and higher for the **uucp** and **news** facilities to the **/var/log/spooler** file:

```
*.info;mail.none;news.none;authpriv.none /var/log/messages
uucp,news.crit /var/log/spooler
```

Actions and Users

In the action field, you can specify files, remote systems, users, or pipes. An action entry for a file must always begin with a **/** and specify its full pathname, such as **/var/log/messages**. To log messages to a remote host, you simply specify the hostname preceded by an @ sign. The following example saves all kernel messages on **rabbit.trek.com**:

```
kern.* @rabbit.trek.com
```

To send messages to users, you list their login names. The following example will send critical news messages to the consoles for the users **chris** and **aleina**:

```
news.=crit chris,aleina
```

You can also output messages to a named pipe (FIFO). The pipe entry for the action field begins with a **|**. The following example pipes kernel debug messages to the named pipe **|/usr/adm/debug**:

```
kern.=debug |/usr/adm/debug
```

An Example for /etc/syslog.conf

The default **/etc/syslog.conf** file for Fedora systems is shown here. Messages are logged to various files in the **/var/log** directory.

/etc/syslog.conf
```
# Log all kernel messages to the console.
#kern.*                          /dev/console
# Log anything (except mail) of level info or higher.
# Don't log private authentication messages!
*.info;mail.none;news.none;authpriv.none;cron.none    /var/log/messages

# The authpriv file has restricted access.
authpriv.*                       /var/log/secure
# Log all the mail messages in one place.
mail.*                           /var/log/maillog
# Log cron stuff.
cron.*                           /var/log/cron
# Everybody gets emergency messages
*.emerg                                  *
# Save mail and news errors of level err and higher in a special file.
uucp,news.crit                   /var/log/spooler
# Save boot messages also to boot.log
local7.*                         /var/log/boot.log
# INN
```

```
news.=crit                    /var/log/news/news.crit
news.=err                     /var/log/news/news.err
news.notice                   /var/log/news/news.notice
```

The Linux Auditing System: auditd

The Linux Auditing System provides system call auditing. The auditing is performed by a server called **auditd**, with logs saved to the **/var/log/audit** directory. It is designed to complement SELinux, which saves its messages to the **auditd** log in the **/var/log/audit/audit.log** file. The audit logging service provides specialized logging for services like SELinux. Logs are located at **/var/log/audit**. To refine the auditing, you can create audit rules to check certain system calls like those generated by a specific user or group.

You can use the **/etc/init.d/auditd** service script to start up and shut down the **auditd** server. Use system-config-services or the **service** command to start and stop the server.

```
service auditd start
```

Configuration for **auditd** is located in both the **/etc/auditauditd.conf** and the **/etd/sysconfig/auditd** files. Primary configuration is handled with **/etc/auditd.conf**, which holds such options as the log file name, the log format, the maximum size of log files, and actions to take when disk space diminishes. See the **auditd.conf** Man page for a detailed description of all options. The **/etc/sysconfig/auditd** file sets server startup options and locale locations such as **en_US**.

The audit package includes the **auditd** server and three commands: **autrace**, **ausearch**, and **auditctl**. You use **ausearch** to query the audit logs. You can search by various IDs; by process, user, group, or event; as well as by filename or even time or date. Check the **ausearch** Man page for a complete listing. **autrace** is a specialized tool that lets you trace a specific process. It operates similar to **strace**, recording the system calls and actions of a particular process.

You can control the behavior of the **auditd** server with the **auditctl** tool. With **auditctl** you can turn auditing on or off, check the status, and add audit rules for specific events. Check the **auditctl** Man page for a detailed description.

Audit rules are organized into predetermined lists with a specific set of actions for system calls. Currently there are three lists: task, entry, and exit, and three actions: never, always, and possible. When adding a rule, the list and action are paired, separated by a comma, as in

```
exit,always
```

To add a rule you use the **-a** option. With the **-S** option you can specify a particular system call, and with the **-F** option you can specify a field. There are several possible fields you can use, such as loginuid (user login ID), pid (process ID), and exit (system call exit value). For a field you specify a value, such as **longinuid=510** for the user with a user login ID of 510. The following rule, as described in the documentation, checks all files opened by a particular user:

```
auditctl -a exit,always  -S open -F loginuid=510
```

Place rules you want loaded automatically in the **/etc/auditaudit.rules**. The **sample.rules** file in the **/usr/share/doc/auditd*** directory lists rule examples. You can also create a specific file of audit rules and use `auditctl` with the `-R` option to read the rules from it.

Performance Analysis Tools and Processes

Linux treats each task performed on your system as a process, which is assigned a number and a name. You can examine these processes and even stop them. Fedora provides several tools for examining processes as well as your system performance. Easy monitoring is provided by the GNOME System Monitor (System | Administration | System Monitor). Other tools are also available, such as GKrellM and KSysguard.

A number of utilities on your system provide detailed information on your processes, as well as other system information such as CPU and disk use (see Table 27-10). Although these tools were designed to be used on a shell command line, displaying output in text lines, several now have KDE and GNOME versions that provide a GUI interface for displaying results and managing processes.

Performance Tool	Description
`vmstat`	Performance of system components
`top`	Listing of most CPU-intensive processes
`free`	Listing of free RAM memory
`sar`	System activity information
`iostat`	Disk usage
GNOME System Monitor	System monitor for processes and usage monitoring (System | Administration | System Monitor)
GKrellM	Stackable, flexible, and extensible monitoring tool that displays information on a wide variety of system, network, and storage operations, as well as services, easily configurable with themes
KDE Task Manager and Performance Monitor	KDE system monitor for processes and usage monitoring
Frysk	Monitoring tool for system processes
System Tap	Tool to analyze performance bottlenecks
GNOME Power Manager	Manage power efficiency features of your system
cpuspeed	Implement CPU speed reduction during idle times (AMD and Intel Cool and Quiet).

TABLE 27-10   Performance Tools

GNOME System Monitor

Fedora provides the GNOME System Monitor for displaying system information and monitoring system processes, accessible from System | Administration | System Monitor. There are four panels, one for the system description, one for processes, one for resources, and one for file systems (see Figure 27-2). The Resources panel displays graphs for CPU, Memory and Swap memory, and Network usage. Your File Systems panel lists your file systems, where they are mounted, and their type, as well as the amount of disk space used and how much is free. The Processes panel lists your processes, letting you sort or search for processes. You can use field buttons to sort by name, process ID, CPU use, and memory. The View menu lets you select all processes, just your own, or active processes. You can easily stop any process by selecting it and then clicking the End Process button. Right-clicking an item displays actions you can take on the process such as stopping or hiding it. The Memory Maps display, selected from the View menu, shows information on virtual memory, inodes, and flags.

The ps Command

From the command line, you can use the **ps** command to list processes. With the **-aux** option, you can list all processes. Piping the output to a **grep** command with a pattern enables you to search for a particular process. A pipe funnels the output of a preceding command as input to a following command. The following command lists all X Window System processes:

```
ps -aux | grep 'X'
```

FIGURE 27-2
GNOME System
Monitor
(Administration |
System Monitor)

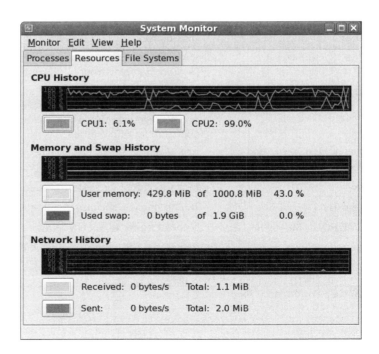

vmstat, free, top, iostat, Xload, and sar

The **vmstat** command outputs a detailed listing indicating the performance of different system components, including CPU, memory, I/O, and swap operations. A report is issued as a line with fields for the different components. If you provide a time period as an argument, it repeats at the specified interval—usually a few seconds. The **top** command provides a listing of the processes on your system that are the most CPU intensive, showing what processes are using most of your resources. The listing is in real time and updated every few seconds. Commands are provided for changing a process's status, such as its priority.

The **free** command lists the amount of free RAM memory on your system, showing how much is used and how much is free, as well as what is used for buffers and swap memory. **Xload** is an X Window System tool showing the load, CPU, and memory; **iostat** displays your disk usage; and **sar** shows system activity information.

System Tap

System Tap is a diagnostic tool for providing information about complex system implementations. It essentially analyzes performance bottlenecks, letting you home in on where a problem could be located. System Tap relies on Kprobes (Kernel Dynamic Probes), which allows kernel modules to set up simple probes.

Frysk

Frysk is a specialized complex monitoring tool for system processes. With Frysk you can set up very specific monitoring tasks, focusing on particular applications and selecting from a set of observer processes to provide information about exit notification, system calls, and execution. You can also create your own customized observers for processes. Find out more about Frysk at **sourceware.org/frysk**. Check **sourceware.org/frysk/javadoc/private/ overview-summary.html** for an overview.

GNOME Power Manager

The GNOME Power Manager is designed to take full advantage of the efficiency features available on both laptops and desktops. It supports tasks like reducing CPU frequency, dimming the display, shutting down unused hard drives, and automatic shutdown or suspension. See **www.gnome.org/projects/gnome-power-manager/index.html** for a detailed description. The GNOME Power Manager is integrated with HAL (Hardware Abstraction Layer) and Dbus to detect hardware states and issue hardware notifications. Hardware notifications are issued using notification icons for devices, such as the battery icon. The notification icons are located on the panel. A tooltip on the battery icon will show how much time you have left.

Power management preferences for laptops lets you set sleep, brightness, and action settings for battery and direct power (AC). For desktops, you can set the inactivity time for putting the display to sleep or suspending the system. You can access the preferences from the System | Preferences | More Preferences | Power Management item.

Features like Cool and Quit for Athlon CPUs and Pentium M frequency controls are handled separately by the cpuspeed service (System | Administration | Server Settings | Services). CPU frequency reporting tools are provided by cpufreq and gkrellm-freq packages.

The cpufreq package installs two applications, cpu-info and cpu-set, which will require Cpu frequency drivers set in the kernel configuration and can be compiled as modules.

GKrellM

GKrellM is a GTK-based set of small stackable monitors for various system, network, and device operations. A title bar at the top of the stack will display the host name of your system. By default, GKrellM will display the host name, system time, CPU load, process chart, disk access, network devices like **eth0**, memory use, and a mail check. You can change the chart display of a monitor, its height, for instance, by right-clicking it to show a display options panel.

Each monitor will have a title bar, showing, for instance, CPU for CPU load, Disk for disk access, and Mem for memory. To configure the monitor, right-click its title bar. This will display the configuration panels for that task. For example, the Disk configuration will let you choose particular hard disks and partitions to monitor. The full configuration window will be displayed, showing a sidebar with configuration menus, with the built-in menu expanded to the selected monitor.

See the **gkrellm** Man page for a detailed description of all monitor configuration options. The GKrellM site, **www.gkrellm.net**, offers resources for documentation, program support, and themes. Fedora comes with GKrellM installed with the built-in plug-ins and with the WiFi plug-in. For added plug-ins and themes, you can download and install the RPM packages for Fedora provided by **freshrpms.net**. These will provide an extensive set of plug-ins and themes for your use, including radio controls, a keyboard LED monitor, and a large list of themes such as marble, Gotham city, and shiny metal blue. There are several plug-in packages: media, misc, and utils. The package may first require other packages; the media package currently requires FFTW (Fourier Transforms), and the misc package needs Imlib2, both available in RPM versions on **freshrpms.net**. You may have to update your version of GKrellM with the most recent package on **freshrpms.net**. Plug-ins can also be downloaded directly from **www.gkrellm.net** and themes from **www.muhri.net**. User themes can be placed in a user's **.gkrellm2/themes** directory.

GKrellM Configuration

You can open the configuration window directly by clicking any monitor and pressing F1. Alternatively, you can open the main menu and select the Configuration entry. To open the main menu, either press F2 or right-click the top monitor. You can use this same menu to move through themes or to quit GKrellM. The configuration window shows a sidebar of configuration entries such as General, Builtins, Plugins, and Themes. Panels to the right let you set the configuration options. The General panel shows global options such as displaying the host name, the overall window size, and window priority.

The Builtins entry will expand to show a list of all the monitors that GKrellM can display. This list is extensive, including monitors as varied as fan and heat sensors, clock, CPU load, Internet connections, mail notification, and battery use.

The Plugins entry will expand to the list of installed plug-ins. To see available plug-ins, click the Plugin entry directly. A list of available plug-ins will be shown with check boxes. To install a plug-in, click its checkbox. Red Hat and Fedora may initially list just the WiFi monitor. As you install other plug-in packages, more will be listed. When installed, a plug-in will appear in the expanded plug-in menu. You can select a plug-in there to display its configuration panels.

Plug-ins for system-wide use are located in the **/usr/lib/gkrellm2/plugins** directory, and themes are located at **/usr/share/gkrellm2/themes**. User GKrellM configuration information and support files are kept in the **.gkrellm2** directory. Here you will find subdirectories for themes and user plug-ins. The **user_config** file holds user configuration settings, listing a monitor, its options, and its settings on each line.

GKrellM Server

You can use GKrellM to monitor hosts remotely using the GKrellM server, **gkrellmd**. You run the server on the system you wish to monitor, letting it allow remote systems to use **gkrellm** clients to gather and display its monitoring statistics. To run **gkrellm** as a client to gather and display information from another system running a **gkrellmd** server, you use the **-s** option and the server's host name. The server has to be configured to allow that remote host to connect. In the next example, a remote host connects to a **gkrellmd** server running on **turtle.mytrek.com** to display information about that the turtle host:

```
gkrellm -s turtle.mytrek.com
```

GKrellM is a service managed by the **/etc/init.d/gkrellmd** script. You can start and stop it with system-config-services or with the **service** command.

```
service gkrellmd start
```

Configuration for the GKrellM server is handled by the **/etd/gkrellmd.conf** configuration file. Here you can specify the hosts to monitor as well as global options such as the frequency of updates, the port to listen on, and the maximum number of simultaneous clients. Options are documented in detail. Check the Man page for **gkrellmd** for a complete listing.

KDE Task Manager and Performance Monitor (KSysguard)

Fedora also provides the KDE Task Manager and Performance Monitor, KSysguard, accessible from the System menu as KSysGuard only on the KDE desktop. This tool allows you to monitor the performance of your own system as well as remote systems. KSysguard can provide simple values or detailed tables for various parameters. A System Load panel provides graphical information about CPU and memory usage, and a Process Table lists current processes using a tree format to show dependencies. You can design your own monitoring panels with worksheets, showing different types of values you want to display and the form you want to display them in, such as a bar graph or a digital meter. The Sensor Browser pane is an expandable tree of sensors for information like CPU System Load or Used Memory. There is a top entry for each host you are connected to, including your own, localhost. To design your own monitor, create a worksheet and drag and drop a sensor onto it.

Grand Unified Bootloader (GRUB)

The Grand Unified Bootloader (GRUB) is a multiboot boot loader used for Fedora and Red Hat Linux. With GRUB, users can select operating systems to run from a menu interface displayed when a system boots up. Use arrow keys to move to an entry and press ENTER. Type **e** to edit a command, letting you change kernel arguments or specify a different kernel. The **c** command places you in a command line interface. Provided your system BIOS supports very large drives, GRUB can boot from anywhere on them. Linux and Unix operating systems are known as multiboot operating systems and take arguments passed to them at boot time. Check the GRUB Man page for GRUB options. You can use the Boot Configuration tool to select your default system or kernel as well as set the timeout limit (accessible from System | Administration menu as Bootloader).

GRUB configuration is held in the **/boot/grub/grub.conf** file. (You can also access this file as **/etc/grub.conf**, which is linked to **/boot/grub/grub.conf**.) You only need to make your entries and GRUB will automatically read them when you reboot. There are several options you can set, such as the timeout period and the background image to use. Check the GRUB info documentation for a detailed description, **info grub** (accessible from System | Help, search on Grub).

Whenever your Package Updater installs a new kernel, or if you install one manually with Yum or from an RPM package, then an entry for the new kernel is automatically placed in your **/boot/grub/grub.conf** file. The new kernel will appear as a boot option when you boot. It will not be made the default. You will still boot by default to your original kernel or operating system. To change the default you can use the Boot loader configuration tool accessible with System | Administration | Bootloader menu entry. This tool lists available operating systems and kernels. Select the one you want as your default. You could select another operating system like Windows for your default (if it is installed on your system and configured in Grub). With this tool you can also set the time delay for displaying the Grub menu before the default is started.

You can manually change the default by editing the **/boot/grub/grub.conf** file directly and changing the value for the default option. The default option selects the default as kernel and operating systems are listed in the grub.conf file, starting from 0. Setting the default to 0 will select the first kernel or operating system entry, 1 will select the second, and so on. Should a new kernel fail, you could just change this option to select a different working kernel by default. The following selects the second entry:

```
default=1
```

The **timeout** option lets you set the time delay before the default is started up, and the **spashimage** option specifies a background image. The **hiddenmenu** option will hide the full menu on bootup. To see the full menu with this option on, press ESC. The boot option specifies the disk to boot from (commented out by default). See the Grub info page for a detailed listing of the Grub commands.

You can specify a system to boot by creating a title entry for it, beginning with the term **title**. You then have to specify where the operating system kernel or program is located, which hard drive to use, and what partition on that hard drive. This information is listed in parentheses following the **root** option. Numbering starts from 0, not 1, and hard drives are indicated with an **hd** prefix, whether they are IDE, SATA, or SCSI hard drives. Thus **root(hd0,2)** references the first hard drive (**sda**) and the third partition on that hard drive (**sda3**). For Linux systems, you will also have to use the **kernel** option to indicate the kernel program to run, using the full pathname and any options the kernel may need. The RAM disk is indicated by the **initrd** option.

```
title Fedora Linux (2.6.21-1.3116)
    root (hd0,2)
    kernel /boot/vmlinuz-2.6.21-1.3116.fc7 ro root=/dev/sda3 rhgb quiet
    initrd /boot/initrd-2.6.21-1.3116.fc7.img
```

The kernel option specifies the kernel to run. The kernel is located in the **/boot** directory and has the name **vmlinuz** with the kernel version number. You can have several kernels in the **/boot** directory and use GRUB to choose the one to use. After the kernel program you specify any options you want for the kernel. This includes an **ro** option that initially starts the kernel as read only. The root option is used to specify the device on which your system was installed, your root directory. In the preceding example, the system was installed on device **/dev/sda3**. If the root directory is on a logical volume, where it is normally installed, the device name would be something like **/dev/VolGroup00/LogVol01**. The **rhgb quiet** option uses the Red Hat Graphical Boot interface to start your system, instead of listing all the startup messages on a text display.

NOTE *If you are having startup problems with your graphic card driver, you may need to remove* **rhgb quiet** *from your kernel option in* **grub.conf***. This starts up Linux using the command line interface.*

If you installed the standard Workstation configuration, your root directory will be installed on a logical volume. Your root option would reference the logical volume, specifying the volume group and the logical volume, as shown here:

```
kernel /vmlinuz-2.6.21-1.3116.fc7 ro root=/dev/VolGroup00/LogVol01 rhgb quiet
```

For another operating system such as Windows, you would use the `rootnoverify` option to specify where Windows is installed. This option instructs GRUB not to try to mount the partition. Use the `chainloader+1` options to allow GRUB to access it. The `chainloader` option tells GRUB to use another boot program for that operating system. The number indicates the sector on the partition where the boot program is located—for example, `+1` indicates the first sector.

```
title Windows XP
      rootnoverify (hd0,0)
      chainloader +1
```

Windows systems will all want to boot from the first partition on the first disk. This becomes a problem if you want to install several versions of Windows on different partitions or install Windows on a partition other than the first one. GRUB lets you work around this by letting you hide other partitions in line, and then unhiding the one you want, making it appear to be the first partition. In this example, the first partition is hidden, and the second is unhidden. This assumes there is a Windows system on the second partition on the first hard drive (**hd0,1**). Now that the first partition is hidden, the second one appears as the first partition:

```
hide (hd0,0)
unhide (hd0,1)
rootnoverify (hd0,1)
```

TIP *If you have problems booting to Fedora, and you can fix the issue by editing the* **grub.conf** *file (as by changing hard drive numbers), you can boot up with your CD/DVD Fedora install disk and type* **linux rescue** *at the boot prompt. Follow the prompts to boot up your system with the command line interface. Issue the* **chroot /mnt/sysimage** *command. You can then change to the* **/boot/grub** *directory and edit your* **grub.conf** *file with an editor like* **vi***.*

A sample **grub.conf** file follows with entries for both Linux and Windows. Notice that kernel parameters are listed in the `kernel` option as arguments to the kernel. The root directory is installed on a logical volume, **/dev/VolGroup00/LogVol01**. There are two kernels in this example, one that is newer (first entry, 0) but not the default (second entry, 1).

```
# grub.conf generated by anaconda
#
# Note that you do not have to rerun grub after making changes to this file
# NOTICE:  You have a /boot partition.  This means that
#          all kernel and initrd paths are relative to /boot/, eg.
#          root (hd0,1)
#          kernel /vmlinuz-version ro root=/dev/VolGroup00/LogVol01
#          initrd /initrd-version.img
#boot=/dev/sda
default=1
timeout=5
splashimage=(hd0,1)/grub/splash.xpm.gz
hiddenmenu
title Fedora (2.6.21-1.3116.fc7)
     root (hd0,1)
     kernel /vmlinuz-2.6.21-1.3116.fc7 ro root=/dev/VolGroup00/LogVol01  quiet
     initrd /initrd-2.6.21-1.3116.fc7.img
title Fedora (2.6.21-1.3116.fc7)
     root (hd0,1)
     kernel /vmlinuz-2.6.21-1.3094.fc7 ro root=/dev/VolGroup00/LogVol01  quiet
     initrd /initrd-2.6.21-1.3084.fc7.img
title Windows XP
     rootnoverify (hd0,0)
     chainloader +1
```

NOTE *Older Red Hat and Fedora versions provide the older Linux Loader (LILO) as its boot manager. It performs the same kinds of tasks as GRUB. You can modify your LILO configuration either by using an administration tool like Boot Manager (LILO-config) or by editing the /etc/ lilo.conf configuration file directly. You can also configure LILO with the KDE Klilo2 tool.*

28

Managing Users

As a system administrator, you must manage the users of your system. You can add or remove users, as well as add and remove groups, and you can modify access rights and permissions for both users and groups. You also have access to system initialization files you can use to configure all user shells. And you have control over the default initialization files copied into a user account when it is first created. You can decide how new user accounts should be configured initially by configuring these files.

> **TIP** *Every file is owned by a user who can control access to it. System files are owned by the root user and accessible by the root only. Services like FTP are an exception to this rule. Though accessible by the root, a service's files are owned by their own special user. For example, FTP files are owned by an **ftp** user. This provides users with access to a service's files without also having root user access.*

User Configuration Files

Any utility to manage a user, such as the system-config-users, makes use of certain default files, called *configuration files*, and directories to set up the new account. A set of pathnames is used to locate these default files or to indicate where to create certain user directories. For example, **/etc/skel** holds initialization files for a new user. A new user's home directory is created in the **/home** directory. Table 28-1 has a list of the pathnames.

> **TIP** *You can find out which users are currently logged in with the **w** or **who** command. The **w** command displays detailed information about each connected user, such as from where they logged in and how long they have been active, and the date and time of login. The **who** command provides less detailed data.*

The Password Files

A user gains access to an account by providing a correct login and password. The system maintains passwords in password files, along with login information like the user name and ID. Tools like the **passwd** command let users change their passwords by modifying these files; **/etc/passwd** is the file that traditionally held user passwords, though in encrypted

Directory and Files	Description
/home	Location of the user's own home directory.
/etc/skel	Holds the default initialization files for the login shell, such as **.bash_profile**, **.bashrc**, and **.bash_logout**. Includes many user setup directories and files such as **.kde** for KDE and **Desktop** for GNOME.
/etc/shells	Holds the login shells, such as BASH or TCSH.
/etc/passwd	Holds the password for a user.
/etc/group	Holds the group to which the user belongs.
/etc/shadow	Encrypted password file.
/etc/gshadow	Encrypted password file for groups.
/etc/login.defs	Default login definitions for users.

TABLE 28-1   Paths for User Configuration Files

form. However, all users are allowed to read the **/etc/passwd** file, which would have allowed access by users to the encrypted passwords. For better security, password entries are kept in the **/etc/shadow** file, which is restricted to the root user.

/etc/passwd

When you add a user, an entry for that user is made in the **/etc/passwd** file, commonly known as the *password file*. Each entry takes up one line that has several fields separated by colons. The fields are as follows:

- **Username**   Login name of the user
- **Password**   Encrypted password for the user's account
- **User ID**   Unique number assigned by the system
- **Group ID**   Number used to identify the group to which the user belongs
- **Comment**   Any user information, such as the user's full name
- **Home directory**   The user's home directory
- **Login shell**   Shell to run when the user logs in; this is the default shell, usually **/bin/bash**

Depending on whether or not you are using shadow passwords, the password field (the second field) will be either an **x** or an encrypted form of the user's password. Fedora implements shadow passwords by default, so these entries should have an **x** for their passwords. The following is an example of an **/etc/passwd** entry. For such entries, you must use the **passwd** command to create a password. Notice also that user IDs in this particular system start at 500 and increment by one. With Fedora, the group given is not the generic User, but a group consisting uniquely of that user. For example, the **dylan** user belongs to a group named **Dylan**, not to the generic **User** group.

```
dylan:x:500:500:Dylan:/home/dylan:/bin/bash
chris:x:501:501:Chris:/home/chris:/bin/bash
```

Tip *If you turn off shadow password support, entries in your passwd file will display encrypted passwords. Because any user can read the /etc/passwd file, intruders can access and possibly crack the encrypted passwords.*

Tip *Although it is technically possible to edit entries in the /etc/passwd file directly, it is not recommended. In particular, deleting an entry does not remove any other information, permissions, and data associated with a user, which opens a possible security breach whereby an intruder could take over the deleted user's ID or disk space.*

/etc/shadow and /etc/gshadow

The **/etc/passwd** file is a simple text file and is vulnerable to security breaches. Anyone who gains access to the **/etc/password** file might be able to decipher or crack the encrypted passwords through a brute-force crack. The shadow suite of applications implements a greater level of security. These include versions of **useradd, groupadd,** and their corresponding update and delete programs. Most other user configuration tools, including system-config-users, support shadow security measures. With shadow security, passwords are no longer kept in the **/etc/password** file. Instead, passwords are kept in a separate file called **/etc/shadow**. Access is restricted to the root user.

The following example shows the **/etc/passwd** entry for a user:

```
chris:x:501:501:Chris:/home/chris:/bin/bash
```

A corresponding password file, called **/etc/gshadow,** is also maintained for groups that require passwords. Fedora supports shadow passwords by default. You can manually specify whether you want to use shadow passwords with the system-config-authentication tool.

Password Tools

To change any particular field for a given user, you should use the user management tools provided, such as the **passwd** command, system-config-users, **adduser, usermod, useradd,** and **chage,** discussed in this chapter. The **passwd** command lets you change the password only. Other tools, such as system-config-users, not only make entries in the **/etc/passwd** file but also create the home directory for the user and install initialization files in the user's home directory.

These tools also let you control users' access to their accounts. You can set expiration dates for users or lock them out of their accounts. Users locked out of their accounts will have their password in the **/etc/shadow** file prefixed by the invalid string, **!!**. Unlocking the account removes this prefix.

Tip *With the Fedora Authentication tool (system-config-authentication; see Chapter 4), you can enable and configure various authentication tools such as NIS and LDAP servers, as well as enable shadow passwords, LDAP, and Kerberos authentication (accessible as Authentication on the System | Administration menu).*

Managing User Environments

Each time a user logs in, two profile scripts are executed, a system profile script that is the same for every user, and a user login profile script that can be customized to each user's needs. When the user logs out, a user logout script is run. In addition, each time a shell is generated, including the login shell, a user shell script is run. There are different kinds of scripts used for different shells. On Fedora and Red Hat Linux, the default shell commonly used is the BASH shell. As an alternative, users could use different shells such as TCSH or the Z shell, both installed with Fedora and Red Hat Linux.

Profile Scripts

For the BASH shell, each user has his or her own BASH login profile script named **.bash_profile** in the user's home directory. The system profile script is located in the **/etc** directory and named **profile** with no preceding period. The BASH shell user shell script is called **.bashrc**. The **.bashrc** file also runs the **/etc/bashrc** file to implement any global definitions such as the **PS1** and **TERM** variables. The **/etc/bashrc** file also executes any specialized initialization file in the **/etc/profile.d** directory, such as those used for KDE and GNOME. The **.bash_profile** file runs the **.bashrc** file and, through it, the **/etc/bashrc** file, implementing global definitions.

As a superuser, you can edit any of these profile or shell scripts and put in any commands you want executed for each user when that user logs in. For example, you may want to define a default path for commands, in case the user has not done so. Or you may want to notify the user of recent system news or account changes.

/etc/skel

When you first add a user to the system, you must provide the user with skeleton versions of their login, shell, and logout initialization files. For the BASH shell, these would be the **.bash_profile, .bashrc**, and **.bash_logout** files. The **useradd** command and other user management tools such as system-config-users add these files automatically, copying any files in the directory **/etc/skel** to the user's new home directory. The **/etc/skel** directory contains a skeleton initialization file for the **.bash_profile, .bashrc**, and **.bash_logout** files or, if you are using the TCSH shell as your login shell, the **.login, .tcshrc,** and **.logout** files. The **/etc/skel** directory also contains default files and directories for your desktops. These include a **.screenrc** file for the X Window System, a **.kde** directory for the KDE desktop, and a **Desktop** directory that contains default configuration files for the GNOME desktop.

As a superuser, you can configure the **.bash_profile** or **.bashrc** file in the **/etc/skel** directory any way you want. Usually, basic system variable assignments are included that define pathnames for commands and command aliases. The **PATH** and **BASH_ENV** variables are defined in **.bash_profile**. Once users have their own **.bash_profile** or **.bashrc** file, they can redefine variables or add new commands as they choose.

/etc/login.defs

System-wide values used by user and group creation utilities such as **useradd** and **usergroup** are kept in the **/etc/login.defs** file. Here you will find the range of possible user and group IDs listed. **UID_MIN** holds the minimum number for user IDs, and **UID_MAX** the maximum number. Various password options control password controls—such as

PASS_MIN_LEN, which determines the minimum number of characters allowable in a password. Options such as **CREATE_HOME** can be set to tell user tools like **useradd** to create home directories for new accounts by default. Samples of these entries are shown here:

```
MAIL_DIR /var/spool/mail
PASS_MIN_LEN          5
CREATE_HOME yes
```

/etc/login.access

You can control user login access by remote users to your system with the **/etc/login.access** file. The file consists of entries listing users, whether they are allowed access, and from where they can access the system. A record in this file consists of three colon-delimited fields: a plus (**+**) or minus (**-**) sign indicating whether users are allowed access, user login names allowed access, and the remote system (host) or terminal (tty device) from which they are trying to log in. The following enables the user **chris** to access the system from the **rabbit.mytrek.com** remote system:

```
+:chris:rabbit.mytrek.com
```

You can list more than one user or location, or use the **ALL** option in place of either users or locations to allow access by all users and locations. The **ALL** option can be qualified with the **EXCEPT** option to allow access by all users except certain specified ones. The following entry allows any valid user to log in to the system using the console, except for the users **larisa** and **aleina**:

```
+:ALL EXCEPT larisa aleina:console
```

Other access control files are used to control access for specific services, such as the **hosts.deny** and **hosts.allows** files used with the **tcpd** daemon for **xinetd**-supported servers.

Controlling User Passwords

Once you have created a user account, you can control the user's access to it. Both the system-config-users and the **passwd** tool let you lock and unlock a user's account. You use the **passwd** command with the **-l** option to lock an account, invalidating its password, and you use the **-u** option to unlock it.

You can also force a user to change his or her password at given intervals by setting an expiration date for that password. Both system-config-users and the **chage** command let you specify an expiration limit for a user's password. A user could be required to change his or her password every month, every week, or at a given date. Once the password expires, the user will be prompted to enter a new one. You can issue a warning beforehand, telling the user how much time is left before the password expires. For accounts that you want to close, you can permanently expire a password. You can even shut down accounts that are inactive too long. In the next example, the password for the **chris** account will stay valid for only seven days. The **-M** option with the number of days sets the maximum time that a password can be valid.

```
chage -M 7  chris
```

Option	Description
-m	Minimum number of days a user must go before being able to change his password
-M	Maximum number of days a user can go without changing her password
-d	The last day the password was changed
-E	Specific expiration date for a password, date in format in yyyy-mm-dd or in commonly used format like mm/dd/yyyy
-I	Allowable account inactivity period (in days), after which password will expire
-W	Warning period, number of days before expiration when the user will be sent a warning message
-l	Display current password expiration controls

TABLE 28-2   Options for the Chage Command

To set a particular date for the account to expire, use the **-E** option with the date specified mm/dd/yyyy:

```
chage -E 07/30/2003   chris
```

To find out what the current expiration settings are for a given account, use the **-l** option:

```
chage -l chris
```

You can also combine your options into one command,

```
chage -M 7 -E 07/30/2003   chris
```

A listing of the **chage** options appears in Table 28-2.

Adding and Removing Users with useradd, usermod, and userdel

Linux also provides the **useradd**, **usermod**, and **userdel** commands to manage user accounts. All these commands take in all their information as options on the command line. If an option is not specified, they use predetermined default values. These are command line operations. To use them on your desktop you first need to open a terminal window (right-click on the desktop and select Open Terminal), and then enter the commands at the shell prompt.

If you are using a desktop interface with Red Hat and Fedora distributions, you should use the system-config-users to manage user accounts (see Chapter 4). You can access system-config-users from the System | Administration | Users and Groups menu entry. It is labeled simply as Users and Groups. Table 28-3 lists the user management tools.

Tool	Description
`system-config-users`	Fedora desktop tool for adding, removing, and modifying users and groups, see Chapter 4 (System | Administration | Users and Groups)
`Kuser`	K Dekstop tool for adding, removing, and modifying users and groups
`useradd` *username options*	Add a user
`userdel` *username*	Delete a user
`usermod` *username options*	Modify a user properties
`groupadd` *groupname options*	Add a group
`groupdel` *groupname*	Delete a group
`groupmod` *groupname options*	Modify a group name

TABLE 28-3   User and Group Managment Tools

useradd

With the **useradd** command, you enter values as options on the command line, such as the name of a user, to create a user account. It then creates a new login and directory for that name using all the default features for a new account.

```
# useradd chris
```

The **useradd** utility first checks the **/etc/login.defs** file for default values for creating a new account. For those defaults not defined in the **/etc/login.defs** file, **useradd** supplies its own. You can display these defaults using the **useradd** command with the **-D** option. The default values include the group name, the user ID, the home directory, the **skel** directory, and the login shell. Values the user enters on the command line will override corresponding defaults. The group name is the name of the group in which the new account is placed. By default, this is **other**, which means the new account belongs to no group. The user ID is a number identifying the user account. The **skel** directory is the system directory that holds copies of initialization files. These initialization files are copied into the user's new home directory when it is created. The login shell is the pathname for the particular shell the user plans to use.

The **useradd** command has options that correspond to each default value. Table 28-4 holds a list of all the options you can use with the **useradd** command. You can use specific values in place of any of these defaults when creating a particular account. The login is inaccessible until you do. In the next example, the group name for the **chris** account is set to **intro1** and the user ID is set to 578:

```
# useradd chris -g intro1 -u 578
```

Once you add a new user login, you need to give the new login a password. Password entries are placed in the **/etc/passwd** and **/etc/shadow** files. Use the **passwd** command to

Option	Description
-d *dir*	Sets the home directory of the new user.
-D	Displays defaults for all settings. Can also be used to reset default settings for the home directory (**-b**), group (**-g**), shell (**-s**), expiration date (**-e**), and password expirations (**-f**).
-e *mm/dd/yy*	Sets an expiration date for the account (none, by default). Specified as month/day/year.
-f *days*	Sets the number of days an account remains active after its password expires.
-g *group*	Sets a group.
-m	Creates user's home directory, if it does not exist.
-m -k *skl-dir*	Sets the skeleton directory that holds skeleton files, such as **.profile** files, which are copied to the user's home directory automatically when it is created; the default is **/etc/skel**.
-M	Does not create user's home directory.
-p *password*	Supplies an encrypted password (crypt or MD5). With no argument, the account is immediately disabled.
-r	A Red Hat–and Fedora–specific option that creates a system account (one whose user ID is lower than the minimum set in **logon.defs**). No home directory is created unless specified by **-m**.
-s *shell*	Sets the login shell of the new user. This is **/bin/bash** by default, the BASH shell.
-u *userid*	Sets the user ID of the new user. The default is the increment of the highest number used so far.

TABLE 28-4   Options for useradd and usermod

create a new password for the user, as shown here. The password you enter will not appear on your screen. You will be prompted to repeat the password. A message will then be issued indicating that the password was successfully changed.

```
# passwd chris
Changing password for user chris
New UNIX password:
Retype new UNIX password:
passwd: all authentication tokens updated successfully
#
```

usermod

The **usermod** command enables you to change the values for any of these features. You can change the home directory or the user ID. You can even change the username for the account. The **usermod** command takes the same options as **useradd**, listed in Table 28-4.

userdel

When you want to remove a user from the system, you can use the **userdel** command to delete the user's login. With the **-r** option, the user's home directory will also be removed. In the next example, the user **chris** is removed from the system:

```
# userdel -r chris
```

Managing Groups

You can manage groups using either shell commands or window utilities like system-config-users. Groups are an effective way to manage access and permissions, letting you control several users with just their group name.

/etc/group and /etc/gshadow

The system file that holds group entries is called **/etc/group**. The file consists of group records, with one record per line and its fields separated by colons. A group record has four fields: a group name, a password, its ID, and the users who are part of this group. The Password field can be left blank. The fields for a group record are as follows:

- **Group name**   The name of the group, which must be unique
- **Password**   With shadow security implemented, this field is an **x**, with the password indicated in the **/etc/gshadow** file
- **Group ID**   The number assigned by the system to identify this group
- **Users**   The list of users that belong to the group, separated by commas

Here is an example of an entry in an **/etc/group** file. The group is called **engines**, the password is managed by shadow security, the group ID is 100, and the users who are part of this group are **chris**, **robert**, **valerie**, and **aleina**:

```
engines:x:100:chris,robert,valerie,aleina
```

As in the case of the **/etc/passwd** file, it is best to change group entries using a group management utility like **groupmod**, **groupadd**, or system-config-users. All users have read access to the **/etc/group** file. With shadow security, secure group data such as passwords are kept in the **/etc/gshadow** file, to which only the root user has access.

User Private Groups

A new user can be assigned to a special group set up for just that user and given the user's name. Thus the new user **dylan** is given a default group also called **dylan**. The group **dylan** will also show up in the listing of groups. This method of assigning default user groups is called the User Private Group (UPG) scheme. UPG is currently used on Red Hat and Fedora systems. The supplementary groups are additional groups that the user may want to belong to. Traditionally, users were all assigned to one group named **users** that would subject all users to the group permission controls for the **users** group. With UPG, each user has its own group, with its own group permissions.

Group Directories

As with users, you can create a home directory for a group. To do so, you simply create a directory for the group in the **/home** directory and change its name to that of the group, along with allowing access by any member of the group. The following example creates a directory called **engines** and changes its group to that of the **engines** group:

```
mkdir /home/engines
chgrp engines /home/engines
```

Then the read, write, and execute permissions for the group level should be set with the **chmod** command, discussed later in this chapter:

```
chmod g+rwx /home/engines
```

Any member of the **engines** group can now access the **/home/engines** directory and any shared files placed therein. This directory becomes a shared directory for the group. You can, in fact, use the same procedure to make other shared directories at any location on the file system.

Files within the shared directory should also have their permissions set to allow access by other users in the group. When a user places a file in a shared directory, the user needs to set the permissions on that file to allow other members of the group to access it. A read permission will let others display it, write lets them change it, and execute lets them run it (used for scripts and programs). The following example first changes the group for the **mymodel** file to **engines**. Then it copies the **mymodel** file to the **/home/engines** directory and sets the group read and write permission for the **engines** group:

```
$ chgrp engines mymodel
$ cp mymodel /home/engines
$ chmod g+rw /home/engines/mymodel
```

Managing Groups with the system-config-users

You can add, remove, and modify any groups easily with system-config-users. First, access system-config-users by clicking the Users and Groups entry in the System | Administration menu. Then click the tabbed panel labeled Groups in the User Manager window. This will list all your current groups. There will be three fields for each entry: Group Name, Group ID, and Group Members.

To add a group, just click the Add Group button. This opens a small window where you can enter the group name. The new group will be listed in the Groups listing. To add users as members of the group, select the group's entry and click the Properties button. This opens a window with tabbed panels for Group Data and Group Users. The Group Users panel lists all current users with checkboxes. Click the checkboxes for the users you want to be members of this group. If you want to remove a user as member, click the checkbox to remove its check. Click OK to effect your changes. If you want to remove a group, just select its entry in the Groups panel and then click the Delete button.

Managing Groups Using groupadd, groupmod, and groupdel

You can also manage groups with the `groupadd`, `groupmod`, and `groupdel` commands. These command line operations let you quickly manage a group from a terminal window.

groupadd and groupdel

With the **groupadd** command, you can create new groups. When you add a group to the system, the system places the group's name in the **/etc/group** file and gives it a group ID number. If shadow security is in place, changes are made to the **/etc/gshadow** file. The **groupadd** command only creates the group category. You need to add users to the group individually. In the following example, the **groupadd** command creates the **engines** group:

```
# groupadd engines
```

You can delete a group with the **groupdel** command. In the next example, the **engines** group is deleted:

```
# groupdel engines
```

groupmod

You can change the name of a group or its ID using the **groupmod** command. Enter **groupmod -g** with the new ID number and the group name. To change the name of a group, you use the **-n** option. Enter **groupmod -n** with the new name of the group, followed by the current name. In the next example, the **engines** group has its name changed to **trains**:

```
# groupmod -n trains engines
```

Controlling Access to Directories and Files: chmod

Each file and directory in Linux contains a set of permissions that determine who can access them and how. You set these permissions to limit access in one of three ways: You can restrict access to yourself alone, you can allow users in a predesignated group to have access, or you can permit anyone on your system to have access. You can also control how a given file or directory is accessed.

NOTE   *See Chapter 17 to learn how to use SELinux to set permissions on users and files.*

Permissions

A file or directory may have read, write, and execute permissions. When a file is created, it is automatically given read and write permissions for the owner, enabling you to display and modify the file. You may change these permissions to any combination you want. A file could also have read-only permission, preventing any modifications.

TIP   *From GNOME you can change permissions easily by right-clicking and selecting Properties. On the Permissions panel you will see options for setting Owner, Group, and Other permissions. These correspond to the Owner, Group, and Other permissions describe here (see Chapter 6).*

Permission Categories

Three different categories of users can have access to a file or directory: the owner, the group, and all others not belonging to that group. The owner is the user who created the file. Any file you create, you own. You can also permit a group to have access to a file. Often, users are collected into groups. For example, all the users for a given class or project could be formed into a group by the system administrator. A user can grant access to a file to the members of a designated group. Finally, you can also open up access to a file to all other users on the system. In this case, every user not part of the file's group could have access to that file. In this sense, every other user on the system makes up the "others" category. If you want to give the same access to all users on your system, you set the same permissions for both the group and the others. That way, you include both members of the group (group permission) and all those users who are not members (others permission).

Read, Write, Execute Permissions

Each category has its own set of read, write, and execute permissions. The first set controls the user's own access to his or her files—the owner access. The second set controls the access of the group to a user's files. The third set controls the access of all other users to the user's files. The three sets of read, write, and execute permissions for the three categories—owner, group, and other—make a total of nine types of permissions.

The **ls** command with the **-l** option displays detailed information about the file, including the permissions. In the following example, the first set of characters on the left is a list of the permissions set for the **mydata** file:

```
$ ls -l mydata
-rw-r--r-- 1 chris weather 207 Feb 20 11:55 mydata
```

An empty permission is represented by a dash, **-**. The read permission is represented by **r**, write by **w**, and execute by **x**. Notice there are ten positions. The first character indicates the file type. In a general sense, a directory can be considered a type of file. If the first character is a dash, a file is being listed. If the first character is **d**, information about a directory is being displayed.

The next nine characters are arranged according to the different user categories. The first set of three characters is the owner's set of permissions for the file. The second set of three characters is the group's set of permissions for the file. The last set of three characters is the other users' set of permissions for the file.

Permissions on GNOME

On GNOME, you can set a directory or file permission using the Permissions panel in its Properties window (see Chapter 6). Right-click the file or directory entry in the file manager window and select Properties. Then select the Permissions panel. Here you will find Access pop-up menus for Owner, Group, and Other where you can set Read, Write, and Execute permissions. You can specify the group you want access provided to from the Group drop-down menu. This displays the groups a user belongs to. The root user can change the owner of the file, listing all possible users from the Owner pop-up menu. You can even change the SELinux security context for the file or directory.

chmod

You use the **chmod** command to change different permission configurations. **chmod** takes two lists as its arguments: permission changes and filenames. You can specify the list of permissions in two different ways. One way uses permission symbols and is referred to as the *symbolic method.* The other uses what is known as a "binary mask" and is referred to as either the absolute or the relative method. Table 28-5 lists options for the **chmod** command.

NOTE *When a program is owned by the root, setting the user ID permission will give the user the ability to execute the program with root permissions. This can be a serious security risk for any program that could effect changes—such as* **rm**, *which removes files.*

Command or Option	Execution
chmod	Changes the permission of a file or directory.
Options	**Execution**
+	Adds a permission.
–	Removes a permission.
=	Assigns entire set of permissions.
r	Sets read permission for a file or directory. A file can be displayed or printed. A directory can have the list of its files displayed.
w	Sets write permission for a file or directory. A file can be edited or erased. A directory can be removed.
x	Sets execute permission for a file or directory. If the file is a shell script, it can be executed as a program. A directory can be changed to and entered.
u	Sets permissions for the user who created and owns the file or directory.
g	Sets permissions for group access to a file or directory.
o	Sets permissions for access to a file or directory by all other users on the system.
a	Sets permissions for access by the owner, group, and all other users.
s	Set User ID and Group ID permission; program owned by owner and group.
t	Set sticky bit permission; program remains in memory.
chgrp *groupname filenames*	Changes the group for a file or files.
chown *user-name filenames*	Changes the owner of a file or files.
ls -l *filename*	Lists a filename with its permissions displayed.
ls -ld *directory*	Lists a directory name with its permissions displayed.
ls -l	Lists all files in a directory with its permissions displayed.

TABLE 28-5 File and Directory Permission Operations

Ownership

Files and directories belong to both an owner and a group. A group usually consists of a collection of users, all belonging to the same group. In the following example, the **mydata** file is owned by the user **robert** and belongs to the group **weather**:

```
-rw-r--r-- 1 robert weather 207 Feb 20 11:55 mydat
```

A group can also consist of one user, however, normally the user who creates the file. Each user on the system, including the root user, is assigned their own group, of which they are the only member, ensuring access only by that user. In the next example, the report file is owned by the **robert** user and belongs to that user's single user group, **robert**:

```
-rw-r--r-- 1 robert robert 305 Mar 17 12:01 report
```

The root user, the system administrator, owns most of the system files that also belong to the root group, of which only the root user is a member. Most administration files, like configuration files in the **/etc** directory, are owned by the root user and belong to the root group. Only the root user has permission to modify them, whereas normal users can read and, in the case of programs, also execute them. In the next example, the root user owns the **fstab** file in the **/etc** directory, which also belongs to the root user group:

```
-rw-r--r-- 1 root root 621 Apr 22 11:03 fstab
```

Certain directories and files located in the system directories are owned by a service, rather than the root user, because the services need to change those files directly. This is particularly true for services that interact with remote users, such as Internet servers. Most of these files are located in the **/var** directory. Here you will find files and directories managed by services like the Squid proxy server and the Domain Name Server (named). In this example, the Squid proxy server directory is owned by the **squid** user and belongs to the **squid** group:

```
drwxr-x--- 2 squid squid 4096 Jan 24 16:29 squid
```

Changing a File's Owner or Group: chown and chgrp

Although other users may be able to access a file, only the owner can change its permissions. If, however, you want to give some other user control over one of your file's permissions, you can change the owner of the file from yourself to the other user. The **chown** command transfers control over a file to another user. This command takes as its first argument the name of the other user. Following the username, you list the files you are transferring. In the next example, the user gives control of the **mydata** file to user **robert**:

```
$ chown robert mydata
$ ls -l mydata
-rw-r--r-- 1 robert weather 207 Feb 20 11:55 mydata
```

You can also, if you wish, change the group for a file, using the **chgrp** command. **chgrp** takes as its first argument the name of the new group for a file or files. Following the new group name, you list the files you want changed to that group. In the next example, the user changes the group name for **today** and **weekend** to the **forecast** group. The `ls -l` command then reflects the group change.

```
$ chgrp forecast today weekend
$ ls -l
-rw-rw-r-- 1 chris forecast 568 Feb 14 10:30 today
-rw-rw-r-- 1 chris forecast 308 Feb 17 12:40 weekend
```

You can combine the **chgrp** operation in the **chown** command by attaching a group to the new owner with a colon.

```
$ chown george:forecast tomorrow
-rw-rw-r-- 1 george forecast 568 Feb 14 10:30 tomorrow
```

Setting Permissions: Permission Symbols

The symbolic method of setting permissions uses the characters **r**, **w**, and **x** for read, write, and execute, respectively. Any of these permissions can be added or removed. The symbol to add a permission is the plus sign, **+**. The symbol to remove a permission is the minus sign, **-**. In the next example, the **chmod** command adds the execute permission and removes the write permission for the **mydata** file for all categories. The read permission is not changed.

```
$ chmod +x-w mydata
```

Permission symbols also specify each user category. The owner, group, and others categories are represented by the **u**, **g**, and **o** characters, respectively. Notice the owner category is represented by a **u** and can be thought of as the user. The symbol for a category is placed before the plus minus sign preceding the read, write, and execute permissions. If no category symbol is used, all categories are assumed, and the permissions specified are set for the user, group, and others. In the next example, the first **chmod** command sets the permissions for the group to read and write. The second **chmod** command sets permissions for other users to read. Notice no spaces are between the permission specifications and the category. The permissions list is simply one long phrase, with no spaces.

```
$ chmod g+rw mydata
$ chmod o+r mydata
```

A user may remove permissions as well as add them. In the next example, the read permission is set for other users, but the write and execute permissions are removed:

```
$ chmod o+r-wx mydata
```

Another permission character exists, **a**, which represents all the categories. The **a** character is the default. In the next example, the two commands are equivalent. The read permission is explicitly set with the **a** character denoting all types of users: other, group, and user.

```
$ chmod a+r mydata
$ chmod +r mydata
```

One of the most common permission operations is setting a file's executable permission. This is often done in the case of shell program files. The executable permission indicates a file contains executable instructions and can be directly run by the system. In the next example, the file **lsc** has its executable permission set and then executed:

```
$ chmod u+x lsc
$ lsc
main.c lib.c
$
```

Absolute Permissions: Binary Masks

Instead of the permission symbols in Table 28-5, many users find it more convenient to use the absolute method. The *absolute method* changes all the permissions at once, instead of specifying one or the other. It uses a *binary mask* that references all the permissions in each category. The three categories, each with three permissions, conform to an octal binary format. Octal numbers have a base 8 structure. When translated into a binary number, each octal digit becomes three binary digits. A binary number is a set of 1 and 0 digits. Three octal digits in a number translate into three sets of three binary digits, which is nine altogether—and the exact number of permissions for a file.

You can use the octal digits as a mask to set the different file permissions. Each octal digit applies to one of the user categories. You can think of the digits matching up with the permission categories from left to right, beginning with the owner category. The first octal digit applies to the owner category, the second to the group, and the third to the others category. The actual octal digit you choose determines the read, write, and execute permissions for each category. At this point, you need to know how octal digits translate into their binary equivalents.

Calculating Octal Numbers

A simple way to calculate the octal number makes use of the fact that any number used for permissions will be a combination derived from adding in decimal terms the numbers 4, 2, and 1. Use 4 for read permission, 2 for write, and 1 for execute. The read, write, execute permission is simply the addition of 4 + 2 + 1 to get 7. The read and execute permission adds 4 and 1, to get 5. You can use this method to calculate the octal number for each category. To get 755, you would add 4 + 2 + 1 for the owner read, write, and execute permission, 4 + 1 for the group read and execute permission, and 4 + 1 again for the other read and execute permission.

Binary Masks

When dealing with a binary mask, you need to specify three digits for all three categories, as well as their permissions. This makes a binary mask less versatile than the permission symbols. To set the owner execute permission on and the write permission off for the **mydata** file and retain the read permission, you need to use the octal digit 5 (101). At the same time, you need to specify the digits for group and other users access. If these categories are to retain read access, you need the octal number 4 for each (100). This gives you three octal digits, 544, which translate into the binary digits 101 100 100.

```
$ chmod 544 mydata
```

Execute Permissions

One of the most common uses of the binary mask is to set the execute permission. You can create files that contain Linux commands, called *shell scripts*. To execute the commands in a shell script, you must first indicate the file is executable—that it contains commands the system can execute. You can do this in several ways, one of which is to set the executable permission on the shell script file. Suppose you just completed a shell script file and you need to give it executable permission to run it. You also want to retain read and write permission but deny any access by the group or other users. The octal digit 7 (111) will set all three permissions, including execute (you can also add 4-read, 2-write, and 1-execute to get 7). Using 0 for the group and other users denies them access. This gives you the digits 700, which are equivalent to the binary digits 111 000 000. In this example, the owner permission for the **myprog** file is set to include execute permission:

```
$ chmod 700 myprog
```

If you want others to be able to execute and read the file, but not change it, you can set the read and execute permissions and turn off the write permission with the digit 5 (101). In this case, you would use the octal digits 755, having the binary equivalent of 111 101 101.

```
$ chmod 755 myprog
```

Directory Permissions

You can also set permissions on directories. The read permission set on a directory allows the list of files in a directory to be displayed. The execute permission enables a user to change that directory. The write permission enables a user to create and remove his or her files in that directory. If you allow other users to have write permission on a directory, they can add their own files to it. When you create a directory, it is automatically given read, write, and execute permission for the owner. You may list the files in that directory, change it, and create files in it.

Like files, directories have sets of permissions for the owner, the group, and all other users. Often, you may want to allow other users to change and list the files in one of your directories, but not let them add their own files to it. In this case, you would to set read and execute permissions on the directory, but not write permission. This would allow other users to change the directory and list the files in it, but not to create new files or to copy any of their files into it. The next example sets read and execute permission for the group for the **thankyou** directory, but removes the write permission. Members of the group may enter the **thankyou** directory and list the files there, but they may not create new ones.

```
$ chmod g+rx-w letters/thankyou
```

Just as with files, you can also use octal digits to set a directory permission. To set the same permissions as in the preceding example, you would use the octal digits 750, which have the binary equivalents of 111 101 000.

```
$ chmod 750 letters/thankyou
```

Displaying Directory Permissions

The **ls** command with the **-l** option lists all files in a directory. To list only the information about the directory itself, add a **d** modifier. In the next example, **ls -ld** displays information about the **thankyou** directory. Notice the first character in the permissions list is **d**, indicating it is a directory:

```
$ ls -ld thankyou
drwxr-x--- 2 chris 512 Feb 10 04:30 thankyou
```

Parent Directory Permissions

If you have a file you want other users to have access to, you not only need to set permissions for that file, you also must make sure the permissions are set for the directory in which the file is located. To access your file, a user must first access the file's directory. The same applies to parents of directories. Although a directory may give permission to others to access it, if its parent directory denies access, the directory cannot be reached. Therefore, you must pay close attention to your directory tree. To provide access to a directory, all other directories above it in the directory tree must also be accessible to other users.

Ownership Permissions

In addition to the read/write/execute permissions, you can also set ownership permissions for executable programs. Normally, the user who runs a program owns it while it is running, even though the program file itself may be owned by another user. The Set User ID permission allows the original owner of the program to own it always, even while another user is running the program. For example, most software on the system is owned by the root user but is run by ordinary users. Some such software may have to modify files owned by the root. In this case, the ordinary user would need to run that program with the root retaining ownership so that the program could have the permissions to change those root-owned files. The Group ID permission works the same way, except for groups. Programs owned by a group retain ownership, even when run by users from another group. The program can then change the owner group's files. There is a potential security risk involved in that you are essentially giving a user some limited root-level access.

Ownership Permissions Using Symbols

To add both the User ID and Group ID permissions to a file, you use the **s** option. The following example adds the User ID permission to the **pppd** program, which is owned by the root user. When an ordinary user runs **pppd**, the root user retains ownership, allowing the **pppd** program to change root-owned files.

```
# chmod +s /usr/sbin/pppd
```

The Set User ID and Set Group ID permissions show up as an **s** in the execute position of the owner and group segments. Set User ID and Group ID are essentially variations of the execute permission, **x**. Read, write, and User ID permission would be **rws** instead of just **rwx**.

```
# ls -l /usr/sbin/pppd
-rwsr-sr-x 1 root root 184412 Jan 24 22:48 /usr/sbin/pppd
```

Ownership Permissions Using the Binary Method

For the ownership permissions, you add another octal number to the beginning of the octal digits. The octal digit for User ID permission is 4 (100) and for Group ID, it is 2 (010) (use 6 to set both—110). The following example sets the User ID permission to the **pppd** program, along with read and execute permissions for the owner, group, and others:

```
# chmod 4555 /usr/sbin/pppd
```

Sticky Bit Permission Using Symbols

The sticky bit permission symbol is **t**. The sticky bit shows up as a **t** in the execute position of the other permissions. A program with read and execute permission with the sticky bit would have its permissions displayed as **r-t**.

```
# chmod +t /home/dylan/myreports
# ls -l /home/dylan/myreports
-rwxr-xr-t 1 root root 4096 /home/dylan/myreports
```

Sticky Bit Permissions

One other special permission provides for greater security on directories, the *sticky bit*. Originally the sticky bit was used to keep a program in memory after it finished execution to increase efficiency. Current Linux systems ignore this feature. Instead, it is used for directories to protect files within them. Files in a directory with the sticky bit set can only be deleted or renamed by the root user or the owner of the directory.

Sticky Bit Permission Using the Binary Method

As with ownership, for sticky bit permissions, you add another octal number to the beginning of the octal digits. The octal digit for the sticky bit is 1 (001). The following example sets the sticky bit for the **myreports** directory:

```
# chmod 1755 /home/dylan/myreports
```

The next example sets both the sticky bit and the User ID permission on the **newprogs** directory. The permission 5755 has the binary equivalent of 101 111 101 101:

```
# chmod 5755 /usr/bin/newprogs
# ls -l /usr/bin/newprogs
drwsr-xr-t 1 root root 4096  /usr/bin/newprogs
```

Permission Defaults: umask

Whenever you create a file or directory, it is given default permissions. You can display the current defaults or change them with the **umask** command. The permissions are displayed in binary or symbolic format as described in the following sections. The default permissions include any execute permissions that would be applied to a directory. Execute permission for a file is turned off by default when you create it. This is because standard data files do not use the executable permissions (for a file that you want to be executable like a script, you will have to manually set its execute permission).To display the current default permissions, use the **umask** command with no arguments. The **-S** option uses the symbolic format.

```
$ umask -S
u=rwx,g=rx,o=rx
```

This default umask provides rw-r--r-- permission for standard files and adds execute permission for directories, rwxr-xr-x.

You can set a new default by specifying permissions in either symbolic or binary format. To specify the new permissions, use the **-S** option. The following example denies others read permission, while allowing user and group read access, which results in permissions of rwxr-x---:

```
$ umask -S  u=rwx,g=rx,o=
```

When you use the binary format, the mask is the inverse of the permissions you want to set. So to set both the read and execute permission on and the write permission off, you would use the octal number 2, a binary 010. To set all permissions on, you would use an octal 0, a binary 000. The following example shows the mask for the permission defaults rwx, rx, and rx (rw, r, and r for files):

```
$ umask
0022
```

To set the default to only deny all permissions for others, you would use 0027, using the binary mask 0111 for the other permissions.

```
$ umask 0027
```

Disk Quotas

You can use disk quotas to control how much disk space a particular user makes use of on your system. On your Linux system, unused disk space is held as a common resource that each user can access as he or she needs it. As users create more files, they take the space they need from the pool of available disk space. In this sense, all the users are sharing a single resource of unused disk space. However, if one user were to use up all the remaining disk space, none of the other users would be able to create files or even run programs. To counter this problem, you can create disk quotas on particular users, limiting the amount of available disk space they can use.

Quota Tools

Quota checks can be implemented on the file system of a hard disk partition mounted on your system. The quotas are enabled using the **quotacheck** and **quotaon** programs. They are executed in the **/etc/rc.d/rc.sysinit** script, which is run whenever you start up your system. Each partition needs to be mounted with the quota options, **usrquota** or **grpquota**. **usrquota** enables quota controls for users, and **grpquota** works for groups. These options are usually placed in the mount entry in the **/etc/fstab** file for a particular partition (see Chapter 30). For example, to mount the **/dev/hda6** hard disk partition mounted to the **/home** directory with support for user and group quotas, you would require a mount entry like the following:

```
/dev/hda6 /home ext2 defaults,usrquota,grpquota 1 1
```

You also need to create **quota.user** and **quota.group** files for each partition for which you enable quotas. These are the quota databases used to hold the quota information for each user and group. You can create these files by running the **quotacheck** command with the **-a** option or the device name of the file system where you want to enable quotas. The following example creates the quota database on the hda1 hard disk partition:

```
quotacheck -a  /dev/hda1
```

edquota

You can set disk quotas using the **edquota** command. With it, you can access the quota record for a particular user and group, which is maintained in the disk quota database. You can also set default quotas that will be applied to any user or group on the file system for which quotas have not been set. **edquota** will open the record in your default editor, and you can use your editor to make any changes. To open the record for a particular user, use the **-u** option and the username as an argument for **edquota** (see Table 28-6). The following example opens the disk quota record for the user **larisa**:

```
edquota -u larisa
```

The limit you set for a quota can be hard or soft. A hard limit will deny a user the ability to exceed his or her quota, whereas a soft limit will just issue a warning. For the soft limit, you can designate a grace period during which time the user has the chance to reduce their disk space below the limit. If the disk space still exceeds the limit after the grace period expires, the user can be denied access to their account. For example, a soft limit is typically 75 megabytes, whereas the hard limit could be 100 megabytes. Users who exceed their soft limit could have a 48-hour grace period.

The quota record begins with the hard disk device name and the blocks of memory and inodes in use. The Limits segments have parameters for soft and hard limits. If these entries are 0, there are no limits in place. You can set both hard and soft limits, using the hard limit as a firm restriction. Blocks in Linux are currently about 1,000 bytes. The inodes are used by files to hold information about the memory blocks making up a file. To set the time limit for a soft limit, use the **edquota** command with the **-t** option. The following example displays the quota record for **larisa**:

```
Quotas for user larisa:
/dev/hda3: blocks in use: 9000, limits (soft = 40000, hard = 60000)
  inodes in use: 321, limits (soft = 0, hard = 0)
```

quotacheck, quotaon, and quotaoff

The quota records are maintained in the quota database for that partition. Each partition that has quotas enabled has its own quota database. You can check the validity of your quota database with the **quotacheck** command. You can turn quotas on and off using the **quotaon** and **quotaoff** commands. When you start up your system, **quotacheck** is run to check the quota databases, and then **quotaon** is run to turn on quotas.

edquota Option	Description
-u	Edits the user quota. This is the default.
-g	Edits the group quota.
-p	Duplicates the quotas of the typical user specified. This is the normal mechanism used to initialize quotas for groups of users.
-t	Edits the soft time limits for each file system.

TABLE 28-6   Options for edquota

quota Option	Description
-g	Prints group quotas for the group of which the user is a member.
-u	Prints the user's quota.
-v	Displays quotas on file systems where no storage is allocated.
-q	Prints information on file systems where usage is over quota.

TABLE 28-7   Options for quota

repquota and quota

As the system administrator, you can use the **repquota** command to generate a summary of disk usage for a specified file system, checking to see what users are approaching or exceeding quota limits. **repquota** takes as its argument the file system to check; the **-a** option checks all file systems.

```
repquota /dev/hda1
```

Individual users can use the **quota** command to check their memory use and how much disk space they have left in their quota (see Table 28-7).

Lightweight Directory Access Protocol

The Lightweight Directory Access Protocol (LDAP) is designed to implement network-accessible directories of information. In this context, the term directory is defined as a database of primarily read-only, simple, small, widely accessible, and quickly distributable information. It is not designed for transactions or updates. It is primarily used to provide information about users on a network, providing information about them such as their e-mail address or phone number. Such directories can also be used for authentication purposes, identifying that a certain user belongs to a specified network. You can find out more information on LDAP at **www.ldapman.org**. You can think of an LDAP directory for users as an Internet-accessible phone book, where anyone can look you up to find your e-mail address or other information. In fact, it may be more accurate to refer to such directories as databases. They are databases of user information, accessible over networks like the Internet. Normally, the users on a local network are spread across several different systems, and to obtain information about a user, you would have to know what system the user is on, and then query that system. With LDAP, user information for all users on a network is kept in the LDAP server. You only have to query the network's LDAP server to obtain information about a user. For example, Sendmail can use LDAP to look up user addresses. You can also use Firefox or Netscape to query LDAP.

NOTE *LDAP is a directory access protocol to an X.500 directory service, the OSI directory service.*

LDAP Clients and Servers

LDAP directories are implemented as clients and servers, where you use an LDAP client to access an LDAP server that manages the LDAP database. Most Linux distributions use

OpenLDAP, an open-source version of LDAP (you can find out more about OpenLDAP at **www.openldap.org**). This package includes an LDAP server (**slapd**), an LDAP replication server (**slurpd**), an LDAP client, and tools. **slurpd** is used to update other LDAP servers on your network, should you have more than one. Once the LDAP server is installed, you can start, stop, and restart the LDAP server (**slapd**) with the **ldap** startup script or system-config-services:

```
service ldap restart
```

TIP *Red Hat and Fedora clients can enable LDAP services and select an LDAP server using the Fedora Authentication tool (system-config-authentication), accessible as the Authentication entry in the System | Administration menu(see Chapter 4).*

LDAP Configuration Files

All LDAP configuration files are kept in the **/etc/openldap** directory. These include **slapd.conf**, the LDAP server configuration file, and **ldap.conf**, the LDAP clients and tools configuration file. To enable the LDAP server, you have to manually edit the **slapd.conf** file and change the domain value (dc) for the suffix and rootdn entries to your own network's domain address. This is the network that will be serviced by the LDAP server.

To enable LDAP clients and their tools, you have to specify the correct domain address in the **ldap.conf** file in the BASE option, along with the server's address in the HOST option (domain name or IP address). For clients, you can either edit the **ldap.conf** file directly or use the system-config-authentication tool (System | Administration | Authentication), clicking the Configure LDAP button on either the User Information or Authentication panel. Here you can enter your domain name and the LDAP server's address. See the **ldap.conf** Man entry for detailed descriptions of LDAP options.

TIP *Keep in mind that the /etc/ldap.conf and /etc/openldap/ldap.conf files are not the same: /etc/ldap.conf is used to configure LDAP for the Nameservice Switch and PAM support, whereas /etc/openldap/ldap.conf is used for all LDAP clients.*

Configuring the LDAP server: slapd.conf

You configure the LDAP server with the **slapd.conf** file. Here you will find entries for loading schemas and for specifying access controls, the database directory, and passwords. The file is commented in detail, with default settings for most options, although you will have to enter settings for several. First you need to specify your domain suffix and root domain manager. The default settings are shown here:

```
suffix          "dc=my-domain,dc=com"
rootdn          "cn=Manager,dc=my-domain,dc=com"
```

In this example, the **suffix** is changed to **mytrek**, for **mytrek.com**. The **rootdn** remains the same.

```
suffix          "dc=mytrek,dc=com"
rootdn          "cn=Manager,dc=mytrek,dc=com"
```

Next you will have to specify a password with **rootpw**. There are entries for both plain text and encrypted versions. Both are commented. Remove the comment for one. In the following example the plain text password option is used, "secret":

```
rootpw              secret
# rootpw            {crypt}ijFYNcSNctBYg
```

For an encrypted password, you can first create the encrypted version with **slappasswd**. This will generate a text encryption string for the password. Then copy the generated encrypted string to the **rootpw** entry. On GNOME you can simply cut and paste from a terminal window to the **/etc/slapd.conf** file in Text Editor (Accessories). You can also redirect the encrypted string to a file and read it in later. SSHA encryption will be used by default.

```
# slappasswd
New password:
Re-enter new password:
{SSHA}0a+szaAwElK57Y8AoD5uMULSvLfCUfg5
```

The **rootpw** root password entry should then look like this:

```
rootpw          {SSHA}0a+szaAwElK57Y8AoD5uMULSvLfCUfg5
```

Use the password you entered at the **slappasswd** prompt to access your LDAP directory.
    The configuration file also lists the schemas to be used. Schemas are included with the **include** directive.

```
include             /etc/openldap/schema/core.schema
include             /etc/openldap/schema/cosine.schema
include             /etc/openldap/schema/inetorgperson.schema
include             /etc/openldap/schema/nis.schema
```

NOTE *LDAP supports the Simple Authentication and Security Layer (SASL) for secure authentication with methods like MD5 and Kerberos.*

LDAP Directory Database: ldif

A record (also known as entry) in an LDAP database begins with a name, known as a *distinguishing name,* followed by a set of attributes and their values. The distinguishing name uniquely identifies the record. For example, a name could be a username and the attribute would be the user's e-mail address, the address being the attribute's value. Allowable attributes are determined by schemas defined in the **/etc/openldap/schema** directory. This directory will hold various schema definition files, each with a **schema** extension. Some will be dependent on others, enhancing their supported classes and attributes. The basic core set of attributes are defined in the **core.schema** file. Here you will find definitions for attributes like country name and street address. Other schemas, like **inetorgperson.schema**, specify **core.schema** as a dependent schema, making its attributes available to the classes. The inetOrgPerson schema will also define its own attributes such as jpegPhoto for a person's photograph.

Schema Attributes and Classes

Attributes and classes are defined officially by RFC specifications that are listed with each attribute and class entry in the schema files. These are standardized definitions and should not be changed. Attributes are defined by an **attributetype** definition. Each is given a unique identifying number followed by a name by which it can be referenced. Fields include the attribute description (DESC), search features such as EQUALITY and SUBSTR, and the object identifier (SYNTAX). See the OpenLDAP administrative guide for a detailed description.

```
attributetype ( 2.5.4.9 NAME ( 'street' 'streetAddress' )
     DESC 'RFC2256: street address of this object'
     EQUALITY caseIgnoreMatch
     SUBSTR caseIgnoreSubstringsMatch
     SYNTAX 1.3.6.1.4.1.1466.115.121.1.15{128} )
```

A class defines the kind of database (directory) you can create. This will specify the kinds of attributes you can include in your records. Classes can be dependent, where one class becomes an extension of another. The class most often used for LDAP databases is inetOrgPerson, defined in the **inetOrgPerson.schema** file. The term inetOrgPerson stands for Internet Organization Person, as many LDAP directories perform Internet tasks. The class is derived from the organizationalPerson class defined in **core.schema**, which includes the original attributes for commonly used fields like street address and name.

```
# inetOrgPerson
# The inetOrgPerson represents people who are associated with an
# organization in some way.  It is a structural class and is derived
# from the organizationalPerson which is defined in X.521 [X521].
objectclass ( 2.16.840.1.113730.3.2.2
    NAME 'inetOrgPerson'
     DESC 'RFC2798: Internet Organizational Person'
    SUP organizationalPerson
    STRUCTURAL
     MAY (
            audio $ businessCategory $ carLicense $ departmentNumber $
            displayName $ employeeNumber $ employeeType $ givenName $
            homePhone $ homePostalAddress $ initials $ jpegPhoto $
            labeledURI $ mail $ manager $ mobile $ o $ pager $
            photo $ roomNumber $ secretary $ uid $ userCertificate $
            x500uniqueIdentifier $ preferredLanguage $
            userSMIMECertificate $ userPKCS12 )
     )
```

You can create your own classes, building on the standard ones already defined. You can also create your own attributes. But each attribute will require a unique object identifier (OID).

Distinguishing Names

Data in an LDAP directory are organized hierarchically, from general categories to specific data. An LDAP directory could be organized starting with countries, narrowing to states, then organizations and their subunits, and finally individuals. Commonly, LDAP directories are organized along the lines of Internet domains. In this format, the top category would be the domain name extension, for instance .com or .ca. The directory would then break down to the network (organization), units, and finally users.

This organization is used to help define distinguishing names that will identify the LDAP records. In a network-based organization, the top-level organization is defined by a domain component specified by the dcObject class, which includes the domainComponent (dc) attribute. Usually you define the network and extension as domain components to make up the top-level organization that becomes the distinguishing name for the database itself.

```
dc=mytrek, dc=com
```

Under the organization name is an organizational unit, such as users. These are defined as an organizationalUnitName (ou), which is part of the organizationalUnit class. The distinguishing name for the user's organizational unit would be

```
ou=users, dc=mytrek, dc=com
```

Under the organizational unit you could then have individual users. Here the user name is defined with the commonName (cn) attribute, which is used in various classes, including Person, which is part of organizationalPerson, which in turn is part of inetOrgPerson. The distinguishing name for the user **dylan** would then be

```
cn=dylan,ou=users,dc=mytrek,dc=com
```

LDIF Entries

Database entries are placed in an LDAP Interchange Format (LDIF) file. This format provides a global standard that allows a database to be accessed by any LDAP-compliant client. An LDIF file is a simple text file with an **.ldif** extension, placed in the **/etc/openldap** directory. The entries for an LDIF record consist of a distinguishing name or attribute, followed by a colon, and its list of values. Each record begins with a distinguishing name to uniquely identify the record. Attributes then follow. You can think of the name as a record and the attributes as fields in that record. You end the record with an empty line.

Initially you create an LDIF file using any text editor. Then enter the records. In the following example, the **mytrek.ldif** LDIF file contains records for users on the network.

First you create records defining your organization and organization units. These distinguishing names will be used in user-level records. You will also have to specify a manager for the database, in this case simply Manager. Be sure to include the appropriate object classes. The organization uses both the dcObject (domain component object) and organization objects. The Manager uses organizationalRole, and users use the organizationalUnit. Within each record you can have attribute definitions, like the organization attribute, o, in the first record, which is set to MyTrek.

```
dn: dc=mytrek,dc=com
objectclass: dcobject
objectclass: organization
dc: mytrek
o: MyTrek

dn: cn=Manager,dc=mytrek,dc=com
cn: Manager
objectclass: organizationalRole
```

```
dn: ou=users,dc=mytrek,dc=com
objectclass: organizationalUnit
ou: users
```

Individual records then follow, such as the following for **dylan**. Here the object classes are organizationalPerson and inetOrgPerson. Attributes then follow, like common name (cn), user ID (uid), organization (o), surname (sn), and street.

```
dn: cn=dylan,ou=users,dc=mytrek,dc=com
objectclass: organizationalPerson
objectclass: inetOrgPerson
cn: dylan
uid: dylan
o: MyTrek
sn: shark
street: 77777 saturn ave
```

An example of an LDIF file is shown here. The organization is mytrek.com. There are two records, one for **dylan** and the other for **chris**:

mytrek.ldif
```
dn: dc=mytrek,dc=com
objectclass: dcobject
objectclass: organization
dc: mytrek
o: MyTrek

dn: cn=Manager,dc=mytrek,dc=com
cn: Manager
objectclass: organizationalRole

dn: ou=users,dc=mytrek,dc=com
objectclass: organizationalUnit
ou: users

dn: cn=dylan,ou=users,dc=mytrek,dc=com
objectclass: organizationalPerson
objectclass: inetOrgPerson
cn: dylan
uid: dylan
o: MyTrek
sn: shark
street: 77777 saturn ave

dn: cn=chris,ou=users,dc=mytrek,dc=com
objectclass: organizationalPerson
objectclass: inetOrgPerson
cn: chris
uid: chris
o: MyTrek
sn: dolphin
street: 99999 neptune way
```

Adding the Records

Once you have created your LDIF file, you can then use the **ldapadd** command to add the records to your LDAP directory. Use the **-D** option to specify the directory to add the records to, and the **-f** option to specify the LDIF file to read from. You could use **ldapadd** to enter fields directly. The **-x** option says to use simple password access, the **-W** will prompt for the password, and the **-D** option specifies the directory manager.

```
# ldapadd -x -D "cn=Manager,dc=mytrek,dc=com" -W -f mytrek.ldif

Enter LDAP Password:

adding new entry "dc=mytrek,dc=com"

adding new entry "cn=Manager,dc=mytrek,dc=com"

adding new entry "ou=users,dc=mytrek,dc=com"

adding new entry "cn=dylan,ou=users,dc=mytrek,dc=com"

adding new entry "cn=chris,ou=users,dc=mytrek,dc=com"
```

Be sure to restart the LDAP server to have your changes take effect.

Searching LDAP

Once you have added your records, you can use the **ldapsearch** command to search your LDAP directory. The **-x** and **-W** options provide simple password access, and the **-b** option will specify the LDAP database to use. Following the options are the attributes to search for, in this case the street attribute.

```
# ldapsearch -x -W -D 'cn=Manager,dc=mytrek,dc=com' -b 'dc=mytrek,dc=com' street
Enter LDAP Password:
# extended LDIF
#
# LDAPv3
# base <dc=mytrek,dc=com> with scope sub
# filter: (objectclass=*)
# requesting: street

# dylan, users, mytrek.com
dn: cn=dylan,ou=users,dc=mytrek,dc=com
street: 77777 saturn ave

# chris, users, mytrek.com
dn: cn=chris,ou=users,dc=mytrek,dc=com
street: 99999 neptune way

# search result
search: 2
result: 0 Success

# numResponses: 6
# numEntries: 5
```

If you want to see all the records listed in the database, you can use the same search command without any attributes.

LDAP Tools

To actually make or change entries in the LDAP database, you use the **ldapadd** and **ldapmodify** utilities. With **ldapdelete**, you can remove entries. Once you have created an LDAP database, you can then query it, through the LDAP server, with **ldapsearch**. For the LDAP server, you can create a text file of LDAP entries using the LDAP Data Interchange Format (LDIF). Such text files can then be read in all at once to the LDAP database using the **slapadd** tool. The **slapcat** tool extracts entries from the LDAP database and saves them in an LDIF file. To reindex additions and changes, you use the **slapindex** utility. See the LDAP Howto at the Linux documentation project for details on using and setting up LDAP databases such as address books (**www.tldp.org**).

TIP   *You can enable and designate LDAP servers with the system-config-authentication tool (Authentication in the System | Administration menu; see Chapter 4). You can also use the LDAP Browser/Editor or the GNOME Directory Administrator to manage and edit LDAP directories.*

LDAP and PAM

With LDAP, you can also more carefully control the kind of information given out and to whom. Using a PAM module (**pam_ldap**), LDAP can perform user authentication tasks, providing centralized authentication for users. Login operations that users perform for different services such as POP mail server logins, system logins, and Samba logins can all be carried out through LDAP using a single PAM-secured user ID and password. To configure PAM to use LDAP, use the system-config-authentication tool (System | Administration | Authentication) and select Enable LDAP Support on the Authentication panel (see Chapter 4). You should also make sure that the LDAP server is correctly specified. To use LDAP for authentication, you need to configure PAM to use it, as well as migrate authentication files to the LDAP format. The **/usr/share/openldap/migration** directory holds scripts you can use to translate the old files into LDAP versions.

LDAP and the Name Service Switch Service

With the **libnss_ldap** module, LDAP can also be used in the Nameservice Switch (NSS) service along with NIS and system files for system database services like passwords and groups. Clients can easily enable LDAP for NSS by using the system-config-authentication tool (System | Administration | Authentication) and selecting Enable LDAP Support in the User Information panel. You also need to make sure that the LDAP server is specified. You could also manually add **ldap** for entries in the **/etc/nsswitch.conf** file.

TIP   *To better secure access to the LDAP server, you should encrypt your LDAP administrator's password. The LDAP administrator is specified in the **rootdn** entry and its password in the **rootpw** entry. To create an encrypted password, use the **slappasswd** command. This prompts you for a password and displays its encrypted version. Copy that encrypted version in the **rootpw** entry.*

Enabling LDAP on Thunderbird

In Thunderbird, open the address book, then select File | New, and choose the LDAPD directory. Here you can enter the LDAP server. This displays a panel where you can enter the address book name, the host name of the LDAP server, the Base DN to search, and the port number, 389 on Fedora.

Pluggable Authentication Modules

Pluggable Authentication Modules (PAM) is an authentication service that lets a system determine the method of authentication to be performed for users. In a Linux system, authentication has traditionally been performed by looking up passwords. When a user logs in, the login process looks up their password in the password file. With PAM, users' requests for authentication are directed to PAM, which in turn uses a specified method to authenticate the user. This could be a simple password lookup or a request to an LDAP server, but it is PAM that provides authentication, not a direct password lookup by the user or application. In this respect, authentication becomes centralized and controlled by a specific service, PAM. The actual authentication procedures can be dynamically configured by the system administrator. Authentication is carried out by modules that can vary according to the kind of authentication needed. An administrator can add or replace modules by simply changing the PAM configuration files. See the PAM Web site at **www .kernel.org/pub/linux/libs/pam** for more information and a listing of PAM modules. PAM modules are located in the **/lib/security** directory.

PAM Configuration Files

PAM uses different configuration files for different services that request authentication. Such configuration files are kept in the **/etc/pam.d** directory. For example, you have a configuration file for logging in to your system (**/etc/pam.d/login**), one for the graphical login (**/etc/pam.d/gdm**), and one for accessing your Samba server (**/etc/pam.d/samba**). A default PAM configuration file, called **/etc/pam.d/other**, is invoked if no services file is present. The **system-auth** file contains standard authentication modules for system services generated by system-config-authentication and is invoked in many of the other configuration files. In addition, Fedora sets up an authentication for its configuration tools, such as system-config-services and system-config-network.

PAM Modules

A PAM configuration file contains a list of modules to be used for authentication. They have the following format:

```
module-type control-flag module-path module-args
```

The *module-path* is the module to be run, and *module-args* are the parameters you want passed to that module. Though there are a few generic arguments, most modules have their own. The *module-type* refers to different groups of authentication management: account, authentication, session, and password. The account management performs account verification, checking such account aspects as whether the user has access and or whether the password has expired. Authentication (**auth**) verifies who the user is, usually through a password confirmation. Password management performs authentication updates such as password changes. Session management refers to tasks performed before a service is accessed and before it is shut down. These include tasks like initiating a log of a user's activity or mounting and unmounting home directories.

TIP *As an alternative to the /etc/pam.d directory, you could create one configuration file called the /etc/pam.conf file. Entries in this file have a service field, which refers to the application that the module is used for. If the /etc/pam.d directory exists, /etc/pam.conf is automatically ignored.*

The *control-flag* field indicates how PAM is to respond if the module fails. The control can be a simple directive or a more complicated response that can specify return codes like **open_err** with actions to take. The simple directives are **requisite, required, sufficient, include,** and **optional**. The **requisite** directive ends the authentication process immediately if the module fails to authenticate. The **required** directive only ends the authentication after the remaining modules are run. The **sufficient** directive indicates that success of this module is enough to provide authentication unless a previous required module has failed. The **include** directive includes lines from a specified configuration file, like the **system-auth** pam configuration file for system authentication. The **optional** directive indicates the module's success is not needed unless it is the only authentication module for its service. If you specify return codes, you can refine the conditions for authentication failure or success. Return codes can be given values such as **die** or **ok**. The **open_err** return code could be given the action **die**, which would stop all authentication and return failure. The **/etc/pam.d/vsftpd** configuration file for the FTP server is shown here:

```
#%PAM-1.0
auth required pam_listfile.so item=user sense=deny
                file=/etc/vsftpd.ftpusers onerr=succeed
auth       required    pam_shells.so
auth       include     system-auth
account    include     system-auth
session    include     system-auth
session    required    pam_loginuid.so
```

29

Software Management

Installing, uninstalling, or updating software packages has always been a simple process in Fedora Linux due to the widespread use of the Red Hat Package Manager (RPM). Instead of using a standard TAR archive, software is packaged in a special archive for use with RPM. An RPM archive contains all the program files, configuration files, data files, and even documentation that constitute a software application. With one simple operation, the Red Hat Package Manager installs all these for you. It also checks for any other software packages that the program may need to run correctly. You can even create your own RPM packages. Fedora now manages its software packages using Fedora repositories. All software is downloaded directly and installed using the Pirut Program Manager and the PUP updater. This approach heralds a move from thinking of most Linux software as included on a few disks, to viewing the disk as just a core from which you can expand your installed software as you like from online repositories. Most software is now located on the Internet-connected repositories. With the integration of Yum into your Fedora system, you can now think of that software as an easily installed extension of your current collection. Relying on disk media for your software becomes, in a sense, obsolete. Check the Fedora documentation on software management for a complete discussion on Yum, "Managing Software with Yum."

```
docs.fedoraproject.org/yum/en/index.html
```

You can update Fedora Linux using Yum repositories, accessible with PUP. You can also use Yum tools like **yum** to download from different Fedora software repositories directly from the command line (**linux.duke.edu/projects/yum**). New Fedora releases can be downloaded with BitTorrent from (**torrent.fedoraproject.org**).

You can also download source code versions of applications and then compile and install them on your system. Where this process once was complex, it has been significantly streamlined with the addition of *configure scripts*. Most current source code, including GNU software, is distributed with a configure script. The configure script automatically detects your system configuration and generates a *Makefile*, which is used to compile the application and create a binary file that is compatible with your system. In most cases, with a few Makefile operations, you can compile and install complex source code on any system.

Software Repositories

You can download Linux software from many online sources. You can find sites for particular kinds of applications, such as GNOME and KDE, as well as for particular distributions, such as Fedora. With Fedora Yum–enabled repositories, Fedora can automatically download and update software installed from RPM packages. You can also download Fedora packages directly from **download.fedora.redhat.com** for the Fedora collection. Two major software repositories are **freshrpms.net** and **rpm.livna.org**. These provide most supplemental software like video card drivers and multimedia codecs. Both are designed to interface directly with Yum and your Pirut and PUP software update tools.

Some sites are repositories for collections of RPM packages, such as **rpmfind.net**, and others like **freshmeat.net** refer you to original sites. A great many of the Open Source Linux projects can be found at **sourceforge.net**. Here you will find detailed documentation and recent versions of software packages. For applications designed for the GNOME desktop, you can check **www.gnomefiles.org**, and you can find KDE applications at **www.kde-apps .org**. For particular database and office applications, you can download software packages directly from the company's Web site, such as **www.oracle.com** for the Oracle database. Table 29-1 lists several popular Linux software sites.

FTP or Web Site	Applications
download.fedora.redhat.com fedoraproject.org/wiki/ Distribution/Download	Software packaged in RPM packages for Fedora and on CD/DVDs (see **repodata** directories in each for package lists, Yum)
rhold.fedoraproject.org/ Download/mirrors.html	List of mirrors for Fedora releases
torrent.fedoraproject.org	Fedora BitTorrent files for ISO and DVD disks
rpm.livna.org	Livna Fedora–sponsored repository (Yum)
jpackage.org	Jpackage Linux/Fedora–compatible Java software (Yum)
freshrpms.net	Customized RPM packages featuring multimedia apps (Yum)
sourceforge.net	Linux Open Source software projects
www.gnomefiles.org	GNOME software
www.kde-apps.org	KDE software
freshmeat.net	Linux software, including RPMs
rpmfind.net	RPM package repository
rpmseek.com	Linux software search site
www.gnu.org	GNU archive

TABLE 29-1   Linux Software Sites

Extension	File
.rpm	A software package created with the Red Hat Software Package Manager, used on Fedora, Red Hat, Caldera, Mandrake, and SuSE distributions
.src.rpm	Software packages that are source code versions of applications, created with the Red Hat Software Package Manager
.gz	A `gzip`-compressed file (use `gunzip` to decompress)
.bz2	A `bzip2`-compressed file (use `bunzip2` to decompress, also use the j option with `tar`, as in `xvjf`)
.tar	A tar archive file, use `tar` with `xvf` to extract
.tar.gz	A `gzip`-compressed `tar` archive file. Use `gunzip` to decompress and `tar` to extract. Use the z option with `tar`, as in `xvzf`, to both decompress and extract in one step
.tar.bz2	A `bzip2`-compressed `tar` archive file. Extract with `tar -xvzj`
.tz	A `tar` archive file compressed with the `compress` command
.Z	A file compressed with the `compress` command (use the `decompress` command to decompress)
.deb	A Debian Linux package
.bin	A self-extracting software file
.torrent	A BitTorrent file for performing BitTorrent-distributed downloads (torrent information only)

TABLE 29-2   Linux Software Package File Extensions

Software Package Types

The software packages on RPM sites like **freshrpms.net** and **rpmfind.net** will have the file extension **.rpm**. RPM packages that contain source code have an extension **.src.rpm**. Other packages, such as those in the form of source code that you need to compile, come in a variety of compressed archives. These commonly have the extension **.tar.gz**, **.tgz**, or **.tar.bz2**. They are explained in detail later in the chapter. Table 29-2 lists several common file extensions that you will find for the great variety of Linux software packages available to you.

Downloading ISO and DVD Distribution Images with BitTorrent

Very large files like distribution ISO images can be downloaded using BitTorrent. BitTorrent is a distributed download operation, where many users on the Internet participate in the same download, each uploading parts that others can in turn download. The file is cut into small IP packets, and each packet is individually uploaded and downloaded as if it were a separate file. Your BitTorrent client will automatically combine the packets into the complete file. There is no shared disk space like what you have in file sharing methods. No access is granted to other uses. A user simply requests that others send him or her a packet. It is strictly a transmission operation, as if many users were participating in the same transmission instead of just one.

You will need to use a BitTorrent client. You have several BitTorrent clients to choose from, such as **azureus, rtorrent, ctorrent, ktorrent**, along with the original BitTorrent. These packages are available from the Fedora repository. For the original BiTorrent, there are two packages, the **bittorrent** and **bittorrent-gui**, which provides a GNOME interface. The original BitTorrent site is now a commercial site for downloading movies that require Windows media player and digital rights management (DRM).

To start a torrent, just click the torrent entry for a file on your Web browser. Firefox will prompt you whether to start up the application directly or download the file. If you run the application, the BitTorrent client will be started and your download will begin. You can stop at any time and restart the torrent later. It will automatically start up where you left off, keeping what you have downloaded so far. For example, to start the Fedora DVD torrent to download the DVD image, click the DVD torrent entry on the **torrent.fedoraproject.org** Web page. The BitTorrent client will automatically adjust to the appropriate download/ upload scale, but you can adjust this as you wish. There are buttons for pausing and stopping the download, as well as for obtaining detailed information about the torrent. An icon bar shows the progress and the estimated time remaining, though this may shorten as the download progresses. The client will show all torrents you have in process, showing how much is downloaded for each and letting you choose which you want active. Configuration entries will let you adjust such behavior as what port to use, the default download directory, and whether to allow torrents to run in parallel.

The file that you would download from **torrent.fedoraproject.org** is not the ISO or DVD image. That will be downloaded by BitTorrent. Instead this is a simple, small BitTorrent file that holds information on how to access and start this particular torrent. You can download the torrent file and later start it to start up the torrent download. You can have a collection of torrent files that you can start and stop as you want. You will have a small torrent file of type **.torrent** on your disk. Double-click it to start a BitTorrent client and the download torrent for the Fedora binary ISO images.

You can use BitTorrent for any file for which you can find an associated torrent file. But downloading is time-sensitive in that it depends on how many users are participating in the torrent. The Linux distribution torrents are usually well maintained, with several users providing constant upload support, known as seeds. Others may die out, if there are no other users participating in the torrent. The speed of the download is directly dependent on the number of users participating in the torrent. This is why the torrent is much more suitable to time-specific distributions such as when a Linux distribution provides a new release.

NOTE *The BitTorrent package also provides the tools for creating your own torrent to distribute a file. Two distribution methods are now available, tracker and trackerless. A trackerless method requires no server support.*

Updating Using yum and PUP

You can update software using the Yum (Yellowdog Update, Modified) repositories that hold Fedora software. Yum uses RPM headers to determine which packages need to be updated. You can find out more about Yum at **linux.duke.edu/projects/yum**.

PUP

To update your packages on Fedora you can use the Package Updater Program (PUP). The RHN update tool used previously is no longer included with Fedora (used for Red that Enterprise Linux. PUP is a graphical update interface for Yum that now performs all updates.

PUP features an update notification applet that will automatically detect when updates are available and notify you of them when you login. The notification will occur on the panel, showing the number of updates (Open Package icon). Clicking on the notification will start up PUP. You can also choose to ignore the notice and even quit the applet. You can also update by manually running PUP. In the Applications | System Tools menu you will find a Software Updater entry with a package (open box) logo.

Once PUP starts up, it will list all the packages in need of updating. All will be selected automatically. The checkboxes for each entry let you de-select any particular packages you may not want to update. Click the Apply button to start updating. Dependencies will be checked first. Then the packages will be downloaded from their appropriate repository. Once downloaded, the packages are updated. All the Yum-compatible repositories that are configured on your system will be checked. Again, software is now seen as a set of collections on different online repositories, rather than particular disks.

Update with the yum Command

Alternatively you can update using the **yum** command with the **update** option. The following would update an already installed **gnumeric** package:

```
yum update gnumeric
```

You can use the **check-update** option to see what packages need to be updated.

```
yum check-update
```

To perform a complete update of all your installed packages, you just use the update option. This would have the same effect of updating with PUP.

```
yum update
```

Automatic Yum Update

Yum also installs a **yum.cron** file in the **/etc/cron.daily** directory, which will automatically update your system. The cron entry will first update the Yum software if needed and then proceed to download and install any updates for your installed packages. It runs **yum** with the **update** option.

The automatic update will run only if it detects a Yum lock file in the **/var/lock/subsys** directory. By default, this is missing. You can add it using the **yum** service script. The **start** option creates the lock file, enabling the cron-supported updates, and the **stop** option removes the file, disabling the automatic update.

```
service yum start
```

Installing Fedora Packages with the yum Command

You can use the **yum** command to access Yum repositories directly, downloading new software. The Fedora repository is already configured for use by Yum. To download any Fedora package, you can either use the Pirut package manager or the **yum** command line with the **install** option. The Pirut Package Manager, accessible as Add/Remove Software in the Applications menu, is a GNOME front end for Yum. The Package Manager is Internet-based, installing from online repositories only, using Yum to download and install. As an alternative to Pirut, you can use **yumex**, the Yum Extender that also provides a desktop interface. The Pirut Package Manager and **yumex** are described in detail in Chapter 4.

> **TIP** *To remove packages with Pirut, just uncheck its entry and then click Apply. All installed packages are checked.*

To use the **yum** command, enter the **yum** command with the **install** option on a command line (on your desktop, right-click and open a terminal window first). The package will be detected, along with any dependent software, and you will be asked to confirm installation. The download and installation will be automatic. You can check the download repository online, as well as the repodata directories to display the available packages on a Web page. The page will include easy access features such as package groups and ad index links based on the first letters of package names.

The following example installs the Xine video player:

```
yum install xine
```

You can also remove packages, as well as search for packages and list packages by different criteria, such as those for updating, those on the repository not yet installed, and those already installed. The following example lists all installed packages:

```
yum list installed
```

The available option shows uninstalled packages.

```
yum list available
```

To search for a particular package you can use the search option.

```
yum search xine
```

> **TIP** *You can use Fedora Yum software repositories like **freshrpms.net** and **rpm.livna.org** to download additional software. Their configuration files will be in **/etc/yum.repos.d**. The **freshrpms.repo** and **livna.repo** files will be installed at **/etc/yum.repos.d**.*

Yum Configuration

Yum options are configured in the **/etc/yum.conf** file, and the **/etc/yum.repos.d** directory holds repository (repo) files that list accessible Yum repositories. The repository files have the extension **.repo**. Check the **yum.conf** Man page for a listing of the different Yum options along with entry formats. The **yum.conf** file consists of different segments separated by bracket-encased headers, the first of which is always the main segment. Segments for different Yum server repositories can follow, beginning with the repository label encased in brackets. On Fedora, however, these are currently placed in separate repository files in the **/etc/yum.repos.d** directory.

/etc/yum.conf

The **yum.conf** file will just have the main segment with settings for Yum options. There are general Yum options like **logfile**, which lists the location of Yum logs, and **distroverpkg**, which is used to determine which release to use. Packages will be downloaded to the directory specified with the **cachdir** option, in this case **/var/cache/yum**. You can elect to keep the downloaded packages or have them removed after they are installed. The **tolerant** option allows for package install errors, and the retries option specifies the number of times to try to access a package. Both **exactarch** and **obsoletes** apply to Yum updating procedures, invoked with the Yum **update** command. The **tolerant** option will allow package list errors such as those for already installed software, enabling installation of other packages in the list to continue. The **obsoletes** option is used for distribution level updates, and **exactarch** will only update packages in your specific architecture, such as i386 instead of i686. **gpgcheck** is a repository option that is set here globally for the **repo** files. It checks for GPG software signatures.

```
[main]
cachedir=/var/cache/yum
keepcache=0
debuglevel=2
logfile=/var/log/yum.log
pkgpolicy=newest
distroverpkg=redhat-release
tolerant=1
exactarch=1
obsoletes=1
gpgcheck=1
plugins=1
metadata_expire=1800

# PUT YOUR REPOS HERE OR IN separate files named file.repo
# in /etc/yum.repos.d
```

Repository Files:/etc/yum.repos.d

The repository entries in the repo files begin with a bracket-enclosed server ID, a single-word unique name. Repository-specific options govern the access of software repositories. These include **gpgcheck**, which checks for GPG software signatures, **gpgkey**, which specifies the location of the signature, and **mirrorlist**, which references URL holding mirror sites. The repository-specific **name** option provides a name for the repository. The URL reference is then assigned to the **baseurl** option. There should be only one **baseurl** option, but you can list several URLs for it, each on its own line. With the **mirrorlist** option you can just list a URL for a list of mirrors, instead of listing each mirror separately in the **baseurl** option. The URL entries often make use of special variables, **releaserver** and **basearch**. The **releaserver** obtains the release information from the **distroverpkg** option set in the main segment. The **basearch** variable specifies the architecture you are using as determined by Yum, such as i386. The enabled option actually turns on access to the repository. By setting it to 0, you choose not to access a specific repository. The **gpgcheck** option specifies that you should perform a GPG authentication check to make sure the download is intact. The **enabled** option will enable a repository, allowing Yum to use it. You can set the enable bit to 0 or 1 to turn off or on access to the repository.

The **gpgkey** option provides an authentication check on the package to make sure you have downloaded the appropriate version. Sometimes downloads can be intercepted and viruses inserted. The GPG key check protects against such attacks. It can also check to make sure the download is not corrupt or incomplete. The Fedora public GPG key may already be installed on your system. If you have already used YUM, you will have already downloaded it. The Fedora GPG key allows you to access Fedora packages. Both Livna and Freshprms repositories use their own public keys, referenced with the **gpgkey** option in their repos files. The keys for all these repositories will be installed in **/etc/pki/rpmgpg** directory.

Fedora

The Fedora repo file shown here lists several repository options. The name is Fedora, with **releaserver** and **basearch** used to determine the release and architecture parts of the name. The **mirrorlist** option is used instead of **baseurl**, which is commented out. Again, the **releaserver** is used to specify the release. The **gpgkey** used, RPM-GPG-KEY-fedora, is already installed in **/etc/pki/rpm-gpg** directory.

```
[fedora]
name=Fedora $releasever - $basearch
#baseurl=http://download.fedora.redhat.com/pub/fedora/linux/$releasever/
$basearch/os
mirrorlist=http://mirrors.fedoraproject.org/mirrorlist/
?repo=$releasever&arch=$basearch
enabled=1
gpgcheck=1
gpgkey=file:///etc/pki/rpm-gpg/RPM-GPG-KEY-fedora
```

Livna

As previously noted, both Livna and Freshrpms.net provide RPM packages that already hold the configuration you need, including GPG keys. Part of the **livna.repo** configuration file installed by the livna-release package is shown here. The configuration specifies several baseurl sites, instead of a mirror list. The failover method option indicates what sequence to use in choosing a site. It can be either priority, in sequence, or round robin, random. The **livna.repo** file also holds a testing configuration to let you access very new untested packages.

```
[livna]
name=Livna for Fedora $releasever - $basearch - Base
baseurl=
        http://rpm.livna.org/fedora/$releasever/$basearch/
ftp://mirrors.tummy.com/pub/rpm.livna.org/fedora/$releasever/$basearch/
failovermethod=priority
```

```
#mirrorlist=http://rpm.livna.org/mirrorlist-7
enabled=1
gpgcheck=1
gpgkey=file:///etc/pki/rpm-gpg/RPM-GPG-KEY-livna
```

Freshrpms

The **freshrpms.repo** file installed by the fresrpms-release package is listed here. Like Fedora, it uses a mirrorlist located at **ayo.freshrpms.net**. The gpgkey is RPM-GPG-KEY-freshrpms, installed by the freshrpms-release package. The gpgkey is also located online at **http://freshrpms.net/RPM-GPG-KEY-freshrpms**.

```
# $Id: freshrpms.repo 3341 2005-06-28 18:40:26Z thias $
[freshrpms]
name=Fedora $releasever - $basearch - Freshrpms
#baseurl=http://ayo.freshrpms.net/fedora/linux/$releasever/$basearch/freshrpms/
mirrorlist=http://ayo.freshrpms.net/fedora/linux/$releasever/mirrors-freshrpms
enabled=1
gpgkey=file:///etc/pki/rpm-gpg/RPM-GPG-KEY-freshrpms
gpgcheck=1
```

jpackage

Jpackage repo file configurations for different Linux distributions are displayed at **www .jpackage.org/yum.php**. Here you will find a listing for the latest Fedora and Red Hat distributions. You can also download the generic version, which will let you enable either Fedora or Red Hat. A sample **jpackage.repo** file is listed here. Like Fedora, it uses a mirrorlist. The gpgkey is online at **http://www.jpackage.org/jpackage.asc**. Due to licensing restrictions, Jpackage cannot freely distribute development tools like the JDK. These you will have to purchase from Jpackage commercially. The JRE is also part of the non-free Java package.

```
name=JPackage 1.6 for Fedora 7
baseurl=MIRROR/VERSION/fedora-2/free/
#mirrorlist=http://www.jpackage.org/jpackage_fedora-$releasever.txt
failovermethod=priority
gpgcheck=1
gpgkey=http://www.jpackage.org/jpackage.asc
```

The Red Hat Enterprise configuration would have a different baseurl.

```
name=JPackage 1.6 for Red Hat Enterprise Linux 4
baseurl=MIRROR/VERSION/redhat-el-4.0/free/
gpgcheck=1
```

If you download the generic jpackage.repo file, you will find repository listings for both Fedora and Red Hat Enterprise Linux, each enabled. You will also have generic configurations for free and non-free repositories, also enabled. Disable the ones that do not apply to your distribution. The **mirrorlist** used in the generic configuration for Fedora is shown in the previous Fedora example, though commented out.

TIP   *Some software projects are electing to distribute updates through Yum and Apt, instead of providing RPMs directly.*

Creating Local Yum Repositories

For local networks where you may have several Fedora systems, each of which may need to update using Yum, you could set up a local repository instead of having each system update from Internet sites directly. In cases where local systems share a single Internet connection, this may significantly increase download times. You can also control what packages can be installed. In effect, you download those packages on a Yum repository you want, and then create from those packages a local repository on one of your local systems. Your local systems then use the local repository to install and update packages. You will have to manually keep the local repository updated. Use the **createrepo** command to create a repository from a directory holding the packages you want. Then it is a simple matter of providing a configuration file for it, specifying its location.

Managing YUM Caches

With the **keepcache** option enabled, Yum will keep its downloaded packages in the **/var/cache/yum** directory. Should you want to save or copy any particular packages, you can locate them there. Caching lets you easily uninstall and reinstall packages without having to download them again. The package is retained in the cache. If caching is disabled, then packages are automatically deleted after they are installed. Packages will be organized into subdirectories according to their respective repositories. Updated packages for each repository will be stored in their own **update** subdirectory.

The size of your cache can increase rapidly, so you may want to clean it out on occasion. If you just want to delete these packages, as they are already installed, you can use the **clean packages** option.

```
yum clean packages
```

YUM also maintains a list of package headers with information on all packages downloaded. The headers are used to update your system, showing what has already been installed. You can opt to remove the headers with the **clean headers** option.

If you want Yum to just access packages in the cache, you use the **-C** option. The following lists just packages in the cache.

```
yum -C list
```

APT

The Advanced Package Tool (APT) is an older installation tool originally based on the Debian version. The current one is modified for use with RPMS packages. APT package management is officially deprecated in Fedora 5 and is not recommended. You can download APT from Fedora repository or **freshrpms.net**. APT places configuration files in the **/etc/apt** directory. The **apt.conf** file contains settings for options, using a more complex format similar to that used for DNS configuration.

Repositories are listed in the **sources.list** file. Each entry consists of type, URL, and path name, along with components identifying the software. The last component is the name of the repository. The following example is the **sources.list** entry for freshrpms:

```
rpm http://ayo.freshrpms.net fedora/linux/7/i386 core updates freshrpms
```

You use the **apt-get** command to install and manage software packages. The **apt-get** tool takes two arguments, the command to perform and the name of the package. The command is a term such as **install** for installing packages or **remove** to uninstall a package. To install a package, you would use

```
apt-get install xine
```

Upgrading is a simple matter of using the **upgrade** command. With no package specified, **apt-get** with the **update** option will upgrade your entire system, downloading from an FTP site or copying from a CD-ROM, and installing packages as needed. Add the **-u** option to list packages as they are upgraded.

```
apt-get -u update
```

Red Hat Package Manager (RPM)

Several Linux distributions, including Fedora, Red Hat, and Mandrake, use RPM to organize Linux software into packages you can automatically install, update, or remove. RPM is a command line–driven package management system that is capable of installing, uninstalling, querying, verifying, and updating software packages installed on Linux systems. An RPM software package operates as its own installation program for a software application. A Linux software application often consists of several files that need to be installed in different directories. The program itself is most likely placed in a directory called **/usr/bin**, online manual files like Man pages go in other directories, and library files in yet another directory. In addition, the installation may require modification of certain configuration files on your system. The RPM software package performs all these tasks for you. Also, if you later decide you don't want a specific application, you can uninstall packages to remove all the files and configuration information from your system. RPM works similarly to the Windows Install Wizard, automatically installing software, including configuration, documentation, image, sample, and program files, along with any other files an application may use. All are installed in their appropriate directories on your system. RPM maintains a database of installed software, keeping track of all the files installed. This enables you to use RPM also to uninstall software, automatically removing all files that are part of the application.

RPM Tools

To install and uninstall RPM packages, you can use the **rpm** command directly from a shell prompt, or the software management tool, system-config-packages. The system-config-packages tool is a GUI front end for the **rpm** command. Although you should download RPM packages for your particular distribution, numerous RPM software packages are designed to run on any Linux system. You can learn more about RPM at its Web site at

www.rpm.org and at **wiki.rpm.org**. The sites contains up-to-date versions for RPM and documentation Also, the Red Hat Linux Customization Guide provides an excellent tutorial for both RPM and system-config-packages. RPM has be reorganized as an independent project, no longer considered just a Red Hat tool.

RPM Packages

The naming conventions for RPM packages vary from one distribution to another. On Fedora, the package name includes the package version along with its platform (**i386** for Intel PCs) and the **.rpm** extension. An example of the Emacs editor's RPM package for Intel systems is shown here:

```
emacs-21.4-3.i386.rpm
```

> **TIP** *RPM packages with the term **noarch** are used for architecture-independent packages. This means that they are designed to install on any Linux system. Packages without **noarch** may be distribution- or architecture-dependent, designed to install on a particular type of machine.*

Installing from the Desktop: rpm

Attempting to install a package from the desktop can be confusing. If you select the package on the GNOME or KDE desktop, and then click Software Installer; the actual package on your desktop is not accessed. Instead, the most current version is downloaded and installed from a Fedora repository by Yum. If you want to use the actual package, you need to open a terminal window and use the **rpm** command.

> **TIP** *You can also install a particular RPM package directly. First display it with the file manager, and then double-click it. This invokes the system-config-packages tool, which installs the package. It also checks for dependent packages and installs those as well. If you are using CD-ROMs instead of the DVD-ROM, you will be prompted to insert any other CD-ROMs as needed.*

Command Line Installation: rpm

If you do not have access to the desktop, or you prefer to work from the command line interface, you can use the **rpm** command to manage and install software packages; **rpm** is the command that actually performs installation, removal, and queries of software packages. In fact, system-config-packages uses the **rpm** command to install and remove packages. An RPM package is an archive of software files that includes information about how to install those files. The filenames for RPM packages end with **.rpm**, indicating software packages that can be installed by the Red Hat Package Manager.

The rpm Command

With the **rpm** command, you can maintain packages, query them, build your own, and verify the ones you have. Maintaining packages involves installing new ones, upgrading to new versions, and uninstalling packages. The **rpm** command uses a set of options to determine what action to take. In addition, certain tasks, such as installing or querying packages, have their own options that further qualify the kinds of action they take. For example, the **-q** option queries a package, but when combined with the **-l** option, it lists all the files in that package. Table 29-3 lists the set of **rpm** options. The syntax for the **rpm** command is as follows (*rpm-package-name* is the name of the software package you want to install):

```
rpm options rpm-package-name
```

Mode of Operation	Effect
rpm **-i***options package-file*	Installs a package; the complete name of the package file is required.
rpm **-e***options package-name*	Uninstalls (erases) a package; you only need the name of the package, often one word.
rpm **-q***options package-name*	Queries a package. An option can be a package name, a further option and package name, or an option applied to all packages.
rpm **-U***options package-name*	Upgrades; same as install, but any previous version is removed.
rpm **-F***options package-name*	Upgrades, but only if package is currently installed.
rpm **-verify***options*	Verifies a package is correctly installed; uses same options as query. You can use **-V** or **-y** in place of **-verify**.
--percent	Displays percentage of package during installation.
--replacepks	Installs an already-installed package.
--replacefiles	Replaces files installed by other packages.
--redhatprovides *dependent-files*	Searches for dependent packages.
--oldfiles	Installs an older version of a package already installed.
--test	Tests installation; does not install, only checks for conflicts.
-h	Displays # symbols as package is installed.
--excludedocs	Excludes documentation files.
--nodeps	Installs without doing any dependency checks (dangerous).
--force	Forces installation despite conflicts (dangerous).
Uninstall Options (to be used with -e)	**Effect**
--test	Tests uninstall. Does not remove, only checks for what is to be removed.
--nodeps	Uninstalls without checking for dependencies.

TABLE 29-3 Red Hat Package Manager (RPM) Options *(continued)*

Uninstall Options (to be used with -e)	Effect
--allmatches	Removes all versions of package.
Query Options (to be used with -q)	**Effect**
package-name	Queries package.
-qa	Queries all packages.
-qf *filename*	Queries package that owns *filename*.
-qR	List packages on which this package depends.
-qp *package-name*	Queries an uninstalled package.
-qi	Displays all package information.
-ql	Lists files in package.
-qd	Lists only documentation files in package.
-qc	Lists only configuration files in package.
-q --dump	Lists only files with complete details.
General Options (to be used with any option)	**Effect**
-vv	Debugs; displays descriptions of all actions taken.
--quit	Displays only error messages.
--version	Displays RPM version number.
--help	Displays detailed use message.
--root*directory*	Uses directory as top-level directory for all operations (instead of root).
--dbpath*directory*	Uses RPM database in the specified directory.
--dbpath *cmd*	Pipes output of RPM to the command **cmd**.
--rebuilddb	Rebuilds the RPM database; can be used with the **-root** and **-dbpath** options.
--initdb	Builds a new RPM database; can be used with the **-root** and **-dbpath** options.
Other Sources of Information	**Effect**
www.rpm.org	The RPM Web site with detailed documentation.
RPM Man page (**man rpm**)	Detailed list of options.

TABLE 29-3   Red Hat Package Manager (RPM) Options

A complete description of **rpm** and its capabilities is provided in the online manual:

```
# man rpm
```

Querying Information from RPM Packages and Installed Software

The **-q** option tells you if a package is already installed, and the **-qa** option displays a list of all installed packages. Piping this output to a pager utility, such as **more**, is best.

```
# rpm -qa | more
```

In the next example, the user checks to see if emacs is already installed on the system. Notice the full filename of the RPM archive is unnecessary. If the package is installed, your system has already registered its name and where it is located.

```
# rpm -q emacs
emacs-22.0.95-1
```

You can combine the **q** option with the **i** or **l** option to display information about the package. The option **-qi** displays information about the software, such as the version number or author (**-qpi** queries an uninstalled package file). The option **-ql** displays a listing of all the files in the software package. The **--h** option provides a complete list of **rpm** options. Common query options are shown in Table 29-4.

TIP *Keep in mind the distinction between the installed software package name and the package filename. The filename ends in an* **.rpm** *extension and can only be queried with a* **p** *option.*

To display information taken directly from an RPM package, you add the **p** qualifier to the **q** options as shown in Table 29-5. The **-qpi** combination displays information about a specific package, and **-qpl** displays a listing of the files a given RPM package contains. In this case, you must specify the entire filename of the RPM package. You can avoid having to enter the entire name simply by entering a unique part of the name and using the * filename-matching character to generate the rest.

Option	Meaning
-q *application*	Checks to see if an application is installed.
-qa *application*	Lists all installed RPM applications.
-qf *filename*	Queries applications that own *filename*.
-qR *application*	Lists applications on which this application depends.
-qi *application*	Displays all application information.
-ql *application*	Lists files in the application.
-qd *application*	Lists only documentation files in the application.
-qc *application*	Lists only configuration files in the application.

TABLE 29-4   Query Options for Installed Software

Option	Meaning
`-qpi` *RPM-file*	Displays all package information in the RPM package.
`-qpl` *RPM-file*	Lists files in the RPM package.
`-qpd` *RPM-file*	Lists only documentation files in the RPM package.
`-qpc` *RPM-file*	Lists only configuration files in the RPM package.
`-qpR` *RPM-file*	Lists packages on which this RPM package depends.

TABLE 29-5   Query Options for RPM Packages

TIP The easiest way to examine the contents of an RPM file is to open the RPM file with File Roller from the GNOME Desktop. Right-click the RPM file icon in the file manager window and select Open With Archive Manager. This displays a File Roller window listing the top install directories for files in the packages. Double-click these entries to see the files or subdirectories. You can double-click text files like README files and have them directly displayed in your text editor.

If your RPM query outputs a long list of data, like an extensive list of files, you can pipe the output to the **more** command to look at it screen by screen, or even redirect the output to a file.

```
# rpm -ql emacs | more
# rpm -qpl emacs-22.0.95-1.i386.rpm  > mytemp
```

Installing and Updating Packages with rpm

You use the **-i** option to install new packages and the **-U** option to update currently installed packages with new versions. With an **-e** option, **rpm** uninstalls the package. If you try to use the **-i** option to install a newer version of an installed package, you will receive an error saying the package is already installed. When a package is installed, RPM checks its signature, using imported public keys from the software vendor. If the signature check fails, an error message is displayed, specifying NOKEY if you do not have the appropriate public key. If you want to install over an already-installed package, you can force installation with the **--replacepks** option. Sometimes a package will include a file, such as a library, that is also installed by another package. To allow a package to overwrite the file installed by another package, you use the **--replacefiles** option. Many packages depend on the libraries installed by other packages. If these dependent packages are not already installed, you will first have to install them. RPM informs you of the missing dependent files and suggests packages to install. If no packages are suggested, you can use the **--redhatprovides** option with the missing files to search for needed packages.

The **-U** option also installs a package if it is not already installed, whereas the **-F** option will only update installed packages. If the package includes configuration files that will overwrite currently installed configuration files, it will save a copy of each current configuration file in a file ending with **.rpmsave**, such as **/etc/mtools.conf.rpmsave**. This preserves any customized configuration changes you may have made to the file. Be sure to also check for configuration compatibilities between the previous and updated versions.

If you are trying to install a package that is older than the one already installed, then you need to use the **--oldpackages** option.

```
# rpm -Uvh emacs-22.0.95-1.i386.rpm
```

If you are installing from a DVD-ROM, you can change to the DVD-ROM's **RPMS** directory, which holds the RPM packages (the **RPMS** directory may be located within a directory like **RedHat** or **Fedora** on the DVD-ROM). An **ls** command lists all the software packages. If you know how the name of a package begins, you should include that with the **ls** command and an attached *****. This is helpful for displaying the detailed name of the package. The list of packages is extensive and does not all fit on one screen. The following example lists most X Window System packages:

```
# ls x*
```

Installation Example

In the next example, the user first installs a new package with the **-i** option and then updates a package with the **-U** option. Including the **-v** and **-h** options is customary. Here, **-v** is the verbose option that displays all files as they are installed, and **-h** displays a crosshatch symbol periodically to show RPM is still working. In the following example, the user installs the software package for the Gnumeric GNOME spreadsheet. Notice the full filename is entered. To list the full name, you can use the **ls** command with the first few characters and an asterisk, **ls gnumeric***. The **rpm** command with the **-q** option is then used to check that the software was installed. For installed packages only, the software name needs to be used—in this case, gnumeric-1.4.3-2. For **gnumeric** you first have to download and install **libgnomedb** and **libgda**, also in Fedora.

```
[root@turtle mypackages]# ls gnumeric*
gnumeric-1.4.3-2.i386.rpm
[root@turtle mypackages]# rpm -ivh gnumeric-1.4.3-2.i386.rpm
warning: gnumeric-1.4.3-2.i386.rpm: Header V3
   DSA signature: NOKEY, key ID 1ac70ce6
Preparing...        ########################################### [100%]
   1:gnumeric        ########################################### [100%]
[root@turtle mypackages]# rpm -q gnumeric
gnumeric-1.4.3-2
```

To display information about the installed package, use **-qi**, and **-ql** displays a listing of the files a given RPM package contains.

```
# rpm -qi gnumeric
# rpm -ql gnumeric
```

If you are worried that a software package will install on your system incorrectly, you can use the test option (**--test**) in the debug mode (**vv**) to see exactly what actions RPM will take.

```
# rpm -ivv --test gnumeric-1.4.3-2.i386.rpm
```

Removing RPM Software Packages

To remove a software package from your system, first use **rpm -q** to make sure it is actually installed. Then use the **-e** option to uninstall it. You needn't use the full name of the installed file. You only need the name of the application. For example, if you decide you do not need Gnumeric, you can remove it using the **-e** option and the software name, as shown here:

```
# rpm -e gnumeric
```

RPM: Verifying an RPM Installation

You can use the verify option (**-V**) to see if any problems occurred with the installation. RPM compares the current attributes of installed files with information about them placed in the RPM database when the package was installed. If no discrepancies exist, RPM outputs nothing. Otherwise, RPM outputs a sequence of eight characters, one for each attribute, for each file in the package that fails. Those that do not differ have a period. Those that do differ have a corresponding character code, as shown in Table 29-6.

The following example verifies the ProFTPD package:

```
[root@turtle mypackages]# rpm -V proftpd
```

To compare the installed files directly with the files in an RPM package file, you use the **-Vp** option, much like the **-qp** option. To check all packages, use the **-Va** option as shown here:

```
# rpm -Va
```

If you want to verify a package, but you only know the name of a file in it, you can combine verify with the **-f** option. The following example verifies the RPM package containing the **ftp** command:

```
# rpm -Vf /bin/ftp
```

Attribute	Explanation
5	MD5 checksum
S	File size
L	Symbolic link
T	File modification time
D	Device
U	User
G	Group
M	Mode (includes permissions and file types)

TABLE 29-6   RPM Discrepancy Codes

Rebuilding the RPM Database

RPM maintains a record of the packages it has installed in its **RPM** database. You may, at times, have to rebuild this database to ensure RPM has current information on what is installed and what is not. Use the **--rebuilddb** option to rebuild your database file:

```
# rpm --rebuilddb
```

To create a new RPM database, use the **--initdb** option. This option can be combined with **--dbpath** to specify a location for the new database.

Installing Software from RPM Source Code Files: SRPMs

Fedora and several other distributors also make available source code versions of their binary RPM-packaged software. The source code is packaged into RPM packages that will be automatically installed into designated directories where you can easily compile and install the software. Source code packages are called SRPMs. The names for these packages end in the extension **.src.rpm**. Source code versions for packages in the Fedora distribution are located in the **SRPMS** directory. Many online sites like **rpmfind.net** also list SRPM packages. Source code versions have the advantage of letting you make your own modifications to the source code, allowing you to generate your own customized versions of RPM-packaged software. You still use the **rpm** command with the **-i** option to install source code packages. In the following example, you install the source code for Freeciv:

```
# rpm -i freeciv-1.14.2-1.src.rpm
```

Source Code RPM Directories

On Fedora, SRPM files are installed in various subdirectories in the **/usr/src/redhat** directory. When SRPMs are installed, a spec file is placed in the **/usr/src/redhat/SPECS** directory, and the compressed archive of the source code files is placed in the **/usr/src/redhat/SOURCES** directory. For Freeciv, a spec file called **freeciv.spec** is placed in **/usr/src/redhat/SPECS**, and a compressed archive called **freeciv-1.14.2-1.tar.gz** is placed in the **/usr/src/redhat/SOURCES** directory.

Building the Source Code

To build the source code files, you need to extract them and run any patches on them that may be included with the package. You do this by changing to the **/usr/src/redhat/SPECS** directory and using the **rpm** command, this time with the **-bp** option, to generate the source code files:

```
# cd /usr/src/redhat/SPECS
# rpm -bp freeciv.spec
```

The resulting source code files are placed in their own subdirectory with the package's name in the **/usr/src/redhat/BUILD** directory. For Freeciv, the Freeciv source code is placed in **/usr/src/redhat/BUILD/freeciv-1.14.2-1** directory. In this subdirectory, you can then modify the source code, as well as compile and install the application. Check the software's **README** and **INSTALL** files for details.

Installing Software from Compressed Archives: .tar.gz

Linux software applications in the form of source code are available at different sites on the Internet. You can download any of this software and install it on your system. Recent releases are often available in the form of compressed archive files. Applications will always be downloadable as compressed archives, if they don't have an RPM version. This is particularly true for the recent versions of GNOME or KDE packages. RPM packages are only intermittently generated.

Decompressing and Extracting Software in One Step

Though you can decompress and extract software in separate operations, you will find that the more common approach is to perform both actions with a single command. The **tar** utility provides decompression options you can use to have **tar** first decompress a file for you, invoking the specified decompression utility. The **z** option automatically invokes **gunzip** to unpack a **.gz** file, and the **j** option unpacks a **.bz2** file. Use the **Z** option for **.Z** files. For example, to combine the decompressing and unpacking operation for a **tar.gz** file into one **tar** command, insert a **z** option to the option list, **xzvf** (see the later section "Extracting Software" for a discussion of these options). The next example shows how you can combine decompression and extraction in one step:

```
# tar xvzf htdig-3.1.6.tar.gz
```

For a **.bz2**-compressed archive, you would use the **j** option instead of the **z** option.

```
# tar xvjf htdig-3.1.6.tar.bz2
```

Decompressing Software

Many software packages under development or designed for cross-platform implementation may not be in an RPM format. Instead, they may be archived and compressed. The filenames for these files end with the extension **.tar.gz**, **.tar.bz2**, or **.tar.Z**. The different extensions indicate different decompression methods using different commands: **gunzip** for **.gz**, **bunzip2** for **.bz2**, and **decompress** for **.Z**. In fact, most software with an RPM format also has a corresponding **.tar.gz** format. After you download such a package, you must first decompress it and then unpack it with the **tar** command. The compressed archives could hold either source code that you then need to compile or, as is the case with Java packages, binaries that are ready to run.

A *compressed archive* is an archive file created with **tar** and then compressed with a compression tool like **gzip**. To install such a file, you must first decompress it with a decompression utility like **gunzip** utility and then use **tar** to extract the files and directories making up the software package. Instead of the **gunzip** utility, you could also use **gzip -d**. The next example decompresses the **htdig-3.2.6.tar.gz** file, replacing it with a decompressed version called **htdig-3.2.6.tar**:

```
# ls
 htdig-3.2.6.tar.gz
# gunzip htdig-3.2.6.tar.gz
# ls
htdig-3.2.6.tar
```

You can download compressed archives from many different sites, including those mentioned previously. Downloads can be accomplished with FTP clients such as NcFTP and gFTP, or with any Web browser. Once downloaded, any file that ends with **.Z**, **.bz2**, **.zip**, or **.gz** is a compressed file that must be decompressed.

For files ending with **.bz2**, you would use the **bunzip2** command. The following example decompresses a **bz2** version:

```
# ls
 htdig-3.2.6.tar.bz2
# bunzip2 htdig-3.2.6.tar.bz2
# ls
htdig-3.2.6.tar
```

Files ending with **.bin** are self-extracting archives. Run the bin file as if it were a command. You may have to use **chmod** to make it executable. The j2sdk software package is currently distributed as a self-extracting bin file.

```
# j2sdk-1.4.2-FCS-linux-i386.tar.bin
# ls
j2sdk-1.3.0-FCS-linux-i386.tar
```

Selecting an Install Directory

Before you unpack the archive, move it to the directory where you want it. Source code packages are often placed in a directory like **/usr/local/src**, and binary packages go in designated directories. When source code files are unpacked, they generate their own subdirectories from which you can compile and install the software. Once the package is installed, you can delete this directory, keeping the original source code package file (**.tar.gz**).

Packages that hold binary programs ready to run, like Java, are meant to be extracted in certain directories. Usually this is the **/usr/local** directory. Most archives, when they unpack, create a subdirectory named with the application name and its release, placing all those files or directories making up the software package into that subdirectory. For example, the file **htdig-3.2.6.tar** unpacks to a subdirectory called **htdig-3.2.6**. In certain cases, the software package that contains precompiled binaries is designed to unpack directly into the system subdirectory where it will be used. For example, it is recommended that **j2sdk-1.4.2-FCS-linux-i386.tar** be unpacked in the **/usr/local** directory, where it will create a subdirectory called **j2sdk-1.4.2**. The **/usr/local/j2sdk-1.4.2/bin** directory holds the Java binary programs.

Extracting Software

First, use **tar** with the **t** option to check the contents of the archive. If the first entry is a directory, then when you extract the archive, that directory is created and the extracted files are placed in it. If the first entry is not a directory, you should first create one and then copy the archive file to it. Then extract the archive within that directory. If no directory exists as the first entry, files are extracted to the current directory. You must create a directory yourself to hold these files.

```
# tar tvf htdig-3.1.6.tar
```

Now you are ready to extract the files from the tar archive. You use **tar** with the **x** option to extract files, the **v** option to display the pathnames of files as they are extracted, and the **f** option, followed by the name of the archive file:

```
# tar xvf htdig-3.2.6.tar
```

The extraction process creates a subdirectory consisting of the name and release of the software. In the preceding example, the extraction created a subdirectory called **htdig-3.2.6**. You can change to this subdirectory and examine its files, such as the **README** and **INSTALL** files.

```
# cd htdig-3.2.6
```

Installation of your software may differ for each package. Instructions are usually provided along with an installation program. Be sure to consult the **README** and **INSTALL** files, if included. See the following section on compiling software for information on how to create and install the application on your system.

Compiling Software

Some software may be in the form of source code that you need to compile before you can install it. This is particularly true of programs designed for cross-platform implementations. Programs designed to run on various Unix systems, such as Sun, as well as on Linux, may be distributed as source code that is downloaded and compiled in those different systems. Compiling such software has been greatly simplified in recent years by the use of configuration scripts that automatically detect a given system's hardware and software configurations and then allow you to compile the program accordingly. For example, the name of the C compiler on a system could be **gcc** or **cc**. Configuration scripts detect which is present and select it for use in the program compilation.

A configure script works by generating a customized Makefile, designed for that particular system. A Makefile contains detailed commands to compile a program, including any preprocessing, links to required libraries, and the compilation of program components in their proper order. Many Makefiles for complex applications may have to access several software subdirectories, each with separate components to compile. The use of configure and Makefile scripts vastly automates the compile process, reducing the procedure to a few simple steps.

First change to the directory where the software's source code has been extracted:

```
# cd /usr/local/src/htdig-3.2.6
```

Before you compile software, read the **README** or **INSTALL** files included with it. These give you detailed instructions on how to compile and install this particular program.

Most software can be compiled and installed in three simple steps. Their fist step is the **./configure** command, which generates your customized Makefile. The second step is the **make** command, which uses a Makefile in your working directory (in this case the Makefile you just generated with the **./configure** command) to compile your software. The final step also uses the **make** command, but this time with the **install** option. The Makefile generated by the **./configure** command also contains instructions for installing the software on your system. Using the **install** option runs just those installation commands. To perform the installation, you have to be logged in as the root user, giving you the ability to add software files to system directories as needed. If the software uses configuration scripts, compiling and installing usually involves only the following three simple commands:

```
#  ./configure
#  make
#  make install
```

In the preceding example, the `./configure` command performs configuration detection. The `make` command performs the actual compiling, using a Makefile script generated by the `./configure` operation. The `make install` command installs the program on your system, placing the executable program in a directory, such as **/usr/local/bin**, and any configuration files in **/etc**. Any shared libraries it created may go into **/usr/local/lib**.

Once you have compiled and installed your application, and you have checked that it is working properly, you can remove the source code directory that was created when you extracted the software. You can keep the archive file (`tar`) in case you need to extract the software again. Use `rm` with the `-rf` options so that all subdirectories will be deleted and you do not have to confirm each deletion:

TIP Be sure to remember to place the period and slash before the `configure` command. The `./` references a command in the current working directory, rather than another Linux command with the same name.

Configure Command Options

Certain software may have specific options set up for the `./configure` operation. To find out what these are, you use the `./configure` command with the `--help` option:

```
#   ./configure --help
```

A useful common option is the `-prefix` option, which lets you specify the install directory:

```
#   ./configure -prefix=/usr/bin
```

---

*TIP Some older X applications use **xmkmf** directly instead of a configure script to generate the needed Makefile. In this case, enter the command **xmkmf** in place of `./configure`. **xmkmf** has been officially replaced. Be sure to consult the **INSTALL** and **README** files for the software.*

Development Libraries

If you are compiling an X-, GNOME-, or KDE-based program, be sure their development libraries have been installed. For X applications, be sure the **xmkmf** program is also installed. If you chose a standard install when you installed your distribution system, these most likely were not installed. For distributions using RPM packages, these come in the form of a set of development RPM packages, usually with the word "development" or "develop" in their names. You need to install them using either **rpm** or system-config-packages. GNOME, in particular, has an extensive set of RPM packages for development libraries. Many X applications need special shared libraries. For example, some applications may need the **xforms** library or the **qt** library. Some of these you may need to obtain from online sites.

Shared and Static Libraries

Libraries can be either static, shared, or dynamic. A *static* library is one whose code is incorporated into the program when it is compiled. A *shared* library, however, has its code loaded for access whenever the program is run. When compiled, such a program simply notes the libraries it needs. Then when the program is run, that library is loaded and the program can access its functions. A *dynamic* library is a variation on a shared library. Like a shared library, it can be loaded when the program is run. However, it does not actually load until instructions in the program tell it to. It can also be unloaded as the program runs, and another library could be loaded in its place. Shared and dynamic libraries make for much smaller code. Instead of a program including the library as part of its executable file, it only needs a reference to it.

Libraries made available on your system reside in the **/usr/lib** and **/lib** directories. The names of these libraries always begin with the prefix **lib** followed by the library name and a suffix. The suffix differs, depending on whether it is a static or shared library. A shared library has the extension **.so** followed by major and minor version numbers. A static library simply has the **.a** extension. A further distinction is made for shared libraries in the old **a.out** format. These have the extension **.sa**. The syntax for the library name is the following:

```
libname.so.major.minor
libname.a
```

The *name* can be any string, and it uniquely identifies a library. It can be a word, a few characters, or even a single letter. The name of the shared math library is **libm.so.5**, where the math library is uniquely identified by the letter **m** and the major version is **5**, and **libm.a** is the static math library. The name of the X Window library is **libX11.so.6**, where the X Window library is uniquely identified with the letters **X11** and its major version is 6.

Most shared libraries are found in the **/usr/lib** and **/lib** directories. These directories are always searched first. Some shared libraries are located in special directories of their own. A listing of these is placed in the **/etc/ld.conf** configuration file. These directories will also be searched for a given library. By default, Linux first looks for shared libraries, then static ones. Whenever a shared library is updated or a new one installed, you need to run the **ldconfig** command to update its entries in the **/etc/ld.conf** file as well as links to it (if you install from an RPM package, this is usually done for you).

Makefile File

If no configure script exists and the program does not use **xmkmf**, you may have to edit the software's Makefile directly. Be sure to check the documentation for such software to see if any changes must be made to the Makefile. Only a few changes may be necessary, but more detailed changes require an understanding of C programming and how **make** works with it. If you successfully configure the Makefile, you may only have to enter the **make** and **make install** commands. One possible problem is locating the development libraries for C and the X Window System. X libraries are in the **/usr/X11R6/lib** directory. Standard C libraries are located in the **/usr/lib** directory.

Command and Program Directories: PATH

Programs and commands are usually installed in several standard system directories, such as **/bin**, **/usr/bin**, **/usr/X11R6/bin**, or **/usr/local/bin**. Some packages place their commands in subdirectories, however, which they create within one of these standard directories or in an entirely separate directory. In such cases, you may be unable to run those commands because your system may be unable to locate them in the new subdirectory. Your system maintains a set of directories that search for commands each time you execute one. This set of directories is kept in a system variable called **PATH** that is created when you start your system. If a command is in a directory that is not in this list, your system will be unable to locate and run it. To use such commands, you first need to add the new directory to the set of directories in the **PATH** variable. Installation tools like RPM will automatically update the **PATH** with the appropriate directories for you.

The PATH variable is added to by different services that start up when the system boots. A safer approach is to add a **PATH** definition in the **/etc/profile** file using that file's **pathmunge** function.

/etc/profile

To make an application available to all users, you can add the software's directory to the path entry in the **/etc/profile** script. The **/etc/profile** script is a system script executed for each user when the user logs in. Carefully edit the **/etc/profile** file using a text editor, such as KEdit, Gedit, Emacs, or Vi (you may want to make a backup copy first with the **cp** command). You can easily add a directory to the **PATH** variable using the pathmung function, which is also defined in /etc/profile. For example, if you install the Java 2 SDK, the Java commands are installed in a subdirectory called **j2sdk-1.4.2/bin** in the **/usr/local** directory. The full pathname for this directory is **/usr/local/j2sdk-1.4.2/bin**. You need to use **pathmunge** to add this directory to the list of directories assigned to **PATH** in the **/etc/profile** file.

```
pathmunge /usr/local/j2sdk-1.4.2/bin
```

You can see other uses **pathmunge** in **/etc/profile** like adding **/sbin** for the root user.

After making your changes, you can execute the profile file to have the changes take effect.

```
$  . /etc/profile
```

NOTE *On older systems you had to create a new assignment entry for the* **PATH** *variable. You had to add a line that begins with* **PATH**, *followed by an* = *sign, and the term* **$PATH**, *followed by a colon, and then the directory to be added. The* **$** *before* **PATH** *extracted the pathname from the* **PATH** *variable. If you added more than one directory, a colon had to separate them. There would also be a colon at the end. The following example shows the* **PATH** *variable with its list of directories and the* **/usr/local/j2sdk-1.4.2/bin** *directory added. Notice the* **$** *before* **PATH** *after the* = *sign:* **PATH=$PATH. PATH=$PATH:/usr/local/j2sdk-1.4.2/bin.**

.bash_profile

Individual users can customize their **PATH** variables by placing a **PATH** assignment in either their **.bashrc** or **.bash_profile** file. In this way, users can access commands and programs they create or install for their own use in their own user directories. User **.bash_profile** files already contain the following **PATH** definition. Notice the use of **$PATH**, which keeps all the directories already added to the **PATH** in previous startup scripts like **/etc/profile**.

```
PATH=$PATH:$HOME/bin
```

The following entry in the **.bash_profile** file adds a user's **newbin** directory to the **PATH** variable. Notice both the colon placed before the new directory and the use of the **$HOME** variable to specify the pathname for the user's home directory.

```
PATH=$PATH:$HOME/bin/:$HOME/newbin
```

For the **root** user, the **PATH** definition also includes **sbin** directories. The **sbin** directories hold system administration programs that the root user would need to have access to. The **root** user **PATH** is shown here:

```
PATH=/usr/local/sbin:/usr/sbin:/sbin:$PATH:$HOME/bin
```

Subversion and CVS

The Subversion and the Concurrent Versions Systems (CVS) are software development methods that allow developers from remote locations to work on software stored on a central server. Subversion is an enhanced version of CVS, designed to eventually replace it. Like CVS, Subversion works with CVS repositories, letting you access software in much the same way. Subversion adds features such as better directory and file access as well as support for metadata information.

CVS sites allow several developers to work on a file at the same time. This means that they support parallel development, so programmers around the world can work on the same task at the same time through a simple Internet connection. It has become popular among Linux developers as a means of creating software using the Internet. CVS sites are also the source for the most up-to-date versions for different software. Ongoing projects like KDE and GNOME use Subversion or CVS servers to post the most recent versions of their desktop applications, primarily because it is easy to use for program development over the Internet. The **sourceforge.net** site provides a CVS repository for many ongoing Linux Projects. Fedora maintains a CVS repository of software under development, **cvs.fedora .redhat.com**. Many CVS sites now support ViewCVS (an enhanced version of WebCVS), a Web browser front end to a CVS repository that lets you browse and select software versions easily. You can find out more about CVS from **www.cvshome.org** and about Subversion from **subversion.tigris.org**.

TIP *You can also use CVS GUI clients on GNOME and KDE, along with ViewCVS, to manage your CVS repositories or access those on the Internet. For GNOME, you can use Pharmacy, and for KDE, you can use Cervisia or LinCVS.*

Using a CVS repository for software development involves procedures for accessing a software version, making your changes locally on your system, and then uploading your changed version back to the CVS repository. In effect, you check out software, make your changes in such a way that they are carefully recorded, and then check your version back in to the repository. CVS was originally developed as a front end to the older Revision Control System (RCS) and shares many of the same commands.

Packaging Your Software with RPM

Many research and corporate environments develop their own customized software for distribution within their organization. Sometimes software packages are downloaded and then customized for use in a particular organization. To more easily install such customized software, administrators pack the programs into their own RPM packages. In such packages, you can include your own versions of configuration files, documentation, and modified source and binaries. RPM automatically installs software on a system in the designated directories, along with any documentation, libraries, or support programs.

The package creation process is designed to take the program through several stages, starting with unpacking it from an archive, then compiling its source code, and finally, generating the RPM package. You can skip any of these stages, up to the last one. If your software is already unpacked, you can start with compiling it. If your software is compiled, you can start with installation. If it is already installed, you can go directly to creating the RPM package.

The build processes for RPM used to be included with the **rpm** command. They are now incorporated into a separate tool called **rpmb**. This tool, along with supporting libraries and documentation, is located in the rpm-build package. Be sure this package is installed before you try to build RPM packages. You can still run the **rpm** command with the build options, but these are simply aliases for corresponding **rpmb** commands.

CHAPTER 30

File System Management

Files reside on physical storage devices such as hard drives, CD-ROMs, or floppy disks. The files on each storage device are organized into a file system. The storage devices on your Linux system are presented as a collection of file systems that you can manage. When you want to add a new storage device, you need to format it as a file system and then attach it to your Linux file structure. Hard drives can be divided into separate storage devices called *partitions,* each of which has its own file system. You can perform administrative tasks on your file systems, such as backing them up, attaching or detaching them from your file structure, formatting new devices or erasing old ones, and checking a file system for problems.

To access files on a device, you attach its file system to a specified directory. This is called *mounting* the file system. For example, to access files on a floppy disk, you first mount its file system to a particular directory. With Linux, you can mount a number of different types of file systems. You can even access a Windows hard drive partition or tape drive, as well as file systems on a remote server. Red Hat Enterprise Linux and Fedora also configure CD-ROM and floppy media to be mounted automatically from GNOME or KDE.

Recently developed file systems for Linux now support *journaling,* which allows your system to recover from a crash or interruption easily. The ext3, ReiserFS, and JFS (IBM) file systems maintain a record of file and directory changes, called a *journal,* which can be used to recover files and directories in use when a system suddenly crashes due to unforeseen events such as power interruptions. Most distributions currently use the ext3 file system as their default, though you also have the option of using ReiserFS or JFS, an independently developed journaling system.

Your Linux system is capable of handling any number of storage devices that may be connected to it. You can configure your system to access multiple hard drives, partitions on a hard drive, CD-ROM discs, DVDs, floppy disks, and even tapes. You can elect to attach these storage components manually or have them automatically mount when you boot. Automatic mounts are handled by configuring the **/etc/fstab** file. For example, the main partitions holding your Linux system programs are automatically mounted whenever you boot, whereas a floppy disk can be manually mounted when you put one in your floppy drive, though even these can also be automatically mounted. Removable storage devices like CD-ROMs, as well as removable devices like USB cameras and printers, are now handled by udev and the Hardware Abstract Layer (HAL), as described in Chapter 32 and partially discussed here.

File Systems

Although all the files in your Linux system are connected into one overall directory tree, parts of that tree may reside on different storage devices such as hard drives or CD-ROMs. Files on a particular storage device are organized into what is referred to as a *file system*. A file system is a formatted device, with its own tree of directories and files. Your Linux directory tree may encompass several file systems, each on different storage devices. On a hard drive with several partitions, you would have a file system for each partition. The files themselves are organized into one seamless tree of directories, beginning from the root directory. For example, if you attach a CD-ROM to your system, a pathname will lead directly from the root directory on your hard disk partition's file system to the files in the CD-ROM file system.

> **TIP** *With Linux you can mount file systems of different types, including those created by other operating systems, including Windows, IBM OS, Unix, and SGI. Within Linux a variety of file systems are supported, including several journaling systems like ReiserFS and ext3.*

A file system has its files organized into its own directory tree. You can think of this as a *subtree* that must be attached to the main directory tree. The tree remains separate from your system's directory tree until you specifically connect it. For example, a floppy disk with Linux files has its own tree of directories. You need to attach this subtree to the main tree on your hard drive partition. Until they are attached, you cannot access the files on your floppy disk.

Filesystem Hierarchy Standard

Linux organizes its files and directories into one overall interconnected tree, beginning from the root directory and extending down to system and user directories. The organization and layout for the system directories are determined by the Filesystem Hierarchy Standard (FHS). The FHS provides a standardized layout that all Linux distributions should follow in setting up their system directories. For example, there must be an **/etc** directory to hold configuration files and a **/dev** directory for device files. You can find out more about FHS, including the official documentation, at **www.pathname.com/fhs**. Linux distributions, developers, and administrators all follow the FHS to provide a consistent organization to the Linux file system.

Linux uses a number of specifically named directories for specialized administrative tasks. All these directories are at the very top level of your main Linux file system, the file system root directory, represented by a single slash, **/**. For example, the **/dev** directory holds device files, and the **/home** directory holds the user home directories and all their user files. You have access to these directories and files only as the system administrator (though users normally have read-only access). You need to log in as the root user, placing yourself in a special root user administrative directory called **/root**. From here, you can access any directory on the Linux file system, both administrative and user.

Root Directory: /

The subdirectories held in the root directory, **/**, are listed in Table 30-1, along with other useful subdirectories. Directories that you may commonly access as an administrator are the

Directory	Function
/	Begins the file system structure—called the root.
/boot	Holds the kernel image files and associated boot information and files.
/home	Contains users' home directories.
/sbin	Holds administration-level commands and any commands used by the root user.
/dev	Holds dynamically generated file interfaces for devices such as the terminal and the printer (see "udev: Device Files" in Chapter 32).
/etc	Holds system configuration files and any other system files.
/etc/opt	Holds system configuration files for applications in **/opt**.
/etc/X11	Holds system configuration files for the X Window System and its applications.
/bin	Holds the essential user commands and utility programs.
/lib	Holds essential shared libraries and kernel modules.
/lib/modules	Holds the kernel modules.
/media	Used to hold directories for mounting media-based removable file systems, like CD-ROMs, floppy disks, USB card readers, and digital cameras.
/mnt	Used to hold directories for additional file systems such as hard disks.
/opt	Holds added software applications (for example, KDE on some distributions).
/proc	Process directory, a memory-resident directory containing files used to provide information about the system.
/sys	The sysfs file system for kernel objects, listing supported kernel devices and modules.
/tmp	Holds temporary files.
/usr	Holds those files and commands used by the system; this directory breaks down into several subdirectories.
/var	Holds files that vary, such as mailbox, Web, and FTP files.

TABLE 30-1   Linux File System Directories

/etc directory, which holds configuration files; the **/dev** directory, which holds dynamically generated device files; and the **/var** directory, which holds server data files for DNS, Web, mail, and FTP servers, along with system logs and scheduled tasks. For managing different versions of the kernel, you may need to access the **/boot** and **/lib/modules** directories as well as **/usr/src/linux**. The **/boot** directory holds the kernel image files for any new kernels you install, and the **/lib/modules** directory holds modules for your different kernels.

System Directories

Your Linux directory tree contains certain directories whose files are used for different system functions. For basic system administration, you should be familiar with the system program directories where applications are kept, the system configuration directory (**/etc**) where most configuration files are placed, and the system log directory (**/var/log**) that holds the system logs, recording activity on your system. Both are covered in detail in Chapter 29. Table 30-2 lists the system directories.

Program Directories

Directories with **bin** in the name are used to hold programs. The **/bin** directory holds basic user programs, such as login, shells (BASH, TCSH, and zsh), and file commands (**cp**, **mv**, **rm**, **ln**, and so on). The **/sbin** directory holds specialized system programs for such tasks as file system management (**fsck**, **fdisk**, **mkfs**) and system operations like shutdown and startup (**init**). The **/usr/bin** directory holds program files designed for user tasks. The **/usr/sbin** directory holds user-related system operation, such as **useradd** for adding new users.

Directory	Description
/bin	System-related programs
/sbin	System programs for specialized tasks
/lib	System libraries
/etc	Configuration files for system and network services and applications
/home	The location of user home directories and server data directories, such as Web and FTP site files
/media	The location where removable media file systems like CD-ROMs and floppy disks are mounted
/var	The location of system directories whose files continually change, such as logs, printer spool files, and lock files
/usr	User-related programs and files. Includes several key subdirectories, such as **/usr/bin**, **/usr/X11**, and **/usr/share/doc**
/usr/bin	Programs for users
/dev	Device files
/sys	The sysfs file system with device information for kernel-supported devices on your system
/usr/X11	X Window System configuration files
/usr/share	Shared files
/usr/share/doc	Documentation for applications
/usr/share/hal	Configuration for HAL removable devices
/etc/udev	Configuration for device files
/tmp	Directory for system temporary files

TABLE 30-2 System Directories

The **/lib** directory holds all the libraries your system makes use of, including the main Linux library, **libc**, and subdirectories such as **modules**, which holds all the current kernel modules.

Configuration Directories and Files

When you configure different elements of your system, such as user accounts, applications, servers, or network connections, you make use of configuration files kept in certain system directories. Configuration files are placed in the **/etc** directory, with more specific device and service configurations located in the **/etc/sysconfig** directory (see Chapter 32 for more details).

The /usr Directory

The **/usr** directory contains a multitude of important subdirectories used to support users, providing applications, libraries, and documentation. The **/usr/bin** directory holds numerous user-accessible applications and utilities; **/usr/sbin** holds user-accessible administrative utilities. The **/usr/share** directory holds architecture-independent data that includes an extensive number of subdirectories, including those for documentation, such as **man**, **info**, and **doc** files. Table 30-3 lists the subdirectories of the **/usr** directory.

The /media Directory

The **/media** directory is used for mountpoints for removable media like CD-ROM, DVD, floppy, or Zip drives, as well as for other media-based file systems such as USB card readers, cameras, and MP3 players. These are file systems you may be changing frequently, unlike partitions on fixed disks. Red Hat Enterprise Linux and Fedora use the Hardware Abstraction Layer (HAL) to dynamically manage the creation, mounting, and device assignment of these devices. As instructed by HAL, this tool will create floppy, CD-ROM, storage card, camera, and MP3 player subdirectories in **/media** as needed. The default subdirectory for mounting is **/media/disk**. Additional drives have a number attached to their name.

Directory	Description
/usr/bin	Holds most user commands and utility programs.
/usr/sbin	Holds administrative applications.
/usr/lib	Holds libraries for applications, programming languages, desktops, and so on.
/usr/games	Holds games and educational programs.
/usr/include	Holds C programming language header files (**.h**).
/usr/doc	Holds Linux documentation.
/usr/local	Holds locally installed software.
/usr/share	Holds architecture-independent data such as documentation.
/usr/src	Holds source code, including the kernel source code.
/usr/X11R6	Holds X Window System–based applications and libraries.

TABLE 30-3 /usr Directories

Tip The ntfs-3g configuration tool will mount NTFS partitions in the /media directory (Applications | System Tools | NTFS Configuration Tool).

The /mnt Directory

The /mnt directory is usually used for mountpoints for other mounted file systems such as Windows partitions. You can create directories for any partitions you want to mount, such as /mnt/windows for a Windows partition.

The /home Directory

The /home directory holds user home directories. When a user account is set up, a home directory is set up here for that account, usually with the same name as the user. As the system administrator, you can access any user's home directory, and so you have control over that user's files.

The /var Directory

The /var directory holds subdirectories for tasks whose files change frequently, such as lock files, log files, Web server files, or printer spool files. For example, the /var directory holds server data directories, such as /var/www for the Apache Web server Web site files or /var/ftp for your FTP site files, as well as /var/named for the DNS server. The /tmp directory is simply a directory to hold any temporary files programs may need to perform a particular task.

The /var directories are designed to hold data that change with the normal operation of the Linux system. For example, spool files for documents that you are printing are kept here. A spool file is created as a temporary printing file and is removed after printing. Other files, such as system log files, are changed constantly. Table 30-4 lists the subdirectories of the /var directory.

The /proc File System

The /proc file system is a special file system that is generated in system memory. It does not exist on any disk. /proc contains files that provide important information about the state of your system. For example, /proc/cpuinfo holds information about your computer's CPU processor. /proc/devices lists those devices currently configured to run with your kernel. /proc/filesystems lists the file systems. /proc files are really interfaces to the kernel, obtaining information from the kernel about your system. Table 30-5 lists the /proc subdirectories and files.

Like any file system, /proc has to be mounted. The /etc/fstab file will have a special entry for /proc with a file system type of proc and no device specified.

```
none    /proc    proc    defaults    0    0
```

---

*Tip You can use **sysctl**, the Kernel Tuning tool, to set proc file values you are allowed to change, like the maximum number of files, or turning on IP forwarding.*

The sysfs File System: /sys

The sysfs file system is a virtual file system that provides a hierarchical map of your kernel-supported devices such as PCI devices, buses, and block devices, as well as supporting kernel modules. The classes subdirectory will list all your supported devices by category,

Directory	Description
/var/account	Processes accounting logs.
/var/cache	Holds application cache data for Man pages, Web proxy data, fonts, or application-specific data.
/var/crash	Holds system crash dumps.
/var/games	Holds varying games data.
/var/lib	Holds state information for particular applications.
/var/local	Used for data that change for programs installed in **/usr/local**.
/var/lock	Holds lock files that indicate when a particular program or file is in use.
/var/log	Holds log files such as **/var/log/messages** that contain all kernel and system program messages.
/var/mail	Holds user mailbox files.
/var/opt	Holds variable data for applications installed in **/opt**.
/var/run	Holds information about the system's running processes.
/var/spool	Holds applications' spool data such as that for mail, news, and printer queues, as well as `cron` and `at` jobs.
/var/tmp	Holds temporary files that should be preserved between system reboots.
/var/yp	Holds Network Information Service (NIS) data files.
/var/www	Holds Web server Web site files.
/var/ftp	Holds FTP server FTP files.
/var/named	Holds DNS server domain configuration files.

TABLE 30-4   /var Subdirectories

such as net and sound devices. With **sysfs** your system can easily determine the device file a particular device is associated with. This is very helpful for managing removable devices as well as dynamically configuring and managing devices as HAL and udev do. The **sysfs** file system is used by udev to dynamically generate needed device files in the **/dev** directory, as well as by HAL to manage removable device files and support as needed (HAL technically provides information only about devices, though it can use tools to dynamically change configurations as needed). The **/sys** file system type is **sysfs**. The **/sys** subdirectories organize your devices into different categories. The file system is used by **systool** to display a listing of your installed devices. The following example will list all your system devices:

```
systool
```

Like **/proc**, the **/sys** directory resides only in memory, but you still need to mount it in the the **/etc/fstab** file. Fedora and Red Hat Enterprise Linux will include such an entry for you.

```
none    /sys      sysfs      defaults    0        0
```

File	Description
/**proc**/*num*	There is a directory for each process labeled by its number. /**proc**/**1** is the directory for process 1.
/**proc**/**cpuinfo**	Contains information about the CPU, such as its type, make, model, and performance.
/**proc**/**devices**	Lists the device drivers configured for the currently running kernel.
/**proc**/**dma**	Displays the DMA channels currently used.
/**proc**/**filesystems**	Lists file systems configured into the kernel.
/**proc**/**interrupts**	Displays the interrupts in use.
/**proc**/**ioports**	Shows the I/O ports in use.
/**proc**/**kcore**	Holds an image of the physical memory of the system.
/**proc**/**kmsg**	Contains messages generated by the kernel.
/**proc**/**loadavg**	Lists the system load average.
/**proc**/**meminfo**	Displays memory usage.
/**proc**/**modules**	Lists the kernel modules currently loaded.
/**proc**/**net**	Lists status information about network protocols.
/**proc**/**stat**	Contains system operating statistics, such as page fault occurrences.
/**proc**/**uptime**	Displays the time the system has been up.
/**proc**/**version**	Displays the kernel version.

TABLE 30-5   /proc Subdirectories and Files

Device Files: /dev, udev, and HAL

To mount a file system, you have to specify its device name. The interfaces to devices that may be attached to your system are provided by special files known as *device files.* The names of these device files are the device names. Device files are located in the **/dev** directories and usually have abbreviated names ending with the number of the device. For example, **fd0** may reference the first floppy drive attached to your system. The prefix **sd** references SCSI hard drives, so **sda2** would reference the second partition on first Serial ATA or SCSI hard drive. In most cases, you can use the **man** command with a prefix to obtain more detailed information about this kind of device. For example, **man sd** displays the Man pages for SCSI devices. A complete listing of all device names can be found in the **devices** file located in the **linux/doc/device-list** directory at the **www.kernel.org** Web site, and in the **devices.txt** file in the **/etc/usr/linux-2.4/Documentation** directory on your system. Table 30-6 lists several of the commonly used device names.

udev and HAL

Device files are no longer handled in a static way. Instead they are now dynamically generated as needed. Previously a device file was created for each possible device, leading

Device Name	Description
sd	IDE hard drives; 1–4 are primary partitions; 5 and up are logical partitions (same drivers and prefix as Serial ATA)
sd	Serial ATA and SCSI hard drives
scd	IDE, Serial ATA, and SCSI CD-ROM drives (SCSI CD/DVD drives may also use **sr**)
fd	Floppy disks
st	SCSI tape drives
nst	SCSI tape drives, no rewind
ht	IDE tape drives
tty	Terminals
lp	Printer ports
pty	Pseudoterminals (used for remote logins)
js	Analog joysticks
midi	Midi ports
ttyS	Serial ports
md	RAID devices
rd/cn**d**n	The directory that holds RAID devices is **rd**; **c**n is the RAID controller and **d**n is the RAID disk for that controller
cdrom	Link to your CD-ROM device file, set in **/etc/udev/rules.d**
dvdwriter	Link to your DVD-R or DVD-RW device file, set in **/etc/udev/rules.d**
modem	Link to your modem device file, set in **/etc/udev/rules.d**
floppy	Link to your floppy device file, set in **/etc/udev/rules.d**
tape	Link to your tape device file, set in **/etc/udev/rules.d**
scanner	Link to your scanner device file, set in **/etc/udev/rules.d**

TABLE 30-6   Device Name Prefixes

to a very large number of device files in the **/etc/dev** directory. Now, your system will detect only those devices it uses and create device files for those only, giving you a much smaller listing of device files. The tool used to detect and generate device files is udev, user devices. Each time your system is booted, udev will automatically detect your devices and generate device files for them in the **/etc/dev** directory. This means that the **/etc/dev** directory and its files are recreated each time you boot. It is a dynamic directory, no longer static. To manage these device files, you need to use udev configuration files located in the **/etc/udev** directory. This means that udev is able to also dynamically manage all removable devices; udev will generate and configure devices files for removable devices as they are attached, and then remove these files when the devices are removed. In this sense, all devices are now considered hotplugged, with fixed devices simply being hotplugged devices that are never removed.

As **/etc/dev** is now dynamic, any changes you would make manually to the **/etc/dev** directory will be lost when you reboot. This includes the creation of any symbolic links like **/dev/cdrom** that many software applications use. Instead, such symbolic links have to be configured using udev rules listed in configuration files located in the **/etc/udev/rules.d** directory. Default rules are already in place for symbolic links, but you can create rules of your own. See Chapter 32 for more details.

In addition to udev, information about removable devices like CD-ROMs and floppy disks, along with cameras and USB printers, used by applications like the desktop to dynamically interface with them, is managed by a separate utility called the Hardware Abstract Layer (HAL). HAL allows a removable device like a USB printer to be recognized no matter what particular connections it may be using. For example, you can attach a USB printer in one USB port at one time and then switch it to another later. The **fstab** file is edited using the **fstab-sync** tool, which is invoked by HAL rules in configuration files in **/usr/share/hal/fdi** directory. See Chapter 32 for more details.

HAL has a key impact on the **/etc/fstab** file used to manage file systems. On Fedora, no longer are entries maintained in the **/etc/fstab** file for removable devices like your CD-ROMs. These devices are managed directly by HAL using its set of storage callouts like **hal-system-storage-mount** to mount a device or **hal-system-storage-eject** to remove one. In effect you now have to use the HAL device information files to manage your removable file systems.(see Chapter 32). Should you want to bypass HAL and manually configure a CD-ROM device, you simply place an entry for it in the **/etc/fstab** file.

Floppy and Hard Disk Devices

The device name for your floppy drive is **fd0**; it is located in the directory **/dev**. **/dev/fd0** references your floppy drive. Notice the numeral **0** after **fd**. If you have more than one floppy drive, additional drives are represented by **fd1**, **fd2**, and so on.

IDE and Serial ATA hard drives use the prefix **sd** (the **hd** prefix for IDE hard drives has been dropped). RAID devices, on the other hand, use the prefix **md**. The prefix for a hard disk is followed by a letter that labels the hard drive and a number for the partition. For example, **sda2** references the second partition on the first IDE hard drive, where the first hard drive is referenced with the letter **a**, as in **sda**. The device **sdb3** refers to the third partition on the second hard drive (**sdb**). RAID devices, however, are numbered from 0, like floppy drives. Device **md0** references the first RAID device, and **md1** references the second. On an IDE hard disk device, Linux supports up to four primary IDE hard disk partitions, numbered 1 through 4. You are allowed any number of logical partitions. To find the device name, you can use `df` to display your hard partitions or examine the **/etc/fstab** file.

NOTE *IDE and SATA drives use the same SATA drivers. The **sd** prefix is also used for IDE drives. The **hd** prefix has been dropped.*

CD-ROM Devices

The device name for your CD-ROM drive varies depending on the type of CD-ROM you have. The device name for an IDE CD-ROM has the same prefix as an IDE hard disk partition, **sd**, and is identified by a following letter that distinguishes it from other IDE devices. For example, an IDE CD-ROM connected to your secondary IDE port may have the name **sdc**. An IDE CD-ROM connected as a slave to the secondary port may have the name **sdd**. The actual name is determined when the CD-ROM is installed, as happened when you installed your Linux system. Serial ATA and SCSI CD-ROM drives the same nomenclature for their device names. They begin with **scd** for a Serial ATA or SCSI drive and are followed by a distinguishing number. For example, the name of a CD-ROM could be **scd0** or **scd1**. The name of your CD-ROM is determined by udev and HAL. SCSI CD/DVD drives may also use the **sr** prefix.

As noted previously, CD-ROM devices are now configured by HAL. HAL does this in a device information file in its policy configuration directory. To configure a CD-ROM device, as by adding user mount capability, you need to configure its entry in the **storage-methods.fdi** configuration file (see Chapter 32 for details). The GNOME Volume Manager uses HAL and udev to access removable media directly, and Samba to provide Windows networking support. Media are mounted by **gnome-mount**, a wrapper for accessing Hal and udev, which perform the mount (/etc/fstab is no longer used).

Mounting File Systems

Attaching a file system on a storage device to your main directory tree is called *mounting* the device. The file system is mounted to an empty directory on the main directory tree. You can then change to that directory and access those files. If the directory does not yet exist, you have to create it. The directory in the file structure to which the new file system is attached is referred to as the *mountpoint*. For example, to access files on a CD-ROM, first you have to mount the CD-ROM.

Mounting file systems can normally be done only as the root user. This is a system administration task and should not usually be performed by a regular user. As the root user, you can, however, make a particular device, like a CD-ROM, user-mountable. In this way, any user could mount a CD-ROM. You could do the same for a floppy drive.

TIP *On GNOME, you can use the Disk Usal Analyzer tool on the Applications | System Tools menu to list your file systems as well as their disk usage. On KDE you can use the KDiskFRee tool.*

Even the file systems on your hard disk partition must be explicitly mounted. When you install your Linux system and create the Linux partition on your hard drive, however, your system is automatically configured to mount your main file system whenever it starts. When your system shuts down, they are automatically unmounted. You have the option of unmounting any file system, removing it from the directory tree, and possibly replacing it with another, as is the case when you replace a CD-ROM.

Once a file system is actually mounted, an entry for it is made by the operating system in the **/etc/mstab** file. Here you will find listed all file systems currently mounted.

File System Information

The file systems on each storage device are formatted to take up a specified amount of space. For example, you may have formatted your hard drive partition to take up 3 GB. Files installed or created on that file system take up part of the space, while the remainder is available for new files and directories. To find out how much space you have free on a file system, you can use the **df** command or, on the desktop, either the GNOME System Monitor (System | Administration | System Monitor) or the Disk Usage Analyzer (Applications | System Tools). On the KDE desktop you can useKDiskFree. For the System Monitor, click the File Systems tab to display a list of the free space on your file systems. KDiskFree displays a list of devices, showing how much space is free on each partition, and the percentage used. The Disk Usage Analyzer performs a complete scan of all your file systems, providing a graphical display for your total usage as well as for each file system.

df

On the command line, you can use the **df** command to display file system disk space usage. It lists all your file systems by their device names, how much disk space they take up, and the percentage of the disk space used, as well as where they are mounted. With the **-h** option, it displays information in a more readable formats; such as measuring disk space in megabytes instead of memory blocks. The **df** command is also a safe way to obtain a listing of all your partitions, instead of using **fdisk** (with **fdisk** you could erase partitions). **df** shows only mounted partitions, however, whereas **fdisk** shows all partitions.

```
$ df -h
Filesystem Size Used Avail Use% Mounted on
/dev/sda3   9.7G 2.8G 6.4G  31%  /
/dev/sda2   99M  6.3M 88M   7%   /boot
/dev/sda2   22G  36M  21G   1%   /home
/dev/sdc    525M 525M 0     100% /media/disk
```

You can also use **df** to tell you to what file system a given directory belongs. Enter **df** with the directory name or **df .** for the current directory.

```
$ df .
Filesystem 1024-blocks Used Available Capacity Mounted on
/dev/sda3 297635 169499 112764 60% /
```

e2fsck and fsck

To check the consistency of the file system and repair it if it is damaged, you can use file system checking tools. **fsck** checks and repairs a Linux file system. **e2fsck** is designed to support ext2 and ext3 file systems, whereas the more generic **fsck** also works on any other file systems. The ext2 and ext3 file systems are the file systems normally used for Linux hard disk partitions and floppy disks. Linux file systems for Fedora and Red Hat Enterprise Linux are normally ext3, which you would use **e2fsck** to check. **fsck** and **e2fsck** take as their argument the device name of the hard disk partition that the file system uses.

```
fsck    device-name
```

Before you check a file system, be sure that the file system is unmounted. **e2fsck** should not be used on a mounted file system. To use **e2fsck**, enter **e2fsck** and the device name that references the file system. The **-p** option automatically repairs a file system without first requesting approval from the user for each repair task. The following examples check the disk in the floppy drive and the primary hard drive:

```
# e2fsck /dev/fd0
# e2fsck /dev/sda1
```

With **fsck**, the **-t** option lets you specify the type of file system to check, and the **-a** option automatically repairs systems, whereas the **-r** option first asks for confirmation. The **-A** option checks all systems in the **/etc/fstab** file.

> ***Tip*** *In earlier distribution versions,* **fsck** *and* **e2fsck** *were also used to recover file systems after disk crashes or reset-button reboots. With recent releases, journaling capabilities were introduced with file systems like ext3 and ReiserFS. Journaling provides for fast and effective recovery in case of disk crashes, so recovering with* **fsck** *or* **e2fsck** *is no longer necessary.*

Journaling

The ext3 and ReiserFS file systems introduced journaling capabilities to Linux systems. Journaling provides for fast and effective recovery in case of disk crashes, instead of using **e2fsck** or **fsck**. With journaling, a log is kept of all file system actions, which are placed in a journal file. In the event of a crash, Linux only needs to read the journal file and replay it to restore the system to its previous (stable) state. Files that were in the process of writing to the disk can be restored to their original state. Journaling also avoids lengthy **fsck** checks on reboots that occur when your system suddenly loses power or freezes and has to be restarted physically. Instead of using **fsck** to manually check each file and directory, your system just reads its journal files to restore the file system.

Keeping a journal entails more work for a file system than a nonjournal method. Though all journaling systems maintain a file system's directory structure (what is known as the *metadata*), they offer various levels of file data recovery. Maintaining file data recovery information can be time-consuming, slowing down the file system's response time. At the same time, journaling systems make more efficient use of the file system, providing a faster response time than the nonjournal ext2 file system.

There are other kind of journaling file systems you can use on Linux. These include ReiserFS, JFS, and XFS. ReiserFS, named after Hans Reiser, provides a completely reworked file system structure based on journaling (**www.namesys.com**). Most distributions also provide support for ReiserFS file systems. JFS is the IBM version of a journaling file system, designed for use on servers providing high throughput such as e-business enterprise servers (**http://jfs.sourceforge.net**). It is freely distributed under the GNU public license. XFS is another high-performance journaling system developed by Silicon Graphics (**oss.sgi .com/projects/xfs**). XFS is compatible with RAID and NFS file systems.

ext3 Journaling

Journaling is supported in the Linux kernel with ext3. The ext3 file system is also fully compatible with the earlier ext2 version it replaces. To create an ext3 file system, you use the **mkfs.ext3** command. You can even upgrade ext2 file systems to ext3 versions automatically, with no loss of data or change in partitions. This upgrade just adds a journal file to an ext2 file system and enables journaling on it, using the **tune2fs** command. Be sure to change the ext2 file type to ext3 in any corresponding **/etc/fstab** entries. The following example converts the ext2 file system on **/dev/sda3** to an ext3 file system by adding a journal file (**-j**):

```
tune2fs -j /dev/sda3
```

Though the ext3 file system maintains full metadata recovery support (directory tree recovery), it offers various levels of file data recovery. In effect, you are trading off less file data recovery for more speed. The ext3 file system supports three options: **writeback**, **ordered**, and **journal**. The default is **writeback**. The **writeback** option provides only metadata recovery, no file data recovery. The **ordered** option supports limited file data recovery, and the **journal** option provides for full file data recovery. Any files in the process of being changed during a crash will be recovered. To specify a ext3 option, use the **data** option in the **mount** command.

```
data=ordered
```

ReiserFS

Though journaling is often used to recover from disk crashes, a journal-based file system can do much more. The ext3, JFS, and XFS file systems only provide the logging operations used in recovery, whereas ReiserFS uses journaling techniques to completely rework file system operations. In ReiserFS, journaling is used to read and write data, abandoning the block structure used in traditional Unix and Linux systems. This gives it the capability to access a large number of small files very quickly, as well as use only the amount of disk space they need. However, efficiency is not that much better with larger files.

Mounting File Systems Automatically: /etc/fstab

File systems are mounted using the **mount** command, described in the next section. Although you can mount a file system directly with only a **mount** command, you can simplify the process by placing mount information in the **/etc/fstab** configuration file. Using entries in this file, you can have certain file systems automatically mounted whenever your system boots. For others, you can specify configuration information, such as mountpoints and access permissions, which can be automatically used whenever you mount a file system. You needn't enter this information as arguments to a **mount** command as you otherwise must. This feature is what allows mount utilities on GNOME or KDE to enable you to mount a file system simply by clicking a window icon. All the mount information is already in the **/etc/fstab** file. For example, when you add a new hard disk partition to your Linux system, you most likely want to have it automatically mounted on startup, and then unmounted when you shut down. Otherwise, you must mount and unmount the partition explicitly each time you boot up and shut down your system.

HAL and fstab

To have Linux automatically mount the file system on your new hard disk partition, you only need to add its name to the **fstab** file, except in the case of removable devices like CD-ROMs and USB printers. Removable devices are managed by HAL, using the storage policy files located in **/usr/share/hal/fdi** and **/etc/hal/fdi** directories. The devices are automatically detected by the **haldaemon** service, and are managed directly by HAL using its set of storage callouts like **hal-storage-mount** to mount a device or **hal-storage-eject** to remove one. In effect you now have to use the HAL device information files to manage your removable file systems. If you want different options set for the device, you should create your own **storage-methods.fdi** file in the **30user** directory. The configuration is implemented using the XML language. Check the default storage file in policy **10osvendors/20-storage-methods.fdi** as well as samples in **/usr/share/doc/hal**_version_**/conf** directory. See Chapter 32 for examples of using HAL to set device options.

fstab Fields

An entry in an **fstab** file contains several fields, each separated from the next by a space or tab. These are described as the device, mountpoint, file system type, options, dump, and **fsck** fields, arranged in the sequence shown here:

```
<device> <mountpoint> <filesystemtype> <options> <dump> <fsck>
```

The first field is the name of the file system to be mounted. This entry can be either a device name or an ext2 or ext3 file system label. A device name usually begins with **/dev**, such as **/dev/sda3** for the third hard disk partition. A label is specified by assigning the label name to the tag **LABEL**, as in **LABEL=/** for an ext3 root partition. The next field is the directory in your file structure where you want the file system on this device to be attached. The third field is the type of file system being mounted. Table 30-7 provides a list of all the different types you can mount. The type for a standard Linux hard disk partition is ext3.

Type	Description
auto	Attempts to detect the file system type automatically.
minux	Minux file systems (filenames are limited to 30 characters).
ext	Earlier version of Linux file system, no longer in use.
ext3	Standard Linux file system supporting long filenames and large file sizes. Includes journaling.
ext2	Older standard Linux file system supporting long filenames and large file sizes. Does not have journaling.
xiaf	Xiaf file system.
msdos	File system for MS-DOS partitions (16-bit).
vfat	File system for Windows 95, 98, and Millennium partitions (32-bit).
reiserfs	A ReiserFS journaling file system.
xfs	A Silicon Graphics (SGI) file system.
ntfs-3g	Windows NT, Windows XP, and Windows 2000 file systems using ntfs-3g file system drivers, included with Fedora.
ntfs	Windows NT, Windows XP, and Windows 2000 file systems. (It affords read access with limited write capability. Install the current version from **rpm-livna.org/fedora**.)
smbfs	Samba remote file systems, such as NFS.
hpfs	File system for OS/2 high-performance partitions.
nfs	NFS file system for mounting partitions from remote systems.
nfs4	NFSv4 file system for mounting partitions from remote systems.
umsdos	UMS-DOS file system.

TABLE 30-7 File System Types *(continued)*

Type	Description
swap	Linux swap partition or swap file.
sysv	Unix System V file systems.
iso9660	File system for mounting CD-ROM.
proc	Used by operating system for processes (kernel support file system).
sysfs	Used by operating system for devices (kernel support file system).
usbfs	Used by operating system for USB devices (kernel support file system).
devpts	Unix 98 Pseudo Terminals (ttys, kernel interface file system).
shmfs and tmpfs	Linux Virtual Memory, POSIX shared memory maintenance access (kernel interface file system).
adfs	Apple DOS file systems.
affs	Amiga fast file systems.
ramfs	RAM-based file systems.
udf	Universal Disk Format used on CD/DVD-ROMs.
ufs	Unix File System, found on Unix system (older format).

TABLE 30-7   File System Types

The next example shows an entry for the main Linux hard disk partition. This entry is mounted at the root directory, /, and has a file type of ext3:

```
/dev/sda3     /      ext3    defaults   0   1
```

The following example shows a **LABEL** entry for the hard disk partition, where the label name is /:

```
LABEL=/      /      ext3    defaults   0   1
```

Auto Mounts

The file system type for a floppy may differ depending on the disk you are trying to mount. For example, you may want to read a Windows-formatted floppy disk at one time and a Linux-formatted floppy disk at another time. For this reason, the file system type specified for the floppy device is **auto**. With this option, the type of file system formatted on the floppy disk is detected automatically, and the appropriate file system type is used.

```
/dev/fd0   /media/floppy   auto    defaults,noauto    0 0
```

mount Options

The field after the file system type lists the different options for mounting the file system. The default set of options is specified by **defaults**, and specific options are listed next to each other separated by a comma (no spaces). The **defaults** option specifies that a device is read/write (**rw**), that it is asynchronous (**async**), that it is a block device (**dev**), that it cannot be mounted by ordinary users (**nouser**), and that programs can be executed on it (**exec**).

Removable devices like your CD-ROMs and floppy disks are now managed by HAL, the Hardware Abstraction Layer. HAL uses its own configuration files to set the options for these devices. You can place your own entries in the **/etc/fstab** file for CD-ROMs to bypass HAL. This will, however, no longer let your CD-ROMs and DVD-ROMs be automatically detected.

In a manual configuration, a CD-ROM should have **ro** and **noauto** options. **ro** specifies that the device is read-only, and **noauto** specifies it is not automatically mounted. The **noauto** option is used with both CD-ROMs and floppy drives, so they won't automatically mount, because you don't know if you have anything in them when you start up. At the same time, the HAL entries for both the CD-ROM and the floppy drive can specify where they are to be mounted when you decide to mount them. The **owner** option is a more secure option used in place of the user option. The **owner** option will only allow the owner of the device to mount or unmount the device, instead of just any user, as the user option does. The **fscontext** option is use by SELinux as discussed in Chapter 17. Table 30-8 lists the options for mounting a file system. An example of a hard drive entry follows:

```
/dev/VolGroup0/LogVol00   /  ext3    defaults       1 1
```

Boot and Disk Check

The last two fields of an **fstab** entry consist of integer values. The first one is used by the **dump** command to determine if a file system needs to be dumped, backing up the file system. The second value is used by **fsck** to see if a file system should be checked at reboot, and in what order with other file systems. If the field has a value of 1, it indicates a boot partition, and 2 indicates other partitions. The 0 value means **fsck** needn't check the file system.

fstab Sample

A copy of an **/etc/fstab** file is shown here. Notice the first line is a comment. All comment lines begin with a **#**. The entries for the **/proc** and **/sys** file systems are special entries used by your Linux operating system for managing its processes and devices; they are not actual devices. To make an entry in the **/etc/fstab** file, you can edit the **/etc/fstab** file directly. You can use the example **/etc/fstab** file shown here as a guide to show how your entries should look. The **/proc** and **swap** partition entries are particularly critical.

/etc/fstab

# <file system>	<mount point>	<type>	<options>	<dump>	<pass>
/dev/sda3	/ ext3	ext3	defaults	1	1
LABEL=/boot	/boot	ext3	defaults	1	2
tmpfs	/dev/shm	tmpfs	defaults	0	0
devpts	/dev/pts	devpts	gid=5,mode=620	0	0
sysfs	/sys	sysfs	defaults	0	0
proc	/proc	proc	defaults	0	0
/dev/sda3	swap	swap	defaults	0	0
/dev/sda1	/media/win	ntfs-3g	defaults,ro,locale=en US.UTF-8 0 0		

Option	Description
async	Indicates that all I/O to the file system should be done asynchronously.
auto	Indicates that the file system can be mounted with the **-a** option. A **mount -a** command executed when the system boots, in effect, mounts file systems automatically.
defaults	Uses default options: **rw**, **suid**, **dev**, **exec**, **auto**, **nouser**, and **async**.
dev	Interprets character or block special devices on the file system.
fscontext	Sets SELinux file system context.
noauto	Indicates that the file system can only be mounted explicitly. The **-a** option does not cause the file system to be mounted.
exec	Permits execution of binaries.
managed	Removable device that is managed by HAL. Options for this device have to be specified in the HAL configuration files.
nouser	Forbids an ordinary (that is, nonroot) user to mount the file system.
owner	Allows only the owner to mount or unmount the device.
remount	Attempts to remount an already-mounted file system. This is commonly used to change the mount flags for a file system, especially to make a read-only file system writable.
ro	Mounts the file system as read-only.
rw	Mounts the file system as read/write.
suid	Allows set-user-identifier or set-group-identifier bits to take effect.
sync	Indicates that all I/O to the file system should be done synchronously.
user	Enables an ordinary user to mount the file system. Ordinary users always have the following options activated: **noexec**, **nosuid**, and **nodev**.
nodev	Does not interpret character or block special devices on the file system.
noexec	Does not allow execution of binaries on the mounted file systems.
nosuid	Does not allow set-user-identifier or set-group-identifier bits to take effect.

TABLE 30-8   Mount Options for File Systems

Partition Labels: e2label

Red Hat Enterprise Linux and Fedora use file system labels for ext2 and ext3 file systems on hard disk partitions. Thus in the **/etc/fstab** file previously shown, the first entry would use a label for its device name, as shown here. In this case, the label is the slash, **/**, indicating the root partition. You could change this device's label with **e2label**, but be sure to also change the **/etc/fstab** entry for it.

```
LABEL=/     /      ext3     defaults     0    1
```

For ext2 and ext3 partitions, you can change or add a label with the **e2label** tool or **tune2fs** with the **-L** option. Specify the device and the label name. If you change a label, be sure to change corresponding entries in the **/etc/fstab** file. Just use **e2label** with the device name to find out what the current label is. In the next example, the user changes the label of the **/dev/sda3** device to **TURTLE**:

```
e2label /dev/sda3  TURTLE
```

Windows Partitions

You can mount MS-DOS; Windows 95/98/ME; or Windows XP, NT, and 2000 partitions used by your Windows operating system onto your Linux file structure, just as you would mount any Linux file system. You have to specify the file type of **vfat** for Windows 95/98/ME, and **msdos** for MS-DOS. Windows XP, NT, and 2000 use either the ntfs-3g or the **ntfs** file types. You may find it convenient to have your Windows partitions automatically mounted when you start up your Linux system. To do this, you need to put an entry for your Windows partitions in your **/etc/fstab** file and give it the **defaults** option, or be sure to include an **auto** option. You make an entry for each Windows partition you want to mount, and then specify the device name for that partition, followed by the directory in which you want to mount it. The **/mnt/windows** directory would be a logical choice (be sure the **windows** directory has already been created in **/mnt**). The next example shows a standard Windows partition entry for an **/etc/fstab** file. Notice the last entry in the **/etc/fstab** file example is an entry for mounting a Windows partition.

```
/dev/sda1 /mnt/windows vfat defaults 0 0
```

The ntfs-3g drivers will provide both write and read support for NTFS file systems used for Windows XP, NT, and 2000. You would specify the **ntfs-3g** type. Be sure to have already installed the ntfs-3g package from Fedora (see Chapter 3). If you use the ntfs-3g NTFS Configuration Tool to configure your NTFS access, then entries for your NTFS partitions will automatically be placed in the **/etd/fstab** file. In the following example, the partition is mounted as read only (**ro**) with the locale specfied as US (**locale**).

```
/dev/sda1 /mnt/win ntfs-3g defaults,ro,locale=en US.UTF-8 0 0
```

For the original NTFS Linux drivers (Linux NTFS Project), you would specify the **ntfs** type. This has to be downloaded separately from **livna.org**. Be sure to have already downloaded and installed the NTFS kernel module (see Chapter 3). The ntfs kernel module from ntfs.org is read only.

```
/dev/sda2 /mnt/windows   ntfs ro,umask=0222 0 0
```

Linux Kernel Interfaces

Your **/etc/fstab** file may also have entries for two special kernel interface file systems, **devpts** and **tmpfs**. Both provide kernel interfaces that are not supported by standard devices. The **/dev/pts** entry mounts a **devpts** file system for pseudoterminals. The **/dev/shm** entry mounts the **tmpfs** file system (also known as **shmfs**) to implement Linux Virtual Memory, POSIX shared memory maintenance access. This is designed to overcome the 4 GB memory limitation on current systems, extending usable memory to 64 GB.

If your **/etc/fstab** file ever becomes corrupt—say, if a line gets deleted accidentally or changed—your system will boot into a maintenance mode, giving you read-only access to your partitions. To gain read/write access so that you can fix your **/etc/fstab** file, you have to remount your main partition. The following command performs such an operation:

```
# mount -n -o remount,rw /
```

noauto

File systems listed in the **/etc/fstab** file are automatically mounted whenever you boot, unless this feature is explicitly turned off with the **noauto** option. If want to manually mount CD-ROM and floppy disks in the fstab file, you whould specfy the **noauto** option. Also, if you issue a **mount -a** command, all the file systems without a **noauto** option are mounted. If you want to make the CD-ROM user-mountable, add the **user** option.

```
/dev/sdc /media/cdrom iso9660 ro,noauto,user 0 0
```

---

*TIP   The "automatic" mounting of file systems from /etc/fstab is actually implemented by executing a **mount -a** command in the /etc/rc.d/rc.sysinit file that is run whenever you boot. The **mount -a** command mounts any file system listed in your /etc/fstab file that does not have a **noauto** option. The **umount -a** command (which is executed when you shut down your system) unmounts the file systems in /etc/fstab.*

Mounting File Systems Manually: mount and umount

You can also mount or unmount any file system using the **mount** and **umount** commands, directly (notice that **umount** lacks an *n*). These opeations are rarely used as mounting is handled automatically for removable devices by HAL and by fstab for fixed devices. These features will invoke mount at some point to perform the actual mounting of the device, but the action remains invisible to the user. In the rare case where you may need to manually mount a file system, you can use the **mount** command in a terminal window to perform the mount. Normally, file systems can be mounted on hard disk partitions only by the root user, whereas CD-ROMs and floppies can be mounted by any user. Table 30-9 lists the different options for the **mount** command.

The mount Command

The **mount** command takes two arguments: the storage device through which Linux accesses the file system, and the directory in the file structure to which the new file system is attached. The *mountpoint* is the directory on your main directory tree where you want the files on the storage device attached. The *device* is a special device file that connects your system to the hardware device. The syntax for the **mount** command is as follows:

```
# mount device mountpoint
```

As noted previously, device files are located in the **/dev** directories and usually have abbreviated names ending with the number of the device. For example, **fd0** may refer to the first floppy drive attached to your system. The following example mounts a hard disk in the

Mount Option	Description
-f	Fakes the mounting of a file system. Use it to check if a file system can be mounted.
-v	Verbose mode. **mount** displays descriptions of the actions it is taking. Use with -f to check for any problems mounting a file system, -fv.
-w	Mounts the file system with read/write permission.
-r	Mounts the file system with read-only permission.
-n	Mounts the file system without placing an entry for it in the **mstab** file.
-t type	Specifies the type of file system to be mounted. See Table 30-7 for valid file system types.
-a	Mounts all file systems listed in **/etc/fstab**.
-o option-list	Mounts the file system using a list of options. This is a comma-separated list of options following -o. See Table 30-8 for a list of the options.

TABLE 30-9   The mount Command

first (**sdc2**) to the **/mymedia** directory. The mountpoint directory needs to be empty. If you already have a file system mounted there, you will receive a message that another file system is already mounted there and that the directory is busy. If you mount a file system to a directory that already has files and subdirectories in it, those will be bypassed, giving you access only to the files in the mounted file system. Unmounting the file system, of course, restores access to the original directory files.

```
# mount /dev/sdc2 /mymedia
```

For any partition with an entry in the **/etc/fstab** file, you can mount the partition using only the mount directory specified in its **fstab** entry; you needn't enter the device filename. The **mount** command looks up the entry for the partition in the **fstab** file, using the directory to identify the entry and, in that way, find the device name. For example, to mount the **/dev/sda1** Windows partition in the preceding example, the **mount** command only needs to know the directory it is mounted to—in this case, **/mnt/windows**.

```
# mount /mnt/windows
```

If you are unsure as to the type of file system that a disk holds, you can mount it specifying the **auto** file system type with the -t option. Given the **auto** file system type, **mount** attempts to detect the type of file system on the disk automatically. This is useful if you are manually mounting a floppy disk whose file system type you are unsure of (HAL would also automatically detect the file system type of any removable media, including floppies).

```
# mount -t auto /dev/fd0 /media/floppy
```

The umount Command

If you want to replace one mounted file system with another, you must first explicitly unmount the one already mounted. Say you have mounted a floppy disk, and now you want to take it out and put in a new one. You must unmount that floppy disk before you can put in and mount the new one. You unmount a file system with the **umount** command. The **umount** command can take as its argument either a device name or the directory where it was mounted. Here is the syntax:

```
# umount device-or-mountpoint
```

The following example unmounts the floppy disk wherever it is mounted:

```
# umount /dev/fd0
```

Using the example where the device was mounted on the **/mydir** directory, you could use that directory to unmount the file system:

```
# umount /mydir
```

One important constraint applies to the **umount** command. You can never unmount a file system in which you are currently working. If you change to a directory within a file system that you then try to unmount, you receive an error message stating that the file system is busy. For example, suppose a CD-ROM is mounted on the **/media/disk** directory, and then change to that **/media/disk** directory. If you decide to change CD-ROMs, you first have to unmount the current one with the **umount** command. This will fail because you are currently in the directory in which it is mounted. You have to leave that directory before you can unmount the CD-ROM.

```
# mount /dev/sdc /media/disk
# cd /media/disk
# umount /media/disk
umount: /dev/sdc: device is busy
# cd /root
# umount /media/disk
```

TIP   *If other users are using a file system you are trying to unmount, you can use the* ***lsof*** *or* ***fuser*** *command to find out who they are.*

Mounting Floppy Disks

As noted previously, to access a file on a floppy disk, the disk first has to be mounted on your Linux system. The device name for your floppy drive is **fd0**, and it is located in the directory **/dev**. Entering **/dev/fd0** references your floppy drive. Notice the number **0** after **fd**. If you have more than one floppy drive, the additional drives are represented by **fd1**, **fd2**, and so on. You can mount to any directory you want. Red Hat Enterprise creates a convenient directory to use for floppy disks, **/media/floppy**. The following example mounts the floppy disk in your floppy drive to the **/media/floppy** directory:

```
# mount /dev/fd0 /media/floppy
```

Remember, you are mounting a particular floppy disk, not the floppy drive. You cannot simply remove the floppy disk and put in another one. The **mount** command has attached those files to your main directory tree, and your system expects to find those files on a floppy disk in your floppy drive. If you take out the disk and put another one in, you get an error message when you try to access it.

To change disks, you must first unmount the floppy disk already in your disk drive. Then, after putting in the new disk, you must explicitly mount that new disk. To do this, use the **umount** command.

```
# umount /dev/fd0
```

For the **umount** and **mount** operations, you can specify either the directory it is mounted on or the **/dev/fd0** device.

```
# umount /media/floppy
```

You can now remove the floppy disk, put in the new one, and then mount it:

```
# mount /media/floppy
```

When you shut down your system, any disk you have mounted is automatically unmounted. You do not have to unmount it explicitly.

Mounting DVD/CD-ROMs

Remember, when you mount a DVD/CD-ROM or floppy disk, you cannot then simply remove it to put another one in the drive. You first have to unmount it, detaching the file system from the overall directory tree. In fact, the DVD/CD-ROM drive remains locked until you unmount it. Once you unmount a DVD/CD-ROM, you can then take it out and put in another one, which you then must mount before you can access it. When changing several DVD/CD-ROMs or floppy disks, you are continually mounting and unmounting them. For a DVD/CD-ROM, instead of using the **umount** command, you can use the **eject** command with the device name or mountpoint, which will unmount and then eject the DVD/CD-ROM from the drive.

To mount a DVD/CD-ROM, all you have to do is insert it into the drive. HAL will detect it and mount it automatically in the **/media** directory and place it in a subdirectory with the same name as the DVD/CD-ROMs title.

If instead, you want to manually mount the drive from the command line with the **mount** command, you will have to first decide on a directory to mount it to (create it if it does not exist). The **/media/ subdirectory for the DVD/CD-ROM disk** is created dynamically when a disk is inserted and deleted when the disk is removed. To manually mount a disk, use the **mount** command, the device name, like **/dev/cdrom**, and the directory it is mounted to.

```
# mount /dev/cdrom   /media/cdrom1
```

If you want to manually unmount the drive, say from the command line, you can use the **unmount** command and the name of the directory it is mounted on.

```
# umount /media/cdrom1
```

Or, if mounted by HAL, you could use

```
# umount /media/mycdromtitle
```

When you burn a CD, you may need to create a CD image file. You could access such an image file from your hard drive, mounting it as if it were another file system (even ripped images could be mounted in this way). For this, you use the **loop** option, specifying an open loop device such as **/dev/loop0**. If no loop device is indicated, **mount** will try to find an open one. The file system type is **iso9660**, a CD-ROM ISO image file type.

```
# mount -t iso9660 -o loop=/dev/loop0 image-file mount-directory
```

To mount the image file **mymusic.cdimage** to the **/mnt/mystuff** directory and make it read-only, you would use

```
# mount -t iso9660 -o ro,loop=/dev/loop0 mymusic.cdimage /mnt/mystuff
```

Once it is mounted, you can access files on the CD-ROM as you would in any directory.

TIP *You use* **mkisofs** *to create a CD-ROM image made up from your files or another CD-ROM.*

Mounting Hard Drive Partitions: Linux and Windows

You can mount either Linux or Windows hard drive partitions with the **mount** command. However, it is much more practical to have them mounted automatically using the **/etc/fstab** file as described previously. The Linux hard disk partitions you created during installation are already automatically mounted for you. As noted previously, to mount a Linux hard disk partition, enter the **mount** command with the device name of the partition and the directory to which you want to mount it. IDE and serial ATA hard drives use the prefix **sd**. The next example mounts the Linux hard disk partition on **/dev/sda4** to the directory **/mnt/mydata**:

```
# mount -t ext3 /dev/sda4 /mnt/mydata
```

You can also mount a Windows partition and directly access the files on it. As with a Linux partition, you use the **mount** command, but you also have to specify the file system type as Windows. For that, use the **-t** option, and then type **vfat** for Windows 95/98/ME (**msdos** for MS-DOS). For Windows XP, 2000, and NT, you would use **ntfs** (full read-only access with limited write access), or ntfs-3g for the **ntfs-3g** drivers. In the next example, the user mounts the Windows hard disk partition **/dev/sda1** to the Linux file structure at directory **/mnt/windows**. The **/mnt/windows** directory is a common designation for Windows file systems (though ntfs-3g uses /media), though you can mount it in any directory (such as **/mnt/dos** for MS-DOS). If you have several Windows partitions, you could create a Windows directory and then a subdirectory for each drive using the drive's label or letter, such as **/mnt/windows/a** or **/mnt/windows/mystuff**. Be sure you have already created the directory before mounting the file system.

```
# mount -t vfat /dev/sda1 /mnt/windows
```

Creating File Systems: mkfs, mke2fs, mkswap, parted, and fdisk

Linux provides a variety of tools for creating and managing file systems, letting you add new hard disk partitions, create CD images, and format floppies. To use a new hard drive, you will have to first partition it and then create a file system on it. You can use either **parted** or **fdisk** to partition your hard drive. To create the file system on the partitions, you use the **mkfs** command, which is a front end for various file system builders. For swap partitions, you use a special tool, **mkswap**, and to create file systems on a CD-ROM, you use the **mkisofs** tool. Linux partition and file system tools are listed in Table 30-10.

Tool	Description
fdisk	Menu-driven program to create and delete partitions.
cfdisk	Screen-based interface for **fdisk**.
parted	GNU partition management tool.
mkfs	Creates a file system on a partition or floppy disk using the specified file system type. Front end to formatting utilities.
mke2fs	Creates an ext2 file system on a Linux partition; use the **-j** option to create an ext3 file system.
mkfs.ext3	Creates an ext3 file system on a Linux partition.
mkfs.ext2	Creates an ext2 file system on a Linux partition.
mkfs.reiserfs	Creates a Reiser journaling file system on a Linux partition (links to **mkreiserfs**).
mkfs.jfs	Creates a JFS journaling file system on a Linux partition.
mkfs.xfs	Creates a XFS journaling file system on a Linux partition.
mkfs.msdos	Creates a DOS file system on a given partition.
mkfs.vfat	Creates a Windows 16-bit file system on a given partition (Windows 95, 98, and ME).
mkfs.cramfs	Creates a CRAMFS compressed flash memory file system, read only (used for embedded devices).
mkfs.ntfs	Creates a Windows NTFS (XP, 2000, NT) file system on a given partition.
mkswap	Tool to set up a Linux swap area on a device or in a file.
mkdosfs	Creates an MS-DOS file system under Linux.
mkisofs	Creates an ISO CD-ROM disk image.
dumpe2fs	Displays lower-level block information for a file system.
gfloppy	GNOME tool to format a floppy disk (Floppy Formatter entry on the System Tools menu).
resize2fs	Tool to extend the size of a partition, using unused space currently available on a disk.
hdparm	IDE hard disk tuner, to set IDE hard disk features.
tune2fs	Tunes a file system, setting features such as the label, journaling, and reserved block space.

TABLE 30-10   Linux Partition and File System Creation Tools

> **TIP** *The easiest way to manage your partitions is to use GParted or QTParted. These are GUI partition tools that operate as front ends to managing partitions. You can use these tools to examine your partitions, create new ones, and to format or mount parititions. You can access them from the Applications | System Tools menu as GParted and QTParted.*

fdisk

To start **fdisk**, enter **fdisk** on the command line with the device name of the hard disk you are partitioning. This brings up an interactive program you can use to create your Linux partition. Be careful using Linux **fdisk**. It can literally erase entire hard disk partitions and all the data on those partitions if you are not careful. The following command invokes **fdisk** for creating partitions on the **sdb** hard drive.

```
fdisk    /dev/sdb
```

The partitions have different types that you need to specify. Linux **fdisk** is a line-oriented program. It has a set of one-character commands that you simply press. Then you may be prompted to type in certain information and press ENTER. If you run into trouble during the **fdisk** procedure, you can press Q at any time, and you will return to the previous screen without any changes having been made. No changes are actually made to your hard disk until you press W. This should be your very last command; it makes the actual changes to your hard disk and then quits **fdisk**, returning you to the installation program. Table 30-11 lists the commonly used **fdisk** commands. Perform the following steps to create a Linux partition.

When you press N to define a new partition, you will be asked if it is a primary partition. Press P to indicate that it is a primary partition. Linux supports up to four primary partitions. Enter the partition number for the partition you are creating. Enter the beginning cylinder for the partition. This is the first number in parentheses at the end of the prompt. You are then prompted to enter the last cylinder number. You can either enter the last cylinder you want for this partition or enter a size. You can enter the size as **+1000M** for 1 GB, preceding the amount with a + sign. Bear in mind that the size cannot exceed your free space. You then specify the partition type. The default type for a Linux partition is 83.

Command	Action
a	Toggle a bootable flag
l	List known partition types
m	List commands
n	Add a new partition
p	Print the partition table
q	Quit without saving changes
t	Change a partition's system ID
w	Write table to disk and exit

TABLE 30-11 Commonly Used fdisk Commands

If you are creating a different type of partition, such as a swap partition, press T to indicate the type you want. Enter the partition number, such as 82 for a swap partition. When you are finished, press W to write out the changes to the hard disk, and then press ENTER to continue.

parted

As an alternative to **fdisk**, you can use **parted** (**www.gnu.org/software/parted**). **parted** lets you manage hard disk partitions, create new ones, and delete old ones. GParted is the Gnome interface for **parted** and QTParted is the KDE interface (System Tools | GParted). Unlike **fdisk**, **parted** also lets you resize partitions. For you to use **parted** on the partitions in a given hard drive, none of the partitions on that drive can be in use. This means that if you wish to use **parted** on partitions located on that same hard drive as your kernel, you have to boot your system in rescue mode and choose not to mount your system files. For any other hard drives, you only need to unmount their partitions and turn your swap space off with the **swapoff** command. You can then start **parted** with the **parted** command and the device name of the hard disk you want to work on. The following example starts **parted** for the hard disk **/dev/sda**:

```
parted  /dev/sda
```

You use the **print** command to list all your partitions. The partition number for each partition will be listed in the first column under the Minor heading. The Start and End columns list the beginning and end positions that the partition uses on the hard drive. The numbers are in megabytes, starting from the first megabyte to the total available. To create a new partition, use the **mkpart** command with either **primary** or **extended**, the file system type, and the beginning and end positions. You can create up to three primary partitions and one extended partition (or four primary partitions if there is no extended partition). The extended partition can, in turn, have several logical partitions. Once you have created the partition, you can later use **mkfs** to format it with a file system. To remove a partition, use the **rm** command and the partition number. To resize a partition, use the **resize** command with the partition number and the beginning and end positions. You can even move a partition using the **move** command. The **help** command lists all commands.

mkfs

Once you create your partition, you have to create a file system on it. To do this, use the **mkfs** command to build the Linux file system and pass the name of the hard disk partition as a parameter. You must specify its full pathname with the **mkfs** command. Table 30-12 lists the options for the **mkfs** command. For example, the second partition on the first hard drive has the device name **/dev/sdb1**. You can now mount your new hard disk partition, attaching it to your file structure. The next example formats that partition:

```
# mkfs -t ext3 /dev/sdb1
```

The **mkfs** command is really just a front end for several different file system builders. A *file system builder* performs the actual task of creating a file system. Fedora and Red Hat Enterprise Linux supports various file system builders, including several journaling file systems and Windows file systems. The name of a file system builder has the prefix **mkfs**

Option	Description
Blocks	Number of blocks for the file system. There are 1,440 blocks for a 1.44 MB floppy disk.
-t *file-system-type*	Specifies the type of file system to format. The default is the standard Linux file system type, ext3.
file-system-options	Options for the type of file system specified. Listed before the device name, but after the file system type.
-V	Verbose mode. Displays description of each action **mkfs** takes.
-v	Instructs the file system builder program that **mkfs** invokes to show actions it takes.
-c	Checks a partition for bad blocks before formatting it (may take some time).
-l *filename*	Reads a list of bad blocks.

TABLE 30-12   The mkfs Options

and a suffix for the name of the type of file system. For example, the file system builder for the ext3 file system is **mkfs.ext3**. For Reiser file systems, it is **mkfs.reiserfs**, and for Windows 16-bit file systems (95, 98, ME), it is **mkfs.vfat**. Some of these file builders are just other names for traditional file system creation tools. For example, the **mkfs.ext2** file builder it just another name for the **mke2fs** ext2 file system creation tool, and **mkfs.msdos** is the **mkdosfs** command. As ext3 is an extension of ext2, **mkfs.ext3** simply invokes **mke2fs**, the tool for creating ext2 and ext3 file systems, and directs it to create an ext3 file system (using the **-j** option). Any of the file builders can be used directly to create a file system of that type. Options are listed before the device name. The next example is equivalent to the preceding one, creating an ext3 file system on the **sdb1** device:

```
mkfs.ext3 /dev/sdb1
```

The syntax for the **mkfs** command is as follows. You can add options for a particular file system after the type and before the device. The block size is used for file builders that do not detect the disk size.

```
mkfs options [-t type] file-sysoptions device size
```

TIP   *Once you have formatted your disk, you can label it with the* **e2label** *command as described earlier in the chapter.*

The same procedure works for floppy disks. In this case, the **mkfs** command takes as its argument the device name. It uses the ext2 file system (the default for **mkfs**), because a floppy is too small to support a journaling file system.

```
# mkfs /dev/fd0
```

mkswap

If you want to create a swap partition, you first use **fdisk** or **parted** to create the partition, if it does not already exist, and then you use the **mkswap** command to format it as a swap partition. **mkswap** formats the entire partition unless otherwise instructed. It takes as its argument the device name for the swap partition.

```
mkswap /dev/sdb2
```

You then need to create an entry for it in the **/etc/fstab** file so that it will be automatically mounted when your system boots.

CD-ROM and DVD ROM Manual Recording

On your desktop, DVD/CD recording is now handled directly by the Gnome Nautilus CD/DVD Creator tool. As described in Chapter 3, you simply insert a blank DVD/CD disk, double-click to open it with the CD/DVD Creator, and drag the files you want to copy to the disk window. Then click the Write button. Alternatively you could use CD/DVD writers like K3b.

To manually record data to DVD/CD-ROM discs from the command line is more complicated. The process involves creating a CD image file of the CD-ROM, and then writing that image file to a CD-R or CD-RW disc in your CD-R/RW drive. With the **mkisofs** command, you can create a CD image file, which you can then write to a CD-R/RW write device. Once you create your CD image file, you can write it to a CD-write device, using the **cdrecord** or **cdwrite** application. The **cdrecord** application is a more powerful application with many options. You can also use GNOME and KDE CD recording applications such as KOnCD and GNOME Toaster to create your CDs easily. Most are front ends to the **mkisofs** and **cdrecord** tools. To record DVD discs on DVD writers, you can use **cdrecord** for DVD-R/RW drives and the dvd+rw tools for DVD+RW/R drives. If you want to record CD-ROMs on a DVD writer, you can just use **cdrecord**.

The **cdrecord** application currently works only on DVD-R/RW drives; it is part of the dvdrtools package. If you want to use DVD+RW/R drives, you would use the dvd+rw tools such as **growisofs** and **dvd+rw-format**. Some dvd+rw tools are included in the dvd+rw-tools package. Check the DVD+RW tools Web site for more information, **http://fy.chalmers.se/~appro/linux/DVD+RW**.

mkisofs

To create a CD image, you first select the files you want on your CD. Then you can use **mkisofs** to create an ISO CD image of them.

mkisofs Options

You may need to include several important options with **mkisofs** to create a data CD properly. The **-o** option is used to specify the name of the CD image file. This can be any name you want to give it. The **-R** option specifies RockRidge CD protocols, and the **-J** option provides for long Windows 95/98/ME or XP names. The **-r** option, in addition to the RockRidge protocols (**-R**), sets standard global permissions for your files, such as read access for all users and no write access because the CD-ROM is read-only. The **-T** option creates translation tables for filenames for use on systems that are not RockRidge compliant.

The **-U** option provides for relaxed filenames that are not standard ISO compliant, such as long filenames, those with more than one period in their name, those that begin with a period such as shell configuration files, and ones that use lowercase characters (there are also separate options for each of these features if you just want to use a few of them). Most RPM and source code package names fall in this category. The **-iso-level** option lets you remove ISO restrictions such as the length of a filename. The **-V** option sets the volume label (name) for the CD. Finally, the **-v** option displays the progress of the image creation.

Disk Image Creation

The last argument is the directory that contains the files for which you want to make the CD image. For this, you can specify a directory. For example, if you are creating a CD-ROM to contain the data files in the **mydocs** directory, you would specify that directory. This top directory will not be included, just the files and subdirectories in it. You can also change to that directory and then use **.** to indicate the current directory.

If you were creating a simple CD to use on Linux, you would use **mkisofs** to first create the CD image. Here the verbose option will show the creation progress, and the **-V** option lets you specify the CD label. A CD image called **songs.iso** is created using the file located in the **newsong** directory:

```
mkisofs -v -V "Goodsongs" -o moresongs.iso  newsongs
```

If you also wanted to use the CD on a Windows system, you would add the **-r** (RockRidge with standard global file access) and **-J** (Joliet) options:

```
mkisofs -v -r -J -V "Goodsongs" -o moresongs.iso  newsongs
```

You need to include certain options if you are using filenames that are not ISO compliant, such as ones with more than 31 characters or ones that use lowercase characters. The **-U** option lets you use completely unrestricted filenames, whereas certain options like **-L** for the unrestricted length will release specific restrictions only. The following example creates a CD image called **mydoc.iso** using the files and subdirectories located in the **mdoc** directory and labels the CD image with the name "Greatdocs":

```
mkisofs -v -r -T -J -U -V "Greatdocs" -o mydocuments.iso   mydocs
```

Mounting Disk Images

Once you have created your CD image, you can check to see if it is correct by mounting it as a file system on your Linux system. In effect, to test the CD image, you mount it to a directory and then access it as if it were simply another file system. Mounting a CD image requires the use of a loop device. Specify the loop device with the **loop** option as shown in the next example. Here the **mydoc.iso** is mounted to the **/media/cdrom** directory as a file system of type **iso9660**. Be sure to unmount it when you finish.

```
mount -t iso9660 -o ro,loop=/dev/loop0 mydocuments.iso /media/cdrom
```

Bootable CD-ROMs

If you are creating a bootable CD-ROM, you need to indicate the boot image file to use and the boot catalog. With the **-c** option, you specify the boot catalog. With the **-b** option, you specify the boot image. The *boot image* is a boot disk image, like that used to start up an installation procedure. For example, on the Fedora CD-ROM, the boot image is **isolinux/isolinux.bin**, and the boot catalog is **isolinux/boot.cat** (you can also use **images/boot.img**. and **boot.cat**). Copy those files to your hard disk. The following example creates a bootable CD-ROM image using Red Hat Linux and Fedora distribution files located on the CD-ROM drive.

```
mkisofs -o rd8-0.iso -b isolinux/isolinux.bin -c isolinux/boot.cat \
  -no-emul-boot -boot-load-size 4 -boot-info-table \
  -v -r -R -T -J -V "Fed4"  /media/cdrom
```

dvdrecord

Once **mkisofs** has created the CD image file, you can use Nautilus (the GNOME file manager) to directly burn an ISO image to a CD/DVD write disk. On the command line interface, you could, instead, use **cdrecord** to write it to a CD/DVD write disc. There is a command called **dvdrcecord**, but this is just a script that calls **cdrecord**, which now writes to both DVD and CD media. If you have more than one CD-writer device, you should specify the DVD/CD-R/RW drive to use by indicating its device name. In this example, the device is an IDE CD-R located at **/dev/sdc**. The **dev=** option is used to indicate this drive. The final argument for **cdrecord** is the name of the CD image file.

```
cdrecord  dev=/dev/sdc  mydocuments.iso
```

In this example, an SATA rewritable CD-RW device with the device **/dev/scd0** is used.

```
cdrecord  dev=/dev/scd0  mydocuments.iso
```

If you are creating an audio CD, use the **-audio** option, as shown here. This option uses the CD-DA audio format:

```
cdrecord  dev=/dev/sdc -audio moresongs.iso
```

TIP The **dummy** *option for* **cdrecord** *lets you test the CD writing operation for a given image.*

dvd+rw Tools

The primary dvd+rw tool is **growisofs**, with which you create DVD+RW/R disks. Two other minor supporting tools are also included, a formatter, dvd+rw-format, and a compatibility tool, dvd+rw-booktype. See the dvd+rw-tools page in **/usr/share/doc** for detailed instructions.

The **growisofs** tool functions like the **mkisofs** tool, except that it writes directly to the DVD+RW/R disc, rather than to an image. It has the same options as **mkisofs**, with a few exceptions, and is actually a front end to the **mkisofs** command. There is, of course, no **-o** option for specifying a disk image. You specify the DVD device instead. For example, to write the contents of the **newsongs** directory to a DVD+RW disc, you would use **growisofs** directly.

```
growisofs -v -V "Goodsongs" -Z /dev/sdc  newsongs
```

PART VI

The device is specified by its name, usually **/dev/scd0** for the first SATA CD/DVD-RW device or **/dev/sdc** for the first secondary IDE drive. Recall that IDE DVD writers are configured as SCSI devices when your system boots up. **growisofs** provides a special **-z** option for burning an initial session. For multi-sessions (DVD-RW), you can use the **mkisofs -M** option. If you want to reuse a DVD-RW disc, just overwrite it. You do not have to reformat it.

To burn an ISO image file to the disc, use the **-z** option and assign the ISO image to the device.

```
growisofs -v -V "Goodsongs" -Z /dev/sdc=moresongs.iso
```

Though **growisofs** will automatically format new DVD+RW discs, the dvd+rw tools also include the dvd+rw-format tool for explicitly performing formats only. You use dvd+rw-format tool only to explicitly format new DVD+RW (read/write) discs, preparing them for writing. This is done only once, and only for DVD+RW discs that have never been used before. DVD+R discs do not need any formatting.

The dvd+rw-booktype tool sets the compatibility setting for older DVD-ROM readers that may not be able to read DVD+RW/R discs.

RAID and LVM

With onset of cheap, efficient, and very large hard drives, even simple home systems may employ several hard drives. The use of multiple hard drives opens up opportunities for ensuring storage reliability as well as more easily organizing access to your hard disks. Linux provides two methods for better managing your hard disks: Logical Volume Management (LVM) and Redundant Arrays of Independent Disks (RAID). LVM is a method for organizing all your hard disks into logical volumes, letting you pool the storage capabilities of several hard disks into a single logical volume. Your system then sees one large storage device, and you do not have to micromanage each underlying hard disk and its partitions. LVM is perhaps the most effective way to add hard drives to your system, creating a large, accessible pool of storage. RAID is a way of storing the same data in different places on multiple hard disks. These multiple hard drives are treated as a single hard drive. They include recovery information that allows you to restore your files should one of the drives fail. The two can be mixed, implementing LVM volumes on RAID arrays. LVM provides flexibility, and RAID can provide data protection.

With LVM you no longer have to keep track of separate disks and their partitions, trying to remember where files are stored on what partitions located in what drive. Partitions and their drives are combined into logical file systems that you can attach to your system directory tree. You can have several logical file systems, each with its own drive and/or partitions.

In a system with several hard drives, with both LVM and RAID, you could combine the hard drives into one logical file system, which accesses the storage as one large pool. Files are stored in a single directory structure, not on directories on a particular partition. Instead of mounting file systems for each individual hard drive, there would be only one file system to mount for all the hard drives. LVM has the added advantage of letting you implement several logical file systems on different partitions across several hard drives.

RAID is best suited to desktops and servers that hold multiple hard drives and require data recovery. The most favored form of RAID, RAID 5, requires a minimum of three hard drives. RAID, with the exception of RAID 0, provides the best protection against hard drive failure and is considered a necessity for storage-intensive tasks like enterprise, database, and Internet server operations. It can also provide peace of mind for smaller operations, providing recovery from hard disk failure. Keep in mind that there are different forms of RAID, each with advantages and weaknesses. RAID 0 provides no recovery capabilities at all. After setting up a RAID array, you could then implement LVM volumes on the array.

In comparison to LVM, RAID can provide faster access for applications that work with very large files, like multimedia, database, or graphics applications. But for normal operations, LVM is just as efficient as RAID. LVM, though, requires running your Linux system and configuring it from your Linux operating system. RAID, which is now supported at the hardware level on most computers, is easier to set up, especially a simple RAID 0 operation that merely combines hard drives into one drive.

Logical Volume Manager

For easier hard disk storage management, you can set up your system to use the Logical Volume Manager (LVM), creating LVM partitions that are organized into logical volumes to which free space is automatically allocated. Logical volumes provide a more flexible and powerful way of dealing with disk storage, organizing physical partitions into logical volumes in which you can easily manage disk space. Disk storage for a logical volume is treated as one pool of memory, though the volume may in fact contain several hard disk partitions spread across different hard disks. Adding a new LVM partition merely increases the pool of storage accessible to the entire system. The original LVM package was developed for kernel 2.4. The current LVM2 package is used for kernel 2.6. Check the LVM HOWTO at **tldp.org** for detailed examples.

LVM Structure

In an LVM structure, LVM physical partitions, also known as *extents,* are organized into logical groups, which are in turn used by logical volumes. In effect, you are dealing with three different levels of organization. At the lowest level, you have physical volumes. These are physical hard disk partitions that you create with partition creation tools such as **parted** or **fdisk**. The partition type will be a Linux LVM partition, code **8e**. These physical volumes are organized into logical groups, known as volume groups, that operate much like logical hard disks. You assign collections of physical volumes to different logical groups.

Once you have your logical groups, you can then create logical volumes. Logical volumes function much like hard disk partitions on a standard setup. For example, on the **turtle** group volume, you could create a **/var** logical volume, and on the **rabbit** logical group, you could create **/home** and **/projects** logical volumes. You can have several logical volumes on one logical group, just as you can have several partitions on one hard disk.

You treat the logical volumes as you would any ordinary hard disk partition. You create a file system on one with the **mkfs** command, and then you can mount the file system to use it with the **mount** command. For Fedora the file system type is **ext3**.

Storage on logical volumes is managed using extents. A logical group defines a standard size for an extent, say 4MB, and then divides each physical volume in its group into extents of that size. Logical volumes are, in turn, divided into extents of the same size, which are then mapped to those on the physical volumes.

Logical volumes can be linear, striped, or mirrored. The mirror option will create a mirror copy of a logical volume, providing a restore capability. The striped option lets you automatically distribute your logical volume across several partitions as you would a RAID device. This adds better efficiency for very large files but is complicated to implement. As on a RAID device, stripe sizes have to be consistent across partitions. As LVM partitions can be of any size, the stripe sizes have to be carefully calculated. The simplest approach is just to use a linear implementation, much like a RAID 0 device, just treating the storage as one large ordinary drive, with storage accessed sequentially.

There is one restriction and recommendation for logical volumes. The boot partition cannot be part of a logical volume. You still have to create a separate hard disk partition as your boot partition with the **/boot** mountpoint in which your kernel and all needed boot files are installed. In addition, it is recommended that you not place your root partition on a logical volume. Doing so can complicate any needed data recovery. This is why a default partition configuration set up during Fedora installation will include a separate **/boot** partition of 100MB of type **ext3**, whereas the root and swap partitions will be installed on logical volumes. There will be two partitions, one for the logical group (LVM physical volume, **pv**) holding both swap and root volumes, and another for the boot partition (**ext3**). The logical volumes will in turn both be **ext3** file systems.

Creating LVMs During Installation

Creating logical volumes involves several steps. First, you create physical LVM partitions, then the volume groups you place these partitions in, and then from the volume groups you create the logical volumes, for which you then specify mountpoints and file system types. You can create LVM partitions during the installation process. Click New and select "physical volume (LVM)" for the File System Type. Create an LVM physical partition for each partition you want on your hard disks. Once you have created LVM physical partitions, you click the LVM button to create your logical volumes. You first need to assign the LVM physical partitions to volume groups. Volume groups are essentially logical hard drives. You could, if you wish, assign LVM physical partitions from different hard disks to the same volume group, letting the volume group span different hard drives. This approach is useful if you are combining several hard disks into one logical group. Once the volume groups are created, you are ready to create your logical volumes. You can create several logical volumes within each group. The logical volumes function like partitions. You will have to specify a file system type and mountpoint for each logical volume you create. The file system type for Fedora is normally **ext3**.

system-config-lvm

The system-config-lvm tool provides a GUI interface for managing your Logical Volume Manager. With it you can obtain information about your logical and physical volumes, as well as perform simple tasks such as deleting and extending logical volumes, or migrating and removing physical volumes. You can invoke system-config-lvm from its menu entry under System | Administration | Logical Volume Management. You can also enter **system-config-lvm** in a terminal window. system-config-lvm will display a window with three panes: one listing all your logical and physical volumes, one showing a graphical representation of a selected volume or volume group, and one that displays information about the selected volumes. Figure 31-1 shows two volume groups. **VolGroup00** is the default volume group set up during installation, whereas **mymedia** is one set up later by the user, as discussed later in the chapter. **VolGroup00** is implemented on a physical volume, a pv partition, which is the third partition on the first hard drive, sda3. The two logical volumes for the group are used for the root and swap partitions, **LogVol01** for the root partition, and **LogVol00** for the swap partition.

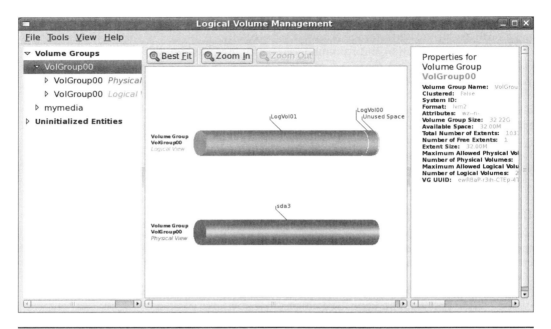

FIGURE 31-1   GUI Logical Volume Manager administration (system-config-lvm)

Selecting a physical volume displays buttons with the options to extend the volume group or remove physical volumes, whereas selecting a particular partition allows you to migrate a particular volume or remove it from the group. When extending a volume group, you will be presented with a list of possible partitions to choose from.

Selecting a logical group shows buttons to create or remove the volume, and selecting a particular volume in that group permits you to remove the logical volume or edit its properties. A logical volume's properties will let you specify its file system type, size, and logical volume name. When adding a new logical volume, you can use properties to set the name, size, and file system type, formatting it appropriately. Space permitting, you can even resize current volumes.

The uninitialized entries are partitions that do not belong to any volume. Recall, though, that the boot partition cannot belong to a volume group; it cannot be a logical volume. Be sure to leave it alone. For other uninitialized partitions, you can select their entries and initialize them to add them to a volume group. Use the Initialize Block Device entry in the Tools menu.

If you have the free space on a logical group you can create a new logical volume. First select the logical group entry on the left-hand pane. Then click Create New Logical Volume (see later Figure 31-4). This opens up a new window with a panel for creating a new logical volume (see Figure 31-2). There are entries for the volume name, its size, the file system you want it formatted with, and where you want it mounted. You also have the option of specifying the size of the extents, though the default normally works well. You can specify whether a logical volume should be linear, mirrored, or striped. These features are similar to the linear, mirrored, or striped implementations used in RAID devices. Normally you would use the linear implementation, which is the default.

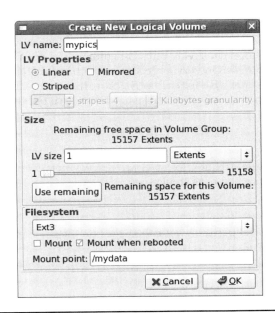

FIGURE 31-2   Creating a new logical volume with LVM

To extend the size of a volume using free space in the volume group, just select the volume group and click the Edit properties button. This opens the same window as displayed in Figure 31-2. You can then use the slider on the volume size to extend the size of the volume. When you click OK, system-config-lvm will unmount your volume group and then resize the volume and check the file system, extending the size while preserving your original data. This capability is a major advantage for LVM devices. Hard disk partitions are fixed, whereas LVM logical disks can easily be expanded. To expand a hard disk partition, you had to destroy the old one and create a new, larger one that in turn was also fixed. With LVM you just add more storage. The logical structure is separated from the physical implementation.

LVM Tools: Using the LVM Commands

Instead of using system-config-lvm, you can use a collection of LVM tools to manage your LVM volumes, adding new LVM physical partitions and removing current ones. The system-config-lvm system tool is actually a GUI interface for the LVM tools. You can either use LVM tools directly or use the **lvm** command to generate an interactive shell from which you can run LVM commands. There are Man pages for all the LVM commands. LVM maintains configuration information in the **/etc/lvm/lvm.conf** directory, where you can configure LVM options such as the log file or the directory for LVM devices (see the **lvm.conf** Man page for more details).

Displaying LVM Information

You can use the **pvdisplay**, **vgdisplay**, and **lvdisplay** commands to show detailed information about a physical partition, volume groups, and logical volumes. **pvscan**, **vgscan**, and **lvscan** list your physical, group, and logical volumes.

Managing LVM Physical Volumes with the LVM Commands

A physical volume can be any hard disk partition or RAID device. A RAID device is seen as a single physical volume. You can create physical volumes either from a single hard disk or from partitions on a hard disk. On very large systems with many hard disks, you would more likely use an entire hard disk for each physical volume.

To initialize a physical volume on an entire hard disk, you use the hard disk device name, as shown here:

```
pvcreate /dev/sdc
```

If you are using a single partition for an entire drive, you create a new physical volume using the partition's device name, as shown here:

```
pvcreate /dev/sdc1
```

This will create one physical partition, pv, called **sdc1** on the **sdc** hard drive (the third Serial ATA drive, drive c).

To initialize several drives, just list them. The following creates two physical partitions, sdc1 and sdd1.

```
pvcreate /dev/sdc1 /dev/sdd1
```

You could also use several partitions on different hard drives. This is a situation in which your hard drives each hold several partitions. This condition occurs often when you are using some partitions on your hard drive for different purposes like different operating systems, or if you want to distribute your logical group across several hard drives. To initialize these partitions at once, you simply list them.

```
pvcreate /dev/hda3 /dev/hdb1 /dev/hdb2
```

Once you have initialized your partitions, you have to create LVM groups on them.

Managing LVM Groups

Physical LVM partitions are used to make up a volume group. You can manually create a volume group using the **vgcreate** command and the name of the group along with a list of physical partitions you want in the group.

If you are then creating a new volume group to place these partitions in, you can include them in the group when you create the volume group with the **vgcreate** command. The volume group can use one or more physical partitions. The default install configuration described previously used only one physical partition for the **VolGroup00**. In the following example, a volume group called **mymedia** is made up two physical volumes, **sdb1** and **sdc1**.

```
vgcreate mymedia  /dev/sdb1 /dev/sdc1
```

The previous example sets up a logical group on two serial ATA hard drives, each with its own single partition. Alternatively, you can set up a volume group to span partitions on several hard drives. If you are using partitions for different functions, this approach gives you the flexibility for using all the space available across multiple hard drives.

The following example creates a group called **rabbit** consisting of three physical partitions, **/dev/hda3**, **/dev/hdb4**, and **/dev/hdb4**:

```
vgcreate rabbit  /dev/hda3 /dev/hdb2 /dev/hdb4
```

If you to later want to add a physical volume to a volume group, you use the **vgextend** command. The **vgextend** command adds a new partition to a logical group. In the following example, the partition **/dev/hda3** is added to the volume group **rabbit**. In effect, you are extending the size of the logical group by adding a new physical partition.

```
vgextend  rabbit  /dev/hda3
```

To add an entire new drive to a volume group, you would follow a similar procedure. The following example adds a fifth serial ATA hard drive, **sde**, first creating a physical volume on it and then adding that volume, **sde1**, to the **mymedia** volume group.

```
pvcreate /dev/sde1
vgextend mymedia /dev/sde1
```

To remove a physical partition, first remove it from its logical group. You may have to use the **pmove** command to move any data off the physical partition. Then use the **vgreduce** command to remove it from its logical group.

You can, in turn, remove a entire volume group by first deactivating it with **vgchange -a n** and then using the **vgremove** command.

Activating Volume Groups

Whereas in a standard file system structure, you mount and unmount hard disk partitions, with an LVM structure, you activate and deactivate entire volume groups. The group volumes are inaccessible until you activate them with the **vgchange** command with the **-a** option. To activate a group, first reboot your system, and then enter the **vgchange** command with the **-a** option and the **y** argument to activate the logical group (an **n** argument will deactivate the group).

```
vgchange -a  y  rabbit
```

Managing LVM Logical Volumes

To create logical volumes, you use the **lvcreate** command and then format your logical volume using the standard formatting command like **mkfs.ext3**. Keep in mind that all these actions can be performed at once by system-config-lvm (see Figure 31-3).

With the **-n** option you specify the volume's name, which functions like a hard disk partition's label. You use the **-L** option to specify the size of the volume. There are other options for implementing features such as whether to implement a linear, striped, or mirrored volume, or to specify the size of the extents to use. Usually the defaults work well. The following example creates a logical volume named **projects** on the **rabbit** logical group with a size of 20GB.

```
lvcreate -n projects  -L 20GB rabbit
```

The following example sets up a logical volume on the **mymedia** volume group that is 540 GB in size. The **mymedia** volume group is made up of two physical volumes, each on 320 GB hard drives. In effect the two hard drives are logically seen as one.

```
lvcreate -n myvideos  -L 540GB mymedia
```

Once you have created your logical volume, you then have to create a file system to use on it. The following creates an ext3 file system on the **myvideos** logical volume.

```
mkfs.ext3 myvideos
```

You can remove a logical volume with the **lvremove** command. With **lvextend**, you can increase the size of the logical volume, and **lvreduce** will reduce its size.

LVM Example for Multiple Hard Drives

With hard drives becoming cheaper and the demand for storage increasing, many systems now use multiple hard drives. To manage multiple hard drives, partitions on each had to individually managed, unless you implemented a RAID system. RAID allows you to treat several hard disks as one storage device, but there are restrictions on the size and kinds of devices you can combine. Without RAID, each hard drive had to be managed separately, with files having to fit into remaining storage as the drives filled up.

With LVM, you no longer have such restrictions. You can combine hard disks into a single storage device. This method is also flexible, letting you replace disks without losing any data, as well adding new disks to automatically increase your storage (or replace smaller disks with larger ones).

For example, say you want to add two hard disks to your system, but you want to treat the storage in both logically, instead of having to manage partitions in each. LVM lets you treat the combined storage of both hard drives as one giant pool. In effect, two 500GB drives could be treated as one 1-Terabyte storage device.

In this example, the Linux system makes use of three hard drives. The Linux system and boot partitions are on the first hard drive, **sda**. Added to this system are two hard drives, **sdb** and **sdc**, which will make up an LVM storage device to be added to the system.

Using the example in Figure 31-3, the steps involved in creating and accessing logical volumes are described in following commands. In this example there are two hard disk drives that will be combined into one LVM drive. The hard drives are Serial ATA drives identified on the systems as **sdb** and **sdc**. Each drive is first partitioned with a single LVM physical partition. Use a partition creation tool like **fdisk** or **parted** to create the physical partitions on the hard disks **sdb** and **sdc**. In this example, you create the partitions **sdb1** and **sdc1**.

Using system-config-lvm

The easiest way to set up and manage LVM drives is with system-config-lvm. The drives will first show up in the Uninitialized entry on the left pane. Select the partitions from the list of Uninitialized Entities under their **sdb** and **sdc** entries, and then select Initialize Disk from the Tools menu. This creates a physical volume partition on each.

You then create a logical group. Open a terminal window and enter the **vgcreate** command to create the logical group. When you restart system-config-lvm, the volume

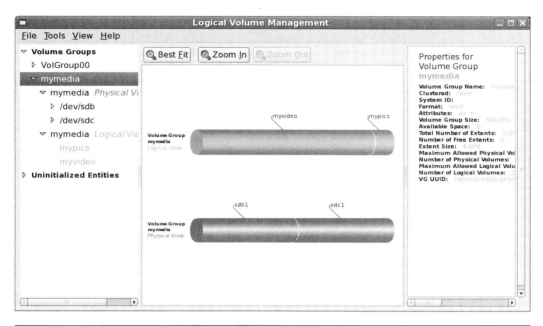

FIGURE 31-3 Logical Volume Management with two hard drives using system-config-lvm

group will then appear on the left pane. Expand it and select its physical view, and then click the Extend Volume Group button to open a window that lists the disks you can add. For this example, the **sdb1** and **sdc1** partitions were added.

You then create your logical volumes. In the example shown in Figure 31-4, two logical volumes have been created, **myvideos** and **mypics**, one at 540 GB and the other at 60 GB. They span two physical hard drives of 320 GB each, **sdb1** and **sdb2**.

To create a logical volume, you first select the logical group entry on the left hand pane. Then click Create New Logical Volume. This opens up a new window with a panel for creating a new logical volume. Figure 31-2 shows the creation of a **mypics** logical volume formatted with an **ext3** file system, mounted at **mydata**, using the remaining available space and a linear storage implementation. File system creation, formatting, and mounting are all specfied on the same screen.

Using LVM Commands

Using the LVM commands you can achieve the same effect.

You first initialize the physical volumes with the **pvcreate** command. The **sda1** and **sda2** partitions in the **sda** entry are reserved for the boot and root partitions and are never initialized.

```
pvcreate /dev/sda1 /dev/sdb1 /dev/sdc1
```

You then create the logical groups you want using the **vgcreate** command. In this case there is one logical group, **mymedia**. The **mymedia** group uses **sdb1** and **sdc1**. If you create

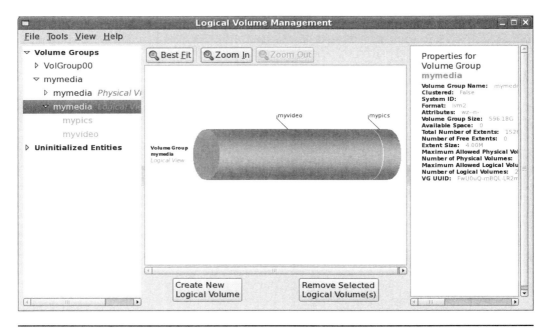

a physical volume later and want to add it to a volume group, you would use the **vgextend** command.

```
vgcreate mymedia   /dev/sdb1 /dev/sdc1
```

You can now create the logical volumes in each volume group, using the **lvcreate** command. In this example two logical volumes are created, one for **myvideos** and another for **mypics**. The corresponding **lvcreate** commands are shown here:

```
lvcreate  -n myvideo   -l 540GB    mymedia
lvcreate  -n mypics    -l 60GB     mymedia
```

Then you can activate the logical volumes. Reboot and use **vgchange** with the **-a y** option to active the logical volumes.

```
vgchange -a y mymedia
```

With system-config-lvm you can now make file systems for each logical volume.

```
mkfs.ext3 myvideo
mkfs.ext3 mypics
```

Then you can mount the logical volumes. In this example they are mounted to subdirectories of the same name in **/mydata**.

```
mount mypics  /mydata/mypics
mount myvideo /mydata/myvideo
```

Using LVM to Replace Drives

LVM can be very useful when you need to replace an older hard drive with a new one. Hard drives are expected to last about six years on the average. You might also want to just replace the older drive with a larger one (available hard drive storage sizes double every year or so). To replace a on-boot hard drive is very easy. To replace a boot drive becomes much more complicated.

To replace the drive, simply incorporate the new drive into your logical volume. The size of your logical volume will increase accordingly. You can use the **pmove** command to move data from the old drive to the new one. Then, issue commands to remove the old one. From the user and system point of view there will be no changes. Files from your old drive will still be stored in the same directories, though the actual storage will be implemented on the new drive.

Replacement with LVM becomes more complicated if you want to replace your boot drive, the hard drive your system starts up from and that holds your Linux kernel. The boot drive contains a special boot partition and the master boot record. The boot partition cannot be part of any LVM volume. You would first have to create a boot partition on the new drive using a partition tool like Parted or fdisk, labeling it as boot. The boot drive is usually very small, about 200 MB. Then mount the partition on your system and copy the contents of your **/boot** directory to it. Then you add the remainder of the disk to your logical volume and logically remove the old disk, copying the contents of the old disk to the new one. You would still have to boot with the linux rescue DVD (or install DVD in rescue mode) and issue the **grub-install** command to install the master boot record on your new drive. You can then boot from the new drive.

LVM Example for Partitions on Different Hard Drives

In a more complex implementation, you can use partitions on different hard drives for the same logical volumes. For example, if you have physical volumes consisting of the hard disk partitions **hda2**, **hda3**, **hdb1**, **hdb2**, and **hdb3** on two hard disks, **hda** and **hdb**, you could assign some of them to one logical group and others to another logical group. The partitions making up the different logical groups can be from different physical hard drives. For example, **hda2** and **hdb3** could belong to the logical group **turtle** and **hda3**, **hdb2**, and **hdb3** could make up a different logical group, say **rabbit**. The logical group name could be any name. For this example, old **hd** prefix for **IDE** is used.

Using the example in Figure 31-5, the steps involved in creating and accessing logical volumes are described in following commands. First use a partition creation tool like **fdisk** or **parted** to create the physical partitions on the hard disks **hda** and **hdb**. In this example, you create the partitions **hda1**, **hda2**, **hda3**, **hdb1**, **hdb2**, **hdb3**, and **hdb4**.

Then you initialize the physical volumes with the **pvcreate** command. The **hda1** and **hda2** partitions are reserved for the boot and root partitions and are not initialized.

```
pvcreate /dev/hda3 /dev/hdb1 /dev/hdb2
pvcreate /dev/hdb3 /dev/hdb4
```

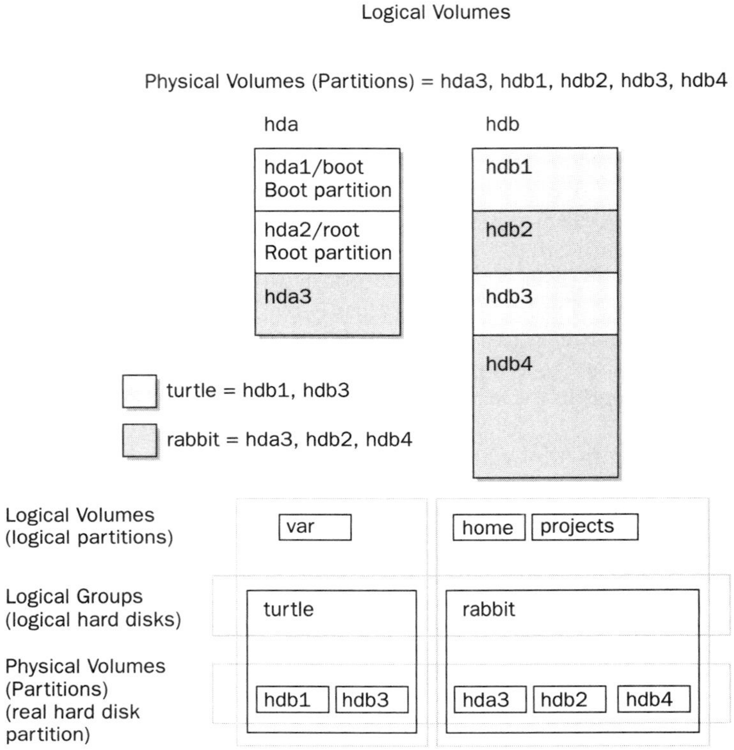

Figure 31-5
Logical volume using
multiple partitions on
different hard drives

Logical Volumes

Physical Volumes (Partitions) = hda3, hdb1, hdb2, hdb3, hdb4

You then create the logical groups you want using the **vgcreate** command. In this case there are two logical groups, **turtle** and **rabbit**. The **turtle** group uses **hdb1** and **hdb3**, and **rabbit** uses **hda3**, **hdb2**, and **hdb4**. If you create a physical volume later and want to add it to a volume group, you would use the **vgextend** command.

```
vgcreate turtle  /dev/hdb1 /dev/hdb3
vgcreate rabbit  /dev/hda3  /dev/hdb2 /dev/hdb4
```

You can now create the logical volumes in each volume group, using the **lvcreate** command.

```
lvcreate  -n var      -l 2000M    turtle
lvcreate  -n home     -l 50000M   rabbit
lvcreate  -n projects -l 20000M   rabbit
```

Then you can activate the logical volumes. Reboot and use **vgchange** with the **-a y** option to activate the logical volumes.

```
vgchange -a y turtle rabbit
```

You can now make file systems for each logical volume.

```
mkfs.ext3 var
mkfs.ext3 home
mkfs.ext3 projects
```

Then you can mount the logical volumes.

```
mount var   /var
mount home /home
mount projects /mnt/myprojects
```

Configuring RAID Devices

RAID is a method of storing data across several disks to provide greater performance and redundancy. In effect, you can have several hard disks treated as just one hard disk by your operating system. RAID then efficiently stores and retrieves data across all these disks, instead of having the operating system access each one as a separate file system. Lower-level details of storage and retrieval are no longer a concern of the operating system. This allows greater flexibility in adding or removing hard disks, as well as implementing redundancy in the storage system to provide greater reliability. With RAID, you can have several hard disks that are treated as one virtual disk, where some of the disks are used as real-time mirrors, duplicating data. You can use RAID in several ways, depending upon the degree of reliability you need. When you place data on multiple disks, I/O operations can overlap in a balanced way, improving performance. Because having multiple disks increases the mean time between failures (MTBF), storing data redundantly also increases fault tolerance.

RAID can be implemented on a hardware or software level. On a hardware level, you can have hard disks connected to a RAID hardware controller, usually a special PC card. Your operating system then accesses storage through the RAID hardware controller. Alternatively, you can implement RAID as a software controller, letting a software RAID controller program manage access to hard disks treated as RAID devices. The software version lets you use IDE hard disks as RAID disks. Linux uses the MD driver, supported in the 2.4 kernel, to implement a software RAID controller. Linux software RAID supports five levels (linear, 0, 1, 4, 5, and 6), whereas hardware RAID supports many more. Hardware RAID levels, such as 7–10, provide combinations of greater performance and reliability.

TIP *Before you can use RAID on your system, make sure it is supported on your kernel, along with the RAID levels you want to use. If not, you will have to reconfigure and install a RAID module for the kernel. Check the Multi-Driver Support component in your kernel configuration. You can specify support for any or all of the RAID levels.*

Hardware RAID Support: dmraid

With kernel 2.6, hardware RAID devices are supported with the *dmraid* module, which currently supports a wide range of hardware RAID devices. This module will map your system to hardware RAID devices such as those provided by Intel, Promise, and Silicon Magic, and often included on motherboards. You use your BIOS RAID configuration utility to set up your RAID devices as instructed by your hardware documentation. During a

Linux installation, the RAID devices are automatically detected and the dmraid module is loaded, selecting the appropriate drivers.

With the **dmraid** command you can detect and activate RAID devices. The following command would display your RAID devices:

```
dmraid -r
```

To list currently supported devices, use **dmraid** with the **-l** option.

```
dmraid -l
```

The dmraid tool is improved continually and may not work well with some RAID devices.

TIP *Keep in mind that many "hardware" RAID devices are, in effect, really software RAID (fakeraid). Though you configure them in the BIOS, the drivers operate as software, like any other drivers. In this respect they could be considered less flexible than a Linux software RAID solution, as well as depending directly on vendor support for any fixes for updates.*

Linux Software RAID Levels

Linux software RAID can be implemented at different levels, depending on whether you want organization, efficiency, redundancy, or reconstruction capability. Each capability corresponds to different RAID levels. For most levels, the size of the hard disk devices should be the same. For mirroring, RAID 1, disks of the same size are required, and for RAID 5 they are recommended. Linux software RAID supports five levels as shown in Table 31-1. RAID 5 does require at least three hard drives. (On Red Hat Enterprise Linux and Fedora, level 4 is implemented as part of level 5.)

RAID Level	Capability	Description
Linear	Appending	Simply treats RAID hard drives as one virtual drive with no striping, mirroring, or parity reconstruction.
0	Striping	Implements disk striping across drives with no redundancy.
1	Mirroring	Implements a high level of redundancy. Each drive is treated as mirror for all data.
5	Distributed parity	Implements data reconstruction capability using parity information. Parity information is distributed across all drives, instead of using a separate drive as in RAID 4. Requires at least three hard drives.
6	Distributed parity	Implements data reconstruction capability using dual distributed parity information. Dual sets of parity information are distributed across all drives. Can be considered an enhanced form of 5.
Multipath	Multiple access to devices	Supports multiple access to the same device.

TABLE 31-1 Linux Software RAID Levels

Linear

The *linear* level lets you simply organize several hard disks into one logical hard disk, providing a pool of continuous storage. Instead of being forced to set up separate partitions on each hard drive, in effect you have only one hard drive. The storage is managed sequentially. When one hard disk fills up, the next one is used. In effect, you are *appending* one hard disk to the other. This level provides no recovery capability. If you had a hard disk RAID array containing two 80 GB disks, after you used up the storage on one, you would automatically start on the next.

RAID 0: Striping

For efficiency, RAID stores data using disk *striping,* where data is organized into standardized stripes that can be stored across the RAID drives for faster access (level 0). RAID 0 also organizes your hard disks into common RAID devices but treats them like single hard disks, storing data randomly across all the disks. If you had a hard disk RAID array containing two 80 GB disks, you could access them as one 160 GB RAID device.

RAID 1: Mirroring

RAID level 1 implements redundancy through *mirroring.* In mirroring, the same data is written to each RAID drive. Each disk has a complete copy of all the data written, so that if one or more disks fail, the others still have your data. Though extremely safe, redundancy can be very inefficient and consumes a great deal of storage. For example, on a RAID array of two 80 GB disk drives, one disk is used for standard storage and the other is a real-time backup. This leaves you with only 80 GB for use on your system. Write operations also have to be duplicated across as many mirrored hard disks as are used by the RAID array, slowing down operations.

RAID 5 and 6: Distributed Parity

As an alternative to mirroring, data can be reconstructed using *parity information* in case of a hard drive crash. Parity information is saved instead of full duplication of the data. Parity information takes up the space equivalent of one drive, leaving most of the space on the RAID drives free for storage. RAID 5 combines both striping and parity (see RAID 4), where parity information is distributed across the hard drives, rather than in one drive dedicated to that purpose. This allows the use of the more efficient access method, striping. With both striping and parity, RAID 5 provides both fast access and recovery capability, making it the most popular RAID level used. For example, a RAID array of four 80 GB hard drives would be treated as one 320 GB hard drive with part of that storage (80 GB) used to hold parity information, giving 240 GB free. RAID 5 does require at least three hard drives.

RAID 6 operates the same as RAID 5, but it uses dual sets of parity information for the data, providing even greater restoration capability.

RAID 4: Parity

Though it is not supported in Red Hat Enterprise Linux and Fedora due to overhead costs, RAID 4, like RAID 5, supports a more compressed form of recovery using parity information instead of mirrored data. With RAID 4, parity information is kept on a separate disk, while the others are used for data storage, much like in a linear model.

TIP *Red Hat Enterprise Linux and Fedora also allow you to create and format RAID drives during installation. At that time, you can create your RAID partitions and devices.*

Multipath

Though not actually a RAID level, Multipath allows for multiple access to the same device. Should one controller fail, another can be used to access the device. In effect, you have controller-level redundancy. Support is implemented on Red Hat Enterprise Linux and Fedora using the **mdadmd** daemon. This is started with the **mdadmd** service script.

```
start mdadmd start
```

RAID Devices and Partitions: md and fd

A RAID device is named an **md** and uses the MD driver. These devices are already defined on your Linux system in the **/etc/dev** directory, starting with **md0**: **/dev/md0** is the first RAID device, and **/dev/md1** is the second, and so on. Each RAID device, in turn, uses hard disk partitions, where each partition contains an entire hard disk. These partitions are usually referred to as RAID disks, whereas a RAID device is an array of the RAID disks it uses.

When creating a RAID partition, you should set the partition type to be **fd**, instead of the 83 for the standard Linux partition. The **fd** type is that used by RAID for automatic detection.

Booting from a RAID Device

As part of the installation process, Fedora lets you create RAID devices from which you can also boot your system. Your Linux system will be configured to load RAID kernel support and automatically detect your RAID devices. The boot loader will be installed on your RAID device, meaning on all the hard disks making up that device.

Fedora does not support booting from RAID 5, only RAID 1. This means that if you want to use RAID 5 and still boot from RAID disks, you will need to create at least two (or more if you want) RAID devices using corresponding partitions for each device across your hard disks. One device would hold your **/boot** partition and be installed as a RAID 1 device. This RAID 1 device would be the first RAID device, **md0**, consisting of the first partition on each hard disk. The second RAID device, **md1**, could then be a RAID 5 device. It would consist of corresponding partitions on the other hard disks. Your system could then boot from the RAID 1 device but use the RAID 5 device.

If you do not create RAID disks during installation, but create them later and want to boot from them, you will have to make sure your system is configured correctly. The RAID devices need to be created with persistent superblocks. Support for the RAID devices has to be enabled in the kernel. On Red Hat Enterprise Linux and Fedora, this support is enabled as a module. Difficulties occur if you are using RAID 5 for your /(root) partition. This partition contains the RAID 5 module, but to access the partition; you have to have already loaded the RAID 5 module. To work around this limitation, you can create a RAM disk in the **/boot** partition that contains the RAID 5 module. Use the **mkinitrd** command to create the RAM disk and the **-with** option to specify the module to include.

```
mkinitrd --preload raid5 --with=raid5 raid-ramdisk 2.6.9-1
```

RAID Administration: mdadm

Red Hat Enterprise Linux and Fedora use the mdadm tool to manage and monitor RAID devices. It replaces the older raid tools used on previous versions of Red Hat Enterprise Linux and Fedora. The mdadm tool is an all-purpose means of creating, monitoring, administering, and fixing RAID devices. You can run commands directly to create and format RAID disks. It also runs as a daemon to monitor and detect problems with the devices.

The mdadm tool has seven different modes of operation, each with its own set of options, including monitor with the -**f** option to run it as a daemon, or create with the -**1** option to set a RAID level for a disk. Table 31-2 lists the different modes of operation. Check the mdadm Man page for a detailed listing of the options for each mode.

Creating and Installing RAID Devices

If you created your RAID devices and their partitions during the installation process, you should already have working RAID devices. Your RAID devices will be configured in the **/etc/mdadm.conf** file, and the status of your RAID devices will be listed in the **/proc/mdstat** file. You can manually start or stop your RAID devices with the **raidstart** and **mdadm** commands. The -**a** option operates on all of them, though you can specify particular devices if you want.

To create a new RAID device manually for an already-installed system, follow these steps:

- Make sure that your kernel supports the RAID level you want for the device you are creating.
- If you have not already done so, create the RAID disks (partitions) you will use for your RAID device.
- Create your RAID device with **mdadm** command in the build or create mode. The array will also be activated.
- Alternatively, you can configure your RAID device (**/dev/md**n) in the **/etc/mdadm .conf** file, specifying the RAID disks to use, and then use the **mdadm** command specifying the RAID device to create.
- Create a file system on the RAID device (**mkfs**) and then mount it.

Adding a Separate RAID File System

If you just want to add a RAID file system to a system that already has a standard boot partition, you can dispense with the first RAID 1 partition. Given two hard disks to use for the RAID file system, you would just need two partitions, one for each disk, **/dev/sda1** and **/dev/sdb1**.

```
ARRAY /dev/md0   devices=/dev/sda1,/dev/sdb1   level=5 num-devices=2
```

Mode	Description
assemble	Assemble RAID array from devices.
build	Build array without per-device superblocks.
create	Build array with per-device superblocks.
manage	Manage array devices, adding or removing disks.
misc	Specific operations on a device, such as making it read only.
monitor	Monitor arrays for changes and act on them (used for RAID 1, 4, 5, 6).
grow	Change array size, as when replacing smaller devices with larger ones.

TABLE 31-2   mdadm Modes

You would then create the array with the following command:

```
mdadm -C /dev/md0 -n2 /dev/sda1 /dev/sdb1 -l5
```

You can then format and mount your RAID device.

Creating Hard Disk Partitions: fd

To add new RAID devices or to create them in the first place, you need to manually create the hard disk partitions they will use, and then configure RAID devices to use those partitions. To create a hard disk partition for use in a RAID array, use **fdisk** or **parted** and specify **fd** as the file system type. You invoke **fdisk** or **parted** with the device name of the hard disk you want to create the partition on. Be sure to specify **fd** as the partition type. The following example invokes **fdisk** for the hard disk **/dev/hdc** (the first hard disk on the secondary IDE connection):

```
fdisk /dev/hdc
```

Though technically partitions, these hard disk devices are referred to as disks in RAID configuration documentation and files.

NOTE *You can also use gparted or qtparted to create your hard disk partitions. These tools provide a GUI interface for* **parted** *(Applications | System Tools menu).*

Configuring RAID: /etc/mdadm.conf

Once you have your disks, you then need to configure them as RAID devices. RAID devices are configured in the **/etc/mdadm.conf** file, with options as shown in Table 31-3. This file will be used by the **mdadm** command in the create mode to create the RAID device. In the **/etc/mdadm.conf** file, you create both DEVICE and ARRAY entries. The DEVICE entries list the RAID devices. The ARRAY entries list the RAID arrays and their options. This example implements a simple array on two disks. Serial ATA drives are used that have a device name prefix **sd** instead of **hd**.

```
DEVICE  /dev/sda1 /dev/sdb1
```

You can list more that one device for a DEVICE entry, as well as have separate DEVICE entries. You can also specify multiple devices using file matching symbols, like *, ?, or []. The following would specify all the partitions on **sda** drive as RAID devices:

```
DEVICE  /dev/sha*  /dev/sdb1
```

For a **ARRAY** entry, you specify the name of the RAID device you are configuring, such as **/dev/md0** for the first RAID device. You then add configuration options such as **devices** to list the partitions that make up the array, **level** for the RAID level, and **num-devices** for the number of devices. The first array holds only the boot partition and uses RAID level 1, whereas the second array uses two partitions and is set to RAID level 5.

```
ARRAY /dev/md0   devices=/dev/sda2,/dev/sdb1  level=5 num-devices=2
```

Directive or Option	Description
DEVICE *devices-list*	Partitions and drives used for RAID devices.
ARRAY	ARRAY configuration section for a particular RAID device.
level=*num*	The RAID level for the RAID device, such as 0, 1, 4, 5, and −1 (linear).
devices=*disk-device-list*	The disk devices (partitions) that make up the RAID array.
num-devices=*count*	Number of RAID devices in an array. Each RAID device section must have this directive. The maximum is 12.
spare-group=*name*	Text name for a spare group, whose devices can be used for other arrays.
auto=*option*	Automatically create specified devices if they do not exist. You can create traditional nonpartitioned (**yes** or **md** option) or the newer partitionable arrays (**mdp** or **part** option). For partitionable arrays the default is 4, which you can change.
super-minor	Minor number of the array superblock, same as md device number.
uuid=*UUID-number*	UUID identifier stored in array superblock, used to identify the RAID array. Can be used to reference an array in commands.
MAILADDR	Monitor mode, mail address where alerts are sent.
PROGRAM	Monitor mode, program to run when events occur.

TABLE 31-3   mdadm.conf Options

The preceding example configures the RAID array **/dev/md0** as two disks (partitions) using **/dev/sda1** and **/dev/sdb1** and is configured for RAID 5 (**level=5**).

Creating a RAID Array

You can create a RAID array either using options specified with the **mdadm** command or using configurations listed in the **/etc/mdadm.conf** file. Use of the **/etc/mdadm.conf** file is not required, though it does make RAID creation more manageable, especially for large or complex arrays. Once you have created your RAID devices, your RAID device will be automatically activated. The following command creates a RAID array, **/dev/md1**, using two devices, **/dev/sda2** and **/dev/sdb1**, at level 5.

```
mdadm --create /dev/md1 --raid-devices=2 /dev/sda1 /dev/sdb1 --level=5
```

Each option has a corresponding short version, as shown in Table 31-4. The same command is shown here with single-letter options.

```
mdadm -C /dev/md1 -n2 /dev/sda1 /dev/sdb1 -l5
```

If you have configured your RAID devices in the **/etc/mdadm.conf** file, you then use the **mdadm** command in the create mode to create your RAID devices. **mdadm** takes as its argument the name of the RAID device, such as **/dev/md0** for the first RAID device. It then locates the entry for that device in the **/etc/mdadm.conf** file and uses that configuration

mdadm –create Option	Description
-n --raid-devices	Number of RAID devices
-l --level	RAID level
-C --create	Create mode
-c --chunk	Specify chunk (stripe) size in powers of 2; default is 64KB
-x --spare-devices	Number of spare devices in the array
-z --size	Size of blocks used in devices, by default set to the smallest device if not the same size
-p --parity	Specify the parity algorithm; left-symmetric is used by default

TABLE 31-4 The mdadm --create Options

information to create the RAID file system on that device. You can specify an alternative configuration file with the **-c** option, if you wish. **mdadm** operates as a kind of **mkfs** command for RAID devices, initializing the partitions and creating the RAID file systems. Any data on the partitions making up the RAID array will be erased.

```
mdadm  --create /dev/md0
```

Creating Spare Groups
Linux Software RAID now allows RAID arrays to share their spare devices. This means that if arrays belong to the same spare group, then should a device in one array fail, it can automatically use the spare in another array. Spare devices from any array can be used in another as needed. You set the spare group that an array belongs to with the **--spare-group** option. The **mdadm** monitoring mode will detect a failed device in an array and automatically replace it with a spare device from arrays in the same spare group. The first command in the next example creates a spare drive called **/dev/hdd1** for the **/dev/md0** array and labels it **mygroup**. In the second command, array **/dev/md1** has no spare drive but belongs to the same spare group as array **/dev/md0**. Should a drive in **/dev/md1** fail, it can automatically use the spare device, **/dev/hdd1**, from **/dev/md0**. The following code lines are really two lines, each beginning with **mdadm**:

```
mdadm --create /dev/md0 --raid-devices=3 /dev/hda1 /dev/hdc1 -x
      /dev/hdd1 --level=5 --spare-group=mygroup
mdadm --create /dev/md1 --raid-devices=2 /dev/hda2 /dev/hdc2 --level=5
      --spare-group=mygroup
```

Creating a File System
Once the RAID devices are activated, you can then create file systems on the RAID devices and mount those file systems. The following example creates a standard Linux file system on the **/dev/md0** device:

```
mkfs.ext3 /dev/md0
```

In the following example, the user then creates a directory called **/myraid** and mounts the RAID device there:

```
mkdir /myraid
mount /dev/md0 /myraid
```

If you plan to use your RAID device for maintaining your user directories and files, you would mount the RAID device as your **/home** partition. Such a mounting point might normally be used if you created your RAID devices when installing your system. To transfer your current home directories to a RAID device, first back them up on another partition, and then mount your RAID device, copying your home directories to it.

Managing RAID Arrays

You can manage RAID arrays with the **mdadm** manage mode operations. In this mode you can add or remove devices in arrays, as well as mark ones as failed. The **--add** option lets you add a device to an active array, essentially a hot swap operation.

```
mdadm /dev/md0 -add /dev/sdd1
```

To remove a device from an active array, you first have to mark it as failed with the **--fail** option and then remove it with **--remove**.

```
mdadm /dev/md0 --fail /dev/sdb1 --remove /dev/sdb1
```

Starting and Stopping RAID Arrays

To start an already existing RAID array, you use **mdadm** with the assemble mode (newly created arrays are automatically started). To do so directly on the command line requires that you also know what devices make up the array, listing them after the RAID array.

```
mdadm -A /dev/md1 /dev/sda2   /dev/sdb1
```

It is easier to configure your RAID arrays in the **/etc/mdadm.conf** file. With the scan option, **-s**, **mdadm** will then read array information from the **/etc/mdadm.conf** file. If you do not specify a RAID array, all arrays will be started.

```
mdadm -As /dev/md0
```

To stop a RAID array, you use the **-S** option.

```
mdadm -S /dev/md0
```

Monitoring RAID Arrays

As a daemon, **mdadm** is started and stopped using the **mdmonitor** service script in **/etc/init.d**. This will invoke **mdadm** in the monitor mode, detecting any problems that arise and logging reports as well as taking appropriate action.

```
service mdadm start
```

You can monitor devices directly by invoking **mdadm** with the monitor mode.

```
mdadm --monitor /dev/md0
```

Monitor-related options can be set in the **/etc/mdadm.conf** file. MAILADDR sets the mail address where notification of RAID events are sent. PROGRAM sets the program to use if events occur.

If you decide to change your RAID configuration or add new devices, you first have to deactivate your currently active RAID devices. To deactivate a RAID device, you use the **mdadm** command in the misc mode. Be sure to close any open files and unmount any file systems on the device first.

```
umount /dev/md0
mdadm -S /dev/md0
```

Configuring Bootable RAID

Once you have your disks, you then need to configure them as RAID devices. RAID devices are configured in the **/etc/mdadm.conf** file, with options as shown in Table 31-3. This file will be used by the **mdadm** command in the create mode to create the RAID device. In the **/etc/mdadm.conf** file, you create both DEVICE and ARRAY entries. The DEVICE entries list the RAID devices. The ARRAY entries list the RAID arrays and their options. This example implements a simple array on two disks, with one partition, sda1, reserved for use as the boot partition. Serial ATA drives are used that have a device name prefix **sd** instead of **hd**. Keep in mind that the two partitions making up the second RAID array have to be the same size.

```
DEVICE  /dev/sda1 /dev/sda2 /dev/sdb1
```

You can list more than one device for a DEVICE entry, as well as have separate DEVICE entries. You can also specify multiple devices using file matching symbols, like *, ?, or []. The following would specify all the partitions on **sda** drive as RAID devices:

```
DEVICE  /dev/sha*  /dev/sdb1
```

For a **ARRAY** entry, you specify the name of the RAID device you are configuring, such as **/dev/md0** for the first RAID device. You then add configuration options such as **devices** to list the partitions that make up the array, **level** for the RAID level, and **num-devices** for the number of devices. The first array holds only the boot partition and uses RAID level 1, whereas the second array uses two partitions and is set to RAID level 5.

```
ARRAY /dev/md0    devices=/dev/sda1  level=1 num-devices=1
ARRAY /dev/md1    devices=/dev/sda2,/dev/sdb1  level=5 num-devices=2
```

The preceding example configures the RAID array **/dev/md0** as a RAID 1 (**level=1**) device. Two disks (partitions) make up second RAID array, **/dev/md1** using **/dev/sda2** and **/dev/sdb1**. It is configured for RAID 5 (**level=5**).

You can create a RAID array either using options specified with the **mdadm** command or using configurations listed in the **/etc/mdadm.conf** file. Use of the **/etc/mdadm.conf** file is not required, though it does make RAID creation more manageable, especially for large or complex arrays. Once you have created your RAID devices, your RAID device will be automatically activated. The following command creates a RAID array, **/dev/md1**, using two devices, **/dev/sda2** and **/dev/sdb1**, at level 5.

```
mdadm --create /dev/md1 --raid-devices=2 /dev/sda2 /dev/sdb1 --level=5
```

Each option has a corresponding short version, as shown in Table 31-4. The same command is shown here with single-letter options.

```
mdadm -C /dev/md1 -n2 /dev/sda2 /dev/sdb1 -l5
```

For the first array in the previous example you would use:

```
mdadm -C /dev/md0 -n2 /dev/sdaa -l1
```

To more efficiently use space, you could use corresponding hard disk partitions as described in the next section.

Corresponding Hard Disk Partitions

The term *device* can be confusing, because it is also used to refer to the particular hard disk partitions that make up a RAID device. In fact, a software RAID device is an array of hard disk partitions, where each partition can, but need not, take up an entire hard disk. In that case, you can think of a RAID device as consisting of a set (array) of hard disks (devices). In practice, the hard disks in your RAID configuration would normally contain several corresponding hard disk partitions, each set having the same size. Each set of corresponding partitions would make up a RAID device. So you could have several RAID devices using the same set of hard disks. This is particularly true for Linux partition configurations, where different system directories are placed in their own partitions. For example, **/boot** could be in one partition, **/home** in another, and **/** (the root) in yet another partition. This approach also lets you set up a RAID5 implementation using just two physical hard drives. In effect you could have three raid devices using partitions on two hard drives (see Figure 31-6). You would, though, loose much of the reliability of a basic three drive RAID5 implementation.

To set up RAID devices so that you have separate partitions for **/boot**, **/home**, and **/** (root), you need to create three different RAID devices, say **md0** for **/boot**, **md1** for **/home**, and **md2** for the root. If you have two hard disks, for example **hda** and **hdc**, each would have three partitions, **/boot**, **/home**, and **/**. The first RAID device, **md0**, would consist of the two **/boot** partitions, the one on **hda** and the one on **hdb**. Similarly, the second RAID device, **md1**, would be made up of the two root partitions, **/**, the one on **hda** and the other on **hdc**. **md3** would consist of the **/home** partitions on **hda** and **hdc** (see Figure 31-6).

When you create the partitions for a particular RAID device, it is important to make sure that each partition has the same size. For example, the **/** partition used for the **md0** device on the **hda** disk must have the same size as the corresponding **md0** partition on the **hdc** disk. So if the **md1** partition on **hda** is 20 GB, then its corresponding partition on **hdc** must also be 20 GB. If **md2** is 100 GB on one drive, its corresponding partitions on all other drives must also be 100 GB.

TIP *During installation, Disk Druid supports the Clone tool that lets you automatically create the corresponding partitions on other hard disks based on one already set up. In effect, you set up the RAID partitions for each RAID device on one hard disk, and then use the Clone tool to create their corresponding partitions on your other hard disks.*

FIGURE 31-6
RAID devices

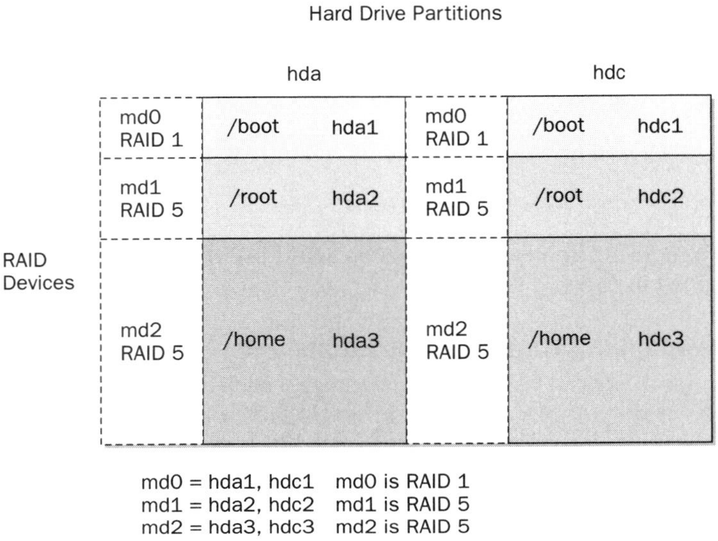

Hard Drive Partitions

md0 = hda1, hdc1   md0 is RAID 1
md1 = hda2, hdc2   md1 is RAID 5
md2 = hda3, hdc3   md2 is RAID 5

RAID Example

Figure 31-6 shows a simple RAID configuration with three RAID devices using corresponding partitions on two hard disks for **/boot**, **/** (root), and **/home** partitions. The boot partition is configured as a RAID 1 device because systems can be booted only from a RAID 1 device, not RAID 5. The other partitions are RAID 5 devices, a more commonly used RAID access method (The example uses the old **hd** prefix for drives).

You could set up such a system during installation, selecting and formatting your RAID devices and their partitions using Disk Druid. The steps described here assume you have your system installed already on a standard IDE drive and are setting up RAID devices on two other IDE disk drives. You can then copy your file from your standard drive to your RAID devices.

First you create the hard disk partitions using a partition tool like **parted** or **fdisk**. Then configure the three RAID devices in the **/etc/mdadm.conf** file.

```
DEVICE  /dev/hda1 /dev/hda2 /dev/hda3 /dev/hdc1 /dev/hdc2 /dev/hdc3

ARRAY /dev/md0    devices=/dev/hda1,/dev/hdc1  level=1 num-devices=2
ARRAY /dev/md1    devices=/dev/hda2,/dev/hdc2  level=5 num-devices=2
ARRAY /dev/md2    devices=/dev/hda3,/dev/hdc3 level=5 num-devices=2
```

Then create your RAID devices with **mdadm**, which will then be automatically activated.

```
mdadm --create /dev/md0 /dev/md1 /dev/md2
```

Create your file systems on the RAID devices.

```
mkfs.ext3 md0 md1 md2
```

You can then migrate the **/boot**, **/**, and **/home** files from your current hard disk to your RAID devices. Install your boot loader on the first RAID device, **md0**, and load the root file system from the second RAID device, **md1**.

Alternatively, you can first create the arrays with the **mdadm** command and then generate the ARRAY entries for an **/etc/mdadm.conf** file from the created RAID information to later manage your arrays, adding or removing components. The following commands would create the three RAID devices in the previous example:

```
mdadm --create /dev/md0 --raid-devices=2 /dev/hda1 /dev/hdc1 --level=1
mdadm -C /dev/md2 -n3 /dev/hda2 /dev/hdc2 -l5
mdadm -C /dev/md2 -n3 /dev/hda3 /dev/hdc3 -l5
```

You can then generate the ARRAY entries for the **/etc/mdadm.conf** file directly using the following command. You will still have to edit **mdadm.conf** and add the DEVICE entries as well as the monitoring entries, like MAILADDR.

```
mdadm --detail --scan > /etc/mdadm.conf
```

PART VI

Devices and Modules: udev, HAL, and MAKEDEV

All devices, such as printers, terminals, and CD-ROMs, are connected to your Linux operating system through special files called *device files*. Such a file contains all the information your operating system needs to control the specified device. This design introduces great flexibility. The operating system is independent of the specific details for managing a particular device; the specifics are all handled by the device file. The operating system simply informs the device what task it is to perform, and the device file tells it how. If you change devices, you have to change only the device file, not the whole system.

To install a device on your Linux system, you need a device file for it, software configuration such as that provided by a configuration tool, and kernel support—usually supplied by a module or support that is already compiled and built into the kernel. Device files are not handled in a static way. They are dynamically generated as needed by udev and managed by HAL. Previously a device file was created for each possible device, leading to a very large number of device files in the **/etc/dev** directory. Now, your system will detect the same devices it uses and create device files for giving you a much smaller listing of device files. Both udev and HAL are hotplug systems, with udev used for creating devices and HAL designed for providing information about them, as well as managing the configuration for removable devices such as those with file systems and those for USB card readers and CD-ROMs.

Managing devices is at the same time easier but much more complex. You now have to use udev and HAL to configure devices, though much of this is automatic. Device information is maintained in a special device file system called sysfs located at **/sys**. This is a virtual file system like **/proc** and is used to keep track of all devices supported by the kernel. Several of the resources you may need to consult and directories that may have to be used are listed in Table 32-1.

Resource	Description
/etc/sysconfig/hwconf	Hardware configuration and listing for your system
/sys	The sysfs file system listing configuration information for all the devices on your system
/proc	An older process file system listing kernel information, including device information
www.kernel.org/pub/linux/docs/ device-list/devices.txt	Linux device names
www.kernel.org/pub/linux/utils/kernel/ hotplug/udev.html	The udev Web site
fedora.redhat.com/docs/udev	Fedora-specific udev information
/etc/udev	The udev configuration directory
www.freedesktop.org/wiki/Software_2fhal	The HAL Web site
/etc/hal	The HAL configuration directory
/usr/share/hal/fdi	The HAL device information files, for configuring HAL information support and policies
/etc/hal/fdi	The HAL system administrator's device information files

TABLE 32-1   Device Resources

Hardware Device Installation: Kudzu

Hardware devices are automatically detected by the hardware probing tool known as Kudzu, a tool that detects and configures new or changed hardware on a system. Kudzu is run when you boot to configure new hardware devices and detect removed ones. You can also run Kudzu manually. When you start Kudzu, it detects the current hardware and checks it against a database stored in **/etc/sysconfig/hwconf**. It then determines if any hardware has been added to or removed from the system. When it detects new or added hardware, Kudzu will, if needed, invoke the appropriate configuration tool for the device, such as system-config-display for video cards, or system-config-keyboard for keyboards. For simple hardware configurations like CD-ROMs, Kudzu just links the **cdrom** device symbolic link to the new device, **/dev/cdrom**.

Kudzu then updates its database in **/etc/sysconfig/hwconf**. If a removed device is detected, the **hwconf** file is updated accordingly. If the device was installed simply with a device link such as **/dev/cdrom** or **/dev/mouse**, that link is removed. In the case of network cards, alias entries like that for **eth0** will be removed.

Device Information: /sys, /proc, and /etc/sysconfig/hwconf

Kudzu maintains a complete profile of all your installed hardware devices in the **/etc/sysconfig/hwconf** file (**/etc/sysconfig** is discussed in Chapter 27). As noted previously, this file is updated by Kudzu (`kudzu`); your new hardware is added and old devices removed. Entries define configuration variables such as a device's class (video, CD-ROM, hard drive, and so on), the bus it uses (PCI, IDE, and so on), its device name (such as **sdd** or **st0**), the drivers it uses, and a description of the device. A mouse entry is shown here:

```
class: MOUSE
bus: PSAUX
detached: 0
device: psaux
driver: generic3ps/2
desc: "Generic 3 Button Mouse (PS/2)"
```

The sysfs File System: /sys

The system file system is designed to hold detailed information about system devices. This information can be used by hotplug tools like udev to create device interfaces as they are needed. Instead of having a static and complete manual configuration for a device, the sysfs system is used to maintain configuration information about the device, which is then used as needed by the hotplugging system to create device interfaces when a device is attached to the system. More and more devices are now removable, and many are meant to be attached temporarily (cameras, for example). Instead of maintaining separate static and dynamic methods for configuring devices, Red Hat Enterprise and Fedora make all devices structurally hotplugged.

The sysfs file system is a virtual file system that provides the a hierarchical map of your kernel-supported devices such as PCI devices, buses, and block devices, as well as supporting kernel modules. The **classes** subdirectory will list all your supported devices by category, such as net and sound devices. With sysfs your system can easily determine the device file a particular device is associated with. This is very helpful for managing removable devices as well as dynamically managing and configuring devices as HAL and udev do. The sysfs file system is used by udev to dynamically generate needed device files in the **/dev** directory, as well as by HAL to manage removable device files as needed. The **/sys** file system type is sysfs. The **/sys** subdirectories organize your devices into different categories. The file system is used by **systool** to display a listing of your installed devices. The tool is part of the **sysfsutils** package. The following example will list all your system devices.

```
systool
```

Like **/proc**, the **/sys** directory resides only in memory, but it is still mounted in the **/etc/fstab** file. Fedora will include such an entry for you.

```
none    /sys        sysfs       defaults    0       0
```

The proc File System: /proc

The **/proc** file system (see Chapter 30) is an older file system that was used to maintain information about kernel processes, including devices. It maintains special information files for your devices, though many of these are now supported by the sysfs file system. The **/proc/devices** file lists your installed character and block devices along with their major numbers. IRQs, DMAs, and I/O ports currently used for devices are listed in the **interrupts**, **dma**, and **ioports** files, respectively. Certain files list information covering several devices, such as **pci**,

File	Description
/proc/devices	Lists the device drivers configured for the currently running kernel
/proc/dma	Displays the DMA channels currently used
/proc/interrupts	Displays the IRQs (interrupts) in use
/proc/ioports	Shows the I/O ports in use
/proc/pci	Lists PCI devices
/proc/asound	Lists sound devices
/proc/ide	Directory for IDE devices
/proc/net	Directory for network devices

TABLE 32-2   Proc Device Information Files

which lists all your PCI devices, and **sound**, which lists all your sound devices. The **sound** file lists detailed information about your sound card. Several subdirectories, such as **net**, **ide**, and **scsi**, contain information files for different devices. Certain files hold configuration information that can be changed dynamically, such as the IP packet forwarding capability and the maximum number of files. You can change these values with the sysctl tool (Kernel Tuning in the System Tools menu) or by manually editing certain files. Table 32-2 lists several device-related **/proc** files (see Chapter 32 for other entries).

udev: Device Files

Devices are now treated as *hotplugged,* meaning they can be easily attached and removed. Their configuration is dynamically detected and does not rely on manual administrative settings. The hotplug tool used to detect device files is udev, user devices. Each time your system is booted, udev will automatically detect your devices and generate device files for them in the **/etc/dev** directory. This means that the **/etc/dev** directory and its files are recreated each time you boot. It is a dynamic directory, no longer static. udev uses a set of rules to direct how device files are to be generated, including any corresponding symbolic links. These are located in the **/etc/udev/rules.d** file. You can find out more about udev at **www.kernel.org/pub/linux/utils/kernel/hotplug/udev.html** and **docs.fedoraproject.org/udev**.

As part of the hotplug system, udev will automatically detect kernel devices that are added or removed from the system. When the device interface is first created, its corresponding **sysfs** file is located and read, determining any additional attributes such as serial numbers and device major and minor numbers that can be used to uniquely identify the device. These can be used as keys in udev rules to create the device interface. Once the device is created, it is listed in the udev database, which keeps track of currently installed devices.

If a device is added, udev is called by hotplug. It checks the sysfs file for that device for the major and minor numbers, if provided. It then uses the rules in its rules file to create the device file and any symbolic links to create the device file in **/dev**, with permissions specified for the device in the udev permissions rules. Once the device file is created, udev runs the programs in **/etc/dev.d**.

NOTE *When the system starts, it invokes **/sbin/udevstart**, which runs udev and creates all the kernel devices making device files in the **/dev** directory. **udevstart** is first run by initrd and then again by rc.sysinit to simulate a hotplug process on system startup.*

As **/etc/dev** is now dynamic, any changes you would make manually to the **/etc/dev** directory will be lost when you reboot. This includes the creation of any symbolic links such as **/dev/cdrom** that many software applications use. Instead, such symbolic links have to be configured udev rules files located in the **/etc/udev/rules.d** directory. Default rules are already in place for symbolic links, but you can create rules to add your own.

udev Configuration

The configuration file for udev is **/etc/udev/udev.conf**. Here are set global udev options such as the location of the udev database; the defaults for device permissions, owner, and group; and the location of udev rules files. The udev tool uses the udev **rules.d** file to dynamically create your device files. Be very careful in making any changes, particularly to rules file locations. Support for all devices on your system relies on these rules. The default **udev.conf** file is shown here:

```
# udev.conf
# The main config file for udev
#
# This file can be used to override some of udev's default values
# for where it looks for files, and where it places device nodes.
#
# WARNING: changing any value can cause serious system breakage!

# udev_root - where in the filesystem to place the device nodes
udev_root="/dev/"

# udev_db - The name and location of the udev database.
udev_db="/dev/.udev.tdb"

# udev_rules - The name and location of the udev rules file
udev_rules="/etc/udev/rules.d/"

#udev_permissions - The name,location of the udev permission file
udev_permissions="/etc/udev/permissions.d/"

# default_mode - set the default mode for all nodes that have no
# explicit match in the permissions file
default_mode="0600"

#default_owner - set the default owner for all nodes that have no
#  explicit match in the permissions file
default_owner="root"

#default_group - set the default group for all nodes that have no
# explicit match in the permissions file
default_group="root"

# udev_log - set to "yes" if you want logging, else "no"
udev_log="no"
```

The location of the device files directory is set by **udev_root** to **/dev**. This is the official device directory on Linux systems and should never be changed. The **udev_rules** file specifies where the rules files that udev uses to generate the device files are located. The **udev_log** option lets you turn logging on and off, useful for detecting errors. The **udev_permissions** option specifies the location of the permission files that hold the permissions to be applied to certain devices. Default permissions are already listed for you. In the case where a device has no permission listed in a permission file, then the defaults set by **default_mode**, **default_owner** and **default_group** are used. These function more like fail-safes. A device permission should be set in a udev permission file.

Device Names and udev Rules: /etc/udev/rules.d

The name of a device file is designed to reflect the task of the device. Printer device files begin with **lp** for "line print." Because you could have more than one printer connected to your system, the particular printer device files are distinguished by two or more numbers or letters following the prefix **lp**, such as **lp0**, **lp1**, **lp2**. The same is true for terminal device files. They begin with the prefix **tty**, for "teletype," and are further distinguished by numbers or letters such as **tty0**, **tty1**, **ttyS0**, and so on. You can obtain a complete listing of the current device filenames and the devices for which they are used from the kernel.org web site at **www.kernel.org/pub/linux/docs/device-list/devices.txt**.

With udev, device names are determined dynamically by rules listed in the udev rules files. These are located in **/etc/udev/rules.d**. The rules files that you will find in this directory are generated by your system during installation. You should never edit them. If you need to add rules of your own, you should create your own rules file. The rules files are named, beginning with a number to establish priority. They are read sequentially, with the first rules overriding any conflicting later ones. All rules files have a **.rules** extension. The primary rules file is **50-udev.rules**. Here you will find the rules for most of your system devices. Other rules files may be set up for more specialized devices like **60-rules-libsane** for scanners, **60-rules-libmtp** for music players, **60-pcmcia.rules** for PCMCIA devices, and **90-alsa.rules** for the sound driver**.**

The rules files already present in the **rules.d** directory have been provided for your Fedora distribution and are designed specifically for it. You should never modify these rules. To customize your setup, create your own separate rules files in **/etc/udev/ruled.d**. In your rules file you would normally define only symlinks, using SYMLINK fields alone, as described in the following sections. These set up symbolic links to devices, letting you access them with other device names. NAME fields are used to create the original device interface, a task usually left to udev itself.

Each line maps a device attribute to a device name, as well as specifying any symbolic names (links). Attributes are specified using keys, of which there may be more than one. If all the keys match a device, then the associated name is used for it and a device file of that name will be generated. Instead of listing a device name, a program or script may be specified instead to generate the name. This is often the case for DVD/CD-ROM devices, where the device name could be a dvdwriter, cdwriter, cdrom, or dvdrom.

The rules consist of a comma-separated list of fields. A field consists of a field name and its assigned valued. The udev fields are listed in Table 32-3. Check the udev Man page for detailed descriptions.

Field	Description
BUS	Match the bus type of the device. (The sysfs device bus must be able to be determined by a "device" symlink.)
DRIVER	Match the device driver name.
ID	Match the device number on the bus, for instance, the PCI bus ID.
KERNEL	Match the kernel device name.
NAME	The name of the node to be created, or the name the network interface should be renamed to.
OWNER, GROUP, MODE	The permissions for the device.
PLACE	Match the location on the bus, such as the physical port of a USB device.
PROGRAM	Use an external program to determine the device. This key is valid if the program returns successful. The string returned by the program may be additionally matched with the RESULT key.
RESULT	Match the returned string of the last PROGRAM call. This key may be used in any following rule after a PROGRAM call.
SYSFS{{*filename*}}	Match the sysfs device attribute, for instance, a label, vendor, USB serial number, SCSI UUID, or file system label.
SYMLINK	The name of the symbolic link (symlink) for the device.
SUBSYSTEM	Match the device subsystem.

TABLE 32-3   udev Rule Fields

The key fields such as KERNEL support pattern matching to specify collections of devices. For example, mouse* will match all devices beginning with the pattern "mouse." The following field uses the KERNEL key to match on all mouse devices as listed by the kernel:

```
KERNEL="mouse*"
```

The next key will match on all printer devices numbered **lp0** through **lp9**. It uses brackets to specify a range of numbers or characters, in this case 0 through 9, **[0-9]**:

```
KERNEL="lp[0-9]*"
```

The NAME, SYMLINK, and PROGRAM fields support string substitution codes similar to the way printf codes work. Such a code is preceded by a % symbol. The code allows several possible devices and names to be referenced in the same rule. Table 32-4 lists the supported codes.

The udev Man page provides many examples of udev rules using various fields. On Fedora, the **50-udev.rules** file holds rules that primarily use KERNEL keys to designate devices. The KERNEL key is followed by either a NAME field to specify the device filename or a SYMLINK field to set up a symbolic link for a device file. The following rule uses the

Substitution Code	Description
%n	The kernel number of the device.
%k	The kernel name for the device.
%M	The kernel major number.
%m	The kernel minor number.
%b	The bus ID.
%c	The string returned by a PROGRAM field (can't be used in a PROGRAM field).
%s {filename}	Content of sysfs attribute.
%e	Used to generate sequentially numbered devices of the same type, such as cdrom1 or cdrom2. The %e adds the next smallest number to the device name, as in 1 or 2.
%%	Quotes the % character in case it is needed in the device name.

TABLE 32-4   udev Substitution Codes

KERNEL key to match on all mouse devices as listed by the kernel. Corresponding device names are placed in the **/dev/input** directory, and the name used is the kernel name for the device (**%k**):

```
KERNEL="mouse*",  NAME="input/%k"
```

This rule uses both a BUS key and a KERNEL key to set up device files for USB printers, whose kernel names will be used to create device files in **/dev/usb**:

```
BUS="usb", KERNEL="lp[0-9]*", NAME="usb/%k"
```

Symbolic Links

Certain device files are really symbolic links bearing common device names that are often linked to the actual device file used. A *symbolic link* is another name for a file that is used like a shortcut, referencing that file. Common devices like printer, CD-ROM, hard drive, SCSI, and sound devices, along with many others, will have corresponding symbolic links. For example, a **/dev/cdrom** symbolic link links to the actual device file used for your CD-ROM. If your CD-ROM is an IDE device, it may use the device file **hdc**. In this case, **/dev/cdrom** would be a link to **/dev/hdc**. In effect, **/dev/cdrom** is another name for **/dev/hdc**. Serial ATA DVD/CD drives will be linked to **scd** devices, like **scd0** for the first Serial ATA CD/DVD drive. If your drive functions both as a CD and DVD writer and reader, you will have several links to the same device. In this case the links **cdrom**, **cdrw**, **cdwriter**, **dvd**, **dvdrw**, **dvdwriter** would all links to the same CD/DVD RW-ROM device.

A **/dev/modem** link file also exists for your modem. If your modem is connected to the second serial port, its device file would be **/dev/ttyS1**. In this case, **/dev/modem** would be a link to that device file. Applications can then use **/dev/modem** to access your modem, instead of having to know the actual device file used. Table 32-5 lists commonly used device links.

Link	Description
cdrom	Link to your CD-ROM device file, set in **/etc/udev/rules.d**
dvd	Link to your DVD-ROM device file, set in **/etc/udev/rules.d**
cdwriter	Link to your CD-R or CD-RW device file, set in **/etc/udev/rules.d**
dvdwriter	Link to your DVD-R or DVD-RW device file, set in **/etc/udev/rules.d**
modem	Link to your modem device file, set in **/etc/udev/rules.d**
floppy	Link to your floppy device file, set in **/etc/udev/rules.d**
tape	Link to your tape device file, set in **/etc/udev/rules.d**
scanner	Link to your scanner device file, set in **/etc/udev/rules.d**
video	Link to your video device file, set in **/etc/udev/rules.d**
audio	Link to your tape audio device file, set in **/etc/udev/rules.d**

TABLE 32-5   Device Symbolic Links

Symbolic links are created by udev using the SYMLINK field. The symbolic links for a device can be listed either with the same rule creating a device file (NAME key) or in a separate rule that will specify only a symbolic link. The inclusion of the NAME key does not have to be specific, if the default device name is used. The + added to the = symbol will automatically create the device with the default name, not requiring an explicit NAME key in the rule. The following rule is for parallel printers. It includes both the default name, and implied NAME key creating the device (+), and a symbolic link, **par**. The **%n** will add a number to the symbolic link like **par1**, **par2**, etc.

```
KERNEL=="lp[0-9]*",      SYMLINK+="par%n"
```

Should you want to create more than one symbolic link for a device, you can list them in the SYMLINK field. The following creates two symbolic links, one **cdrom** and another named **cdrom-** with the kernel name attached (**%k**).

```
SYMLINK+="cdrom cdrom-%k"
```

Should you decide to set up a separate rule that specifies just a symbolic link, the symbolic link will be kept on a list awaiting the creation of its device. This also allows you to add other symbolic links for a device in other rules files. This situation can be confusing because symbolic links can be created for devices that are not yet generated. The symbolic links will be defined and held until needed, when the device is generated. This is why you could have many more SYMLINK rules than NAME rules in udev that actually set up device files. In the case of removable devices, they will not have a device name generated until they are connected.

In the **50-rules.udev** file you will find several SYMLINK rules for optical devices, one of which is shown here, using the implied default name:

```
KERNEL="scd[0-9]*",              SYMLINK+="cdrom cdrom-%k"
```

In most cases, you will only need symbolic links for devices, using the official symbolic names. Most of these are already defined for you. Should you need to create just a symbolic link, you can create a SYMLINK rule for it. However, a new SYMLINK rule needs to be placed before the name rules that name that device. The SYMLINK rules for a device are read by udev and kept until a device is named. Then those symbolic names can be used for that device. You can have as many symbolic links for the same device as you want, meaning that you could have several SYMLINK rules for the same device. When the NAME rule for the device is encountered, the previous SYMLINK keys are simply appended.

Most standard symbolic names are already defined in the **50-udev.rules** file, such as **audio** for the audio device. In the following example, the device is referenced by its KERNEL key and the symbolic link is applied with SYMLINK key. This is only a SYMLINK rule. The NAME key is implied:

```
KERNEL="audio0", SYMLINK+="audio"
```

Program Fields and /lib/udev

Several kinds of devices use special scripts to determine the name to be used for the device. This is particularly true of CD/DVD readers or writers, for which there can be multiple devices of very different types, such as CD-ROMs, DVD-RWs, or CD-RWs. The symbolic link used can be **cdwriter** for a CD-RW, **cdrom** for a CD-ROM, or even **dvd** for a DVD-ROM. To determine the correct symbolic link the **50-udev.rules** use a **PROGRAM** field to invoke a script to determine the device. Many of these programs are specialized scripts kept in the **/lib/udev** directory, such as **check-cdrom.sh**, which determines the cdrom type.

In the following rule, the **check-cdrom.sh** script is used to see if an IDE device (hd) is DVD. The script is passed the kernel name and the DVD parameter and will return a positive value if the device is a DVD-ROM. It is then assigned a **dvd**n symbolic link, as in **dvd1**. Two other keys are used in this example. The BUS key checks to see if the device is an IDE CD-ROM, and **ATTRS{removable}=="1"** confirms whether it is removable.

```
KERNEL="sd[a-z]", BUS="ide", ATTRS{removable}=="1",
PROGRAM="check-cdrom.sh %k DVD", SYMLINK+="dvd dvd-%k"
```

The following rule is used for simple CD-ROMs. The ATTRS field will return the name of the IDE device in the **sys** filesystem and its output is tested to see if it is a CD-ROM. Then a symbolic link is assigned, as in **cdrom** or **cdrom-** with its kernel name attached. The following lines are one line.

```
KERNEL="hd[a-z]", BUS="ide", ATTRS{media}== cdrom, SYMLINK+="cdrom cdrom-%k"
```

Creating udev Rules

Default rules for your devices are placed by udev in the **/etc/udev/rules.d/50-udev.rules** file. You should never edit this file, though you can check it to see how device naming is handled. This file will create the device files using the official kernel names. These names are often referenced directly by applications that expect to find devices with these particular names, such as **lp0** for a printer device.

If you want to create rules of your own, you should place them in a separate rules file. The NAME rules that name devices are read lexically, where the first NAME rule will take precedence over any later ones. Only the first NAME rule for a device will be used. Later NAME rules for that same device will be ignored. Keep in mind that a SYMLINK rule with a += includes a NAME rule for the default device, even though the NAME field is not explicitly shown. Check **www.reactivated.net/writing_udev_rules.html** for a tutorial on writing udev rules.

Since rules are being created that are meant to replace the default rules, they would have to be run first. To do this, you would place them in a rules file that begins with a very low number, say 10. Such a rules file would be executed before the **50-udev.rules** file, which holds the default rules. Rules files are read in lexical order, with the lower numbers read first. You could create a file called **10-user.rules** in the **/etc/udev/rules.d** directory. Here you would place your own rules. Conversely, if you wanted rules that would run only if the defaults failed for some reason, you would use a rules file numbered after 50, like **90-mydefaults.rules**.

The upcoming section "Persistent Names: udevinfo," describes how to create a canon-pr rule to replace the default printer rule for that printer. The new user canon-pr rule would be placed in a **10-user.rules** file to be executed before the printer rules in the **50-udev.rules** file, thereby taking precedence. The default printer rule in the **50-udev.rules** file (shown here) would not be applied to the Canon printer.

```
BUS="usb", KERNEL="lp[0-9]*", NAME="usb/%k"
```

SYMLINK Rules

In most cases, you will only need to create symbolic links for devices, using the official name. You can also create rules that just create symbolic links. However, these need to be placed before the name rules that name the devices. These SYMLINK rules are read by udev and kept until a device is named. Then all the symbolic names will be used for that device. You can have as many symbolic links for the same device as you want, meaning that you could have several SYMLINK rules for the same device. When the NAME rule for the device is encountered, the previous SYMLINK keys are simply appended.

Most standard symbolic names are already defined in the **50-udev.rules** file, such as audio for the audio device. In the following example, the device is referenced by its KERNEL key and the symbolic link is applied with SYMLINK field. The NAME field for the default device is implied:

```
KERNEL="audio0",  SYMLINK+="audio"
```

If you always know the name for a device, you can easily add a SYMLINK rule. For example, if you know your DVD-ROM is attached to the first secondary SATA connection (**sdc**), you can create a symbolic name of your own choosing with a SYMLINK rule. In the next example a new symbolic link, **mydvdrom**, is created for the DVD-ROM on the **/dev/sdc** device.

```
KERNEL="sdc",    SYMLINK="mydvdrom"
```

For a SYMLINK rule to be used, it must occur before a NAME rule that names the device. You should place these rules in a file that will precede the **50-udev.rules** file, such as **10-user.rules**.

Persistent Names: udevinfo

The default udev rules will provide names for your devices using the official symbolic names reserved for them, for instance, lp*n* for printer, where *n* is the number of the printer. For fixed devices, such as fixed printers, this is normally adequate. However, for removable devices, such as USB printers, that may be attached in different sequences at different times to USB ports, the names used may not refer to the same printer. For example, if you have two USB printers, an Epson and Canon, and attach the Epson first and the Canon second, the Epson will be given the name **usb/lp0** and the Canon will have the name **usb/lp1**. If, however, you later detach them and reattach the Canon first and the Epson second, then the Canon will have the name **usb/lp0** and the Epson will have **usb/lp1**. If you want the Epson to always have the same name, say **epson-pr**, and likewise the Canon, as in **canon-pr**, you would have to create your own rule for detecting these printers and giving them your own symbolic names.

The key task in creating a persistent name is to use unique information to identify the device. You then create a rule that references the device with the unique information, identifying it, and then name it with an official name, but giving it a unique symbolic name. You can then use the unique symbolic name, like **canon-pr**, to always reference just that printer and no other, when it is plugged in. In this example, unique information such as the Canon printer serial number is used to identify the Canon printer. It is next named with the official name, **usb/lp0** or **usb/lp1**, depending on whether another printer was plugged in first, and then it is given a unique symbolic name, **canon-pr**, which will reference that official name, whatever it may be. Keeping the official name, like **lp0**, preserves standard access to the device as used by many applications.

You use **/sys** file system information about the device to detect the correct device to reference with the symbolic link. Unique **/sys** device information such as the vendor serial number or the vendor name can be used to uniquely reference the device. To obtain this information, you need to first query the **/sys** file system. You do this with the **udevinfo** command.

First you will need to know where the device is located in the **/sys** file system. You plug in your device, which will automatically configure and name it, using the official name. For example, plugging in the USB printer will create a **/dev/usb/lp0** device name for it. You can use this device name to find out where the USP printer information is in **/sys**. Use the **udevinfo** command with the **-q path** option to query for the **/sys** pathname, and add the **-n** option with the device's full pathname to identify the device you are searching for. The following command will display the **/sys** path for the printer with the device name **lp0**. In this case, the device is in the **class** subdirectory under **usb**. The path will assume **/sys**.

```
udevinfo -q path -n  /dev/usb/lp0
  /class/usb/lp0
```

One you have the device's **/sys** path, you can use that path to display information about it. Use the **udevinfo** command again with the **-a** option to display all information about the device and the **-p** option to specify its path in the **/sys** file system. The listing can be extensive, so you should pipe the output to **less** or redirect it to a file.

```
udevinfo -a  -p  /sys/class/usb/lp0 | less
```

Some of the key output to look for is the BUS used and information such as the serial number, product name, or manufacturer. Look for information that would uniquely identify the device, such as serial number. Some devices will support different buses, and the information may be different for each. Be sure to use the information for that bus when setting up your keys in the udev rule.

```
BUS="usb"
ATTRS{serial}="300HCR"
ATTRS{manufacturer}="Canon"
ATTRS{idproduct}="1074"
ATTRS{product}="S330"
```

You can use much of this information in an ATTRS key in a udev rule to identify the device. The ATTRS key (attributes) is used to obtain **/sys** information about a device. You use the ATTRS key with the field you want referenced placed in braces. You can then match that field to a value to reference the particular device you want. Use the = sign and a valid field value to match against. Once you know the **/sys** serial number of a device, you can use it in ATTRS keys in udev rules to uniquely reference the device. The following key checks the serial number of the devices field for the Canon printer's serial number:

```
ATTRS{serial}="300HCR"
```

A user rule can now be created for the Canon printer.

In another rules file you can add your own symbolic link using **/sys** information to uniquely identify the printer, and name the device with its official kernel name. The first two keys, BUS and ATTRS, specify the particular printer. In this case the serial number of the printer is used to uniquely identify it. The NAME key will name the printer using the official kernel name, always referenced with the **%k** code. Since this is a USB printer, its device file would be placed in the **usb** subdirectory, **usb/%k**. Then the SYMLINK key defines the unique symbolic name to use, in this case **canon-pr** in the **/dev/usb** directory.

```
BUS="usb", ATTRS{serial}="300HCR", NAME="usb/%k", SYMLINK="usb/canon-pr"
```

The rules are applied dynamically in real time. To run a new rule, simply attach your USB printer (or detach and reattach). You will see the device files automatically generated.

Permission Fields: MODE, GROUP, OWNER

Permissions that will be given to different device files are determined by the permission fields in the udev rules. The MODE field is an octal bit permission setting, the same as used for file permissions. Usually this is set to 660, owner and group read/write permission. Pattern matching is supported with the *, ?, and [] operators. The following example sets audio devices to the owner and group with read/write owner and group permission:

```
KERNEL=="audio*",      MODE="0660"
```

The floppy device entry specifies a floppy group.

```
KERNEL=="fd[01]*",      GROUP="floppy", MODE="0660"
```

USB printer devices use the **lp** group with Mode 660.

```
KERNEL=="usb/lp*",      GROUP="lp", MODE="0660"
```

Tape devices use the disk group.

```
KERNEL=="npt*",     GROUP="disk", MODE="0660"
```

The default settings set the OWNER and GROUP to root with owner read/write permissions (600).

```
KERNEL=="*",     OWNER="root" GROUP="root", MODE="0600"
```

Hardware Abstraction Layer: HAL

The purpose of the Hardware Abstraction Layer (HAL) is to abstract the process of applications accessing devices. Applications should not have to know anything about a device, even its symbolic name. It should just have to request a device of a certain type, and then a service, like HAL, should provide what is available. Device implementation becomes hidden from applications.

HAL makes devices easily available to desktops and applications using a D-BUS (device bus) structure. Devices are managed as objects that applications can easily access. The D-BUS service is provided by the HAL daemon, **haldaemon**. Interaction with the device object is provided by the freedesktop.org HAL service, which is managed by the **/org/freedesktop/HAL/Manager**.

HAL is an information service for devices. The HAL daemon maintains a dynamic database of connected hardware devices. This information can be used by specialized callout programs to maintain certain device configuration files. This is the case with the managing removable storage devices. HAL will invoke the specialized callout programs that will use HAL information to dynamically manage devices. Removable devices like CD-ROM discs or USB card readers are managed by specialized callouts with HAL information, detecting when such disks are attached. The situation can be confusing. Callout programs perform the actual tasks, but HAL provides the device information. For example, though the callout hal-system-storage-mount mounts a device, the options and mountpoints used for CD-ROM entries are specified in HAL device information files that set policies for storage management.

HAL has a key impact on the **/etc/fstab** file used to manage file systems. On Fedora, no longer are entries maintained in the **/etc/fstab** file for removable devices like your CD-ROMs. These devices are managed directly by HAL using its set of storage callouts like **hal-storage-mount** to mount a device or **hal-storage-eject** to remove one. In effect you now have to use the HAL device information files to manage your removable file systems.

HAL is a software project of **freedesktop.org**, which specializes in open source desktop tools. Check the latest HAL specification documentation at **www.freedesktop.org** under the software/HAL page for detailed explanations of how HAL works (the **specifications** link on the HAL page, Latest HAL Specification). The documentation is very detailed and complete.

The HAL Daemon and hal-device-manager (hal-gnome)

The HAL daemon, **hald**, is run as the **haldaemon** process. You can start and stop it using the **haldaemon** service script, as well as with system-config-services.

```
service haldaemon start
```

Information provided by the HAL daemon for all your devices can be displayed using the HAL device manager. The HAL device manager is part of the hal-gnome package. You can access it, once installed, from the System | Administration | Hardware menu entry. The actual Hal device manager program is named **hal-device-manager.**

When you run the manager, it will display an expandable tree of your devices arranged by category, in the left panel. The right panel will display information about the selected device. A Device pane will list the basic device information such as the vendor and the bus type. The Advanced pane will list the HAL device properties defined for this device, as described in later sections, as well as **/sys** file system paths for this device. For device controllers there will also be a USB or PCI panel. For example, a DVD writer could have an entry for the **storage.cdrom.cdr** property that says it can write CD-R discs. For an IDE CD/DVD-ROM device you may find this under IDE (some third party IDE controllers may be labeled as SCSI devices). A typical entry would look like this. The **bool** is the type of entry, namely boolean:

```
storage.cdrom.cdr     bool      true
```

Numerical values may use an **int** type or an **strlist** type. The following **write_speed** property has a value 7056:

```
storage.cdrom.write_speed      strlist      7056
```

The **/sys** file system path will also be a string. It will be preceded by a linux property category. Strings will use a **strlist** type for multiple values and **string** for single values. The following entry locates the **/sys** file system path at **/sys/block/sdc**:

```
linux.sysfs_path     strlist    /sys/block/sdc
```

HAL Configuration: /etc/hal/fdi, and /usr/share/hal/fdi

Information about devices and policies to manage devices are held in device information files in the **/etc/hal/fdi** and **/usr/share/hal/fdi** directories. These directories are where you would set properties such as options that are to be used for CD-ROMs in **/etc/fstab**.

The implementation of HAL on Fedora configures storage management by focusing on storage methods for mountable volumes, instead of particular devices. Volume properties define actions to take and valid options that can be used. Special callouts perform the actions directly, such as **hal-storage-mount** to mount media, or **hal-storage-eject** to remove it.

Device Information Files: fdi

HAL properties for these devices are handled by device information files (fdi) in the **/usr/share/hal/fdi** and **/etc/hal/fdi** directories. The **/usr/share/hal/fdi** directory is used for configurations provided by the distribution, in this case, Fedora, whereas **/etc/hal/fdi** is used for setting user administrative configurations. In both are listed subdirectories for the different kinds of information that HAL manages, such as **policy**, whose subdirectories have files with policies for how to manage devices. The files, known as device information files, have rules for obtaining information about devices, as well as detecting and assigning options for removable devices. The device information files have the extension **.fdi**, as in **storage-methods.fdi**. For example, the **policy** directory has two subdirectories: **10osvendor** and **20thirdpary**. The **10osvendor** holds the fdi files that have policy rules for managing removable devices on Fedora (10osvendor replaces 90defaultpolicy in Fedora 3). This directory holds the **20-storage-methods.fdi** policy file used for storage devices. Here you will find the properties that specify options for removable storage devices such as CD-ROMs. The directories begin with numbers; lower numbers are read first. Unlike with udev, the last property read will override any previous property settings, so priority is given to higher-numbered directories and the fdi files they hold. This is why the default policies are in **10osvendor**, whereas the user policies, which would override the defaults, would be in a higher-numbered directory like **30user**, as are third-party policies, **20thirdpolicy**.

There are currently three device information file directories set up in the device information file directories, each for different kinds of information: information, policy, and preprobe.

- **Information**   The **information** directory is for information about devices.
- **Policy**   The **policy** directory is for setting policies such as storage policies. The default policies for a storage device are in a **20-storage-methods.fdi** file in the **policy/10osvendor** directory.
- **Preprobe**   The **preprobe** directory handles difficult devices such as unusual drives or drive configurations, for instance, those in **preprobe/10osvendor/10-ide-drives .fdi**. This contains information needed even before the device is probed.

Within these subdirectories are still other subdirectories indicating where the device information files come from, such as **vendor**, **thirdparty**, or **user**, and their priority. Certain critical files are listed here:

- **information/10freedesktop**   Information provided by freedesktop.org
- **policy/10osvendor**   Default policies (set by system administrator and OS distribution)
- **preprobe/10usevendor**   Preprobe policies for difficult devices

Properties

Information for a device is specified with a *property* entry. Such entries consist of a key/value pair, where the key specifies the device and its attribute and the value is the value for that attribute. There are many kinds of values, such as Boolean true/false, string values such as those use to specify directory mountpoints, or integer values.

Properties are classified according to metadata, physical connection, function, and policies. Metadata provides general information about a device, such as the bus it uses, its driver, or its HAL ID. Metadata properties begin with the key info, as in info.bus. Physical properties describe physical connections, namely the buses used. The IDE, PCI, and SCSI bus information is listed in ide, pci, and scsi keys. The usb_device properties are used for the USB bus; an example is usb_device.number.

The functional properties apply to specific kinds of devices. Here you will find properties for storage devices, such as the **storage.cdrom** keys that specify if an optical device has writable capabilities. For example, the **storage.cdrom.cdr** key set to true will specify that an optical drive can write to CD-R discs.

The policies are not properties as such. They indicate how devices are to be handled. They are, in effect, the directives that callout programs will use to carry out tasks. Policies for storage media are handled using Volume properties, specifying methods (callouts) to use and valid options such as mount options. HAL uses scripts in the **/usr/share/hal/scripts** directory to actually manage media. The following abbreviated entries come from the **20-storage-methods.fdi** policy file. The first specifies the action to take and the second the callout script to execute, **hal-storage-mount**.

```
<append key="Volume.method_names" type="strlist">Mount</append>
<append key="Volume.method_execpaths" type="strlist">hal-storage-mount</append>
```

Mount options are designated using volume.mount.valid_options as shown here for ro (read only). Options that will be used will be determined when the mount callout is executed.

```
<append key="volume.mount.valid_options"type="strlist">ro</append>
```

Several of the commonly used volume policy properties are listed in Table 32-6.

Device Information File Directives

Properties are defined in directives listed in device information files. As noted, device information files have **.fdi** extensions. A directive is encased in greater- and less-than symbols. There are three directives:

- The **merge** directive will merge a new property into a device's information database.
- The **append** directive will append or modify a property for that device already in the database.
- The **match** directive will test device information values.

A directive will include a type attribute designating the type of value to be stored such as string, bool, int, and double. The **copy_property** type will copy a property.

Property	Description
`volume.method.execpath`	Callout script to be run for a device
`volume.policy.desired_mount_point` (string)	The preferred mountpoint for the storage device
`Volume.mount.valid_options.*` (bool)	Mount options to use for specific device, where * can be any mount option, such as **noauto** or **exec**
`volume.method_names`	Action to be taken
`volume.policy.mount_filesystem` (string)	File system to use when mounting a volume
`volume.mount.valid.mount_options.*` (bool)	Default mount options for volumes, where * can be any mount option, such as **noauto** or **exec**

TABLE 32-6   HAL Storage Policies

The following discussion of the **storage-methods.fdi** file shows several examples of merge and match directives.

storage.fdi

The **20-storage-methods.fdi** file in the **/usr/share/hal/fdi/policy/10osvendor** directory lists the policies for your removable storage devices. Here is where your options for storage volumes (e.g., CD-ROM) entries are actually specified. The file is organized in sections beginning with particular types of devices to standard defaults. Keys are used to define options, such as **volume.mount.valid_options**, which will specify a mount option for a storage device such as a CD-ROM. Keys are used to specify exceptions like hotplugged devices.

The **20-storage-methods.fdi** file begins with default properties and then lists those for specific kinds of devices. Unless redefined in a later key, the default will remain in effect. The options you will see listed for the default storage volumes will apply to CD-ROMs. For example, the **noexec** option is set as a valid default. The following sets **noexec** as a default mount option for a storage device. There are also entries for **ro** and **quiet**. The append operation adds the policy option.

```
<append key="volume.mount.valid_options"type="strlist">noexec</append>
```

The default mountpoint root directory for storage devices is now set by the mount callout script, **hal-storage-mount**. Currently this is **/media**. The default mountpoint is disk. HAL will try to use the Volume property information to generate a mountpoint.

The following example manages blank disks. Instead of being mounted, such disks can only be ejected. To determine possible actions, HAL uses **method_names**, **method_signatures**, and **method_execpaths** for the Volume properties (the org.freedesktop.Hal prefix for the keys has been removed from this example to make it more readable, as in **org.freedesktop.Hal.Volume.method_names**).

```
<match key="volume.disc.is_blank" bool="true">

<append key="info.interfaces"type="strlist">Volume</append>
<append key="Volume.method_names" type="strlist">Eject</append>
<append key="Volume.method_signatures" type="strlist">as</append>
<append key="Device.Volume.method_execpaths" type="strlist">hal-storage-
eject</append>

</match>
```

After dealing with special cases, the file system devices are matched as shown here:

```
<match key="volume.fsusage" string="filesystem">
```

Storage devices to ignore like vfat are specified.

```
<merge key="volume.ignore" type="bool">false</merge>
```

Then the actions to take and the callout script to use are specified such as the one for Unmount that uses hal-storage-mount.

```
<append key="Device.Volume.method_names" type="strlist">Mount</append>
<append key="Device.Volume.method_signatures" type="strlist">ssas</append>
<append key="Device.Volume.method_execpaths" type="strlist">hal-storage-mount</append>
```

Options are then specified with Volume.mount.valid_options, starting with defaults and continuing with special cases, like **ext3** shown here.

```
<!-- allow these mount options for ext3 -->

<match key="volume.fstype" string="ext3">
<append key="volume.mount.valid_options"type="strlist">data=</append>
 </match>
```

HAL Callouts

Callouts are programs invoked when the device object list is modified or when a device changes. As such, callouts can be used to maintain system-wide policy (that may be specific to the particular OS) such as changing permissions on device nodes, managing removable devices, or configuring the networking subsystem. There are three different kinds of callouts for devices, capabilities, and properties. *Device* callouts are run when a device is added or removed. *Capability* callouts add or remove device capabilities, and *property* callouts add or remove a device's property. In the current release, callouts are implemented using info.callout property rules, such as which invokes the **hal-storage-mount** callout when CD/DVD-ROMs are inserted or removed as shown here:

```
<append key="org.freedesktop.Hal.Device.Volume.method_execpaths"
type="strlist"> hal-storage-mount</append>
```

Callouts are placed in the /usr/libexec directory with the HAL callouts prefixed with **hal-**. Here you will find many of the storage callouts used by HAL such as **hal-storage-eject** and **hal-storage-mount**. HAL uses these callouts to manage removable devices like DVD/CD-ROMs directly instead of editing entries in the **/etc/fstab** file (**fstab-sync** is no longer used). The **gnome-mount** tool used for mounting CD/DVD disk on the Gnome desktop uses the HAL callouts. Other supporting scripts can be found in the **/usr/lib/hal/scripts** directory.

Manual Devices

Several devices still need to be created manually; printer parallel ports, for example. Most of these devices are already configured with MAKEDEV and the **/etc/makedev.d** files. To have these devices created by udev, their names are placed in configuration files in the **/etc/udev/makedev.d** directory. The **50-udev.nodes** file contains a list of device names that udev will use MAKEDEV to manually construct when udev generates the **/dev** device directory. Here you will find entries for parallel ports like **paraport0** through **parport3**.

You can, if you wish, create device file interfaces manually yourself using the **MAKEDEV** or **mknod** commands. To have them added to the **/dev** directory by udev, place them in the **/etc/udev/devices** directory; udev will copy them for you to the **/dev** directory when it generates them. For some devices, such as ISDN devices, you may have to do this. The following example makes an ISDN device using **MAKEDEV** and places it in the **/etc/udev/devices** directory.

```
/sbin/MAKEDEV -d /etc/udev/devices isdn
```

Device Types

Linux implements several types of devices, the most common of which are block and character. A *block device,* such as a hard disk, transmits data a block at a time. A *character device,* such as a printer or modem, transmits data one character at a time, or rather as a continuous stream of data, not as separate blocks. Device driver files for character devices have a *c* as the first character in the permissions segment displayed by the **ls** command. Device driver files for block devices have a *b.* In the next example, **lp0** (the printer) is a character device and **sda1** (the hard disk) is a block device:

```
# ls -l sda1 lp0
brw-rw---- 1 root disk 3, 1 Jan 30 02:04 sda1
crw-rw---- 1 root lp   6, 0 Jan 30 02:04 lp0
```

The device type can be either *b, c, p,* or *u.* As already mentioned, the *b* indicates a block device, and *c* is for a character device. The *u* is for an unbuffered character device, and the *p* is for a FIFO (first in, first out) device. Devices of the same type often have the same name; for example, serial interfaces all have the name **ttyS**. Devices of the same type are then uniquely identified by a number attached to the name. This number has two components: the major number and the minor number. Devices may have the same major number, but if so, the minor number is always different. This major and minor structure is designed to deal with situations in which several devices may be dependent on one larger device, such as several modems connected to the same I/O card. All the modems would have the same major number that references the card, but each modem would have a unique minor number. Both the minor and major numbers are required for block and character devices (*b, c,* and *u*). They are not used for FIFO devices, however.

Valid device names along with their major and minor numbers are listed in the **devices .txt** file located in the **/Documentation** directory for the kernel source code, **/usr/src/ linux-*ver*/Documentation**. When you create a device, you use the major and minor numbers as well as the device name prefix for the particular kind of device you are creating. Most of these devices are already created for you and are listed in the **/etc/dev** directory.

MAKEDEV

You use **MAKEDEV** to create device files. **MAKEDEV** uses device configuration files located in the **/etc/makedev.d** directory to determine device options like the major or minor number of the device or any symbolic links that should be created for it. For example, the **/etc/ makedev.d/01sound** file lists sound devices. A **MAKEDEV** configuration file can have three different kinds of records, each beginning with a different operator:

- **b or c**   Create a block (b) or character (c) device. These entries hold several options: mode (permissions), owner, group, major and minor numbers, inc, count (number of devices created), and fmt (the name of the device). The fmt option is technically a format string, which can include a format specifier for numerically incrementing names of the similar devices, such as **cdrom%d** for **cdrom0**, **cdrom1**, and so on. The inc option sets an increment.

- **l**   Creates a symbolic link for a device.

- **a**   An alias applies the commands used for one device for those of another. This lets you create a sound device, which in turn automatically creates audio, midi, and mixer devices, and so on.

In the **/etc/makedev.d/01sound** file, there are numerous alias entries for sound, such as the following:

```
a   sound audio
```

A link entry will create a symbolic link called **audio0** for the audio device file.

```
l audio0 audio
```

The actual sound device file creation is configured in the **alsa** file. Sound devices use ALSA sound drivers. Here you will find numerous c entries with permission, owner, group values, etc.

With so much of the configuration handled in the **MAKEDEV** device configuration files, the command to create a device is very simple. However, bear in mind that with udev, device files cannot be created in **/dev**. This directory is automatically regenerated by udev. To have udev place your device file in **/dev** when it generates it, you place the device file you made in **/etc/udev/devices**. Use the **-d** option to specify the udev device directory. The following would create an ISDN device:

```
MAKEDEV -d /etc/udev/devices   isdn
```

mknod

Though the **MAKEDEV** command is preferable for creating device files, it can only create files for which it is configured. For devices not configured for use by **MAKEDEV**, you will have to use the **mknod** command. This is a lower-level command that requires manual configuration of all its settings. With the **mknod** command you can create a device file in the traditional manner without any of the configuration support that **MAKEDEV** provides.

The **mknod** command can create either a character or block-type device. The **mknod** command has the following syntax:

```
mknod options device device-type major-num minor-num
```

As most devices are easily covered by **MAKEDEV** as well as automatically generated by udev, you will rarely if ever need to use **mknod**. As a simple example, creating a device file with **mknod** for a printer port is discussed here. Linux systems usually provide device files for printer ports (**lp0–2**). As an example, you can see how an additional port could be created manually with the **mknod** command. Printer devices are character devices and must be owned by the root and daemon. The permissions for printer devices are read and write for the owner and the group, 660. The major device number is set to 6, while the minor device number is set to the port number of the printer, such as 0 for LPT1 and 1 for LPT2. Once the device is created, you use **chown** to change its ownership to the **root** user, since only the administrator should control it. Change the group to **lp** with the **chgrp** command.

Most devices belong to their own groups, such as **disks** for hard disk partitions, **lp** for printers, **floppy** for floppy disks, and **tty** for terminals. In the next example, a printer device is made on a fourth parallel port, **lp3**. The **-m** option specifies the permissions—in this case, 660. The device is a character device, as indicated by the **c** argument following the device name. The major number is 6, and the minor number is 3. If you were making a device at **lp4**, the major number would still be 6, but the minor number would be 4. Once the device is made, the **chown** command then changes the ownership of the parallel printer device to **root**. For printers, be sure that a spool directory has been created for your device. If not, you need to make one. Spool directories contain files for data that varies according to the device output or input, like that for printers or scanners.

As with all manual devices, the device file has to be placed in the **/etc/udev/devices** directory; udev will later put it in **/dev**.

```
# mknod -m 660 /etc/udev/devices/lp3 c 6 3
# chown root /etc/udev/devices/lp3
# chgrp lp /etc/udev/devices/lp3
```

Mono and .NET Support

With Mono, Fedora now provides .NET support, along with .NET applications like the Beagle desktop search tool and the F-Spot photo management tool. Mono provides an open source development environment for .NET applications. The Mono project is an open source project supported by Novell that implements a .NET framework on Unix, Linux, and OS X systems. Currently Mono 1.2 and 2.0 are included. 1.2 corresponds generally with .NET 1.1 features, and 2.0 with .NET 2.0. See **www.mono-project.com** for detailed information.

Mono is implemented on Fedora using several RPM packages. The mono-core package contains the basic Mono .NET application, including Mono tools like the Mono certification manager (certmgr), the Global Assemblies Cache Manager tool (gacutil) for making assemblies available at runtime, and mcs—the Mono C# compiler. There are several separate packages for distinct features like mono-basic for visual basic support, mono-data for SQL database queries, and mono-web and web-forms for .NET Web support, which include the disco Web services discovery tool, along with the soapsuds and wsdl for WSDL management. The Mono language testing tool, NUnit, and java script packages are also included. Documentation is provided in the monodoc package.

Configuration is found in the **/etc/mono/config** file, which is an XML-like file that maps DLL references to Linux libraries. The **/etc/mono** file also contains configuration files for 1.0 and 2.0 versions of Mono. Mono is installed in **/usr/lib/mono**. In the corresponding 1.0 and 2.0 directories you will find the DLL and EXE .NET support assemblies for different Mono applications. Other directories will hold .NET DLLs and configuration for different applications and services, including evolution, dbus, and gtk.

Local configuration information and runtime applications are placed in the user's **.config** directory.

Installing and Managing Terminals and Modems

In Linux, several users may be logged in at the same time. Each user needs his or her own terminal through which to access the Linux system, of course. The monitor on your PC acts as a special terminal, called the *console,* but you can add other terminals through either the serial ports on your PC or a special multiport card installed on your PC. The other terminals can be stand-alone terminals or PCs using terminal emulation programs. For a detailed explanation of terminal installation, see the **Term-HOWTO** file in **/usr/share/doc/HOWTO** or at the Linux Documentation Project site (**www.tldp.org**). A brief explanation is provided here.

Serial Ports

The serial ports on your PC are referred to as COM1, COM2, COM3, and COM4. These serial ports correspond to the terminal devices **/dev/ttyS0** through **/dev/ttyS3**. Note that several of these serial devices may already be used for other input devices such as your mouse, and for communications devices such as your modem. If you have a serial printer, one of these serial devices is already used for that. If you installed a multiport card, you have many more ports from which to choose. For each terminal you add, udev will create the appropriate character device on your Linux system. The permissions for a terminal device are normally 660. *Terminal devices* are character devices with a major number of 4 and minor numbers usually beginning at 64.

TIP *The /dev/pts entry in the /etc/fstab file mount a **devpts** file system at /dev/pts for Unix98 Pseudo-TTYs. These pseudoterminals are identified by devices named by number.*

mingetty, mgetty, and agetty

Terminal devices are managed by your system using the `getty` program and a set of configuration files. When your system starts, it reads a list of connected terminals in the **inittab** file and then executes an appropriate `getty` program for each one, either `mingetty`, `mgetty`, or `agetty`. Such `getty` programs set up the communication between your Linux system and a specified terminal. `mingetty` provides minimal support for virtual consoles, whereas `agetty` provides enhanced support for terminal connections. `agetty` also includes parameters for the baud rate and timeout. `mgetty` is designed for fax/modem connections, letting you configure dialing, login, and fax parameters. `mgetty` configuration files are held in the **/etc/mgetty+sendfax** directory. Modem connection information is held in the **/etc/mgetty+sendfax/mgetty.config** file. All `getty` programs can read an initial message placed in the **/etc/issue** file, which can contain special codes to provide the system name and current date and time.

termcap and inittab Files

The **/etc/inittab** file holds instructions for your system on how to manage terminal devices. A line in the **/etc/inittab** file has four basic components: an ID, a runlevel, an action, and a process. Terminal devices are identified by ID numbers, beginning with 1 for the first device. The runlevel at which the terminal operates is usually 1. The action is usually *respawn*, which means to run the process continually. The process is a call to the `mingetty`, `mgetty`, or `agetty` with the terminal device name. The **/etc/termcap** file holds the specifications for different terminal types. These are the different types of terminals users could use to log in to your system. Your **/etc/termcap** file is already filled with specifications for most of the terminals currently produced. An entry in the **/etc/termcap** file consists of various names that can be used for a terminal separated by a pipe character (|) and then a series of parameter specifications, each ending in a colon. You find the name used for a specific terminal type here. You can use `more` to display your **/etc/termcap** file, and then use a search, /, to locate your terminal type. You can set many options for a terminal device. To change these options, use the `stty` command instead of changing configuration files directly. The `stty` command with no arguments lists the current setting of the terminal.

tset

When a user logs in, having the terminal device initialized using the **tset** command is helpful. Usually the **tset** command is placed in the user's **.bash_profile** file and is automatically executed whenever the user logs in to the system. You use the **tset** command to set the terminal type and any other options the terminal device requires. A common entry of **tset** for a **.bash_profile** file follows. The **-m dialup:** option prompts the user to enter a terminal type. The type specified here is a default type that is displayed in parentheses. The user presses ENTER to choose the default. The prompt looks like this: **TERM=(vt100)?**.

```
eval 'tset -s -Q -m dialup:?vt00'
```

Input Devices

Input devices, such as mice and keyboards, are displayed on several levels. Initial detection is performed during installation where you select the mouse and keyboard types. Keyboard and mice will automatically be detected by HAL. You can peform detailed configuration with your desktop configuration tools, such as the Gnome or KDE mouse configuration tools. On Gnome, select System | Preferences | Hardware | Mouse to configure your mouse. There is a Keyboard entry on that same menu for keyboards. (To detect new keyboards you can use system-config-keyboard in System | Administration | Keyboard.)

Installing Sound, Network, and Other Cards

For you to install a new card, your kernel must first be configured to support it. Support for most cards is provided in the form of modules that can be dynamically loaded into the kernel. Installing support for a card is usually a simple matter of loading a module that includes the drivers for it. For example, drivers for the Sound Blaster sound card are in the module **sb.o**. Loading this module makes your sound card accessible to Linux. Most Linux distributions, including Red Hat and Fedora, automatically detect the cards installed on your system and load the needed modules. If you change sound cards, the new card is automatically detected, invoking system-config-soundcard to configure it. For network cards, system-config-network is invoked to perform the configuration. You could also load modules you need manually, removing an older conflicting one. The section "Modules" later in this chapter describes this process.

Device files for most cards are already set up for you in the **/dev** directory by **udev**. For example, the device name for your sound card is **/dev/audio**. However, the device names for network cards are aliases for network modules instead of device files. For example, the device name for your Ethernet card begins with **eth,** with the numbering starting from **0**, as in **eth0** for the first Ethernet card on your system. An alias is used to reference the module used for that particular card; for example, a 3Com Etherlink card aliases the 3c59x network module, whose alias would be **eth0** if it is the first Ethernet card. The modules themselves are kept in the kernel's module directory located at **/lib/modules**, as described in the last section.

Sound Devices

On Fedora, you can use the system-config-soundcard utility to install most sound cards on Linux. A listing of the different sound devices is provided in Table 32-7. Some sound cards may require more specialized support. For sound cards, you can tell what your current sound configuration is by listing the contents of the **/proc/asound/oss/sndstat** file. You can test your card by simply redirecting a sound file to it, as shown here:

```
cat sample.au > /dev/audio
```

For the 2.4 kernel, most Linux sound drivers were developed as part of the Open Sound System (OSS) and freely distributed as OSS/Free. These are installed as part of Linux distributions. The OSS device drivers are intended to provide a uniform API for all Unix platforms, including Linux. They support Sound Blaster– and Windows Sound System–compatible sound cards (ISA and PCI). OSS is also available for a nominal fee and features configuration interfaces for device setup.

The Advanced Linux Sound Architecture (ALSA) replaced OSS in the 2.6 Linux kernel; it aims to be a better alternative to OSS, while maintaining compatibility with it. ALSA provides a modular sound driver, an API, and a configuration manager. ALSA is a GNU project and is entirely free; its Web site at **www.alsa-project.org** contains extensive documentation, applications, and drivers. Currently available are the ALSA sound driver, the ALSA Kernel API, the ALSA library to support application development, and the ALSA manager to provide a configuration interface for the driver. ALSA evolved from the Linux Ultra Sound Project. The ALSA project currently supports most Creative sound cards.

The Linux Musical Instrument Digital Interface (MIDI) and Sound Pages, currently at **www.linux-sound.org**, includes links to sites for Linux MIDI and sound software.

Video and TV Devices

Device names used for TV, video, and DVD devices are listed in Table 32-8. Drivers for DVD and TV decoders have been developed. mga4linux (**marvel.sourceforge.net**) is developing video support for the Matrox Multimedia cards. The General ATI TV and Overlay Software (GATOS) (**gatos.sourceforge.net**) has developed drivers for the currently unsupported features of ATI video cards, specifically TV features. The BTTV Driver Project has developed drivers for the Booktree video chip. Creative Labs sponsors Linux drivers for the Creative line of DVD DXR2 decoders (**opensource.creative.com**).

TABLE 32-7
Sound Devices

Device	Description
/dev/sndstat	Sound driver status
/dev/audio	Audio output device
/dev/dsp	Sound sampling device
/dev/mixer	Control mixer on sound card
/dev/music	High-level sequencer
/dev/sequencer	Low-level sequencer
/dev/midi	Direct MIDI port

Device Name	Type of Device
/dev/video	Video capture interface
/dev/vfx	Video effects interface
/dev/codec	Video codec interface
/dev/vout	Video output interface
/dev/radio	AM/FM radio devices
/dev/vtx	Teletext interface chips
/dev/vbi	Data services interface

TABLE 32-8 Video and TV Device Drivers

PCMCIA Devices

PCMCIA devices are card readers commonly found on laptops to connect devices like modems or wireless cards, though they are becoming standard on many desktop systems as well. The same PCMCIA device can support many different kinds of devices, including network cards, modems, hard disks, and Bluetooth devices.

PCMCIA support is now managed by udev and HAL. You no longer use the cardmgr/pcmcia service. PCMCIA devices are now considered hotplugged devices managed by HAL and udev directly. Card information and control is now managed by pccardctl. The PCMCIA udev rules are listed in **60-pcmcia.rules**, which automatically probes and installs cards. Check **www.kernel.org/pub/linux/utils/kernel/pcmcia/pcmcia.html** for more information.

You can obtain information about a PCMCIA device with the **pccardctl** command, as well as manually eject and insert a device. The **status**, **config**, and **ident** options will display the device's socket status and configuration, and the identification of the device. The **insert** and **eject** options will let you add and remove a device. The **cardinfo** command also provides device information.

It is not advisable to hot-swap IDE or SCSI devices. For these you should first manually shut down the device using the **pccardctl** command.

```
pccardctl eject
pccardctl scheme home
```

Modules

The Linux kernel employs the use of modules to support different operating system features, including support for various devices such as sound and network cards. In many cases, you do have the option of implementing support for a device either as a module or by directly compiling it as a built-in kernel feature, which requires you to rebuild the kernel. A safer and more robust solution is to use modules. *Modules* are components of the Linux kernel that can be loaded as needed. To add support for a new device, you can now simply instruct a kernel to load the module for that device. In some cases, you may have to recompile only that module to provide support for your device. The use of modules has the added advantage of reducing the size of the kernel program as well as making your system more stable. The kernel can load modules in memory only as they are needed. Should a module fail, only the module stops running, and it will not affect the entire system. For example, the module for the PPP network interface used for a modem needs to be used only when you connect to an ISP.

Kernel Module Tools

The modules your system needs are usually determined during installation, according to the kind of configuration information you provided and the automatic detection performed by Kudzu. For example, if your system uses an Ethernet card whose type you specified during installation, the system loads the module for that card. You can, however, manually control what modules are to be loaded for your system. In effect, this enables you to customize your kernel whatever way you want. You can use several commands, configuration tools, and daemons to manage kernel modules. The 2.6 Linux kernel includes the Kernel Module Loader (Kmod), which has the capability to load modules automatically as they are needed. Kernel module-loading support must also be enabled in the kernel, though this is usually considered part of a standard configuration and is included with Fedora distributions. In addition, several tools enable you to load and unload modules manually, if you must. The Kernel Module Loader uses certain kernel commands to perform the task of loading or unloading modules. The **modprobe** command is a general-purpose command that calls **insmod** to load modules and **rmmod** to unload them. These commands are listed in Table 32-9. Options for particular modules, general configuration, and even specific module loading can specified in the **/etc/modprobe.conf** file. You can use this file to automatically load and configure modules. You can also specify modules to be loaded at the boot prompt or in **grub.conf**.

Module Files and Directories: /lib/modules

The filename for a module has the extension **.o**. Kernel modules reside in the **/lib/modules/** *version* directory, where *version* is the version number for your current kernel with the extension FC7. The directory for the 2.6.20-1.2054_FC7 kernel is **/lib/modules/**2.6.20-1.2054_FC5. As you

Command	Description
`lsmod`	Lists modules currently loaded.
`insmod`	Loads a module into the kernel. Does not check for dependencies.
`rmmod`	Unloads a module currently loaded. Does not check for dependencies.
`modinfo`	Displays information about a module: `-a` (author), `-d` (description), `-p` (module parameters), `-f` (module filename), `-v` (module version).
`depmod`	Creates a dependency file listing all other modules on which the specified module may rely.
`modprobe`	Loads a module with any dependent modules it may also need. Uses the file of dependency listings generated by `depmod`: `-r` (unload a module), `-l` (list modules).

TABLE 32-9   Kernel Module Commands

install new kernels on your system, new module directories are generated for them. One method to access the directory for the current kernel is to use the **uname -r** command to generate the kernel version number. This command needs to have backquotes.

```
cd /lib/modules/`uname -r`
```

In this directory, modules for the kernel reside in the **/kernel** directory. Within the **/kernel** directory are several subdirectories, including the **/drivers** directory that holds subdirectories for modules like sound drivers or video drivers. These subdirectories serve to categorize your modules, making them easier to locate. For example, the **kernel/drivers/ net** directory holds modules for your Ethernet cards, and the **kernel/drivers/sound** directory contains sound card modules.

TIP *You will notice that there are no entries for the Ethernet devices in the /dev file, such as **eth0** or **eth1**. That is because these are really aliases for kernel modules defined in the /etc/modprobe .conf file, or devices handled by the kernel directly. They are not device files.*

Managing Modules with /etc/moprobe.conf

As noted previously, there are several commands you can use to manage modules. The **lsmod** command lists the modules currently loaded into your kernel, and **modinfo** provides information about particular modules. Though you can use the **insmod** and **rmmod** commands to load or unload modules directly, you should use only **modprobe** for these tasks. Often, however, a given module requires other modules to be loaded. For example, the module for the Sound Blaster sound card, **sb.o**, requires the **sound.o** module to be loaded also.

The depmod Command

Instead of manually trying to determine what modules a given module depends on, you use the **depmod** command to detect the dependencies for you. The **depmod** command generates a file that lists all the modules on which a given module depends. The **depmod** command generates a hierarchical listing, noting what modules should be loaded first and in what order. Then, to load the module, you use the **modprobe** command using that file. **modprobe** reads the file generated by **depmod** and loads any dependent modules in the correct order, along with the module you want. You need to execute **depmod** with the **-a** option once, before you ever use **modprobe**. Entering **depmod -a** creates a complete listing of all module dependencies. This command creates a file called **modules.dep** in the module directory for your current kernel version, **/lib/modules/***version*.

```
depmod -a
```

The modprobe Command

To install a module manually, you use the **modprobe** command and the module name. You can add any parameters the module may require. The following command installs the Intel high definition sound module. **modprobe** also supports the use of the ***** character to enable you to use a pattern to select several modules. This example uses several values commonly used for sound cards. You would use the values recommended for your sound card on your system. Most sound card drivers are supported by the ALSA project. Check their Web site for find what driver module is used for your card.

```
modprobe  snd-hda-intel
```

To discover what parameters a module takes, you can use the **modinfo** command with the **-p** option.

You can use the **-l** option to list modules and the **-t** option to look for modules in a specified subdirectory. Sound modules are arranged in different subdirectories according to the device interface they use, like **pci**, **isa**, or **usb**. Most internal sound cards use **pci**. Within the interface directory, there may be further directories like emu10k1 used for the Creative Audigy cards and hda for high definition drivers. In the next example, the user lists all modules in the **sound/pci/hda** directory:

```
# modprobe -l -t sound/pci/hda
/lib/modules/2.6.15-1.3059_FC7/kernel/sound//pci/hda/snd-hda-intel.o
/lib/modules/2.6.15-1.3059_FC7/kernel/sound//pci/hda/snd-hda-codec.o
/lib/modules/2.6.15-1.2054_FC5/kernel/drivers/sound/sound.o
/lib/modules/2.6.15-1.2054_FC5/kernel/drivers/sound/soundcore.o
```

Options for the **modprobe** command are placed in the **/etc/modprobe.conf** file. Here, you can enter configuration options, such as default directories and aliases. An alias provides a simple name for a module. For example, the following entry enables you to reference the **3c59x.o** Ethernet card module as **eth0** (Kmod automatically detects the 3Com Ethernet card and loads the 3c59x module):

```
alias eth0 3c59x
```

On Nvidia systems, the forcedeth module is used.

```
alias eth0 forcedeth
```

The insmod Command

The **insmod** command performs the actual loading of modules. Both **modprobe** and the Kernel Module Loader make use of this command to load modules. Though **modprobe** is preferred, because it checks for dependencies, you can load or unload particular modules individually with **insmod** and **rmmod** commands. The **insmod** command takes as its argument the name of the module, as does **rmmod**. The name can be the simple base name, like **sb** for the **sb.o** module. You can specify the complete module filename using the **-o** option. Other helpful options are the **-p** option, which lets you probe your system first to see if the module can be successfully loaded, and the **-n** option, which performs all tasks except actually loading the module (a dummy run). The **-v** option (verbose) lists all actions taken as they occur. In those rare cases where you may have to force a module to load, you can use the **-f** option. In the next example, **insmod** loads the **sb.o** module:

```
# insmod -v sb
```

The rmmod Command

The **rmmod** command performs the actual unloading of modules. It is the command used by **modprobe** and the Kernel Module Loader to unload modules. You can use the **rmmod** command to remove a particular module as long as it is not being used or required by other modules. You can remove a module and all its dependent modules by using the -**r** option. The -**a** option removes all unused modules. With the -**e** option, when **rmmod** unloads a module, it saves any persistent data (parameters) in the persistent data directory, usually **/var/lib/modules/persist**.

The /etc/modprobe.conf File

Module loading can require system renaming as well as specifying options to use when loading specific modules. Even when removing or installing a module, certain additional programs may have to be run or other options specified. These parameters can be set in the **/etc/modprobe.conf** file. The **mobprobe.conf** file supports four actions: alias, options, install, and remove.

- **alias** *module name*   Provides another name for the module, used for network and sound devices.
- **options** *module options*   Specifies any options a particular module may need.
- **install** *module commands*   Uses the specified commands to install a module, letting you control module loading.
- **remove** *module commands*   Specifies commands to be run when a module is unloaded.
- **include** *config-file*   Additional configuration files.

Among the more common entries are aliases used for network cards. Notice that there is no device name for Ethernet devices in the **/dev** directory. This is because the device name is really an alias for a Ethernet network module that has been defined in the **modprobe.conf** file (this was called **modules.conf** in previous releases). If you were to add another Ethernet card of the same type, you would place an alias for it in the **modprobe.conf** file. For a second Ethernet card, you would use the device name **eth1** as the alias. This way, the second Ethernet device can be referenced with the name **eth1**. A **modprobe.conf** entry is shown here:

```
alias eth1 ne2k-pci
```

---

*TIP   After making changes to /etc/modprobe.conf, you should run **depmod** again to record any changes in module dependencies.*

If you had added a different model Ethernet card, you would have to specify the module used for that kind of card. In the following example, the second card is a standard PCI Realtek card. Kmod has already automatically detected the new card and loaded the **ne2k-pci** module for you. You only need to identify this as the **eth1** card in the **/etc/modprobe.conf** file.

```
alias eth0 forcedeth
alias eth1 ne2k-pci
```

Note *Instead of a single **modprobe.conf** file, modprobe configuration can be implemented using separate files in an **/etc/modprobe.d** directory.*

A sample **modprobe.conf** file is shown here. Notice the aliases for the Nvidia Serial ATA controller, **sata_nv** and the AMD parallel ATA adapter, **pata_amd**. Both are aliased as SCSI host adapaters. controller, the FireWire connection, and the sound card. The sound card is referenced by its module name, snd-hda-intel, in later install and remove operations. The last two lines are one line, beginning with **remove**.

```
alias eth0 forcedeth
alias eth1 ne2k-pci
alias scsi_hostadapter sata_nv
alias scsi_hostadapter1 pata_amd
alias snd-card-0 snd-hda-intel
options snd-card-0 index=0
options snd-hda-intel index=0
remove snd-hda-intel { /usr/sbin/alsactl store 0 >/dev/null 2>&1 || : ; };
        /sbin/modprobe -r --ignore-remove snd-hda-intel
```

Tip *In some cases, Kmod may not detect a device in the way you want, and thereby not load the kernel module you would like. In this case, kernel parameters were specified to the GRUB boot loader to load the correct modules.*

Installing New Modules from Vendors: Driver Packages

Often you may find that your hardware device is not supported by current Linux modules. In this case you may have to download drivers from the hardware vendor or open source development group to create your own driver and install it for use by your kernel.

The drivers could be in RPM or compressed archives. The process for installing drivers differs, depending on how a vendor supports the driver. Different kinds of packages are listed here:

- **RPM packages**   Some support sites will provide drivers already packaged in RPM files for direct installation on Fedora. For these you can just run system-config-packages or **rpm** to install the module.

- **Drivers compiled in archives**   Some will provide drivers already compiled for Fedora, but packaged in compressed archives. In this case a simple install operation will place the supporting module in the **modules** directory and make it available for use by the kernel.

- **Source code**   Others provide just the source code, which, when compiled, will detect your system configuration and compile the module accordingly.

- **Scripts with source code**   Some will provide customized scripts that may prompt you for basic questions about your system and then both compile and install the module.

For drivers that come in the form of compressed archives (**tar.gz** or **tar.bz2**), the compile and install operations normally make use a Makefile script operated by the **make** command.

A simple install would usually just require running the following command in the driver's software directory:

```
make install
```

In the case of sites that just supply the source code, you may have to perform both configure and compile operations as you would for any software.

```
./configure
make
make install
```

For packages that have no install option, compiled or source, you will have to manually move the module to the kernel module directory, **/lib/modules/**_version_, and use **depmod** and **modprobe** to load it (see the preceding section).

If a site gives you a customized script, you would just run that script. For example, the Marvel gigabit LAN network interfaces found on many motherboards use the SysKonnect Linux drivers held in the sk98lin.o module. The standard kernel configuration will generate and install this module. But if you are using a newer motherboard, you may need to download and install the latest Linux driver. For example, some vendors may provide a script, **install .sh**, that you run to configure, compile, and install the module.

```
./install.sh
```

If you are only provided a source code file for the module, such as a **.c** file, you can use the kernel files in the **/lib/modules/**_version_**/build** directory to compile the module. See the Release Note on the DVD/CD-ROM for details on how to create a customized Makefile for creating modules. You will not have to download and install the source code.

Kernel Header Files: /lib/modules/version/build

If you need to compile modules, your module source code will make use of kernel headers. The location of these headers was changed with Fedora 3. Normally most module source expects to find the kernel headers along with the kernel source code in the **/usr/src/linux** directory. This usually required installing the entire kernel source code on your system, which seemed excessive just to compile a downloaded module.

With Fedora 4 the kernel headers were placed in the **/usr/src/kernels/**_version_ directory, where _version_ is the kernel name. If your system has more than one kernel installed, you will find the header directories for each here. In the **modules** directory for an installed kernel there is a link to its headers, named **build**, **/lib/modules/**_version_**/build** (**/lib/modules/** _version_**/source** is a link to the **build** directory). This link can be used in the source code for kernel modules to reference the kernel headers. The headers are installed as part of the kernel binary packages, and the kernel source is now maintained solely as a source code package to be downloaded separately if needed. To compile modules, you just need to use the kernel headers in **/lib/modules/**_version_ **/build**. The **/lib/modules/**_version_**/build** link is actually a link to **/lib/modules/**_version_**/build**, which in turn links to **/usr/src/linux/**_version_**.c**.

Problems occur when module source code expects to find the kernel headers in **/usr/src/ linux**. In this case you would receive missing kernel header errors when you tried to compile. To remedy the problem, you can just create **/usr/src/linux** as a link to the kernel header directory in **/usr/src/kernels/**_version_ or to the link in **/lib/modules/**_version_**/source**. The following example creates **/usr/src/linux** as a symbolic link to **/usr/src/kernels/2.6.21-1.3116.fc7-686**.

```
ln -s  /usr/src/kernels/2.6.21-1.3116.fc7-686 /usr/src/linux
```

You can then compile your module or run your script.

If you have more than one kernel installed on your system, be sure to make the **/usr/src/ linux** symbolic link reference the kernel you want to create the module for. Each kernel binary RPM package will include its own source subdirectory with its own kernel headers. These are used for creating modules for its kernel. You cannot mix module and headers for one kernel with another. Be sure **kernel-devel** package is installed.

Installing New Modules from the Kernel

The source code for your Linux kernel contains an extensive set of modules, of which not all are actually used on your system. The kernel binaries provided by Fedora come with an extensive set of modules already installed. If, however, you install a device for which kernel support is not already installed, you will have to configure and compile the kernel module that provides the drivers for it. This involves using the kernel source code to select the module you need from a list in a kernel configuration tool, and then regenerating your kernel modules with the new module included (see Chapter 33). Then the new module is copied into the module library, installing it on your system. You can also enter it in the **/etc/modprobe.conf** file with any options, or use **modprobe** to install it manually.

First, make sure you have installed the kernel source code in the **/usr/src/redhat/BUILD** directory. If not, simply use the **rpm** tool to install the kernel source RPM package for Fedora. This can be found with the SRPMS for your distribution. To generate the source code, you then use the **rpmbuild** command with the kernel spec file and specify the type of architecture you want. Change to the **/usr/src/redhat/SPECS** directory and run the **rpmbuild** command with the **-bp** option (build) and the **--target** option to specify the architecture. The following command will extract the i686 version of the kernel:

```
rpmbuild -bp --target=i686  kernel-2.6.spec
```

If instead you are using the original source code version of the kernel in the compressed archive from kernel.org, then unpack it in any directory (but do not use **/usr/src/linux**).

Now change to the kernel directory. For the RPM source package this will be in **/usr/src/ redhat/BUILD/kernel-**_version_**/linux-**_version_, where _version_ is the kernel version. Then use the **make** command with the **gconfig** or **menuconfig** argument to display the kernel configuration menus, invoking them with the following commands. The **make gconfig** command starts an X Window System interface that needs to be run on your desktop from a terminal window.

```
make gconfig
```

Using the menus select the modules you need. Make sure each is marked as a module, clicking the Module check box in **gconfig** or typing **m** for **menuconfig**. Once the kernel is configured, save it and exit from the configuration menus. Then you compile the modules, creating the module binary files with the following command:

```
make modules
```

This places the modules in the kernel source modules directory. You can copy the one you want to the kernel modules directory, **/lib/modules/***version***/kernel**, where *version* is the version number of your Linux kernel. A simpler approach is to reinstall all your modules, using the following command. This copies all the compiled modules to the **/lib/modules/***version***/kernel** directory:

```
make modules_install
```

TIP *To easily change to a kernel header library you can use a match on the patch name, like cd **/usr/**src/kernels/*3116*.*

Kernel Administration: Virtualization

The *kernel* is the operating system, performing core tasks such as managing memory and disk access, as well as interfacing with the hardware that makes up your system. For example, the kernel makes possible such standard Linux features as multitasking and multiuser support. It also handles communications with devices like your CD-ROM or hard disk. Users send requests for access to these devices through the kernel, which then handles the lower-level task of actually sending appropriate instructions to a device. Given the great variety of devices available, the kind of devices connected to a Linux system will vary. When Linux is installed, the kernel is appropriately configured for your connected devices. However, if you add a new device, you may have to enable support for it in the kernel. This involves reconfiguring the existing kernel to support the new device through a procedure that is often referred to as *building* or *compiling the kernel.* In addition, new versions of the kernel are continuously made available that provide improved support for your devices, as well as support for new features and increased reliability for a smoother-running system. You can download, compile, and install these new versions on your system.

Kernel Versions

The version number for a Linux kernel consists of four segments: the major, minor, revision, and security/bug fix numbers. The *major number* increments with major changes in the kernel. This is rarely changed. The *minor number* indicates a major revision of the kernel. The revision number is used for supporting new features. The security/bug number is used for security and bug fixes. New development versions will first appear as release candidates, which will have an **rc** in the name. As bugs are discovered and corrected, and as new features are introduced, new revisions of a kernel are released. For example, kernel **2.6.21.7** has a major number of 2 and a minor number of 6, with a revision number of 20, and a securit/bug fix number of 7. The release candidate version would have a name like **2.6.22-rc7**.

Distributions often add another number that refers to a specific set of patches applied to the kernel, as well as a distribution initial. For example, for Fedora, the kernel is **2.6.21-1.3116.f7**, where **3116** is the patch number and b refers to the Fedora 7 distribution.

On distributions that support RPM packages, you can use an RPM query to learn what version is installed, as shown here:

```
rpm -q kernel
```

You could have more than one version of the kernel installed on your system. To see which one is running currently, you use the **uname** command with the **-r** option (the **-a** option provides more detailed information).

```
uname -r
```

The Linux kernel is being worked on constantly, and new versions are released when they are ready. Distributions may include different kernel versions. Fedora includes the most up-to-date stable kernel in its releases. Linux kernels are available at **kernel.org**. Also, RPM packages for a new kernel are often available at distribution update sites. One reason you may need to upgrade your kernel is to provide support for new hardware or for features not supported by your distribution's version. For example, you may need support for a new device not provided in your distribution's version of the kernel. Certain features may not be included in a distribution's version because they are considered experimental or a security risk.

NOTE *In many cases, you don't need to compile and install a new kernel just to add support for a new device. Kernels provide most device support in the form of loadable modules, of which only those needed are installed with the kernel. Most likely, your current kernel has the module you need; you simply have to compile it and install it.*

TIP *Many modules can be separately compiled using sources provided by vendors, such as updated network device drivers. For these you only need the Kernel headers, which are already installed in the /usr/lib/modules/version/build directory, where version is an installed kernel version. In these cases, you do not have to install the full kernel source to add or modify modules.*

References

You can learn more about the Linux kernel from **kernel.org**, the official repository for the current Linux kernels. The most current source code, as well as documentation, is there. Your distribution Web site will also provide online documentation for installing and compiling the kernel on its systems. Several Linux HOW-TOs also exist on the subject. The kernel source code software packages also include extensive documentation. Kernel source code files are always installed either directly in a local directory or in the Fedora **/usr/src/redhat/BUILD** directory (the **/usr/src/kernels** directory is used for library headers, not the kernel source). The source itself will be in a directory labeled **linux-***version*, where *version* is the kernel release, as in **linux-2.6.21**. In this directory, you can find a subdirectory named **/Documentation,** which contains an extensive set of files and directories documenting kernel features, modules, and commands. The following listing of kernel resources also contains more information:

- **kernel.org**   The official Linux kernel Web site. All new kernels originate from here
- **www.linuxhq.com**   Linux headquarters, kernel sources, and patches
- **kernelnewbies.org**   Linux kernel sources and information
- **en.tldp.org**   Linux Documentation Project

Kernel Tuning: Kernel Runtime Parameters

Several kernel features, such as IP forwarding or the maximum number of files, can be turned on or off without compiling and installing a new kernel or module. These tunable parameters are controlled by the files in **/proc/sys** directory. Parameters that you set are made in the **/etc/sysctl.conf** file. Fedora installs this file with basic configuration entries such as those for IP forwarding and debugging control. You use the **sysctl** command directly. The **-p** option causes **sysctl** to read parameters from the **/etc/sysctl.conf** file (you can specify a different file). You can use the **-w** option to change specific parameters. You reference a parameter with its key. A *key* is the parameter name prefixed with its **proc** system categories (directories), such as **net.ipv4.ip_forward** for the **ip_forward** parameter located in **/proc/sys/net/ipv4/**. To display the value of a particular parameter, just use its key. The **-a** option lists all available changeable parameters. In the next example, the user changes the domain name parameter, referencing it with the **kernel.domainname** key (the **domainname** command also sets the **kernel.domainname** parameter):

```
# sysctl -w kernel.domainname="mytrek.com"
```

The following example turns on IP forwarding:

```
# sysctl -w net.ipv4.ip_forward=1
```

If you use just the key, you display the parameter's current value:

```
# sysctl net.ipv4.ip_forward
 net.ipv4.ip_forward = 1
```

Installing a New Kernel Version

To install a new kernel, you need to download the software packages for that kernel to your system. You can install a new kernel either by downloading a binary version from your distribution's Web site and installing it or by downloading the source code, compiling the kernel, and then installing the resulting binary file along with the modules. For the binary version of the kernel is provided in an RPM package. You can install a new kernel, just as you would any other RPM software package.

The easiest way to install a new kernel on Fedora is to use Pirut. Pirut will automatically download and install a new kernel. The installation will create a GRUB entry so that when you boot, the new kernel will be listed as one of the options, usually the default.

If you want to download kernel RPM packages manually, keep in mind that the complete kernel installation usually includes a series of RPM packages, all beginning with the word *kernel*. There are also other packages you may need, which contain updated system configuration files used by the new kernel. You can use the packages already installed on your system as a guide. Use the **rpm** command with the **-qa** option to list all packages and then pipe that list through the **grep** command with the **kernel** pattern to display only the kernel packages:

```
rpm -qa | grep kernel
```

The kernel source code version is available for download from distribution FTP sites in the source directory and is included on distribution source code CD-ROM. You can also download the latest source directly from **www.kernel.org**. Wherever you download a kernel version from, it is always the same. The source code downloaded for a particular kernel version from a distribution site is the same as the one for **www.kernel.org**. Patches for that version can be applied to any distribution.

CPU Kernel Packages

Fedora and Red Hat provide different kernel packages optimized for various popular CPUs. Choose the appropriate one for your machine. All the kernels include multiprocessor support. The x86 distribution will include the x86 versions, and the 64-bit distribution will hold the x86_64 versions. Each package is named kernel, but each has a different qualifier. For the x86, there are two different kernel packages, one for the newer Pentium 2, 3, and 4 CPUs, and one for the older Pentiums, AMD K6 CPUs, and other older systems. Each package will have a CPU reference in its filename: 686 for Pentium 2, 3, and 4; 586 for Pentium, K6, and other systems.

```
kernel-2.6.version.i586.rpm
kernel-2.6.version.i686.rpm
```

For 64-bit systems, like the Athlon 64 series, the 64-bit distribution will include only an x86_64 package.

```
kernel-2.6.version.x86_64.rpm
```

There are also kernel packages for the Xen virtualization and the PAE kernel for extended system memory support (kdump support is included in 32 bit kernels).

```
kernel-xen
kernel-PAE
```

For each kernel, there are also corresponding kernel header packages (also known as builds), denoted with the term **devel**, that contain only the kernel headers. These are used for compiling kernel modules or software applications that do not need the full kernel source code, just the headers. The headers for your current kernel are already installed. The kernel headers will be installed in the **/etc/src/kernels** directory with a **build** link to it in the kernel's **/lib/modules** directory.

Installing Kernel Packages: /boot

You will not need all of these packages. For example, for a simple kernel upgrade for a basic Pentium computer, you would need only the 686 package. You can download and install easily using Pirut, and searching for "kernel." Also, the PUP Package updater will automatically download and install new kernels as they become available, selecting the version appropriate for your system.

Should you want to install manually, you can the **rpm** command in a terminal window. To make sure a kernel RPM package was downloaded without any errors and to verify its authentication, you can use the **rpm** command with the **-K** option (to authenticate the package, you need the public key):

```
rpm -K *rpm
```

You can now install the kernel. As a safety precaution, you should preserve your old kernel in case the new one does not work out for some reason. This involves installing with the install (`-i`) option instead of the update (`-U`) option, creating a separate RAM disk for the new kernel, and then modifying **grub.conf** to have GRUB start up using the new kernel.

```
# rpm -ivh kernel-2.6.version.i686.rpm
```

If your system has a SCSI controller or any other specialized hardware, RPM will also create a RAM disk to hold appropriate support modules (you can create a RAM disk manually with the **mkinitrd** command). The RAM disk is named **initrd-***kernel-version***.img** and is located in the **/boot** directory, as in **/boot/initrd-2.6.***version***.img**.

On most distributions, kernels are installed in the **/boot** directory. Performing an `ls -l` operation on this directory lists all the currently installed kernels. A file for your old kernel and a file for your new one now exist. If you took the precautions described in the preceding section, you may have already renamed the older kernel. If you are using a boot loader such as GRUB, you need not change its configuration file (**/boot/grub.conf**) to add the entry to invoke the new kernel. The kernel boots using the selected **/boot/vmlinuz-***version* kernel file. In your **grub.conf** file, you need a kernel line to reference this kernel file. You also need to include a line for the RAM disk, `initrd`.

```
kernel /boot/vmlinuz-version ro root=/dev/hda3
initrd /boot/initrd-version.img
```

TIP *Although it is not included with Fedora, user-mode Linux (UML) is an optional version of the kernel designed to run as a stand-alone program separate from the kernel. In effect, it creates a virtual machine with disk storage implemented on a user file. UML is often used to test software or experiment with kernel configurations, without harming the real system. You can also use UML to implement virtual hosting, by running several virtual machines on one physical host. With a virtual machine, you can control the access to the host system, providing greater security. You can find out more about user-mode Linux at **user-mode-linux.sourceforge.net**.*

Precautionary Steps for Modifying a Kernel of the Same Version

If you want to modify your kernel configuration and build a new one, you should retain a copy of your current kernel. In case something goes wrong with your modified version, you can always boot from the copy you kept. You do not have to worry about this happening if you are installing a new version of the kernel. New kernels are given different names, so the older one is not overwritten.

To retain a copy of your current kernel, you can make a backup copy of it, letting the original be overwritten. An installed version of a kernel makes use of several files in the **/boot** directory. Each file ends with that kernel version's number. These include the **vmlinuz** file, which is the actual kernel image file, along with several support files, **System.map**, **config**, and **initrd**. This **System.map** file contains kernel symbols needed by modules to start kernel functions. For example, the kernel image file is called **vmlinuz-***version*, where *version* is the version number attached, as in **vmlinuz-2.6.***version*. The **System.map** file for this kernel called **System.map-2.6.***version*. Here are the kernel files for version **2.6.v**:

```
/boot/vmlinuz-2.6.version
/boot/System.map-2.6.version
/boot/initrd-2.6.version.img
/boot/config-2.6.version
```

If, on the other hand, you are creating a modified version of the same kernel, the kernel file, here called **vmlinuz-2.6.***version,* will be overwritten with the new kernel image file, along with the **System.map** and **config** files. To keep your current working version, you first have to make a copy of these files. You would make a copy of the **/boot/vmlinux-2.6.***version* file, giving it another name, as shown here:

```
cp /boot/vmlinuz-2.version /boot/vmlinuz-2.6.version.orig
```

You would also make backups of the **System.map** and **config** files. You should also back up your modules located in the **/lib/modules/***version* directory, where *version* is the version number of the kernel. Otherwise, you will lose the modules already set up to work with the original kernel. For version 2.6.*version*, the libraries are located in **/lib/modules/2.6.***version*. If you are compiling a different version, those libraries are placed in a new directory named with the new version number.

Boot Loader

Installation of a kernel package will automatically create a GRUB boot loader entry for the new kernel. You will be able to select it on startup. Entries for your older kernel will remain. Should you create a customized version of the current kernel, while keeping the original versions as a backup, you would then need to create a new entry for the original kernel in the boot loader configuration file. Leaving the entry for the original kernel is advisable in case something goes wrong with the new kernel. This way, you can always reboot and select the original kernel. For example, in **/boot/grub.conf**, add a new entry, similar to the one for the old kernel, which references the new kernel in its kernel statement. The **grub.conf** entry would look something like the following code. You could then select the entry with the title "Old Linux (2.6.*version*.orig)" at the GRUB menu to launch the original kernel.

```
title Original Linux (2.6.version.orig)
 root (hd0,2)
 kernel /boot/vmlinuz-2.6.version.orig root=/dev/hda3
 initrd /boot/initrd-2.6.version.orig.img
```

If you use a label for the boot partition, the **root** option for the **kernel** statement would look like this for a boot partition labeled **/**:

```
kernel /boot/vmlinuz-2.6.version.orig ro root=LABEL=/
```

Boot Disk

You should also have a boot CD-ROM ready, just in case something goes wrong with the installation (normally you created one during installation). With a boot CD-ROM, you can start your system without using the boot loader. You can create a boot CD-ROM using the **mkbootdisk** utility. To create a boot CD-ROM, you need to know the full version number for your kernel. You can, in fact, have several kernels installed, and create boot CD-ROMs for each one (your **grub.conf** file lists your kernel version number). If the kernel version is 2.6.*version*, use it as the argument to the **mkbootdisk** command to create a boot CD-ROM for your system.

To make a boot CD-ROM, you can use the **--iso** option with the **--device** option to specify the CD image file. You can then burn the image file to a CD-ROM with an application like K3b. In the next example, the user creates a CD-ROM image file, called **myimage.iso**, for a boot CD-ROM of the 2.6.*version* kernel:

```
mkbootdisk --iso --device myimage.iso   2.6.version
```

Compiling the Kernel from Source Code

Instead of installing already-compiled binary versions of the kernel, you can install the kernel source code on your system and use it to create the kernel binary files yourself. Kernel source code files are compiled with the **gcc** compiler just as any other source code files are. One advantage to compiling the kernel is that you can enhance its configuration, adding support for certain kinds of devices such as Bluetooth devices.

Installing Kernel Sources with Fedora Core SRPM

You can obtain a recent version of the kernel source code from the Fedora distribution's **SRPMS** directory. It is no longer included with the binary RPMS files. It will have the name **kernel-source**. New versions of the Fedora source can be downloaded by directly accessing the Fedora distribution's FTP site. You simply install them as you would any RPM package. You can also use Firefox to download the package. You have use the **rpm** command in a terminal window as shown here:

```
# rpm -ivh kernel- 2.6.version.src.rpm
```

Building the Kernel Source

Since Fedora Linux 3, the management of Fedora kernel source RPM packages has changed significantly. Fedora RPM sources are now managed through the Fedora RPM build directories, not in the traditional **/usr/src** directory. When you install the Fedora kernel RPM, the RPM spec file, **kernel-2.6.spec**, is placed in the **/usr/src/redhat/SPEC** directory. Configuration information, patches, and the compressed archive for the kernel source are placed in the **/usr/src/redhat/SOURCES** directory.

To generate the source code, you then use the **rpmbuild** command with the kernel spec file and specify the type of architecture you want. Change to the **/usr/src/redhat/SPECS** directory and run **rpmbuild** with the **-bp** option (build) and the **--target** option to specify the architecture. The following command will extract the i686 version of the kernel:

```
rpmbuild -bp --target=i686   kernel-2.6.spec
```

The extracted kernel source will be placed in the **/usr/src/redhat/BUILD** directory under **kernel-2.6.21/linux-2.6.21**. You can then run commands like **make xconfig** to configure the kernel source.

Often, when compiling software using the kernel source, the software expects to find the kernel source in the **/etc/src/linux** directory. To accommodate this situation, you can create a link named **/etc/src/linux** to your Linux kernel source directory. This is the directory to which you expanded the Linux source package.

```
ln -s /usr/src/redhat/BUILD/linux-2.6.21/  /usr/src/linux
```

Different Kernel System Configurations

Should you want to use a different configuration, you need to configure your kernel source for that particular system. To do this, you use the appropriate configuration file for your systems. These are located in the kernel source's **configs** directory. For the i386 RPM source you will find kernel configuration files for x86 systems, i586 and i686.

The **.config** file will already be the version you specified in the target option when you extracted the source with **rpmbuild**. For a different configuration, you copy the config file you want as the **.config** file in the top kernel source directory. The following example copies the i686 configuration file as the kernel source configuration file:

```
cp configs/kernel.2.6.21-i686.config  .config
```

Then update your kernel source with the new configuration by issuing the following command:

```
make oldconfig
```

Installing Kernel Sources: Kernel Archives and Patches

You can also download the original kernel source from **www.kernel.org**. This version will not be optimized for Fedora. It should be placed in directory of your choosing, but not in the **/usr/src/linux** directory.

These versions are normally much more recent than those available on your distribution site, but they may not have been thoroughly tested on the distribution platform. The kernel source is in the form of compressed archives (**.tar.gz**). They have the prefix **linux** with the version name as the suffix. You decompress and extract the archive with the following commands. You first change to the local directory you chose and then unpack the archive with either File Roller or the tar command. It creates a directory with the prefix **linux** where the source files are placed. The following example extracts the 2.6.21.7 kernel:

```
cd mykernel
tar -xzvf linux-2.6.21.7.tar.gz
```

Be sure to unpack the archive for the kernel.org version in a directory you choose, like **mykernel** in a home directory. The source will reside within a subdirectory that has the prefix **linux** and a suffix consisting of the kernel version, as in **linux-2.6.21** for kernel 2.6, revision 21. The local directory in this example would be **mykernel/linux-2.6.21**.

TIP If you are using the original kernel source, you should also check for any patches.

Configuring the Kernel

Once the source is installed, you must configure the kernel. Configuration consists of determining the features for which you want to provide kernel-level support. These include drivers for different devices, such as sound cards and SCSI devices. You can configure features as directly included in the kernel itself or as modules the kernel can load as needed. You can also specifically exclude features. Features incorporated directly into the kernel make for a larger kernel program. Features set up as separate modules can also be easily updated. Documentation for many devices that provide sound, video, or network support can be found in the **/usr/share/doc** directory. Check the kernel-doc package to find a listing of the documentation provided.

```
rpm -ql kernel-doc
```

NOTE *If you configured your kernel previously and now want to start over from the default settings, you can use the* **make mrproper** *command to restore the default kernel configuration.*

Kernel Configuration Tools

You can configure the kernel using one of several available configuration tools: `config`, `menuconfig`, `xconfig` (qconf), and `gconfig` (gkc). You can also edit the configuration file directly. These tools perform the same configuration tasks but use different interfaces. The `config` tool is a simple configure script providing line-based prompts for different configuration options. The `menuconfig` tool provides a cursor-based menu, which you can still run from the command line. Menu entries exist for different configuration categories, and you can pick and choose the ones you want. To mark a feature for inclusion in the kernel, move to it and press the SPACEBAR. An asterisk appears in the empty parentheses to the left of the entry. If you want to make it a module, press M and an *M* appears in the parentheses. The `xconfig` option runs qconf, the QT (KDE)-based GUI kernel configuration tool, and requires that the QT libraries (KDE) be installed first. The `gconfig` option runs the gkc tool, which uses a GTK interface, requiring that GNOME be installed first. Both qconf and gkc provide expandable menu trees, selectable panels, and help windows. Selectable features include check buttons you can click. All these tools save their settings to the **.config** file in the kernel source's directory. If you want to remove a configuration entirely, you can use the `mrproper` option to remove the **.config** file and any binary files, starting over from scratch.

```
make mrproper
```

You start a configuration tool by preceding it with the **make** command. Be sure you are in the kernel directory (either **/usr/src/redhat/BUILD** for RPM kernel packages, or the local directory you used for the compressed archive, such as **tar.gz**). The process of starting a configuration tool is a **make** operation that uses the Linux kernel Makefile. The `xconfig` tool should be started from a terminal window on your window manager. The `menuconfig` and `config` tools are started on a shell command line. The following example lists commands to start **xconfig**, **gconfig**, **menuconfig**, and **config**:

```
make gconfig
make xconfig
make menuconfig
make config
```

gconfig (gkc)

The GTK kernel configuration tool (gkc) is invoked with the **gconfig** option. This uses a GNOME-based interface that is similar to qconf (**xconfig**). The gkc tool opens a Linux Kernel Configuration window with expandable submenus like those for qconf. Many categories are organized into a few major headings, with many now included under the Device Drivers menu. The Load and Save buttons and File menu entries can be used to save the configuration or to copy it to a file. Single, Split, and Full view buttons let you display menus in one window, in a display panel with another panel to containing an expandable tree to select entries, or as a single expandable tree of entries. The Expand button will expand all headings and subheadings, whereas Collapse will let you expand only those you want displayed. Use the down and side triangles for each entry to expand or collapse subentries.

Clicking an entry opens a window that lists different features you can include. Entries are arranged in columns listing the option, its actual name, its range (yes, module, or no), and its data (yes, no, or module status). Entries in the Options menu let you determine what columns to display: Name for the actual module name; Range for the selectable yes, no, and module entries; and Data for the option status, titled as Value.

The Range entries are titled N, M, and Y and are used to select whether not to include an option (N), to load it as a module (M), or to compile it directly into the kernel (Y). Entries that you can select will display an underscore. Clicking the underscore will change its entry to Y for module or direct kernel inclusion, and N for no inclusion. The Value column will show which is currently selected.

The Options column will include a status showing whether the option is included directly (check mark), included as a module (line mark), or not included at all (empty). To quickly select or deselect an entry, double-click the option name in the Options field. You will see its check box checked, lined (module), or empty. Corresponding N, M, and Y entries for no inclusion, module, or kernel inclusion are selected. The default preference for either module or direct kernel inclusion for that option is selected automatically. You can change it manually if you wish.

xconfig (qconf)

The **xconfig** option invokes the qconf tool, which is based on KDE QT libraries. KDE has to first be installed. The qconf tool opens a Linux Kernel Configuration window listing the different configuration categories. It has a slightly simpler interface, without the expand or collapse buttons or the columns for module and source status.

Important Kernel Configuration Features

The **xconfig**, **menuconfig**, and **gconfig** tools provide excellent context-sensitive help for each entry. To the right of each entry is a Help button. Click it to display a detailed explanation of what that feature does and why you would include it either directly or as a module, or even exclude it. When you are in doubt about a feature, always use the Help button to learn exactly what it does and why you would want to use it. Many of the key features are described here. The primary category for a feature is listed in parentheses.

TIP *As a rule, features in continual use, such as network and file system support, should be compiled directly into the kernel. Features that could easily change, such as sound cards, or features used less frequently should be compiled as modules. Otherwise, your kernel image file may become too large and slower to run.*

- **Loadable Module Support**   In most cases, you should make sure your kernel can load modules. Click the Loadable Module Support button to display a listing of several module management options. Make sure Enable Loadable Module Support is marked Yes. This feature allows your kernel to load modules as they are needed. Kernel Module Loader should also be set to Yes, because this allows your daemons, such as your Web server, to load any modules they may need.

- **Processor Type And Features**   The Processor Type And Features window enables you to set up support for your particular system. Here, you select the type of processor you have (486, 586, 686, Pentium III, Pentium IV, and so forth), as well as the amount of maximum memory your system supports (up to 64GB with the 2.4 kernel).

- **General Setup**   The General Setup window enables you to select general features, such as networking, PCI BIOS support, and power management, as well as support for ELF and **a.out** binaries. Also supported is `sysctl` for dynamically changing kernel parameters specified in the **/proc** files. You can use redhat-config-proc (the Kernel Tuning tool in the System Tools menu) to make these dynamic changes to the kernel. In the additional device driver support menu, you can enable specialized features like Crypto IP Encapsulation (CIPE) and accelerated SSL.

- **Block Devices (Device Drivers)**   The Block Devices window lists entries that enable support for your IDE, floppy drive, and parallel port devices. Special features, such as RAM disk support and the loopback device for mounting CD-ROM image files, are also there.

- **Multi-Device Support (RAID and LVM) (Device Drivers)**   The Multi-Device Support window lists entries that enable the use of RAID devices. You can choose the level of RAID support you want. Here you can also enable Logical Volume Management support (LVM), which lets you combine partitions into logical volumes that can be managed dynamically.

- **Networking Options (Device Drivers/Networking Support)**   The Networking Options window lists an extensive set of networking capabilities. The TCP/IP Networking entry must be set to enable any kind of Internet networking. Here, you can specify features that enable your system to operate as a gateway, firewall, or router. Network Packet Filtering enables support for an IPtables firewall. Support also exists for other kinds of networks, including AppleTalk and IPX. AppleTalk must be enabled if you want to use NetTalk to connect to a Macintosh system on your network (Filesystems).

- **ATA/IDE/MFM/RLL Support (Device Drivers)**   In the ATA/IDE/MFM/RLL Support window, you can click the "IDE, ATA, and ATAPI Block Device" button to open a window where you can select support for IDE ATA hard drives and ATAPI CD-ROMs.

- **SCSI Support (Device Drivers)**   If you have any SCSI devices on your system, make sure the entries in the SCSI Support window are set to Yes. You enable support for SCSI disks, tape drives, and CD-ROMs here. The SCSI Low-Level Drivers window displays an extensive list of SCSI devices currently supported by Linux. Be sure the ones you have are selected.

- **Network Device Support (Device Drivers/Networking Support)**   The Network Device Support window lists several general features for network device support. There are entries here for windows that list support for particular types of network devices, including Ethernet (10 or 100Mb) devices, token ring devices, WAN interfaces, and AppleTalk devices. Many of these devices are created as modules you can load as needed. You can elect to rebuild your kernel with support for any of these devices built directly into the kernel.

- **Multimedia Devices (Device Drivers)**   Multimedia devices provide support for various multimedia cards as well as Video4Linux.

- **File Systems**   The File Systems window lists the different types of file systems Linux can support. These include Windows file systems such as DOS, VFAT (Windows 95/98), and NTFS, as well as CD-ROM file systems such as ISO and UDF. Network file systems such as NFS, SMB (Samba), and NCP (NetWare) are included, as well as miscellaneous file systems such as HFS (Macintosh).

- **Character Devices (Device Drivers)**   The Character Devices window lists features for devices such as your keyboard, mouse, and serial ports. Support exists for both serial and bus mice.

- **Sound (Device Drivers)**   For the 2.4 kernel, the Sound window lists different sound cards supported by the kernel. Select the one on your system. For older systems, you may have to provide the IRQ, DMA, and Base I/O your sound card uses. These are compiled as separate modules, some of which you could elect to include directly in the kernel if you want. For the 2.6 kernel, you can select the Advanced Linux Sound Architecture sound support, expanding it to the drivers for particular sound devices (the Open Sound System is also included, though deprecated).

- **Bluetooth Devices (Device Drivers/Networking Support)**   Support is here for Bluetooth-enabled peripherals, listing drivers for USB, serial, and PC card interfaces.

- **Kernel Hacking**   The Kernel Hacking window lists features of interest to developers who work at the kernel level and need to modify the kernel code. You can have the kernel include debugging information, and also provide some measure of control during crashes.

Once you set your options, save your configuration. Selecting the Save entry on the File menu overwrites your **.config** configuration file. The Save As option lets you save your configuration to a particular file.

Compiling and Installing the Kernel

Now that the configuration is ready, you can compile your kernel. You first need to generate a dependency tree to determine what part of the source code to compile, given your configuration. Use the following command in the kernel source directory:

```
make dep
```

You also have to clean up any object and dependency files that may remain from a previous compilation. Use the following command to remove such files:

```
make clean
```

You can use several options to compile the kernel (see Table 33-1). The **bzImage** option simply generates a kernel file called **bzImage** and places it in the **arch** directory. For Intel and AMD systems, you find **bzImage** in the **i386/boot** subdirectory, **arch/i386/boot**. For a kernel source, this would be in **arch/i386/boot**.

```
make bzImage
```

The options in Table 33-1 create the kernel, but not the modules—those features of the kernel to be compiled into separate modules. To compile your modules, use the **make** command with the **modules** argument.

```
make modules
```

To install your modules, use the **make** command with the **modules_install** option. This installs the modules in the **/lib/modules/**_version-num_ directory, where _version-num_ is the version number of the kernel. You should make a backup copy of the old modules before you install the new ones.

```
make modules_install
```

The **install** option both generates the kernel files and installs them on your system as **vmlinuz**, incorporating the **make bzImage** step. This operation will place the kernel files such as **bzImage** in the **/boot** directory, giving them the appropriate names and kernel version numbers.

```
make install
```

Option	Description
zImage	Creates the kernel file called `zImage` located in the **arch** or **arch/i386/boot** directory.
install	Creates the kernel and installs it on your system.
zdisk	Creates a kernel file and installs it on a floppy disk (creates a boot disk, 1.44MB).
bzImage	Creates the compressed kernel file and calls it `bzImage`.
bzdisk	Creates the kernel and installs it on a floppy disk (creates a boot disk). Useful only for smaller kernel builds, 1.44MB.
fdimage	Creates floppy disk image with the kernel, 1.44MB (bootable).
fdimage288	Creates floppy disk 2.88 image with the kernel (bootable).

TABLE 33-1 Compiling Options for Kernel make Command

If you are booting Linux from DOS using `loadlin`, you will need to copy the **bzImage** file to the **loadlin** directory on the DOS partition where you are starting Linux from. The commands for a simple compilation and installation are shown here:

```
make dep
make clean
make bzImage
make modules
make modules_install
make install
```

If you want, you could enter these all on fewer lines, separating the commands with semicolons, as shown here:

```
make dep; make clean; make bzImage; make modules
make modules_install; make install
```

A safer way to perform these operations on single lines is to make them conditionally dependent on one another, using the **&&** command. In the preceding method, if one operation has a error, the next one will still be executed. By making the operations conditional, the next operation is run only if the preceding one is successful.

```
make dep && make clean && make bzImage
make modules
make modules_install &&  make install
```

Installing the Kernel Image Manually

To install a kernel **bzImage** file manually, copy the **bzImage** file to the directory where the kernel resides and give it the name used on your distribution, such as **vmlinuz-2.6.**_version_. Remember to first back up the old kernel file, as noted in the precautionary steps. **vmlinuz** is a symbolic link to an actual kernel file that will have the term **vmlinuz** with the version name. So, to manually install a **bzImage** file, you copy it to the **/boot** directory with the attached version number such as **vmlinuz-2.6.**_version_.

```
make bzImage
cp arch/i386/boot/bzImage /boot/vmlinuz-2.6.version
```

TIP _The_ `bzImage` _option, and those options that begin with the letter b, create a compressed kernel image. This kernel image may not work on older systems. If not, try using the_ `zImage` _option to create a kernel file called_ _zImage. Then install the_ _zImage file manually the same way as you would do with_ **bzImage.** _Bear in mind that support for_ `zImage` _will be phased out eventually._

You will also have to make a copy of the **System.map** file, linking it to the **System.map** symbolic link.

```
cp arch/i386/boot/System.map  /boot/System.map-2.6.version
```

The following commands show a basic compilation and a manual installation. First, all previous binary files are removed with the **clean** option. Then the kernel is created using the **bzImage** option. This creates a kernel program called **bzImage** located in the **arch/i386/boot** directory. This kernel file is copied to the **/boot** directory and given the name **vmlinuz-2.6.***version.* Then a symbolic link called **/boot/vmlinuz** is created to the kernel **vmlinuz-2.6.***version* file. Finally, the modules are created and installed:

```
make dep
make clean
make bzImage
make modules
make modules_install
cp arch/i386/boot/bzImage /boot/vmlinuz-2.6.version
cp System.map /boot/System.map-2.6.version
```

Kernel Boot Disks

Instead of installing the kernel on your system, you can simply place it on a boot disk or CD-ROM and boot your system from that disc. For a CD-ROM you can first create the kernel as a **bzImage**, install the kernel, and then use **mkbootdisk** to create a bootable CD-ROM. For a boot disk you have the option of creating either a floppy disk directly or a floppy disk image.

If you are using a stripped-down configured version of the kernel that will fit on a 1.44MB floppy disk, you can use the **bzdisk** or **zdisk** options to compile the kernel and install directly on a floppy. You will be need a floppy disk placed in your floppy drive. A standard kernel 2.6 configuration is too large to fit on a floppy, though 2.4 versions will.

For a floppy disk image you can create either a 1.44 or 2.88 image (which will hold the 2.6 kernel). Use the **fdimage** option for a 1.44 image and **fdimage288** for the 1.88 image. Both **fdimage** and **fimage288** create corresponding floppy disk images in the **arch/i386/boot** directory. They use their own **mtools.conf** configuration located in that directory to generate the letters for the floppy disk image, which **mcopy** can then use to create the images. The **fdimage288** image is often used for virtual users.

```
make bzdisk
make fdimage
make fdimage288
```

TIP *If you are experimenting with your kernel configurations, it may be safer to put a new kernel version on a boot CD-ROM, rather than installing it on your system. If something goes wrong, you can always boot up normally with your original kernel still on your system (though you can always configure your boot loader to access previous versions).*

Boot Loader Configurations: GRUB

If you are using a boot loader such as GRUB or LILO, you can configure your system to enable you to start any of your installed kernels. As seen in the earlier section "Precautionary Steps for Modifying a Kernel of the Same Version," you can create an added entry in the boot loader configuration file for your old kernel. As you install new kernel versions, you could simply add more entries, enabling you to use any of the previous kernels. Whenever you boot, your boot loader will then present you with a list of kernels to choose from. For example, you could install a developmental version of the kernel, along with a current stable version, while keeping your old version. In the image line for each entry, you specify the filename of the kernel. You can create another boot loader entry for your older kernel.

In the next example, the **/boot/grub.conf** file contains entries for two Linux kernels, one for the kernel installed earlier, **2.6.20-1.2869.fc7**, and one for a more recent kernel, **2.6.21-1.3116.fc7**. With GRUB, you only have to add a new entry for the new kernel.

```
# grub.conf generated by anaconda
#
#boot=/dev/hda
default=0
timeout=30
splashimage=(hd0,2)/boot/grub/splash.xpm.gz
title New Linux (2.6.21-1)
    root (hd0,2)
    kernel /boot/vmlinuz-2.6.21-1.3116.fc7 ro root=/dev/hda3
    initrd /boot/initrd-2.6.21-1.3116.fc7.img
title  Old Linux (2.6.20-1)
    root (hd0,2)
    kernel /boot/vmlinuz-2.6.20-1.2869.fc7 ro root=/dev/hda3
    initrd /boot/initrd-2.6.20-1.2869.fc7.img
title Windows XP
    rootnoverify (hd0,0)
    chainloader +1
```

A default configuration will set up a logical LVM partition on which to install the root directory, like Logical01 volume on the Logical01 volume group. Your **kernel** entry will look something like this.

```
kernel /vmlinuz-2.6.20-1.3104.fc7 ro root=/dev/Logical00/Logical01 rhgb quiet
```

Module RAM Disks

If your system uses certain block devices unsupported by the kernel, such as some SCSI, RAID, or IDE devices, you will need to load certain required modules when you boot. Such block device modules are kept on a RAM disk that is accessed when your system first starts up (RAM disks are also used for diskless systems). For example, if you have a SCSI hard drive or CD-ROMs, the SCSI drivers for them are often held in modules that are loaded whenever you start up your system. These modules are stored in a RAM disk from which the startup process reads. If you create a new kernel that needs to load modules to start up, you must create a new RAM disk for those modules. You need to create a new RAM disk only if your kernel has to load modules at startup. If, for example, you use a SCSI hard drive but you incorporated SCSI hard drive and CD-ROM support (including support for the specific model) directly into your kernel, you don't need to set up a RAM disk (support for most IDE hard drives and CD-ROMs is already incorporated directly into the kernel).

If you need to create a RAM disk, you can use the **mkinitrd** command to create a RAM disk image file. The **mkinitrd** command incorporates all the IDE, SCSI, and RAID modules that your system uses, including those listed in your **/etc/modules.conf** file. See the Man pages for **mkinitrd** and RAM disk documentation for more details. **mkinitrd** takes as its arguments the name of the RAM disk image file and the kernel that the modules are taken from. In the following example, a RAM disk image called **initrd-2.6.***version***.img** is created in the **/boot** directory, using modules from the 2.6.21 kernel. The 2.6.21 kernel must already be installed on your system and its modules created.

```
# mkinitrd /boot/initrd-2.6.version.img 2.6.21-1.3116.fc7
```

You can select certain modules to be loaded before or after any SCSI module. The **--preload** option loads before the SCSI modules, and **--with** loads after. For example, to load RAID5 support before the SCSI modules, use **--preload=raid5**:

```
mkinitrd --preload=raid5 raid-ramdisk 2.6.21-1.3116.fc7
```

In the **grub.conf** segment for the new kernel, place an **initrd** entry specifying the new RAM disk:

```
initrd /boot/initrd-2.6.21-1.3116.fc7.img
```

Virtualization

There are now several methods of virtualization available for use on Fedora. These range from the para-virtualization implementation employed by Xen to the hardware acceleration used by the Kernel-base Virtualization Machine (KVM) for Intel and AMD processors with hardware virtualization support. You can even use software emulation. All of these can be installed and managed easily with the Virtual Machine Manager, a GNOME base tool that provides a simple GUI interface for managing your virtual machines and installing new ones. Fedora also provides the GNOME VM applet, **gnome-applet-vm**, a panel applet that can monitor your virtual machines. See Table 33-2 for a listing of virtualization resources. All virtualization packages are available from the Fedora repository. See **virt.kernelnewbies.org** for general virtualization links and overview.

Resource	Description
fedoraproject.org/wiki/Docs/Fedora7VirtQuickStart	Virtualization on Fedora, both KVM and Xen with details on Virtual Machine Manager
fedoraproject.org/wiki/Tools/Virtualization	Fedora virtualization resources
virt-manager.et.redhat.com/	Virtual Machine Manager, virt-manager
fedoraproject.org/wiki/Tools/Xen	Fedora Xen documentation
www.xensource.com	Xen para-virtualization Web site
fabrice.bellard.free.fr/qemu/	QEMU software virtualization
kvm.qumranet.com/kvmwiki	KVM hardware virtualization
libvirt.org/	vibvirt tool kit for accessing Linux virtualization capabilities

TABLE 33-2   Virtualization Resources

All virtualization methods can be installed and managed with the Virtual Machine Manager. The Virtual Machine Manager greatly simplifies the process of installing and managing virtual operating systems (guest OS). With just a few steps you can install Windows or other Linux distributions on your Fedora system, and run them as guest operating systems whenever you need them. KVM virtual hosts will run directly from the processor, running almost as fast and as stable as if you installed it separately with a dual boot configuration.

There are two major methods currently used for virtualization, full and para virtualization. Full virtualization (KVM or QEMU) runs a guest OS independently, whereas para-virtualzation (Xen) requires that you first boot up a Xen Linux kernel from which to launch para-virtualized guest OS systems. This means that a fully virtualized OS can be started with the Virtual Machine Manager from a normal Linux kernel, whereas a para-virtualized OS requires booting up with a Xen kernel.

Virtual Machine Manager: virt-manager

You can easily manage and set up KVM or Xen virtual machines using the Virtual Machine Manager (virt-manager). Be sure that virt-manager is installed. Select Virtual Machine Manager from the Applications | System Tools menu. This will display a window listing your virtual machines (see Figure 33-1). Features like the machine ID, name, stats, CPU, and memory usage will be displayed. You can use the View menu to determine what features to display. Click the Help entry in the Help menu to show a detailed manual for Virtual Machine Manager.

For detailed information about the host machine, click Host Details from the Edit menu. The Overview panel will show information like the host name, the number of CPUs it has, and the kind of hypervisor it can launch. The Virtual Network panel shows your virtual networks, listing IPv4 connection information, the device name, and the network name (default already set up). Select guest and click Details button for guest information.

To create a virtual machine, select New Machine from the File menu. This will start up virt-install wizard. You will be prompted for name, the kind of virtualization, the location of the Operating System install disk or files, the storage to use for the guest operating system, and the amount of system memory to allocate for the guest OS.

After entering a name, you then choose your virtualization method. If you are running a standard kernel, you will only have the option to use a fully virtualized method.

FIGURE 33-1
The Virtual Machine Manager

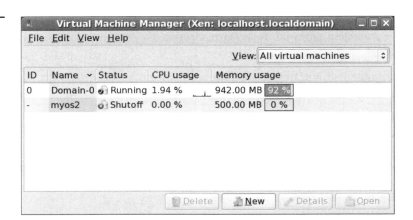

On systems with Intel VT and AMD SVM processors you will also have the option to enable hardware acceleration. This means using KVM (kernel-based virtual machine) support that will provide processor-level hardware virtualization. For processors without hardware virtualization support, a software emulation is used.

If, instead, you are running Virtual Machine Manager from the Xen kernel (as Domain 0), you can use Para-virtualization. For versions of a guest OS specially modified for use by Xen, that guest OS can be run with virtualization employed as required. In addition, for Intel VT and AMD SVM, Xen HVM methods can be used to employ hardware virtualization when virtualization is needed.

TIP   *With a system with extensive memory and processor support, you can even run or install guest operating systems simultaneously using KVM from the Virtual Machine Manager.*

You then choose the location of the OS install media. For a fully virtualized OS, this can either be a disk image or a CD/DVD-ROM, like a Windows install disk. You then choose the type of operating system you are installing, first selecting a category like Linux or Windows, and then a particular distribution or version like Centos Linux or Windows XP. For a para-virtualized OS (Xen), you choose a network location for the install media.

You then choose the storage method. This can be either an existing partition or a file. If you choose a file, you can either set a fixed size (like a fixed partition), or have the file expand as needed. Should the file be on partition with a great deal of free space, this may not be an issue.

You then choose a virtual network or a physical device for your network connection. Then choose the amount of system memory to allocate to each virtual machine, as well as the number of virtual CPUs to use. A final screen displays all your configuration information for the new virtual machine before you start installation. You can still cancel at this point. When you start installation, the install window for the guest OS is displayed and you install as you normally would. An installed OS is run in the virtual machine condole window. There are buttons to run, pause, and shutdown the OS.

TIP   *You can also manage your virtual machines from the command line with* **virsh**.

Kernel-based Virtualization Machine (KVM): Hardware Virtualization

With kernel version 2.6.20, hardware virtualization is now directly supported in the kernel (previous versions used a kernel module). Hardware virtualization is implemented by Intel and AMD as Hardware Virtual Machine abstraction layer. Intel processors that have hardware virtualization support are labeled VT (Virtualization Technology), and AMD processors are labeled SVM (Secure Virtual Machine). An HVM system has the capability to provide full virtualization, not requiring a specially modified version of an OS kernel like Xen's para-virtualization method uses. You can even run Windows XP directly from Linux using the HVM capability. KVM is a open source project developed by Qumranet, **kvm .qumranet.com/kvmwiki**. Be sure to check the KVM entries in Fedora Project virtual quick start guide for details on how to implement KVM, **fedoraproject.org/wiki/Docs/ Fedora7VirtQuickStart**.

Kernel-based Virtual Machine (KVM) uses the hardware virtualization in a processor to run virtual machine directly from hardware. There is no underlying software translation. Whereas Xen will work through an underlying domain 0 kernel, KVM operates directly with the processor.

Hardware requirements are as follows:

- An Intel (VT) or AMD (SVM) virtualization enabled-processor (like AMD AM2 socket processors or Intel Core2Duo processors). You may need to enable virtualization support in your motherboard. Some motherboards will work better than others. In some cases you may have to disable ACPI support in the motherboard BIOS to allow Windows XP to run.

- At least 1 GIG of system memory to allow space for the virtual OS to run. The hardware virtual OS requires its own memory.

KVM is launched as a process directly from the Linux kernel, as if booting to a new OS. As a process it can be managed like any Linux process. KVM adds a quest process mode with its own user and kernel mode. This is in addition to the Linux kernel and user modes. KVM uses the kernel modules **kvm-intel** or **kvm-amd** to interface with the processor's virtualization hardware. A modified version of a software emulator QEMU is used to run the OS guest. QEMU was originally designed as an emulator and is also available as such for processors without hardware virtualization. See **fabrice.bellard.free.fr/qemu** form more information on QEMU.

NOTE *KVM is run with a modified version of QEMU which has limited virtual device support, like the graphics driver (Xen has full native device driver access).*

On Fedora, to install KVM open the Add/Remove Software Browse panel and select Base System, and then Virtualization. Make sure all optional packages are selected, particularly kvm, qemu, virt-manager, and Gnome-applet-vm. You do not have to install Xen to run KVM. KVM can be run separately, though installing Xen will not interfere with KVM installs. Once installed, you can use the Virtual Machine Manager to install a KVM guest OS.

Be sure to boot into the standard kernel, not into the Xen kernel. Start the Virtual Machine Manager on your Gnome desktop (Applications | System Tools | Virtual Machine Manager). Choose New Machine for the File menu. This starts the virt-install wizard. When choosing the type of virtualization to use, select Fully Virtualized and make sure hardware acceleration is selected (Enabled kernel/hardware acceleration. You are then prompted for various features like the name, the amount of system memory to use, whether to use a given partition or an image file along with the file size, graphics support, and where the install image is located (this can be a CD/DVD-ROM disk , though a disk image is preferred for Windows)).

Once installed, you can use the Virtual Machine Manager to start up your guest OS at any time. Your guest OK is run in a virtual machine console.

NOTE *To access data directly on your virtual disks or files, you can use **lomount** or **kpartx**.*

Xen Virtualization Kernel

Fedora includes versions of the kernel that incorporate Xen Virtualization. Xen Virtualization technology allows you to run different operating systems on a Linux system, as well as running virtual versions of the kernel to test new applications. Xen is an open source project originally developed by the University of Cambridge Computer Laboratory in coordination with the Open Source Development Labs and several Linux distributors, including Fedora. You can find more about Xen at **www.cl.cam.ac.uk/Research/SRG/netos/xen**. Xen development is currently managed by Xen.source, a commercial service that provides both free open source versions of Xen and commercial implementations with support. Here you can find detailed documentation on the latest Xen releases, **www.xensource.com**.

Fedora provides its own Xen kernel versions in RPM packages. These are included with the distributions, and updated versions can be easily obtained from Fedora update sites. To learn how to use Xen on Fedora, you can consult the Fedora Xen documentation at **fedoraproject.org/wiki/Tools/Xen**. Just to learn the basic procedures for running Xen, check the startup guide for your distribution, like **fedoraproject.org/wiki/Docs/ Fedora7VirtQuickStart**.

On a single Xen server you can run several virtual machines to run different operating systems at the same time. Commercial virtualization is currently provided by VMware. Xen is a para-virtualized system, meaning that the guest operation system has to be modified to run on Xen. It cannot run without modification as it could on a fully virtualized system like VMware. Xen uses a para-virtualization approach to increase efficiency, giving its virtual machines nearly the same level of efficiency as the native kernel. This makes virtualization practical for enterprise-level systems. Some of the advantages cited for Xen are setting up a separate test system, isolating servers in virtual machines on the same system, and letting virtual machines access the hardware support provided by the native kernel. For an operating system to work on Xen, it must be configured to access the Xen interface. Currently only Unix and Linux operating systems are configured to be Xen compatible, though work is progressing on Windows.

To use the Xen kernel, you first have to install the Xen kernel package as well as the Xen server, tools, and documentation. There is one Xen kernel package, which incorporates support for running Xen in domain 0 (xen0), as a server, and for unprivileged (xenU), user access. Detailed documentation will be in **/usr/share/doc/xen**-*version*. Configuration files will be placed in the **/etc/xen** directory, and corresponding kernels in the **/boot** and **/lib/modules** directories. In the **/etc/xen** directory you will find the **xend-config** file for configuring the Xen **xend** server, as well as example Xen configuration files.

Once the package is installed, reboot and select the Xen kernel from the GRUB screen. Your standard original kernel will also be listed, which you can select to return to a normal kernel. Selecting Xen will start up the Xen kernel with the ability to create your Xen-based virtual systems. Everything will look exactly the same. If you have the GNOME VM monitor applet running, it will now detect a 0 domain.

NOTE *If you want to set up KVM based virtual machines, then you would boot into your standard kernel and use the Virtual Machine Manager to set up the fully virtualized system with hardware acceleration.*

Xen sets up separate virtual machines called domains. When the Xen kernel starts up, it creates a primary domain, domain0, which manages your system and sets up virtual machines for other operating systems. Management of the virtual machines is handled by the **xend** server. Your native kernel is installed on domain0, which will handle most of the hardware devices for all the other virtual machines.

You control the domains with the **xend** server. **xend** messages are placed in the **/var/log/ xend.log** file. The **xend** server should automatically be started when you start up with the Xen kernel. A **xend** service script on Fedora lets you start the **xend** server manually with the following command. You can also manage **xend** from system-config-services:

```
service xend start
```

NOTE *Xen also provides support for the Hardware Virtual Machine, HVM. This is the Hardware Virtual Machine abstraction layer that Intel is implementing in its new processors as Intel VT-x. AMD will implement HVMas SVM. The example configuration file for HVM in the /etc/xen directory has the extension .hvm. In this file, options are set to detect and use HVM. The* `virt-install` *script also checks for HVM.*

---

virt-install

Instead of configuring a file directly or using the Virtual Machine Manager, you can use the `virt-install` script from other Xen–compatible operating systems. It currently can only install from a remote network location using an **http://**, **nfs://**, or **ftp://** prefix. This script will not allow you to use less than 256 MB for each virtual machine. If you want to use less memory than that, say for a scaled-down version of Fedora, you will have to use the configuration files directly as described in the preceding section. For Fedora, you can use the online Fedora repository.

If you have a limited amount of RAM memory, you may need to limit the amount the **domain 0** virtual machine is using. You can reduce this to the recommended 256 MB with the following command:

```
xm mem-set 0 256
```

To start **virt-install** script, open a terminal window and enter the script name.

```
virt-install
```

You will be prompted to set different parameters, and then a configuration file will be automatically generated. You will first be prompted to name the virtual machine. This is your host name. Then you are asked how much RAM to allocate. A minimum of 256 is required. This means that for just one virtual machine you would have to have at least 500 MB of RAM, 256 MB for the Xen0 server (Domain 0) and 256 MB for the guest/user machine (Domain 1). More virtual machines would use correspondingly more RAM.

You are then prompted for the disk path for the virtual machine image file. Enter the path with the image filename. You are then prompted for the size of the image file in Gigabytes. Virtual machines use an image file where its entire system is kept. Finally you are prompted for the location of installation files for the operating system you want to install. Here you can enter an FTP, Web, or NFS site, such as the online Fedora repository.

Keep in mind that the script looks for the Xen-compatible kernel images in the **images/Xen** directory of the distribution. Your download location has to prefix this directory. The online Fedora 7 directory is shown in the next example:

```
# virt-install
What is the name of your virtual machine? my-newvm1
 How much RAM should be allocated (in megabytes)? 256
 What would you like to use as the disk (path)? /home/my-newvm1
  How large would you like the disk to be (in gigabytes)? 8
Would you like to enable graphics support?(yes or no) yes
What is the install location?
http://download.fedora.redhat.com/pub/fedora/linux/7/i386/os/
```

Once the files have been downloaded, the text-based install interface will start up, asking for keyboard and language. If you enabled graphics support, the standard Fedora graphical install will start up.

Creating Xen Virtual Machines with Configuration Files

For advanced users, you can create a virtual machine bys setting up and editing the machine Xen configuration file directly. Instead of using the Virtual Machine Manager or virt-install to generate your configuration and install your OS, you can set more refined options. You first have to create the machine's configuration file in the **/etc/xen** directory. In this directory you will find sample configuration files you can use as a template. There are standard Xen configuration examples, as well as configuration for Xen HVM implementations. Here are settings you may want to change:

- **kernel**   The path to the kernel image used by the virtual machine.
- **root**   The root device for the domain.
- **memory**   The amount of memory you will allow the domain to use.
- **disk**   The block devices (partitions) you want the domain to use.
- **dhcp**   Have the domain use DHCP to set networking. For manual configuration, you can set netmask and gateway parameters.
- **hostname**   The host name for the virtual machine.
- **vif**   The MAC address to use (random ones will be generated if none is specified).
- **extra**   Additional boot parameters.
- **restart**   Automatic restart options: always, never, onreboot.

You will have to set the kernel. This is the location of the xenU kernel. The root entry specifies the partition where the boot image is stored. The disk entry lets you specify disks that the new domain will use. These can be logical volumes or disk image files. These cannot be already mounted by the primary domain. Note that **xenguest-install** described later will set up a disk image file to be used by the virtual machine, instead of a logical volume. The following uses a disk image **/home/mynewvm1**, which will appear to the virtual machine as **xvda** and have read/write access:

```
disk = [ 'phy:/home/mynewvm1,xvda,w' ]
```

You may also want to enable **dhcp** if your network uses that to set up a network connection. For example the kernel setting would look like this:

```
kernel = "/boot/vmlinuz-2.6.20-1.3104-f7
```

You use the **xm** command with the **create** option, followed by the configuration file. In this example there is a configuration file in **/etc/xen** called **my-unewvm1**, which is the same name as the virtual machine. Check the Man page for **xmdomain.cfg** for detailed configuration options and examples.

```
xm create my-newvm1
```

You can then connect to it with the **console** option.

```
xm console my-newvm1
```

You can combine the two **xm commands** using the **-c** option for the console connection.

```
xm create -c my-newvm1
```

You will still have to install the operating system you want to use. You can do this on a designated partition or logical volume, or use **virt-install**. You can install with a text-based system or use VNC for a virtual install.

Managing Xen Virtual Machines with xm

After you have installed the system, you can then create a connection to it with **xm** command. To access a particular domain, use the **console** option and the domain name.

```
xm console my-newvm1
```

If the domain no longer exists, you have to also create it and then connect.

```
xm create -c my-newvm1
```

Check the **xm** options on the **xm** Man page for other operations you can perform on your virtual machines.

To access domains, you use the **xm** command. The **list** option lists your domains. The listing will include detailed information such as its domain ID, the CPU time used, memory used, and the domain state. The following lists your domains:

```
xm list
```

The **xm save** and **restore** options can be used to suspend and restart a domain.

Block devices such as partitions and CD-ROMs can be exported from the main domain to virtual domains. This allows a given virtual domain to use a particular partition. You can even share block devices between domains, though such shared devices should be read only.

To start and stop your domains, you can use the **xendomains** service script. The **xendomains** script will use **xm** with the **create** option to create a domain configured in the **/etc/xen/auto** directory. Place Xen domain configuration files in this directory for

xendomains to start. These domains will be started automatically when the kernel for domain0 is started. The following command manually starts your domains:

```
service xendomains start
```

To have your domains start automatically at boot, use **chkconfig** with the **xendomains** script to add the script.

```
chkconfig --add xendomains
```

NOTE *To more efficiently use block memory (hard disk partitions), you could implement dynamically allocated space using either file VBDs (virtual block devices implemented as files) or LVM VBDs.*

TIP *The Virtual Machine Manager runs the guest OS in a virtual machine console. This console will grab the mouse pointer at times when using the mouse for the guest OS, locking the mouse to the console window. You can use CTRL-ALT key combination to unlock the mouse, restoring mouse usage on the rest of your Linux desktop.*

NOTE *When installing Windows systems on KVM, there may be difficulty detecting your CD/DVD drive on reboot. You may have to use a disk (ISO) image of the install disk instead of the CD disk.*

NOTE *You can create disk image files for KVM directly using qemu-img.*

Backup Management: rsync, Amanda, and dump/restore

Backup operations have become an important part of administrative duties. Several backup tools are provided on Linux systems, including Anaconda and the traditional dump/restore tools, as well as the **rsync** command for making individual copies. Anaconda provides server-based backups, letting different systems on a network back up to a central server. The dump tools let you refine your backup process, detecting data changed since the last backup. Table 34-1 lists Web sites for Linux backup tools.

Individual Backups: archive and rsync

You can back up and restore particular files and directories with archive tools like **tar**, restoring the archives later. For backups, **tar** is usually used with a tape device. To automatically schedule backups, you can schedule appropriate **tar** commands with the **cron** utility. The archives can be also compressed for storage savings. You can then copy the compressed archives to any medium, such as a DVD disc, a floppy, or tape. On GNOME you can use File Roller to create archives easily (Archive Manager under System Tools). The Kdat tool on KDE will back up to tapes, a front end to **tar**. See Chapter 10 for a discussion of compressed archives.

If you want to remote-copy a directory or files from one host to another, making a particular backup, you can use **rsync**, which is designed for network backups of particular directories or files, intelligently copying only those files that have been changed, rather than the contents of an entire directory. In archive mode, it can preserve the original ownership and permissions, providing corresponding users exist on the host system. The following example copies the **/home/george/myproject** directory to the **/backup** directory on the host **rabbit**, creating a corresponding **myproject** subdirectory. The **-t** specifies that this is a transfer. The remote host is referenced with an attached colon, **rabbit:**.

```
rsync -t /home/george/myproject   rabbit:/backup
```

Web Site	Tools
rsync.samba.org	rsync remote copy backup
www.amanda.org	Amanda network backup
dump.sourceforge.net	dump and restore tools

Table 34-1   Backup Resources

If, instead, you wanted to preserve the ownership and permissions of the files, you would use the **-a** (archive) option. Adding a **-z** option will compress the file. The **-v** option provides a verbose mode.

```
rsync -avz  /home/george/myproject    rabbit:/backup
```

A trailing slash on the source will copy the contents of the directory, rather than generating a subdirectory of that name. Here the contents of the **myproject** directory are copied to the **george-project** directory.

```
rsync -avz  /home/george/myproject/   rabbit:/backup/george-project
```

The **rsync** command is configured to use SSH remote shell by default. You can specify it or an alternate remote shell to use with the **-e** option. For secure transmission you can encrypt the copy operation with ssh. Either use the **-e ssh** option or set the **RSYNC_RSH** variable to ssh.

```
rsync -avz -e ssh  /home/george/myproject   rabbit:/backup/myproject
```

As when using **rcp**, you can copy from a remote host to the one you are on.

```
rsync -avz  lizard:/home/mark/mypics/  /pic-archice/markpics
```

You can also run rsync as a server daemon. This will allow remote users to sync copies of files on your system with versions on their own, transferring only changed files rather than entire directories. Many mirror and software FTP sites operate as rsync servers, letting you update files without having to download the full versions again. Configuration information for rsync as a server is kept in the **/etc/rsyncd.conf** file. On Fedora, rsync as a server is managed through **xinetd**, using the **/etc/xinetd.d/rsync** file, which starts **rsync** with the **--daemon** option. In the **/etc/services** file, it is listed to run on port 873. It is off by default, but you can enable it with system-config-services On Demand Services panel or **chkconfig**.

```
chkconfig rsync on
```

Tip   *Though it is designed for copying between hosts, you can also use **rsync** to make copies within your own system, usually to a directory in another partition or hard drive. In fact there are eight different ways of using **rsync**. Check the **rsync** Man page for detailed descriptions of each.*

Amanda

To back up hosts connected to a network, you can use the Advanced Maryland Automatic Network Disk Archiver (Amanda) to archive hosts. Amanda uses `tar` tools to back up all hosts to a single host operating as a backup server. Backup data is sent by each host to the host operating as the Amanda server, where it is written out to a backup medium such as tape. With an Amanda server, the backup operations for all hosts become centralized in one server, instead of each host having to perform its own backup. Any host that needs to restore data simply requests it from the Amanda server, specifying the file system, date, and filenames. Backup data is copied to the server's holding disk and from there to tapes. Detailed documentation and updates are provided at **www.amanda.org**. For the server, be sure to install the amanda-server package, and for clients you would use the amanda-clients package.

Amanda is designed for automatic backups of hosts that may have very different configurations, as well as operating systems. You can back up any host that supports GNU tools, including Mac OS X and Windows systems connected through Samba.

Amanda Commands

Amanda has its own commands corresponding to the common backup tasks, beginning with "am," such as `amdump`, `amrestore`, and `amrecover`. The commands are listed in Table 34-2. The `amdump` command is the primary backup operation.

Command	Description
amdump	Perform automatic backups for the file systems listed in the disklist configuration file.
amflush	Use to directly back up data from the holding disk to a tape.
amcleanup	Clean up if there is a system failure on the server.
amrecover	Select backups to restore using an interactive shell.
amrestore	Restore backups, either files or complete systems.
amlabel	Label the backup medium for Amanda.
amcheck	Check the backup systems and files as well as the backup tapes before backup operations.
amadmin	Back up administrative tasks.
amtape	Manage backup tapes, loading and removing them.
amverify	Check format of tapes.
amverifyrun	Check the tapes from the previous run, specify the configuration directory for the backup.
amrmtape	Remove a tape from the Amanda database, use for damaged tapes.
amstatus	Show the status of the current Amanda backup operation.

TABLE 34-2   Amanda Commands

The `amdump` command performs requested backups; it is not designed for interactive use. For an interactive backup, you would use an archive tool like `tar` directly. The `amdump` is placed within a cron instruction to be run at a specified time. If, for some reason, `amdump` cannot save all its data to the backup medium (tape or disk), it will retain the data on the holding disk. The data can then later be directly written with the with the `amflush` command.

You can restore particular files as well as complete systems with the `amrestore` command. With the `amrecover` tool, you can select from a list of backups.

Amanda Configuration

Configuration files are placed in **/etc/amanda**, and log and database files in **/var/lib/amanda**. These are created automatically on Fedora when you install the Amanda RPM package. You will also need to create a directory to use as a holding disk where backups are kept before writing to the tape. This should be on a file system with very large available space, enough to hold the backup of your largest entire host.

/etc/amanda

Within the **/etc/amanda** directory are subdirectories for the different kind of backups you want to perform. Each directory will contain its own **amanda.conf** and **disklist** file. By default a daily backup directory is created called **DailySet1**, with a default **amanda.conf** and a sample **disklist** file. To use them, you will have to edit them to enter your system's own settings. For a different backup configuration, you can create a new directory and copy the **DailySet1 amanda.conf** and **dislist** files to it, editing them as appropriate. When you issue Amanda commands like `amdump` to perform backups, you will use the name of the **/etc/amanda** subdirectory to indicate the kind of backup you want performed.

```
amdump DailySet1
```

The **/etc/amanda** directory also contains a sample cron file, **crontab.sample**, that shows how a cron entry should look.

amanda.conf

The **amanda.conf** file contains basic configuration parameters such as the tape type and logfile as well as holding file locations. In most cases you can just use the defaults as listed in the **DailySet1/amanda.conf** file. The file is commented in detail, telling you what entries you will have to change. You will need to set the tapedev entries to the tape device you use, and the tape type entry for your tape drive type. In the holding disk segment, you will need to specify the partition and the directory for the holding disk you want to use. See the amanda Man page and documentation for detailed information on various options.

disklist

The **disklist** file is where you specify the file systems and partitions to be backed up. An entry lists the host, the partition, and the dump-type. The possible dump-types are defined in **amanda.conf**. The dump-types set certain parameters such as the priority of the backup and whether to use compression or not. The comp-root type will back up root partitions with compression and low priority, whereas the always-full type will back up an entire partition with no compression and the highest priority. You can define other dump-types in **amanda.conf** and use them for different partitions.

Backups will be performed in the order listed; be sure to list the more important ones first. The **disklist** file in **DailySet1** provides detailed examples.

Enabling Amanda on the Network

To use Amanda on the network, you need to run two servers on the Amanda server as well as an Amanda client on each network host. Access must be enabled for both the clients and the server.

Amanda Server

The Amanda server runs through **xinetd**, using **xinetd** service files located in **/etc/xinetd.d**. The two service files are **amidxtape** and **amandaidx**. You can turn these on with `chkconfig` or with system-config-services On Demand Services panel. You only need to do this once.

```
chkconfig amidxtape on
chkconfig amandaidx on
```

Then restart the **xinetd** daemon to have it take immediate effect.

```
service xinetd restart
```

For clients to be able to recover backups from the server, the clients' host names must be placed in the **.amandahosts** file in the server's Amanda users' directory. On Red Hat Enterprise Linux and Fedora, this is **/var/lib/amanda**. On the server, **/var/lib/amanda/.amandahosts** will list all the hosts that are backed up by Amanda.

Amanda Hosts

Each host needs to allow access by the Amanda server. To do this, you place the host name of the Amanda server in each client's **.amandahosts** dot file. This file is located in the client's Amanda user home directory. On Fedora systems, this is the **/var/lib/amanda** directory.

Each host needs to run the Amanda client daemon, **amanda**, which also runs under **xinetd**. Use either `chkconfig` or system-config-services On Demand Services panel to turn it on.

```
chkconfig amanda on
```

TIP   *If your server and hosts have firewalls, you will need to allow access through the ports that Amanda uses, usually 10080, 10082, and 10083.*

Using Amanda

Backups are performed by the **amdump** command.

```
amdump DailySet1
```

An **amdump** command for each backup is placed in the Amanda **crontab** file. It is helpful to run an **amcheck** operation to make sure that a tape is ready.

```
0 16 * * 1-5 /usr/sbin/amcheck -m DailySet1
45 0 * * 2-6 /usr/sbin/amdump DailySet1
```

Before you can use a tape, you will have to label it with **amlabel**. Amanda uses the label to determine what tape should be used for a backup. Log in as the Amanda user (not root) and label the tape so that it can be used.

```
amlabel DailySet DailySet1
```

A client can recover a backup using **amrecover**. This needs to be run as the root user, not as the Amanda user. The **amrecover** command works through an interactive shell much like **ftp**, letting you list available files and select them to restore. Within the **amrecover** shell the **ls** command will list available backups, the **add** command will select one, and the extract operation will restore it. The **lcd** command lets you change the client directory; **amrecover** will use **DailySet1** as the default, but for other configurations you will need to specify their configuration directory with the **-C** option. Should you have more than one Amanda server, you can list the one you want with the **-t** option.

```
amrecover -C DailySet1
```

To restore full system backups, you use the **amrestore** command, specifying the tape device and the host name.

```
amrestore  /dev/rmt1  rabbit
```

To select certain files, you can pipe the output to a recovery command such as **restore** (discussed in the next section).

```
amrestore -p /dev/rmt1  rabbit mydir  |  restore  -ibvf 2 -
```

Backups with dump and restore

You can back up and restore your system with the dump and restore utilities. dump can back up your entire system or perform incremental backups, saving only those files that have changed since the last backup. dump supports several options for managing the backup operation, such as specifying the size and length of storage media (see Table 34-3).

NOTE *Several disk dump tools are also available. The* **diskdumpfmt** *command can be used to format tapes for use by dump.* **diskdumpctl** *registers a dump partition with the system.* **savecore** *saves a* **vmcore** *file from the data in a dump partition. Dumped cores can be read by the* **crash** *tool. Check the* **crash** *Man page for details.*

The dump Levels

The dump utility uses *dump levels* to determine to what degree you want your system backed up. A dump level of 0 will copy file systems in their entirety. The remaining dump levels perform incremental backups, backing up only files and directories that have been created or modified since the last lower-level backup. A dump level of 1 will back up only files that have changed since the last level 0 backup. The dump level 2, in turn, will back up only files that have changed since the last level 1 backup (or 0 if there is no level 1), and so on up to dump level 9. You could run an initial complete backup at dump level 0 to back up

Option	Description
-0 through -9	Specifies the dump level. A dump level 0 is a full backup, copying the entire file system (see also the -h option). Dump level numbers above 0 perform incremental backups, copying all new or modified files new in the file system since the last backup at a lower level. The default level is 9.
-B records	Lets you specify the number of blocks in a volume, overriding the end-of-media detection or length and density calculations that dump normally uses for multivolume dumps.
-a	Lets dump bypass any tape length calculations and write until an end-of-media indication is detected. Recommended for most modern tape drives and is the default.
-b blocksize	Lets you specify the number of kilobytes per dump record. With this option, you can create larger blocks, speeding up backups.
-d density	Specifies the density for a tape in bits per inch (default is 1,600 BPI).
-h level	Files that are tagged with a user's nodump flag will not be backed up at or above this specified level. The default is 1, which will not back up the tagged files in incremental backups.
-f file/device	Backs up the file system to the specified file or device. This can be a file or tape drive. You can specify multiple filenames, separated by commas. A remote device or file can be referenced with a preceding hostname, *hostname:file.*
-k	Uses Kerberos authentication to talk to remote tape servers.
-M file/device	Implements a multivolume backup, where the *file* written to is treated as a prefix and the suffix consisting of a numbered sequence from 001 is used for each succeeding file, *file001*, *file002*, etc. Useful when backup files need to be greater than the Linux **ext3** 2 GB file size limit.
-n	Notifies operators if a backup needs operator attention.
-s feet	Specifies the length of a tape in feet. dump will prompt for a new tape when the length is reached.
-S	Estimates the amount of space needed to perform a backup.
-T date	Allows you to specify your own date instead of using the **/etc/dumpdates** file.
-u	Writes an entry for a successful update in the **/etc/dumpdates** file.
-W	Detects and displays the file systems that need to be backed up. This information is taken from the **/etc/dumpdates** and **/etc/fstab** files.
-w	Detects and displays the file systems that need to be backed up, drawing only on information in **/etc/fstab**.

TABLE 34-3   Options for dump

your entire system, and then run incremental backups at certain later dates, having to back up only the changes since the full backup.

Using dump levels, you can devise certain strategies for backing up a file system. It is important to keep in mind that an incremental backup is run on changes from the last lower-level backup. For example, if the last backup was 6 and the next backup was 8, then the level 8 would back up everything from the level 6 backup. The sequence of the backups is important. If there were three backups with levels 3, then 6, and then 5, the level 5 backup would take everything from the level 3 backup, not stopping at level 6. Level 3 is the next-*lower*-level backup for level 5, in this case. This can make for some complex incremental backup strategies. For example, if you want each succeeding incremental backup to include all the changes from the preceding incremental backups, you could run the backups in descending dump level order. Given a backup sequence of 7, 6, and 5, with 0 as the initial full backup, 6 would include all the changes to 7, because its next lower level is 0. Then 5 would include all the changes for 7 and 6, also because its next lower level is 0, making all the changes since the level 0 full backup. A simpler way to implement this is to make the incremental levels all the same. Given an initial level of 0, and then two backups both with level 1, the last level 1 would include all the changes from the backup with level 0, since level 0 is the next *lower* level—not the previous level 1 backup.

Recording Backups

Backups are recorded in the **/etc/dumpdates** file. This file will list all the previous backups, specifying the file system they were performed on, the dates they were performed, and the dump level used. You can use this information to restore files from a specified backup. Recall that the **/etc/fstab** file records the dump level as well as the recommended backup frequency for each file system. With the **-w** option, dump will analyze both the **/etc/dumpdates** and **/etc/fstab** files to determine which file systems need to be backed up. The **dump** command with the **-w** option just uses **/etc/fstab** to report the file systems ready for backup.

Operations with dump

The **dump** command takes as its arguments the dump level, the device it is storing the backup on, and the device name of the file system that is being backed up. If the storage medium (such as a tape) is too small to accommodate the backup, **dump** will pause and let you insert another. **dump** supports backups on multiple volumes. The **u** option will record the backup in the **/etc/dumpdates** file. In the following example, an entire backup (dump level 0) is performed on the file system on the **/dev/sda3** hard disk partition. The backup is stored on a tape device, **/dev/tape**.

```
dump -0u -f /dev/tape /dev/sda5
```

NOTE *You can use the* **mt** *command to control your tape device;* **mt** *has options to rewind, erase, and position the tape. The* **rmt** *command controls a remote tape device.*

The storage device can be another hard disk partition, but it is usually a tape device. When you installed your system, your system most likely detected the device and set up **/dev/tape** as a link to it (just as it did with your CD-ROMs). If the link was not set up, you have to create it yourself or use the device name directly. Tape devices can have different device names, depending on the model or interface. SCSI tape devices are labeled with the prefix **st**, with a number attached for the particular device: **st0** is the first SCSI tape device. To use it in the **dump** command, just specify its name.

```
dump -0u -f /dev/st0 /dev/sda5
```

Should you need to back up to a device located on another system on your network, you would have to specify that hostname for the system and the name of its device. The hostname is entered before the device name and delimited with a colon. In the following example, the user backs up file system **/dev/sda5** to the SCSI tape device with the name **/dev/st1** on the **rabbit.mytrek.com** system:

```
dump -0u -f rabbit.mytrek.com:/dev/st0 /dev/sda5
```

The **dump** command works on one file system at a time. If your system has more than one file system, you will need to issue a separate **dump** command for each.

TIP *You can use the system **cron** utility to schedule backups using dump at specified times.*

Recovering Backups

You use the **restore** command either to restore an entire file system or to just retrieve particular files. **restore** will extract files or directories from a backup archive and copy them to the current working directory. Make sure you are in the directory you want the files restored to when you run **restore**. **restore** will also generate any subdirectories as needed. **restore** has several options for managing the restore operation (see Table 34-4).

To recover individual files and directories, you run **restore** in an interactive mode using the **-i** option. This will generate a shell with all the directories and files on the tape, letting you select the ones you want to restore. When you are finished, **restore** will then retrieve from a backup only those files you selected. This shell has its own set of commands that you can use to select and extract files and directories (see Table 34-5). The following command will generate an interactive interface listing all the directories and files backed up on the tape in the **/dev/tape** device:

```
restore -ivf /dev/tape
```

This command will generate a shell encompassing the entire directory structure of the backup. You are given a shell prompt and can use the **cd** command to move to different directories, and the **ls** command to list files and subdirectories. You use the **add** command to tag a file or directory for extraction. Should you later decide not to extract it, you can use the **delete** command to remove from the tagged list. Once you have selected all the items you want, you enter the **extract** command to retrieve them from the backup archive. To quit the restore shell, you enter **quit**. The **help** command will list the restore shell commands.

If you need to restore an entire file system, you would use restore with the **-r** option. You can restore the file system to any blank formatted hard disk partition of adequate size, including the file system's original partition. It may be advisable, if possible, to restore the file system on another partition and check the results.

Restoring an entire file system involves setting up a formatted partition, mounting it to your system, and then changing to its top directory to run the **restore** command. First you should use **mkfs** to format the partition where you are restoring the file system, and then mount it onto your system. Then you use restore with the **-r** option and the **-f** option to specify the device holding the file system's backup. In the next example, the user formats

Operation	Description
-C	Lets you check a backup by comparing files on a file system with those in a backup.
-i	The interactive mode for restoring particular files and directories in a backup. A shell interface is generated where the user can use commands to specify file and directories to restore (see Table 34-5).
-R	Instructs **restore** to request a tape that is part of a multivolume backup, from which to continue the restore operation. Helpful when multivolume restore operations are interrupted.
-r	Restores a file system. Make sure that a newly formatted partition has been mounted and that you have changed to its top directory.
-t	Lists the contents of a backup or specified files in it.
-x	Extracts specified files or directories from a backup. A directory is restored with all its subdirectories. If no file or directory is specified, the entire file system is restored.
Additional Option	**Description**
-b *blocksize*	Use a specific block size; otherwise, restore will dynamically determine it from the block device.
-f *file/device*	Restores the backup on the specified file or device. Specify a hostname for remote devices.
-F *script*	Runs a script at the beginning of the restore.
-k	Uses Kerberos authentication for remote devices.
-h	Extracts only the specified directories, without their subdirectories.
-M *file/device*	Restores from multivolume backups, where the *file* is treated as a prefix and the suffix is a numbered sequence, *file001*, *file002*.
-N	Displays the names of files and directories, does not extract them.
-T *directory*	Specifies a directory to use for the storage of temporary files. The default value is **/tmp**.
-v	The verbose mode, where each file and its file type that **restore** operates on is displayed.
-y	By default, **restore** will query the operator to continue if an error occurs, such as bad blocks. This option suppresses that query, allowing **restore** to automatically continue.

TABLE 34-4   Operations and Options for restore

and mounts the **/dev/sda5** partition and then restores on that partition the file system backup, currently on a tape in the **/dev/tape** device.

```
mkfs /dev/sda5
mount /dev/sda5 /mystuff
cd /mystuff
restore -rf /dev/tape
```

Command	Description
add [*arg*]	Adds files or directories to the list of files to be extracted. Such tagged files display an * before their names when listed with ls. All subdirectories of a tagged directory are also extracted.
cd *arg*	Changes the current working directory.
delete [*arg*]	Deletes a file or directory from the extraction list. All subdirectories for deleted directories will also be removed.
extract	Extracts files and directories on the extraction list.
help	Displays a list of available commands.
ls [*arg*]	Lists the contents of the current working directory or a specified directory.
pwd	Displays the full pathname of the current working directory.
quit	Exits the restore interactive mode shell. The quit command does not perform any extraction, even if the extraction list still has items in it.
setmodes	Sets the owner, modes, and times for all files and directories in the extraction list. Used to clean up an interrupted restore.
verbose	In the verbose mode, each file is listed as it is extracted. Also, the ls command lists the inode numbers for files and directories.

TABLE 34-5   Interactive Mode Shell Commands for restore

To restore from a backup device located on another system on your network, you would have to specify that hostname for the system and the name of its device. The hostname is entered before the device name and delimited with a colon. In the following example, the user restores a file system from the backup on the tape device with the name **/dev/tape** on the **rabbit.mytrek.com** system:

```
restore -rf rabbit.mytrek.com:/dev/tape
```

PART VI

VII

PART

Network Administration

CHAPTER 35
Administering TCP/IP
Networks

CHAPTER 36
Domain Name System

CHAPTER 37
Network Autoconfiguration:
IPv6, DHCPv6, and DHCP

CHAPTER 38
NFS, NIS, and GFS

CHAPTER 39
Samba

Administering
TCP/IP Networks

L inux systems are configured to connect into networks that use the TCP/IP protocols. These are the same protocols that the Internet uses, as do many local area networks (LANs). TCP/IP is a robust set of protocols designed to provide communications among systems with different operating systems and hardware. The TCP/IP protocols were developed in the 1970s as a special DARPA project to enhance communications between universities and research centers. These protocols were originally developed on Unix systems, with much of the research carried out at the University of California, Berkeley. Linux, as a version of Unix, benefits from much of this original focus on Unix. Currently, the TCP/IP protocol development is managed by the Internet Engineering Task Force (IETF), which, in turn, is supervised by the Internet Society (ISOC). The ISOC oversees several groups responsible for different areas of Internet development, such as the Internet Assigned Numbers Authority (IANA), which is responsible for Internet addressing (see Table 35-1). Over the years, TCP/IP protocol standards and documentation have been issued in the form of Request for Comments (RFC) documents. Check the most recent ones for current developments at the IETF Web site at **www.ietf.org**.

TCP/IP Protocol Suite

The TCP/IP protocol suite actually consists of different protocols, each designed for a specific task in a TCP/IP network. The three basic protocols are the Transmission Control Protocol (TCP), which handles receiving and sending out communications, the Internet Protocol (IP), which handles the actual transmissions, and the User Datagram Protocol (UDP), which also handles receiving and sending packets. The IP protocol, which is the base protocol that all others use, handles the actual transmissions, handling the packets of data with sender and receiver information in each. The TCP protocol is designed to work with cohesive messages or data. This protocol checks received packets and sorts them into their designated order, forming the original message. For data sent out, the TCP protocol breaks the data into separate packets, designating their order. The UDP protocol, meant to work on a much more raw level, also breaks down data into packets but does not check their order. The TCP/IP protocol is designed to provide stable and reliable connections that ensure that all data is

Group	Title	Description
ISOC	Internet Society	Professional membership organization of Internet experts that oversees boards and task forces dealing with network policy issues **www.isoc.org**
IESG	Internet Engineering Steering Group	Responsible for technical management of IETF activities and the Internet standards process **www.ietf.org/iesg.html**
IANA	Internet Assigned Numbers Authority	Responsible for Internet Protocol (IP) addresses **www.iana.org**
IAB	Internet Architecture Board	Defines the overall architecture of the Internet, providing guidance and broad direction to the IETF **www.iab.org**
IETF	Internet Engineering Task Force	Protocol engineering and development arm of the Internet **www.ietf.org**

TABLE 35-1   TCP/IP Protocol Development Groups

received and reorganized into its original order. UDP, on the other hand, is designed to simply send as much data as possible, with no guarantee that packets will all be received or placed in the proper order. UDP is often used for transmitting very large amounts of data of the type that can survive the loss of a few packets—for example, temporary images, video, and banners displayed on the Internet.

Other protocols provide various network and user services. The Domain Name Service (DNS) provides address resolution. The File Transfer Protocol (FTP) provides file transmission, and the Network File System (NFS) provides access to remote file systems. Table 35-2 lists the different protocols in the TCP/IP protocol suite. These protocols make use of either the TCP or UDP protocol to send and receive packets, which, in turn, uses the IP protocol for actually transmitting the packets.

In a TCP/IP network, messages are broken into small components, called *datagrams,* which are then transmitted through various interlocking routes and delivered to their destination computers. Once received, the datagrams are reassembled into the original message. Datagrams themselves can be broken down into smaller packets. The *packet* is the physical message unit actually transmitted among networks. Sending messages as small components has proved to be far more reliable and faster than sending them as one large, bulky transmission. With small components, if one is lost or damaged, only that component must be resent, whereas if any part of a large transmission is corrupted or lost, the entire message has to be resent.

The configuration of a TCP/IP network on your Linux system is implemented using a set of network configuration files (Table 35-6 provides a complete listing). Many of these can be managed using administrative programs, such as system-config-network as well as third-party tools like Webmin, on your root user desktop (see Chapter 5). You can also use the more specialized programs, such as netstat, ifconfig, Wireshark, and route. Some configuration files are easy to modify yourself using a text editor.

Transport	Description
TCP	Transmission Control Protocol; places systems in direct communication
UDP	User Datagram Protocol
IP	Internet Protocol; transmits data
ICMP	Internet Control Message Protocol; status messages for IP
Routing	**Description**
RIP	Routing Information Protocol; determines routing
OSPF	Open Shortest Path First; determines routing
Network Addresses	**Description**
ARP	Address Resolution Protocol; determines unique IP address of systems
DNS	Domain Name Service; translates hostnames into IP addresses
RARP	Reverse Address Resolution Protocol; determines addresses of systems
User Service	**Description**
FTP	File Transfer Protocol; transmits files from one system to another using TCP
TFTP	Trivial File Transfer Protocol; transfers files using UDP
Telnet	Remote login to another system on the network
SMTP	Simple Mail Transfer Protocol; transfers e-mail between systems
RPC	Remote Procedure Call; allows programs on remote systems to communicate
Gateway	**Description**
EGP	Exterior Gateway Protocol; provides routing for external networks
GGP	Gateway-to-Gateway Protocol; provides routing between Internet gateways
IGP	Interior Gateway Protocol; provides routing for internal networks
Network Service	**Description**
NFS	Network File System; allows mounting of file systems on remote machines
NIS	Network Information Service; maintains user accounts across a network
BOOTP	Boot Protocol; starts system using boot information on server for network
SNMP	Simple Network Management Protocol; provides status messages on TCP/IP configuration
DHCP	Dynamic Host Configuration Protocol; automatically provides network configuration information to host systems

TABLE 35-2   TCP/IP Protocol Suite

TCP/IP networks are configured and managed with a set of utilities: ifconfig, route, and netstat. The ifconfig utility operates from your root user desktop and enables you to configure your network interfaces fully, adding new ones and modifying others. The ifconfig and route utilities are lower-level programs that require more specific knowledge of your network to use effectively. The netstat utility provides you with information about the status of your network connections. Wireshark is a network protocol analyzer that lets you capture packets as they are transmitted across your network, selecting those you want to check.

IPv4 and IPv6

Traditionally, a TCP/IP address is organized into four segments, consisting of numbers separated by periods. This is called the *IP address.* The IP address actually represents a 32-bit integer whose binary values identify the network and host. This form of IP addressing adheres to Internet Protocol, version 4, also known as IPv4. IPv4, the kind of IP addressing described here, is still in wide use.

Currently, a new version of the IP protocol called Internet Protocol, version 6 (IPv6) is gradually replacing the older IPv4 version. IPv6 expands the number of possible IP addresses by using 128 bits. It is fully compatible with systems still using IPv4. IPv6 addresses are represented differently, using a set of eight 16-bit segments, each separated from the next by a colon. Each segment is represented by a hexadecimal number. A sample address would be

```
FEC0:0:0:0:800:BA98:7654:3210
```

Advantages for IPv6 include the following:

- IPv6 features simplified headers that allow for faster processing.
- IPv6 provides support for encryption and authentication along with virtual private networks (VPN) using the integrated IPsec protocol.
- One of its most significant advantage lies in its extending the address space to cover 2 to the power of 128 possible hosts (billions of billions). This extends far beyond the 4.2 billion supported by IPv4.
- IPv6 supports stateless autoconfiguration of addresses for hosts, bypassing the need for DHCP to configure such addresses. Addresses can be generated directly using the MAC (Media Access Control) hardware address of an interface.
- IPv6 provides support for Quality of Service (QoS) operations, providing sufficient response times for services like multimedia and telecom tasks.
- Multicast capabilities are built into the protocol, providing direct support for multimedia tasks. Multicast addressing also provides that same function as IPv4 broadcast addressing.
- More robust transmissions can be ensured with anycast addressing, where packets can be directed to an anycast group of systems, only one of which needs to receive them. Multiple DNS servers supporting a given network could be designated as an anycast group, of which only one DNS server needs to receive the transmission, providing greater likelihood that the transmissions will go through.
- IPv6 provides better access for mobile nodes, like PDAs, notebooks, and cell phones.

TCP/IP Network Addresses

As noted previously, the traditional IPv4 TCP/IP address is organized into four segments, consisting of numbers separated by periods. This kind of address is still in widespread use and is what people commonly refer to as an *IP address*. Part of an IP address is used for the network address, and the other part is used to identify a particular interface on a host in that network. You should realize that IP addresses are assigned to interfaces—such as Ethernet cards or modems—and not to the host computer. Usually a computer has only one interface and is accessed using only that interface's IP address. In that regard, an IP address can be thought of as identifying a particular host system on a network, and so the IP address is usually referred to as the *host address*.

In fact, though, a host system could have several interfaces, each with its own IP address. This is the case for computers that operate as gateways and firewalls from the local network to the Internet. One interface usually connects to the LAN and another to the Internet, as by two Ethernet cards. Each interface (such as an Ethernet card) has its own IP address. For example, when you use the Fedora Network Configuration tool to specify an IP address for an Ethernet card on your system, the Devices panel lists an entry for each Ethernet card installed on your computer, beginning with **eth0** for the first. Opening up a Device window, you can select the TCP protocol in the Protocols panel to open a TCP/IP setting window where you can enter the card's IP address. Other Ethernet cards have their own IP addresses. If you use a modem to connect to an ISP, you would set up a PPP interface that would also have its own IP address (usually dynamically assigned by the ISP). Remembering this distinction is important if you plan to use Linux to set up a local or home network, using Linux as your gateway machine to the Internet (see the section "IP Masquerading" in Chapter 20).

IPv4 Network Addresses

The IP address is divided into two parts: one part identifies the network, and the other part identifies a particular host. The network address identifies the network of which a particular interface on a host is a part. Two methods exist for implementing the network and host parts of an IP address: the original class-based IP addressing and the current Classless Interdomain Routing (CIDR) addressing. Class-based IP addressing designates officially predetermined parts of the address for the network and host addresses, whereas CIDR addressing allows the parts to be determined dynamically using a netmask.

Class-Based IP Addressing

Originally, IP addresses were organized according to classes. On the Internet, networks are organized into three classes depending on their size—classes A, B, and C. A class A network uses only the first segment for the network address and the remaining three for the host, allowing a great many computers to be connected to the same network. Most IP addresses reference smaller, class C networks. For a class C network, the first three segments are used to identify the network, and only the last segment identifies the host. Altogether, this forms a unique address with which to identify any network interface on computers in a TCP/IP network. For example, in the IP address 192.168.1.72, the network part is 192.168.1 and the interface/host part is 72. The interface/host is a part of a network whose own address is 192.168.1.0.

In a class C network, the first three numbers identify the network part of the IP address. This part is divided into three network numbers, each identifying a subnet. Networks on the Internet are organized into subnets, beginning with the largest and narrowing to small subnetworks. The last number is used to identify a particular computer, referred to as a *host*. You can think of the Internet as a series of networks with subnetworks; these subnetworks have their own subnetworks. The rightmost number identifies the host computer, and the number preceding it identifies the subnetwork of which the computer is a part. The number to the left of that identifies the network the subnetwork is part of, and so on. The Internet address 192.168.187.4 references the fourth computer connected to the network identified by the number 187. Network 187 is a subnet to a larger network identified as 168. This larger network is itself a subnet of the network identified as 192. Here's how it breaks down:

192.168.187.4	IPv4 address
192.168.187	Network identification
4	Host identification

Netmask

Systems derive the network address from the host address using the netmask. You can think of an IP address as a series of 32 binary bits, some of which are used for the network and the remainder for the host. The *netmask* has the network set of bits set to 1s, with the host bits set to 0s (see Figure 35-1). In a standard class-based IP address, all the numbers in the network part of your host address are set to 255, and the host part is set to 0. This has the effect of setting all the binary bits making up the network address to 1s. This, then, is your netmask. So, the netmask for the host address 192.168.1.72 is 255.255.255.0. The network part, 192.168.1, has been set to 255.255.255, and the host part, 72, has been set to 0. Systems can then use your netmask to derive your network address from your host address. They can determine what part of your host address makes up your network address and what those numbers are.

For those familiar with computer programming, a bitwise AND operation on the netmask and the host address results in zeroing the host part, leaving you with the network part of the host address. You can think of the address as being implemented as a four-byte integer, with each byte corresponding to a segment of the address. In a class C address, the three network segments correspond to the first three bytes and the host segment corresponds to the fourth byte. A netmask is designed to mask out the host part of the address, leaving the network segments alone. In the netmask for a standard class C network, the first three bytes are all 1s and the last byte consists of 0s. The 0s in the last byte mask out the host part of the address, and the 1s in the first three bytes leave the network part of the address alone. Figure 35-1 shows the bitwise operation of the netmask on the address 192.168.1.4. This is a class C address to the mask, which consists of twenty-four 1s making up the first three bytes and eight 0s making up the last byte. When it is applied to the address 192.168.1.4, the network address remains (192.168.1) and the host address is masked out (4), giving you 192.168.1.0 as the network address.

The netmask as used in Classless Interdomain Routing (CIDR) is much more flexible. Instead of having the size of the network address and its mask determined by the network class, it is determined by a number attached to the end of the IP address. This number simply specifies the size of the network address, how many bits in the address it takes up.

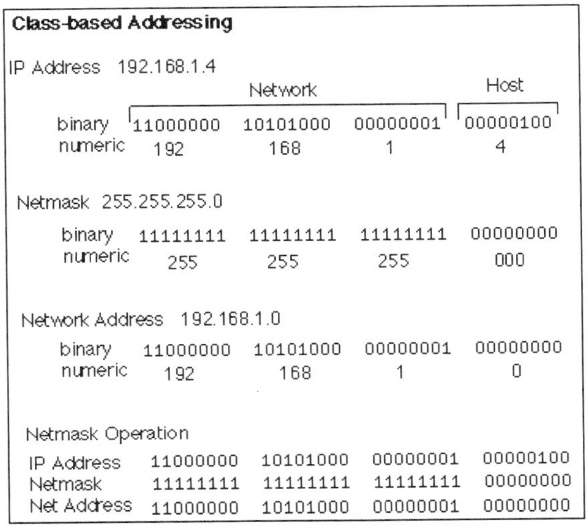

FIGURE 35-1
Class-based netmask
operations

```
Class-based Addressing

IP Address   192.168.1.4
                          Network                        Host
         binary  11000000   10101000   00000001  00000100
         numeric    192        168          1        4


Netmask  255.255.255.0

         binary   11111111   11111111   11111111  00000000
         numeric    255        255        255        000


Network Address   192.168.1.0

         binary   11000000   10101000   00000001  00000000
         numeric    192        168          1         0


Netmask Operation
IP Address    11000000   10101000   00000001   00000100
Netmask       11111111   11111111   11111111   00000000
Net Address   11000000   10101000   00000001   00000000
```

For example, in an IP address whose network part takes up the first three bytes (segments), the number of bits used for that network part is 24—eight bits to a byte (segment). Instead of using a netmask to determine the network address, the number for the network size is attached to the end of the address with a slash, as shown here:

```
192.168.1.72/24
```

CIDR gives you the advantage of specifying networks that are any size bits, instead of only three possible segments. You could have a network whose addresses takes up 14 bits, 22 bits, or even 25 bits. The host address can use whatever bits are left over. An IP address with 21 bits for the network can cover host addresses using the remaining 11 bits, 0 to 2,047.

Classless Interdomain Routing (CIDR)

Currently, the class-based organization of IP addresses is being replaced by the CIDR format. CIDR was designed for midsized networks, those between a class C and classes with numbers of hosts greater than 256 and smaller than 65,534. A class C network-based IP address using only one segment for hosts uses only one segment, an 8-bit integer, with a maximum value of 256. A class B network-based IP address uses two segments, which make up a 16-bit integer whose maximum value is 65,534. You can think of an address as a 32-bit integer taking up four bytes, where each byte is 8 bits. Each segment conforms to one of the four bytes. A class C network uses three segments, or 24 bits, to make up its network address. A class B network, in turn, uses two segments, or 16 bits, for its address. With this scheme, allowable host and network addresses are changed an entire byte at a time, segment to segment. With CIDR addressing, you can define host and network addresses by bits, instead of whole segments. For example, you can use CIDR addressing to expand the host segment from 8 bits to 9, rather than having to jump it to a class B 16 bits (two segments).

CIDR addressing notation achieves this by incorporating netmask information in the IP address (the netmask is applied to an IP address to determine the network part of the address). In the CIDR notation, the number of bits making up the network address is

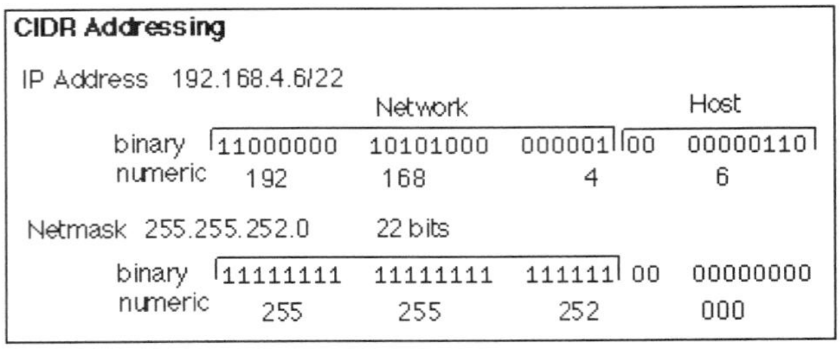

Figure 35-2
CIDR addressing

```
CIDR Addressing

IP Address   192.168.4.6/22
                              Network                    Host
          binary  11000000   10101000   000001 00   00000110
          numeric    192        168        4           6

Netmask  255.255.252.0        22 bits

          binary  11111111   11111111   111111 00   00000000
          numeric    255        255        252         000
```

placed after the IP address, following a slash. For example, the CIDR form of the class C 192.168.187.4 IP address is

```
192.168.187.4/24
```

Figure 35-2 shows an example of a CIDR address and its network mask. The IP address is 192.168.1.6 with a network mask of 22 bits, 192.168.1.6/22. The network address takes up the first 22 bits of the IP address, and the remaining 10 bits are used for the host address. The host address is taking up the equivalent of a class-based IP address's fourth segment (8 bits) and 2 bits from the third segment.

Table 35-3 lists the different IPv4 CIDR network masks available along with the maximum number of hosts. Both the short forms and the full forms of the netmasks are listed.

Short Form	Full Form	Maximum Number of Hosts
/8	/255.0.0.0	16,777,215 (A class)
/16	/255.255.0.0	65,535 (B class)
/17	/255.255.128.0	32,767
/18	/255.255.192.0	16,383
/19	/255.255.224.0	8,191
/20	/255.255.240.0	4,095
/21	/255.255.248.0	2,047
/22	/255.255.252.0	1,023
/23	/255.255.254.0	511
/24	/255.255.255.0	255 (C class)
/25	/255.255.255.128	127
/26	/255.255.255.192	63
/27	/255.255.255.224	31
/28	/255.255.255.240	15
/29	/255.255.255.248	7
/30	/255.255.255.252	3

Table 35-3   CIDR IPv4 Network Masks

IPv4 CIDR Addressing

The network address for any standard class C IPv4 IP address takes up the first three segments, 24 bits. If you want to create a network with a maximum of 512 hosts, you can give them IP addresses where the network address is 23 bits and the host address takes up 9 bits (0–511). The IP address notation remains the same, however, using the four 8-bit segments. This means a given segment's number could be used for both a network address and a host address. Segments are no longer wholly part of either the host address or the network address. Assigning a 23-bit network address and a 9-bit host address means that the number in the third segment is part of both the network address and the host address, the first 7 bits for the network and the last bit for the host. In this following example, the third number, 145, is used as the end of the network address and as the beginning of the host address:

```
192.168.145.67/23
```

This situation complicates CIDR addressing, and in some cases the only way to represent the address is to specify two or more network addresses. Check RFC 1520 at **www.ietf.org** for more details.

NOTE *A simple way to calculate the number of hosts a network can address is to take the number of bits in its host segment as a power of 2, and then subtract 2—that is, 2 to the number of host bits, minus 2. For example, an 8-bit host segment would be 2 to the power of 8, which equals 256. Subtract 2 (1 for the broadcast address, 255, and 1 for the zero value, 000) to leave you with 254 possible hosts.*

CIDR also allows a network administrator to take what is officially the host part of an IP address and break it up into subnetworks with fewer hosts. This is referred to as *subnetting.* A given network will have its official IP network address recognized on the Internet or by a larger network. The network administrator for that network could, in turn, create several smaller networks within it using CIDR network masking. A classic example is to take a standard class C network with 254 hosts and break it up into two smaller networks, each with 64 hosts. You do this by using a CIDR netmask to take a bit from the host part of the IP address and use it for the subnetworks. Numbers within the range of the original 254 addresses whose first bit would be set to 1 would represent one subnet, and the others, whose first bit would be set to 0, would constitute the remaining network. In the network whose network address is 192.168.187.0, where the last segment is used for the hostnames, that last host segment could be further split into two subnets, each with its own hosts. For two subnets, you would use the first bit in the last 8-bit segment for the network. The remaining 7 bits could then be used for host addresses, giving you a range of 127 hosts per network. The subnet whose bit is set to 0 would have a range of 1 to 127, with a CIDR netmask of 25. The 8-bit segment for the first host would be 00000001. So the host with the address of 1 in that network would have this IP address:

```
192.168.187.1/25
```

For the subnet where the first bit is 1, the first host would have an address of 129, with the CIDR netmask of 25, as shown here. The 8-bit sequence for the first host would be 10000001.

```
192.168.187.129/25
```

Each subnet would have a set of 126 addresses, the first from 1 to 126, and the second from 129 to 254; 127 is the broadcast address for the first subnet, and 128 is the network address for the second subnet. The possible subnets and their masks that you could use are shown here:

Subnetwork	CIDR Address	Binary Mask
First subnet network address	.0/25	00000000
Second subnet network address	.128/25	10000000
First subnet broadcast address	.127/25	01111111
Second subnet broadcast address	.255/25	11111111
First address in first subnet	.1/25	00000001
First address in second subnet	.129/25	10000001
Last address in first subnet	.126/25	01111110
Last address in second subnet	.254/25	11111110

IPv6 CIDR Addressing

IPv6 CIDR addressing works much the same as with the IPv4 method. The number of bits used for the network information is indicated by number following the address. A host (interface) address could take up much more than the 64 bits that it usually does in an IPv6 address, making the network prefix (address) section smaller than 64 bits. How many bits that the network prefix uses is indicated by the following number. In the next example the network prefix (address) uses only the first 48 bits of the IPv6 address, and the host address uses the remaining 80 bits:

```
FEC0:0000:0000:0000:FEDC:BA98:7654:3210/48
```

You can also use a two-colon notation (::) for the compressed version:

```
FEC0::FEDC:BA98:7654:3210/48
```

Though you can use CIDR to subnet addresses, IPv6 also supports a subnet field that can be used for subnets.

Obtaining an IP Address

IP addresses are officially allocated by IANA, which manages all aspects of Internet addressing (**www.iana.org**). IANA oversees Internet Registries (IRs), which, in turn, maintain Internet addresses on regional and local levels. The Internet Registry for the Americas is the American Registry for Internet Numbers (ARIN), whose Web site is at **www.arin.net**. These addresses are provided to users by Internet service providers (ISPs). You can obtain your own Internet address from an ISP, or if you are on a network already connected to the Internet, your network administrator can assign you one. If you are using an ISP, the ISP may temporarily assign one from a pool it has on hand with each use.

IPv4 Reserved Addresses

Certain numbers are reserved. The numbers 127, 0, or 255 cannot be part of an official IP address. The number 127 is used to designate the network address for the loopback interface on your system. The loopback interface enables users on your system to communicate with each other within the system without having to route through a network connection. Its network address would be 127.0.0.0, and its IP address is 127.0.0.1. For class-based IP addressing, the number 255 is a special broadcast identifier you can use to broadcast messages to all sites on a network. Using 255 for any part of the IP address references all nodes connected at that level. For example, 192.168.255.255 broadcasts a message to all computers on network 192.168, all its subnetworks, and their hosts. The address 192.168.187.255 broadcasts to every computer on the local network. If you use 0 for the network part of the address, the host number references a computer within your local network. For example, 0.0.0.6 references the sixth computer in your local network. If you want to broadcast to all computers on your local network, you can use the number 0.0.0.255. For CIDR IP addressing, the broadcast address may appear much like a normal IP address. As indicated in the preceding section, CIDR addressing allows the use of any number of bits to make up the IP address for either the network or the host part. For a broadcast address, the host part must have all its bits set to 1 (see Figure 35-3).

A special set of numbers is reserved for use on non-Internet LANs (RFC 1918). These are numbers that begin with the special network number 192.168 (for class C networks), as used in these examples. If you are setting up a LAN, such as a small business or a home network, you are free to use these numbers for your local machines. You can set up an intranet using network cards, such as Ethernet cards and Ethernet hubs, and then configure your machines with IP addresses starting from 192.168.1.1. The host segment can go up to 256. If you have three machines on your home network, you could give them the addresses 192.168.1.1, 192.168.1.2, and 192.168.1.3. You can implement Internet services, such as FTP, Web, and mail services, on your local machines and use any of the Internet tools to make use of those services. They all use the same TCP/IP protocols used on the Internet. For example, with FTP tools, you can transfer files among the machines on your network. With mail tools, you can send messages from one machine to another, and with a Web browser, you can access local Web sites that may be installed on a machine running its own Web servers. If you want to have one of your machines connected to the Internet or some other network, you can set it up to be a gateway machine. By convention, the gateway machine is usually given the address 192.168.1.1. With a method called *IP masquerading,* you can have any of the non-Internet machines use a gateway to connect to the Internet.

Numbers are also reserved for class A and class B non-Internet local networks. Table 35-4 lists these addresses. The possible addresses available span from 0 to 255 in the host segment

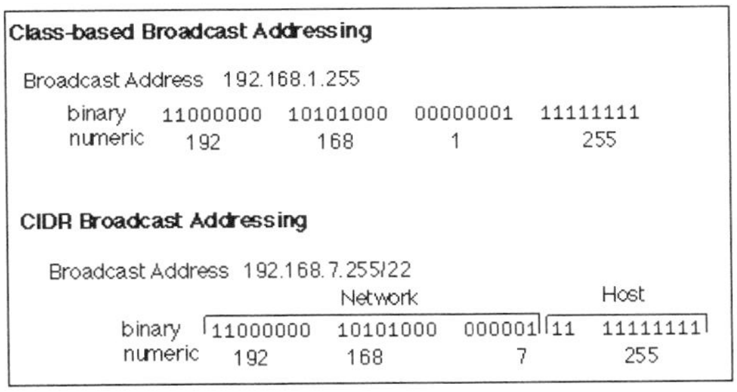

FIGURE 35-3
Class-based and CIDR broadcast addressing

```
Class-based Broadcast Addressing

Broadcast Address  192.168.1.255
     binary    11000000   10101000   00000001   11111111
     numeric      192        168         1         255


CIDR Broadcast Addressing

Broadcast Address  192.168.7.255/22
                         Network                           Host
     binary    11000000   10101000   000001 11   11111111
     numeric      192        168         7          255
```

IPv4 Private Network Addresses	Network Classes
10.0.0.0	Class A network
172.16.0.0–172.31.255.255	Class B network
192.168.0.0	Class C network
127.0.0.0	Loopback network (for system self-communication)

TABLE 35-4   Non-Internet IPv4 Local Network IP Addresses

of the address. For example, class B network addresses range from 172.16.0.0 to 172.31.255.255, giving you a total of 32,356 possible hosts. The class C network ranges from 192.168.0.0 to 192.168.255.255, giving you 256 possible subnetworks, each with 256 possible hosts. The network address 127.0.0.0 is reserved for a system's loopback interface, which allows it to communicate with itself, enabling users on the same system to send messages to each other.

Broadcast Addresses

The broadcast address allows a system to send the same message to all systems on your network at once. With IPv4 class-based IP addressing, you can easily determine the broadcast address using your host address: the broadcast address has the host part of your address set to 255. The network part remains untouched. So the broadcast address for the host address 192.168.1.72 is 192.168.1.255 (you combine the network part of the address with 255 in the host part). For CIDR IP addressing, you need to know the number of bits in the netmask. The remaining bits are set to 1 (see Figure 35-3). For example, an IP address of 192.168.4.6/22 has a broadcast address of 192.168.7.255/22. In this case, the first 22 bits are the network address and the last 10 bits are the host part set to the broadcast value (all 1s).

In fact, you can think of a class C broadcast address as merely a CIDR address using 24 bits (the first three segments) for the network address, and the last 8 bits (the fourth segment) as the broadcast address. The value 255 expressed in binary terms is simply 8 bits that are all 1s. 255 is the same as 11111111.

IP Address	Broadcast Address	IP Broadcast Number	Binary Equivalent
192.168.1.72	192.168.1.255	255	11111111
192.168.4.6/22	192.168.7.255/22	7.255 (last 2 bits in 7)	1111111111

Gateway Addresses

Some networks have a computer designated as the gateway to other networks. Every connection to and from a network to other networks passes through this gateway computer. Most local networks use gateways to establish a connection to the Internet. If you are on this type of network, you must provide the gateway address. If your network does not have a connection to the Internet, or a larger network, you may not need a gateway address. The gateway address is the address of the host system providing the gateway service to the network. On many networks, this host is given a host ID of 1: the gateway address for a network with the address 192.168.1 would be 192.168.1.1, but this is only a convention. To be sure of your gateway address, ask your network administrator.

Name Server Addresses

Many networks, including the Internet, have computers that provide a Domain Name Service (DNS) that translates the domain names of networks and hosts into IP addresses. These are known as the network's *domain name servers.* The DNS makes your computer identifiable on a network, using only your domain name, rather than your IP address. You can also use the domain names of other systems to reference them, so you needn't know their IP addresses. You must know the IP addresses of any domain name servers for your network, however. You can obtain the addresses from your system administrator (often more than one exists). Even if you are using an ISP, you must know the address of the domain name servers your ISP operates for the Internet.

IPv6 Addressing

IPv6 addresses introduces major changes into the format and method of addressing systems under the Internet Protocol (see RFC 3513 at **www.ietf.org/rfc** or **www.faqs.org** for more details). There are several different kinds of addressing with different fields for the network segment. The host segment has been expanded to a 64-bit address, allowing direct addressing for a far larger number of systems. Each address begins with a type field specifying the kind of address, which will then determine how its network segment is organized. These changes are designed not only to expand the address space but to also provide greater control over transmissions at the address level.

NOTE   *Red Hat Enterprise Linux and Fedora are distributed with IPv6 support already enabled in the kernel. Kernel support for IPv6 is provided by the IPv6 kernel module. Kernel configuration support can be found under Device Drivers | Networking Support | Networking Options | The IPv6 Protocol.*

IPv6 Address Format

An IPv6 address consists of 128 bits, up from the 32 bits used in IPv4 addresses. The first 64 bits are used for network addressing, of which the first few bits are reserved for indicating the address type. The last 64 bits are used for the interface address, known as the interface identifier field. The amount of bits used for subnetting can be adjusted with a CIDR mask, much like that in IPv4 CIDR addressing (see the preceding section).

An IPv6 address is written as eight segments representing 16 bits each (128 bits total). To more easily represent 16-bit binary numbers, hexadecimal numbers are used. Hexadecimal numbers use 16 unique numbers, instead of the 8 used in octal numbering. These are 0–9, continuing with the characters A–F.

In the following example the first four segments represent the network part of the IPv6 address, and the following four segments represent the interface (host) address:

```
FEC0:0000:0000:0000:0008:0800:200C:417A
```

You can cut any preceding zeros, but not trailing zeros, in any given segment. Segments with all zeros can be reduced to a single zero.

```
FEC0:0:0:0:8:800:200C:417A
```

The loopback address used for localhost addressing can be written with seven preceding zeros and a 1.

```
0:0:0:0:0:0:0:1
```

Many addresses will have sequences of zeros. IPv6 supports a shorthand symbol for representing a sequence of several zeros in adjacent fields. This consists of a double colon (::). There can be only one use of the :: symbol per address.

```
FEC0::8:800:200C:417A
```

The loopback address 0000000000000001 can be reduced to just the following:

```
::1
```

To ease the transition from IPv4 addressing to IPv6, a form of addressing incorporating IPv4 addresses is also supported. In this case, the IPv4 address (32 bits) can be used to represent the last two segments of an IPv6 address and can be written using IPv4 notation.

```
FEC0::192.168.0.3
```

IPv6 Interface Identifiers

The identifier part of the IPv6 address takes up the second 64 bits, consisting of four segments containing four hexadecimal numbers. The interface ID is a 64-bit (four-segment) Extended Unique Identifier (EUI-64) generated from a network device's Media Access Control (MAC) address.

IPv6 Address Types

There are three basic kinds of IPv6 addresses, unicast, multicast, and anycast. These, in turn, can have their own types of addresses.

- A *unicast* address is used for a packet that is sent to a single destination.
- An *anycast* address is used for a packet that can be sent to more than one destination.
- A *multicast* address is used to broadcast a packet to a range of destinations.

In IPv6, addressing is controlled by the format prefix that operates as a kind of address type. The format prefix is the first field of the IP address. The three major kinds of unicast network addresses are global, link-local, and site-local. Global, site-local, and link-local are indicated by their own format prefix (see Table 35-5).

- Global addresses begin with the address type 3, site local with FEC, and link-local with FE8. Global addresses can be sent across the Internet.
- Link-local addresses are used for physically connected systems on a local network.
- Site-local can be used for any hosts on a local network. Site-local addresses operate like IPv4 private addresses; they are used only for local access and cannot be used to transmit over the Internet.

IPv6 Addresses Format Prefixes and Reserved Addresses	Description
3	Unicast global addresses
FE8	Unicast link-local addresses, used for physically connected hosts on a network
FEC	Unicast site-local addresses, comparable to IPv4 private addresses
0000000000000001	Unicast loopback address (for system self-communication, localhost)
0000000000000000	Unspecified address
FF	Multicast addresses

TABLE 35-5   IPv6 Format Prefixes and Reserved Addresses

In addition, IPv6 has two special reserved addresses. The address 0000000000000001 is reserved for the loopback address used for a system's localhost address, and the address 0000000000000000 is the unspecified address.

IPv6 Unicast Global Addresses

IPv6 global addresses currently use four fields: the format prefix, a global routing prefix, the subnet identifier, and the interface identifier. The format prefix for a unicast global address is 3 (3 bits). The global routing prefix references the network address (45 bits), and the subnet ID references a subnet within the site (16 bits).

IPv6 Unicast Local Use Addresses: Link-Local and Site-Local Addresses

For local use, IPv6 provides both link-local and site-local addresses. Link-local addressing is used for interfaces (hosts) that are physically connected to a network. This is usually a small local network. A link-local address uses only three fields, the format prefix FE8 (10 bits), an empty field (54 bits), and the interface identifier (host address) (64 bits). In effect, the network section is empty.

IPv6 site-local addresses have three fields: the format prefix (10 bits), the subnet identifier (54 bits), and the interface identifier (64 bits). Except for any local subnetting, there is no network address.

IPv6 Multicast Addresses

Multicast addresses have a format prefix of FF (8 bits) with flag and scope fields to indicate whether the multicast group is permanent or temporary and whether it is local or global in scope. A group identifier (112 bits) references the multicast group. For the scope, 2 is link-local, 5 is site-local, and E is global. In addition to their interface identifiers, hosts will also have a group ID that can be used as a broadcast address. You use this address to broadcast to the hosts. The following example will broadcast only to those hosts on the local network (5) with the group ID 101:

```
FF05:0:0:0:0:0:0:101
```

To broadcast to all the hosts in a link-local scope, you would use the broadcast address:

```
FF02:0:0:0:0:0:0:1
```

For a site-local scope, a local network, you would use

```
FF05:0:0:0:0:0:0:2
```

IPv6 and IPv4 Coexistence Methods

In the transition from IPv4 to IPv6, many networks will find the need to support both. Some will be connected to networks that use the contrary protocol, and others will have to connect through other network connections that use that protocol. There are several official IETF methods for providing IPv6 and IPv4 cooperation, which fall into three main categories:

- **Dual-stack**   Allows IPv4 and IPv6 to coexist on the same networks.
- **Translation**   Enables IPv6 devices to communicate with IPv4 devices.
- **Tunneling**   Allows transmission from one IPv6 network to another through IPv4 networks as well as allowing IPv6 hosts to operate on or through IPv4 networks.

In the dual-stack methods both IPv6 and IPv4 addresses are supported on the network. Applications and DNS servers can use either to transmit data.

Translation uses NAT tables (see Chapter 37) to translate IPv6 addresses to corresponding IPv4 address and vice versa as needed. IPv4 applications can then freely interact with IPv6 applications. IPv6-to-IPv6 transmissions are passed directly through, enabling full IPv6 functionality.

Tunneling is used when one IPv6 network needs to transmit to another through an IPv4 network that cannot handle IPv6 addresses. With tunneling, the IPv6 packet is encapsulated within an IPv4 packet, where the IPv4 network then uses the outer IPv4 addressing to pass on the packet. Several methods are used for tunneling, as shown here, as well as direct manual manipulation:

- **6-over-4**   Used within a network to use IPv4 multicasting to implement a virtual LAN to support IPv6 hosts, without an IPv6 router (RFC 2529)
- **6-to-4**   Used to allow IPv6 networks to connect to and through a larger IPv4 network (the Internet), using the IPv4 network address as an IPv6 network prefix (RFC 3056)
- **Tunnel brokers**   Web-based services that create tunnels (RFC 3053)

TCP/IP Configuration Files

A set of configuration files in the **/etc** directory, shown in Table 35-6, are used to set up and manage your TCP/IP network. These configuration files specify such network information as host and domain names, IP addresses, and interface options. The IP addresses and domain names of other Internet hosts you want to access are entered in these files. If you configured your network during installation, you can already find that information in these files.

Address	Description
Host address	IP address of your system; it has a network part to identify the network you are on and a host part to identify your own system
Network address	IP address of your network
Broadcast address	IP address for sending messages to all hosts on your network at once
Gateway address	IP address of your gateway system, if you have one (usually the network part of your host IP address with the host part set to 1)
Domain name server addresses	IP addresses of domain name servers your network uses
Netmask	Used to determine the network and host parts of your IP address
File	**Description**
/etc/hosts	Associates hostnames with IP addresses, lists domain names for remote hosts with their IP addresses
/etc/sysconfig/network-scripts	Network connection configurations
/etc/host.conf	Lists resolver options
/etc/nsswitch.conf	Name Switch Service configuration
/etc/resolv.conf	Lists domain name server names, IP addresses (nameserver), and domain names where remote hosts may be located (search)
/etc/protocols	Lists protocols available on your system
/etc/services	Lists available network services, such as FTP and Telnet, and the ports they use
/etc/sysconfig/networking	Holds network configuration files managed by system-config-network
/etc/sysconfig/network	Network configuration information

TABLE 35-6   TCP/IP Configuration Addresses and Files

Identifying Hostnames: /etc/hosts

Without the unique IP address the TCP/IP network uses to identify computers, a particular computer cannot be located. Because IP addresses are difficult to use or remember, domain names are used instead. For each IP address, a domain name exists. When you use a domain name to reference a computer on the network, your system translates it into its associated IP address. This address can then be used by your network to locate that computer.

Originally, every computer on the network was responsible for maintaining a list of the hostnames and their IP addresses. This list is still kept in the **/etc/hosts** file. When you use a domain name, your system looks up its IP address in the **hosts** file. The system administrator is responsible for maintaining this list. Because of the explosive growth of the Internet and the development of more and more large networks, the responsibility for associating domain names and IP addresses has been taken over by domain name servers. The **hosts** file is still used to hold the domain names and IP addresses of frequently accessed hosts, however. Your system normally checks your **hosts** file for the IP address of a domain name before taking the added step of accessing a name server.

The format of a domain name entry in the **hosts** file is the IP address followed by the domain name, separated by a space. You can then add aliases for the hostname. After the entry, on the same line, you can enter a comment. A comment is always preceded by a **#** symbol. You can already find an entry in your **hosts** file for localhost.localdomain and localhost with the IP address 127.0.0.1; localhost is a special identification used by your computer to enable users on your system to communicate locally with each other. The IP address 127.0.0.1 is a special reserved address used by every computer for this purpose. It identifies what is technically referred to as a *loopback device*. The corresponding IPV6 localhost address is **::1**, which has the host name **localhost6**. You should never remove the **localhost** and **localhost6** entries. A sample **/etc/hosts** file is shown here:

/etc/hosts
```
127.0.0.1            localhost.localdomain localhost turtle.mytrek.com
::1                  localhost6.localdomain6   localhost6
192.168.0.1          turtle.mytrek.com
192.168.0.2          rabbit.mytrek.com
192.168.34.56        pango1.mytrain.com
```

/etc/resolv.conf

As noted in Chapter 36, the **/etc/resolv.conf** file holds the IP addresses for your DNS servers along with domains to search. A DNS entry will begin with the term nameserver followed by the name server's IP address. A search entry will list network domain addresses. Check this file to see if your network DNS servers have been correctly listed. I you have a router for a local network, DHCP will automatically place an entry for it in this file. The router in turn will reference your ISP's nameserver.

/etc/resolv.conf
```
search  mytrek.com    mytrain.com
nameserver  192.168.0.1
nameserver  192.168.0.3
```

/etc/sysconfig/network-scripts

The **/etc/sysconfig/network-scripts** directory holds configuration information for different network connection devices such the IP address and network address used. For a detailed discussion, see the section "Network Interfaces and Routes: ifconfig and route" later in this chapter.

/etc/sysconfig/networking

The **/etc/sysconfig/networking** directory holds configuration information set up with system-config-network (Network on the System Settings menu and window). These files should not be edited manually. The profiles directory holds configurations for the different profiles you set up. Different profiles directories will include the hosts file listing host domain names and IP addresses, the network file holding your system's host name, and the **resolv.conf** file, which contains your domain name servers. The device configuration file for the connection you use for that profile will also be listed, such as **ifcfg-eth0** for the first Ethernet device. These are all configurations that may change depending on the profile you use. For example, at the office you may use an Ethernet connection on a company network with its own DNS servers, whereas at home you may use a modem connection to an ISP with its own Internet DNS servers. Your hostname and domain name may vary depending on the networks your different profiles connect to.

/etc/services

The **/etc/services** file lists network services available on your system, such as FTP and Telnet, and associates each with a particular port. Here, you can find out what port your Web server is checking or what port is used for your FTP server. You can give a service an alias, which you specify after the port number. You can then reference the service using the alias.

/etc/protocols

The **/etc/protocols** file lists the TCP/IP protocols currently supported by your system. Each entry shows the protocol number, its keyword identifier, and a brief description. See **www .iana.org/assignments/protocol-numbers** for a complete listing.

/etc/sysconfig/network

The **/etc/sysconfig/network** file contains system definitions for your network configuration. These include definitions for your domain name, gateway, and hostname, as shown here:

```
NETWORKING=yes
HOSTNAME=turtle.mytrek.com
GATEWAY=192.168.0.1
```

Domain Name System (DNS)

Each computer connected to a TCP/IP network, such as the Internet, is identified by its own IP address. IP addresses are difficult to remember, so a domain name version of each IP address is also used to identify a host. As described in Chapter 35, a domain name consists of two parts, the hostname and the domain. The hostname is the computer's specific name, and the domain identifies the network of which the computer is a part. The domains used for the United States usually have extensions that identify the type of host. For example, **.edu** is used for educational institutions and **.com** is used for businesses. International domains usually have extensions that indicate the country they are located in, such as **.de** for Germany or **.au** for Australia. The combination of a hostname, domain, and extension forms a unique name by which a computer can be referenced. The domain can, in turn, be split into further subdomains.

As you know, a computer on a network can still be identified only by its IP address, even if it has a hostname. You can use a hostname to reference a computer on a network, but this involves using the hostname to look up the corresponding IP address in a database. The network then uses the IP address, not the hostname, to access the computer. Before the advent of large TCP/IP networks, such as the Internet, it was feasible for each computer on a network to maintain a file with a list of all the hostnames and IP addresses of the computers connected on its network. Whenever a hostname was used, it was looked up in this file and the corresponding IP address was located. You can still do this on your own system for remote systems you access frequently.

As networks became larger, it became impractical—and, in the case of the Internet, impossible—for each computer to maintain its own list of all the domain names and IP addresses. To provide the service of translating domain addresses to IP addresses, databases of domain names were developed and placed on their own servers. To find the IP address of a domain name, you send a query to a name server, which then looks up the IP address for you and sends it back. In a large network, several name servers can cover different parts of the network. If a name server cannot find a particular IP address, it sends the query on to another name server that is more likely to have it.

If you are administering a network and you need to set up a name server for it, you can configure a Linux system to operate as a name server. To do so, you must start up a name server daemon and then wait for domain name queries. A name server makes use of several configuration files that enable it to answer requests. The name server software used on Linux systems is the Berkeley Internet Name Domain (BIND) server distributed by the Internet Software Consortium (**www.isc.org**). Chapter 36 describes the process of setting up a domain name server in detail.

Name servers are queried by resolvers. These are programs specially designed to obtain addresses from name servers. To use domain names on your system, you must configure your own resolver. Your local resolver is configured with your **/etc/host.conf** and **/etc/resolv .conf** files. You can use **/etc/nsswitch** in place of **/etc/host.conf**.

host.conf

Your **host.conf** file lists resolver options (shown in Table 35-7). Each option can have several fields, separated by spaces or tabs. You can use a **#** at the beginning of a line to enter a comment. The options tell the resolver what services to use. The order of the list is important. The resolver begins with the first option listed and moves on to the next ones in turn. You can find the **host.conf** file in your **/etc** directory, along with other configuration files.

Option	Description
`order`	Specifies sequence of name resolution methods: `hosts` Checks for name in the local **/etc/host** file `bind` Queries a DNS name server for an address `nis` Uses Network Information Service protocol to obtain an address
`alert`	Checks addresses of remote sites attempting to access your system; you turn it on or off with the **on** and **off** options
`nospoof`	Confirms addresses of remote sites attempting to access your system
`trim`	Checks your local host's file; removes the domain name and checks only for the hostname; enables you to use only a hostname in your host file for an IP address
`multi`	Checks your local hosts file; allows a host to have several IP addresses; you turn it on or off with the **on** and **off** options

TABLE 35-7   Resolver Options, **host.conf**

In the next example of a **host.conf** file, the `order` option instructs your resolver first to look up names in your local **/etc/hosts** file, and then, if that fails, to query domain name servers. The system does not have multiple addresses.

/etc/host.conf
```
# host.conf file
# Lookup names in host file and then check DNS
order bind host
# There are no multiple addresses
multi off
```

/etc/nsswitch.conf: Name Service Switch

Different functions in the standard C Library must be configured to operate on your Linux system. Previously, database-like services, such as password support and name services like NIS or DNS, directly accessed these functions, using a fixed search order. For GNU C Library 2.*x*, used on current versions of Linux, this configuration is carried out by a scheme called the Name Service Switch (NSS), which is based on the method of the same name used by Sun Microsystems Solaris 2 OS. The database sources and their lookup order are listed in the **/etc/nsswitch.conf** file.

The **/etc/nsswitch.conf** file holds entries for the different configuration files that can be controlled by NSS. The system configuration files that NSS supports are listed in Table 35-8. An entry consists of two fields: the service and the configuration specification. The service consists of the configuration file followed by a colon. The second field is the configuration specification for that file, which holds instructions on how the lookup procedure will work. The configuration specification can contain service specifications and action items. Service specifications are the services to search. Currently, valid service specifications are nis, nis-plus,

File	Description
aliases	Mail aliases, used by Sendmail
ethers	Ethernet numbers
group	Groups of users
hosts	Hostnames and numbers
netgroup	Network-wide list of hosts and users, used for access rules; C libraries before glibc 2.1 only support netgroups over NIS
network	Network names and numbers
passwd	User passwords
protocols	Network protocols
publickey	Public and secret keys for SecureRPC used by NFS and NIS+
rpc	Remote procedure call names and numbers
services	Network services
shadow	Shadow user passwords

TABLE 35-8   NSS-Supported Files

Service	Description
files	Checks corresponding **/etc** file for the configuration (for example, **/etc/ hosts** for hosts); this service is valid for all files
db	Checks corresponding **/var/db** databases for the configuration; valid for all files except **netgroup**
compat	Valid only for **passwd**, **group**, and **shadow** files
dns	Checks the DNS service; valid only for **hosts** file
nis	Checks the NIS service; valid for all files
nisplus	NIS version 3
hesiod	Uses Hesiod for lookup

TABLE 35-9 NSS Configuration Services

files, db, dns, and compat (see Table 35-9). Not all are valid for each configuration file. For example, the dns service is valid only for the **hosts** file, whereas nis is valid for all files. The following example will first check the local **/etc/password** file and then NIS.

```
passwd:  files nisplus
```

An action item specifies the action to take for a specific service. An action item is placed within brackets after a service. A configuration specification can list several services, each with its own action item. In the following example, the entry for the network file has a configuration specification that says to check the NIS service and, if not found, to check the **/etc/protocols** file:

```
protocols: nisplus [NOTFOUND=return] files
```

An action item consists of a status and an action. The status holds a possible result of a service lookup, and the action is the action to take if the status is true. Currently, the possible status values are SUCCESS, NOTFOUND, UNAVAIL, and TRYAGAIN (service temporarily unavailable). The possible actions are return and continue: return stops the lookup process for the configuration file, whereas continue continues on to the next listed service. In the preceding example, if the record is not found in NIS, the lookup process ends.

Shown here is a copy of the **/etc/nsswitch.conf** file, which lists commonly used entries. Comments and commented-out entries begin with a **#** sign:

/etc/nsswitch.conf
```
#
# /etc/nsswitch.conf
#
# An example Name Service Switch config file.
passwd:         db files nisplus nis
shadow:         db files nisplus nis
group:          db files nisplus nis
hosts:          files nisplus dns
```

```
bootparams:        nisplus [NOTFOUND=return] files
ethers:            files
netmasks:          files
networks:          files
protocols:         files
rpc:               files
services:          files
netgroup:          nisplus
publickey:         nisplus
automount:         files
aliases:           files nisplus
```

Network Interfaces and Routes: ifconfig and route

Your connection to a network is made by your system through a particular hardware interface, such as an Ethernet card or a modem. Data passing through this interface is then routed to your network. The **ifconfig** command configures your network interfaces, and the **route** command sets up network connections accordingly. If you configure an interface with a network configuration tool, such as system-config-network, you needn't use **ifconfig** or **route**. However, you can directly configure interfaces using **ifconfig** and **route**, if you want. Every time you start your system, the network interfaces and their routes must be established. This is done automatically for you when you boot up by **ifconfig** and **route** commands executed for each interface by the **/etc/rc.d/init.d/network** initialization file, which is executed whenever you start your system. If you are manually adding your own interfaces, you must set up the network script to perform the **ifconfig** and **route** operations for your new interfaces.

Network Startup Script: /etc/rc.d/init.d/network

Your network interface is started up using the **network** script in the **/etc/rc.d/init.d** directory. This script will activate your network interface cards (NICs) as well as implement configuration information such as gateway, host, and name server identities. You can manually shut down and start your network interface using this script and the **restart**, **start**, or **stop** options, as well as system-config-services. You can run the script with the **service** command. The following commands shut down and then start up your network interface:

```
service network stop
service network start
```

If you are changing network configuration, you will have to restart your network interface for the changes to take effect:

```
service network restart
```

To test if your interface is working, use the **ping** command with an IP address of a system on your network, such as your gateway machine. The **ping** command continually repeats until you stop it with a CTRL-C.

```
ping 192.168.0.1
```

Interface Configuration Scripts: /etc/sysconfig/network-scripts

The **/etc/rc.d/init.d/network** file performs the startup operations by executing several specialized scripts located in the **/etc/sysconfig/network-scripts** directory. The **network** script uses a script in that directory called **ifup** to activate a network connection, and **ifdown** to shut it down; **ifup** and **ifdown** will invoke other scripts tailored to the kind of device being worked on, such as **ifup-ppp** for modems using the PPP protocol, or **ifup-ipv6** for network devices that use IP Protocol version 6 addressing.

NOTE *You can activate and deactivate network interfaces using system-config-network accessible from the System | Administration | Network.*

The **ifup** and **ifdown** scripts make use of interface configuration files that bear the names of the network interfaces currently configured, such as **ifcfg-eth0** for the first Ethernet device. These files define shell variables that hold information on the interface, such as whether to start them at boot time. For example, the **ifcfg-eth0** file holds definitions for NETWORK, BROADCAST, and IPADDR, which are assigned the network, broadcast, and IP addresses that the device uses.

The **ifdown** and **ifup** scripts, in turn, hold the **ifconfig** and **route** commands to activate scripts using these variables defined in the interface configuration files. If you want to manually start up an interface with **ifup**, you simply use the interface configuration file as its argument. The following command starts up the second Ethernet card:

```
cd /etc/sysconfig/network-scripts
ifup ifcfg-eth1
```

Interface configuration files are automatically generated when you configure your network connections, such as with a Red Hat and Fedora's system-config-network administrative tool . You can also manually edit these interface configuration files, making changes such as whether to start up the interface at boot or not (though using a configuration tool such as system-config-network is easier). A sample **ifcfg-eth0** file is shown here using a static IP address:

/etc/sysconfig/network-scripts/ifcfg-eth0
```
DEVICE=eth0
BOOTPROTO=static
BROADCAST=192.168.0.255
IPADDR=192.168.0.1
NETMASK=255.255.255.0
NETWORK=192.168.0.0
ONBOOT=yes
```

A DHCP-based interface would look something like this, where BOOTPROTO is assigned dhcp:

/etc/sysconfig/network-scripts/ifcfg-eth0
```
DEVICE=eth0
BOOTPROTO=dhcp
HWADDR=00:00:00:00:00:01
TYPE=Ethernet
ONBOOT=yes
```

ifconfig

The `ifconfig` command takes as its arguments the name of an interface and an IP address, as well as options. The `ifconfig` command then assigns the IP address to the interface. Your system now knows that such an interface exists and that it references a particular IP address. In addition, you can specify whether the IP address is a host address or a network address. You can use a domain name for the IP address, provided the domain name is listed along with its IP address in the **/etc/hosts** file. The syntax for the `ifconfig` command is as follows:

```
# ifconfig interface -host_net_flag address options
```

The *host_net_flag* can be either **-host** or **-net** to indicate a host or network IP address. The **-host** flag is the default. The `ifconfig` command can have several options, which set different features of the interface, such as the maximum number of bytes it can transfer (**mtu**) or the broadcast address. The **up** and **down** options activate and deactivate the interface. In the next example, the `ifconfig` command configures an Ethernet interface:

```
# ifconfig eth0 192.168.0.1
```

For a simple configuration such as this, `ifconfig` automatically generates a standard broadcast address and netmask. The standard broadcast address is the network address with the number 255 for the host address. For a class C network, the standard netmask is 255.255.255.0, whereas for a class A network, the standard netmask is 255.0.0.0. If you are connected to a network with a particular netmask and broadcast address, however, you must specify them when you use `ifconfig`. The option for specifying the broadcast address is **broadcast**; for the network mask, it is **netmask**. Table 35-10 lists the different `ifconfig` options. In the next example, `ifconfig` includes the netmask and broadcast address:

```
# ifconfig eth0 192.168.0.1 broadcast 192.168.0.255 netmask 255.255.255.0
```

Once you configure your interface, you can use `ifconfig` with the **up** option to activate it and with the **down** option to deactivate it. If you specify an IP address in an `ifconfig` operation, as in the preceding example, the **up** option is implied.

```
# ifconfig eth0 up
```

Point-to-point interfaces such as Parallel IP (PLIP), Serial Line IP (SLIP), and Point-to-Point Protocol (PPP) require you to include the **pointopoint** option. A PLIP interface name is identified with the name **plip** with an attached number. For example, **plip0** is the first PLIP interface. SLIP interfaces use **slip0**. PPP interfaces start with **ppp0**. Point-to-point interfaces are those that usually operate between only two hosts, such as two computers connected over a modem. When you specify the **pointopoint** option, you need to include the IP address of the host. In the next example, a PLIP interface is configured that connects the computer at IP address 192.168.1.72 with one at 204.166.254.14. If domain addresses were listed for these systems in **/etc/hosts**, those domain names could be used in place of the IP addresses.

```
# ifconfig plip0 192.168.1.72 pointopoint 204.166.254.14
```

Option	Description
Interface	Name of the network interface, such as **eth0** for the first Ethernet device or **ppp0** for the first PPP device (modem)
`up`	Activates an interface; implied if IP address is specified
`down`	Deactivates an interface
`allmulti`	Turns on or off the promiscuous mode; preceding hyphen (-) turns it off; this allows network monitoring
`mtu` *n*	Maximum number of bytes that can be sent on this interface per transmission
`dstaddr` *address*	Destination IP address on a point-to-point connection
`netmask` *address*	IP network mask; preceding hyphen (-) turns it off
`broadcast` *address*	Broadcast address; preceding hyphen (-) turns it off
`point-to-point` *address*	Point-to-point mode for interface; if address is included, it is assigned to remote system
`hw`	Sets hardware address of interface
Address	IP address assigned to interface

Table 35-10   The ifconfig Options

If you need to, you can also use `ifconfig` to configure your loopback device. The name of the loopback device is **lo**, and its IP address is the special address 127.0.0.1. The following example shows the configuration:

```
# ifconfig lo 127.0.0.1
```

The `ifconfig` command is useful for checking on the status of an interface. If you enter the `ifconfig` command along with the name of the interface, information about that interface is displayed:

```
# ifconfig eth0
```

To see if your loopback interface is configured, you can use `ifconfig` with the loopback interface name, **lo**:

```
# ifconfig lo
```

Routing

A packet that is part of a transmission takes a certain *route* to reach its destination. On a large network, packets are transmitted from one computer to another until the destination computer is reached. The route determines where the process starts and to what computer your system needs to send the packet for it to reach its destination. On small networks, routing may be static—that is, the route from one system to another is fixed. One system knows how to reach another, moving through fixed paths. On larger networks and on the

Internet, however, routing is dynamic. Your system knows the first computer to send its packet off to, and then that computer takes the packet from there, passing it on to another computer, which then determines where to pass it on. For dynamic routing, your system needs to know little. Static routing, however, can become complex because you have to keep track of all the network connections.

Your routes are listed in your routing table in the **/proc/net/route** file. To display the routing table, enter **route** with no arguments (the **netstat -r** command will also display the routing table):

```
# route
Kernel routing table
Destination Gateway       Genmask       Flags Metric Ref Use  Iface
192.168.0.0    *          255.255.255.0 U      0       0   0    etho
127.0.0.0      *          255.0.2055.0  U      0       0   0    lo
default      192.168.0.1  0.0.0.0       UG     0       0   0    eth0
```

Each entry in the routing table has several fields, providing information such as the route destination and the type of interface used. The different fields are listed in Table 35-11.

With the **add** argument, you can add routes either for networks with the **-net** option or with the **-host** option for IP interfaces (hosts). The **-host** option is the default. In addition, you can then specify several parameters for information, such as the netmask (**netmask**), the gateway (**gw**), the interface device (**dev**), and the default route (**default**). If you have more than one IP interface on your system, such as several Ethernet cards, you must specify the name of the interface using the **dev** parameter. If your network has a gateway host, you use the **gw** parameter to specify it. If your system is connected to a network, at least one entry should be in your routing table that specifies the default route. This is the route taken by a message packet when no other route entry leads to its destination. The following example is the routing of an Ethernet interface:

```
# route add 192.168.1.2 dev eth0
```

Field	Description
Destination	Destination IP address of the route
Gateway	IP address or hostname of the gateway the route uses; * indicates no gateway is used
Genmask	The netmask for the route
Flags	Type of route: U = up, H = host, G = gateway, D = dynamic, M = modified
Metric	Metric cost of route
Ref	Number of routes that depend on this one
Window	TCP window for AX.25 networks
Use	Number of times used
Iface	Type of interface this route uses

TABLE 35-11   Routing Table Entries

If your system has only the single Ethernet device as your IP interface, you could leave out the **dev eth0** parameter:

```
# route add 192.168.1.2
```

You can delete any route you establish by invoking **ifconfig** with the **del** argument and the IP address of that route, as in this example:

```
# route del 192.168.1.2
```

For a gateway, you first add a route to the gateway interface, and then add a route specifying that it is a gateway. The address of the gateway interface in this example is 192.168.1.1:

```
# route add 192.168.1.1
# route add default gw 192.168.1.1
```

If you are using the gateway to access a subnet, add the network address for that network (in this example, 192.168.23.0):

```
# route add -net 192.168.23.0 gw dev eth1
```

To add another IP address to a different network interface on your system, use the **ifconfig** and **route** commands with the new IP address. The following command configures a second Ethernet card (**eth1**) with the IP address 192.168.1.3:

```
ifconfig eth1 192.168.1.3
route add 192.168.1.3 dev eth1
```

Monitoring Your Network: ping, netstat, tcpdump, EtherApe, Ettercap, and Wireshark

Several applications are available on Linux to let you monitor your network activity. Graphical applications like EtherApe, Ettercap, and Wireshark provide detailed displays and logs to let you analyze and detect network usage patterns. Other tools like ping offers specific services.

The EtherApe, Ettercap, and Wireshark tools can be accessed on the Applications | Internet menu. Tools like ping, tracerout, and netstat can be accessed with the Gnome Network Tools application accessible on the Applications | System Tools menu, as well as being rung individually on a command line (Terminal window).

EtherApe provides a simple graphicial display for your protocol activity. The Preferences dialog lets you set features like the protocol to check and the kind of traffic to report.

ping

With the ping program, you can check to see if you can actually access another host on your network. The ping program sends a request to the host for a reply. The host then sends a reply back, and it is displayed on your screen. The ping program continually sends such a request until you stop it with a **break** command, CTRL-C. You see one reply after another scroll by on your screen until you stop the program. If ping cannot access a host, it issues a message saying the host is unreachable. If ping fails, this may be an indication that your network connection is not working. It may be only the particular interface, a basic configuration problem, or a bad physical connection. The ping utility uses the Internet Control Message Protocol (ICMP), discussed in Chapter 20. Networks may block these protocols as a security measure, also preventing ping from working. A ping failure may simply indicate a security precaution on the part of the queried network.

To use ping, enter **ping** and the name of the host.

```
$ ping ftp.redhat.com
```

Ettercap

Ettercap is a sniffer program designed to detect Man in the Middle attacks. In this kind of attack, packets are detected and modified in transit to let an unauthorized user access a network. You can use either its graphical interface or its command line interface. Ettercap can perform Unified sniffing on all connections, or Bridged sniffing on a connection between network interfaces. Ettercap uses plugins for specific tasks, like dos_attack to detect Denial of Service attacks and dns-spoof for DNS spoofing detection. Check the plugins Help panel, or enter **ettercap -P list** for a complete listing. Ettercap can be run in several modes, including a text mode, a command line cursor mode, a script mode using commands in a file, and even as a daemon logging results automatically.

Wireshark

Wireshark is a network protocol analyzer that lets you capture packets transmitted across your network, selecting and examining those from protocols you want to check. You can examine packets from a particular transmissions, displaying the data in readable formats. The Wireshark interface displays three panes: a listing of current packets, the protocol tree for the currently selected packet, a display of the selected packets contents. The first pane categorizes entries by time, source, destination, and protocol. There are button headers for each. To sort a set of entries by a particular category, click its header. For example, group entries by protocol, click the Protocol button; for destinations, use the Destination button.

Capture Options

To configure Wireshark, you select the Options entry from the Capture menu. This opens an options window where you can select the network interface to watch. Here you can also select options such as the file to hold your captured information in and a size limit for the capture, along with a filter to screen packets. With the promiscuous mode selected, you can see all network traffic passing through that device, whereas with it off, you will see only those packets destined for that device. You can then click the start button to start Wireshark. To stop and start Wireshark, you select the Stop and Start entries on the Capture menu.

- The Capture Files option lets you select a file to save your capture in. If no file is selected, then data is simply displayed in the Wireshark window. If you want to keep a continuous running snapshot of your network traffic, you can use ring buffers. These are a series of files that are used to save captured data. When they fill up, the capture begins saving again to the first file, and so on. Check Use multiple file to enable this option.

- Display options control whether packets are displayed in real time on the Wireshark window.

- Limits let you set a limit for the capture packet size.

- Capture filter lets you choose the type of protocol you want to check.

- Name resolution enables the display of host and domain names instead of IP addresses, if possible.

Wireshark Filters

A filter lets you select packets that match specified criteria, such as packets from a particular host. Criteria are specified using expressions supported by the Packet Capture Library and implemented by **tcpdump**. Wireshark filters use similar expressions to those used by the **tcpdump** command. Check the **tcpdump** Man page for detailed descriptions.

You can set up a either a Search filter in the Find panel (Edit menu) to search for certain packets, or set up a Capture filter in the Options panel (Capture menu) to select which packets to record. The filter window is the same for both. On the filter window you can select the protocol you want to search or capture. The Filter name and string will appear in the Properties segment. You can also enter your own string, setting up a new filter of your own. The string must be a filter expression.

To create a new filter, enter the name you want to give it in the Filter Name box. Then in the Filter String box, enter the filter expression, like **icmp**. Then click New. Your new filter will appear in the list. To change a filter, select it and change its expression in the Filter String box, then click Change.

A filter expression consists of an ID, such as the name or number of host, and a qualifier. Qualifiers come in three types: type, direction, and protocol. The type can reference the host, network, or port. The type qualifiers are **host**, **net**, and **port**. Direction selects either source or destination packets, or both. The source qualifier is **src**, and the destination, **dst**. With no destination qualifier, both directions are selected. Protocol lets you specify packets for a certain protocol. Protocols are represented using their lowercase names, such as **icmp** for ICMP. For example, the expression to list all packets coming in from a particular host would be **src host** *hostname*, where *hostname* is the source host. The following example will display all packets from the 192.168.0.3 host:

```
src host 192.168.0.3
```

Using just **host** will check for all packets going out as well as coming in for that host. The **port** qualifier will check for packets passing through a particular port. To check for a particular protocol, you use the protocol name. For example, to check for all ICMP packets you would use the expression

```
icmp
```

There are also several special qualifiers that let you further control your selection. The **gateway** qualifier lets you detect packets passing through a gateway. The **broadcast** and **multi-cast** qualifiers detect packets broadcast to a network. The **greater** and **less** qualifiers can be applied to numbers such as ports or IP addresses.

You can combine expressions into a single complex Boolean expression using **and**, **or**, or **not**. This lets you create a more refined filter. For example, to capture only the ICMP packets coming in from host 192.168.0.2, you can use

```
src host 192.168.0.3 and icmp
```

tcpdump

Like Wireshark, **tcpdump** will capture network packets, saving them in a file where you can examine them. **tcpdump** operates entirely from the command line. You will have to open a terminal window to run it. Using various options, you can refine your capture, specifying the kinds of packets you want. **tcpdump** uses a set of options to specify actions you want to take, which include limiting the size of the capture, deciding which file to save it to, and choosing any filter you want to apply to it. Check the **tcpdump** Man page for a complete listing.

- The **-i** option lets you specify an interface to listen to.

- With the **-c** option, you can limit the number of packets to capture.

- Packets will be output to the standard output by default. To save them to a file, you can use the **-w** option.

- You can later read a packet file using the **-r** option and apply a filter expression to it.

The **tcpdump** command takes as its argument a filter expression that you can use to refine your capture. Wireshark uses the same filter expressions as **tcpdump** (see the filters discussion in Wireshark).

netstat

The netstat program provides real-time information on the status of your network connections, as well as network statistics and the routing table. The **netstat** command has several options you can use to bring up different sorts of information about your network:

```
# netstat
Active Internet connections
Proto Recv-Q Send-Q Local Address Foreign Address (State) User
tcp 0 0 turtle.mytrek.com:01 pango1.mytrain.com.:ftp ESTABLISHED dylan
Active UNIX domain sockets
Proto RefCnt Flags Type State Path
unix 1 [ ACC ] SOCK_STREAM LISTENING /dev/printer
unix 2 [ ] SOCK_STREAM CONNECTED /dev/log
unix 1 [ ACC ] SOCK_STREAM LISTENING /dev/nwapi
unix 2 [ ] SOCK_STREAM CONNECTED /dev/log
unix 2 [ ] SOCK_STREAM CONNECTED
unix 1 [ ACC ] SOCK_STREAM LISTENING /dev/log
```

The **netstat** command with no options lists the network connections on your system. First, active TCP connections are listed, and then the active domain sockets are listed. The domain sockets contain processes used to set up communications among your system and other systems. You can use **netstat** with the **-r** option to display the routing table, and **netstat** with the **-i** option displays the uses of the different network interfaces.

IP Aliasing

In some cases, you may want to assign a single Linux system that has only one network interface to two or more IP addresses. For example, you may want to run different Web sites that can be accessed with separate IP addresses on this same system. In effect, you are setting up an alias for your system, another address by which it can be accessed. In fact, you are assigning two IP addresses to the same network interface—for example, assigning a single Ethernet card two IP addresses. This procedure, referred to as *IP aliasing,* is used to set up multiple IP-based virtual hosts for Internet servers. This method enables you to run several Web servers on the same machine using a single interface (or more than one on each of several interfaces). See Chapters 22 and 23 for FTP and Web server information about virtual hosts, and Chapter 36 for Domain Name System configuration.

Setting up an IP alias is a simple matter of configuring a network interface on your system to listen for the added IP address. Your system needs to know what IP addresses it should listen for and on what network interface. You set up IP aliases using the **ifconfig** and **route** commands, or a network administrative tool.

To add another address to the same interface, you need to qualify the interface by adding a colon and a number. For example, if you are adding another IP address to the first Ethernet card (**eth0**), you would add a **:0** to its interface name, **eth0:0**. The following example shows the **ifconfig** and **route** commands for the Ethernet interface 192.168.1.2 and two IP aliases added to it: 192.168.1.100 and 192.168.1.101. To add yet another IP address to this same interface, you would use **eth0:1**, incrementing the qualifier, and so on. The first **ifconfig** command assigns the main IP address, 192.168.1.2, to the first Ethernet device, **eth0**. Then, two other IP addresses are assigned to that same device. In the first **route** command, the network route is set up for the Ethernet device, and then routes are set up for each IP interface. The interfaces for the two aliases are indicated with **eth0:0** and **eth0:1**:

```
ifconfig eth0 192.168.1.2
ifconfig eth0:0 192.168.1.100
ifconfig eth0:1 192.168.1.101
route add -net 192.168.1.0 dev eth0
route add -host 192.168.1.2 dev eth0
route add -host 192.168.1.100 dev eth0:0
route add -host 192.168.1.101 dev eth0:1
```

IP aliasing must be supported by the kernel before you can use it. If your kernel does not support it, you may have to rebuild the kernel (including IP aliasing support), or use loadable modules to add IP aliasing.

36

CHAPTER

Domain Name System

The Domain Name System (DNS) is an Internet service that locates and translates domain names into their corresponding Internet Protocol (IP) addresses. As you may recall, all computers connected to the Internet are addressed using an IP address. As a normal user on a network might have to access many different hosts, keeping track of the IP addresses needed quickly became a problem. It was much easier to label hosts with names and use the names to access them. Names were associated with IP addresses. When a user used a name to access a host, the corresponding IP address was looked up first and then used to provide access.

With the changeover from IPv4 to IPv6 address, DNS servers will have some configuration differences. Both are covered here, though some topics will use IPv4 addressing for better clarity, as they are easier to represent. IPv4 and IPv6 addressing are discussed in detail in Chapter 35.

DNS Address Translations

The process of translating IP addresses into associated names is fairly straightforward. Small networks can be set up easily, with just the basic configuration. The task becomes much more complex when you deal with larger networks and with the Internet. The sheer size of the task can make DNS configuration a complex operation.

Fully Qualified Domain Names

IP addresses were associated with corresponding names, called fully qualified domain names. A *fully qualified domain name* is composed of three or more segments. The first segment is the name that identifies the host, and the remaining segments are for the network in which the host is located. The network segments of a fully qualified domain name are usually referred to simply as the domain name, while the host part is referred to as the hostname (though this is also used to refer to the complete fully qualified domain name). In effect, subnets are referred to as domains. The fully qualified domain name **www.linux.org** could have an IPv4 address 198.182.196.56, where 198.182.196 is the network address and 56 is the host ID. Computers can be accessed only with an IP address, so a fully qualified domain name must first be translated into its corresponding IP address to be of any use. The parts of the IP address that make up the domain name and the hosts can vary. See Chapter 35 for a detailed discussion of IP addresses, including network classes and Classless Interdomain Routing (CIDR).

IPv4 Addresses

The IP address may be implemented in either the newer IPv6 (Internet Protocol Version 6) format or the older and more common IPv4 (Internet Protocol Version 4) format. Since the IPv4 addressing is much easier to read, that format will be used in these examples. In the older IPv4 format, the IP address consists of a number composed of four segments separated by periods. Depending on the type of network, several of the first segments are used for the network address and one or more of the last segments are used for the host address. In a standard class C network used in smaller networks, the first three segments are the computer's network address and the last segment is the computer's host ID (as used in these examples). For example, in the address 192.168.0.2, 192.168.0 is the network address and 2 is the computer's host ID within that network. Together, they make up an IP address by which the computer can be addressed from anywhere on the Internet. IP addresses, though, are difficult to remember and easy to get wrong.

IPv6 Addressing

IPv6 addressing uses a very different approach designed to provide more flexibility and support for very large address spaces (see Chapter 35). There are three different types of IPv6 addresses, unicast, multicast, and anycast, of which unicast is the most commonly used. A unicast address is directed to a particular interface. There are several kinds of unicast addresses, depending on how the address is used. For example, you can have a global unicast address for access through the Internet or a site-level unicast address for private networks.

Though consisting of 128 bits in eight segments (16 bits, 2 bytes, per segment), an IPv6 address is made up of several fields that conform roughly to the segments and capabilities of an IPv4 address, networking information, subnet information, and the interface identifier (host ID). The network information includes a format prefix indicating the type of network connection. In addition, a subnet identifier can be used to specify a local subnet (see Chapter 35). The network information takes up the first several segments; the remainder are used for the interface ID. The interface ID is a 64-bit (four-segment) Extended Unique Identifier (EUI-64) generated from a network device's Media Access Control (MAC) address. IP addresses are written in hexadecimal numbers, making them difficult to use. Each segment is separated from the next by a colon, and a set of consecutive segments with zero values like the reserved segment can be left empty.

Manual Translations: /etc/hosts

Any computer on the Internet can maintain a file that manually associates IP addresses with domain names. On Linux and Unix systems, this file is called the **/etc/hosts** file. Here, you can enter the IP addresses and domain names of computers you commonly access. Using this method, however, each computer needs a complete listing of all other computers on the Internet, and that listing must be updated constantly. Early on, this became clearly impractical for the Internet, though it is still feasible for small, isolated networks as well as simple home networks.

DNS Servers

The Domain Name System has been implemented to deal with the task of translating the domain name of any computer on the Internet to its IP address. The task is carried out by interconnecting servers that manage the Domain Name System (also referred to as DNS servers or name servers). These DNS servers keep lists of fully qualified domain names and their IP addresses, matching one up with the other. This service that they provide to a network is referred to as the Domain Name System. The Internet is composed of many connected subnets called *domains*, each with its own DNS servers that keep track of all the fully qualified domain names and IP addresses for all the computers on its network. DNS servers are hierarchically linked to root servers, which, in turn, connect to other root servers and the DNS servers on their subnets throughout the Internet. The section of a network for which a given DNS server is responsible is called a *zone*. Although a zone may correspond to a domain, many zones may, in fact, be within a domain, each with its own name server. This is true for large domains where too many systems exist for one name server to manage.

DNS Operation

When a user enters a fully qualified domain name to access a remote host, a resolver program queries the local network's DNS server requesting the corresponding IP address for that remote host. With the IP address, the user can then access the remote host. In Figure 36-1, the user at **rabbit.mytrek.com** wants to connect to the remote host **lizard.mytrek.com**. **rabbit .mytrek.com** first sends a request to the network's DNS server—in this case, **turtle.mytrek .com**—to look up the name **lizard.mytrek.com** and find its IP address. **turtle.mytrek.com** then returns the IP address for **lizard.mytrek.com**, 192.168.0.3, to the requesting host, **rabbit.mytrek.com**. With the IP address, the user at **rabbit.mytrek.com** can then connect to **lizard.mytrek.com**.

DNS Clients: Resolvers

The names of the DNS servers that service a host's network are kept in the host's **/etc/resolv .conf** file (see Chapter 35). When setting up an Internet connection, the name servers provided by your Internet service provider (ISP) were placed in this file. These name servers resolve any fully qualified domain names that you use when you access different Internet sites.

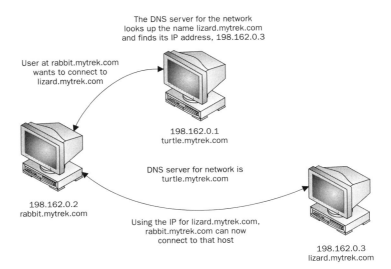

FIGURE 36-1
DNS server
operation

The DNS server for the network
looks up the name lizard.mytrek.com
and finds its IP address, 198.162.0.3

User at rabbit.mytrek.com
wants to connect to
lizard.mytrek.com

198.162.0.1
turtle.mytrek.com

DNS server for network is
turtle.mytrek.com

198.162.0.2
rabbit.mytrek.com

Using the IP for lizard.mytrek.com,
rabbit.mytrek.com can now
connect to that host

198.162.0.3
lizard.mytrek.com

For example, when you enter a Web site name in your browser, the name is looked up by the name servers and the name's associated IP address is then used to access the site.

/etc/resolv.conf
```
search   mytrek.com    mytrain.com
nameserver  192.168.0.1
nameserver  192.168.0.3
```

Local Area Network Addressing

If you are setting up a DNS server for a local area network (LAN) that is not connected to the Internet, you should use a special set of IP numbers reserved for such local networks (also known as *private networks* or *intranets*). This is especially true if you are implementing IP masquerading, where only a gateway machine has an Internet address, and the others make use of that one address to connect to the Internet. Though structurally the same, IPv4 and IPv6 use different addressing formats for local addresses. Many local and home networks still use the IPv4 format, and this is the format used in the following local addressing example.

IPv4 Private Networks

IPv4 provides a range of private addresses for the three classes supported by IPv4. As you have seen, class C IPv4 network numbers have the special network number 192.168. Numbers are also reserved for class A and class B non-Internet local networks. Table 36-1 lists these addresses. The possible addresses available span from 0 to 255 in the host segment of the address. For example, class B network addresses range from 172.16.0.0 to 172.16.255.255, giving you a total of 65,534 possible hosts. The class C network ranges from 192.168.0.0 to 192.168.255.255, giving you 254 possible subnetworks, each with 254 possible hosts. The number 127.0.0.0 is reserved for a system's loopback interface, which allows it to communicate with itself, as it enables users on the same system to send messages to each other.

These numbers were originally designed for class-based addressing. However, they can just as easily be used for Classless Interdomain Routing (CIDR) addressing, where you can create subnetworks with a smaller number of hosts. For example, the 254 hosts addressed in a class C network could be split into two subnetworks, each with 125 hosts. See Chapter 35 for more details.

IPv6 Private Networks

IPv6 supports private networks with site-local addresses that provide the same functionality of IPv4 private addresses. The site-local addresses have no public routing information. They cannot access the Internet. They are restricted to the site they are used on. The site-local addresses use only three fields: a format prefix, subnet identifier, and interface identifier.

Address	Networks
10.0.0.0	Class A network
172.16.0.0–172.31.255.255	Class B network
192.168.0.0	Class C network
127.0.0.0	Loopback network (for system self-communication)

TABLE 36-1   Non-Internet Private Network IP Addresses

A site-level address has the format prefix **fec0**. If you have no subnets, it will be set to 0. This will give you a network prefix of **fec0:0:0:0**. You can drop the set of empty zeros to give you **fec0::**. The interface ID field will hold the interface identification information, similar to the host ID information in IPv4.

```
fec0::                 IPv6 site-local prefix
```

The loopback device will have special address of **::1**, also known as localhost.

```
::1                    IPv6 loopback network
```

Rather than using a special set of reserved addresses as IPv4 does, with IPv6 you only use the site-local prefix, **fec0**, and the special loopback address, **::1**.

TIP *Once your network is set up, you can use ping6 or ping to see if it is working. The ping6 tool is designed for Ipv6 addresses, whereas ping is used for IPv4.*

Local Network Address Example Using IPv4

If you are setting up a LAN, such as a small business or home network, you are free to use class C IPv4 network (254 hosts or less) that have the special network number 192.168, as used in these examples. These are numbers for your local machines. You can set up a private network, such as an intranet, using network cards such as Ethernet cards and Ethernet hubs, and then configure your machines with IP addresses starting from 192.168.0.1. The host segment can range from 1 to 254, where 255 is used for the broadcast address. If you have three machines on your home network, you can give them the addresses 192.168.0.1, 192.168.0.2, and 192.168.0.3. You can then set up domain name services for your network by running a DNS server on one of the machines. This machine becomes your network's DNS server. You can then give your machines fully qualified domain names and configure your DNS server to translate the names to their corresponding IP addresses. As shown in Figure 36-2, for example,

FIGURE 36-2
DNS server and
network

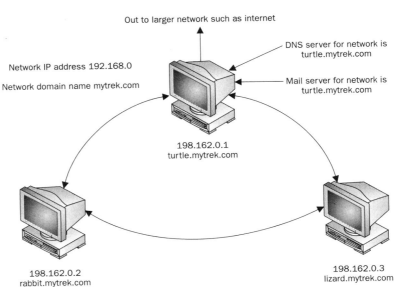

Out to larger network such as internet

DNS server for network is
turtle.mytrek.com

Network IP address 192.168.0

Mail server for network is
turtle.mytrek.com

Network domain name mytrek.com

198.162.0.1
turtle.mytrek.com

198.162.0.2
rabbit.mytrek.com

198.162.0.3
lizard.mytrek.com

you could give the machine 192.168.0.1 the name **turtle.mytrek.com** and the machine 192.168.0.2 the name **rabbit.mytrek.com**. You can also implement Internet services on your network such as FTP, Web, and mail services by setting up servers for them on your machines. You can then configure your DNS server to let users access those services using fully qualified domain names. For example, for the **mytrek.com** network, the Web server could be accessed using the name **www.mytrek.com**. Instead of a Domain Name Service, you could have the **/etc/hosts** files in each machine contain the entire list of IP addresses and domain names for all the machines in your network. But for any changes, you would have to update each machine's **/etc/hosts** file.

BIND

The DNS server software currently in use on Linux systems is Berkeley Internet Name Domain (BIND). BIND was originally developed at the University of California, Berkeley, and is currently maintained and supported by the Internet Software Consortium (ISC). You can obtain BIND information and current software releases from its Web site at **www.isc.org**. Web page documentation and manuals are included with the software package. At the site you can also access the BIND Administration Manual for detailed configuration information. RPM packages are available at distribution FTP sites. The BIND directory in **/usr/share/doc** contains extensive documentation, including Web page manuals and examples. The Linux HOW-TO for the Domain Name System, DNS-HOWTO, provides detailed examples. Documentation, news, and DNS tools can be obtained from the DNS Resource Directory (DNSRD) at **www .dns.net/dnsrd**. The site includes extensive links and online documentation, including the *BIND Operations Guide (BOG)*. See Table 36-2 for a list of DNS resources.

Alternative DNS Servers

Several alternative DNS servers are now available. These include djbdns, noted for its security features, CustomDNS, a dynamic server implemented in Java (**customdns.sourceforge.net**), and Yaku-NS, an embedded server. The djbdns server (**cr.yp.to/djbdns.html**), written by D.J. Bernstein, is designed specifically with security in mind, providing a set of small server daemons, each performing specialized tasks. In particular, djbdns separates the name server, caching server, and zone transfer tasks into separate programs: tinydns (tinydns.org) implements the authoritative name server for a network, whereas dnscache implements a caching server that will resolve requests from DNS clients such as Web browsers. In effect, dnscache operates as the name server that your applications will use to resolve addresses. dnscache will then query tinydns to resolve addresses on your local network. Zone transfers are handled separately by axfrdns and asfget.

Web Site	Resource
www.isc.org	Internet Software Consortium
www.dns.net/dnsrd	DNS Resource Directory
www.nominum.com	Nominum, BIND support and consulting

TABLE 36-2   BIND Resources

BIND Servers and Tools

The BIND DNS server software consists of a name server daemon, several sample configuration files, and resolver libraries. As of 1998, a new version of BIND, beginning with the series number 8.*x*, implemented a new configuration file using a new syntax. Version 9.0 adds new security features and support for IPv6. Older versions, which begin with the number 4.*x*, use a different configuration file with an older syntax. Most distributions currently install the newer 9.*x* version of BIND.

The name of the BIND name server daemon is **named**. To operate your machine as a name server, simply run the **named** daemon with the appropriate configuration. The **named** daemon listens for resolution requests and provides the correct IP address for the requested hostname. You can use the Remote Name Daemon Controller utility, **rndc**, provided with BIND to start, stop, restart, and check the status of the server as you test its configuration. **rndc** with the **stop** command stops **named** and, with the **start** command, starts it again, reading your **named.conf** file. **rndc** with the **help** command provides a list of all **rndc** commands. Configuration is set in the **/etc/rndc.conf** file. See the Red Hat Reference Guide (Red Hat Enterprise documentation) for detailed information on configuring **rndc** access to your DNS server. Once your name server is running, you can test it using the **dig** or **nslookup** utility, which queries a name server, providing information about hosts and domains. If you start **dig** with no arguments, it enters an interactive mode where you can issue different **dig** commands to refine your queries.

To check the syntax of your DNS server configuration and zone files, BIND provides the **named-checkconfig** and **named-checkzone** tools: **named-checkconfig** will check the syntax of DNS configuration file, **named.conf**, and **named-checkzone** will check a zone file's syntax. Other syntax checking tools are also available, such as **nslint**, which operates like the programming tool **lint**.

Numerous other DNS tools are also available. Check the DNS Resource Directory at **www.dns.net/dnsrd** for a listing. Table 36-3 lists several DNS administrative tools.

Tool	Description
dig *domain*	Domain Information Groper, tool to obtain information on a DNS server. Preferred over **nslookup**
host *hostname*	Simple lookup of hosts
nslookup *domain*	Tool to query DNS servers for information about domains and hosts
named-checkconf	BIND tool to check the syntax of your DNS configuration file, **/etc/named.conf**
named-checkzone	BIND tool to check the syntax of your DNS zone files
nslint	Tool to check the syntax of your DNS configuration and zone files
rndc *command*	Remote Name Daemon Controller, an administrative tool for managing a DNS server (version 9.*x*)
ndc	Name Daemon Controller (version 8.*x*)
system-config-bind	Fedora Core Bind DNS server configuration tool

TABLE 36-3   BIND Diagnostic and Administrative Tools

Starting and Stopping the BIND Server

The **named** daemon is started using a startup script in the **/etc/rc.d/init.d** directory called **named**. You can use this script to start, stop, and restart the daemon using the **stop**, **start**, and **restart** arguments. You can invoke the script with the **service** command as shown here:

```
service named restart
```

On most distributions, **named** runs as a stand-alone daemon, starting up when the system boots and constantly running. If you don't want **named** to start up automatically, you can use system-config-services or **chkconfig** to change its status.

Domain Name System Configuration

You configure a DNS server using a configuration file, several zone files, and a cache file. The part of a network for which the name server is responsible is called a *zone*. A zone is not the same as a domain, because in a large domain you could have several zones, each with its own name server. You could also have one name server service several zones. In this case, each zone has its own zone file.

DNS Zones

The zone files hold resource records that provide hostname and IP address associations for computers on the network for which the DNS server is responsible. Zone files exist for the server's network and the local machine. Zone entries are defined in the **named.conf** file. Here, you place zone entries for your master, slave, and forward DNS servers. The most commonly used zone types are described here:

- **Master zone**   This is the primary zone file for the network supported by the DNS server. It holds the mappings from domain names to IP addresses for all the hosts on that network.

- **Slave zone**   These are references to other DNS servers for your network. Your network can have a master DNS server and several slave DNS servers to help carry the workload. A slave DNS server automatically copies its configuration files, including all zone files, from the master DNS server. Any changes to the master configuration files trigger an automatic download of these files to the slave servers. In effect, you only have to manage the configuration files for the master DNS server, as they are automatically copied to the slave servers.

- **Forward zone**   The forward zone lists name servers outside your network that should be searched if your network's name server fails to resolve an address.

- **IN-ADDR.ARPA zone**   DNS can also provide reverse resolutions, where an IP address is used to determine the associated domain name address. Such lookups are provided by **IN-ADDR.ARPA** zone files. Each master zone file usually has a corresponding **IN-ADDR.ARPA** zone file to provide reverse resolution for that zone. For each master zone entry, a corresponding reverse mapping zone entry named **IN-ADDR.ARPA** also exists, as well as one for the localhost. This entry performs reverse mapping from an IP address to its domain name. The name of the zone entry uses the domain IP address, which is the IP address with segments listed starting from the host, instead of the network. So for the IP address 192.168.0.4, where 4 is the host address, the corresponding domain IP address is 4.0.168.192, listing the segments in reverse order. The reverse mapping for the localhost is 1.0.0.127.

- **IP6.ARPA zone**   This is the IPv6 equivalent of the **IN-ADDR.ARPA** zone, providing reverse resolution for that zone. The IP6.ARPA zone uses bit labels the provide a bit-level format that is easier to write, requiring no reverse calculation on the part of the DNS administrator.

- **IP6.INT zone**   This is the older form of the IPv6 IP6.ARPA zone, which is the equivalent of the IPv4 **IN-ADDR.ARPA** zone, providing reverse resolution for a zone. IP6.INT is meant to be used with the older AAAA IPv6 address records. IP6.INT uses a nibble format to specify a reverse zone. In this format, a hexadecimal IPv6 address is segmented into each of its 32 hexadecimal numbers and listed in reverse order, each segment separated by a period.

- **Hint zone**   A hint zone specifies the root name servers and is denoted by a period (.). A DNS server is normally connected to a larger network, such as the Internet, which has its own DNS servers. DNS servers are connected this way hierarchically, with each server having its root servers to which it can send resolution queries. The root servers are designated in the hint zone.

NOTE   *You can use system-config-bind, the BIND Configuration Tool, to configure a DNS server for a simple local network (see Chapter 5). system-config-bind (accessible from Server Settings window or menu) provides a GNOME interface for setting up the master, slave, forward, and IN-ADDR.ARPA zones you would need for a server. Be aware, though, that it will overwrite your **named.conf** file. system-config-bind can be accessed from the Server Settings menu.*

DNS Server Types

There are several kinds of DNS servers, each designed to perform a different type of task under the Domain Name System. The basic kind of DNS server is the *master* server. Each network must have at least one master server that is responsible for resolving names on the network. Large networks may need several DNS servers. Some of these can be slave servers that can be updated directly from a master server. Others may be *alternative master* servers that hosts in a network can use. Both are commonly referred to as *secondary* servers. For DNS requests a DNS server cannot resolve, the request can be forwarded to specific DNS servers outside the network, such as on the Internet. DNS servers in a network can be set up to perform this task and are referred to as *forwarder* servers. To help bear the workload, local DNS servers can be set up within a network that operate as caching servers. Such a server merely collects DNS lookups from previous requests it sent to the main DNS server. Any repeated requests can then be answered by the caching server.

A server that can answer DNS queries for a given zone with authority is known as an *authoritative* server. An authoritative server holds the DNS configuration records for hosts in a zone that will associate each host's DNS name with an IP address. For example, a master server is an authoritative server. So are slave and stealth servers (see the list that follows).

A caching server is not authoritative. It only holds whatever associations it picked up from other servers and cannot guarantee that the associations are valid.

- **Master server**   This is the primary DNS server for a zone.

- **Slave server**   A DNS server that receives zone information from the master server.

- **Forwarder server**   A server that forwards unresolved DNS requests to outside DNS servers. Can be used to keep other servers on a local network hidden from the Internet.

- **Caching only server**   Caches DNS information it receives from DNS servers and uses it to resolve local requests.

- **Stealth server**   A DNS server for a zone not listed as a name server by the master DNS server.

Location of Bind Server Files: /etc/named/chroot

Both the configuration and zone files used by BIND are placed in a special subdirectory called **chroot** located within the **/var/named** directory, **/var/named/chroot**. The **chroot** directory sets up a chroot jail, creating a virtual root directory for any users of the DNS service. This prevents access by DNS users to any other part of the system. When the BIND server starts up, the **chroot** command is run on the **named** service making **/var/named/chroot** the root directory for any users of the DNS service. Check the Chroot-BIND HOWTO at the Linux Documentation site for more information (**www.tldp.org**).

Within the **/var/named/chroot** directory are subdirectories that hold the BIND files on your system. These include **var**, **etc**, and **dev**. The **var** subdirectory has a **named** subdirectory within which are the zone files used by the BIND DNS server. Links to these files are located in the **/var/named** directory. The **named.conf** configuration files is located in the **/var/named/chroot/etc** directory. The **/etc/named.conf** file is just a link to this file. The links allow your configuration files and tools to reference zone files using the standard BIND DNS directory names, as in **/etc/named**. For new configuration and zone files you would create new links.

```
/etc/named/chroot/etc/named.conf              BIND configuration file
/etc/named/chroot/var/named                   BIND zone files
```

named.conf

The configuration file for the **named** daemon is **named.conf**. A link to it is located in the **/etc** directory, with the original file located in the **/var/named/chroot/etc** directory. It uses a flexible syntax similar to C programs. The format enables easy configuration of selected zones, enabling features such as access control lists and categorized logging. The **named. conf** file consists of BIND configuration statements with attached blocks within which specific options are listed. A configuration statement is followed by arguments and a block that is delimited with braces. Within the block are lines of option and feature entries. Each entry is terminated with a semicolon. Comments can use the C, C++, or Shell/Perl syntax: enclosing **/* */**, preceding **//**, or preceding **#**. The following example shows a **zone** statement followed by the zone name and a block of options that begin with an opening brace (**{**). Each option entry ends with a semicolon. The entire block ends with a closing brace, also followed by a semicolon. The format for a **named.conf** entry is shown here, along with the different kinds of comments allowed. Tables 36-5, 36-6, and 36-7 list several commonly used statements and options.

```
// comments
/* comments */
# comments

statements {
 options and features; //comments
};
```

The following example shows a simple caching server entry:

```
// a caching only nameserver config
//
zone "." {
        type hint;
        file "named.ca";
        };
```

Once you have created your configuration file, you should check its syntax with the **named-checkconfig** tool. Enter the command on a shell command line. If you do not specify a configuration file, it will default to **/etc/named.conf**.

```
named-checkconfig
```

The zone Statement

The **zone** statement is used to specify the domains the name server will service. You enter the keyword **zone**, followed by the name of the domain placed within double quotes. Do not place a period at the end of the domain name. In the following example, a period is within the domain name, but not at the end, "**mytrek.com;**" this differs from the zone file, which requires a period at the end of a complete domain name.

After the zone name, you can specify the class **in**, which stands for Internet. You can also leave it out, in which case **in** is assumed (there are only a few other esoteric classes that are rarely used). Within the zone block, you can place several options (see Table 36-6). Two essential options are **type** and **file**. The **type** option is used to specify the zone's type. The **file** option is used to specify the name of the zone file to be used for this zone. You can choose from several types of zones: master, slave, stub, forward, and hint. *Master* specifies that the zone holds master information and is authorized to act on it. A master server was called a primary server in the older 4.*x* BIND configuration. *Slave* indicates that the zone needs to update its data periodically from a specified master name server. You use this entry if your name server is operating as a secondary server for another primary (master) DNS server. A *stub zone* copies only other name server entries, instead of the entire zone. A *forward zone* directs all queries to name servers specified in a **forwarders** statement. A *hint zone* specifies the set of root name servers used by all Internet DNS servers. You can also specify several options that can override any global options set with the **options** statement.

Type	Description
master	Primary DNS zone
slave	Slave DNS server; controlled by a master DNS server
hint	Set of root DNS Internet servers
forward	Forwards any queries in it to other servers
stub	Like a slave zone, but holds only names of DNS servers

TABLE 36-4   DNS BIND Zone Types

Table 36-4 lists the BIND zone types. The following example shows a simple **zone** statement for the **mytrek.com** domain. Its class is Internet (in), and its type is master. The name of its zone file is usually the same as the zone name, in this case, "**mytrek.com**."

```
zone "mytrek.com" in {
        type master;
        file "mytrek.com";
        };
```

Configuration Statements

Other statements, such as **acl**, **server**, **options**, and **logging**, enable you to configure different features for your name server (see Table 36-5). The **server** statement defines the

Statement	Description
`/* comment */`	BIND comment in C syntax.
`// comment`	BIND comment in C++ syntax.
`# comment`	BIND comment in Unix shell and Perl syntax.
`acl`	Defines a named IP address matching list.
`include`	Includes a file, interpreting it as part of the **named.conf** file.
`key`	Specifies key information for use in authentication and authorization.
`logging`	Specifies what the server logs and where the log messages are sent.
`options`	Global server configuration options and defaults for other statements.
`controls`	Declares control channels to be used by the ndc utility.
`server`	Sets certain configuration options for the specified server basis.
`sortlists`	Gives preference to specified networks according to a queries source.
`trusted-keys`	Defines DNSSEC keys preconfigured into the server and implicitly trusted.
`zone`	Defines a zone.
`view`	Defines a view.

TABLE 36-5   BIND Configuration Statements

Option	Description
type	Specifies a zone type.
file	Specifies the zone file for the zone.
directory	Specifies a directory for zone files.
forwarders	Lists hosts for DNS servers where requests are to be forwarded.
masters	Lists hosts for DNS master servers for a slave server.
notify	Allows master servers to notify their slave servers when the master zone data changes and updates are needed.
allow-transfer	Specifies which hosts are allowed to receive zone transfers.
allow-query	Specifies hosts that are allowed to make queries.
allow-recursion	Specifies hosts that are allowed to perform recursive queries on the server.

TABLE 36-6   Zone Options

characteristics to be associated with a remote name server, such as the transfer method and key ID for transaction security. The **control** statement defines special control channels. The **key** statement defines a key ID to be used in a **server** statement that associates an authentication method with a particular name server (see "DNSSEC" later in this chapter). The **logging** statement is used to configure logging options for the name server, such as the maximum size of the log file and a severity level for messages. Table 36-6 lists the BIND statements. The **sortlists** statement lets you specify preferences to be used when a query returns multiple responses. For example, you could give preference to your localhost network or to a private local network such a 192.168.0.0.

The options Statement

The **options** statement defines global options and can be used only once in the configuration file. An extensive number of options cover such components as forwarding, name checking, directory path names, access control, and zone transfers, among others (see Table 36-7). A complete listing can be found in the BIND documentation.

The directory Option

A critically important option found in most configuration files is the **directory** option, which holds the location of the name server's zone and cache files on your system. The following example is taken from the **/etc/named.conf** file. This example specifies the zone files are located in the **/var/named** directory. In this directory, you can find your zone files, including those used for your local system. The example uses IPv4 addresses.

```
options {
        directory "/var/named";
        forwarders { 192.168.0.34;
                192.168.0.47;
                };
      };
```

Option	Description
`sortlist`	Gives preference to specified networks according to a queries source.
`directory`	Specifies a directory for zone files.
`forwarders`	Lists hosts for DNS servers where requests are to be forwarded.
`allow-transfer`	Specifies which hosts are allowed to receive zone transfers.
`allow-query`	Specifies hosts that are allowed to make queries.
`allow-recursion`	Specifies hosts that are allowed to perform recursive queries on the server.
`notify`	Allows master servers to notify their slave servers when the master zone data changes and updates are needed.
`blackhole`	Option to eliminate denial response by **`allow-query`**.

TABLE 36-7   Bind Options for the options Statement

The forwarders Option

Another commonly used global option is the **`forwarders`** option. With the **`forwarders`** option, you can list several DNS servers to which queries can be forwarded if they cannot be resolved by the local DNS server. This is helpful for local networks that may need to use a DNS server connected to the Internet. The **`forwarders`** option can also be placed in forward zone entries.

The notify Option

With the **`notify`** option turned on, the master zone DNS servers send messages to any slave DNS servers whenever their configuration has changed. The slave servers can then perform zone transfers in which they download the changed configuration files. Slave servers always use the DNS configuration files copied from their master DNS servers. The **`notify`** option takes one argument, **yes** or **no**, where **yes** is the default. With the **no** argument, you can have the master server not send out any messages to the slave servers, in effect preventing any zone transfers.

An IPv4 named.conf Example

The following example is a simple **named.conf** file based on the example provided in the BIND documentation. This example shows samples of several of the configuration statements. The file begins with comments using C++ syntax, **//**. The **options** statement has a directory entry that sets the directory for the zone and cache files to **/var/named**. Here, you find links to your zone files, such as **named.local** and reverse mapping files, along with the cache file, **named.ca**. The original files will be located in **/var/named/chroot/var/named**. The first **zone** statement (**.**) defines a hint zone specifying the root name servers. The cache file listing these servers is **named.ca**. The second **zone** statement defines a zone for the **mytrek.com** domain. Its type is master, and its zone file is named "**mytrek.com**." The next zone is used for reverse IP mapping of the previous zone. Its name is made up of a reverse listing of the **mytrek.com** domain's IP address with the term **IN-ADDR.ARPA** appended.

The domain address for **mytrek.com** is 192.168.0, so the reverse is 1.168.192. The **IN-ADDR
.ARPA** domain is a special domain that supports gateway location and Internet address-to-
host mapping. The last **zone** statement defines a reverse mapping zone for the loopback
interface, the method used by the system to address itself and enable communication
between local users on the system. The zone file used for this local zone is **named.local**.

named.conf

```
//
// A simple BIND 9 configuration
//

logging {
        category cname { null; };
        };

options {
        directory "/var/named";
        };

zone "." {
        type hint;
        file "named.ca";
        };

zone "mytrek.com" {
            type master;
            file "mytrek.com";
            };
zone "1.168.192.IN-ADDR.ARPA" {
            type master;
            file "192.168.0";
            };

zone "0.0.127.IN-ADDR.ARPA" {
            type master;
            file "named.local";
            };
```

An IPv6 named.conf Example

The IPv6 version for the preceding **named.conf** file appears much the same, except that the
IN-ADDR.ARPA domain is replaced by the IP6.ARPA domain in the reverse zone entries
(IP6.INT is an older, deprecated version). IP6.ARPA uses bit labels providing bit-level
specification for the address. This is simply the full hexadecimal address, including zeros,
without intervening colons. You need to use IP6.ARPA format of the IPv6 address for both
the **mytrek.com** domain and the localhost domain. The IPv6 address for the localhost
domain is 0000:0000:0000:0001, a special reserved address. IP6.INT is an older version of
IP6.ARPA that uses a nibble format for reverse addresses (discussed later).

named.conf

```
//
// A simple BIND 9 configuration
//
```

```
logging {
        category cname { null; };
        };

options {
        directory "/var/named";
        };

zone "." {
         type hint;
         file "named.ca";
        };

zone "mytrek.com" {
                type master;
                file "mytrek.com";
                };
zone "\[xFEC0000000000000/64].IP6.ARPA" {
                type master;
                file "fec.ip6.arpa";
                };

zone "\[x00000000000000000000000000000001/128].IP6.ARPA" {
                type master;
                file "named.local";
                };
```

Caching-Only Server

When BIND is initially installed, it creates a default configuration for what is known as a caching-only server. A *caching-only* server copies queries made by users and saves them in a cache, for use later if the queries are repeated. This can save DNS lookup response times. The cache is held in memory and lasts only as long as **named** runs. The caching-only server configuration file is named.caching-nameserver.conf file. This file contains basic options for managing the caching server. It includes the named.rfc1912.zones file (also in /etc) which contains the zone configurations for the caching server.

Resource Records for Zone Files

Your name server holds domain name information about the hosts on your network in resource records placed in zone and reverse mapping files. Resource records are used to associate IP addresses with fully qualified domain names. You need a record for every computer in the zone that the name server services. A record takes up one line, though you can use parentheses to use several lines for a record, as is usually the case with SOA records. A resource record uses the Standard Resource Record Format as shown here:

name [*<ttl>*] [*<class>*] *<type> <rdata>* [*<comment>*]

Here, *name* is the name for this record. It can be a domain name or a hostname (fully qualified domain name). If you specify only the hostname, the default domain is appended. If no name entry exists, the last specific name is used. If the @ symbol is used, the name server's domain name is used. *ttl* (time to live) is an optional entry that specifies how long the record is to be cached ($TTL directive sets default). *class* is the class of the record. The class used in most resource record entries is IN, for Internet. By default, it is the same as that specified for the domain in the **named.conf** file. *type* is the type of the record. *rdata* is the resource record data. The following is an example of a resource record entry. The name is **rabbit.mytrek.com**, the class is Internet (IN), the type is a host address record (A), and the data is the IP address 192.168.0.2.

```
rabbit.mytrek.com.    IN    A    192.168.0.2
```

Resource Record Types

Different types of resource records exist for different kinds of hosts and name server operations (see Table 36-8 for a listing of resource record types). A, NS, MX, PTR, and CNAME are the types commonly used. A is used for host address records that match domain names with IP addresses. NS is used to reference a name server. MX specifies the host address of the mail server that services this zone. The name server has mail messages sent to that host. The PTR type is used for records that point to other resource records and is used for reverse mapping. CNAME is used to identify an alias for a host on your system.

Time To Live Directive and Field: $TTL

All zone files begin with a Time To Live directive, which specifies the time that a client should keep the provided DNS information before refreshing the information again from

Type	Description
A	An IPv4 host address, maps hostname to IPv4 address
A6	An IPv6 host address
NS	Authoritative name server for this zone
CNAME	Canonical name, used to define an alias for a hostname
SOA	Start of Authority, starts DNS entries in zone file, specifies name server for domain, and other features such as server contact and serial number
WKS	Well-known service description
PTR	Pointer record, for performing reverse domain name lookups, maps IP address to hostname
RP	Text string that contains contact information about a host
HINFO	Host information
MINFO	Mailbox or mail list information
MX	Mail exchanger, informs remote site of your zone's mail server
TXT	Text strings, usually information about a host
KEY	Domain private key
SIG	Resource record signature
NXT	Next resource record

TABLE 36-8   Domain Name System Resource Record Types

the DNS server. Realistically this should be at least a day, though if changes in the server are scheduled sooner, you can temporarily shorten the time, later restoring it. Each record, in fact, has a Time To Live value that can be explicitly indicated with the TTL field. This is the second field in a resource record. If no TTL field is specified in the record, then the default as defined by the $TLL directive can be used. The $TTL directive is placed at the beginning of each zone file. By default it will list the time in seconds, usually 86400, 24 hours.

```
$TTL 86400
```

You can also specify the time in days (d), hours (h), or minutes (m), as in

```
$TTL 2d3h
```

When used as a field, the TTL will be a time specified as the second field. In the following example, the turtle resource record can be cached for three days. This will override the default time in the TTL time directive:

```
turtle      3d      IN     A       192.168.0.1
```

Start of Authority: SOA

A zone or reverse mapping file always begins with a special resource record called the Start of Authority (SOA) record. This record specifies that all the following records are authoritative for this domain. It also holds information about the name server's domain, which is to be given to other name servers. An SOA record has the same format as other resource records, though its data segment is arranged differently. The format for an SOA record follows:

```
name {ttl} class SOA Origin Person-in-charge (
                              Serial number
                              Refresh
                              Retry
                              Expire
                              Minimum )
```

Each zone has its own SOA record. The SOA begins with the zone name specified in the **named.conf** zone entry. This is usually a domain name. An @ symbol is usually used for the name and acts like a macro expanding to the domain name. The *class* is usually the Internet class, IN. *SOA* is the type. *Origin* is the machine that is the origin of the records, usually the machine running your name server daemon. The *person-in-charge* is the e-mail address for the person managing the name server (use dots, not @, for the e-mail address, as this symbol is used for the domain name). Several configuration entries are placed in a block delimited with braces. The first is the *serial number.* You change the serial number when you add or change records, so that it is updated by other servers. The serial number can be any number, as long as it is incremented each time a change is made to any record in the zone. A common practice is to use the year-month-day-number for the serial number, where number is the number of changes in that day. For example, 1999120403 would be the year 1999, December 4, for the third change. Be sure to update it when making changes.

Refresh specifies the time interval for refreshing SOA information. *Retry* is the frequency for trying to contact an authoritative server. *Expire* is the length of time a secondary name server keeps information about a zone without updating it. *Minimum* is the length of time records in a zone live. The times are specified in the number of seconds.

The following example shows an SOA record. The machine running the name server is **turtle.mytrek.com**, and the e-mail address of the person responsible for the server is **hostmaster.turtle.mytrek.com**. Notice the periods at the ends of these names. For names with no periods, the domain name is appended. **turtle** would be the same as **turtle.mytrek .com**. When entering full hostnames, be sure to add the period so that the domain is not appended.

```
@ IN SOA turtle.mytrek.com. hostmaster.turtle.mytrek.com. (
                          1997022700 ; Serial
                          28800 ; Refresh
                          14400 ; Retry
                          3600000 ; Expire
                          86400 ) ; Minimum
```

Name Server: NS

The name server record specifies the name of the name server for this zone. These have a resource record type of NS. If you have more than one name server, list them in NS records. These records usually follow the SOA record. As they usually apply to the same domain as the SOA record, their name field is often left blank to inherit the server's domain name specified by the @ symbol in the previous SOA record.

```
        IN    NS      turtle.mytrek.com.
```

You can, if you wish, enter the domain name explicitly as shown here:

```
mytrek.com.  IN    NS      turtle.mytrek.com.
```

Address Record: A and A6

Resource records of type A are address records that associate a fully qualified domain name with an IP address. Often, only their hostname is specified. Any domain names without a terminating period automatically have the domain appended to them. Given the domain **mytrek.com**, the **turtle** name in the following example is expanded to **turtle.mytrek.com**:

```
rabbit.mytrek.com. IN    A       192.168.0.2
turtle             IN    A       192.168.0.1
```

BIND supports IPv6 addresses. IPv6 IP addresses have a very different format from that of the IPv4 addresses commonly used (see Chapter 37). Instead of the numerals arranged in four segments, IPv6 uses hexadecimal numbers arranged in seven segments. In the following example, **turtle.mytrek.com** is associated with a site-local IPv6 address: **fec0::**. Recall that there are only three fields in a site-local address: format prefix, subnet identifier, and interface identifier. The empty segments of the subnet identifier can be represented by an empty colon pair (::). The interface identifier follows, **8:800:200C:417A**.

```
turtle.mytrek.com. IN    A6     FEC0::8:800:200C:417A
```

IPv6 also supports the use of IPv4 addresses as an interface identifier, instead of the MAC-derived identifier. The network information part of the IPv6 address would use IPv6 notation, and the remaining interface (host) identifier would use the full IPv4 address.

These are known as mixed addresses. In the next example, **lizard.mytrek.com** is given a mixed address using IPv6 network information and IPv4 interface information. The IPv6 network information is for an IPv6 site-local address.

```
lizard.mytrek.com. IN    A6       fec0::192.168.0.3
```

The AAAA record is an older and deprecated version of an IPv6 record. It is still in use in many networks. An AAAA record operates much like a standard A address record, requiring a full IPv6 address. You can do the same with an A6 record. An A6 record, though, can be more flexible, in that it does not require a full address. Instead you chain A6 records together, specifying just part of the address in each. For example, you could specify just an interface identifier for a host, letting the network information be provided by another IPv6 record. In the next example, the first A6 record lists only the address for the interface identifier for the host **divit**. Following the address is the domain name, **mytrek.com**, whose address is to be used to complete **divit**'s address, providing network information. The next A6 record provides the network address information for **mytrek.com**.

```
divit.mygolf.com. IN   A6    0:0:0:0:1234:5678:3466:af1f  mytrek.com.
mytrek.com.       IN   A6    3ffe:8050:201:1860::
```

Mail Exchanger: MX

The Mail Exchanger record, MX, specifies the mail server that is used for this zone or for a particular host. The mail exchanger is the server to which mail for the host is sent. In the following example, the mail server is specified as **turtle.mytrek.com**. Any mail sent to the address for any machines in that zone will be sent to the mail server, which in turn will send it to the specific machines. For example, mail sent to a user on **rabbit.mytrek.com** will first be sent to **turtle.mytrek.com**, which will then send it on to **rabbit.mytrek.com**. In the following example, the host 192.168.0.1 (**turtle.mytrek.com**) is defined as the mail server for the **mytrek.com** domain:

```
mytrek.com. IN    MX   10   turtle.mytrek.com.
```

You could also inherit the domain name from the SOA record, leaving the domain name entry blank.

```
            IN    MX   turtle.mytrek.com.
```

You could use the IP address instead, but in larger networks, the domain name may be needed to search for and resolve the IP address of a particular machine, which could change.

```
mytrek.com. IN    MX   10   192.168.0.1
```

An MX record recognizes an additional field that specifies the ranking for a mail exchanger. If your zone has several mail servers, you can assign them different rankings in their MX records. The smaller number has a higher ranking. This way, if mail cannot reach the first mail server, it can be routed to an alternate server to reach the host. In the following example, mail for hosts on the **mytrek.com** domain is first routed to the mail server at

192.168.0.1 (**turtle.mytrek.com**), and if that fails, it is routed to the mail server at 192.168.0.2 (**rabbit.mytrek.com**).

```
mytrek.com.  IN MX 10 turtle.mytrek.com.
             IN MX 20 rabbit.mytrek.com.
```

You can also specify a mail server for a particular host. In the following example, the mail server for **lizard.mytrek.com** is specified as **rabbit.mytrek.com**:

```
lizard.mytrek.com.  IN      A       192.168.0.3
                    IN      MX  10  rabbit.mytrek.com.
```

Aliases: CNAME

Resource records of type CNAME are used to specify alias names for a host in the zone. Aliases are often used for machines running several different types of servers, such as both Web and FTP servers. They are also used to locate a host when it changes its name. The old name becomes an alias for the new name. In the following example, **ftp.mytrek.com** is an alias for a machine actually called **turtle.mytrek.com**:

```
ftp.mytrek.com.  IN CNAME turtle.mytrek.com.
```

The term CNAME stands for canonical name. The canonical name is the actual name of the host. In the preceding example, the canonical name is **turtle.mytrek.com**. The alias, also known as the CNAME, is **ftp.mytrek.com**. In a CNAME entry, the alias points to the canonical name. Aliases cannot be used for NS (name server) or MX (mail server) entries. For those records, you need to use the original domain name or IP address.

A more stable way to implement aliases is simply to create another address record for a host or domain. You can have as many hostnames for the same IP address as you want, provided they are certified. For example, to make **www.mytrek.com** an alias for **turtle.mytrek.com**, you only have to add another address record for it, giving it the same IP address as **turtle.mytrek.com**.

```
turtle.mytrek.com.  IN A 192.168.0.1
www.mytrek.com.  IN A 192.168.0.1
```

Pointer Record: PTR

A PTR record is used to perform reverse mapping from an IP address to a host. PTR records are used in the reverse mapping files. The name entry holds a reversed IP address, and the data entry holds the name of the host. The following example maps the IP address 192.168.0.1 to **turtle.mytrek.com**:

```
1.1.168.192 IN PTR turtle.mytrek.com.
```

In a PTR record, you can specify just that last number segment of the address (the host address) and let DNS fill in the domain part of the address. In the next example, 1 has the domain address, 1.168.192, automatically added to give 1.1.168.192:

```
1 IN PTR turtle.mytrek.com.
```

Host Information: HINFO, RP, MINFO, and TXT

The HINFO, RP, MINFO, and TXT records are used to provide information about the host. The RP record enables you to specify the person responsible for a certain host. The HINFO record provides basic hardware and operating system identification. The TXT record is used to enter any text you want. MINFO provides a host's mail and mailbox information. These are used sparingly, as they may give too much information out about the server.

Zone Files

A DNS server uses several zone files covering different components of the DNS. Each zone uses two zone files: the principal zone file and a reverse mapping zone file. The *zone file* contains the resource records for hosts in the zone. A *reverse mapping file* contains records that provide reverse mapping of your domain name entries, enabling you to map from IP addresses to domain names. The name of the file used for the zone file can be any name. The name of the file is specified in the **zone** statement's file entry in the **named.conf** file. If your server supports several zones, you may want to use a name that denotes the specific zone. Most systems use the domain name as the name of the zone file. For example, the zone **mytrek.com** would have a zone file with the same name and the extension **zone**, as in **mytrek.com.zone** (system-config-bind saves zone file using a **.db** extension). These could be placed in a subdirectory called **zones** or **master**. The zone file used in the following example is called **mytrek.com**. The reverse mapping file can also be any name, though it is usually the reverse IP address domain specified in its corresponding zone file. For example, in the case of **mytrek.com.zone** zone file, the reverse mapping file might be called **192.168.0.zone**, the IP address of the **mytrek.com** domain defined in the **mytrek.com.zone** zone file. This file would contain reverse mapping of all the host addresses in the domain, allowing their hostname addresses to be mapped to their corresponding IP addresses. In addition, BIND sets up a cache file and a reverse mapping file for the localhost. The cache file holds the resource records for the root name servers to which your name server connects. The cache file can be any name, although it is usually called **named.ca**. The localhost reverse mapping file holds reverse IP resource records for the local loopback interface, localhost. Although localhost can be any name, it usually has the name **named.local**. The IPv6 version is **named.ip6.local**.

Once you have created your zone files, you should check their syntax with the **named-checkzone** tool. This tool requires that you specify both a zone and a zone file. In the following example, in the **/var/named** directory, the zone **mytrek.com** in the zone file **mytrek.com.zone** is checked:

```
named-checkzone  mytrek.com mytrek.com.zone
```

Zone Files for Internet Zones

A zone file holds resource records that follow a certain format. The file begins with general directives to define default domains or to include other resource record files. These are followed by a single SOA record, name server and domain resource records, and then resource records for the different hosts. Comments begin with a semicolon and can be placed throughout the file. The @ symbol operates like a special macro, representing the domain name of the zone to which the records apply. The @ symbol is used in the first field of a resource or SOA record as the zone's domain name. Multiple names can be specified using the * matching character. The first field in a resource record is the name of the domain to which it applies. If the name is left blank, the previous explicit name entry in another resource record is automatically used. This way, you can list several entries that apply to the same host without having to repeat the hostname. Any host or domain name used throughout this file that is not terminated with a period has the zone's domain appended to it. For example, if the zone's domain is **mytrek.com** and a resource record has only the name **rabbit** with no trailing period, the zone's domain is automatically appended to it, giving you **rabbit.mytrek.com.**. Be sure to include the trailing period whenever you enter the complete fully qualified domain name, **turtle.mytrek.com.**, for example.

Directives

You can also use several directives to set global attributes. $ORIGIN sets a default domain name to append to address names that do not end in a period. $INCLUDE includes a file. $GENERATE can generate records whose domain or IP addresses differ only by an iterated number. The $ORIGIN directive is often used to specify the root domain to use in address records. Be sure to include the trailing period. The following example sets the domain origin to **mytrek.com** and will be automatically appended to the **lizard** host name that follows:

```
$ORIGIN   mytrek.com.
lizard    IN   A    192.168.0.2
```

SOA Record

A zone file begins with an SOA record specifying the machine the name server is running on, among other specifications. The @ symbol is used for the name of the SOA record, denoting the zone's domain name. After the SOA, the name server resource records (NS) are listed. Just below the name server records are resource records for the domain itself. Resource records for host addresses (A), aliases (CNAME), and mail exchangers (MX) follow. The following example shows a sample zone file, which begins with an SOA record and is followed by an NS record, resource records for the domain, and then resource records for individual hosts:

```
; Authoritative data for turle.mytrek.com
;
$TTL 86400
@ IN SOA turtle.mytrek.com. hostmaster.turtle.mytrek.com. (
                        93071200 ; Serial number
                           10800 ; Refresh 3 hours
                            3600 ; Retry 1 hour
                         3600000 ; Expire 1000 hours
                           86400 ) ; Minimum 24 hours

              IN     NS        turtle.mytrek.com.
              IN     A         192.168.0.1
              IN     MX    10  turtle.mytrek.com.
              IN     MX    15  rabbit.mytrek.com.

turtle        IN     A         192.168.0.1
              IN     HINFO     PC-686 LINUX
gopher        IN     CNAME     turtle.mytrek.com.
```

```
ftp          IN      CNAME     turtle.mytrek.com.
www          IN      A         192.168.0.1

rabbit       IN      A         192.168.0.2

lizard       IN      A         192.168.0.3
             IN      HINFO     MAC MACOS
localhost    IN      A         127.0.0.1
```

The first two lines are comments about the server for which this zone file is used. Notice that the first two lines begin with a semicolon. The class for each of the resource records in this file is IN, indicating these are Internet records. The SOA record begins with an @ symbol that stands for the zone's domain. In this example, it is **mytrek.com**. Any host or domain name used throughout this file that is not terminated with a period has this domain appended to it. For example, in the following resource record, **turtle** has no period, so it automatically expands to **turtle.mytrek.com**. The same happens for **rabbit** and **lizard**. These are read as **rabbit.mytrek.com** and **lizard.mytrek.com**. Also, in the SOA, notice that the e-mail address for hostmaster uses a period instead of an @ symbol; @ is a special symbol in zone files and cannot be used for any other purpose.

Nameserver Record

The next resource record specifies the name server for this zone. Here, it is **mytrek.com.**. Notice the name for this resource record is blank. If the name is blank, a resource record inherits the name from the previous record. In this case, the NS record inherits the value of @ in the SOA record, its previous record. This is the zone's domain, and the NS record specifies **turtle.mytrek.com** as the name server for this zone.

```
             IN   NS    turtle.mytrek.com.
```

Here the domain name is inherited. The entry can be read as the following. Notice the trailing period at the end of the domain name:

```
mytrek.com.  IN    NS     turtle.mytrek.com.
```

Address Record

The following address records set up an address for the domain itself. This is often the same as the name server, in this case 192.168.0.1 (the IP address of **turtle.mytrek.com**). This enables users to reference the domain itself, rather than a particular host in it. A mail exchanger record follows that routes mail for the domain to the name server. Users can send mail to the **mytrek.com** domain and it will be routed to **turtle.mytrek.com**.

```
             IN    A     192.168.0.1
```

Here the domain name is inherited. The entry can be read as the following:

```
mytrek.com.  IN    A     192.168.0.1
```

Mail Exchanger Record

The next records are mail exchanger (MX) records listing **turtle.mytrek.com** and **fast.mytrek.com** as holding the mail servers for this zone. You can have more than one mail exchanger record for a host. More than one host may exist through which mail can be routed. These can be listed in mail exchanger records for which you can set priority rankings (a smaller number ranks higher). In this example, if **turtle.mytrek.com** cannot be reached, its mail is routed through **rabbit.mytrek.com**, which has been set up also to handle mail for the **mytrek.com** domain:

```
IN      MX      100     turtle.mytrek.com.
IN      MX      150     rabbit.mytrek.com.
```

Again the domain name is inherited. The entries can be read as the following:

```
mytrek.com.     IN      MX  100     turtle.mytrek.com.
mytrek.com.     IN      MX  150     rabbit.mytrek.com.
```

Address Record with Host Name

The following resource record is an address record (A) that associates an IP address with the fully qualified domain name **turtle.mytrek.com**. The resource record name holds only **turtle** with no trailing period, so it is automatically expanded to **turtle.mytrek.com**. This record provides the IP address to which **turtle.mytrek.com** can be mapped.

```
turtle   IN    A     192.168.0.1
```

Inherited Names

Several resource records immediately follow that have blank names. These inherit their names from the preceding full record—in this case, **turtle.mytrek.com**. In effect, these records also apply to that host. Using blank names is an easy way to list additional resource records for the same host (notice that an apparent indent occurs). The first record is an information record, providing the hardware and operating system for the machine.

```
IN      HINFO     PC-686 LINUX
```

Alias Records

If you are using the same machine to run several different servers, such as Web, FTP, and Gopher servers, you may want to assign aliases to these servers to make accessing them easier for users. Instead of using the actual domain name, such as **turtle.mytrek.com**, to access the Web server running on it, users may find using the following is easier: for the Web server, **www.mytrek.com**; for the Gopher server, **gopher.mytrek.com**; and for the FTP server, **ftp.mytrek.com**. In the DNS, you can implement such a feature using alias records. In the example zone file, two CNAME alias records exist for the **turtle.mytrek.com** machine: FTP and Gopher. The next record implements an alias for **www** using another address record for the same machine. None of the name entries ends in a period, so they are appended automatically with the domain name **mytrek.com**. **www.mytrek.com**, **ftp.mytrek.com**, and **gopher.mytrek.com** are all aliases for **turtle.mytrek.com**. Users entering those URLs automatically access the respective servers on the **turtle.mytrek.com** machine.

Loopback Record

Address and mail exchanger records are then listed for the two other machines in this zone: **rabbit.mytrek.com** and **lizard.mytrek.com**. You could add HINFO, TXT, MINFO, or alias records for these entries. The file ends with an entry for localhost, the special loopback interface that allows your system to address itself.

IPv6 Zone File Example

This is the same zone file using IPv6 addresses. The addresses are site-local (FEC0), instead of global (3), providing private network addressing. The loopback device is represented by the IPv6 address `::1`. The A6 IPv6 address records are used.

```
; Authoritative data for turle.mytrek.com, IPv6 version
;
$TTL 1d
@ IN SOA turtle.mytrek.com. hostmaster.turtle.mytrek.com.(
                                93071200 ; Serial number
                                   10800 ; Refresh 3 hours
                                    3600 ; Retry 1 hour
                                 3600000 ; Expire 1000 hours
                                   86400 ) ; Minimum 24 hours


              IN      NS        turtle.mytrek.com.
              IN      A6        FEC0::8:800:200C:417A
              IN      MX   10   turtle.mytrek.com.
              IN      MX   15   rabbit.mytrek.com.

turtle        IN      A6        FEC0::8:800:200C:417A
              IN      HINFO     PC-686 LINUX
gopher        IN      CNAME     turtle.mytrek.com.
ftp           IN      CNAME     turtle.mytrek.com.
www           IN      A6        FEC0::8:800:200C:417A

rabbit        IN      A6        FEC0::FEDC:BA98:7654:3210

lizard        IN      A6        FEC0::E0:18F7:3466:7D
              IN      HINFO     MAC MACOS
localhost     IN      A6        ::1
```

Reverse Mapping File

Reverse name lookups are enabled using a reverse mapping file. *Reverse mapping* files map fully qualified domain names to IP addresses. This reverse lookup capability is unnecessary, but it is convenient to have. With reverse mapping, when users access remote hosts, their domain name addresses can be used to identify their own host, instead of only the IP address. The name of the file can be anything you want. On most current distributions, it is the zone's domain address (the network part of a zone's IP address). For example, the reverse mapping file for a zone with the IP address of 192.168.0.1 is 192.168.0. Its full pathname would be something like **/var/named/192.168.0**. On some systems using older implementations of BIND, the reverse mapping filename may consist of the root name of the zone file with the extension **.rev**. For example, if the zone file is called **mytrek.com**, the reverse mapping file would be called something like **mytrek.rev**.

IPv4 IN-ADDR.ARPA Reverse Mapping Format

In IPv4, the zone entry for a reverse mapping in the **named.conf** file uses a special domain name consisting of the IP address in reverse, with an **IN-ADDR.ARPA** extension. This reverse IP address becomes the zone domain referenced by the **@** symbol in the reverse mapping file. For example, the reverse mapping zone name for a domain with the IP address of **192.168.43** would be **43.168.192.IN-ADDR.ARPA**. In the following example, the reverse domain name for the domain address **192.168.0** is **1.168.192.IN-ADDR.ARPA**:

```
zone "1.168.192.IN-ADDR.ARPA" in {
        type master;
        file "192.168.0";
        };
```

A reverse mapping file begins with an SOA record, which is the same as that used in a forward mapping file. Resource records for each machine defined in the forward mapping file then follow. These resource records are PTR records that point to hosts in the zone. These must be actual hosts, not aliases defined with CNAME records. Records for reverse mapping begin with a reversed IP address. Each segment in the IP address is sequentially reversed. Each segment begins with the host ID, followed by reversed network numbers. If you list only the host ID with no trailing period, the zone domain is automatically attached. In the case of a reverse mapping file, the zone domain as specified in the **zone** statement is the domain IP address backward. The 1 expands to 1.1.168.192. In the following example, **turtle** and **lizard** inherit the domain IP address, whereas **rabbit** has its address explicitly entered:

```
; reverse mapping of domain names 1.168.192.IN-ADDR.ARPA
;
$TTL 86400
@ IN SOA turtle.mytrek.com. hostmaster.turtle.mytrek.com. (
                        92050300 ; Serial (yymmddxx format)
                          10800 ; Refresh 3hHours
                           3600 ; Retry 1 hour
                        3600000 ; Expire 1000 hours
                          86400 ) ; Minimum 24 hours


@               IN    NS      turtle.mytrek.com.
1               IN    PTR     turtle.mytrek.com.
2.1.168.192     IN    PTR     rabbit.mytrek.com.
3               IN    PTR     lizard.mytrek.com.
```

IPv6 IP6.ARPA Reverse Mapping Format

In IPv6, reverse mapping can be handled either with the current IP6.ARPA domain format, or with the older IP6.INT format. With IP6.ARPA, the address is represented by a bit-level representation that places the hexadecimal address within brackets. The first bracket is preceded by a backslash. The address must be preceded by an x indicating that it is a hexadecimal address. Following the address is a number indicating the number of bits referenced. In a 128-bit address, usually the first 64 bits reference the network address and the last 64 bits are for the interface address. The following example shows the network and interface addresses for lizard.

```
FEC0:0000:0000:0000:00E0:18F7:3466:007D   lizard IPv6 address
\[xFEC0000000000000/64]                    lizard network address
\[x00E018F73466007D/64]                    lizard interface address
```

The zone entry for a reverse mapping in the **named.conf** file with an **IP6.ARPA** extension would use the bit-level representation for the network address.

```
zone "\[xfec0000000000000/64].IP6.ARPA" in {
        type master;
        file "fec.ip6.arpa";
        };
```

A reverse mapping file then uses the same bit-level format for the interface addresses.

```
$TTL 1d
@ IN SOA turtle.mytrek.com. hostmaster.turtle.mytrek.com. (
                        92050300 ; Serial (yymmddxx format)
                           10800 ; Refresh 3hHours
                            3600 ; Retry 1 hour
                         3600000 ; Expire 1000 hours
                           86400 ) ; Minimum 24 hours

@                               IN   NS       turtle.mytrek.com.
\[x00080800200C417A/64]         IN   PTR      turtle.mytrek.com.
\[xFEDCBA9876543210/64]         IN   PTR      rabbit.mytrek.com.
\[x00E018F73466007D/64]         IN   PTR      lizard.mytrek.com.
```

IPv6 IP6.INT Reverse Mapping Format

The older IP6.INT format uses a nibble format for the IPv6 address. This has since been replaced by the IPv6.ARPA format. The hexadecimal address is segmented into each hex number, separated by a period and written in reverse. This gives you 32 hex numbers in reverse order. The IP6.INT version for the lizard address are shown here:

```
FEC0:0000:0000:0000:00E0:18F7:3466:007D    lizard IPv6 address
0.0.0.0.0.0.0.0.0.0.0.0.0.0.c.e.f          lizard network address
D.7.0.0.6.6.4.3.7.F.8.1.0.E.0.0            lizard interface address
```

The zone entry for a reverse mapping in the **named.conf** file with an **IP6.INT** extension would use the reverse nibble format for the network address.

```
zone "0.0.0.0.0.0.0.0.0.0.0.0.0.c.e.f.IP6.INT" in {
        type master;
        file "fec.ip6.int";
        };
```

The reverse zone file then uses the reverse nibble format for each interface address.

```
$TTL 1d
@ IN SOA turtle.mytrek.com. hostmaster.turtle.mytrek.com. (
                        92050300 ; Serial (yymmddxx format)
                           10800 ; Refresh 3hHours
                            3600 ; Retry 1 hour
                         3600000 ; Expire 1000 hours
                           86400 ) ; Minimum 24 hours
$ORIGIN 0.0.0.0.0.0.0.0.0.0.0.0.0.c.e.f  IN  NS   turtle.mytrek.com.
A.7.1.4.C.0.0.2.0.0.8.0.8.0.0.0          IN   PTR      turtle.mytrek.com.
0.1.2.3.4.5.6.7.8.9.A.B.C.D.E.F          IN   PTR      rabbit.mytrek.com.
D.7.0.0.6.6.4.3.7.F.8.1.0.E.0.0          IN   PTR      lizard.mytrek.com.
```

Localhost Reverse Mapping

A localhost reverse mapping file implements reverse mapping for the local loopback interface known as *localhost,* whose network address is 127.0.0.1. This file can be any name. localhost is given the name **named.local** for IPv4 and **named.ip6.local** for IPv6 addressing. On other systems, localhost may use the network part of the IP address, 127.0.0. This file allows mapping the domain name localhost to the localhost IP address, which is always 127.0.0.1 on every machine. The address 127.0.0.1 is a special address that functions as the local address for your machine. It allows a machine to address itself. In the **zone** statement for this file, the name of the zone is **0.0.127.IN-ADDR.ARPA**. The domain part of the IP address is entered in reverse order, with **IN-ADDR.ARPA** appended to it, **0.0.127.IN-ADDR.ARPA**. The **named.conf** entry is shown here:

```
zone "0.0.127.IN-ADDR.ARPA" {
        type master;
        file "named.local";
        };
```

IPv4 Locahost

The name of the file used for the localhost reverse mapping file is usually **named.local**, though it can be any name. The NS record specifies the name server localhost should use. This file has a PTR record that maps the IP address to the localhost. The 1 used as the name expands to append the zone domain—in this case, giving you 1.0.0.127, a reverse IP address. The contents of the **named.local** file are shown here. Notice the trailing periods for localhost:

```
$TTL 1d
@ IN SOA localhost. root.localhost. (
                        1997022700 ; Serial
                            28800 ; Refresh
                            14400 ; Retry
                          3600000 ; Expire
                            86400 ) ; Minimum


        IN      NS      turtle.mytrek.com.
1       IN      PTR     localhost.
```

IPv6 Locahost

In IPv6, localhost reverse mapping is specified using the reverse of the IPv6 localhost address. This address consists of 31 zeros and a 1, which can be written in shorthand as **::1**, where :: represents the sequence of 31 zeros. With IPv6 IP6.ARPA format, these can be written in a bit-level format, where the first 64 bits consist of a network address of all zeros, and the interface address has the value 1.

```
0000:0000:0000:0000:0000:0000:0000:0001    locahost IPv6 address
\[x00000000000000000000000000000001/128]    localhost address
```

In the **named.conf** file, the IP6.ARPA localhost entry would look like this:

```
zone "\[x00000000000000000000000000000001/64].IP6.ARPA" in {
        type master;
        file "named.ip6.local";
        };
```

In the localhost reverse mapping file, the localhost entry would appear like this:

```
\[x0000000000000001/64]     IN      PTR    localhost.
```

Subdomains and Slaves

Adding a subdomain to a DNS server is a simple matter of creating an additional master entry in the **named.conf** file, and then placing name server and authority entries for that subdomain in your primary DNS server's zone file. The subdomain, in turn, has its own zone file with its SOA record and entries listing hosts, which are part of its subdomain, including any of its own mail and news servers.

Subdomain Zones

The name for the subdomain could be a different name altogether or a name with the same suffix as the primary domain. In the following example, the subdomain is called **beach .mytrek.com**. It could just as easily be called **mybeach.com**. The name server to that domain is on the host **crab.beach.mytrek.com**, in this example. Its IP address is 192.168.0.33, and its zone file is **beach.mytrek.com**. The **beach.mytrek.com** zone file holds DNS entries for all the hosts being serviced by this name server. The following example shows zone entries for its **named.conf**:

```
zone "beach.mytrek.com" {
        type master;
        file "beach.mytrek.com";
        };

zone "1.168.192.IN-ADDR.ARPA" {
        type master;
        file "192.168.0";
        };
```

Subdomain Records

On the primary DNS server, in the example **turtle.mytrek.com**, you would place entries in the master zone file to identify the subdomain server's host and designate it as a name server. Such entries are also known as *glue records*. In this example, you would place the following entries in the **mytrek.com** zone file on **turtle.mytrek.com**:

```
beach.mytrek.com.    IN    NS    beach.mytrek.com.
beach.mytrek.com.    IN    A     192.168.0.33.
```

URL references to hosts serviced by **beach.mytrek.com** can now be reached from any host serviced by **mytrek.com**, which does not need to maintain any information about the **beach.mytrek.com** hosts. It simply refers such URL references to the **beach.mytrek.com** name server.

Slave Servers

A slave DNS server is tied directly to a master DNS server and periodically receives DNS information from it. You use a master DNS server to configure its slave

DNS servers automatically. Any changes you make to the master server are automatically transferred to its slave servers. This transfer of information is called a *zone transfer*. Zone transfers are automatically initiated whenever the slave zone's refresh time is reached or the slave server receives a notify message from the master. The *refresh time* is the second argument in the zone's SOA entry. A notify message is automatically sent by the master whenever changes are made to the master zone's configuration files and the **named** daemon is restarted. In effect, slave zones are automatically configured by the master zone, receiving the master zone's zone files and making them their own.

Slave Zones

Using the previous examples, suppose you want to set up a slave server on **rabbit.mytrek.com**. Zone entries, as shown in the following example, are set up in the **named.conf** configuration file for the slave DNS server on **rabbit.mytrek.com**. The slave server is operating in the same domain as the master, and so it has the same zone name, **mytrek.com**. Its SOA file is named **slave.mytrek.com**. The term "slave" in the filename is merely a convention that helps identify it as a slave server configuration file. The **masters** statement lists its master DNS server—in this case, 192.168.0.1. Whenever the slave needs to make a zone transfer, it transfers data from that master DNS server. The entry for the reverse mapping file for this slave server lists its reverse mapping file as **slave.192.168.0**.

```
zone "mytrek.com" {
        type slave;
        file "slave.mytrek.com";
        masters { 192.168.0.1;
        };

zone "1.168.192.IN-ADDR.ARPA" {
         type slave;
         file "slave.192.168.0";
         masters { 192.168.0.1;
         };
```

Slave Records

On the master DNS server, the master SOA zone file has entries in it to identify the host that holds the slave DNS server and to designate it as a DNS server. In this example, you would place the following in the **mytrek.com** zone file:

```
        IN          NS          192.168.0.2
```

You would also place an entry for this name server in the **mytrek.com** reverse mapping file:

```
        IN          NS          192.168.0.2
```

Controlling Transfers

The master DNS server can control which slave servers can transfer zone information from it using the **allow-transfer** statement. Place the statement with the list of IP addresses for the slave servers to which you want to allow access. Also, the master DNS server should be sure its `notify` option is not disabled. The `notify` option is disabled by a "notify no" statement in the options or zone **named.conf** entries. Simply erase the "no" argument to enable notify.

Incremental Zone Transfers

With BIND versions 8.2.2 and 9.0, BIND now supports incremental zone transfers (IXFR). Previously, all the zone data would be replaced in an update, rather than changes such as the addition of a few resource records simply being edited in. With incremental zone transfers, a database of changes is maintained by the master zone. Then only the changes are transferred to the slave zone, which uses this information to update its own zone files. To implement incremental zone transfers, you have to turn on the `maintain-ixfr-base` option in the options section.

```
maintain-ixfr-base yes;
```

You can then use the `ixfr-base` option in a zone section to specify a particular database file to hold changes.

```
ixfr-base "db.mytrek.com.ixfr";
```

IP Virtual Domains

IP-based virtual hosting allows more than one IP address to be used for a single machine. If a machine has two registered IP addresses, either one can be used to address the machine. If you want to treat the extra IP address as another host in your domain, you need only create an address record for it in your domain's zone file. The domain name for the host would be the same as your domain name. If you want to use a different domain name for the extra IP, however, you have to set up a virtual domain for it. This entails creating a new `zone` statement for it with its own zone file. For example, if the extra IP address is 192.168.0.42 and you want to give it the domain name **sail.com**, you must create a new `zone` statement for it in your **named.conf** file with a new zone file. The `zone` statement would look something like this. The zone file is called **sail.com**:

```
zone "sail.com" in {
        type master;
        file "sail.com";
        };
```

In the **sail.com** file, the name server name is **turtle.mytrek.com** and the e-mail address is **hostmaster@turtle.mytrek.com**. In the name server (NS) record, the name server is **turtle .mytrek.com**. This is the same machine using the original address that the name server is running as. **turtle.mytrek.com** is also the host that handles mail addressed to **sail.com** (MX). An address record then associates the extra IP address 192.168.0.42 with the **sail.com** domain name. A virtual host on this domain is then defined as **jib.sail.com**. Also, **www** and **ftp** aliases are created for that host, creating **www.sail.com** and **ftp.sail.com** virtual hosts.

```
; Authoritative data for sail.com
;
$TTL 1d
```

```
@ IN SOA turtle.mytrek.com. hostmaster.turtle.mytrek.com. (
                                93071200 ; Serial (yymmddxx)
                                   10800 ; Refresh 3 hours
                                    3600 ; Retry 1 hour
                                 3600000 ; Expire 1000 hours
                                   86400 ) ; Minimum 24 hours

        IN      NS          turtle.mytrek.com.
        IN      MX    10    turtle.mytrek.com.
        IN      A           192.168.0.42 ;address of the sail.com domain

jib     IN      A           192.168.0.42
www     IN      A           jib.sail.com.
ftp     IN      CNAME       jib.sail.com.
```

In your reverse mapping file (**/var/named/1.168.192**), add PTR records for any virtual domains.

```
42.1.168.192      IN      PTR     sail.com.
42.1.168.192      IN      PTR     jib.sail.com.
```

You also have to configure your network connection to listen for both IP addresses on your machine (see Chapter 5).

Cache File

The *cache file* is used to connect the DNS server to root servers on the Internet. The file can be any name. On many systems, the cache file is called **named.ca**. Other systems may call the cache file **named.cache** or **roots.hints**. The cache file is usually a standard file installed by your BIND software, which lists resource records for designated root servers for the Internet. You can obtain a current version of the **named.ca** file from the **rs.internic.net** FTP site. The following example shows sample entries taken from the **named.ca** file:

```
; formerly NS.INTERNIC.NET
;
. 3600000 IN NS A.ROOT-SERVERS.NET.
A.ROOT-SERVERS.NET. 3600000 A 198.41.0.4
;
; formerly NS1.ISI.EDU
;
. 3600000 NS B.ROOT-SERVERS.NET.
B.ROOT-SERVERS.NET. 3600000 A 128.9.0.107
```

If you are creating an isolated intranet, you need to create your own root DNS server until you connect to the Internet. In effect, you are creating a fake root server. This can be another server on your system pretending to be the root or the same name server.

Dynamic Update: DHCP and Journal Files

There are situations where you will need to have zones updated dynamically. Instead of your manually editing a zone file to make changes in a zone, an outside process updates the zone, making changes and saving the file automatically. Dynamic updates are carried out both by master zones updating slave zones and by DHCP servers providing IP addresses they generated for hosts to the DNS server.

A journal file is maintained recording all the changes made to a zone, having a **.jnl** extension. Should a system crash occur, this file is read to implement the most current changes. Should you want to manually update a dynamically updated zone, you will need to erase its journal file first; otherwise, your changes would be overwritten by the journal file entries.

You allow a zone to be automatically updated by specifying the **allow-update** option. This option indicates the host that can perform the update.

```
allow-update {turtle.mytrek.com;};
```

Alternatively, for master zones, you can create a more refined set of access rules using the **update-policy** statement. With the **update-policy** statement, you can list several grant and deny rules for different hosts and types of hosts.

TSIG Signatures and Updates

With BIND 9.*x*, TSIG signature names can be used instead of host names or IP addresses for both **allow-update** and **update-policy** statements (see the following sections on TSIG). Use of TSIG signatures implements an authentication of a host performing a dynamic update, providing a much greater level of security. For example, to allow a DHCP server to update a zone file, you would place an **allow-update** entry in the zone statement listed in the **named.conf** file.

The TSIG key is defined in a key statement, naming the key previously created by the **dnssec-keygen** command. The algorithm is HMAC-MD5, and the secret is the encryption key listed in the **.private** file generated by **dnssec-keygen**.

```
key mydhcpserver {
algorithm HMAC-MD5;
secret "ONQAfbBLnvWU9H8hRqq/WA==";
};
```

The key name can then be used in an **allow-update** or **allow-policy** statement to specify a TSIG key.

```
allow-update { key mydhcpserver;};
```

Manual Updates: nsupdate

You can use the update procedure to perform any kind of update you want. You can perform updates manually or automatically using a script. For DHCP updates, the DHCP server is designed to perform dynamic updates of the DNS server. You will need to configure the DHCP server appropriately, specifying the TSIG key to use and the zones to update.

You can manually perform an update using the **nsupdate** command, specifying the file holding the key with the **-k** option.

```
nsupdate -k myserver.private
```

At the prompt, you can use **nsupdate** commands to implement changes. You match on a record using its full or partial entry. To update a record, you would first delete the old one and then add the changed version, as shown here:

```
update delete rabbit.mytrek.com. A 192.168.0.2
update add rabbit.mytrek.com. A 192.168.0.44
```

DNS Security: Access Control Lists, TSIG, and DNSSEC

DNS security currently allows you to control specific access by hosts to the DNS server, as well as providing encrypted communications between servers and authentication of DNS servers. With access control lists, you can determine who will have access to your DNS server. The DNS Security Extensions (DNSSEC), included with BIND 9.*x*, provide private/public key–encrypted authentication and transmissions. TSIGs (transaction signatures) use shared private keys to provide authentication of servers to secure actions such as dynamic updates between a DNS server and a DHCP server.

Access Control Lists

To control access by other hosts, you use access control lists, implemented with the **acl** statement. **allow** and **deny** options with access control host lists enable you to deny or allow access by specified hosts to the name server. With **allow-query**, you can restrict queries to specified hosts or networks. Normally this will result in a response saying that access is denied. You can further eliminate this response by using the **blackhole** option in the **options** statement.

You define an ACL with the **acl** statement followed by the label you want to give the list and then the list of addresses. Addresses can be IP addresses, network addresses, or a range of addresses based on CNDR notation. You can also use an ACL as defined earlier. The following example defines an ACL called **mynet**:

```
acl mynet { 192.168.0.1; 192.168.0.2; };
```

If you are specifying a range, such as a network, you also add exceptions to the list by preceding such addresses with an exclamation point (!). In the following example, the mynetx ACL lists all those hosts in the 192.168.0.0 network, except for 192.168.0.3:

```
acl myexceptions {192.168.0.0; !192.168.0.3; };
```

Four default ACLs are already defined for you. You can use them wherever an option uses a list of addresses as an argument. These are **any** for all hosts, **none** for no hosts, **localhost** for all local IP addresses, and **localnet** for all hosts on local networks served by the DNS server.

Once a list is defined, you can then use it with the **allow-query**, **allow-transfer**, **allow-recursion**, and **blackhole** options in a **zone** statement to control access to a zone. **allow-query** specifies hosts that can query the DNS server. **allow-transfer** is used for master/slave zones, designating whether update transfers are allowed. **allow-recursion** specifies those hosts that can perform recursive queries on the server. The **blackhole** option will deny contact from any hosts in its list, without sending a denial response. In the next example, an ACL of mynet is created. Then in the **mytrek.com** zone, only these hosts are allowed to query the server. As the server has no slave DNS servers, zone transfers are disabled entirely. The **blackhole** option denies access from the myrejects list, without sending any rejection notice.

```
acl mynet { 192.168.0.0; };
acl myrejects { 10.0.0.44; 10.0.0.93; };

zone "mytrek.com" {
        type master;
        file "mytrek.com";
        allow-query { mynet; };
        allow-recursion { mynet; };
        allow-transfer { none; };
        blackhole {myrejects};
        };
```

Secret Keys

Different security measures will use encryption keys generated with the **dnssec-keygen** command. You can use **dnssec-keygen** to create different types of keys, including zone (ZONE), host (HOST), and user (USER) keys. You specify the type of key with the **-n** option. A zone key will require the name ZONE and the name of the zone's domain name. A zone key is used in DNSSEC operations. The following example creates a zone key for the **mytrek.com** zone:

```
dnssec-keygen -n ZONE mytrek.com.
```

To create a host key, you would use the HOST type. HOST keys are often used in TSIG operations.

```
dnssec-keygen -n HOST turtle.mytrek.com.
```

You can further designate an encryption algorithm (**-a**) and key size (**-b**). Use the **-h** option to obtain a listing of the **dnssec-keygen** options. Currently you can choose from RSA, DSA, HMAC-MD5, and DH algorithms. The bit range will vary according to the algorithm. RSA ranges from 512 to 4096, and HMAC-MD5 ranges from 1 to 512. The following example creates a zone key using a 768-bit key and the DSA encryption algorithm:

```
dnssec-keygen -a DSA -b 768 -n ZONE mytrek.com.
```

The **dnssec-keygen** command will create public and private keys, each in corresponding files with the suffixes **.private** and **.key**. The **.key** file is a KEY resource record holding the public key. For DNSSEC, the private key is used to generate signatures for the zone, and the public key is used to verify the signatures. For TSIG, a shared private key generated by the HMAC-MD5 algorithm is used instead of a public/private key pair.

DNSSEC

DNSSEC provides encrypted authentication to DNS. With DNSSEC, you can create a signed zone that is securely identified with an encrypted signature. This form of security is used primarily to secure the connections between master and slave DNS servers, so that a master server transfers update records only to authorized slave servers and does so with a secure encrypted communication. Two servers that establish such a secure connection do so using a pair of public and private keys. In effect, you have a parent zone that can securely authenticate child zones, using encrypted transmissions. This involves creating zone keys for each child and having those keys used by the parent zone to authenticate the child zones.

Zone Keys

You generate a zone key using the **dnssec-keygen** command and specifying the zone type, ZONE, with the **-n** option. For the key name, you use the zone's domain name. The following example creates a zone key for the **mytrek.com** zone:

```
dnssec-keygen -n ZONE mytrek.com.
```

You can further designate an encryption algorithm (**-a**) and a key size (**-b**). Use the **-h** option to obtain a listing of the **dnssec-keygen** options. Since you are setting up a public/private key pair, you should choose either the RSA or DSA algorithm. The bit range will vary according to the algorithm. RSA ranges from 512 to 4096, and DSA ranges from 512 to 1024. The following example creates a zone key using a 768-bit key and the DSA encryption algorithm:

```
dnssec-keygen -a DSA -b 768 -n ZONE mytrek.com.
```

The **dnssec-keygen** command will create public and private keys, each in corresponding files with the suffixes **.private** and **.key**. The private key is used to generate signatures for the zone, and the public key is used to verify the signatures. The **.key** file is a KEY resource record holding the public key. This is used to decrypt signatures generated by the corresponding private key. You add the public key to the DNS configuration file, **named.conf**, using the **$INCLUDE** statement to include the **.key** file.

DNSSEC Resource Records

In the zone file, you then use three DNSSEC DNS resource records to implement secure communications for a given zone: KEY, SIG, and NXT. In these records, you use the signed keys for the zones you have already generated. The KEY record holds public keys associated with zones, hosts, or users. The SIG record stores digital signatures and expiration dates for a set of resource records. The NXT record is used to determine that a resource record for a domain does not exist. In addition, several utilities let you manage DNS encryption. With the **dnskeygen** utility, you generated the public and private keys used for encryption. **dnssigner** signs a zone using the zone's private key, setting up authentication.

To secure a DNS zone with DNSSEC, you first use **dnskeygen** to create public and private keys for the DNS zone. Then use **dnssigner** to create an authentication key. In the DNS zone file, you enter a KEY resource record in which you include the public key. The public key will appear as a lengthy string of random characters. For the KEY record, you enter in the domain name followed by the KEY and then the public key.

```
mytrek.com. KEY 0x4101 3 3 (
AvqyXgKk/uguxkJF/hbRpYzxZFG3x8EfNX3891 7GX6w7rlLy
BJ14TqvrDvXr84XsShg+OFcUJafNr84U4ER2dg6NrlRAmZA1
jFfV0UpWDWcHBR2jJnvgV9zJB2ULMGJheDHeyztM1KGd2oGk
Aensm74NlfUqKzy/3KZ9KnQmEpj/EEBr48vAsgAT9kMjN+V3
```

```
NgAwfoqgS0dwj5OiRJoIR4+cdRt+s32OUKsclAODFZTdtxRn
vXF3qYV0S8oewMbEwh3trXi1c7nDMQC3RmoY8RVGt5U6LMAQ
KITDyHU3VmRJ36vn77QqSzbeUPz8zEnbpik8kHPykJZFkcyj
jZoHT1xkJ1tk )
```

For authentication, you can sign particular resource records for a given domain or host. Enter the domain or host followed by the term **SIG** and then the resource record's signature.

```
mytrek.com. SIG KEY 3 86400 19990321010705 19990218010705 4932 com. (
Am3tWJzEDzfU1xwg7hzkiJ0+8UQaPtlJhUpQx1snKpDUqZxm
igMZEVk= )
```

The NXT record lets you negatively answer queries.

```
mytrek.com. NXT ftp.mytrek.com. A NS SOA MX SIG KEY NXT
```

Signing Keys

To set up secure communications between a parent (master) DNS server and a child (slave) DNS server, the public key then needs to be sent to the parent zone. There, the key can be signed by the parent. As you may have more than zone key, you create a keyset using the **dnssec-makekeyset** command. This generates a file with the extension **.keyset** that is then sent to the parent. The parent zone then uses the **dnssec-signkey** command to sign a child's keyset. This generates a file with the prefix **signedkey-**. This is sent back to the child and now contains both the child's keyset and the parent's signatures. Once the child has the **signedkey-** files, the **dnssec-signedzone** command can be used to sign the zone. The **dnssec-signedzone** command will generate a file with the extension **.signed**. This file is then included in the **named.conf** file with the INCLUDE operation. The **trusted-keys** statement needs to list the public key for the parent zone.

TSIG Keys

TSIG (transaction signatures) also provide secure DNS communications, but they share the private key instead of a private/public key pair. They are usually used for communications between two local DNS servers, and to provide authentication for dynamic updates such as those between a DNS server and a DHCP server.

NOTE *For BIND 8.0, you use **dnskeygen** instead of **dnssec-keygen**.*

Generating TSIG keys

To create a TSIG key for your DNS server, you use the **dnssec-keygen** command as described earlier. Instead of using the same keys you use for DNSSEC, you create a new set to use for transaction signatures. For TSIG, a shared private key is used instead of a public/private key pair. For a TSIG key you would use an HMAC-MD5 algorithm that generates the same key in the both the **.key** and **.private** files. Use the **-a** option to specify the HMAC-MD5 algorithm to use and the **-b** option for the bit size. (HMAC-MD5 ranges from 1 to 512.) Use the **-n** option to specify the key type, in this case HOST for the host name. The bit range will vary according to the algorithm. The following example creates a host key using a 128-bit key and the HMAC-MD5 encryption algorithm:

```
dnssec-keygen -a HMAC-MD5 -b 128 -n HOST turtle.mytrek.com
```

This creates a private key and a public key, located in the **.key** and **.private** files. In a TSIG scheme, both hosts would use the same private key for authentication. For example, to enable a DHCP server to update a DNS server, both would need the private (secret) key for a TSIG authentication. The HMAC-MD5 key is used as a shared private key, generating both the same private and public keys in the **.key** and **.private** files.

The Key Statement

You then specify a key in the **named.conf** file with the **key** statement. For the algorithm option, you list the HMAC-MD5 algorithm, and for the secret option, you list the private key. This key will be listed in both the **.private** and **.key** files. The preceding example would generate key and private files called **Kturtle.mytrek.com.+157.43080.key** and **Kturtle .mytrek.com.+157.43080.private**. The contents of the **.key** file consist of a resource record shown here:

```
turtle.mytrek.com.  IN KEY 512 3 157 ONQAfbBLnvWU9H8hRqq/WA==
```

The contents of the private file show the same key along with the algorithm:

```
Private-key-format: v1.2
Algorithm: 157 (HMAC_MD5)
Key: ONQAfbBLnvWU9H8hRqq/WA==
```

Within the **named.conf** file, you then name the key using a **key** statement:

```
key myserver {
algorithm HMAC-MD5;
secret "ONQAfbBLnvWU9H8hRqq/WA==";
};
```

The key's name can then be used to reference the key in other named statements, such as **allow-update** statements:

```
allow-update myserver;
```

The DNS server or DHCP server with which you are setting up communication will also have to have the same key. See the earlier section "Dynamic Update: DHCP and Journal Files" and Chapter 37 for more information on DHCP and TSIG. For communication between two DNS servers, each would have to have a server statement specifying the shared key. In the following example, the **named.conf** file for the DNS server on 192.168.0.1 would have to have the following server statement to communicate with the DNS server on 10.0.0.1, using the shared myserver key. The **named.conf** file on the 10.0.0.1 DNS server would have to have a corresponding server statement for the 192.168.0.1 server.

```
server 10.0.0.1 {  keys (myserver;}; };
```

Split DNS: Views

BIND 9.*x* allows you to divide DNS space into internal and external views. This organization into separate views is referred to as *split DNS*. Such a configuration is helpful to manage a local network that is connected to a larger network, such as the Internet. Your internal view would include DNS information on hosts in the local network, whereas an external view would show only the part of the DNS space that is accessible to other networks. DNS views are often used when you have a local network that you want to protect from a larger network such as the Internet. In effect, you protect DNS information for hosts on a local network from a larger external network such as the Internet.

Internal and External Views

To implement a split DNS space, you need to set up different DNS servers for the internal and external views. The internal DNS servers will hold DNS information about local hosts. The external DNS server maintains connections to the Internet through a gateway as well as manages DNS information about any local hosts that allow external access, such as FTP or Web sites. The gateways and Internet-accessible sites make up the external view of hosts on the network. The internal servers handle all queries to the local hosts or subdomains. Queries to external hosts such as Internet sites are sent to the external servers, which then forward them on to the Internet. Queries sent to those local hosts that operate external servers such as Internet FTP and Web sites are sent to the external DNS servers for processing. Mail sent to local hosts from the Internet is handled first by the external servers, which then forward messages on to the internal servers. With a split DNS configuration, local hosts can access other local hosts, Internet sites, and local hosts maintaining Internet servers. Internet users, on the other hand, can access only those hosts open to the Internet (served by external servers) such as those with Internet servers like FTP and HTTP. Internet users can, however, send mail messages to any of the local hosts, internal and external.

You can also use DNS views to manage connections between a private network that may use only one Internet address to connect its hosts to the Internet. In this case, the internal view holds the private addresses (192.168...), and the external view connects a gateway host with an Internet address to the Internet. This adds another level of security, providing a result similar to IP masquerading (see Chapter 20).

Configuring Views

DNS views are configured with the allow statements such as **allow-query** and **allow-transfer**. With these statements, you can specify the hosts that a zone can send and receive queries and transfers to and from. For example, the internal zone could accept queries from other local hosts, but not from local hosts with external access such as Internet servers. The local Internet servers, though, can accept queries from the local hosts. All Internet queries are forwarded to the gateway. In the external configuration, the local Internet servers can accept queries from anywhere. The gateways receive queries from both the local hosts and the local Internet servers.

In the following example, a network of three internal hosts and one external host is set up into a split view. There are two DNS servers: one for the internal network and one for external access, based on the external host. In reality these make up one network but they are split into two views. The internal view is known as **mygolf.com**, and the external as **greatgolf.com**. In each configuration, the internal hosts are designated in ACL-labeled internals, and the external host is designated in ACL-labeled externals. Should you want to designate an entire IP address range as internal, you could simply use the network address, as in 192.168.0.0/24. In the options section, **allow-query**, **allow-recursion**, and **allow-transfers** restrict access within the network.

Split View Example

The following example shows only the configuration entries needed to implement an internal view. In the **mygolf.com** zone, queries and transfers are allowed only among internal hosts. The global **allow-recursion** option allows recursion among internals.

Internal DNS server
```
acl internals { 192.168.0.1; 192.168.0.2; 192.168.0.3; };
acl externals {10.0.0.1;};
options {
        forward only;
        forwarders {10.0.0.1;}; // forward to external servers
        allow-transfer { none; };
        // allow-transfer to no one by default
        allow-query { internals; externals; };// restrict query access
        allow-recursion { internals; };
        // restrict recursion to internals
        }
zone "mygolf.com" {
        type master;
        file "mygolf";
        forwarders { };
        allow-query { internals; };
        allow-transfer { internals; }
        };
```

In the configuration for the external DNS server, the same ACLs are set up for internals and externals. In the **options** statement, recursion is now allowed for both externals and internals. In the **mygolf.com** zone, queries are allowed from anywhere, and recursion is allowed for externals and internals. Transfers are not allowed at all.

External DNS server
```
acl internals { 192.168.0.1; 192.168.0.2; 192.168.0.3; };
acl externals {10.0.0.1;};
options {
        allow-transfer { none; }; // allow-transfer to no one
        allow-query { internals; externals; };// restrict query access
        allow-recursion { internals; externals };
        // restrict recursion
        };

zone "greatgolf.com" {
        type master;
        file "greatgolf";
        allow-query { any; };
        allow-transfer { internals; externals; };
};
```

37

CHAPTER

Network Autoconfiguration: IPv6, DHCPv6, and DHCP

Many networks now provide either IPv6 autoconfiguration or the DHCP (Dynamic Host Configuration Protocol) service, which automatically provides network configuration for all connected hosts. Autoconfiguration can be either stateless, as in the case of IPv6, or stateful, as with DHCP. Stateless IPv6 autoconfiguration requires no independent server or source to connect to a network. It is a direct plug-and-play operation, where the hardware network interfaces and routers can directly determine the correct addresses. DCHP is an older method that requires a separate server to manage and assign all addresses. Should this server ever fail, hosts could not connect.

With the DHCP protocol, an administrator uses a pool of IP addresses from which the administrator can assign an IP address to a host as needed. The protocol can also be used to provide all necessary network connection information such as the gateway address for the network or the netmask. Instead of having to configure each host separately, network configuration can be handled by a central DHCP server. The length of time that an address can be used can be controlled by means of leases, making effective use of available addresses. If your network is configuring your systems with DHCP, you will not have to configure it.

There are currently two versions of DHCP, one for the original IPv4 protocol and another, known as DHCPv6, for the IPv6 protocol. The IPv6 protocol includes information for dynamic configuration that the IPv4 protocol lacks. In this respect, the IPv4 protocol is much more dependent on DHCP than IPv6 is. This chapter covers primarily DHCP for the IPv4 protocol.

IPv6 Stateless Autoconfiguration

In an IPv6 network, the IPv6 protocol includes information that can directly configure a host. With IPv4 you either had to manually configure each host or rely on a DHCP server to provide configuration information. With IPv6 configuration information is integrated into the Internet protocol directly. IPv6 address autoconfiguration is described in detail in RFC 2462.

IPv6 autoconfiguration capabilities are known as stateless, meaning that it can directly configure a host without recourse of an external server. Alternatively, DHCP, including DHCPv6, is stateful, where the host relies on an external DHCP server to provide configuration information. Stateless autoconfiguration has the advantage of hosts not having to rely on a DHCP server to maintain connections to a network. Networks could even become mobile, hooking into one subnet or another, automatically generating addresses as needed. Hosts are no longer tied to a particular DHCP server.

Generating the Local Address

To autoconfigure hosts on a local network, IPv6 makes use of the each network device's hardware MAC address. This address is used to generate a temporary address, with which the host can be queried and configured.

The MAC address is used to create a link-local address, one with a link-local prefix, **FE80::0**, followed by an interface identifier. The link-local prefix is used for physically connected hosts such as those on a small local network.

A uniqueness test is then performed on the generated address. Using the Neighbor Discovery Protocol (NDP), other hosts on the network are checked to see if another host is already using the generated link-local address. If no other host is using the address, then the address is assigned for that local network. At this point the host has only a local address valid within the local physical network. Link-local addresses cannot be routed to a larger network.

Generating the Full Address: Router Advertisements

Once the link-local address has been determined, the router for the network is then queried for additional configuration information. The information can be either stateful or stateless, or both. For stateless configuration, information such as the network address is provided directly, whereas for stateful configuration, the host is referred to a DHCPv6 server where it can obtain configuration information. The two can work together. Often the stateless method is used for addresses, and the stateful DHCPv6 server is used to provide other configuration information such as DNS server addresses.

In the case of stateless addresses, the router provides the larger network address, such as the network's Internet address. This address is then added to the local address, replacing the original link-local prefix, giving either a complete global Internet address or, in the case of private networks, site-local addresses. Routers will routinely advertise this address information, though it can also be specifically requested. The NDP protocol is used to query the information. Before the address is officially assigned, a duplicate address detection procedure checks to see if the address is already in use. The process depends on the router's providing the appropriate addressing information in the form of router advertisements. If there is no router, or there are no route advertisements, then a stateful method like DHCPv6 or manual configuration must be used to provide the addresses.

Figure 37-1 shows a network that is configured with stateless address autoconfiguration. First each host determines its interface identifier using its own MAC hardware address. This is used to create a temporary link-local address for each host using the **FE08::0** prefix. This allows initial communication with the network's router. The router then uses its network prefix to create full Internet addresses, replacing the link-local prefix.

Router Renumbering

With IPv6, routers have the ability to renumber the addresses on their networks, by changing the network prefix. Renumbering is carried out through the Router Renumbering Protocol, RR. (See RFC 2894 for a description of router renumbering.) Renumbering is often

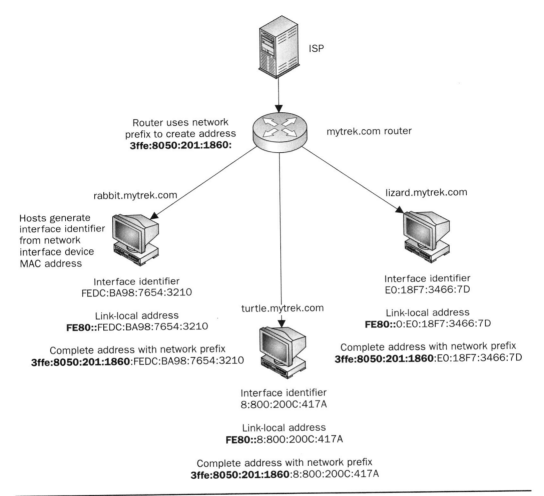

Router uses network
prefix to create address
3ffe:8050:201:1860:

mytrek.com router

ISP

rabbit.mytrek.com

Hosts generate
interface identifier
from network
interface device
MAC address

Interface identifier
FEDC:BA98:7654:3210

Link-local address
FE80::FEDC:BA98:7654:3210

Complete address with network prefix
3ffe:8050:201:1860:FEDC:BA98:7654:3210

turtle.mytrek.com

Interface identifier
8:800:200C:417A

Link-local address
FE80::8:800:200C:417A

Complete address with network prefix
3ffe:8050:201:1860:8:800:200C:417A

lizard.mytrek.com

Interface identifier
E0:18F7:3466:7D

Link-local address
FE80::0:E0:18F7:3466:7D

Complete address with network prefix
3ffe:8050:201:1860:E0:18F7:3466:7D

FIGURE 37-1   Stateless IPv6 address autoconfiguration

used when a network changes ISP providers, which requires the net address for all hosts to
be changed (see Figure 37-2). It can also be used for mobile networks where a network can
be plugged in to different larger networks, renumbering each time.

With renumbering, routers place a time limit on addresses, similar to the lease time in
DHCP, by specifying an expiration limit for the network prefix when the address is generated.
To ease transition, interfaces still keep their old addresses as deprecated addresses, while the
new one are first being used. The new ones will be the preferred addresses used for any new
connections while deprecated ones are used for older connections. In effect a host could have
two addresses, one deprecated and one preferred. This regeneration of addresses effectively
renumbers the hosts.

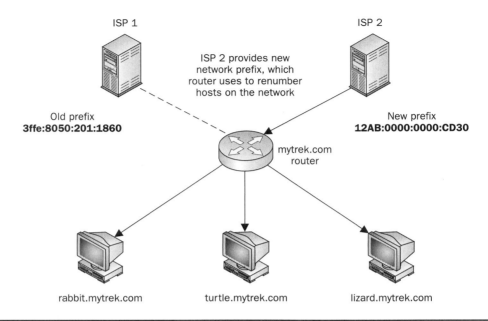

ISP 1

ISP 2 provides new
network prefix, which
router uses to renumber
hosts on the network

ISP 2

Old prefix
3ffe:8050:201:1860

New prefix
12AB:0000:0000:CD30

mytrek.com
router

rabbit.mytrek.com   turtle.mytrek.com   lizard.mytrek.com

FIGURE 37-2   Router renumbering with IPv6 autoconfiguration

IPv6 Stateful Autoconfiguration: DHCPv6

The IPv6 version of DHCP (DHCPv6) provides stateful autoconfiguration to those networks that still want a DHCP-like service on IPv6 networks. DHCP IPv6 provides configuration information from a server, just like DHCP. But it is a completely different protocol from the IPv4 version, with different options and capabilities. As a stateful configuration process, information is provided by an independent server. DHCPv6 is still under development, though a version is distributed with Fedora and Red Hat Enterprise Linux.

DHCPv6 uses a its own set of options for both the client and the server. The DHCP server for IPv6 is called **dhcp6s**, and the DHCP client for IPv6 is **dhcp6c**. Their corresponding configuration files are **/etc/dhcp6c** and **/etc/sysconfig/dhcp6s**. A service script, **/etc/init .d/dhcp6s**, can be used to manage the **dhcp6s** server.

As with IPv6 autoconfiguration, the host identifier for a local address is first automatically generated. This is a local-link address containing a host identifier address generated from the host interface's MAC address.

Once the local-link address is determined, the router is queried for the DHCPv6 server. This information is provided in router advertisements that are broadcast regularly. At this point the two different kinds of stateful information can be provided by the server: addresses and other configuration information. The host is notified which kinds of stateful information are provided. If address information is not given by the DHCPv6 server, then addresses will be determined using the stateless autoconfiguration method described in the preceding section. If address information is provided, then an address will then be obtained from the server, instead of being directly generated. Before leasing an address, the server will run a duplicate address detection procedure to make sure the address is unique.

> **NOTE** *DHCPv6 stateful addressing is useful for situations in which strict control needs to be maintained over the IP address of a host, whereas stateless IPv6 addressing is suitable for situations where the actual IP address is not important, just that connections be effective.*

Linux as an IPv6 Router: radvd

For a Linux system that operates as a router, you use the **radvd** Router ADVertisement Daemon to advertise addresses, specifying a network prefix in the **/etc/radvd.conf** file. The **radvd** daemon will detect router network address requests from hosts, known as router solicitations, and provide them with a network address using a router advertisement. These router advertisements will also be broadcast to provide the network address to any hosts that do not send in requests. For **radvd** to work, you will have to turn on IPv6 forwarding. Use **sysctl** and set **net.ipv6.conf.all.forwarding** to 1. To start up the **radvd** daemon, you use the **radvd** startup script. To check the router addresses **radvd** is sending, you can use **radvdump**.

You will have to configure the **radvd** daemon yourself, specifying the network address to broadcast. Configuration, though, is very simple, as the full address will be automatically generated using the host's hardware address. A configuration consists of interface entries, which in turn list interface options, prefix definitions, and options, along with router definitions if needed. The configuration is placed in the **/etc/radvd.conf** file, which would look something like this:

```
interface eth0 {
    AdvSendAdvert on;
        prefix fec0:0:0:0::/64
        {
        AdvOnLink on;
        AdvAutonomous on;
        };
};
```

This assumes one interface is used for the local network, eth0. This interface configuration lists an interface option (AdvSendAdvert) and a prefix definition, along with two prefix options (AdvOnLink and AdvAutonomous). To specify prefix options for a specific prefix, add them within parentheses following the prefix definition. The prefix definition specifies your IPv6 network address. If a local area network has its own network address, you will need to provide its IPv6 network prefix address. For a private network, like a home network, you can use the site-local IPv6 prefix, which operates like the IPv4 private network addresses, 192.168.0. The preceding example uses a site-local address that is used for private IPv6 networks, fec0:0:0:0::, which has a length of 64 bits.

The AdvSendAdvert interface option turns on network address advertising to the hosts. The AdvAutonomous network prefix option provides automatic address configuration, and AdvOnLink simply means that host requests can be received on the specified network interface.

A second network interface is then used to connect the Linux system to an ISP or larger network. If the ISP supports IPv6, this is simply a matter of sending a router solicitation to the ISP router. This would automatically generate your Internet address using the hardware address of the network interface used to connect to the Internet and the ISP router's advertised network address. In Figure 37-2, a local network, the eth0 network interface connects to the local network, whereas eth1 connects to the Internet.

DHCP for IPv4

DHCP provides configuration information to systems connected to an IPv4 TCP/IP network, whether the Internet or an intranet. The machines on the network operate as DHCP clients, obtaining their network configuration information from a DHCP server on their network. A machine on the network runs a DHCP client daemon that automatically receives its network configuration information from its network's DHCP server. The information includes its IP address, along with the network's name server, gateway, and proxy addresses, including the netmask. Nothing has to be configured manually on the local system, except to specify the DHCP server it should get its network configuration from. This has the added advantage of centralizing control over network configuration for the different systems on the network. A network administrator can manage the network configurations for all the systems on the network from the DHCP server.

NOTE *DHCP is based on the BOOTP protocol developed for diskless workstations. Check DHCP documentation for options specific to machines designed to work with BOOTP.*

A DHCP server also supports several methods for IP address allocation: automatic, dynamic, and manual. Automatic allocation assigns a permanent IP address for a host. Manual allocation assigns an IP address designated by the network administrator. With dynamic allocation, a DHCP server can allocate an IP address to a host on the network only when the host actually needs to use it. Dynamic allocation takes addresses from a pool of IP addresses that hosts can use when needed and release when they are finished.

The current version of DHCP now supports the DHCP failover protocol, in which two DHCP servers support the same address pool. Should one fail, the other can continue to provide DHCP services for a network. Both servers are in sync and have the same copy of network support information for each host on the network. Primary and secondary servers in this scheme are designated with the primary and secondary statements.

A variety of DHCP servers and clients are available for different operating systems. For Linux, you can obtain DHCP software from the Internet Software Consortium (ISC) at **www.isc.org**. The software package includes a DHCP server, a client, and a relay agent. Linux includes a DHCP server and client. The DHCP client is called **dhclient**, and the IPv4 server is called **dhcpd**.

Configuring DHCP IPv4 Client Hosts

Configuring hosts to use a DHCP server is a simple matter of setting options for the host's network interface device, such as an Ethernet card. For a Linux host, you can use a distribution network tool to set the host to automatically access a DHCP server for network information. On a network tool's panel for configuring the Internet connection, you will normally find a check box for selecting DHCP. Clicking this box will enable DHCP. For Fedora and Red Hat Enterprise Linux, you can use the system-config-network tool: Select the network device on the Devices panel and edit it. On the General panel, click the entry labeled Automatically Obtain IP Address Settings With, and be sure DHCP is selected from the pop-up menu. If you are connecting to an Internet service provider (ISP), under DHCP Setting, click Automatically Obtain DNS Information From Provider. The **BOOTPROTO** entry to DHCP will be set in that interface's network script in the **/etc/sysconfig/network-**

scripts directory, such as **ifcfg-eth0** for the first Ethernet card. You could also manually make this entry:

```
BOOTPROTO=dhcp
```

Be sure to restart your network devices with the network script to have the changes take effect.

Client support is carried out by the **dhclient** tool. When your network starts up, it uses **dhclient** to set up your DHCP connection. Though defaults are usually adequate, you can further configure the DHCP client using the **/etc/dhclient.conf** file. Consult the **dhclient .conf** Man page for a detailed list of configuration options. **dhclient** keeps lease information on the DCHP connection in the **/var/lib/dhcp/dhclient.leases** file. You can also directly run **dhclient** to configure DHCP connections.

```
dhclient
```

On a Windows client, locate the TCP/IP entry for your network interface card, and then open its properties window. Click the box labeled Obtain IP Address Automatically. Then locate the WINS panel (usually by clicking the Advanced button) and select DHCP as the protocol you want to use.

Configuring the DHCP IPv4 Server

You can stop and start the DHCP server using the **dhcpd** command in the **/etc/rc.d/init.d** directory. Use the redhat-config-services tool or the **service** command with the **start**, **restart**, and **stop** options. The following example starts the DHCP server. Use the **stop** option to shut it down and **restart** to restart it.

```
service dhcpd start
```

Dynamically allocated IP addresses, known as *leases*, will be assigned for a given time. When a lease expires, it can be extended or a new one generated. Current leases are listed in the **dhcpd.leases** file located in the **/var/lib/dhcp** directory. A lease entry will specify the IP address and the start and end times of the lease along with the client's hostname.

DHCP server arguments and options can be specified in the **/etc/sysconfig/dhcpd** file. Network device arguments specify which network device the DHCP server should run on. You can also specify options such as the configuration file to use or the port to listen on. Network device arguments are needed should you have two or more network interfaces on your system but want the DHCP server to operate on only selected connections. Such arguments are listed in the **/etc/sysconf/dhcpd** file using the DHCPARGS setting. The following example says to run the DHCP server only on the Ethernet network device **eth0**:

```
DHPCARGS=eth0
```

This kind of configuration is useful for gateway systems that are connected to both a local network and a larger network such as the Internet through different network devices. On the Internet connection, you may want to run the DCHP client to receive an IP address from an ISP, and on the local network connection, you would want to run the DHCP server to assign IP addresses to local hosts.

The configuration file for the DHCP server is **/etc/dhcpd.conf**, where you specify parameters and declarations that define how different DHCP clients on your network are accessed by the DHCP server, along with options that define information passed to the clients by the DHCP server. These parameters, declarations, and options can be defined globally, for certain subnetworks, or for specific hosts. Global parameters, declarations, and options apply to all clients, unless overridden by corresponding declarations and options in subnet or host declarations. Technically, all entries in a **dhcpd.conf** file are statements that can be either declarations or parameters. All statements end with a semicolon. Options are specified in **options** parameter statements. Parameters differ from declarations in that they define if and how to perform tasks, such as how long a lease is allocated. Declarations describe network features such as the range of addresses to allocate or the networks that are accessible. See Table 37-1 for a listing of commonly used declarations and options.

Entries	Description
Declarations	
`shared-network` *name*	Used to indicate if some subnets share the same physical network.
`subnet` *subnet-number netmask*	References an entire subnet of addresses.
`range` [*dynamic-bootp*] *low-address* [*high-address*] ;	Provides the highest and lowest dynamically allocated IP addresses.
`host` *hostname*	References a particular host.
`group`	Lets you label a group of parameters and declarations and then use the label to apply them to subnets and hosts.
`allow unknown-clients;` `deny unknown-clients;`	Does not dynamically assign addresses to unknown clients.
`allow bootp; deny bootp;`	Determines whether to respond to **bootp** queries.
`allow booting; deny booting;`	Determines whether to respond to client queries.
Parameters	
`default-lease-time` *time;*	Length in seconds assigned to a lease.
`max-lease-time` *time;*	Maximum length of lease.
`hardware` *hardware-type hardware-address;*	Network hardware type (Ethernet or token ring) and address.
`filename` "*filename*";	Name of the initial boot file.
`server-name` "*name*";	Name of the server from which a client is booting.
`next-server` *server-name;*	Server that loads the initial boot file specified in the filename.
`fixed-address` *address* [, *address* ...] ;	Assigns a fixed address to a client.
`get-lease-hostnames` *flag;*	Determines whether to look up and use IP addresses of clients.

TABLE 37-1   DHCP Declarations, Parameters, and Options *(continued)*

Entries	Description
`authoritative;` `not authoritative;`	Denies invalid address requests.
`server-identifier hostname;`	Specifies the server.
Options	
`option subnet-mask` *ip-address;*	Client's subnet mask.
`option routers` *ip-address* [, *ip-address...*] ;	List of router IP addresses on client's subnet.
`option domain-name-servers` *ip-address* [, *ip-address...*] ;	List of domain name servers used by the client.
`option log-servers` *ip-address* [, *ip-address...*] ;	List of log servers used by the client.
`option host-name` *string;*	Client's hostname.
`option domain-name` *string;*	Client's domain name.
`option broadcast-address` *ip-address;*	Client's broadcast address.
`option nis-domain` *string;*	Client's Network Information Service domain.
`option nis-servers` *ip-address* [, *ip-address...*] ;	NIS servers the client can use.
`option smtp-server` *ip-address* [, *ip-address...*] ;	List of SMTP servers used by the client.
`option pop-server` *ip-address* [, *ip-address...*] ;	List of POP servers used by the client.
`option nntp-server ip-address` [, *ip-address...*] ;	List of NNTP servers used by the client.
`option www-server` *ip-address* [, *ip-address...*] ;	List of Web servers used by the client.

TABLE 37-1   DHCP Declarations, Parameters, and Options

Declarations provide information for the DHCP server or designate actions it is to perform. For example, the **range** declaration is used to specify the range of IP addresses to be dynamically allocated to hosts:

```
range 192.168.0.5 192.168.0.128;
```

With parameters, you can specify how the server is to treat clients. For example, the **default-lease-time** declaration sets the number of seconds a lease is assigned to a client. The **filename** declaration specifies the boot file to be used by the client. The **server-name** declaration informs the client of the host from which it is booting. The **fixed-address** declaration can be used to assign a static IP address to a client. See the Man page for **dhcpd.conf** for a complete listing.

Options provide information to clients that they may need to access network services, such as the domain name of the network, the domain name servers that clients use, or the broadcast address. See the Man page for **dhcp-options** for a complete listing. This information is provided by **option** parameters as shown here:

```
option broadcast-address 192.168.0.255;
option domain-name-servers 192.168.0.1, 192.168.0.4;
option domain-name "mytrek.com";
```

Your **dhcpd.conf** file will usually begin with declarations, parameters, and options that you define for your network serviced by the DHCP server. The following example provides router (gateway), netmask, domain name, and DNS server information to clients. Additional parameters define the default and maximum lease times for dynamically allocated IP addresses.

```
option routers 192.168.0.1;
option subnet-mask 255.255.255.0;
option domain-name "mytrek.com ";
option domain-name-servers 192.168.0.1;
default-lease-time 21600;
max-lease-time 43200;
```

With the subnet, host, and group declarations, you can reference clients in a specific network, particular clients, or different groupings of clients across networks. Within these declarations, you can enter parameters, declarations, or options that will apply only to those clients. Scoped declarations, parameters, and options are enclosed in braces. For example, to define a declaration for a particular host, you use the **host** declaration as shown here:

```
host rabbit {
        declarations, parameters, or options;
        }
```

You can collect different subnet, global, and host declaration into groups using the **group** declaration. In this case, the global declarations are applied only to those subnets and hosts declared within the group.

Dynamic IPv4 Addresses for DHCP

Your DHCP server can be configured to select IP addresses from a given range and assign them to different clients. Given a situation where you have many clients that may not always be connected to the network, you could effectively service them with a smaller pool of IP addresses. IP addresses are assigned only when they are needed. With the **range** declaration, you specify a range of addresses that can be dynamically allocated to clients. The declaration takes two arguments, the first and last addresses in the range.

```
range 192.168.1.5 192.168.1.128;
```

For example, if you are setting up your own small home network, you would use a network address beginning with 192.168. The range would specify possible IP addresses with that network. So for a network with the address 192.168.0.0, you would place a **range** declaration along with any other information you want to give to your client hosts. In the following example, a range of IP addresses extending from 192.168.0.1 to 192.168.0.128 can be allocated to the hosts on that network:

```
range 192.168.0.5 192.168.0.128;
```

You should also define your lease times, both a default and a maximum:

```
default-lease-time 21600;
max-lease-time 43200;
```

For a small, simple home network, you just need to list the **range** declaration along with any global options as shown here. If your DHCP server is managing several subnetworks, you will have to use the **subnet** declarations.

In order to assign dynamic addresses to a network, the DHCP server will require that your network topology be mapped. This means it needs to know what network addresses belong to a given network. Even if you use only one network, you will need to specify the address space for it. You define a network with the **subnet** declaration. Within this **subnet** declaration, you can specify any parameters, declarations, or options to use for that network. The **subnet** declaration informs the DHCP server of the possible IP addresses encompassed by a given subnet. This is determined by the network IP address and the netmask for that network. The next example defines a local network with address space from 192.168.0.0 to 192.168.0.255. The **range** declaration allows addresses to be allocated from 192.168.0.5 to 192.168.0.128.

```
subnet 192.168.1.0 netmask 255.255.255.0 {
        range 192.168.0.5 192.168.0.128;
}
```

Versions of DHCP prior to 3.0 required that you even map connected network interfaces that are not being served by DHCP. Thus each network interface would have to have a corresponding **subnet** declaration. Those not being serviced by DHCP would have a **not authoritative** parameter as shown here (192.168.2.0 being a network not to be serviced by DHCP). In version 3.0 and later, DHCP simply ignores unmapped network interfaces:

```
subnet 192.168.2.0 netmask 255.255.255.0 {
     not authoritative;
}
```

The implementation of a very simple DHCP server for dynamic addresses is shown in the sample **dhcpd.conf** file that follows:

/etc/dhcpd.conf
```
option routers 192.168.0.1;
 option subnet-mask 255.255.255.0;
 option domain-name "mytrek.com ";
 option domain-name-servers 192.168.0.1;

subnet 192.168.1.0 netmask 255.255.255.0 {
    range 192.168.0.5 192.168.0.128;
    default-lease-time 21600;
    max-lease-time 43200;
    }
```

DHCP Dynamic DNS Updates

For networks that also support a Domain Name Server, dynamic allocation of IP addresses currently needs to address one major constraint: DHCP needs to sync with a DNS server. A DNS server associates hostnames with particular IP addresses, whereas in the case of dynamic allocation, the DHCP server randomly assigns its own IP addresses to different hosts. These may or may not be the same as the IP addresses that the DNS server expects to associate with a hostname. A solution to this problem is being developed, called Dynamic DNS. With Dynamic DNS, the DHCP server is able to automatically update the DNS server with the IP addresses the DHCP server has assigned to different hosts.

NOTE *Alternatively, if you want to statically synchronize your DHCP and DNS servers with fixed addresses, you would configure DHCP to assign those fixed addresses to hosts. You can then have the DHCP server perform a DNS lookup to obtain the IP address it should assign, or you can manually assign the same IP address in the DHCP configuration file. Performing a DNS lookup has the advantage of specifying the IP address in one place, the DNS server.*

The DHCP server has the ability to dynamically update BIND DNS server zone configuration files. As noted in Chapter 36, you enable dynamic updates on a DNS server for a zone file by specifying the `allow-update` option for it in the **named.conf** file. Furthermore, it is strongly encouraged that you use TSIG signature keys (see Chapter 36) to reference and authenticate the BIND and DHCP servers. Currently DHCP uses the Interim DNS Update Scheme to perform dynamic DNS updates, replacing an earlier Ad-Hoc DNS Update Scheme. A finalized version will be implemented in future DHCP releases. You can find detailed information about dynamic DNS in the **dhcpd.conf** Man page.

Enabling the use of a TSIG key involves syncing configurations for both your DHCP and DNS servers. Both have to be configured to use the same key for the same domains. First you need to create a shared secret TSIG signature key using **dnssec-keygen**, as described in Chapter 36. In the DNS server, you place TSIG key declarations and **allow-update** entries in the server's **named.conf** file, as shown in this example:

```
key mydhcpserver {
algorithm HMAC-MD5;
secret "ONQAfbBLnvWU9H8hRqq/WA==";
};


zone "mytrek.com" {
      type master;
      file "mytrek.com";
      allow-update {key mydhcpserver;};
 };

zone "1.168.192.IN-ADDR.ARPA" {
      type master;
      file "192.168.0";
      allow-update {key mydhcpserver;};
};
```

In the DHCP server, you place a corresponding TSIG key declaration and **allow-update** entries in the server's **dhcpd.conf** file, as shown in this example. The **key** declaration has the same syntax as the DNS server. DHCP **zone** statements are then used to specify the IP address of the domain and the TSIG key to use. The domain names and IP addresses need to match exactly in the configuration files for both the DNS and DHCP servers. Unlike in the **named.conf** file, there are no quotes around the domain name or IP addresses in the **dhcpd .conf** file. In the **dhcpd.conf** file, the domain names and IP addresses used in the **zone** statement also need to end with a period, as they do in the DNS zone files. The **key** statement lists the key to use. Though the DHCP server will try to determine the DNS servers to update, it is recommended that you explicitly identify them with a primary statement in a **zone** entry.

```
key mydhcpserver {
    algorithm HMAC-MD5;
    secret "ONQAfbBLnvWU9H8hRqq/WA==";
    };

zone mytrek.com. {                  #DNS domain zone to update
        primary 192.168.0.1;        #address of DNS server
        key mydhcpserver;           #TSIG signature key
 };

zone 1.168.192.IN-ADDR.ARPA. {      #domain PTR zone to update
        primary 192.168.0.1;        #address of DNS server
        key mydhcpserver;           # TSIG signature key
};
```

To generate a fully qualified hostname to use in a DNS update, the DHCP server will normally use its own domain name and the hostname provided by a DHCP client (see the **dhcpd.conf** Man page for exceptions). Should you want to assign a specific hostname to a host, you can use the **ddns-hostname** statement to specify it in the host's hardware section. The domain name is specified in the **domain-name** option:

```
option domain-name "mytrek.com"
```

The DNS update capability can be turned on or off for all domains with the **ddns-update-style** statement. It is on by default. To turn off DNS updates for particular domains, you can use the **ddns-updates** statement. This is also on by default.

A simple DNS update configuration for a DHCP server in the **dhcpd.conf** file is shown here:

/etc/dhcpd.conf
```
option routers 192.168.0.1;
 option subnet-mask 255.255.255.0;
 option domain-name "mytrek.com ";
 option domain-name-servers 192.168.0.1;
 key mydhcpserver {
     algorithm HMAC-MD5;
     secret "ONQAfbBLnvWU9H8hRqq/WA==";
     };

subnet 192.168.1.0 netmask 255.255.255.0 {
     range 192.168.0.5 192.168.0.128;
     default-lease-time 21600;
```

```
        max-lease-time 43200;
        zone mytrek.com. {
            primary 192.168.0.1;
            key mydhcpserver;
            }
        zone 1.168.192.IN-ADDR.ARPA. {
            primary 192.168.0.1;
            key mydhcpserver;
            }
}
```

DHCP Subnetworks

If you are dividing your network space into several subnetworks, you could use a single DHCP server to manage them. In that case, you would have a **subnet** declaration for each subnetwork. If you are setting up your own small network, you would use a network address beginning with 192.168. The range would specify possible IP addresses within that network. So for a network with the address 192.168.0.0, you would create a **subnet** declaration with the netmask 255.255.255.0. Within this declaration, you would place a **range** declaration along with any other information you want to give to your client hosts. In the following example, a range of IP addresses extending from 192.168.0.1 to 192.168.0.75 can be allocated to the hosts on that network:

```
subnet 192.168.0.0 netmask 255.255.255.0 {
 range 192.168.0.5 192.168.0.75;
}
```

You may want to specify different policies for each subnetwork, such as different lease times. Any entries in a **subnet** declaration will override global settings. So if you already have a global lease time set, a lease setting in a **subnet** declaration will override it for that subnet. The next example sets different lease times for different subnets, as well as different address allocations. The lease times for the first subnet are taken from the global lease time settings, whereas the second subnet defines its own lease times:

```
default-lease-time 21600;
max-lease-time 43200;

subnet 192.168.1.0 netmask 255.255.255.0 {
     range 192.168.0.5 192.168.0.75;
     }
subnet 192.168.1.128 netmask 255.255.255.252 {
     range 192.168.0.129 192.168.0.215;
     default-lease-time 56000;
     max-lease-time 62000;
       }
```

If your subnetworks are part of the same physical network, then you need to inform the server of this fact by declaring them as shared networks. You do this by placing subnet declarations within a **shared-network** declaration, specifying the shared network's name.

The name used can be any descriptive name, though you can use the domain name. Any options specified within the **shared-network** declaration and outside the subnet declarations will be global to those subnets. In the next example, the subnets are part of the same physical network and so are placed within a **shared-network** declaration:

```
shared-network mytrek.com
{
default-lease-time 21600;
max-lease-time 43200;
subnet 192.168.1.0 netmask 255.255.255.0 {
        range 192.168.0.5 192.168.0.75;
        }
subnet 192.168.1.128 netmask 255.255.255.252 {
        range 192.168.0.129 192.168.0.215;
        default-lease-time 56000;
        max-lease-time 62000;
        }
}
```

NOTE *Within a network, you could have subnets that run DHCP servers and some that don't. In that case, you can use the DHCP Relay Agent to let DHCP clients on a subnet without a DHCP server use a DHCP server running on another subnet. The DHCP Relay Agent, **dhcrelay**, can be managed with the **service** command. It is configured with the **/etc/sysconfig/dhcrelay** file, where you can specify the network interfaces to receive requests from and the DHCP servers to use.*

DHCP Fixed Addresses

Instead of using a pool of possible IP addresses for your hosts, you may want to give each one a specific addresses. Using the DHCP server still gives you control over which address will be assigned to a given host. However, to assign an address to a particular host, you need to know the hardware address for that host's network interface card (NIC). In effect, you have to inform the DHCP server that it has to associate a particular network connection device with a specified IP address. To do that, the DHCP server needs to know which network device you are referring to. You can identify a network device by its hardware address, known as its MAC address. To find out a client's hardware address, you log in to the client and use the **ifconfig** command to find out information about your network devices. To list all network devices, use the **-a** option. If you know your network device name, you can use that. The next example will list all information about the first Ethernet device, **eth0**:

```
ifconfig eth0
```

This will list information on all the client's network connection devices. The entry (usually the first) with the term **HWaddr** will display the MAC address. Once you have the MAC address, you can use it on the DHCP server to assign a specific IP address to that device.

In the **dhcpd.conf** file, you use a **host** declaration to set up a fixed address for a client. Within the **host** declaration, you place a **hardware** option in which you list the type of network connection device and its MAC address. Then you use the **fixed-address** parameter to specify the IP address to be assigned to that device. In the following example, the client's network device with a MAC address of 08:00:2b:4c:29:32 is given the IP address 192.168.0.2.

```
host rabbit {
            option host-name "rabbit.mytrek.com"
            hardware ethernet 08:00:2b:4c:29:32;
            fixed-address 192.168.0.2;
            }
```

You can also have the DHCP server perform a DNS lookup to obtain the host's IP address. This has the advantage of letting you manage IP addresses in only one place, the DNS server. Of course, this requires that the DNS server be operating so that the DHCP server can determine the IP address. For example, a proxy server connection (which can provide direct Web access) needs just an IP address, not a DNS hostname, to operate. If the DNS server were down, the preceding example would still assign an IP address to the host, whereas the following example would not:

```
host rabbit {
            option host-name "rabbit.mytrek.com"
            hardware ethernet 08:00:2b:4c:29:32;
            fixed-address rabbit.mytrek.com;
            }
```

You can also use the **host** declaration to define network information for a diskless workstation or terminal. In this case, you add a **filename** parameter specifying the boot file to use for that workstation or terminal. Here the terminal called **myterm** obtains boot information from the server **turtle.mytrek.com**:

```
host myterm {
            option host-name "myterm.mytrek.com"
            filename "/boot/vmlinuz";
            hardware ethernet 08:00:2b:4c:29:32;
            server-name "turtle.mytrek.com";
            }
```

The implementation of a very simple DHCP server for fixed addresses is shown in the sample **dhcpd.conf** file that follows. In the second **host** declaration, the DHCP will perform a DNS lookup to obtain the IP address of **rabbit.mytrek.com**:

/etc/dhcpd.conf
```
option routers 192.168.0.1;
option subnet-mask 255.255.255.0;
option domain-name "mytrek.com ";
option domain-name-servers 192.168.1.1;

subnet 192.168.1.0 netmask 255.255.255.0 {
host turtle {
            option host-name "turtle.mytrek.com"
            hardware ethernet 08:00:2b:4c:29:32;
            fixed-address 192.168.0.1;
            }
```

```
host rabbit {
            option host-name "rabbit.mytrek.com"
            hardware ethernet 00:80:AD:30:17:2A;
            fixed-address rabbit.mytrek.com;
            }
host lizard {
            option host-name "lizard.mytrek.com"
            hardware ethernet 00:70:2b:4b:29:14;
            fixed-address 192.168.0.3;
            }
}
```

A **host** declaration can also be placed within the **subnet** declaration to provide information about particular hosts in that subnet.

A common candidate for a fixed address is the DNS server for a network. Usually, you would want the DNS server located at the same IP address, so that it can be directly accessed. The DHCP server can then provide this IP address to its clients.

NFS, NIS, and GFS

L inux provides several tools for accessing files on remote systems connected to a network. The Network File System (NFS) enables you to connect to and directly access resources such as files or devices like CD-ROMs that reside on another machine. The new version, NFS4, provides greater security, with access allowed by your firewall. The Network Information Service (NIS) maintains configuration files for all systems on a network. With GFS you can set up a network file system, accessing disk space across a network.

Network File Systems: NFS and /etc/exports

NFS enables you to mount a file system on a remote computer as if it were local to your own system. You can then directly access any of the files on that remote file system. This has the advantage of allowing different systems on a network to access the same files directly, without each having to keep its own copy. Only one copy would be on a remote file system, which each computer could then access. You can find out more about NFS at its Web site at **nfs.sourceforge.net**.

NOTE *Mac OS X for Macintosh computers, which is based on BSD Unix, now supports NFS for file sharing. To access Apple file systems and printers using older Apple operating systems, you can use Netatalk. Netatalk implements the classic AppleTalk and AppleShare IP network protocols on Unix and Linux systems. The current Netatalk Web site is **netatalk.sourceforge.net**, with links to the FAQ and the HOW-TO sections.*

NFSv4

NFS version 4 is a new version of the NFS protocol with enhanced features like greater security, reliability, and speed, currently supported on Fedora and Red Hat Linux. Most of the commands are the same with a few changes. For example, when you mount an NFSv4 file system, you need to specify the **nfs4** file type. Also, for NFSv4, in the **/etc/exports** file, you can use the **fsid=0** option to specify the root export location.

```
/home/richlp          *(fsid=0,ro,sync)
```

The preceding entry lets you then mount the file system to the **/home/richlp** directory without having to specify it in the mount operation.

```
# mount -t nfs4  rabbit.mytrek.com:/  /home/dylan/projects
```

NFS Daemons

NFS operates over a TCP/IP network. The remote computer that holds the file system makes it available to other computers on the network. It does so by exporting the file system, which entails making entries in an NFS configuration file called **/etc/exports**, as well as by running several daemons to support access by other systems. These include **rpc.mountd**, **rpc.nfsd**, and **rpc.portmapper**. Access to your NFS server can be controlled by the **/etc/hosts.allow** and **/etc/hosts.deny** files. The NFS daemons are listed here:

- **rpc.nfsd**   Receives NFS requests from remote systems and translates them into requests for the local system.
- **rpc.mountd**   Performs requested mount and unmount operations.
- **rpc.portmapper**   Maps remote requests to the appropriate NFS daemon.
- **rpc.rquotad**   Provides user disk quota management.
- **rpc.statd**   Provides locking services when a remote host reboots.
- **rpc.lockd**   Handles lock recovery for systems that have gone down.

NOTE *It is advisable to use NFS on a local secure network only. If used over the Internet, NFS would open your system up to nonsecure access. NSF4 does provide protection.*

Starting and Stopping NFS

You can start up and shut down the NFS daemons using the **/etc/rc.d/init.d/nfs** service, which you can invoke with the **service** command, **service nfs start**. To have NFS started automatically, you can use **chkconfig** or the system-config-services tool to specify the runlevels at which it will operate. The following example will have NFS start up automatically at runlevels 3 and 5:

```
chkconfig -level 35  nfs on
```

The **nfs** script will start up the **portmapper**, **nfsd**, **mountd**, and **rquotad** daemons. To enable NFS locking, you use the **nfslock** script. This will start up the **statd** and **lockd** daemons. NFS locking provides for better recovery from interrupted operations that can occur from system crashes on remote hosts.

To see if NFS is actually running, you can use the **rpcinfo** command with the **-p** option. You should see entries for **mountd** and **nfs**. If not, NFS is not running.

Configuring NFS with the NFS Configuration Tool

Instead of manually mounting and configuring NFS directories, you can use the NFS Configuration tool (system-config-nfs). Select NFS entry from the System │ Administration │ Server Settings menu. This opens the NFS Server Configuration Tool window. Be sure your

NFS server software is installed (system-config-packages) and that the NFS server is running (system-config-services).

To add a directory to share, click the Add button to open an Add NFS Share dialog window. You can browse for or enter the directory to be shared in the Directory box. You then list the host where it is located, and specify the access permissions. On the General Options tab, you can set basic security and update features such as insecure file locking or immediate syncing of write operations. By default, the Sync Write Operations On Request option is set. On the User Access tab, you can treat users as local root users or as anonymous users with specific user or group IDs.

When you click OK, the entry will be listed in the NFS Server Configuration window. Changes do not take effect until you click Apply. This will create an entry in the **/etc/exports** file for the shared directory. You can later change any of these settings by selecting the entry and clicking Properties to open an Edit dialog box. To save your settings, click Apply. Should a firewall require the use of specific ports to access NFS directories, you can specify them in the Server Setting window.

The following example has the same entries that are used in the **/etc/exports** file described in the next section. The **/etc/exports** file generated by the NFS Server Configuration tool using this example is shown here:

```
/home/foodstuff/       lizard.mytrek.com(rw,sync)
/media/cdrom           rabbit.mytrek.com(ro,sync)
/home/richlp           *(ro,sync)
/pub                   *(ro,insecure,sync,all_squash)
```

Options set in the Basic, General Options, and User Access panels show up as options listed for each entry. For example, Read access is ro and Read/Write access is rw. Check the NFS Server Configuration help documents for a complete listing. Options are listed in Table 38-1.

NFS Configuration: /etc/exports

An entry in the **/etc/exports** file specifies the file system to be exported and the hosts on the network that can access it. For the file system, enter its *mountpoint,* the directory to which it was mounted on the host system. This is followed by a list of hosts that can access this file system along with options to control that access. A comma-separated list of export options placed within a set of parentheses may follow each host. For example, you might want to give one host read-only access and another read and write access. If the options are preceded by an * symbol, they are applied to any host. A list of options is provided in Table 38-1. The format of an entry in the **/etc/exports** file is shown here:

```
directory-pathname     host-designation(options)
```

NFS Host Entries

You can have several host entries for the same directory, each with access to that directory:

```
directory-pathname     host(options)  host(options)   host(options)
```

You have a great deal of flexibility when specifying hosts. For hosts within your domain, you can just use the hostname, whereas for those outside, you need to use a fully qualified domain name. You could also just use the host's IP address. Instead of just a single host,

General Option	Description
`secure`	Requires requests originate on secure ports, those less than 1024. This is on by default.
`insecure`	Turns off the `secure` option.
`ro`	Allows only read-only access. This is the default.
`rw`	Allows read/write access.
`sync`	Performs all writes when requested. This is the default.
`async`	Performs all writes when the server is ready.
`no_wdelay`	Performs writes immediately, not checking to see if they are related.
`wdelay`	Checks to see if writes are related, and if so, waits to perform them together. Can degrade performance. This is the default.
`hide`	Automatically hides an exported directory that is the subdirectory of another exported directory. The subdirectory has to be explicitly mounted to be accessed. Mounting the parent directory does not allow access. This is the default.
`no_hide`	Does not hide an exported directory that is the subdirectory of another exported directory (opposite of `hide`). Only works for single hosts and can be unreliable.
`subtree_check`	Checks parent directories in a file system to validate an exported subdirectory. This is the default.
`no_subtree_check`	Does not check parent directories in a file system to validate an exported subdirectory.
`insecure_locks`	Does not require authentication of locking requests. Used for older NFS versions.
User ID Mapping	**Description**
`all_squash`	Maps all UIDs and GIDs to the anonymous user. Useful for NFS-exported public FTP directories, news spool directories, and so forth.
`no_all_squash`	The opposite option to `all_squash`. This is the default setting.
`root_squash`	Maps requests from remote root user to the anonymous UID/GID. This is the default.
`no_root_squash`	Turns off root squashing. Allows the root user to access as the remote root.
`anonuid` `anongid`	Sets explicitly the UID and GID of the anonymous account used for `all_squash` and `root_squash` options. The defaults are nobody and nogroup.

TABLE 38-1   The /etc/exports Options

you can reference all the hosts within a specific domain, allowing access by an entire network. A simple way to do this is to use the * for the host segment, followed by the domain name for the network, such as *.mytrek.com for all the hosts in the **mytrek.com** network. Instead of domain names, you could use IP network addresses using a CNDR format where you specify the netmask to indicate a range of IP addresses. You can also use an NIS netgroup name to reference a collection of hosts. The NIS netgroup name is preceded by a @ sign.

```
directory       host(options)
directory       *(options)
directory       *.domain(options)
directory       192.168.1.0/255.255.255.0(options)
directory       @netgroup(options)
```

NFS Options

Options in **/etc/exports** operate as permissions to control access to exported directories. Read-only access is set with the **ro** option, and read/write with the **rw** option. The **sync** and **async** options specify whether a write operation is performed immediately (**sync**) or when the server is ready to handle it (**async**). By default, write requests are checked to see if they are related, and if so, they are written together (**wdelay**). This can degrade performance. You can override this default with **no_wdelay** and have writes executed as they are requested. If two directories are exported, where one is the subdirectory of another, the subdirectory is not accessible unless it is explicitly mounted (**hide**). In other words, mounting the parent directory does not make the subdirectory accessible. The subdirectory remains hidden until also mounted. You can overcome this restriction with the **no_hide** option (though this can cause problems with some file systems). If an exported directory is actually a subdirectory in a larger file system, its parent directories are checked to make sure that the subdirectory is the valid directory (**subtree_check**). This option works well with read-only file systems but can cause problems for write-enabled file systems, where filenames and directories can be changed. You can cancel this check with the **no_subtree_check** option.

NFS User-Level Access

Along with general options, there are also options that apply to user-level access. As a security measure, the client's root user is treated as an anonymous user by the NFS server. This is known as *squashing* the user. In the case of the client root user, squashing prevents the client from attempting to appear as the NFS server's root user. Should you want a particular client's root user to have root-level control over the NFS server, you can specify the **no_root_squash** option. To prevent any client user from attempting to appear as a user on the NFS server, you can classify them as anonymous users (the **all_squash** option). Such anonymous users would only have access to directories and files that are part of the anonymous group.

Normally, if a user on a client system has a user account on the NFS server, that user can mount and access his or her files on the NFS server. However, NFS requires the User ID for the user be the same on both systems. If this is not the case, he or she is considered to be two different users. To overcome this problem, you could use an NIS service, maintaining User ID information in just one place, the NIS password file (see the following section for information on NIS).

NFS /etc/exports Example

Examples of entries in an **/etc/exports** file are shown here. Read-only access is given to all hosts to the file system mounted on the **/pub** directory, a common name used for public access. Users, however, are treated as anonymous users (**all_squash**). Read and write access is given to the **lizard.mytrek.com** computer for the file system mounted on the **/home/foodstuff** directory. The next entry would allow access by **rabbit.mytrek.com** to the NFS server's CD-ROM, using only read access. The last entry allows anyone secure access to **/home/richlp**.

/etc/exports

```
/pub                   *(ro,insecure,all_squash,sync)
/home/foodstuff        lizard.mytrek.com(rw,sync)
/media/cdrom           rabbit.mytrek.com(ro,sync)
/home/richlp           *(secure,sync)
```

Applying Changes

Each time your system starts up the NFS server (usually when the system starts up), the **/etc/exports** file will be read and those directories specified will be exported. When a directory is exported, an entry for it is made in the **/var/lib/nfs/xtab** file. It is this file that NFS reads and uses to perform the actual exports. Entries are read from **/etc/exports** and corresponding entries made in **/var/lib/nfs/xtab**. The **xtab** file maintains the list of actual exports.

If you want to export added entries in the **/etc/exports** file immediately, without rebooting, you can use the **exportfs** command with the **-a** option. It is helpful to add the **-v** option to display the actions that NFS is taking. Use the same options to effect any changes you make to the **/etc/exports** file.

```
exportfs -a -v
```

If you later make changes to the **/etc/exports** file, you can use the **-r** option to re-export its entries. The **-r** option will resync the **/var/lib/nfs/xtab** file with the **/etc/exports** entries, removing any other exports or any with different options.

```
exportfs -r -v
```

To both export added entries and re-export changed ones, you can combine the **-r** and **-a** options.

```
exportfs -r -a -v
```

Manually Exporting File Systems

You can also use the **exportfs** command to manually export file systems instead of using entries for them in the **/etc/exports** file. Export entries will be added to the **/var/lib/nfs/xtab** file directly. With the **-o** option, you can list various permissions, and then follow them with the host and file system to export. The host and file system are separated by a colon. For example, to manually export the **/home/myprojects** directory to **golf.mytrek.com** with the permissions **ro** and **insecure**, you would use the following:

```
exportfs -o rw,insecure golf.mytrek.com:/home/myprojects
```

You can also use **exportfs** to unexport a directory that has already been exported, either manually or by the **/etc/exports** file. Just use the **-u** option with the host and the directory exported. The entry for the export will be removed from the **/var/lib/nfs/xtab** file. The following example will unexport the **/home/foodstuff** directory that was exported to **lizard.mytrek.com**:

```
exportfs -u lizard.mytrek.com:/home/foodstuff
```

NFS File and Directory Security with nfs4 Access Lists

With NFS4 you can set up access control lists for particular directories and files, ACL. You use the NFS4 FACL tools to manage these lists (nfs4-acl-tools package). The NFS4 ACL tools include **nfs4_getfacl**, **nfs4_setfacl**, and **nfs4_editfacl**. Check the Man page for each for detailed options and examples. **nfs4_getfacl** will list the access controls for a specified file or directory. **nfs4_setfacl** will create access controls for a directory or file, and **nfs4_editfacl** will let you change them. **nfs4_editfacl** simple inovkes **nfs_setfacl** with the **-e** option. When editing access controls you are placed in an editor where you can make your changes. For setting access controls you can read from a file, the standard input, or list the control entries on the command line.

The file and directory access controls are more refined than the standard permissions described in Chapter 28. The ACL entries follow the syntax described in detail on the **nfs4_acl** Man page. An ACL entry begins with an entry type like an accept or deny entry (**A** or **D**), followed by an ACL flag which can specify group or inheritance capabilitiy, then principal to which the ACL is applied, and finally the list of access options like **r** for read or **w** for write. The principal is usually a user URL that is to be permitted or denied access. You can also specify groups, but you need to set the **g** group flag. The special URLs OWNER@, GROUP@, and EVERYONE@ correspond to the owner, group, and other access used on standard permissions. The following example provides full access to the owner, but only read and execute access to the user george@rabbit.com. Group write and execute access is denied.

```
A::OWNER@:rwadtTnNcCy
A::george@rabbit.com:rxtncy
D:g:GROUP@:waxtc
```

In addition to read, write, and execute permissions (**r**,**w**,**x**), ACL lists also provide attribute reads (**t**,**n**) and attribute writes (**T**,**N**) as well as ACL read (**c**) and write (**C**) access. NFS read and write synchronization is enabled with the **y** option. The ability to delete files and directories is provided by the **d** option and for subdirectories with the **D** option. The **a** option lets you append data and create subdirectories. Keep in mind that **rtncy** are all read options, wheras **wadDTNC** are write options, while **x** remains the execute option. You will need y for any synchronized access. The **C** option in particular is very powerful as it allows the user to change the access controls (lowercase **c** only allows reading of the access controls).

Controlling Accessing to NFS Servers

You can use several methods to control access to your NFS server like using hosts.allow and hosts.deny to permit or deny access, as well as using your firewall to intercept access.

/etc/hosts.allow and /etc/hosts.deny

The **/etc/hosts.allow** and **/etc/hosts.deny** files are used to restrict access to services provided by your server to hosts on your network or on the Internet (if accessible). For example, you can use the **hosts.allow** file to permit access by certain hosts to your FTP server. Entries in the **hosts.deny** file would explicitly deny access to certain hosts. For NFS, you can provide the same kind of security by controlling access to specific NFS daemons.

NOTE *You can further secure your NFS transmissions by having them operate over TCP instead of UDP. Use the **tcp** option to mount your NFS file systems (UDP is the default). However, performance does degrade for NFS when it uses TCP.*

Portmapper Service

The first line of defense is to control access to the portmapper service. The portmapper tells hosts where the NFS services can be found on the system. Restricting access does not allow a remote host to even locate NFS. For a strong level of security, you should deny access to all hosts except those that are explicitly allowed. In the **hosts.deny** file, you would place the following entry, denying access to all hosts by default. ALL is a special keyword denoting all hosts.

```
portmap:ALL
```

In the **hosts.allow** file, you would then enter the hosts on your network, or any others that you would want to permit access to your NFS server. Again, you would specify the portmapper service and then list the IP addresses of the hosts you are permitting access. You can list specific IP addresses or a network range using a netmask. The following example allows access only by hosts in the local network, 192.168.0.0, and to the host 10.0.0.43. You can separate addresses with commas:

```
portmap: 192.168.0.0/255.255.255.0, 10.0.0.43
```

The portmapper is also used by other services such as NIS. If you close all access to the portmapper in **hosts.deny**, you will also need to allow access to NIS services in **hosts.allow**, if you are running them. These include ypbind and ypserver. In addition, you may have to add entries for remote commands like **ruptime** and **rusers**, if you are supporting them.

In addition, it is also advisable to add the same level of control for specific NFS services. In the **hosts.deny** file, you would add entries for each service, as shown here:

```
mountd:ALL
rquotad:ALL
statd:ALL
lockd:ALL
```

Then, in the **hosts.allow** file, you can add entries for each service:

```
mountd:   192.168.0.0/255.255.255.0, 10.0.0.43
rquotad:  192.168.0.0/255.255.255.0, 10.0.0.43
statd:    192.168.0.0/255.255.255.0, 10.0.0.43
lockd:    192.168.0.0/255.255.255.0, 10.0.0.43
```

Netfilter Rules

You can further control access using Netfilter to check transmissions from certain hosts on the ports used by NFS services. (See Chapter 20 for an explanation of Netfilter.) The portmapper uses port 111, and nfsd uses 2049. Netfilter is helpful if you have a private network that has an Internet connection, and you want to protect it from the Internet. Usually a specific network device, such as an Ethernet card, is dedicated to the Internet connection. The following examples assume that device **eth1** is connected to the Internet. Any packets attempting access on port 111 or 2049 are refused.

```
iptables -A INPUT -i eth1 -p 111 -j DENY
iptables -A INPUT -i eth1 -p 2049 -j DENY
```

To enable NFS for your local network, you will have to allow packet fragments. Assuming that **eth0** is the device used for the local network, you could use the following example:

```
iptables -A INPUT -i eth0 -f -j ACCEPT
```

NOTE *A root user on a remote host can try to access a remote NFS server as a root user with root level permissions. The* **root_squash** *option (a default) will automatically change the remote root user to the nobody (anonymous) user.*

Check the **nfs** Man page for NFSv4 options.

Mounting NFS File Systems: NFS Clients

Once NFS makes directories available to different hosts, those hosts can then mount those directories on their own systems and access them. The host needs to be able to operate as an NFS client. Current Linux kernels all have NFS client capability built in. This means that any NFS client can mount a remote NFS directory that it has access to by performing a simple mount operation.

Mounting NFS Automatically: /etc/fstab

You can mount an NFS directory either by an entry in the **/etc/fstab** file or by an explicit **mount** command. You have your NFS file systems mounted automatically by placing entries for them in the **/etc/fstab** file. An NFS entry in the **/etc/fstab** file has a mount type of NFS. An NFS file system name consists of the hostname of the computer it is located on, followed by the pathname of the directory where it is mounted. The two are separated by a colon. For example, **rabbit.trek.com:/home/project** specifies a file system mounted at **/home/project** on the **rabbit.trek.com** computer. The format for an NFS entry in the **/etc/fstab** file follows. Notice that the file type is **nfs**.

```
host:remote-directory    local-directory    nfs    options    0    0
```

You can also include several NFS-specific mount options with your NFS entry. You can specify the size of datagrams sent back and forth, and the amount of time your computer waits for a response from the host system. You can also specify whether a file system is to be hard-mounted or soft-mounted. For a *hard-mounted* file system, your computer continually tries to make contact if for some reason the remote system fails to respond. A *soft-mounted* file system, after a specified interval, gives up trying to make contact and issues an error message. A hard mount is the default. A system making a hard-mount attempt that continues to fail will stop responding to user input as it tries continually to achieve the mount. For this reason, soft mounts may be preferable, as they will simply stop attempting a mount that continually fails. Table 38-2 and the Man pages for **mount** contain a listing of these NFS client options. They differ from the NFS server options indicated previously.

An example of an NFS entry follows. The remote system is **rabbit.mytrek.com**, and the file system is mounted on **/home/projects**. This file system is to be mounted on the local system as the **/home/dylan/projects** directory. The **/home/dylan/projects** directory must already be created on the local system. The type of system is NFS, and the **timeo** option specifies the local system waits up to 20 tenths of a second (two seconds) for a response. The mount is a soft mount and can be interrupted by NFS.

```
rabbit.mytrek.com:/home/projects /home/dylan/projects  nfs
soft,intr,timeo=20
```

Mounting NFS Manually: mount

You can also use the **mount** command with the **-t nfs** option to mount an NFS file system explicitly. For a NFSv4 file system you would use **-t nfs4**. To mount the previous entry explicitly, use the following command:

```
# mount -t nfs -o soft,intr,timeo=20   \
        rabbit.mytrek.com:/home/projects   /home/dylan/projects
```

Option	Description
rsize=n	The number of bytes NFS uses when reading files from an NFS server. The default is 1,024 bytes. A size of 8,192 can greatly improve performance.
wsize=n	The number of bytes NFS uses when writing files to an NFS server. The default is 1,024 bytes. A size of 8,192 can greatly improve performance.
timeo=n	The value in tenths of a second before sending the first retransmission after a timeout. The default value is seven-tenths of a second.
retry=n	The number of minutes to retry an NFS mount operation before giving up. The default is 10,000 minutes (one week).
retrans=n	The number of retransmissions or minor timeouts for an NFS mount operation before a major timeout (default is 3). At that time, the connection is canceled or a "server not responding" message is displayed.
soft	Mount system using soft mount.
hard	Mount system using hard mount. This is the default.
intr	Allow NFS to interrupt the file operation and return to the calling program. The default is not to allow file operations to be interrupted.
bg	If the first mount attempt times out, continue trying the mount in the background. The default is to fail without backgrounding.
tcp	Mount the NFS file system using the TCP protocol, instead of the default UDP protocol.

TABLE 38-2 NFS Mount Options

You can, of course, unmount an NFS directory with the **umount** command. You can specify either the local mountpoint or the remote host and directory, as shown here:

```
umount /home/dylan/projects
umount  rabbit.mytrek.com:/home/projects
```

> **NOTE** *You can also mount and unmount all your NFS file systems at once with the **/etc/rc.d/**
> **init.d/netfs** script, which you can invoke with the **service** command. This script reads
> the NFS entries in the /etc/fstab file, using them to mount and unmount NFS remote
> directories. Using the **stop** argument unmounts the file systems, and with the **start**
> argument, you mount them again. The **restart** argument first unmounts and then remounts
> the file systems.*

Mounting NFS on Demand: autofs

You can also mount NFS file systems using the automount service, autofs. This requires added configuration on the client's part. The autofs service will mount a file system only when you try to access it. A directory change operation (**cd**) to a specified directory will trigger the mount operation, mounting the remote file system at that time.

The autofs service is configured using a master file to list map files, which in turn lists the file systems to be mounted. The **/etc/auto.master** file is the autofs master file. The master file will list the root pathnames where file systems can be mounted along with a map file for each of those pathnames. The map file will then list a key (subdirectory), mount options, and the file systems that can be mounted in that root pathname directory. On some distributions, the **/auto** directory is already implemented as the root pathname for file systems automatically mounted. You could add your own file systems in the **/etc/auto.master** file along with your own map files, if you wish. You will find that the **/etc/auto.master** file contains the following entry for the **/auto** directory, listing **auto.misc** as its map file:

```
/auto    auto.misc    --timeout 60
```

Following the map file, you can add options, as shown in the preceding example. The **timeout** option specifies the number of seconds of inactivity to wait before trying to automatically unmount.

In the map file, you list the key, the mount options, and the file system to be mounted. The key will be the subdirectory on the local system where the file system is mounted. For example, to mount the **/home/projects** directory on the **rabbit.mytrek.com** host to the **/auto/projects** directory, you would use the following entry:

```
projects  soft,intr,timeo=20   rabbit.mytrek.com:/home/projects
```

You could also create a new entry in the master file for an NFS file system, as shown here:

```
/myprojects    auto.myprojects    --timeout 60
```

You would then create an **/etc/auto.myprojects** file and place entries in it for NFS files system mounts, like the following:

```
dylan     soft,intr,rw   rabbit.mytrek.com:/home/projects
newgame   soft,intr,ro   lizard.mytrek.com:/home/supergame
```

***

NOTE *The autofs service can be used for any file systems, including floppy disks and CD-ROMs. See Chapter 30.*

***

Network Information Service: NIS

On networks supporting NFS, many resources and devices are shared by the same systems. Normally, each system would need its own configuration files for each device or resource. Changes would entail updating each system individually. However, NFS provides a special service called the Network Information System (NIS) that maintains such configuration files for the entire network. For changes, you only need to update the NIS files. NIS works for information required for most administrative tasks, such as those relating to users, network access, or devices. For example, you can maintain user and password information with an NIS service, having only to update those NIS password files.

***

NOTE *NIS+ is a more advanced form of NIS that provides support for encryption and authentication. However, it is more difficult to administer.*

***

NIS was developed by Sun Microsystems and was originally known as Sun's Yellow Pages (YP). NIS files are kept on an NIS server (NIS servers are still sometimes referred to as YP servers). Individual systems on a network use NIS clients to make requests from the NIS server. The NIS server maintains its information on special database files called *maps*. Linux versions exist for both NIS clients and servers. Linux NIS clients easily connect to any network using NIS.

The NIS client is installed as part of the initial installation on most Linux distributions. NIS client programs are ypbind (the NIS client daemon), ypwhich, ypcat, yppoll, ypmatch, yppasswd, and ypset. Each has its own Man page with details of its use. The NIS server programs are ypserv (the NIS server), ypinit, yppasswdd, yppush, ypxfr, and netgroup—each also with its own Man page. You can start and stop the **ypbind** client daemon and the **ypserv** NIS server with the `service` command. Alternatively, you can use system-config-services to start and stop the NIS client and server daemons.

```
service ypbind start
service ypserv start
```

***

NOTE *You can use system-config-authentication to specify the remote NIS server on your network.*

***

NIS Servers

You have significant flexibility when setting up NIS servers. If you have a small network, you may need only one NIS domain, for which you would have one NIS server. For larger networks, you can divide your network into several NIS domains, each with its own server. Even if you only have one domain, you may want several NIS slave servers. For an NIS domain, you can have a master NIS server and several NIS slave servers. The slave servers can act as backups, in case the master server goes down. A slave server only contains copies of the configuration files set up on the NIS master server.

Configuring an NIS server involves several steps, listed here:

1. Define the NIS domain name that the NIS server will work for.

2. Start the **ypserv** daemon.

3. In the **/var/yp/Makefile** file, set any NIS server options and specify the configuration files to manage.

4. Use **/usr/lib/ypinit** to create the NIS versions of the configuration files.

Defining NIS Domain

You first have to define an NIS domain name. You can have the NIS domain defined whenever you start up your system, by defining the NIS_DOMAIN variable in the **/etc/sysconfig/network** file. To this variable, you assign the name you want to give your NIS domain. The following example defines the NIS domain called **myturtles.nis**:

```
NIS_DOMAIN=myturtles.nis
```

When first setting up the server, you may want to define your NIS domain name without having to restart your system. You can do so with the **domainname** command, as shown here:

```
domainname myturtles.nis
```

NIS server options are kept in the **/etc/ypserv.conf** file. Check the Man page for that file for details. You can start the NIS server with the **ypserv** startup script:

```
service ypserv start
```

Setting NIS Server Options

Next edit the **/var/yp/Makefile** file to select the configuration files that the NIS server will maintain, along with setting any NIS server options. Standard options as well as most commonly used configuration files are usually already set up.

NIS server options are listed first. The **NOPUSH** option will be set to true, indicating that there are no slave NIS servers. If you are setting up any slave NIS servers for this domain, you will have to set this option to false:

```
NOPUSH = true
```

The minimum user and group IDs are set to 500. These are set using the **MINUID** and **MINGID** variables:

```
MINUID=500
MINGID=500
```

Most distributions use a shadow password and shadow group files to encrypt passwords and groups; the **MERGE_PASSWD** and **MERGE_GROUP** settings will be set to true. NIS will merge shadow password information into its password file:

```
MERGE_PASSWD=true
MERGE_GROUP=true
```

The directories where NIS will find password and other configuration files are then defined using the **YPSRCDIR** and **YPPWDIR** variables. Normally, the **/etc** directory holds your configuration files:

```
YPSRCDIR = /etc
YPPWDDIR = /etc
```

Then the configuration files that NIS can manage are listed. Here, you will find entries like **PASSWD** for password, **GROUP** for your groups, and **PRINTCAP** for your printers. A sample of the entries is shown here:

```
GROUP       = $(YPPWDDIR)/group
PASSWD      = $(YPPWDDIR)/passwd
SHADOW      = $(YPPWDDIR)/shadow
GSHADOW     = $(YPPWDDIR)/gshadow
ALIASES     = /etc/aliases
ETHERS      = $(YPSRCDIR)/ethers       # ethernet addresses (for rarpd)
BOOTPARAMS  = $(YPSRCDIR)/bootparams # for booting Sun boxes (bootparamd)
HOSTS       = $(YPSRCDIR)/hosts
NETWORKS    = $(YPSRCDIR)/networks
PRINTCAP    = $(YPSRCDIR)/printcap
PROTOCOLS   = $(YPSRCDIR)/protocols
```

Specifying Shared Files

The actual files that are shared on the network are listed in the **all:** entry, which follows the list of configuration files. Only some of the files defined are listed as shared, those listed in the first line after **all:**. The remaining lines are automatically commented out (with a preceding **#** sign). You can add files by removing the **#** sign or moving their entries to the first line.

```
all:  passwd group hosts rpc services netid protocols mail \
      # netgrp shadow publickey networks ethers bootparams printcap \
      # amd.home auto.master auto.home auto.local passwd.adjunct \
      # timezone locale netmasks
```

Be sure not to touch the remainder of the Makefile.

Creating the NIS Database

You then enter the **ypinit** command with the **-m** option to create the NIS database consisting of the NIS configuration files. Your NIS server will be detected, and then you will be asked to enter the names of any slave NIS servers used on this NIS domain. If there are any, enter them. When you are finished, press CTRL-D. The NIS database files are then created.

```
ypinit -m
```

For an NIS slave server, you would use

```
ypinit -s masterhost
```

Should you receive the following error, it most likely means that your NIS server was not running. Be sure to start ypserv before you run **ypinit**.

```
failed to send 'clear' to local ypserv: RPC: Program not registeredUpdating
```

If you later need to update your NIS server files, you would change to the **/var/yp** directory and issue the **make** command.

```
cd /var/yp
make
```

Controlling Access

The **/var/yp/securenets** file enables access by hosts to your NIS server. Hosts can be referenced by network or individually. Entries consist of a subnet mask and an IP address. For example, you could give access to all the hosts in an local network with the following entry:

```
255.255.255.0  192.168.1.0
```

For individual hosts, you can use the mask 255.255.255.255 or just the term "host," as shown here:

```
host    192.168.1.4
```

Controlling how different hosts access NIS shared data is determined in **/etc/ypserv.conf**.

Netgroups

You can use NIS to set up netgroups, which allow you to create network-level groups of users. Whereas normal groups are created locally on separate hosts, an NIS netgroup can be used for network-wide services. For example, you can use NIS netgroups to control access to NFS file systems. Netgroups are defined in the **/etc/netgroup** file. Entries consist of a netgroup name followed by member identifiers consisting of three segments: the host, the user, and the NIS domain:

```
group    (host, user, NIS-domain) (host, user, NIS-domain) ...
```

For example, in the NIS domain **myturtles.nis**, to define a group called **myprojects** that consist of the user **chris** on the host **rabbit**, and the user **george** on the host **lizard.mytrek .com**, you would use the following:

```
myprojects (rabbit, chris, myturtles.nis) \
                    (lizard.mytrek.com, george, myturtles.nis)
```

A blank segment will match on any value. The following entry includes all users on the host **rabbit**:

```
newgame (rabbit,,myturtles.ni)
```

If your use of a group doesn't need either a user or a host segment, you can eliminate one or the other using a hyphen (-). The following example generates a netgroup consisting just of hostnames, with no usernames:

```
myservers (rabbit,-,) (turtle.mytrek.com,-,)
```

You can then reference different netgroups in various configuration files by prefixing the netgroup name with an **@** sign, as shown here:

```
@newgame
```

NIS Clients

For a host to use NIS on your network, you first need to specify your NIS domain name on that host. In addition, your NIS clients need to know the name of your NIS server. If you installed Linux on a network already running NIS, you may have already entered this information during the installation process.

Specifying the NIS Domain and Server

You can specify your NIS domain name and server with the authconfg-gtk tool, which you can access from the System Settings window. In that window, select Authentication. This opens the Authentication Configuration window. On the User Information panel, click the Configure NIS button to open a dialog where you can enter the name of the NIS domain as well as the NIS server. Be sure to also enable NIS on the User Information panel. The NIS domain will be saved in the **/etc/sysconfig/network** file, and the NIS server, in the **/etc/yp.conf** file.

Accessing the Server

Each NIS client host on your network then has to run the ypbind NIS client to access the server. In the client's **/etc/yp.conf** file, you need to specify the NIS server it will use. The following entry would reference the NIS server at 192.168.1.1:

```
ypserver 192.168.1.1
```

Alternatively, you can specify the NIS domain name and the server it uses:

```
domain mydomain.nis  server servername
```

The authconfg-gtk tool will make the following entry in **/etc/yp.conf** for the **myturtle.nis** NIS domain using the **turtle.mytrek.com** server:

```
domain myturtles.nis server turtle.mytrek.com
```

To start the NIS client, you run the **ypbind** script:

```
service ypbind start
```

Then, to check that all is working, you can use **ypcat** to try to list the NIS password file:

```
ypcat passwd.
```

You can use **ypcat** to list any of the NIS configuration files. The **ypwhich** command will display the name of the NIS server your client is using. **ypmatch** can be used to find a particular entry in a configuration file.

```
ypmatch cecelia passwd.
```

Users can change their passwords in the NIS **passwd** file by using the **yppasswd** command. It works the same as the **passwd** command. You will also have to have the **yppasswdd** daemon running.

Specifying Configuration Files with nsswitch.conf

To ensure that the client accesses the NIS server for a particular configuration file, you should specify **nisplus** in file's entry in the **/etc/nsswitch.conf** file. The **nisplus** option refers to the NIS version 3. The **nis** option is used to refer to the older NIS version 2. The **/etc/nsswitch.conf** file specifies where a host should look for certain kinds of information. For example, the following entry says to check the local configuration files (**files**) first and then the NIS server (**nisplus**) for passwords data:

```
passwd:    files nisplus
```

The **files** designation says to first use the system's own files, those on the local host. **nis** says to look up entries in the NIS files, accessing the NIS server. **nisplus** says to use NIS+ files maintained by the NIS+ server. **dns** says to perform DNS lookups; it can only be used on files like **hosts** that contain hostnames. These are some standard entries:

```
passwd:       files nisplus
shadow:       files nisplus
group:        files nisplus

hosts:        files nisplus dns
bootparams:   nisplus [NOTFOUND=return] files

ethers:       files
netmasks:     files
networks:     files
protocols:    files nisplus
rpc:          files
services:     files nisplus
netgroup:     files nisplus
publickey:    nisplus
automount:    files nisplus
aliases:      files nisplus
```

Distributed Network File Systems

For very large distributed systems like Linux clusters, Linux also supports distributed network file systems, such as Coda, Intermezzo, Red Hat Global File System (GFS and GFS 2), and the Parallel Virtual File System (PVFS2). These systems build on the basic concept of NFS as well as RAID techniques to create a file system implemented on multiple hosts across a large network, in effect, distributing the same file system among different hosts at a very low level (see Table 38-3). You can think of it as a kind of RAID array implemented across network hosts instead of just a single system. Instead of each host relying on its own file systems on its own hard drive, they all share the same distributed file system that uses hard drives collected on different distributed servers. This provides far more efficient use of storage available to the hosts, as well as providing for more centralized management of file system use.

Web Site	Name
fedoraproject.org/wiki/Tools/GFS	Fedora GFS resources and links
www.pvfs.org	Parallel Virtual File System, PVFS2 (open source)
sourceware.org/gfs	Global File System (Fedora and commercial versions)
www.coda.cs.cmu.edu **ftp.coda.cs.cmu.edu/pub/coda/linux**	Coda File system, disconnected mobile access (experimental)
www.inter-mezzo.org	Intermezzo (open source)
clusterfs.com	Lustre

TABLE 38-3   Distributed File Systems

Parallel Virtual File System (PVFS)

The Parallel Virtual File System (PVFS) implements a distributed network file system using a management server that manages the files system on different I/O servers. Management servers maintain the file system information, including access permissions, directory structure, and metadata information. Requests for access to a file are submitted by a client of the management server. The management server then sets up a connection between the client and the I/O servers that hold the requested file's data. Access operations such as read and write tasks are then carried out directly between the client and the I/O servers. PVFS can be implemented transparently using a kernel module to make use of the kernel's virtual file system. The PVFS file system can then be mounted by a client like any file system. In a PVFS implementation, the file system is organized into stripes of data, similar to a RAID array, but the stripes are distributed to different hosts on the network. Files are accessed as a collection of stripes that can be distributed across this network.

A new version of PVFS, known as PVFS2, is currently available from **www.pvfs.org**. You can download the source code from there. PVFS is a joint project with the Parallel Architecture Research Laboratory at Clemson University and the Mathematics and Computer Science Division at Argonne National Laboratory.

The PVFS manager server uses two configuration files, **pvfs2-fs.conf** and **pvfs2-server.conf**. You create these files using a configuration script, **pvfs2-genconfig**. The script will prompt you for configuration information such as the protocol, port, log file, and storage directory. To configure a cluster network, be sure to enter the hosts that will operate as I/O servers.

The management server is **pvfs2-server**. To manage the server, first place the **pvfs2-server** service script in the **/etc/init.d** directory. Then you can use the script with the **service** command to start and stop the server. To have the server run automatically, use **chkconfig** or system-config-services to turn it on.

On I/O servers, you run the **pvfs2-server** script to create storage space, and then start the server. The I/O servers use the **/etc/pvfs2-fs.conf** configuration file. You can use the **pvfs2-server** server script to turn the server on automatically.

On the clients that will use the PVFS system, you need to install file system configuration information and access tools. Each client will need a PVFS daemon, **pvfs2-client**, and its supporting module and library. File systems mount configuration can be held in **/etc/pvf2stab**, though you can place entries directly in the **/etc/fstab** file. To mount a PVFS file system, you can also use the pvfs2 type in the **mount** command with the **-t** option. PVFS2 provides its own set of file commands, such as **pvfs2-ping, pvfs2-cp**, and **pvfs2-ls**, to list and access files on its file system.

A PVFS2 file system can be accessed by the client either through a kernel module to provide direct Linux file system access, or with the MPI-IO interface, which requires recompiling using the libpvfs2 library but provides better performance for parallel applications. Parallel support in PVFS2 is implemented with the message passing interface (MPI) as supported by ROMIO (**www-unix.mcs.anl.gov/romio**) and MPICH2 (**www-unix.mcs.anl.gov/mpi/mpich2**), available from the MCS division of the Argonne National Laboratory.

NOTE *For applications to take full advantage of PVFS, they should be PVFS-enabled, which will stripe their file data for better use on PVFS systems.*

Coda

Coda is developed by Carnegie Mellon University as an experimental project, though freely available. Some of its features include support for mobile computing, access controls, and bandwidth adaptation. You can obtain information about Coda from **www.coda.cs.cmu .edu**. You can download Fedora and Red Hat RPM packages for some releases from **ftp .coda.cs.cmu.edu/pub/coda/linux**.

Using a kernel module to interface with the virtual file system, distributed Coda files can be accessed from the Coda directory on a client, usually **/coda**. Coda will maintain a cache of frequently accessed files on the client to improve efficiency. The cache is maintained by a cache manager called venus that handles all file system requests. The use of a cache allows for a disconnected operation on a file, letting users work on a file locally and then update it later with the main servers. A disconnected operation works well for mobile computing, where laptops may be disconnected from the network for periods of time. Corresponding databases for frequently used files by users, known as hoards, are also maintained on the server to facilitate updates.

To configure clients, you will need the coda-debug-client package. Use the **venus-setup** script to configure the client, and then start up Coda with the **venus** daemon. For the server, you will need to install the coda-dbug-server package and run **venus-setup** to configure your server.

Red Hat Global File System (GFS and GFS 2)

Red Hat has released its Global File System (GFS) as an open source freely available distributed network file system. The original GFS version was included with Fedora 4 and 5. Starting with Fedora Core 6, the new version of GFS, GFS 2, is included, using a similar set of configuration and management tools, as well as native kernel support. Instead of a variety of seemingly unrelated packages, GFS 2 is implemented with just three: **gfs2-utils**, **cman**, and **lvm-cluster**. Native kernel support for GFS 2 provides much of the kernel-level operations.

A distributed network file system builds on the basic concept of NFS as well as RAID techniques to create a file system implemented on multiple hosts across a large network, in effect, distributing the same file system among different hosts at a very low level. You can think of it as a kind of RAID array implemented across network hosts instead of just a single system. In effect, instead of each host relying on its own file systems on its own hard drive, they all share the same distributed file system that uses hard drives collected on different distributed servers. This provides far greater efficient use of storage available to the hosts, as well as providing for more centralized management of file system use. GFS can be run either directly connected to a SAN (storage area network) or using GNBD (Global Network Block Device) storage connected over a LAN. The best performance is obtained from a SAN connection, whereas a GNBD format can be implemented easily using the storage on LAN (Ethernet)-connected systems. As with RAID devices, mirroring, failover, and redundancy can help protect and recover data.

GFS separates the physical implementation from the logical format. A GFS file system appears as a set of logical volumes on one seamless logical device that can be mounted easily to any directory on your Linux file system. The logical volumes are created and managed by the Cluster Logical Volume Manager (CLVM), which is a cluster-enabled LVM. Physically, the file system is constructed from different storage resources known as cluster nodes distributed across your network. The administrator manages these nodes, providing needed mirroring or storage expansion. Should a node fail, GFS can fence a system off until it has recovered the node. Setting up a GFS file system requires planning. You have to determine ahead of time different settings like the number and names of your GFS file systems, the nodes that will be able to mount the file systems, fencing methods, and the partitions and disks to use.

For detailed information check the Cluster Project Page site at **sourceware.org/ cluster**. Listed are the pacakges used in both GFS (Cluster Componenets -Old) and GFS 2 (Cluster Componenets - New). Here you will find links for documentation like the clustering FAQ. The Red Hat GFS Administrators Guide can be helpful but may be dated. The guide can be found on the Red Hat documentation page located at www.redhat.com. (Bear in mind that GFS now uses logical volumes instead of pools to set up physical volumes.)

Web Site	Name
www.redhat.com/software/rha/gfs	Global File System (Red Hat commercial version)
www.redhat.com/docs/manuals/csgfs/	Global File System Red Hat manuals (Red Hat Enterprise implementation)
sourceware.org/cluster	Cluster Project Web site, which includes links for GFS documentation
/etc/cluster.conf	GFS cluster configuration file (css)

system-config-cluster

With the system-config-cluster tool you can configure and manage your GFS cluster. When you first start the tool, it will create an **/etc/cluster.conf** file if one does not exist. On the Cluster Configuration tab you can create cluster nodes and fence devices. For the fence device you specify the fence method along with the name, IP address, and login and password. In the Managed Resources section you can specify the name, mountpoint, and device of your GFS file systems. system-config-cluster is included with Fedora.

GFS 2 Packages (Fedora Core 6 and on)

The original GFS, GFS 1, as implemented by Fedora, used a variety of separate packages for cluster servers and management tools, which did not appear related just by their names. With GFS 2, these have been combined into the **cman** package. Here you will find tools such as fence, cman cluster manager, dlm locking control, and **ccs** cluster configuration. Cluster configuration is supported by the Cluster Configuration System, **ccs**. Fencing is used to isolate failed resources. It is supported by in the **fence** server. LVM cluster support is located in a separate package, the **lvm2-cluster**.

To run a cluster, you need both a cluster manager and locking mechanism. **cman** with the Distributed Lock Manager (**dlm**) implements cluster management and locking. **cman** manages connections between cluster devices and services, using **dlm** to provide locking. The **dlm** locking mechanism operates as a daemon with supporting libraries.

All these services are invoked by the **cman** script, which checks the **/etc/cluster.conf** file for cluster configuration.

GFS 2 Service Scripts

To start the GFS file system, you run the **cman** script to start the needed daemon and implement your configuration. The **cman** script will run the **ccsd** to start up configuration detection, **fenced** for fencing support, **dlm_controld** for cluster management **dlm** locking, and **cman** for cluster management. The script will check for any GFS configuration settings in the **/etc/sysconfig/cluster** file. You the use the **gfs2** script to mount your GFS 2 file systems. To shut down the GFS file system service, you use the **cman** script with the **stop** option.

```
service cman start
service gfs2 start
```

The **gfs2** service script will mount GFS file systems to the locations specified in the **/etd/ fstab** file. You will need entries for all the GFS file systems you want to mount in **/etc/fstab**. The stop option will unmount the file systems. You can use **cman_tool** to have a node join a cluster or remove a node from the cluster.

Implementing a GFS 2 File System

To set up a GFS 2 file system, you first need to create cluster devices using the physical volumes and organizing them into logical volumes. You use the CLVM (Clustering Logical Volume Manager) to set up logical volumes from physical partitions (in the past you used a volume manager called pool to do this). You can then install GFS file systems on these logical volumes directly. CLVM operates like LVM, using the same commands. It works over a distributed network and requires that the **clvmd** server be running.

You then configure your system with the Cluster Configuration System. Create a **/etc/ cluster.conf** file and set up your configuration. The configuration will include information like the nodes used, the fencing methods, and the locking method used. Consult the **cluster. conf** Man page for configuration details. For configuration you can also use the system-config-cluster tool, which provides an easy-to-use GUI interface for setting up your GFS file system. You can select locking and fence methods as well as mountpoints and devices. You then test the configuration with the **ccs_test** tool.

```
ccs_test mygfs
```

You then use the **ccs_tool** to create **cluster.ccs**, **fence.ccs**, and **node.ccs** configuration files. These files are organized into a CCS archive that is placed on each node and cluster device.

On each node, you then start the **ccsd** configuration, the **fenced** fencing server, and the locking method you want to use, such as **dlm**. Check the respective Man pages for details on the locking servers. You can start the servers with their service scripts as noted previously.

To create new file systems on the cluster devices, you use the **gfs2_mkfs** command, and then mount them with the **-t gfs2** option. The following command creates a GFS file system on the **/dev/gv0/mgfs** and then mounts it to the **/mygfs** directory. For **gfs2_mkfs**, the **-t** option indicates the lock table used and the **-p** option specifies the lock protocol. The **-j** option specifies the number of journals.

```
gfs2_mkfs  -t mycluster:mygfs  -p lock_dlm  -j 2   /dev/vg0/mgfs
mount -t gfs /dev/vg0/mgfs /gfs1
```

To have the **gfs** service script mount the GFS file system for you, you need to place an entry for it in the **/etc/fstab** file. If you do not want the file system automatically mounted, add the **noauto** option.

```
/dev/vg0/mgfs    /mygfs    gfs2    noauto,defaults    0    0
```

With GFS **/etc/fstab** entries, you can then use the **gfs2** script to mount the GFS file system.

```
service gfs start
```

GFS Tools

GFS has several commands in different categories, such as those that deal with fencing, like **fence_node**, **gulm_tool** to manage gulm locking, and those used for configuration, like **ccs_tool**. The GFS commands for managing GFS file systems are listed in Table 38-4. Check their respective Man pages for detailed descriptions.

GFS File System Operations

GFS has several commands in different categories, such as those that deal will fencing, like **fence_tool** to manage gulm locking, those used for configuration, like **ccs_tool**, and those for cluster management, like **cman_tool**. Several GFS commands manage the file system, such as **gfs2_mount** for mounting file systems, **gfs2_mkfs** to make a GFS file system, **gfs2_fsck** to check and repair, and **gfs2_grow** to expand a file system. Check their respective Man pages for detailed descriptions.

NOTE *For GFS 1, you use the same names for the GFS tools without the number 2, **gfs** instead of **gfs2**.*

To mount a GFS file system, you use the **mount** command specifying **gfs2** as the mount type, as in

```
mount  -t gfs2  /dev/vg0/mgfs  /mygfs
```

This will invoke the **gfs2_mount** tool to perform the mount operation. Several GFS-specific mount options are also available, specified with the **-o** option, such as **lockproto** to specify a different lock protocol and **acl** to enable ACL support .

Command	Description
ccs	CCS service script to start Cluster Configuration Service server
ccs_tool	CCS configuration update tool
ccs_test	CCS diagnostic tool to test CCS configuration files
ccsd	Daemon run on nodes to provide CCS configuration data to cluster software
clvmd	Cluster Logical Volume Manager daemon, needed to create and manage LVM cluster devices; also a service script to start **clvmd**
cman	The Cluster Manager, **cman**, startup script, uses dlm for locking (**cman** is run as a kernel module directly)
cman_tool	Manages cluster nodes; requires **cman**
dlm	Distributed Lock Manager, implemented as a kernel module, invoked by the **cman** script
fence	Fence overview
fenced	Fencing daemon; also a service script for starting the fenced daemon
fence_tool	Manages fenced
fence_node	Invokes a fence agent
Fencing Agents	Numerous fencing agents available for different kinds of connections; see **fence** Man page
fence_manual	Fence Agent for manual interaction
fence_ack_manual	User interface for fence_manual
gfs2	GFS 2 service script to mount GFS 2 file systems; also a Man page overview
gfs2_mount	Invoked by mount; Use **-t gfs2** mount option
gfs2_fsck	The GFS 2 file system checker
gfs2_grow	Grow a GFS 2 file system
gfs2_jadd	Add a journal to a GFS 2 file system
mkfs.gfs2	Make a GFS 2 file system
gfs2_quota	Manipulate GFS 2 disk quotas
gfs2_tool	Manage a GFS 2 file system
getfacl	Get the ACL permissions for a file or directory
setfacl	Set access control (ACL) for a file or directory
rmanager	Resource Group Manager, manage user services

TABLE 38-4   GFS Tools, Daemons, and Service Scripts

To check the status of a file system, you can use **gfs2_fsck**. This tool operates much like fsck, checking for corrupt systems and attempting repairs. You must first unmount the file system before you can use **gfs2_fsck** on it.

Should you add available space to the device on which a GFS file system resides, you can use **gfs2_grow** to expand the file system to that available space. It can be run on just one node to expand the entire cluster. If you want journaling, you first have to add journal files with the **gfs2_jadd** tool. **gfs2_grow** can only be run on a mounted GFS file system.

Journal files for GFS are installed in space outside of the GFS file system, but on the same device. After creating a GFS file system, you can run **gfs2_add** to add the journal files for it. If you are expanding a current GFS file system, you need to run **gfs2_add** first. Like **gfs2_grow**, **gfs2_add** can only be run on mounted file systems. With the **setfacl** command you can set permissions for files and directories.

As noted previously, to create a GFS file system you use the **gfs2_mkfs** command. The **-t** option specifies the lock table to use, the **-j** options indicates the number of journals to create, and the **-p** option specifies the lock protocol to use.

The Resource Group Manager, **rgmanager**, provides a command line interface for managing user services and resources on a GFS file system, letting you perform basic administrative tasks like setting user quotas, shutting down the system (**clushutdown**), and getting statistics on GFS use (**clustat**). The primary administrative tool is **clusterfs**. Options can be set in the **/etc/sysconfig/cluster** file. You start up **rgmanager** with the **rgmanager** script. This starts up the **clurgmgrd** daemon, providing access to the GFS system.

GFS also supports access controls. You can restrict access by users or groups to certain files or directories, specifying read or write permissions. With the **setfacl** command you can set permissions for files and directories. You use the **-m** option to modify an ACL permission, and **-x** to delete it. The **getfacl** obtains the current permissions for file or directory. The following sets read access by the user **dylan** to **myfile**.

```
setfacl -m u:dylan:r myfile
```

GFS 1 Packages (Red Hat Enterprise Linux 4, Fedora Core 4/5)

Red Hat Enterprise Linux 4, as well as Fedora Core 4 and 5, use GFS 1, which implements GFS with a series of separate packages, seemingly unrelated. To use GFS 1, you would have to install a number of different packages that include the GFS 1 tools, the locking method you would want to use, and configuration tools. The GFS 1 tools and locking methods also have several corresponding kernel module and header packages. See **sourceware.org/ cluster** under the heading "Cluster Components - Old" for a listing of GFS 1 tools. There were kernel module packages for the different types of kernels: i586, i686, SMP, and Xen. T.

Samba

With Samba, you can connect your Windows clients on a Microsoft Windows network to services such as shared files, systems, and printers controlled by the Linux Samba server and, at the same time, allow Linux systems to access shared files and printers on Windows systems. Samba is a collection of Linux tools that allow you to communicate with Windows systems over a Windows network. In effect, Samba allows a Linux system or network to act as if it were a Windows server, using the same protocols as used in a Windows network. Whereas most Unix and Linux systems use the TCP/IP protocol for networking, Microsoft networking with Windows uses a different protocol, called the Server Message Block (SMB) protocol, that implements a local area network (LAN) of PCs running Windows. SMB makes use of a network interface called Network Basic Input Output System (NetBIOS) that allows Windows PCs to share resources, such as printers and disk space. One Windows PC on such a network can access part of another Windows PC's disk drive as if it were its own. SMB was originally designed for small LANs. To connect it to larger networks, including those with Unix systems, Microsoft developed the Common Internet File System (CIFS). CIFS still uses SMB and NetBIOS for Windows networking. Wanting to connect his Linux system to a Windows PC, Andrew Tridgell wrote an SMB client and server that he called Samba. Samba allows Unix and Linux systems to connect to such a Windows network as if they were Windows PCs. Unix systems can share resources on Windows systems as if they were just another Windows PC. Windows PCs can also access resources on Unix systems as if they were Windows systems. Samba, in effect, has become a professional-level, open source, and free version of CIFS. It also runs much faster than CIFS. Samba effectively enables you to use a Linux or Unix server as a network server for a group of Windows machines operating on a Windows network. You can also use it to share files on your Linux system with other Windows PCs, or to access files on a Windows PC from your Linux system, as well as between Windows PCs. On Linux systems, a **cifs** file system enables you, in effect, to mount a remote SMB-shared directory on your own file system. You can then access it as if it were a directory on your local system.

Samba Documentation

You can obtain extensive documentation and current releases from the Samba Web and FTP sites at **www.samba.org** and **ftp.samba.org**. Samba HOW-TO documentation is also available at **www.tldp.org**. Other information can be obtained from the SMB newsgroup,

comp.protocols.smb. RPM packages can be obtained from Fedora repositories and are included as part of Fedora Linux.

Extensive documentation is provided with the software package and installed on your system, usually in the **/usr/share/doc** directory under a subdirectory bearing the name of the Samba release. The directory will include the version name:

```
/usr/share/doc/samba-version
```

The **htmldocs** subdirectory holds various documentation including the Samba HOWTO, Samba By Example, the Samba developers guide, the Man pages, and Using Samba. All are in Web page format. The examples include sample **smb.conf** files for different kinds of configuration. PDF versions for the HOWTO, By Example, and Developers Guide are in the top directory.

The home page of the SWAT configuration utility also provides Web page-based Samba documentation, as well as context-level help for different features.

Samba Applications

The Samba software package consists of two server daemons and several utility programs (see Table 39-1). One daemon, **smbd**, provides file and printer services to SMB clients and other systems, such as Windows, that support SMB. The nmbd utility is a daemon that provides NetBIOS name resolution and service browser support. The smbclient utility provides FTP-like access by Linux clients to Samba services. mount.cifs and umount.cifs enable Linux clients to mount and unmount Samba shared directories (used by the **mount** command with the **-t samba** option). The smbstatus utility displays the current status of the SMB server and who is using it. You use testparm to test your Samba configuration. **smbtar** is a shell script that backs up SMB/CIFS-shared resources directly to a Unix tape drive. You use nmblookup to map the NetBIOS name of a Windows PC to its IP address. Also included with the package is the Samba Web administration tool (SWAT) and system-config-samba. This enables you to use a Web page or GUI interface to create and maintain your Samba configuration file, **/etc/samba/smb.conf**. Samba configuration files are kept in the **/etc/samba** directory.

NOTE *To use Add/Remove Software (system-config-packages) to install Samba, select the Windows File Server entry from the Servers list on the Browse panel.*

Samba provides four main services: file and printer services, authentication and authorization, name resolution, and service announcement. The SMB daemon, **smbd**, provides the file and printer services, as well as authentication and authorization for those services. This means users on the network can share files and printers. You can control access to these services by requiring users to provide a password. When users try to access a shared directory, they are prompted for a password. Control can be implemented in share mode or user mode. The *share* mode sets up one password for the shared resource and then enables any user who has that password to access it. The *user* mode provides a different password for each user. Samba maintains its own password file for this purpose: **/etc/samba/smbpasswd**.

Application	Description
smbd	Samba server daemon that provides file and printer services to SMB clients
nmbd	Samba daemon that provides NetBIOS name resolution and service browser support
smbclient	Provides FTP-like access by Linux clients to Samba services
mount.cifs	Mounts Samba share directories on Linux clients (used by the **mount** command with the **-t cifs** option)
smbpasswd	Changes SMB-encrypted passwords on Samba servers
smbstatus	Displays the current status of the SMB network connections
smbrun	Interface program between **smbd** and external programs
testparm	Tests the Samba configuration file, **smb.conf**
smbtar	Backs up SMB/CIFS-shared resources directly to a Unix tape drive
nmblookup	Maps the NetBIOS name of a Windows PC to its IP address
system-config-samba	Samba GUI configuration tool (System I Administration I Server Setttings I Samba)
SWAT	Samba Web administration tool for configuring **smb.conf** with a Web browser; enables you to use a Web page interface to create and maintain your Samba configuration file, **smb.conf**
winbindd	Uses authentication services provided by Windows domain

TABLE 39-1　Samba Applications

Name resolution and service announcements are handled by the nmbd server. Name resolution essentially resolves NetBIOS names with IP addresses. Service announcements, also known as *browsing,* are the way a list of services available on the network is made known to the connected Windows PCs (and Linux PCs connected through Samba).

Samba also includes the **winbindd** daemon, which allows Samba servers to use authentication services provided by a Windows domain. Instead of a Samba server maintaining its own set of users to allow access, it can make use of a Windows domain authentication service to authenticate users.

Starting Up Samba

For a simple Samba setup, you should be able to use the default **/etc/samba/smb.conf** file installed with the Linux distribution package of Samba. If you need to make changes, however, you must restart the Samba server to have the changes take effect. Starting, stopping, and restarting the Samba server is managed by the **smb** and **nmb** scripts in the **/etc/rc.d/init.d/** directory, using the options **start**, **stop**, and **restart**. You can run the scripts using nmb and smb entries on the system-configi-services Background

Services panel (System | Administration | Server Settings | Services). You can also start them directly as shown here:

```
service smb restart
service nmb restart
```

To ensure name resolution, you can enter the name of your host and its IP address in the **/etc/samba/lmhosts** file. On Windows systems, **lmhosts** entries consist of an IP address and the system's NetBIOS name, the name it is known by on a Microsoft network. For your Linux system, you can enter the IP address and the Linux system's hostname.

TIP *Be sure that you also start up the **nmb** server, not just the **smb** server. Without the **nmb** server, Windows cannot detect your Samba server.*

Firewalls

The IPtables firewall prevents browsing Samba and Windows shares from your Linux desktop. To work around this restriction, you use system-config-security level (System | Administration | Firewall and SElinux). Select the Samba entry in the Trusted services section. Firewall on your Windows computer and on your network router could, in turn, block Samba server access. Be your Windows and router firewalls are configured to accept local IP addresss assigned by the router for computers on your network.

Testing Samba from Linux

To test your connection from a Linux system, you can use the `smbclient` command to query the Samba server. To access the home directory of a user on the Samba server, use the IP or hostname address of the Samba server. With the `-U` option, specify a user to connect to on the system, as shown here:

```
smbclient -L //turtle.mytrek.com -U dylan
```

You are then prompted for a password. If the client password is different from the server password, use the server password. Once connected, you are presented with the SMB client prompt as shown here. You can then access the files on the user's home directory:

```
smb: \>
```

Configuring Samba Access from Windows

To set up a connection for a Windows client, you need to specify the Windows workgroup name and configure the password. The workgroup name is the name that appears in the My Network Places on Windows 2000, NT, and XP (the Entire Network window in the Network Neighborhood on earlier Windows versions). To set the workgroup name on Windows XP, open System on the Control Panel, and on the Computer Name panel, click the Change button for the Rename Or Change Domain Entry. This opens a dialog window with a setting for the Workgroup, where you can enter the workgroup name. The default may be WORKGROUP or MSHOME. You can set up your own workgroup name, but all your computers would have to be configured to use that name.

On your Linux Samba server, in the **smb.conf** file, you specify the workgroup name in the **workgroup=** entry in the **global** section. The workgroup name should be uppercase and contain no spaces. The default name used on Windows XP systems is simple WORKGROUP. The **smb.conf workgroup** entry would then look like this:

```
workgroup = WORKGROUP
```

You can then restart the Samba server. On a Windows client, you see the Samba server listed when you select View Workgroups Computers from My Network Places. (On older Windows versions, use the Entire Network folder in your Network Neighborhood.) The Samba server will have as a name the description you gave it in your Samba configuration. Opening the icon will display a window with all the configured shares and printers on that Samba server.

To add a network place, in effect a shared Linux directory on the Samba server, click on the Add a Network Place entry in the Network Tasks panel for the My Network Places window. This starts the Add network place wizard, where, on the second dialog, you select Choose another network location. The following panel displays a Browse button and a text box for the network place. Click the Browse button, then in My Network Places, expand the Entire Network entry, and then Microsoft Windows Network. Here you should find listed your workgroup networks. Expand the you set up to use Samba. It should list both your Windows and Linux computers. Expand your Linux computer and select the shared directory you want to have listed in your My Network Places window.

Samba Configuration File and Tools

Samba configuration options are kept in the **/etc/samba/smb.conf** file. You edit this file to make changes to the configuration. Once you finish making any changes, you should test your **smb.conf** file using the testparm program. The testparm program checks the validity of your configuration entries and lists your server definitions. By default, testparm uses the **/etc/samba/smb.conf** file, although you can supply a different configuration file as an argument:

```
testparm
```

To check your network connections, use the **smbstatus** command. This command returns a listing of all active SMB connections, showing the Windows computers you are connected to and your Linux shares.

NOTE *The /etc/samba/smbusers file associates Windows network usernames with corresponding users on your Linux Samba server. For example, **admin** and **administrator** are made equivalent to the Linux root user.*

User Level Security

Samba primarily provides user level security, requiring users on remote systems to log in using Samba registered passwords. Samba still provides share and server level access, but these methods have been deprecated and are not recommended. User level security requires the use of Windows encrypted passwords. Windows uses its own methods of encryption. For Samba to handle such passwords, it has to maintain its own Windows compatible password database. It cannot use the Linux password databases. Windows also uses additional information for the login process like where the user logged in.

User level security requires that each user that wants to login to a Samba share from a Windows system has to have a corresponding user account on the Samba server. In addition, for this account, you have to have a separate Samba password with which to login to the Samba share. In effect they become Samba users. The account on the Samba server does not have to have the same name as the one on the Windows system. A Windows user name can be specified for a Samba user. This mapping of Windows users to Samba (Linux) users is listed in the **/etc/smbusers file**. The following maps the Windows user **rpetersen** to the Samba (Linux) user **richard**.

```
richard = rpetersen
```

In the system-config-samba tool, you are allowed only to use users already created on your Samba server, but can specify a different Windows user. You also then enter the Samba password to use for that user. This is not the same as the password the user would ordinarily use for login on Linux.

When the Windows user in Windows tries to access the Samba share, the user will be prompted to log in. The Windows user would then enter **rpetersen** as the user name and the Samba password that was set up for **richard**.

User level security is managed by password backend databases. By default the **tdbsam** back end database is used. This is a **tdb** database file (trivial data base) that stores Samba passwords along with Windows extended information. The tdbsam database is designed for small networks. For systems using LDAP to manage users, you can use the LDAP enabled back end, **ldbsam**. The **ldbsam** database is designed for larger networks. The **smbpasswd** file previously used is still available, but is included only for backward compatibility. The default configuration entries for user access in the **smb.conf file** are shown here.

```
security = user
passdb backend = tdbsam
```

The **username map** option specifies the file used to associate Windows and Linux users. Windows users can use the Windows user name to log in as the associated user. The username map file is usually /etc/samba/smbusers. This is the file that both SWAT and system-config-samba use when setting up Samba users.

```
username map = /etc/samba/smbusers
```

If you are using an LDAP enabled Samba database, ldbsam, you would use special LDAP Samba tools to manage users. These are provided in the smbldap-tools package. They are prefixed with the term smbldap. There are tools for adding, modifying, and deleting users and groups like **smbldap-useradd**, **smbldap-userdelete**, and **smbldap-groupmod**. You use the **sbmldap-passwd** command to manage Samba passwords with LDAP. The **smdbldap-userinfo** to obtain information about a user. You configure your LDAP Samba tools support using the **/etc/smbldap-tools/smbldap.conf** file.

Samba also provides its own Samba password PAM module, **pam_smbpass.o**. With this module, you provide PAM authentication support for Samba passwords, enabling the use of Windows hosts on a PAM-controlled network. The module could be used for authentication and password management in your PAM **samba** file. The following entries in the PAM **samba** file would implement PAM authentication and passwords using the Samba password database:

```
auth required pam_smbpass.so nodelay
password required pam_smbpass.so nodelay
```

Be sure to enable PAM in the **smb.conf** file:

```
obey pam restrictions = yes
```

Samba Passwords: smbpasswd

With user-level security, access to Samba server resources by a Windows client is allowed only to users on that client. Each user on the Windows client has to have a corresponding account on the Samba server. A user logs in to his or her Windows account and then, when accessing a Samba share or printer, has to log in using the Windows account name specified for Samba server access. A The User name and password used to access the Samba server has to be registered in the Samba password database. Note: If you are using the older smbpasswd file, you can use the **mksmbpasswd.sh** script to generate an smbpasswd file made up of all the users listed in your **/etc/passwd** file. You pipe the contents of the passwd file to **mksmbpasswd.sh** and then use redirection (**>**) to create the file.

Adding and Changing Passwords

You use the **smbpasswd** command to add, or later change, passwords. To add or change a password for a particular user, you use the **smbpasswd** command with the username:

```
# smbpasswd dylan
New SMB Password: new-password
Repeat New SMB Password: new-password
```

Users can use **smbpasswd** to change their own password. The following example shows how you would use **smbpasswd** to change your Samba password. If the user has no Samba password, that user can just press the ENTER key.

```
$ smbpasswd
Old SMB password: old-password
New SMB Password: new-password
Repeat New SMB Password: new-password
```

Should you want to use no passwords, you can use smbpasswd with the **-n** option. The **smb.conf** file will have to have the **null passwords** option set to yes. Note: If you are using the older smbpasswords file, be sure that Samba is configured to use encrypted passwords. Set the **encrypt passwords** option to **yes** and specify the SMB password file.

Managing Samba Users: smbasswd and pdbedit

The easiest way to manage Samba users is to use the system-config-samba tool. Click Preferences to select Samba Users. In this window you can then add, edit, or remove Samba users. In the SWAT tool you would use the Password panel.

To manage users you can either use the smbpasswd command or the pdbedit tool. The **smbpasswd** command with the **-a** option will add a user and the **-x** option will remove one.

```
smbpasswd -a aleina
```

To enable or disable users you would use the **-e** and **-d** options.

The smbpasswd command will operate on both the older smbasswd file or the newer tdbsam backend database files. For just the tdbsam backend database files you can use **pdbedit** instead. To add a user you would use the **-a** option and to remove a user you use the **-x** option.

```
pdbedit -a larisa
```

This is a command line tool with options for adding and removing users, as well as features like changing password and setting the home directory. You can also import or export the user entries to or from other backend databases.

The **pdbedit** command lets you display more information about users. To display users from the backend database you could use the **-L** option. Add the **-v** option for detailed information. For a particular user add the user name.

```
pdbedit -Lv richard
```

For domain policies like minimum password length or retries, you use the -P option.

```
pdbedit -P
```

You use the **-i** and **-e** options to import and export database entries. The following will import entries from the old **smbpasswd** file to the new **tdbsam** backend database.

```
pdbedit -i smbpasswd -e tdbsam
```

If your system is using LDAP-enabled Samba database, then use the smbldap tools to manage users and groups.

Configuring Samba with system-config-samba

The system-config-samba tool provides a simple means to configure your Samba server, adding Samba users and specifying Samba shares. It will also automatically configure all the printers on your Linux system as Samba shared printers, allowing you to use them from a connected Windows system. You can start system-config-samba from the Samba entry in the Server Settings menu, accessible from the System Setting menu. The system-config-samba tool will list all the shares for your server. You can use buttons at the top to manage your shares, adding new ones or deleting current ones. If you delete, the actual directories are not removed; they just lose their status as shared directories.

Server Configuration with system-config-samba

To configure your Samba server, select Server Settings from the Preferences menu. This opens a window with two panels, Basic and Security. On the Basic panel, you enter the Samba server workgroup name. This will be the same name used as the workgroup by all your Windows systems. For example, if you are using the group name, WORKGROUP, for your Windows systems, you would enter WORKGROUP here. The description is the name you want displayed for your Samba server on your Windows systems. On the Security panel, you specify the authentication mode, the password encryption option, and the name of the guest account, along with the authentication server.

- As explained in detail later, the authentication mode specifies the access level, which can be user, share, server, or domain. User-level access restricts access by user password, whereas share access opens access to any guest.

- Normally, you would elect to encrypt passwords, rather than have them passed over your network in plain text.

- The Guest user is the name of the account used to allow access to shares or printers that you want open to any user, without having to provide a password. The pop-up menu will list all your current users, with nobody as the selected default.

Adding Samba Users with system-config-samba

With system-config-samba, you can add users and shares easily. User-level access restricts Windows users to those that are assigned corresponding account on the Samba server. Samba maintains its own password listing for users. To provide a user Samba access, you need to register the user as a Samba user, giving them a Samba password. Select Samba Users from the Preferences menu to open the Samba Users window, clicking the Add User button. Here you enter the Unix Username, the Windows Username, and the Samba Password. There is an additional box for confirming the Samba password. The Unix Username is a pop-up window listing all the users on your Samba server.

Specifying Samba Shares with system-config-samba

Click Add to add a share, or select Add Share from the File menu. On the Basic panel, you can then enter the directory on the Samba server that you want to share, specifying the full pathname. The Browse button lets you search and select a directory. You can also set permissions to either read-only or read/write. On the Access panel, you can restrict access to certain users or allow access to all users. All Samba users on your system will be listed with check boxes where you can select those you want to give access.

The Samba smb.conf Configuration File

You configure the Samba daemon using the **smb.conf** file located in the **/etc/samba** directory. The file is separated into two basic parts: one for global options and the other for shared services. A shared service, also known as *shares*, can either be filespace services (used by clients as an extension of their native file systems) or printable services (used by clients to access print services on the host running the server). The filespace service is a directory to which clients are given access; they can use the space in it as an extension of their local file system. A printable service provides access by clients to print services, such as printers managed by the Samba server.

The **/etc/samba/smb.conf** file holds the configuration for the various shared resources, as well as global options that apply to all resources. Linux installs an **smb.conf** file in your **/etc/samba** directory. The file contains default settings used for your distribution. You can edit the file to customize your configuration to your own needs. Many entries are commented with either a semicolon or a **#** sign, and you can remove the initial comment symbol to make them effective. Instead of editing the file directly, you may want to use the SWAT configuration utility, which provides an easy-to-use, full-screen Web page interface for entering configurations for shared resources. The SWAT configuration utility also provides extensive help features and documentation. For a complete listing of the Samba configuration parameters, check the Man page for **smb.conf**. An extensive set of sample **smb.conf** files is located in the **/usr/share/doc/samba*** directory in the **examples** subdirectory.

In the **smb.conf** file, global options are set first, followed by each shared resource's configuration. The basic organizing component of the **smb.conf** file is called a *section*. Each resource has its own section that holds its service name and definitions of its attributes. Even global options are placed in a section of their own, labeled **global**. For example, each section for a filespace share consists of the directory and the access rights allowed to users of the filespace. The section of each share is labeled with the name of the shared resource. Special sections, called **printers** and **homes**, provide default descriptions for user directories and printers accessible on the Samba server. Following the special sections, sections are entered for specific services, namely access to specific directories or printers.

A section begins with a section label consisting of the name of the shared resource encased in brackets. Other than the special sections, the section label can be any name you want to give it. Following the section label, on separate lines, different parameters for this service are entered. The parameters define the access rights to be granted to the user of the service. For example, for a directory, you may want it to be browsable, but read-only, and to use a certain printer. Parameters are entered in the format *parameter name = value*. You can enter a comment by placing a semicolon at the beginning of the comment line.

A simple example of a section configuration follows. The section label is encased in brackets and followed by two parameter entries. The **path** parameter specifies the directory to which access is allowed. The **writeable** parameter specifies whether the user has write access to this directory and its filespace.

```
[mysection]
 path = /home/chris
 writeable = true
```

A printer service has the same format but requires certain other parameters. The path parameter specifies the location of the printer spool directory. The **read-only** and **printable** parameters are set to **true**, indicating the service is read-only and printable. **public** indicates anyone can access it.

```
[myprinter]
 path = /var/spool/samba
 read only = true
 printable = true
 public = true
```

Parameter entries are often synonymous but different entries that have the same meaning. For example, **read only = no**, **writeable = yes**, and **write ok = yes** all mean the same thing, providing write access to the user. The **public** parameter is a synonym for **guest ok**. SWAT will use **guest ok** instead of **public**, and **read only** in place of **writeable**.

SWAT and smb.conf

SWAT is a network-based Samba configuration tool that uses a Web page interface to enable you to configure your **smb.conf** file. SWAT is an easy way to configure your Samba server, providing the full range of configuration options rather than the defaults provided by system-config-samba. SWAT provides a simple-to-use Web page interface with buttons, menus, and text boxes for entering values. A simple button bar across the top enables you to select the sections you want to configure. A button bar is even there to add passwords. To see the contents of the **smb.conf** file as SWAT changes it, click View. The initial screen (HOME) displays the index for Samba documentation. One of SWAT's more helpful features is its context-sensitive help. For each parameter and option SWAT displays, you can click a Help button to display a detailed explanation of the option and examples of its use.

Activating SWAT

SWAT is normally installed with Samba. SWAT is an xinetd service. As an xinetd service, it will be listed in the **/etc/services** and **/etc/xinetd.d/swat** files. The SWAT program uses port 901, as designated in the **/etc/services** file and shown here:

```
swat 901/tcp # Samba Web Administration Tool
```

As an xinetd service, SWAT will have its own xinetd file in the **/etc/xinetd.d** directory, **/etc/xinetd.d/swat**. SWAT is turned off by default, and its **disable** option is set to **yes**. To use SWAT, you will have to change the **disable** option to **no** as shown here:

```
# default: off
# description: SWAT is the Samba Web Admin Tool. Use swat \
#      to configure your Samba server. To use SWAT, \
#      connect to port 901 with your favorite web browser.
service swat
{
        disable = no
        port = 901
        socket_type = stream
        wait = no
        only_from = 127.0.0.1
        user = root
        server = /usr/sbin/swat
        log_on_failure += USERID
}
```

You can do this by using either **chkconfig** or the Service Configuration tool to turn on the SWAT service or by manually editing the **/etc/xinetd.d/swat** file and changing the

disable option to **no**. **chkconfig** will edit the **/etc/xinetd.d/swat** file for you, making this change (see Chapter 21 for more information about **chkconfig**). The following example shows how you would enable SWAT with the **chkconfig** command:

```
chkconfig swat on
```

With **chkconfig**, you will not have manually restart the xinetd server. However, if you manually edit the file, you will also have to restart the server to have the change take effect. You can do this simply using the **xinetd** script, as shown here:

```
service xinetd restart
```

Before you use SWAT, back up your current **smb.conf** file. SWAT overwrites the original, replacing it with a shorter and more concise version of its own. The **smb.conf** file originally installed lists an extensive number of options with detailed explanations. This is a good learning tool, with excellent examples for creating various kinds of printer and directory sections. Simply make a backup copy:

```
cp /etc/samba/smb.conf /etc/samba/smb.bk
```

Accessing SWAT

You can start SWAT by opening your browser and enter the IP address 127.0.0.1 with port 901 to access SWAT.

```
http://127.0.0.1:901
```

Instead of 127.0.0.1 you can use **localhost.localdomain**.

```
http://localhost.localdomain:901
```

You can start SWAT from a remote location by entering the address of the Samba server it is running on, along with its port (901), into a Web browser. However, you will first have to enable this feature in the **/etc/xinetd.d/swat** file. Currently, the **only_from** line in this file restricts access to just localhost. To enable access from any remote system, just remove this line. If you want to provide access to certain specific hosts, you can list them after 127.0.0.1 on the **only_from** line. Be sure to restart SWAT after any changes. The following example enables access from both 127.0.0.1 and **rabbit.mytrek.com**:

```
only_from  127.0.0.1  rabbit.mytrek.com
```

The following URL entered into a Web browser on a remote system would then display the Web page interface for SWAT on the **turtle.mytrek.com** Samba server:

```
http://turtle.mytrek.com:901
```

You are first asked to enter a username and a password. To configure Samba, you need to enter **root** and the root password. (If you are connecting from a remote system, it is *not* advisable to enter the root password in clear text—see Chapter 29.)

SWAT Configuration Pages

The main SWAT page is displayed with a button bar, with buttons for links for HOME, GLOBAL, SHARES, PRINTERS, STATUS, VIEW, and PASSWORD (see Table 39-2). You can use STATUS to list your active SMB network connections.

For the various sections, SWAT can display either a basic or advanced version. The basic version shows only those entries needed for a simple configuration, whereas the advanced version shows all the possible entries for that type of section. Buttons labeled Advanced and Basic appear at the top of the section page for toggling between the advanced or basic versions. Section pages for printers and shares have added buttons and a menu for selecting the particular printer or share you want to configure. The term "share," as it's used here, refers to directories you want to make available through Samba. When you click the SHARES button, you initially see only a few buttons displayed at the top of the SHARES page. You use these buttons to create new sections or to edit sections already set up for shares. To set up a new Share section, you enter its name in the box next to the Create Share button and then click that button. The new share name appears in the drop-down menu next to the Choose Share button. Initially, this menu is blank. Click its drop-down symbol to display the list of current Share sections. Select the one you want, and then click the Choose Share button. The page then displays the entries for configuring a share. For a new share, these are either blank or default values. For example, to select the Homes section that configures the default setting for user home directories, click the drop-down menu, where you find a Homes entry. Select it, and then click the Choose Share button. The entries for the Homes section are displayed. The same process works for the Printers page, where you can select either the Printers section or the Create sections for particular printers.

NOTE *For Samba to use a printer, it first has to be configured on your system as either a local or network printer (see system-config-printer in Chapter 4). Keep in mind that a network printer could be a printer connected to a Windows system.*

Page	Description
HOME	SWAT home page listing documentation resources.
GLOBALS	Configures the global section for Samba.
SHARES	Selects and configures directories to be shared (shares).
PRINTERS	Sets up access to printers.
WIZARD	Quick server setup, rewrites original smb.conf file removing all comments and default values.
STATUS	Checks the status of the Samba server, both smbd and nmbd; lists clients currently active and the actions they are performing. You can restart, stop, or start the Samba server from this page.
VIEW	Displays the **smb.conf** configuration file.
PASSWORD	Sets up password access for the server and users that have access.

TABLE 39-2 SWAT Configuration Pages

There is a Help link next to each entry. Such a link displays a Web page showing the Samba documentation for **smb.conf**, positioned at the appropriate entry.

When you finish working on a section, click the Commit Changes button on its page to save your changes. Do this for each separate page you work on, including the GLOBALS page. Clicking Commit Changes generates a new version of the **smb.conf** file. To have the Samba server read these changes, you then have to restart it. You can do this by clicking the Restart SMB button on the Status page.

Creating a New Share with SWAT

The basic procedures for creating a new share using SWAT include the following steps:

1. Select the Share page and, in the Create Share text box, enter the name of the new share.

2. Click the Create Share button to open a configuration page for the new share. The name of the new share will appear in the pop-up menu next to the Choose Share button.

3. Enter various options. For the Basic Options, you will have to specify the directory for the share in the Path text box. In the Comment text box, you enter the label that will appear on Windows for the share.

4. Click Commit Changes to save your share entry to the Samba configuration file, **smb.conf**. Then restart the Samba server to effect your changes (click the Restart SMB button on the Status page).

You can follow a similar procedure to add a new printer, but make sure the printer is also configured on the system with the Samba server.

You can, of course, edit the **/etc/samba/smb.conf** file directly. This is a simple text file you can edit with any text editor. You still must restart the SMB server to have the changes take effect, which you can do manually with the following command:

```
service smb restart
```

A SWAT-Generated smb.conf Example

The following example shows an **smb.conf** file generated by SWAT for a simple configuration. This is much smaller than the comment-intensive versions originally installed with Samba. In this configuration, share-level security is implemented and password encryption is enabled. A share called **myprojects** is defined that has guest access and is writable. A printer share called **myhp** is also defined that supports guest access.

```
# Samba config file created using SWAT
# from localhost.localdomain (127.0.0.1)
# Date:

# Global parameters
[global]
    server string = richard5
    security = SHARE
    log file = /var/log/samba/%m.log
    max log size = 50
```

```
      dns proxy = No
      hosts allow = 192.168.0., 192.168.1., 192.168.2., 127.
      cups options = raw

[homes]
         comment = Home Directories
         path = /home
         read only = No
         guest ok = Yes

[printers]
         comment = All Printers
         path = /var/spool/samba
         guest ok = Yes
         printable = Yes
         browseable = No

[myprojects]
         path = /myprojects
         read only = No
         guest ok = Yes

[myhp]
         path = /var/spool/samba
         read only = No
         guest ok = Yes
         printable = Yes
         printer = myhp
         oplocks = No
         share modes = No
```

TIP *The **writeable** option is an alias for the inverse of the **read only** option. The **writeable** = **yes** entry is the same as **read only** = **no** entry.*

Global Section

The Global section determines configuration for the entire server, as well as specifying default entries to be used in the home and directory segments. In this section, you find entries for the workgroup name, password configuration, and directory settings. Several of the more important entries are discussed here.

Specifying the Workgroup and Server

The Workgroup entry specifies the workgroup name you want to give to your network. This is the workgroup name that appears on the Windows client's Network Neighborhood window. The default Workgroup entry in the **smb.conf** file is shown here:

```
[global]

# workgroup = NT-Domain-Name or Workgroup-Name
  workgroup = MYGROUP
```

The workgroup name has to be the same for each Windows client that the Samba server supports. On a Windows client, the workgroup name is usually found on the Network Identification or General panel in the System tool located in the Control Panel window. On many clients, this is defaulted to WORKGROUP. If you want to keep this name, you have to change the Workgroup entry in the **smb.conf** file accordingly. The Workgroup entry and the workgroup name on each Windows client have to be the same.

```
workgroup = WORKGROUP
```

The server string entry holds the descriptive name you want displayed for the server on the client systems. On Windows systems, this is the name displayed on the Samba server icon. The default is Samba Server, but you can change this to any name you want.

```
# server string is the equivalent of the NT Description field
 server string = Samba Server
```

Security Level

Samba resources are normally accessed with either share- or user-level security. On a share level, any user can access the resource without having to log in to the server. On a user level, each user has to log in, using a password. Furthermore, Windows 98, ME, NT, and XP clients use encrypted passwords for the login process. Passwords are encrypted by default and managed by the password database, as noted previously

```
security = user
passdb backend = tdbsam
```

If you want share-level security, specify **share** as the security option. However this option is deprecated. User level security is considered the standard:

```
security = share
```

On the SWAT Globals page, select the security level from the Security pop-up menu, either User or Share. Then select Yes for the encrypt passwords entry.

Network Access Control

As a security measure, you can restrict access to SMB services to certain specified local networks. On the host's network, type the network addresses of the local networks for which you want to permit access. To deny access to everyone in a network except a few particular hosts, you can use the EXCEPT option after the network address with the IP addresses of those hosts. The localhost (127) is always automatically included. The next example allows access to two local networks:

```
hosts allow = 192.168.1. 192.168.2.
```

Printing

To enable printing, specify Cups options and load printer configurations.

```
cups options = raw
load printers = yes
```

Other options like **printing** let you specify a different printing server (CUPS is the default).

Guest User Access

You can use a guest user login to make resources available to anyone without requiring a password. A guest user login would handle any users who log in without a specific account. On Linux systems, by default Samba will use the **nobody** user as the guest user. Alternatively, you can set up and designate a specific user to use as the guest user. You designate the guest user with the Guest Account entry in the **smb.conf** file. The commented **smb.conf** file provided with Samba currently lists a commented entry for setting up a guest user called **pcguest**. You can make this the user you want to be used as the guest user. Be sure to add the guest user to the password file:

```
guest account = pcguest
```

On SWAT, you can specify a guest account entry on the GLOBALS page. By default, this is already set to the **nobody** user.

Passwords

As noted previously, user-level security requires that each user log in to the Samba server using a password. Samba can use either clear text or encrypted passwords, though current Windows clients support encrypted passwords. You can use the **smbpasswd** command to add and change Samba passwords. On SWAT, you enable password encryption on the Globals page and manage passwords on the Passwords page. In the Server Password Management section, you can add, change, remove, enable, or disable users. To add a new user, enter the username and password, and then click Add New User. As the root user on the Samba server, you can add new passwords as well as enable or disable current ones. Normal users can use the Client/Server Password Management section to change their own passwords.

Homes Section

The Homes section specifies default controls for accessing a user home directory through the SMB protocols by remote users. To access the Homes section on SWAT, you simply select the SHARES page, select the Homes entry from the drop-down menu, and click Choose Share. Setting the **browseable** entry to **no** prevents the client from listing the files in a file browser. The **writeable** entry specifies whether users have read and write control over files in their home directories. The **create mode** and **directory mode** set default permissions for new files and directories (on SWAT, these are create mask and directory mask). The **valid users** entry uses the %S macro to map to the current service.

```
[homes]
 comment = Home Directories
 browseable = no
 read only = no
 valid users = %S
 create mode = yes
 directory mode = 775
```

Printer Section

The Printers section specifies the default controls for accessing printers. These are used for printers for which no specific sections exist. In this case, Samba uses printers defined in the server's **printcap** file.

In this context, setting **browseable** to **no** simply hides the Printers section from the client, not the printers. The **path** entry specifies the location of the spool directory Samba will use for printer files. To enable printing at all, the **printable** entry must be set to yes. To allow guest users to print, set the **guest ok** entry to **yes**. On SWAT, select the PRINTER page and the Printers entry in the drop-down menu, and then select Choose Printers. A standard implementation of the Printers section is shown here:

```
[printers]
 comment = All Printers
 path = /var/spool/samba
 browseable = no
 guest ok = yes
 writable = no
 printable = yes
```

If you can't print, be sure to check the Default Print entry. This specifies the command the server actually uses to print documents.

Shares

Sections for specific shared resources, such as directories on your system, are usually placed after the Homes and Printers sections. For a section defining a shared directory, enter a label for the system. Then, on separate lines, enter options for its pathname and the different permissions you want to set. In the **path** = *option*, specify the full pathname for the directory. The **comment** = *option* holds the label to be given the share. You can make a directory writable, public, or read-only. You can control access to the directory with the Valid Users entry. With this entry, you can list those users permitted access. For those options not set, the defaults entered in the Global, Homes, and Printers segments are used.

On SWAT, you use the SHARES page to create and edit shared directories. Select the one you want to edit from the drop-down menu and click Choose Share. The Basic View shows the commonly used entries. For entries such as Valid Users, you need to select the Advanced View. Be sure to click Commit Changes before you move on to another Share or Printer section.

The following example is the **myprojects** share generated by SWAT from a share page. Here the **/myprojects** directory is defined as a share resource that is open to any user with guest access.

```
[myprojects]
     comment = Great Project Ideas
     path = /myprojects
     read only = no
     guest ok = yes
```

To limit access to certain users, you can list a set of valid users. Setting the **guest ok** option to **no** closes it off from access by others.

```
[mynewmusic]
 comment =  New Music
 path = /home/specialprojects
 valid users = mark
 guest ok = no
 read only = no
```

To allow complete public access, set the **guest ok** entry to **yes**, with no valid user's entry.

```
[newdocs]
 comment =  New Documents
 path = /home/newdocs
 guest ok = yes
 read only = no
```

To set up a directory that can be shared by more than one user, where each user has control of the files he or she creates, simply list the users in the Valid Users entry. Permissions for any created files are specified in the Advanced mode by the Create Mask entry (same as create mode). In this example, the permissions are set to 765, which provides read/write/execute access to owners, read/write access to members of the group, and only read/execute access to all others (the default is 744, read-only for group and other permission, see Chapter 30):

```
[myshare]
 comment = Writer's projects
 path = /usr/local/drafts
 valid users = justin chris dylan
 guest ok = no
 read only = no
 create mask = 0765
```

For more examples, check those in the original **smb.conf** file that shows a Shares section for a directory **fredsdir**.

Printers

Access to specific printers is defined in the Printers section of the **smb.conf** file. You can also configure printers in the SWAT Printers page. For a printer, you need to include the Printer and Printable entries, as well as specify the type of Printing server used. With the Printer entry, you name the printer, and by setting the Printable entry to yes, you allow it to print. You can control access to specific users with the valid users entry and by setting the Public entry to no. For public access, set the Public entry to yes. For the CUPS server, set the printing option cups. On SWAT, you can create individual Printer sections on the Printers page. Default entries are already set up for you.

The following example sets up a printer accessible to guest users. This opens the printer to use by any user on the network. Users need to have write access to the printer's spool directory, located in **/var/spool/samba**. Keep in mind that any printer has to first be installed on your system. The following printer was already installed as myhp and has an **/etc/printcap** entry with that name. You can use system-config-printer to install an LPRng printer, giving it a name and selecting its driver (see Chapters 4 and 26). You use the CUPS administrative tool to set up printers for the CUPS server (see Chapter 26). The Printing option can be inherited from general Printers share.

```
[myhp]
     path = /var/spool/samba
     read only = no
     guest ok = yes
```

```
        printable = yes
        printer = myhp
        oplocks = no
        share modes = no
        printing = cups
```

As with shares, you can restrict printer use to certain users, denying it to public access. The following example sets up a printer accessible only by the users **larisa** and **aleina** (you could add other users if you want). Users need to have write access to the printer's spool directory.

```
[larisalaser]
        path = /var/spool/samba
        read only = no
        valid users = larisa aleina
        guest ok = no
        printable = yes
        printing = cups
        printer = larisalaser
        oplocks = no
        share modes = no
```

Variable Substitutions

For string values assigned to parameters, you can incorporate substitution operators. This provides greater flexibility in designating values that may be context-dependent, such as usernames. For example, suppose a service needs to use a separate directory for each user who logs in. The path for such directories could be specified using the **%u** variable that substitutes in the name of the current user. The string **path = /tmp/%u** would become **path = /tmp/justin** for the **justin** user and **/tmp/dylan** for the **dylan** user. Table 39-3 lists several of the more common substitution variables.

Variable	Description
%S	Name of the current service
%P	Root directory of the current service
%u	Username of the current service
%H	Home directory of the user
%h	Internet hostname on which Samba is running
%m	NetBIOS name of the client machine
%L	NetBIOS name of the server
%M	Internet name of the client machine
%I	IP address of the client machine

TABLE 39-3 Samba Substitution Variables

Testing the Samba Configuration

After you make your changes to the **smb.conf** file, you can then use the testparm program to see if the entries are correctly entered. testparm checks the syntax and validity of Samba entries. By default, testparm checks the **/etc/samba/smb.conf** file. If you are using a different file as your configuration file, you can specify it as an argument to testparm. You can also have testparm check to see if a particular host has access to the service set up by the configuration file.

With SWAT, the Status page will list your connections and shares. From the command line, you can use the **smbstatus** command to check on current Samba connections on your network.

To check the real-time operation of your Samba server, you can log in to a user account on the Linux system running the Samba server and connect to the server.

Domain Logons

Samba also supports domain logons whereby a user can log on to the network. Logon scripts can be set up for individual users. To configure such netlogon capability, you need to set up a **netlogon** share in the **smb.conf** file. The following sample is taken from the original **smb.conf** file. This share holds the **netlogon** scripts—in this case, the **/var/lib/samba/ netlogon** directory—which should not be writable but should be accessible by all users (Guest OK):

```
[netlogon]
 comment = Network Logon Service
 path = var/lib/samba/netlogon
 guest ok = yes
 writeable = no
 share modes = no
```

The Global section would have the following parameters enabled:

```
domain logons = yes
```

With netlogon, you can configure Samba as an authentication server for both Linux and Windows hosts. A Samba username and password need to be set up for each host. In the Global section of the **smb.conf** file, be sure to enable encrypted passwords, user-level security, and domain logons, as well as an operating system level of 33 or more:

```
[global]
 encrypt passwords = yes
 security = user
 domain logons = yes
 os level = 33
```

NOTE *You can also configure Samba to be a Primary Domain Controller (PDC) for Windows NT networks. As a PDC, Samba can handle domain logons, retrieve lists of users and groups, and provide user-level security.*

Accessing Samba Services with Clients

Client systems connected to the SMB network can access the shared services provided by the Samba server. Windows clients should be able to access shared directories and services automatically through the Network Neighborhood and the Entire Network icons on a Windows desktop. For Linux systems connected to the same network, Samba services can be accessed using the GNOME Nautilus file manager and KDE file manager, as well as special Samba client programs.

With the Samba smbclient, a command line client, a local Linux system can connect to a shared directory on the Samba server and transfer files, as well as run shell programs. Using the **mount** command with the **-t cifs** option, directories on the Samba server can be mounted to local directories on the Linux client. The **cifs** option invokes **mount.cifs** to mount the directory.

Accessing Windows Samba Shares from GNOME

You can use Nautilus (the GNOME file manager) to access your Samba shares. You can open the My Computer icon and then the Network icon. This will display the icons for your network. The Windows Network icon will hold the Windows workgroups that your Windows hosts are part of. Opening up the Windows Network icon will list your Windows network groups, like WORKGROUP. Opening up the Windows group icon will list the hosts in that group. These will show host icon for your shared Windows hosts. Clicking a host icon will list all the shared resources on it. The following steps access your Windows shares:

1. Click My Computer to open a window with a Network icon.
2. Click the Network icon to open a window with a Windows network icon.
3. Click the Windows network icon to list your Windows network groups, such as workgroup.
4. Click the workgroup icon to list all your Windows hosts.

Alternatively, you can start Nautilus in browser mode and enter the **smb:** protocol to display all the Samba and Windows networks, from which you can access the Samba and Windows shares.

smbclient

The smbclient utility operates like FTP to access systems using the SMB protocols. Whereas with an FTP client you can access other FTP servers or Unix systems, with smbclient you can access SMB-shared services, either on the Samba server or on Windows systems. Many smbclient commands are similar to FTP, such as **mget** to transfer a file or **del** to delete a file. The smbclient program has several options for querying a remote system, as well as connecting to it. See the **smbclient** Man page for a complete list of options and commands. The smbclient program takes as its argument a server name and the service you want to access on that server. A double slash precedes the server name, and a single slash separates it from the service. The service can be any shared resource, such as a directory or a printer. The server name is its NetBIOS name, which may or may not be the same as its IP name. For example, to specify the **myreports** shared directory on the server named **turtle.mytrek.com**, use **//turtle.mytrek.com/myreports**. If you must specify a pathname, use backslashes for Windows files and forward slashes for Unix/Linux files:

```
//server-name/service
```

You can also supply the password for accessing the service. Enter it as an argument following the service name. If you do not supply the password, you are prompted to enter it.

Accessing Shares with smbclient

You can then add several options to access shares, such as the remote username or the list of services available. With the **-I** option, you can specify the system using its IP address. You use the **-U** option and a login name for the remote login name you want to use on the remote system. Attach **%** with the password if a password is required. With the **-L** option, you can obtain a list of the services provided on a server, such as shared directories or printers. The following command will list the shares available on the host **turtle.mytrek.com**:

```
smbclient -L turtle.mytrek.com
```

To access a particular directory on a remote system, enter the directory as an argument to the **smbclient** command, followed by any options. For Windows files, you use backslashes for the pathnames, and for Unix/Linux files, you use forward slashes. Once connected, an SMB prompt is displayed and you can use smbclient commands such as **get** and **put** to transfer files. The **quit** or **exit** commands quit the smbclient program. In the following example, smbclient accesses the directory **myreports** on the **turtle.mytrek.com** system, using the **dylan** login name:

```
smbclient //turtle.mytrek.com/myreports -I 192.168.0.1 -U dylan
```

In most cases, you can simply use the server name to reference the server, as shown here:

```
smbclient //turtle.mytrek.com/myreports -U dylan
```

If you are accessing the home directory of a particular account on the Samba server, you can simply specify the **homes** service. In the next example, the user accesses the home directory of the **aleina** account on the Samba server, after being prompted to enter that account's password:

```
smbclient //turtle.mytrek.com/homes -U aleina
```

You can also use smbclient to access shared resources located on Windows clients. Specify the computer name of the Windows client along with its shared folder. In the next example, the user accesses the **windata** folder on the Windows client named **lizard**. The folder is configured to allow access by anyone, so the user just presses the ENTER key at the password prompt.

```
$ smbclient //lizard/windata
```

Once logged in, you can execute smbclient commands to manage files and change directories. Shell commands can be executed with the **!** operator. To transfer files, you can use the **mget** and **mput** commands, much as they are used in the FTP program.

The **recurse** command enables you to turn on recursion to copy whole subdirectories at a time. You can use file-matching operators, referred to here as *masks,* to select a certain collection of files. The file-matching (mask) operators are *****, **[]**, and **?** (see Chapter 8). The default mask is *****, which matches everything. The following example uses **mget** to copy all files with a **.c** suffix, as in **myprog.c**:

```
smb> mget *.c
```

During transfers, you can have smbclient either prompt you for each individual file or simply transfer all the selected ones. The **prompt** command toggles this file prompting on and off.

   To access a particular printer on a remote system, enter the printer name as an argument to the **smbclient** command, followed by any options. In the following example, smbclient accesses the myepson printer on the **turtle.mytrek.com** system, using the **dylan** login name:

```
smbclient //turtle.mytrek.com/myepson -U dylan
```

   Once connected, an smb prompt is displayed and you can use smbclient commands such as **print** to print files and **printmode** to specify graphics or text. In the next example, the user prints a file called **myfile**, after having accessed the myepson printer on **turtle.mytrek.com**:

```
smb> print myfile
```

mount.cifs: mount -t cifs

Using the **mount** command with the **-t cifs** option., a Linux or Unix client can mount a shared directory onto its local system. The **cifs** option invokes the **mount.cifs** command to perform the mount operation. The syntax for the **mount.cifs** command is similar to that for the **smbclient** command, with many corresponding options. The **mount.cifs** command takes as its arguments the Samba server and shared directory, followed by the local directory where you want to mount the directory. The following example mounts the **myreports** directory onto the **/mnt/myreps** directory on the local system:

   Instead of using **mount.cifs** explicitly, you use the **mount** command with the file system type **cifs**. **mount** will then run the **/sbin/mount.cifs** command, which will invoke **smbclient** to mount the file system:

```
mount -t cifs //turtle.mytrek.com/myreports /mnt/myreps -U dylan
```

   To unmount the directory, use the **cifs.umount** command with the local directory name, as shown here:

```
umount /mnt/myreps
```

   To mount the home directory of a particular user on the server, specify the **homes** service and the user's login name. The following example mounts the home directory of the user **larisa** to the **/home/chris/larisastuff** directory on the local system:

```
mount -t samba //turtle.mytrek.com/homes /home/chris/larisastuff -U larisa
```

You can also mount shared folders on Windows clients. Just specify the computer name of the Windows client along with its folder. If the folder name contains spaces, enclose it in single quotes. In the following example, the user mounts the **windata** folder on **lizard** as the **/mylinux** directory. For a folder with access to anyone, just press ENTER at the password prompt:

```
$ mount -t cifs //lizard/windata  /mylinux
Password:
$ ls /mylinux
_hi_mynewdoc.doc_myreport.txt
```

To unmount the shared folder when you are finished with it, use the `cifs.umount` command.

```
umount /mylinux
```

You could also specify a username and password as options, if user-level access is required:

```
mount -t cifs -o username=chris passwd=mypass //lizard/windata /mylinux
```

You can also use the cifs type in an **/etc/fstab** entry to have a Samba file system mounted automatically:

```
//lizard/windata /mylinux cifs defaults 0 0
```

Sharing Windows Directories and Printers with Samba Clients

To manage directory shares, open the Computer Management tool in the Administrative window in the Control Panel. Click Shared Folders and there you can see the Shares, Sessions, and Open folders. To add a new share, click the Shares folder and then click the Action menu and select New File Share. The Sessions and Open folders' Action menus let you disconnect active sessions and folders.

To allow share-level open access by users on other clients or on the Samba server, be sure to enable the guest user on your Windows client. It is not enabled by default. Access the Users and Passwords tool in the Control Panel to a set up the guest user. Guest access is particularly important for providing access to a printer connected to a Windows client. The Linux system that wants to access a printer on a Windows system will configure the printer on its own system as a remote Samba printer. The user normally entered to access the printer is **guest**. For the Linux system to access the Windows printer, that Windows system has to have a guest user.

Sharing Windows Directories

To share a directory, right-click the directory and select Sharing from the pop-up menu (Sharing And Security on Windows XP). Click Share This Folder and then enter the share name, the name by which the directory will be known by Samba. You can specify whether you want to allow others to change files on the share. You can also specify a user limit (maximum allowed is the default). You can further click the Permissions button to control access by users. Here, you can specify which users will have access, as well as the type of access. For example, you could allow only read access to the directory.

Sharing Windows Printers

To share a printer, locate the printer in the Printers window and right-click it, selecting the Sharing As option. This opens the Sharing panel, where you can click the Shared As button and enter the name under which the printer will be known by other hosts. For example, on the Windows client named lizard, to have a printer called Epson Stylus Color shared as myepson, the Sharing panel for this printer would have the Shared As button selected and the name myepson entered. Then when the user double-clicks the lizard icon in the Computers Near Me window, the printer icon labeled myepson will appear.

For a Linux system to use this printer, it will have be first configured as a remote Windows printer on that Linux system. You can do this easily with system-config-printer (Printing on the System | Administration menu). You can also use the CUPS Print Configuration tool.

To configure your remote printer, you give the printer a name by which it is known on your Linux system, the Windows client computer name, and the name of the printer as it is accessed on the Windows client, along with the username for access (usually **guest**). Once configured, your printing commands can access it using just the printer name, as they would any other printer. For example, the **myepson** printer installed on the Windows client has to also be installed for CUPS on the Linux system operating as the Samba server. For the CUPS print server, you can use system-config-printer to configure your Windows printer. You can give the printer the same name, if you wish. In the New Printer window, you select the Windows Printer via Samba entry in the Select Connection panel. In the facing panel you enter the SMB share name, such as **//lizard/myepson**. You can also use the share browser below this entry to locate your printer. Here you also select the workgroup used. Once selected, the SMB share name will be entered for you. For Authentication, enter **guest** for the user.

Once it is installed, you can restart the CUPS server. Then an `lpr` command can access the remote Windows printer directly. The next example prints the **mydoc** file on the Windows client's Epson printer:

```
lpr -P myepson mydoc
```

Windows Clients

To access Samba resources from a Windows system, you will need to make sure that your Windows system has enabled TCP/IP networking. This may already be the case if your Windows client is connected to a Microsoft network. If you need to connect a Windows system directly to a TCP/IP network that your Linux Samba server is running on, you should check that TCP/IP networking is enabled on that Windows system. This involves making sure that the Microsoft Network client and the TCP/IP protocol are installed, and that your network interface card (NIC adapter) is configured to use TCP/IP. The procedures differ slightly on Windows 2000 and XP, and Windows 95, 98, and ME.

Once connected, your Samba shares and printers will appear in the Windows network window. On Windows XP you can select My Network Places and it will list the Samba shares on your Linux Samba server. If you open View Workgroup Computers, it will list your Samba server (along with any other Samba or Windows systems in your workgroup). The Samba server will have the name given it in the **server string** option along with the netbios name (the host name). Follow the instructions on your particular Windows system for accessing remote shared resources such as printers and directories.

Index

Numbers

0-6 Linux software RAID levels, explanations of, 706–708

0-6 runlevels, descriptions of, 578–579

64-bit machines, creating Fedora distributions for, 51

Symbols

- (standard input) argument, using with commands, 210

! operator, using with packet rules, 426, 430

\! shell prompt code, description of, 237

(pound sign) prompt, use of, 194

prompt, explanation of, 58–59

\# shell prompt code, description of, 237

$ (dollar) sign
    at command line prompt, explanation of, 58–59
    referencing arguments for shell scripts with, 218–219
    referencing variable values with, 215
    use with BASH (Bourne again) shell, 194
    using with variables, 197

\$ shell prompt code, description of, 237

$? special variable, example of, 219

$TTL directive, using with zone files, 841–842

% (percent) field specifier, using with Apache logs, 502

% (percent) prompt, use of, 194

% (percent) symbol, referencing background jobs with, 212

& (ampersand)
    executing background jobs with, 212
    using with lftp client, 341
    using with Mail utility, 314

&& (ampersands), using with commands, 195

* (asterisk)
    using in BASH (Bourne again) shell, 203, 207
    using with filename searches, 261

. (dot) command
    using with .bash_profile script, 240
    using with .bashrc file, 243

. (dot) files
    displaying, 90
    use of, 248

. command, using, 217

.. symbol, referencing files in parent directory with, 257

.bash_profile file, using, 658

/ (root directory)
    role in FHS (File System Hierarchy Standard), 662–663
    setting with chroot command, 49
    significance of, 250

/ (slash), placing after directory names, 228

/etc/login.access file, contents of, 605

/etc/nsswitch.conf file, relationship to DNS (domain name service), 813–815

? (question) mark, using in BASH (Bourne again) shell, 203–204, 207

@ (at) sign, using with host names, 197

[] (brackets), using in BASH (Bourne again) shell, 204, 207

\ (backslash)
    using in BASH (Bourne again) shell, 207
    using with commands, 194

\ [\] shell prompt code, description of, 237

\\ shell prompt code, description of, 237

{} (curly braces), using in BASH (Bourne again) shell, 205

| (pipes), using in BASH (Bourne again) shell, 207, 209–210

~ (tilde), using with user names, 197

= (assignment) operator, using with variables, 215

= (equal) sign, using with aliases, 228

> (greater-than sign), use with Mail utility, 315

> and >> (redirection operators), using in BASH (Bourne again) shell, 206–208

>& and 2> symbols, using in BASH (Bourne again) shell, 210–211

; (semicolon)
    purpose in wvdial, 129
    separating commands with, 195

' (single quote)
    versus back quote (`), 216–217
    using with aliases, 228–229

/ directory, function of, 253

` (back quote) versus single quote ('), 216–217

A

A type addresses, using, 843–844

AbiWord word processor
    description of, 288
    features of, 283

AbiWord word processor (*continued*)
  installing from command
    line, 81
  installing with Yum, 104
About Me preferences dialog,
  configuring, 66
absolute versus relative
  pathnames, 252
accept and reject tools, using with
  CUPS (Common Unix Printing
  System), 558
ACCEPT target, using with packets,
  424, 426
access control lists (ACLs), using
  with Squid proxy server, 516–517
access controls
  in Apache Web server, 498
  types of, 369–371
access vector rules with allow,
  managing in SELinux, 386–387
AccessFileName directive, using
  with Apache Web server, 497
acl entries in squid proxy server,
  patterns of, 519
ACLs (access control lists)
    using in DNS (Domain
      Name System),
      859–860
    using with Squid proxy
      server, 516–517
Acrobat Reader for Linux document
  viewer, description of, 284
actions and users, specifying in
  system logs, 591–592
Add New Device Type window,
  displaying, 126
AddHandler directive, using with
  Apache Web server, 506
address records, using,
  843–844, 848
administrative access, controlling,
  572–573
administrative tasks, performing, 92
Advanced Intrusion Detection
  Environment (AIDE) tool,
  using, 367
Advanced Linux Sound
  Architecture (ALSA), Web site
  for, 296
Advanced Maryland Automatic
  Network Disk Archiver
  (Amanda). *See* Amanda
  (Advanced Maryland Automatic
  Network Disk Archiver)
Advanced Package Tool (APT),
  features of, 642–643
Advanced Platform of Red Hat
  Enterprise Linux, features of, 6–7
AFE (Affix Frontend Environment),
  Web site for, 117
Affix Frontend Environment (AFE),
  Web site for, 117
agetty program, using with terminal
  connections, 741

AH (authentication header)
  protocol, relationship
  to IPsec, 396
AH payload, encrypting in IPsec
  connections, 399
AIDE (Advanced Intrusion
  Detection Environment) tool,
  using, 367
AIM (AOL Instant Messenger),
  features of, 347
Alacarte, using in GNOME 2.x, 142
alias command, creating command
  names with, 228–229
Alias directive, using with Apache
  Web server, 497
alias records, using, 849
aliases
    IP aliasing, 824
    removing, 229
    support in Sendmail, 532–533
    using command names as, 229
    using with modules, 748
    using with resource
      records, 845
allow access control directive, using
  with Apache Web server, 498
allow keyword, using in SELinux,
  386–387
AllowOverrride directive, using
  with Apache Web server, 497
allow-transfer statement, using in
  DNS, 855–856
--all-stages option, using with
  Pungi, 54
ALSA (Advanced Linux Sound
  Architecture)
    using with sound
      devices, 742
    Web site for, 296
ALT key. *See* keyboard shortcuts
Amanda (Advanced Maryland
  Automatic Network Disk
  Archiver)
    commands for, 781–782
    configuring, 782–783
    enabling on networks, 783
    features of, 781
    using, 783–784
ampersand (&)
    executing background jobs
      with, 212
    using with lftp client, 341
    using with Mail utility, 314
ampersands (&&), using with
  commands, 195
anacron, supplementing cron
  service with, 578
Anonymous directive, using with
  Apache Web server, 501
anonymous FTP
    allowing access for, 476
    features of, 475
    files for, 477
    server directories for, 477

anonymous logins, using .netrc
  feature with, 339–340
AOL Instant Messenger (AIM),
  features of, 347
ap parameter, using with iwconfig
  Wireless Tool, 132
Apache Configuration Tool,
  using, 508
Apache Jakarta Project, significance
  of, 489–490
Apache Web server
    access control in, 498
    alternatives to Apache, 488
    authentication in, 500–501
    configuration files for, 491–492
    configuration operations
      for, 493
    configuring, 120, 496
    configuring individual
      directories, 497
    directives used with, 493
    features of, 489
    files and directories for, 491
    global configuration of, 494
    installations of, 490
    and IP addressing, 506
    log files in, 501–503
    MPMs (multiprocessing
      modules) for, 490
    service scripts for, 491
    starting and stopping, 490–492
    starting and stopping
      manually, 453
    support for interpolated
      strings in, 505–506
    using automatic directory
      indexing with, 500
    using CGI files with, 499–500
    using MIME types with, 499
    using modules with, 494–495
    using URL pathnames with,
      498–499
    virtual hosting on, 503–506
apachectl control tool, features of, 492
Apache-SSL Web server, Web site
  for, 488, 509
appconfig, using in SELinux, 391
Appearance pane, using in KDE
  panel (Kicker), 181
applets. *See also* GNOME applets
    relationship to panels in
      GNOME, 162
    support in KDE panel
      (Kicker), 180
application launchers
    adding to panels, 163
    creating in GNOME desktop,
      147–148
    creating with Nautilus file
      manager, 157
applications. *See also* programs
    accessing from KDE
      (K Desktop Environment),
      182

grouping under Drawer
icons, 163
starting at start up in KDE
(K Desktop Environment),
183
starting in KDE (K Desktop
Environment), 181
starting in Nautilus file
manager, 156
APT (Advanced Package Tool),
features of, 642–643
arch option, specifying 32- and
64-bit versions with, 50
Archive Manager, using, 110
archived tar files, compressing with
gzip, 272
archives
compressing, 270–271
creating with File Roller,
266–267
creating with tar (tape
archive), 268
displaying contents of, 268
extracting, 268–269
extracting contents of, 272
extracting for source code
applications, 110
extracting in Konqueror, 184
updating, 270
use of, 247
archiving to tape, 271
Area Code variable, using with
wvdial, 130
arguments
including command names
with, 229
referencing for shell scripts,
218–219
using in Linux commands,
72–73
ARIN (American Registry for
Internet Numbers), Web site
for, 802
Arrangement pane, using in KDE
panel (Kicker), 181
ARRAY entry, specifying name of
RAID device for, 710, 714
ascii command, using with ftp
program, 338
assignment (=) operator, using with
variables, 215
asterisk (*)
using in BASH (Bourne
again) shell, 203, 207
using with filename
searches, 261
at (@) sign, using with host names,
197
AT&T Unix Korn shell, description
of, 227
ATI drivers, packages for, 101
attacks, protecting systems from,
111–114

attributetype definition, using with
LDAP directory databases, 625
ATTRS key, using with udev
rules, 731
audio CDs, playing in Fedora, 70
audit2allow tool, using with
SELinux, 376–377, 380–381
auditd system, features of, 592–593
AUTH command, using with
Sendmail, 542
AuthConfig directive, using with
Apache Web server, 497
authentication
in Apache Web server,
500–501
configuring, 113–114
of packages, 109
in Samba, 84–85
with SSH (Secure Shell), 407
use of, 111
authentication header (AH)
protocol, relationship
to IPsec, 396
authentication header payload,
encrypting in IPsec
connections, 399
Authentication tool, configuring
Kerberos with, 418
AuthName directive, using with
Apache Web server, 500
auto mounts, implementing, 676
Auto Reconnect variable, using with
wvdial, 130
autofs service, mounting NFS on
demand with, 895

B

back quote (`) versus single quote
('), 216–217
backslash (\)
using in BASH (Bourne
again) shell, 207
using with commands, 194
backups
making with dump and
restore, 784–789
recording, 786
recovering, 787–789
restoring from, 789
scheduling automatically,
779
Balsa mail client, using with
GNOME desktop, 311–312
BASH (Bourne again) shell. *See also*
command line; jobs in BASH
(Bourne again) shell
command line editing in,
195–196
conditional control
structures in, 221–223
configuring, 242–243
configuring history in, 201

default prompt for, 237
defining environment
variables in, 231
description of, 227
editing capabilities of, 195
editing history events in,
200–201
ending processes in, 214
filters and regular
expressions in, 224–226
generating patterns in, 205
history list kept by, 197–201
initialization and
configuration files for, 244
job management operations
in, 211
loop control structures in,
223–224
matching multiple characters
in, 203
matching range of characters
in, 204
matching shell symbols in,
204–205
matching single characters
in, 203–204
navigating between
characters in, 195
operators in, 207
redirecting and piping
standard errors in,
210–211
redirecting standard output
in, 206, 208
redisplaying commands
in, 198
referencing events in, 200
running background jobs
in, 212
searching files in, 225
special characters used for
filenames in, 201–202
special features of, 230
standard input in, 205–206,
208–209
standard output in, 205–206
symbols used in, 202
test operators for, 220
using pipes (|) in, 209–210
variables in, 214–217
bash command, description of, 228
BASH command line
command line completion
in, 196–197
file name completion in,
196–197
command line, identifying,
194
BASH profile script
editing, 239–240
reexecuting manually, 240
BASH_ENV shell variable,
specifying, 236

.bash_logout file, using, 243–244
.bash_profile file, significance of, 238
BASH shell variable, description of, 232
BASH_VERSION shell variable, description of, 232
.bashrc, configuring BASH (Bourne again) shell with, 242–243
bashrc file, contents and location of, 243
Basic panel in Nautilus Properties box, explanation of, 157
Baud variable, using with wvdial, 130
Behavior preferences, setting in Nautilus file manager, 159
Bell Labs, popularity of Unix at, 14
Berkeley Internet Name Domain (BIND), features of, 830–832
Berkeley Software Distribution (BSD), development of, 14
Beryl compositing window manager, using, 148
bg command, using with jobs, 213
biff utility, Mail Notification feature of, 316
/bin directory
    contents of, 584, 663–664
    function of, 253
binary masks, using with permissions, 616–617
binary method, using with ownership permissions, 618–619
BIND (Berkeley Internet Name Domain), features of, 830–832
BIND configuration statements, descriptions of, 836
BIND server files, location of, 834
BIND servers, starting and stopping, 832
BIND zone types, descriptions of, 836
bit or rate parameter, using with iwconfig Wireless Tool, 132
BitTorrent, downloading ISO and DVD distribution images with, 635–636
BitTorrent files for Fedora, location of, 28
Bluetooth
    configuring, 117–118
    support for, 117
BlueZ
    alternative to, 117
    features of, 118
bookmarks, using with directories in Konqueror, 186
boot, specifying with title, 598
boot CD-ROM, creating, 758–759
/boot directory, contents of, 663
boot disk
    creating, 49
    placing kernel on, 767

boot loader
    configurations for, 767–768
    creation of, 758
    installing, 43
    reinstalling, 50
boot partition, setting up, 41
boot source options, choosing, 34–35
bootable CD-ROMs, creating, 690–691
bootable RAID, configuring, 714–715
booting from RAID devices, 708
booting up, troubleshooting, 49
brackets ([]), using in BASH (Bourne again) shell, 204, 207
broadcast addresses, using, 804
Browser view in Nautilus
    explanation of, 153
    navigating, 154
browser view, using in GNOME desktop, 62
browsers
    Epiphany, 328
    features of, 325
    Firefox, 326–328
    Galeon, 328
    Konqueror, 328
    line-mode browsers, 328–329
    Mozilla framework, 326
    Nautilus, 328
BSD (Berkeley Software Distribution), development of, 14
bsh command, description of, 228
bye command, using with ftp program, 338
byte stream, explanation of, 249
bytes, examining files by, 249
bzip utility, using with compressed files, 271
bzip2 utility, compressing files with, 273–274

━━ C ━━

cache memory, configuring in Squid proxy server, 520
cache_peer, using with Squid proxy server, 519
caches, using with Squid Proxy server, 519–520
caching-only server, using with DNS, 840
Cairo images, compliance with TANGO style guidelines, 140
Calc program in OpenOffice, features of, 280
case command, using esac keyword with, 221
cat command
    effect of, 253
    listing files with, 254
    using, 197
    using with parent directory, 257

CD burners and rippers, availability of, 302
cd command
    moving between directories with, 49
    navigating directories with, 256–257
    using with lftp client, 341
    using with source code applications, 110
CDPATH system environment variable, description of, 232
CD-ROM boot disk image, location of, 35
CD-ROM drives, device name for, 670–671
CD-ROMs
    booting Linux from, 38
    burning with GNOME Volume Manager, 150
    burning with GNOME, 71
    creating boot CDs, 49
    creating file systems on, 685
    displaying contents of, 183
    ejecting, 183
    installing Fedora from, 30–31
    mounting manually, 683–684
    obtaining for Fedora installation, 27–28
    playing in Fedora, 70
    recording manually, 689–692
    unmounting, 183
CD-R/RW discs, copying files to, 261
cedega drivers, playing Windows games with, 86
CENTOS (Community Enterprise Operating System), using, 7
certificates, using in IPsec configuration, 402
CGI programs versus PHP, 507
chage command, specifying password expirations with, 605–606
chain rules, adding and changing, 423–424
chains
    creating for firewalls, 443–444
    in NAT (Network Address Translation), 431–432
    relationship to Netfilter firewalls, 422
channel parameter, using with iwconfig Wireless Tool, 132
characters. See also special characters
    matching in BASH (Bourne again) shell, 203
    matching with regular expressions, 225
chcon command, using in SELinux, 392

checkmodule command, using in SELinux, 391
checkpolicy command, using in SELinux, 391
chgrp command, using, 614–615
chkconfig tool
    configuring xinetd services for use by, 4601
    enabling and disabling xinetd services with, 460, 470–471
    function of, 461
    listing services with, 458
    managing services with, 582–583
    options for, 459
    removing and adding services with, 460
    starting and stopping services with, 459
    using, 452
    using with CUPS (Common Unix Printing System), 551
    using with Network Manager, 122
chmod command
    changing permissions with, 612–613
    using, 615–616
    using +x option with, 217
chown command, using, 614–615
chron command, using with SELinux troubleshooter, 381
chrond service, starting, 574
chroot command
    relationship to FTP servers, 473
    setting root directory with, 49
CIDR (Classless Interdomain Routing), relationship to netmasks, 798–802
class B network, segments in, 799
class-based IP addressing, explanation of, 797–798
Classless Interdomain Routing (CIDR), relationship to netmasks, 798–802
clear command, using with .bash_logout file, 244
clearlooks theme, using with Fedora desktop, 140
Clock applet, setting preferences for, 164
Clone tool, using with RAID devices, 715
close command, using with ftp program, 338
CNAME records, using, 845
Coda distributed network file system, using, 903
color backgrounds, creating for panels in GNOME, 161–162

COM ports, relationship to terminal devices, 741
command history, keeping in BASH (Bourne again) shell, 198–200
command line. *See also* BASH (Bourne again) shell
    accessing PPP from, 129–131
    editing operations for, 198
    explanation of, 193
    installing AbiWord from, 81
    installing MPlayer from, 82–83
    marking beginning of, 194
    shutting down Linux from, 59
    starting GUIs from, 66
command line editing, performing in BASH (Bourne again) shell, 195–196, 200
command line installation, performing, 644–651
command line interface
    accessing Linux from, 58
    logging in and out with, 58
    using, 72–73
command line mail clients
    Mail utility, 314–315
    Mutt, 314
command names
    including with arguments, 229
    using as aliases, 229
command options, configuring for software, 655
command results, assigning to variables, 216–217
commands
    entering on several lines, 194
    executing in background, 212
    for invoking shells, 228
    location of, 657
    redisplaying, 73
    redisplaying in BASH (Bourne again) shell, 198
    renaming with alias command, 228–229
    repeating with while loops, 223
    running on same line, 195
    running within command lines, 195
    sending data between, 209–210
    separating with semicolons (;), 195
    substituting with aliases, 228–229
    using arguments and options with, 194
Common Unix Printing System (CUPS). *See* CUPS (Common Unix Printing System)

Community Enterprise Operating System (CENTOS), using, 7
comparisons, making with test command, 219–220
compiler configuration, generating, 111
Compiz compositing window manager, using, 148
compiz window manager, features of, 60
compress command, using, 273
compressed archives
    extracting, 110
    installing software from, 652–656
compressing archives, 270–271
compressing files, 272–274
Computer folder, contents of, 69
Concurrent Versions System (CVS), explanation of, 658–659
conditional control structures, using, 219, 221–223
configuration directories and files
    descriptions of, 586
    /etc directory, 585
    /etc/sysconfig, 587
configuration files
    advisory about editing of, 90
    creating Xen virtual machines with, 775–776
    editing directly, 90
    listing in home directory, 245
    locating, 258
    location of, 585, 665
configurations. *See also* system configuration
    resolving conflicts in, 49
    selecting for Fedora installation, 29
configure scripts, use of, 633
connection tracking modules, using with IPtables, 429–431
console, monitor as, 740
constraint rules, managing in SELinux, 387
contact application, availability in KOffice, 281
-context option, using with find command, 260
context-sensitive help, availability of, 73
Control Center in KDE. *See* KDE Control Center
control structures
    conditional control structures, 221–223
    functions of, 221–222
    types of, 219
copying
    directories, 263
    files, 259–262
cp command
    effect of, 261

cp command (*continued*)
    meaning of, 257
    syntax for, 260
    using, 351
    using backslash (\) with, 194
    using with directories, 263
CPU kernel packages, availability
    of, 756
CPU usage, displaying, 164
Create Launcher tool, using in
    Nautilus file manager, 157
CREATE TABLE command,
    using, 563
Create User panel, features of, 48
cron directory names, using, 578
cron directory scripts, running,
    577–578
cron service
    editing in BASH shell, 576
    environment variables
        for, 575
    files and directories for,
        577–578
    scheduling tasks with,
        574–578
    supplementing with
        anacron, 578
cron.d directory, contents of, 576
crontab command, using, 576
crontab entries, fields in, 575
CrossoverOffice program
    features of, 278
    running, 278–279
    running Windows
        applications with, 87
    Web site for, 277
csh command, description of, 228
.csh extension, explanation of, 241
CTRL key. *See* keyboard shortcuts
CUP printer classes, using, 553
CUPS (Common Unix Printing
    System)
    configuration files for, 554
    configuring, 553–554
    configuring remote printers
        on, 552–553
    downloading, 549
    installing printers with,
        551–553
    printer configuration file
        for, 550
    using directives with, 554
    using xinetd with, 551
CUPS command line administrative
    tools
    accept and reject, 558
    enable and disable, 558
    features of, 556–557
    lpadmin tool, 557
    lpinfo, 558
    lpoptions, 558
CUPS command line print clients
    features of, 554–555
    lpc client, 555–556

    lpq and lpstat clients, 556
    lpr client, 555
    lprm client, 556
CUPS printers, configuring shared
    CUPS printers, 553
CUPS server, starting, 551
cupsd.conf file, using, 554
curl client, features of, 335–336
curly braces ({}), using in BASH
    (Bourne again) shell, 205
CustomLog directive, using with
    Apache Web server, 502
CVS (Concurrent Versions System),
    explanation of, 658–659
CVS archives, displaying and
    examining in Konqueror, 185

D

\d shell prompt code, description
    of, 237
DAC (discretionary access control),
    explanation of, 369–370
daemon, relationship to FTP server
    software, 473
daemon function, using with httpd
    service script, 461–462
database connectivity, in GNOME
    Office, 282–283
database front ends, availability in
    OpenOffice, 279–280
database integration capability,
    availability in KOffice, 281
database management systems
    categories of, 285
    DB2, 287
    GNU SQL, 287
    MaxDB, 287
    SQL databases (RDBMS),
        286–287
    Sybase, 287
database servers
    features of, 561
    MySQL, 563–566
    PostgreSQL, 566
database versions of Linux,
    availability of, 19–20
databases, creating in SQL, 562
datagrams, transmission of, 794
Date And Time Configuration
    panel, features of, 47–48
date and time, setting, 92
date command, using, 573–574
DB2 database management system
    features of, 287
    Web site for, 285
deny access control directive, using
    with Apache Web server, 498
dependencies, detecting with
    depmode command, 746
depmode command
    detecting dependencies with, 746
    using with driver
        modules, 114

Desktop Configuration Wizard,
    running, 174
Desktop directory, contents
    of, 190
DESKTOP directory in GNOME,
    contents of, 166
desktop editors, descriptions
    of, 288
desktop operations
    accessing file systems,
        devices, and remote
        hosts, 69–70
    configuring personal
        information, 66–67
    configuring sessions, 67
    searching files with Beagle,
        67–69
    setting font sizes, 66
desktop publisher, availability in
    KOffice, 282
Desktop Switcher, accessing, 66
desktops. *See also* Fedora desktop;
    GNOME desktop; KDE (K
    Desktop Environment); XFce4
    desktop
    starting from command
        line, 66
    starting up, 57
/dev directory
    contents of, 663–664
    function of, 253
development libraries, using,
    655–656
device drivers, support for,
    114–115
device filenames, obtaining list of,
    724–726
device files
    for cards, 742
    CD-ROM devices,
        670–671
    contents of, 719
    creating with MAKEDEV
        command, 738–739
    creating with mknod
        command, 739–740
    floppy and hard disk
        devices, 670
    managing, 668–670
    udev and HAL, 668–670
device icon display, enabling on
    desktop, 175
device information
    obtaining, 719–722
    specifying with properties,
        734–735
device information files, directives
    for, 735–737
device names
    prefixes for, 669
    and udev rules,
        724–726
device types, implementation
    of, 738

devices. *See also* udev hotplug tool
    accessing, 69–70
    creating manually, 737–740
    mounting from desktop, 183
    resources for, 720
    symbolic links for, 727
    using HAL (Hardware
        Abstraction Layer)
        with, 732
Devices panel, using with system-
    config-network tool, 124–125
/dev/modem link file, using, 726
df command, using, 672
DHCP (Dynamic Host
    Configuration Protocol)
    configuration of, 34
    declarations, parameters,
        and options for IPv4
        servers, 874–875
    dynamic IPv4 addresses for,
        876–877
    support for, 119
DHCP and journal files, using in
    DNS (Domain Name System),
    857–859
DHCP dynamic DNS updates,
    performing, 878–880
DHCP fixed addresses, using,
    881–883
DHCP IPv4 client hosts,
    configuring, 872–873. *See also*
    IPv4
DHCP IPv4 servers, configuring,
    873–876
DHCP subnetworks, implementing,
    880–881
DHCPv6, performing IPv6 stateful
    autoconfiguration with, 870–871
Dia drawing program, features
    of, 283
diagnostic tools. *See* performance
    analysis tools and processes
Dial Command variable, using with
    wvdial, 130
Dial Prefix variable, using with
    wvdial, 130
digiKam photo management tool,
    features of, 296
digital signatures
    checking for software
        packages, 109, 365–367
    combining with encryption,
        357
    decrypting with GPG (GNU
        Privacy Guard), 364
    using, 356
Digital Subscriber Line (DSL),
    configuring, 127
dir command, using with NcFTP
    client, 342
directives
    for device information files,
        735–737

using with Apache Web
    server, 493
using with CUPS (Common
    Unix Printing System),
    554
directories. *See also* system
    directories
    accessing, 251
    adding to PATH shell
        variable, 239
    changing, 110
    commands for, 255
    configuring Apache Web
        servers with, 496
    contents of, 250
    copying and moving, 263
    creating and deleting, 256
    creating in KDE (K Desktop
        Environment), 176
    displaying contents of, 256
    displaying in KDE (K
        Desktop Environment),
        183
    erasing, 263
    expanding and shrinking in
        Nautilus, 152
    for groups, 610
    locating, 259
    moving through, 256–257
    navigating, 49
    navigating in Konqueror, 186
    navigating in Nautilus file
        manager, 153–154
    organization of files in, 15
    ownership of, 614
    referencing parent
        directories, 257
    searching, 258–259
    searching working
        directories, 259
    setting global attributes
        with, 847
    system KDE directories, 191
    for system startup files, 452
Directory directive, using with
    Apache Web server, 497
.directory file, contents of, 187
directory names, placing slashes
    after, 228
directory paths, adding to PATH
    variable, 235
directory properties, viewing in
    Nautilus file manager, 157–158
DirectoryIndex directive, using with
    Apache Web server, 497
discretionary access control (DAC),
    explanation of, 369–370
Disk Druid, using with RAID
    devices, 715
disk images
    creating with mkisofs, 690
    mounting with mkisofs, 690
disk packages, installing, 106

disk quota databases, checking
    validity of, 621
disk quotas
    commands for, 621–622
    features of, 620
    setting with edquota
        command, 621
    tools for, 620
diskboot.img file, using, 35
Display Manager in GNOME,
    features of, 56–57
Display Preferences, setting in
    Nautilus file manager, 159
display settings, changing with
    system-config-display, 99–100
distributed network file systems
    Coda, 903
    features of, 901
    PVFS (Parallel Virtual File
        Systems), 902–903
distributed parity (RAID Levels 5
    and 6), explanation of, 707
divert command, using with
    Sendmail, 537
DivX 6, availability of, 83
DivX files, playing in Fedora, 70–71
DivX video compressor, features
    of, 305
DKMS (Dynamic Kernel Module
    Support)
    generating NTFS modules
        with, 117
    updating kernel modules
        with, 107
DKMS versions, using with video
    graphics card drivers, 102
dmraid module, using, 705–706
DNAT and SNAT targets, using,
    431–432
dnl command, using with
    Sendmail, 537
DNS (Domain Name System). *See
    also* resource records; zone files
    for Internet zones
    and $TTL directive, 841–842
    and address records, 843–844
    and BIND (Berkeley Internet
        Name Domain), 830–832
    and cache files, 857
    and CNAME aliases, 845
    configuring, 135
    and dynamic update, 857–859
    and /etc/nsswitch.conf file,
        813–815
    and host information, 846
    and hosts.conf file, 812–813
    incremental zone transfers
        in, 856
    and IP virtual domains,
        856–857
    LAN addressing in, 828–830
    and MX (Mail Exchanger),
        844–845

DNS (*continued*)
name server addresses
for, 805
and named.conf file, 834–837
and NS (name server) record
type, 843
operation of, 827
and options statement,
837–840
overview of, 811–812, 825
and PTR (pointer)
records, 845
and resource record
types, 841
resource record types for, 841
restarting, 136
and SOA (Start of Authority),
842–843
and subdomain zones, 854
using caching-only server
with, 840
using options statement
with, 837–840
using subdomains and
slaves in, 854–856
and zone files, 846–854
DNS address translations
and DNS server, 826–827
and fully qualified domain
names, 825
and IPv4 addresses, 826
and IPv6 addressing, 826
manual translations, 826
DNS clients, use of, 827–828
DNS security methods. *See also*
security
ACLs (access control lists),
859–860
DNSSEC, 860—862
secret keys, 860
TSIG keys, 862–863
DNS servers
availability of, 830
configuring, 832–834
connecting to root servers on
Internet, 857
purpose of, 826–827
types of, 833–834
zones used by, 846
DNS settings, using with system-
config-network tool, 123
DNS space, dividing into views,
863–865
DNS zones, types of, 832–833
do keyword, using with while
loops, 223
document viewers, availability
of, 284
documentation
accessing files for, 73–74
availability of, 7–8
for Linux, 21–23

Documentation pane in GConf
configuration editor, description
of, 168
DocumentRoot directive, using with
Apache Web server, 496
dollar ($) sign
at command line prompt,
58–59
referencing arguments for
shell scripts with,
218–219
referencing variable values
with, 215
use with BASH (Bourne
again) shell, 194
using with variables, 197
domain logons, support
in Samba, 929
domain name service (DNS). *See*
DNS (Domain Name System)
domain names, entering in /etc/
hosts file, 826
domains
listing in Squid proxy
server, 518
in SELinux, 373
dot (.) command
using with .bash_profile
script, 240
using with .bashrc file, 243
dot (.) files
displaying, 90
use of, 248
Dovecot, capabilities of, 545–546
Draw program in OpenOffice,
features of, 280–281
drawers
adding to panels, 163
versus menus, 164
drawing applications
in GNOME Office, 283
in OpenOffice, 279–280
drawing applications, availability in
KOffice, 281
driver modules
checking for dependent
modules, 114
discovering parameters
for, 115
installing, 114
listing, 114
updating dependencies
for, 114
driver packages, installing modules
with, 749–750
driver releases, installation of, 107
drivers, support for, 114–115
drives, replacing with LVM, 703
DROP policy, setting up for Netfilter
firewall, 440
DROP target, denying packets with,
424, 426

DSL (Digital Subscriber Line),
configuring, 127
dual-boot systems
installing Fedora on, 30
setting up, 92
dual-head connections, configuring
for video cards, 100
dump command, operations with,
786–787
dump levels, using with system
backups, 784–786
DVD boot disk image, location
of, 35
DVD distribution images,
downloading, 635–636. *See also*
image files
DVD files, playing in Fedora, 70–71
DVD players, accessing, 303–304
dvd+rw tools, using, 691–692
dvdrecord command, using, 691
DVD::rip project, Web site for, 304
DVD-R/RW discs, copying files
to, 261
DVDs
booting Linux from, 38
burning with GNOME, 71
burning with GNOME
Volume Manager, 150
installing Fedora from, 30–31
mounting manually, 683–684
obtaining for Fedora
installation, 27–28
plug-ins required for, 81–82
recording manually, 689–692
support for, 83
Dynamic Host Configuration
Protocol (DHCP). *See* DHCP
(Dynamic Host Configuration
Protocol)
dynamic IPv4 addresses, using with
DHCP, 876–877. *See also* IPv4
addresses
Dynamic Kernel Module Support
(DKMS)
generating NTFS modules
with, 117
updating kernel modules
with, 107
dynamic update, relationship to
DNS (Domain Name System),
857–859
dynamic virtual hosting,
implementing on Apache,
504–506

E

-e option, using with rpm
command, 108
e2fsck command, using, 672
e2label, use in mounting file
systems, 678–679
echo command, using, 216

editors, features of, 288

edquota command, setting disk quotas with, 621

Eikga VoIP application, features of, 346–347

ELinks line-mode browser, features of, 329

elsels script, example of, 222–223

Emacs, Web site for, 313

Emacs command line editor, using with BASH (Bourne again) shell, 200

Emacs editor
features of, 289–290
use of keyboard with, 291

Emacs mail clients, features of, 313

emblems, adding in Nautilus, 153

Emblems panel in Nautilus Properties box, explanation of, 157

enable and disable tools, using with CUPS (Common Unix Printing System), 558

encryption
combining with digital signatures, 357
with SSH (Secure Shell), 406–407
use of, 111

encryption (ESP) protocol, relationship to IPsec, 396

encryption payload, encrypting in IPsec connections, 399

end-user discussion support forum, accessing, 73

enigmail extension, using with Thunderbird, 358

environment component of Linux, significance of, 15

environment variables. *See also* variables
defining in shells, 231
using with cron service, 575

Epiphany Web browser, features of, 328

-eq option, using with test command, 219

equal (=) sign, using with aliases, 228

err priority, components of, 589

error messages
appearance of, 210
specifying in Sendmail, 543

error redirection symbols in BASH (Bourne again) shell, execution of, 202

esac keyword, using with case command, 221

ESP (encryption) protocol, relationship to IPsec, 396

ESP payload, encrypting in IPsec connections, 399

essid parameter, using with iwconfig Wireless Tool, 132

/etc directories, contents of, 663–664

/etc directory
contents of, 585
function of, 253

/etc/exports file for NFS configuration, contents of, 887–891

/etc/fstab file, mounting NFS directories with, 893–895

/etc/group and /etc/gshadow files, contents of, 609

/etc/hosts file
contents of, 809–810
entering IP addresses and domain names in, 826

/etc/inputrc file, running, 241

/etc/login.defs file, contents of, 604–605

/etc/mdadm.conf file, configuring RAID with, 710–711

/etc/modprobe.conf file
actions supported by, 748
managing modules with, 746

/etc/named/chroot director, contents of, 834

/etc/passwd file, fields in, 602

/etc/profile file
adding software directories to, 657
significance of, 241

/etc/protocols file, contents of, 811

/etc/rc.d system startup file, initialization files in, 451

/etc/rc.d/init.d directory
purpose of, 452–455
service scripts in, 453

/etc/rc.d/initd.iptables script, using, 435–436

/etc/rc.d/init.d/network directory, contents of, 815

/etc/services file, contents of, 811

/etc/shadow and /etc/gshadow files, using, 603

/etc/skel directory, contents of, 604

/etc/slapd.conf file, using, 623–624

/etc/sysconfig directory, contents of, 587

/etc/sysconfig startup file, description of, 452

/etc/sysconfig/hwconf file, contents of, 720–721

/etc/sysconfig/iptables script, using, 434–435

/etc/sysconfig/iptables-config script, using, 435–436

/etc/sysconfig/network file, contents of, 811

/etc/sysconfig/networking file, contents of, 810–811

/etc/sysconfig/network-scripts file, contents of, 810, 816

/etc/syslog.conf, example of, 591–592

/etc/systemconfig/network-scripts directory, contents of, 128–129

/etc/wvdial.conf file, example of, 129–130

/etc/X11/xorg.conf file, purpose of, 100

/etc/xinetd.d directory, contents of, 469

/etc/yum.conf file, contents of, 639

/etc/yum.repos.d file, contents of, 639–640

Ethernet cards, configuring with system-config-network tool, 126

Ethernet devices, troubleshooting connections with, 124

Ettercap sniffer program, using, 821

EUID system environment variable, description of, 233

events
checking /var/log/messages file for, 367
editing in BASH (Bourne again) shell, 200–201
referencing in BASH (Bourne again) shell, 200

Evince document viewer, description of, 284

Evolution mail client
features of, 309–310
using with GNOME desktop, 311–312

-exec option, using with find command, 260

exec SSI element, use of, 507

execute permissions, using, 612

EXINIT system environment variable, description of, 232

exit command, returning to user login with, 571

export command, using with environment variables, 231, 238, 240

ext3 journaling, 673–674

extensions for files, selecting in BASH (Bourne again) shell, 203

extract command, using with backups, 787

F

F keys. *See* keyboard shortcuts

Faces images, changing, 66

FancyIndexing directive, using with Apache Web server, 500

FAQ with help topics, accessing, 73

fc command option, using in BASH (Bourne again) shell, 200–201

.fc policy configuration files, using in SELinux, 387–388

FCEDIT system environment variable, description of, 232

fd file system type, using with hard
    disk partitions, 710
fd partition type, using
    with RAID, 708
fdisk commands
    partitioning hard disks with,
        686–687
    using, 672
    using with hard drives,
        684–685
FEATURE macro, using with
    Sendmail, 534, 536–537
Fedora
    adding new users on, 93–94
    administration tools for,
        90–91, 583–584
    availability of, 6
    boot source options for,
        34–35
    booting to, 599
    documentation for, 7–8
    downloading, 6
    enabling and disabling write
        support for, 17–18
    FTP site for, 6
    hardware requirements for, 32
    install methods for, 35
    installation procedures for,
        29–30
    installing from CDs or
        DVDs, 30–31
    installing sources and
        configurations for, 29
    multimedia applications
        available for, 104
    network configuration tools
        for, 120
    network servers and security
        available on, 20
    playing MP3, DVD, and
        DivX files in, 70
    updates in, 5
    updating, 17, 102–103
    Web sites related to, 8, 75, 104
Fedora 7, features of, 9–11
Fedora BitTorrent files, location of, 28
Fedora CD/DVD-ROM ISO images,
    downloading, 103
Fedora Community Portal,
    accessing, 73
Fedora core SRPM, installing kernel
    sources with, 759–762
Fedora depository, checking for
    software, 3–4
Fedora desktop, features of, 60,
    140–141. See also desktops
Fedora desktop spins, performing
    minimal installs with, 26
Fedora documentation, accessing
    online, 73
Fedora download site, accessing, 27
Fedora Extras repository, features
    of, 79
Fedora FAQ, Web site for, 8

Fedora GNOME interface, panels
    in, 145
Fedora install spins, creating with
    Pungi, 50–55
Fedora Installation
    accessing guide for, 25, 28
    features of, 25–26
    minimal install strategies for,
        26–27
Fedora Live CD
    contents of, 11–12
    performing minimum install
        with, 26
Fedora network tools. See also
    networks
    features of, 122
    system-config-network,
        123–126
Fedora news and developments,
    accessing information about, 73
Fedora packages
    downloading, 79
    updating with Yum, 638
Fedora Portal page, Web address
    for, 21
Fedora Project
    explanation of, 5–6
    Web site for, 8, 73
Fedora repo file, contents of, 640
Fedora repositories, features of, 79
Fedora Re-Spin disks, installing and
    updating with, 102
Fedora Software Manager,
    accessing, 45
Fedora software repositories. See
    also repositories
    completing installations
        with, 76–77
    features of, 75–76
    Freshrpms, 80–81
    Livna, 79–80
    Pirut, 77
    yumex Yum Extender, 77–79
Fedora system administration tools,
    accessing in KDE, 173–174
Fedora User Manager, features of,
    93–94
Fetchmail, using, 317
FFmpeg, downloading and
    installing, 83
fg command
    bringing jobs to foreground
        with, 213
    using with lftp client, 341
fglrx, using with ATI drivers, 101
fgrep, searching files with, 225
FHS (File System Hierarchy
    Standard), adherence of Linux
    to, 15
FHS components
    device files, 668–671
    /home directory, 666
    /media directory, 665
    /mnt directory, 666

/proc file system, 666
root directory (/),
    662–663
/sys sysfs file system,
    666–667
system directories, 664
/usr directory, 665
/var directory, 666
fi keyword, using with if-then
    command, 221
Figures
    About Me information, 68
    Add New Device Type
        window, 126
    Beagle search, 68
    CIDR addressing, 800
    class-based and CIDR
        broadcast addressing, 803
    class-based netmask
        operations, 799
    DNS server and network, 829
    DNS server operation, 827
    Fedora GNOME desktop, 60
    Fedora User Manager, 93
    file information displayed
        using -l option with ls
        command, 249
    file manager in GNOME
        desktop, 62
    file properties in Nautilus, 158
    File Roller, 267
    file structure with root
        directory, 250
    firewall rules applied to local
        network, 439
    Font Preferences dialog, 67
    GConf editor, 168
    Gedit text editor and
        configuration files, 92
    GNOME applets, 65
    GNOME panel, 159
    GNOME System Monitor, 594
    GNOME themes, 166
    GNOME Volume
        Manager, 149
    GNOME with Preferences
        menu, 144
    IPsec on system-config-
        network, 398
    KDE Control Center, 189
    KDE desktop, 174
    KDE file manager, 183
    KDE panel (Kicker), 180
    Kerberos authentication, 416
    Konqueror Configure
        window, 188
    logical volume, 697
    Logical Volume Manager
        GUI, 696
    logical volume using
        multiple partitions on
        different hard drives, 704
    logical volumes with system-
        config-lvm, 702

LVM with two hard drives, 701
Nautilus window in Browser view, 152
Nautilus window in Spatial view, 151
network with firewall, 438
New Printer Select Connection dialog, 96
OpenOffice.org's Writer word processor, 280
Panel Add To box in GNOME, 160
panel with Workspace Switcher and Window List, 160
pathnames, 251–252
Pirut Package Manager, 105
printer model for new printers, 97
Printer Options panel, 97
public-key encryption and digital signatures, 357
RAID devices, 716
removable devices, Computer folder, and shared network folders, 69
router renumbering with IPv6 autoconfiguration, 870
SSH setup and access, 409
stateless IPv6 address autoconfiguration, 869
system resources access from file manager in KDE, 177
system-config network DNS panel, 124
system-config-date utility, 573
system-config-display Display settings window, 99
system-config-network device configuration, 125
system-config-network Network Configuration window, 123
system-config-printer tool, 95
system-config-securitylevel tool, 134
system-config-selinux, 378–379
system-config-services tool, 458
Virtual Machine Manager (virt-manager), 770
Yum Extender group view, 78
file command, using, 249
file contexts policy rule, managing in SELinux, 386
file expansion symbols in BASH (Bourne again) shell, execution of, 202

file extensions, identifying, 635
file interface files, managing in SELinux, 390
File Manager in GNOME 2.x, features of, 143
file manager windows. *See also* Konqueror
    accessing KDE Control Center entries from, 190
    opening, 69
    opening in GNOME desktop, 61
    opening in KDE (K Desktop Environment), 176–177
file operations, execution of, 261
file properties
    displaying in Konqueror, 187
    viewing in Nautilus file manager, 157–158
File Roller application
    archiving and compressing files with, 266–267
    starting, 272
file sharing, setting up on Linux systems, 85
file sizes
    listing in blocks, 228
    using human-readable format for, 229
file structure of Linux, explanation of, 15
file system and partition creation tools, descriptions of, 685
file system directories, functions of, 663
file system hierarchy standard (FHS), adherence of Linux to, 15
File System view in Nautilus, explanation of, 152
file systems
    accessing, 69–70
    accessing with GNOME Volume Manager, 149–150
    adding RAID file systems, 709–710
    checking consistency of, 672
    creating, 684–689
    creating for RAID, 712–713
    creating on CD-ROMs, 685
    creating on partitions, 685
    determining amount of space on, 671–672
    exporting manually, 890–891
    getting information about, 671–672
    mounting, 668
    mounting automatically, 674–680
    organization of files in, 662
    repairing, 672
    types of, 675–676
    using mkfs command with, 687–688

file test operators, functions of, 220
filenames, using wildcard characters with, 261
filenames in BASH (Bourne again) shell
    referencing, 205
    special characters for, 201–202
files. *See also* Linux files; Web file types
    adding to panels, 163
    archiving and compressing, 266–267
    changing owners and groups for, 614–615
    compressing, 272–274
    copying, 259–262
    copying and moving in Konqueror, 187
    copying between hosts, 412–413
    copying in Nautilus file manager, 155
    copying to GNOME desktop, 147
    creating multiple names for, 263–265
    creating on KDE desktop, 176
    decompressing with gzip, 272
    deleting in Konqueror, 187
    displaying, 254
    displaying contents of, 73, 252
    erasing, 263
    erasing with rm command and asterisk (*), 203
    examining byte by byte, 249
    grouping in Nautilus file manager, 156
    listing, displaying, and printing, 253
    managing in Nautilus file manager, 154–156
    moving, 262
    opening in Konqueror, 184
    organization of, 15
    ownership of, 614
    printing, 254
    reinstalling, 49
    renaming in Konqueror, 187
    renaming in Nautilus file manager, 155–156
    searching in Konqueror, 185
    searching with Beagle, 67–69
    searching with grep and fgrep, 225
    selecting in Konqueror, 187
    viewing, 49
files with extensions, selecting in BASH (Bourne again) shell, 203
files with hard links, erasing, 265
files with symbolic links, erasing, 264
filters
    using in BASH (Bourne again) shell, 224
    using with commands, 209

finance application, availability in GNOME Office, 283
find command
 effect of, 257
 options for, 260
 searching directories with, 258–259
 using -name option with, 258
 using -print option with, 258
 using -type option with, 259
finger network tool, features of, 345
Firefox FTP client, features of, 334
Firefox Web browser
 enabling JRE (Java Runtime Environment) for, 331
 features of, 326–328
firewall chains, use by kernel, 423
Firewall Configuration screen, options on, 47
firewalls. *See also* Netfilter firewalls
 allowing access to, 441
 creating user-defined rules for, 443–444
 illustration of, 438
 implementing, 113
 setting up with system-config-securitylevel tool, 133–134
 use of, 111, 419–420
fixfiles command
 relabeling in SELinux with, 374
 setting security contexts with, 392
Flagship compiler
 features of, 287–288
 Web site for, 285
Flask architecture, relationship to SELinux, 370–371
Flickr Web site, address for, 296
floppy disks
 accessing, 183
 archiving to, 270
 device name for, 670
 mounting manually, 682–683
flow chart generator, availability in KOffice, 281
folders
 adding to panels, 163–164
 creating in Nautilus, 153
 creating on KDE desktop, 176
 opening as tabs in Konqueror, 184
font sizes, setting, 66
for control structure, function of, 222
for structure, using with while loops, 223–224
Force Address variable, using with wvdial, 130
for-in structure, using with while loops, 223

FormatLog directive, using with Apache Web server, 502
FORWARD chains
 defining user chains for, 443
 use by kernel, 423
 using with IPtables, 427
frag parameter, using with iwconfig Wireless Tool, 132
free command, using, 595
freeciv package, listing files in, 108
-freeciv-2.0.8-7.tar.bz2 file, meaning of, 110
freq parameter, using with iwconfig Wireless Tool, 132
Freshrpms repository
 features of, 80–81
 Web site for, 4
freshrpms.rep file, contents of, 641
Frysk monitoring tool, features of, 595
fsck command, using, 672
F-Spot Photo Manager, features of, 295–296
fstab entry, using with NTFS Project read-only access, 116
fstab file
 adding file systems to, 674
 example of, 677
 fields in, 675–676
 integer values in, 677
FTP access, allowing anonymous FTP access, 476–477
FTP browser, using Nautilus file manager as, 159
FTP clients
 comparing smbclient utility to, 930–931
 curl, 335–336
 features of, 332–333
 Firefox, 334
 gFTP, 335
 Konqueror, 334
 lftp program, 341
 Nautilus, 334–335
 NcFTP, 342
 network file transfer, 333–334
 wget, 335
ftp configuration file, .netrc file in, 339–341
ftp downloads, resuming with regret command, 338
FTP (File Transfer Protocol), accessing with Konqueror, 187–188
FTP files secured by encryption, transferring, 413
ftp program
 commands for, 337
 features of, 336–339
FTP server directories, creating, 474–475

FTP server software, components of, 473
FTP servers
 availability of, 474
 configuring for rsync, 478–479
 Web resources for, 474
ftp sessions, ending, 338
FTP sites
 accessing, 339
 accessing with rsync, 478
 components of, 475
FTP users
 access available to, 475
 creating, 476
fully qualified domain names, relationship to DNS, 825

G

Galeon Web browser, features of, 328
gateway addresses, using, 804
gateway connections, configuring with racoon, 404
gateways, encrypting, 403–404
GATOS (General ATI TV and Overlay Sofware), Web site for, 743
GCConf configuration editor
 features of, 166–167
 panes in, 168
gconfig (gkc) kernel configuration tool, using, 762
GDM (GNOME Display Manager), features of, 56–57
Gedit desktop editor
 description of, 288
 features of, 289
 using with configuration files, 90
get command
 using with ftp program, 338
 using with lftp client, 341
 using with NcFTP client, 342
getty program, managing terminal devices with, 741
GFS (Global File System)
 features of, 903–904
 references for, 904
 tools, daemons, and service scripts for, 907
GFS 1 packages, using, 908
GFS 2 file systems, implementing, 905–906
GFS 2 packages, using, 905
GFS 2 service scripts, using, 905
GFS clusters, configuring and managing, 904
GFS file system operations, performing, 906–908
GFS tools, using, 906
gFTP client, features of, 335

-gid option, using with find
command, 260
GIF images, MIME type for, 191
GIMP (GNU Image Manipulation
Program), features of, 297
GKrellM monitors, features of,
596–597
Global File System (GFS)
features of, 903–904
references for, 904
GNOME 2.x features
File Manager, 143
overview of, 141–143
GNOME applets. *See also* applets
adding, 164
features of, 65
Window List, 165
Workspace Switcher, 165
GNOME applications
compatibility with iPods, 301
configuring, 167
using GTK+ widget set with,
143–144
GNOME binaries, location of, 166
GNOME CD Player, using, 301
GNOME configuration directories,
contents of, 167
GNOME Control Center,
organization of, 140–141
GNOME desktop. *See also* desktops
accessing Windows Samba
shares from, 930–932
advisory about removing
icons from, 147
applications on, 147–148
burning CDs and DVDs
with, 71
CD burners and rippers for,
302
components of, 139, 145
configuring, 165–166
configuring keyboard
shortcuts in, 64
copying files to, 147
creating links between files
in, 147
displaying with themes, 145
downloading source code
for, 139
dragging and dropping files
to, 146–147
features of, 15–16
File Management
configuration in, 64
graphics tools for, 297–298
versus KDE (K Desktop
Environment), 59–60
mail clients for, 311–312
MIME associations on, 309
Mouse and Keyboard
preferences in, 64
moving windows in, 62
multimedia support for, 298

obtaining applications
for, 634
opening file manager
window in, 61
panels and menus in, 61
permissions on, 612
preferences in, 63–65
quitting, 62, 146
resources for, 140
setting volume control in,
64–65
sound configurations in,
64–65
starting programs in, 145
user directories in, 166
using browser view in, 62
using Gedit editor with, 289
using PDAs on, 284–285
using with window
managers, 148–149
Web site for, 3
Windows configuration in, 64
GNOME desktop Live CD,
creating, 12
GNOME desktop menu, items
on, 148
GNOME developers, Web site for, 21
GNOME Display Manager (GDM),
features of, 56–57
GNOME Help browser, description
of, 74, 146
GNOME interface
Applications menu in, 144
configuring, 165–166
menus in, 144
panels in, 145
GNOME libraries, location of, 166
GNOME multimedia applications,
Web site for, 296
GNOME Office
downloading, 283
features of, 282–283
Web site for, 277
GNOME panels. *See* panels
GNOME Power Manager, features
of, 595–596
GNOME System Log Viewer,
accessing, 588
GNOME System Monitor, features
of, 594
GNOME Volume Manager, features
of, 149–150
GNOME-DB database connectivity
program, features of, 282–283
gnome-nettool, features of, 343
GNU Emacs editor, features of,
288–289
GNU General Public License (GPL),
explanation of, 4, 16–17
GNU Image Manipulation Program
(GIMP), features of, 297
GNU info pages, accessing, 73
GNU software, explanation of, 16

GNU SQL database management
system
features of, 287
Web site for, 285
GnuCash finance application,
features of, 283
gnumeric package, updating, 637
Gnumeric spreadsheet
features of, 282–283
installing, 79
GNUPro development tools, Web
site for, 5
GPG (GNU Privacy Guard). *See also*
security
commands and options for,
359–360
decrypting digital signatures
with, 364
decrypting messages with,
363–364
encrypting messages
with, 363
features of, 358
generating private and
public keys for, 358
making public keys available
in, 360–361
obtaining public keys with,
361–362
protecting keys in, 360
signing messages with, 364
using, 109, 112, 363
validating keys with, 362
gpg command, using with
GnuPG, 358
GPG key, installing manually, 80
gpgcheck option, relevance to
repository configuration files, 109
gPhoto project, Web site for, 297
GPL (GNU General Public License),
explanation of, 16–17
Grand Unified Bootloader (GRUB).
See GRUB (Grand Unified
Bootloader)
graphic programs, availability for X
Window System, 297
graphic projects, Web site for, 295
graphical logins, handling of, 56–57
graphics drivers, obtaining, 76
graphics programs, availability in
KOffice, 281
graphics tools
availability of, 298
for GNOME, 297
for KDE, 297
for photo management,
295–296
greater-than sign (>), use with Mail
utility, 315
grep, searching files with, 225
Greylisting Policy Server in Postfix,
features of, 528
group directories, using, 610

group name, specifying for sudo
command, 572
-group option, using with find
command, 260
groupadd and groupdel commands,
using, 611
groupmod command, using, 611
groups
adding, modifying, and
deleting, 610–611
changing for files,
614–615
managing, 609–611
managing with system-
config-users, 610
ownership of files and
directories by, 614
GROUPS shell variable, description
of, 232
growisofs dvd+rw tool, using,
691–692
GRUB (Grand Unified Bootloader)
displaying after rebooting,
46–47
features of, 597–600
installing, 43
reinstalling, 50
using, 767–768
grub.conf file, example of, 600
GStreamer framework
features of, 299–300
MP3 compatibility of, 301
Multimedia Systems Selector
component of, 300
plug-ins for, 81–82, 300
.gtckrc file in GNOME, explanation
of, 166
GTK kernel configuration tool,
using, 762
GTK+ widget set, using with
GNOME applications,
143–144
GUI interface
forcing exit from, 57
starting from command
line, 66
GUI-based Fedora tools,
accessing, 90
gunzip utility, decompressing files
with, 652
gv document viewer, description
of, 284
gvim desktop editor
description of, 288
using as alternative to
Vim, 294
gzip utility
compressing files with,
272–273
options for, 273
using with compressed files,
270–271, 652

H

\h shell prompt code, description
of, 237
HAL (Hardware Abstract Layer)
configuring, 733
managing removable devices
with, 674
purpose of, 732
relationship to udev, 670
HAL callouts, using, 737
HAL connections, using with
printers, 96
HAL daemon, using, 733
HAL storage policies, descriptions
of, 735
halt command, shutting down
system with, 49, 59
halt file, contents of, 451
hard disk partitions, creating, 710
hard drive, configuring for Linux, 33
hard drive names, determining for
NTFS partitions, 116
hard drive partitions
mounting manually, 684
separating for RAID devices,
715–716
hard drives
LVM example for, 700–703
partitioning, 685
partitioning with fdisk
command, 686–687
prefix for, 670
hard links
erasing, 265
support for, 263
Hardware Abstract Layer (HAL),
managing removable devices
with, 674
hardware configuration, registering
with Fedora Project, 48
hardware detection, installing, 39
hardware devices, installation
of, 720
hardware RAID support,
availability of, 705–706
hardware requirements, for Linux
installation, 32
hardware virtualization,
implementing, 771–772
HDTV reception, using PCHDTV
video card for, 303
header files for KDE applications,
system KDE directory for, 192
Help Center in KDE, features of, 181
help resources
application documentation,
73
context-sensitive help, 73
Info pages, 75
Man pages, 73
hidden files, displaying in
Konqueror, 184

hiddenmenu option in GRUB,
using, 598
Hiding pane, using in KDE panel
(Kicker), 181
HINFO records, using, 846
HISTCMD shell variable,
description of, 232
HISTFILE system environment
variable, description of, 232–233
history events, editing in BASH
(Bourne again) shell, 200–201
history lists, keeping with BASH
(Bourne again) shell, 197
history utility in BASH (Bourne
again) shell, using, 198–200
HISTSAVE variable, configuring in
BASH (Bourne again) shell, 201
HISTSIZE system environment
variable
configuring in BASH
(Bourne again) shell, 201
description of, 232
/home directory
contents of, 663–664, 666
function of, 253
listing configuration files
in, 245
listing files in, 253–254
locating pathname of,
234–235
name of, 250
searching, 239
HOME shell variable
description of, 232
using, 234–235
host address, form in mail address,
524–525
host names, using @ (at) sign
with, 197
host network tool, features of, 345
HOSTFILE system environment
variable, description of, 232
HOSTNAME shell variable,
description of, 232
hostnames
use in mail addresses,
524–525
use with URL addresses, 324
hosts
adding principals for, 418
copying files between,
412–413
IP masquerading of, 447
masquerading in Sendmail,
538–539
receipt of encrypted IPsec
transmissions by, 400
Hosts panel, using with system-
config-network tool, 123–124
hosts with shared directories,
listing, 69
hosts.allow file, contents of, 472

hosts.conf file, relationship to DNS (domain name service), 812–813
HOSTTYPE system environment variable, description of, 232–233
hotplugged devices, explanation of, 722
.htaccess file, using with Apache Web server, 492
http_access options, ordering in Squid proxy server, 518
HTTP/1.1 protocol, using with Apache virtual hosting, 503
httpd daemon, calling for Apache Web server, 492
httpd service script, using, 461–462
httpd.conf configuration file, contents of, 492
hypertext database, components of, 323

-i option, using with rm, cp, and mv commands, 229
-I option, using with rpm command, 108
IANA, allocation of IP addresses by, 802
ICMP (Internet Control Message Protocol) packets, using, 427–428
ICMP packets, controlling, 442
Icon view in Nautilus, explanation of, 153
ICP (Internet Cache Protocol), using with Squid proxy server, 519
ICQ protocol, features of, 347
IDE hard drives, prefix for, 670
identities in SELinux, purpose of, 373
if condition, using, 221–222
ifcfg-eth0 file, example of, 129
ifconfig command, using, 815, 817–818
ifdown script, using, 816
IFS system environment variable, description of, 232
if-then command, using fi keyword with, 221
ifup script, using, 816
ignoreeof feature, using, 230
IGNOREEOF system environment variable, description of, 232
IKE (IPsec Key Exchange) protocol, using, 401
image files, downloading for Fedora installation, 28. See also DVD distribution images; ISO distribution images
IMAP (Internet Mail Access Protocol), capabilities of, 544–545
IMAP and POP servers, availability of, 546

IN-ADDR.ARPA reverse mapping format, using in IPv4, 850–851
include directories, use with GNOME, 166
Indexes directive, using with Apache Web server, 497
InfiniBand, support for, 134–135
Info pages, accessing, 75
Informix database management system
    features of, 286–287
    Web site for, 285
Inherits variable, using with wvdial, 130
init script functions, descriptions of, 462
Init1...Init9 variable, using with wvdial, 130
initab, runlevels in, 580
initialization files
    use of, 248
    using with shell parameter variables, 234
initrd.img file, booting from, 35
inittab files, components of, 741
INN (InterNetNews) news server
    configuration files for, 559–560
    features of, 559
    implementing, 561
    inn.conf file for, 560
    storage formats for, 560
    support for overviews in, 560–561
    Web site for, 558
INPUT chains
    defining user chains for, 443
    use by kernel, 423
    using with IPtables, 427
input devices, displaying, 742
INPUTRC system environment variable, description of, 233
install directory, selecting, 653
install guides. See also Linux installation
    for Fedora, 25
    for Red Hat Enterprise, 25
install sources, selecting
    for Fedora, 29
Install to Hard Drive process, starting for Fedora, 27
installation
    automating with kickstart, 36–37
    from command line, 644–651
    finishing, 46–48
installation process, completing with repositories, 76–77
installation program, starting for Linux, 38
installed software, querying information from, 647–648

Instant Messenger (AOL), features of, 347
integer comparisons, functions of, 220
integrity checks
    tools for, 367
    use of, 111, 356–357
interface configuration scripts
    network configurations saved in, 128–129
    using, 816
Internet Cache Protocol (ICP), using with Squid proxy server, 519
Internet Control Message Protocol (ICMP) packets, using, 427–428
Internet Mail Access Protocol (IMAP), capabilities of, 544–545
Internet Mail Consortium, Web site for, 309
Internet Protocol Security (IPsec)
    description of and Web site for, 112
    features of, 113
Internet Relay Chat (IRC), features of, 347
Internet resources, accessing with URLs, 324
Internet Security Protocol (IPsec). See IPsec (Internet Security Protocol)
Internet zones, zone files for, 846–865
interpolated strings, support in Apache, 505–506
intrusion detection
    tools for, 367
    use of, 111
I/O architecture, InfiniBand as, 134–135
iostat command, using, 595
IP addresses
    and Apache Web server, 506
    assigning with ifconfig command, 817–818
    association with fully qualified domain names, 825
    entering in /etc/hosts file, 826
    obtaining, 120–121, 802–804
    specification of, 404
    specifying, 426
    translating for DNS, 825–828
    using static IP addresses with wireless connections, 128
IP aliasing, using, 824
IP forwarding, turning on, 447
IP masquerading. See also masquerading
    implementing, 445–446
    of local networks, 446
    of NAT rules, 446
    of selected hosts, 447

IP Payload Compression Protocol (IPComp), relationship to IPsec, 396
IP spoofing, protecting private networks from, 440–441
IP virtual domains, relationship to DNS (Domain Name System), 856–857
IP6.ARPA reverse mapping format, using in DNS, 851–852
IP6.INT reverse mapping format, using in DNS, 852
ip6tables, support for, 437
ip6tables package, using with Netfilter firewalls, 421
IP-based virtual hosting, implementing on Apache, 503
IPComp (IP Payload Compression Protocol), relationship to IPsec, 396
iPods, compatibility with GNOME applications, 301
IPsec (Internet Security Protocol). *See also* security
        configuring with racoon (IKE), 401–403
        configuring with system-config-network, 397–398
        description of and Web site for, 112
        features of, 113
        net traversal in, 403
        overview of, 395
        resources for, 396
        setting up VPNs with, 128
IPsec connections
        configuring with setkey, 399–401
        setting up secure two-transmissions for, 400–401
IPsec Key Exchange (IKE) protocol, using, 401
IPsec keys, implementation of, 401
IPsec modes, overview of, 396
IPsec packets, passing, 403
IPsec protocols, explanations of, 396
IPsec security databases, overview of, 397
IPsec tools, availability of, 397
IPsec transmissions, receipt by hosts, 400
IPsec tunnel mode, using with VPNs, 403–404
IPtables
        enabling to pass IPsec packets, 403
        options for, 424–426
        support for, 434
        targets for, 422
        using connection tracking modules with, 430–431
        using FORWARD and INPUT chains with, 427

IPtables commands
        chain names in, 422
        functions of, 424
        using with Netfilter firewalls, 420–422
IP-tables file, loading for firewalls, 134
iptables options, listing, 442–443
IPtables package, contents of, 421
IPtables rules
        applying, 426
        saving, 436–437
        using, 434–435
        using inverse of, 426
IPtables scripts, example of, 437–445
iptables service scripts
        /etc/rc.d/initd.iptables, 435–436
        /etc/sysconfig/iptables, 434–435
        /etc/sysconfig/iptables-config, 435–436
        features of, 433–434
iptables-config, configuration parameters for, 435
IPv4, using with LAN addressing, 829–830. IPv4. *See also* DHCP
IPv4 client hosts
        IPv4 addresses, implementing, 826. *See also* dynamic IPv4 addresses
IPv4 and IPv6
        coexistence methods for, 808
        support for, 44, 794
IPv4 CIDR addressing, overview of, 801–802
IPv4 CIDR network masks, forms of, 800
IPv4 example IPtables script, 437–445
IPv4 IN-ADDR.ARPA reverse mapping format, using, 850–851
IPv4 localhost reverse mapping, using in DNS, 853
IPv4 named.conf example, 838–839
IPv4 network addresses, components of, 797
IPv4 private networks, relationship to LAN addressing, 828
IPv4 reserved addresses, overview of, 803–804
IPv6
        advantages of, 796
        support for, 119
IPv6 addressing
        format of, 805–806
        implementing, 826
        interface identifiers for, 806
        types of, 806–808
IPv6 CIDR addressing, overview of, 802
IPv6 localhost reverse mapping, using in DNS, 853–854

IPv6 named.conf example, 839–840
IPv6 private networks, relationship to LAN addressing, 828–829
IPv6 router, Linux as, 871
IPv6 stateful autoconfiguration, performing with DHCPv6, 870–871
IPv6 stateless autoconfiguration tasks
        generating full address, 867
        generating local address, 867
        router renumbering, 867–868
IPv6 zone file example, 850
IRC (Internet Relay Chat), features of, 347
ismod command, loading modules with, 747
ISO distribution images, downloading, 635–636. *See also* image files
ISO images
        downloading, 103
        using with Fedora installations, 28
ISP connections, configuring Sendmail workstations for, 541
iwconfig Wireless Tool
        description of, 131
        features of, 131–132
        parameters used with, 132
iwlist Wireless Tool
        description of, 131
        features of, 133
iwpriv Wireless Tool
        description of, 131
        features of, 132
iwspy Wireless Tool
        description of, 131
        features of, 133

J

Jakarta project, Web site for, 332
Java 2 SDK (Software Development Kit), features of, 332
Java applications
        availability of, 332
        downloading, 83–84
        and Web applications, 330
Java Runtime Environment (JRE)
        enabling for Mozilla/Firefox, 331
        installing, 331
job management operations in BASH (Bourne again) shell, execution of, 211
job notification in BASH (Bourne again) shell, implementing, 212–213
jobs command
        versus ps command, 214
        using with lftp client, 341

jobs in BASH (Bourne again) shell.
See also BASH (Bourne again)
shell
bringing to foreground, 213
cancelling, 213
referencing, 212
running in background, 212
suspending and stopping,
213–214
journal files and DHCP, using in
DNS (Domain Name System),
857–859
journaling, 673–674
JPackage, downloading Java and
Java applications from, 331
JPackage Project, Web site for, 332
Jpackage rep file, contents of, 641
J-Pilot application, using with
PDAs, 285
JRE (Java Runtime Environment)
enabling for Mozilla/Firefox,
331
installing, 331

K

K Desktop editors, using, 289
K Desktop Environment (KDE),
significance of, 15–16
-K option, using with rpm
command, 108–109
.k5login, obtaining remote access
permission with, 350–351
KAME project, Web site for, 395
Kate desktop editor, features of,
288–289
KDE (K Desktop Environment). *See
also* desktops
accessing applications
from, 182
accessing Fedora system
administration tools
in, 173
accessing home directory
in, 176
accessing system resources
from file manager in,
176–177
Active Desktop Borders
feature in, 180
application desktop links
in, 182
application standard links
in, 182
changing settings for, 175
configuration and
administration access
with, 173–174
configuring, 177–178
creating directories on, 176
creating folders and files
on, 176
displaying selected
directories in, 183

enabling device icon display
in, 175
features of, 65
versus GNOME desktop,
59–60
graphics tools for, 297–298
installation directories
for, 191
link files on, 178
mail client for, 312
menus in, 175
MIME associations on, 309
mounting devices from, 183
multimedia support for, 298
navigating, 179
overview of, 171–172
Qt library used by, 173
quitting, 175–176
selecting themes for, 178
significance of, 15–16
starting applications in, 181
Web site for, 172
KDE applications
accessing, 175
downloading, 635
KDE components category, options
in, 190
KDE configurations, accessing, 174
KDE Control Center
accessing entries in, 190
description of, 173
panes in, 189–190
setting up MIME types
with, 190
KDE Desktop Pager, features of,
179–180
KDE developers library, Web site
for, 21
.kde directory, contents of, 191
KDE file manager. *See* Konqueror
KDE Help Center, features of,
74, 181
KDE Help system, system KDE
directory for, 192
KDE interface, configuring behavior
of, 190
KDE libraries, system KDE
directory for, 192
KDE links files, location of, 190
KDE main menu, keyboard shortcut
for, 175
KDE menu, creating desktop files
on desktop in, 182
KDE multimedia applications, Web
site for, 296
KDE panel (Kicker), features of,
180–181. *See also* panels
KDE programs, system KDE
directory for, 192
KDE Web Dev, Web site for, 329
KDE windows. *See also* windows
configuring appearance and
operation of, 179
functionality of, 178

minimizing, maximizing,
and closing, 179
switching to, 179
KDEDIR system environment
variable, description of, 233
kdenetworkmanager, starting, 121
kdestroy command, destroying
tickets with, 417
KDiskFree, using, 671
KDVI document viewer, description
of, 284
KEdit desktop editor
description of, 288
features of, 289
KeepAlive directive, using with
Apache Web server, 494
KeepAliveTimeout directive, using
with Apache Web server, 494
Kerberized services, setting up, 417
Kerberos application, description of
and Web site for, 112
Kerberos authentication
managing passwords in, 416
overview of, 414–415
process of, 416–417
viewing tickets in, 415
Web resource for, 406
Kerberos servers
configuring, 417–418
using, 415
Kerberos Ticket Manager,
availability of, 415
kernel
advisory about modifying
versions of, 757–759
compiling and installing,
764–767
compiling from source code,
759–762
configuring, 760–761
definition of, 753
determining version of,
753–754
explanation of, 15
firewall chains used by, 423
installation during
updates, 103
installing modules from,
751–752
installing new version of,
755–757
placing on boot disk, 767
resource for, 754
runtime parameters for, 755
kernel configuration, features of,
762–764
kernel configuration tools, using,
761–762
kernel drivers, availability of,
106–107
kernel header files, location of,
750–751
kernel image, installing manually,
766–767

kernel interfaces, use in mounting file systems, 679–680
kernel make command, compiling options for, 765
kernel modules
  commands for, 745
  tools for, 745
  updating, 107
kernel option for GRUB, location of, 599
kernel packages
  CPU kernel package, 756
  installing, 756–757
kernel source
  building, 759–760
  installing, 760
kernel system configurations, using, 760
Kernel-based Virtualization Machine (KVM), using, 771–772
key or enc parameter, using with iwconfig Wireless Tool, 132
keyboard shortcuts
  BASH (Bourne again) shell history operations, 199
  BASH (Bourne again) shell navigation, 195
  command line editor for BASH (Bourne again) shell, 200
  command-line editing operations, 196, 198
  configuring in GNOME desktop, 64
  copying files to GNOME desktop, 147
  Emacs command line editor, 200
  for forcing exit from GUI interface, 57
  KDE main menu, 175
  for Konqueror, 186
  leaving shells, 227
  logging out of user shell, 230
  online help in Vi Editor, 293
  Run Command in KDE, 181
  suspending and stopping jobs, 213
  switching to KDE windows, 179
  user-login access, 571
keyboards, use with Vim and Emacs editors, 291
keys. See also private keys; public keys
  creating for GPG (GNU Privacy Guard), 358, 360
  creating with ssh-keygen command, 409–410
  loading in SSH (Secure Shell), 411
  protecting in GPG (GNU Privacy Guard), 360

signing in DNS security, 862
using in IPSec configuration, 401–402
using with GConf configuration editor, 167–169
validating with GPG (GNU Privacy Guard), 362
keys file, using in IPsec configuration, 398
keys imported, displaying list of, 109
keyservers
  accessing, 361
  downloading, 365
KGet tool for Konqueror, features of, 188
KGhostView document viewer, description of, 284
Kicker (KDE panel), features of, 180–181. See also panels
kickstart, automating installation with, 36–37
kill command, using with jobs, 213–214
killproc function, using with service scripts, 462
kinit command, using in Kerberos, 416
KJots desktop editor
  description of, 288
  features of, 289
klist command, viewing Kerberos tickets with, 415
KMail mail client, using with KDE, 312
Knemo network device monitor, configuring, 175
KNetworkManager, description of, 120
KOffice Suite for KDE
  applications in, 281–282
  features of, 280–281
  KParts component model in, 282
  Web site for, 277
Konqueror. See also file manager windows
  configuring, 188–189
  copy, move, delete, rename, and link operations in, 187
  displaying hidden files in, 184
  extracting tar archives in, 184
  features of, 183
  keyboard shortcuts for, 186
  navigating directories in, 186
  Navigation panel in, 185
  opening files in, 184
  searching for files in, 185
  tabbed displays in, 184
  Web and FTP access in, 187–188

Konqueror FTP client, features of, 334
Konqueror Web browser, features of, 328
Konqueror window, components of, 184
Korn shell, initialization and configuration files for, 244
KPDF document viewer, description of, 284
KPilot application, using with PDAs, 285
ksh command, description of, 228
KSysguard (KDE Task Manager and Performance Monitor), features of, 597
Kudzu tool
  hardware-device information maintained by, 720–722
  installing hardware devices with, 720
KVM (Kernel-based Virtualization Machine), using, 771–773
KWord desktop editor, description of, 288
Kyum, using instead of Pirut, 173

L

-l option, using with ls command, 194
labeling and transitions in SELinux, purpose of, 374
LAME
  downloading, 83
  playing MP3 files with, 301
LAN addressing
  example using IPv4, 829–830
  and IPv4 private networks, 828
  and IPv6 private networks, 828–829
LANs (local area networks)
  configuring with Internet services on firewall systems, 444–445
  creating firewall script for, 444
LANs (local area networks), configuring, 135–136
launchers
  creating in Nautilus file manager, 157
  relationship to panels in GNOME, 162
lcd command
  using with ftp client, 336
  using with lftp client, 341
LDAP (Lightweight Directory Access Protocol)
  clients and servers for, 622–623
  configuration files for, 622–623

description of and Web site for, 112

enabling on Thunderbird, 630

features of, 622

and NSS (Nameservice Switch) service, 629

and PAM, 629

and PAMs (Pluggable Authentication Modules), 630

support in Sendmail, 532–533

LDAP databases, records in, 624

LDAP directory database

adding records to, 628

distinguishing names in, 625–626

LDIF entries in, 626–627

schema attributes and classes in, 625

searching, 628–629

LDAP servers

configuring, 623–624

securing, 629

LDAP tools, using, 629

ldapsearch command, using, 628–629

LDIF (LDAP Interchange Format), significance of, 626–627

LDP (Linux Documentation Project)

explanation of, 21

guides and formats available in, 22

less command

effect of, 253

listing files with, 254

viewing files with, 49, 73

Lesser General Public License (LGPL), explanation of, 16

lftp client, features of, 341

LGPL (Lesser General Public License), explanation of, 16

/lib directories, contents of, 663–664

/lib/modules version directory, contents of, 745–746

/lib/modules/version/source directory, using, 750–751

libraries

development libraries, 655–656

shared and static libraries, 656

/lib/udev directory, contents of, 728

licenses, protection of open source software by, 16

licensing restrictions, being aware of, 72

lighthttpd Web server, Web site for, 488

Lightweight Directory Access Protocol (LDAP). *See* LDAP (Lightweight Directory Access Protocol)

Limit directive, using with Apache Web server, 497

line-mode browsers, features of, 328–329

lines, referencing with special characters, 226

link files, using in KDE (K Desktop Environment), 178

links

creating between files in GNOME desktop, 147

creating on KDE desktop, 176

support for, 263–265

Linux. *See also* Red Hat Enterprise Linux

accessing from command line interface, 58

components of, 3, 15

development of, 3

documentation for, 21–23

enabling temporarily, 116

features of, 3–4

hard-drive configuration for, 33

history of, 14–15

initial setup for, 39

installing hardware detection for, 39

Internet clients and servers for, 19–20

logging into, 58

open source applications available for, 3

as open source software, 16–17

and operating systems, 12–13

organization of files in, 15

setting up Windows software on, 85–87

shutting down and rebooting, 59

shutting down from command line, 59

starting installation program for, 38

as version of Unix, 13

Linux commands, format for, 72

Linux compilers and tools, Web site for, 21

Linux Documentation Project (LDP)

explanation of, 21

guides and formats available in, 22

Linux file structure

home directories, 250–251

pathnames, 251–252

system directories, 252

Linux file system, formatting, 183

Linux files. *See also* files

byte-stream format of, 249

displaying detailed information about, 248–249

including extensions with, 248

initialization files used with, 248

naming, 248

types of, 249

Linux Foundation, Web site for, 8, 15

Linux installation. *See also* install guides

custom and review partitioning options for, 40–43

hardware requirements for, 32

information requirements for, 33

partition, RAID, and logical volume options for, 39

processes involved in, 37–38

Linux kernel interfaces, use in mounting file systems, 679–680

Linux programming, Web sites related to, 21

Linux software

availability of, 17

downloading, 17, 634

Fedora software repositories, 17–18

RAID levels for, 706–708

third-party repositories for, 18–19

Web sites for, 104

Linux systems

accessing, 56–59

setting up file sharing on, 85

shutting down, 57

Linux Usenet newsgroups, accessing, 23

linux-wlan project, wireless drivers available from, 133

List Columns preferences, setting in Nautilus file manager, 159

Live CD. *See* Fedora Live CD

livecd-creator, creating Fedora Live CD with, 11

Livna

enabling temporarily, 101

precompiled kernel modules from, 106–107

using for NTFS Project read-only access, 116

Livna repository

features of, 80

Web site for, 4

Livna versions, using with vendor graphics drivers, 100–101

livna.repo file, contents of, 640–641

ln command

effect of, 257, 261

-s option used with, 264

using with hard links, 265

using with symbolic links, 264

-lname option, using with find command, 260

LoadModule directive, using with Apache Web server, 494–495
local area networks (LANs)
   configuring, 135–136
   configuring with Internet services on firewall systems, 444–445
   creating firewall script for, 444
localhost reverse mapping, using in DNS, 853–854
log files, using with Apache Web server, 501–503
LogFormat directive, using with Apache Web server, 502
logged in users, identifying, 601
logging in, 58–59
logging out, 57–59
logical comparisons, functions of, 220
Logical Volume Management (LVM). *See* LVM (Logical Volume Management)
logical volumes, configuring during installation, 39
login prompt, appearance of, 48
Login Prompt variable, using with wvdial, 130
login screen, changing, 93
Login Screen, configuration tools for, 92
login shell, configuring, 238–242. *See also* shells
Login variable, using with wvdial, 130
login window, example of, 58
logins, handling of graphical logins, 56–57
LOGNAME system environment variable, description of, 233
logresolve utility, using with Apache, 502
logs
   creating for Pungi actions, 54
   displaying, 92
   keeping in Squid proxy server, 520
loop control structures
   explanation of, 219
   functions of, 222
loop control structures, using, 223–224
loopback records, using, 849
lpadmin tool, using with CUPS (Common Unix Printing System), 557
lpc client, using with CUPS (Common Unix Printing System), 555–556
lpinfo tools, using with CUPS (Common Unix Printing System), 558
lpoptions tool, using with CUPS (Common Unix Printing System), 558

lpq and lpstat clients, using with CUPS (Common Unix Printing System), 556
lpq command
   effect of, 253
   printing files with, 254
lpr client, using with CUPS (Common Unix Printing System), 555
lpr command
   effect of, 253
   explanation of, 252
   printing files with, 254
lprm client, using with CUPS (Common Unix Printing System), 556
lprm command
   effect of, 253
   printing files with, 254
LPRng (Line Printer, Next Generation), Web resource for, 550
ls command
   -a option used with, 245
   effect of, 253
   -F option used with, 228, 254, 256
   -h option used with, 229
   -l option used with, 194, 229, 248–249
   -R option used with, 254
   -s option used with, 228
-ls option, using with find command, 260
lsc shell script, executing, 217–218
lsmod command, listing modules with, 746
lvcreate command, using in LVM, 699, 702
lvextend command, using in LVM, 700
LVM (Logical Volume Management). *See also* volumes
   GUI interface for, 694–695
   replacing drives with, 703
   structure of, 694–695
   support for, 42–43, 693–694
LVM commands, using, 701–703
LVM examples
   for multiple hard drives, 700–703
   for partitions on different hard drives, 703–705
LVM groups, managing, 698–699
LVM information, displaying, 697
LVM logical volumes, managing, 699–700
LVM physical volumes, managing, 698
LVMs, creating during installation, 695
lvremove command, using in LVM, 700

Lynx line-mode browser, features of, 328–329

M

MAC (mandatory access control), explanation of, 369–370
mail
   accessing on remote POP mail servers, 316–317
   notifications of receipt of, 316
mail address, components of, 524–525
mail clients
   command line mail clients, 313–315
   configuring with Sendmail, 539–540
   Emacs, 313
   Evolution, 309–310
   for GNOME, 311–312
   for KDE, 312
   MIME (Multipurpose Internet Mail Extensions), 308–309
   SquirrelMail, 313
   Thunderbird, 310–311
Mail command line mail client, features of, 314–315
mail delivery agents (MDAs), explanation of, 523
Mail Exchanger (MX) records, using, 845–846, 848–849
mail servers
   configuring with Sendmail, 539–540
   functions of, 523
MAIL system environment variable, description of, 233
mail transfer agents (MTAs)
   explanation of, 523
   features of, 523–524
   Postfix, 525–530
mail user agents (MUAs), explanation of, 523
MAILCHECK system environment variable, description of, 233
MAILER macro, using with Sendmail, 534, 536
mailer tables, using with Sendmail, 541–542
MAILERS macro, using with Sendmail, 537
mailing lists, subscribing to, 317–318
Mailman program, availability of, 318
MAILPATH system environment variable, description of, 233
main.cf Postfix file, using, 526–528
Majordomo program, Web site for, 318
make certificate command, using with snakeoil, 511

make command
    compiling software with, 111
    using with driver modules,
        114
    using with kernel, 765
make install command, using, 111
make policy command, using in
    SELinux, 391
MAKEDEV command, creating
    device files with, 738–739
Makefiles
    editing, 656
    use of, 633
Man pages, accessing, 73
mandatory access control (MAC),
    explanation of, 369–370
mangle table, using in Netfilter
    firewalls, 433
masquerading. *See also* IP
    masquerading
        implementing for
            networks, 442
        in Postfix MTA (mail transfer
            agent), 528
        in Sendmail, 537–539
MaxClients directive, using with
    Apache Web server, 495
MaxDB database management
    system
        features of, 287
        Web site for, 285
MaxKeepAlive directive, using with
    Apache Web server, 494
MaxRequestsPerChild directive,
    using with Apache Web
    server, 495
mcopy command, using with
    MS-DOS disks, 266
MCS (multicategory security), use
    in SELinux, 375, 383
md RAID device, use of, 708
MD5 value, significance
    to security, 357
mdadm, administering RAID with,
    708–709
mdadm.conf file, options
    for, 711
MDAs (mail delivery agents),
    explanation of, 523
mdir command, using with
    MS-DOS disks, 266
mdmonitor service script,
    monitoring RAID arrays with,
    713–714
/media directory, contents of,
    663–664, 665
media players, accessing, 303–304
menus
    adding to panels, 164
    versus drawers, 164
    editing in GNOME 2.x, 142
Menus pane, using in KDE panel
    (Kicker), 181

messages
    checking in SELinux, 382
    decrypting with GPG (GNU
        Privacy Guard), 363–364
    encrypting with GPG (GNU
        Privacy Guard), 363
    signing with GPG (GNU
        Privacy Guard), 364
Metacity compositing window
    manager, using, 149
mget command
    using with ftp program,
        338–339
    using with lftp client, 341
    using with NcFTP client, 342
mgetty configuration files, location
    of, 741
Microsoft Office, running on Linux,
    278–279
MIDI & sound software, Web site
    for, 296
MIME (Multipurpose Internet Mail
    Extensions), features of, 308–309
MIME type for GIF images,
    explanation of, 191
MIME types, using with Apache
    Web server, 499
MINFO records, using, 846
mingetty program, using with
    virtual consoles, 741
minimal-manifest file for Pungi,
    copy of, 52–53
Minix program, origin of, 14
mirror command, using with lftp
    client, 341
mirror sites
    downloading Fedora CD/
        DVD-ROM ISO images
        from, 103
    downloading Linux software
        from, 17
    for Fedora installation, 27
    linking to, 21–22
mirroring (RAID Level 1),
    explanation of, 707
mkbootdisk command, creating
    boot disk with, 49
mkdir command
    effect of, 255
    using, 256
mkfs command, using with file
    systems, 687–688
mkinitrd command, creating RAM
    disks with, 768
mkisofs tool
    creating bootable CD-ROMs
        with, 691
    recording CDs with, 689–691
    using, 685
mknod command, creating device
    files with, 739–740
mkswap command, using with
    partitions, 685, 689

MLS (multilevel security), use in
    SELinux, 370–371, 375, 382–383
/mnt directory, contents of, 663, 666
mod_ssl, configuring for Apache,
    510–511
mode parameter, using with
    iwconfig Wireless Tool, 132
Modem variable, using with wvdial,
    130
modems
    configuring, 127
    installing and managing,
        740–742
    using /dev/modem link file
        with, 726
Modification pane in GConf
    configuration editor, description
    of, 168
modprobe command
    installing driver modules
        with, 114
    installing modules with,
        746–747
    storing options for, 115
    using with packets, 431
    using with unsupported
        Ethernet cards, 126
modprobe.conf file, example of, 749
module files
    and directories, 745–746
    managing in SELinux, 390
module RAM disks, using, 768–769
modules
    compiling, 750–751
    installing, 749–750
    installing for kernel, 765
    installing from kernel,
        751–752
    installing with driver
        packages, 749–750
    installing with modprobe
        command, 746–747
    listing, 746
    loading, 748
    loading and unloading, 746
    loading with ismod
        command, 747
    managing with /etc/
        moprobe.conf, 746
    unloading with rmod
        command, 748
    use by Linux kernel, 744–745
    using aliases with, 748
monitor settings, changing, 100
monitoring tools. *See* performance
    analysis tools and processes
monitors, automatic configuration
    of, 33
Mono, implementation of, 740
more command
    displaying file contents
        with, 73
    listing files with, 254

mount command
mounting file systems
manually with, 680–681
mounting NFS with
manually, 894–895
using with GFS file
systems, 906
using with NTFS Project
read-only access, 116
mounting DVDs and CD-ROMs
manually, 683–684
mounting file systems, 661, 671
mounting file systems automatically
boot and disk checks for, 677
e2label used in, 678–679
Linux kernel interfaces used
in, 679–680
noauto option used in, 680
options for, 676–678
partition labels used in,
678–679
Windows partitions used
in, 679
mounting file systems manually
with mount command,
680–681
with umount command, 682
mounting floppy disks manually,
682–683
mountpoint, specifying, 41
mouse, automatic configuration
of, 33
move operation, using with
GNOME desktop, 146–147
moving directories, 263
Mozilla framework
enabling JRE (Java Runtime
Environment) for, 331
use of, 326
MP3 files
playing in Fedora, 70–71
playing with LAME, 301
plug-ins required for, 81–82
MPlayer multimedia player
features of, 304
installing from command
line, 82–83
MPM prefork, configuration
settings for, 495
MPMs (multiprocessing modules),
using with Apache Web server,
490
mput command, using with ftp
program, 338
MS-DOS disks, using mtools with,
265–266
MTAs (mail transfer agents)
explanation of, 523
features of, 523–524
Postfix, 525–530
-mtime option, using with find
command, 260
mtools, using with MS-DOS disks,
265–266

MUAs (mail user agents),
explanation of, 523
multicast addresses, using with
IPv6, 807–808
multicategory security (MCS), use
in SELinux, 375, 383
multilevel security (MLS), use in
SELinux, 370–371, 375, 382–383
multimedia support
availability of, 295–296, 298
FFmpeg and DivX, 83
GStreamer framework,
299–301
GStreamer plug-ins, 81–82
installing, 71
MP3 with LAME, 83
resources for, 76
Xine, 83
Multipath, relationship to RAID
levels, 708
multiprocessing modules (MPMs),
using with Apache Web
server, 490
music, playing with Xine, 83
music applications, playing, 301–302
Mutt command line mail client,
features of, 314
mv command
effect of, 261
-i option used with, 261
using, 257, 262
MX (Mail Exchanger) record, using,
845–849
MX records, use with mail
addresses, 525
myfilter script example, 437–445
MySQL database management
system
features of, 286
tools for, 565
Web site for, 285
MySQL database server
commands for, 565
configuring, 563–564
global configuration of, 564
managing, 565–566
starting and stopping, 565
structure of, 562–563
user configuration of, 565

<hr>

N

\n shell prompt code, description
of, 237
-name option, using with find
command, 260
name server addresses, using, 805
name server (NS) records, contents
of, 843
name-based virtual hosting,
implementing on Apache, 503
named.conf file
IPv4 example of, 838–839
IPv6 example of, 839–840

using configuration
statements with, 836–837
using zone statement with,
834–836
nameserver records, using, 848
NAT (Network Address Translation)
overview of, 431
targets and chains in, 431–432
NAT operations, types of, 431–432
NAT rules
adding, 431
IP masquerading of, 446
NAT tables, implementing packet
redirection with, 433
Nautilus file manager
burning CDs and DVDs
with, 150
changing background of File
Manager window in, 153
as desktop shell, 151–152
displaying files and folders
in, 153
features of, 143, 150–151
as FTP browser, 159
grouping files in, 156
managing files in, 154–156
navigating directories in,
153–154
opening subdirectories
in, 154
renaming files in, 155–156
setting preferences in, 158–159
sidebar views in, 152
starting applications in, 156
View menu options in, 153
viewing file and directory
properties in, 157–158
Views panel in, 158
Nautilus file manager menu
displaying, 153
options on, 154
Nautilus file pop-up menu, option
son, 155
Nautilus FTP client, features of,
334–335
Nautilus Web browser, features
of, 328
Nautilus windows, views of,
151–152
Navigation panel in Konqueror,
configuring, 185
NcFTP client, features of, 342
NCSA Web server, Web site for, 488
.NET, support for, 740
Netfilter (iptables) security
application, description of and
Web site for, 112
Netfilter firewalls. See also firewalls;
packet filtering
adding and changing chain
rules for, 423–424
and chains, 422
controlling port access with,
428–429

firewall and NAT chains
related to, 423
and ICMP packets, 427–428
ip6tables package for, 421
iptables command used
with, 420–421
modules for, 421
and packet mangling
tables, 433
setting up, 419
setting up DROP policy
for, 440
and targets, 422–423
using with NFS servers, 893
netgroups, setting up with NIS
(Network Information
Service), 899
netmasks
obtaining, 121
relationship to TCP/IP
network addresses,
798–799
.netrc file, inclusion in ftp
configuration file, 339–341
Netscape Enterprise Web server,
Web site for, 488
netstat program, monitoring
network connections with,
823–824
network configuration tools, 120
network configurations, saving in
interface configuration scripts,
128–129
network connections
configuring, 34
detecting, 121–122
monitoring with netstat
program, 823–824
network devices
configuring manually,
126–128
specifying in KDE, 175
Network File System (NFS). See NFS
(Network File System)
Network Information Service (NIS).
See NIS (Network Information
Service)
Network Manager
description of, 120
features of, 121–122
network monitors
Ettercap sniffer program, 821
netstat program, 823–824
ping, 820–821
tcpdump, 823
Wineshark protocol analyzer,
821–823
network packets, capturing, 821–823
network security applications, Web
sites for, 420
network servers, availability to
Fedora, 20
network services, availability in
local network, 136

network startup script, using, 815
network talk and messenger clients
AIM (AOL Instant
Messenger), 347
descriptions of, 346
Eikga VoIP, 346–347
ICQ protocol, 347
Network Time Protocol, using, 47–48
network tools
finger, 345
gnome-nettool, 343
host, 345
ping, 344–345
traceroute, 345–346
who, 345
networks. See also Fedora network
tools
allowing local access to, 442
blocking outside initiated
access to, 441
configuring, 43–44
descriptions of, 344
dynamic configuration
of, 119
enabling Amanda on, 783
IP masquerading local
networks, 446
masquerading, 442
obtaining static network
information, 120–121
protecting from IP spoofing,
440–441
new servers, using, 558–560
newaliases command, using with
Sendmail, 533
-newer option, using with find
command, 260
news servers, specifying, 237–238
news transport agents, features of,
320–321
Newsbin Windows-based
newsreader, using, 320
newsgroups
accessing, 23
topics associated with, 319
newsreaders
accessing, 560
descriptions of, 315
reading Usenet articles with,
319–320
using with Usenet news, 318
NFS (Network File System)
configuring, 887, 889–891
distributed network file
systems, 901–903
features of, 885
mounting on demand with
autofs, 895
starting and stopping, 886
NFS Configuration tool, using,
886–887
NFS daemons, using, 886
NFS file systems, mounting,
893–895

NFS host entries, configuring,
887, 889
NFS mount options, descriptions
of, 894
NFS servers, controlling access to,
891–893
NFS shares, configuring, 120
nfs4 access lists, implementing
security with, 891
NFSv4, features of, 885–886
NIS (Network Information Service)
features of, 896
setting up netgroups
with, 899
specifying shared files
for, 898
NIS clients, setting up, 900–901
NIS database, creating,
898–899
NIS domains, defining, 897
NIS servers
controlling access to, 899
setting up, 896–897
setting up options for,
897–898
specifying, 896
specifying configuration files
for, 901
\nnn shell prompt code, description
of, 237
NNTPSERVER shell parameter
variable, using, 237–238
noauto option, use in mounting file
systems, 680
noclobber feature
preventing redirection
with, 230
using with standard output
in BASH (Bourne again)
shell, 206
--nosignature option, using with
rpm -K command, 110
Notes view in Nautilus, explanation
of, 152
notify command, using with jobs in
BASH (Bourne again) shell,
212–213
NS (name server) records, contents
of, 843
NSS (Nameservice Switch) service,
relationship to LDAP, 629
NSS configuration services,
descriptions of, 814
NSS-supported files, descriptions
of, 813
nsswitch.conf, specifying NIS server
configuration files with, 901
nsupdate command, using with
DNS (Domain Name System),
858–859
NTFS, drivers for, 279
NTFS modules, generating with
DKMS (Dynamic Kernel Module
Support), 117

NTFS partitions, determining hard drive names for, 116. *See also* partitions

NTFS project read-only access, using Livna for, 116

NTFS read/write access, obtaining, 115–116

NTFS support, availability to Fedora, 17–18

ntfs-3g NTFS driver, using, 115–116

NTP servers, enabling, 574

NVIDIA drivers, packages for, 100–101

nwid or domain parameter, using with iwconfig Wireless Tool, 132

O

objects. *See* panel objects

octal numbers, calculating, 616

Office suites, descriptions of, 278–279

office versions of Linux, availability of, 19–20

OLDPWD shell variable, description of, 232

OO (OpenOffice). *See* OpenOffice (OO)

OP RPIntegrated power management, controlling in GNOME 2.x, 142

open command, using with NcFTP client, 342

Open Sound System, Web site for, 296

Open Source Development Network (OSDN), Web site for, 3

open source software, overview of, 16–17

Open With panel, using in Nautilus file manager, 156, 158

OpenHBCI home banking interface, Web site for, 283

OpenLDAP, Web site for, 623

OpenOffice (OO)
database files available in, 280
features of, 279–280
support for, 277
Web site for, 277

OpenPGP Public Keyserver project, Web site for, 361

OpenSSH application, description of and Web site for, 112

OpenSSH packages, availability of, 407–408

OpenSSL, obtaining open source version of, 509

Openswan (Open Secure/Wide Area Network) project, Web site for, 395

Openwriter desktop editor, description of, 288

operating systems
kernel as, 753
relationship to Linux, 12–13

operators for test command, functions of, 220

/opt directory, contents of, 663

options, using in Linux commands, 72–73

Options directive, using with Apache Web server, 497

options statement
forwarders option for, 838
notify option for, 838
using directory option with, 837
using with DNS (Domain Name System), 837–840

Oracle database management system
features of, 286
Web site for, 285

OSDN (Open Source Development Network), Web site for, 3

OSTYPE macro, using with Sendmail, 537

OSTYPE shell variable, description of, 232

OUTPUT chain, use by kernel, 423

overviews, support in INN (InterNetNews) news server, 560–561

owners, changing for files, 614–615

ownership of files and directories, significance of, 614

ownership permissions, setting, 618–619

P

package files
obtaining list of, 108
querying, 108

package groups, specifying in Pungi, 53

package integrity, checking with rpm command, 109–110

Package Manager
accessing, 45
features of, 105–106

package security check, performing, 109–110

Package Updater Program (PUP), using, 102–103

packages, 654–655. *See also* RPM packages; software
authenticating, 109
installing, 81–83
installing and uninstalling, 107–108
installing with software repositories, 76
selecting with yumex, 78

packet filtering. *See also* Netfilter firewalls
executing in Netfilter firewalls, 420–421
explanation of, 11–23, 419–420
implementation of, 421–422

packet mangling tables, using in Netfilter firewalls, 433

packet redirection, implementing, 433

packet states, specifying, 429–430

packets
accepting and denying, 424, 426
defining rules for, 430
routing, 818–820
tracking, 430–431

paint and image program, availability in KOffice, 281

Palm PDAs, accessing, 284–285

PAM module, relationship to LDAP, 629

PAM service, using with vsftpd, 485

PAMs (Pluggable Authorization Modules)
description of and Web site for, 112
relationship to LDAP, 630–631

pand network configuration tool, description of, 120

panel objects
adding, 162–163
adding menus to, 164
application launchers, 163
drawers, 163
folder and file launchers, 163
moving, removing, and locking, 162
types of, 162, 164

panels. *See also* KDE panel (Kicker)
adding directory folders to, 164
changing backgrounds of, 161–162
configuring and adding in GNOME, 160
displaying in GNOME, 161
features of, 159–160
moving, removing, and locking objects in, 162
moving and hiding in GNOME, 161
properties of, 160
relationship to applets, 162

PANs (Personal Area Networks), implementing with Bluetooth, 118

parent directories, referencing, 257

parent directory permissions, setting, 618

parity (RAID Level 4), explanation of, 707

parted command, using with hard drives, 684–685, 687

partition and file system creation tools, descriptions of, 685
partition configuration, example of, 41
partition labels, use in mounting file systems, 678–679
partition management packages, examples of, 33
partitions. *See also* NTFS partitions
configuring during installation, 39–40
creating, 42
creating, editing, and deleting, 40–41
creating manually, 41
editing, 42
formatting, 41
separating for RAID devices, 715
setting up boot partition, 41
passphrase, changing for SSH keys, 410
passwd command, use by root user, 570
password files
/etc/passwd, 602
/etc/shadow and /etc/gshadow, 603
maintaining for users, 601–603
Password Prompt variable, using with wvdial, 130
Password variable, using with wvdial, 130
passwords. *See also* shadow passwords
changing, 66, 94
controlling, 605–606
entering, 58
entering for printers, 98
managing in Kerberos, 416
specifying expiration dates for, 605–606
tools for, 603
using with Samba, 915–916
using with SWAT Samba configuration tool, 925
PATH variables
adding directories to, 239
contents of, 657
customizing, 658
description of, 232
using, 235–236
pathmunge function, using with PATH variable, 240
pathnames
identifying in URLs, 324
relationship to directories, 251–252
for user configuration files, 601–602
pax, using as alternative to tar, 267
PCHDTV video card, using for HDTV reception, 303

PCMCIA devices, support for, 744
PDAs
accessing, 284–285
device name for, 285
pdfedit document viewer, description of, 284
percent (%) field specifier, using with Apache logs, 502
percent (%) prompt, use of, 194
percent (%) symbol, referencing background jobs with, 212
performance analysis tools and processes
features of, 593
Frysk monitoring tool, 595
GKrellM, 596–597
GNOME Power Manager, 595–596
GNOME System Monitor, 594
KSysguard, 597
ps command, 594
System Tap, 595
Perl, Web site for, 21
-perm option, using with find command, 260
permission fields, using with udev rules, 731–732
permissions
absolute permissions, 616–617
categories of, 611–612
changing with chmod command, 612–613
defaults for, 619–620
directory permissions, 617–618
on GNOME, 612
indicating empty status of, 612
operations for, 613
ownership permissions, 618–619
read, write, and execute permissions, 612
setting for application desktop links in KDE, 182
setting with symbols, 615–616
sticky bit permissions, 619
using binary masks with, 616–617
Permissions panel in Nautilus Properties box, explanation of, 157–158
persistent names, creating, 730
Personal Area Networks (PANs), implementing with Bluetooth, 118
personal information, configuring, 66–67
PGP (Pretty Good Privacy) sites, descriptions of, 356

Phone variable, using with wvdial, 130
photo management tools
digiKam, 296
F-Spot Photo Manager, 295–296
photographs, selecting from Pictures folder, 66
PHP (PHP: Hypertext Preprocessor), features of, 507–508
Pictures folder, selecting photographs from, 66
pilot-link package, features of, 284
ping command, using with network startup scripts, 815
ping network tool, features of, 344–345
ping operations, controlling for ICMP packets, 427–428
ping program, monitoring networks with, 820–821
pipes (|), using in BASH (Bourne again) shell, 207, 209–210
Pirut
features of, 77
using Kyum instead of, 173
Pirut Package Manager
accessing, 45
features of, 105–106
pixmaps directory in Nautilus, contents of, 157
Places view in Nautilus, explanation of, 152
Pluggable Authentication Modules (PAMs), relationship to LDAP, 630–631
pmove command, using with LVM, 703
pointer (PTR) records, using, 845
policies, listing for removable storage devices, 736–737
policies in SELinux
creating, 391–392
implementation of, 383–384
purpose of, 375
using apol tool with, 382
Policies panel, using with printers, 98
policy methods, using in SELinux, 383–384
policy module tools, using in SELinux, 391
POP (Post Office Protocol), capabilities of, 544–545
POP and IMAP servers, availability of, 546
POP mail servers, accessing mail on, 316–317
port access, controlling with Netfilter firewalls, 428–429
Port directive, using with Apache Web server, 496
port forwarding, using, 413–414

portmapper service, using with NFS servers, 892
POSIX (Portable Operating System Interface for Computer Environments) standard, significance of, 14–15
Post Office Protocol (POP), capabilities of, 544–545
Postfix Greylisting Policy Server, features of, 528
Postfix MTA (mail transfer agent)
    commands in, 526
    configuration of, 526–528
    configuring for use with SpamAssassin, 547
    controlling user and host access in, 528–530
    features of, 525–526
    masquerading in, 528
    parameters used with, 529–530
    virtual domains in, 528
PostgreSQL database management system
    features of, 286
    Web site for, 285
PostgreSQL database server, structure of, 562
POSTROUTING chain, using to masquerade hosts, 447
pound sign (#) prompt, use of, 194
power parameter, using with iwconfig Wireless Tool, 132
PowerDVD player, Web site for, 304
PPID shell variable, description of, 232
PPP, accessing from command line with wvdial, 129–131
ppp connections, listing modem devices, 127
pref command, using with NcFTP client, 342
preferences
    in GNOME desktop, 63–65
    setting for Clock applet, 164
    setting in Nautilus file manager, 158–159
Preferred Applications tool, using in Nautilus file manager, 156
PREROUTING chain, using to masquerade hosts, 447
presentation programs
    availability in KOffice, 281
    in OpenOffice, 279
Preview preferences, setting in Nautilus file manager, 159
print job, explanation of, 551
-print option, using with find command, 260
printer connections, selecting, 95
printers
    accessing in Samba, 927–928
    adding and editing, 95

configuring, 94
configuring remote printers on CUPS, 552–553
device files for, 550
displaying configurations for, 94
editing, 96, 98
installing with CUPS, 551–553
setting up remote printers, 98
printing
    enabling in Samba, 924
    sites and resources for, 550
    using spool directories in, 551
printing features, selecting defaults for, 98
printing files, 254
priorities, listing for system logs, 589–591
private groups, using, 609
private keys. See also keys; public keys
    creating with ssh-keygen command, 409–410
    generating for GPG (GNU Privacy Guard), 358
    in SSH authentication, 406–407
/proc directory, contents of, 663
/proc file system
    contents of, 666, 721–722
    subdirectories and files of, 668
processes
    ending in BASH (Bourne again) shell, 214
    listing, 594
procmail, configuring to use SpamAssassin, 547
.profile file, significance of, 238
profile scripts
    managing user environments with, 604
    using with shells, 240–242
profiles, support in system-config-network tool, 125
program directories, contents of, 584, 664–665
program fields, relationship to /lib/udev directory, 728
programs. See also applications
    installing, 111
    locating, 258
    location of, 657
project management capability, availability in KOffice, 281
prompt, marking beginning of command line with, 194. See also shell prompt
prompt command, using with ftp program, 339–341

PROMPT_COMMAND system environment variable, description of, 233
properties, specifying device information with, 734–735
Properties box in Nautilus, panels in, 157–158
proxies
    use of, 420
    use with browsers, 327–328
proxy servers, features of, 513–514
ps command
    listing processes with, 594
    obtaining system process number with, 214
PS1 system environment variable
    configuring shell prompt with, 236–237
    description of, 233
PS2 system environment variable
    configuring shell prompt with, 236–237
    description of, 233
PSOTROUTING rule, using with SNAT targets, 432
PTR (pointer) records, using, 845
public keys. See also keys; private keys
    authenticating RPM packages with, 109
    creating with ssh-keygen command, 409
    generating for GPG (GNU Privacy Guard), 358
    importing for software packages, 365
    making available in GPG (GNU Privacy Guard), 360–361
    obtaining with GPG (GNU Privacy Guard), 361–362
    in SSH authentication, 406–407
    using in SSH (Secure Shell), 411
    validating for software packages, 366
public licenses, protection of open source software by, 16
public-key encryption, using, 356
Pungi
    creating Fedora install spins with, 50–55
    editing Yum configuration file for, 53
    stages for creating spins, 54
Pungi actions, creating log for, 54
pungi.conf file, default for, 51
PUP (Package Updater Program)
    updating software with, 636–637
    using, 102–103
Pure FTPD server, features of, 474

PVFS (Parallel Virtual File Systems), using, 902–903
pwd command, effect of, 255
PWD shell variable, description of, 232
PXE (Pre-Execution Environment), booting from, 35

Q

-qi option, using with rpm command, 108
-ql option, using with rpm command, 108
-qpi option, using with rpm command, 108
-qpl option, using with rpm command, 108
Qt library, using in KDE (K Desktop Environment), 173
Qt Public License (QPL), explanation of, 16
QTDIR system environment variable, description of, 233
quataoff command, using, 621
question (?) mark, using in BASH (Bourne again) shell, 203–204, 207
queue command, using with lftp client, 341
quit command, using with ftp program, 338
quota command, using, 622
quotacheck command, using, 621
quotaon command, using, 621
quotas. *See* disk quotas
quotes, single quote (') versus back quote (`), 216–217

R

r (read) permissions, setting, 615, 618
-r option, using with shutdown command, 59
racoon tool
    configuring gateway connections with, 404
    configuring IPsec with, 401–403
radvd Router ADVertisement Daemon, using, 871
RAID (Redundant Arrays of Independent Disks)
    administration with mdadm, 708–709
    configuring, 710–711
    configuring bootable RAID, 714–715
    creating spare groups for, 712
    example of, 716–718
    features of, 705

hardware RAID support, 705
    support for, 693–694
RAID arrays
    creating, 711–712
    managing, 713
    monitoring, 713–714
    starting and stopping, 713
RAID devices
    booting from, 708
    configuring during installation, 39
    creating and installing, 709
    and partitions, 708
    setting up with separate partitions, 715
RAID disks, creating, 43
RAID file systems, adding, 709–710
RAID levels, explanations of, 706–708
RAM disks, using, 768–769
RANDOM shell variable, description of, 232
rar archives, using unrar tool with, 267
Raven and Stronghold licensing, Web site for, 487
RBAC (role-based access control) security model, use by SELinux, 370–371, 383
rbac file, using in SELinux, 390
rc.local file, contents of, 451
rcp command, using, 349–351
rc.sysinit file, contents of, 451
read permissions, using, 612
Readline editing operations, using with BASH (Bourne again) shell, 195
RealPlayer, downloading, 302
rebooting, 49
records
    adding to LDAP directory database, 628
    creating and inserting in SQL, 562
recovery, implementing via journaling, 673–674
Red Hat
    documentation for, 7–8
    FTP site for, 7
Red Hat Enterprise Linux. *See also* Linux
    accessing documentation and help resources for, 73
    downloading, 6
    install guides for, 25
    updating, 102–103
    versions of, 6–7
Red Hat Enterprise Linux, features of, 5
red hat graphical boot (rhgb) tool, troubleshooting, 46–47
Red Hat Linux
    popularity of, 5
    Web sites related to, 8

Red Hat Package Manager (RPM). *See* RPM (Red Hat Package Manager)
redirection
    of packets, 433
    and piping of standard errors in BASH (Bourne again) shell, 210–211
    preventing with noclobber feature, 230
redirection operators (> and >>), using in BASH (Bourne again) shell, 206–208
redirection symbols in BASH (Bourne again) shell, execution of, 202
Redundant Arrays of Independent Disks (RAID). *See* RAID (Redundant Arrays of Independent Disks)
regret command, using with ftp program, 338
regular expressions, using in BASH (Bourne again) shell, 224–226
ReiserFS, journaling in, 674
relabel option, using with security contexts, 392
relational database structure, use by MySQL and PostgreSQL, 562
relative versus absolute pathnames, 252
remote access commands, effects of, 349
remote access permission, obtaining, 350–351
remote anonymous stanza, using in IPsec configuration, 402
remote hosts, accessing, 69–70
remote locations, developing from, 658–659
remote login, performing with ssh client, 411–412
remote POP mail servers, accessing mail on, 316–317
remote printers, setting up, 98
removable devices
    accessing with GNOME Volume Manager, 149–150
    listing, 69
    listing policies for, 736–737
    managing with HAL (Hardware Abstract Layer), 674
    using, 70
repodata directory page, accessing Fedora packages from, 79
report generator, availability in KOffice, 281
repositories. *See also* software repositories
    disabling, 77
    for Fedora, 17–18

repositories (*continued*)
  incompatibilities with, 77
  for third-party Linux
    software, 18–19
  using for minimal install of
    Fedora, 26
repository configuration files, listing
  with yumex, 79
repquota command, using, 622
rescue CD, creating, 49
rescue mode, booting Linux in, 49
resolvers, use with DNS (Domain
  Name System), 827–828
resource records. *See also* DNS
  (Domain Name System)
  format used by, 840
  types of, 841
  using aliases with, 845
  using in DNSSEC, 861–862
restore command
  interactive mode shell
    commands for, 789
  using, 787–788
restorecon command, using with
  security contexts, 392
Results pane in GConf configuration
  editor, description of, 168
reverse mapping files, using SOA
  records with, 842–843
reverse name format
  for IPv4, 850–851
  for IPv6, 851–853
reverse proxy cache, configuring in
  Squid proxy server, 521
Review option for partitions,
  choosing during installation, 40
RFC 3513 (IPv6 addresses), Web site
  for, 805
rhgb (red hat graphical boot) tool,
  troubleshooting, 46–47
rlogin, availability of, 350
rlogin command, effect of, 349, 351
rm command
  effect of, 261
  meaning of, 257
  using asterisk (*) with, 203
  using with files and
    directories, 263
rmdir command
  effect of, 255
  using, 256
rmod command, unloading
  modules with, 748
roaming, setting on with iwpriv
  Wireless Tool, 132
role allow rules, managing in
  SELinux, 387
role and type declarations,
  managing in SELinux, 384–385
role-based access control (RBAC)
  security model, use by SELinux,
  370–371, 383
roles in SELinux, purpose of, 374

root directory (/)
  role in FHS (File System
    Hierarchy Standard),
    662–663
  setting with chroot
    command, 49
  significance of, 250
root partition, contents of, 41
root password, changing, 92
root servers, connecting DNS
  servers to, 857
root user
  becoming, 570
  changing passwords for, 94
  definition of, 569
  logging in as, 48
  password for, 570
root user access, obtaining, 570–571
root user account, logging into, 570
root user security levels,
  determining in SELinux, 394
rootnoverify option, using with
  GRUB, 599
rootpw command, using with
  LDAP servers, 624
rotatelogs utility, using with
  Apache, 502
routers, renumbering with IPv6
  autoconfiguration, 869–870
routes
  deleting, 820
  location of, 819
routing rules, 818–820
routing table, entries in, 819
RP records, using, 846
RPM (Red Hat Package Manager)
  features of, 643
  options for, 645–646
  packaging software
    with, 659
RPM archives, contents of, 633
RPM binary packages, repository
  for, 296
rpm command
  installing and updating
    packages with, 648–649
  installing packages with,
    107–109
  options used with, 108
  reinstalling files with, 49
  using, 644–645
RPM databases, rebuilding, 651
RPM directory, importing Red Hat
  public keys from, 365
RPM discrepancy codes,
  explanations of, 650
RPM files, examining contents
  of, 648
RPM installation, verifying, 650
RPM packages. *See also* packages;
  software
  authenticating with public
    keys, 109

  checking public keys
    with, 366
  installation example, 649
  installing, 108
  installing and uninstalling,
    643–644
  installing and updating,
    648–649
  installing from desktop, 644
  query options for, 648
  querying information from,
    647–648
  removing, 650
  using, 103, 644
  for video applications,
    302–303
  for XviD, 305
RPM source code files, installing
  software from, 651
RPM tools, using, 643–644
rpmbuild operation, using with
  SELinux, 388
rpm.livna.org, configuring Yum
  for, 80
rsh command, using, 350, 352
rsync command
  accessing FTP sites with, 478
  making backups with,
    779–780
rsync mirroring, implementing, 479
rsync servers, configuring, 478–479
rules, defining for packets, 430
rules.d file, using with udev
  hotplug tool, 723
Run Command, selecting in
  KDE, 181
runlevel command, using, 581
runlevels
  changing with telinit, 580
  in initab, 580
  for service scripts, 455
  states of, 578–579
runtime configurations, using in
  SELinux, 383–384
runtime parameters, using with
  kernel, 755
ruptime command, effect of, 350
rwho command, effect of, 350

■■■■■ **S** ■■■■■

\s shell prompt code, description
  of, 237
SA (security associations), using
  with IPsec connections, 399
sainfo anonymous section, using in
  IPsec configuration, 402
Samba. *See also* SWAT Samba
  configuration tool
  accessing printers in,
    927–928
  allowing guest user access
    to, 925

applications for, 910–911
configuring firewalls for, 912
configuring with system-config-samba, 916–917
documentation for, 909–910
enabling printing in, 924
features of, 909
mounting shared directories in, 932–933
Printers section of, 925–926
services provided by, 910
setting up Windows network access with, 84–85
shares in, 926–927
starting up, 911–913
support for domain logons in, 929
testing from Linux, 912
user level security provided by, 913–916
using with Windows systems on GNOME, 149–150
variable substitutions in, 928
Samba access, configuring from Windows, 912–913
Samba clients, sharing Windows directories and printers with, 933–934
Samba configuration options for, 913
testing, 929
Samba daemon, configuring, 917–919
Samba passwords, using, 915–916
Samba resources, accessing from Windows systems, 934
Samba services, accessing with clients, 930–934
Samba shares. *See also* shares
accessing with smbclient utility, 931–932
configuring, 120
specifying with system-config-samba, 917
Samba users
adding with system-config-samba, 917
managing, 916
sar command, using, 595
SASL (Simple Authentication and Security Layer), using with Sendmail, 542–544
/sbin directory
contents of, 663–664
function of, 253
scheduled tasks, organizing, 576–577
scp client, using, 412–413
scp command, using, 351
Scribus desktop publishing tool, 277, 284

search operations, performing in SQL, 562
search servers, using, 558–560
Search tool in GNOME desktop, using, 258
seaudit tool, using with SELinux, 382
secret keys, using in DNS security, 860
Secure Shell (SSH). *See* SSH (Secure Shell)
Secure Sockets Layer (SSL). *See* SSL (Secure Sockets Layer)
security. *See also* DNS security methods; GPG (GNU Privacy Guard); IPsec (Internet Security Protocol); SELinux (Security-Enhanced Linux); SSH (Secure Shell); system-config-securitylevel
configuring, 111–114
digital signatures, 356
in Fedora, 20
implementing with nfs4 access lists, 891
implementing xinetd network security, 468–469
integrity checks, 356–357
public-key encryption, 356
in Samba, 913–916, 924
in Sendmail, 542–544
of Squid proxy server, 516–519
of Web servers, 508–511
security applications, descriptions of, 74
security associations (SA), using with IPsec connections, 399
security check, performing on packages, 109–110
security context files, managing in SELinux, 390
security contexts
checking in SELinux, 376
determining for security identity, 373
locating defaults for, 394
relationship to Flask architecture, 370–371
setting up defaults for, 394
using in SELinux, 392
using relabel option with, 392
using restorecon command with, 392
security in SELinux, purpose of, 374
security issues, finding out about, 113
security models, use by SELinux, 370–371
security policy (SP), relationship to setkey in IPsec, 399–400
security services, availability of, 112–113

Security-Enhanced Linux (SELinux). *See* SELinux (Security-Enhanced Linux)
select control structure, function of, 222
SELinux (Security-Enhanced Linux). *See also* security
adding new users in, 392–393
checking messages in, 382
checking security context in, 376
checking status and statistics in, 376
configuration for, 384
configuring, 377–379
features of, 369–370
managing users in, 383
MCS (multicategory security) in, 375, 383
MLS (multilevel security) in, 375, 382–383
obtaining system administration access under, 372
policy methods in, 383–384
resources for, 370
runtime security contexts and types in, 383–384
security models used by, 370–371
turning off, 375
using security contexts in, 392
SELinux management tools
audit2allow, 376–377, 380–381
descriptions of, 377
setools packages, 376
system-config-selinux, 377–379
SELinux modules, compiling, 388
SELinux Policy Analysis tool, features of, 382
SELinux policy configuration files
application configuration and appconfig, 391
changing, 387–388
file interface files, 390
module files, 390
policy module tools, 391
security context files, 390
types files, 390
user configuration and roles, 390–391
SELinux policy packages, availability of, 371–372
SELinux policy rules
access vector rules with allow, 386–387
constraint rules, 387
file contexts, 386
role allow rules, 387

SELinux policy rules (*continued*)
transition and vector rule
macros, 387
type and role declarations,
384–385
user roles, 386
SELinux reference policies, using,
382–383
SELinux screen, options on, 47
SELinux security application,
description of and Web site
for, 112
SELinux source configuration,
using, 388–389
SELinux terminology
domains, 373
identities, 373
policies, 375
roles, 374
security context, 374
transitions and labeling, 374
types, 374
SELinux troubleshooter, using,
380–381
semanage, using with SELinux, 381
semanage_module command, using
in SELinux, 388, 391–392
semicolon (;)
purpose in wvdial, 129
separating commands
with, 195
semodule command, using with -i
option in SELinux, 392
Sendmail
access actions in, 543
configuring, 533–534,
536–537
configuring for centralized
mail server, 540–541
configuring for simple
network configuration,
540
configuring mail servers and
mail clients with, 539–540
configuring workstations
with direct ISP
connections, 541
defining virtual domains
in, 542
distribution of, 366
features of, 530, 532, 535–536
files and directories for, 531
LDAP support in, 532–533
mailer table in, 541–542
masquerading in, 537–539
security in, 542–544
specifying errors messages
in, 543
SSL support in, 542
support for aliases in,
532–533
using divert command
with, 537

using dnl command with, 537
using FEATURE macros
with, 534, 536–537
using MAILER macro with,
534, 536–537
using OSTYPE macro
with, 537
sens parameter, using with iwconfig
Wireless Tool, 132
serial ports, relationship to terminal
devices, 741
server daemons, managing startup
and shutdown of, 453
ServerAlias directive, using with
Apache Web server, 504
ServerName directive, using with
Apache Web server, 496
ServerRoot directive, using with
Apache Web server, 494
servers
designating for printers, 98
listing, 45
server-side includes (SSIs), features
of, 505–506
ServerTokens directive, using with
Apache Web server, 494
service command
starting and stopping
Bluetooth with, 117
using, 583
using with Network
Manager, 122
service management tools
chkconfig, 458–461
system-config-services,
457–458
service script tags, using, 462–463
service scripts
for Apache Web server, 491
in /etc/rc.d/init.d directory,
453–454
example of, 463–464
functions of, 461–462
installing, 465
runlevels for, 455
running, 454
starting and stopping
services with, 456
services
configuring to start up
automatically at boot, 452
listing with chkconfig
tool, 458
managing, 582–583
removing and adding
services with, 460
starting and stopping
manually, 453
starting and stopping with
chkconfig, 459
starting automatically,
456–457
starting directly, 455

sessions
saving, 67
starting for services, 455
sestatus command, using in
SELinux, 376
set command
using, 216
using with ignoreeof
feature, 230
setenforce command, turning of
SELinux with, 375
setkey, configuring IPsec
connections with, 399–401
Settings option in KDE, using, 173
Setup Agent, running, 47
seuser command, using in
SELinux, 393
seusers file, contents of, 394
sftp and sftp-server clients,
using, 413
sh command, description of, 228
sh command, using, 217
.sh extension, explanation of, 241
shadow passwords. *See also*
passwords
description of and Web site
for, 112
turning off, 603
share directories, contents of, 190
shared keys, using in IPsec
configuration, 402
shares. *See also* Samba shares
configuring in Samba,
926–927
setting up, 85
using with printers, 98
shell command interpreter, features
of, 193
shell feature variables, case of, 233
shell operations, controlling, 230
shell parameter variables
assigning, 238–239
BASH_ENV, 236
EXINIT, 234
exporting, 238
features of, 233–234
HOME, 233–235
MAIL, 234
PATH, 234–235
PS1, 234
PS2, 234
SHELL, 234
using initialization files
with, 234
using with news servers,
237–238
shell prompt, configuring, 236–237.
See also prompt
shell scripts
arguments for, 218–219
executing, 217–218
SHELL system environment
variable, description of, 233

shell variables, 232
shell-based programs, running in KDE (K Desktop Environment), 182
shells. *See also* login shell
commands for invocation of, 228
configuration directories and files for, 245
defining environment variables in, 231
definition of, 214–215
initialization and configuration files for, 244–245
leaving, 227
preventing logging out of, 230
system environment variables for, 232–233
types of, 227
using profile script with, 240–242
Web sites for, 194
SHLVL shell variable, description of, 232
shortcuts, use of symbolic links as, 263–264
shutdown command
options for, 582
using, 581
using -h option with, 59
shutting down Linux systems, 49, 57
signature files, relationship to mail clients, 307
Simple Authentication and Security Layer (SASL), using with Sendmail, 542–544
single quote (')
versus back quote (`), 216–217
using with aliases, 228–229
sites. *See* Web sites
-size option, using with find command, 260
slappasswd command, using with LDAP servers, 624
slash (/), placing after directory names, 228
slave records, using in DNS, 854–856
slave servers, using in DNS, 854–856
slave zones, using in DNS, 855
slogin command, using, 351
slrn newsreader, features of, 320
slrnpull utility, features of, 320
SMB services, restricting access to, 924
SMB shared remote printers, accessing, 98
smbclient utility
accessing Samba shares with, 931–932

comparing to FTP clients, 930–931
smb.conf file
example of, 922–923
SSL version of Apache Web server in, 510
using, 917–919
smbpasswd command, using, 915–916
Smolt hardware profile screen, features of, 48
snakeoil certificate, installing, 511
SNAT and DNAT targets, using, 431–432
SOA (Start of Authority) records, using with zones and reverse mapping files, 842–843
SOA records, using with zone files, 847–848
software. *See also* packages; RPM packages
checking digital signatures for, 365–367
compiling, 111, 654–655
configuring command options for, 655
decompressing and extracting, 652
determining installation of, 108
downloading, 104
extracting, 653–654
file extensions for, 635
installing, 44–46, 103–104
installing from compressed archives, 652–656
installing from RPM source code files, 651
installing manually with rpm command, 107–109
installing with Yum, 104–105
listing with Pirut Package Manager, 106
packaging with RPM, 659
removing, 108–109
types of, 635
updating with Yum and PUP, 636–637
software depositories, Web sites for, 3
software directories, adding to /etc/profile file, 657
software repositories. *See* Fedora software repositories; repositories
downloading software from, 634–635
using Yum on, 76
sort command, using, 209
sound & MIDI software, Web site for, 296
sound applications
availability of, 298
LAME, 301

for music, 301–302
sound cards
detecting and testing, 92
installing, 742
sound drivers, selecting in GNOME desktop, 65
Sound panel, features of, 48
source code applications
configuring, compiling, and installing, 110–111
extracting archives for, 110–111
source code, compiling kernel from, 759–762
source code packages (SRPMs), installing software from, 651
SourceForge hosting site, Web address for, 16, 296
sources, selecting for Fedora installation, 29
SP (security policy), relationship to setkey in IPsec, 399–400
space on file systems, determining, 671–672
SpamAssassin, features of, 546–547
spashimage option in GRUB, using, 598
Spatial view in Nautilus
explanation of, 153
navigating, 154
special characters. *See also* characters
for regular expressions, 225
using in file searches, 225
spins
downloading, 103
using with Fedora installations, 28
split DNS
configuring views in, 864
internal and external views in, 864
spool directories, using printing, 551
spreadsheet applications
in GNOME Office, 282–283
in KOffice, 281
in OpenOffice, 279–280
spreadsheet applications, availability in KOffice, 281
SQL databases (RDBMS)
Informix, 286–287
MySQL database management system, 286
Oracle, 286
PostgreSQL, 286
SQL query language
commands in, 562
use by database servers, 562–563
SQL-based databases, explanation of, 285

squashing users in NFS, explanation of, 889
Squid application, description of and Web site for, 112
Squid proxy server
ACL (access control list) options for, 517
administrative settings in, 520
caches used by, 519–520
configuring cache memory in, 520
configuring client browsers for, 514–515
features of, 513–514
listing domains in, 518
logs in, 520
memory and disk configuration in, 520
order of http_access options in, 518
protocols supported by, 514
security of, 516–519
using reverse proxy cache in, 520–521
Web server acceleration in, 520–521
Web site for, 513
squid.conf file, location of, 516
SquirrelMail mail client, features of, 313
SRPMs (source code packages), installing software from, 651
SSH programs, use of, 113
SSH (Secure Shell). *See also* security
authentication mechanics of, 407
authorized keys in, 411
configuration files for, 410
encryption methods used by, 406–407
functions of, 406
implementations of, 405
loading keys in, 411
and port forwarding (tunneling), 413–414
setup of, 408–409
versus SSL (Secure Sockets Layer), 509
ssh client, using, 411–412
SSH clients
scp, 412–413
sftp and sftp-server, 413
ssh, 411–412
SSH Communications Security, Web site for, 405
SSH configuration files, managing, 414
SSH keys, creating with ssh-keygen, 409–410
SSH tools, using, 407–408
ssh-keygen command, using, 409–410

SSIs (server-side includes), features of, 505–506
SSL (Secure Sockets Layer)
features of, 509–511
mod_ssl implementation of, 510
versus SSH (Secure Shell), 509
support in Sendmail, 542
standard errors, redirecting and piping in BASH (Bourne again) shell, 210–211
standard input (-) argument, using with commands, 210
standard input in BASH (Bourne again) shell
explanation of, 205–206
receiving data from, 208–209
standard output in BASH (Bourne again) shell
explanation of, 205–206
redirecting, 206, 208
Standard Resource Record Format, using with resource records, 840
StarOffice suite, Web site for, 277
Start of Authority (SOA) records, using with zones and reverse mapping files, 842–843
STARTTLS command, using with Sendmail, 542
startx command, starting desktops with, 66
state extension, detecting packet tracking information with, 429–430
static IP addresses, using with wireless connections, 128
static network information, obtaining, 120–121
steganography, definition of, 365
sticky bit permissions, setting, 619
storage devices, attaching file systems on, 671
Storage Media option, using in KDE, 177
storage.fdi file, contents of, 736–737
string comparisons, functions of, 220
striping (RAID Level 0), explanation of, 707
Stronghold and Raven licensing, Web site for, 487
Stronghold Enterprise Web server, Web site for, 488
stty command, listing terminal settings with, 741
Stupid Mode variable, using with wvdial, 130
su command, use by root user, 570–571
subdomain records, using in DNS, 854

subdomain zones, using in DNS, 854
Subversion software development, explanation of, 658–659
sudo command, controlling administrative access with, 572–573
suffix command, using with LDAP servers, 623
Sun Java System Web server, Web site for, 488
Sun Java, Web site for, 21, 331
superuser
becoming, 570
changing passwords for, 94
definition of, 569
logging in as, 48
password for, 570
swap partitions
allocating space for, 33
creating, 685
SWAT configuration pages, displaying, 921–922
SWAT Samba configuration tool, 920. *See also* Samba
accessing, 920
activating, 919–920
creating shares with, 922
features of, 919
Global section of, 923–925
Homes section of, 925
security levels of, 924
using passwords with, 925
SWAT-generated smb.conf example, 922–923
switchdesk command, using, 66
Sybase database management system
features of, 287
Web site for, 285
symbolic links
support for, 263–264
using with udev hotplug tool, 726–728
SYMLINK rules, adding, 729
/sys directory, contents of, 663–664
/sys sysfs file system, contents of, 666–667, 721
sysconfig files, relationship to Fedora system administration tools, 588
sysctl, running for IP forwarding, 447
syslogd, facilities, priorities, and operators for, 590
syslogd and syslog.conf files, features of, 589
syslogd.conf files, features of, 589
system administration operations, performing, 569
system administration tools, descriptions of, 571
system administrator
becoming, 570
changing passwords for, 94

definition of, 569
  logging in as, 48
  password for, 570
system bashrc file, contents and
  location of, 243
system configuration. *See also*
  configurations
    tools for, 91
    troubleshooting, 89
system directories. *See also*
  directories
    configuration directories and
      files, 665
    contents of, 252
    descriptions of, 585, 664
    functions of, 253
    program directories, 584,
      664–665
system environment variables,
  using with shells, 232–233
system GNOME directories,
  contents of, 167
system logs
    features of, 588
    priorities for, 589–591
    specifying actions and users
      in, 591–592
    syslogd and syslog.conf, 589
    syslogd.conf, 589
    viewing, 588
System menus, explanations of, 141
System Monitor, using, 671
System option in KDE, using,
  173–174
system process number,
  obtaining, 214
system resources, accessing from
  file manager in KDE, 176–177
system runlevels. *See* runlevels
system startup files
    and directories, 452
    /etc/rc.d, 451
    /etc/rc.d/init.d, 452–455
    /etc/sysconfig, 451
    rc.local, 451
    rc.sysinit, 451
System Tap diagnostic tool, features
  of, 595
system time and date, setting,
  573–574
system time, setting, 44
system tools, accessing in KDE, 173
System V init script tags,
  descriptions of, 463
system-config-authentication tool,
  description of and Web site
  for, 112
system-config-bind, description
  of, 120
system-config-cluster, managing
  GFS clusters with, 904
system-config-date utility, using,
  573–574

system-config-display, changing
  display settings with, 99–100
system-config-httpd, description
  of, 120
system-config-lvm
    entering in terminal window,
      695–697
    using, 700–701
system-config-netboot, description
  of, 120
system-config-network
    configuring Ethernet cards
      with, 126
    configuring IPSec with,
      397–398
    Devices panel in, 124–125
    DNS panel in, 123
    Hosts panel in, 123–124
    profiles support in, 125
system-config-network, description
  of, 120
system-config-nfs, description
  of, 120
system-config-printer, starting, 94
system-config-samba
    adding Samba users
      with, 917
    configuring Samba with,
      916–917
    description of, 120
    specifying Samba shares
      with, 917
system-config-securitylevel. *See also*
  security
    description of, 120
    setting up firewalls with,
      133–134
system-config-selinux
    description of and Web site
      for, 112
    using, 377–379
system-config-services
    description of, 120
    starting and stopping xinetd
      services with, 465–466
    using, 452, 457–458, 583
    using with network
      services, 136
system-config-services ON Demand
  panel, 466
system-config-users, managing
  groups with, 610

T

\t shell prompt code, description
  of, 237
tables, creating in SQL, 562
tabs in Konqueror, opening folders
  as, 184
TANGO style guidelines,
  compliance of Cairo images
  with, 140

tape, archiving to, 271
tar (tape archive) tool
    creating archives with, 268
    decompressing software
      with, 652
    displaying archive contents
      with, 268
    extracting archives with,
      268–269
    extracting software with,
      653–654
    features of, 267
    versus pax, 267
tar archives, extracting in
  Konqueror, 184
tar command
    c option used with, 268
    f option used with, 268
    options for, 269
    r option used with, 269
    scheduling automatic
      backups with, 779
    u option used with, 270
    updating archives with, 270
    using, 110
    using to archive to floppy
      disks, 270
    using with driver
      modules, 114
    x option used with, 268
    z option used with, 270, 272
targets
    in NAT (Network Address
      Translation), 431–432
    relationship to Netfilter
      firewalls, 422–423
tasks
    organizing scheduled tasks,
      576–577
    scheduling with cron service,
      574–578
TCP wrappers, using with xinetd-
  managed servers, 471–472
tcpdump, capturing network
  packets with, 823
TCP/IP configuration files
    addresses for, 809
    /etc/hosts file, 809–810
    /etc/protocols file, 811
    /etc/services file, 811
    /etc/sysconfig/network file,
      811
    /etc/sysconfig/networking
      file, 810–811
    /etc/sysconfig/network-
      scripts file, 810
TCP/IP network addresses
    and class-based IP
      addressing, 797–798
    IPv4 addresses, 797
    and netmasks, 798–799
TCP/IP protocol development
  groups, Web sites for, 794

TCP/IP protocol suite, components of, 793–796
tcsh command, description of, 228
TCSH shell
    defining environment variables in, 231
    description of, 227
    initialization and configuration files for, 244
TCSH Web site, accessing, 194
TE (type enforcement) security model, use by SELinux, 370–371
.te policy configuration files, using in SELinux, 387–388
telinit command
    changing runlevels with, 580
    using, 348–349
    using with vendor drivers for video cards, 101–102
TERM system environment variable, description of, 233
termcap files, contents of, 741
terminals, installing and managing, 740–742
test command, using, 219–220
TeX typesetting tool, features of, 284
text files, editing, 90
themes
    clearlooks, 140
    displaying GNOME desktop with, 145
    selecting for KDE (K Desktop Environment), 178
    using with Fedora desktop, 60
    using with GDM (GNOME Display Manager), 57
third-party kernel drivers, availability of, 106–107
ThreadsPerChild directive, using with Apache Web server, 495
Thunderbird mail client
    enabling LDAP on, 630
    using enigmail extension with, 358
Thunderbird mail client, features of, 310–311
tickets
    destroying, 417
    viewing in Kerberos, 415
tilde (~), using with user names, 197
time, setting, 44
time and date, setting, 92, 573–574
Time To Live directives, using with zone files, in zone files, 841–842
Timeout directive, using with Apache Web server, 494
timeout option in GRUB, using, 598
TMOUT system environment variable, description of, 233
/tmp directory, contents of, 663–664
top command, using, 595
torrents, starting with BitTorrent, 636

Torvalds, Linus, 14
TOS targets, using, 432
traceroute network tool, features of, 345–346
transfer protocol, use with URL addresses, 324
TransferLog directive, using with Apache Web server, 502
transfers, controlling in DNS, 855–856
transition and vector rule macros, managing in SELinux, 387
transitions and labeling in SELinux, purpose of, 374
transmissions, tunneling, 403–404
Trash folder, system KDE directory for, 192
Tree pane in GConf configuration editor, description of, 168
tree structure, explanation of, 250
Tree view in Nautilus, explanation of, 152
Tripwire integrity checker, using, 367
troubleshooting, performing with audit2allow tool, 380–381
tset command, initializing terminal devices with, 742
TSIG keys, using in DNS security, 862–863
TSIG signatures and updates, using in DNS (Domain Name System), 858
tunneling, 403–404, 413–414
Tux Content Accelerator, features of, 487–488
TV devices
    device name for, 743
    drivers for, 744
TV players, features of, 304–305
TXT records, using, 846
type and role declarations, managing in SELinux, 384–385
type enforcement (TE) security model, use by SELinux, 370–371
-type option, using with find command, 260
type structure, use in SELinux, 383
types files
    managing in SELinux, 390
    and runtime security contexts in SELinux, 383–384
types in SELinux, purpose of, 374

U

-U option, using with rpm command, 108
\u shell prompt code, description of, 237
udev, relationship to HAL (Hardware Abstract Layer), 670

udev hotplug tool. *See also* devices
    configuring, 723–724
    features of, 722–723
    substitution codes for, 726
    using symbolic links with, 726–728
udev rules
    creating, 728–729
    fields for, 725
    relationship to device names, 724–726
    using ATTRS key with, 731–732
    using permission fields with, 731–732
udevinfo command, using, 730–731
-uid option, using with find command, 260
UID shell variable, description of, 232–233
umask command, displaying permission defaults with, 619–620
UML (user-mode Linux), purpose of, 757
umount command
    mounting file systems manually with, 682
    using with DVDs and CD-ROMs, 683
unalias command, using, 229
uncompress command, using, 273
unicast global addresses, using with IPv6, 807
unicast local use addresses, using with IPv6, 807
Universal Resource Locators (URLs), accessing Internet resources with, 324
Unix operating system
    development of, 4
    editors in, 291
    history of, 13–14
    Linux as version of, 13
unrar tool, accessing, 267
unset command, using, 216
until control structure, function of, 222
URL desktop files, creating in KDE (K Desktop Environment), 178
URL pathnames, using with Apache Web server, 498–499
URLs (Universal Resource Locators), accessing Internet resources with, 324
USB drives, booting from, 35
UseCanonicalName directive, using with Apache Web server, 496, 504
Usenet articles, reading with newsreaders, 319–320
Usenet news, features of, 318–319

user accounts
  creating, 48
  creating and deleting, 94
  locking and unlocking, 605
user and group management tools,
  descriptions of, 607
user authentication, requirement in
  Samba, 84
user configuration and roles,
  managing in SELinux, 390–391
user configuration files, pathnames
  for, 601–602
user environments, managing,
  604–606
user interface, purpose of, 12
user login, returning to, 571
user names, using ~ (tilde) with, 197
user passwords, controlling,
  605–606
user roles, managing in SELinux, 386
User Switcher, features of, 57–58
USER system environment variable,
  description of, 233
useradd command, using,
  94, 607–608
user-defined rules, creating for
  firewalls, 443–444
userdel command, using, 94, 609
usermod command, using, 608
user-mode Linux (UML), purpose
  of, 757
usernames
  entering, 58
  entering for printers, 98
users
  adding, 607–608
  adding in SELinux (Security-
    Enhanced-Linux),
    392–393
  configuring, 93–94
  identifying logged-in status
    of, 601
  managing in SELinux, 383
  modifying, 608
  password files for, 601–603
  removing from system, 609
users and actions, specifying in
  system logs, 591–592
using CGI files, using with Apache
  Web server, 499–500
/usr directory
  contents of, 663–665
  functions of, 253

V

\v shell prompt code, description
  of, 237
values of variables, referencing, 215
/var directory
  contents of, 663–664, 666
  function of, 253
  subdirectories of, 667

variables. *See also* environment
  variables
  assigning command results
    to, 216–217
  assigning values to, 215
  defining and evaluating in
    BASH (Bourne again)
    shell, 215–216
  listing, 216
  referencing values of, 215
  removing, 216
  substituting in Samba, 928
  using $ (dollar) sign
    with, 197
/var/log/messages file, checking
  for events, 367
vgchange command, using in LVM,
  699, 702, 704
vgcreate command, using in LVM,
  698, 700–702, 704
vgextend command, using in LVM,
  699, 702
Vi (visual) editor
  a (append) command for, 293
  command and input modes
    in, 291
  commands for, 292–293
  entering text in, 293
  exiting, 293
  features of, 290–291
  :help command for, 293
  :q command for, 293
  ZZ command for, 293
video applications, availability of,
  302–305
video cards
  automatic configuration of, 33
  changing settings for, 100
video CDs, playing in Fedora, 70
video devices
  device names for, 743
  drivers for, 744
video graphics card drivers
  installing with Yum, 101
  support for, 100–102
videoLAN project, Web site for, 303
vim command, executing, 291
Vim editor
  features of, 290
  jumping to command mode
    in, 291
  using gvim instead of, 294
virt-install, using with Xen
  Virtualization kernel, 774
virtual desktops
  changing number of, 180
  support in KDE (K Desktop
    Environment), 179–180
virtual domains, configuring in
  Sendmail, 542
virtual hosting
  on Apache, 503–506
  logs for, 506

using with vsftpd (Very
  Secure FTP Server),
  485–486
Virtual Machine Manager (virt-
  manager), using, 770–771
Virtual Network Computing (VNC)
  installation, performing, 36
virtual private networks (VPNs). *See*
  VPNs (virtual private networks)
VirtualDocumentRoot directive,
  using with Apache Web
  server, 504
virtualization, support for, 769–770
vmstat command, using, 595
VMware, features of, 279
VNC (Virtual Network Computing)
  installation, performing, 36
volume control, setting in GNOME
  desktop, 64–65
volume groups, activating in LVM
  (Logical Volume
  Management), 699
volumes, managing with GNOME
  Volume Manager, 149–150. *See
  also* LVM (Logical Volume
  Management)
VPN Consortium, Web site for, 395
vpnc client, availability of, 395
VPNs (virtual private networks)
  features of, 128
  implementation relative to
    IPSec, 397–398
  using IPsec tunnel mode
    with, 403–404
vsftpd (Very Secure FTP Server)
  anonymous user permissions
    for, 482–483
  configuring, 480–483
  connection time limits
    for, 483
  enabling login access in, 482
  files for, 484
  implementing virtual users
    in, 486
  local user permissions
    for, 482
  logging in, 483
  messages in, 483
  restricted command usage
    in, 485
  running, 480
  running as stand-alone
    server, 482
  starting, stopping, and
    restarting, 480
  using PAM service with, 485
  virtual hosting in,
    485–486
vsftpd access controls
  chroot_list_enable option, 484
  deny_email_enable
    option, 484
  userlist_enable option, 484

vsftpd server package
and anonymous FTP, 475
using, 474–475
vsftpd.conf, configuration options
for, 481

━━━ **W** ━━━

w (write) permissions, setting,
615, 618
\w shell prompt code, description
of, 237
\W shell prompt code, description
of, 237
wait command, using with lftp
client, 341
Web, accessing with Konqueror,
187–188
Web browsers. *See* browsers
Web clients
browsers, 325–329
and URL addresses, 324
Web file types, descriptions of, 325.
See also files
Web protocols, descriptions of, 324
Web servers
allowing access to, 441
alternatives to Apache, 488
security of, 508–511
Web sites
AbiSource project, 283
AFE (Affix Frontend
Environment), 117
AIM (AOL Instant
Messenger), 347
ALSA (Advanced Linux
Sound Architecture), 296
Apache Software
Foundation, 489
Apache Web server
resources, 489–490
Apache-SSL Web server, 488
ARIN (American Registry
for Internet Numbers), 802
backup resources, 780
BASH (Bourne again) shell
information, 193
Beryl compositing window
manager, 148
BIND resources, 830
CD burners and rippers, 302
CENTOS (Community
Enterprise Operating
System), 7–8
Compiz compositing
window manager, 148
creating, 329
CrossoverOffice
program, 278
CUPS (Common Unix
Printing System), 549
database and office software
for Linux, 19–20

database resources, 561
DB2 database management
system, 285, 287
device resources, 720
documentation for Fedora,
7–8
DVD::rip project, 304
Emacs, 313
Emacs editor, 289
Epiphany Web browser, 328
Fedora CD/DVD-ROM ISO
images, 103
Fedora download, 6
Fedora download site, 27
Fedora FAQ, 8
Fedora Installation Guide,
25, 28
Fedora Live CD, 11
Fedora Portal page, 21
Fedora Project, 8
Fedora repositories, 18
Fedora software, 104
Fedora support, 75
Flagship compiler, 285, 288
Flickr, 296
Freshrpms repository, 4
F-Spot Photo Manager, 295
FTP servers, 474
GATOS (General ATI TV and
Overlay Sofware), 743
GFS (Global File System)
references, 904
GNOME, 3
GNOME 2.x features, 141
GNOME desktop, 16
GNOME graphics tools, 297
GNOME Office project, 282
GNOME resources, 140
GNOME source code, 139
GNOME User's Guide, 143
GNU SQL database
management system,
285, 287
GNUPro development
tools, 5
GPG (GNU Privacy Guard)
encryption tool, 112
gPhoto project, 297
graphic projects, 295
graphics tools, 298
GStreamer, 300
GStreamer framework, 299
HAL specification
documentation, 732
IANA, 802
ICQ protocol, 347
IMAP and POP servers, 546
InfiniBand Project, 135
Informix database
management system,
285–287
INN (InterNetNews) news
server, 558

Internet Mail Consortium, 309
IPsec (Internet Security
Protocol) resources, 395
Jakarta project, 332
Java packages and Web
applications, 330
JPackage Project, 332
K Desktop themes, 178
KAME project, 395
KDE (K Desktop
Environment), 16, 172
KDE Web Dev, 329
Kerberos, 112
Kerberos authentication, 406
kernel resources, 754
KOffice Suite for KDE, 281
KVM (Kernel-based
Virtualization Machine)
implementation, 771
LDAP (Lightweight
Directory Access
Protocol), 112
LDP (Linux Documentation
Project), 21
lighthttpd Web server, 488
Linux Foundation, 8
Linux Foundations, 15
Linux information and
news, 22
Linux office and database
software, 19
Linux Office suites, 278
Linux programming, 21
Linux software, 104, 634
Linux software downloads, 17
linux-wlan project, 133
Livna repository, 4
LPRng (Line Printer, Next
Generation), 550
Majordomo program, 318
MaxDB database
management system,
285, 287
mirror sites for Fedora
installation, 27
Mozilla project for
Thunderbird mail
client, 310
MPlayer multimedia
player, 304
multimedia, 296
multimedia and sound
applications, 299
multimedia applications, 298
multimedia applications for
Fedora, 104
music applications, 301–302
MySQL database
management system,
285–286
NCSA Web server, 488
Netfilter (iptables) security
application, 112

Netfilter Project, 420
Netscape Enterprise Web server, 488
network security applications, 420
ntfs-3g NTFS driver, 115
office and database software for Linux, 19–20
Open Source movement, 16
OpenHBCI home banking interface, 283
OpenLDAP, 623
OpenOffice, 279
OpenPGP Public Keyserver project, 361
OpenSSH security application, 112
OpenSSL, 509
Openswan (Open Secure/Wide Area Network) project, 395
Oracle database management system, 285–286
Perl, 21
PGP (Pretty Good Privacy), 356
PHP (PHP: Hypertext Preprocessor), 507
pilot-link package, 284
POP and IMAP servers, 546
PostgreSQL database management system, 285–286
PowerDVD player, 304
printing sites and resources, 550
Pure FTPD servers, 474
RealPlayer, 302
Red Hat Enterprise Linux download, 6
for Red Hat Linux and Fedora resources, 8
RFC 3513 (IPv6 addresses), 805
Scribus desktop publisher, 284
SELinux (Security-Enhanced Linux), 112
SELinux resources, 370
Sendmail, 530
Smolt registration of hardware configuration, 48
software depositories, 3
sound and multimedia applications, 299
SourceForge hosting site, 16
Squid proxy server, 513
Squid security application, 112
SSH Communications Security, 405

Stronghold and Raven licensing, 487
Stronghold Enterprise Web server, 488
Sun Java, 21
Sun Java site, 331
Sun Java System Web server, 488
Sybase Adaptive Server Enterprise server, 287
Sybase database management system, 285
TANGO style guidelines, 140
TCP/IP protocol development groups, 794
TCSH, 194
third-party Linux software repositories, 19
TV players, 304–305
unrar tool, 267
video applications, 302–303
videoLAN project, 303
virtualization resources, 769
VMware, 279
VPN Consortium, 395
window managers, 60
Wine, 278
XBase database management system, 285
Xine player, 304
Zope application Web server, 488
Webalizer tool, generating reports on Web logs with, 501
wget client, features of, 335
while control structure function of, 222
using, 223–224
who network tool, features of, 345
wildcard matching symbols searching files with, 185
using with filenames, 261
using with TCP wrappers, 471
Window List applet, features of, 165
window managers starting up, 57
using with GNOME desktop, 148–149
Web sites for, 60
windows, moving in GNOME desktop, 62. See also KDE windows
Windows directories, sharing with Samba clients, 933–934
Windows games, playing on Linux, 86
Windows network access, setting up with Samba, 84–85
Windows partitions, use in mounting file systems, 679
Windows printers, sharing with Samba clients, 934

Windows Samba shares, accessing from GNOME, 930–932
Windows software, running on Linux, 85–87
Windows systems, accessing Samba resources from, 934
Wine
downloading and installing, 320
running Windows applications with, 85–87
Web site for, 278
Wineshark protocol analyzer, using, 821–823
wireless connections configuring, 127–128
configuring manually, 131–133
wireless devices displaying information about, 133
displaying statistics for, 132
wireless drivers, availability of, 133
Wireless Tools, descriptions of, 131
word processors, 281
in GNOME Office, 282–283
in OpenOffice, 279
Workgroup entry in smb.conf file, displaying, 923–924
working directory, searching, 259
Workspace Switcher applet, features of, 165
write permissions, using, 612
write support, enabling and disabling for Fedora, 17–18
Writer word processor in OpenOffice, features of, 280
wvdial network configuration tool accessing PPP from command line with, 129–131
description of, 120
starting, 131
variables for, 130
www hostname, significance of, 324

X

x (execute) permissions setting, 615
setting with binary masks, 616–617
x (execute) permissions, setting, 618
X Window System graphic programs for, 297
graphics tools for, 298
Xbase database management system features of, 287–288
Web site for, 285
Xbase language, explanation of, 285–286
xconfig (qconf) kernel configuration tool, using, 762

XEmacs desktop editor, description of, 288
Xen virtual machines
  creating with configuration files, 775–776
  managing with xm command, 776–777
Xen Virtualization kernel, using, 773–777
XFce4 desktop, features of, 65. *See also* desktops
Xine player, features of, 83, 304
xinetd attributes, using, 469–470
xinetd daemon, configuring for services, 456–457
xinetd network security, implementing, 468–469
xinetd program, internal services for, 469
xinetd services
  attributes for, 467–468
  configuration files for, 469
  configuring, 466
  configuring for use by chkconfig, 4601
  disabling and enabling, 470–471
  enabling and disabling with chkconfig, 460
  logging, 466
  starting and stopping, 465–466
  using with CUPS (Common Unix Printing System), 551
xinetd.conf file, using, 466–469
xinetd-managed servers, using TCP wrappers with, 471–472
Xload command, using, 595

xm command, managing Xen virtual machines with, 776–777
xmkmf, using, 655–656
X.org, using with Fedora, 99
xpdf document viewer, description of, 284
XviD, running DivX files with, 305

Y

Yelp GNOME Help browser, features of, 146
Yum (Yellowdog Update, Modified)
  accessing tips on use of, 105
  configuring, 638–643
  configuring to access rpm.livna.org, 80
  installing Fedora packages with, 638
  installing software packages with, 104–105
  installing video graphics card drivers with, 101
  repository files for, 639–640
  updating software with, 636–637
  using on software repositories, 76
Yum caches, managing, 642–643
yum command, updating software with, 637
Yum configuration file, editing for Pungi, 53
Yum repositories, creating, 642
yum updates, automating, 637
yumconf option, using with Pungi, 50–51
yumex Yum Extender, features of, 77–79

Z

Z shell
  description of, 227
  initialization and configuration files for, 244
Zip utility, compressing and decompressing files with, 274
zone files for Internet zones. *See also* DNS (Domain Name System)
  address records, 848
  address records with host names, 849
  alias records, 849
  directives, 847
  inherited names, 849
  loopback records, 849
  MX (Mail Exchanger) records, 848–849
  nameserver records, 848
  resource records for, 840–846
  SOA records, 847–848
  Time To Live directives in, 841–842
zone keys, using in DNSSEC, 861
zone statement
  options for, 837
  using with named.conf file, 834–836
zones, using SOA records with, 842–843
Zope application Web server, Web site for, 488
zsh command, description of, 228